RATIONALE

OF THE

DIRTY JOKE

AN ANALYSIS OF SEXUAL HUMOR
FIRST SERIES

G. LEGMAN

Simon & Schuster Paperbacks
New York London Toronto Sydney

SIMON & SCHUSTER PAPERBACKS
Rockefeller Center
1230 Avenue of the Americas
New York, NY 10020

First Simon & Schuster paperback edition 2006

SIMON & SCHUSTER PAPERBACKS and colophon are
registered trademarks of Simon & Schuster, Inc.

For information about special discounts for bulk purchases,
please contact Simon & Schuster Special Sales:
1-800-456-6798 or business@simonandschuster.com.

Manufactured in the United States of America

10 9 8 7 6 5 4 3 2 1

Library of Congress Catalog Card Number: 68-29924

ISBN-13: 978-0-7432-9252-8
ISBN-10:   0-7432-9252-9

TO

THE *MANES*

OF

POGGIO BRACCIOLINI

LOVER OF BOOKS,

FOLK HUMOR,

AND

WOMEN

No story has been encountered, in the thirty-five or more years of this research, that makes this point so absolutely frank, yet with what worlds of unspoken sardonic criticism, as the following: *A vaudeville performer is describing his act to a skeptical booking-agent. "It's very simple. My wife and I shit on the stage, and then the kids come out and wallow in it." Agent, thunderstruck: "What kind of act do you call that?" Vaudevillian, polishing his fingernails on his lapel: "We call it — 'The Aristocrats'!"* (N.Y. 1953. Compare the actual theatre-of-cruelty stage act, "Sexy Goose," which tops this, as described in section II.III.2, "Orgies and Exhibitions.")

G. Legman,
No Laughing Matter: Rationale of the Dirty Joke, Second Series

CONTENTS

For a complete Analytic Table of Contents,
see the Subjects & Motifs following the text.

RATIONALE
OF THE
DIRTY JOKE

FIRST SERIES

"I laugh, so that I may not cry."
—BEAUMARCHAIS,
The Barber of Seville

INTRODUCTION

I

UNDER the mask of humor, our society allows infinite aggressions, by everyone and against everyone. In the culminating laugh by the listener or observer — whose position is often really that of victim or butt — the teller of the joke betrays his hidden hostility and signals his victory by being, theoretically at least, the one person present *who does not laugh.* Compulsive story-tellers and jokesters express almost openly the hostile components of their need, by forcing their jokes upon frankly unwilling audiences among their friends and loved ones, and upon every new person they meet. Often they proffer this openly as their only social grace. The listener's expected laughter is, therefore, in a most important but unspoken way, a shriving of the teller, a reassurance that he has not been caught, that the listener has partaken with him, willy-nilly, in the hostility or sexuality of the joke, or has even acceded in being its victim or butt.

This is particularly clear in the type of rambling or pointless anecdote, nowadays known as the 'talking horse' or 'shaggy dog' story and mistakenly believed to be a new genre, though it is a special art in, for example, *Joe Miller's Jests* (1739) No. 79 — modelled on Apuleius' *Golden Ass,* and Balaam's ass centuries earlier — in Laurence Sterne's *Tristram Shandy* (1767), which confesses itself a 'Cock & Bull story' at the end, and in many of the best stories and lectures of Mark Twain, such as "The Celebrated Jumping Frog" and "His Grandfather's Old Ram" in Twain's *Autobiography*. In such tales and jokes, the dénouement or 'punch-line' is improportionately small or absurd (or even simply evaded) by comparison with the long and complex development or 'build-up' of the listener's expectation; and the avowed butt of the joke is simply the person who has been tricked into listening.

Erotic humor is far & away the most popular of all types, and an extremely large percentage of the jokes authentically in oral circulation, in this and apparently in all centuries and cultures, is concerned

9

with the humor — often unwilling, unpleasant, and even purposely macabre — of the sexual impulse. The humor of scatology must be assimilated to this, if only because both operate under the same physiological and verbal taboos. Rather than attempt here a general synthesis of the forms of erotic humor, each chapter and section of the present work is prefaced with a few paragraphs attempting to indicate the particular way in which the specific aggressions (sometimes self-directed, as it would appear) of various types of jokes are expected to slough off the fear or uneasiness that the teller feels, consciously or unconsciously, about the subject matter of his or her favorite jokes, by exposing the listener to precisely the same fear or uneasiness.

The editor is very conscious that, in presenting so large and so varied a collection of what this culture calls frankly and appreciatively 'dirty jokes,' he is himself falling into every kind of aggression in the book, and is almost certain to cause every reader, without exception, some sort of uneasiness in one chapter or another. The reader is not advised in that case simply to skip the jokes found offensive and to proceed to the next, but rather, as Norman Douglas truculently suggests, in the Introduction to his annotated collection, *Some Limericks* (Florence, 1928), to any reader suffering 'from that trying form of degeneracy which is horrified at coarseness,' to 'close the book at once and send it back to me, in the hope that I may be simple enough to refund him the money.' For the present work is not only purposely so titled as to warn off all persons not really interested in the subject, but is furthermore so arranged that the jokes which are most likely to offend susceptible readers fall at the end of their respective chapters. In the same way, the presumably more 'offensive' chapters and themes increase as one approaches the end of the book. The materials have also been so selected as to give the same relative length and prominence, to each chapter, as jokes about the subject of such chapters have been more frequently or less frequently encountered, both in books and 'in the field.' It is of obvious significance, therefore, that Chapter 8, "Marriage," is almost twice as long as any other; suggesting — since, after all, most of the inventors and tellers of jokes must unquestionably be men and not women — that monogamic marriage, as practiced in the West, is actually the principal focus of male sexual anxiety.

The present volume or series, containing the first nine of the fifteen main subject-groupings into which erotic and scatological jokes may be divided, is intended to be followed by a Second Series (already completed) covering, in equal detail, jokes on the following themes: Homosexuality, Prostitution, Venereal Disease, Castration, Dysphemism & Cursing, and Scatology. These are subjects presumably of less ordinary occurrence or of greater psychological danger or violence, and are therefore theoretically of greater anxiety-content than those in this First Series. Their jokes are certainly both more graphic and more cruel, to match the more extreme anxieties they are intended to express and allay. It might be said, therefore, that the present series contains the *'clean'* dirty jokes, while the Second Series will contain the *'dirty'* dirty jokes. Actually, as with the similar distinction between 'black humor' and 'good humor,' such divisions are purely relative and to a degree meaningless. The jokes that any specific reader will consider 'clean' or 'dirty' are almost entirely so judged subjectively, on the basis of that reader's own life experience and anxieties. There are just as many tellers-of and listeners-to jokes — I am one of them — in whom great anxiety is precipitated (or alleviated) as much by jokes about sexual sadism or marital humiliation as by jokes on such theoretically more 'nasty' or unsettling subjects as homosexuality, prostitution, venereal disease, castration, or scatology, which have been reserved for the Second Series, along with the many dysphemistic jokes turning strictly on 'obscene' vocabulary or cursing.

Formidable difficulties in both the collection and arrangement of the present text have been solved, more or less well, by the use of the format already consecrated to the analysis of jokes in Sigmund Freud's *Wit and Its Relation to the Unconscious* (1905), as translated into English by A. A. Brill in 1916. A more recent continuation of Freud's approach, and psychoanalytic point of view, is Dr. Martha Wolfenstein's deeply compassionate *Children's Humor* (1954). I am proud to have learned a great deal from both these works. In the format here, the jokes are given in *italics,* with the historical and analytic discussion in Roman type. This serves the double purpose of 'ventilating' the analytic text — which would otherwise be far too ponderous and compact, especially on such a subject as bawdy and scatological jokes and folklore — and of making it possible to present an inordinately large body of field-collected jokes and library-researched analogues in a subject arrangement that can, if necessary, stand on its own logic, without recourse to the textual discussion. That is to say, perfectly frankly, that the editor has been given to understand that there are many people who will confine themselves strictly to the *italic jokes,* and will skip all the laborious discussion, the way readers are known impatiently to skip the 'descriptions' of scenery and the weather in novels. I only hope that there will be no one so unutterably stuffy as to read only the discussion — of such a subject as this — and to skip all the jokes. Actually, it has not been my intention either to offend anyone or to entertain anyone, though I am sure I will be guilty of both.

II

The clearest general statement as to the social and psychological function of erotic humor is that of Freud, in *Wit and Its Relation to the Unconscious,* chap. 3, significantly grouping "Hostile and Obscene Wit." 'The smutty joke,' says Freud, 'is like a denudation of a person of the opposite sex toward whom the joke is directed. Through the utterance of obscene words, the person attacked is forced to picture the parts of the body in question, or the sexual act, and is shown that the aggressor himself pictures the same thing. There is no doubt that the original motive of the smutty joke was the pleasure of seeing the sexual displayed.' That the 'attacked' and 'denuded' person is, generally, a woman, when the joke-teller is a man, shows clearly that the telling of jokes in this way is actually intended as a modified form of rape: verbal rape rather than physical — a sort of seduction or preparation of the woman for the man's actual physical approach.

Freud also observes that if the woman shows herself unwilling, or if the social situation is such — owing to the presence of third parties — that the affair cannot readily be brought to any physical conclusion, the man's jokes will become more and more hostile, and more insistent in their denudation and even degradation of the woman. In such cases, the feint will often be engaged in of directing the jokes presumably to the (male) third party present, instead of to the woman herself. When the male third party happens to be the woman's husband, lover, or companion, the situation of joke-telling becomes then a covert form of *verbal adultery,* with the husband or lover as unconscious confederate. As Freud describes the process: 'As soon as the libidinal impulse of the first person [the man], to gratify himself through the woman, is blocked, he immediately develops a hostile attitude towards this second person [the woman], and takes the originally intruding third person as his confederate. Through the obscene speech of the first person, the woman is exposed before the third person, who now as a listener is bribed by the easy gratification of his own libido.' D. H. Lawrence develops this passage into the standard parlor-scene it creates, in *Lady Chatterley's Lover* (Florence, 1928), in an early chapter showing Lady Chatterley being required to sit quietly at her needle-work while her impotent husband and his friends talk anti-woman bawdy before her.

This is not, however, the only function of erotic humor and of bawdy jokes, and is not the function of scatological humor at all. The frequent occurrence of excrementitious substances, such as feces, urine, and even vomit, and of ghastly images, horrible accidents, genital injuries and mutilations — in a word, the castration theme — in 'dirty' jokes and poems known to many thousands of men and women in our culture, requires a further word of explanation as to the function of sexual humor.

The ordinary dirty joke (or limerick, or ballad) engages directly and apparently therefore pleasurably with taboo themes: sex, scatology, incest, and the sexual mocking of authority-figures, such as parents, teachers, policemen, royalty, nobility (Englishmen, millionaires, and movie-stars), clergymen, and gods. The telling of dirty jokes, like the whispering of bawdy words to strange women in the street or by telephone, or the chalking of genital monosyllables on walls, serves in its simplest form — as shown by Freud — as a sort of vocal and inescapable sexual relationship with other persons of the desired sex. It is for this reason that listeners not wanting such relationships will agree to listen to dirty jokes only with the proviso '. . . If they're *clever.*' 'Clever' means that all taboo words and graphic descriptions will be avoided in the telling, thus allowing the listener either to accept, or (by not laughing or 'not understanding') to refuse to accept, the intimacy of any particular *double entendre.* Jokes not conforming to this rule are the opposite of clever: they are 'stupid.' That is to say, they are unavoidably clear, and lacking in indirection — verbal rape, as opposed to verbal seduction.

There is, however, an entirely different function that the retailing of obscenities performs. For this function, the grosser the vocabulary and the more horrible and excruciating the actual content of the joke or poem, the better it seems to serve. The purpose here is to absorb and control, even to slough off, by means of jocular presentation and laughter, the great anxiety that both teller and listener feel in connection with certain culturally determined themes. The really fearful themes, in our society, are, above all: venereal disease, homosexuality, and castration. A non-sexual example of this same technique would be the "My Most Embarrassing Moment" columns vying for popularity with the "Clever (*i.e.* unrepressed) Sayings of Children" in newspapers, where the anxiety allayed is concerned with socially rather than sexually taboo behavior. Actually, the "Clever Sayings of Children" appearing in the public prints are pitifully expurgated, or pre-selected by parents (and editors) to be nothing other than charming and cuddly-cute. The reality of the life of the child is very different, and often bitterly frightened and sad, and the real humor of children turns largely on their two main taboo themes: scatology, and attempts to deal with the knowledge or suspicion of the sexual intercourse of the parents. Both these themes are dealt with at some length in the opening chapter of the present work, and, in particular analytic detail, in Dr. Wolfenstein's *Children's Humor,* to which the reader is referred.

Scatological themes, which will be treated in the closing chapters of the Second Series (to follow later), clearly fall into the anxiety-laden group too, if only from the dysphemistic grossness of their vocabulary and the graphic images employed. It is noticeable, however, that jokes, limericks, &c., wildly tossing around and finally eating — the "Food-Dirtying" theme — vomit, feces, and other bodily excrements thought to be particularly indelicate (as hair, nasal mucus, preputial smegma, and 'toe-punk': all frequent motifs), actually concern materials that are not, in themselves, of fearful nature, but are rather of daily familiarity, though surrounded with taboos. It is the explosive flaunting of these taboos that the scatological joke attempts, along with a foisting-off of the terror at breaking the taboo on the unwilling listener.

In many jokes on themes more taboo than simple sexuality, the person 'denuded' by the joke is really the teller himself — or herself. In fact, most joke-tellers have their own personal styles, not only of treatment and vocabulary, but of preferred subjects. Many of their stories, or their favorite stories, circle insistently about a single taboo theme, such as castration or homosexuality, and it is not difficult to see that they are, in such stories, allowing their own conscious or unconscious problems a socially acceptable avenue of expression and petcock of release. Listeners also have their styles: the 'dirty' stories over which they invariably break up in gales of laughter, where jokes of other types leave them untouched and often contemptuous.

There are also national styles to be discerned, though it is necessary to go cautiously here. Germans and the Dutch, for example, are obviously far more susceptible to scatology in humor than to any other theme. This is doubtless a reaction to excessively strict and early toilet-training, and general rigidity and compulsiveness in the Teutonic upbringing and character, and is an open release for the resultant 'cleanliness complex' in later life, common in all Anglo-Saxon cultures. A clever joke-teller can bring the usual German audience to quite a high pitch of screaming entertainment, rolling out of their seats, and so forth, just by *preparing* to tell a joke of which the inevitable punchline must include the word 'shit' (sometimes built up to the reduplicative '*Scheissdreck*'), without ever even beginning the joke. This is essentially the technique of the shaggy dog story, playing entirely on the listeners' nervous expectation and unconscious involvement. I was myself once witness to such a story-telling session, at Cagnes-sur-Mer, France, in 1955, at which a German prince of the most exquisite manners and courtesy evinced only a quite refined amusement, but later expressed his real appreciation by sending me a whole series of scatological postal cards from Italian spas, all turning on the humor of persons unable to get into toilet-cubicles when 'taken short,' and be-shitting themselves gloriously (shown printed in brown ink).

In the very interesting *Four-Letter Word Games: The Psychology of Obscenity* (New York, 1967) by the Dutch psychiatrist, Dr. Renatus Hartogs, and Hans Fantel, the concluding chapter, "Dirty Humor," p. 163–77, notes Dr. Hartogs' life-long collecting in this field in many countries, and opens with some autobiographical anecdotes demonstrating the anal concentration or touchiness of Dutch and German humor. With this should of course be compared the humor of 'goosing,' or tickling the anus of another person with the finger as an allusion to pedication, both in the rough horse-play of men and boys, and on the vaudeville stage for many centuries. The Dutch social historian, J. M. Huizinga, in his *Confessions of a European in England* (London, 1958) p. 44–5, also gives an anecdote — almost too 'innocent' to have been wholly accidental — of having destroyed his own social career in England by erroneously saying *pump shit* when he meant to use the polite euphemism for urination: *pump ship*. (The passage is quoted in full in Edward Sagarin's *The Anatomy of Dirty Words,* New York, 1962, p. 58–60.) Dr. Hartogs goes on to attempt to typify national characters according to their favorite themes in jokes, p. 167–9, stating:

The main concern in Gallic off-color stories is the refinement and variation of sexual technique . . . Aside from its main focus on sexual technique, the French dirty joke concerns itself with such corollary subjects as cuckolding and the more amiable aspects of seduction. Amiability, in fact, is the key word in describing most French obscenities. This stands in marked contrast to their Anglo-Saxon equivalents, whose principal trait is one of nastiness and disguised aggression. . . .

Sexual maturation in the context of such a culture [France] is relatively non-traumatic for both men and women. This may well account for the aura of pleasantness in most French sex jokes and their concentration on adult satisfaction, in contrast to the anal-regressive, adolescent, and often cruel sex jokes heard elsewhere.

In England, for example, I was struck by the high proportion of jokes referring to homosexuality. The incestuous component also seems to figure prominently in English jokes, mother-fixations of confirmed bachelors being a standard ingredient.

Oral-genital jokes enjoy high currency in the United States. . . . The racial antagonisms peculiar to the American environment also find frequent expression in dirty humor.

It may be stated axiomatically that: *a person's favorite joke is the key to that person's character,* a rule-of-thumb all the more invariable in the case of highly neurotic persons. The artless directness with which the joke-teller's deepest problem is sometimes expressed, under the transparent gauze of the 'favorite joke,' is like the acting out of a charade of self-unveiling, or like the sending of a psycho-telegraphic S.O.S. to the audience, whose sympathy and understanding are being unconsciously courted. A woman who had lost a leg during World War II and had to wear an artificial limb, with the unexpected result that perverted men began following her in the subway and whispering sexual invitations to her (that is, *to the leg she had lost* — as she put it — since they had never paid her any attention before), told as her favorite joke, or rather as the only one she could remember, with the apology: 'It's really just a play on words: *"Anybody can make a mistake," as the hedgehog said when he got down off the hairbrush.'* (Paris, 1954.) Her whole sexual tragedy is unconsciously summed up in that one foolish Wellerism, apologizing for the wooden leg that had destroyed her erotic image of herself.

The writing of the present book was inspired, in fact, by another such experience, many years ago, in which again the person telling the joke was a woman, in this case a very respectable Jewish woman of middle age, encouraged to add something at a joke-telling session by her grown-up children and their friends. It should be noted that this woman's life with her husband was gruellingly unhappy, an unhappiness the children and neighbors all knew about and shared. As usual with amateur joke-tellers, particularly women, she stated that she did not know (or could not remember) any jokes, but finally agreed that she did know one. In fact, it was her favorite, she admitted, but it was 'too awful' to tell. On being urged, she told this story, obviously of Middle European origin, though the same story is well known in the United States, with a judge or a marriage counsellor replacing the original rabbi. *A man goes to the village rabbi and says he wants to divorce his wife "because she has such filthy habits." "What are these habits?" the rabbi asks. "Oh, I can't tell you," says the man; "it's too filthy to describe!" The rabbi refuses, under those circumstances, to grant him the divorce. "Well, if I must I must," says the man. "I'll tell you. Everytime I go to piss in the sink, it's always full of dirty dishes."* (Scranton, Pa., 1936.) Other than the obvious level of self-unveiling here, of the woman's unhappiness with her brutal and egoistic husband, there is perhaps a further level, even better concealed, in which the joke complains of woman's woes concerning the household chores that make her too tired and unready to enjoy her sexual life, here alluded to in almost infantile terms as her husband's 'pissing in the sink.' It is in this fashion, and from this analytic viewpoint, that the present collection has been transcribed and interpreted.

III

What we are dealing with here, in a large number of cases, and what is probably one of the main functions of folk-humor, is an interesting folklore mechanism of great importance and relative frequency, which, as I have never seen it directly discussed, may well be worth a brief comment. It is the *rationalization* — the attempt to make understandable, or at least believable, even endurable, if only as a 'joke' — of some highly-charged neurotic situation into which the original folk-teller of the tale has stumbled, or has found himself forced to live, perhaps out of his own (or her own) psychological need. The folktale or joke therefore represents a protective mechanism whereby the seriousness, and even the physical *reality*, of the situation can be denied and made light of, by telling it — or by accepting some serious original anecdote describing it — simply as a joke; as something allowing the accumulated tension of living this situation, or telling about it, or listening to it, to relieve itself in the harmless but necessary explosion of laughter. This is perhaps the principal function of the creation of humor, and certainly of the accepting of things as humorous, such as cuckoldry, seduction, impotence, homosexuality, castration, death, disease, and the Devil, which are obviously not humorous at all. Sexual humor is a sort of whistling in the dark, like Beaumarchais' Figaro, who "laughs so that he may not cry."

An extreme example of the transmutation of what is unendurable in life into the pleasurable experience of humor — of what is a matter of anxiety to believe could really happen, into what is a matter of laughter as an 'impossibility' or a 'joke' — is the ancient and famous folktale, "*Cocu, battu et content.*" This story first appears in Europe in Boccaccio's *Decameron* (1353) Day VII, Tale 7, and was given the above title, by which it is usually known and which ticks off perfectly each of its three essential 'traits,' in the *Contes et Nouvelles* of La Fontaine in 1665. It is one of the most widespread and popular of European folktales, and a Russian version appears as the final story in the *Russian Secret Tales* (1872) of Aleksandr N. Afanasyev, an erotic supplement to his standard collection *Narodnye russkie skazki* (Popular Russian Tales, 1855–64). A very full bibliographical note on other European versions of the same story, in many languages, appears in the notes to Afanasyev [attributed to Prof. Giuseppe Pitrè] in *Kryptádia* 1888, IV. 250–52, now translated in the American edition of *Russian Secret Tales* (New York: Brussel & Brussel, 1968). Further references to this widespread tale will be found in D. P. Rotunda's *Motif-Index of the Italian Novella* (Bloomington, Indiana, 1942) at Motif K1514.4.1, appropriately hidden among Motifs K1210–1599, "Deceptions," along with several hundred other erotic jokes and folktales that Dr. Rotunda was not permitted to index otherwise under Prof. Stith Thompson's Motif-Index system at X700, "Humor concerning Sex," the model on which his Index was based.

From any psychological viewpoint, the story "*Cocu, battu et content*" is nothing other than a straight description — as though seen by a mocking outsider — of a very obvious sado-masochistic 'game' or insincere comedy, involving eventually, as the final situation or 'pay-off,' the willing submission to transvestism and flagellation on the part of the husband, elaborately set up by the victim himself (though rationalized, in the Russian version, as being set up by the wife instead: her 'game' instead of his), on the pretext of testing the wife's virtue with the presumed lover, who has intercourse with the wife and administers the beating to the husband. The victim also significantly comes home, half-dead, rejoicing at the mistreatment he has suffered, since this 'proves' his wife's virtue; and he expresses not only his contentment with what has happened to him, but his contentment with her. This is apparently folk-shorthand or expurgation, for the hidden but necessarily implied part of the story, that the husband is now able to be sexually potent with his wife, after he has been desexed (in women's clothing) and flagellated, as he was *not* able to be until "cuckolded, beaten and content," which is presumably why she was unfaithful to him in the first place.

This would be a very good example, if it were a true story instead of a folktale — but it probably *was* originally a true story, and may even repeat itself spontaneously in real life from time to time, in various countries, including this one — of Dr. Eric Berne's summing-up, in his sardonically humorous *Games People Play* (1964), of "The Players," that: 'Many games are played most intensely by disturbed [*i.e.* prepsychotic] people; generally speaking the more disturbed they are, the harder they play.' By 'harder' Dr. Berne means dangerously and mercilessly, whether to oneself or others. The excuse for this 'hard-playing' in the *commedia dell'arte* con-games of daily life that Dr. Berne describes with desperately penetrating gallows-wit is also to be discerned in the contrary rule that he candidly notes: 'Curiously enough, some schizophrenics seem to refuse to play games, and demand candidness from the beginning.' They are not, of course, for all their candidness, any the less schizophrenic. One is reminded of the current beatnik or hippie pose, or 'beat-Zen' *ethos,* of dogged and inconvenient impulsiveness and truth-telling — especially when these hurt or destroy everyone involved — on the pretext of a theoretically total but actually quite false revolt against the 'conventional lies of civilization' (Nordau), for which other conventional lies, of anti-civilization, have simply been substituted, such as that the roaring of mountain lions or meaningless vocables strung together are poetry, and that the Marquis de Sade was a great philosopher. (Zen-Sadism?)

As to folktales or jokes, a good rule of thumb might be that those stories in particular may be considered *folk-rationalizations,* of psychologically disturbed behavior and 'games,' which are concerned in their main and pivotal traits with behavior obviously opposed to the cultural norms, or opposed to the individual's own actual advantage, and regularly appearing only in psychopathic personalities as they are now understood. (See the excellent study by Dr. Hervey Cleckley, *The Mask of Sanity,* 1950.) Among these abnormal and anti-cultural traits are, for instance, practically all of those appearing in "*Cocu, battu et content,*" and in the pornographic fantasies and real case histories which are the truth hidden behind it, and the details it cannot give: the assuming of the clothing of the opposite sex (very common now among Western women, on one pretext or another, in impersonation of men; but still not generally allowed to men), the conniving at sado-masochistic humiliations and tortures, and all the palette of comedy cuckoldry, from wife-sharing to seminal exsufflation. ("*Oho!*" *cries the husband of the barren wife* [in another joke], "*I'm planting them, but that bugger of a bishop eats them up!*") Eventually the relationship with the 'other man' is seen to bulk significantly larger, on a proto-homosexual basis, than the relation with the woman herself, as will be discussed much more fully in Chapter 9, "Adultery."

Another important area of this sort of folk-rationalization in humor, which cannot be covered in the present volume, is the use of comedy-insanity — 'nut' or 'bop' jokes, 'sick' jokes, and all the elaborate *non sequiturs,* as to shaggy dogs, elephants, &c. (Sometimes these are only half-rationalized, as mere lies or tall-tale exaggerations, or the temporary delirium of drunkenness, as in the 'nonsense' rigmaroles and 'impossibility' songs of the older folklore.) One such story-type has been excellently handled by Brian Sutton-Smith, " 'Shut Up and Keep Digging': The Cruel Joke Series," in *Midwest Folklore* (1960) x. 11–22, and a few specifically sexual examples of this type will be given at the opening of Chapter 14 (Second Series), in the section on "Dysphemism." Any story is relevant that involves the actual *mise-en-scène* of the insane asylum itself, or any equivalent of it, such as an army induction center, a marriage-counsellor's (formerly rabbi's) or physician's office, or a psychoanalyst's couch, this last tacitly replacing the older stories' confessional booth, for only in these may the 'hidden horrors of the human heart' be openly avowed, and even there without having to *face* the analyst or confessor.

In all these stories and lesser forms, the rationalizing purpose of the humorous insanity is to excuse or explain *the inexplicable irrationalities of the sane,* which are obviously felt by the folk-tellers to be more serious, somehow, and more disturbing — more necessary to be *laughed off,* in the popular and very exact phrase — than mere insanity. A striking example of this is given in the article, "Texture, Text, and Context," by Dr. Alan Dundes, in *Southern Folklore Quarterly* (1964) XXVIII. 259–61, in a joke on three comedy-lunatics who — as the joke carefully spells out its hidden colloquial phrase — literally cannot 'tell their ass from their elbow,' or 'from a hole in the ground.' (The folklore of the elbow — also the knee, especially of girls — remains to be charted, from the superstitions and divinations connected with kissing one's elbow, or the proto-masturbatory admonitions about putting nothing larger than the elbow into one's eye — nor beans up one's nose: the whole Struwwelpeter set of cautionary horrors — to its appearance in Shakespeare's *Henry V,* in the comedy scene, Act II.v, of the French princess' mispronunciations of obscene Anglo-French homonyms . . . and 'elbow.')

As it happens, this joke is of much earlier provenance than the text collected by Dr. Dundes in 1961. In an earlier form, which I collected from an Italian scientist, it is anti-German (as also in a Yiddish form, on *tochus,* even older), and the scientific Teuton finally betrays the hollowness of his boasted linguistic science in the punchline: "*Must be scientific! Systematic! German! Got to use your* ASS!" (*Tapping himself on the forehead.*) Many of us, who refuse to forget the 'scientific' *Vernichtung* by the Nazis of six million Jews — and a nearly equal number of Poles, Gypsies, and others — would be glad to believe that the scientific irrationality of our German friends, and their current imitators, is *only* insanity.

Dr. Dundes follows his version of this story with an extraordinary flyting or 'crossing' of horrible castration jokes by two real informants, a husband and wife, in which — in jocular form, *of course,* and in in each other's presence — each describes having castrated the other by means of a pretended foolish literalism, and further pretends to be carrying around the other's cut-out organ, which is then offered 'insanely' to the listener's view! The leading line, certainly, in all these insane and insane-asylum variants and charades, as in the older wise-fool jokes, is the idea that one can get away with anything if only one acts crazy enough (*Hamlet, Goha, Schweik*), and that simply and actually being insane is perhaps the best rationalization of all. We are now becoming aware of the dangerously anti-rational currents in modern life, as a mute and largely unconscious resistance against the dehumanizations of a scientifically-oriented, technocratic society. This is one of them.

The approach to folk-humor suggested here, involving, as it does, difficult assessments of motive and pretext, and at least an attempt at psychological and sociological insight, may nevertheless prove useful in bringing some order out of the chaos of that very large category of folktales and folksongs involving anti-social or anti-natural behavior, especially in the areas of food, sex, scatology, sado-masochism, and their various combinations. Exactly in the style of modern war comic-books and the almost identical secret-agent movies, it is observable that many of the more ferocious Italian *novellieri* of past centuries, such as Bandello, and the more ruthless *fabliaux* and folk-ballads, such as "The Eaten Heart" (Child Ballad 269), do not present their materials as jokes or made-up stories at all, but as factual relations concerning the violent and insensate actions of real persons, generally named, and implied to be historical, such as Bluebeard and Rasputin.

What is suggested here is not that all these stories are necessarily true, and personages such as Bluebeard truly historical. (Yet what about Gilles de Retz, an historical psychopath certainly, pinpointed by legend as the original Bluebeard?) What is meant is that these stories and individuals do personify what the tellers and singers well know to be real but inexplicable peculiarities of human behavior, which they are attempting somehow to fit into a rational view of the world, whether as horror or as humor. The original horrible anecdote, secret gossip, or historical fact, working its way down slowly to innocuousness, as nothing more than a nursery rhyme or laughable tale — as with Charles Perrault's incorporating the legend of Bluebeard into his *Contes de ma Mère l'Oye* (Mother Goose Tales) — represents an effective and time-tested folk method of dealing with the unbearable abnormalities of human conduct, of which the emotional impact and scars cannot in any other way easily be sloughed off, either by the innocent or sometimes by the guilty.

Nothing further will be said here, in a general way, on these matters. A very full and elaborate chapter, which will in many ways serve as a further historical introduction to the whole field of erotic folk-humor, has already been published in my collection of essays,

The Horn Book: Studies in Erotic Folklore and Bibliography (1964) p. 454–93, under the title "Toward a Motif-Index of Erotic Humor." As to the psychological elements of various jokes and kinds of jokes, it will be necessary to refer to the separate chapters here. As has already been observed, every kind of joke has its own special amateurs, both among tellers and listeners. The reader is forewarned that there is not one Rationale of the Dirty Joke, but many.

IV

The basic float of modern American and British bawdy jokes and other erotic folklore, on which this work is based, has only rarely been recorded in print, and then only in very small part. The principal documentary records are all, without exception, rare or even unique printed volumes and manuscripts, which cannot by any stretch of the imagination be considered to have had any effect whatsoever on the actual oral transmission of their jokes among the thousands or millions of people telling such jokes, of whom only an infinitesimal percentage (or sometimes none) can be presumed to have had access to the printed or manuscript works. The principal printed documents include the erotic British magazine, *The Pearl* (1879–80), and its various sequels — on which, and on all the following, see the Bibliography at the end of the Second Series — and the very rare printed books, *Forbidden Fruit: A Collection of Popular Tales* [Scotland, about 1890, only one copy known], *The Stag Party* [Boston? about 1888, only one copy known], and the unexpurgated *Anecdota Americana,* Series 1 and 2, of Fliesler and of Smith [New York, 1927–34], both with the fictitious imprint 'Boston: Humphrey Adams.'

A particular effort has been made to search out manuscript joke-collections which have never been published because of their forthright unexpurgaiety. Many of these have been found and others are known to exist, though buried in the files of jealous collectors who will not allow them to be seen. Still others have been destroyed by the shocked widows, finding them among their husbands' papers after their deaths, though it is my studied impression that the widows — for whom everyone has a hard word — do not cause half as much trouble as the jealous and privative book-collectors and *soi-disant* bibliophiles. Among the manuscripts which have nevertheless been unearthed, the most valuable have been *A Treasury of Erotic and Facetious Memorabilia* [America, about 1910? — Kinsey Library]; the brief *Anecdota Erotica, or Stable Stories* (New York, 1924—NYPL: 3*), compiled by the American philologist, Frank J. Wilstach; the exceedingly important *"Unprintable" Ozark Folklore* volumes (1949–57: Library of Congress, Music Division) of Vance Randolph, and Idaho *Barnyard* collections (1952) of Kenneth Larson (Indiana University Folklore Archive); and the valuable British compilation, *Union Jack* (Chelmsford, Essex, 1954), made specifically for the present work by a very good friend. Many more recent collections have been made by students, in the form of Masters' theses or archived materials, for the Department of Folklore of Indiana University (where the extraordinarily valuable materials of the Institute for Sex Research will now also be found), and of the University of California at Los Angeles, as well as several others, in particular the University of Texas at Austin.

In addition to these primary printed and manuscript collections of modern Anglo-American materials, the entire literature of erotic folklore and folk-humor in other languages has also been very carefully explored, and mapped in part (in *The Horn Book*, 1964), though certainly not exhaustively researched and collated, which is obviously a bigger job than any one person can reasonably be expected to undertake. As will be seen in certain cases — of which the number could easily be very much increased — historical analogues and Levantine or European 'originals' of the jokes here presented are traced as far back, on occasion, as the Greek *Astéia* or *Philogelos,* attributed to Hierocles and Philagrius in the 9th century A.D.; the *Arabian Nights* (10th century), and the derivative Italian *novellieri,* such as Boccaccio. Most crucial, in the printed history of erotic jokes and humor, are the earliest European jestbook compilers, beginning with Poggio Bracciolini, Heinrich Bebel, and Girolamo Morlini (15th and 16th centuries), all three of whom translated into Latin, the Esperanto of their time — not as expurgation, but for ease of international transmission — the folk-jests they had collected 'in the vulgar tongue.'

I have already noted, in *The Horn Book*, p. 462–8, that: One of the most striking characteristics of the jestbooks, their wholesale and inveterate copying from one another, has often been observed, but without ever drawing the clear inference that these collections — which derive mainly from one another, and seldom from coeval folk sources — are not so much being alimented by folk sources as constituting, themselves, a main source of the jokes in oral transmission. As to their copying from one another, that is only one intermediate step in their migrations: from one mouth to another, one book to another, one land to another. Almost the entire French belletristic literature and poetry of the crucial sixteenth century stem from Italy, just as the English literature and poetry of the sixteenth and seventeenth centuries take their inspiration from France (only occasionally directly from Italy, *via* translations, as in Shakespeare's sources). Of nothing is this more true than of the popular or sub-literary art of humorous tales and jokes, arriving in Italy and Spain in the first place from and during the centuries of the Arab conquest. That is the main bridge for western European folktales and jokes, and any such tale or joke that can be traced at all will generally be found to follow backward this same itinerary: through France, to Italy (or Spain), and thence to the Levant. The Slavonic and Germanic tales do not even make this Western detour, but pass directly up through Asia Minor, via Turkey and Greece, to eastern Europe. This answers the question, tiresomely reiterated, *"Who invents jokes?"* Jokes are not invented; they are evolved. And they arrive to us from other countries and older civilizations, by way of oral and printed infiltrations over a period of centuries, and along certain massive and rather well delimited cultural highways . . .

Particular attention should be drawn to three rare works presenting Modern Greek, Arabic, and other Levantine erotic tales and fool-stories: *La Fleur Lascive Orientale* ('Oxford' [Bruxelles: Gay & Mlle. Doucé], 1882), anonymously translated from the originals by J.-A. Decourdemanche, an even rarer English retranslation also existing ('Athens' [Sheffield: Leonard Smithers], 1893); *Contes Licencieux de Constantinople et de l'Asie Mineure,* collected before 1893 by Prof. Jean Nicolaidès, and published after his sudden and mysterious death as the opening volume of a series imitating *Kryptádia*: *"Contributions au Folklore Erotique"* (Kleinbronn & Paris: G. Ficker [!], 1906–09, 4 vols.); and especially two modern French chapbooks, one entitled *Histoires Arabes* (Paris: A. Quignon, 1927), ascribed to an admittedly pseudonymous 'Khati Cheghlou,' and its sequel or supplement, *Les Meilleures Histoires Coloniales* (about 1935). Badly typeset and wretchedly printed, on miserable newsprint paper which will require photographic reduplication to preserve these invaluable works, this truly remarkable collection by the *rawi* or tale-teller 'Khati Cheghlou' (who

is believed to have been Albert Josipovici, secretary to the Khedive of
Egypt, and co-author with Albert Adès of the superb *Livre de Goha le
Simple*) is the last bloom in the grand proliferation of Levantine humorous tales, other than those included in the *Arabian Nights* themselves. In the hands of a scholarly annotator, of the stature of the 19th
century giants, Child, Chauvin, Pitrè, Wesselski, Bolte, Köhler (but
whither are they flown?!) the above works could serve as the Rosetta
Stone of the transmission of the extraordinary erotic stories of Ancient
Greece to the Arab world, and from the Arab world to Spain, Italy,
and the rest of Europe, probably via Jewish migrants and converts,
such as 'Pedro Alfonsi' (Moshè Sephardi), author of the *Disciplina
Clericalis,* about 1108 A.D., which started the modern Western vogue
of fiction.

Owing to the extraordinary increase in chapbook publishing facili-
ties in the seventeenth and eighteenth centuries, the paradoxical position was quickly reached where the native or 'original' folk content of
the jestbooks had most conspicuously dried up and was lacking, at exactly the period of their heaviest printing and greatest circulation, from
about 1700 to 1820. This is very similar to the present disaffected position in the popular arts, where, at the very moment of the greatest
technological possibility of mass circulation, in print, movies, television,
and so forth, the materials so circulated are of an almost total folk
falsity wherever they touch, or purport to touch, upon folklore, folksong, and the like. This situation has been developing generally since
the parodying of folksongs in the ballad-operas of the 1730's, if not
since much earlier with the "sacred contrefacts" or religious parodies
set to folk tunes at the very beginning of the Protestant Reformation.
The influence of the later jestbooks must, in the same way, be assessed
as in large measure bogus or fakeloristic—to use the term that has now
'passed into the language' — pumping tired and undesired jokes into a
disgruntled audience that would really have preferred something native
and 'new.'

Not until the Wild West humor of the American almanacs of the
1850's, and slightly earlier, and the frontier journalism of the John
Phoenix and Mark Twain type, was this 'new' element rediscovered:
the ancient art of telling tales and spinning whoppers in a droll and
leisurely fashion. But by then it was impossible to re-inject this element
into the jokebooks, which continued to retail all the ancient chestnuts
without any but unimportant dialect or costume changes, as for in-

stance the burnt-cork blackface of the bogus 'Nigger' minstrels; while the Twains, the Nasbys, and the other authentic native humorists had to make their careers in journalism and on the lecture platform (now radio and TV) instead.

The almost total disaffection of the audience came rapidly, after the expurgation of the jestbooks in the Anglo-Saxon culture in about the 1830's, on the wave of moralistic reaction and repression preceding and attempting to avert the revolutions of the 1840's. The expurgated jokes thereafter to be found in the English-language jokebooks and chapbook series (such as those of Wehman and the Ottenheimers until World War I, and Haldeman-Julius and Shomer until World War II) and in the dreary joke-columns of humorous journals of the period, such as *Punch*, later *Life*, the *Literary Digest*, and the college-humor magazines, have become increasingly different — not only in matter but in form — from the older tales and jokes. The folk nerve has been almost completely cut. Page after page and at machine-gun speed, these publications shoot out their hopeless puns and 'one-liners,' with less and less emphasis on art in the telling, or in fact on almost any verbal art; and with more and deeper reliance on improbable and even maniacal situations (the modern "sick" and "bop" jokes), on the accompanying illustration — which finally becomes everything, as in the comic books and *The New Yorker* — on hostile repartee and the 'quickie' format, and most of all on the brief and unsatisfying climactic pleasure of the verbal explosion or punch-line. Visibly dying, this sort of shrill and counterfeit slapstick is almost unrecognizable as the reliques or effluvia of folktales.

V

Very recently, and in response to the 'New Freedom' stemming from the 1930's U.S. court decisions liberating James Joyce's *Ulysses*, then— after a long pause — D. H. Lawrence's *Lady Chatterley's Lover*, Henry Miller's *Tropic of Cancer*, and even the two-century-old secret classic, Cleland's *Fanny Hill* (on the first day of Spring, 1966); the chapbook purveyors and jokebook compilers have attempted a comeback for erotic humor, realizing finally that it had now at last become possible, in the United States, openly to publish the unexpurgated folk-humor which had been exiled from their pages for over a century, since the great pre-Revolutionary cleanup of the 1830's in England. (French jokebooks were never cleaned up. See my collection of 120 modern items at Ohio State and s.f.p.l.) Thus it comes about that most of the current 'men's magazines,' and their side-publications of *Adult Stag Humor* books and so forth, now resolutely attempt a men's joke column, of theoretically sexual 'stag' jokes, which are, however, excruciatingly expurgated and still at the pussyfooting level of the large colored photographs of nude women, in which the same magazines actually specialize, still hiding their pubic hair as in the worst mid-Victorian kitsch of Biedermeyer and Bouguereau.

The truth of the matter seems to be that folk materials, and especially folk-humor of any authentic kind, do not and cannot flourish in the grubby environments of competitive and exploitative fakelore publication, of which the whole art has been nothing other than grotesque falsification for centuries. Whether dressed up in printed disguise, in the floppy quarto format and glossy paper of the 'quality' magazines, or soaring through the bullshit empyrean of movies, radio, television, and the other frankly propagandistic 'mass media' (for which the advertisers pay the freight and call the tune), folk-humor of this synthetic type has no real audience, no viability, and no future. It is relevant to quote here, I think, the conclusion of my article "Who Owns Folklore?" (1962), the applicability of which has certainly not diminished, but rather increases daily:

> The replacement of the arts of literature and the stage, since the First World War, by movies, radio, television, disc- and tape-recordings, and other mechanical substitutes and succedanea for the living experience, still in the womb of Time, has operated principally as a mass premium for mass illiteracy and passivity, and has had the effect, owing to the monumental and reduplicative censorships under which it staggers, not of making human communication more easy, more broad and instantaneous — as advertised — but of making it *impossible,* except for sexless and synthetic art, sadistic entertainments, and falsified information that no rational person wants to see broadcast at all. . . . When every human emotion or folk expression must be broken on the wheel beforehand, as the *sine qua non* of public performance, and forcibly reduced to the simultaneously watered-down and jazzed-up fakelore and kitsch, until nothing remains but pre-

fabricated human process cheese, wafted over with a garlic belch about the 'common man,' it seems almost unnecessary to observe that what passes for folklore and folksong — and of this *folk* — cannot possibly be anything under these circumstances but the most pitiful travesty.

Prof. Marshall McLuhan of Fordham University has lately made himself the St. Peter of the so-called mass media. Having denied them thrice, in the pages of Dwight Macdonald's *Politics* and my own magazine, *Neurotica,* in the 1950's, anatomizing and anathematizing them in slashing style; he has now heard the cock crow, where he sits warming himself by the fire (*Luke,* xxii. 55–60), and he has gone out and wept bitterly and publicly for his past lack of faith. He has made himself now the arch-disciple — and eventual Pope? — of these same mass media, in several works of which the most popular is entitled *Understanding Media* (1964), and of which the actual message — delightedly received by the 'media' whipmasters — is that nobody (least of all Prof. McLuhan) can understand them, and that they had jolly well better be taken on faith because they *exist* and are *electrical,* and also there is a hell of a lot of money tied up in them. In other words, like Tertullian in his reply to the Emperor Septimius Severus, he believes in them *because they are absurd.*

Thus, like a new Dr. Pangloss, Prof. McLuhan finds that all the cultural atrocities he once excoriated now somehow add up to a gloriously rosy future and the 'Best of all possible worlds.' And he accepts implicitly as gospel — and thus begs all of us faithfully to accept as the new and evolving human culture — not only all the worst and most anti-human mechano-cultural drivel and detritus of our century, and every kind of advertising propaganda and mass-muddlification technique (at their sinister best in wartime, of course), but also every new and as-yet unborn form of Pop-culch, Pop-art, Put-On art, and down to the lowest varieties of electro-mechanical kitsch and *quatsch* — which is the stuff that even people who like kitsch admit is lousy. Understandably phrased (something at which Prof. McLuhan does not shine, for all his titular pretensions), what 'The medium is the message' *really* means is, as Mary McCarthy has put it — and better — though not referring specifically to McLuhan (in *Fact,* 1964, No. 1, p. 7): *'Writing about mass culture for a mass audience [is] the mirror on the ceiling of the whorehouse.'*

With these fruity exotica of the popular-culture industry, which is a good deal older than Gutenberg's mere five hundred years, and at least as old as organized religion (note, for example, the profitable sale of silver shrines of the decayed 'virgin-mother' goddess, Diana of Ephesus, recorded in the *Acts of the Apostles,* xix. 24–7, as competing with the new Christian religion about the year A.D. 55), we have fortunately hardly to concern ourselves. Almost nothing of what has appeared publicly in print in English, until the last half dozen years, in the way of sexual folklore and humor — and certainly even less of what has been offered by the competing 'media' (*read:* religions) of motion pictures, radio, television, and mere printed paper — has had in it even the slightest truth or validity as the folklore it might pretend to be; and precious little humor either, if the truth be told, for all the laughs laboriously milked out of pre-warmed audiences by means of large signs held up out of TV-camera range, marked "LAUGHTER" and "APPLAUSE," in cynical contempt for the slob mentality of such audiences.

Of the rest — the authentic material — all of it has appeared either in privately printed quasi-pornographica obviously out of the economic reach of the real folk audience, or else in gruellingly expurgated form in the humor columns of magazine-digest magazines, and in the 'men's' leg-art and humor reviews directed to post-adolescent male readers, by whom in fact these very materials have usually been sent in (in *un*expurgated form), and to whom this watered-down retransmission can only be considered a form of adulterated industrial feedback.

It should be particularly observed that remarkable materials can still be collected in the Hispanic cultures of Mexico and of South America, and particularly in Greece and the Levant, in the way of erotic — and other — humor and folklore. These would well repay any folklorist who will set out to find them. The drying up of folk-sources which is so palpable at many levels in the English-speaking world (and not only as to erotic folklore, *bien entendu*), has 'progressed' much more slowly in these other cultures, owing specifically to their jealous clinging to their national heritage, language, and peculiarities, and to their purposeful rejection of the American melting-pot ideal of the turn of the 20th century. It is precisely this mistaken ideal, and its frightened rejection of all non-American national and historical past, that has so badly enfeebled American folklore — as the one outstanding example of this enfeeblement — in the struggle to hold its own against the encroachments and replacements by the popular-culture synthetic kitsch of movies, radio, television, the entertainment industry in general, and almost all the pop-level 'printed matter' offered for sale, from fakelore 'treasuries' both textual and pictorial, right down to humorous hate-cards and fake-*révolté* or fake-sentimental lapel-buttons, bumper-stickers, and the patriotico-propagandistic postage stamp cancellations, such as the never-to-be-forgotten government-sponsored "REPORT OBSCENE MAIL TO YOUR POSTMASTER" of the early 1960's in the United States. And the equally insincere and mock-religious official stamp-cancellation: "PRAY FOR PEACE" — meanwhile assiduously making war.

VI

A word as to the transcription system used for the jokes in the present work, and the indexing system intended to be their key.

As almost no collection of jokes has ever been published, in any language, in the exact words in which they were heard told, even in the case of very recent works based on phonographic and magnetic-tape transcriptions, it has not seemed essential to devote the great amount of space necessary to quoting all the jokes at full length, either as collected in the field (usually in ornately long form), or as given in the printed sources where versions (usually expurgated) may have appeared. The loss of many various authentic personal and humorous touches thus occasioned is of course regretted, but again the real intention here is not to entertain, but to record and interpret. Certain stories have been supplied in manuscript by other collectors, and are here printed verbatim, in particular the baker's dozen of stories — written down within a few hours of hearing them told, by the outstanding Ozark folklorist, Mr. Vance Randolph, for his unpublished collection, *Pissing in the Snow, and Other Ozark Folktales* (MS. 1954), from which he has given his special and very kind permission to select and to quote in full these extraordinary texts, and one other, "The Magic Walking Stick," a 'talking-vagina' story collected since.

Unless, therefore, a joke text in the present volume is set off from the rest of the page by indentation at both sides, or is printed in whole or in part within single quotation marks, it is *always* to be construed as rewritten in the present tense — and usually very much abbreviated — by the editor, even though cited to a printed work. Touches not appearing in the printed sources are added (parenthetically) from field-collected texts. Though this has been done quite sparingly, it is admitted to here so that there will be no semblance of falsifying the historical record. It should be understood very clearly that any printed sources not unmistakably signboarded as having been quoted verbatim, by means of indentation or by single quotation marks, are cited only for the terminal value of their DATE, as proving that a given joke was certainly then in existence — and probably in oral circulation — in a form reasonably close to that printed here. The correct and complete original text is, of course, available in the printed work cited, for anyone who cares to look it up.

All citations will be found fully amplified in the Bibliography at the end of the Second Series. The frequent citations '1:' and '2:' refer to the most important modern American published collection of erotic jokes, *Anecdota Americana,* issued in New York in 1927 with the fictitious imprint of 'Boston,' a work which in this original edition was collected and written by Mr. Joseph Fliesler, at that time publicity director for UFA Films. The second series, issued with the same title and 'Boston' imprint [by Smith, in New York] but with the date 1934, was not edited by Mr. Fliesler and is entirely different in tone, being far less broadly humorous and much more prone to the merely nasty. The *expurgated* work under the same title, edited and published by Mr. Samuel Roth, with imprint 'New York,' in 1933 (revised further as *The New Anecdota Americana,* 1944), has been referred to as infrequently as possible, and is mentioned here only to avoid any confusion with the original work that it imitates.

Aside from texts from print, field-collected jokes in the present work are indicated by the place and date of collection in parentheses at the end of each text. The two most common locations, New York City and Washington, D.C., are indicated by the initials N.Y. and D.C. respectively. Other than these necessary precisions as to source, both printed and oral, the scholarly apparatus will be found to have been kept here to a minimum. The real and intended emphasis of this research has been throughout on *the authentic and unexpurgated presentation of the jokes,* and on the serious interpretation of them thus made possible from the socio-analytic and psychoanalytic points of view.

American folklorists and many abroad have long been hampered, both in their researches and in communication with one another, by the lack of a motif-index or tale-type analysis of erotic folktales, jokes, and humor generally. This is mainly due to the fact that the whole erotic and scatologic area of folklore has been evaded in print by almost all academic English-speaking folklorists until very recently, in fact until the "Symposium on Obscenity in Folklore," delivered before the combined American Folklore Society and Modern Language Association in Philadelphia, December 28, 1960, and published — with regrettable and inappropriate expurgations — in the *Journal of American Folklore* (July 1962) vol. 75: p. 187–265. My own address, delivered at this Symposium *in absentia* as its principal portion (though very much abridged), is printed in full in *The Horn Book,* p. 237–88, under the title "Misconceptions in Erotic Folklore." The fact is there emphasized in some detail that not only the English-speaking folklorists and journal-editors have been recalcitrant to publish the unfalsified folk-record where the collected material is verbally erotic or 'obscene,' but that the open prudery of the Finnish folklore movement since the turn of the 20th century, and especially of its followers in America, has been even more debilitating.

As is well known, the *Motif-Index of Folk-Literature* by Prof. Stith Thompson of Indiana, in both its original edition (1932–36) and later revision (Copenhagen, 1955–58, in six volumes), and the many other motif-indexes based on the Thompson system, rigorously omit — or appear to omit — all classification of motifs in erotic and scatologic humor, allotting to this subject the numbers X700-799, "Humor Concerning Sex," but leaving these almost entirely *blank,* with the following note refusing any further responsibility:

> Thousands of obscene motifs in which there is no point except the obscenity itself might logically come at this point, but they are entirely beyond the scope of the present work. They form a literature to themselves, with its own periodicals and collections. In view of the possibility that it might become desirable to classify these motifs and place them within the present index, space has been left . . . for such motifs.

D. P. Rotunda, in reprinting this note in his *Motif-Index of the Italian Novella in Prose* (1942) p. 214n, adds the somewhat restive codicil: 'I quote this note from Professor Thompson . . . upon whose classification this Index is based. I agree that some line must be drawn, although some may question its allocation, and I leave the space free.' The question of allocation is evidently difficult. Another culture than our own might prefer to include the obscene motifs, and omit the hundreds of descriptions of horrible murders and sadistic mutilations at the sigla Q400, "Kinds of Punishment," and "S. — Unnatural Cruelty", "Revolting Murders or Mutilations", "Abandoned or Murdered Children," in the work of both Thompson and Rotunda, in which motifs there is certainly no point except the sadism itself. As I have made this particular cultural contradiction and intellectual blindspot the subject of an independent work, *Love & Death: A Study in Censorship* (1949), with fuller details of its application to the subjects of folksong and folklore in *The Horn Book,* p. 347–52, there seems no point in pursuing it further here.

It has proved entirely impossible to fit the sprawling body of erotic and scatologic folktales and jokes — even those of America and Britain over the last century — into the exact hundred index-numbers or sigla, X700–799, reserved for the world literature of this subject in Prof. Thompson's *Motif-Index of Folk-Literature,* with an unnavigable break in the exact middle, at X750–760, for jokes on old maids and courtship. Nevertheless, so far as has been practicable, without making the present text unreadably clumsy and plodding, the effort has seriously been made to organize the entire collection of over five thousand jokes (of which only about one-third are given here, selected as most representative) on a framework roughly of a tale-type or motif-index character. The indexing, and thus the sequence of the text, turns however on the psychological *nexus* or key to each story — the essential element without which it cannot exist — rather than solely on such merely formal or fortuitous elements as the age, nationality, or profession ascribed to the actors in the particular version of the story collected, which is the one worst fault of most existing folktale indexes. The approach is closest to Aarne's *Types of the Folktale* (Helsinki, 1961), with its invaluable bibliographical references.

In any case, the sterility of any *un*organized presentation of the jokes by themselves, without any systematic framework or attempted analytic annotation, has always been clear, particularly in regard to sexual humor. Without some such framework or logical sequence, and some meaningful approach to the evident historical and psychological undercurrents, so difficult and emotionally-charged a subject matter cannot easily be brought into understandable form. Any single chapter here will demonstrate the logical development made possible by means of this approach, and, I think, its superiority to the usual helter-skelter compilation.

No competition is intended with the usual unorganized collections of tales and jokes, whether 'clean' or 'dirty.' Of these, the proposed audience — and the compilers' purpose — has always been signally obscure, since the *Astéia* of Hierocles and Philagrius in the 9th century A.D. It is possible that such collections simply represent their compilers' repertoire and other collectanea, and that the act of publication is intended as a method of telling their jokes to audiences larger than those available in person, with all the usual satisfactions. Anyone who has seen professional music-hall and nightclub comedians 'working' — as, earlier, in vaudeville and burlesque — for example the late Lenny Bruce, whose specialty was the purposely shocking and obscene, will understand the obvious *need* that the performer has for the audience, whose presence and response (that shriving laughter!) are a precondition of the joke-teller's inspiration, the same mechanism whereby a bird soars on rising currents of air.

Few jokebook compilers, whether professional humorists or among the academic folklorists, have ever been able to resist the temptation of taking personal possession of the jokes, by adding a few flowers of their own rhetoric, or wry and imaginative touches of their own brand, to their orally-collected texts. This is certainly their right — 'Even folklorists are a kind of folk,' as has been said—but few of them have ever had the *echt* folk touch. Best of all, and least intrusive, was perhaps the great Humanist and bibliophile, Poggio, private secretary (*i.e.* ghost-writer) to seven Popes in the 15th century, who travelled all over Europe on the eve of the invention of printing, searching fervidly in the libraries of medieval monasteries 'after the manuscripts of lost works by ancient authors,' to be delivered eventually to the LIFE BEYOND LIFE (Milton's *Areopagitica*) of the printed page; and who at the age of fifty-five — after having had fourteen illegitimate children — married an eighteen-year-old girl, the beautiful Vaggia de' Buondelmonti, with whom he was exceedingly happy and by whom he had five further sons and a daughter. Poggio is remembered today for none of his great works, but for the *Facetiæ* he wrote at the age of seventy (the manuscript is dated 1451 at No. 240), in which he showed himself the first and most important joke-collector and editor of modern times. In this collection of two hundred and seventy-three tales, gathered in his travels and told in the *Bugiale*, or 'laboratory for fibs' of the papal secretaries, the older Arab-Italian *novella*, or lengthy folktale, is seen changing to the brief modern *facezia* or joke — punch-line and all.

VII

Duplications of jokes are inevitable in such a work as this, where the main effort has not been to present the jokes simply as humor, but to create a logical and analytic framework on which these and other jokes — to be collected later, possibly by other researchers — might be brought together. There has been no hesitation about giving the same story twice, under two different subject headings, where two or more important elements were involved, but in such cases different texts have generally been selected from different printed works or field-collections, rather than printing exact duplicates. Few jokes are really ever exact duplicates, not only because of minor variations over the centuries, or from mouth to mouth, but because of conscious refashioning by the tellers to suit their own psychological bent. A good example is the story with the verbal climax "*Ad-lib!*" or "*Fake it!*" in Series Two, in the chapter on Prostitution, section III, part 3, "Oragenital Acts," where, in two versions of what is visibly the same story, the entire meaning is shifted: one version is of the ultimate humiliation of a blonde prostitute by a blasé Indian prince; the other is an amusing misadventure in a perfectly mutual love-passage between a musician and a woman in the audience who has sought him out after being excited by his playing of the lovers' pastoral during a performance of *Tristan & Isolde*. These two versions do not appeal to the same sort of person — or even to the same sexes! — and certainly were not evolved by the same sort of persons, though both may very well have been musicians. The two versions are nevertheless printed together and confronted, since their *nexus* or pivotal turning point (the oragenital and musical lapse) is identical.

In the following chapter (12), in Series Two, the opposite situation will be seen. One tale reprinted in all editions of the *Oeuvres badines* of the 18th-century French erotic poet, Alexis Piron, which is still often collected in English, is that which he presents in *conte-en-vers* form as "Le Placet" (The Petition): *A nobleman, to whom a petition is submitted by a pretty young girl, will not stay to read it but seduces her forthwith, only to find — on finally reading her 'placet' — that it is a complaint against the doctor who was not able to cure her of venereal disease.* This same story is retold by François de Neufchâteau, at the time of the French Revolution, as "*La Consultation épineuse,*" with the nobleman modified to a mere lawyer, and the crashing venereal disease climax softened down to: *The girl sobs continuously that the man she is complaining of had done "that and more, and more, and more" — to wit, he had started all over, which the lawyer finds himself unable to do.* Neufchâteau's version has in turn been reprinted as the first piece in *Le Parnasse Hippocratique* of "Docteur Minime" (1884), omitting the poet's name in the reprint of 1896 and in various other sly ways palming off the *consultation* referred to as medical rather than legal. As collected in America in recent years, the story is invariably told about a priest in confession, with the 'more, and more' or 'worse, and worse' element taken precisely from Neufchâteau, but returning to the venereal disease dénouement of the Piron tale. *Priest: "What worse could he do than* that?!" *"Father," says the weeping girl, shaking down her skirt, "he gave me the clap."*

This is again a very good example of the difficulty of teasing out the really essential or pivotal point of any joke, a difficulty often due (as here) to the changes in protagonist undergone during the transmission and migrations of the joke. It is obvious that this tale, as nowadays told and collected in America, could and probably would be motif-indexed under Thompson's system at V20, "Confession of Sins," owing to the recent and irrelevant turn of its being cast in anti-clerical and anti-confessional form. It is equally obvious that it does not really belong there. Even if indexed not by personnel, but by the particular form of the climax collected, the Piron 'original' and the Neufchâteau modification of this identical tale might easily be widely separated under the Thompson system, at Q240, "Sexual Sins Punished," for the first, and possibly J1367, "Impotent Suitor Rejected," for the second.

From the operative point of view, of *the nexus on which the story unchangingly turns,* the real subject is seen to gravitate around the sudden climactic surprise or reversal, the Greek *para prosdokian,* the *unexpected,* closely related to Thompson's motifs X0-99, "Humor of Discomfiture." From the same position, *all* of the Thompson sigla, X200-599, "Humor of Social Classes," and X600-699, "Humor Concerning Races or Nations," and much of P400, "Trades and Professions" — representing about half of his whole treatment of the section "X. — Humor," other than those motifs taken bodily from the manuscript of Ernest Baughman's *Type/Motif Index of the Folktales of England and North America* (The Hague, 1966) — ought probably to be withdrawn and reclassified by the operative element, instead of the largely irrelevant and fluid personnel of nations, classes, and professions.

One particularly valuable result of the historical and geographical method in dealing with jokes — as opposed to the shotgun multiplication of motif-listings from various sources and disparate cultures — is the light it sheds and the assistance it very often provides, as in the "Placet" example, in integrating and tracing the real or *pivotal* motif, and separating this from the merely confusing background elements of personnel, punch-lines, and other adventitious trappings and 'gimmicks' forming part of the tellers' private art, which are transmitted later by the audience in good faith as somehow essential to the tale itself. This is the identical problem, or mystery, of the transmission of folksongs, in which every singer clings to, and generally imagines he is repeating, his version of a song word-for-word and note-for-note as he learned it — this being the only 'right' version — yet every version is different.

It should be clearly understood that the present collection has, in all cases of conflict, sacrificed textual length of the jokes to brevity, and the motif-index approach to the superior necessities of the parallel socio-psychological annotation. The identification of types and mechanisms of folk-humor has also been given precedence over any strict index approach. Undeniably, therefore, a good many of the jokes given here — intended to illustrate either the introductory portions of the chapters or special points as to form or technique of humor, rather than of subject-matter — at unlikely locations in the text must frankly be considered 'misplaced' even on their own system. But it has been thought more important for the present work — which is, after all, the first extended interpretive effort in this difficult field — to carry its own cross-references with it in this way, rather than try to create a rigidly patterned index system which might be of use, or even interest, only to specialists in folktale classification, or to persons mainly interested in 'safely' handling the living experience of erotic folklore *in a non-living fashion,* by means of the classificational pigeon-holes and jargonesque tongs which have been the curse of folklore study until now. A great deal more is said about this matter, and with a great deal more violent detail, in *The Horn Book* (1964) p. 237–88: the article "Misconceptions in Erotic Folklore," especially in its last twenty-four pages, to which the interested reader is urgently referred.

VIII

The motif-index or framework proposed here employs only two numbers, or at most three, separated by periods, to designate each specific subject, joke-type, or group of themes. These are the Arabic chapter-number, followed by a Roman numeral indicating the main sections of each chapter. If necessary, a final (decimal) number is added referring to the subsection. The complete reference or motif-index number, for any given subject or joke-type, is, for example, 4.III, or 10.V.6, depending on whether or not subsections have been made. This is not complicated and will be found easy to use. Obviously it will not lead directly to any specific joke, but it is not intended to do so. It is intended to index joke-themes and motifs. *It does not index the jokes.*

This system also leaves room for the supplementary or omitted motifs that will certainly be discovered later, which can then be added at the open ends of the main (Roman-numeralled) sections, in the relevant chapters, in the form of additional decimal subsections, such as 10.V.7, 10.V.8, and so forth. The exact logical position in the thematic development will not always be possible to achieve in this way, but for practical purposes it is close enough. The definitive and 'complete' motif-index of erotic humor still remains for the future. The caution must already be voiced that additional motif-numberings such as those just proposed, by means of new decimal subsections, should be conscientiously distinguished from any attempt at *numbering the jokes,* which is neither necessary nor desirable. An example of what should perhaps be avoided is Prof. Thompson's inclusion at X910–1815, "Humor of Lies and Exaggerations," of several hundred tall-tales picked up bodily from Baughman's manuscript, where they are simply consecutively numbered. This is not motif-indexing, or, if it is, it goes much too far in the direction of simply *numbering the jokes.* From that to mock-systematic boondoggling with one's materials, or running them through Hollerith hole-punching machines (the dehumanized 'Finnish system' of studying folklore) with the notion that one is learning something in that way, is but a step.

If it should ever really seem useful to coördinate the present index-system of erotic humor with the Thompson *Motif-Index,* at the blank purposely left there to receive it at X700, this can perhaps be done most simply by translating the present Roman numerals into Arabic form, and then adding — or imagining — the sigla 'X70' (NOT 'X700') at the beginning of each subject-reference of which the chapter number is below 10, and 'X7' for chaps. 10 and above: 4.111 thus becoming X704.3, and 10.v.6 becoming X710.5.6. (The two section-titles ventured in this area by Prof. Thompson, X750 "Jokes on old maids," and X760, "Jokes on courtship," would thus not be disturbed. Unfortunately, it is their obtrusive existence that has made it impossible to use the allotted hundred numbers X700–799 in a straightforward way, owing to the interruption they create at the exact center of any logical development, in which for example, "Jokes on courtship" would certainly come much closer to the beginning of any systematic presentation of sexual folklore. The six old-maid stories Prof. Thompson details, as his only subheadings, X751–756, are also far more fully documented in his own edition of Antti Aarne's *Types of the Folktale,* Helsinki, 1961, at Types 1475–1499, there including a dozen further old-maid stories — for which he proposes no motif-numbers at all.)

It will be observed that the present system really only employs the first fifteen digits available to it in the Thompson system, one for each chapter-number here, which can thus be added to the Thompson system, if desired, as sections X701–715. The sigla X700 and all the others from X716 through X799 (excepting always those old maids being courted at X750–760), are left open for introductory or supplementary materials that it may seem desirable to add later. Actually, the first fifteen digits have proved quite sufficient, and should continue to do so, by means of the decimal additions proposed above.

To assist as unobtrusively as possible with the subject or index framework offered here, every left-hand page of text carries its *chapter* number in the inner corner of the top margin, with the *section* numeral (in Roman numerals), and the subsection number, if any, following along in the top margin of the right-hand page facing. Thus, the upper inner corners of every two facing pages show the complete subject-reference or index-number for the subject being treated at that point. This is as invisible as an index system can be, and still be of any practical use. It is also less complicated than it may sound, as a glance at any page-opening in the text will show. These index-numbers are further set off [in square brackets] to avoid any possible confusion with the page-numbers at the outer corners of the same running headlines, and they can simply be overlooked unless needed, exactly as page-numbers are overlooked.

This is certainly all very clumsy, though perhaps not any more so than the whole idea of indexing or referring to Cinderella's symbolic slipper or Hans Carvel's even more symbolic ring *by numbers* in the first place. Some of the existing indices on the Aarne-Thompson system also add half the alphabet of capital letters after the number (for example, Types 1698A-through-N), sometimes with sub-coefficients in addition (Types $1525H_{1-4}$), and up to three asterisks, as in Types 1539**, "Truth-telling Member" [*i.e.* vagina!] and 1542**, 'formerly 1542*,' "The Maiden's Honor" — which the tailor-trickster promises to sew on for her — as well as Motifs of such numerical complexity as G303.16.19.17.1, for Rabelais' *"Papefiguière."* (K83.1). Prof. Thompson also notes, p. 8, that without the improved amenities of his new edition of Aarne, 'these asterisks might occasionally increase to twelve or fifteen.' This obviously requires only the addition of the area- and zip-codes, and possibly the joke-teller's social security number and checkbook (magnetic) code as well, to become a joke itself.

This has already been seen happening, as long ago as Octave Mirbeau's *La 628-E8,* in 1908 — with its scandalous and gruesome dossier concerning the death of Balzac, suppressed in most copies — and Hugo Gernsback's early utopian science-fiction hero, Ralph 124C41+. (A rebus.) Even more to the point are the *numbered* hero and heroine of Cyril Connolly's "Year Nine" (1938, reprinted in Dwight Macdonald's *Parodies: An Anthology,* 1960, p. 386–91), the brief and powerful satire on which Orwell's *1984* is based — Orwell's other 'sources' are listed in my *The Fake Revolt,* 1967, p. 20, and in *The Horn Book,* p. 317. Connolly's "Year Nine" is itself certainly the masterpiece of 20th-century black humor, quite aside from its quality as parody, of which another recent high-point is the same writer's "Bond Strikes Camp," which rips the mask off the endemic homosexuality of spy-thrillers — and spies. Openly presented as humor, there is also at the folk level the *joke about jokes told by their numbers,* satirizing the anti-human mechanization and intended total numeralization and soul-eating of modern technocratic culture — IBM syndrome, or 'technosis,' the new disease.

A variant of this theme also exists in which: *The efficiency-expert compulsively counts the number of cows in a herd, as seen from a moving train, by counting their teats and dividing by four.* (Collected: Minneapolis, Minn. 1944.) Many other anti-mathematical and anti-machine folktales of a non-erotic kind are also now being created such as: *The high-speed computer that is pitted against a Japanese abacus — and loses,* which is stated to have been a true occurrence in the 1950's (but that's all been 'bugged out' now), and: *The professor at Princeton demonstrating the use of the slide-rule to his class in Atom-Bomb Engineering I, by multiplying together at high speed — always at high speed — any two numbers called out. A 'voice from the back of the room'* [that anonymous folk-hero] *calls out, "Two times two!" The professor zips this into his slide-rule and announces, "Three, point, nine, nine, nine, nine, eight; but let's call it four."* (N.Y. 1952.)

This is in any case a lot less funny than some of the perfectly serious manifestations of the new disease, 'mathematical technosis,' now being impressed upon us, such as zip-codes and check-routing magnetic numbers a foot long, against which the grass-roots rebellion has already started, among the folknik or folklore-revival young people, of inventing sardonic or obscene telephone-exchanges, such as MEgalith-2 or FUckhead-7, to replace the demanded three-number substitution for human names, and having these on their stationery.

Lest it be thought that the present writer foolishly imagines himself free of any taint of this disease (struggling daily, as he must, under the gross tonnage of sixty thousand index-cards and some ten thousand books!) it should be observed that the present work is also provided with its own seven-number identification band, eventually replacing both its name and the author's — as are most books now openly published in the United States — under the polite euphemism of the 'Library of Congress Catalog Card Number' on the back of the title-page. In the same way (if small things may be compared with great) the *Third New International Merriam-Webster Dictionary,* the biggest in the world, is outfitted with heavy, ugly typographical dots at the end of each definition. All this for the diplomatically unavowed and perhaps partly unconscious purpose of eventually 'processing' every printed piece of paper in the world for feeding, in microfilm form, into reading machines which have unfortunately not yet been invented, but which — when they *are* invented — are presumably going to do every bit of the world's library-reference work automatically and AT HIGH SPEED (while the machine-tenders go out for a smoke in the toilet, and tell dirty jokes), including not only all necessary mechanical collating and confrontation, but also the psychological and sociological interpretation, not to mention the artistic and human evaluation, of course.

IX

An apology is perhaps necessary for some of the more allusive section-titles and subject headings used in the present work. Where these are not entirely self-explanatory, the opening pages of the material involved will generally show just what is meant. Such allusive and colloquial titles are not intended to be witty or extravagant, and are certainly not offered with the intention of creating a new jargon, or gobbledygook terminology, of a purported new science. They have simply been found, over the course of many years of working with these materials and attempting to make some *sense* out of the chaotic literature of jestbooks and erotic folktales, to be quite superior on any mnemonic basis to the usual, more precise anthropological or psychoanalytic terms. They are certainly more likely to be recollected when searching for a specific joke, or trying to 'place' one in the system; and that is their purpose. Every assistance is necessary in dealing with a subject-matter so complex, and no numerical system alone — no matter how simple or how complete — will be found as helpful as such classic popular iconologies or subject-typifications as "Father Time," "The Widow of Ephesus," "The Weeping Bitch" (Type 1515), "Cinderella's slipper," or "Hans Carvel's ring." In any case, as all language and communication is based on the arbitrary allotment and recognition of certain conventional meanings for, and responses to, chosen combinations of sounds or signs, it has seemed desirable in the present first attempt at analyzing this difficult subject-matter to *get there fastest with the mostest* in creating the necessary descriptive or allusive labels.

As a substitute for any further joke-index, and to avoid creating too cluttered a typographical presentation, the full analytic Table of Contents is given, in the form of a Subject-Index, at the end of each volume or series here. It is hoped that this will be found to offer a self-sustaining and coherent key to the principal themes of erotic jokes and humorous erotic folklore in the Anglo-Saxon culture (America and Great Britain) since about 1870, the modern era beginning with the end of the American Civil War. It will also perhaps offer at least a working basis for indexing, eventually, the erotic and scatologic humorous folklore of other European cultures since the 15th century, including that of Russia (recorded in major part from oral tradition, in Prof. Friedrich S. Krauss' yearbooks of erotic folklore, *Kryptádia* and *Anthropophytéia,* and their various supplementary volumes), as the many historical parallels and cognate tales given here from non-English-speaking countries certainly imply. Much remains to be done in the drawing of such parallels, but, again, this has proved extremely difficult owing to the omission of almost all the materials as to sexual humor from the motif-indexes hitherto published on the Thompson system. Aside from the study of Krauss' series and his imitators', there are all the *novellieri* and the European jestbooks, many of these superbly edited by Wesselski and others, and the endless folktale collections to which the key is Bolte & Polívka's *Anmerkungen zu Grimm* (1913–31).

The interpretations offered in the present text, and the side-subjects explored (with their own bibliographical references included), are the only contribution the editor has attempted to make, other than the collecting and subject-organization of the material itself. The reader who is interested only in the jokes will find the interpretations intrusive; the psychoanalytically trained or oriented reader may very well find them over-simplified. It has nevertheless seemed important to make this first analytic attempt as to erotic folk-humor, an attempt for which the much superior models have been, as already stated, Freud's *Wit and Its Relation to the Unconscious* (1905), and Dr. Martha Wolfenstein's *Children's Humor.*

The defect has long been observed in the existing folktale collections and indexes, that their logical organization — when such exists — is essentially their only advance over the earlier jestbooks, and over the spoken repertoires of the living tale-tellers from which they are ultimately drawn, and which are, at all levels, a far more vital and illuminating experience. Except for their organization, therefore, the purely index works are really only boondoggling, or marking time, waiting for the *meaning* of their indexed materials to be discovered, or even discussed, by someone else. This deeply important work, of the *interpretation of folklore* and its psychological and sociological assessment *vis-à-vis* the people who transmit it and who respond to it, remains for the folklorists of the future. Those of us who are conscious of the great gulf separating us from Sigmund Freud, and who have neither his trenchant insights and intuitions, nor the imperturbable simplicity of his style, will find this work of interpretation difficult indeed, and nowhere more difficult than in erotic folklore.

X

In coming now to the end of this very long and very laborious research, which has taken over three decades in the collecting and has proved the exact opposite of the experience hoped for in undertaking lightheartedly to *write a book about dirty jokes,* as the publisher who originally commissioned this work frankly phrased it, I should admit — despite the motto on the half-title, quoted from Beaumarchais' Figaro, or perhaps in accordance with it — that the book has been written almost as often in tears as in laughter. As every folklore research must be, it is visibly an unruly combination of field- and library-research, in proportions varying according to the writer's available time and luck, in the thirty years of spare moments and evenings' entertainment that it has involved. (As opposed to what might be imagined, it was the spare moments that were devoted to the field-collection, and the library-research that was the evenings' entertainment . . .) In addition to the jokes found in earlier printed and manuscript sources, it has been possible therefore to supplement these with an equal or slightly larger number of modern joke texts, which are in fact the central matter of this work, and to select for publication only the most representative examples — hardly more than a third of the materials actually on hand — on the important principle enunciated for all collectors three centuries ago by La Fontaine: *'Far from exhausting your subject, learn to take only its flower.'*

The modern joke texts here presented have been collected since about 1935 'in the field' — mostly the urban American *milieu* of parlor, bedroom, and beer-joints, which are among the places where they will be found — with the assistance of many friends and more than a few enemies, notable among them: Miss Christine Conrad (the former Mrs. Legman), Mr. Robert Ash, Mr. Mahlon Blaine, Mr. Richard Buehler, Sr. Ismael Adolfo Cerceda, Mr. David Eisendrath — who has not missed a trick in twenty years — Mr. Joseph Fliesler, Mr. Martin Gardner, Mr. Harry Johnson, Mr. Jan Kindler, Dr. Martin Kamen, Mr. Jay Marshall, Mr. John Newbern, Mr. Fred Petras, Mr. Roderick Roberts, Mr. Joseph Rosner (like Miss Conrad, Sr. Cerceda, Mr. Fliesler, and Mr. Marshall, a superb *raconteur*), Dr. Charles Winick, for many favors; and above all the late Henry Schuman, publisher, to whose encouragement — long before the New Freedom

— the original undertaking of this book is due. To all of these, and especially to Dr. Roger Abrahams, Prof. Richard Dorson, Mr. Frank Hoffmann, Dr. Kenneth Goldstein, Mr. Kenneth Larson, Mr. Vance Randolph, Prof. D. K. Wilgus, and the Trustees of the Institute for Sex Research (Kinsey Library), for access to the archived materials of all these last, and to the many authors — and their publishers — whose works are quoted here, I must and do express my deeply grateful indebtedness.

It seems wise also to express one final caution. The references throughout this work to parallel jokes and 'originals,' in languages other than English, are solely for the purpose of indicating, and tracing in part, the historical continuity of the present basic collection of erotic and scatological jokes of recent currency in the English language. Any attempt to create a complete motif-index for the entire literature of erotic humor, since its beginnings (?) and in all countries, is evidently too vast and would be foolishly optimistic at the present time. Every effort must still be made to trace the English-language materials as far back and as far afield as possible, through their earlier transformations and transmigrations, and so to *place* them in their historical and human context, and help to determine what it is about them that has proved universal to, and expressive of, the human condition in all cultures in which they are encountered.

That is at present the best approach to the non-English-language materials as well, and would allow of moving outward in expanding circles from the present index and collection, and the present interpretation, to the many books and manuscript collections — including those of the future! — that it has obviously not been possible to consult. The starting point for any such future study and enlargement, and the *broadening of the interpretation* to include the erotic jokes, folklore, and similar taboo materials of other cultures, must and can only be the forty or more volumes published in the various sexual folklore series edited and inspired by Prof. Friedrich S. Krauss, from 1883 to 1931, under the collective titles of *Kryptádia* and *Anthropophytéia:* "Secret Things," and "The Sexual Life of Humanity." It is hoped also to undertake the necessary continuation of these yearbooks, specifically for the publication of the enormous erotic folklore of the English language, toward which project large amounts of material have already been collected by the present editor and others.

There remains only to say, as has become something of a formula but is here sincerely meant, that the editor will be grateful for any additions or corrections, whether of jokes or of the interpretations, and for criticisms of any kind, that might improve the Second Series or further editions of the present work, and the whole series of later volumes — already far advanced in preparation — in which will be presented other portions of the tremendous field of erotic folklore in the English language. Materials are urgently sought, to complete the very large collections already in hand, of erotic and scatological folksongs, ballads, folk-poems, limericks, riddles, recitations and toasts, proverbs, comparisons, tricks, 'new' jokes, graffiti, puns and word-plays, children's rhymes and games, customs, superstitions, curses and blasphemies, and especially erotic synonyms and *slang;* as well as printed or manuscript novelties and scrimshaw, and other ephemeral or pictorial materials, of a humorous sexual or scatological nature, defying classification. The identity of contributors will be carefully concealed, or just as carefully acknowledged — whichever is preferred. Please address all communications to the editor:

G. LEGMAN

La Clé des Champs
Valbonne (Alpes-Maritimes)
FRANCE

I

CHILDREN

NOTHING in the sexual education of the child is so difficult for it to absorb as the fact of the parents' intercourse: overhearing it, worrying about it, coming upon its traces, or possibly actually observing it and then misapprehending its nature as a sadistic or anal act, and finally arguing bitterly with playmates as to whether such a thing exists at all, by what bodily aperture it is effected, and whether one's *own* parents could conceivably do anything of the kind. All this in addition to, and even in defiance of, whatever real or pretended sex education of a merely verbal kind the child may be offered by these same parents, or by the teachers who are their surrogates and substitutes.

To add to the difficulty, the parents' various sexual prohibitions — at whatever level of silence or of speech these are transmitted — lose all rational force after the child's discovery of the parents' own sexual life, and such prohibitions can then be understood only as arbitrary unfairness, if not as plain lying and hypocrisy. The parents have been discovered to do these things, and often, and seem to enjoy them very much. But they forbid the child to do the very same things, or to be present while they are going on, under some social or hygienic explanation or another, all of which adds up to: "You're not old enough yet — you're too small." And most parents will still generally punish a child of either sex, if only by grim facial expressions and the dreaded 'withdrawal of love,' if the child is caught engaging in the same sexual acts as the parents, or artlessly admits to this, or even trustingly asks the parents' advice.

Little Johnny Jones, age 7, is in love with Mary Smith, the little girl next door, and comes to confide to his father that they plan to get married. Mr. Jones is amused. "What are you going to do about money?" he asks with pretended gravity. "I have my allowance, and

49

Mary has nearly a dollar in the piggy-bank." "*That's all right for now,*" says his father, "*but what will you do when the children come?*" "*Well, we've had pretty good luck so far.*" (N.Y. 1963.) This is only a joke, of course, and the point is not really the child's 'innocence' but his knowingness, and the sudden mocking unveiling of both his own and all adults' sexual life, in the framework of the equally mocking adult pretense of accepting him as an equal in money and family responsibilities. The scene is not really likely to occur, though it conceivably could. It is a *joke,* made up probably by an adult, and intended to achieve its effect as humor by freshening and recalling the tragic reality and massive sexual and personal defeats of being a child.

Sex classically becomes involved for the child at a very early age, in Western civilization, with the realization that parents are hypocritical and unfair; that there is one law for the big and another for the little. That the only thing worth being is *big,* and strong; and that later, when one is big and strong, one will have one's innings and one's revenge not only by doing all the forbidden things, but by forbidding them in turn to one's own children, who will be littler than oneself and therefore proper to dominate and harass. Underneath this not-so-innocent dream of 'growing up' runs along the hopeless admission that one is still pretty little, and the anxious realization that one's sexual life is a dangerous matter indeed. Like playing with food or feces, or refusing to do what one is told, or speaking in a loud and demanding way (as do adults), sex can cause one to be unfairly rejected or severely punished by those whose love one very much needs. This is the real sexual enlightenment of the child, and of just as serious a nature as that concerning the birds & bees, or even human genitalia and what they do. *At what age does enlightenment come? — For me, sir, there was no Santa at six, no stork at nine, no God at twelve!* (Quoted by John Kempner as motto to his 1930's novel, *No Stork at Nine.*)

I. MOCK IGNORANCE

The principal weapon at the child's disposal, to punish the parents for their insincerity, is the public denuding of the parents' own sexual lives by means of mock-ignorant questions and the classic embarrassing — *i.e.* inconveniently candid — remarks of children. This is the main theme about which sexual jokes concerning children really turn. It is also noticeable that the farther the child gets from home, in the jokes, the more open is the expression of this mocking exposure of the sexuality of adults. Mere parent-substitutes, such as older sisters and lady teachers, are ruthlessly cut down and stripped naked before fiancés, strangers, mass-audiences, and the like. Naturally, these jokes are not to be construed as the records of real events, and few of them are either originated or TOLD by children. But the people who do tell them were once children, and it is clearly an indigestible memento of childhood that the child-voyeuristic joke attempts to resolve. *The child as voyeur:* what's in a name? Let us say, rather, the child as exhibitionist — a reality everyone either recollects or can observe — and here exhibiting not its own sexual organs and actions, but those of the parents.

As the opening item in a work called *Your Slip Is Showing* (1953), pocket-reprinted as *Pardon My Blooper* (1959) — a collection of authentic errors, spoonerisms, and embarrassing moments in radio broadcasting, as monitored by radio-producer Kermit Schafer — the following incident is recorded as having really happened:

> On "Strike It Rich," popular television program produced by Walt Framer; Warren Hull, Master of Ceremonies, interviewed a five year old child whose father was in the United States Army serving in Korea. She wanted to Strike it Rich for an apartment where she would have her own bedroom; whereupon the surprised Hull asked: "With Daddy away in Korea, isn't the apartment you live in with Mommy big enough?" The child's reply was, "During the week I sleep in the bedroom with Mommy, but on the week-ends, when Uncle Charlie comes, they make me sleep on a cot in the kitchen. Anyway, he's not really my uncle."

The perfection of this story *as humor* rises from its not being a humorous story at all, and the five-year-old girl's knowing revenge drives into her mother's flank like an arrow. That her anger is not so much the result of her own sleeping accommodations as of the adults' waking activities is perfectly clear. And though the mother is the obvious victim of this public denuding, it is also clear that the child's animosity is more particularly jealousy, directed against the man who replaces her in her mother's bed. The mother is punished not only for her sexuality but by means of it. The real animus against her is for having rejected the child.

It may also be observed, as a technical point, that this story goes on past the usual hostile 'punch-line' to a further *clincher* or harpoon-line, after which there is no getting the hook out. In calling such secondary endings 'toppers,' there is a tendency to think of them as somehow searching or competing for higher peaks of humorousness: to force the already-smiling listener to outright laughter. The fact of the matter is that MOST JOKES MUST HAVE A BUTT OR VICTIM, even if it is only the listener — as in 'shaggy dog' stories. The real meaning of the topper or clincher, as very strikingly in the present example, is to supply the positive *coup de grâce* and to make sure that the butt or victim has really been destroyed.

A particular object of the child's hostility, in jokes, is the parent's sexual lies or evasions, and these are attacked by turning them against the parents themselves through a pretended or mock-ignorant lit-eralism. The joke that is unquestionably the best known, and one of the earliest learned by children in the United States, is never found in printed collections, not as being too 'obscene,' but more likely as being too childish to make an adult laugh. Yet it is one of the few jokes of this type actually told by children, who obviously find it highly satisfying. *A little girl and boy are being bathed together. The little girl points to her brother's penis, and asks, "What's that, Mama?" "That's Johnny's hot dog," says the mother. "And what's that?" asks the little boy. "That's Mary's bun." An hour later the little girl comes running in crying, "Mama, Johnny put his hot dog in my bun!"* (Scranton, Pa. 1925.) This is the first joke I believe I ever heard. Variants encountered before 1935 include *horse and stable* (or *barn*), *automobile* (or *roadster*) *and garage,* and *roll of bills and purse.*

As is usual in incestuous situations, the sister and brother are sub-stitutes here for the parents, and, in questions about the anatomy of the smaller male or female, knowledge of the larger is expected and gained. The version most recently collected, before declining to record further examples, expresses this element unmistakably. *A child sees its parents in the bathtub, and asks what their genitals are. The mother says: "That's my harbor." The father: "That's my boat." Child: "Daddy, why don't you set your boat in Mama's harbor?"* (N.Y. 1952.) This seems impossibly weak as humor to an adult, but is precisely the image used three centuries earlier in Thomas Carew's heavily symbolized "A Rapture," in his *Poems* (1640):

> Yet my tall pinnace shall, in the Cyprian strait,
> Ride safe at anchor and unload her freight.

(Carew's effeminization of the punned-upon *penis,* as seen in the pronoun 'her,' is presumably in response to the inevitable femaleness of ships; but compare the similar sex reversal in the French *la pine,* but *le con.* The reversal also exists in Latin, as complained of in a neo-classical Latin "Epigram," attributed to Joannes Secundus, and printed at the end of the Elzevirian editions of Nicolas Chorier's pseudonymous *Dialogues of Luisa Sigea,* 1659:)

> *Dicite Grammatici, cur mascula nomina cunnus,*
> *Et cur fœmineum mentula nomen habet.*

In all forms of the preceding joke, the wonderful humor to the child is the mocking of the parents' evasions, which are somehow so foolishly phrased, inevitably, that precisely the action that is intended to be hidden or prevented is the one that must logically follow. A whole chapterful of matching euphemisms or metaphors of this type will be found in Rabelais' chapter on the voyage to the Island of Ennasin, in *Pantagruel,* Bk. IV, chap. 9, originally published in 1548. The suggestive 'novelty' song, "My Handy-Man," by Andy Razaf, about 1930, turns entirely on images of this kind, as do many of the Negro blues of the type Razaf was vulgarizing. Probably the most extreme modern example is in Bk. III, "The Book of the Thousand Sacred Names," in a privately published American poem, *The Hell of the Good* by 'Edouard de Verb' [Arthur Davison Ficke: *ficken* being the German 'verb' for sexual intercourse], printed for the author, also about 1930. Here eighteen full sestets are devoted to elaborate erotic metaphors of this almost childish type: '*One plied his Night-stick up a girl's Dark Alley; Another's Plough worked in a lady's valley;*' not forgetting '*One filled her empty Purse with his Bank-roll,*' which may very well have been taken from the joke here under discussion. This entire metaphoric section of Ficke's poem is reprinted in my Introduction to the revised volume I of John S. Farmer & William Ernest Henley's *Dictionary of Slang & Its Analogues* (New Hyde Park, N.Y. 1966) part IX, covering several pages, lxix–lxxii. Essentially, all jokes of this kind derive from the metaphoric folk-element behind Boccaccio's "Putting the Devil in Hell" (III.10), the most famous example. Compare *Russian Secret Tales,* Nos. 14 and 36, on 'horse' and 'well,' also in the English folksong, "The Trooper."

I. PENIS-ENVY

Explicit penis-envy is very common in jokes. *A little girl demands "boy candies" in buying chocolate "nigger-babies," because she gets more that way.* (2:14.) — *The same little girl asks for a "male choco-late bar — one with nuts."* (2:214. That this *is* the very same little girl in both cases is insisted upon by the anonymous editor of *Anecdota Americana II,* on the last text page, p. 205, though the "male Hershey bar" line is U.S. folk-wit.) A didactic work, *Step by Step in Sex Education,* by Dr. Edith Hale Swift (New York, 1938) presents the classic situation of small children being bathed together, though one certainly cannot agree with the author that lisping toddlers should be taught neo-Latin terms like 'labia' and 'urinate,' nor yet that the mother should herself engage in the sexual exploration of the two children's bodies, with them as spectators (instead of letting them do it themselves) as is made very specific by Dr. Swift:

BERT (*aged two years and a quarter*). All fru?

MOTHER. Just one more little job. I must pull this skin of your penis back a little way, and clean it carefully. There you are. . . . Now let's powder Sister.

BERT. Bert see what she has.

MOTHER. Surely. Just these little soft labia. Mother will part them carefully and put powder in the groove here. Would you like Mother to find the little hole where her urine comes from, which gets her diapers wet so often? Here it is — just a wee little opening from a bag inside her body. She hasn't learned yet to hold her urine till she gets to the chair, as you do.

BERT. My little hole way out here.

MOTHER. Yes, you have something like a hose. The urine has to come a long way to get out. Now into bed . . . (*aside to Father*) Enough for one day, eh?

The rest of Dr. Swift's book is written in the same style — only more so — and the amateur of this type of unconscious humor is recommended to look up the original. Equally unlikely, as the true conversation of children, are the repartees given in jokes. *A little girl is being bathed with her little brother. She points to his penis and begins to cry. "I want one of those!" "If you're a good little girl," says her mother, "you'll get one later." "Yes," says her father, "and if you're a bad little girl you'll get lots of them."* (1:223.) Variant: *"Mama, when I get big will I get a dickey like Willie's got?" Mother: "When you get big, honey, you'll get plenty of it."* (D.C. 1943.) These repartees were obviously never made up by a child. In an even more sophisticated variant on the bathtub situation, *The mother tells the little girl that the little boy's penis is a whistle. "No it ain't. I blew it all afternoon and I couldn't get a sound out of it."* (Joe "Miller" Murray, *Smoker Stories*, 1942, p. 5; told as a 'Little Audrey' or female-fool joke.) — *An old man meets a little girl who is crying, "I want one of those things like my brother's got, that sticks out and lays down and sticks out again!" The old man begins to cry too.* (2:162.)

In the old man here introduced we have the 'grandfather' or 'voice from the upper berth' or other evasive father-figure so common in jokes, as will be seen. Explicit viewing of the actual father's or mother's genitals is not, however, uncommon in jokes. *A little girl sees her father urinating while out driving in the country. "How many of those have you got, Daddy?" "Only one, why?" "Well, what did you do with the great big one you stuck in Mama this morning?"* (2:314.) The idea of loss, the hidden notion of the vagina as harming or devouring the penis, is quite evident here. The overcompensatory matching notion, that a man might have two penises (see the Female Fool jokes, later) is also present. *Bathtub situation: the little girl asks about the father's testicles. He tells her they are his "apples." She runs to tell her mother. "Did he tell you anything about that dead limb they're hanging on?"* (Transcontinental train, U.S. 1943.)

A father is bending over arranging presents under the Christmas tree in his nightshirt. Little boy's voice: "Hey, Pop, who gets the bagpipes?" (Murray, *Smoker Series*, 1942.) A doggerel poem in Pennsylvania Dutch dialect, on seeing the mother in the same situation, has been commonly printed and circulated as a novelty, under the titles "Dot Leedle Fur Cap" and "Der Nite B4 Xmas," in which *the mother lifts her nightgown apronwise to hold the presents, and tells the little boy who inquires as to who gets the "little fur cap," "I tink I give dot to your fadder tonight!"* (*Folk Poems and Ballads*, 'Mexico

City, 1945' [Cleveland, Ohio 1948] p. 56.) This poem also exists, and
may have originated, in French form, in an anonymous volume of
contes-en-vers entitled *Histoires Naturelles,* 'Par Un Membre de
plusieurs sociétés savantes' (Paris, 1883) p. 87–9, *"Le Bonnet à poil,"*
ending with the mother answering the boy that: *'C'est le Noël à petit
père.'* (Copy: Ohio State. This volume also includes a modern version
of Béroalde de Verville's "Sea Crab" *vagina dentata* tale, as *"Le Crabe,"*
p. 39–45, and several other items worth tracing.)

The substitution of a large, strong animal (the horse, or the elephant with its phallic trunk, for choice) to represent the fearful
father with his hirsute body and parts appears in the many animal-
voyeurism stories, of which the following is typical: *Little French boy
at the zoo, to Nurse: "What's that?" "That's the elephant's trunk."
"No, not that — that!" "Oh, you mean the tail?" "No, that thing right
there!" "Oh, that! That's nothing."* Bystander, tipping his hat:
"Mam'selle is blasée." (1:381.) — Variant: *Child at the zoo with his
parents sees the elephant with an enormous erection, and asks his
mother what it is. "It's nothing," she says; "shhh!" The boy then asks
his father, who says, "Why don't you ask your mother?" "I did ask
her — she said it's nothing." "Well, she's been spoiled."* (N.Y. 1945.)

The only small-child story collected concerning the genitals of any
female person other than the mother, appears to be adapted from a
better-known fool story, and expresses the infantile notion of the castratory origin of the female genitals: *A little boy and girl are sleighriding and tumble into the snow. Girl: "I hurt my belly — look."* She
*unzips her playsuit and pulls down her panties. Little boy: "Whew!
you snapped it right off!"* (N.Y. 1952.) An important variant of the
bathtub situation expresses the female-castration fantasy far more
cynically: *The mother is drying herself after a bath, with one foot on
the edge of the tub. Little boy: "Mama, what's that?" "That's where
Daddy hit me with the axe." "Got you right in the cunt, didn't he?"*
(1:15, also 2:234; one of the few repetitions in *Anecdota II.*) This
would appear to be a 'topper' to the first joke given above, and was
heard so used, in Michigan, 1935, to put a stop to a set of variations
being run on the boy-&-girl-in-bathtub joke by two girls of about
seventeen. Actually, however, it is a folk idea, dating from at least the
16th century in France, and the unchanged motif of the *axe* has required a number of rationalizations in the telling, such as changing

"That's where Daddy hit me . . ." to *"That's where the Indian hit me"* (N.Y. 1953), or, taking refuge in the Sense of Nonsense: *"That's where an angel hit me with a little golden hatchet"* (*to which the boy replies, "Gee whiz, the angel must have hit Grandmaw with a broadaxe."* D.C. 1950.)

The original folktale is alluded to by Rabelais in *Pantagruel*, Bk. II, chap. 15 (1533), and again, with the 'hatchet' changed to a demonic fingernail, in the story of the Devil of Papefiguière, Bk. IV, chap. 47 (published in 1552), where it is combined with the ancient belief that the devil can be frightened off by the sight of a woman's genitals. (See the 'brainpicker' story under "Female Fools.") The original tale, which has been heard in America as late as 1950, is one of those just-so stories that explain the origin of all things, in this case the presumable peculiarity that little women have bigger vaginas than big women (given as an 'old Andalusian proverb' in *Anecdota* 1:192). *When God first made men and women, he left it to the devil to make their genitals. This the devil did, in the case of women, by having them stand over a pit in which he crouched with a scythe.* [Cf. the fingernail in Rabelais.] *The tall women got only a nick. The women with short legs coming closer to the ground, they received a deeper gash.* The great antiquity of the idea of a castrating scythe (Kronos') will be discussed in the following section here, "The Diaper and the Scythe." See further on this story under "Misunderstandings," 2.v.

On infantile and sadistic theories of this type generally, see Freud's *Three Contributions to the Theory of Sex* (1905), end of chapter 2. One which crops up very often is that babies are born from the rectum. *A little boy (or Englishman) maintains that his baby brother was born from his mother's rectum. He is forced to admit that he is wrong, but mutters, "Well, it was only this far away!" — gesturing with thumb and forefinger.* (N.Y. 1942.) In a more elaborate version, *A "mindreading druggist" is being tried out. He hands a box of Kotex to the first woman who walks in, but she refuses it and says she wants toilet paper. "Well," he explains, gesturing, "I only missed it by that much!"* (N.Y. 1949.) A particularly straightforward form, told of a Negro child and his mother: *A boy asks where he came from, and is shown. "That's where you came from," his mother says. "Uhm, uhm!" he marvels. "Another inch and I'd 'a been a turd."* (Cleveland, Ohio 1938.)

2. THE PRIMAL SCENE

The mocking tone becomes more prominent as the child in the stories drops the fact or pretense of wanting information as to the nature and purpose of the genitals, and begins to twit the parents on overheard or overseen sexual acts, particularly those that are unequivocally sinful as being adulterous as well. Overheard remarks being more difficult for the parent to deny, and easier for the child to pretend to be confused by, these are the principal opportunities taken to make the parents the butt of humor. Hidden somewhere underneath there is a tone of 'reality testing' by the child — or, rather, by the child that the story-teller once was — begging to be told it isn't so, but this is generally overwhelmed in the flood of ridicule.

A little girl objects to the long prayers she has to recite and asks why she can't use the short prayers she overheard her parents say. "What prayers do you mean?" *her mother asks.* "Last night I heard you just as plain. You were saying, 'Oh, God, I'm coming!' And Papa said, 'Jesus Christ, wait for me!'" (*A Treasury of Erotic and Facetious Memorabilia*, MS. 1910.) As collected several times in the 1940's, the father is given the first speech. (*Eppur si muove.*) Variant: "*Mama, do people go to heaven feet first?*" "*Why, no. Why do you ask?*" "*Well the maid was laying on the bed with her feet up, hollering, 'Oh, God, I'm coming!' And she would have, too, if Daddy hadn't held her down.*" (2:346, collected earlier in Idaho, 1932.) Very funny, but observe the child's undisguised fright: *A little boy is explaining to a policeman why he is running away at midnight with his belongings in a bindle over his shoulder.* "Papa was hollering, 'Here I go!' and Mama was screaming, 'Wait for me!' and I figured why should I get stuck with a $20,000 *mortgage?*" (N.Y. 1964. Compare *Kryptádia*, 1907, x. 174, of a landlord.)

Mere wisecracks on the same theme are common. *Little Girl:* "Mama, I know why Daddy has such a big belly. I saw Nurse blowing it up this morning." (1:197.) This is apparently the original, or background fantasy, of Al Capp's 'trumpappy,' in his "Li'l Abner" comic-strip (*N.Y. Sunday Mirror*, January 25, 1953), in which Pappy Yokum is blown by Mammy, 'triple-tongued,' through the ear. (See Ernest Jones, "The Madonna's Conception Through the Ear," 1914, in his *Essays in Applied Psycho-Analysis*, ed. 1951, II. 266–357.) — *Little boy:*

"Mama, can Papa eat glass?" "No, what makes you think so?" "Well I just heard him tell Nurse that if she'd put out the light he'd eat it." (1:216. Compare 1:487, *"I'm always a Goblin under de sheets . . . If anybody guesses the right answer I'll put out the lights."*) Finally, from World War II, *The little boy who tells his mother his father can take a Wac apart, because "I overheard Daddy say that last night he screwed the ass off a Wac."* (D.C. 1945.)

These flimsy gags have almost nothing in common with the realities of childhood. Here is a story that has everything: *Little boy: "Papa, I want a drink!" "Shh!" "Papa, I want a drink!" "Hush up!" Long pause, then very determinedly: "Papa, I'll shake the bed for Mama if you'll get me a drink!"* (Idaho, 1932.) World War II variant (Calif. 1942), on *A little boy bragging of his father's bravery in going out during the air-raids, while the cowardly man next door hurried over without even waiting to dress, got into bed with the mother, "and was so scared that the bed shook something terrible."*

The classic story on the theme of overhearing parental intercourse is recorded in *Anecdota* 2:297, and earlier in Paul Haines' "A Critique of Pure Bawdry," in *The Modern Thinker* (Sept. 1933) III. 293. The punch-line has become a conversational tag among people who often do not know the story itself. *The mountaineer and his wife and their three little boys all sleep in the same bed together, the boys wearing their coon-skin hats to keep warm. During the parents' intercourse the bed collapses several times, the boys' hats flying in all directions. The parents wait till the children are asleep and try again. Just as their orgasm is approaching a tiny voice shouts, "Hold onto your hats, boys! Here we go again!"* (Variant: *Kryptádia*, 1907, x. 133, to mother!)

All pretense of any emotion other than malice in the child's intervention is dropped as the jokes about the primal scene progress from overhearing to seeing, as in the following Machiavellian example: *"Oh, Mama, guess what I saw Daddy and the maid doing on the bed!" "Be quiet!"* Then, after a moment's reflection, *"You wait till Mama asks you."* At the supper table that night she says, *"Now, Johnnie, what were you going to tell me this morning?" "Nothing; only that I saw Daddy and the maid on the bed together, doing just like you and Uncle John did last summer when Daddy was away fishing."* (Idaho, 1952.) It is observable that the pretense of ignorance is still preserved: the child does not quite understand what has been seen, and under this innocent subterfuge can humiliate and ridicule the parents *ad lib.* In a printed novelty recitation sometimes called "How to Kill an Eel" and circulated since at least the 1920's, *A little boy describes to his horrified mother how he has watched his older sister and her beau kill an eel which "popped out of his pants and dug its way into her." The mother faints.* The theme of the little brother — *i.e.* the identification-image of the teller — who hides behind the davenport to spy on his older sister's love-making, is the subject of much cartoon humor, cover-illustrations for popular magazines, etc., where the same situation with the mother instead of the sister would be considered outrageous. At Lake Winola, Pennsylvania, about 1927, the children (mostly girls) sang a leering little song on this theme in the evenings, drawing out the refrain in the most knowing way:

> *My sister has a fella, comes to see her every night,*
> *I wonder why, I wonder why.*
> *They sit in the parlor and turn out the light,*
> *I wonder why, I wonder why.*
> *Last night through the keyhole I heard my sister say,*
> *"Stop, Charlie! Don't, Charlie! Take your hand away!"*
> *I wonder why, I wonder why.*

When grown-ups were within hearing distance, 'hand' in the last line became 'arm.' In the original "Hey Baba Leeba" jazz-song (before 1942) which, by a mispronunciation of the last word, gave its name to the later 'bebop,' or decadent jazz music, the same message is transmitted with all subterfuges of older sister, parlor-petting, &c., gone. (This version collected D.C. 1945):

> *Mama's on the bottom,*
> *Papa's on the top,*
> *Baby's in the cradle*
> *Hollerin', "Put it to her, Pop."*

The little children in New Rochelle, New York, about 1930, had a similar chant, to the tune of Wagner's "Ride of the Valkyrie": "*Oh, Papa and Mama, Papa and Mama, Papa and* MAMA, *Do it all night!*"

The usual cartoon solution to the problem of getting rid of the little brother is to give him a quarter to go to the movies. In one orally transmitted joke, *The little brother refuses all monetary offers to leave the parlor so his sister and her beau can pet. "Well, what* do *you want?" the sister finally asks. "I wanna watch."* (N.Y. 1946; also D.C. 1951, as a pun on *The little Scots boy who wanted a watch for Christ-*

mas, so his parents let him.) Lacking quite this permissiveness, in another story *A little boy is told by his mother to follow his sister and her boyfriend on a stroll in the woods "to find out what love is." Next day he reports, "Well, I watched them for a while, but when they began taking their pants off I figured they were going to take a shit. I didn't have to, so I came home."* (D.C. 1946.) In a nonsense version: *A boy reports to his parents that he saw his sister and her music-teacher kissing and then taking off their pants. "Well, what happened, what happened?" the parents urge. "I dunno. I figured they were going to shit in the piano, so I left."* (Berkeley, Calif. 1965, and earlier.) A variant in *Kryptádia* (1907) XI. 283, 285, shows its origin in a child's fear of punishment for fecal incontinence.

On the same theme, similarly identifying sex and excretion in a way treated much more fully in Series Two (12.IV.1, "Cloacal Intercourse"), but here leaving more for the listener to *translate* from the displaced or symbolized allusion to snot: *A little boy is peeping through the keyhole of his sister's bedroom on her wedding night. "And she's the one that bawled me out for picking my nose!"* (N.Y. 1942.) Also seen as a ceramic 'novelty' item in France — in French — about 1955, publicly for sale to tourists in Cannes, along with toilet-shaped mustard-jars, etc. (with the toilet-mop as serving-spoon). A version of the joke collected on a transcontinental train in the west, 1943, combined this (with end-line: *"And they bawl me out for sucking my thumb!"*) with a further joke in which *The grandmother berates the little boy for peeping through the keyhole of his parents' bedroom and muttering "God damn . . . God damn!" Then she bends to peep too, and mutters "God damn!"* The interesting projection here, in which it is the parents who peep on their children, and not the reverse, will be treated fully in the later chapter on Marriage.

In the most permissive story collected — so much so, that it shades off into the fool category, though really only based on the crowded living-quarters of the poor — *An Armenian (or hillbilly) is told about coitus from behind, tries it, but complains later, "It was all right, but the kids all laughed at me."* (1:96.) In a version collected in 1943, this posture is used purposely "to amuse the kids." Seen from the child's point of view: *In a poor family with only one bed, the little boy has to sleep at his parents' feet, and one night he gets kicked onto the floor. He climbs back in bed muttering, "You and your fancy fucking'll make a cripple out of me yet!"* (N.Y. 1953.)

The animal-voyeuristic stories of children tend to have their point in the drawing of an analogy between the animals' activities and those of grown-ups, particularly to support the rectal theory of coitus. *A little boy runs home shouting, "Grandpa, Grandpa, guess what I saw! The ole bull tried to jump clear over the cow. And he would have, too, only a big red thing came out of his belly and caught her in the ass-hole!"* (Idaho, 1910.) *Three children are watching two dogs in the street. 6-year-old child: "Look at those dogs playing around." 8-year-old child: "They're fucking." 10-year-old child: "Dog-fashion too."* (Calif., 1944.) This also exists in French (1966) with end-line: *"And badly too!"*

3. EMBARRASSMENTS

In the duel between the parent and the child, as envisaged by jokes, the standard humorous device of the question-answered-wrongly or equivocally is commonly employed. The parent (or teacher) uses it to evade a true answer; the child uses it to force one. *Mother: "Why, John, this is the same train we took on our honeymoon to Niagara Falls." Little Boy: "Papa, was I with you on that trip?" Father: "Yes, son. You went up with me and came back with your mother."* (Memorabilia, 1910; also Murray, 1942.) — *"Daddy, what's a eunuch?" "A eunuch is a man that's, er, bald." "You're bald, Daddy. Are you a eunuch?" "No, son, I'm TOO BALD!"* (New York State, 1942, told by an old man, slapping his thigh uproariously to indicate the pun.) — *A woman runs out of rubbers while canning tomatoes and sends her little boy to the store to buy a dozen. He comes back with the wrong kind of rubbers. "That's not the kind I wanted," says his mother. "Those are for cucumbers."* (D.C. 1944.)

The child responds to this evasiveness of adults, however clever, with unappreciative hostility; and counters with mock-innocent literalism or embarrassing frankness, concentrating first on those scatological acts for which a certain childish allowance can be safely expected. This also allows of an amount of anal-sadistic insulting of the parents that becomes even more striking later in connection with sexual permissiveness. *A little girl comes stamping into a roomful of guests, dripping wet. She points angrily to each of the men present, saying, "You, or you, or you, or you, left the toilet seat up, and I fell in!"* (Minn. 1935.) This habit men have of leaving the toilet seat up after urination is particularly annoying to women, as they sense the implied insult to them (as non-phallic beings) but cannot quite bring it to consciousness in their complaints. The split-front toilet seat is probably the simplest solution. *A boy is told by his mother not to say "piss" before guests, but to use the euphemism "whisper." At the reception he tells his father, who has not been briefed, "Daddy, I want to whisper." "All right, son, do it in my ear."* (D.C. 1950.) *A little girl is taught to signal by waving her hand instead of saying "pee-pee." She waves her hand frantically behind the guests' backs. "I understand, dear," says her mother. "Run along." "But, Mama, shit too!"* (2:17.)

Again, animal-incidents are a perfect opening for the child to express either secret knowledge or an even more secret hostility without fear of punishment. *A little boy is looking at a milkman's horse and wagon. "Mister, that horse will never get you home." "Why not?" "He just lost all his gasoline."* (Bennett Cerf, *Good for a Laugh*, 1952, p. 39.) — *A city boy on the farm sees his mother about to pour a glass of milk from a milking-can. "Don't drink that, Mother! The cow pissed it!"* (2:409.) Observe the perfect reversal here. In the publicly published version, Cerf's, the tabooed image is hidden by the everyday metaphor (of gasoline). In the privately published folk example, the everyday fact of milking a cow is presented in taboo (scatological) metaphors.

In the sexual sphere, the child's knowingness is expressed — as in many examples already given — under the guise of ignorance. That is to say, it is not the child who is really knowing, but the adult who is making up these 'children's stories' who manipulates the situation and the actors so as to create the image of the knowing child he wishes he had dared to be, twitting the parent by means of pretended ignorance. *Boy, in zoo, to his father, while both of them are watching the monkeys. "Say, Pop, how long does it take to make a baby monkey?" "Oh, about six months." "Well then, what's their hurry?"* (2:415.) Another form of this will be given in a later chapter, elaborately set up as of Martians and human beings observing each other's methods of reproduction.

Most pointedly of all, the child's cautious stupidity makes possible some really cruel embarrassments of the parents, but the canon of poetic justice is usually observed in its being their own lies that come home to roost. *A wedding. The groom kisses the bride long and passionately. Child's voice: "Now is he sprinkling the pollen on her,*

Mama?" (2:421.) — Father: "My new stenographer looks like a French doll." Little girl: "Papa, does she shut her eyes when you lay her down on her back, like my doll?" (2:349. There is also a doll that drinks through a real nipple and wets its didy-pants, which then have to be changed, but this has not yet been made the subject of humor.) Varying the situation here, the embarrassing slip is frankly projected on the adult, with the child merely as the excuse. Little girl: "Me slept with Daddy last night." "That's not right," says the governess; "you mean 'I slept with Daddy'." (1:403.)

Out of the house — among strangers, store-keepers, and the like — the child reels off all the family sexual secrets without the slightest pretense of not understanding what they mean, but rather with brag-gartly-tough cynicism. A little girl asks in a store for toilet paper, and says, "Charge it." Storekeeper: "Who is it for?" Little girl, haugh-tily: "For all of us." (1:61.) — A visitor is waiting impatiently. "When will your parents be down, little boy?" "Pretty soon now. Dad said if we had stew again he'd shove it up Ma's ass, and he has everything up there now but two potatoes." (N.J. 1942. 'Potatoes,' as meaning testicles, also occurs in the phrase concerning eunuchs, "All that meat and no potatoes.") In an earlier form recorded in Anecdota 1:220, A customer in a restaurant tells the waiter that the steak is tough and to stick it up the chef's ass. "You'll have to take your turn, sir. There's a beef stew and a cocoanut pie ahead of you."

The older sister and other only quasi-parental figures again receive the brunt of most of the embarrassments. A small boy asks in a drug-store for condoms. "What size?" "Gimme assorted sizes. They're for my sister. She's going to the country." (1:6. Collected again, D.C. 1951, of a colored girl who is 'going on a picnic.') A number of rather con-trived jokes exist on the older-sister theme. A little boy is polishing an apple industriously but refuses to sell it to the minister who happens to pass by. "I'm saving it to buy a dog. I figure if my sister got a Cadillac for a cherry, I ought to be able to get a greyhound for this apple." (N.Y. 1952.) The machinery creaks even worse in the follow-ing, reprinted from Judge and Magazine Digest (1944): A grand-mother has been cheating on her diabetes diet and is hospitalized. She is given a room in the maternity ward owing to overcrowding. Her granddaughter comes to visit. "I want to see my grandmother." "Grandmother? What's she doing here?" "Oh, she's been cheating again." The aunt, once so common a figure in erotic literature (as in

Eugene Field's *Only a Boy*), appears in a joke of which the main interest here is the clarity of her position as euphemised or substitute mother: *A little boy tells a welfare worker that he has neither father nor mother. "Never had any," he adds. "Then how were you born?" "Some damn gorilla knocked up my aunt."* (1:483. 'Gorilla': *guerilla*, slang of the period for a gangster.) Two *cante fables* not often collected in America make the father-surrogate of priest or king into the butt whose sexual secrets are told: "The Wrong Song" (Type 1735A: a French version in *Kryptádia*, 1884, II. 143, notes that it is much older); and "The Bag of Lies" (Type 570), in the Randolph MS., No. 29, as "Fill, Bowl, Fill."

Miscellaneous examples of embarrassing or other frankness by children: *Two cats in coitus on the roof of a whore-house fall off together. A small boy rushes in and shouts to the madam, "Hey, lady, your sign fell off!"* (1:40.) Probably old, but untraced. Jokes on signboards occur at least as far back as John Mottley's *Joe Miller's Jests,* 1739, No. 25, on the lady who objects to 'the Sign of the *Cock* and *Leather-Breeches*' at her lodgings, and says to the young landlord, "I'll tell you how you may satisfy both me and my Daughter: *Only take down your* Breeches *and let your* Cock *stand.*" — *A boy watching the birth of a baby brother sees the doctor slap the baby's bottom to make it breathe. "Hit him again, Doc! He didn't have no business being up there in the first place!"* (N.Y. 1942.) — *A farmer showing two old ladies around the farm sees a boy fishing. "Catchin' any big 'uns?" Boy: "Big as your pecker!" Farmer, to ladies: "He sure is catchin' some whoppers."* (N.Y. 1939.)

II. SCHOOL

I. TORMENTING THE TEACHER

School days, as the jokesmiths pretend to remember them, are strictly pandemonium, with the lady school-teacher leading the rout. Not being a blood relative, she is considered fair game. School jokes divide themselves into three clear groups: those concerned with arriving at class and settling down to study (or not); the problems posed by the teacher, and the punning sexual answers with which the children torment her; and finally the jokes about the sexual relations of the bad boy — always the bad boy — with the teacher. Sunday-school jokes are no longer collected, their catechism milieu being changed to college, but they must once have been an important category. The first joke given here, concerning arriving at school, is a direct descendant of one of *Joe Miller's Jests* (1739) No. 96, of a 'poor dirty Shoe-Boy' at Sunday-evening catechism, who is asked his name by the parson. "*Rugged* and *Tough,* answered he, *who gave you that Name?* says Domine: *Why the Boys in our Alley,* reply'd poor *Rugged* and *Tough, Lord d–mn them.*"

A girl and her little brother arrive hand in hand the first day at a country school. "Your name?" "Stinky Slocum," says the girl. "None of your impertinence, you hillbilly. You go right home and tell your mother to teach you some manners." The girl turns to her brother. "Come on, Shitass, if she don't believe me, she'll never believe you." (N.Y. 1952.) In the same way, *Two little twin boys are sent home from school with a note saying: "Dear Mrs. Smith, Your boys say their names are Hitler and Mussolini. Is this true or are they making fun of me?" Answer: "Dear Teacher, The name is Miss Smith, not Mrs. Smith, and if you had two little bastards what would* you *call them?"* (N.Y. 1942.) The wistful recollection here, of the disabilities — particularly as regards unobtrusive names, unpatched clothing, and other luxuries — with which children are often sent off to school by their parents, to be ridiculed by other children, is perhaps overcompensated in the following variation on the preceding theme: *Boy triplets at school, two of the same size but one much larger. "You see, Teacher," the largest explains, "my old lady only had two tits, so I had to suck on the old man."* (2:133.)

The principal method of milking humor out of the schoolroom situation is the reverse of the evasive answering of sexual questions by the parents, and consists of answering sexually every innocent question of the teacher's. It seems clear that she is suffering for them. In exactly this vein, in Shakespeare's *Merry Wives of Windsor* (Folio text only, 1623) IV.i.52–70, when the Welsh schoolmaster pronounces 'vocative' as 'focative,' adding that "*Focative* is *caret,*" Dame Quickly underlines his mispronunciation by remarking, "And that's a good roote." ("O'man, forbeare," says the schoolmaster.) Then she is horrified by the Latin exercises, 'Genitive, *horum, harum, horum,*' crying "Vengeance of Ginyes case; fie on her; never name her (childe) if she be a whore." This is the error or device usually called *omne ignotum pro obscœno*, 'everything unknown is taken for obscene' (itself punning on a remark by the British general Galgacus in A.D. 84, as reported by Tacitus), but everything *possible* would be closer.

A little boy excuses himself for being late to school by saying that he had to take the bull to the cow. Teacher: "Couldn't your father do that?" "No, you got to have the bull." (1:269, also in John Steinbeck's *The Grapes of Wrath,* 1939, p. 214, with the variant ending: "Sure he could, but not as good as the bull.") This is known in various other languages: *Kryptádia,* x. 16. On the same theme, using the same trick, *A farmer leaves his youngest son in charge of the stud animals, telling him to collect $30 for the use of the horse, $20 for the bull, and $10 for the boar. A neighbor comes to complain that the farmer's oldest son, Elmer, has made his daughter pregnant. "You'll have to wait till Dad gets home," says the boy. "I don't know what he charges for Elmer."* (D.C. 1942–45.)

The tiresome spelling and arithmetic problems have naturally not been overlooked. *A teacher writes the word "foot" on the blackboard, asking "What's that?" Students: "Twelve inches." "But what else is it?" They don't know. "What has a cow got four of that I have two of?" "Teats."* (N.Y. 1942.) In a rather strained variant: *Lady teacher: "What does a clock have that I have too?" Class: "A face . . . hands . . ." "Now, what has a clock got that I don't have?" Bad little boy: "You ain't got no pendulum."* (Elgart, *Over Sexteen,* 1951, p. 136.) A good deal more will be said about clock and watch jokes, shortly, in the section "The Diaper and the Scythe." *A teacher is explaining an arithmetic problem to a little boy. "Now suppose I lay 5 eggs here and 3 eggs there," she says, "how many will I have altogether?" "Bunk," says the little boy. "I don't believe you can do it."* (Minneapolis, 1949.) — *Teacher: "Johnny, give me a sentence with the word 'fiddle' in it." Johnny: "If the bed is too short my fiddle-stick out."* (Minneapolis, 1949.) Purposely strained puns of this type had a short fad in the middle 1930's, being formalized quickly into a still-surviving pun-game called "Knock-knock," in which the propounder of the impossible pun also answers it, as no one else usually can do so. *"Knock-knock." "Who's there?" "Jeeter." "Jeeter who?" "Jeeter get off the pot."*

The tutorial formula that is most particularly objectionable to students of all ages is the asking of pat questions to which the teacher knows one certain correct answer and will accept no other. (This is particularly prevalent in European schools, even at college level.)

Framed as a written examination it is suffered silently, but in recitation form its insincerity and its superego intention of inculcating dutiful rather than intelligent replies are infuriatingly clear. It is probably no accident that the three school-jokes encountered handling the teacher most sadistically all stem from this situation. *The teacher asks what is the most interesting thing the children saw on their vacation. One saw a big tree, lake, suspension bridge, etc. Little Johnny Jones, the bad boy, says he saw nothing. Teacher: "But there must have been something." Johnny: "Yeah, Teacher, I remember now. I saw a chicken, and Jesus Christ, Teacher, she laid an egg this big!" Teacher, horrified: "What did you say, Johnny Jones?" "I said 'Goodbye, asshole!'"* (2:208.) The pretended freedom of choice in answering does not fool the bad boy — the classroom hero — in the slightest. His pure 'id' replies are directed not only against the teacher, by way of rebellion against the situation that dominates him, but against the good children as well, their letter-perfect recitations, noble sentiments, and generally priggish falling into the demanded pattern.

The teacher asks what is the fastest thing in the world. Good little boy: "Thought." Good little girl: "Lightning." Bad little boy: "Shit." Teacher: "What!" Bad little boy: "Yep. Yesterday on the way home from school, without a thought and quicker than lightning, I shit in my pants." (2:319.) Same situation: *The children are to say what is the most wonderful thing in the world. Good little girl: "The sunset." Too-good little boy: "The love of God." Bad little boy: "Fucking is the most wonderful thing in the world." Teacher: "Oh! Johnny Jones, you go right home, and don't come back without a letter from your father!" Next day. Teacher: "Have you got a letter from your father?" Bad little boy: "No. My father says he thinks fucking is the most wonderful thing in the world too. And he says anybody that doesn't think so must be a cocksucker, and with them he don't correspond!"* (N.Y. 1942.) In a drugstore, rather than schoolroom version, the mother is the permissive parent: *A little boy rushes into a drugstore and shouts, "Gimme a pisspot!" Druggist: "You can't come in here hollering things like that. Go home and get a note from your mother. And furthermore, what size?" Five minutes later the boy is back. "My mother says if it'll fit your face it'll fit her ass, and she won't write no fuckin' note!"* (N.Y. 1953.)

The following burlesque recitation so utterly turns back against the teacher the standard virtues of self-help, inventiveness, and thrift, so carefully inculcated into the poor, that even the final gesture of handing her the regained penny — and with it the rejected lesson — is not missing. *Three Cockney kids are each given a penny by the teacher and told to spend it and tell the class what they got for it. Next day the first boy recites: "I bought two chocolates for my penny, and I gave my sister one." Teacher: "Very good, Alfred. And what did you get, Henry?" "I bought warnuts. I cracked them in half very carefully, and I ate out the meats. Then I made sails out of cancelled postage stamps that I soaked off envelopes, and put them on the warnut shells with matchsticks, and I sold them to the other boys for boats. I got two farthings for them." "Oh, wonderful, Henry! That shows a real self-reliant spirit, self-help, inventiveness and thrift. And what did you do, Willie?" "I bought a sossidge. I untied one end and ate out the meat — then I gave the skin to my father — he used it on my mother — I shit in the skin — took it back to the butcher and told him it was bad — he bit it — said it was — and gave me my penny back." Hands the penny to the teacher.* (N.Y. 1953. Type 1339A, with 2034C.)

The disembodied 'voice from the peanut gallery' or 'someone in the crowd,' that anonymous hero who openly represents the teller's identification-image in so many situations, is not common in the schoolroom joke, where, instead, the bad boy and the somewhat more mature bad girl usually proudly identify themselves. There are, however, a few 'voice' jokes. *A little boy in school cannot spell "sheet" correctly, and is asked by the teacher what his father does for a living. "He's a storekeeper." "Well then, you'd better learn how to spell 'sheet.' Go up and write it on the blackboard one hundred times." Voice from the back row (or, the bad boy asked next what his father does): "My father's a bookie, and six'll get you ten that kid's gonna write 'shit' on the blackboard."* (London, 1954, from an American.) Variant: *A little boy is told to write "sheet" on the blackboard, and writes "shit" instead. For this he is made to write "I will learn to spell 'sheet' correctly" five hundred times. The next day the teacher again tells him to write "sheet" on the blackboard, and this time he writes "shiet." "Gee whiz," says a voice, "now he can't even spell 'shit'."* (N.Y. 1953.) — *The teacher marvels when a girl announces that her mother is having another baby. "But your father has been overseas for two years, hasn't he?" "Well yes," the girl concedes, "but he writes to her every day." "Whew," whistles a boy in the rear of the room, "he must have a long pencil."* (D.C. 1947.)

The blackboard recitation has called into existence a number of pictographic jokes rather difficult to reduce to words. *The teacher tells the children to draw the most exciting thing they know of. One boy draws a lion, "because it roars and eats people." Another draws a train, "because it goes fast and makes a big noise." A third boy draws a line of dots . . . explaining that they are periods, "And around our house when my sister misses one, there's always a lot of excitement."* (D.C. 1952.) The lion and railroad engine, both well-established father-figures to the child (see *The Locomotive God* of William Ellery Leonard, with whose Oedipal agoraphobia compare Freud's), are merely touched upon here in passing. In a more famous pictographic joke, the father-figure is the whole point. *The class is drawing a progressive picture on the blackboard, each child explaining what the picture represents at the step he has drawn. One draws a straight line representing the horizon, the second draws an Indian tepee on this horizon, the third a half-moon decoration near the top of the tepee, the fourth a wisp of smoke rising from the top, the fifth makes a small circle higher up representing the sun, and the sixth draws a set of rays all around the sun. Seventh is the bad boy* [that seventh son of a seventh son!] *He says he doesn't know what to make of it, but that it looks to him (drawing a large half-circle over the whole thing, beginning and ending at the horizon) like his father washing out the bathtub on a Saturday night.* (Scranton, Pa. 1935.) In another version, collected D.C. 1944, a somewhat different drawing is identified as *"My sister wiping herself after her Saturday night bath."* Various modern pictographic jokes of this kind, including both of those just noted, are illustrated in Jiménez' *Picardía Mexicana* (1960) p. 255–66.

The most famous blackboard joke says everything: *The teacher comes into the classroom to find* SHIT *written on the blackboard. "Now I'm not going to scold," she says. "We're going to take care of this on the Honor System. We're all going to shut our eyes while I count out loud to a hundred, and when we open them I want that to be erased." They all close their eyes and she counts. Pitter-patter. Pitter-patter. Squeak-squeak. "One hundred!" They open their eyes and look. On the floor below the blackboard is a fresh pile of shit, and chalked above it:* "THE PHANTOM STRIKES AGAIN." (N.Y. 1950. Urinary cleanup, as 'a suspicious puddle,' in Bennett Cerf's *Good for a Laugh*, 1952, p. 41.) On this fecal 'calling-card,' see Theodor Reik's *The Unknown Murderer* (1936) chap. 8, and the Second Series here (15.III.3 and 5, "Where Is It?" and "Feces as Gift").

The hero of the preceding joke has entered American naval folklore as "The Phantom Asshole" or "Phantom Shitter," who makes mysterious piles on deck during the night to infuriate disliked officers. A number of the stories in Chapter 15, "Scatology" (Second Series) give the otherwise unexplained *mise-en-scène* of a sailor trying to explain such a pile to the captain. ("*It weren't a sea-faring man made that, Cap'n.*" "*How do you know?*" "*You can see it isn't coiled!*" N.Y. 1937, from an ex-sailor who had been at sea during the 1920's.) The explanation is now given in J. S. Fagan's manuscript collection, "*Folklore and the Modern Sailor*" (Indiana University, 1966) p. 19:

> The Phantom Shitter is a person who goes his merry way around the ship, defecating in some of the most unlikely places. Some of his favorite spots, according to the stories, are the executive officer's stateroom, the captain's cabin, and down the hatches leading to the engine-rooms. [I.e. "*Where were you when the shit hit the turbine?*"] Phantom Shitters have also been known to leave poetic, or threatening notes along with . . . other leavings.
>
> One such person was said to have kept the skipper and the XO on the *Fox* in fits for about two months. According to the stories, he was never caught. To the sailor, the Phantom Shitter is a Robin Hood figure. He never performs any of his pranks to harm the common sailor. All of his actions are directed at the officers. . . . A Phantom Shitter always seems to appear in times of severe oppression of the common sailor. When the trouble has subsided he disappears, not to be heard from again until the need for his services arises.

Obviously, the Phantom Shitter is a hero indeed, and his Oedipo-fecal exploits express without disguise the sailors' dreamed-of anal-sadistic revenge against oppressive officers. As a former U.S. marine explained it to me: "*Just when you least expect it, the Phantom Asshole sneaks up in back of the Old Man and slugs him with a sockful of shit.*" (Paris, 1965.)

The idea of such mythical figures or ghosts fits very well with the typical superstitious fears of sailors concerning mythical ships and beings, *e.g.* the "Flying Dutchman." These stem, of course, from the eeriness and the relative helplessness of being off land for long periods, and represent an appeal to quasi-religious powers for protection against the merciless sea. Sailors on protracted submarine duty are attacked even more specifically by this eerieness, and invent mythical pets, such as the "Invisible Dog," for diversion. In one case, during World War II, the Invisible Dog 'scam' or 'put-on' was purposely begun by the medical officer of a submarine to restore the crew's buckling morale after a record period without surfacing. That the Invisible Dog will also leave piles of his droppings — this is the main part of the fun — makes him an evident surrogate of the Phantom Shitter. He is also in the tradition of the mythical or mystical Arkansas "Sooner Dog" (or Druther Dog), who would 'Sooner [or Druther] shit in the house than go outside.' Little metal 'novelty' dogs are also sold in the United States under this name, with chemical tablets to be placed into their rectum, and then lit, causing a long whitish serpentine representing feces to emerge. Jiménez' *Picardía Mexicana* (1960) p. 138, shows such a "Sooner" figure in the shape of a squatting monk, as tailpiece to the chapter on toilets and graffiti.

2. SEX IN THE SCHOOLROOM

The sexually dominant female appears first in jokes as the precocious little girl, then as the sex-starved teacher. Few jokes represent the little boy as taking the initiative. However, since most jokes appear to be originated by men and not by women, the modified incest theme of the dominant schoolgirl or schoolmarm can only be interpreted as a retroactive fantasy — desirable or fearful as the case may be. A filler from the English magazine *Countryman* (Autumn 1946) p. 114, perfectly expresses the little boy's hopeful confusion. *Small boy of five and one-half on his way home from school asks if he might have a lift in the car. "Why, Jimmie, it's not far; you can quite well walk." "No," he replies, "they's two girls what chases me." "Why do they chase you?" "I don't know, they've never caught me yet."*

Open advertisement of their nascent sexuality is put into the little girls' mouths in the classroom. *The girls have been combing their hair in class and putting the combings in the desks. Teacher: "All girls with hair in their drawers raise their hands." 11-year-old girl: "Does fuzz count?"* (N.J. 1942.) — *The little boys' spelling team fails to spell "Peter" correctly. The first little girl asked, rattles off "P-e-t-e-r. How's that, Teacher? They can't come too long or too hard for us!"* (2:320.) — *A boy asking about his older sister's pubic hair is told that it is a sign* of "having religion." *Asked in Sunday school, "What is religion?" he answers, "Religion is hair on your belly."* (Penn. 1930. French versions: *Kryptádia*, 1884, II. 282; XI. 232.) Note the non-religious 'gag' form:

A little girl on the way to school sees a little boy urinating in back of a tree. "What's that?" she says. "That's my natural parts." "What?" "It's just my nature." In school later the teacher asks, "What is nature?" Little girl: "It's that long thing Johnny Jones has between his legs." Teacher: "Oh! How can you say such a thing? I never would have thought you had it in you!" "I didn't. The damn bell rang too soon." (N.Y. 1942.) This is a real children's joke. Its artless use of coincidence is noticeable, also its forcing of humor out of the meaning of 'dictionary words.' In the school I went to, in Scranton, Pa., in the early 1920's, the definition of 'friction' given in the *Wonders of Nature* book as 'the rubbing of two bodies together' seemed so privately and hilariously indecent to the whole class that one little girl, who was my particular sweetheart, ran out of the classroom crying rather than answer the teacher's question "What is friction?" I remember this particularly because I got into several fistfights thereafter, to protect her honor when the incident was mentioned, and lost all of them.

The little boy's first overtures to the teacher are made, in jokes, strictly in a negative sense — he does not like her, he is afraid of her, she is a dumbbell, etc. *A little boy brings a squirrel to school. It runs up the teacher's skirt, and she shrieks, "Get it out, get it out!" "Don't worry, Teacher, when he finds out there aren't any nuts up there he'll come out all right."* (1:383.) This symbolization of the squirrel here as penis — in the up-the-skirt terror, usually the *mouse* — hardly conceals the underlying attraction toward, rather than the stated rejection of, the female genitals. In the following little comedy-pretense of a similar rejection, the actual fascinated attention the boy pays to any mother-surrogate's breasts is not even concealed. *A little boy asks for a turtle-neck sweater for Christmas on the ground that a V-neck sweater is dangerous. "Dangerous?" his mother asks him; "how?" "Teacher has a sweater like that, and every time she bends down, her lungs fall out."* (Idaho, 1932.) In another negative identification of teacher and mother, *The teacher calls up a boy's mother on the phone and says, "Your little boy is masturbating in class, and he'll have to stop it." The mother does not understand. "He's playing with his virile organ," the teacher explains. "Well, take it away from him!"* (N.Y. 1952.) Where 'bad' boys, or those who are not studying well, are demoted to seats at the back of the classroom, masturbation among them — basically as a defiance of the teacher — is common. On a wholesale occurrence of this kind, see Sonia Stirt, "Mass Masturbation in a Public School," in *American Journal of Orthopsychiatry* (1940).

The standard punishment of 'staying after school' is inevitably construed as an intended sexual relation between the teacher and the 'bad boy' being punished in this way. Such incidents are persistently described and retailed as true incidents, especially concerning teen-aged boys, and it seems probable that they did occasionally occur in small American country schools. In weakly modified (urinary) form: *Little boy, waving hand: "Please, Teacher, may I be excused?" Teacher: "No, you stay in and fill up the inkwells."* ("Purple Cow," in *The Cherub*, Jan. 1937, p. 11.) Merely punning on the situation: *During recess Willie Jones, the bad boy, has chalked on the board, "Willie Jones has the biggest prick in school." The teacher indignantly orders him to stay after school. The gang wait an hour for him to appear, and anxiously ask him what happened. He merely winks and says, "It pays to advertise."* (1:451.) — *The biggest boy in class is kept after school by the pretty young teacher for being bad. His friends are waiting for him. "What did she do to you? Did she hit you? Or what?" "I don't know what it was," he says, "but it sure beats pissing all to hell!"* (2:366.) Sexual relations with the teacher will be given under the subject of permissiveness, where the essence is the child's activity and not his passivity as here.

The growing obsolescence of religion in English-speaking countries over the last century, certainly since Darwin, and the *Encyclopædia Britannica's* higher critical handling of the Bible in its ninth edition (1875–89), has reduced the Sunday-school story, as noted above, to hardly more than a relic, but it may still be possible to collect examples from older informants. Most of the few on hand have been collected both in Sunday-school forms and in variants with the religious background completely lacking. *Minister: "Do you know where little boys and girls go when they do bad things?" Bad Boy: "Sure, back of the churchyard."* (1:247. Compare, "The Mess Line," *Army Times* July 1, 1944, p. 18: '*"Where do good girls go?" asked the teacher. "To heaven." "And where do bad girls go?" "Down to the docks when the fleet comes in," chorused the class.'*) Nothing but heaven is left.

With the following relic, reset in a 'college' background, compare the original forms — given below — all based on the famous Sunday-school question as to human and divine origins: "Who made you?" *College professor to young co-ed: "Who made you, little girl?" Co-ed: "Originally or recently?"* (*Smile and the World Smiles With You*, Guam, 1952, p. 18.) An orally collected version of this (D.C. 1944) arrives only halfway, in changing the meaning of 'make' from strict progenitorship to coitus: the story is told of *two little girls who are going to tell an even littler girl 'the facts of life' and who begin with the routine question, "Well, do you know who made you?"* in precisely the sexual sense that the Sunday-school question is intended to wrap up in teleological disguise.

Here are the more authentic forms of the story, both being carefully worked-out situations as compared to the 'college' wise-crack. These are the 'pre-arranged answers that go awry' (Motifs J1741.3, and 3.1), a trick of the 'stupid scholar' in 16th-century joke collections in both English and French (Des Périers' *Nouvelles récréations*, 1558, No. 7). *Sunday-school children are taught to answer the stock questions, "Who made Adam and Eve?" "What did Adam say to Eve?" etc. At the recitation before the bishop, the teacher jogs the students' memories by jabbing them privately with a hatpin. "What did Eve say to Adam?" the bishop asks a little girl, while the teacher draws back the pin to jab. "Don't you stick that thing in me!"* (2:233.) Same situation, with the *Sunday-school stock questions and replies: "Who made you? — God made me." "Who were the first man and woman? — Adam and Eve." The little boy who is to answer the first question has been "excused to go to the basement" just before the arrival of the bishop, who therefore begins with the second boy: "Who made you?" "Adam and Eve." The bishop is horrified. Teacher: "No, no! God made you." "He did not. The boy God made is downstairs taking a shit."* (N.Y. 1940. Anti-Virgin in *Kryptádia*, XI. 205.)

This is extremely close to a French text given in the Alsatian patois in *Kryptádia* (1884) II. 278, "*Le Tout est de bien commencer.*" In this version (in translation), which is obviously older than the American form and perhaps its origin: *The visiting ecclesiastic is examining the best pupil in the village school. "Well, my boy," he says, "what is your first thought and deed every morning?" The boy does not know the expected answer. To help him along the examiner says, "The first thing you do is to say your prayers to your Father in heaven, isn't it?"* "No," *says the boy, finding his tongue: "first I go behind the barn and shit."* Note how the European clerically-dominated 'village school' has become the American 'Sunday school,' the religious element in both cases being the story-tellers' main scatological target. Here is a true story, not a joke: *A little girl whose mother had just had a baby was extremely disappointed to learn that the baby was a girl instead of the boy she had expected. She was told patiently that the parents would have preferred a boy too* [obviously the origin of her sexual self-hatred], *but that it was "God's will." She disappeared into the bathroom and did not come out for some time. "What are you doing in there so long?" her father asked her finally. "Shitting on God."* (N.Y. 1965.)

III. THE DIAPER AND THE SCYTHE

Human aggregations differ from those of most of the other mammals in the continuing presence of the male in the entourage of the female after she has become pregnant. With the exception of certain species of apes and the horned & hooved animals, such as deer and mountain sheep, that are powerful enough to gather harems and to drive away all younger males, the peculiar and continuing sexual possessiveness displayed by the human male for the female is quite rare in the mammalian orders. This avoidance of anything that might be called a 'family' effectively protects the nursing young from the sexual jealousy of the father (who cannot assist in feeding them, as can birds), and where quasi-families are set up among mammals, the father tends to eat or otherwise destroy the children unless the female is strong enough to prevent him. The harem system protects the young slightly, partly by their very number and partly by the continuing sexual busy-ness of the father; but when monogamy is approached — as, sometimes, among the larger cats and human beings — the infant is in no small danger from the mother's consort.

Nothing that is said here is intended to be humorous, nor is it humorous. Little boys in Anglo-Germanic countries have only within living memory ceased to be dressed protectively in girls' clothes, such as pinafores, kilts, and the semi-dresses of Fauntleroy collars and Buster Brown belted suits, with long curls to match, until a special initiatory rite at puberty allows them to drop girls' clothing and act the part of men. This particular rite ('confirmation': the *'bar mitzvah'* or 'son of the commandment' of religious Jews) is itself a modification at fourth or fifth hand of a ceremony clearly intended not to make the child the social and sexual equal of the father, but to deprive him physically of the ability to compete sexually with the father at all. It is the subliminal realization of this original reversal of the pre- tended meaning of 'confirmation' among Christians and Jews that makes the boy's soprano announcement, "Today I am a man," so richly humorous to the adult.

This is certainly not the place to trace at full length the history of the origin of human patriarchy and of the killing of the male (*i.e.* sexually uninteresting) children by the father, through the historical stages of plain killing and eating, through ceremonial offering to the god before killing and eating, then the sacrificing and eating of the god or the god's son (still current), the substitution of an animal or money- payment for the son (the Jewish 'redemption of the son' or *pidyon ha-ben*), and finally the mere cutting off of the child's penis, or some part of it, to dissuade him from competing for the mother or other harem-females.

For those interested, this whole history will be seen briefly, as in a lightning flash, in the story of Abraham and his sons, one of whom he drives into the desert with his mother to die (*Genesis,* xxi. 14–16), the other of whom he sets out to kill personally (xxii. 6–10), but satis- fies himself instead, at God's suggestion, with killing a ram, and cut- ting off only the tips of the boys' penis-skins with a special knife. (See *Exodus,* iv. 24–26, as to the bird-goddess Zipporah's circumcision knife of *stone,* implying the ancientness of these castratory practices as harking back beyond the human use of metal tools.) Judæo- Christian groups have since reduced the date of circumcision from the beginning of the boy's sexual maturation at thirteen (*Genesis,* xvii. 23–25) when it does him the most irreparable emotional damage, to eight days (xxi.4, baptism among Christian sects), and have ex- changed the religious rationalization for the even more tenuous one of 'hygiene.' But they still enact a token recollection of the original killing or castration, in the confirmation ceremonial at the age of thirteen; and retain with inordinate and inexplicable dread the autumn circumcision festival (Yom Kippur) still observed by Mohammedan groups in the form of a wholesale roundup of all the pubescent boys — once with camels, now with jeeps — to circumcise them *en masse.*

I. FATHER TIME

Far older recollections of this history still survive. The one oldest mythic survival still the subject of ritual in Western civilization is unquestionably the festival of Kronos, the titan who castrated his father Saturn with a scythe, on New Year's Eve. Kronos, or 'Father Time' (appearing in the combined characters of both Death and Time, with the scythe, hourglass, and cloaked wings common to both), not only still wanders with his scythe once a year, but he has changed places in the drama with the father he castrated and killed — in order to marry his sister — and, for his rebellion, is cut down with his own scythe at the very stroke of midnight by a small, naked boy wearing only a large, well-filled diaper and a chest-banner reading "Happy New Year!" In the street, in New York City, for instance, the Saturnalia is observed by several million or more hysterical worshippers, who shuffle about screaming and blowing horns for reasons they are unable to explain, in a special area (called Times Square) in which storewindows are barricaded with wooden fences to prevent damage — and looting — by the overexcited natives.

This double displacement of the castratory struggle between the father and the son, to the bearded grandfather and naked grandson who can enact it with easier identification and less feeling of sin, and dread of punishment, on the part of the spectator, is discussed at some length in Otto Rank's *Inzest-Motif* (1912) chapters 6 and 9.*ii*, though he does not make mention of the New Year's survival. That the winter solstice is, however, the focus of most of this anxiety, any study of the Christmas – New Year's week, with its Saturnalia and Feast of Fools observances, will immediately demonstrate. All the material points so unmistakably in the same direction that it is remarkable it has never been collected: the Phoenician baby-eating god Baal, who became the Greek Saturn-Kronos, and, with the blood wiped off his chops, Zeus; the Saturnalia itself, especially in the later forms with the father-castrating and father-defying titan appearing as the Lord of Misrule (see Frazer's *Golden Bough*), the Jewish anti-chorus of Purim, and the Irish Beltane; even the solemn religious calendaring to this day among Catholics, of the first day of spring as the day the Virgin became pregnant, of Christmas, nine months later, as the day She gave birth to Jesus, and of the eighth day thereafter, January 1st, as the Feast of the Circumcision. (Now expurgated on French saints' day calendars to the allusive '*Octave de Noël.*' I am waiting for some innocent French mother to name a child born on New Year's day after precisely that 'saint'!) Santa Claus himself is only Saturn in a red suit (but with the same old whiskers), dealing out toys exclusively to good children nowadays. The 'switches' for bad children that he once dealt out as Father Nicholas are now forgotten, with such similar Teutonic castration lore as the Daumenabschneider or Thumb-cutter of *Struwwelpeter* (on whom see *Neurotica,* 1951, No. 9).

Readers of science fiction — and particularly of the readers' own mimeographed fan-magazines, which are so much more revealing than the stereotyped professional pulp — will find endless lore since H. G. Wells' *The Time Machine* (1895) on that science-fictional on-slaught against Time that rivals even the similarly endless war on the father-god's planet, Mars. (Martians, in the science-fiction illustrators' pantheon, as codified by Edgar Rice Burroughs, are red, stiff, tall, robust, heavy-chested, and really good at heart. Venusians, on the other hand, are female, green, shapeless, slimy, diseased, batrachian, steam-ing hot, with sagging breasts, and truly evil.) The principal problem in the war on Time — the problem frankly avowed and recalculated innumerable times — is *to go back in time and kill your own grand-father, and yet somehow manage to be born (without a grandfather) in order to go back in time and kill him.* Mark Twain fumbled his way much closer to the real problem in his equally jocular discussion of the boy and his father who marry a mother and daughter (the boy marrying the mother — *ha ha ha* — and the father marrying the daugh-ter), and the complicated relationships then ensuing when the daugh-ter has a baby, with the net result somehow that the boy ends up being *his own grandfather.* Other paradoxes of this kind (since the 1790's) flirt even more openly with the symbolized incest.

As useful references on the subject of Time are difficult to find, I will mention here, for the use of anyone who cares to follow this very rich furrow, at least the following in addition to those above: Joost Meerloo's "Father Time," in *Psychiatric Quarterly* (Oct. 1948, and Oct. 1950), with his further references to the psychoanalytic lit-erature, XXII. 608, and XXIV. 671; John W. Dunne's *An Experiment with Time* (1927, later revised); Freud on the clock as conscience, in his *Collected Papers,* II. 158-9; Marie Bonaparte's "Time and the Unconscious," in *International Journal of Psycho-analysis* (1940); and much other material on Father Time and on watches and clocks: for instance, the automata of Greece and the Middle Ages, both lethal (Leonardo da Vinci) and merely horological, and the clock that turns all to smiles on welcoming Alice through the Looking-Glass. On Time, as identical with Death, see especially Erwin Panofsky's *Studies in Iconology* (1939), or even the identical representations in so informal a source as the *Pequeño Larousse Ilustrado* (Buenos Aires, 1943) at "Alegoría," p. 42, and "Tiempo," Suppl. p. 1482. Hogarth's bitter caricature, captioned "As Statues Moulder into Worth," showing Time smoking a clay pipe while he dismembers a statue and slashes a painter's canvas with his scythe, should also not be overlooked.

One folklore survival in which the whole drama is realistically enacted, of the father's attempted killing or castration of the son — not with one knife but many — and the son's miraculous escape, is the famous Hindu Rope Trick, which no one has ever seen (or will), but which a friend-of-a-friend has been swearing to since the century when it was first slightingly mentioned in the *Vedanta Sutras*. In a provocative but very condensed page in *American Imago* (1951) VIII. 287–8, William H. Desmonde notes some of the psychoanalytic implications of the related folktale of "Jack and the Beanstalk," which — although Dr. Desmonde does not mention this — is the Hindu Rope Trick told frankly as a fairy-tale (Aarne Type 328), with the pie-in-the-sky heaven that the climbing boy goes to, the ogre's wife that he commits some type of adultery with there, and all. On the identity of the ogre, see the joke, below, on the little girl and boy playing sexually under the very tree in which their Father — as in *Genesis,* iii.8 — is hiding.

2. THE STOPPED CLOCK

Where several thousand years of mythology, religion, mass-hysterical ceremonials (like New Year's Eve), and mass-neurotic literatures (like science fiction) have not been able to allay successfully the fear of being killed and eaten by one's father, or, at the very least, castrated by him by way of punishment for one's sexual urges toward the mother, sister, or other women of the father's harem (such as the maid), it is hardly to be expected that a handful of dirty jokes can do the job. Nevertheless, two remarkable stories may be cited identifying the timepiece with the penis in circumcision-castration themes.

Both stories are based on impossible situations, and may therefore be assumed to exist simply to allay — by means of humorous treatment — the anxiety focussed in this subject for both the originators of the stories and those who repeat them. The first is a Jewish story. *A man in a small town finds that his watch has stopped. He goes into a shop displaying a large watch outside, and asks the man to fix his watch. "I don't fix watches." "But you have a big watch hanging outside." "I know, but I don't fix watches. I'm a mohel (circumciser)." "So why do you have a watch outside?" "Nu, so what should I have — a putz?"* (N.Y. 1940.) It is self-evident that the hypothetical 'putz' (penis) sign would involve at least symbolic castration (of the penis-sign's former 'owner') as an advertisement for circumcision. *A man is smuggling a valuable watch into England. In order to hide it he hangs it on his penis [!] and would have gotten it through successfully except that when the customs inspector asks him, "Do you have the time on you, old cock?" the man faints.* (N.Y. 1953.)

With this may be compared the following, in *Joe Miller's Jests* (1739) No. 107, following a joke on a 'devout Gentleman' whose watch was stolen from him 'while he was at Prayers.' It should be understood that ladies at this period — as gentlemen now, in a 'fob' pocket — wore their watches *en chatelaine* just over the pubis. *George Ch—n, who was always accounted a very blunt Speaker, asking a young Lady one Day, what it was o'Clock, and she telling him her Watch stood, I don't wonder at that, Madam, said he, when it is so near your ——.* The suspicion raised by the first story above, and strengthened here, that the *stopped watch* represents impotence, becomes a certainty when one observes the third story in *Joe Miller's* train of associations from the stolen watch to the stopped watch:

> 108. A modest Gentlewoman being compelled by her Mother to accuse her Husband of Defect, and being in the Court, she humbly desired of the Judge, that she might write her Mind, and not be obliged to speak it, for Modesty's sake; the Judge gave her that Liberty, and a Clerk was immediately commanded to give her Pen, Ink, and Paper, whereupon she took the Pen without dipping it into the Ink, and made as if she would write; says the Clerk to her, Madam, there is no Ink in your Pen. *Truly, Sir,* says she, *that's just my Case, and therefore I need not explain myself any further.* (Taken from *Comedians Tales,* 1729; reissued as *Spiller's Jests,* p. 7.)

In its modern form this is told as of *an American in Paris who refuses the egg in his whiskey that will 'put lead in his pencil,' on the grounds that he has 'no one to write to.'* (1:299.) Other material on the identification of impotence with castration will be found in Chapter 13.

A large amount of material could be collected, if wanted, on the clock as conscience, as noted above in Freud's *Collected Papers,* II. 158–9, where the meaning of conscience (the superego) as the internalization of parental prohibitions concerning sex and hostility will also be found discussed. The inevitable presents of a fountain pen and wristwatch at the modern Jewish boy's *bar-mitzvah* confirmation — on which, see above — draw their equally inevitable humor ("Today I am a fountain pen!") strictly from their symbolic level. Less humorously, a remarkable incident appearing in an AP dispatch of Feb. 27, 1951, is reprinted in *Neurotica* No. 8: p. 39, of a boy who killed himself by means of a home-made electrocution device attached to his arm and leg while he slept, and set off by an alarm clock at 6 A.M. The sin, in his sleep, for which he felt he deserved death, is not hard to discern. There is also the masochist novel, *The Big Clock,* by Kenneth Fearing ('name-fatality'?), made into a popular movie, about a man who is hired to chase himself — all unbeknownst — for seducing the 'boss's' wife; but it is difficult to take seriously these grown-up proliferations of childish fantasies of sexual sin and parental punishment.

Folk materials come closer to the point, at least in the identification of the wound-up clock and male potency, if not of the clock as the censorious and all-seeing father's face. (Grandville's, and much later Magritte's, sky-floating *eye,* which has recently become the single most popular paranoid theme in derivative advertising art. Compare De Chirico's "Enigma of the Hour," 1914, and Dali's famous *limp watches* in "The Persistence of Memory," 1931.) As to male potency, in a long mock 'debtor letter,' in which an old farmer explains why getting any money out of him to pay his bills 'would be like trying to ram a pound of melted butter up a wildcat's ass with a red-hot poker' (or, 'with a wilted noodle'), the recounting of the farmer's sexual troubles ends with him being left with nothing but "*A Waterbury watch and a stricture . . . I was kept busy winding my watch and running to piss.*" (D.C. 1945–48.) In another version he is left with "*A dollar watch and the clap. The clap ran; the watch wouldn't.*" (N.Y. 1953.) Similarly, *A sailor in Atlantic City naïvely refuses a streetwalker's invitation, "Do you want your watch fixed?" He is told by a buddy that this is simply a form of solicitation, and accepts the next such offer. A year later, when another streetwalker asks him if he wants his watch fixed, he replies, "I had it fixed a year ago, and it's been running ever since."* (On the concept of venereal disease as a punishment for sexual sin, see Chapter 12, in Series Two.)

The clock image is also reported as a gag-line worked into a conversation: *A man recently married was asked how his wedding present, an alarm clock, worked. "Fine! The clock, my wife, and I all go off at the same time."* (Calif. 1941. If this is anything like a telephone ringing at the same time, it can be added to all definitions of pandemonium.) Exactly matching, on the dust-jacket prepared for the publisher Grayson in 1952, in taking over Elgart's *Over Sixteen* (1951), a single cartoon is added to the new issue, noted as 'an overflow' making the book 'gay from cover to cover and flap-happy besides,' and showing a bride and groom lying in bed with the covers rounded in a tent over his sleeping erection, while nearby three alarm clocks are set to go off at two-hour intervals beginning at midnight, to reconsummate his marriage. This is, of course, only a dream. In a woman's conversational complaint of her husband, recorded D.C. 1949, the more usual identification is made: "*Why, the goddamn sonofabitch takes more time to wind his watch.*" This naturally brings to mind the famous opening of Sterne's *Tristram Shandy* (1760) in which the wife interrupts the husband in coitus to ask *whether he has wound the clock.* Much more evidence could be cited, but enough has been given to identify with some certainty Time (Kronos) as the castrator, the scythe that he shares with Death as the instrument of the operation, and the clock — formerly the hourglass — as his *memento mori.*

IV. MASTURBATION

1. THE CASTRATORY THREAT

Children are very clever and very forlorn, but — in this culture at least — they do not have a chance. Whatever the pretense of freedom or 'modernity' in its training, the child very soon understands that its sexual experimentations, whether with its own body or with anyone else's, are considered wrong by adults and are usually punished, if not by castration then by the specific threat of castration or some equivalent such as circumcision. This last, though adults find it easy to agree to (for the child) under some 'hygienic' or other rationalization, is guaranteed not to fool any child.

However cleverly hidden, the threat may always be discerned by its effect. In the following story, the dénouement, as given, does not at all explain the child's terror and sudden obedience, and it may confidently be assumed that the ending is a mere veiling of the castration threat — probably from the originator of the story as well as from its tellers. As it stands, the story is really in the class with the "Sleeve Job" story (Chapter 8.III.3-4) and that other "Most Maddening Story in the World," in which we are left wondering *what* was on the paper, or in store for the young man on his wedding night. That it is Santa Claus, whose jolly, fat fraud has been discussed above, who is chosen here as the custodian of the great secret — castration — seems significant indeed.

A little boy makes a pest of himself by refusing to get off the department store hobby-horse when taken to see Santa Claus. When the mother gives up, Santa Claus offers to help out. He whispers a few words in the little boy's ear. The little boy pales and immediately jumps off and leaves dutifully with his mother. In the street the mother asks him what it was that Santa said that made him so obedient. The child's lip trembles, but he will not say. "Did he say he'd bring you presents if you were a good boy?" "No, Mummy, he didn't say anything about presents." "Then what did he say, darling?" "He said, 'You little son of a bitch, if you don't get off that horse this minute, I'll kick the living piss out of you!'" (Anecdota Americana II, 1934, No. 109.)

The compiler of *Anecdota II*, and almost every other teller of this story, piles on the profanity hard, to try to invent a threat that will have some possible relation to the observed effect, but their profanity is the measure of their failure, as bad little boys are quite used to being sworn at. Actually, in this terrific unveiling, Santa Claus drops the mask, and is again — not just Father Christmas with his 'switches' for bad children, but Saturn-Kronos with his still-living scythe. (The author faithfully promises that 'what song the Syrens sang, or what name Achilles assumed when he hid himself among women' will not be solved in the present volume; but on the first of these other classic problems see Henry Alden Bunker's "The Voice as (Female) Phallus," in *Psychoanalytic Quarterly*, 1934, III. 391-429. The Indian Rope

Trick has already been identified above as the folktale of "Jack and the Beanstalk," Aarne Type 328, with extensive references, not one of which draws this obvious parallel.) Compare now the similar story in which the disobedient little boy is tamed by exactly the opposite method to castration — but one still closely related: *A guest at a bridge-party, "a gray-haired man," offers to get an unruly boy child to be quiet. He takes the boy upstairs, and when he comes down a few minutes later all is quiet. Asked after the party, by the boy's mother, what the secret method was, he explains: "It was really very simple. I taught him how to masturbate."* (2:184.)

A little boy is told that if he bites his fingernails he will get "a great big stomach like that lady" — his mother points, as she says this, to a pregnant woman on the streetcar. The boy stares at the woman and when she angrily asks him why, he whispers, "I know what you've been doing!" (2:343.) The form of the story, and the end-line used, are the same as those in the well-known medieval story of the magpie that had all its feathers pulled out for telling the husband that his wife ate a 'good morsell' (namely, an eel) in his absence; and 'ever after, whanne the [mag]pie sawe a balled [*sic*] or a pilled man, or a woman with an high forhede, the pie saide to *t*hem, "ye spake of the ele"; (Geoffroy de La Tour-Landry, *The Book of the Knight of La Tour-Landry*, 1372, ed. Thomas Wright, 1906, chap. 16; and Wright's note, p. 208, mentioning that the story 'is often repeated by the medieval *conteurs*' and that 'it is the subject of a much more modern story,' which, however, he does not give. Motif J551.5.)

So much for the form. The actual matter is obviously that of *Struwwelpeter* by Dr. Heinrich Hoffmann (1845), in which the little boy — called Conrad, but clearly the Struwwelpeter of the title-page — has his thumbs cut off by a tailor with an enormous shears for no worse sin than sucking them. Again, the utter disparity of cause & effect indicates that the child's real sin is masturbation and the real punishment castration. The psychoanalytic literature aside (see Dr. Rudolph Friedmann's remarkable "Struwwelpeter," in *Neurotica*, 1951, No. 9; p. 25–32; enlarged and reprinted in Dwight Macdonald's *Parodies: An Anthology*, 1960, p. 493–501), the equivalence of nail-biting or thumb-sucking to masturbation, and of the measures or threats — here pregnancy! — intended to prevent these to threats of castration, is baldly and unequivocally stated in the joke intended to follow immediately after the one above in *Anecdota II: 'Another young ster was in the habit of pissing on the streets, a habit of which his mother wished to break him. She called him and chastized him severely, telling him that if he continued she would be forced to cut his prick off. "Aw," said he, "what the hell do I care! All the girls have theirs cut off and tucked in".'* (2:353, quoted exactly. 2:343, above, is the first joke preceding to which the prefatory 'Another youngster' can refer.) As castration is a ridiculous punishment for urination, the following joke will make clear both what is meant and what is being punished: *"What are you doing behind that tree?" "Just pissing." "Well stop this minute. You know good and well you don't have to pump it out!"* (Idaho, 1919, told in Negro dialect.)

A boy masturbating in a tree is reprimanded by an old lady who tells him that this wastes a possible president, baseball player, aviator, or similar. The boy continues anyhow, and the ejaculate lands at the old lady's feet. "I guess you're right," he says. "There goes an acrobat." (2:42.) Actually this is only a wisecracked version of the story, with the inner emphasis shifted to the exhibitionistic relation with the 'old lady.' *Anecdota I* gives the original form, opening with the phrase, 'Everybody is familiar with the story . . .' *The little boy is masturbating, looks at the semen in his hand and says, "You might have been a barber, a farmer . . . or even President. But now, well . . ." suddenly swallowing it down, "I'll give you another chance."* (1:149.)

There is finally the threat of death, on which H. A. Bunker makes the following parallel:

> For the patient, death and castration were interchangeable terms; they were one and the same thing. Not only did he have many fantasies of death and of suicide (simultaneously with a terror of death) and numerous dreams involving various appurtenances of death (cemeteries, etc.) . . . but his equating of death and castration was unequivocally proved to him by an occasion on which, seeing a young man stretched out naked on a table in the morgue, his instantaneous thought was, "It will never rise again." (*Psychoanalytic Quarterly*, 1934, III.405. Compare the Egyptian depictions of the dead Osiris with an erection, and the folk and other materials given in Chapter 13, in Series Two, identifying erection and resurrection.)

A little boy going to a party is told by his mother that he will die if he kisses a girl. He kisses a girl anyhow, but suddenly runs away. The girl pursues him and asks why. "Because I'm going to die. My mother said so and now I know she's right — I could feel myself starting to get stiff while I was kissing you." (*Clean Dirt,* Addendum, 1938.) To intrude a personal example of the minced castration-threat, I was told when small that if I played the 'pee-pee' doctor-game any more with the little girl next door, my mother would hit me with a broom and then I could never 'get married.' I took this very seriously, at the time, and am still made nervous by the sound of a broom sweeping. This idea of being unfitted for marriage is perhaps only a Hungarian superstition (compare the medieval accusation against witches that they could *nouer l'aiguillette,* or hex the codpiece); but the same misfortune is believed by some, in America, to result from walking under a ladder. (On the broom see, of course, the witch's phallic-flying broom, classically illustrated in Goya's *Los Caprichos,* No. 68, "Pretty Mistress," quite Lesbian in tone; and in the forthright illustration of flying coitus on the witches' broom — with the Lesbian tone studiously avoided — in Alexander King's illustrations to Samuel Putnam's translation of *All the Extant Works of Rabelais,* 1929, II.632 and 708.)

The atmosphere now begins to lighten somewhat for the child. In the death-threat the parent has gone too far, for experience in 'falling from grace' quickly shows the child that the threat is hollow. The parental prohibition is defied, neither death nor castration is found actually to follow, and the child turns at once to ridiculing the forbidding parent, to masturbation without feelings of wrong, and, eventually — at least in jokes — to the incest with the sister or mother that is really what is being forbidden behind the shibboleth of masturbation.

A little boy is told that if he continues to masturbate he will die. His mother listens at his bedroom door. "I'll die! I'll die! I'll die, diddle-diddle, dee-die, dee-die!" (*Tune: "The Campbells Are Coming"* or *"Over the Hills and Far Away."* N.Y. 1952.) The 'diddle-diddle' element, here slyly imported to refer to masturbation, was, in Shakespeare's time, a popular refrain, as in Autolycus' peddler's pack that 'has the prettiest love-songs for maids; so without bawdry, which is strange; with such delicate burthens of dildos and fadings, "jump her and thump her" . . . where some stretch-mouthed rascal would, as it were, mean mischief and break a foul gap into the matter' — *A Winter's Tale* (MS. 1610) IV. iii. 193–98. It has fallen away since to the purposeful 'nonsense' of a nursery-rhyme refrain, as in "Hey Diddle-

Diddle, the Cat and the Fiddle," or, perhaps more relevantly, in "Lavender's Green" (before 1685):

> Some to make hay, Diddle diddle,
>   some to the Corn,
> Whilst you and I, Diddle diddle,
>   keep the bed warm.

(Reprinted from the broadside, in Iona & Peter Opie's *Oxford Dictionary of Nursery Rhymes*, 1951, p. 266 and pl. x.)

"There are those in this congregation," shouts the revivalist, *"who have committed the unutterable sin of heing-and-sheing. Stand up and repent!" Three-quarters of the congregation stand up. "And there are those who have committed that double sin of sins, heing-and-heing. Stand up!" The rest of the men stand up. "And I positively know that there are those that have committed that triplest of triple sins, sheing-and-sheing!" The rest of the women all rise, sobbing hysterically. No one is left sitting but one little boy. "Elder Hogmouth," he quavers, "how do you stand on meing-and-meing?"* (N.Y. 1942.)

2. GROUP PERMISSION

Searching for permission to experiment sexually, at least with its own body, the child turns to every possible authority-figure: the brother, father, doctor, playmates, even to the mysterious stranger who answers Yes when everyone else says No. (The 'gray haired man' who explains calmly, *"I taught him how to masturbate."* — 2:184.) A male teacher in the New York primary schools reported (1953) that he was chosen by the little boys of his class to give them this needed permission — or to be the butt of the necessary defiance of authority — in the following repeated pantomime: *"Hey, teach'! Man sees a duck — he shoots it (pointing the hand upward at penis level as though a gun) — stabs it ten times — it's dead!"* Even a mock-religious justification is adduced. *A man finds a boy masturbating in a public toilet. "Say, stop that!" "Let me alone, mister. I'm a Christian Scientist, and I'm screwing my girl in Chicago."* (N.Y. 1949. Also an elaborate variant, 1953, in which a whole parade of clergymen — rabbi, minister, and priest — are defied by the boy before topping them with his own 'permissive' religious affiliation.)

Swimming-pool jokes, with their implied exhibition of the genitals, offer a surprising corroboration of the identification between circumcision and the punishment for sexual acts. *Two poor boys and two rich boys (or two country boys and two city boys) are swimming naked in the same pool. "Did you notice the small pricks on the rich kids?" says one of the poor boys. "They have toys to play with," the other explains.* (N.Y. 1952.) Collected also as a bare gag-line, in Minneapolis, 1946, about *the Scotsman who cut the pockets out of his son's pants so he wouldn't have to buy him any toys.* Here the permissive and castratory (the cutting) elements are mixed. In a version collected in Monterey about the same time, the connection with circumcision is directly stated: *"I told her to do like they did in the old days — not give them any toys, and you won't have to circumcise them."* Similarly: *"Twenty dollars to have Junior circumcised?" objects the father. "Let him wear it off, the way I did!"* (N.Y. 1945.)

The most common appeal for permission, in fact as well as in jokes, is the child's own contemporaries: brothers not too much older, and playmates. *Two little boys are standing urinating together. "I wish I had a big prick like my brother," says one; "he has to use four fingers to hold it." "Well you're using four fingers." "Yes, but I'm pissing on three of them."* (N.Y. 1953.) The whole manipulatory tone here — lacking only the mention of urinating at a target or for height — suggests that the ostensible subject, urination, is simply the usual masturbational screen.

The so-called 'orgies' of children and adolescents, plugged very hard by the newspapers over the last twenty years or more (quite aside from the recent infantile hippie 'group gropes'), are by no means the enactments of 'unbridled lust' that parent-teacher associations and police authorities tend to announce, but rather the child's attempt to achieve group approval — and therefore individual permission — for acts which are powerfully urgent but almost equally powerfully forbidden. That *"Everybody does it"* (the title of a Mozart comic opera, *Così fan tutte,* 1790, and of a more recent James M. Cain pocket-reprint) is still the best available permission for what are felt to be disapproved acts. The mass formalizations of hostile impulses in games and other public entertainments, such as football, wrestling, TV murder-dramas, war, lynching, etc., necessary before American adults can enjoy these without mental reservation, are an even better example of the same mechanism of permission. In a more childish and probably more normally sexual form: *A club of boys are playing "ring-jerk poker." Each boy puts in a dime, and the one who finishes masturbating first wins the pot. Leader: "All right, everybody stop now. The fellow in the corner came." Boy: "Uh-uh, I got a good hand and I'm playing it out."* (N.Y. 1949. On the obvious homosexual element here, and its formalization into publicly accepted hostile forms in gambling, wrestling, etc., see Ralph R. Greenson, in *American Imago,* 1947, IV, No. 2: p. 61–77; and the further material in Dr. John Del Torto's "On Gambling," in *Neurotica,* 1950, No. 6: p. 11–22.)

Group sexual activities are always essentially masturbatory, for all their plural pretense. This is the paradox, or mathematical nature, of orgies. As I have noted in *The Fake Revolt* (1967) p. 31: 'the actual 3-in-1 oil orgy, involving kissing-HER-while-screwing-HIM, or screwing several other people (and the dog) simultaneously, under the excuse of drugged drunkenness, not only necessarily and permutationally must involve sexual perversion, but is also, in the deepest sense, the setting up of a sexual hall of mirrors, or a thinning-out and cooling-down of the sexual charge and sexual relationship, to the point where there is really nobody present but the drugged orgiast, whose main emotion is an intense and frightened narcissistic concern *to touch no one,* except with the necessary tip of his or her penis or clitoris, and sometimes not even with that. The masturbator's dream. Obviously, a better solution would be a vibrating scalp-massage motor.' The exhibitionistic or show-off element is also very prominent, whether under the hoary pretext of religion (or *anti*-religion), as in the so-called 'Black Mass' and other devil-worshipping rites, or in the modern 'group grope' and 'street fucking' proposed by the current mock-révolté and drug-addicted hippies. (Hitting *Time* magazine, July 7, 1967, p. 17/3, in a brief and permissive publicity reference to the hippies' 'group grope,' of which the essential difference from the more solid citizens' 'wife-swapping' is really only its simultaneity — but that will come.)

In Scranton, Pa., in 1930, the little girls of about ten reported a secret 'clothespin club,' in which each girl put a piece of candy in the pot, and the winner was determined by the depth of entry achieved on a clothespin. Public performances like these give rise to fancy virtuosity, recollected in such lines as the boy's jeer: *"Can you change hands without missing a stroke?"* (Pa. 1934.) One is reminded somehow of the efficiency-expert father's single-stroke method of taking a bath, as described in Frank Gilbreth Jr.'s *Cheaper by the Dozen*. A similar narcissistic lavishing of a long-drawn caress on the body — under the guise of cutting down the amount of body-handling to an absolute minimum — was the winning of a radio shaving-contest for college boys (N.Y. 1940), in which chorus-girls whisked up the lather, held the mirrors, etc., by a young man who completed the whole job in a single stroke, in the *boustrophedon* or ox-turn fashion of ancient Greek writing. Compare the 'trip around the world' or prolonged body-tonguing, considered the ultimate oragenital caress.

The wet dream represents the complete but innocent failure of repression, and, whatever pretenses are made about it, is welcomed by the young boy as a safe way out of an impossible conflict between impulse and interdict. In *Geraldine Bradshaw* (1950) chap. 20, Calder Willingham catches, with the most remarkable ear for dialogue, the once-a-year school lecture 'for the benefit of pubescent juniors and seniors,' in which the fake-friendly 'Old Doc' begins with 'the dirty nightmare . . . the foul, noxious weed of night, a weeeeeeed in the garden of the soul,' ending, of course, with the stereopticon slides of the 'spotted victims' of tertiary syphilis, caught somehow in a dream. The more permissive approach of the general practitioner is roughly approved in the following: *High-strung Young Man: "Doctor, I suffer from wet dreams and loss of manhood." Old-Time Doctor: "Why hell, that's not a disease. That's a pastime!"* (Minneapolis, 1946.)

V. INCEST

There is finally the question of the content of the dream. Who is the dreamer fantasying in his sleep, if one may be so unkind as to inquire? Is it really just movie-stars, innocently attained in a new *Hypnerotomachia Poliphili-Perversi*, as with *The messenger boy who delivers flowers to the actress naked in her dressing room, and stays to stare. "Run along now,"* she says, giving him a quarter; *"I hear somebody coming." "You have marvellous hearing,"* he says. *"That's me."* (2:161. This is also the subject of the best-known modern limerick, on the young man of Dee, 'who was plumbing his girl by the sea.' *The Limerick*, Paris, 1953, no. 60–63, gives English, French, German, and modern-Latin versions dating since 1927.) The dreamer keeps his secret close, but he is not averse to letting on that the illusion is prefer-able to the reality, or at least safer: *The boy who would rather have a wet dream than a woman, because "You meet a better class of women that way."* (2:239.)

Frankly approaching, if not identifying, the woman actually dreamed of — and compare the 'old lady' above, to whom the mastur-bating boy's semen is presented as an acrobatic gift — *A boy who has had a wet dream throws back the covers and says, "Look, Ma, no hands!"* (N.Y. 1941), the irreproachable achievement. A pantomime joke difficult to classify — it is not quite a fool joke — probably belongs here, in its subterfuge sexual approach to the mother figure. *A woman in a department store sees a shoplifter putting something into his pocket and denounces him to the floorwalker. The shoplifter denies it. "But I saw you put it in your pocket myself!" the woman insists, and reaches into his pocket to prove it. She faints. "What have you got in your pocket?" the floorwalker demands. "Pockets? Who's got pock-ets?"* (N.Y. 1942. Compare the Scotsman, above.)

The first actual physical approach to incest is usually with the sis-ter, as in the real life cases of Nietzsche, Byron and Beardsley. In life the initiative is usually the boy's, as witness that the sister tends to be younger, but in jokes the sexually aggressive little girl is a cherished fantasy. *One little girl asks the other her age. The second little girl doesn't know. "Have you been with a boy?" "No." "Then you must be eight, 'cause I'se nine."* (Transcontinental train, 1943.) Little girls have their problems too, with forbidding mothers, just as do boys with their fathers. But subterfuges can be found, to evade most prohibitions, without shocking the childish conscience. *A little girl is told before going out that her mother will be disgraced if she lets a boy lay on top of her. She lays on top of the boy. "Now his mother is disgraced."* (2:448.) The rationalization here is double in that, for the purposes of the joke, it evades the parent's prohibition, while for the purposes of the jokester it explains away the little girl's dominance. This is also told of a big girl (D.C. 1942) as a fool story, but with a good deal less meaning. More graphically, on the theme of the child's grappling with the problems of sexual anatomy — as in the fool story, given later, of the nose — *A little girl cautions a little boy: "My mother says I mustn't let you put your hand up my dress. But you can put your hand down my dress in back, if you want. It's the second hole you come to."* (1:303.)

A joke that has remained popular for twenty or more years sums up the real usefulness of the fantasy of the sexually aggressive little girl. It may usefully be compared with Adam's explanation of why he ate the 'apple.' *A little boy is accused of stealing a girl's bicycle. "I didn't steal it, Judge," he says. "She gave it to me. She was riding me home from school on the handlebars, and she stopped in the woods and took off her blue jeans and her panties and said I could have anything she had. Well, the panties were girl things and the blue jeans wouldn't fit me, so I took the bicycle."* (This form, Norfolk, Va., 1953. Versions without the blue jeans since 1935. The wearing of identical clothing currently by adolescents of both sexes in America — in particular the dungarees that were formerly the mock-virile badge of the homosexual prostitute — is noted briefly in my book *Love & Death*, 1949, p. 77; and is satirized in "Al Capp's America," in *Pageant*, March 1953. It has since then passed far beyond satire, with 'Twiggy' 'look-alike' contests for couples, 1967, in which the boy may have hair longer than the girl.) There is also a homosexual version of this joke in which *A fairy is picked up by a movie-star in her car. She takes him to a hotel, undresses, and tells him he can have anything he wants. He takes the car. "And you did right, dear," says the other fairy. "Her clothes would never have fit you."* (N.Y. 1953.) Even more briefly: *The homosexual's wedding night, as told by the bride: "He took off all my clothes — then he took off all his clothes — then he put on my clothes — and I haven't seen him since."* (N.Y. 1950.)

That the rejection of women means the acceptance of homosexuality is a truism that does not need to be supported by jokes. To continue in the normal pattern, the little boy must eventually accept both the initiative and the guilt of his sexual attempts, if they are to succeed. *Little boy, to little girl: "Wanna peanut?" "Thanks." "Wanna go down in the cellar?" "No." "Gimme back my peanut."* (N.Y. 1943.) A fuller version of this 'cute-kid' parody of adolescent seduction has been heard principally from women. It is one of the few stories in which a woman can identify with the winner and not with the villain. *A little boy hides in the rumble seat of his brother's car to find out how to handle girls. The next day he pedals down the street in his kiddie-car to try his own hand. He sees a little girl. "Wanna ride?" "Yeh." "Det in." Pedals around the corner. "Now pull up your dwess." "I won't." "Det out." This is repeated several times. Finally one little girl agrees but says, "What'll you gimme?" "All I got's two jelly beans an' a nickel." They go down into the cellar and the little girl pulls up her dress. Little boy: "Aw gee, no hair!" Little girl: "What do you want for a nickel — turls?"* (N.Y. 1939.)

The sexual approach to the sister and mother is made circumspectly in jokes, by way of cousins, maids, cooks, and other surrogates of the actual female relative. The poor, the Negroes, and other 'inferior' groups are used here in the traditional belief that they are 'practically animals' in their sexual unrepression. *A farmer boy is sent to bring his city cousin from the train with the horse & buggy, but is cautioned not to use any bad language or make any indecent proposals. On the way back to the farm they pass a clump of horse-dung on the road. "What's that?" asks the little city girl. "That's, er, road-apples," he explains. "Where I come from we call it horse-shit," she says. He drops the reins and turns to her eagerly, crying, "Honey, let's fuck!"* (Transcontinental train, 1943.)

Of the many elements in the following story available to psychoanalytic interpretation, one has already been noted — that of the mother-tree in which the father hides to spy (*Genesis*, iii. 8). The rest are left to the reader to gloss. I am indebted for this remarkable story to Mr. Kenneth Larson, of Idaho, where the story was collected in 1919. *A little boy and girl are late to school every day. The teacher complains, and the father decides to go early and hide somewhere to see what they do. Soon they arrive under a big tree and stop to play. "You be the mare and I'll be the stud," says the little boy. The little girl obligingly pulls down her pants, and the boy begins prancing around her on his hands and knees with his penis out. "Now you pee a little," he says. She tries but can't. Suddenly the little boy tosses his head and sees his father watching from up in the tree. "Do you want me to pee a little for you now?" the girl asks. "No!" replies the boy in desperation. "But if you'll look up in that tree, you'll shit!"*

Finally, the mother-figure. First as the Negro mammy or maid. *A small boy cajoles the Negro washerwoman to let him have intercourse with her, and after many refusals, on the grounds that he is too small and she is too busy, she allows him to do so while she bends over the washtub and continues to work. Suddenly she says, "C'mon in bed, chile. You got talent."* (1:373.) As compared to this achieving of adult male potency, there is the wishful dream of the child who impregnates his mother against his father's will. *"My four-year-old son knocked up the maid." "Impossible!" "Yes sir, the little son-of-a-bitch punctured all my condoms with a pin."* (2:331.) An unpleasant Lesbian-fecal variation on this idea occurs in Pierre Louÿs' *Trois Filles de leur Mère* (1926), of which two English manuscript translations have been made, and a third published in Paris as *The She-Devils,* by 'Peter Lewys.'

The theme of 'the mother and the penis of her son' is one of the various approaches of the two made possible by sickness, the law-courts, etc. *An 11-year-old boy is accused of rape. His mother takes out his penis to show the judge the absurdity of the charge. "Why this tiny organ, your Honor, this little bauble! How could my boy even be suspected of raping this woman with his undeveloped little . . ." Boy: "Hey, Ma, better quit stroking that or we're gonna lose this case sure."* (N.Y. 1939.) Mark Twain tells a story containing a number of similar elements, explaining that it is a true incident that had occurred in a law-court in Hartford, Conn., 'about a dozen years before I went there, in 1871.' *A lawyer who is famous for two things, his diminutive-ness and his persecuting of witnesses, is questioning a vast Irishwoman who has testified that she awoke in the morning and found the ac-cused lying beside her, and discovered that she had been raped. The little lawyer elaborately measures her figure with his eyes. "Now, Madam, if one may take so preposterous a thing as that seriously, you might even charge it upon me. Come now, suppose you should wake up and find me lying beside you? What would you think?" She meas-ures him critically and at her leisure with her eyes, and says, "I'd think I'd had a miscarriage!"* (*Mark Twain in Eruption,* 1940, p. 44, in a passage on Andrew Carnegie's small size, dated 1907.)

The emphasis on the smallness of the accused male, as compared to the largeness of the woman in all such rape stories, makes it per-fectly clear that he is really a child. *"How does it happen,"* asks the judge in a rape case, *"that a little bit of a fellow like that was able to attack a large woman like you? It seems to me that standing against a tree, as you say you were, he could barely reach you." "Well, Judge,"* says the woman, *"maybe I did stoop a little."* (1:281. In Carnoy's "Contes Picards," in *Kryptádia,* 1907, x. 118.)

Occasionally, the accused rapist is actually a midget. *The midget is accused of raping the fat woman by standing on a bucket. His de-fense lawyer stands him on a bucket and shows how, with one kick, the woman could have knocked over both the bucket and him. The midget is acquitted but the judge still has his doubts. He takes him aside after and says, "It's all over now and you can't be tried twice, but I know damn well you did it. How?" The midget winks. "The bucket." "But didn't your lawyer . . . couldn't the woman . . ." "I didn't stand on it," says the midget. "I put it over her head and hung on to the handle."* (N.Y. 1942. Compare Motif J2372.)

As these comedy routines with midgets and buckets should indicate, stories baldly describing acts of incestuous intercourse between a mother or sister and son are not common. There is one, however, and it is very commonly collected, and from all over the world (English-speaking informants in Denmark, West Africa, etc.). It is the only joke in *Anecdota I* indexed under "Incest," and is prefaced in the text by the statement that it is 'The dirtiest story ever told,' though only the first half is given. As it is not particularly funny, its great popularity certainly suggests that it serves a need for the tellers. It is generally called "The Happy Family," as in the earliest version found, in the McAtee MS. (1912) envelope 7, noting that it is 'Based on a story heard in Grant County [Indiana], in the '90's.' (Compare, in the final chapter of Series Two, "The Aristocrats.") *Mother: "My, Jimmy, your prick is bigger than Dad's!" Jimmy: "Yes, that's what Sister always says."* (1:225, and many variants to 1962, changing the speakers to sister and brother. A complex variant, in *Anecdota* 2:37, has the father speaking to the daughter, with extended dysphemistic trills on the abilities of members of a fine old Southern family at anilinctus, etc.) Other versions of this story will be found in Chapter 12, "Disease & Disgust," in Series Two, where its hands-around effect is made use of to transmit venereal disease to the father-enemy. The disease-bearing form is probably the original and can be traced at least as far back as Voltaire's *Candide* in 1759.

One item of evidence as to its date is perhaps the strictly logical structure of the "Happy Family" joke, which displays the classical rhetorical inversion of *hipallage,* or perhaps *chiasmus.* In the same way, the oldest traced incest joke turns on a similar reversal with true medieval logic. *A boy is given a dollar by his father to go to town and have a woman. On the way he meets his grandmother, who offers to do it for half price. "Back so soon?" asks the father. The son explains what happened. "What!" shouts the father. "You screwed my mother?" "Why not? Didn't you screw mine?"* (2:280.) This exact story will be found in the *Cent Nouvelles Nouvelles,* written in Burgundy, between 1456 and 1461, to entertain the Dauphin of France, in exile for trying to kill his father, Charles VII, an Oedipal expression not really very different from that in the story itself. This is Tale No. 50, and is signed by the editor of the collection, Antoine de La Sale, who caps the climax with the remark that *the father wants to kill his son for having tried to do, once, what he himself had done (with the son's mother) more than five hundred times without the son saying a single word!* The English translator, Robert B. Douglas (text entitled *One Hundred Merrie and Delightsome Stories,* Paris: Carrington, 1899, offset-reprint [New York, 1929] II. 530) notes, probably after Thomas Wright's standard edition of the French text in 1858, that the story is taken from the 14th Tale of Sacchetti, who died in 1400, or from Poggio (MS. 1451) No. 143, adding: 'The idea has suggested itself to many writers, including Laurence Sterne, in *Tristram Shandy* [1760–67].' This implies a spontaneous re-creation of the story, which is probably not the case. Further conscious imitations, as by La Fontaine, are noted in the more recent English translation by Rossell Hope Robbins, entitled *The Hundred Tales* (1960) p. 384, No. 50. Rotunda T423.

VI. PEDOPHILIA

It cannot be overlooked that the Oedipus complex, of sexual attraction to the parent or parent-surrogate, is only half the story. The Laïus and Jocasta complexes — to call them by the names of the parents of Oedipus (see *Jocasta's Crime,* 1933, by Lord Raglan) — are at least as important. In their hostile aspects the father resists and resents the attention the mother is paying to the boy-child, and exposes the child to death with its feet pierced (Laïus' crime, though no one has written a book about it yet), or to some other expression of paternal jealousy and displeasure. That this drives the boy who wishes to stay at peace with (*i.e.* uncastrated by) his father into homosexuality and the pretended rejection of women, and drives the girl — who wishes to stay at peace with her mother in her matching Electra complex — into Lesbianism and the pretended detestation of men, will be discussed further in the chapter on Homosexuality in Series Two. What is of more particular interest here is the erotic element in the parent's relationship with its own or someone else's child.

No child can possibly actually have sexual relations with a parent or older sister or brother except by the parent's or sibling's express desire, and probably at their instigation (being older). Pedophilia, as the sexual attraction to children, is particularly common among older men, actual sexual exhibitionism being enacted principally before small girls (or boys), seldom before grown women. This represents a probable regression to the sexual goals and attractions of childhood on the part of the aging individual. In older women the expression of sexual interest in extremely young men — 'she's old enough to be his mother' — or emotional dominance over them, on some social, fad-religious, or intellectual pretext, is considered practically respectable if the woman is divorced, rich or cultured (the 'salon'), or otherwise quasi-available. The use of homosexuals in this way by aging, per-verted, or unattractive female 'fag-hags' is particularly common. The greater freedom allowed to women in this, where the rich 'sugar-daddy' or 'Dirty Old Man' (the *lobster* of the 1900's) is an object of ridicule, is clearly due to the woman's necessarily greater closeness to the child, her handling of the child's genitals, etc. In fiction and folk-lore she is invariably shown as the aggressive party (La Putiphara, in *Genesis*, xxxix. 6–22), but this appears to represent, at least in part, a shifting of the guilt for the incestuous dream from the male author to the mother-figure.

Most of the jokes about dominant women and sexually subservient young men are not cast in terms of incest, but simply of male 'folly.' They are therefore given in Chapter 2, under the subject of Fools. (Actually such young men are usually masochists or homosexuals or both.) In the same way, however, that the midget-&-fat-woman jokes are interpreted above as disguises for mother-son incest, the numerous jokes about the rustic fool and the tough young flapper from the city in her expensive roadster (with condoms in the glove compartment) must also be interpreted as fantasies of incest. Masochism in the male inevitably involves a sexual, and usually an oral (food or sex) relation-ship with a dominant mother-image. It is certain, too, that the 'fool' is simply the child who has grown up without learning what sex means, or who pretends to have done so in order to facilitate otherwise taboo sexual activities. Only one joke can be given here in which the mother-figure actually seduces the child, and this has the built-in apology of completely rejecting her for doing so. (Compare the similar treatment of sexual relations with the schoolteacher, above.) *A small boy is sitting on the curb with an erection, using it to snap pebbles into the air. A woman observes him from the window, invites him upstairs, and seduces him. An hour later, seeing him in the street, she invites him to come up again. "Aw, go to hell, you busted my bean shooter!"* (2:361, illustrated.) Also as of a fool on a desert island using his penis as a clam-digger. (N.Y. 1953.)

Most pedophilic jokes involve older men and young girls. In no case so far collected (except the dysphemistic variant of the "Happy Family" in *Anecdota* 2:37) are a father and daughter actually named as the participants in incest. The whole point of the "Happy Family" story is to express this only by means of an elaborate implication. One well-known permissive example does, however, turn on a father's reminding his daughter of the sexual hospitality due to strangers. *"Lift up yo' ass, daughter, an' get that gen'leman's balls up off'n that cold marble floor!"* (This is actually a catch-phrase, or punch-line-without-a-joke.)

Sleeping arrangements in poor and farm communities, on which the classic travelling-salesman-&-farmer's-daughter jokes turn, are also made use of in pedophilic terms. *A circuit-riding minister is to sleep over in a Scots farmer's house. The farmer's wife tells the smallest daughter that after she has finished her chores she should lie in the minister's bed to warm it. The child falls asleep there. The minister comes up to bed, sees the tousled head on his pillow, and says, "Weel, that was a wunnerful souper, an' the whuskey was great, but eh Gad, this is the height o' hospitality!"* (Minn. 1946.) In a joke on the same situation, in *Tom Brown's Jester* (1755, ed. New York, 1850's, p. 39), '*A citizen more tender of his wife than himself, used to make her go to bed first in the winter-time, and lie in his place to warm it, and then called her his warming-pan; which she not well relishing ... left something smoking in the place; he suddenly leaped into it, and finding himself in a stinking pickle, Wife, said he, I am bes–t; No, husband, said she, it is but a coal dropped out of your warming-pan.'* (This is copied verbatim from *Tom Brown* in the American manuscript collection, *A Treasury of Erotic and Facetious Memorabilia*, c. 1910.)

Where the two-in-a-bed situation is made use of in another joke for relations with a child, not only the first move is made to seem hers (as with the Scots minister, preceding), but the man sleeps innocently through the whole action — a pretense which, in a woman, would invariably be considered absurd. *A travelling salesman stops at a farmer's house overnight, and is given a bed with the farmer's small daughter. She watches him undress and asks what his penis is. "Oh, that's my dolly."* In the morning he asks, *"Well, how did you sleep?"* She says, *"I didn't sleep. I played with your dolly all night. It's funny though. When I touched it, it sat up, then it stood up, then it threw up, and then it fainted."* (*Clean Dirt*, 1938, Addendum; told of the comedian Joe Penner and his mythical 'duck,' in the 1930's. Text form, Minn. 1946.) In another story in which the little girl is practically the aggressor: *A barber leans over the shoulder of the little girl whose hair he is cutting to get at an unruly forelock. "Oh look," he says, "you have hair on your lollypop." "Yes, and I'm not even twelve yet."* (N.Y. 1941. Also collected N.Y. 1953, as of *a little girl eating a cookie and spitting. "Do you have hair on your cookie?" "Don't be silly. I'm only eleven."*)

The pre-pubescent girl — the word itself refers to her lack of pubic hair — is frankly described as desirable only by a foreigner (in this case a Russian, apparently even lower than a Frenchman), the standard stalking-horse under which the 'id' expression of taboo desires becomes allowable in jokes. The clean young non-foreign interlocutor, or stooge, represents of course the superego or conscience. *Diplomatic attaché: "And what would you like to do tonight, General?" Russian general: "I vould like a vooman, a yong vooman." "Well, how young — eighteen, nineteen?" "No, yong! Tvalff — tirteen." "But migod, General, a kid that young — why she wouldn't even have any hair between her legs!" "Pozzibly, pozzibly," says the General, stroking his beard, "bot* TONIGHT!!!" (N.Y. 1941.) Pedophilia of this kind has been made a household word in America in recent years by the novel *Lolita* (Paris, 1955) by the Russian emigrant author, Vladimir Nabokov.

A veiled homosexual element is present in the two following jokes, but they are of more particular interest as leading into the mocking of father- and authority-figures which will be seen to follow immediately upon sexual permissiveness. *A man left to look after the little boy, takes him to the burlesque show with him. During one of the stripper's bumps and grinds the boy shouts, "Hey, Pop, somebody is pushing me off your lap!"* (Pa. 1940; also told of a ventriloquist and his wooden dummy watching chorus-girls rehearse.) — *The vicar comes to visit, and the little boy of the family sits on his lap while his mother and older sisters discuss ways of raising money for the foreign missions. They show their silk hose, silk petticoats, silk panties, etc., suggesting that if they would replace these with cotton the money saved could be given to charity. Suddenly the little boy jumps off the vicar's* lap. "*I'm not going to sit on your lap any more. You have something live in your pants pocket.*" (Minn. 1946. Often collected as of an elderly man giving a girl a seat on his lap on a crowded bus. *Kryptádia*, 1907, x. 38.) Compare in Chapter 8.VI.3, p. 603, *The 'fool' who gives the baby his penis to play with, as the climax of his efforts to do his wife's housework for her.*

VII. PERMISSIVENESS AND RIDICULE

The almost total prohibitiveness of our culture toward the three primary impulses of the newborn and growing child — the oral, anal, and genital, in that order — contrasts worse than almost anything else about us with the total permissiveness, in regard to these same impulses in children, in more advanced societies, such as that of the natives of Okinawa, an island in the Pacific. Dr. James Clark Moloney, in an article in *Psychiatry* (Nov. 1945, abstracted in *Neurotica*, No. 9: p. 36–7), has scathingly compared the rock-like emotional stability of the Okinawans after the dreadful traumata of years of bombing, annihilation, starvation, living in caves, infestation of open wounds with vermin, maggots, etc. etc. etc., during World War II, at the end of which only an inconsequential few of the people to whom this had happened had 'developed mental diseases of sufficient severity to warrant institutionalization,' while, in the American society, simultaneously, with nothing worse for civilians to suffer than standing in line for cigarettes, the reduction of exotic ice-cream flavors to only fourteen, and the necessity of counting red points for the juicier cuts of beef, 'over fifty percent of all hospital beds [were and] are allocated to those suffering from mental disease.'

Dr. Moloney has been prominent in the movement to allow children in Western civilization at least the advantage the Okinawan child has in being well-mothered (by its own mother) from the time of birth, and in being fed thereafter on human, rather than bovine, milk. This pre-historic, but also somehow incredibly advanced and radical permissiveness, beginning at birth, has shown some signs of advancing to include infancy (with a relaxation of forcible toilet-'training,' and of rubbing the child's nose in accidental vomit, almost achieved in certain specially-educated classes). That it will be allowed to include sexual experimentation in childhood and early puberty —

also as on Okinawa — is most unlikely, and the jocular folkloristic thrusts at our own repressive rather than permissive sexual control of children seem slated for a long life still ahead.

The lag between the token permissiveness of sex-enlightenment lectures (to parents: 'Children under sixteen not admitted'), and the actual experimentation engaged in privately by the children, is so great as to be beyond absurdity. One may quote an editorial, harbinger-ing the New Freedom and fearlessly entitled at the time, "All Sex Isn't Bad," in a Sunday tabloid, the *New York Enquirer* (Jan. 12, 1953) p. 11, defending a Maryland schoolteacher 'who was forced to quit his job . . . after teaching his pupils how to play Postoffice. . . . Many people, no doubt, were shocked that a teacher would send boys and girls into a cloakroom to kiss each other. But really, what's so awful about that? Kids have been doing it at perfectly proper parlor parties [*all those p's and no petting?*] for generations!' This editorial broad-mindedness is intended to show that the publishers are not really prudes, for the series of articles beginning in the same issue, p. 4, and entitled, with hopeful sensationalism, "$ex $mut in Best $ellers," in which, however, four words accidentally reprinted in a horrified ex-cerpt from James Jones' *From Here to Eternity* are *erased by hand* in every copy of the newspaper released.

One is reminded of *The skywriter who got so mad that he went behind the cloud and wrote "shit."* (N.Y. 1953.) Or of *The two children home alone. "Let's talk dirty — you first." "Hair under your arm." "That's enough. I came."* (N.Y. 1946. This is also told as of two homo-sexuals.) Compare the little poem Robert Graves quotes, in *Lars Porsena: The Future of Swearing and Improper Language* (London, 1927, ed. 1936, p. 42), after mentioning the little girl and boy who de-cided to test the reality of God in the hearing of (the modern) Sir Wal-ter Raleigh. ' "Let's say something awful and see what happens," said the little girl. "He might bang out on us from a cloud," said the little boy nervously, "and frighten us to death!" But the little girl did not care. She looked up into the sky, put out her tongue and said provocatively, "*Piggy* God!" ' With this Graves compares 'the refrain that nasty little East-enders sometimes sing in the [London] streets to embarrass passing clergymen and old ladies:

' "*Pa's out and Ma's out, let's talk dirt!*
Pee-poh-belly-bottom-drawers." '

It is extremely difficult to separate the jokes turning strictly on permissiveness and those in which the child immediately makes use of the achieved sexual permission to mock the authority of the parent-figure — human or divine. In a transitional group, the mocking and physical hostility are put into the mouth of the parent instead of the child. *A little boy whose modern parents have told him the sexual truth at all times, comes home at the age of nine announcing to his mother, "Well, I had my first piece of tail today!" When the father comes home she sobbingly tells him the news. He reaches for a heavy frying-pan. "Don't hit him, dear!" cries the mother; "it's really our own fault." "Hit him? I'm not going to hit him. I'm going to fry him a couple of eggs. He can't begin that way on cornmeal mush."* (2:197.) In a current joke, more popular than its modicum of humor would seem likely to have made it, *A soldier just back from the war is asked by his father to tell his little brother "the facts of life, you know, nothing rough, just about the birds and the bees." He takes the boy aside and says, "Ya remember them two McCafferty girls we used to take in that old packing-case under the porch and screw the asses off?" Boy: "Yeah . . ." "Well, Pop wants me to tell you that the birds and the bees do it too."* (N.Y. 1944.) A version collected the next year has *The tough Marine telling Junior, in a loud voice: "Lissen kid, when a man and a woman want a baby, they* FUCK *— just like the birds and the bees."*

The word-taboo has also been made the object of some humor. I do not refer here to the endemic humor of long articles on the 'four-letter words' carefully not using a single one, such as Allen Walker Read's otherwise remarkable "An Obscenity Symbol," in *American Speech* (1934) IX. 264–78; Bernard De Voto on "Mr. Roberts," in *Harper's* (Dec. 1948) p. 98–101; Henry Bosley Woolf's *The G.I.'s Favorite Four Letter Word* (Baton Rouge, La. 1948?) 7 pages; David Kahn's "The Dirtiest Word," in the men's magazine *Nugget* (New York, August 1961) pp. 21 and 68; and the similar but less serious short article quoted in part in Benjamin C. Bowker's *Out of Uniform* (New York, 1946) p. 119–21, chapter 8, "Full of Strange Oaths." Of all of these — and I am sure others equally titillatory will be written — one might say, as does the father of *the boy with an arithmetic problem about butter, who asks, "Say, pop, how do you spell 'firkin'?" "Spell it? Why, son, you can't even pronounce it!"* (N.Y. 1938. Variant: *"Do you think that girl would let me suck her kumquat?" "Suck it?*

You can't even say *it!"* — Nice, France, 1967, colloquy overheard between two American sailors.) One might also cite the most staggering example of modern lexicographical nincumpoopery — in the original sense of the word — in the omission from Eric Partridge's *Shakespeare's Bawdy* (London, 1947) of all of Shakespeare's punning references to the word *'cunt.'* (Detailed in my Introduction to John S. Farmer & Henley's *Dictionary of Slang & Its Analogues,* ed., New Hyde Park, 1966, p. xc.)

The permissive parent is seldom the father, or, if he is, he is so permissive as to be imbecilic. For the non-comedy father the position is reserved of being mocked by the child's new-found freedom. The permissiveness tends therefore to be described as coming from a roughly good-natured brother, an earthy farmer, or a fond mother or grandmother. A little joke or catch of this type collected remarkably often, and obviously a favorite, is that of: *A little boy and girl who are making a great noise up in the attic. Jewish grandmother: "Votcha doin', kids, you fighting?" "No, grandma, we're fucking." "Dot's nice. Dun't fight."* (N.Y. 1940.) This is the franker origin of the hippie anti-war motto of the 1960s: "MAKE LOVE — NOT WAR." The form I originally suggested, taken directly from the joke, was "DON'T FIGHT — FUCK!" but this does not seem to have been used, as yet, on any lapel-button. The relationship is also clear of the late Wilhelm Reich's excellently-taken point that people who have satisfactory orgasms in normal intercourse do not want to make war.

The 'Jewish grandmother' is, of course, a sort of hopelessly innocent Lady-from-Philadelphia or permissive fairy godmother, and gives permissions that no one else would. The White Anglo-Saxon Protestant father with his flat-top haircut (nor even the two other American types matching the WASP: the GCC and NJB — Good Clean Catholic, and Nice Jewish Boy) cannot be expected to give his children any such permissive advice, though — in actual fact — he often does so nowadays, sometimes with even greater imbecility than the fathers in jokes. I recollect one seventeen-year-old American girl very recently who told me that her mother made her wear girdles *up to here* as a chastity-belt (and pulled me into a dressing-cubicle, where she was trying on a psychedelically-patterned dress, to show me), while her more broad-minded father had told her that she should *'save it* [her virginity] *for her husband by going down on her boy-friends.'* Compare the variant of the Jewish grandmother story, here with a farmer-father: *"Whatcha*

doin' up there in the hayloft, Tessie?" "*I'm screwin' the hired man,*
pop." "*Goddamit, Tessie, you'll be chewin' gum next!*" (N.Y. 1953.)
This is the *Tobacco Road* tradition or influence, of the farmer or
mountain hill-billy or Arkansawyer as an utterly amoral '*gun-totin',*
granny-jazzin', whiskey-swillin' pig,' with only three entertainments:
'*fightin', fuckin', an' fishin'* — (*an' in the winter there ain't no fishin'*).'
These catch-phrases are not insults but brags!

　　In the same tradition, or even beyond, is the ultra-permissive story
of *the Ozark father coming charging out of his ramshackle cabin and*
saying angrily to his little boy, "Would you mind coming inside and
fucking out — *we're having supper.*" (N.Y. 1953. Revenge for life
in the womb?) Compare some of Randolph's 'unprintable' Ozark jokes,
with which may also be compared the joke-relic printed by Elgart in
Over Sexteen (1951) p. 105, of the mountaineer who says to his wife
at dinner, "*Maw, how old is Zeke now?*" "*Nigh onto twenty I reckon,*
Paw." Paw, very seriously: "*Maw, it appears to me we better start put-*
ting pants on Zeke. Did you see what he dragged through the soup?"
(To make up for his inexplicit presentation, Elgart entitles this "Soup
to Nuts.") In a semi-incestuous hillbilly joke, *The half-grown son*
rushes in at meal time, jumps into his mother's lap, pulls out one of
her breasts, sucks at it, and then says disgustedly, "Hey Pop, Ma's been
eating wild onions again!" (N.Y. 1942.) The usual rejection covers the
otherwise taboo intimacy — even in the mountains — between the adolescent boy and his mother. In another fond-mother joke, the permissive parent is again made out as practically an idiot. *The nouveau-*
riche family is entertaining the vicar. Just as the mother is pouring
the vicar's tea, a cat comes screaming through the parlor and leaps
out the bay-window. Right after it, in hot pursuit, comes a little boy.
He stops in the middle of the parlor and announces, "If I catch that
cat, I'll fuck it!" and then dives out the window after it. "He will too,"
says the mother. "He's a manly little fellow. (Or: horny little bastard.)
— More cream?" (N.Y. 1953.)

　　A well-known motif in folktales is the trickster's deception, usually
for purposes of theft, by which he tells his intended victim that his
name is Who-Shit? or Kick-Me-Arse, or similar. The end situation is
then that the victim is chasing the trickster, who has robbed him,
shouting "Who-Shit?" or "Kick-Me-Arse!" while helpful passers-by
prevent him from ever catching the trickster by matching insults, or
by doing what the presumable name suggests. In *Kryptádia* (1884)

II. 70 and 117 ff., three quite clever 'sells' of this type are given, from Brittany and Picardy, on the names *'Je Chie'* and *'J'ai Chié'*: *("Alors, dit le passeur, débarbouillez-vous dans la rivière"*), *'Attrape-mes-couilles,'* and *'J'ai-trois-poils-au-con;'* with note of a similar story in Afanasyev's *Russian Secret Tales* (collected about 1865), No. 72, "Les Noms étranges," of the *Je Chie* and *J'ai Chié* type. This is No. 71 in the English translation of Afanasyev, published by Carrington in Paris (1897) and recently reprinted, p. 245–8, in which the scatological names are disguised in Arabic [!] and in Latin, as *Cacabo* and *Cacavi.* Afanasyev observes that this is 'a pleasantry of the type of Ulysses in the cave of Polyphemus, taking the name of *Outis* [No-one].' This would refer it (Type 1138, Motif K602) to the Homeric legends, gathered by the *diacévastes* under Pisistratus in the 5th century B.C., though then much older, making this probably one of the oldest recorded joke-types in the world, and connected of course with even more ancient ideas of 'ineffable' name-magic.

A current American story uses the same device to achieve both sexual permission — at least verbally — and an opening for the ridicule of parents. (This is Type 1545, Motif K1399.2:) *A boy hires himself out as a farm-hand, telling the farmer that his name is Johnnie Fuckerfast. "Well, go down to the pasture and get the cows," says the farmer. "My daughter will show you the way." Darkness comes, but neither the boy, the cows, nor the daughter is back. The farmer goes to the window and shouts, "Oh, Johnnie Fuckerfast! Oh, Johnnie Fuckerfast!" The boy raises up out of the ditch nearby and replies, "Shut up, you old fool! I'm fucking her as fast as I can!"* (Idaho, 1919.) Variant: *A boy is nicknamed Johnnie Fuckerfast by his mother* [!] *She comes home and hears him up in the attic, but does not know he is there with a little girl. "Oh, Johnnie Fuckerfast!" she calls. The boy sticks his head out the attic window. "If you think you can fuck her any faster," he says, "you can come on up and try."* (Indiana, 1936. Also collected from a ten-year-old New England girl on a transatlantic liner, 1964. She knew many other erotic jokes, and used them as part of her attempted seductiveness to at least one adult man.)

As in the *'Piggy'* God' defiance quoted above from Raleigh, vicars, ministers, priests, and clergymen generally (with the exception of rabbis, who are presumably fiendishly clever) are a favorite target of displaced resistance or mockery actually intended against the father or father-god. In at least one joke — a mere catch, but very pointed

— the fatherhood is shared in more than the clergyman's title. *Minister: "And how is my little lad today?" Little lad: "Shh! Not so loud. Dad might hear!"* (1:51.) Another catch, again of displaced aggression, as the druggist must accept all the hostility no one dares express against doctors: *A boy goes into a drugstore and asks, "Do you handle contraceptives?"* (or: *"Do you fit diaphragms?"*) *"Sure," says the druggist. "O.K., wash your hands and get me an ice cream cone."* (D.C. 1952.) The nameless man, who also substitutes for the father as 'the voice from the upper berth' on the honeymoon trip, appears in the character of he-who-gets-slapped in the following joke, which harks back to the child's earlier pretense of anatomical ignorance. *A man at Coney Island has to take the last bathing suit in the bathhouse. It is too small but he squeezes into it, all but his testicles. These he holds in his hand, and makes a run for the water. Little boy, shouting: "Hey mister, if you're going to drown those puppies, can I have one?"* (*Memorabilia*, 1910.) A modified version, making the man's testicles into a woman's breasts — an unconscious equivalence commonly felt but seldom noted — was printed several times in the popular magazines during the 1940's. (Also Elgart, 1951, p. 102.) As is usual with mother-figures in humor, except mothers-in-law, who are skinny or else simply overbearingly big, the woman is almost always carefully stated to be fat. That is why she does not fit in the bathing suit, etc.

In the following story, which has been repeatedly collected in both forms given, the first form concentrates on the achieving of sexual permission by means of a trick (as with the "Johnnie Fuckerfast" story, above); the other moves on to the pederastic rape of the father-figure — the ultimate insult. *A boy is always betting, and his father asks the schoolteacher to help him get the boy to stop by making him lose at least one bet. Next day the boy sniffs peculiarly at the teacher when alone in the schoolroom with her, and offers to bet fifty cents that she is menstruating. Knowing that she is not, she bets, pulls up her skirt, shows him, and takes his money, later that day telling the boy's father that she believes the boy now must be cured of betting. "Cured, hell!" says the father, on hearing the details. "Only this morning he bet me five dollars he'd see your cunt before tonight!"* (1:371.)

The homosexual variant involves grown-ups: *A cardsharp on a ship bets the captain $10,000 that he has piles. The captain cannot resist the size of the bet, and takes down his pants to let the cardsharp* *see he is wrong. Considering the size of the bet, again, the cardsharp insists on feeling with his finger too. He then admits he has lost and pays the bet. The captain goes back to the ship's salon to brag of his victory. He finds everyone there in a dead faint but the waiter. The cardsharp has bet them* $50,000 *that he'd have his finger up the captain's ass inside of twenty minutes.* (N.Y. 1942.) On the ship-captain, specifically, as a father-figure worth defying, note the activities of the "Phantom Shitter," described earlier, and see the description of an incident during World War II, recounted by an army nurse, in which the prohibition by the captain, 'an unpleasantly strict disciplinarian,' of social intercourse or any other between the women and men on the ship completely collapsed after the inscription "Kilroy Was Here" appeared 'on the most sacrosanct spot on the whole ship . . . the captain's bridge, visible to everyone.' (Richard Sterba, "Kilroy Was Here," in *American Imago,* Nov. 1948, v. 177–8, with a remarkable nasophallic illustration of Kilroy, of a banana type, with the usual testicle-hands at both sides, p. 181.)

The grandparents are, of course, useful substitutes for the real parents in ridicule-jokes, a point that will be discussed at greater length in the chapter on Animals, concerning humorous greeting cards. In the simplest form the joke merely states the grandfather's impotence, tantamount to wishing the same for the father. *"What'cha doin', Granpa? Jerkin' off?" "No, Son. Just jerkin'."* (N.Y. 1939.) A much more dysphemistic version of the following occurs in *Anecdota II* (1934) No. 71, punning on the child's request for a 'fairy-story.' *"Grandma, tell us a bedtime story." "Oh well, once upon a time there was an old son-of-a-bitch . . ." "Oh Grandma, don't tell us about Grandpa. Tell us about that time you were a whore in Chicago."* (*Smile and the World Smiles with You,* Guam, 1948.) The presumably humorous figures of the prostitute mother and bawdy-talking grandmother (educating her granddaughter) are made the central matter of Victoria Lincoln's novel, *February Hill* (1936), with every possible quasi-Lesbian overtone of the manless family situation capitalized.

The actual father is finally reached in the form of a tree! *A little pine tree loses all its needles when winter comes, and none of the other little pine trees will talk to it. A big pine tree nearby looks down and says, "Cheer up, sonny, you'll get your needles back in the spring, and I ought to know — I'm your father." "Gee, are you sure?" says the little pine tree. "But you have all your needles. What's the matter with me? Was there something wrong with my mother?" "Your mother? Son, your mother was the finest piece of ash in this whole damn forest!"* (N.Y. 1942.) In a later and more strained version the little tree is trying to find out whether it's "a son of a beech or a son of a birch" (Elgart, 1951, p. 118), and is cheered up by a woodpecker who tells him, *"Your mother was the finest piece of ash anybody ever drove his pecker into."* (N.Y. 1952.) Compare, in W. L. McAtee's *Grant County, Indiana, Speech and Song: Supplement 2* (1946, the materials collected in the 1890's), the bit of 'Doggerel certainly learned in early school years':

> *The woodpecker pecked on the schoolhouse door,*
> *And he pecked and he pecked till his pecker was sore.*

Two jokes sexually ridiculing the father and directly naming him have been collected, but in the first of these the son dares this only after the father is dead, as with the ancient defiance of defecating on the dead father's grave. Noted in Horace's *Ars Poetica*, before 8 B.C., as given in Ben Jonson's translation; and collected several times in the late 1940's, in connection with columnist Westbrook Pegler's crusade against the already-dead F. D. Roosevelt, *e.g.* "He won't be satisfied till he digs up Roosevelt's grave and pisses on him." The caution, according to Horace, that this is certain to cause insanity is an interesting sidelight on the castratory paternal punishment hidden in the superstition that masturbation will also cause insanity. *A dying father calls his children to his bedside and tells them, "Children, your mother and I loved each other very dearly, but we were never married." He then dies. Long silence. Finally the youngest son says, "Well, I don't know about you bastards, but I'm going to the movies."* (Minn. 1946.) Elgart gives two variants (1951, pp. 66 and 42), in one of which *the parents do not die but are bickering over what people will say when they learn that the clergyman who married them was an impostor. "Never mind about you two!" says Junior. "How about* ME*?"* In the other, *several college boys are attempting to force an old lady to leave their restaurant table by bragging about how few months after their parents' marriage they were born. The old lady finally looks up and says pleasantly, "Will one of you bastards please pass the salt?"*

As actual sexual ridicule of the father is so uncommon, a variant should be mentioned here of a joke given earlier about the children who laughed at their father for trying coitus from behind (1:96). In a version collected in 1953, *The new position attempted is not from behind but upside down,* i.e. *with the mother on top, and the father complains to the friend who made the suggestion,* "*Well, it was all right, but the kids ran around the house singing, 'Daddy is a sissy! Daddy is a sissy!'*" Again in the following example the ability to ridicule the father sexually is predicated on the mother's dominance. *A little boy playing out in the back yard gets mad and kicks a chicken.* "*Just for that,*" *says his mother,* "*you don't get any eggs for two weeks.*" *Later the boy kicks a dog and is told he will not get any hot dogs for two weeks. The father then comes home, drunk, gets mad, and kicks the cat.* "*O.K., Mom,*" *says the boy,* "*are you going to tell him, or shall I?*" (D.C. 1952.) Miss Maya Deren's excellent *avant-garde* film, *At Land* (1945?), concerning herself as a fish cast confusedly ashore, similarly lands in unexpected bathos when the lady-fish, after a polyandrous courtship in which she rejects all male human proposals with an understanding smile, finally comes upon a gentleman laid out with a white sheet over him in a deserted house, and suddenly produces a *pussy-cat* from nowhere, held hip-high, which she drops before him in a gesture of rejection. Mr. Manny Farber, in an indignant review of this and other of Miss Deren's films in the *New Republic,* at the time, saw in them the Lesbian propaganda and homosexual hi-jinks, but there is perhaps more to all the avant-garde movies — even now — than the simple sexual 'camp' and degeneracy they so openly offer.

Five jokes directly and unmistakably mocking the father-figure bring this chapter to a close. What is particularly striking about all of them is their use of scatological (anal-sadistic) insults, especially the first story, which has, however, been publicly published a number of times as 'cute.' *A man in a streetcar feels a dripping on his nose from a basket above him in the bundle rack. He licks up a drop, and winks knowingly at the smiling boy whose basket it is.* "*Pickles?*" *says the man.* "*No, puppies.*" (N.Y. 1940. A variant, in which a 'quiet little man' achieves a similar victory over a 'federal agent' during Prohibition, is given by Elgart, 1951, p. 142.) — "*My father can blow smoke rings out of his ass.*" "*Did you see him do it?*" "*No, but I seen the nicotine on his underpants.*" (N.Y. 1942.) A relic of the 'Pétomane'? The pickles-or-puppies story is a much softened relic of a horrible revenge-tale of the "Entrapped Lovers" variety (Type 1730, itself modified to a mere joke as Types 1355A–C), of which the Levantine original will be found in *Histoires Arabes,* pp. 132, 223.

Dominant figures from the outside, superior in strength to the father, such as policemen, burglars, etc., are of course welcomed, when identification with them is possible. *A burglar enters a bedroom and points his gun at a little boy who is in bed with his father. The father has already ducked under the bedclothes. "Get your head under the covers and keep it there!" the burglar threatens the boy, brandishing his gun. "All right, all right! Don't shoot!" This happens three times. The third time the boy begs the burglar to let him keep at least his nose out. "You have no idea how scared Pop is!"* (Minn. 1947.)

The doctor with whose visits the child was once threatened for such significant sins as fingernail biting, thumb-sucking, and masturbation, has given way — so far as the adults who make up kid jokes are concerned — to the psychoanalyst. A whole book of American anti-psychiatric jokes and magazine cartoons could easily be collected, and it is interesting to observe that the hostility to psychoanalysis rises not from any denial or frustration expected from the analyst (who is usually shown as of an almost idiot permissiveness and inattention), but from the presumed fearfulness of analytic techniques which will force or shame the patient into sexual self-realization, and thereby into further repression by his or her own conscience. On this basis it is clear that the 'anti-analytic jitters prevailing in almost all strata in America' (according to *Neurotica,* 1951, No. 9: p. 3) are perfectly justifiable, and that the psychoanalyst is rapidly replacing both the father and minister as the forbidding parent. *A boy is sent to the psychiatrist for playing pattycake all the time with nothing in his hands. "What are you doing?" says the psychiatrist as the boy pats his hands back and forth. "I'm making psychiatrists." "What are you making them out of?" "Shit!" The psychiatrist refers the patient to another psychiatrist, whom he forewarns by phone. This time when the boy begins playing pattycake the psychiatrist says, "I know what you're doing." "Yeah? What?" "You're making psychiatrists." The boy peeks between his cupped hands. "Uh-uh," he says, shaking his head. "Not enough shit."* (N.Y. 1952. Motif J2186, American Indian.)

With this may be compared a joke, or possibly a true incident, given in Sándor Ferenczi's *Further Contributions to Psycho-analysis* (1926) p. 325, under the forgiving title, "Childish Ideas of Digestion" (1913): '*Three-year-old boy: "Uncle Doctor, what have you got in your stomach that makes you so fat?" The family physician's joking reply: "Ka-ka!"* [a German nursery word for feces]. *The boy: "Do you eat so much Ka-ka?"'* On the same page, in an article or brief paper on

"Flatus as an Adult Prerogative" (1913), Ferenczi remarkably adumbrates the following joke, which was apparently entirely unknown to him. *At dinner at a Pennsylvania Dutch farmer's house, one of the children breaks wind noisily. Guest: "Do you allow the children to do this before you?" Farmer: "Ve haf no rules aboud it. Sometimes dem first, sometimes me first."* (1:379.) Says Ferenczi: 'It sometimes occurs that patients being analyzed have to resist the inclination to pass a clearly audible and also noticeable amount of flatus in the course of the hour; this usually happens when they are being refractory with the doctor. This symptom, however, is intended not only to insult the doctor but to intimate that the patient intends to allow himself things that his father forbade him, but permitted himself. The licence referred to here represents all the prerogatives which parents arrogate to themselves but strictly deny to their children, and which the patient now wishes to appropriate for himself.' That sexual as well as hostile 'prerogatives' are included is obvious.

2

FOOLS

PROBABLY the most important element in understanding any joke is to grasp clearly and from the beginning, *who is the butt*. This not only means determining which of the characters in the story receives the hostile impact of the punch-line (so well named), but whether, for that matter, the butt is actually any character in the story at all. The listener, in particular, may well suspect that *he* is the butt, as in shaggy dog and other interminable stories, and in all riddles. Beyond this, there is also a deeper identification to seek. The surface identity of the butt may be wholly symbolic. Where the butt is Woman, or the Negro, or the Jew, their ridicule as, respectively, sexually greedy, sexually overdeveloped, or sexually sly, suggests that their specific identification in the joke, by race, religion, or sex, may usually be trusted. In fool jokes the surface identity is entirely misleading. Women exist, and so do Negroes and Jews, but there are no fools to be encountered of quite the sort one meets in jokes.

Where the fool is allowed some unwitting freedom of speech or damaging frankness, it is obvious that he is not the butt of the joke at all, but the victor, and that the butt is the father, teacher, officer, doctor, druggist, judge, or other authority-figure who is, as it were, defied or denuded by the fool's frankness in which the listener identifies. But where the fool is shown as egregiously ignorant of sexual matters, no identification is possible. It is then certainly the fool who is the butt. But who is the fool? The great similarity between themes of sexual ignorance in stories of children and stories of fools makes the identification clear: the fool is the child who has grown up without learning the meaning of sex. The frank-fool story allows a pleasant recapture of the verbal freedom presumably accompanying childish innocence. The ignorant-fool story ridicules those who have allowed themselves to remain in sexual darkness, to their own detriment, and

113

thus congratulates both teller and listener on the sexual enlightenment they themselves have achieved.

The famous and quite absurd theory once held among anthropologists, under the leadership of Sir James Frazer, that human societies exist in Australia and Melanesia in which the relationship between sexual intercourse and the birth of the child is unknown, is a remarkable example of the projection of the self-congratulatory benefits of the fool story into an ostensible science. The fact has now been lost sight of, though it was clear enough in 1911 during the last battles in England between religion on the one hand and science (as represented by the 9th and 11th editions of the *Encyclopædia Britannica* and its 'higher criticism' of the Bible) on the other, that the whole point behind Frazer's avowal of the 'nescience' theory of sexual ignorance, in his *Totemism and Exogamy* (1911) IV. 98 *ff.*, was religious in nature. The presumable sexual ignorance of the most backward of the Australian tribes was to be used to shore up the religious dogma of the Virgin Birth, the last of the prepared positions to which the religious mind was, at that time, prepared to retreat.

In Walter Heape's *Sex Antagonism* (1913), a book-length criticism of Frazer's work, the biologist Heape forced Frazer to admit candidly (in manuscript) that he had avoided giving due prominence to the fact, recorded earlier by the North Queensland ethnologist W. E. Roth, that among the selfsame Australian natives 'sexual connection as a cause of conception . . . is admitted as true for all animals — indeed this idea confirms them in their belief of superiority over the brute creation [!]' But on the following page (in *Sex Antagonism,* p. 90) Heape finally brought into the open the whole background purpose of the 'nescience' theory in the then-raging war between religion and science:

> In effect [says Heape] Dr. Frazer imagines a peculiar kind of wall around the mind of the savage; he declares the savage cannot be judged by the civilised man because his methods of thought and his power of reasoning are on an entirely different [*i.e.* 'lower'] plane. . . . And yet there would not seem to be any great, any fundamental difference between this refusal of the Queensland natives to admit of equal comparison between themselves and the lower animals, and the belief held by a vast proportion of Christian men and women to-day in the immacu-

late conception [*sc.* Nativity] of the Virgin Mary. The Christian religion requires that in this one particular instance conception was induced by a spirit, the religion of the Queensland natives demands that spirit conception is universal amongst human beings. But both the Queenslander and the Christian know the truth, it is only superstition which compels them to deny it for a special reason or for a particular case. In this matter I can see no essential difference between savage and civilised man.

Recent attempts to salvage, or at least excuse, the Frazerian theory, by explaining that the backward Australian 'blacks' do not understand causality in connection with *any* subject, and that even our most famous logical error of *post hoc ergo propter hoc* is beyond them, are doubtless gallantly intended, but quite unnecessary. Actual investigation, as that of Geza Róheim, of the "Nescience [of paternity] of the Aranda," has shown that the so-called ignorance of paternity in Australia is an almost open pretense, with florid symbolic equivalents in speech — as truly meaningful as our 'Your obedient servant' — such as the explanation that women are made pregnant by the blossom of the banana! (Roscoe, *The Baganda, their Customs and Belief,* 1911; cited by Frazer, II. 507, and, more pointedly, by Heape, p. 100.)

The origin of this pretended ignorance of paternity has not yet been studied, but one may venture to suggest that when it is, it will be found to involve a formalized recollection, in the neo-patriarchal societies of the South Pacific, of the recent status of man as the unimportant parent in the matriarchal society that preceded. The quasi-castratory Australian rite of subincision of the penis — the *mika-mika* operation, called by the natives 'male menstruation' — is clearly a striving toward the achievement of former honorific status (or freedom from paternal attack) by imitating the female organs. (Compare the skirt-like clothing of Western priests, and their former self-castration.) In comparison to the *fact* of splitting the penis up the bottom and flattening it into a practically useless mass, the mere *pretense* of male uselessness is obviously nothing. For persons of strong stomach, and rock-like emotional security, the following articles on the subincision rite may be useful to consult: Theodor Reik's *Ritual* ("Puberty Rites of Savages"), Felix Bryk's *Circumcision,* the relevant writings of H. Basedow, Geza Róheim, and M. F. Ashley Montagu, and the illustrated article by R. M. Berndt in *American Imago* (June 1951).

I. NINCUMPOOPS

In falling away to a mere synonym for fool, the original meaning of the word 'nincumpoop' has been entirely forgotten and might usefully be revived. The word is apparently a corruption of *non compos mentis,* the legal description of an imbecile, and became popular in Restoration slang as meaning 'a silly soft, Uxorious Fellow.' ('B. E[dwards], Gent.' *A New Dictionary of the Canting Crew,* 1699, *s.v.* Nickumpoop. Farmer & Henley's *Slang and Its Analogues* quotes, from the earlier playwrights of the 1670's, Shadwell's *Epsom Wells* and Wycherley's *Plain Dealer.*) But there is more to it than mere uxoriousness — a peculiar word, by the way, English being almost the only language having an insulting term for a man who loves his wife. In Captain Francis Grose's *Classical Dictionary of the Vulgar Tongue* (1785) the rest of the story is told, in the definition '*Nickumpoop* or *Nincumpoop,* one who never saw his wife's ——.' Badcock, the plagiarist of Grose (under the expurgatory pseudonym of 'John Bee'), modifies this somewhat, but the idea is clearly there, in his *Dictionary of the Turf* (1823), as 'a term of derision, applied by a young lass to her lover, who presses not his suit with vigour enough.' It is that idea which still gives the insulting force, and the meaning of sexual ignorance or fumbling incompetence to the word.

In the jokes actually concerning nincumpoopery, in the sense of a man's never having seen the female genital and not knowing what it is, fear rather than ignorance is the emotion the fool displays. What he sees, or thinks he sees, is a castrated male. This idea, that a woman is simply a castrated man, has long been known to be a fantasy of children, but that it still retains operative force among adults has only recently been proved on the widest possible scale in the undesirable publicity given in America and Britain to the so-called sex change of George into Christine Jorgensen during the 1950's. The public, and particularly the homosexual public, is willing to define a woman as a man without a penis or testicles, and to imagine that a man can become a woman by castration. That there are such things as a womb, a vagina, and specifically female rather than male secretions involved in being a woman — not to mention breasts, for which rubber appliances or forced hormonal enlargement will presumably do — is quite overlooked.

The privative and castratory tone in the real nincumpoop jokes is unmistakable. *A farmer boy is being seduced by a slick city girl. She shows him her breasts. He does not know what they are, so she tells him. She then takes off her skirt and shows him her genitals. "Do you know what that is?" she says. "Gee, I don't know," he says, "but grab a club and I'll help you kill it."* (Transcontinental train, 1943.) In another form, *The moron on a double date is told just to say "How about it?" to which the girl answers, "Sorry, not tonight. I have the rag on." "The rag?" "You know; I'm bleeding." "Bleeding?" She shows him. Moron: "Gee, no wonder you're all bloody. They cut your cock off."* (Calif. 1942, and collected several times since.) One variant which is particularly interesting, since castratory fantasies and fears usually concern the penis and not the testicles: *Two young boys see a girl playmate crying. One asks her why and she tells him that she is menstruating for the first time, and shows him her sanitary pad. He goes back to the other boy. "Well, why's she crying?" "You'd cry too if your balls were cut off."* (N.Y. 1953.) In all of these the child or 'moron' — *i.e.* fool — is used interchangeably by various tellers.

Two relevant points that may be touched upon here are, first, that the British horror of the word 'bloody' certainly derives from this identification of menstruation and castration (unknown to Partridge and Graves in their discussions of the word). In fact, the sickening dread that many men feel on seeing blood flowing profusely, or the clots of menstrual blood, can only be considered a revival of traumatic castration fear. The joy in watching bare-knuckle boxing and the bleeding faces of the pugilists (similarly in German university-style saber duelling, with its 'displacement upward' of homosexual interest in the pelvis to the face and head), or Japanese sword-killing (*samurai* sadism, also entirely homosexual) especially as seen in Japanese 19th century woodblock-books and 20th century horror-films, is a typical mastering of such fears by projecting them on the bloodied victims. This is likewise the explanation of the new American (post-Atom Bomb) total castratory and annihilatory fears, expressed on the one hand by the bogus and panicky 'Sexual Revolution,' of wildcat orgiastic and homosexual activities, and on the other hand in the delight in the goriest possible blood-sadism — in full color — in the war-movies, crime-movies, outright horror-films, and in the public prints. Note (but do not see!) in particular the July 1967 issue of *Esquire* magazine, purportedly an exposé of "Violence: The New Pornography," but actually, as I have remarked in *Models of Madness* (1968), 'quite the most nauseating exploitation of full-color sadism . . . ever printed on paper since the world began.'

Second, and specifically linguistically, the male *fear* of the female genitals as the 'proof' that castrated beings can exist (and "*You're next!*" as in barber-shops), is also partly the basis of the peculiar usage, throughout the American south and southwest, of the word '*cock*' — the principal colloquial term for the penis — as meaning the female genitals. This is not ignorance: it is a terminological way of refusing to accept the existence of 'beings without a penis.' The actual linguistic origin is the French *coquille,* cockleshell, as referring to the female genitals (vulviform shellfish are immemorially sacred to Venus), noted in Ph.-J. Leroux' *Dictionnaire comique* in the 18th century, citing Sorel's *Histoire comique de Francion* (1622). In Allen Walker Read's excellent *Lexical Evidence from Folk Epigraphy* (Paris, 1935) p. 42, the very first entry under '*cock*,' as meaning the penis, erroneously quotes a California epigraph, dated 1928, in which the vagina is meant: 'Ashes to ashes dust to dust if it wasnt for your cock my prick would rust.' (Read's first entry under '*crap*' is similarly in error for 'crabs': 'This is no fish market So leave youre crape [*sic*] at home.')

The pubic hair is sometimes used to rationalize the nincumpoop's ignorance of the female genitals. *The fool on his wedding morning sees his naked bride lift her arms to brush her hair, and notices the tufts of hair in her armpits. "Oh boy," he chortles, "two more!"* (1: 484.) The wedding-night ignorance is displaced in the following story on the bellboy. The build-up is also somewhat strained. *A bride in a hotel bedroom is practising contortionistic positions for intercourse while waiting for her husband to return. Her legs become locked behind her head and under the bedposts and she cannot untangle herself. She finally has to call for help. A bellboy rushes in, takes one look, rushes out again and down to the manager's desk. "Quick!" he shouts, "there's been a murder in Room 27. It's a man with curly black whiskers, and his throat's been cut from ear to ear!"* (*Waggish Tales,* 1947, p. 241.) Note the open identification of the female genitals as a *mortal wound* (castration), and compare the "Mad Barber of Fleet Street" in Chapter 13, in the Second Series, following.

Ignorance is also the first excuse in an important group of fool stories in which, by one method or another, the woman's sexual overtures are rejected and her dominance resisted. *The moron in bed with*

*his bride does nothing, so she says, "Honey, my feet are cold." He gets
her a towel. "My shoulders are cold too," she says. He gets another
towel. "Listen," she says disgustedly, "don't you know there's a hole
between my legs?" "Oh, maybe that's where the draft is coming from."*
(N.Y. 1953. With this 'wise fool' response, compare the folk-witticism
to a man who has a cold: "You been sleeping by a crack?" Pa. 1936.)
*The town fool is getting advice on how to conduct his affair with the
schoolteacher — when to hold hands with her, when to kiss her, etc.
Finally he is told to take her sleighriding and put his hand inside her
bloomers under the lap robe. "Did you do like I said?" his mentor
asks, next day in the barber shop. "Yup. Shore did." "Well, how did
it feel?" "I dunno. I had my mittens on."* (2:172.)

The rejection stories now begin in earnest, with ignorance of the
sexual act rather than of the sexual organs of the woman as the crux.
*A girl is having intercourse with a fool, and has to tell him exactly
what to do. "Put it in here," she says. He does so. "Now push it in
deep. Now pull it out. Push it in, pull it out, push it in, pull it out!"
she orders. "Now wait a minute," he says, panting; "make up your
mind."* (Calif. 1942.) In a form of Hungarian or Russian origin, *A
sleeping girl wakes up to find herself being raped by an importunate
lover whom she has often refused. "What are you doing?" she cries.
"Shall I take it out?" he asks. "Well," she says, "take it out and put it
in, and then take it out and put it in again, and I'll make up my mind."*
In an older form she says, *"No, I'm just asking what you're doing."*
(N.Y. 1939.) Giving it a practical twist, *A city girl in an automobile
sees a plow-boy stop to urinate against a tree. Intrigued by the size of
his penis she pulls up her car and seduces him. "Put it in," she says,
seeing that he does not know what to do. "Now pull it out. Now push
it in." "Goddamit, lady," he says, "make up your mind. I still got four
acres of land to plow."* (D.C. 1943.)

In what is clearly a variant of the last form given, the pretense of
ignorance is almost dropped in favor of the insult direct. *The teacher
is seducing the farmer boy. She lifts her dress and says, "Do you think
you can slip it in through my corset?"* (or: *under panties*) *"Sure thing,
lady. Just this morning I put it in the old gray mare, in harness."* (D.C.
1943.) The element of the harmful or disgusting 'cure' for erection in
the following joke, displaced upon the woman, will be seen in a later
chapter to be a modified form of castration, in the later case the ham-

mering of the boy's penis on the blacksmith-father's anvil. It is of course the background fear of castratory punishment that makes necessary the anal-sadistic rejection of the woman. This is clear in all anti-woman literature since the middle ages, particularly that by homosexual authors. *A hired boy on a farm is bothered by persistent erections every morning. The farmer advises him to cure it by going to the barn whenever it happens and putting his penis into two shovelfuls of cow manure. Finding him doing so one morning, the farmer's wife suggests she knows a better way to cure it, and takes him upstairs with her. She strips, lies down on the bed, and opens her legs. "Now put it in," she says. "You mean the whole two shovelfuls?" the boy asks.* (D.C. 1951.)

The city flapper in her automobile and other virile appurtenances has already been introduced as the type of the dominant female, *vis à vis* the fool or ignorant farm-boy. His folly, however, vacillates between real and pretended. *Two farm-boys working in the field are picked up by two city girls in a roadster who show them how to use condoms, "to prevent disease," before having intercourse. Two weeks later. "Zeke, have you got a disease?" "No, I ain't got any disease." "Neither have I. Let's take these damn things off."* (N.Y. 1940.) This is pure ignorance, as is also another form in which the boys are told that the condoms will prevent both disease and pregnancy, and then ask each other, *"You pregnant?" "No." "You got a disease?" "No."* etc. (Calif. 1941.) With the change of a single word, however, the women are punished for their dominance. In the changed form, *They show the farm-boys how to put on the condoms by rolling them down their thumbs. Two weeks later. "You got a disease?" "No." "Neither have I. Let's take these damn things off our thumbs."* (N.Y. 1942.) A version of this without the farm-boy background had appeared in *Anecdota Americana II* in 1934. *A boy in a brothel for the first time is shown how to put on a condom by the madam rolling it down her thumb. After intercourse the girl says, "That rubber must have broken. I feel all wet." "No it didn't," says the boy, holding up his thumb; "it's just as good as new."* (2:250.) As collected again in Washington, D.C., 1952, the illogical element here, of attempting to 'punish' a prostitute with pregnancy, is edited out by making the girl a clerk in a drugstore.

The mistakes of foreigners, which will be treated more fully in the last section of this chapter, can also be made to serve the purposes of rejection by the fool. *An American in Paris picks up a French girl.*

He draws a picture of a cab, and they go for a drive in the park. Then he draws a picture of a table and chair, and they go to a restaurant. Finally she takes his pencil and pad and draws a four-poster bed. "Now I ask you," he concludes, "how did she know I was in the furniture business?" (Elgart, 1951, p. 52.) The element of rejection here seems to have been imported into an earlier joke of the exactly opposite intent. *The fool on the ocean liner is flirting with a French girl by means of an English-French dictionary. He looks up the words to ask her to go to dinner; she looks up the words to ask him to dance. Afterwards, going down the passageway, she pulls him into her stateroom and begins taking off his clothes.* "And there I was," he says, "without the damn dictionary. I didn't know what to say." (N.Y. 1940.) In another story, similarly on the value of ignorance, *A fool is renowned for his inability to get on with the ladies. His friends are amazed to see him coming out of a hotel one morning with the town beauty.* "How did it happen?" they ask. "We were at a dance," says the fool, "and after I danced with her three times she said, 'Say something!' and I couldn't think of anything else to say." (Curran, 1938, p. 136.)

The substitution of food pleasure for sexual pleasure has created two very famous jokes of rejection. *A man is shipwrecked on a desert island for ten years. A beautiful naked young woman is washed ashore on a beer barrel. He revives her and she says,* "Now that you've been so good to me I'm going to give you something you haven't had for ten years." He: "You mean to tell me there's some beer in that barrel?" (Va. 1952.) Even more famous is *The travelling salesman who stops at the farmer's house when they are having beans for supper. He is put to bed between the farmer and the farmer's wife. In the middle of the night the barn catches on fire and the farmer rushes out to save it.* "Now's your chance," *the farmer's wife whispers to the salesman. So he rushes downstairs and eats the rest of the beans.* (Curran, 1938, p. 82. Given in Parke Cummings' "The Art of the Off-color Story," in *American Mercury,* Sept. 1939, p. 27, as of cole-slaw, noting that it is also told of rice-pudding.) In a gag revision given by Elgart, *The couple are hugging with the lights very low.* "What are you thinking about, darling?" *he whispers.* "The same thing you are," *she answers shyly.* "Then I'll race you to the ice-box!" *he shouts.* (Elgart, 1951, p. 137, captioned "Belly Laugh.") The same basic story was made the subject of a superb brief movie-skit in the French motion picture, *The Seven Deadly Sins,* just after World War II, with the benighted traveller leaving the flirtatious farmer's wife yearning in bed while he races to the kitchen for the cream-cheese he wanted at supper.

The bedroom accommodation situation is crucial in most of the travelling salesman jokes, and it is not well known that the jokes actually concerning travelling salesmen and farmers' daughters or wives are more often of sexual rejection than of sexual achievement. The 'dolly' or 'duck' (Joe Penner) joke given in the section on Pedophilia in the preceding chapter has to make the girl-child the aggressor before anything can happen. *A young widow is putting up a travelling salesman for the night, his car having broken down. "You know," she says coyly, "the door between our rooms doesn't lock." "Don't you worry about that, ma'm. I'll just jam a chair up against the knob."* (Minneapolis, 1935.) In another version the rejection is put into the woman's mouth. *A travelling salesman's car breaks down. He is given a room for the night by an attractive woman living alone. He cannot sleep. Suddenly he hears a light rapping at the door. "Would you like some company?" she asks, appearing at the door in her dressing-gown. "You bet I would!" he says. "That's good, because here's another gentleman whose car broke down and who wants a room for the night."* (Curran, 1938, p. 81.)

In two complex and not very funny examples the rigorous chastity of the fool is rationalized as religious principles rather than pure folly, but in both cases the punch-line re-emphasizes the accusation of being a fool. *A minister travelling in his car picks up a girl hitch-hiker and allows her to sleep in the car while he takes a bed in a tourist cabin. Little by little she gets into the cabin and finally in bed with him. After lying silently by him for an hour she says, "Mister, here we are alone. Nobody knows we're here. Couldn't we put on one little party and then go to sleep together?" "What!" he shouts, "after all I've done for you, now you want me to go out for ice cream and cake? You've driven me to the point where I absolutely refuse to do anything more for you!"* (Minn. 1946.) The phrase 'to put on a party' is a folk euphemism for coitus, dating at least from the 1920's, as in *The Party Book,* by 'Keith K. Knight' (Hollywood, privately issued about 1929; later re-issued as *How to Love, or The Art of Intercourse,* by 'Douglass McK. MacDougall,' 1930, and other titles), which appears to have been the first perfectly serious manual of sex technique illustrated with *photographs* showing positions, a format finally appearing publicly, in Germany and Japan — with photographs of doll-figures! — in the 1960's.

A clergyman's young assistant tells him that the women of the con-
gregation are tempting him sorely. He is told "Resist, young man, and
you'll get your reward in Heaven." This happens several times. When
it is the red-headed girl in the choir, the assistant says, "Reverend, I
don't know how much longer I can resist. And by the way, what do
you figure the reward will be that I'll get in Heaven?" "A bale of hay,
you jackass!" (Baker, 1945, vol. II. Elgart, 1951, p. 44, piously changes
the ministry to 'a large accounting firm.') A similar situation is made
the theme of an extremely funny Trinidadian Calypso ballad of the
1930's, "Resisting Temptation," sung by Wilmoth Houdini on Victor-
Bluebird record B-10619, ending with the climactic:

> *Little girl, I'm going to tell you the trut',*
> *I don't intend to eat the forbidden fruit.*
> *I rather commit suicile*
> *Than to make love to a little chile —*
> *Oh little girl! please leave my bachelor room!*

In the standard travelling salesman routine this becomes rejection
by accident or misunderstanding rather than design. *The travelling*
salesman is told he will have to sleep either with the baby or in the
barn. Having visions of the baby wetting him in his sleep, etc., he picks
the barn. In the morning a beautiful young girl comes in to milk the
cow. "Who are you?" he asks. "I'm the baby of the family. Who are
you?" "I'm the jackass that slept in the barn." (Pa. 1936.) I heard the
following joke first in eastern Pennsylvania about 1930 as of just a
girl and a boy, but it is given in *Waggish Tales* (1947) p. 169, roughly
as follows: *The travelling salesman is given a bed with the farmer's*
daughter, but the farmer (or his wife) officiously puts a rolled-up
pillow between them as a bundling-board. During the night the girl
rolls and tosses, and touches him with her toes, and says, "You know,
I've never been in bed with a man before. I'm so scared I'll bet I
couldn't even scream if anything happened." "Don't worry," he says
gallantly, "nothing's going to happen." In the morning she walks him
to the gate. Her hat blows over the fence, and he says, "I'll jump over
the fence and get it for you." "Never mind," she says, "last night you
couldn't even jump over a pillow." At Aarne Type 1445 — and compare
Type 1351A — Thompson notes a German version before 1954, and
observes that he heard this story himself 'in Kentucky about 1906
(told of a local character).' While it might seem fanciful to im-

agine this story actually to be drawn or surviving from ancient Celtic legends, it is interesting to compare it with the following trait from a legend of the Arthurian or Tristan & Isolde cycles, as noted in Robert Briffault's magistral work, *The Mothers* (1927) III.441:

Masculine jealousy is in the early romantic literature of Europe, both in its primitive and more sophisticated forms, what it is in savage societies; husbands are jealous of lovers lest they run away with their wives, but there is no hint of lovers ever being jealous of husbands. Of any delicacy, of any reticence, whether in words, deeds, or sentiments, there is not a trace. The women almost invariably do the wooing, and they do it with a directness and determination that ignore rebuffs. Deidre springs at Naisi like a wild beast, seizes him by his ears, refusing to release him till he has promised to elope with her. The terms in which they make their advances will scarcely bear repeating. Deidre tells Naisi that she is a young cow and wants him as her bull. Grainne urges on the hesitating Diarmaid by an obscene jest, which is reproduced in Tristan and Iseult. ("The Pursuit of Diarmaid and Grainne," *Revue Celtique*, XXXIII, p. 48. *As she walks by her lover's side through some water, it splashes up to her thighs; she remarks: "A plague on thee, streaky splash, thou art bolder than Diarmaid."* Iseult 'of the white hands' makes a similar remark. — Eilhart von Oberge, *Tristan*, v. 6134)

Two travelling sales*woman* jokes will end this group. *The travelling saleswoman stops at the farmer's house. There is no extra room so she must sleep with the farmer's son. During the night she nudges him and says, "Do something." "Huh?" "Do something!" He (vibrating his lower lip with one finger): "Bubba-bubba-bubble."* (*Anecdota* 2:300, ending, so he 'took out his harmonica and played "Yankee-Doodle".' Text form, N.Y. 1938.) *The travelling saleswoman in bed with the farmer's son says to him, "How about trading sides with me? You roll over me and I'll roll over you, and we'll be more comfortable." "Oh, that's all right, lady, I'll just walk around the bed." He does so. This happens several more times with the same result. Finally she says, "You know, I don't believe you know what I really want." "The hell I don't," he replies, "you want the whole damn bed, but you ain't a-goin' to get it!"* (D.C. 1949.)

Generally, as above, it is only with his folly that the fool is punished. *The old fool is telling of his son's conquests. The boy has been to the big city and spent the night in bed with a burlesque queen.* "Yup," says the father, "and if he'd 'a played his cards right I believe he could 'a screwed her." (1:476.) More extreme punishments are also suggested, of which only the modified forms of breaking a leg or being kicked will be noted here. *A policeman stops a younger man from kicking an older.* [Compare the preceding joke.] *But the older man explains that he asked him to do it. Twenty years ago, he says, a woman invited him to sit on a couch with her, changed into a negligée, let it fall open on the grounds that she was too warm, and finally let him leave saying that someday when he remembers it he'll ask somebody to kick him* "where it will do the most good." "And just today," *he finishes,* "it came to me like a flash what she meant." "Hey you," *says the policeman to the young man,* "start kicking him again — quick!" (*Waggish Tales,* 1947, p. 318.) Elgart gives this (1951, p. 84) as of an old Swedish carpenter, who, while shingling a roof twenty years later, suddenly understands, and is telling his story in the hospital with a broken leg. That both these punishments are modified castrations will be seen more clearly in Chapter 13, in Series Two, where *the recalcitrant penis is tied with a string, made to kiss its owner's buttocks, prevented from urinating etc., with agonized, self-directed screams of* "Revenge! Revenge!"

II. PURE FOOLS

The ultimate fool is one who does not understand how to perform sexual intercourse, or who does not recognize it when he sees it being engaged in (by his own wife with someone else). As compared to this depth of folly, the mere not recognizing of the female sexual organs, or not being awake to one's sexual opportunities, are simply halfway stages. The *Oldest Stories in the World,* as Dr. Theodor Gaster calls them, are the Babylonian and Assyrian tales composed nearly four thousand years ago in Mesopotamia, and written down on clay tablets in the 7th century B.C. for the library of the great King Ashurbanipal, at Nineveh (the modern Kouyunjik) — a library first unearthed only about a hundred years ago. These stories have been published in English adaptation by Dr. Gaster (1952), and among them will duly be found, mixed in with the legends of the wars of the gods, the story of the quintessential fool, *Appu,* who does not know how to perform sexual intercourse and must ask. Naturally he gets the directions all wrong. This is the standard folktale trait of the 'literal fool' (Aarne Type 1685, "The Foolish Bridegroom," and Thompson Motif J2462, "Literal Fools.") Thompson gives further motifs on this theme at J1744, "Absurd Ignorance," particularly J1744.-1.1, from India: '*The numskull groom on his wedding night does not know how to get [in]to the bed, the curtains being drawn. He scales one of the posts, clambers to the canopy, falls upon his bride below, who screams for help.*' Though not exactly a joke, this is of course high comedy, probably intended in part as a travesty of the complex coital positions in the Hindu love-books such as Vatsyayana's *Kama Sutra.* In an American erotic comic-book (seen Ann Arbor, Michigan, 1935), entirely devoted to mock coital positions, one very similar to this Indian story shows the bridegroom maniacally swan-diving from the wooden foot of the bed upon his frightened but expectant bride. A joke on this very 'posture' (considered an ultimate refinement of erotic technique) will be given later.

The foolish bridegroom does not know how to perform coitus. The bride complains to her mother, who tells her, "Just take his hand and put it on your affair." Next morning the bride complains again, "It didn't work. I put his hand on my pussy, and he got up and washed himself!" (1:352.) Again, it will be seen, the foolishness amounts to a rejection of the woman, quite unmistakable in both the preceding and following examples: *A moron ignorant of what to do on his wedding night is told to "watch the animals." Next morning the bride complains, "Oh, it was terrible. All he kept doing was smell my asshole and piss against the leg of the bed."* (D.C. 1943. *Kryptádia,* x. 125.)

In a version of this situation which has all the earmarks of age, *A foolish bridegroom is told by his mother, "Tonight when you go to bed, put your hand on Mary's head and feel down till you come to the first hole. Then put your hand on your head and feel down till you come to the first long thing. Then take the long thing and shove it into the hole hard." The fool feels down his wife's head and along her back until he comes to her anus, then down his own face till he comes to his nose. He promptly plunges his head under the covers and makes connection. "Sure is fun," he exclaims, coming up for air, "only it smells kind of spoiled."* (Idaho, 1919, with MS. caption "The Half-wit.") In a shorter version, collected D.C. 1945, the fool — here some-what unusually identified as 'A jew' (the Jew-nose stereotype?) — is told by the doctor *"To put the longest thing he had in the hairiest thing his wife had," in order to make her pregnant. Weeks later he complains, "Well, I stick my nose in her armpit every night, but no luck yet."* (*Kryptádia*, 1884, II. 15, and 139. Also in *Russian Secret Tales*, c. 1865, No. 14, with other traits.)

The fool may also be ignorant of the pelvic motions or other tech-nique of intercourse. *The fool describes his bride to the corner loafers as dumb, on the grounds that on their wedding night she put the pillow under her buttocks instead of under her head.* (2:123.) In Austria a bride is — or was, at the turn of the century — given a small embroidered cushion for just this purpose called the *Brautkisse,* or bridal pillow. *The office (formerly village) fool gets married. Next day his friends ask him, "How many times?" "Five." "Good work." Next day they ask him again. "Twelve." They look dubious. "Really? We'll see tomorrow." The next day he says, "Sixty-six. Honest to God,"* he adds, seeing their doubting faces, and counts (*motion of the hips back and forth*): *"One-two, three-four . . ."* (N.Y. 1941.) This is per-haps not so utterly foolish as it seems. Many young people of both sexes believe that the insertion of the penis constitutes the entire act of intercourse, and are surprised to learn of the necessity for reciprocating motions in order to arrive at orgasm — and this in spite of what they might have been able to infer from their probable experience with masturbation. Relevant here is the story of *The mountaineer who brings back his bride to her father the morning after the wedding. "What's the matter, Zeke? Weren't she a virgin?" "Wal,"* says the bridegroom, *"I dunno. That up-and-down motion may come natural, but that round-and-round motion was learned!"* (Penna. 1936.)

The inability to recognize sexual intercourse on seeing it is usually pivotal in stories of adultery with the fool's wife, but is also encoun-tered strictly as ignorance. *A backwoodsman brings his son to town for the first time. They look into a machine shop and see holes being bored in boilers; and see holes being bored in chair seats in a carpentry shop. They then separate and when they meet later, the son, who has been looking in the door of a whore-house crib, says, "I saw them making people." "You what?" says the father. "I saw them making people. The workman was just finishing a woman. She was all done except her asshole, and he had her down on the floor boring that out."* (Idaho, 1919. In *Kryptádia*, 1907, x. 134, "La Fabrique du Monde.")

The punch-line of the following anecdote has long since become a catch-phrase. *Two yokels looking for a roof-garden movie get on the wrong roof by mistake, sit down on a cornice, and see, opposite, one lighted hotel window in which a young woman in a kimono gets a man to throw away his cigar and come to bed with her. She then goes to the bathroom while he sits down and smokes another cigar. She comes back and starts kissing him again. He throws away the cigar. "Let's go," says one yokel to the other. "This is where we came in."* (2:218.) There is a clean version of this in John Mottley's *Joe Miller's Jests* (1739) No. 188, also on a theatrical background.

The following group of stories might perhaps better be given under Adultery, particularly for the prominence in them of the proto-homosexual *relationship with the other man* which is so significant in jokes on adultery. However, the fool's ignorance of coitus when he sees it, leading to his allowing or even assisting at adultery by his own wife, is one of the standard fool situations at least since the time of Boccaccio (1353). See the whole series of motifs in Thompson and especially Rotunda, K1500–1549, particularly those stemming from the Enchanted Pear Tree (*Decameron,* Day VII, Tale 9; and see the literature on the sources of this motif noted by Rotunda, K1518), in which the husband is made to deny the evidence of his senses.

At the wedding the fool finds the best man in bed with the bride. He goes down and brings up all the wedding guests to see, chortling, "Why he's so drunk he thinks he's me!" (Elgart, 1951, p. 48, as of a comedy Mexican, one of the more recent avatars of the fool.) Similarly, in a variant of the famous "Let him make his own coffee!" story quoted in a later chapter, *The cuckold who has lost his key* [!] *says to the policeman, "Sure it's my house. This is my hall, that's my carpet, this is my bedroom, that's my bed, that's my wife, and you see that man on top of her? — that's me!"* (N.Y. 1942.) — *"I've got a good joke on you,"* says one friend to the other. *"Last night you forgot to pull down the shade, and I could see you laying your wife." "Ha ha,"* says the other, *"the joke is on you. I wasn't home last night!"* (Curran, 1938, p. 116.) A variant, with the standard midwest fool character of the Swede: *"I got a good yoke on Ole. He pay my wife five dollar to foke her, and I foke her for nothing."* (Curran, 1938, p. 222.) The same collection gives a third example of the self-satisfied fool, wise in his own eyes, who projects his folly on everyone else: *The office fool is late to work. "I got up late,"* he says; *"got dressed in a hurry, and just as I was reaching for the bedroom door-handle, it opened, and the iceman walked in.*" "*What did you do?*" "*Do? I nearly laughed myself to death. Can you imagine anybody so dumb he thinks we keep the icebox in the bedroom?*" (Curran, 1938, p. 118.)

In the American standardization of existing fool stories, about 1940, as 'Little Moron' jokes, one remaining sub-type was the foolish question or *non sequitur,* usually on the bleeding-hearts framework: "Now my question, Mr. Anthony, is . . ." *The fool comes home and finds his wife and her lover on the couch together. They beat him, they spit on him, they make him bring towels and cook supper for them.* "*Now my question, Mr. Anthony, is . . . can they make trouble for me if I sell the couch?*" (N.Y. 1945.) A variant of this is quoted by Dr. Frederic Wertham, in *American Journal of Psychotherapy* (1949) III. 587, as illustrating the similarity between the poetry prize for Ezra Pound and the Nobel Prize due to Ilse Koch for her artistic work on lamp-shades (of human skin) in the Belsen concentration camp: 'The Senate-House Library Committee . . . instead of doing something about the Pound award itself, has ordered the Library of Congress to discontinue all other future awards . . . like the proverbial husband who found his wife with a man on the couch in the living-room, asked no questions — and threw out the couch.' This is nothing other than Rotunda's Motif K1569.2*, cited to the *Cent Nouvelles Nouvelles* (1460) No. 71, and to various Spanish and Italian *novellieri:* 'Husband surprises wife and paramour. Rebukes them for not shutting the door.'

Even the trait of the *door* has survived, in a version (to be discussed again later, under "The Relationship with the Other Man," 9.II.6) in which: *The homosexual who has found his wife in adultery is telling another homosexual about it.* "*But, Bunny, what did you* DO?" "*Do? The way I* thlammed *the door when I went out, they knew I* wathn't pleathed!" (1:310, heard with affected homosexual lisp on the burlesque stage, N.Y. 1937.) This folktale has all the air of being a true incident, 'rationalized' originally by telling it as a joke, in the way discussed in the Introduction, section III.

The various replies and pretenses of the adulterer to the deceived husband move out of the adultery category, and into that of the fool, when the husband believes them. *The husband comes home and finds his wife on a rumpled bed, and the child crying,* "*Papa, there's a boogie-man in the closet.*" "*Nonsense! There's no such thing as a boogie-man.*" "*But Papa, there's a boogie-man in the closet!*" "*Look,*

I'll show you there's no such thing," he says, *pulling the door open. Inside a naked man is cowering behind the clothes. The husband is dumbfounded.* "What the hell is the big idea going around scaring kids!?" (N.Y. 1940.) The genealogy of this story may be traced to the *Cent Nouvelles Nouvelles* (1461) No. 23, *"La Procureuse passe la raye,"* of the child who tells his father not to cross the chalk-line the adulterer has made in sporting with the wife, "or he'll tumble you as he did mother." In the boogie-man element one may also perhaps discern No. 72, *"La Nécessité est ingénieuse,"* which still exists in much clearer form in the stories and poems of the head or tail caught in the toilet-seat, on which see Chapter 15, "Scatology," in Series Two.

Another story, or set of stories, even older is that of the adulterer disguised as a doctor. (Rotunda, K1514.11*, citing only Grazzini 1: No. 10.) This is clearly Boccaccio's story, Day IX, Tale 10, of *the wife who is being changed into a mare by a magician* [compare the *Golden Ass* of Apuleius, and *Joe Miller's Jests,* No. 79], *but her husband ruins the spell by objecting when the magician is about to apply the tail.* The identification of the penis as a *tail* is common in most Romance languages (Latin *cauda,* French *queue*), though the 'tail' in the English 'piece of tail,' as meaning sexual intercourse, actually refers to the buttocks or pelvic area of the woman. In a nudist-camp or wild-party version of the children's game, "Pin the Tail on the Donkey," suggested in a cartoon in the bawdy-joke magazine, *Sex to Sexty* (Arlington, Texas, 1967), the target-board or 'donkey' is the figure of a naked man without genitals, and the women players are supplied with long paper penises which they are to pin, blindfolded, at the proper position. Boccaccio's story is indexed by Rotunda at K1315.3.2, "Seduction by posing as magician," with numerous folktale references, and a significant cross-reference to his K1963.2, the sham magician (or gypsy) whose real stock in trade is always either alchemy — as with Cagliostro, the last of the magicians — or aphrodisiacs ('love-potions'), or both.

Rotunda does not, however, refer to his own closely connected K1363.2*, in which not a magician but a *"Friar adds missing nose (fingers) to unborn child. Tells pregnant woman that foetus is imperfect and offers to substitute for absent husband."* This joke, cited to Poggio, No. 222, and Francesco Delicado's *La Lozana Andaluza* (Venice, 1528; unique copy rediscovered and reprinted by Pascual de Gayángos, Madrid, 1871) No. 61, p. 309–10, is still alive today; the gypsy or trickster — no longer always a friar, as in Afanasyev's *Russian Secret Tales* No. 43, "The Pope [priest] and the Peasant" — promising to make the baby into a violinist, bishop, and so forth. The wittol husband is now seen either congratulating himself on his future fortune, with so fine a child, and objecting only if the trickster farts (*"Hey, I said a violinist, not a trumpeter!"*), or helping matters along by a well-placed kick in the rump, to push the trickster even deeper into his wife's vagina (to get a cardinal, not just a bishop: Type 1547).

In the six hundred years, almost exactly, since Boccaccio wrote, the magician in these stories has simply changed the black robe of occult science, or the habiliments of a monk — even the rags of that hedge-priest, the gypsy tinker — for the white or frock coat of the physician. As I have already observed, in *Neurotica* (1951) No. 8: p. 25, 'Fondling the purple mantle of philosophy as he laid it down, and fingering the white coat of psychological "science" as he took it up,' William James, at the turn of this century — himself a physician — took the obvious next step. *A man comes home unexpectedly, and finds the doctor in bed with his wife. "What do you think you're doing, Doc?" "I'm, er, taking your wife's temperature." "O.K., Doc, but that thing better have numbers on it when you take it out!"* (N.Y. 1940.) In what is probably an older and less gagged-up version, *The doctor prescribes "intercourse" for the ailing wife, and demonstrates for the benefit of the husband, who does not understand the word. "Intercourse, hah? If I didn't know you was the doctor, I'd think you were fucking my wife!"* (N.Y. 1953.) In a variant, with the same conclusion, the prescription is of a white powder to be rubbed into the wife's spine "from inside," the doctor giving a personal application when the husband's attempts do not seem to give the wife relief. Some of the manipulations of present-day 'faith healers' are not a whit less cynical, their sexuality being probably the least harmful part.

Ignorance of paternity, and, therefore, of methods of birth control, are standard equipment for the fool — a fact which makes particularly absurd the anthropological gullibility concerning the 'nescience of paternity' among the South Sea islanders. One really begins to wonder who fooled who. *An Ozark mountaineer tells the census-taker that he and his wife have eighteen children, but that he reckons they won't be having any more. "Found out about birth control, eh?" "Hell no. I think I found out what's causin' 'em."* (2:386.) — *The doctor tells a foreigner to put a condom on his organ before intercourse, but his family continues to increase. "I got no organ," he explains, "but I put it on the piano every time."* (N.Y. 1945.)

Pure ignorance of paternity is sometimes modified to an ignorance not of the total relationship but of the exact details, particularly of the relationship between the time or number of times of intercourse, and the time of birth or number of children. The total ignorance contemplated by Sir James Frazer regarding the Pacific islanders seems, to the folk mind, almost too much to ascribe even to a fool. *A travelling salesman returns home after a nine months' trip to find himself the father of twins. " But, Doctor," he protests, "I remember that I only spent one night home when I was here last."* (*Anecdota,* expurgated ed. 1933, No. 282. The 'one night' is apparently an expurgation for one act of intercourse.) — *A father in the waiting-room at a hospital is told his wife has just had a baby boy. He looks at the clock. "9:20," he says. "Ain't nature wonderful!" Half an hour later the nurse announces twins. "Well well," he says. "Ten to ten. Ain't nature wonderful!" He starts to leave. "Where are you going?" the nurse asks. "Just for a little stroll. The next one ain't due till midnight."* (Elgart, 1951, p. 104.) To end the cycle, there is finally ignorance of the technique of maternity as well. *Over the telephone: "Never mind coming out to the farm, Doctor. My wife had the baby already." "Is she all right?" "Well, I guess so, but I had to twist her arm pretty bad before I could make her eat the afterbirth."* (N.Y. 1942. Compare Motif J1919.9.)

III. MISTAKES BY WOMEN

It will be observed later that the most common verbal technique of the male approach, as visualized or dreamed of by jokes, is the twisting by a man of something that a woman has said in such a way as to make what she has said seem sexual. As something of a historical example, there might be cited the following, from the manuscript *Treasury of Erotic and Facetious Memorabilia* (N.Y. 1910) f. 52: 'Bill (*meeting her on the street*): "What makes you walk so stiff, Mame?" Mame: "'Cause I've got on patent-leather shoes, and patent-leather draws." Bill: "Oh, you have, eh?" Mame (*indignantly*): "It does!"' Examples of the reverse technique, in which it is the woman who purposely imports the sexual tone into the man's innocent remark, are extremely rare, and are usually ascribed to some dominant female figure such as the already semi-mythical Mae West, the Hollywood 'Venus of Willersdorf.'

When a woman in a joke twists what a man says into sexuality, it is generally a 'mistake.' She blushes, she is covered with confusion. She has not meant it, she has not been trying to leer at him and seduce him — as he would be doing in the same situation — but her presumable sexual yearnings, and dreamed-of readiness at all times, have tricked her into self-betrayal. Her mistake seduces her, as effectively as would the man's purposeful jest.

This ever-ready willingness not only to be raped but to like it too, is of course the wet-dream ideal of womanhood — that is to say, of all other women but one's own — remarked upon bitterly in Ruth Herschberger's *Adam's Rib* (1948) chap. 3, "Is Rape A Myth?" It represents a fantasy escape by men from the rigorous female chastity demanded by patriarchy. These jokes of female self-rape, by 'mistake,' may be lumped with the endless novelistic tales of adultery written by men — in which the woman is always at fault. Basically the jokes and tales are the same dream, and both are of great age. The "Devil in Hell" story of Boccaccio (III.10), which is the most famous story in what is unquestionably the most famous book in European literature, is based squarely on the humor of a woman's misunderstanding a phrase, *"putting the Devil in Hell"* (Rotunda, K1363.1, K1631.1). It is admitted that the phrase has been picked by the man for the purpose of seducing her. Two centuries later, in Fortini's *Tales of the Novices* (1562) Day I.2, the story reappears completely in its modern form, in which a husband teaches his wife the foreign erotic phrase, *"Ansi visminere?"* — which he has learned from a prostitute — telling her that it means "Do you want to eat?" She repeats it, out the window, to a pilgrim from the foreign country, who takes it as a sexual invitation. (Rotunda, J1749.3*. This tale is translated in Dr. John Del Torto's unpublished English version of Fortini's tales.) Compare the French maid, later.

As most current jokes on women's mistakes are still strictly verbal, and hardly more than puns, they will be given in abbreviated form. *The girl student who confuses "femmes de guerre" with "hors de combat."* (N.Y. 1938.) — *A Frenchwoman visiting America in the 1920's asks to meet the "Mrs. O'Bitch who sent so many brave sons to help France."* (Baker, 1945, v. 2) — *A woman orders a "sexual sofa" when an interior decorator tells her that her living-room needs "an occasional piece."* (D.C. 1952.) — *At a baseball game the umpire shouts, "Three balls!" "What does that mean?" the girl asks her escort. "It means that batter's got three balls on him." "Some man, I'll tell the world!" she exclaims.* (1:378. Very contrived. Variant given of a country girl asking about moth-balls in a drugstore window. "Some moths!" she says. — *Waggish Tales*, 1947, p. 314; followed by the "*I see you shot another golf*" woman's error given later under Castration, in Series Two.) — *A man is describing Lady Luck to his girl. "She has dice for earrings," he says, "and eight-balls for a bra . . ." "My God!" says the girl, "eight?"* (Elgart, 1951, p. 114.) — *Reporter to the town spinster on her ninetieth birthday: "And have you ever been bedridden at all, Miss Lucy?" "Yes twice," she says, "and once in a horse and buggy — but land's sakes, don't put that in the papers!"* (Baker, 1947, vol. III.)

The misunderstanding may be even less than verbal, and based simply on pronunciation. *Two Swedish housemaids are having their picture taken. "Why is he lookin' at us like that?" "He's got to focus." "No, tell him yust take the picture first."* (1:108.) — *Aviator: "I shot down the first Fokker at five thousand feet, but another Fokker was diving at me at twelve o'clock —" Interested Lady: "Was it a Messerschmidt?"* (N.Y. 1953.) In another form, the over-eager beaver is not a female fool but a male prude. *A German atom-bomb scientist, formerly an officer in the Luftwaffe, is telling his new American associates about his wartime experiences, at a banquet in his honor on Operation Overkill. "I was coming in on the Russians at twelve o'clock, strafing the bastards and dropping my eggs at the same time. Well, these two fuckers were supposed to be covering me at my right, when suddenly I see this other fucker —" General Blowhole, smoothly: "Dr. Schmierkäse is referring of course to the old German fighter-plane, the Fokker, similar to our PU-2." "Well, maybe you're right, General, but this fucker was a Russian Mig."* (La Jolla, Calif. 1965, from an Italian scientist.)

In a presumably authentic recollection of Queen Victoria's household during the Boer War, we are told that in the German newspapers being read there, the English troops were reported as advancing on the Boers shouting "Kill the buggers!" whereupon the ladies of the court entered into a spirited discussion as to whether this was a misprint for 'burghers.' In a mythical accretion to this tale, *The butler or some gentleman court-official present and trying with difficulty to re-*

strain his smiles, on being asked what a bugger was, covered himself with glory forever by answering, "A bugger is a man who does another man an injury behind his back." (*The Pearl*, No. 15, Sept. 1880.)

Even a mere slip of the tongue — actually a neat 'return of the repressed' — has been collected in the mispronunciation category. *A woman who worked for Funk-Brentano (the German historian) for forty years is fired suddenly without warning. "Mr. Funk," she says, gathering up her erasers, "I think you're a prink!"* (N.Y. 1953.) The most famous joke of this type was a popular burlesque routine in the 1930's. *An American in London asks the waitress what's on the menu. "Rhubarb, rutabagas, ravioli, rice, and roast," she says. "Say, you sure do roll your r's." "Oh, it's just the high heels I'm wearing wot does that, sir."* (Elgart, 1951, p. 100.) In a topper version, *The waitress has a peculiar walk. "Pardon me, miss, do you have hemorrhoids?" "No, sir, just what's on the menu."* (Minn. 1946.)

The woman's misunderstanding of a word may lead her into embarrassing admissions, or acceptances of sexual propositions not yet made. *Dance-hall girl: "Aren't you going to take me home?" Sailor: "Is there anything in it?" "Just a little dust from dancing."* (*Anecdota Americana*, 1933, No. 336. In a more recent variant, on a bathing-beach background, the girl's reply is less purely silly, with a *vagina dentata* tone: *"Well maybe a little sand."* N.Y. 1953.) — *Soldier, saying goodbye to his girl in a car (or wagon): "Will you correspond with me?" Girl: "Sure I will, honey, but do you think there's room enough in back?"* (Curran, 1938, p. 184.) — *New stenographer: "I suppose you begin the day here in New York the same way they do in Los Angeles?" Boss: "Sure thing." She lies down on the desk. "All right. Hurry up and screw me, and let's get to work."* (Canada, 1940.) — *A travelling salesman takes a girl up to his hotel room. He pours her a glass of whiskey and as he adds the soda he looks up and says, "Say when." "Can't I even have my drink first?" she asks.* (Calif. 1942.) Compare *"He's got to focus,"* above.

The embarrassing admissions into which the woman's mistake tricks her are, in the same way, self-seductions, but projected into her past rather than promising for the future. *The Swedish maid has been entertaining her sailor boyfriend. Mrs. Johnson, the mistress, wanting to be polite, asks: "And how long is his furlough?" The maid blushes furiously. "Not so long as Mr. Yohnson's — but it's ticker!"* (Idaho, 1920.) A very similar Scottish story is given in *Kryptádia* (1884) II.

262, with the girl's foolish frankness again rationalized simply as that of an upcountry maid: *The mistress is suspicious of her two sons casting an eye on her maid. One day when they are working together she becomes quite confidential and asks the girl which of her sons she likes the best. The girl answers: "I like baith the laddies weel enough; but commend me for a straucht (straight) stroke to your ain man (own husband").* A Turkish version from Smyrna is given by Jean Nicolaidès, *Contes Licencieux de Constantinople* (1906) p. 196.

In a World War II revision, the furlough story has been much worked up, especially on the hateful side. *A soldier on furlough makes love to his wife so unrelentingly that she sues for divorce. Judge: "How long is your husband's furlough?" "Seven inches," she replies. Judge: "I mean, how long does he get off?" "Just long enough for a cigarette and a cup of coffee."* (D.C. 1944.) — *A man is complaining of his wife's sexual appetite. They went to bed at nine, he explains, and at eleven she says, "Well how about it?" Then at twelve, "Well how about it?" Again at two* A.M, *"Well, honey, how about it?" At this point he becomes angry and snaps, "How about what?" "How about getting off me so I can go and take a piss?"* (2:213.)

As the final self-betrayal through ignorance there is the accidental or erroneous admission of adultery. *A woman farts a good deal, and feels she should mention it at confession. She asks a neighbor what the polite word for it is, and is told "Oh, say you commit adultery." She does so, and the confessor asks, "How often?" "About a hundred times a day." "A hundred times a day! What does your husband say?" "He says, 'More power to your big fat ass!'"* (N.Y. 1942.) This occurs in a very similar form in *Fun upon Fun, or The Jolly Fellow's Budget Broke Open, being A Choice Collection of Monstrous Good Jests* (London, 1797) p. 45, of a child who asks her mother what fornication is, and is told 'in a pet [!] — *a fart.*' The child then tells her confessor that she commits fornication all day. Where? "In bed — in the garden — in the greenhouse" etc. A variant, in which 'adultery' is erroneously used to describe the sin *"de pisser entre la grand' messe et les vêpres,"* collected in Brittany in 1881, is given in *Kryptádia* (1884) II. 84. Dropping the pretense of error, *A woman confesses to the priest that she has committed adultery. "Was it against your will?" "No," she says, "it was against the cupboard, and you should have heard the china rattle!"* (D.C. 1949.)

IV. THE FEMALE FOOL

The female fool exactly matches her male counterpart. Where he is ignorant of the female genitals, she is ignorant of the male, and both are ignorant, though not equally, of the technique of intercourse and other matters of tabooed knowledge. *A little old lady on shipboard sees a whale spouting. "'Pears to me like it could quit laying on its back and showing off like that," she complains.* (Elgart, 1951, p. 86.) — *The schoolmarm's heifer wants bulling, so they bring her to the bull. Great commotion. The owner of the bull runs out, shouting "What's the trouble?" Schoolmarm: "We can't make her lay down."* (N.Y. 1939.) It may be noted that it is widely believed by children (and some adults) that elephants — always a prime parental image owing to their size, phallic trunk, etc. — have intercourse with the cow elephant lying on her back and all four legs uplifted like tree-trunks. Note the chapter on the serving and pregnancy of an elephant (not covering this particular point, however) in Gene Fowler's *Timber Line* (1933) p. 355–69, "The Royal Family." The famous story of the female fool and the elephant, printed in many collections: *A woman phones the zoo and says, "Come quick, your elephant is loose in my garden, and he's pulling up all the cabbages with his tail." "What's he doing with them, lady?" "You wouldn't believe me if I told you!"* (2:418. Randolph No. 96, "The Circus Come to Town," the teller apologizing for the implied Ozark ignorance. Most recently reprinted in Elgart, 1951, p. 44, with the hinting caption, "Stuffed Cabbage.") The horticultural synonyms for the female genitals are overdetermined here — garden, and the cabbages in which 'babies are found.' See the interesting list of Latin agricultural and horticultural sexual synonyms given in Leonard Smithers' translation of the *Priapeia* (Erotika Biblion Society, 1888 [Sheffield, 1889]) p. 135–8.

In a children's story, collected in Michigan, 1932, *A man in an old-fashioned hotel has no bathrobe and takes a chance on running to the bathroom down the hall naked. On the way back three old maids step off the elevator as he is halfway down the hall, and he freezes and pretends to be a piece of statuary. One old maid puts a penny in his mouth. The second puts in a nickel. The third puts in a dime and shakes his penis.* "*Look, girls,*" *she says,* "*hand lotion.*" This strikes the adult as rather stupid, but it is no more than a modernization of the *Heptameron* (1558) No. 65, given in *Kryptádia* (1884) II. 133, under the title "Le Soldat au Couvent," in which a soldier, caught in a nun's cell stark naked is passed off as a statue of "*un nouveau saint pour la chapelle.*" One of the nuns — the modern 'old maid' — examining his erect penis, says, "*Ah! la jolie invention! Nous pourrons y suspendre nos chapelets entre les offices!*" Moving on from mock ignorance to mere unsophistication, a well-known joke on *the housemaid who thinks a condom is a "skinned penis"* will be found in the chapter on Castration in Series Two.

Similarly castratory and aggressive, under the disguise of ignorance, *A man complains of suffering from a stiff neck because his wife has forgotten to sew a button on his collar. Next morning he finds that she has sewed the button on his collar but has cut all the buttons off his fly!* (Curran, 1938, p. 103.) This is a reversal of the form found in *Memorabilia* (1910), in which: *One man observes to another that his fly is unbuttoned.* "*I did it on purpose,*" *the other replies.* "*I left my collar off last night and got a stiff neck.*" (Also in *Anecdota*, 2:173.) Here the tone is more exhibitionistic, with allusion to the impotence that makes exhibitionism the inevitable protective reaction. The intense need many men feel to inform another man of his disarray, if his fly happens to be open (as after urinating), seems also to involve a fear of — because an identification with — his unconscious exhibitionism. Note the signs prominent in men's public toilets in England and America: "KINDLY ARRANGE YOUR CLOTHING BEFORE LEAVING," and other phrasings of the same message. Though opposite to, this is clearly connected, in its excessive focal interest on the male genitals, with the schoolboy prank of 'ripping another boy's fly,' modified to whipping out his tie (displacement upward) when adults are present, and now becoming passé owing to zipper-flies.

In a carefully logical joke on presumable female ignorance, *A woman complains that a man has taken out his penis to urinate in public. The policeman rubs his chin in puzzlement and says,* "*Lady, if you've seen one before, you got no complaint against him. And if you've never seen one before, you don't know what it is!*" (N.Y. 1942, told in Irish brogue.) The classic female folly, however, involves not so much pure ignorance of the male genitalia, as an overexpectation in the matter of size or of the possibilities of enlargement. Poggio's *Face-*

tiae (1451) No. 43 gives the classic form, in which *The foolish girl complains of the size of her husband's penis. He shows it to the wedding guests who find it "egregiously" large. But the girl says that after all it is only half as long as that of a jackass, "which is nothing but a beast."* La Sale's *Cent Nouvelles Nouvelles* (1461) No. 80, "La Bonne Mesure," improves on the logic here by having the girl point out that the ass is only six months old and her husband is twenty-four. In the *Cazzaria* of Antonio Vignale (1530) ed. 'Cosmopoli,' 1863, p. 38, in the section captioned "Why Women Get Knocked Up" in the unpublished translation (MS. 1931) attributed to Samuel Putnam, this story is repeated in the *Cent Nouvelles'* logical form, and is topped with another about *A man who, to please his wife, offers to have the end of a horse's penis grafted onto his own. She tries to dissuade him, but when he pretends to insist she says, "Dear heart, if you must take such a terrible risk as all that, have them graft on that black piece too; for even if it should be too much, we will find some place to stow it away."*

In the modern version of Poggio's and La Sale's joke, all the elements of the foolish wife's dissatisfaction are retained, and the public display of the husband's very long penis to a court (of relatives or of matrons, in the original) is retained. Only the punch-line has changed, again to a more 'rational' form. This is a particularly good example of the fact that the punch-line, which is nowadays believed to be the heart & soul of the joke, is actually just a modern accretion, capable of a good deal of radical change. The important and universal elements of the joke have all been delivered before the punch-line is reached. *A woman complains to the judge that she wants a divorce because her husband's penis is too small. The judge has the man take down his pants, and is shown a truly enormous penis. "Why that's the biggest tool I ever saw," he says. "Maybe so," says the woman, whirling her husband around, "but look at that scrawny ass, Judge. You can't drive a spike with a tack-hammer!"* (2:84.) In a variant collected N.Y. 1953, she says simply, *"Maybe so, but he just hasn't got the ass to swing it!"* The original of this story will be found, rather unexpectedly, in an anonymous scandal-work published on the eve of the French Revolution, *L'Espion dévalisé* ('Londres,' 1782), chap. 15, p. 189, attributed to Bauduoin de Quémadeuc, or to Mirabeau, author of the first serious historical study of sex, *Erotika Biblion* (1783). The joke is given as a quotation from a letter from the encyclopedist, Diderot, to Catherine the Great. (*In translation:*)

Dider[ot] wrote to the Empress of Russia: "When we were young, we sometimes used to go to a brothel, Montesquieu, Buffon, President de Brosse, & myself. Of us all, when he had got himself good and ready, President de Brosse was the one who presented the most imposing figure; & this merit couldn't help but be contrasted with his short stature of four-&-a-half feet [*pieds du Roi*], slender & delicate. Well, as every short man is vain, he was boasting to the nymphs of the place about the one end that gave him a certain superiority over the rest of us. One of them turned him around, & said to him: THAT'S ALL VERY WELL; BUT WHERE IS THE ARSE THAT WILL DRIVE IT?

"In the same way, when I see the sketch of a picture, the draft of a poem, the plan of a tragedy, or a political enterprise; I always think of that devil of a girl. I look at the man, & I say: THAT'S ALL VERY WELL; BUT WHERE IS THE ARSE?"

A famous mock-schoolroom joke (that it is the student and not the teacher who is the butt would alone prove that it is not a real schoolroom joke) is similarly concerned with female estimates of penis size and erectibility. *A college professor of anatomy asks, "What organ of the body enlarges to six times its natural size?" No one answers. "You, Miss Smith," he says. "Well, I . . . I don't see why I should be called on to answer such a question!" Professor: "Everybody gets zero for not studying today's lesson. The only organ of the body that can enlarge to six times its natural size is the pupil of the eye. And as for you, Miss Smith, you're due for a terrible disappointment."* (2:324.) In a variant collected N.Y. 1942, the question is: *"What portion of the body becomes harder than steel?"* The answer is, *"the fingernails. And as for you, Miss Smith, you're nothing but an idle dreamer."* Note how little importance there is to the actual *form* of the punch-line. This is the case with all real jokes, of powerfully worked-out 'situational humor.' Real life has its pathetic ignorances too, but they tend to be quite different from what is contemplated in jokes. In an authentic incident (discussed later in another context in the chapter on Marriage, 8.1.1), which took place at Western Reserve College, Cleveland, Ohio, in the 1930's, *a woman teacher giving a sex lecture to a class of girls was asked during the question period, "How far does it go in?" to which she resolutely answered, "About an inch."*

The idea that the penis is detachable from the man's body, and can be replaced with other penises (preferably larger), occurs in a number of the older jokes on female fools, and is a good-humored riposte to the problem of the enlargement of the vagina after the birth of several children. In one form, *the trickster promises to buy a penis for his girl at the fair, taking money from her for this purpose; and later makes love to her, telling her that his testicles are her change.* The Breton tale, "La Frênolle," given in *Kryptádia* (1884) II. I, is of this type, and the editor notes, p. 4–5, several other French versions as well as that in Afanasyev's *Russian Secret Tales* (Russian text: Geneva, 1872) No. 46, "The Comb," which ends with elements taken from "The Maiden's Honor," to be discussed in a moment. "La Frênolle" is translated into English as "The Instrument," in *The Way of a Virgin* by 'L. and C. Brovan' [Raymond Thompson?], with imprint 'London, 1922' [actually: New York, c. 1928] p. 55–8, along with a far older version from Béroalde de Verville's superlatively important folktale source, *Le Moyen de Parvenir* (c. 1600). This will be found in chap. 23, "Problême," I. 96–7, in what is the best edition of Béroalde's remarkable book, with charmingly bawdy wood-engravings [by Gilbert?] and *an index to the folktales included* [by Prosper Blanchemain], also with a supplementary volume of many of the same tales in *conte-en-vers* form (Paris: Willem, 1870–74, 3 vols.) I have not examined the two English translations, as *The Way to Attain,* made by Arthur Machen and Oliver Stonor (Hesperides Press, 1928), except to note that the second is better. (Buying the new penis: Motif J1919.8.)

The similar story of "The Maiden's Honor" (Aarne Type 1542**) will be found in Blanchemain's edition of Béroalde, I. 141–3, chap. 31, "Cause," *ad fin.* Here, *when the man tells the former virgin that he cannot "sew on her honor" again because he has no more thread, she exclaims, "Hey, hey! And what have you done then with those two little balls of yarn that were hanging between your legs?"* There is some connection here with the famous 'just-so' story of how *The bellies of Adam and Eve were sewn up at the Creation with uneven lengths of leather cord, or whang-string, Adam getting too long a piece and Eve too short — and they have been struggling over the piece ever since.* This, in turn, is Béroalde's chap. 43, "Annotation," told by Sapho (ed. 1870, I. 217), and is still current in English as a poem or recitation, "That Little Piece of Whang."

In Béroalde's version of the "Frênolle" story (chap. 23, "Problême," I. 96–7), *A husband gets money from his unsatisfied wife to buy a better penis. "What did you do with the old one?" she asks, after trying out the "new" one. "I threw it away, sweetheart." "Oh, you shouldn't have done that. It would have been just right for my mother."* (The only really perfect anti-mother-in-law squelch. On the daughter's resistance to her mother's control of her sexual life, breaking into open contempt after the daughter's marriage, see "The Forbidding Mother" section in the chapter on Marriage, 8.1.1.) Poggio's *Facetiæ*, written in 1451, No. 62, give an earlier form of the story: *The husband pretends to have two penises of different sizes: one specially small for defloration. He then cannot supply the larger one when his wife asks for it.* This story, too, is still very much alive, still concentrating on the wife's being dissatisfied. *A young man is petting his fiancée on his lap. She feels his penis stirring under her, and, when he shifts it to the other side of his pants, feels it there too. He explains that he has two penises. On their wedding night, after intercourse, she suggests that he should now use the second penis, but he explains that he has given it to a friend who didn't have one. A few days later he finds her coming out of the friend's house. "Aaah," she says forlornly, "you gave away the best one!"* (1:71.) Note that the punch-line here is really a 'topper' of the original story, the trickster falling into his own trap.

A more recent rationalization of the girl's mistake is the sailor's pants-flap (the older 'ballap') with the buttons on each side. I collected a form of this in New York, 1944, but it will not compare to that given by Vance Randolph, in *Pissing in the Snow* (MS. 1954) No. 42, "The Double-Action Sailor," noting that he collected it in Argenta, Arkansas, 1940, from a male informant, and adding that: 'Before World War II, enlisted men in the Navy did wear bell-bottom trousers that opened at the sides.'

One time there was a sailor come to this town, and he had ribbons on his uniform. And also his pants was buttoned at both sides, instead of in front. Pretty soon he propositioned one of the town girls, but she says no. "I don't never fool with strangers," says she. "What could you give me, that the home boys ain't got?"

The Navy fellow looked kind of surprised. "Lady," says he, "it must be you don't know about sea-faring men. These farmer boys ain't got only one pecker apiece, but I've got two." The girl never heard of such a thing before. "You've got two tallywhackers?" she says. The fellow told her yes, and he says all sailors is built double-action that way, on account of the government regulations. "This I've got to see," says the girl, and down the road they went.

Soon as she comes to the brickyard the girl rolled over and pulled up her clothes. The sailor unbuttoned his pants on the right side, and he sure did give her a good screwing. Then they both laid there and rested awhile. Pretty soon she says, "Well, let's try the other one." So he unbuttoned his pants on the left side, and pulled it out. But the goddam thing just hung down, limp as a rag. "Look at that now," says the sailor, "a-sulking because he didn't get to go first!" The girl just set there a minute, and then she laughed till the tears run down her face.

She busted out laughing the next night too, when the Navy fellow wanted to take her out again. But she wouldn't go with him. "Sailors is educational, and I wouldn't have missed it for anything," she says. "But when it comes to steady company, these single-action country boys is good enough for me."

Note the built-in contradiction that the "Double-Action Sailor" can only make love to her once, but what the girl wants is the 'single-action country boys' who can make love to her twice at a séance, or possibly more. Compare also the story of: *The hobo or gypsy in old, torn clothes, whose penis keeps falling out various holes in his unpatched pants while the kind housewife is feeding him in the kitchen. Later she tells another woman, "I never in my life saw a beast with so many pricks!"* (N.Y. 1950). This leads to the whole subject of frankly mythical 'critters' with multiple genitalia. These are essentially riddles, and it is observable in all the preceding stories of female fools that a prominent element is that of the male trickster sexually fooling the gullible woman. Note, for example, the riddling *"Gormagon,"* in Francis Grose's *Classical Dictionary of the Vulgar Tongue* (1785), which is defined as: *'a monster with six eyes, three mouths, four arms, eight legs, five on one side and three on the other, three arses, two tarses* [penises] *and a* **** [cunt] *upon its back.'* Solution: *'a man on horseback with a woman behind him.'* (The woman is riding side-saddle.) Compare the 'Yogi' or 'oogly-booger' magic-penis stories.

There are also various limerick versions of a favorite concerning the man with two penises. *The Limerick* (Paris, 1953) No. 202, gives:

There was a young fellow named Locke
Who was born with a two-headed cock.
When he'd fondle the thing
It would rise up and sing
An antiphonal chorus by Bach.

This is dated 1939, and paired with a limerick on a young lady of Natchez, possessing 'equipment that matches,' with a long note on an actual case of diphallus from *The Lancet* (London, 1865) II. 124. As to the joke, a version even older than that of Béroalde de Verville or of Poggio will be found in *The History of the Forty Viziers,* a Turkish collection ascribed to Sheikh-Zada and dedicated to Murad II, who reigned from 1421 to 1451. This particular story, of the man who makes the woman believe he has two penises, is the Fortieth Vizier's tale, but is omitted from the translation by E. J. W. Gibbs (London, 1886.) It will be found printed as Appendix B to Burton's *Arabian Nights*, vol. XIV, surviving in *Histoires Arabes*, pp. 61, 147, 168, 201, in various fanciful forms. Nicolaidès, p. 163, gives a Greek version from the Isle of Chios, with a 'topper' in which *the first penis is said to be for the legitimate wife, and the other (which the wife finally demands) "is just for bitches and whores."*

The contrast between these real jokes, of great age and universality, and the weak and silly modern puns of the 'Little Audrey' — the female 'Little Moron' — type, is really brutal. *The foolish bride who does not take off her wedding gown because her husband said they would be "going to town about eleven o'clock."* (Elgart, 1951, p. 46.) — *The foolish bride who spends her wedding night looking out the window because her mother told her it would be the most beautiful night of her life, and she doesn't want to miss a minute of it.* (Elgart, 1951, p. 30.) — *The bride on the train who asks her husband if he has their "intercourse tickets," after she hears a man say, "I can't find my fucking ticket."* In a variant, *The bride is worried about the slowness of the train when she hears a man say, "By the time this train gets to Florida, the fucking season will be over."* (N.Y. 1953.)

One of the essentials of the wise-fool story is that the fool's cocksure ignorance ends in some sort of self-harm. *A woman locks out her drunken husband on a Saturday night. By the time he rolls home, it is Sunday morning and people are passing on their way to church. To disgrace her he begins a serenade: "Oh Flora dear, I love my beer,*

and I slept with you before we got marrrr—ied." His wife angrily
flings up the window and sings back, *"And so did every other boy in
town, and so did every other boy in town!"* (Curran, 1938, p. 108.) In
a similar story in the *Cent Nouvelles Nouvelles* (1461) No. 8, *A bridegroom's ex-mistress attempts to disgrace him at his wedding by telling
her mother of their intimacy. "What?" says the bride, "do you mean to
say she told her mother you slept with her? How stupid! Why the
waggoner at our house slept with me more than forty times, and you
can be sure I never told my mother anything!" The husband immediately returns to the ex-mistress.* With this whole matter of sexual recrimination, compare Bessie Breuer's *The Daughter* (New York,
1938), an important and courageous handling of the problem of Electra's frigidity; especially the climactic scene, p. 342, in which the inferior male with whom the daughter, Katy, has been able to have an
affair, gets drunk and shouts the details of their intimacy under the
hotel window, where her mother and everyone else must hear: "Katy?
I don't want Katy. I want Elvira. I want a girl with big bubs and
plenty to hold onto. I don't want Katy — to hell with Katy. She's got
fangs. I can't get it up with Katy no more. Lemme go . . . God damn
you, I'm going to Elvira. Katy's a man! She —— the first night, that
snatching box . . . " This was probably the first such passage of colloquial frankness publicly printed in English on the 'New Freedom,'
following the re-publication of Joyce's *Ulysses* in America, and it is
significant that it is by a woman.

Ignorance of the mechanism of birth represents the ultimate folly in
a woman. *A woman gets on a train with nine children, in three sets of
triplets. Conductor: "Do you get three every time?" "Oh no, sometimes we don't get any at all."* (Elgart, 1951, p. 10.) — *1st Woman:
"Did you hear about the woman that had quadruplets? I understand
that only happens once every sixty thousand times." 2nd Woman: "My
goodness! When does she get her housework done?"* (N.Y. 1940. Also
in *The Medicoban,* University of Manitoba, Canada, Jan. 16, 1953; this
issue banned by the authorities and largely reprinted in *Justice Weekly,*
Toronto, Feb. 7, 1953, p. 5/3.) Both of these, it will be noted, are of
the type in which an erotic image is imported into a superficially non-
erotic conversation. Also of the same type: *A poor woman bribes the
parson with a dozen fresh-baked scones, which she delivers to him
personally at the rectory one evening, not to embarrass her with hard
questions at catechism class. But he forgets and the next week asks her*

a particularly hard question. "Your Reverence," she says, struggling to her feet, "I don't think you ought to ask me such a question, after what passed between us the other night at the rectory." (Curran, 1938, p. 38.)

Ignorance of the mechanism of intercourse very rarely occurs in jokes on female fools, though it is one of the most prominent themes in connection with male fools. In one of the few examples collected the woman's ignorance is not even of ordinary intercourse, but only of a special position and a misleading slang term to describe it. *A girl working in a laundry takes night work at a whore-house to increase her income. The madam impresses on her the necessity of "giving it to the men any way they want it." Her first customer says he will give her double the usual fee if she will do it "dog fashion." "All right," says the girl, "but for heaven's sake, don't drag me past the laundry."* (1:97.) Re-collected several times as of a man offering his wife sums and presents up to a mink coat for the same privilege, with the same simile, *"Just like a couple of dogs." "All right," she says finally, unable to refuse the mink coat, "but for God's sake, not on our block!"* (N.Y. 1952.)

In an artful old example of the misunderstanding joke, *A man makes a hit at a stag party with the toast, "To the happiest moments of my life — spent between the legs of my wife." He tells his wife he has said, "To the happiest moments of my life — spent in church beside my wife." Next day a neighbor at the market congratulates her on her husband's toast, saying it was very nice. "Yes," she says, "if it were only true. But it's only happened twice. Once before we were married and once after. And the second time I had to wake him up after it was all over."* (D.C. 1951) This is given as collected — which is the paramount rule of folklore collecting — though it seems obvious that the *"spent between the legs of my wife"* was the teller's dysphemistic personal or 'nonce' variation of the standard formula *"spent in the arms of my wife,"* since no one would congratulate the wife the next day on a toast actually given in the form stated. I have already noted, in *The Horn Book* (1964) p. 361-2: 'The song "(When) Once I Lay with Another Man's Wife," parodied in *The Beggar's Opera,* [by John Gay, 1728, a song which] was either based on a play on words, or has since been so disguised, as it survives in the form of a toast, still sometimes heard:

> Here's to the happiest hours of my life,
> Spent in the arms of another man's wife —
>   My Mother!

After which, little more need be said as to the Oedipal strivings, in the strict Freudian sense, involved in these songs and jests.'

A strange story, combining many themes, is given here under Female Fools as being frankly unclassifiable elsewhere. *In a certain town in Russia during the war with Germany, aeroplanes were entirely new to the inhabitants, and were identified by them as enormous birds called "brainpickers." During an air-raid one woman, in terror, sticks her head in a pile of straw, leaving her buttocks exposed in the air, and a passing man takes the opportunity to have intercourse with her from behind. "Pick away, pick away," she chortles from underneath the straw. "You'll never get to my brains that way!"* (N.Y. 1953.) This story, which was offered and accepted as 'typically Russian' etc., when told, will be found under the title "L'Oiseau Frouc Frouc," in *Kryptádia* (1884) II. 150, having been collected in Picardy. There the bird is a fiction by which the young man seduces a girl, whom he assures that the bird is very dangerous as it will put its beak in her eyes. Her face hidden under her skirt, she feels the young man in intercourse with her, and laughs, at the 'Frouc Frouc' bird: *"Mets ton bec dans mon con si tu veux, tu ne pourras pas le mettre dans mes yeux!"* Also in *Sex to Sexty* (1967) 14:14, as of an Ozark 'Dumb Dora.' This is basically a reference to the idea that the display of the genitals will put the Devil to flight, which is also probably hidden in the Levantine story of *The woman who is caught bathing by a strange man, and who covers her face rather than her genitals.* (Given as winner of a 'bad wife' contest, in *Histoires Arabes*, p. 214. Poggio, No. 136/7, rationalized version: Motif J2521.2.)

V. MISUNDERSTANDINGS

Aside from the misunderstandings ascribed to foreigners, which will be discussed in the next section, the simple misunderstanding of words through ignorance or mis-hearing is a common theme, in which the fool often turns the tables on the wise by the twist his error gives to the situation. *An ignorant alderman votes against the city urinal project until they explain to him exactly what a urinal is. "Why didn't you tell me before?" he says. "I wouldn't have voted against the arsenal last week."* (N.Y. 1953.) — *A company of women soldiers are being inspected stripped to the waist. The captain appears and shouts, "My God, sergeant, I said* kits!*"* (Elgart, 1951, p. 38.) — *A handyman misses getting a good job because he misunderstands when the lady of the house says, "And now let me see your testimonials."* (Pa. 1935. *Histoires Coloniales,* p. 165.) See, in Bennett Cerf's *Laughter Incorporated* (1950) p. 22, a frantic cleanup about a butler displaying his legs to the queen to see if he will look well in knee-breeches, in which every effort is made to swim, crawl, or fly to the missing punch-line, without actually reaching it. *A man is arrested for assaulting a girl sexually at a dance. He explains that it was all an accident. He mis-heard when the fiddler called out, "Everybody truck!"* (Curran, 1938, Addendum.)

Among the newspaper columnists who have been 'livening up' their daily stints with refurbished sex jokes over the last few decades, and the magazines (such as *Time*) and comic-strippers (Al Capp, etc.) who have gone so far as to venture allusions to well-known bawdy jokes, such as "Don't make any waves!" and "Lucky Pierre," nothing quite so brave has yet been seen as the half-page ad for Gimbels department store in *The New York Times,* Sunday, August 14, 1949, p. 72, in which all possible changes are rung — for advertising purposes — on the following variation on the *Omne ignotum pro obscœno* theme: *A dying Irishman who has become rich, though uneducated, leaves half his fortune to the church, intending to leave the other half to the state coeducational college. "Devil's work!" cries the priest. "They take decent boys and girls and make them* matriculate *together. They even have to use the same* curriculum!" *The bequest to the college is cancelled.* (N.Y. 1942.) The Gimbels ad changes the priest to an 'old lad,' though with a hint of a brogue — 'Sure and he's got a point' — to serve as reminder; adding, 'But with 480 coed colleges dotting the smirking face of this land, with some 585,431 *wimmen* shamefully lurking with the lads in same, leave us face it. Matriculate together they will, says *Gimbels* — so you gals might just as well relax and enjoy it.' (The modern proverbial advice on rape. Compare the even more crudely cynical: *'If you can't lick 'em,* JOIN *'em!'*) Baker, 1947, v.3, gives this as a political speech by Senator Claghorn to his backwoods constituents (*cf.* V. Randolph, *Hot Springs & Hell,* No. 300). Also, at the period, Earl Wilson, in the New York *Post,* April 6, 1950, p. 17, about *The politician who is forced by his opponent's underhand tactics to reveal "that he is, secretly, an* EXTROVERT *... But the worst thing is this, much as I hesitate to say it: His wife was once a* THESPIAN *in Greenwich Village."*

This is perhaps the original of (or derived from) the classic 'boo-boo' or moronism attributed to movie-producer Samuel Goldwyn — the presumable humorless Joe Miller or Mrs. Malaprop of the 20th Century (or was that Willie Fox?) — *who wanted to buy the movie rights to 'Radclyffe Hall's' novel* The Well of Loneliness. *"But Sam," an underling tried to warn him, "you don't want to make a movie out of that. It's all about Lesbians!" "Lissen, get me the book. So we'll make 'em into Chinks."* (N.Y. 1937, heard — as usual — from someone who swore he personally knew the vice-president at MGM to whom the remark was made.) The date of first collection of this story suggests that it was probably created *de toutes pièces* after the success of Lillian Hellman's play about a Lesbian accusation in a girls' school, *The Children's Hour* (1934). There is also a theory — and a strong likelihood — that all or most of the superb moronisms attributed to Goldwyn were actually invented and put into circulation by his principal screen-writer, Ben Hecht, a good newspaperman gone Hollywood, co-author with Charles MacArthur of the marvellous typifications in satirical form of the true milieux of the American newspaper office, and the theatre, in the plays *The Front Page* (1928) and *Twentieth Century* (1933), documents not to be overlooked by cultural historians of the future. As is, or should be, well known, the satirical theatre and ephemera of the 16th and 17th centuries (the plays, for example, of Ben Jonson and John Marston; the pamphlets of Robert Greene and Taylor the Water-Poet; and the biographical notes of John Aubrey's *Brief Lives,* and, in France, of Brantôme and Bussy-Rabutin) are by far the most authentic historical materials on their period, owing to the crushing censorship under which more formal historians had then to operate. This is certainly even more true of the 19th and 20th centuries, for all our bogus exposés.

Sheer misunderstandings seem to center around drug-stores, plumbers, and other sub-sexual professions of that sort. *A farmer (or foreign actress), wanting a cigarette holder asks in a drug-store for "one of those long round rubber things the fellows use." "What size?" the druggist asks. "Oh, give me one to fit a Camel."* (Penna. 1930. *Anecdota Americana II,* 1934, No. 196. Usually told of Greta Garbo. Condom stories are much less common nowadays, owing to the undertaking of birth-control *by women themselves,* in the form of diaphragms, the ovulation thermometer, the Pill invented by Dr. Gregory

Pincus, etc.) I trust that the company manufacturing this particular brand of cigarettes — the last successful holdover from the *Arabian Nights* names of many of the earlier American brands, such as "Fatima," etc. — will not disagree that most of the 'blue' gags in impromptu magic and puzzlery that concern cigarettes center around the "Camel" brand. (See Martin Gardner's "Blue Magic: I. Penis Pricks," for publication in the first volume of *Kryptádia: The Yearbook of Erotic Folklore.*) Most of these are not jokes, but 'quickies' and other obscœna, such as: *"Nine out of ten doctors who tried Camels — preferred women."* (N.Y. 1953, on the format of a radio announcement 'scientifically' proving the superiority of one brand over all others.) More common are spelling-out riddles on the letters of the name: *"Can A Man Ever Live, without his hump?"* — *pointing to the package illustration of the camel's hump:* 'once a fashionable word for copulation,' said Grose, in 1785, obviously laying away the word as passé far too soon! Or, on another cigarette brand's slogan, 'LS/MFT': *"Let's Suck — My Finger's Tired."* (N.Y. 1953.)

Another such bit of folk-wit may perhaps be seen, *in statu nascendi,* in a letter by Mr. Brian McNaulty, in *Playboy* (November 1967) p. 69, in response to an earlier column, "The Phallic Fallacy," intended to reassure *Playboy's* readers that their penises are NOT really too small (as every high-school boy is persuaded of himself). Said Mr. McNaulty: 'A recent cigarette advertisement states the case almost as well . . . "It's not how long you make it — it's *how* you make it long".' Whatever cigarette brand this slogan may refer to, it is highly unlikely that the ad-writers were unaware of the possible *double entendre.* (On sex exploitation in current advertising, see *Printer's Ink,* issue of February 1967, and J. F. Held's remarkably frank *"L'Escalade de l'érotisme,"* in *Le Nouvel Observateur,* Dec. 1967, No. 160: p. 28–30.) The full-page advertisement facing, in the same issue of *Playboy,* p. 68, showing a fight-it-out-for-top-banana 'modern couple,' both in pants, the male with its legs nervously crossed [!] and the fallaciously-phallic red-headed female with its legs widely spread (to prove that it *does* have a penis — of whatever length), is an even more cynical type of modern advertising sex-gag, of obviously destructive nature. Thousands like this could be culled. This one is captioned candidly: 'Comes the "look-alike" generation — they dress alike, work alike, play alike.' Yes, and *if you can't lick 'em, join 'em and cash in!*

A city girl visiting the country leaves behind a box of kotex [a brand-name — become generic in America — of disposable paper menstrual napkins, introduced during the 1920's from Japan, where they are of immemorial use]. *The farmer, not knowing what they are, uses them to bandage a cow who has torn her side on a barb-wire fence. When he runs out of pads he goes into town and asks for more at the drug-store. "What size?" asks the druggist; "they come in four sizes." The farmer marks off his whole right forearm, with a chopping gesture of his left hand: "Gimme some for a gash this big."* (N.Y. 1953.) Note the standard identification of 'cow' as woman. 'Gash' is, of course, one of the more cruel and castratory synonyms for the female genitals. It is related to folktales of the type of Rabelais' *"Diable de Papefiguière"* and Béroalde de Verville's "Little Piece of Whang," especially *the just-so story explaining the proverb, "Big woman, big cunt; little woman,* ALL *cunt!" as the result of the creation of the female genitals by the Devil* [the anti-Creator or Creator of Evil], *who stood in a deep hole with a scythe cutting open the vaginas of all the women in the world, standing spread-legged over the hole — those with the shortest legs getting the deepest gashes.* (N.Y. 1938, given by an educated teller, and probably drawn from a much older printed European source rather than from folk-transmission in English.)

The hand-gesture of the farmer (which is essentially a retort to his being mocked), marking off his whole right forearm with a chopping motion of the left hand, is the ancient Roman *digitus impudicus* or 'shameless finger,' the middle finger being held up, with the others curled down, to represent the penis & testicles, as an apotropaion or warding-off of the 'evil eye.' American female mock-soldiers ('servicewomen') during World War II were often surprised by the little Italian ragamuffins rushing to meet their boats or tourist busses, at Pompeii, with little metal *ex votos* either of the upraised finger or, frankly, of the male genitals, with the cry (in English!): *"Prick & balls, lady? Prick & balls?"* The hand-gesture is still very much alive, and nowadays usually includes the whole arm (the modern Italian form), often accompanied with the spoken catch-phrases, courageously glossing the gesture: *"Up your ass!" "Up your gig!" "Up your poop-a-doop!" "Up your fur-lined shit-shoot!"* and the like; or simply retorting to mockery or intended cheating (while twisting the upraised middle finger back & forth, with a look of hatred): *"Up* YOURS!"

Meaning: *"Stick it* [my penis] *up your ass!"* and sometimes adding: *" – and give it a left-hand turn!"* or *" – and break it off and let it stay!"* The gesture is nowadays (1968) known and used among American college-girls, as a virile vulgarism. The sadistic spy-movie *Goldfinger* was advertised, in New York in 1965, in a theatre just off lower Fifth Avenue, with an enormous cardboard hand, the size of a human being, with the middle finger painted 'gold,' (*i.e.* shit-colored) uplifted in this gesture, facing the street.

Prof. Archer Taylor has recorded – with certain pudibund omissions, as was his habit – the history of the related gesture of nose-thumbing, in his monograph, *The Shanghai Gesture* (Helsinki, 1956: FF Communications, No. 166). Of Italian origin, it is variously called *'la fica,'* the fig; *'fa'n'gul'* (dialectal Italian for *"I fuck* [you] *in the ass"*); 'biting the thumb' (*Romeo & Juliet,* I. i), 'cocking snooks,' 'taking a grinder,' and, most commonly nowadays, 'thumbing the nose,' and has a long and interesting history. Rabelais (Bk. IV, chap. 45) gives the usual etymologizing story, of the defeated Milanese who had to remove the fig from a mule's anus with their teeth (the story is taken from Paradin's *De antiquo Burgundiæ statu,* Lyons, 1542; and see Albert Kranz, *Saxonia,* vi.6), and it is remarkable that the thumbed nose is still perfectly well understood to derive its insulting quality from the implied invitation "Kiss my ass!" The gesture is, however, far older, as noted above, being the Roman *digitus impudicus.*

The 'thumb-biting,' or 'nose-thumbing' gesture refers – in the form in which the thumb is thrust between the index and second fingers, and used to pick the front teeth – to the clitoris, with an implied accusation of female dominance. (Leonard Smithers, in *Priapeia,* '1888,' p. 180; and see the peculiar story in La Sale's *Cent Nouvelles Nouvelles,* 1460, No. 66, in which both husband and wife are publicly shamed by their son's referring to the large size of his mother's clitoris as seen in the bath, with special emphasis on the masculine pronoun for the female genitals in French: "Mother had the finest and biggest — but *he* had such a big nose!") The related gesture of the forefinger of one hand being put through a circle made from the thumb and forefinger of the other hand, and agitated back & forth, is international for coitus (see the illustration in *Private Memoirs of a Profiteer,* New York, 1939, translated from the French of 'Marcel Arnac' [Bodereau], p. 13), as noted in the following joke: *The foolish bridegroom does not produce the ring when called for. The minister makes the gesture of a ring put on a finger. Bridegroom: "Tonight! Tonight!"* (Picard version in *Kryptádia,* XI. 234.)

The theme of the Fortunate Fool, which has also an ancient lineage, is touched upon in only one collected example, other than that of "The Fortunate Fact" (2.VII.2, below). *A fraternity brother or lodge member gets into the wrong meeting house, and is refused entrance as he does not know the password. "Get out of here," he is told, "this is a secret meeting of the Society of Khrap." "The Society of Khrap?" he marvels; "well I'm a son of a bitch!" "Why didn't you say so the first time? Enter, brother."* (*Waggish Tales,* 1947, p. 189.) This is the Dr. Know-all story — Grimm, No. 98, Aarne type 1641 — which exists almost everywhere in the world, and has been traced as far back as the Indian *Ocean of Story* (A.D. 1070) in the Tale of the Brahman Harisharman. It also occurs in Poggio (1451) Nos. 4 and 87, and the *Cent Nouvelles Nouvelles* (1460) No. 79, where the fool's fortune rises from some lucky accident occurring when he, or a patient to whom he has administered a laxative, turns aside to defecate. (Thompson-Rotunda, L141.2* and K1956.1, citing also Malespini, I. No. 81.) In the present sub-type the essential element is the discovery of a hidden word or name owing to an accidental pun. This is Type 1700, Motif J1802.1, in a Jewish folktale, on the Passover house-that-Jack-built song, with the repeated refrain *"Dayeinu!"* (It would have been enough!) which the evil minister, named Dayeinu — for purposes of the story — listening at the door, believes to be a recital of his endless crimes by the Jews.

I. FRANKNESS

Whether accidental or otherwise, frankness represents in jokes the deep anti-social urge to say what one truly means instead of being diplomatically polite and insincere. Everything that follows in this chapter — involving a large percentage of all the jokes collected presumably on 'fools' — turns on the fool's or lunatic's socially sacrosanct ability to *tell the truth* and blame it on his folly or madness. This is an essential part of the current 'beatnik' or 'hippie' pose of compulsive truth-telling (to others). One of the really authentic children's stories comes to grips directly with the traditionally required social falseness: *A bellboy is being instructed in courtesy and tact. If, for instance, he finds a woman naked in a bathtub, he is to say "Excuse me, sir!" The "excuse me" is courtesy, but the "sir" is tact.* (Pa. 1930. *Anecdota Americana II,* 1934,

No. 183.) The topper to this was first collected in New York, 1952: *The ship steward (in this version) is sent for a martini for the Duke. He is delayed, and on getting back to the Duke's stateroom, finds him in intercourse with the Duchess. Remembering in the nick of time his lesson in tact, he says: "Pardon me, which one of you gentlemen ordered the martini?"* The gratuitous homosexual implication here suggests an intended satire on a real duke, unnamed.

The following joke, often reprinted, recollects the eulogies of medieval Mariolatry, though no such age is suggested for the joke itself: *In a debate on what is a woman's greatest attraction, one speaker eulogizes her hair, another her eyes, a third her lips, etc. Fourth speaker: "I move this meeting be adjourned before some damn fool tells the truth."* (2:150.) In another form, *the last man observes that "There has been some disagreement as to the most beautiful part of a woman: certain people spell it with a K."* (Fredericksburg, Virginia, 1952, also collected much earlier, in the 1930's.) *The Limerick,* No. 1379, gives the traditional form of this from *The Pearl* (1879), and, at No. 914, a better-known modern variant from *Immortalia* ('Philadelphia' [New York: Macy-Masius], 1927):

> There was a young girl of Bombay
> Who was put in the family way
>   By the mate of a lugger,
>   An ignorant bugger
> Who always spelled CUNT with a K.

Swift's *Tale of a Tub* (1704, MS. 1697) Sect. II, begins with three sons who, attempting to find the letters of the word 'shoulder-knot' in their father's will, cannot find a K anywhere in it, and finally satisfy themselves that 'it was a gross mistake in our language to spell "knot" with a K; but that from henceforward . . . it should be writ with a C.' — which leaves it perilously close (*totidem literis,* as Swift puts it) to 'cunt.' This may indicate that the joke was already in existence then, or else was developed from Swift's jibe against religious factionalism in the character of the three sons, representing the three main religions. Another spelling limerick, which does not get any farther than "C-U-", is discussed in *The Limerick,* Note 1141.

Not concerned with verbal games, but on unexpectedly sexual replies, is a related story, *At a repertory performance in a western town, when the hero cries, "What shall I do with her body?" a voice from the gallery shouts back, "Fuck it before it gets cold!"* At the next per-

formance the sheriff is stationed prominently in the gallery with two guns to prevent disturbance. The danger point is safely passed, but in the following scene when the hero asks the resuscitated heroine, "What can be sweeter than your lips? What can be softer than your heart?" the sheriff leaps to his feet and shouts, "I'll shoot the first son-of-a-bitch that answers that!" (2:245.) — Wartime cleanup: *A nice old lady phones the USO and offers to entertain a group of Marines. The entertainment consists of several trays of crumpets, and the Marines begin edging toward the door. "But boys," says the old lady, "if you leave now what can I do with all these lovely crumpets?" Tough sergeant: "Anybody that answers that question gets thirty days in the brig!"* (Baker, 1945, v.2.)

Purposeful mockery, rather than the pretended ignorance, is quite prominent. *A soldier is reprimanded by the doctor for saying "prick" in the presence of the nurse, and is told to say "thumb" (or "ear"). "All right, now what's the matter with your thumb?" the doctor continues. "I don't know, sir. I can't piss through it."* (D.C. 1949.) — *At the college anti-sex lecture. Speaker: "One pint of seminal fluid is equal to a gallon of blood!" Student: "Doctor, if a man needs bleeding in a hurry, is it all right to jerk him off?"* (1:331.) — *A woman at a party is telling about a dream she had. "I put my fingers in my mouth," she says, "but I couldn't feel any teeth." Everyone leaves in a huff when the fool asks, "Are you sure it was your mouth?"* (McAtee MS. 1913, env. 7, "The Dream," versified from 'a popular yarn,' as he notes in 1944. Prose version in *Waggish Tales*, 1947, p. 60.) This is of course the 'toothed vagina' or *vagina dentata* motif (Thompson, F547.1), about which much more will be said in the chapter on Castration, 13.1, in Series Two. It is very significant that the dream of losing one's teeth — or the fear of actually losing them — is one of the most standard substitutes for castration fears, in this case the idea of woman as a 'castrated man.' The *vagina dentata* and castration themes are combined in the clearest possible way in the mythology of various American Indian tribes, in which the first men in the world are being killed by teeth in the women's vaginas, until the male hero inserts a stick instead of his penis. This is chewed up, but he then uses a harder stick with which he knocks out all the vaginal teeth, or all except one (*i.e.,* the clitoris). According to certain tribal myths, the woman does not have teeth inside, but a carnivorous fish. (*Standard Dictionary of Folklore*, 1950, p. 1152.) See the section on the culture-hero, "Tooth Breaker," in chapter 13.1.2, in Series Two.

Exactly this story of the stick and teeth has been collected as an *echt*-American joke, making fun of the comedy Englishman. *Young Lord Nauseous is about to be married, and knows nothing of sex. "Practice, m'boy, practice," says his father, the Duke. "Go out and stick your tool in a hollow tree, y'know, and get the hang of the thing." On his wedding night the young man shoves a cane into his bride's vagina, and scrapes out the sides with the ferrule in spite of her agonized screams. "Sorry, m'dear," he says. "Got to make damn sure there isn't a hornet's nest in this one."* (Calif. 1952. *Kryptádia,* 1907, x. 182.)

In spite of the ultra-sensitiveness of audiences in recent years about anti-Jewish and anti-Negro jokes and phrases, even so gruesomely anti-woman a nightmare as the above will pass without particular comment in joke-telling sessions. That the hero of the Indian myth is, in the American story, made the fool, is perhaps a step in the direction of greater sensitiveness, but seems more probably a mere disguise or sop. See further, on the myth of the *vagina dentata,* Verrier Elwin's *Myths of Middle India* (1949), and the excellent analytic article "Dragon Lady," by Jacques Schnier, in *American Imago* (July 1947), reprinted in *Yearbook of Psychoanalysis,* iv, particularly the discussion of the personification of this tooth-breaking stick or cane in the character of the spike-armored hero swallowed by the dragon to kill it from inside. Note also the peculiarly phallic fitting out of the ugly-woman ideal with horrible protuberant nose and teeth, as in *all* the "Lena the Hyena" portraits awarded prizes by Mr. Al Capp and reproduced in *Life,* October 28, 1946, p. 14–15, far and away the two most repulsive pages of pictures ever printed.

Self-betrayals through frankness are usually put into the mouths of male fools, where female fools betray themselves only through ignorance, as above. *The efficient hired hand: "Well, I got all the hay in,"* *he tells the farmer, who has been away; "chickens layin' double, vegetables comin' up triple strong; and you know them bleeding spells your daughter used to have? — I got them stopped."* (2:204.) *- A beggar is told to introduce himself as the son of some well-known family, depending on the prospect's religion. He is thrown out of the first place he comes to for saying he is the Cardinal's son.* (*Waggish Tales,* 1947, p. 114.) *— The court fool finds the King bending over and gooses him. He is told he will be forgiven only if he makes an excuse even more outrageous than his deed. "That's easy," he says. "I thought it was the Queen."* (*Histoires Arabes,* 1927, p. 189. *Anecdota,* 1933:

320.) — *A baker's assistant is found by the baker trimming a cake with his false teeth (or slapping the cookie-dough against his belly-button to make peaks). "What's the matter with you?" the baker rages; "why don't you use your tool?" "That I use for doughnuts," says the assistant.* (Minn. 1946.)

Absent-minded professor jokes, of the usual anti-intellectual type, have not been found. One exception, probably inauthentic: *An absent-minded professor is asked the difference between adultery and fornication. "Bless me," he says, "they both seem very much the same to me."* (Elgart, 1951, p. 156, with another obviously contrived p. 168). A more hateful version: *The absent-minded professor who fucked the door and slammed his wife.* (N.Y. 1953.) This is on the format of 'spoonerisms,' often attributed to absent-minded professors as a logical peg for them, as with the opening of an allocution purportedly given before Queen Victoria at Oxford, the unfortunate speaker beginning: "*I have in my bosom a half-warmed fish . . .*" The following joke will be referred to again in Series Two, Chapter 11.II.4, under "Male Prostitution," but is here considered to be of the wandering-innocent type (the near-Eastern "Goha the Fool"), which is closest to the harmless-fool category into which the absent-minded professor jokes fall. *A rag-peddler is shouting "Rags — paper!" A woman calls him up to her apartment, has intercourse with him, and gives him fifty cents to buy a drink with. He trudges up the street shouting "Rags — paper — focking!"* (N.Y. 1953.) The absent-minded student is also perhaps intended to substitute. *Student: "I want a nice room for me and my wife." Clerk: "Yes, sir, just sign the register. Anything else, sir?" Student: "Yeah, gimme a pack of cigarettes." Clerk: "What brand, sir?" Student (turning to wife): "What kind of cigarettes do you smoke, babe?"* (Elgart, 1951, p. 165.)

The remarkable obscene *gaffes* and howlers so often reported as having been broadcast over the radio generally are fictitious. (See the collection of authentic boners in Kermit Schafer's *Your Slip Is Showing,* 1953.) Famous slips of the tongue have certainly occurred, and one quite mild broadcast by Mae West in a "Garden of Eden" skit was objected to. But the dream of spouting erotic jokes on the radio, under the guise of error, is strictly only a dream, broadening out to a wider audience the fantasy of the fool's frankness. *A man wins a beer-naming contest with the name "Love in a Canoe" (or "Romance on the Beach"). Asked to explain his choice over a national hookup he* says, "*It's fucking close to water.*" (D.C. 1952.) There is also a certain amount of half-believed lore about national contests nearly, but never quite won with erotic entries, *e.g.* one for evaporated canned milk: "*No shit to pitch — No tits to twitch — Just punch a hole in the son-of-a-bitch!*" (N.Y. 1940), and advertising campaigns which have had to be cancelled because of hidden eroticisms in the script. It would be too much to say that there is no truth in any of this (I myself heard a comedy character in a radio-broadcast 'Negro' soap-opera say, of a pie, "*Mmm, tastes just like pussy — willow!*" N.Y. 1944), but there is not much. Sex comedians, like the late Lenny Bruce, are not allowed on radio or t.v., and must 'do their thing' in nightclubs or on the burlesque (or lecture) stage.

Slips of the tongue and spoonerisms (metathesis) are the final types of general mistakings and frankness. *A patron in a bar angers the bartender by staring hungrily at the bartender's girl. "I'm sorry," the patron apologizes. "Gimme a piece of beer."* (N.Y. 1953.) — *Church announcements: Clergyman, "There will be a meeting of the Little Mothers after the service. Anyone interested in becoming a Little Mother, please see me in my office."* (N.Y. 1940.) — *Nervous Young Curate: "Thursday night there will be a peter-pulling contest at St. Taffy's Church."* (Curran, 1938, Addendum.) — *Toastmaster, introducing a man named Hotchkiss: "And now I want to introduce a man — a man who (etc. etc.) — a man whose very name breathes romance — the last syllable of whose name all of us would willingly press upon the lips of the beautiful ladies present. I take great pleasure in presenting — Mr. Hitchcock!"* (1:344.) A reminiscence of this joke is used as one of the cacoëmphatonic climaxes in the article "Not for Children," in my book *Love & Death* (1949) p. 52.

2. THE COURTROOM

Under the heading of "Incest" (1.v) a group of stories has already been given concerning boys and midgets accused of raping much larger women. The point was made, and I do not think it can be denied, that these stories are actually disguises for mother-son incest themes, and that the boy and the midget are one and the same. The publicity marriages arranged between the midget and fat woman in circus side-shows, and the audience ah's & ooh's over his 'cuteness' as he poses with his head between her ample breasts, leave little to be guessed at as to the actual appeal of the situation. Joking courtroom stories seldom concern the achievement or exculpation of longed-for sexual sins, but only the taunting of the judge — as the supreme father-figure — by the blundering sexual frankness of the fool. Only one courtroom joke has been collected in which anyone but the judge, or his surrogate as the prosecuting attorney, is the sole butt, and even here the importing of an unexpected sexual element to the confusion of the attorney is more important than the actual denigration of character. *A farmer is testifying as to the character of the woman defendant. "What about her veracity?" asks the prosecutor. "Wa-a-al," says the farmer, scratching his head, "some sez she does and some sez she don't."* (Elgart, 1951, p. 137.) Usually the attack on the judge is perfectly direct. *"Judge, I hit him because he called me a dirty Polack son of a bitch." "Why I wouldn't hit a man for calling me something I knew I really wasn't." "But Judge, what if he called you the kind of a son of a bitch you really are?"* (N.Y. 1940.) — *A woman beats up her husband because, as she tells the judge, "When he finally got me all hot an' bothered, I pulled up my wrapper, and Judge, he wasn't ready! — he wasn't no more ready than you are this minute, Judge!"* (2:59.)

The commonest trick is that of ignorance of a word, particularly of some sonorous Latin euphemism for a tabooed organ or act. *"Judge, he just reached over with the axe and hit him in the ass." "You mean 'rectum'?" "Well, it didn't do him no real good."* (N.J. 1942.) — *The fool in the courtroom is testifying in a rape case, and is cautioned, after using the word "prick," that he must modify his language or he will be held in contempt. "All right, Judge, but before I go on, what's the polite word for cunt?"* (1:210.) Compare the similar story in the preceding section on the man who is told to say 'thumb' (or 'ear') instead of 'prick.' In a story often collected, the witness' defiance of the demanded polite speech is given in the form of a *cante fable* (variant in 2:224): *The witness in the rape case horrifies the court by saying, "I don't know if he was raping her, Judge, but they sure were fucking."* *He is asked if he has anything to say in explanation before he is fined for contempt. He says:*

> *His pants were down, his ass was bare,*
> *His balls were hanging in midair,*
> *His you-know-what was you-know-where;*
> *If that wasn't fucking, then I wasn't there!*

(Apparently of Welsh origin, given in *Kryptádia*, 1884, II. 344*n*, 'evidence of an eyewitness to a rape ... versified.' Arabic version in *Histoires Coloniales*, p. 78. Compare Motif J2667.)

Nothing could be more precise than the contrast between real, as opposed to merely verbal, contempt displayed in the final story of this type: *A witness in a rape case uses the word "fuck" and is told to say "intercourse" instead. "What's that, Judge?" "That's a technicality of speech you wouldn't know anything about." Witness continues: "Well, he had her up against the door intercoursing her, and suddenly he gives her the Chicago stroke (or: cross-jostle) ..." Judge: "What's the Chicago stroke?" "Why Judge, that's a technicality of fucking that you wouldn't know anything about."* (1:408.)

3. MUTES, STUTTERERS, IDIOTS

Mutes, stutterers and spastics are considered in jokes to be close kin to idiots, and the pretended agonies of stammering, and cruel imitation of the spastic's clutching gait, engaged in by the tellers of stories of this type are not pleasant to watch. Nevertheless it is significant that even real idiots in jokes are always considered to be sane enough to understand the meaning of sexual intercourse (compare Frazer on Australian ignorance of paternity); the humor of the stories generally turning on this point. *A city slicker sees an ugly, hare-lipped country girl sitting on a fence. He stops his car and engages her in conversation, meanwhile feeling her legs and genitals, while she snickers and mumbles, "Oh, what ya doin'?" Finally he begins having intercourse with her. She laughs and says, "Oh, I know — you're screwing me."* (Calif. 1942, the collector marking this 'Seduction — so he thought!')

The mute's attempts to communicate by gestures are also made the subject of jokes, the point again being the 'semi-idiot's' knowledge of intercourse and unfailing ability to communicate this knowledge. *A deaf-mute is witness in a rape case. "How did the girl go into the barn?" the attorney writes on the blackboard. The mute walks his fore- and middle-fingers trippingly across the table. The man goes in as the fore- and ring-fingers with the middle finger sticking straight out between. The girl then comes out as fingers held wide apart and stumbling, and the man as he went in but with the middle finger now drooping. The girl is pronounced raped.* (Pa. 1927. *Anecdota* 1:466, in the same year, gives a variant ending in which: 'Then the deaf-mute, gurgling and pointing excitedly to himself, made two fingers walk with the middle finger sticking up, rigid.') *A man is accused of raping a deaf & dumb girl. He denies it vigorously in court, saying "Why I didn't even touch her with the tip of my finger! (marking off the last joint of his baby finger with his thumb)." "Unnh unnh!" snorts the girl excitedly, and marks off her whole arm in the fa'n'gul gesture.* (N.Y. 1945.) Again Rabelais' "contest in gestures."

In the only stutterer story collected, except one on the Castration theme (in Series Two), the element of stuttering is irrelevant — any peculiarity would have served — and may have been added simply to draw out the build-up of a standard 'catch': *A stutterer is being mocked at for his impediment. "B-b-but everyb-body has some p-p-peculiarity like that," he says. "N-n-now y-y-you f-f-for instance. W-w-which hand do you w-w-wipe your ass with?" "The left hand." "Well, th-th-that's your p-p-peculiarity. M-m-m-most people y-y-use paper."* (N.Y. 1942.)

Actual idiots, as the insane are called, figure in a type of story quite different from the abysmal 'Little Moron' gags of the 1940's, such as *The Little Moron who cut off his prick because it got in his way when he made love* (N.Y. 1949) and *The Little Moron who went around eating the pink candy out of all the urinals* (Minn. 1946. Referring to the colored camphor cakes placed in urinals as a deodorant.) The real idiot stories concern the traditional sexual unrepression of the insane, and their efforts to get out of the insane asylum *without* submitting to the demanded sexual repression. *The village idiot is masturbating before an audience of idlers. He does not come for so long that they begin throwing money. Finally there is seventy-five cents on the floor. "A dollar, a dollar," the idiot chants in time with his strokes, "o—n—e, d—o—ll—a—r. All right, let 'er go for seventy-five!"* (2:303.) — *The lunatic confides to the visiting minister in the insane asylum that he is being persecuted by attendants who rub off with a white eraser what he writes with coal, and with a black eraser what he writes with chalk. "But I'll fool them yet," he tells the minister. "In fact, I'm ahead of them. I have a shit and a fuck on the white wall, two big pricks on the black wall, and I just scribbled cunt on your collar."* (2:68.)

The jokes on trying to get out of the asylum had a long run during World War II, when they were assimilated to the many jokes on the draftee attempting to stay out (or get out) of the Army. *The "readjust-*

ment interview" in the asylum. Doctor: "What's the first thing you're going to do when you get out of here?" Lunatic: "I'm going to get a slingshot, and break all the windows in this goddam dump!" "Take him back." The next time, having been briefed to talk about women, he answers: "I'm going to walk down Broadway and pick up a girl." Doctor: "And then what?" "Then, uh, I'm going to take her to a hotel." "And then?" "And then I'm going to, uh, throw her on the bed." "And then?" "And then I'm going to pull off her bloomers and take out the elastic and make me a slingshot and break all the windows in this goddam dump!" (N.Y. 1942, the end-line being delivered at breakneck speed. A patriotic cleanup is reprinted from *Judge* in *Magazine Digest,* Toronto, 1944, with '*shooting Japs*' rather than breaking the asylum windows with the slingshot.) Note the similarity to a story, probably earlier in origin, on the confessional. *Girl: "Father, I want to confess that I let my boy-friend kiss me." Priest: "Is that all you did?" Girl: "Well, no; I let him put his hand on my leg too. "And then what?" "And then I let him pull down my panties." "And then?" "Then he took out his thing and put it in my hand." "And then, and then?!" "And then my mother walked into the room." Priest: "Oh, shit!"* (N.Y. 1965, from a young Greek woman.)

The "readjustment interview" again. *Doctor: "Now I want you to free associate. Just say the first thing that comes into your mind. What's the first thought you'd have if a stark naked woman walked into this room with the biggest pair of breasts you ever saw?" "Windshield wipers!" "All right, take him back." On the way back to the ward the attendant asks, "Why in hell did you say windshield wipers?" Patient, turning his head slowly from side to side: "You know (sound effect): kiss — kiss; kiss — kiss."* (N.Y. 1953.) This tends immediately to the army medical examination stories, since in both types the desire of the individual being examined is not to succeed — as usual in our culture — but to *fail.* Compare other such negative strivings in folk use, as for instance the 'Dutch auction,' in which the bids *descend from* an impossible estimate, rather than *rise to* an improbable price; and the 'limbo stick' game, in which the contestants must crawl under a consecutively lower and lower bar, rather than jump over one that is higher and higher. Note that in both of these the idea of *winning-by-failing* (less and less, or lower and lower) is nevertheless re-imported. An extreme example of the socially-disapproved 'will to fail,' in connection with the army medical examination, is the black-humor codification of *1001 Ways To Beat the Draft* (New York, 1966; enlarged and illustrated edition, Grove Press, 1967) by Tuli Kupferberg & Robert Bashlow, a continuation of hippie-poet Kupferberg's earlier similar *1001 Ways To Live Without Working*. These represent the draftee's (or asylum-inmate's) violent and profane ripostes to the physician's trick questions and superior medical 'gen.' The idea throughout is that the best way to succeed — under the circumstances — is to fail, and the best way to fail is to be, or pretend to be, insane. (See further, Section III of the Introduction here.)

The imaginary display of a woman's breasts to the asylum-inmate, being asked to free-associate, is sometimes presented as the actual display of the breasts of that 'sacred prostitute,' the nurse — after all, the essential nature of a *nurse* is to have breasts — but for the doctor's evil purposes. *The pretendedly half-blind draftee is unmasked by having the nurse strip off her blouse at a signal from the doctor. "What do you see?" the doctor asks. "Not a thing. Just a blur." "Your eyes may not be much good, son, but your pecker is pointing straight to Fort Dix!"* (Orangeburg, New York, 1944.) Randolph has a version of this in *Pissing in the Snow*, No. 14, "He Didn't Get No Pension," collected in Noel, Missouri, in 1923, from a teller who 'said it was one of many "old soldier jokes" that circulated in McDonald county, Mo., about 1895.' He also cites a 'related yarn' in *Waggish Tales of the Czechs* (1947) p. 47–50, a work having no relationship whatsoever with Czech folklore.

VI. FOREIGNERS

Certainly one of the most ancient of human prejudices is that against the foreigner. The real expression of this prejudice is in war, where the foreigner is killed, his women raped, and his property seized. Between wars, this purely feral form is modified in certain formalized gestures of economic (tariff), diplomatic and spying (unmentionable), and purely folkloristic forms. Sexual vilification of the foreigner is the natural accompaniment of the desire for his women when in his country, and the desire to prevent him for competing for one's own women when he is here. Thus it is humorously believed in America — without the slightest germ of humor — that all, or practically all, Englishmen are homosexuals, and that all Frenchmen prefer oral sexual relations with their women. The birth rate in both countries is presumably kept up by visiting Americans, who are all gloriously normal.

As more lethal expressions of the xenophobic fear & hatred of the foreigner do not come to their fullest expression more than once or twice every twenty years, in war (declared or otherwise), the pilot expressions in folk beliefs and humor are never in danger of flickering out. The standard disguise for the xenophobic urge is to displace the hostility upon the mere accoutrements of the foreigner's foreignness: his clothes, his accent, his misunderstandings of national customs and speech. The Greeks had their Boeotians, the English have the Welsh and Irish (see, for example, Fluellen and Pistol in Shakespeare's *Henry V*), and the Americans have the English — and others. Over the last few years, the attempt has been made to 'clean up' these jokes by assimilating them to in-groups instead of foreigners or 'inferiors.' But no one is really fooled when jokes about Texans or 'Aggies' are prettified as concerning 'wasps,' especially in the scatological forms that will be seen in Chapter 14, "Dysphemism," in Series Two. In a courageous article by Roger L. Welsch, "American Numskull Tales: The Polack Joke," in *Western Folklore* (1967) xxvi. 183-6, though the title refers to jokes, the examples given are all insulting riddles concerning invidious nationality or *blasons populaires* (ethnic insults).

I. SWEDES AND CHINAMEN

With the exception of the Negro, the typical butts of anti-national humor in America have almost entirely ceased to be 'inferiors,' and in fool jokes certainly the concentration is all on the deposed authority-figure of the Englishman. In the Mid-west, from Minnesota on out, the Swede or Polack is the local butt, and a few relics of the anti-Chinese era of the 19th century are still to be found, but neither of these bulk very large in fool jokes. *A couple are applying for a marriage license.* "*Your name?*" "*Ole Oleson.*" "*And yours?*" "*Lena Oleson.*" "*Any connection?*" *The bride blushes.* "*Only vunce. He yumped me.*" (*Memorabilia*, 1910. Also collected without significant change, in Minnesota, 1939 and 1946.) In a variant, with a religious twist, *Abie wants to marry his Irish Rose, and the rabbi agrees to officiate only if he can be assured that Rose has "a little Jew in her." "Oh, I do,"* she says. "*Abie couldn't wait.*" (D.C. 1943.) The folly here is clearly Irish, but the sexual sin is that of the Jew. In the only other fool joke collected on Jewish themes, it is again the gentile who is the actual butt. *Butler, to the new chauffeur: "Yes, these Jewish people have very quaint customs. For instance, on Rosh Hashanah they blow the shofar." "What a wonderful way to treat the help!"* (N.Y. 1952.)

This was collected again, told by a 'modern rabbi' at a dinner-party in his garden (Passaic, New Jersey, 1964), told with several other such jokes in a compulsive fashion, apparently excited in part by the presence of three handsome young women, including the rabbi's wife. The telling of bawdy jokes is not forbidden by the Jewish religion, in the sense that Paul the Apostle's *Epistle to the Ephesians,* v. 3-4 (about 60 A.D.) forbids it to Christians, grouping it with '*fornication, and all uncleanness, or covetousness, let it not be once named among you, as becometh saints; Neither filthiness, nor foolish talking, nor jesting which are not convenient: but rather giving of thanks.*' Just as gambling is a feature of the Jewish observance of the winter solstice (*Chanukah*) under the rationalization of an all-night vigil (*Nittel-nacht,* December 24th) against the usual Christmas pogroms; the telling of bawdy jokes is a feature of the permitted licence of *Purim,* the Jewish festival of the vernal equinox, similar to the Saturnalia and Lupercalia of the Romans, or other licentious pagan festivals of the midwinter solstice or springtime equinox, such as the derivative Christian 'Carnival' preceding Lent, which was rejected by the strait-laced Protestants. At the Purim 'Feast of Fools,' playing of pranks is even allowed with the liturgy, in the synagogue itself, as for example the drowning out of certain taboo names (of the evil Haman, at the reading of *Esther,* ix. 24-25) by means of noise-maker toys, and stamping — Haman's name being written in chalk on the soles of the shoes — and the setting up by himself of a mock- or anti-cantor, who prays faster than the real cantor, finishing far ahead of him and dismissing the congregation ahead of the rabbi with a loud "Amen!" (Scranton, Pa. 1930, a prank learned in Hungary.) See also the note on erotic riddles at funerals, at the end of the present chapter, 2.VII.2, under "The Fortunate Fart."

As has been seen earlier, the sexual ignorance of the male fool is translated into, or balanced against, the sexual complaisance of the female fool. The 'Swedish housemaid,' in particular, has been saddled in America with this libel (as in the "focus" joke earlier), an obvious enough projection of the immemorial sexual exploitation of servants so bitterly excoriated in Octave Mirbeau's *Celestine: The Diary of a*

Chambermaid. (English translation, by Benjamin Tucker, in the 1900's, reprinted 1930; expurgated pocket-reprint, 1945. I have the original galley proofs of this pocket-reprint, showing the expurgations demanded by the distributing company, and made. All English translations, in any case, omit the chapter on the phallic saint.) *Mrs. Johnson's Swedish maid refuses to be vaccinated on the grounds that she has been already. "How many times?" asks her mistress. "Tvice. Vunce in the kitchen and vunce in the voodshed." "What doctor?" "No doctor! Vas Mr. Yohnson."* (Idaho, 1918, obviously stemming from the World War I epidemics.)

Impromptu times & places for sexual intimacy are the subject of much backwoods humor. Compare "Once in a Sedan and Twice Standing Up," by Julian Shapiro, in *Contact* (New York, 1932) No. 3, p. 37–45, reprinted in the magnificent novel *Seventy Times Seven* by John Sanford (1939, later pocket-reprinted as *Make My Bed in Hell!*), which I have reviewed retrospectively, in *Fact* (New York, July 1965) p. 43, as the 'Great American Novel' it was, as differentiated from the pretentious works hopefully offering themselves for that title, such as John Dos Passos' trilogy, *U.S.A.,* and the yearly doses of flatulent book-club garbage, puffed to the skies. *A Swedish housemaid, at her friend's suggestion, decides to go out with the travelling man to make extra money. "How did you make out?" asks the friend, next day. "I went out with him, like you said," says the maid, "and I did like he said. Then in the morning I said, 'Giff me five dollars,' like you said. And he said, 'Go take a shit for yourself.' And vhen I come back he was gone!"* (1:169. Compare the 'party record' song-title, about 1942, "Columbus Took a Ship for Himself.") This joke will be treated again, under Prostitution.

Of all discriminated-against groups in America — until the Negroes very recently — the Chinese have always expressed the most open hostility toward 'white Gentile Americans,' or 'white Anglo-Saxon Protestants' (WASPS), as the phrase has it. This unashamed aversion is no longer reciprocated, although in the period following the mass importation and exploitation of the Chinese in building the railroads of the American west, a good deal of anti-Chinese feeling was carefully generated. The comedy 'Chinaman,' as the foolish foreigner, appears in only a few jokes nowadays, and there only in the capacity of laundryman or other body servant. *A woman who keeps a Chinese serving boy is embarrassed by his walking into her bedroom while she is undressed, and insists that he knock before entering. He never again embarrasses her, but he also never knocks. She asks how.* "Velly simple. Beflore come in, me look thlough keyhole. If you no dlessed, me no come in." (1:467.) — *An army officer's wife has come to visit him at the station in the Orient where he has been for several years. In the morning his Chinese valet wakes her by slapping her on the buttocks, and says,* "All light, missy, time fo' bleakfast, then you go home." (N.Y. 1948. Cf. Picard anti-clerical version in *Kryptádia*, 1907, XI. 258.) — *Tough movie-actress, phoning the laundry:* "Now I don't want any more of your nonsense. Get that laundry up here, and licketysplit." "Bling laundly o.k. lady. No licketysplit." (N.Y. 1942.) One of the most chastening experiences of the present writer's career was in connection with his first book, *Oragenitalism* (1940), a term invented by himself but which no one seemed willing to try to pronounce: Prof. Kinsey and other sexologists popularizing it as 'oral-genital,' while the booksellers searched for the work — most of the edition having been destroyed — under the simpler title, "Lickety-split."

2. BLOODY ENGLISHMEN

The various shifts in the national identity of the butt in English humor are noted by F. P. Wilson in his article on "The English Jest-books," in *Huntington Library Quarterly* (1939) II. 128–9, though his treatment stops short in the 17th century and thereby avoids treatment of the use of the American as butt in England for the full century from the Revolution of 1776 to well after the Civil War. The full record will best be seen in the articles by Allen Walker Read on the acceptance of the 'American language' in England, and much more material along this line will be found in H. L. Mencken's *The American Language* (3 vols.) and William J. Burke's *The Literature of Slang* (New York Public Library, 1939) p. 14–58.

This historical basis for the American folk prejudice against the 'superior' English makes it possible to understand the great peculiarity that while national butts are usually chosen from among groups of inferior strength and subjected status — Negroes, women, Jews, the Irish and the immigrant Swedish and Chinese come immediately to mind as typical butts of humor in no position to butt back — the English are, far & away, considered a superior group and of commanding authority in America on every other level but that of jokes. The deference that the "U" British accent creates, and the excruciatingly funny aping of it by radio announcers and other aspirants to culture, would alone be sufficient to prove this, quite apart from its more serious expressions in the political and snob-import (*e.g.* automobile) fields.

The upper-class (and caste) "U" Englishman is by no means the 'inferior' group in America that might be expected of the butt of so many jokes and so much comic — as opposed to snobbish and serious — mimicry. It is the Englishman's authority position, as arbiter of elegance, speech, literature, etc., that makes him so awesome to certain Americans and so infuriating to others. This has been going on certainly since the early 19th century when visiting Englishmen (and Frenchmen, such as De Tocqueville) came to America to see — with a hardly hidden yearning under the pose of patrician acerbity — whether the long-awaited democratic Utopia had, indeed, been achieved, as a model for decadent Europe sick of its rotted monarchy. It is this strain — of looking to America for a model — that has now won out, with the new inundation of Europe and the Orient with Coca-Cola, rock-&-roll, and other aspects of American culture. (Rock-&-roll is, in any case, a gross Italian form of popular music-hall singing, concentrating on a machine-like sexual rhythm, and reimported to Europe via the United States. See further, my discussion of its frankly 'totalitarian' or fascistic emotional meaning, in *Models of Madness,* 1968.)

During the middle period, at the turn of the 20th century, the pose of the godlike Englishman or contemptuous European still had a few takers, and it is unquestionably significant that the three super-English Englishmen of modern literature — Henry James, T. S. Eliot, and Logan Pearsall Smith — have all been nothing other than Americans, from Boston, St. Louis, and Philadelphia, respectively, in glorious self-exile in London, where, presumably, they found the needed reconciliation with the forbidding father-figure. It is certainly equally significant that all three are also believed to have been homosexual, though, on the first two, their most recent biographers among the 'New Critics' have preferred to take the line that they were 'merely' impotent or asexual. (See my *On the Cause of Homosexuality,* 1950, for the relationship between the feared and angry or castratory father-figure — here represented by the England against which America rebelled — and the conciliatory homosexual boy.)

Most silly-ass Englishmen jokes concern the haughty English character as the American sees it. Jokes simply turning on English pronunciation (inevitably the dropped 'h') concern Cockneys only — that is to say, working-class Englishmen — whom the tonier Englishmen also, of course, affect to despise. *The champion speller of London loses the match. "Now 'ow was I supposed to know 'ow to spell 'auspices'?"* (N.Y. 1953.) Also with a complex variant on the same term, collected in the 1930's: *A young Englishman and his girl are in a midget automobile, which stalls under a guardsman's horse. The horse takes the opportunity to piss on the automobile by way of expressing his contempt. "Well," the young man apologizes, "I only 'opes we meet agyne under better orspices."* Puns of this kind are not the real stuff of folk-humor.

The attempt to milk humor out of mere British phraseology is nowadays dreary indeed. *An Englishman is confused by the American prostitute. "We went upstairs," he says, "and had a bit of old narsty, and she looked up at me and said, 'Are you through?' not meaning was I through to the other side, but simply had I finished. Haw!"* (Minn. 1946.) The humor here may be entirely obscure to most Americans, being based on British telephone etiquette, in which 'Some quick-witted hello girls . . . go so far now as to tell a Yank "Here's your party," rather than "You're through, sir." ' (Quoted from *Yank,* Oct. 7, 1942, by Thomas Pyles, *Words and Ways of American English,* 1952, p. 221.) On the other hand, a well-timed thrust at the affectations of British pronunciation may come off much better. *A Cockney girl is arrested for having intercourse on a public thoroughfare. She explains in court that it wasn't her fault, that this American soldier simply grabbed her, threw her in the gutter, "and fawked me." The judge asks her to repeat her statement several times, which she does verbatim, emphasizing that the soldier had "fawked" her. The judge looks at the jury. "Wonderful word, isn't it?"* (Calif. 1942.)

The marrow of the anti-British joke is in its view of the British character, particularly in its objection to British reserve and understatement. The American immediately senses in these habits the notion of superiority, though he is seldom able to see, in his own opposite habits of flamboyance and overstatement, an anxious uncertainty as to whether he might not actually be inferior. The interplay of the caricatured British and American characters is the real point of all these jokes. Compare the grotesquely anti-gallant, anti-mother joke, given in Chapter 9.11.6, "Conniving at Adultery," with the punchline to the Englishman with the hearing-aid: "*He knows Mother.*"

As has been seen, not to understand sexual intercourse is the folk-tale mark of the fool, but not to enjoy it or feel strongly about it is felt to be something even worse — the mark of an Englishman. *A young English nobleman is being fellated by a male prostitute in his parlor, when a friend is ushered in. They engage in animated conversation as to who has been invited to Lady Windemere's party and who has been snubbed. The male prostitute interrupts. "I beg pardon, your Ludship, but you've come." "Why so I have, so I have. Here's a shilling for you, my good man."* (N.Y. 1940.) In the vein of ignorant rather than unfeeling folly: *Englishman, to a prostitute who has just given him a moist tongue-kiss: "Now, I say, don't get personal, Miss, or I jolly well shan't fawk you!"* (1:93.)

The railroad train, an important prop in wedding-night and wedding-trip jokes, is also common in jokes on Englishmen, as a natural area of encounter with travellers. This even includes 'clean' jokes, *e.g. The Englishman on his third day on a slow train through Texas: "You know, this Columbus chap that discovered America; what I mean is — how could he have missed it?!"* The following joke is a pantomime, which is a very popular type of bawdy joke among certain tellers because it allows the miming of various taboo gestures as part of the necessary presentation of the story. (Often this very subterfuge is itself the point of the joke, as with the just-so story among children as to why policemen have a stripe down the side of their pants, involving a policeman on parade with a nasal drip, who says "Look at the moon!" pointing with his finger, and then "P'liceman wipes it down his pants." Penna. 1927.) — *A drunk on an English train scandalizes the compartment passengers by picking his nose, scraping the fur off his tongue and putting it under the seat, reaching into his fly and elaborately adjusting his genitals, etc. (All gestures being acted out). An Englishman has been watching him coldly from the seat facing, and finally says, "Do you suppose, old chap, that you could conclude the entertainment with a rousing good fart?"* (N.Y. 1953.) With this apparent nadir of ideas of entertainment may be compared the even greater depth reached in the music-hall joke: *Actor: "To be or not to be . . ." Voice from the balcony: "Sing something!" The actor begins over, with dignity: "To be or not to be . . ." Voice: "You heard him — sing something!" "But gentlemen, I cahn't sing!" "Well, then, show us your cock!"* (N.Y. 1952.) Unexpected, and almost ununderstandable as this seems, for all its drollness, it is actually a reference to a folk-forfeit — to be discussed more fully later — in which workmen once challenged each other, during *'breakdowns,' 'hoe-downs,'* or other rest periods: *"Whistle or sing, Or show your thing."* (Louie Attebery, "Rural Traditions of the Snake River Valley," in *Northwest Folklore,* Winter 1965/66, vol. 1, No. 2, p. 28-9, denying that the challenge was ever really expected to be taken literally.)

The theme of defecation in and from trains, in hotel rooms, saloons, and other unlikely locations will be noted in Chapter 15, "Scatology," in Series Two, where the 'cigar' mentioned below will also appear in quite a different context. It is touched upon here as involving the most hostile joke about the English character yet encountered, which sums up, for Americans, everything hated in the pose of snobbish superiority covering the endemic mad-dog egoism of that particular kind of snob. *An Englishman in a locked compartment on a train without a toilet asks his American seat-companion's permission to relieve himself on a spread newspaper, which he then folds up and flings out the window. The American, who cannot avoid watching the entire procedure, lights up a long black cigar to cover some of the fecal odor. "I say!" says the Englishman, "you know, this isn't a smoking compartment!"* (1:407.) The symbolic elements here, as to what the standard Englishman's elevated ways add up to in dealing with the sub-human American, and what the American would really like to do to the Englishman (with the lighted cigar) are not too difficult to discern. This joke did not originally concern either Englishmen or trains, being given in *Histoires Arabes,* p. 118-19, concerning *A fool masturbating (or having intercourse with a jackass) in front of a mosque. When a passer-by spits in disgust, the fool cries, "Aren't you ashamed to spit in this sacred place?"* Another form, p. 23, has the passer-by *whistling,* as already seen under "Female Fools" as to *The Scottish girl who "will na fornicate wi' a mon that whustles on the Sabbath!"*

3. WATER WIT (THE DOZENS)

A little-known survival of the ancient 'flytings,' or contests-in-insult of the Anglo-Scottish bards, is the type of xenophobic humor once known as 'water wit,' in which passengers on small boats crossing the Thames (and perhaps other rivers) would insult each other grossly, in all the untouchable safety of being able to get away fast. The flytings were more formal engagements, with the opponents knee-to-knee against each other as in a sort of trial by ordeal, and a remarkable record of this poetic and usually alliterative form of word-battle will be found in the great "Flyting betwixt Polwart and Montgomery," printed in James Watson's *Choice Collection of Comic and Serious Scots Poems* (Edinburgh, 1706–11; private facsimile reprint, Glasgow, 1869) III. 1–32, which is overlooked, or perhaps simply not dared to reprint, in the various Anthologies "of Invective and Abuse", "Whips and Scorpions", etc. of modern times.

This appears to have been one of the elements of the older British folklore transmitted to the Negro slaves in America, during the Colonial period, and it is still very common among modern Negroes both in the United States and the British Caribbean islands, under the name of "The Dozens" (possibly from the Saxon word, 'doze,' to stun or overwhelm, as in 'bulldozer').

Some have held that it is actually a survival of African verbal contests, and, though this would leave the mystery of the *name* "The Dozens" unsolved, color is given to this contention by the record of the existence of similar customs among other non-white primitives, in the article, "The *Poele* (Gross Insult) among the Mono People, Western Solomon Island," by Gerald Camden Wheeler, in *Anthropophytéia* (1913) x. 310–14. The *poele* include, and in fact specialize in, the same sexual and scatological insults against the mother and other female relatives — modestly translated by Wheeler into Latin as: '*Cum mulieris tuæ stercore (de more) cois,*' and '*Cum matre tua (de more) cois*' — as are the common coin of the American Negro "dozens," with their endless 'mother-fuckers.' See further Dr. John Dollard's pioneering study of the "dozens" in *American Imago* (1939) I. 3–24, and Dr. Roger Abrahams' article in *Journal of American Folklore* (1962) vol. 75: p. 209–20, and especially his *Deep Down in the Jungle* (1964) with wholly unexpurgated texts.

I have noted, in the Introduction to Farmer & Henley's *Dictionary of Slang and Its Analogues* (rev. ed., New Hyde Park, 1966, p. xxix–xl, the very similar Russian ultimate-insult, "*Idy v kibini matri*" ('Go fuck your mother!' sometimes unconsciously translated into the anti-Russian, "*Why don't you go back where you came from?*" and compare the English folk-phrase of insult: "*Does your mother know you're out?*") Near-Eastern parallels are also cited in the same Introduction, from the Arabic stylist and rhetorician, Al-Jahiz (died A.D. 869), involving a cross-biting or topping of such insults, as in the interchange in which '*Abu-l-Harit Gummain asked of a certain great personage: "Can you tell me, I pray you, what this basket contains?"* — *"Your mother's cunt!"* (Vulva matris tuæ!) — *"Make me bite into it," he replied.'* (Compare the similar formula replies of superstitious or apotropaic character, such as "*Gesundheit!*" or "*Santé!*" when another person sneezes; "*Bread & butter!*" (with the reply, "*Slice it and spread it!* or similar) when two people walking together are temporarily separated by a tree or other obstacle; and the riddling question, "*What goes up a chimney?*" to which the 'correct' reply, "*Smoke!*" must be given when two people accidently pronounce the same word at the same time, so that "their wishes should come true," wishing then over linked baby-fingers.)

Even more similar to the modern Negro insults of the "dozens" are the "Turco-Mongolian Curses and Obscenities," recorded by John R. Krueger in *Journal of American Folklore* (1964) vol. 77: p.78–9, in which the writer interestingly compares the Mongolian '*ecegé alsan*' ('Father-killer!') and the 'corresponding curse involving the *mater familias,*' with the American supreme opprobrium, "Mother-fucker!" 'Among the Turks . . . as the insult *par excellence,* one may . . . make the grand curse of "I urinate on your father's head and have intercourse with your mother!" ' With this perfectly direct Oedipal statement — diverted simply upon the *other* person's parents — may be compared the Roman superstition, translated by Ben Jonson, as mentioned elsewhere, that a man who pisses upon his father's grave goes mad.

An Englishman punting on the Thames loses his pole. He calls to a man in a boat with two ladies, "I say, may I borrow one of your oars?" "Gorn with you, you barstard! These ayn't 'ores! One of 'em's me muvver, an' the other me bloody sister!" (1:156. Text version from Minnesota, 1946.) This joke is of course very well known, and so is a cruder form, which does not even pretend to involve any humorous 'misunderstanding.' *A young gentleman boating on Sunday with two young ladies finds their way barred at a narrow lock in the river by a great dirty barge. "I say, my good man," he calls imperiously to the bargee, "can you let us pass?" "Can't do it, guv'nor," the bargee responds lazily; "got to get this load o' shrimps to Wigan before dark." "Dammitall! Let us pass, I say!" the young gentleman shouts, losing his temper. "Oh, so it's cursin', is it?" replies the bargee. "Well, I won't sye nuffin* narsty, *seein' as you've got a load o' cunt aboard. All I'll sye is 'Bloody fuckin' arseholes to* you!' " (Chelmsford, Essex, 1954.)

What is specifically to be observed in these is the clear survival — including the *mise en scène* of river-boats — of the older 'water wit' already mentioned. This is described in Boswell's *Life of Johnson,* under date 1780, as 'formerly a rude custom for those who were sailing upon the Thames, to accost each other as they passed, in the most abusive language they could invent, generally, however, with as much satirical humour as they were capable of producing. Addison gives a specimen of this ribaldry in Number 383 of the *Spectator,* when Sir Roger de Coverly and he are going to Spring-garden.' A far better example, as being less tittivated up for the polite ears of the period, will be found in *Tom Brown's Jester* (1755; ed. New York, *c.* 1860, p. 16) under the heading "Water Dialect: Being Tom Brown's humorous voyage up the River Thames, in company with an Indian," which opens without preamble:

> No sooner had my Indian and I took water at Black Friars, and got into the middle of the stream, but our two watermen began to attack a couple of fine ladies with a footman, as follows: How now, you two confederate brimstones [*whores*], where are you swimming with your fine top-knots? I'll warrant your poor cuckolds are hovering about Change, to hear what news from Flanders, whilst you, like a couple of hollow-belly'd whores, are sailing up to Vauxhall to cram one end with roasted fowls, and the other with raw sausages.

The ladies of course answer in kind, and a 'western boat, stowed with a mixture of both sexes' (compare *Westward for Smelts,* 1620, a satire attributed by Henrietta Bartlett to Taylor the Water-Poet) begins to attack Tom Brown's Indian companion as 'that king of the gipsies . . . why he looks as if he had painted his face with a child's surreverence [*feces*], to make his countenance shine. Out you nasty turd-coloured dog! born upon a dunghill without a head, that your mother was forced to supply the defect with a yellow pumpkin!' This custom of water wit, still recollected in the term 'Billingsgate,' is touched upon only very lightly a few years later in "A Letter from a French Gentleman," probably by Oliver Goldsmith, in *The New Boghouse Miscellany, or A Companion for the Close-stool* (1761) pp. 50, also 60, in two rather guarded passages on the 'water-language' and other affronts addressed to the French Gentleman by 'two young ladies extremely handsome,' etc. Boswell's introductory passage quoted above serves, in his *Life of Johnson* (indexed under "Thames, ribaldry," in modern editions), to introduce an unpublished recollection of Bennet Langton's, omitted from Rogers' *Boswelliana,* in which Dr. Johnson himself is shown engaged ponderously in this folk-sport.

> Mr. Samuel Johnson was one day upon the Thames when the fashion of people on the river trying who should give each the worst language prevailed. Johnson's figure was a good subject for an attack of this kind from a rude fellow. Johnson thought he would for once try to give a Broadside, which he did thus, "Sir, your wife *under pretence of keeping a Bawdy-house,* is a receiver of stolen goods." (Boswell's italics. The Langton MS. is quoted from C. B. Tinker's Introduction to the Oxford Standard edition of Boswell, 1933, p. xii.)

As can hardly be misunderstood, 'water wit' had and still has its principal use as a weapon of class-struggle, in which fellow Englishmen of the 'laborious classes' ('rude Fellow' means, of course, rustic and uncouth, not the more modern unmannerly) scathelessly let fly at the heads of their 'betters' under cover of folk-custom. Their targets, in turn, try to answer back in the more elegant armamentarium of their higher education, in the style of the sword-bearing, aristocratic Mohocks, also of the pre-Revolutionary 18th century, the lineal ancestors of our own juvenile delinquents (the French *'jeunesse pourrie,'* or 'rotted youth') of good family, out terrorizing the town. Actually, the quoted examples here are picked for their relative mildness. A few cruder examples of 'water wit,' as it has survived more modernly in the repartees attributed to cab-drivers — the Thames boatmen of later centuries — will be found in the opening section, "Dysphemism," of Chapter 14 in the Second Series.

4. LITERALISM

The principal actual folly of which the visiting Englishman is accused, in America, is literalism. This is the one sin out of which his misunderstanding of American customs must be made to rise, since he cannot really be lampooned as a foreigner of different tongue. At most he can be said to misunderstand and horribly mispronounce his native language: he cannot actually be presumed to be ignorant of it. For example: *An Englishman in America is called a "lucky dog" when he wins at cards. On being assured that this is not an insult, when his hostess wins he calls her a "lucky bitch."* (1:355.) — *An Englishman is told that skin condoms are better than rubber because they are thinner, and can be washed and used again. Later he complains, "They were all right, you know — thinner and all that — but I got quite a narsty note from the laundry."* (1:4.)

Americans abroad are always more fortunate in their gaucherie, as the jokes see it. *The American attending a banquet in London is surprised to notice that when the dowager hostess breaks wind, one of the male guests rises gallantly and says, "I beg your pardon!" The nicety of etiquette being explained to him, the next time the hostess breaks wind the American leaps up, restraining another Englishman who is about to rise. "It's all right," he says, "this one is on me."* (1:460.) This has completely changed accent since its 16th-century original, in which it is not the man who is a fool, but the woman who is made a fool of by the man. It is the final joke or mythical adventure in the *Merrie Conceited Jests of George Peele,* 1607 (reprinted in Charles Hindley's *Old Book Collector's Miscellany,* 1871, 1. ad fin.), "How George served a Gentlewoman," in which '*as she put out her arm to take the capon,* George *sitting by her, jerks me out a huge fart, which made all the company in a maze, one looking upon the other, yet they knew it came that way. Peace, quoth* George, *and jogs her on the elbow, I will say it is I. At which all the company fell into a huge laughter, she into a fretting fury . . .*' This is also the 'plot' of Mark Twain's *1601.* A similar de-pantsing of his audience by the 'fool' is achieved in the following: *An American is being shown through a hall full of ancestral portraits in an English castle. The guide explains that this was Lord Henry who fought the Armada, this was Lord Humphrey who escaped with Bonnie Prince Charlie in women's clothes, etc. "And this," says the guide, stopping before the largest portrait, "this is Sir Gyles, the founder of the family." "What did he do?" asks the American. "He was the founder of the family!" "Yes, but what did he do in the daytime?"* (Curran, 1938, p. 239.) Compare the now-famous recitation, called "How Fights Begin in Saloons," about two drunks in an English pub discussing a portrait of Gladstone over the bar, with the repeated question, "*Well, wot did 'E do?*" leading finally to blows. This was recorded in the 1930's, by Cyril Smith, as interlocutor: *Rudy Vallée's Surprises No. 2* (Victor-Bluebird B.10069).

The element of hating and defying the 'Britisher' as authority-figure comes very close to the surface in the materials in the preceding paragraph. In the following example the abdicated king becomes the mouthpiece of this defiance. *George VI, telephoning before the coronation:* "*I say, David, you know we can't find the crown anywhere. Do you suppose Wally might have wrapped it up in an old towel or something?*" *David:* "*I'll take a look around and call you back.*" *Later:* "*Sorry, George, can't find it anywhere. Do you suppose the Archbishop could have taken me seriously when I told him to shove it up his arse?*" (Baker, 1945, vol. II. Also collected, Calif. 1952, of the royal orb.) Even allowing for satirical intent, there is a far more subtle expression here of the American attitude toward the ex-king than in the equally authentic psycho-biography, *Lese Majesty* [sic]: *The Private Lives of the Duke & Duchess of Windsor,* by 'Norman Lockridge,' New York, 1952, principally alleging early homosexuality, and ending with an excruciating imaginary dialogue between the two. (See the review, captioned "An outrageous insult to our Royal Family," and giving the author's actual name, Samuel Roth, in the London *Sunday Pictorial,* Oct. 26, 1952, p. 1, col. 1.)

The Oedipal understructure of the defiance of authority merely because it is authority — i.e. *patria potestas* restraining one from sexual enjoyment of the mother or mother-figure — is neatly shown in the best known of all jokes on English literalism. *Englishman, at the coronation:* "*'Ere comes the Queen!*" *American:* "*Oh, fuck the Queen!*" "*Fuck 'er? Why you cawn't even approach 'er!*" (1:445, noted as 'A story that deservedly takes its place with the hoary antiquities,' apparently at least temp. Victoria Regina — a name inevitably spoonerized during the Broadway run of the play of the same name in the 1930's.) There are at least two modernizations: *An Englishman admires an American's overcoat and asks where he got it.* "*Browning Kings.*" "*I sye! And 'ere I've been fucking Queens for years and never got so much as a necktie!*" (N.Y. 1942.) More important than the Englishman's literalism, in the other modernization, is the American's pure 'Id' expression of what he really wants, in a way usually allowed only to fools and, in this case, Americans. *The airliner is about to crash. The American grabs the last parachute and starts buckling it on. Englishman:* "*I say, old chap, what about the ladies?*" *American:* "*Fuck the ladies!*" *Englishman:* "*Do you think we'll have time?*" (Curran,

1938, p. 193, in a section marked "Expurgated," with the key word given as '*kiss*.')

This appears to be a condensation of the "Queen's Coronation" story with a much longer tale, almost without punch-line, collected N.Y. 1939: *On a troopship coming back from Africa a young Victoria Cross hero is paying marked attention to a pretty young nurse, and everyone on board is talking about the slow progress of their affair. Bad weather. The lifeboats are being swept overboard. The V.C. man pokes his head up on the captain's bridge and says, "Are we in any danger, sir?" This happens three times. The third time the astonished captain says, "Danger? Lots of it. But why are you bothering me at a time like this? Are you afraid, Major?" "Not at all, Captain, but I was only thinking if the ship is going down I ought to profit by my last five minutes and fuck that nurse."* (Compare with the VC's heroism, the "*I'm scared stiff!*" joke, later under Adultery.) There is a brilliantly written short story, "When the Vestilinden Was Lost," on the same theme — more or less — with the last descendant of a noble family taking the last few minutes before the ship sinks to consummate his affair with the healthy young cabin-girl and then throw her into the departing lifeboat. This appears in the volume *Stories of Strange Women* by J. Y. F. Cooke (London: John Long, 1906) at p. 109. This story has been reprinted several times in America. 'Cooke' has been said to be a pseudonym of the late Norman Douglas, and a transvestist story in the same volume, "The Garments of a Girl," seems to lend color to the ascription of authorship, but Douglas specifically denied this some months before his death when asked by his latest bibliographer, Cecil Woolf.

One final story on the misunderstanding of sexual terms combines just about every possible element of the fool story: the female fool, the foreigner fool, and the English fool, with an obvious connection to the embarrassment situations rising from telling sexual lies to children. *A French maid asks her mistress what the word "fuck" means and is told that it means "to serve." At the next formal dinner the maid haughtily announces to the butler, "James, fuck the duck." Visiting Englishman: "How jolly! Do you mind if I stick my prick in the mashed potaytoes?"* (1:328) In spite of its utterly modern appearance this is a very old joke, and will be found in the second English jestbook published, *Tales, and Quicke Answeres* (about 1535) No. 95 — actually 96 — "*Of the wydowes daughter that was sent to the abbot with a couple of capons . . . And so he made her to be sette downe atte his owne table to eate some meate. Amonge other meates, the abbotte had than a grene goose with sorell sauce, whereof he dyd eate. So one that sat at the abbottes table, gave the rompe of the goose to the mayde to picke theron. She toke the rompe in her hande, and bycause she sawe the abbot and other wete their meate in the sorell sauce, she sayde. My lorde, I pray thee gyve me leve to wete myn arse in thy grene sauce."* Note that the girl's joke here is only verbal: she is mocking the goose's rump or 'Pope's nose' with which she has been fobbed off. The story of the French maid and visiting Englishman involves, instead, two fools proud in their folly. In another analogous modern form, collected in Brittany in 1881 (*Kryptádia,* II. 28), it is the trickster who teaches the visiting stranger to use obscene words unknowingly.

VII. RIDDLES WRONGLY RETOLD

The marred anecdote, or riddle wrongly retold, is the fool tale *par excellence.* Almost all of those collected in the present research have been told as of silly-ass Englishmen, or on theatrical backgrounds. A short selection will be found in Charles Bombaugh's *Facts and Fancies for the Curious* (1905) and in Grenville Kleiser's *Humorous Hits* (1908), as noted in *The Humor of Humor* (1952) p. 264, by Evan Esar [Levine], who discusses only the non-erotic types. Here is the complete standard framework of the erotic anecdote marred, which almost always includes *An Englishman about to return home from America who asks for a typical American joke he can repeat in England. He is given a riddle: "A girl is standing on a street corner and three men go by, one on a horse, one on a bicycle, and one on foot. One of the men knows the girl. Which one?" "I give up," says the Englishman; "which one?" "The horse-manure!" "Oh, ripping!" He goes back to England and tries it out: "A young lady is standing at an intersection — this is in America, you know — and three gentlemen pass by: an equestrian, a pedestrian, and a velocipedist. One of them is acquainted with the young lady. Now which one?" "We give up, Reggie. Which?" "Well, I don't know* how *that American chap did it, but the answer is horse-shit!"* (N.Y. 1942.)

Occasionally the misremembered joke or riddle is a little poem (with which compare the courtroom *cante fable* earlier). *An Englishman is taught the following parody:*

> "Mary had a little skirt
> 'Twas split just right in half,
> And everywhere that Mary went,
> She showed her little calf."

He goes back to England and repeats it as follows, "to amuse the ladies": "Mary had a little skirt, 'Twas split, er . . . don'tcherknow, just in front, And everywhere that Mary went, She showed her little — My Gawd, that can't be right!" (1:80.) In a variant, collected Minneapolis, 1946, the poem is given in two verses, without any Englishman, the second verse being:

> "Mary had another dress,
> The skirt was split in front —
> She never wore that one."

Of marred theatrical anecdotes, types both with and without poems have been collected. *The prompter is reading out the stage directions at rehearsal: "Enter the Duchess with a candle, right upper entrance." "No, no, no!" the director shouts, as all the ballet-girls begin to laugh. The prompter tries again: "Enter the Duchess with a candle, left upper entrance."* (N.Y. 1940.) *— An old actor is given his last chance in a walk-on part with only one line: "My God, Duchess, what have you done?" Overjoyed, he gets stinking drunk, sleeps all night in the gutter, and arrives at curtain time with a terrible cold, to deliver his line: "My God, Duchess (sniff, sniff), what have you done!"* (N.Y. 1940.) *— The star is sick, and the understudy is having difficulty memorizing the lines:*

> "Ah, she sleeps and dreams of peace,
> Her soul is full of hope.
> So I shall quickly snatch a kiss,
> And fly off in the air."

At the performance he comes out onstage, becomes confused at the sight of the beautiful heroine lying on the grass in her white gown, and recites:

> *"Ah, she sleeps and dreams of a piece,*
> *Her hole is full of soap.*
> *So I shall quickly kiss her snatch,*
> *And shoot off in the air."*

(Curran, 1938, p. 197, rationalizing the last line of the poem by having the actor dressed in aviator costume. Compare: *The Soldier's Farewell: He kissed her goodbye, and went off in his uniform (or) and shot across the lawn.* — N.Y. 1941.)

1. SPOONERISMS AND RIDDLES

The theatrical joke, preceding, plays entirely on a special form of 'marred' repetition called the spoonerism or *contrepéterie*. The form is quite old, and has been taken farthest in the French language. The English name, spoonerism, is taken from that of a quite modern English clergyman and educator, William Archibald Spooner, dean and warden of New College, Oxford, who died in 1930, and on whom a whole slew of such lapses — in public speeches — has been fathered, some perhaps authentically, such as *"kinkering congs"* for *"conquering kings"* (in announcing the name of a hymn), *"blushing crow"* for *"crushing blow,"* and the unforgettable, *"I have in my bosom a half-warmed fish,"* allegedly in a speech of welcome to Queen Victoria. The anal element — of looking at the *other side,* or back-side of everything — is very prominent in spoonerisms, and generally in the people who like working out their permutations, or who actually do 'accidentally' fall into them in a habitual way. This is very common when one is tired (as with other erroneous right-&-left gestures, opening things instead of closing them, etc.), and I have myself heard a very reserved young woman say in irritation, walking home in the snow at the end of a long evening, *"Oh, shit quivering!"* apparently accidentally. (N.Y. 1948.) Even so, the anal or scatological element gives the main pith to her reproach.

The spoonerism is essentially the ancient rhetorical form of *metathesis* (transposition) or *chiasmus* (the crossing), and many more forms are possible than those simply permutating the initial sounds, as is usual in English. Even in English, it is understood that other forms are possible, as in the whole sets of changes rung, in jokes, on the mispronounced phrases, "*Horn-rimmed spectacles,*" "*As the crow flies,*" and especially the mock book-title, *Memoirs of a Milkmaid, or Forty Years of Scum-Creaming,* I mean *Scream Coming,* I mean *Cream-Skimming . . .*! As early as the 17th century in England, the spoonerism had been adapted to the uses of the fool joke or foolish character. F. P. Wilson in *Huntington Library Quarterly,* 1939, II. 133, notes an example from Henry Peacham's *Compleat Gentleman,* 1634 (ed. 1906, p. 231): 'A melancholy Gentleman sitting one day at a table, where I was, started up upon the sudden, and meaning to say, *I must goe buy a dagger,* by transposition of the letters, said: "Sir, *I must goe dye a beggar.*" Erotic examples comprise a whole category of sexual humor, and are now usually delivered as riddles or 'differences': "*What's the difference between a sharpshooter and a constipated owl? — The sharpshooter shoots and shoots and never hits . . .*" (The erotic or scatological balancing version is usually left for the listener to work out.) In the theatrical poem just given, the second line is adapted from a well-known spooneristic 'difference' dating from at least the 1920's.

The form is international, being known in Germany as '*Schüttelreime*' (a few erotic examples in the collection of *Mikosch-Anekdoten,* Pressburg, 1892, p. 42), and in French as '*contrepéteries,*' of which Rabelais' two examples in *Pantagruel* (1533) Bk. II. chap. 16 and 21, standardized the simple transpositional type: "*A Beaumont le Vicomte — A beau con le vit monte*" "*Femme folle à la messe. — Femme molle à la fesse.*" The art has been taken so far as to begin drawing some of its humor not only from the sexuality of the images, but from the marvellous improbability of the transpositions made. I can think of only one English example of this complexity: a parody (Los Angeles, 1947) of the famous American vaudeville patter-song of the early 20th century, "Mr. Gallagher and Mr. Sheen," in which Mr. Gallagher is complaining to Mr. Sheen about the excessive shortness of the girls' skirts (a brief fad in the 1920's, which returned and reached its climax — if that's the word I'm looking for — with the mini-skirts of 1967: "*one inch below the water-line*"). Gallagher explains that it takes a man's mind off what he is doing, in this case 'reading Pushkin's verse,' when

> "The sight of her behind
> Forces Pushkin from your mind — "
> "Forces Pushkin, Mr. Gallagher?"
> "Pushes foreskin, Mr. Sheen!"

In France, complexity of this kind — and worse! — is now *de rigueur.* Many examples in the main French collection, *La Redoute des Contrepéteries* (1934, and enlarged and illustrated in later editions), by the bibliographer of erotic literature, Louis Perceau [Guitteau], whose very rare first book, *Le Trésor des Equivoques* ('Gélatopolis,' 1909), was also on the same subject, would really be quite impossible to solve — only the non-erotic halves being given — were it not for the disposition of the materials into chapters according to the type of inversion or controversion, which usually gives the necessary hint. (See further, Luc Étienne [Perin], *L'Art du Contrepet,* Paris, 1957, and the same author's *L'Art de la Charade à tiroirs,* 1965, both remarkable performances, as also *L'Album de la Comtesse,* 1967.)

The riddle element is the heart of the marred anecdote, and without it the spoonerism or *contrepéterie* remains merely a verbal trick. In *Anecdota Americana* (1927) 1:423, one story of a riddle wrongly retold is given as of a Jewish anti-hero, and not the Englishman usual in this situation in America. *A son comes home from college and tells his father a riddle: "What is it that's hard, and long, and leaks?" His father begins to berate him. "Don't get excited, Pop. It's a fountain pen." The father repeats the riddle the next night in company. The women present raise their hands in horror. "Don't get excited, ladies. It ain't a prick. It's a fountain pen."* Stories of this type are sometimes outfitted with 'toppers' in which: *The fool revenges himself on his audience by repeating the same riddle, after its innocent solution has been given. When he is told, "Yes, we know, it's a fountain pen;" he says, "No, this time it's what you thought it was the first time!"* (Paris, 1965.) This is the 'persistent-fool' type of the "Mr. Perkins-Smith of the London *Times*" version of the Fortunate Fart, which has been traced to the *Arabian Nights,* as will be seen. (Compare the Egyptian "Goha the Fool," the Tunisian Bahloul in *The Perfumed Garden,* and Karaghuez, the Near-Eastern puppet figure, of which the best study is Prof. Sabri Esat Sivayusgil's *Karagöz: Son histoire, ses personnages, son esprit mystique et satirique* [Istanbul, 1961], an illustrated work which, however, much plays down the purposeful obscene posing of the ithyphallic puppet in these popular folk-*guignols* — now a thing of the past — as in the probably derivative Italian *commedia dell' arte,* shown in Jacques Callot's remarkable series of engravings, *Balli di Sfessania,* 1622. See also Wesselski's edition of *Der Hodscha Nasr'eddin,* Weimar, 1911, on this and other Levantine 'fools.')

In a similar Jewish story, *The uneducated father has been told not to say a single word while the family is entertaining the elegant parents of his daughter's fiancé. Tea is served and he is accidentally not given a spoon. He sits fuming silently for fifteen minutes, until the mother-in-law-to-be suddenly notices. "Why, you're not drinking your tea,"* she says. *"So what am I supposed to stir it with,"* he bursts out, *"my* putz?" (N.Y. 1953.) Here the riddle element is lacking, and the humor is left to turn strictly on the unexpected candor of the fool or 'sacred lunatic.' Compare the other in 8.vi.3, p. 603 below.

Erotic riddles which can be politely or innocently resolved are at least as old as the Renaissance, and will be found used as the framework of certain of the imitators of Boccaccio among the *novellieri,* particularly in Straparola's *Most Delectable Nights* (1550; unexpurgated English translation, Paris, 1906). It is not possible to pursue this interesting subject at greater length here. Mention should, however, be made of the extremely rare set of engravings by the Dutch artist Jan van Halbeeck, *Énigmes joyeuses pour les bons esprits* (*c.* 1615) of which an example, possibly unique, was offered by J. L. Beijers of Utrecht, Holland, in 1966, Catalogue 130: no. 69. Each engraving is accompanied by a sonnet — lacking in the Beijers copy — which is 'extremely scabrous, filled with double-meanings, posing an enigma to which the illustration furnishes a perfectly innocent solution.' The same sonnet texts appear in the equally rare *Incogniti scriptoris nova poemata* (1618), of which only two copies are known to exist, both in the Royal Library of The Hague.

It is unfortunate that the great comparative study of *English Riddles from Oral Tradition* (Berkeley, Calif. 1951) by Professor Archer Taylor, as also Professor Taylor's various works on the proverb, have been expurgated of almost all discernible sexual materials — which are among their most striking and important components — before publication. Numerous scholars have protested to Professor Taylor against his expurgation of his own (and their!) materials in this way, despite their admiration for his enormous and far-reaching erudition in the fields of folklore and linguistics, an erudition unparalleled in America since the days of Child and Kittredge. His *English Riddles* are even outfitted with a reverse-expurgated concluding section, Nos. 1739–49, "Erotic Scenes," p. 687–8, in which the innocuous answers to the erotic riddles, but not the riddles themselves, are given! A certain amount of sexual material is, however, available elsewhere in the riddle text, for

instance a group on the penis, No. 1572*a–c,* subject-indexed only under
the 'cover'-solutions of *radish* and *carrot.* Professor Taylor observes, p.
637–8, concerning this group, that 'riddlers either have failed to per-
ceive the import of the comparison or have deliberately obscured it,'
but how anyone could seriously attempt to obscure "*Stiff standing on
the bed, First it's white, an' then it's red; There's not a lady in the land,
That would not take it in her hand,*" passes the understanding.

2. THE FORTUNATE FART

Far & away the most interesting erotic story of the riddle type has
a long history, which I will attempt to indicate, and numerous progeny, some of them quite pure, such as the Bateman cartoon of the boy
who was sent to jail for breathing heavily on the glass of one of the
cases in the British Museum, and who comes back, on being let out
years later, an old man broken of body but not of spirit, to breathe
his last on the very same case in the British Museum! (Type 1271.)
Note that this is the transitional story to that, earlier, of the man in
the insane asylum, who, driven too far by the examining psychiatrist's
persistent questioning, admits that he only wants the girl to "*pull off
her bloomers and take out the elastic and make me a slingshot and
break all the windows in this goddam dump!*" (The present chapter,
2.v.3.) — *A London hostess invites the drama critic of* The Times *to a
party, but he cannot go and an obscure assistant named Perkins (or
Smith) is sent instead. They are playing riddles, and when it comes
Perkins' turn he asks, "What is it that's round, and hot, with hair on
both sides, and it gets wet when you stick your finger in?" Horrified,
the others give up. "It's a cunt," Perkins says simply. "James," says the
hostess icily, "give this man his hat and coat." Perkins loses his job, is
black-balled, and goes to India in disgrace. Years later he returns covered with medals, as a major-general, and his welcoming banquet is by
some accident tendered by the same hostess. "Major-General Perkins,"
she simpers, "is there anything you'd specially like to do?" "Yes," he
says, "I'd like to play riddles. What is it that's round, and hot, with hair
on both sides, and it gets wet when you stick your finger in?" Everyone
waits breathlessly for what they expect this time will be the right answer (the eye). "We give up," says the hostess; "what is it?" "James,"
he says, "get my hat and coat. It's still a cunt!"* (1:464, not noting the
correct answer.)

I am indebted to Dr. Alan Barnert for the observation that the ancestor of this story — that is to say of the motif of the public disgrace and its repetition on returning years later — is the *Arabian Nights* story (about 1450) "How Abu Hasan Brake Wind," which is one of the only two stories in Burton's *Nights* (Night 410 — the other being the "Tale of the Husband and the Parrot" in vol. 1) which Burton did not plagiarize from John Payne's earlier and better translation. Abu Hasan farts at his wedding feast, just as he is about to enter the bride's chamber, whereupon "each guest turned to his neighbour and talked aloud and made as though he had heard nothing." Nevertheless Abu Hasan realizes he is disgraced, leaves the house on the logical pretense of "answering a call of nature," and goes to India. (Compare Perkins.) Years later he returns, expecting that his lapse will have been long since forgotten, but overhears on the outskirts of town a woman telling her daughter she was born "on the night when Abu Hasan farted!"

This motif also occurs in Burton's Supplemental Night 390, vol. XIV, a 'male-motherhood' story in which the Kazi is led to believe that he has given birth to a baby rectally, leaves in disgrace, and returns many years later expecting it to be forgotten, only to find that the street urchins reckon time from the "year when our Kazi was brought to bed." (*Histoires Arabes,* p. 256–8. See the excellent motif-index of the *Arabian Nights,* Nikita Elisséeff's *Thèmes et Motifs des "Mille et Une Nuits,"* Beyrouth: Institut Français de Damas, 1949, which unfortunately suffers from a lack of attention to what the compiler euphemistically calls, p. 81, *'la trivialité de certains contes.'* J2321.2.)

The motif of the stubborn fool has been common at least since the time of Poggio — also 1450 — who gives a story, No. 59, of the stubborn wife who is drowned by her husband for calling him lousy, and who goes under for the last time, unable to speak but making the gesture of pinching lice with her fingernails. (Compare *Joe Miller's Jests,* 1739, No. 6, of the man who told his 'termagant Wife . . . if she spoke one more *crooked* Word he'd beat her Brains out: Why then *Ram's Horns,* you Rogue, said she, if I die for't.') Poggio's related No. 60, of the man who sought his stubborn wife *up*stream when she drowned, was translated into English about 1535 in *Tales, and Quicke Answeres,* No. 55. (This is largely a translation of Poggio — 43 out of 114 stories being taken over directly.) *Tales, and Quicke Answeres* has the wife falling off a bridge, but the juxtaposition of the stories in Poggio makes it much more likely that she was pushed.

The transitional story between Abu Hasan's breaking wind and Perkins' "It's still a cunt!" will be found in *Tom Brown's Jester* (1755, ed. 1860? p. 40), and is so remarkable an example of the joke *in statu nascendi* — before the modern punch-line has been added — that it is given here complete:

A lawyer's clerk was in love with an extreme pretty girl, courted her and agreed to marry her. The wedding entertainment was provided, and among others, the clerk's master was invited. In the heat of dancing, a sigh, caused by indigestion or windy food, escaped the bride the contrary way, and loud enough to be heard by all the company, who burst into laughter: She blushed, and the bridegroom was so confounded and enraged, that he instantly broke off the match, to which no remonstrance nor intreaties could reconcile him; he imagined his acquaintance would jeer him for ever upon this accident, and he left the house in a pet [!] Great was now the disorder of the guests! The clerk's master, who was one of them, and though a man in years, had eyed the girl with great attention, and was smitten with her beauty, not only condemned his clerk's excessive delicacy, but proposed to repair the injury he had done the girl, and offered her marriage on the spot. Piqued at her lover's desertion, and pressed by her friends, who foresaw the advantages of such a match, she consented, and they were married immediately. After marriage, she behaved to him with so much modesty and discretion, that dying soon after, he left her mistress of a very opulent fortune. Being now a widow, handsome, young and rich, she had many offers of marriage, but accepted only the Marshal de L'Hospital's, Governor of Paris! who also dying soon after, left her once more a widow, though with greater additions of honour than of fortune. Her person and character were now so amiable, that Casimir, King of Poland, residing in France, after his abdication of the throne [1668], fell in love with her and married her. So great a fortune perhaps never took its rise from so burlesque an incident.

Other transitional forms of this story are discussed in *The Horn Book*, p. 465-6, including the retelling in John Aubrey's *Brief Lives*, in the late 17th century, with no other change from the original 'than to transform Abu Hassan into a courtier of Queen Elizabeth's, Edward de Vere, Earl of Oxford, who spends seven years in proud disgrace in Italy after a gastric lapse at court. In this form, which Aubrey tells as historical fact, the tale is now first fitted out as a joke, with a sardonic punch-line or verbal climax put into the mouth of the Queen: "My lord, I had forgot the Fart." Mark Twain's famous *1601, or Tudor Conversation* turns on an identical scene in the presence of Queen Elizabeth, as recounted by a mythical Aubrey or Pepys.' The form given in *Tom Brown's Jester,* as of an 'extreme pretty girl,' is retold by the late 18th-century erotic poet, Vincent Lombard de Langres, in *Berthe, ou le Pet mémorable* (1807, with other *contes-en-vers*), the subtitle referring to the tale — possibly jocularly — as an 'anecdote of the ninth century,' suggesting a fabliau origin, which I have not been able to trace. Ex-King Casimir of Poland is not mentioned.

It is perfectly clear that it is the incident of the embarrassment that 'makes' the story for both the *Arabian Nights'* Abu Hassan and for Tom Brown's 'extreme pretty girl.' The specific riddle that is Perkins-Smith's downfall is not the point at all. There is also a minor connection between the marriage feast in the two earlier forms, and the London dinner-party in the modern joke. For the telling of erotic riddles is a standard *rite de passage,* still well-known at weddings, and also (in Hispanic countries) at wakes over the coffin of a dead person. The erotic riddles at wakes must also once have been the case in other parts of Europe. *The Limerick,* Note 536, cites the Scottish poet, Thomas Hamilton, Earl of Haddington's *Select Poems on Several Occasions* (about 1730), "The Dying Toast," on 'two virtuous virgins' arguing at the death-bed of a third (the 'toast' referred to) over whether the parson or the curate has the longer penis. Even more relevantly here might be mentioned the Hispanic-American joking song, "*El Bobo en el Velorio*" (The Fool at the Funeral), formerly recorded for the phonograph on the Victor 78-rpm label, in which the fool pesters the guests at the wake by propounding double-entendre riddles on the style of Perkins-Smith's eye-riddle, *e.g.:* "*Lo muto blando, lo tengo duro — divina me!*" (I put it in soft, I took it out hard — riddle me that!) The answer being: biscuits. With this may be compared the white American children's riddle — anatomically reversed and therefore somewhat more credible — "*It goes in hard and comes out soft. What is it?*" (Chewing-gum: also "goes in hard and dry, and comes out soft and wet.") See Jiménez' *Picardía Mexicana,* p. 47–63.

As with the telling of bawdy jokes, and other 'licentious' acts, at the various Feast of Fools celebrations, at the winter solstice and vernal equinox — in the northern countries, such as Scandinavia, also on midsummer night — as discussed earlier in the present chapter, 2.VI.1, in connection with the joke on "blowing the *shofar*," the ritual Jewish ram's-horn; it is clear that the formal telling of erotic riddles as a *rite de passage,* at wakes and the like, can only be for the purpose of bringing into play the ritual power of verbal obscenity, replacing physical sexual exhibition or erotic acts, which may be presumed to have preceded mere verbal displays historically. It is this that I have referred to in the article "The Bawdy Song" (in *The Horn Book,* 1964, p. 426), noting: 'In the days when priests ordained ritual public coitus at dawn, at the winter solstice, under the mistletoe-laden boughs of sacred trees, to bring back the dying sun from fearfully remembered glacial night; in those days there was no need of bawdy song, yet that was perhaps its heyday. The remnant that we have of it is strange and misshapen, more often monstrous and repellent — as the world it mirrors becomes monstrous and repellent — than simple and unashamed as it once was, in the days of the *Song of Songs*.' This same magical sexual power is that which is invoked at wakes, evidently for the purpose of driving away lurking evil spirits (*i.e.* the dead themselves, who *must not* be allowed to return, as in W. W. Jacobs' "The Monkey's Paw"). There is also perhaps a rationalized purpose, of accentuating the sexual theme as the 'cure' or contrary of death: "*Thus have we lost them, and thus we must replace them.*" Eros against Thanatos. Sexual love — and therefore life — even in the midst of death: an almost-conscious folk-reversal of the *Book of Common Prayer*'s solemn invocation over the grave, but now reading: "*In the midst of Death we are in Life!*" In the world of prefabricated sentiments and emotions, that will make a great lapel-button motto after the Atom Bomb.

One final observation as to Fool jokes should be made. This ancient Levantine form, which is one of the most popular among the older tales, and will be found to include the largest group of motifs (J and K) appearing in jokes, is intended to serve two purposes. First, it exhorts the child to grow up, to learn — especially about sex and the wisdom of life — and to be a fool no more. But simultaneously it identifies with the protracted childhood we all would love to live, and even shows it as somehow sacrosanct and above danger. I have already noted, in the Introduction, section III, the anti-rational aspirations in which anything is forgiven if only one acts crazy enough: *Goha, Hamlet, Schweik,* and now the 'moron' and 'bop' jokes. For it is essential to realize that, by and large, *the Fool never comes to any harm: he is saved by his folly.* In fact, he is himself the Trickster, wiser than his persecutors. And only the heroic trickster or fool characters ever appear in more than one joke: Pat & Mike, Speedy Pedro (the French colonial Foutindouha), and all the small-brained supermen of the Paul Bunyan type. All other actors in jokes *are destroyed by the punch-line,* and no further existence for them can be imagined. Only the Trickster or Fool survives — God's fool, he who has been 'touched' — saved precisely by his folly-that-is-wisdom, and that is the wishful dream of every child.

3

ANIMALS

SURELY as anthropomorphic as the milder sex gags of the comic postcards are the animal jokes in oral tradition, in which, by the same rule of thumb as that under which the comic cards are manufactured — 'If it's too dirty to do it with children [or Negroes, or little old grandpas], do it with animals' — the animals are shown doing everything that human beings do not dare to do. No one needs to be told that Aesop's fables are not really about wolves and lambs. "*Quid rides?*" asks Horace. "*Mutato nomine, de te fabula narratur.*" (Why do you laugh? Change the names, and the tale is told of you. — *Satires,* I.i.69.) And compare with this the story of David and Uriah's wife, represented to King David by the prophet Nathan, also as a parable concerning 'one little ewe lamb' (2 *Samuel,* xii. 1-9), but here the repressed intention finally bursts through at end of the story — as never in the similar Aesopic fictions of lambs and wolves — with the prophet Nathan's bold *de te fabula narratur:* "Thou art the man!" That is all that is lacking in the animal tales.

As with murder-mystery detectives and fictional spies, what makes any specific animal protagonist popular is the ease with which the human audience can identify with it. Dogs and cats are conspicuously absent from most erotic animal jokes, as it appears to be much too difficult to identify with their sexual characters. The tomcat would be an exception to this, but in the patriarchal folk-mind all cats are she's, and, as such, feared and disliked, and traditionally connected with witchcraft. (Most recently in the *vagina dentata* horror-story, by W. W. Jacobs I believe, in which a man who has wantonly killed one of a mother-cat's kittens while visiting a tower filled with torture instruments, *is killed by the mother-cat,* who leaps at and frightens the person holding the rope when the murderer of her kitten gets into the "Iron Maiden" — the heavy toothed cover being held up by that rope.)

Dogs, on the other hand, are so openly sold to human owners on a slave basis, being dragged out to defecate on city streets with a rope around their necks, and made available for any amount of ruthless sadistic whipping (with heavy braided leather and metal leashes) and other mistreatment on the part of sexually perverted owners, that it is practically impossible to identify with them except on a masochistic basis. ("It's a dog's life," being "put in the dog-house" [*i.e.* sexually starved], etc.) Even their cute urinary activities — which are actually the dogs' main method of sexual approach and advertisement, though this factor is usually toned down — are so rigorously controlled that it is difficult to identify with this animal as really male. Compare, however, the exceptional "Shoot Blue!" story, at the end of the section on "Rape by Animals," in the chapter on Homosexuality, 10.v.5, in Series Two, all of which section is of course relevant here.

Shaggy dog and talking horse stories, as already noted at the opening of the Introduction, are an ancient form, appearing at least as early as *Joe Miller's Jests* (1739) No. 79, an ensorcellment tale copied from Apuleius' *Golden Ass* in the 2nd century A.D., in both of which the talking by the animal is rationalized as the result of necromancy and conjuration. Such explanations are dropped by modern shaggy dog stories, which take refuge in total 'nonsense' instead. The same is true even in parrot stories, where the parrot's speech (always to tattle on the human owners) is made a rational activity by the bird, and not a matter of rote, as though the parrot too contained an ensorcelled human being in its skin. Such stories have best been handled by Dr. Martha Wolfenstein, in the chapter, "Riddles and the Legend of the Moron," in her work on *Children's Humor* (1954) p. 151–6, observing that 'The formula of this type of joke is that something very far-fetched happens and that someone grossly underreacts to it,' and, even more centrally, that 'The animals who behave like human beings in these jokes may be interpreted in the reverse sense as representing human beings who behave like animals. Thus we are brought back to the initial occasion of the child's amazement, the sexual behavior of adults. . . . We are shown that an amazing event can be taken entirely casually, and besides we realize it never happened.' Most such stories have also almost no direct sexual component, and are in any case so completely anthropomorphised that they are evidently not really animal stories at all, and are not included here.

It has been possible to examine an extensive series of jokes and limericks recited, or possibly composed, by a well-known West Coast literary critic during the 1940's, at a limerick club, and it is interesting to note that although all of these without exception are on the sexual lives and misadventures of little anthropomorphic animals, none include dogs or cats. The Piddling Pup, Squirting Skunk (*i.e.* cat), and Satisfied Persian Cat recitations are admitted exceptions to what has been said above, but it is fairly definite that the ballad-reciting and joke-telling groups are completely different sets of individuals, apparently of far different tastes. Omitting all animal jokes on scatological themes, which will be found in the final chapter, in Series Two, only two dog or cat examples have been collected, both notably weak. *Pampered little Peppermint, a Pekinese, escapes from her kennel one night and returns in the morning bedraggled, scratched, and with her pink ribbon in shreds. "Poor little Peppermint, where have you been?" asks her mistress. "Peppermint, hell. From now on just call me Little Whorehound."* (D.C. 1944.) — *Two old maids live with a tabby cat. One wins a free trip to Paris. Her second morning there she cables back: "Dear Aggie: Wonderful town. Let out the cat."* (N.Y. 1950.) To which might be added the perfect anthropomorphism of, *Male cat: "Nee-e-ouw?" Female cat: "Not nee-e-ouw."* (D.C. 1944.) In a similar sexual decoding of animal cries, *A mountaineer is told he has consumption and that he must rise early, run up the mountainside, clap his hands, and yodel at the top of his voice. Another mountaineer shoots him, explaining, "He got too damned cocky for his pants! Every morning he ran up the mountainside, flapping his arms like a rooster, and crowing: 'I diddled the old lady too! I diddled the old lady too!' Couldn't have that sort of thing going on with my wife!"* (Idaho, 1946. Compare Motif J1811.4: rooster's crow interpreted.)

The identification with rabbits and monkeys is, by contrast, extremely strong. In the case of rabbits the identification is with the animal's well-known brevity of intercourse — jokes on its "multiplying rapidly" are strictly Easter egg stuff for the kiddies. *Male rabbit, to female: "That won't take long, did it?"* (N.Y. 1945. Also, "It won't hurt, did it?") — *A male and female rabbit are hiding in a thicket from a pack of wolves. "Shall we make a run for it, or outnumber them?"* (Calif. 1941.) A riddle: *"How long is the hair [hare] on a rabbit?" "This long: (snaps fingers)."* (Calif. 1942.) It is not to be thought that the tellers take pride in the minute-man status they feel they share with the rabbit. The most commonly collected rabbit joke — encountered six times by one collector, and four times by another — gruesomely punishes the poor rabbit for his rapid and egoistic habits in intercourse: *A little rabbit whose method with his girl friends is "Wham bam, thank you, Mam," accidentally attempts to mount a concrete rabbit in a graveyard. "Wham bam, God damn!"* (Calif. 1942.) The dialogue line, but not the situation, is given in William M. Camp's *Retreat, Hell!* (1943) p. 524, and in Thomas Heggen & Joshua Logan's popular war play, *Mr. Roberts.* Homosexual variant: *Two male rabbits each take a line of females one evening, calling out the wham-bam tag-line to each other as they go. Suddenly, at the end of the line, "God damn! Is that you, Sam?"* (Fla. 1949.) The rabbit's castratory misadventure is somewhat modified — that is to say, made only a threat rather than an actuality — in a highly anthropomorphic (child-*vs.*-adult) story of a squirrel, a practically identical animal to city dwellers. *A male squirrel is running frantically around the base of a tree while a female squirrel on a high branch flirts her tail at him. Bystander: "Why don't you go up and get her, sonny?" Squirrel (in a tiny voice): "Listen, mister, did you ever try to climb a tree with a hard on?"* (N.Y. 1951.)

I. MONKEYS AND ELEPHANTS

The near-humanity of the monkey is too well understood to need discussion here. Its use to represent the human vices in certain philosophical contexts in Renaissance and archaizing modern art (Titian's parody of the Laocoön, for instance, and the work of Beardsley and Bayros) is beautifully documented and illustrated in a careful study, *Apes and Ape Lore in the Middle Ages and the Renaissance,* by H. W. Janson (London, 1952). In jokes the monkey appears as both clever and yet pathetic, particularly when paired off with a much larger female mammal or mama, as in the midget and fat-woman jokes. The special intelligence of the monkey is presumed to reside (as with the equally 'sub-human' lunatic) in the difficulty of dissuading it from its traditional eroticism. The most famous monkey joke, and an old familiar burlesque routine: *A young man takes his girl to the zoo to see the monkeys, but goes inside first to make sure they are not "misbehav-*

ing." He finds half the tribe in intercourse and the other half [i.e. the human half?] *masturbating as they watch. "Do you suppose they'd stop if I gave them peanuts?" he asks the keeper. Keeper: "Would you?"* (2:406.) The sexual exploitation of monkeys in zoos – the young man here only pretending to refuse what everyone else demands to see (with a notable relaxation of the usual taboos about body odors) – has nowhere in the modern world been taken further than in Col. William T. Hornaday's Bronx Zoo, with its well-publicized natural habitat 'open' enclosures for lions, etc. Whatever the lions may get, the monkey-house in the Bronx Zoo is today a darkened auditorium with a theatre-pitched floor, through which a mad crush of Sunday spectators is kept circulating by a special staff of assistants, while the monkeys perform their proto-hippie 'group grope' under spotlights and behind glass – the well-known natural habitat of monkeys.

The monkey itself, owing to its hairiness, lasciviousness, and perhaps other 'cute' traits, is a common symbolic equivalent of the female sexual parts, and, like the cat ('*pussy*': compare the French *chat*), a slang synonym for the vulva. This fact lends much greater depth to the jokes on the clever monkey (or Pekinese, Chihuahua, or other toy dog) as the wife's pet. *A man is complaining to a friend about his wife's monkey, which she insists on taking to bed with them. "But what about the smell?" says the friend. "It'll just have to get used to it, the way I did."* (N.Y. 1942.) Really only the occasion for the standard anti-woman slur on the vaginal odor, as will be seen later in the chapter on Women. *A man decides to get rid of his wife's pet monkey by tricking it into cutting its throat. He gives the monkey a lathering brush, soap, and a straight razor, and goes through the motions of lathering up, while the monkey apes his every gesture. The man then makes a terrific pretended slash across his own throat with his razor. The monkey thumbs his nose (or makes the fa'n'gul gesture with the razor).* (N.Y. 1953. Des Périers, 1558, No. 19. Motif J2413.4.)

The monkey's amours with the elephant (or giraffe) show with the utmost clarity the absolute human identification in all such stories. Even with the disparity of size going in the opposite direction, the intention as parable cannot be mistaken. In Céline's anti-Semitic dithyramb, *Bagatelles pour un massacre* (1938), the very first page of text explains: 'I could, I could become – even I – a real stylist, a "significant" academic. It's a matter of work, of application for months . . . perhaps years. . . . Nothing's impossible. As the 'old Spanish proverb' says: "Plenty of vaseline, even more patience, and the Elephant bugger-luggers (*encugule*) the Ant".' (Varying *Matthew,* xix. 24, on the camel going through the eye of a needle. The actual proverb that Céline is quoting is French: *"Patience et saindoux* [lard], *et l'éléphant encule le pou* [louse]." This is usually expurgated and reduced to the aposiopoetic *"Patience et longueur de temps . . ."*) — *The monkey is in love with the giraffe. She finally succumbs to his blandishments. The monkey staggers home to the zoo, hours after the giraffe arrives, explaining: "Between kissing her and screwing her, I wore myself completely out."* (2:92, illustrated. And compare, in *Anecdota I,* The man who objected to intercourse with a mule "because you got to go such a long way round to kiss her." 1:271.) — *The monkey has done a good deed for the lady-elephant, and asks to be allowed to have intercourse with her as pay. A coconut falls from a nearby tree and hits the elephant on the head, making her bellow fiercely. The monkey agitates his hips excitedly: "Am I hurting you, honey?"* (2:450, illustrated; the last joke in the collection.) As with the prematurely ejaculating rabbit jokes, one can see here only too clearly the damaged sexual self-esteem of the originator and tellers of this joke, in their certainty that their orgasm is too soon, women's organs too big, and their own penises too childishly small anyway.

Like the bull or stallion, the elephant is a standard symbol of virility and fatherhood, owing to its largeness, phallic trunk, and so forth. (Its cryptorchidism is a well-kept secret.) The story of P. T. Barnum's elephant is a fascinating outcropping in the history of the American unconscious — with its special song, *Oh! Have You Seen the Elephant?* 'as sung by Mrs. Barney Williams' (New York, 1855), and with the tradition, still alive in the novelty trade, that the first shipments of carved ivory elephants from the Orient in the mid-19th century did not sell until the down-hanging trunks were sawed off and turned upward to make them 'lucky'! The less symbolized frankness of modern TV-top bric-à-brac, concentrating on the ceramic bull's testicles and the blond wooden doe's scut, has already been mentioned.

An elephant voyeuristic story involving a child (*"Mademoiselle is blasé!"*) has been given in Chapter 1. An even better known example: *Curious Lady: "Keeper, is that the elephant's penis or has he got five legs?" Keeper: "You were right the first time, Madam." "Well tell me, is it like his trunk or does it really get, you know — stiff?" Keeper: "Madam, I should think that would be of interest only to another ele-*

phant." (N.Y. 1940.) A modified version, in which the woman inquires merely as to the elephant's sex, is often printed. — *A group of circus elephants are crossing a railroad track, trunks holding tails as circus 'critters' go. A locomotive coming around the curve hits the last elephant and kills it. The circus sues for twenty times the cost of the elephant killed, because when the railroad train hit her "it pulled the assholes out of the other nineteen."* (2:130.) Apparently a pedication fantasy reversed, with the dominant male figure — locomotive and twenty elephants — greatly overdetermined. (In a similar Negro story on the super-strong folk-hero, *John Henry, when a drink is refused him in a San Francisco barroom because he is black, he wrenches the water-faucet from the bar, thus causing the Earthquake, "because all the pipes was connected."*)

The female animal, like the female human being in jokes, is considered hardly more than a walking sexual appetite. *A farmer takes his sow in a wheelbarrow to the boar day after day, expecting a litter of pigs every morning. "Any pigs this morning?" he calls down to his wife. "No pigs," she calls back, "but the sow's sitting in the wheelbarrow waiting for you."* (D.C. 1944.) — *A farmer buys a young mare and puts her in the same corral with a stallion, but not wanting her to be bred he ties a bedsheet around her buttocks for the night. In the morning she is gone. He trails her, and asks a neighbor if he saw a mare run by with a sheet tied around her back. "No," says the neighbor, "but I saw one dash past with a handkerchief sticking out of her ass."* (D.C. 1950.)

Dr. Roger Abrahams has published, in *Deep Down in the Jungle* (1964) pp. 136–57, and 211–13, a series of texts of the most popular American Negro recitation or 'toast,' which is concerned with the adventures of the identification-hero, the "Signifying Monkey." 'Signifying' is an older British term, brought to America during the Colonial period and now surviving only in the South, particularly among or in connection with Negroes, as is also the case with such British terms as 'boy' and 'wench,' referring once to any young man-and maid-servants, but now principally to a Negro man or woman, especially if a servant, of any age. The word 'Signifying' is glossed by Dr. Abrahams as meaning now, in specifically Negro usage: 'To imply, goad, beg, boast by indirect verbal or gestural means. A language of implication.' As good as his name, the Signifying Monkey sets the Elephant and Lion at loggerheads by way of revenging himself:

> Down in the jungle near a dried-up creek,
> The signifying monkey hadn't slept for a week
> Remembering the ass-kicking he had got in the past
> He had to find somebody to kick the lion's ass. . .

This long recitation will not be given here, as Dr. Abrahams' texts are superlative, and worth examining for their power and drollery. He gives four texts (p. 147–57) of "The Lion and the Monkey" adventure, which is the most interesting, as showing the Negro identification with the monkey, and against the power figure of the Lion, using the Elephant as cat's paw — to mix all zoological metaphors! An earlier text is cited p. 139, from another scatological adventure of the Monkey with the Elephant himself, from a single verse (the rest being omitted as expurgation, of course) sung on an early 'race record,' "Can't You Read?" recorded by Big Maceo Merriweather in 1941 (Bluebird recording 8772; Victor 3209). This seems to be the earliest reference, though these recitational 'toasts' are certainly much older.

Negro 'signifying' tactics — based on a long history as slave and underdog — should be borne in mind in connection with the new American 'Black Power' or 'Black Revolt' movement of the 1960's, especially in its suicidal riots against whites, its carnival-style looting, and the bragging announcements by certain militant Negro leaders that they plan to 'burn down America' with Molotov-cocktails, to poison the reservoirs before they are jailed, and to kill all the 'honkies' [whites], and rape all the white women. The white host-group unfortunately takes such obvious posturing and playing of the 'dozens' as serious revolutionary pronunciamento, and reacts with the far more dangerous 'white backlash' or counter-threat of planning seriously — though silently — to lock up in concentration-camps (and doubtless eventually to gas) all the millions of American Negroes 'protectively.' "Playing the Dozens" and "Signifying Monkeys" — even with Russia cast as the big-brother Elephant — need not really go so desperately far. See the prefiguration of the genocidal plot against the American Negroes, as a top-secret government plan, "KING ALFRED," in John A. Williams' *The Man Who Cried I Am* (Boston, 1967, p. 371–6, especially the closing paragraph or punch-line!

As the voice of the white backlash is much heard in the land, but seldom printed, everyone preferring simply to deplore (publicly) that it exists at all; here is a minor sample, possibly its theme-song. It was performed for his buddies by an American sailor from Fort Worth,

Texas, in Cannes, France, in 1967, at a whore-pickup bar, at a time when the newspapers were filled with accounts of the 'Burning of Detroit' by Negro rioters. He also proudly, if prematurely, announced that concentration-camps were already set up in the west for 'the Nigras, if push comes to shove.' (The same premature statement was made by the Negro militant leader, Hubert Rap Brown, in an extraordinary interview with the Italian journalist, Oriana Fallaci, published in French as *"Je suis prêt à tuer! . . ."* in *Le Nouvel Observateur,* Sept. 11th, 1967, p. 16–20.) The sailor sang his little song mockingly, in a husky, rasping voice — a sort of lynch-mob disguise — in exaggerated Southern accent, with the *'fa'n'gul-até'* middle-finger gesture rising and reaming climactically at the last three words; ending in tableau as the Statue of Liberty. (Tune: *Little Brown Jug*.)

> Black-hearted nigger, hating me,
> Under the excuse that "Man Is *Free!*"
> Lookin' for my wimmen, lookin' for a screw —
> Black-hearted nigger . . . I FUCK YOU!

II. PARROTS AND OTHER FOWL

It is a necessary part of the anthropomorphism of the animal story that, where possible, the animal should make use of human language. This can be dispensed with entirely, as in the last four stories given, or it may be done with such simplicity and naturalness that its impossibility is hardly noticed. Part of the bogus quality of the shaggy dog stories — I think every sensitive listener must feel the strained note in all of these, as in the even less credible bop or moron jokes of the last few years — is that too much is made of the animal's talking or other anthropomorphic trait, just as far too much is made of the bopster's or hippie's marihuana daze.

In order to raise a laugh, the shaggy dog and bop jokes must be told with daggers drawn at the punch-line, the listener being given to understand that this is it, and he must either laugh or else! As, in at least one case, a story of this type can be shown historically to have lost its point, and to have none as currently told, the suspicion that most of them are pointless, and that they are merely aggressive exercises on the tellers' part (*no* one likes to listen to them), is strengthened. The defective story referred to is that of the horse that is smuggled upstairs into the bathtub for the stated purpose of saying "Yes, I know," when the wife (or landlady) will excitedly say in the morning, "There's a horse in the bathtub." The prototype story is to be found in La Sale's *Cent Nouvelles Nouvelles* (1460) No. 61, "Le Cocu dupé," where a jackass is brought into the house and substituted by the wife for her lover, whom her husband has locked in a bin or trough (*huche*) — the bathtub, in the modern form — while her husband is away gathering relatives and witnesses for her intended public humiliation. Just the comparison of the dramatic situation of the *Cent Nouvelles Nouvelles* story with the paltering shaggy-bathtub tale, is sufficient to show how much the latter has lost, even aside from its defective conclusion.

The parrot-story type imports the desired anthropomorphism in the most natural possible way, since parrots do talk. The fantasy element in the story is therefore always that the parrot not only speaks but speaks to the point, or, frankly, that it has thought out the situation and is commenting upon it. The parrot is used as background in this way all over the Orient. The fine Persian collection of tales, the *Tuti-Namah,* or "Tales of a Parrot" (written about 1306, English translation by George Small, 1875) is entirely recounted by the parrot of the title, and derives from a far older Sanskrit original now called the *Shuka-Saptati,* or "Seventy Tales of a Parrot" (German translation by R. Schmidt, 1894), in which the tales of the parrot are specifically to prevent a wife's adultery, by keeping her interested until her husband's return! (Aarne Type 1352A.) The formal similarity is obvious to the well-known frame story of the *Arabian Nights,* in which the stories are told by Shahrazade to her husband, the Sultan Shahryar, night after night, each time ending in the middle of a story at dawn, to keep him from having her strangled in the morning to 'prevent' her from committing adultery — since all women are bad. In the important ethnographical work, *Japanisches Geschlechtsleben* (Japanese Sexual Life), by Friedrich S. Krauss and Dr. Tamio Satow, the final edition published in Leipzig, 1931, in two volumes, to end the great *Anthropophytéia* set of erotic folklore monographs, a series of reproductions are given in volume 1: ills. 93*a-m,* of a 'pillowbook,' or erotic posture picture-book for newlyweds, titled simply "The Bird," and dating from about 1850 (school of Kunisada), in which the bird — a parrot — is framed on its perch in the background corner of each of the twelve coital posture illustrations, apparently telling the surrounding story text. The narrating animal or object, as the thread upon which to string a disorderly series of tales, appeared in France somewhat after Galland's translation of the *Arabian Nights,* with loquacious canopies, mirrors, sofas (Crébillon), and cab-drivers, and, in England, Charles Johnstone's *Chrysal, or the Adventures of a Guinea* (1760–5) and Smollett's far more interesting *Adventures of an Atom* (1769) with its peculiar passages on the history of pants — a monograph on which subject would be well worth doing — and on fanny-kicking, as it is now politely called. (Modern proverb: *"Never get into an ass-kicking contest with a three-legged man."*)

The medieval prototype of all the modern parrot tales has been quoted earlier, in the section "The Castratory Threat," p. 85, but may be recollected here. It concerns a 'magpie' that had all its feathers pulled out for telling the husband that his wife ate a 'good morsell' (*i.e.* the symbolic eel) in his absence, and 'ever after, whanne the [mag]pie sawe a balled or a pilled man, or a woman with an high forhede, the pie saide to *t*hem, "ye spake of the ele." ' (Geoffrey de La Tour-Landry, *The Book of the Knight of Tour-Landry,* 1372, English translation edited by Thomas Wright, 1906, p. 208. Motif J551.5.) I trust I will not be suspected of improving on the facts if I mention that I was called to the telephone while working on this section only to have the following story told to me by a complete stranger, stemming from her unsolicited observation that the noise in the background was her parrakeet chattering. *A parrot has the habit of jumping on the hens, and the farmer tells him that if does it again he will pull out every feather on its head. The parrot jumps on the hens again, and his head-feathers are all pulled out. Meanwhile, the farmer's wife, who has pretentions to culture, is having a formal dinner. She appoints the parrot to be butler and to tell the guests where to put their hats and coats. "Ladies to the right!" the parrot announces. "Gentlemen to the left." Suddenly two bald-headed men enter, and the parrot says, "You two chicken-fuckers come out in the hen-house with me."* (N.Y. 1953. Motif J2211.2, citing Pauli, No. 669.)

In a variant retaining neither the baldness nor the sexual element, *A parrot sees the minister walk naked through the house to take a bath, and cries, "I see your ass!" He is doused with water in punishment for swearing. Later, when the pastor's daughter comes in from the rain and shakes off her wet raincoat, the parrot says, "Whose ass*

did YOU *see?"* (D.C. 1944.) Varying the sexual element, *A farmer with
an order for four dozen chickens finds he has only forty-seven, so he
puts a parrot in the last coop. A mile from town he finds all forty-
seven chickens walking in the road behind the wagon, and the parrot
standing on the tail-board shouting, "If any of you girls change your
minds, let me know and you can ride."* (2:108.)

The principal element in parrot stories is of course the parrot's
swearing, for which it takes the entire blame, while the person who
has taught it to swear takes none. This forgotten culprit is usually
referred to, if at all, as a former owner who was a sailor or a prostitute,
but the practice of teaching bawdy words to children and foreigners
as a joke, and to young women as a part of their seduction, is almost
universal. An embarrassingly exact rendition of such a verbal seduction
scene is given in Bessie Breuer's superb *The Daughter* (1938), p. 276,
at the opening of chapter 19. Parrot stories turning on the word 'ass,'
like the minister story above, seem to be thought of as the mildest, and
several others exist. *A preacher is buying a parrot. "Are you sure it
doesn't swear?" "Oh, absolutely. It's a religious parrot," the proprietor
assures him. "Do you see the string on his leg? When you pull on that
he recites the Lord's Prayer, and when you pull the string on the other
leg he recites the 23rd Psalm." "Wonderful!" says the preacher, "but
what would happen if I pulled on both strings?" "Why you stupid
son of a bitch," the parrot squawks, "I'd fall on my ass!"* (Baker, 1945,
J2721.) — *The birds are having a race; running, not flying. The favorites are the Argentine condor and the American eagle, but the Brazilian parrot wins. He steams up to the finish line screaming, "Who put
that firecracker up my ass!"* (N.Y. 1953.) Compare the earlier remarks
on *negative contests* and the 'will to fail,' end of section 2.v.3.

One of the conventions of the parrot story is that the bird will stop
swearing if it is given sexual satisfaction. *An old maid has a parrot
that swears terribly. She borrows the minister's parrot, which never
does anything but pray, and puts them together in the cage hoping to
influence her parrot to be good. The minute they are alone together
the swearing parrot says, "How about a little loving?" "Hell yes," says
the holy bird. "What do you think I've been praying for all these
years?"* (D.C. 1945.) — *A young woman is worried by her parrot's
swearing before her fiancé. She tries to get a mate for it, to quiet it,
but has to settle for an owl. That evening as her fiancé walks in, the
parrot begins shrieking, "Somebody's going to get screwed! Some-*

body's going to get screwewewed!" "Who-o?" cries the owl, "Who-o?"
"Not you, you flat-faced son of a bitch!" (2:399.)

Other than sailors' parrots who simply swear, parrots who have been former whore-house pets are a standard source of embarrassment. This may even appear before they are bought. *A Hollywood madam has died and all her ornate furnishings are being auctioned off, including a magnificent parrot. "Now what am I bid for this beautiful bird?" "Three dollars." "Five dollars." "Seven-fifty!" At this point the parrot speaks up. "Don't be a piker, Daddy," it croaks. "Make it ten and I'll give you a blow-job too."* (N.Y. 1946.) The parrot who will not talk at all balances against those who talk too much. *The new parrot cannot be made to talk. Everything is tried, beginning with "Polly wants a cracker?" but with no result. That afternoon at the wife's bridge party, the discussion turns on the current quality of silk underwear. "Look at this wonderful petticoat," says one, turning up the corner of her dress. "And look at these wonderful bloomers," says another, pulling up her skirt all the way. "Home at last," says the parrot. "One of you whores give me a cigarette."* (1:46.) In another version, *The father brings home a parrot in a cloth-covered cage where it is kept for two weeks hoping to make it forget its vocabulary. When the cage is finally uncovered the parrot looks around at the parlor and the family, and says, "Awwrk! New house. New madam. New whores. Same old customers. Hello, Charlie!"* (D.C. 1945.)

The cage-cover that quiets the parrot also appears in the connected story of *The woman who gets up, puts up the shade, takes the cover off the parrot's cage, makes coffee, has a cigarette. Suddenly the phone rings. Her boyfriend is coming over. She puts out her cigarette, pulls down the shade, puts the cover back on the parrot's cage, and gets back into bed. Parrot, from under the cloth: "Well, that was a short fuckin' day!"* (N.Y. 1953.) Other punishments and dissuasions of the parrot's swearing are not quite so mild, as with the pulled out head-feathers of the original 14th-century magpie tale. *A pet-shop owner warns that a parrot has the habit of swearing, but that this can be stopped by taking it by the feet and swinging it in a circle. At its first meal it spits the food on the floor, screaming, "Whale shit! Man the life-boats, we must be sinking! Shit! Shit!" The new owner hurriedly seizes it by the legs and begins swinging it in a circle. Slowly, in time with the swinging, the parrot chants, "What — a — fuckin' — breeze!"* (N.Y. 1946.)

The perfect appropriateness here of the parrot as the identification-object of the child (the reminiscent or would-be child who is telling the story!) is particularly clear in the touch of *spitting the food on the floor,* as anyone who knows anything about babies will understand. Also, for all its modern appearance, and its allusion to an American folk-simile: *"lower than whale shit — and that's on the bottom of the ocean,"* this is actually one of the oldest of the parrot stories, and is the transitional tale from the Sanskrit *Shuka-Saptati,* or "Seventy Tales of a Parrot." All that is left of the original is the trait of *the storm* which the parrot is made to believe is raging, by swinging it in circles: *"What — a — fuckin' — breeze!"* This is Aarne's Tale Type 1422 (with extensive references), of which the Italian *novella* versions are cited by Rotunda at Motif J1154.1: *'Parrot (or magpie) unable to tell husband details as to wife's infidelity. Wife has it describe a storm very realistically. Husband observes contrast in the two tales.'* Note on the one hand the concern with the wife's adultery (the Sanskrit "Seventy Tales of a Parrot," Aarne Type 1352A), and on the other the interchangeability of parrot and magpie, as in the French version of *The Book of the Knight of La Tour-Landry.* It is surprising, in fact, that the English version has clung to the parrot, by preference, suggesting a direct borrowing of the tale from the Far East.

It is also to be observed that the parrot is, in most of the jokes, alleging an erotic 'past' for its former owner — the ex-sailor or ex-prostitute — and this too is an essential element of the older stories, such as "The Tell-Tale Parrot" (Aarne Type 243.1.b). Finally, the element of discrediting the witness by tricking him — or her — into talking nonsense, is central to a whole group of folktales listed by Aarne-Thompson from a tremendous area of collection, at Type 1381 and its subtypes A through E*. The "Tell-Tale Parrot" type (243) generally has the indiscreet parrot condemned to death — but it escapes — as in the most famous, the most ruthless, and the earliest recorded of the modern erotic parrot jokes. This also involves the castration-(death)-&-resurrection theme, which will be discussed further in chapter 13, "Castration," in Series Two. Observe the drawing of reassurance, rather than dread, from the fact of the woman's genital 'castration': *i.e.* her menstrual bleeding. *A wife complains of the parrot's swearing, so her husband cuts its throat and throws it in the toilet. A few minutes later the wife, who is menstruating, goes to the toilet. A voice issues from the depths of the china bowl: "If she can live with a gash like that, so can I."* (2:11.) This story appears in Conrad Aiken's *Blue Voyage* (1927).

Another version omits the element of menstruation — thus, blood — and ends in *cante fable* form with a little poem or chant in which the parrot mocks the autosuggestion therapy of Doctor (of pharmacy) Emile Coué, which had a brief fad during the 1920's: "*I'm gonna get well, I'm gonna get well. If you can live with a gash like that,* I'M *gonna get well!*" (N.Y. 1953.) See other examples in Neil Rosenberg's *An Annotated Collection of Parrot Jokes* (M.A. thesis, 1964, Indiana University Folklore Archive).

The woodpecker appears to be a sort of cousin to the parrot, in the matter of speech, though most of the humor about it (see in the chapter on Children, "*the finest piece of ash anyone ever drove his pecker into*") rises from its name. McAtee, in *Grant County, Indiana, Speech and Song: Supplement 2* (1946) records from the 1890's the following bit of doggerel, still current:

> *The woodpecker pecked on the schoolhouse door*
> *And he pecked and he pecked till his pecker was sore.*

With the variant conclusion, from Iowa: —

> *And whenever he thinks of the schoolhouse yard,*
> *His head gets red and his pecker gets hard.*

The woodpecker joke hardly more than retells this, but with a wry twist taking it completely out of the childhood background. *A frustrated woodpecker, disgusted with the runt-sized trees in Texas, migrates to California's giant redwood forest. Just as he starts pecking on a huge sequoia, lightning strikes the tree and splits it right down the middle. The woodpecker looks at it in amazement and says, "Gee, you never know how hard your pecker will get till you're away from home!*" (D.C. 1952.)

Chicken stories are completely anthropomorphic. Hardly a grain of the bird's real nature is essential to the jokes about it, except perhaps in the matter of the eggs. *A hen finds a group of Easter eggs and sits on them. When the rooster sees the eggs he rushes across the yard and beats up the peacock.* (N.Y. 1952.) — *A duck is lording it over a hen on the grounds that duck eggs bring forty-five cents a dozen and hen's eggs only thirty-five cents. "Huh," says the hen, "I should stretch my ass for ten cents?*" (2:137.)

The persistent note of cross-breeding struck again and again in the bird stories — parrot and hen, parrot and owl, woodpecker and redwood(!), etc. — seems to hint at the zoöphilic attraction of human beings to animals that is the subject of so many animal jokes. An extreme and rather confused example, satisfying itself with a merely verbal point: *A bird-breeder is showing off his hybrids to visitors. "This is a cross between a chicken and a turkey — we call it a churkey. And this is a cross between a chicken and a goose — we call it a choose. And this, this is my masterpiece — a cross between a pheasant and a duck. We call it George."* (Minn. 1935. Collected N.Y. 1948, with the variant hybrids of a crow and a magpie: *cragpie;* and a vulture and an eagle: *veagle.*)

Of the strictly anthropomorphic type, but still concerned with eggs and unorthodox breeding, *A farmer whose hens are laying sterile eggs rushes out to the chicken-coop, and pointing a shotgun at the line of roosters shouts, "All right, now, which one of you bastards has been using rubbers?"* (Calif. 1941.) — *Two old maids see a rooster chasing a chicken-hen to mount her. The hen runs out into the middle of the road and is run over by a trolley car. "How beautiful," says one old maid to the other. "Death before dishonor!"* (1:133.) — *Two brassière manufacturers with ulcers retire to a chicken farm to regain their health. No eggs. A neighboring farmer explains to them that they have to get a rooster. One of the partners goes to town and comes back with a scrawny rooster for which he paid $10. It pays no attention whatsoever to the hens unless two of them get together and put him on top of the third. The second partner is disgusted, goes to town and buys the finest rooster available, for $50. He brings it back and puts it out in the henyard, where it immediately descends upon the first rooster, leaps on its back, and begins striking at it with its talons. "Fifty dollars he spends," cries the first partner, "and he had to get a homosexual rooster!"* (N.Y. 1952. I am indebted for this hilarious story to Dr. Charles Winick.)

III. ZOÖPHILY

I. LOVES OF THE BEASTS

Two things about animal jokes that seem to come as a surprise even to people who have been telling them all their lives, is that most of them are not of the cute, anthropomorphic animal type, but concern the sexual intercourse of human beings with other animals, and that furthermore an appreciable group of these involve intercourse with the animal dominant. In other folklore-forms the percentage of zo-öphilic examples is even higher. In *The Limerick* (Paris, 1953), Limericks 574 through 665, or ninety out of the some eighteen hundred limericks in the main text, are concerned with animal sexuality, and almost none of these are without human participants; many of the best known examples turning on the monstrous births alleged to be the products of such intercourse. The Græco-Roman legends of the loves of Jupiter in animal form always stress the resulting monstrous births: such as Leda (and the Swan) laying eggs!

Voyeurism at the zoo has already been discussed in 3.1 above, and the folk-belief that the observation of the intercourse of other animals or of human beings has an aphrodisiacal or permissive effect on the viewers is firmly rooted in fact. There is of course an element of projecting one's own fantasies upon the animal. *A young man and his girl at the racetrack go through the paddock before the races to pick a horse. The first stall they look into contains a young stallion who is waving his yard and slapping it against his leg in fine fettle. "Don't bet on him, honey," says the girl. "He won't win. He ain't got his mind on business."* (1:402.) A pantomime joke, difficult to reduce to print: *A farmer's young wife is aroused sexually by a combination of beating eggs with a whisk and looking out the kitchen window at the animals' antics in the spring. "Gee, I'm glad I married a farmer," she says, beating the eggs. "It's so nice to live on a farm and see all the fields and things, and oh, look at those horses, that stallion (beating the eggs furiously); oh yes, it's so nice, the crops, and the fields, and the pigs, oh look at that boar (beating faster and faster until she has an orgasm); and oh, the chickens, look at that rooster, and —" Just then her little boy comes in and asks, "Where's Papa?" "Oh, I don't know, Johnnie. He's NEVER around when I want him!"* (Transcontinental train, U.S. 1943.)

The dominant animal is, above all, the bull. The whole sub-homosexual literature of bull-loving and bull-killing that we have been treated to in America since the mid-1930's, beginning with Ernest Hemingway's nauseating *Death in the Afternoon* (1932), and in quite a renewed gush in the last five or ten years, takes its rise strictly from the traditional identification of the bull with the feared and submitted-to father. (This also includes the buffalo, so murderously dear to Cols. Cody and Roosevelt.) The history of the bull as the patriarchal father is of great interest, and it is easy to trace — at least to the animal sacrifices of the Semitic Levant, the bull-leaping dances of Crete and the goddess-queen Pasiphaë (Aphrodite) and her seduction of, and triumph over, the baby-eating bull-god (Moloch) disguised as a cow — and need not be discussed further here. The alternation of dominance between the experienced old father-bull and the Oedipal young son is very striking in the two following jokes. *An old bull and a young bull are standing on a hillside looking down at a herd of young heifers. "Look at that pretty little red heifer," says the young bull. "Let's run down and fuck her!" "No," says the old bull, "lets walk down and fuck 'em all."* (N.Y. 1939.) Given in *Smile and the World Smiles with You,* Guam, 1948, reversed, with the old bull saying "Let's walk down and screw one of them," and the young bull replying, "No, let's run down and screw them all." This leads even more clearly into the other joke: *A farmer who has only two impotent old bulls buys a new, young, and vigorous bull, who is industriously mounting one cow after another in the pasture. One of the old bulls begins pawing the ground and snorting. "What's the matter," says the other. "You getting young ideas?" "No," says the first bull, "but I don't want that young fellow to think I'm one of the cows."* (D.C. 1951.) Compare with this the joke on the "homosexual rooster" ending the preceding section.

By comparison the relationship with the female is quite mild. *A city girl is chased by a bull. As the hired man helps her down from the tree he says, "What's the matter, can't you take it?" "Sure I can take it,"* she says belligerently, *"but what the hell would I do with a calf in Chicago?"* (Fla. 1953.) The same theme is evident in the some-what milder stories, both printed in *Charley Jones' Laugh Book* (Wichita, Kans., May 1951): *An old hen is walking down the road when she is hit from behind by a jeep. She gets up, shakes her feathers, and says coyly, "Do you have to be so rough?"* Charley Jones' version of the other story uses the standard movie and radio euphemism of 'kissing': *During the war, a girl is bent over a washtub scrubbing clothes, and a passing soldier has intercourse with her from behind. She continues with her washing. Another soldier follows, then several more. Finally an old mule (or bear) ambles over and has intercourse with her in the same way. Without turning around the girl says, "Will that last gentleman please leave his name and address?"* In a variant *She says languishingly, "If you were a gentleman, you'd take off that fur coat.* (N.Y. 1953. Generally told as of a Negro woman.)

What is sauce for the goose is psychological collapse for the gander. The two following stories have been observed to raise the most hysterical laughter among audiences of men. The idea of homosexual rape propounded is clearly too anxiety-laden to be endured. *Pat and Mike are escaping from the battlefield in the skin of a cow. Mike, in front, begins to run faster and faster, with Pat bringing up the rear. Suddenly Mike stops, and gasps, "It's no use, Pat, brace yourself — here comes the bull!"* (1:32.) — *An actor is told that he can have the part in the play if he loses forty pounds before the next night. He goes to a deluxe health salon, and is told this can easily be done by means of either a $500 treatment taking twenty-four hours, or a $1000 treatment taking twelve hours. He picks the $500 treatment and is ushered into a large room in which he finds a naked girl wearing a sign reading:* "YOU CATCH ME, YOU FUCK ME." *He begins thinking, if this is the $500 treatment, what must the $1000 treatment be? And rushes back to the office and asks to change to the more expensive treatment. This time he is ushered into a small room and the door is locked behind him. A door opens at the other side of the room and a gorilla with an enormous erection enters wearing a sign:* "I CATCH YOU, I FUCK YOU." (N.Y. 1952.) Other versions, and further stories on this theme of the pedicatory rape of men by animals, will be found in Series Two, Chapter 10.V.5, under Homosexuality, in particular the story with the punchline, *"Shoot Blue!"*

2. ZOÖPHILY

The usual situation in zoöphilic jokes is naturally that of the dominant human being and exploited animal. The animal of choice is traditionally the sheep, as in the definition: *"Texas — where men are men, and sheep are scared to death."* (Minn. 1946.) — *A farmhand has insomnia. A friend tells him to count sheep. He counts: "One, two, three, hello sweetheart; five, six . . ."* (End-line only, without the situation, in Parke Cummings' "The Art of the Off-Color Story," in *American Mercury*, Sept. 1939, p. 29.) — *A ventriloquist at a summer camp is amazing the neighboring farm-hands with his abilities. He has the horse say, "Hello, Captain," and the cow moo, "Oh, my aching tits!" He then is looking thoughtfully at the flock of sheep nearby when one of the hired hands bursts out, "Listen, if that little ewe at the end says anything, she's a goddam liar!"* (N.J. 1942. Talking dog version, *Kryptádia,* 1907, XI. 268. Motif J1895, Type 1750.)

The last great folklore-producing period in America ended just after the final conquering of the west about 1910. One of the standard situations in jokes is that of the tenderfoot out west who either cannot find a woman or is looking for the toilet. As to the first problem, the proffered solution is usually either an animal or another man, usually a Chinaman. *A man in a gold-rush town asks the hotel clerk where he can find a woman, and is told there are no women but that he can use the mule in Perkins' barn for a dollar. After much wrestling with his conscience he goes to the barn, where he finds the mule all decked in ribbons and smelling of perfume. His dollar is refused. "Nothin' doin',"* says the guardian, waving him away. *"Jim McCann, the gambler, is keepin' her now."* (1:31.) In a variant developing the Oedipal conflict here, *A tenderfoot out west in need of a woman is told by the bartender to find himself a sheep. He does so and ends up in jail. He goes back to berate the bartender. "Didn't you say just to get myself a sheep and go to work?" "Sure, but you didn't have to screw the sheriff's personal sheep."* (N.Y. 1949.)

The relationship here with the hotel clerk or bartender, or in general *some other man,* suggests that bestiality always seems somehow less of a natural choice, under the circumstances, than homosexual practice would be. *Sheep-herder: "Did you wash those sheep?" "Yep." "And did you take the blue ribbon off that little ewe?" "Yep." "You mean to say I got to fuck through that whole herd again?"* (N.Y. 1949.) — *A sheep-herder is terribly embarrassed at his army medical examination (or on his visit to the town whore-house). "It was awful,"* he says. *"When I skinned back my prick, two sheep-turds fell out."* (Transcontinental train, 1943.) The complex relationship between the inevitable two men in this type of joke may even go so far as becoming brother-husbands, as will be discussed more fully in the chapter on Adultery. *The wife of an African chief has an albino baby, and suspicion fastens on the white missionary. When he sees that things are beginning to look bad for him, he takes the chief aside and says, "Look, chief, see up on that hill, all those white sheep?" "Unnh." "And see that one little black lamb — ?" "O.K.,"* says the chief, *"You no tell, I no tell."* (N.Y. 1952, told by a young woman.)

Although the cow has as much reason to be a mother-figure as the bull to be a father-figure, and is certainly sometimes so identified in folklore, it occurs much less often in zoöphilic contexts than the sheep. Perhaps its paramount motherliness, as milk-giver etc., fortifies the taboo against bestiality with incestuous taboos as well. The guilt-laden Jewish system of food taboos involving milk, which is not generally understood to be the rejected offering, under patriarchy, of the sacrifice to the matriarchal goddess of a young goat seethed in the milk of its mother, *Exodus* xxiii.19, is even taken so far as learned discussions on whether a cow's udder is to be considered milk or meat. With this may be compared the equal ambivalence of simultaneously prohibiting the use of blood, except sacrificially (*Exodus,* xii.7), but allowing the eating of the heart.

Jokes about sexual relations with cows do, of course, exist. *An old farmer attempts to get into a whore-house with sixty-five cents which he fishes out of an old snap purse. He is told curtly by the madam that the price is "two dollars, including towels, and don't you put your dirty boots on my clean sheets!" "Now lookie here, lady," he complains, "don't you be getting so dern independent about a job thet c'n be done almost ez good by a caow."* (Minn. 1935.) — *Two soldiers see a cow (or pig) ambling across the battlefield. 1st Soldier: "Oh boy, if it was only a woman!" 2nd Soldier: "Oh, boy, if it was only dark!"* (1:23.) The identification here of woman and cow is absolutely direct, and even more so in: *The cowboy on his wedding night who rolls all his clothes in a bundle and puts them on a high shelf, explaining to his curious bride, "I ain't never had a woman before, but if it's anything like with a cow this place is going to be ass-high in shit."* (2:168.) Compare the burlesque demonstration by Leonardo da Vinci, in his *Quaderni d'anatomia* (Dybwad edition) folio 7 *recto,* note 5, that the sexual parts of a woman are, proportionately, three times as large as those of a cow!

In corroboration of the mother-image element in the cow stories may be cited two curious reversals or projections in which it is the human being who gives nurse, sexually, to the cow. *A man allows himself to be tied up in a haunted barn all night to prove there are no ghosts. In the morning he is found in a state of collapse. "Now do you believe in ghosts?" "Ghosts, my ass; why don't you wean that calf of yours?"* (N.Y. 1945. Revenge-version in *Kryptádia,* xi. 307.) — *A little boy going to urinate in a cow pasture calls out in a progressively fading voice: "Mama, come get this calf away! Ma—mm-aa, co—ome get th—is ca—lf a—way!" Then silence.* (2:310.) — *A young farmer about to be married is told by the doctor that he can enlarge his penis by dipping it in milk every day and allowing a calf to suck it. Two months later the farmer and doctor meet in the street. "Well, I suppose you're married and settled down now, eh?" says the doctor. "Well not exactly, Doc. I bought the calf instead."* (2:414. Sometimes heard with the 'nonsense' ending, *"I married the calf."*) Many 'true anecdotes' of men putting their penises in a cow-milking device, *i.e.*, pulsating artificial vagina. *A farmer is having trouble milking a cow, who keeps swishing his face with her tail. He ties the tail to one side of the stall. Then she starts licking his face. He ties her head to the stall, also her back legs, which she is putting into the milk-pail. Just then his wife walks in.* (N.Y. 1949. Motif J2119.8.)

Jokes on sexual relations of women with animals have not been collected, unless a punning reference to a woman's pet cat that dies of a pubic hair-ball can be considered a joke. Stories of this type are generally told, not as jokes, but as true anecdotes demonstrating the sexual greediness and depraved appetites of women in general. One such 'true anecdote' very frequently heard almost exactly duplicates the *vagina dentata* fantasy (quoted in Chapter 13, "Castration," in Series Two) of the man who becomes locked in coitus with a woman when her vagina goes into spasm owing to fright. In the reverse, zoöphilic form, it seems quite clear that the whole idea rises from the observation of coital locking in dogs — *A woman is having intercourse with a large dog. It becomes frightened by the slamming of a door and pulls away from the woman suddenly, which "turns her organs inside out like a glove." A gynecologist has to be called in to put her prolapsed organs back inside again, and he hushes the story up. The narrator himself heard the story from the gynecologist.* (N.Y. 1938.)

The idea that women are particularly interested sexually in asses or mules seems to stem in part from the very large penises of these animals and from the breeding of jackasses 'above themselves' with mares. The intercourse of a woman with a jackass is the climactic scene in Apuleius' *Golden Ass* (2nd century A.D.) with the saving grace that the ass is really a human male in magical disguise. A similar scene, without any such pretense, occurs in *Gamiani* (1833) by Alfred de Musset, and it is interesting that both of these works are overwhelmingly masochist in tone — as was De Musset in his life, and in his famous affair with the Lesbian writer 'George Sand' — even aside from the identification with the animal. The jackass scene in Nerciat's erotic *Diable au Corps* (1803) is played as a comedy of manners!

Survivals of sexual superstitions about jackasses are still encountered in the southern United States. One of Erskine Caldwell's short
stories turns completely on the idea, apparently seriously held in the
south, that the braying of a rutting jackass will excite women sexually
in the most uncontrollable way. That the jackass is specifically attracted
to human females is also suggested in this peculiar joke, with overtones of the apotropaic display of the genitals to ward off evil. *A mule
gets into a colored woman's cabbage patch, and she rushes out, shooing
him away by flapping up her skirt. The mule continues feeding on
the cabbages, good-naturedly swinging his tool. "Look out, Maria," a
man calls over the fence; "first thing you know, that mule'll think you
want to put a collar on him."* (1:495.) A variant of this story, in free
verse, is given as "The Ass and the Fat Lady" in the *Red-Bone Legends*
of 'Mason Jordan Mason,' printed in *Neurotica* (1951) No. 9: p. 46,
in which the Ass says to the Fat Lady, who 'got no drawers on underneath', ' "I only scared you put that fur-lined horse-collar on around
my neck," That he never see anything like before.' Rabelais' story, in
Pantagruel Bk. II. chap. 15, printed in 1533, of the old woman whose
vagina the lion and fox attempt to fill with moss, has certain elements
in common; and see also IV. 47, the "Diable de Papefiguière," in
which the demon-frightening use of the vaginal 'wound' is even more
clearly stated. (Compare *Ocean of Story*, A.D. 1070, omitted in Tawney's
translation; see ed. Penzer, III.32–5.)

The intercourse of men with horses, mules, and assorted animals,
insects, etc., as seen in jokes, involves quite a parade of excuses, rang-
ing from mere laziness to the lack of human females. *The Laziest
Man: he is found sitting on a barrel, having intercourse with a mule
by saying "Giddap, whoa, back up! Giddap, whoa, back up!"* (1:34,
with a human variant, 1:42, on *A man with so large a penis that he
tells the woman, "Put in the head. All ready? Now walk slowly
towards me!"*) Then, mere errors of accent or implication: *Tongue-
tied man, buying a horse: "Now let's see her twot." "Giddap, Es-
meralda."* (N.Y. 1939.) — *"What's a taxidermist?" "A man that mounts
animals." "That's not what they call him in Montana."* (N.Y. 1940.)

Nonsense jokes, such as the following, are usually done with
drunks, which allows of slurring over almost any insufficiently clear
point of the action or motivation. As with the taxidermist in Montana,
however, there is certainly something odd about putting a duck in
one's pants, on any excuse, drunk or sober. *A man wins a live duck in
a barroom drawing at Christmas, and wanders into a theatre carrying*

it. He is told he cannot bring the duck in with him, and goes out and hides it inside his pants. In the darkened theatre the woman next to him clutches her escort's sleeve and whispers, "The man next to me has his prick out." "Oh, so what?" says her escort, "you've seen one before." "But this one is eating popcorn!" (N.Y. 1953.) Variant in which: *A golfer misses a crucial putt on happening to look up the skirt of a woman sitting in the audience with a pet lamb under her dress. When he explains how it happened his backer says, "Well hell, you've seen a woman's snatch before." "Yes, but this one was eating grass!"* (N.Y. 1953.) The oragenital, and not castratory, tone of these stories is rather hidden in this form, but that it is there cannot be doubted when they are compared with the original, or at least the earliest collected version: *A man smuggles a puppy with him on an air-liner by hiding it inside his pants. During the flight the hostess sees him grinning broadly and asks him why. He explains what he has done. Hostess: "But is the puppy, uh, house-broken?" Passenger, grinning even more broadly: "Hell, he ain't even weaned yet!"* (N.Y. 1942. Compare the calf jokes above.)

A well-known octopus story (shaggy octopus?) is generally accepted at its face value. *A sailor has a pet octopus that keeps whistling "Embraceable You" as it mops the decks, cooks in the galley, and so forth, so he buys it a set of bagpipes. After an hour below decks struggling with them, the octopus slithers back up and says, "Listen, how do you fuck this thing?"* (N.Y. 1948.) What is suspicious here is not just the grotesquerie, but that the octopus is more generally a symbol for the fearsome vagina. (Wall-epigraph: an eight-tentacled female genital, captioned *"Octopussy."* – N.Y. 1940). This suggests that the real problem behind the joke is how to get into the 'octopus' successfully, and not the reverse.

Sexual approaches made to animals and to persons of the same sex are accepted in jokes as practically forgivable in persons whose occupations close off normal avenues of sexual expression, as in the army, in jail, on ships, in logging camps, etc. A very popular joke over the last two decades combines, and sometimes confuses, the permissible bestiality or homosexuality here. *A man confesses to his psychiatrist that he is sexually interested in horses. "Male or female horses?" the psychiatrist asks. The patient bristles. "You think I'm queer?"* (N.Y. 1948. "Queer" being the commonest euphemism for homosexual.) This has also been collected in the form of a dialogue between two stuffy

British majors: *"Heard about Squidgely?" "No." "Been drummed out of the army." "Gad, what for?" "Caught in the act with a horse." "Ghastly! Mare or stallion?" "Stallion, of course — nothing queer about Squidgely!"* (Fla. 1952.) This seems a bit overdone, of course, and yet compare — as to the British background of homosexual *horror feminæ* — the remarkable 'humorous' passage on sisters and mothers in E. M. Forster's *Two Cheers for Democracy* (New York, 1951), p. 12:

> Long, long ago, while Queen Victoria reigned, I attended two preparatory schools. At the first of these, it was held to be a disgrace to have a sister. Any little boy who possessed one was liable to get teased. The word would go round: "Oh, you men, have you seen the Picktoes' sister?" The men would then reel about with sideway motions, uttering cries of "sucks" and pretending to faint with horror, while the Picktoes . . . found themselves banished into the wilderness. . . . It was a very different story at my second school. Here, sisters were negligible, but it was a disgrace to have a mother. Crabbe's mother, Gob's mother, eeugh! No words were too strong, no sounds too shrill. . . . Nearly every little boy had a mother in a cupboard, and dreadful revelations occurred. . . . Many tried to divert suspicion by being aggressive and fastening female parents upon the weak.

As the French have never been suspected of national homosexuality, the matching French Foreign Legion story veers toward pure zoöphily. *Sergeant Leclerc is being drummed out of the Foreign Legion for having had intercourse with an ostrich. After hours of documents being read, affidavits of witnesses, and beratings by his superior officers, Leclerc cracks under the strain. "All right," he screams, "all right! I'll marry the bird!"* (N.Y. 1952.) A satirical story based on intercourse with ostriches, "Even the Beasts and the Birds" by Ridgely Cummings, is published in the literary magazine *The Deer and Dachshund* (Taos, 1952) No. 2, with the ostriches given the pig-Latin name 'Ockfahs,' and the unworldly professor who falls in love with the female Ockfah being blinded by her beak in punishment. Less unpleasantly, from World War I: *A soldier swears fidelity to his wife, but after months at the front without relief he has intercourse with a pig. On his return home his wife asks, "Have you been faithful to me, honey?" "I sure have." "In a pig's ass, you have!" "*DAMN *them German spies!"* (Cleveland, Ohio, 1939.)

A few unclassifiable and pansexual examples will end the subject here. The ad-parody already mentioned under Misunderstandings, 2.v: *"Nine out of ten doctors who tried Camels — preferred women"* (N.Y. 1953). — *A schoolteacher on a train going through the west sees an Indian on the platform at a desert stop. "Are you a real Indian?" "Ugh." "How many wives do you have?" "Eight." "But what do you do with so many wives?" "Fuckum." "Why, you dog!" "Fuckum dog too." "But my dear!" "No can fuckum deer. Deer run too fast."* (2:433, illus.) The humor mechanism here is that used in Panurge's colloquy with the Semiquaver Friar (Rabelais' Bk. v, chap. 28, published in 1553) where, no matter what Panurge asks, the Friar answers only in monosyllables. A polite version of this, with the wife sent on a sea-voyage by her husband who tells her to answer all questions with ad-verbs — "Possibly ... occasionally ... certainly — " is used in the Sacha Guitry motion picture, *The Crown Diamonds.* This is merely a sophisti-cation of the folksong formula, "No, John, No!" (Type 853A.) Also in *Russian Secret Tales,* No. 23, "No!"

Even sexual relations with insects are the subject of folklore, gen-erally sadistic, as in the pretended masturbatory technique involving tearing one wing off a fly while lying altogether submerged in a bathtub except for the head of the penis. *Two men are lying in bed side by side totally naked one morning, in hot weather. One has an erection, and a fly is crawling about on it. "There's a fly crawling on your dick," says the other man; "shall I flick it off?" "No, just jerk it a few times and I'll plaster him to the ceiling."* (Okla. 1915; text form, Minn. 1946.) That this is homosexual and not zoöphilic is obvious.

As the statement is often made, and the historical materials alluded to throughout the present text seem also to suggest, that no new jokes exist or can be created; at least one completely topical and presumably new example may be cited in closing. (Another, on the author who writes a book entitled *I Fucked a Gorilla,* will be found in the later chapter on Homosexuality, in Series Two.) *First Farmer: "Did you hear about this fellow Kinsey, that's been going around saying things against us farmers?" Second Farmer: "What's he been saying?" First Farmer: "He says us farmers go around fucking sheep — and goats — and chickens — and snakes — " Second Farmer: "Snakes?"* (N.Y. 1953.)

4

THE MALE APPROACH

ONE FACT strikingly evident in any collection of modern sexual folklore, whether jokes, limericks, ballads, printed 'novelties,' or what-not, is that this material has all been created by men, and that there is no place in it for women except as the butt. It is not just that so preponderant an amount of the material is grossly anti-woman in tendency and intent, but also that the situations presented almost completely lack any protagonist position in which a woman can identify herself — *as a woman* — with any human gratification or pride.

No one at all conversant with ordinary life today, especially in the Anglo-Saxon Western world, can be ignorant of the fact that women tell dirty jokes, and can listen to them — if they will listen at all (many will not) — without the slightest apparent shock, however crude the language or images presented. On women who themselves tell dirty jokes see the very incisive paragraph, headed "Four-Letter Words," by Dr. Theodor Reik, quoted in Series Two at the end of Section 11.II.4, in the chapter on Prostitution, as to such women's unconscious and hostile attempt to parody or impersonate men — as they imagine them to be — by such verbal means. Nevertheless, there is generally a noticeable slackening off, in the presence of women listeners, of those jokes concentrating mainly on insulting generalizations, or even more insulting particularities, concerning the odor or size of the female genitals, and other unmistakable affronts to the woman listener. Certain women, of the most obvious castratory and reclamatory type, actually specialize in telling horrible and insulting anti-woman jokes, in the same way that Jews have often been observed (as by Freud, during the broadly anti-Semitic period of the Dreyfus Trial and the rest of the prologue to World War I in Europe) to be uncontrollably given to telling anti-Semitic jokes; or Negroes — at the present embattled moment of their struggle for social equality in the white host-nations,

217

particularly in America, where they find themselves exiled — who affect the telling of Negro-White jokes. (See, for a group of these, and a rather poor analysis, D. J. Bennett's "The Psychological Meaning of Anti-Negro Jokes," in *Fact,* New York, March 1964, vol. 1, no. 2: p. 53–9.) Most jokes of this type told by Negroes are, in any case, virulently anti-white.

As noted in the Introduction, it cannot, of course, be overlooked that the telling of sexual jokes *to* women by men is certainly and inevitably a preliminary sexual relation and represents a definite sexual approach, just as listening to (or telling) such jokes by women implies a readiness for or acceptance of such an approach. The telling of jokes in company also assists in this, since the permissive group often present at joke-telling sessions also allows of a much greater sexual denudation of all concerned than a woman might permit to a more or less strange man alone. When the group or party then breaks up into the usual twosomes, it is more difficult for the woman to backtrack to a shocked or virginal pose of sexual refusal. A refusal at that point cannot be couched in moral terms and must be based on a more insulting personal rejection, which is not always easy to negotiate. Both sexes count on this contractational value of public sexual discussion or humor in making easier the male 'attack' and female 'submission,' if the whole thing has not been achieved in some satisfactory symbolic way during the joke-telling itself. In this latter sense, the persistent anti-woman tone of so many jokes may be considered to serve the neurotic homosexual need implied in the rejection of the woman, but difficult for men operating under the virile ideals of this culture to express publicly in any other way than as a joke.

The British poet, Herbert Farjeon, puts the matter of the permissive situation in a bitter little poem on music-hall and 'cabaret' singers:

> To the bees and the breeze and the trees, no doubt,
>   A kitchenmaid heart responds,
> But when men who are really men go out
>   With blondes who are really blondes,
>
>> You give 'em smut,
>> You give 'em dirt,
>> In a nice white tie
>> And a nice white shirt,

> And they'll clap you loud,
> They'll clap you long,
> Till you give 'em a dirtier
> Dirty song.

(This possibly refers to the singing of limericks with the audience chorus-line, "*Sing us another one — worse than the other one!*" and itself seems to take its opening from just such a song, of the 1920's, satirizing short skirts: "*The breezes, the breezes, they blow through the treeses, They blow the chemises, and through the girls' kneeses; The college boy seeses* [seizes?] *and dooes what he pleases, Which causes diseases, by Jesus, by Jesus!*") Quoting Farjeon's verse, in *The Sense of Humour* (London, 1954), Stephen Potter — of *Gamesmanship* fame — sums the matter up acidly: 'We do not laugh at sex jokes if they are not funny, unless other people are present. It is possible to roar with laughter at a very minute impropriety if it is delivered from the stage to an auditorium the size of the Palladium. We laugh even at bad sex jokes if we are young and virginal, to show we are not young and virginal . . .'

Sexual conversation or discussion *in public* is always felt, and often used, to create a permissive sexual situation. The attack on the theatre has always been based in part on the quasi-aphrodisiacal tone imparted to the audience by any free & easy handling of sexual materials on the stage, from the waving of monster-sized leather penises painted red on the Greek comic stage and in the Italian *commedia dell'arte* street performances (see Jacques Callot's *Balli di Sfessania,* 1622, as the most open modern illustration of this), to the bedroom farce and theatrical burlesque that have become standard in the European and English theatre since the mid-17th century. There is also the historical connection between prostitution and the theatre, once perfectly open, as late as the orange-girl period of the Restoration and after, but now more expensively disguised as the sinful availability of chorus-girls, moving-picture extras, and models of all sexes.

The sexual approach, as the theatrical skit and modern joke view it, consists primarily of a veering of the conversation into jestingly sexual channels by the man. Hamlet's jokes to Ophelia about lying in her lap, and 'country matters' (1st Quarto: 'contrary matters' — the pronunciation hardly matters at all), are typical of the style in which this is done. (*Hamlet,* III.ii.120–130.) Whole interludes of this type, in rude metre, were commonly inserted in Elizabethan plays, under the name of 'jigs,' to keep the audience interested — "he's for a jig or a tale of bawdry, or he sleeps," Hamlet complains, II.ii.522. The study of the form by C. R. Baskervill, *The Elizabethan Jig and related Song Drama* (Chicago, 1929), hardly gives sufficient notice to the jigging scenes of cross-biting conversation throughout Shakespeare's lighter comedies, such as *As You Like It* and *The Taming of the Shrew* (in which latter a number of the jests are given in much less expurgated form in the unrevised First Quarto). As there is some question whether the first *Taming of a Shrew* (1594) is by Shakespeare at all, it may be mentioned that jigging passages of witty insults and interruptions will be found throughout the drama of the period, for instance in the Shakespeare source-play, *The Troublesome Raigne of John, King of England* (1591). The passage referred to is that between Philip and the 'fat Franciscan' friar, which falls at once into the unmistakable stamping rhythm of the jig metre:

> *In nomine Domini,* make I my homily,
> Gentle Gentilitie grieve not the Cleargie . . .

(*Miscellaneous Pieces of Antient English Poesie,* 'by Shakespeare and Marston,' London, 1764, p. 49; also reprinted in the "Bankside" Shakespeare, 1892, XVIII.144.) This type of cross-banter, more often than not still in rhyme, survives in the song & dance interludes of modern comedies. A particularly neat example was the male-protest song "I Can Do Anything You Can Do Better Than You" ('. . . *In nomine Domini,* make I my homily . . .' even the metre hasn't much changed) in the musical-comedy *Annie Get Your Gun,* in which, when the masochist male lead attempts to floor the female-gunner (Annie Oakley) by reminding her that at least she can't fill his pants, she retorts with the sub-scatological "In your hat!"

It is understood that an Ophelia-like innocence in the woman sets off the conversational sexual bravado of the male far better than any knowing acceptance, let alone the eagerness of a gun-toting, man-quelling heroine, as above, to get into the act. In the excursus on "Ophelia's Crime" in Chapter 6. III following, the utter unacceptableness of the character of the sexually dominant female to the patriarchal male will be considered at greater length. It is sufficient to observe here only that the woman is expected to be coy and shamefast while the man reconnoiters her sexual territory with leers and wisecracks;

willing and incautious to the point of imbecility when he progresses to seduction, and capable of experiencing orgasm during rape, when he descends to that. This last point is of far greater importance than may appear on the surface, and has only once, to my knowledge, been ventilated in print, in Ruth Herschberger's blisteringly angry *Adam's Rib* (1948).

I. THE MALE APPROACH

The male approach — to borrow a title from Heinrich Wolf — is based in the English-speaking countries, in jest and in fact, on a number of distressing vulgarities and practicalities, the first of which is that all women are 'available' and have only to be asked. Sexual selection is presumably left entirely in the woman's hands, and is to consist of saying "yes" to all comers. The male superiority which, in a state of biological health, the female demands (obviously inferior males with weak eyes and heavy, horn-rimmed spectacles are now all the decadent rage, as mock-virile), is striven for in jokes almost entirely on a conversational level of the wise-guy, or straw-hat drummer type, vintage 1910. The drummer, or travelling salesman himself, it may be mentioned, has been so much maligned sexually, in his presumable penchant for moronic waitresses and hare-lipped farmers' daughters, that he has fallen away from his super-virile status as conversational rapist to practically a butt. A typical *Saturday Evening Post* cover by Norman Rockwell, August 19, 1950, deals the final blow of depicting him sitting up forlornly in a hotel-room bed, playing symbolic *solitaire* on the side of his sample-case, but one can hardly believe things have changed quite so much as that.

The male approach, in its conversational phase — before rape is attempted — involves a certain parade of sexual notions, representing the still-hidden male genitalia, before the woman's attention. In jokes this is generally done under the humorous pretense that the eroticism lies in what the woman has said, and that the man is merely replying to her lead. Straight verbal rape, or the 'proposition' — there is only one kind of proposition, and it is not a proposal — is apparently the real dream, and everything less forthright represents a concession to female coyness and selectivity. Other forms, the punning proposition, the proposition-in-error, etc., are also encountered in jokes and will be quoted, but they are clearly only *faute de mieux*. Here is the complete dream: *Salesman: "Listen, I'm only in town for a couple of hours, and I can't kid around. Do you screw or don't you?" Girl, shyly: "Well, I don't usually, but you talked me into it."* (N.Y. 1939.)

Modifications are possible, as, for instance, for a favored male. The same dream, but putting even more of the responsibility on the woman: *He: "How's about a quick fuck?" She: (no answer). He: "I said, how's about a quick fuck?" She: (no answer). He: "Whatsamatter, you deef?" She: "Whatsamatter? You tied hand and foot?"* (N.Y. 1953.) The once-famous Ford jokes and Tin-Lizzie labels are represented in the present collection by only one example, demonstrating this point: *A Ford car stops on the highway and will not start. The owner is standing helplessly by when a big Lincoln comes along, stops, and out of it steps Henry Ford. He lifts the hood of the little car, whispers a few words to it, and the motor immediately starts. "How did you do it? What did you say to it?" the owner asks, as Ford gets back into his limousine. "I just said, 'Lizzie, this is Henry. Turn over'."* (1:121.)

Unquestionably the most popular erotic folk-poem in America during World War II was a sort of ode on the impossibility of verbal rape entitled "Ode to the Four Letter Word." This was first encountered in 1942, and the various reproductions of it collected since are an object-lesson in the transmission of erotic folklore. I have seen a typed copy on official stationery of the Canadian Department of National Defence – Army, with printed date '12–43;' two variant mimeographings, a violet ditto copy, and a brownprint, all from typewriting and apparently emanating, on the evidence of the reproduction methods used, from business offices, though of course informally. The "Ode" is printed in *Folk Poems and Ballads* ('Mexico City: Cruciform Press, 1945' [U.S. 1948]) p. 53–4, with the compiler's note, p. 113: 'The present version was given to me by a professor of a large college, on a mimeograph sheet.' (This probably does not refer to two scatological verses printed in this version, but not present in any other form collected.) The climactic fifth verse of the original makes the problem entirely clear, though the dreamed-of solution is replaced by four chaste hyphens:

> *Though a lady repel your advance, she'll be kind*
> *As long as you intimate what's on your mind.*
> *You may tell her you're hungry, you need to be swung;*
> *You may ask her to see how your etchings are hung;*

You may mention the ashes that need to be hauled,
Put the lid on her saucepan; *even* lay's *not too bald.*
But the moment you're forthright, get ready to duck,
For the girl isn't born yet who'll stand for "Let's ----."

Here, according to the evidence of the jokes, are a few girls who did: *An ex-prizefighter who is very successful with women is asked his secret.* "*I just stand on the corner and when the girls pass by I say,* '*Do you fuck?*'" "*Don't you get plenty of slaps in the face?*" "*Sure, but you'd be surprised how much fucking I get too.*" (1:76.) In a variant, *An Indian stands on the street corner saying* "*When*" *to all the good-looking girls. An onlooker asks,* "*Joe, I thought you Indians always said* '*How*'." *The Indian replies:* "*I know how. What I want to know is* when." (Va. 1953.) A connected joke takes a somewhat more realistic view. "*Gee, I feel like screwing that dame again.*" "*What! you mean to tell me you screwed that swell dame?*" "*No, but I felt like it before.*" (1:38. Encountered in magazines several times in a cleaned-up aggressive variant: "*I feel like punching that guy in the nose again.*") Even more self-pitying: "*I wish I had a nickel for every girl I ever laid.*" "*What would you do?*" "*Buy a pack of gum.*" (N.Y. 1946. Nightclub squelch line, collected the same year: "*Here's a nickel. Go call up all your friends.*")

As the "Ode" quoted above indicates, nothing but the barest monosyllabic proposition really satisfies the requirements of verbal rape. The rationalization offered is that the male is tired of seduction and its endless skirmishing in the outskirts, or even more frankly, in Ogden Nash's line, that '. . . seduction is for sissies, but a he-man wants his rape!' *Fast worker, in taxi:* "*Let's go up to my apartment and fuck.*" *Chorus-girl, lifting her eyebrow:* "*What, no build-up?*" (2:358.) — *A young man disgraces himself when his first words to his blind date are* "*Let's fuck.*" *His friend takes him behind the car to explain things.* "*First you talk about books, the theatre,*" *he says;* "*and* then *you lead into the proposition.*" *The young man gets back into the car and tries again.* "*Read any good books lately?*" "*No,*" *says the girl.* "*Seen any shows?*" "*No, I haven't.*" "*Neither have I. Let's fuck.*" (1:374.) Same situation: *The young man in the rumble seat says nothing to his blind date while the couple in front are necking madly. Finally the girl taps the other couple on the shoulder.* "*Say, what kind of a dummy did you fix me up with? I thought you said he went to college.*" "*Sure he goes to college. Hey, Harry, say something to the girl." Harry, with marked rising inflection: "Fuck?"* (Penna. 1935, stated to be a true incident.) Finally, a semi-patriotic version, fixing the verbal ungallantry on: *A Russian soldier riding through New England next to a Wac. "Nize country, America." The Wac nods disinterestedly. Miles later, "Nize trees." She nods again. "Nize cow." An indifferent glance. Finally he says, "Enough of dis loff-making. Let's fock."* (D.C. 1945.)

I. BEATING AROUND THE BUSH

Shakespeare points out, in *As You Like It,* V.iv.100, how even those worst of quarrels stemming from the Lie Direct can be avoided, 'with an If . . . as "If you said *so,* then I said *so"* . . . Your If is the only peace-maker; much virtue in If.' This is just as true of the sexual proposition as of the 'unconsciously' homosexual duelling proposition. It can be so phrased that it is only a proposition if . . . All responsibility can be placed upon the woman. Her innocent remark is not innocent, or has been misconstrued by elaborate accident, and so forth. The man is ready to apologize if . . . There are possibilities of danger and embarrassment to the man in the unprovoked, monosyllabic Proposition Direct. The punning proposition is the second line of attack. Even this is not altogether safe. Not all women can be counted on to reply with only the pointedly modest unknowingness of Ophelia, who answers Hamlet's "Do you think I meant country matters?" with "I think nothing, my Lord," and when he puns further on her 'nothing': "That's a fair thought to lie between maids' legs." "What is, my Lord?" "Nothing" — probably holding up his thumb & forefinger in the yonijic *O,* as noted by Professor Thomas Pyles in "Ophelia's 'Nothing'," *Modern Language Notes,* 1949, vol. 64: p. 322–3 — satisfies herself simply with "You are merry, my Lord." Swift, in his *Polite Conversation* (1738), an almost untapped treasury of folk-wit and catch-phrases, shows a later Miss of quite a different cut.

> *Miss:* If you please, my Lord, a Bit of Undercrust.
> *Neverout* (whispers to Miss): I find you love to lie under.
> *Miss* (aloud): What does the Man mean? Sir, I don't understand you at all. (Dialogue I, ed. 1743, p. 111.)

And again, when Neverout presumes to ask her, "Pray Miss, how do you look when you lye?" (Dialogue III, ed. 1743, p. 142), she snaps him up in rhyme:

Miss: Better than you when you cry. Manners, indeed! I find you mend like sour Ale in summer.

Neverout: I beg your pardon, Miss; I only meant, when you lie alone.

Miss: That's well turn'd; one turn more would have turn'd you down stairs.

In the same way, a whole group of jokes on punning sexual propositions exists in which the ostensible point of the joke (in some versions) is to explain how the man got a black eye. *A man is asked how he got his black eye. "Well," he explains, "my stenographer came in today and said she had a new position." "So?" "So I said, 'Did you lock the door?'"* (1:101. Black-eye version, N.Y. 1939.) — *The Widow Brown is talking to Mr. Murphy. "I was looking at my stomach the other day," she says, "and there's hardly a wrinkle in it, outside the one I was born with." Mr. Murphy observes that his stomach has no wrinkles at all. "Well mine is nicer," snaps the widow. "Oh, is it?" says Murphy; "I'll put mine against it any day!"* (1:347, the editor adding: *Please omit flowers.*) In a modified form, this sort of situation is used to explain a broken engagement. *A young man and his fiancée are sitting on a sofa. He notices the cat playing with a tassel and says daringly, "After we're married that's what you'll be doing to me." She looks down, and slaps him in the face. The cat is now licking its tail.* (1:283.)

Here is a simple jigging misinterpretation into sexuality of something a woman has said, followed by a variant (probably the original form) in which the conversational 'honors' go to the woman instead. Both are based on an animal-voyeuristic situation similar to the preceding. *Farm-hand: "How do you like the country?" City girl: "Oh, just grand. I milked the cows and everything!" Farm-hand: "Golly, that must have been a surprise to the bulls!"* (Minn. 1935.) Compare: *A young man in the country takes his father's cow to the neighboring farmer's bull. As he is watching the animals mating, he sees the farmer's daughter watching too. "Some bull," he says. The girl nods. "Sure does a good job." She nods again. "Believe me, I'd like to be doing what that bull is doing!" "Why don't you?" she says, "it's your cow."* (1:416. Compare also, for the form, the Russian soldier and the Wac.)

The punch-line is supposed to floor and destroy the person spoken to. This point has been made before, but must not be lost sight of. The old standbys in the punning proposition field do not give this weapon to the woman. Sometimes she hardly speaks at all. *A woman leans out the window just before dawn and calls to the milkman: "Have you the time?" "Sure, lady, but who'll hold my horse?"* (Pa. 1935. Also collected as a catch-phrase reply to the same question: *"Yes, but not the inclination."* The possible reference here to the angle of erection is doubtless accidental.) — *Scene, a Scottish stagecoach with two girls on top. It begins to rain. The driver sticks his head over the side and calls out to the men inside: "Is there a mackintosh in there to cover a couple of girls up here in the rain?" "No, but there's a MacGregor that's willing to try!"* (*Memorabilia*, 1910. The same pun occurs in John Donne's Elegie XIX, "To his Mistris Going to Bed" (MS. 1595): 'To teach thee, I am naked first; why then, What needst thou have more covering than a man.') — *A painter, arriving the second day on the job, is met by the lady of the house in negligée. "Oh, Mr. Painter," she says, "I'd like you to come upstairs and see where my husband put his hand last night." "If it's all the same to you, lady," says the painter, "I got a day's work to do on that ladder. Couldn't we just settle for a cigar?"* (Baker, 1945, vol. II.) In a Yiddish form, collected earlier, *the painter replies, "Look, lady, I'm an old man. How about just gimme a gless tea?"*

2. PROPOSITIONS IN ERROR

There is a nice distinction to be made between errors and misunderstandings of the pure fool type, and those in which we have merely the pretense of folly as a cover under which an erotic proposition is made or prepared. "If you said *so*, then I said *so* . . . much virtue in If." Certain jokes purportedly about fools or children are perfectly obvious importations of sexual images by the presumable fool. *"Mama, may I go out to play?" "What! With those holes in your pants?" "No, with the girl next door."* (*Happy Days*, Nov. 20, 1937, p. 8. There is possibly an additional masturbatory implication on 'playing with oneself' through the holes in one's pants — 'pocket pool.') In a connected joke, often publicly printed in the 1940's, the child and adult-in-error both subserve the hidden sexual approach: *A little boy has torn his pants climbing a tree and is ordered upstairs by his mother while she mends them. Some time later she hears a noise in the cellar and calls down, "Are you running around down there without your pants on?" "No, Ma'am," replies a male voice, "I'm reading the gas-meter."* Purposeful perversions of this kind will be discussed further in the following section. The *cellar* is always sexually toned in folklore.

During the 1950's, a 'new' type of *sick-joke* became popular in America, almost always beginning with a child's question similar to the formula-line, *"Mama* (or *Daddy), can I go out and play?"* as in the joke just quoted from *Happy Days,* of date 1937. But now there is no real colloquy, the travesty-parent's reply being invariably some crushing gruesomeness, unveiling an entirely different situation than the innocent one which the child's question implies. That these sick-jokes are intended as bitter criticisms of parents' authority, and *'the mess they've made of things,'* does not need to be underlined; but it should not be overlooked that the jokes conjure up, and revel and grovel in much worse messes than any normal parent ever contemplates. (Yes, yes, the Atom Bomb.) Brian Sutton-Smith has presented some of these jokes in "'Shut Up and Keep Digging': The Cruel Joke Series," in *Midwest Folklore* (1960) x. 11–22, and some rather less expurgated examples will be found at the opening of Chapter 14, in the Second Series here, in the section on Dysphemism. The form is no longer strictly American, one of the nastiest appearing in the Scottish folklife magazine, *Chapbook* (Aberdeen, 1967) vol. IV, No. 3, p. 6, in an article, "Bawdry, Cancer or Cure?" by James Addison, noting that 'if we laugh at good, honest bawdry, surely this must be chalked to the credit side, particularly at the expense of "sick" jokes such as: *"Mummy, mummy, may I lick the bowl out?" "No, pull the chain like everyone else".'*

When used as seductions, tendentious errors require situations in which a man and a woman strange to each other, and therefore presumably erotically desirable and exciting to each other, can reasonably meet, and thus set off to best effect the somewhat unseasonable candor of the man's remarks. Shops of all types, and services (such as the telephone) are particularly apt locales. *A girl in a florist's shop is shocked when a customer asks for a bastard, and is told that this is the scientific name of a certain flower.* (Obviously a *hardware* shop and a certain kind of *file* are intended.) *The next customer who asks for this flower simply points to it. "You mean you want one of those bastards?" she says helpfully. "Yes, and while you're at it, give me that son-of-a-bitch over there."* (Calif. 1952.) This is not a proposition, of course, but the direction of the conversation is unmistakable. Perfectly openly: *Manicurist, to her male customer: "Shall I skin back the cuticle for you?" "No, just kiss me, honey, and it'll take care of itself."* (D.C. 1952. The metaphor of 'pushing his cuticle back' is also used in a party record, *"Rasputin,"* made about 1946.)

Cognizance is taken in jokes of the fact that women feel insulted by the sexual overtures of strangers to them. Like such formerly neutral words as 'intercourse' and 'toilet,' the word 'insult' (in reference to a woman) is nowadays immediately assumed to involve some tabooed phrase or activity. *A Negro woman mistakes a photographic ad, "Use Relox Paper," as meaning toilet paper, and asks for it in a drugstore. Clerk: "What size is your Brownie?"* (1:480.) In a related joke, *A drugstore clerk is slapped by a woman customer who cannot decide between two pastel shades of toilet paper, when he says, "Take the green. It goes good with brown."* (Illinois, 1930. Note the Negro reference has been omitted, but only by moving on to strict scatology.) — *A man becomes angry at the telephone operator and tells her to stick the telephone up her ass. The next day two workmen appear and begin disconnecting the phone. He pleads with them that he needs the phone in his business. They suggest that he call up the operator and apologize. After much difficulty he gets the insulted operator on the wire. "Are you the operator I told to stick the telephone up your ass?" Operator, very icily: "Yes . . . ?" "Well, there's two men here to take it out."* (1:452.)

The anonymous and obscene telephone-call — an exhibitionist or verbal or mechanized poison-pen letter — has been a public problem ever since the invention of the telephone, and became an uncontrollable menace in large cities such as New York by the middle 1960's if not earlier. Mark Twain had already alluded, at the turn of the century, to the convenience of the telephone for saying *inconvenient* things (in "Travelling with a Reformer"), and this 'safe' format has an obvious appeal to the sado-masochists who make the obscene phone-calls. The modern French poet, Pierre Louÿs, who is believed to have died insane from the use of drugs (this is probably intended as an excuse!), is reported to have made endless such calls toward the end of his life, in the 1920's, to women whose names he picked *for their beauty* from the Paris telephone directory. A poet to the last. With this is to be compared his gruellingly sado-masochistic erotic poetry, written in the 1890's, none of which was published until after his death, and his very similar erotic novel, *Trois Filles de leur mère.* Almost all of Louÿs' erotica is in the form of obscene banter with (or by) women, and his openly-published *Adventures of King Pausole* is hardly more than a polite version of the same.

The party records of the 1940's leaned heavily on the *double-entendre* shop or service situation. Many earlier recitations and printed
novelties or obscœna were dressed up in dialogue form, when not already so cast, and were recorded for the phonograph with suitable
sound-effects and label names, such as T.N.T. (for "Tunes 'n' Titters")
and similar. Examples: *The photographer who is mistaken by the
housewife for a state inseminator, and who offers to do the desired job
on top of a bus, or even in the park if the squirrels don't nibble at his
equipment. — The girl who wants to buy a rake but does not know its
name, and describes it as "a long thing, about this thick around, and it
has teeth at one end," to which the storekeeper replies, "Well, you can
put teeth on it."* There are at least half a dozen real jokes, transmitted
as jokes, cast in this burlesque dialogue form, which survives since at
least the days of the Elizabethan jig. *A man accidentally gets into a
sewing-machine office instead of a call-house. "What kind would you
like?" asks the girl attendant. "Well, how much are they?" he counters. "Some are fifty dollars and some are a hundred." "Go on," he says,
"I got one last time for twenty bucks." "Oh," says the girl, "that must
be the kind you screw on the table." "No, ma'am! I screwed this one
in bed!"* (1:132. Actually made into a party record, about 1942. In the
earliest form collected, from Idaho, 1919, a variant ending is given:
*"Oh, those," says the girl, "they're the ones that don't have any legs.
You have to screw them on the table." "Shucks," says the man, "I
don't object to the table part, but durned if I can stomach screwing one
without legs."*) Mostly this joke remains current in the completely decayed version of a mere definition: WIFE, *A gadget you screw on the
bed to get the housework done.* This has also been collected redone in
pidgin English as a "Confucius say . . ."

*Woman customer in record store: "Do you have Hot-Lips on a ten-
inch Decca?" Fresh salesman: "No, but I've got hot nuts on a ten-inch
pecker." "Is that a record?" "Maybe not, but it's well above average."*
(Calif. 1942, and collected also D.C. 1944, and N.Y. 1952. In the form
originally collected, the recording wanted is called "Hot Lips and
Seven Kisses," and the mistake rises from crossed telephone wires giving her a garage instead of a record store, a typical situational dodge
in novelty obscœna of the 1920's.) Another pun on the same word,
'pecker,' is based on its use in polite circles — as also 'spunk,' and sometimes even 'gism,' both actually referring to the semen — as meaning

courage or strength. *A boatload of American soldiers is met by British girls shouting, "Keep your pecker up, chum!" American soldier: "Keep my pecker up? Listen, babe, if I don't get the old meat dunked pretty soon, they'll be using it for a radio antenna."* (Minn. 1946.) The absolute end in the conversational male approach in the shop or service situation is quoted here exactly as collected from a spastic in California, 1940: '*A war-veteran in a perpetual palsy ordered a sundae in a drugstore. "Chocolate?" asked the waitress, and he quivered horribly, leered, and stuttered, "Y-yes." "Lots of syrup?" Shaking hideously, he replied: "Y-yes." "Whipped cream?" "Y-yes." "Crushed nuts?" The veteran shook insanely, as he answered: "No. Shell-shock."*' One is reminded of the sage advice given by the booking agent to the desperate vaudevillian who offered to commit suicide on the stage. "It's no good," said the agent. *"What would you do for an encore?"* (For the original mock-handbill as to suicide on the stage, see William Jefferson's *Selection of Curiosities of Literature,* York, 1795, p. 276.)

In situations that are actually sexual, or that involve sexual organs or institutions, such as marriage, it is not necessary to go to such excruciating lengths to import the erotic tone into the conversation. *A drunk stumbles into the women's toilet by mistake, and pulls open the door of an occupied booth. The woman sitting there cries, "This is for ladies only." " So is this," says the drunk, waggling his penis at her, "but do you mind if I pass a little beer through it?"* (D.C. 1943, collected as a wall inscription in a U.S.O. French form, earlier.) This is a very good example of the greater power of the situation in jokes than of the mere pun or gag used as punch-line. The whole joke has really been delivered here before a word is said. Compare the mere froth of: *Visitor at a nudist camp: "Isn't that Dick Brown?" Guide: "No, just a little sunburned"* (Fla. 1949), with the far more subtle 'importation of the erotic' in a joke printed publicly several times in the 1940's: *Young man at dinner with his maiden aunt: "You don't want a drink, do you, Auntie?" "Yes, thank you, I'll have a martini." "Why I thought you belonged to the W.C.T.U." "No, dear boy; it's the Society for the Suppression of Vice." "I knew there was something I shouldn't offer you!"*

Many other examples could be given on all subjects used in jokes to show this continuous battle between the really meaningful situation, and the shallow verbal wit of the punch-line accepted nowadays as the crucial part of the joke. *A young man phones to cancel a date, explaining that he mashed his finger at work. "The whole finger?" asks his girl anxiously. "No, the one next to the hole finger."* (N.Y. 1942.) As with the crushed-nuts 'joke' above, this actually belongs in the chapter on the castration theme, and it is that theme, and not the pun, that makes both examples meaningful to the tellers.

Compare again the far richer background elements in the following stories than the punning end-lines would warrant if they were really the essential part. *A girl at college gets the money out of her father to buy a pet monkey by pretending that she wants to buy a bicycle. Later the animal gets sick, and she forgets her story and telegraphs:* SEND TWENTY DOLLARS FOR THE DOCTOR. THE HAIR IS COMING OUT OF MY MONKEY. *Her father telegraphs back:* SELL THE GODDAM BICYCLE. (Minn. 1946.) Is this a building up to a pun on the word 'monkey,' or is it a little chiaroscuro drama of the Elektra relation between the pubescent daughter and her father — of his incestuous fantasies about her changing body, and the little lies she must tell, and the medical attentions pay for, in the process of moving away from her father and toward some younger man?

In the same way, is the next story really only an elaborately built-up pun on a transient colloquial phrase (as will be seen), or is it a mocking, with the probability of failure, of the sub-erotic conversation of high-ranking brass presuming to deny erotic relief to the lower ranks? Which is the real point? *Marine Officer to Wac Major: "I want you to keep those Wacs of yours locked up when we bring in those two thousand Marines tonight. They haven't seen a woman for eleven months." Wac Major: "You don't have to worry about my girls. They've got it up here (tapping herself on the forehead)." Marine Officer: "I don't care where they've got it — those boys will find it."* (N.Y. 1952.)

3 · PURPOSEFUL PERVERSION

Purposeful perversion of what a woman has said, without any pretense of error or misunderstanding, is a long step closer to a direct attempt at seduction or rape. The man no longer hides behind an If, he no longer pretends that it is she who is bringing sex onstage and trying to seduce him. Jokes of this type generally are somewhat flatfooted, and lacking in wit, being based on simple homonymous puns. As has been noted, they also operate on the vulgarian principle that all women are willing, at all hours of the day, and have only to be asked. As such, they do not deal in nuance, but offer what is actually a knock-down-&-drag-out insult to the woman on the assumption that its sexual nature makes it a seductive remark. An older example of this technique, or lack of technique, may be quoted again: *"What makes you walk so stiff, Mame?"* *"I've got on patent-leather shoes, and patent-leather draws."* *"Oh you have, eh?"* *"It does!"* (*Memorabilia*, 1910. This antiquated, *r*-dropping pun still survives in the humorous postcard caption, under a picture of an individual in long winter underwear: 'The nights are getting longer — winter draws on.')

Certain ostensible fool-jokes or children jokes far too purposely pervert the 'teacher's' remarks to be accepted at face value. *Teacher: "Yes, children, a cold shower every morning will make you feel rosy all over. Now are there any questions?" Voice from the back: "Yeah, teacher, tell us more about Rosie."* (Baker, 1947, v.3.) In a reversal of the usual sexual rôles, equally improbable: *Two M.P.'s* [Military Police] *notice two Wacs strolling along the street after midnight, and stop them, asking: "Aren't you out after hours?" "I don't know,"* says one of the *Wacs, "but I'll bet you're out after ours."* (D.C. 1944.) This simply revamps, on a wartime background, a college-humor line of some five years earlier. With it may be compared another college joke of the same period, which simply rolls in the pea-green sophomoric pleasures of homonymy. *Two college boys take two college girls twenty miles out of town in their car. They park, and explain that this is a "Hereafter" date: "If you aren't here after what we're here after, you're going to be here after we're gone."* (Revived by Davis, *Playgirls, U.S.A.*, 1956, p. 14, as of a movie-director and 'unsuspecting playgirl,' whatever that may mean.) More will be said later on these standard alternatives of highway rape.

The standard semi-prostitute of folklore is the waitress, with the manicurist running a poor second. As the new American Lesbianism progresses we must expect a similar development of folklore about the hairdresser or beauty-operator, the standard Lesbian prostitute since classical antiquity. The profession is at the moment still dominated by male homosexuals, on an identification basis. — *Waitress, bending over the counter: "What'll you have?" 1st Customer: "Raisin pie." 2nd Customer: "Same here." 3rd Customer, looking at her breasts: "Mine's raisin' too."* (1:141. Variant, collected D.C. 1944, with the waitress asking the last customer, *"Is yours raisin?" "Check and double-check!"*) That these perversions of what has been said are really assaults and not seductions — and assaults in the aggressive rather than erotic sense —

is made rather clear in the most commonly collected waitress joke, in which the point is strictly one of sexual rejection, presumably just for the sake of a wisecrack. *A steady customer always studies the menu carefully and then orders ham & eggs. The waitress hands him the menu one morning, after marking his favorite dish, saying: "I scratched something you like." Customer, without looking up: "Go wash your hands and bring me some ham & eggs."* (1:278.)

In a number of older jokes the technique of purposeful perversion is used in conversations between men, strictly as insults or conversational victories, on the style of the 18th-century 'catches' in which the victim is artfully led to ask a question that can be answered with the insulting "My arse!" The following is one of many stories invariably ascribed to Lincoln, as modern erotic ballads are usually ascribed, with equal improbability, to A. P. Herbert. *"Permit me to introduce my family, Mr. Lincoln,"* says an admirer. *"My wife, Mrs. Bates. My daughter, Miss Bates. My son, Master Bates." Lincoln: "Make him stop. It's a bad habit."* (1:340. Variant, 1933: *"Why brag about it?"*) — *Two men are in a boat that starts to leak. One tries to plug up the hole, but complains that he has trouble finding it under water. The other: "You wouldn't have any trouble if it had hair around it."* (N.Y. 1939. Also in *Kryptádia*, 1884, vol. II, from Wales. This is used as a catch-phrase to anyone fumbling with a keyhole, and the keyhole situation has often been milked for laughs by older male comics, as W. C. Fields' funnel device for getting the key into the hole when drunk, and, most recently, by Charlie Chaplin, in the drunk scene opening his next-to-last movie, *Limelight.* 'Novelty' fur-covered car-ignition keyhole, U.S. 1968.)

The utter uselessness, in seduction, of offensive remarks — again understanding the word in the aggressive rather than erotic sense — makes it unnecessary to underline the element of verbal sadism in these approaches. In the section following, on "The Sadistic Concept of Coitus," the more aggravated verbal violences in connection with sexual acts will be considered. Such examples as are given here are apparently just love-taps. *The inspector in a war factory hears a woman say to a man, "Hand me that wrench, jerk." He objects to her swearing and she says, "Why that's his name. He's my husband." Inspector: "You shouldn't have told me that. It's against the rules for a husband and wife to work together here. Now I'll either have to lay you or Jerk off."* (N.Y. 1944. Also as Jack and Jill, by 1965.) In *The Hills Beyond* (1941) by Thomas Wolfe, who died in 1938, a Negro plantation story is given of *A woman who evinces an interest in a wagonload of peanuts being hauled by a jackass. The planter calls to the driver: "Hey boy, back your ass over here and show the lady your nuts."*

In a pretended reversal of this sort of erotic conversation, done in pantomime, *A streetcar conductor is conversing in gestures with a deaf & dumb woman. She thumbs her nose. He double-thumbs his. He points to her breast and genitals. She points to her buttocks. Later one of the other passengers asks what it meant. "She asked me if the fare was five cents," says the conductor, "and I said it was ten. Then I asked her if she wanted to get off at the dairy or the ballpark, and she said to let her off at the gas works."* (N.Y. 1941.) This is a very old formula, the contest-in-gestures, and Jewish anti-Christian stories of the kind still exist (Aarne Types 924A and B), presumably dating from the period of the Spanish Inquisition and the expulsion of the Arabs and Jews from Spain in 1492. Neither Aarne (Type 924) nor Thompson, *Motif-Index,* H607, makes any reference to what is really the *locus classicus* on the subject, Rabelais' two entire chapters devoted to the contest-in-gestures, which are masterpieces of drollery and of utterly correct folk-observation: *Pantagruel* (published in 1532) Bk. II, chap. 19, "How Panurge put to a non-plus the Englishman, that argued by signs;" and Bk. III, chap. 20, "How Goatsnose by signs maketh answer to Panurge." The latter takes off from a discussion of the sign-language of the dumb, in chapter 19, with a joke concerning *Sister Fatbum, a nun who is found to be pregnant and claims she was raped, but did not dare to cry for help owing to the convent rule of silence. Instead she tried to call the other nuns by means of gestures . . . 'with her buttocks she made a sign unto them as vigorously as she could, yet never one of them did so much as offer to come to her help and assistance.'* Possibly original with Rabelais, this joke is still very much alive in English. The modern form, on *the girl who claims to the lawyer that she was raped, but did not cry out so as not to wake her mother,* will be found in the chapter on "The Sadistic Concept," 5.1.

Another formula, of the story told in mis-applied brand names (usually of whiskeys or cigarettes), or in the titles of popular songs or plays taken in a *double-entendre* sense, which dates from the 1890's at the latest, is made use of in a different streetcar story-without-words. *A woman, obviously pregnant, complains to the conductor that a male passenger is laughing at her. The passenger explains that the woman sat down first under an advertising poster saying: "The Gold-Dust Twins Are Coming." When he smiled, she moved away and sat under a sign saying: "Johnson's Shaving Stick Did This." When he tittered, she moved under a sign reading: "Kelly's Rubbers Could Have Prevented It." Then he burst out laughing.* (Printed novelty card, U.S. 1940, probably dating originally about 1920.)

Since the woman in both of these does not even speak, it is difficult to pretend that she has provoked erotic insult. Observe how a built-in provocation is created in order to excuse the verbal annihilation of the woman chosen as the butt: *A woman bothers the greengrocer for onions during a wartime scarcity. She refuses to believe there are none, and accuses him of hiding them for the better-spending customers. Exasperated, he finally says, "Listen, lady, it ain't up to me. Who put the straw in strawberries? Who put the punk in punkins, and the bees in beeswax? And who put the fuck in onions?" Woman: "There ain't no fuck in onions." Grocer: "That's what I been trying to tell you!"* (N.Y. 1943.) On the same background: *A woman pulls a pickle out of the pickle-barrel three times, and each time asks to have it weighed and priced, hoping to beat the grocer down. The third time he says: "Lady! It's a pickle; it ain't a putz. It don't get bigger and it don't get smaller. The price is fifteen cents!"* (N.Y. 1940.)

Finally, pretended provocations by the woman. In the first example, mere effeteness: *Sporting Woman (soprano): "Waiter, wipe my plate off with a lemon peel. And give me a cup of coffee mild as a lily. And won't you please tell me what* hard-*workin' guy that is sitting over there?" Cowboy (basso robusto): "Waiter, scrub my ass with a brickbat. Gimme a cup of coffee strong as jackass piss, with the foam farted off. 'N' tell me who that damn whoor is sittin' over there."* (Brooklyn waterfront lunchroom, 1949, marvellously recited by a Texas Negro laborer on a barge.) — *A man has the habit of telling dirty jokes to women. They decide to cure him by all walking away the next time he starts. He joins the group and begins at once: "A boatload of whores is sailing for Italy ——" They all walk away. "Don't leave," he shouts after them, "the boat doesn't sail till* 10 A.M." (N.Y. 1948.) A version of this is reported to have been worked into an auditorium lecture by a New York college professor, resulting in his near-dismissal. *"We don't use books for this course,"* the professor announced. *"We use maps. Here, for instance (touching the map of Africa): the men in this country have penises ten inches long. (A girl student gets up and starts to leave.) Where are you going? The boat doesn't leave till morning!"* (N.Y. 1949.)

II. THE PRIMACY OF COITUS

The primacy of coitus, the idea that it is more important than anything else in the world, is the second of the folklore principles of the male approach, the first being that all women are available as partners, and have only to be asked. The best statement of this principle is the joke quoted in the chapter on Children, earlier, about the boy who is sent home from school for announcing that "Fucking is the most wonderful thing in the world," and who cannot get a letter of apology from his father because his father agrees — *and so must everyone else.* As generally presented, however, the idea of primacy is not concerned with the comparative value of sexual pleasure, but with having it precede and replace every other interest at all times. As such, it is seen to be more a part of the super-virile pose than an unrepressed expression of the sexual urge, in the sense implied by the burlesque comedian's dropping whatever he is doing, erecting his red fright-wig, and pursuing the passing blonde. Harpo Marx' comedy specialty was this 'id' routine, yet everyone knew that — certainly in his film character — he would really drop the blonde for a harp. The truest view of the facts is probably that taken by: *The American being shown the portrait of the founder of the family who asks, "What did he do in the daytime?"* Everyone does something in the daytime, and the sex life as it is really lived begins to shape up only as the sun goes down.

So much for the facts. The jokes insist flatly on the primacy principle. *Two stately Southern colonels alight from a train in Alabama, their white beards blowing in the wind. "Well, Stephen," says one, "shall we check in at a hotel, or go directly to the whore-house?"* (2:38.) The original *Anecdota Americana* [1927] opens with a key anecdote — it is hardly a joke — making the same point. *"All aboard!" the conductor calls, and the train starts. A salesman enters the pullman smoking compartment. "Gentlemen," he says, "is there any reason why we shouldn't begin to talk cunt right away?"* (1:1.)

These are the travellers away from home. The returning traveller is, if anything, even more definite about it. *"Am I a good cook?" says the wife. "Why, my husband is crazy about my apple pie. When he comes home from the road it's the second thing he asks for!"* (1:320, a *fleischige* version on pot roast.) A spelled-out variant or allusion appears in the *Leatherneck* for February 1945, p. 53: '*Hot showers head the list of luxuries Marines want most when they go home. Yes, we said first on the list — since when is a girl a luxury?'* Similarly, in an obscœnum circulated at about the same period (and also recorded for the phonograph) in which: *The heroic aviator, Lieut. Rudder (jg) is being interviewed by the press, with Cmdr. Eager Beaver of Navy Public Relations interpreting for him, when the press asks: "What's the first thing you're going to do in New York, Lieutenant?" Jaygee: "Get laid." As rephrased for publication by Cmdr. Beaver, this becomes: "Yes, Lt. Rudder can't wait to get back to his mother's apple pie."* The whole parody interview is excellently done, and it is a pity it does not exist in print.

The most popular joke on primacy of coitus during World War II was first collected in California, 1942, on a neutral background, but is principally retold in a Russian ski-trooper form given in Bennett Cerf's *Pocket Book of War Humor* (1943) p. 184. *Two Russian ski-troopers are conversing. "What's the first thing you're going to do when you get home?" "Do you have to ask?" "Well, what's the second thing you're going to do?" "I'm going to take off these goddam skis!"* (In Milton Caniff's servicemen's comic-strip, "Male Call," one sequence published in 1944 shows two sailors walking down the dock from their ship. One is saying, "And the SECOND thing I'm gonna do is to get into a pair of LOOSE PANTS.")

These are not strictly World War II jokes. At least one can be shown to have been revived from World War I: *A soldier is returning home, and his wife is waving to him from the dock. He shouts, "F.F." She shakes her head and calls back, "E.F." This goes back and forth several times. F.F. E.F. — F.F. E.F. Finally one of his buddies asks, "What's this F.F., E.F. business?" "Oh, you know how women are. She wants to eat first."* (N.Y. 1941. This joke is alluded to, by the code letters only, in Robert Paul Smith's *Because of My Love*, in the 1940's, a sort of mechanized Lizzie Borden love-story about a girl who accidentally cuts open her father's head with a buzz-saw.)

Another popular World War II number of earlier date: *A newcomer to Washington, confused by the red tape, phones down to the hotel desk: "Send me up a blonde, a bedpan, and a violin — I don't know whether I want to diddle, piddle, or fiddle."* (N.Y. 1942.) First collected, California, 1941, as a simple riddle: *"If Nero fiddled while Rome burned, what did he do to put it out? — He piddled."* A version from Guam, 1948, changes the bedpan to a block of wood (whittle, not piddle). In Washington, D.C., in the summer of 1952, and since, the

most popular novelty item, offered at the change counter in practically
every downtown drugstore-luncheonette, was a realistic little figurine
— sometimes a plaque — showing a man sitting on the toilet, with the
caption: "The only man in Washington who knows what he's doing."

*A lieutenant, a sergeant, and a corporal are arguing about sexual
intercourse. The lieutenant says it's ninety percent work and ten percent pleasure. The sergeant says it's ten percent work and ninety percent pleasure. The corporal says it's about fifty-fifty. They decide to ask
the first person who comes along. A buck private comes along, and
answers their question without hesitation: "It's a hundred percent
pleasure, because if there was any work to it, at all, you'd make us
privates do it for you."* (N.Y. 1939.) In a similar decision dating from
the 16th century, *A man is told that he will lose his hearing if he continues to have relations with women. A few months later the doctor
examines him again and finds his hearing even worse. "Well," says the
man, "I laid off women for two months, but nothing I was hearing
made me feel half as good."* (N.Y. 1942. This is Rotunda's novella-motif
J2567*, "Thankful Fools," citing Carbone's *Facezie,* No. 100.)

Many jokes current among non-Jews involve simple Yiddish words
for the sexual organs and acts, but few discuss any religious practice
of Judaism other than circumcision. The following story is very exceptional in its involving the Jewish method of silently rocking back
& forth on the heels — *dovening* — while praying. *A salesman is given
a room in a crowded hotel with a rabbi. He finds the rabbi dovening
in a corner, rocking on his heels and praying in an undertone. "I'm
your new roommate," says the salesman. The rabbi nods without
speaking. "Which bed shall I take?" The rabbi points to one of the
beds, continuing to pray. The salesman unpacks his suitcase, and then
blurts out, "Say, do you mind if I bring up a girl?" The rabbi holds up
two fingers.* (Minn. 1946.) Compare Panurge's contests-in-gestures
with Goatsnose and the Englishman, *Pantagruel* (1532) II.19, and
III.20.

III. SEDUCTION

The word 'contrectation,' revived by Albert Moll from its medieval
desuetude, usefully combines all those activities whereby the male and
female attempt to *approach* each other sexually, whether by sight,

smell, touch, or any other sense. The orphan sense, in any such analysis, is generally speech, though in men this is as important for sexual display as bodily ornamentation has become for women. The oafish propositions and jests scheduled above are, in their way, closely related to the more artistic sexual displays of speech in poetry, sermonizing, singing (and music generally), all of which are known, and have always been known, to be of great use in attracting and exciting the woman. This much of the sexual reputation of poets, fashionable ministers, and even tenors, is probably based on fact.

The frontier brags recorded by Mark Twain in *Life on the Mississippi* (1883) and by other writers, solely concern the death-dealing abilities of the braggarts. None of the sexual brags that must have existed concurrently have come down to us except in the matter of penis length (as in the recitation, "Our Lil," discussed in *The Horn Book,* '*And when he laid it on the bar, Stranger, it stretched from thar — to thar!*'), but perhaps some may yet be found. The closest thing to it is the famous burlesque oration, "Change the Name of Arkansaw? God Almighty Damn!" of which all available versions have been courageously recorded in James R. Masterson's *Tall Tales of Arkansas* (Boston, 1942) p. 352–8, with the beginnings of a case for attributing it to Mark Twain. But the Arkansaw speech is strictly a volcanic outporing of verbal sadism and sacrilege — hardly of any use in, or relation to, contrectation. Though nowadays one never knows . . .

Leaving aside, for the moment, brags about penis length, very few contrectational speeches will be found in jokes that could possibly be intended to arouse the woman. The main impulse seems to be to shock and, if possible, frighten her; and were it not for the matching folklore notion that women delight in absorbing the greatest possible length of penis, brags of this type might also be construed as intended to appall. One thing is certain: there is no verbal love-making in jokes (as with the Russian soldier and the Wac, earlier). It is all hate. The closest thing to a reasonable proposition as yet encountered is obviously couched in terms of rape. *Young Man: "I'm tired of this fooling around. I'm coming over to your house tonight and I'm going to throw you on the sofa and pull off your pants —" Girl: "Oh no, you're not!" Young Man: "And I'm going to lay you so hard you won't be able to walk straight." Girl: "Oh no, you're not!" Young Man: "And what's more, I'm not even going to wear a cundrum!" Girl: "Oh yes, you are!"* (N.Y. 1940.)

The excuse is sometimes made or implied that the man's violence stems from uncontrollable sexual appetite, as in a bridegroom or returned soldier. In jokes, as in fact, a certain amount of reasonable violence of this kind can only be flattering to the woman. *A soldier arriving home on furlough says, "Honey, get your sweeping done around the house, because for the next two weeks you're not going to see anything but the ceiling!"* (Calif. 1942. In the earliest form collected, McAtee, 1913, env. 7, *A bride writes to a friend that she can't describe the scenery on her honeymoon trip, because "In hotels by day and trains by night, in the three weeks we've been gone the only scenery I've seen was the flowers on the ceiling."*) The violence of the man's approach is charitably displaced from the women to her clothing in an equally well known example: *A returning soldier (or a Scotsman who has been charged fifty dollars in advance by a prostitute) begins throwing all the girl's clothes out the window. When she expostulates he says, "Don't worry. When I get through with you, the styles will have changed."* (2:420. Very commonly encountered during World War II.) In another displacement of hatred and rejection from the woman to the clothing — in this one the man's own clothing being used as the symbol — *A beautiful brunette has a red-headed baby. "Ah," says the doctor, "father red-headed?" "I don't know," says the brunette. "He didn't take off his hat."* (1:253.) James Gibbons Huneker, in his musical novel, *Painted Veils* (1919), makes a good deal of *fin de siècle* stock humor out of the unlikely situation in which a man forgets to take his top hat off during intercourse. The symbolism of the hat, as representing phallic strength for decayed politicians and superannuated generals, is too well known to require further discussion here.

The concentration of verbal sadism increases sharply after intercourse, or when men are depicted in the jokes as speaking privately among themselves about their feelings about women. *A master-sergeant points out to a group of young recruits the actions of a dog to whom he throws a piece of inner tube, as a lesson in handling themselves in foreign territory: "If you can't eat it or screw it, piss on it!"* (Minn. 1946.) A really climactic example of male post-coital repugnance for the woman perfectly typifies the self-hatred, projected upon the woman, that men feel when forced by sexual need to make some concessions in the matter of the ideal beauty, age, etc., of the temporary sexual partner. *A man in a small hotel calls the desk and says, "Send*

*me up a whore." The proprietor's wife is shocked and demands that
her husband throw the man out. He is afraid, and so the wife goes up
to throw him out herself. Great racket: sounds of furniture breaking,
screams, curses. The guest comes downstairs panting, his face scratched
and his shirt torn, dusting off his hands. "Well," he confides to the
proprietor, "that was a tough old bitch you sent up, but I fucked her,
God damn her!"* (2:317.) The 'sadistic concept of coitus' in its pure
form.

This is seldom the aspect of the male approach that the woman
is allowed to see in advance. It is, in any case, largely verbal, since
people generally feel a great deal less guilt about sadistic speech than
they would about physically violent acts such as striking the other person. Also, the verbal affront is likely to be answered only in kind, and
is therefore not as dangerous to the challenger. Approaches made to
the woman by means of senses or abilities other than that of speech are
mild by comparison. Physical approaches in particular seldom involve
more, even in jokes, than such simili-sexual acts as touching the breasts,
slapping the buttocks, goosing, and — most importantly — bold staring.
The magical idea that what one says can physically harm the person
one says it to, which survives in our law of libel and in the nervous
shiftings of real and assumed names that many modern people engage
in, especially when young — not to mention emperors and noblemen —
has always had its counterpart in the idea of the evil eye. (See Selig-
mann's *Der böse Blick*, 1910, the standard source on the subject.) The
principal modern survival involves the phallic symbolism of the eye,
in which men compete at staring each other down in public vehicles,
and women call the police if a man stares at them too fixedly. J. Redding Ware in *Passing English* (1909) s.v. 'aspect,' gives some interesting notes on the use of the word *'aspetto!'* in the Italian quarter of
London, to chide too eager a look of love. 'A fiery youth looking too
fiercely into the eyes of a gutter donzella [!]' says Ware, 'she observes,
"aspetto — aspetto!" ' Nothing could be clearer than: *"If you don't
stop looking at me like that I'll call a cop!" "Lady, you're just lucky.
If I had a cock-eye, you'd be the mother of triplets by now!"* (1:263.)
This is exactly the Scottish 'pintle-keek,' or Shakespeare and Cleland's
'looking goats and monkeys.' (*Othello*, III.iii.403, IV.i.261.)

The jokes on sexual approach through sight are as strange as they
are uncommon, for the reason that the sexual nature of the steady gaze
is clearly felt — even when not obviously directed at the woman's

breasts or under her skirt — but is seldom verbalized at a folk level. *A man is urinating behind a bush after a beer party, when he notices a girl who has also been at the party doing the same thing. Neither can stop. Recognizing him, but embarrassed, she says, "Well, here's to you!" "What do you say we clink glasses?"* (2:362. Earlier in various modern French collections, on *'trinquer,'* to clink glasses.) The visual approach has to be fortified by the verbal to satisfy the teller, though again we have an example here of the joke in which all the universality and humor lies in the situation, while the verbal 'snapper' is weak, though witty enough in its relevance, and could be changed for any one of a dozen others.

The strange, repressed joke that follows has been used to illustrate the scholarly problem of 'internal evidence,' in connection with the recent flush of Bowdlerian editing of the *Poems* of the Earl of Rochester, in which even in the truly startling Princeton facsimile, done in 1950, of the first edition of 1680 — a landmark in the history of university press publishing freedom — a drone-bass of editorial hedging has to follow, in which every possible erotic and semi-erotic poem is ascribed, on 'internal evidence,' to someone other than Rochester. *A woman in a maternity ward begs of the nearest man in white to examine her, as she thinks her labor has begun. He pulls up the sheet, turns up her nightgown, examines her pubis carefully, and then turns down the sheet again with a thoughtful air. "Well, Doctor," the woman implores, "has my time come?" "I don't know, lady," he says. "I'm only the plumber."* (N.Y. 1951. The end-line only, in the form "I'm one of the painters down the hall," is given in 'Evan Esar's' *The Humor of Humor,* 1952, p. 28-9.) The eeriness here clearly stems from the sexual exploitation of a woman in labor, or even — in other forms — simply of a woman in the hospital. Not sporting.

IV. BREASTS

No one needs to be told that the female breast has become in America the principal fetich of male attraction. A literature is even growing up, principally composed of attacks on mothers, in which the oral-neurotic and masochistic overtones of this concentration on breasts are discovered — every week anew — by startled writers, who blame mothers for not breast-feeding their children and yet manage to insist that this deprivation is simultaneously the cause of the breast-fetich of the adult American male. Fetich attractions do not work that way. The ascendancy of the breast, and the advance of oral neurosis, represent an increased turning toward the mother-figure and a conscious rejection of the father. The bare-breasted mother-goddess (sometimes even multi-breasted like a cat, as in the statue of the great Diana of Ephesus — now assimilated to the Virgin Mary) is returning. It is only unfortunate that her sons tend to be masochistic, in their oral dependence, as, until recently, they tended to be homosexual in their fear of and dependence upon the father — now disappearing from the scene.

I have made the point elsewhere, and would like to make it again here, as its importance cannot be underestimated in prefiguring the coming Western neuroses, that 'It may be observed in all periods of history where patriarchy collapses, that the predominantly male homosexual and female masochist characters — in the life of the culture, as in its literature and art — rapidly disappear, and are replaced by the similarly matching female homosexual and male masochistic characters. Examples of the latter in English literature, from Herrick on through Keats and Swinburne, are the rule rather than the exception. One may also see signs of another such period close at hand.' (*The Horn Book*, p. 66, as originally published in *American Aphrodite*, No. 9, 1953. For a fuller discussion see my pamphlets, *Love & Death*, 1949, p. 78-9, and *On the Cause of Homosexuality*, 1950, p. 31.) To this formulation I have added, in a brief series of "Notes on Masochism," interpolated between Nos. 5 and 6 in *The Compleat Neurotica* (New York, 1963), the tentative conclusion that: *castration anxieties rising from the father or father-surrogate lead to homosexuality in the male (and masochism in the female). In the same way, castration anxieties rising from the mother or mother-surrogate lead to homosexuality in the female (and masochism in the male)*. This could be developed at great length, with typical examples from literature and life.

The "Notes on Masochism" analyze a series of sado-masochistic letters, "Answers to an Ad," published in *Neurotica*, No. 5, these being authentic letters — though making incredible reading — in answer to a 'classified advertisement' in No. 4: 'STRAPPING *young woman interested in works of Marquis de Sade would meet young man interested in Sacher-Masoch. State height and weight. Box* 124.' As a result of this exposé, advertisements for perverts, which had been running openly in various American magazines, literary and other, ceased appearing for a number of years. Very similar *graffiti* have, during the middle 1960's, reappeared massively in the hippie or 'far-out' news-papers, in particular the *Los Angeles Free Press* and New York *East Village Other*, of which latter a staff-writer, Mr. Stephen Kraus, has announced (in a classified ad) a study of such ads in progress, at this late date. "The Degenerates' Corner" — as it was called in *Neurotica* — rides again. But this time there is little concealment, and the hippie newspaper ads blatantly announce that the advertisers wish 'instruction in cunnilingus' and the like. The breast-fetich is too mild even to men-tion; also probably too standard a fare in commercial photographic advertisements and 'men's magazines.' Mr. Kraus' eventual column on the subject, in *East Village Other* (Feb. 23, 1968) p. 10, says precisely nothing, but the facing column, "Filming the Two-Backed Beast," by another writer, on pornographic movies' finding their perverted actors in the sex-ads, p. 16 (and "Pearl the Intimate Sadist," pp. 6, 15) says everything — and more.

Jokes about attraction to the breast allow of at least some expression of regard for the woman's body, in the process of approaching her sexually, since almost all types of folklore concerning the vagina itself express only the most direct hatred and fear. This may seem overstated, but is actually the opposite, as an examination of the materials in the next chapter, on Women, and the sub-section *"Vagina Dentata,"* in Chapter 13 (Series Two), will prove. Even the jokes on the breast move rather rapidly from attraction to rejection and sadistic harm.

A father is explaining the business to his son. "The most important thing," he says, "is getting the right people to work for you. First I'll show you how to hire a stenographer." They interview three girls: one is an attractive brunette with three years' experience, one is a drab little woman with twenty years' experience in the best firm in the field, and the third is a ravishing blonde with no experience. "Now which one do you pick?" says the father. "I don't know," says the son. "The one with the biggest tits, naturally!" (N.Y. 1951.) — *A draftee taking his army physical examination stark naked claims to have trouble with his eyesight. The doctor holds up two fingers and asks, "What do you see?" "A picket fence, sir." The doctor beckons to the nurse, unbuttons her blouse, and exposes her breasts. "Now what do you see?" "Noth-ing, sir." "The hell you don't! You see four big tits, and there's your pecker sticking up in front of you to prove it."* (Transcontinental train, 1943, with a variant, collected the same year, with the doctor ending:

"That's what you *say, but your indicator is pointing to Fort Dix!"* Another version, said to date from the 1890's, has already been given in the chapter on Fools, 2.v.3.)

As remarked before, all other breast jokes collected fall away rapidly from the forthright attraction and acceptance of the above, to varieties of contemptuous rejection and harm. *Abraham Lincoln (according to the story) attended a charity bazaar, and tendered a twenty-dollar bill in payment for a bunch of violets. Receiving no change, he reached over the counter to pat the girl's breasts. "What are these, my dear?" he asked. "Why they're my breasts, Mr. Lincoln." "I see," he said; "everything is so high around here, I thought they might be your buttocks."* (Calif. 1942. Ascription to Lincoln in *The New Anecdota Americana,* 1944, No. 491, an expurgated version, with the original form implied in No. 413: 'Wall Street Tillie says her boss always used to grab her by the knee, "but yesterday he reached a new high!"')

A soldier on leave finds his wife exposing her breasts alluringly. "I haven't time to chew the fat," he says, *"just to come and go."* (D.C. 1945.) This expression of the ideal of minimum contact is a punning revision of an older joke in which the oral-dependent identification of the wife's breasts and the mother's milk is strikingly made. *A husband rushes his wife into bed, showing no interest in her romantically exposed breasts. "I just thought maybe you'd like a bite to eat first,"* she *apologizes.* (Minn. 1935. Also a part-Yiddish variant, presumably adding to the poignancy: *"I thought maybe you'd like a* knash *first."* Compare the novelty card, N.Y. 1950, showing a man's head with enormously opened mouth, wholly engulfing a woman's breast, and the caption: OUT TO LUNCH. Oragenital lapel-button reported from hippie California, 1967: DOWN TO LUNCH.) The soldier story has also been collected with the breast element omitted, leaving nothing but the forced pun on the word 'come,' and the minimum-contact rejection. *A soldier is passing through his home town on a train that will stop over for only thirty minutes. He phones his girl friend. "I'm in town and I'll be right over. Have all your clothes off." "Even my panties?" "Everything. I just have time to come and go."* (Minn. 1946.)

The element of insult may be somewhat covert, as in this example of the standard mocking identification of woman and cow, at least as old as the 15th century, of Leonardo da Vinci, as noted earlier. *A statistician on a train tabulates the number of cows he sees out the window in an impossibly short time, explaining: "Oh, I don't count the cows. I*

count the number of tits, and divide by four." (N.Y. 1939.) Also collected with a long build-up in which the statistician is observed snap-
ping his fingers and mumbling numbers to himself. The social background of this joke has already been discussed in the Introduction,
section VIII. *A waiter assists a lady in extreme décolletage to put back
one of her breasts when it pops out as she bends over to pick up her
napkin. He is berated by the headwaiter. "Where did you ever work
before, in a pastrami joint? In a restaurant like this when that occurs
we use two warm spoons.*" (Baker, 1945, vol. II.) As the whole point
of the story is to achieve the utmost in absurd over-solicitousness, it
seems clear that it is really to be understood with a minus sign before
it — as animosity toward the breast — instead of the indicated double-
plus. In case there is any doubt of this, a shorter version collected
about the same period makes the real meaning clear. *A woman in a
restaurant in extreme décolletage complains to her escort of heartburn.
"Heartburn, hell! Your left tit is hanging in the soup.*" (Minn. 1946.)

The slightest hint of pendency in the breast — the background element of *falling* breasts in the two preceding stories — is construed as
an affront to him by the man. In the novelty pictorial catalogues of
breast types current since about 1943, the presumably ideal 'Dream
Boats' and 'Super-Bloopers' are not only as round and over-plump as
on a Hindu mother-goddess, but actually point upward like howitzers
(one type being called by that name). The merely human and moderately pendant breast is hated. *A woman is told that the best way to
commit suicide is to shoot herself two inches below her left breast. She
goes home and blows off her kneecap.* (N.Y. 1940.) The reason for her
attempted suicide, that is to say the crime for which she is condemned
to death, is unquestionably the state of her breasts. See further, on breast
types, *Bisba* by Timothy Burr (Trenton, 1965) p. 64, a peculiar work
ending with an *anti-woman glossary,* pp. 303–449.

*A woman at a banquet puts two handkerchiefs in the bosom of her
dress. They fall through and she cannot find them. Suddenly she finds
everyone silently observing her as she fumbles in both sides of her
bosom, murmuring, "I'm sure I had two when I left home.*" (N.Y.
1946.) This was picked up by several newspaper columnists, and retailed as a 'true occurrence.' *A woman has her first two lovers' faces
tattooed on her breasts* [!] *On her wedding night her husband takes
the matter laughingly, saying, "Ten years from now, what long faces
they'll have.*" (Elgart, back flap of 1952 dust-jacket.) This is the ancient motif of the Italian *novellieri,* of the husband's painting — usu-

ally a jackass — on the wife's belly, as a test of her chastity while he is absent: Rotunda H439.1.1. — *A drunk is picked up in a bar by a girl who insists they have met before. He does not recognize her until they are undressing in her apartment. She has her brassière half off, with one breast dangling. "I got it!" he cries. "You're Wiley Post!"* (N.Y. 1940. Mr. Post was a famous one-eyed aviator of the period. Elgart, 1951, p. 172, referring to Floyd Gibbons.) This whole theme of the rejected breast — Jimmy Cagney's grapefruit in the early gangster movie, *Public Enemy* — comes much more clearly into focus in the light of the homosexual tone of the last example. See further in the sub-section "Food-Dirtying," in the Second Series following, 12.IV.2, under "Narsty-Narsties."

A pantomime joke, which rather surprised me in its openly self-directed hostility in the matter of the pendency of the breasts, was told me by a young woman (with very lovely breasts) when I expressed surprise at the lesbian handling of the women customers' breasts by the saleswomen in a brassière shop. *A woman whose breasts are too small, and whose husband is therefore running around with other women, is told by the doctor to massage her breasts every day to the tune of "The Farmer in the Dell." As he has forgotten to tell her when to stop, she continues with the massage for three years. When she finally goes back to the doctor he is amazed by the condition of her breasts, and asks if she has been doing the massage exercises the whole time. "Sure," she says. "Like this: (Singing) 'The farmer in the dell' (rubs inward around and around at both breasts), 'The farmer in the dell' (same motion but outward); 'Heigh-o' (one breast thrown over the right shoulder), 'the cherry-o' (other breast over the left shoulder); 'The farmer' (kick back and up with right heel) 'in the dell' (kick with left)!"* (Scranton, Pa. 1942.) Among other things, this is a very good example of the doctor-as-priest, since the prescribed exercises which go wrong, by being continued too long, are obviously in the tradition of the erroneously or excessively appealed-to magical spell or charm: "The Sorcerer's Apprentice," Tale-Type 325*, and many associated motifs.

The present section was intended to discuss the principal element of attraction in the male approach. Women are more or less neutral about breasts; they are a problem only to men. This makes them a problem to women. But as even the pretense of attraction to the breasts is dropped when they become pendant, there is now almost no way of modulating back to the theme of seduction and the sexual approach unless the following mixed example of love and harm will do it. *A woman complains to the doctor that her breasts hurt, and mentions that her husband likes to sleep with her nipple in his mouth. "Oh that wouldn't cause it," says the doctor. "Lots of husbands do that." "Well, would twin beds make any difference?"* (Pa. 1941.)

V. CASH ON DELIVERY

The unromantic male generally comes to realize that 'dating' in America, as visiting sociologists are shocked to find, is a sort of formalized anti-sexual dance, in which the male and female circle warily looking for the advantage, the man attempting to get the maximum of physical pleasure out of the woman for a minimum of emotional investment, while the woman tries to get the maximum of emotional (and monetary) involvement out of the man for a minimum of physical investment. The only music suitable for a dance like this is the clatter of money, as even Jupiter found in wooing Danaë. As every dollar spent in this way represents an unabsorbable blow to the man's self-esteem — in spite of the Veblenian swathe of conspicuous consumption it helps him cut — he tends to part with every penny reluctantly, at least in jokes, and to bilk the woman of it if he can. The most penetrating discussion of the hostilities inherent in modern 'dating' will be found in Dr. Jules Henry's magistral *Culture Against Man* (New York, 1963) p. 165-9. A book beyond superlatives.

Again, the very jokes about sex and money that purport to show how money eases the necessary approach and desired conquest, tend actually to express detestation of women and sex, and of the loveless situation in which, as the advice for finding a woman in a strange town phrases it, *"You stand on a street corner with your prick in one hand and a twenty-dollar bill in the other."* (N.Y. 1944.) That even this might not work is beyond men's believing. One of the few shaggy dog stories on erotic themes makes the point definite. *A man has a trained dog that he gives twenty cents to go to the corner and buy him a newspaper and a bucket of beer. One day he has no change and gives the dog a five-dollar bill. The dog does not return, and the man finally finds him in the alley mounted on a female. "I'm surprised at you,"* says the man. *"You never did anything like this before." The dog looks up at him. "I never had the money."* (Minn. 1946.) Masochistic jokes like this, in which one has no choice but to identify with the underdog—in a manner of speaking—are extremely rare, and the reader may find it of interest to search for them.

The idea is, of course, not that any-old woman is available for money, but that *all* women are available. A story that has been told of almost every modern celebrity beginning with President Wilson and H. G. Wells: *A famous man at a charity banquet asks the beautiful young woman next to him, "Assuming that we gave the money to charity, would you sleep with me for ten thousand dollars?" After some thought she says, "Yes." "And would you for two dollars?" "Why, what do you think I am!" "We've already decided that. Now we're just haggling about price."* As male listeners are sometimes blinded to the unfairness of this swindle, in admiring the neatness with which it is sprung, a variant may be of interest in which: *A beautiful young woman at a charity banquet asks H. G. Wells, "Assuming that we gave the money to the victims of Nazi atrocities, would you kiss Hitler's (or my) ass in Macy's window for ten thousand dollars?" After some thought, etc. etc.* (N.Y. 1945.) In a slightly less hostile variant of the original: *After the woman agrees to the ten-thousand-dollar price, the man begins to feel her leg under the table, saying,"All right, I'll take a nickel's worth."* (N.Y. 1952.)

Many men are perfectly capable of confusing the plain buying of women with seducing them, and many others—who can afford it—simply do not give a damn which method they use. In my Introduction to the public reprint (1966) of what is probably one of the largest autobiographies ever written, and certainly the largest purely sexual autobiography, *My Secret Life* (1888–94?), I try to make the point, in the reprint edition, p. xliii, concerning the well-to-do Victorian writer of these memoirs, whom I believe to have been the collector and bibliographer of erotica, H. Spencer Ashbee:

> His principal form of sexual experimentation or search for novelty is not in sex technique at all—as it must be, with monogamists—but, as with almost all Don Juans, in *varietism*. In his youth, in particular, he is all of a jumble, in a sort of massive Oedipal search for incest substitutes: aunts, cousins, nursing women's legs, old women, young girls, fat girls, thin girls, women of all other countries (except Lapland), and the like. He also suffers from one very important peculiarity, and though he is quite conscious of it, he does not at all see the

ruinous effect it has on any possibility of real emotional relations with the women and girls he frequents: HE IS TOO RICH,
too prone to cut impatiently through the delay about seducing
a woman by simply buying her. It is for this reason that the
roll-call of his "conquests" shows the same rather high percentage of women of low social caste as do the *Mémoires* of
Casanova. Too many of them have been bought. That is also
perhaps why he so seldom speaks of love.

As I have been told that I am too hard on the author, that 'it
wasn't his fault he was rich,' and that, at bottom, I am simply expressing the anti-snobbery of the have-nots against the haves, and not a
little puritanism as well (I particularly object to the child-rapes and
paid 'seductions' of little girls with which the volumes are frighteningly alive); I would like also to quote a brief assessment of the same
author and the same question by another Englishman, Wayland Young,
Lord Kennet, who has this to say about him in *Eros Denied* (1964)
p. 291–2, published with imperturbable fairness by Grove Press, publishers also of the integral reprint of *My Secret Life*. Says Lord Kennet:

> The author appears to have been a rich Englishman. . . . His
> obliviousness to the tears, disasters and muddles he caused with
> his stupid money — he did not even take a sadistic pleasure in
> them — makes the book painful to read. It is a compulsively
> long and factual account of what it is like to be a compulsive
> collector of physical contacts. Although he paid for most of his
> experiences in money, he was a thief of touch; it is full of near
> rapes and surreptitious fumbles, and whenever a woman liked
> it, he was astonished.

The easiest victims of sexual exploitation are, naturally, the poor.
If they are not poor, you make them poor. *A Negro girl is parading the
main street of an Alabama town in fine new clothes. "Where'd you get
all them beautiful togs?" "Ain't you heard? I been ruined!"* (1:84.) As
the editor of *Anecdota* notes, this same story is told in verse, on a Wes-
sex background, as "The Ruined Maid," in Thomas Hardy's *Collected
Poems* (ed. 1923) p. 145. Or it can be done in a dream: *"Dear Flo, I
dreamt of you last night. Enclosed find check. Harold."* (*Anecdota*,
expurgated ed. 1933, No. 418.) Then too, as the young man says, *"I'd
rather have a wet dream than a woman. You meet a much better class*

of women that way." (2:239.) On the probable secret of the preference for such dreams, see the handling of this same joke earlier, under "Incest," I.V. But the strange women are best of all. There are so many of them. And besides, one of them might be a much nearer relative than you suspect. Who has not heard of the young man who found an ex-schoolteacher of his (read *mother?*) working as a strip-teaser in a burlesque show. Etc. *A preacher tells a man who does a great deal of cursing that every time he does so he should hand a dollar to the nearest stranger, and that will cure him soon enough. The man stubs his toe leaving, and silently hands a dollar to a woman just entering the church. "O.K.," she whispers, "but can you wait till after the services?"* (N.Y. 1935.)

The price is terribly important, you see. It is not that one is a tight-wad. By no means. But one hates to have to pay for what should really be given freely, simply because one is such a fine fellow and has had the nerve to ask. "*Say, I know a place where you can get a glass of beer and a screw all for a dime!" "I don't believe it." "No, honest; it happened to my sister."* (N.Y. 1939, usually given an extremely long build-up about a foreigner or a stranger in town.) The longest story I have ever heard, and I have sat through it several times, can be reduced to the following shaggy blonde elements: *A rich young college boy who has never had a woman finally manages, after driving around the block several times with the door of his roadster swung open, to pick up a demure little blonde in a trim blue suit. She says very little, but agrees with a murmured "Mmm," to his various suggestions: a drive in the park, a trip upstairs to see his Persian hooked rugs, and finally to go to bed. The third day he manages to crawl out of bed and pull up the Venetian blinds, and crawls back to her feet to offer her his fortune, a Broadway show of her own, or even the family name of Van Rensselaer. She refuses everything with a murmured "Um-umh." He finally becomes irritated. "Well what do you want?" "A dime," she mumbles. "Stop mumbling," he says; "have you got something in your mouth?" She nods and says, "Dimes."* (N.Y. 1941.) This has been reduced to about one-seventh of its original length, but I am still unable to be sure I have uncovered the kernel of humor I have been assured it possesses. Other versions of both this and the following story will be found, in a different context, in Chapter 11, "Prostitution," in the Second Series.

Somewhere in the background — even in exploiting pre-psychotic blondes at a dime a head — there lurks the real dream, of being asked nothing, of 'getting it for love.' (Not money.) *An inexperienced young man is taken by a taxi-driver to a whore-house. He is struck by the politeness of the girl, who calls her mother "Madam," and so forth. In the morning he dresses carefully and is about to leave. "What about some money?" says the girl. "Oh, no, you've been more than kind already."* (Minn. 1946.) Or: *"Certainly not! But if you like, you can buy me a couple of ties."* (N.Y. 1953.) The necktie here as obvious phallic symbol, as in much joke- and prank-lore, such as the pre-zipper fly-ripping (*tie*-ripping when teachers are present), and in the current exploitation of nubile girls to wear massive clip-on neckties over fetichistic plastic skirts or fly-front pants. In a later chapter will be discussed a version of the preceding joke made central to the plot in Norman Krasna's play, *Sunday in New York*, of which the movie version (1963) ushered in the same 'New Freedom' for sexual conversation in motion pictures as had been available on the public stage since at least the 1920's. In the *Sunday in New York* form, the would-be seducer tells this joke to his intended 'victim' — an aging young virgin, anxious to get laid — who runs away owing to this unveiling of his intentions. To the man, of course, this joke would be intended in such a situation, not to soften up the girl by means of dirty jokes (as the author pretends), but to indicate, in a not-uncharming way, that this is all to be for 'love,' not money. It is a question of pride. The man who so elaborately misunderstands is here a proud Hungarian army-officer, and: *"A Hungarian officer* never *accepts money!"*

The standard victim is the stenographer, as shown in Jerome Weidman's *I Can Get It For You Wholesale* (a 1930's novel made into a 1960's play), represented in the most brutally exact detail. This is an extension of the idea that a woman is really a sexual chattel (*feme covert*), and that whatever else she is hired to do, her sexual complaisance should go with it, just as a wife is expected to work all day, though it is her sexual complaisance that was originally 'bought.' Further, the concept of every woman servant or employee as an ancillary or auxiliary wife must be very ancient. It unquestionably survives from the earliest periods and legends of patriarchy, as in the case — already cited — of the patriarchs Abraham and Jacob's wives, Sarah, Rachel, and Leah, giving them their handmaids (of other colors or nationalities) to 'go in unto' for the purpose of fathering extra progeny to be credited not to the maid-servants but to the barren wives.

The modern female office-worker is clearly assimilated to the maid-servant group. The usual 'men's magazine' cartoons show the boss's wife endlessly on the prowl to catch him with the stenographer on his lap (cartoon-shorthand for making love with him during the after-noon 'sex break,' now increasingly popular to match the morning 'coffee break'). But the truth seems to be that the actual wives of busi-nessmen are aware of and take for granted the relay-activity of the 'office wives,' and of the simple prostitutes whom the same men fre-quent at magniloquently styled business fairs and conferences, always somehow taking place in towns famous for the plentiful supply and good quality (also reasonable *price*) of the local prostitutes, such as Atlantic City formerly, and Hamburg, Germany, and various capitals of the Caribbean islands now. I have put this perhaps a bit stronger in *The Fake Revolt* (1967) p. 24:

> The dream of the New Freedom and the New Revolt is al-ready being savantly squibbed off into something of no danger whatsoever to the R.O.F. (Rotten Old Futzes) Organization. Into something indistinguishable, in fact, from what the big-shots of that very Organization also openly dream of: a sort of crude moral holiday, with gimmicked sex, drugs, and sports-cars speeding one to an at least temporary freedom from all human restraints, especially the ones against cruelty and ego-mania, as on business weekends — on tax-deductible expense ac-counts and swindle-sheets — with their sexier secretaries at hunt-ing lodges and ocean resorts, or "trade fairs" (ho-ho) in Puerto Rico, Hamburg, or Las Vegas, or some other gook country where prostitution and drugs are wide-open, and underage ass of both sexes is pitifully cheap.

The jokes make no bones about the secretary's availability. *A man jumps out of an office window and his secretary explains that he has been acting peculiar for weeks. Three weeks ago he gave her a hun-dred dollars to parade around the office in her petticoat; two weeks ago two hundred dollars to wear just her panties & brassière. Finally, he gave her three hundred dollars to sit on his lap naked. "And now,"* he said, *"how much do you want for the monkey business?" And when she told him, "Just the usual two dollars," he jumped out the window.* (N.Y. 1938.)

The method of selecting a stenographer by breast size has been detailed above. There is also the matter of haggling about price. *A stenographer asks for thirty dollars a week.* "I'll give you that with pleasure," says the boss. "With pleasure that'll be forty dollars." (N.Y. 1940, or more subtly, "Making forty dollars altogether.") Same situation: *A stenographer asks for thirty dollars a week but is offered twenty.* "The girl that left told me you gave her thirty dollars." "Yes, but I went in the hole on that." (N.Y. 1945. Hardly more than a pun; also in Guam mimeo, 1948, of *A girl who wants a brassière tattooed on for five dollars. The tattooer asks ten.* "Oh, you tattooed a pair of panties on my girl friend not long ago for five dollars." "Yes, but I went in the hole on that job.") — *A politician is trying to seduce his new secretary, and asks her if twenty-five dollars will be enough.* "If you can raise my dress as high as you've raised taxes," she says, "and pull my pants down as low as wages, and screw me as good as you've screwed the public, you can have it free." (D.C. 1951.) Usually told of the President of the United States.

The word 'bilk' has long been reserved exclusively for cheating prostitutes and cab-drivers of their hackney earnings, and I have seen a letter of furious expostulation when the word was applied to bilking a poor typist of her fee. The motive in refusing to pay afterward what one has offered to pay before is not parsimony but hurt vanity. The opportunity offering, the man attempts to punish the woman for asking for payment in the first place, instead of offering herself 'for love' even though neither of them *feels* any love. 'Love' perhaps means here the equivalent of zero, or nothing, as in tennis. There is also a strong element of projecting on the woman the feelings of guilt and self-hatred that overwhelm the man after sordid intercourse. (Observe the faces in Hogarth's well-known "Before & After" engravings.) *A man taking a girl to his room passes many shop windows with her, and promises her all the fur coats, hats, shoes, and so forth that strike her fancy. After intercourse he refuses everything, explaining,* "When I'm hard I'm soft, but when I'm soft I'm hard." (1:222.) In a modified version, *A man seduces a girl by telling her she can go to the best store in town and pick out any fur coat she wants and any jewellery. After intercourse he repeats his promise and gives her his card, saying,* "If there's any question, have them phone me at this number." "Is that your home phone or your office?" *the girl asks.* "It's the candy-store on the corner, but they'll call me." (N.Y. 1944.) I have often told this joke publicly, in discussing humor, and the 'candy-store' form invariably seems to break up any mixed audience.

Post-coital cynicism is for some reason particularly ascribed to actors, who are presumably besieged by women at all times and can afford to be frank. *An actor-director is bawling out a chorus-girl for being late. "But, Ben . . . " she says. " 'Ben' in bed. Mr. Neale here!"* (1:329.) The hostility is only a trifle more hidden — considering the situation implied — in the line ascribed to Caruso: *"I never make love in the morning: it's bad for the voice, it's bad for the health, and you never know who you might meet during the afternoon!"* (*Anecdota,* 1933, No. 326, not as of Caruso.) Ascriptions of jokes to theatrical notables, and literary and Bohemian luminaries of the moment, are persistently made and often believed. This is part of the quasi-royal or cynosure status of people who get their names in the papers, who are expected to do all the sinful and illegal things that the people reading the papers are afraid to do. This apparently includes post-coital insults, where lesser mortals attempt to live up to the 'glow of mutual satisfaction' remarked upon by the manuals of sex technique. *A girl comes to a famous actor's dressing room to ask for a part in his next play. He has intercourse with her on the couch and then tells her that the play won't be cast until the next year. "Gee," she says, "I'm dead broke. Could you give me a couple of dollars meanwhile?" "A couple of dollars! What for?" "I'm hungry. I want to buy some bread." "Bread? Fuck a baker. I'm an actor. I give passes."* (N.Y. 1939.) Invariably told of the late Boris Thomashefsky or John Barrymore.

5

THE SADISTIC
CONCEPT

I. RAPE

IN THE examination of witches, as everyone knows, the suspected witch was thrown into the water trussed hand & foot. If she floated she was adjudged guilty, and was fished out and burnt. If she drowned she was innocent. This is called giving somebody a choice. In the same way, the automobile-age alternative *"Fuck or Walk"* (1:306) is conceived of as the halfway point between seduction and rape. To the man it is just a practical way of making it easy for the girl to accept the sexual intimacy she probably had in mind in the first place in accepting the ride. To the girl it is rape. This tends to be clearest only to those men who have had the same alternatives offered to them while hitch-hiking, by homosexual truck drivers of the wolf or 'tough fag' variety, some of whom are not above hefting a tire-iron in one hand while making the seductive suggestion. Even a girl more or less willing to be seduced may prefer the standard techniques of seduction (on which see Emily Hahn's delightful *Seductio ad Absurdum,* New York, 1930), to being given the alternatives of promptly succumbing or of finding herself alone on the highway at 2 A.M. in a party dress and high heels, with the cars zooming by with blazing headlights at fifty miles an hour.

The standard excuse for rape — that the woman really wanted it — will be found in all the "Fuck or Walk" jokes, and in most of those on other types of rape as well. *A man is rattling along on the highway in an old Ford, and picks up a girl who is crying. She explains, "I was out with a man in a big Packard, and he tried to make me do something and I wouldn't and he told me to get out and walk." "Jump in,"* says the man. *"I'll take you back to town." The car bumps and jolts along for a few miles, and finally the girl taps her benefactor on the shoulder. "Please let me out," she says. "I'd rather be raped in a Packard than jerked off in a Ford."* (1:442.) Shorter versions of the same idea exist. *A man leaves his girl in a Ford car with the motor running while he goes into a store to get cigarettes. When he comes back she says, "K-k-kiss me, Ch-charlie! I'm c-c-coming!"* (1:398.) Compare the folk definition of a 'lead-pipe cinch': *"If you take a girl out for a ride, and you stop the car in front of a drugstore, and you say, 'Pardon me while I go in and get some condoms,' and she's still there when you get back — that's a lead-pipe cinch."* (Canada, 1944. The actual etymology of the phrase is disputed. It may refer to the bendability of lead pipe, making plumbing with it very easy, or it may refer to its use as a club. The second etymon seems probable here.)

A woman's joke: *A man takes a girl out in his car, stops seven miles out of town, and propositions her. She walks back. The second night he takes her fifteen miles. She walks back. The third night he takes her thirty miles, and she gives in. Afterwards he asks why, and she explains, "I'll walk seven miles, or even fifteen miles, to save a friend of mine from a dose of clap. But not thirty."* (1:306.) A weak modification, collected D.C. 1944, drops the whole point for a pun: *The first two nights the girl says, "Legs, you are my best friends," and the third night, "Even the best of friends must part."*

The point is almost always made that the woman is really willing, or, at the very least, that her unwillingness somehow changes to an uncontrollable yea-saying and 'giving way' during the actual rape, when biological deep calls to deep, when the falsities of civilization are stripped away, etc. etc. — the usual sound-track so dear to physical weaklings like D. H. Lawrence, dreaming of rape. This is the point on which Ruth Herschberger grows so justifiably bitter in *Adam's Rib* (1948) chapter 3, "Is Rape A Myth?", but she ruins the purity of her anger by intruding a vengeful sub-section, "Can Women Rape Men?", on the technique of what she envisages as forced 'extravaginal masturbation,' doubtless at the point of a gun. (Compare the adulterer who is 'scared stiff' when he hears the husband knocking at the door.) The cases of exactly this sort of rape of men by women, reported in the American papers since 1950, give very few details of technique. Presumably the sub-virile or masochist type of male chosen for rape is specially excited by the woman-rapist's violence, and biological deep calls — as advertised — to deep. In a letter from a young lady, in the

New York *Village Voice* (Aug. 10, 1967), on a more recent article by Miss Herschberger on more or less the same anti-man theme as twenty years ago, the explanation seems to be given of the real technique of raping the male: *he is castrated* by knife-toting girl gangsters, who plan to form a secret 'Society for Cutting Up Men' (scum). The sadistic concept of coitus taken to its ultimate conclusion, but this time with the female as the sadistic and castratory 'rapist.' Though obviously merely a hateful fantasy (as yet), this is a lot franker than the majority of the anti-man screeds now being published, which are for some reason good, noble, and right where the anti-woman attacks of the past have been evil, ignoble, and wrong.

In her original statement, Miss Herschberger did not go anywhere near so far, and closed her discussion, "Is Rape a Myth?" p. 24–6, with a word of logical warning to the romantic (male) rapist who 'at the same time cannot bear to think that the woman is not actually enjoying herself': 'It is difficult to know how often the resistance of an unwilling woman is merely an attempt to whet the vigor of a mutual experience . . . Where a strong and beautiful subject is selected, it might be necessary to render her unconscious first, in which case it is difficult to presume that she is psychologically implicated in the act.' No one could disagree with this sardonic statement, of course, but why would being strong *and beautiful* (italics supplied) make it more necessary to knock the girl unconscious than if she were, say, strong *and ugly*? Maybe the ugly girls really *are* more likely to be willing to 'whet the vigor of a mutual,' etc. Hard to know. Certainly many insecure seducers prey on fat girls — without any question of rape — and are cynically advised to do so, on the grounds that fat girls are easy lays (because nobody pays any sexual attention to them), in a volume of beer-joint and nightclub adviseering, largely composed of hilarious put-ons and other scams, *New York Unexpurgated,* by 'Petronius' (Julian Press, 1966), which has been ascribed by Robert Wolf, in *The Realist* (May 1967), p. 16, to Miss Joyce Greller.

These merely technical questions, as to the rape-victim's being willing or not, are no longer as paramount as they may have seemed in Miss Herschberger's faraway 1948. The direct appeal to the *chemical violence* of drugs has now become standard, particularly among the psychopathic fringe-group known as 'hippies.' A large percentage of these pitiful and disorganized adolescents are conked completely out of their minds on psychomimetic drugs such as LSD, DMT, and mescaline. As such, it does not seem too wrong, perhaps, to conk somebody else out similarly. It was once the ultimate in the definition of a human swine or cad, that he would drug a girl to have sexual intercourse with her. This is, for instance, made into quite a gentlemanly little scene in *The Big Sleep* (1939) by the mock-American — actually British — murder-mystery writer, Raymond Chandler, when the detective smells *ether* in the wine-glass of the naked and unconscious girl he has stumbled upon. Today such subterfuges are utterly common among all classes of American society, alcohol and marihuana being the usual drugs of choice. The girl is later referred to as having been 'seduced.' One of the main problems in such 'seduction' — that there is little or no vaginal lubrication in the drugged girl, which may make coitus painful for the man — is solved in part by gang-rape or 'gang-shagging.' This has been picked up by the hippies and their 'plastic' imitators from the delinquent motorcycle gangsters, among whom it is a ritual initiation, or sharing-of-guilt. (Initiation of the men, not the girl.) In the gang-shag, only the first man has the problem of insufficient lubrication. The others, as I have heard it elegantly expressed, *'skid in on some other guy's scum.'* (El Cerrito, Calif. 1965. Also known as *'riding a wet deck'* among sailors; Grose's *'buttered bun'* in 1785.)

The obvious homosexual elements in the gang-shag are, of course, denied by most such rapists, who see nothing unmanly in eight or ten burly young men standing in line with their penises out, masturbating 'slightly' to get ready for their turn, if the sadistico-sexual spectacle somehow lacks aphrodisiacal effect on them. The hippie gang-bangers do not give a damn, and proclaim themselves *proud* of their advertised 'group-grope,' which is simply a drugged bisexual circus. Here is the rape scene, as reported matter-of-factly by Chester Anderson, in a 'Digger' or 'Communications Company' flying-sheet (reprinted in *Underground Digest,* No. 1 [October 1967], headed "Uncle Tim's Children," referring to Timothy Leary, head propagandist for LSD), which gets right down to the nitty-gritty in the opening line:

Pretty little 16 year-old middle-class chick comes to the Haight [*the hippie slum in San Francisco*] to see what it's all about and gets picked up by a seventeen year-old street dealer [*drug-peddler*] who spends all day shooting her full of speed [*Meth-edrine*] again and again, then feeds her 3000 mikes [*micrograms of LSD: ten or twelve times the usual dose*] and raffles her temporarily unemployed body for the biggest Haight Street gang bang since the night before last. The politics and ethics of ecstasy. Rape is as common as bullshit on Haight Street. The Love Generation never sleeps.

(The meaning of the last line, which is perhaps obscure, is that drug-addicts and psychotics — the 'Love Generation' — seldom sleep regular hours, but reel about in a vague daze much of the time, looking for a 'connection.' This is referred to as 'dropping out' of society, on pre-sumed philosophical and libertarian pretexts.) A similar gang-bang — or perhaps the same one, but here with the specification that the gang-bangers were Negroes — is described in an angry and unusually frank newspaper article, "Love Is Dead [in San Francisco]," by Earl Shorris, appearing in the *New York Times,* Magazine section (October 29th, 1967) pp. 27, 113–16: 'Negroes are blamed for the increasing use of Methedrine: "They get some nice white chick [girl], the kind your mother would want you to go out with, and they shoot her full of speed. Then they gang her, 14, 15 of them, and she never knows what's happening." At the end of the Methedrine jag, when she crashes, she will know.' Only a few weeks earlier, at the other end of the country, an eighteen-year-old Connecticut society-girl was bludgeoned to death with 'her hippie boyfriend after a Lower East Side LSD party.' (*New York Post,* October 10th, 1967: headline story. The 'Lower East Side' is now the New York hippie slum.) According to the coroner's ex-amination of her nude dead body, she 'had been raped four times.' There's scientific exactitude for you! Two Negro suspects were held.

By comparison with the way life is actually lived (and died) in the U.S.A. at the present time, the jokes and weak puns about rape are pitifully mild. *A boy and girl argue about the possibility of rape. They try it, and he wins. "You didn't win fair," says the girl. "My foot slipped. Let's try it again."* (N.Y. 1939. Printed in E. Haldeman-Julius' *American Freeman,* 'Feb. 1951' [1950], p. 3/3.) In a related poetic fancy (*cf.* Lyly's masochistic "Cupid and Campaspe played"), *The girl complains of stolen kisses, and demands that the man give them back.* — Briefest modern form: *He: "I'll rape you, so help me!" She: "I'll help you, so rape me."* (D.C. 1944. Variant or gag-ending: *"But if I help you, will it be rape?"* N.Y. 1953.) Note that the implied situation is that the woman is not only willing, but is leading the man on, with her resistance, in 'merely an attempt to whet the vigor of a mutual ex-perience.'

A girl rushes into a lawyer's office. "I want him arrested! He threw me on the bed. He . . . oh, it was awful!" *Lawyer:* "Now calm down. Let's get the story straight. What did he do first?" *Girl:* "He locked the door." *Lawyer:* "Aha, kidnapping! (He makes a note.) Ten years. Then what did he do?" "He pulled up my dress." "Indecent exposure. Two more years. (Making a note.) Then what?" "He put his hand on my . . . my . . ." "It's all right. I understand. Attempted assault. Five years. And then what?" "He threw me on the bed." "Ah hah! Mayhem and felonious constraint. Ten to fifteen years. And then?" "Then . . . he did it to me." "That does it! Rape! Twenty years — maybe we can get him the chair! And meanwhile you were screaming and struggling . . ." *Girl:* "Well-l-l. Not exactly. You see, it was kind of late, and I didn't want to disturb everybody, and . . ." *Lawyer (tearing up his notes in disgust):* "Oh, for Christ's sake, that's just a plain ordinary fuck!" (N.Y. 1942, told at a lawyers' convention.) This is Rabelais' "Sister Fatbum" story, in *Pantagruel,* 1532, III.19, quoted above: 4.1.3. The real humor of this story will be made more clear by confronting it with several others of the same type, in the section following on "Displaced Aggressions": the crossed-whips wallpaper, the man who insults the Quaker, and so forth, where the story offers all the pleasure of the taboo act — in the present case, rape — but also offers a miraculous happy ending in which it all turns out to be an almost-innocent mistake. This is the only kind of story that a properly repressed sadist (or rapist) can really enjoy.

Most rape stories do not describe the act itself, but its legal sequelæ, in court. This is the real area of anxiety — not that the girl's body or emotions will be outraged. The jokes turn the accusation of rape, in court, to the desired farce by having the woman complainant accidentally betray her essential willingness. *The bellboy is accused of having raped the chambermaid by catching her with her head out the window watching a parade, locking her head there by pulling down the window, and having intercourse with her from behind.* "Why didn't you call for help?" *asks the judge.* "Well, Judge, I didn't want people to think I was cheering for a Republican parade." (1:411.) The situation of being locked in place erotically by a window-blind also occurs in *Tristram Shandy,* while Casanova describes a real incident of exciting himself and a woman by watching a public execution from a window overlooking the scene, and having intercourse with the woman from behind while she is gobbling up the scene optically, leaning out the window. This is also a favorite situation or pose in European jokes and folktales in which the woman *speaks* to someone (the husband) outside, who cannot see that someone is making love to her inside. This is similarly the pose of the 'vat' story in Boccaccio, Day VII, Tale 2, of which Rotunda notes as source the *Golden Ass* of Apuleius, chap. 38, with other interesting parallels (K1517.3). In a quite unashamedly sadistic Turkish story, translated by Decourdemanche in *La Fleur Lascive Orientale* (Bruxelles, 1882) No. 9, p. 98, a man has intercourse with a girl from behind while she is leaning out a window, as she 'does not want to miss a single detail of the beating the two cuckolds are giving each other' in the courtyard below. Casanova's incident is identical. A revenge story of this kind from Picardy is given in *Kryptádia* (1907) XI. 307, with a lubricious priest caught in his own mechanical confessional-box, and his penis given to a calf to suck. A chair of this kind is central to the plot of an English-language sadistic eroticum, *The Way of a Man With a Maid* (Paris, *c.* 1900). The motif seems to have entered Europe through the *Novelle* (1573) IV. 27, of the Dominican friar, Matteo Bandello, whose specialty was cruel revenges. (Motifs D1413.6–8 and K984, with further references in Thompson's index-volume, VI. 127, at "Chair." Type 571A.) In the most recent form, both are watching television.

Same situation: *A man is accused of raping a woman leaning over the railing of her front porch. The judge asks the woman, "What did you do when he started pushing you?" "I pushed right back, Judge. Nobody's going to push me off my own front porch!"* (2:211.) This has also been collected in connection with the proverb (*Confucius say . . .*): *"Rape is impossible. A woman can run faster with her dress up than a man with his pants down."* (N.Y. 1948.) Again the courtroom situation: *The accused rapist is very short; the woman whom he is accused of having raped up against a tree is very large. The judge is dubious. "I don't really see how he could have done it." "Well, Judge," says the woman, "maybe I did stoop a little."* (1:281.) Several other jokes on the theme of the midget raping the fat woman have been given in Chapter 1.V in the section, "Incest," with the various sleights and subterfuges used. It seems obvious, as in Mark Twain's 'miscarriage' example, and in that in which the midget rapist hangs by the handle of a bucket put over the woman's head, that the 'midget' is to be interpreted as a child, and the 'fat woman' or 'large woman' as his mother. (Helping the rapist: *Cent Nouvelles*, No. 25.)

Behind the idea that rape never occurs at all, and that the woman is invariably willing, is, first, the realization that many false accusations of rape have been made over the centuries (as the woman's excuse, where she is surprised with her lover, especially if he is a Negro or other social inequal); and, second, the fairly clear idea, in the folk mind, of the rape-fantasies in which women often engage, not out of fear but by way of casting all responsibility for the sexual acts in which they do wish to engage on the presumed 'rapist,' who then must carry all the blame. In more than one joke on a courtroom background, the whole intention is to ridicule the mere idea of rape, and to insist that the woman was willing. ' "*Your Honor, I wasn't within a mile of the place where this woman says she was raped. Besides, I didn't rape her, she asked me to fuck her. And anyway, that ain't the woman I fucked!*" ' (1:415.) As collected again, Berkeley, Calif. 1965, the end-line is even more openly farcical: "*— And besides, Judge, that ain't the girl I raped!*" (*Cf.* Randolph, *Hot Springs &c.*, Nos. 75, 317.)

It is observable that the male judge is expected to be grossly prejudiced in favor of the accused rapist's innocence, as understanding the improbability, or even impossibility, of the charge. As a matter of fact, rape is very easy to perform, it being necessary merely to put the woman *hors de combat* by means of stunning her with a blow with a club, or with intoxicant drugs, but in such cases, as Ruth Herschberger bitterly observes, it is difficult to pretend that she is really willing and enjoying every minute of it. Women judges would perhaps not be quite so charitable in such cases as the jokes expect of men. *A mountaineer about to be sentenced for statutory rape objects that the girl consented and was over sixteen anyhow. He is told that the law has been changed, and that the legal age of consent is now eighteen. "Well, before you sentence me, Judge, can I have a week out on bail? I want to tell a couple of my friends that're working under the old ruling."* (2:405.) The note here, of Damon & Pythias solidarity with the other man in his attempts at rape, is also the real source of the humor — with the additional overtones of incest and homosexuality — in the World War I classic: *A conscientious objector is asked, "What would you do if a Hun tried to rape your sister?" "I'd get between them."*

Old maids are presumably very grateful for the sinless opportunities of rape. In a joke usually ascribed to the American Civil War, but actually international: *A young girl and her maiden aunt are captured by enemy soldiers, who prepare to rape them. The girl begins to plead, but her aunt interrupts her:* "*Don't holler. Them soldiers have their orders. War is war.*" (1:201. Also, on a European background: "*A pogrom is a pogrom.*" N.Y. 1953.) *Train robbery.* "*All right now,*" *says the first robber,* "*we're going to rob all the men and fuck all the women.*" "*Now wait a minute,*" *says the second robber.* "*Let's just grab the dough and beat it.*" *Old maid:* "*Who's robbing this train, I'd like to know!*" (1:159.)

In a homosexual version: *Jesse James gets rattled while robbing a train with his henchman, and announces,* "*Line up against the wall, folks. We're gonna fuck all the men and rob all the women!*" "*Wait a minute, Jesse,*" *says his henchman,* "*ain't you got that backwards?*" "*Now just* YOU *wait a minute,*" *pipes up a homosexual passenger in a flutey accent;* "*you heard what Mr. James said!*" (Bloomington, Ind. 1963.) This is in the line of the jokes on pedicatory 'rape' as *courted* by the homosexual, given later in Chapter 10, in Series Two, in which the homosexual appears — as here — as a sort of wheedling child, trying to achieve the gratification he seeks by means of provocation, willful misunderstanding, and other childish techniques. *Riveter, to homosexual trying to flirt with him,* "*Get away from me, ya fuckin' fag, or I'll give you this jack-hammer up the ass!*" *The homosexual bends over, and looks back over his shoulder smiling:* "*A pwomise is a pwomise!*"

The identification of robbery and rape is standard in dreams, particularly with the phallic overdeterminants of the mask or hood (foreskin) and gun. The endless magazine cartoons of the old maid looking hopefully under the bed for a 'robber' make unmistakable the folk cognizance taken of this symbol. *A girl complains to the police that a man went up to her room with her, threw her on the bed, tore her clothes, and then ran off with her purse.* "*Did you scream?*" "*Of course not. How did I know he was going to rob me?*" (Transcontinental train, 1943.) Or: *The man has stolen her money out of her stocking in a theatre.* "*How did I know he was after my money?*" (Paris, 1958.)

Very few stories have been collected about rape as seen from the man's point of view. One often printed publicly: *A man has married one of twin sisters.* "*How do you tell them apart?*" "*I don't try. The other one just has to look out for herself.*" (McAtee, 1933, env. 8, with a variant giving the last line to the unmarried twin.) A case could probably be made for this particular joke having the oldest genealogy of almost any yet collected, as the situation is very similar to that in *Genesis,* xxix. 21–30 (Ezraic redaction, about 430 B.C.) in which Laban cheats Jacob by substituting Leah for Rachel on their wedding night.

*A man finds a girl naked in the woods tied to a tree. "A man tied
me to this tree so I can't move a muscle," she sobs, "and he raped me."
"Are you sure you can't move a muscle?" her rescuer asks. "No I
can't, so please untie me." "The hell I will! I'm going to rape you
myself."* (Minn. 1935.) This also has the earmarks of a very old story,
but the attempt has not been made to trace it. The obvious 'source' is
the Greek myth of Andromeda and Perseus, and the overcompensatory *looking away* by the chaste knight in Burne-Jones' saccharine
painting of "Andromeda Liberata" also suggests a not-too-well suppressed urge toward rape. A homosexual version of the joke, illustrated
in later editions, is in *La Légende Joyeuse* (1749) I, No. 51.

The woman tied to a tree by a robber, or stripped of her clothes,
is also the central plot-element of Fielding's *Tom Jones* (1749), made
into one of the finest English-speaking motion pictures since *Citizen
Kane*. Here *the young man, a foundling, who saves the half-naked
woman from the rapist (not robber) is strangely excited by her bared
breasts himself, and later has intercourse with her at an inn, neither
of them knowing that he is her son.* Copping out to the bogus morality
of his century — *Tom Jones* was published the same year as *Fanny
Hill!* — Fielding explains all this away by an absurd plot-gimmick, in
which the boy turns out not to be the woman's son at all, after the
flavor of the 'accidental' incest has been well savored by the reader.
This is known as eating your pornographic cake, and having it too.
Like looking at horror-pictures of war victims, or printing these in
magazines, to express one's righteous indignation about war. Tortured
dogs for 'anti'-vivisectionist magazines (in some cases posed and faked
for the good of the crusade), and the like. *Rainy day in heaven. Saint
Peter suggests to God that He go down to earth for one of those good
old times. "No, Peter, no more of that. I knocked up a Jewish girl two
thousand years ago, and they still haven't stopped talking about it."*
(1:499. This joke seems to have inspired the format of Charles Erskine
Scott Wood's *Heavenly Discourse*, 1927.) In spite of Ogden Nash's
'Seduction is for sissies; A he-man wants his rape!' most civilized men
have given it up as a bad job. Except during war, of course. But that
is what war is for, and why it has not been given up long ago: a moral
vacation for the exercising of all the horrible and destructive impulses
one feels, but cannot safely engage in except against helpless 'natives'
somewhere safely far from home — and against their women. As in the
story preceding. Why doesn't Jehovah pick on a handsome lady-angel,
somewhere around heaven? (Motif K1301, seduction by god.)

II. THE SADISTIC CONCEPT OF COITUS

Freud's remarkable analysis of the dream of the 'white wolves' ("The Dream and the Primal Scene," in "From the History of an Infantile Neurosis," 1918, *Collected Papers*, III. 499–508) gives us the patient's ultimate recollection that at the age of perhaps four, on waking up from an afternoon nap, 'he witnessed coitus *a tergo*, three times repeated; he was able to see his mother's genitals as well as his father's member; and he understood the process as well as its significance.' Freud returns to this astounding recollection some eight pages later (p. 516*n*), and although he then expresses some doubt as to whether what the patient actually saw was coitus from behind, 'three times repeated,' or whether the ordinary attitude may not have been used, he observes that in either case the sight of parental intercourse 'cannot fail to produce [on the child] the impression of being a sadistic act.' The reinforcement of this idea, as the child grows older, by similar impressions everywhere to be encountered in colloquial speech, folklore, and particularly in the violent expression of sexual taboo to which children are exposed, creates the almost inexpugnable belief that intercourse is a form of sadistically wreaking punishment upon another person.

Otto Fenichel, in what is virtually the encyclopedia or bible of psychoanalysis, *The Psychoanalytic Theory of Neurosis* (1945) p. 92, re-emphasizes the importance of childhood observations and of fantasies based on hints tantamount to observation:

> The observation of sexual scenes between adults (between the parents) by the child, simultaneously creates a high degree of sexual excitement — the nature of which varies according to the child's age — and the impression that sexuality is dangerous. This impression is caused by the fact that the quantity of excitement is beyond the child's capacity to discharge and is therefore experienced as traumatically painful; the child may also sadistically misinterpret what he perceives. . . . Instead of a primal scene all kinds of primal-scene substitutes may have been experienced: observations of animals, or nude adults, and even of scenes that objectively are entirely nonsexual but that are subjectively experienced as sexual. . . . Arguments between the parents are often equated with sexual scenes by children, and thus create a sadistic idea of sexuality.

This substitution is given every possible support by the anti-sexual culture in which the child finds himself. I have tried to show, in my monograph *Love & Death* (1949), how, in the decadence of a culture that has immolated itself on the anti-sexual ethic, the tabooed sexuality is given mass facilitation to express itself freely as sadism in all the popular arts or 'media,' with children not yet old enough to read encouraged to steep themselves in thousands upon thousands of scenes of horror and death. I will not attempt to rewrite that book here, but I could not in any case express the whole cultural ethic and intention better than the following little encapsulation, taken from a cute-kid comic-strip: *A movie screen shows the cowboy and blonde heroine locked in an embrace. The cowboy's horse looks sullenly on from one corner. The audience of little boys are turned backwards in their seats, and otherwise express their disapproval. In the foreground one is remarking to another:* "Ya gotta use your imagination, Herbie ... pretend they're engaged in mortal combat and they're locked in a deathgrip." (1952.) This is picked up and worked even more unmistakably into prose, signed Al Spong, in Charley Jones' *Laugh Book* (Wichita, Kan. May 1953), p. 28, as follows: 'Two small boys had just seen a romantic movie. "Wasn't it terrible?" said one in disgust. "I didn't think it was too bad," said the other. "During the kissing scenes I just closed my eyes and made believe he was choking her." ' (Observe that the woman is now named as the loser in what was originally just a 'mortal combat.') *Bonnie & Clyde* vomiting blood, yes; sex, no!

A good deal of material is scattered through the present volume bearing on the sadistic concept, for instance the ruthless propositions and gloats in the sub-section "The Male Approach" and "Seduction," above; the discussions of rectal intercourse as forced homosexual submission in the chapters on Animals, Homosexuality, and Castration; and the notes on the use of various synonyms for sexual intercourse, as meaning 'to cheat,' in the section "Dysphemism" in Chapter 14 (Series Two). These cannot all be repeated here, but should be consulted for the fullest presentation of even this small corner of the current float of folklore that so powerfully reinforces the sadistic concept of coitus. The materials in the next two sections: "*Mort Douce*" and "Displaced Aggressions," are also integral parts of the present treatment.

Much more could be said, of course, as to the expression of these various ideas in certain sub-literatures now very prominent, such as the American Mickey Spillane killer-volumes, and the British 'Hank Janson' (author's pseudonym). The 'James Bond' thrillers of the late

Ian Fleming, immediately spawn an equally popular set of imitations, like "The Man from U.N.C.L.E.," both in comic-book, and motion-picture or television form. These are all essentially modern folklore, as I have argued in *The Horn Book* (1964) in the article, "Folk Literature and Folklore: With a Few Words on Science-Fiction," p. 313-31, and are in fact very significant and influential folklore; but they are not *humorous*. Nor are they intended to be, for all the sullen 'sick' gags with which the killers in these products do their killing. It is worth observing, in the present context, that these sub-literatures of crime (they are always and only about crime, now cravenly *on the side of the law,* or at least of 'the Government') powerfully express the feelings of impotence and helplessness from which their audiences visibly suffer. This is done by overaccentuating the phallic attributes of guns, long lithe sports cars (secretly fitted up as motile weapons), rockets, etc., and, for that matter, the long lean phallicism of the heroes themselves, who are essentially nothing more than living penises. Superman becomes *Penisman!*

The penis is almost invariably understood in folklore to be primarily a weapon, and not an instrument of pleasure. For any one joke, limerick, or even synonym for the penis, in which it is described as having some special facility or even excrescent growth — such as a row of warts — which will specially please a woman, ten jokes or limericks or synonyms will be found in which the penis is used to harm, impale or, plainly, kill her. *Mata Hari appears at her execution naked under a fur coat. At the order to fire, she drops the coat and is killed by flying pants buttons.* (2:221. Limerick version in *The Limerick,* No. 285, omitting the lethal element.) — *A druggist is selling a farmer a French tickler. "Before I sell you this," he says, "do you know what that rubber barb on the end will do to a woman?" "No, but I know it'll make a plow-mule jump a ten-foot fence."* (N.Y. 1941.) — *The god Thor is bored drinking mead in Valhalla and comes down to earth and goes to bed with a chorus-girl, staying with her for three days and nights.* [Jupiter and Alcmene, mother of Hercules.] *On leaving, the fourth morning, he decides to tell her how signally she has been honored. "I'm Thor," he says. "You're Thor! I'm tho thore I can't even pith!"* (N.Y. 1942.) In a variant, *A woman wants a divorce because of her husband's inordinate sexual demands. "Have you filed your affidavit?" says her lawyer. "Filed it? It's so sore I can't even touch it!"* (D.C. 1944). Both female-fool jokes, of course, and set up on rather weak puns.

Where the penis cannot be counted on to cause sufficient pain, substitutes will do. *An old man is pleased when the girl screams during intercourse. "Am I hurting you, honey?" he beams. "Yes, you're stepping on my foot!"* (1:145. Numerous variants on the method of harm: the girl's pubic hair caught in his fly-buttons, etc. Compare also the more poignant version, earlier, of the monkey asking the same question of the female elephant.) — *A woman travelling in India falls in love with an Indian prince, and begs him to come back to America with her. He assures her that this is impossible, as the color of his skin would cause her to be ostracized, but he gives her a magic penis carved of ivory which, by saying to it the mystic word "Yogi," will solace her in his absence. Back in America, her sister finds her writhing on the bed one afternoon, under the ministrations of the magic penis, but does not believe a word of the story. "Ridiculous," she says. "Yogi, my ass! — Eek!!"* (N.Y. 1938.) Set up in a rather expurgated revenge version, in *Sex to Sexty* (1966) 6:44, as concerning a: *"Wooley Booger," a living but 'weird' animal, not magical but trained to destroy anything named in combination with its own name; which animal a woman buys from a bartender to punish her mean husband with, as, when he is told what it is, he is sure to growl the magic words, "Wooley Booger, my bohind* [sic]*!"* With items that have been so heavily manipulated by their chapbook editor, one is not really sure of the real folk-provenance of anything about them, least of all their vocabulary, and much is obviously and unfortunately being lost for the folklore record in this way. The reversal of the sexes in this version, in which it is the woman who magically attacks or rapes the man rectally, by means of the trained (magical) penis-demon, is its most significant feature. The "Woogly Booger" (ugly bugger) is originally Levantine: see *Histoires Arabes*, 1927, p. 25. This magic-penis story is the real prototype of that large family of Indo-European folktales slightly expurgated as the "Magic Cudgel" or "Whimwham" (Aarne Types 563 and 571-through-571c, with extensive references). It is also obviously connected with the "Mechanical Man" or sex-machine stories, to be discussed later.

Passive rectal urges such as those expressed by the man (assuming it was a man) who invented the 'oogly-booger' version, and by the men who repeat it, are almost impossible for men to admit to frankly in our society, being construed as specifically homosexual. Straining coincidence, but perfectly true, as I sit typewriting these pages in the farthest corner of France, a slender business envelope arrives in the mail (post-marked: Los Angeles, California — needless to say! — Oct. 27 [19]67), offering me — or, for that matter, anyone interested — for the absurdly low price of $9.95, plus 5% sales-tax for California residents, *'Exciting Stimulation with the Vibrex Cordless Massager,'* for both ladies AND gentlemen. 'Featherlight,' 'streamlined shape' (guess what), seven and one-quarter inches long (oh, come *on!*), and batteries included — well, accept no substitutes at any price! *'There is only one Vibrex . . . Can be carried in pocket or purse! — A joy to use anytime, on virtually any portion of the body . . . Older men feel young again as their body re-discovers youthful sensations and active energy!'* 'Cleopatra's secret' is the name earlier given to rectal stimulation of the man during inter-course, in a rare and curious American work of the 1930's, J. V. Wynn's *The Naked Truth About Sex.* It is this same manipulation which the French Mark Twain, Henry Monnier, is satirizing as *'The American corkscrew'* (also known in France as *'the secret of Marseille,'* being a specialty of the famous brothel-district of this ancient Greek port in France), in the original of the mysterious and significant "Sleeve Job" story, to which an entire section is devoted in the later chapter on Mar-riage, 8.III.3. The 'Vibrex' is certainly only an ethical and authentic massage device. (Say! I wonder if it would recharge on the 220-volt current here?) But what was frankly a vibrating dildo of milk-rubber was perfected and produced in 1937 by a famous anatomical model-maker, the late Dr. Vladimir Fortunato, in New York, being connected to a vibrating scalp-massage motor. Three sizes of replaceable phallic shafts (beautifully modelled in rubber) were available, specifically for women: *Large, Medium,* and *Very Large.* For my assistance in inspir-ing this invention, I was presented by Dr. Fortunato with the Medium size.

So much emphasis is placed, in later parts of the present chapter, on brags and lies and anti-brags concerning the length of the penis, that it should be borne in mind at all times in considering this lore that the enormous penises bragged of are seldom even pretended to be of use in pleasing the woman. The brags are intended as reassurance against the castratory notion that one's own penis is too small. This reassur-ance is also reinforced by projecting the idea of castration on the woman — the real use of all the proud inches beyond a reasonable five or six being to injure or impale her.

The following story is very unusual in its overcompensatory em-ployment of the long penis to cure rather than harm the woman, and it is observable that the cure is achieved accidentally, the man assuming rather that he has killed her. *An old maid goes to the doctor with vaginal complaints. He understands the problem at once, and tells her to get a goose egg, insert it in her vagina, and then get a man with the longest penis she can find to break it. She puts up a sign over her gate asking for a man with a very long penis to call, inserts the goose egg, and waits. Pat & Mike see the sign, measure penises, and Mike wins by four inches. Pat waits outside. Mike inserts his penis, the egg breaks, and the yolk comes running out. He dashes out of the house yelling,* "Run, Pat, run! I busted her shit-bladder!" (Idaho, 1919.) Also in *Anecdota* 2:294, in an almost meaningless variant with all pretense of sense dropped, in which: *A prostitute puts an egg into her vagina before intercourse because she 'had no opportunity' to dispose of it elsewhere!* (Compare Type 1464A, and *Kryptádia*, 1907, XI. 291 & 278.)

This is by no means a modern story, and it will be found in Béroalde de Verville's *Moyen de Parvenir* (1610) chapter 18, "Metaphrase;" in the translation by Arthur Machen as *Fantastic Tales* (1890, repr. 1923) p. 69. There is another translation of this one story as "The Breaker of Eggs," in *The Way of a Virgin*, by 'L. and C. Brovan' ('London, 1922' [New York, 1928?]) p. 237. The theme is also recollected in a peculiar semi-limerick entitled "Berries," printed in *Immortalia* (1927) p. 98:

> *Berries, berries, all kinds of berries,*
> *Chancres on her ass like California cherries,*
> *The first time I hit her*
> *I nearly broke her shitter,*
> *Down where the Hasiampa flows.*

With this one exception — if it is an exception at all — the other stories of the sexual use of the ultra-long penis, so much desired, are all of the undisguised sadistic variety. *Bride:* "Be careful, dear; remember my weak heart." *Groom:* "I'll go easy passing the heart." (1:177. Meaning, of course, that he will *not* go easy. See the next section, "MORT DOUCE," on the fantasy of killing the wife by means of intercourse.) In a burlesque routine, recorded D.C. 1945, *The comedian approaches a lady with a long account of his troubles. "That man's tale has touched my heart," she says. Straight man: "What a heart." Comedian: "What a tale!"* Another wedding-night colloquy: "Deep enough? — No, deeper. — Deep enough now? — No, deeper! — Now is it deep enough? — Ugg ugg." (2:163, in a homosexual version in which: *A man is pedi-*

cated by a stranger in a hotel bed; answering his rough inquiry, "Is that all right?" with "I guess so" — and finally, "I ghec gho.")

A prostitute accepts a customer with a very long penis only after putting a wad of chewing gum on the tip. "When I start chewing again," she says, "you'll know I've had enough." (D.C. 1945.) In an animal story on the same theme, A man's penis is too long for any woman to accept. He pays a farmer fifty dollars for the use of a ewe. Sounds of scuffling and agonized bleating from the barn. "Put a couple more sheep on in front," the man cries; "it's gone through!" (Calif. 1937.) In a well-known limerick exactly similar, a young man of Tibet can 'bugger six Greeks en brochette.' (The Limerick, No. 351, dating this 1941; with other limericks on impalement themes, Nos. 350 and 1722.)

Wedding-night sadism is naturally connected with the idea of defloration as a cutting or tearing — basically, a castrating — of the woman by means of the phallic weapon. A man who is overcharged five dollars in a whore-house has the girl stand naked against the wall while he runs at her several times from across the room with his erect penis (or attempts intercourse in her navel), explaining, "At these prices I'll make my own hole!" (2:49, the navel version. Text form, 1953. Also a punishment version, collected N.Y. 1952, in which: The man finally misses the girl, shatters a window, and lacerates his penis with shreds of glass. See further the chapter on Marriage, 8.III.5, "The Taboo of Virginity.") That even a fantasy as gruesome as this can be turned into fact is seen in the actual achievement of 'a hole of his own' by a male patient, through abdominal operation on himself, with the transfer of sexual interest from the penis to this, recorded by S. Mouchly Small, "Validation of Libido Theory," in Psychiatric Quarterly (1952–3) XXVII.: p. 38–51. As already noted, the ugly international self-castration scandal of the George ("Christine") Jorgensen case in the 1950's seriously revived this fantasy among homosexuals apparently ignorant of the actual nature of the vagina, and even of the existence of the female uterus, ovaries, and breasts.

III. MORT DOUCE

Unless he dies in the act of intercourse — the French mort douce, or 'sweet death' — no man is ever assumed in jokes to be sexually satisfied. The man's ability to satisfy and oversatisfy the woman is, however, taken for granted. One would imagine that this is intended to give her pleasure, but the jokes make very clear that there is no such intention. She is forcibly oversatisfied to prove the man's virile status, and, if possible, to kill her in the process. Oversatisfaction is therefore strictly sadistic, in an extension of the idea of the penis as a weapon that harms and may destroy the woman. *A man leaves a girl in a hotel room and goes down for a smoke in the lobby. She lays writhing naked on the bed. A bellboy sees and goes down and tells the man, "Say mister, your girl is laying on the bed moving around like someone was on her. Ain't you worried leaving her like that?" "No sir-ee, sonny. When I fuck 'em, they stay fucked!"* (1:229.) The sexual brag, invariably made to other men, can also be phrased more politely. *Two men in the lobby of a honeymoon hotel. "Where's your wife?" says one. "She's upstairs smoking." "Gee, mine is upstairs too, but she's not that hot."* Compare the similar purposeful perversion or misunderstanding: *Man, worried about disease, to a friend: "Say, does your penis burn after inter-course?" "I don't know; I never thought of lighting it."* (N.Y. 1965.) Female version: *One woman asks another: "Do you smoke after inter-course?" "I don't know; I never looked."* (San Francisco, 1968.) Note the reassuring change from fear of disease to female sexual 'heat.'

Peculiar accidents sometimes assist in oversatisfying the woman, with the element of bodily harm to her not even disguised. *A man is having intercourse with a prostitute standing up in an alley. She keeps nodding as he thrusts. "You like it, eh?" he says. She nods vigorously. "Yes, but you've got a bit of me scarf tucked in."* (D.C. 1951.) Various sadistic cleanups of this have circulated recently in the public prints, in which an obnoxious woman in a theatre is punished by immobilizing her head with her scarf, or in an interestingly guilty reversal of direction, by having all the hairpins removed from her head by means of a magnet. (Compare also the mare and handkerchief at the end of the section "Monkeys and Elephants," 3.1, above.) — *An iceman is having intercourse with the maid standing up against a door in the hall. After he is finished he notices that she is still wiggling and writhing. "What's the matter, honey," he asks; "didn't I satisfy you?" "Oh, you satisfied me, all right," she replies. "I just can't get the door-knob out."* (D.C. 1943.)

Nihilistic ideas of bodily dissolution and destruction, of everything rotting or disappearing and becoming dust and ashes, are common in childless or menopausal women, and in men at the climacteric who are beginning to worry about their potency. The urge to create a monu-ment for oneself — a child, a pyramid, or some other try at immortality

— is the humanly constructive side of this common symptom of depression in the late 40's or 50's of one's age. The inhuman side is the projection of the fears of bodily dissolution, impotence, and death upon someone else. This is the real explanation of the insane technological destruction of millions of human victims by the Nazis when they knew their régime was doomed, and, to come no closer to home, is also seen in the killing of horses, wives, and other chattels (*suttee*) on the pyre, in India, or in the tomb of kings of the Levant.

Failing any handy supply of Jews, 'gooks,' horses, or other convenient victims on whom to displace pre-impotent fears of bodily dissolution, women are an easily available substitute, particularly when the fantasy can be dressed up as a joke. In a bit of British blackout humor about 1940, often reprinted in America during the war, *Two Cockney women are talking in a communal bomb shelter during an aerial bombardment. "Ain't it awful,"* says one; *"we might get blasted into maternity any minute." "Yes,"* says the other, *"and the worst of it is, we'd never know who done it."* Possibly related: *The old maid who is finally convinced by the doctor that she is pregnant, says "Damn that air-raid warden, anyhow! He said it was artificial respiration."* This joke has, of course, been given a whole new lease on life by the 'mouth-to-mouth' artificial respiration launched in the 1960's, but actually only to be operated — on men at least — by policemen and other sacerdotal personages. Surely related: bomb-shelter joke in 6.ii.1, p, 344.

A man takes a woman to a hotel room, and she removes a false leg saying she hopes he won't mind. While she is in the bathroom he takes the leg all apart, and can't get it together again. He runs out in the hall distractedly and explains his predicament to the first man he sees. "That's nothing," says the man, *"I've got a girl with both legs apart, and I can't even remember which room she's in."* (D.C. 1952.) The attempted modulation back into simple eroticism at the punch-line does not quite come off, as the ugly situation of bodily dissolution is too clearly the real point of the joke. Also, all such jokes on wooden legs, blindness and other mutilations are obvious surrogates of castration — here projected on the women. One of the sources of this story is evidently the much more complete 'dismantling' tale: *A man in an upper berth on a train is watching an old maid undressing in the berth below. She unscrews a wooden arm, wooden leg, takes off her wig, removes false teeth, and a glass eye. Suddenly she sees him watching her. "What do you want?" she cries. "You know damn well what I want,"* he says; *"unscrew it and throw it up here."* (1:261. Type 1379*.)

Stories about cripples, prosthetic limbs, wigs, and the like have a special fascination for persons — especially adolescents — suffering from castration ideas. Normal adults generally find them repulsive, unless they are like the army officer in one of Hemingway's last and worst novels — but then, all his novels were exceedingly poor, despite his great reputation — who carries small testicular objects in his pockets, to rub together reassuringly, 'a sucker for crips.'

One solution of the guilts implicit in stories such as this is to die together with one's victim, as in the legend of the blinded, sexually-enslaved Samson (according to rabbinic legend, his 'grinding' really refers to forced sexual use by the Philistine women, *Judges,* xvi. 21) dragging down the pillars of the house to destroy himself and the Philistines together. In a sexual sense, this exactly expresses the ideal *mort douce,* as of Tristan & Isolde. *A Marine and a girl retire to a hotel room, hanging out a "Do not disturb" sign on the door. After three days the manager breaks in, but finds no one in the room. He staggers down the stairs to tell his tale. "All there was," he says, "was two quivering assholes on the bedspread!"* (D.C. 1952, with a variant in which these are the winners of the 'International Fucking Contest' as found by the judges.) The Kilkenny cats, their tails tied together and then thrown over a clothesline, who fought until nothing was left but the knot, belong to this same sado-nihilistic group, as also the impacted version — very similar to the joke just given — in which two snakes start swallowing each other simultaneously, beginning at the tail. (Given as a riddle.)

The sexual version, of the 'quivering ass-holes,' is connected with the important puzzle-stories, "The Sleeve Job" and "The Mysterious Card," which are treated at length in the chapter on Marriage, 8.III.3 and 4, below. Note especially the form given in *La Diligence de Lyon* (Brussels, 1882) by 'Le Grand Jacques' [Richard Lesclide, the secretary of Victor Hugo], in which Henry Monnier's original recitation or joke, which has become "The Sleeve Job" in America, is inflated into an occult horror-story on a man and woman who finally disappear in an explosion at some sort of Black Mass, searching for a higher wisdom, *à la* Faust. This is of course a standard fantasy of death and dissolution, as the punishment for over-vaunting ambition of divine knowledge or power by a human being, as for instance the myth of Prometheus, or more particularly of Dædalus and Icarus, in which, as noted in *The Horn Book,* p. 330, the parallel is very distinct, 'since here the father actually figures in the tragedy, though only in debilitated form, the real Father-God being evidently the Sun, who both is challenged by Icarus' flight, and deals out the ultimate punishment.' In modern forms, certainly since the alchemical legend of Faust, the death or disappearance is understood as being dragged off, or 'summoned' to Hell by the Devil, as in the tremendous climax of Mozart's masterpiece, *Don Giovanni* (the libretto written by Emanuele Conegliano, called 'Lorenzo Da Ponte'). It is worth noting also, as to the sexual aspect of the transgression punished by diabolical death, that Don Juan, in this version, is not punished for any of his sexual sins against his 'thousand and three' female victims — and those only in Spain! — but for the Oedipal crime of murder of the father-figure, compounded by mocking and defying the heroic statue of the Commander: an even more obvious father-god figure, who actually drags him off to Hell. Compare Hamlet's verbal and pretended subservience to his murdered father's Ghost, promising to 'sweep to his revenge,' but his actual flaunting and evading of the Ghost's demand for vengeance.

There is also straight sexual murder. Fantasies of this are more popular than is suspected. The whole following section, of "Displaced Aggressions," records what are essentially only minced forms of the fantasy of killing the woman with the penis. Of undisguised forms: *A prostitute dies in a client's embrace* [the reverse of the usual *mort douce*]. *He is put on trial for murder.* "*How did it happen?*" *asks the judge.* "*I can't figure it out, your Honor. I had my thumb up her ass, my tongue down her throat, and two pounds of cock in her cunt. How the breath of life got out of her, God only knows.*" (2:334.) This appears as female-fool story (on the 'Pétomane' or anal-aspiration of air Yoga principle) in *Histoires Arabes,* p. 83; and the original in the important French poetic 'drollery,' *Le Cabinet Satyrique* (1618), "Un Compagnon, par charité."

The subsidiary fantasy of intercourse with the corpse is always expressed as simply an accident, or as the wife's fault for being habitually so cold in intercourse that the husband does not know when she is dead. (1:429.) See also the sections on sex-hostility in the chapter on Adultery, 9.1.4. *A man in a crowded hotel is given a room in which a woman has just died, the body being behind a screen. He rushes down to the desk and says, "Say, that woman in Room 33 is dead!" "I know," says the room clerk, "but how did you find out?"* (1:285.) Modified even further, with the lethal wish hidden behind a mere mispronunciation and projected on the usual Jewish scapegoat: *A Jewish couple register at a hotel for their silver wedding anniversary. An hour later the wife is heard shouting, "Murder! Fire! Police!" As the detective is about to burst in, he hears her more plainly, crying: "Furder, Meyer, p'lease!"* (2:372.) Projected on the victim — the best method — as suicide: *Girl: "I think I'm knocked up." Playboy: "What are you going to do?" Girl, emotionally: "Kill myself!" Playboy: "Good sport!"* (N.Y. 1953.)

In a very popular story, *A big powerful man with a tiny wife is disgusted with her slovenly ways and decides to kill her with love. He goes to bed with her on getting home from work Friday and can barely stagger to work Monday morning, leaving his wife exhausted on the bed. When he gets home he sees fresh curtains in all the windows, and decides that the neighbors have come in to lay out the body and clean up the place. In the kitchen he finds his wife stark naked except for a little apron, happily preparing a six-course dinner. "But, honey . . .?" he says. She points an admonishing finger at him. "You treat me right, I'll treat you right."* (N.Y. 1938, enlarged to a two-page storiette in "Wife Torture — A Fine Art," in *For Men Only*, in the same year.) In a self-punishing variant: *After months of this, the man is a broken hulk while his wife is blossoming gloriously. "Heh heh," he confides to a friend, in a cracked voice, "she may not look it but she's only got two more weeks to live."* (N.Y. 1951.)

All this is doubtless very amusing, but the reality behind these humorous notions and tales is the unbearable gruesomeness of the lust-murder, and sexual intercourse with the lacerated corpse. I remember seeing Dr. Robert Latou Dickinson, dean of American gynecologists, in a towering rage over what he called 'German medical pornography,' set off by the four pages of photographs of lust-murder victims that, as he felt, disgrace the four massive volumes and 3,680 text pages of the *Bilder-Lexikon der Erotik* edited by Leo Schidrowitz (1928–31). I wondered what he would have thought — but did not have the heart to show him, as he was a very old man — of the volume, *The Sexual Criminal,* by Dr. J. Paul de River, which had just appeared in Springfield, Illinois, under the imprint of a very respectable medical publisher, in 1949.

This interesting work, of some three hundred pages, contains exactly thirty pages on sexual crime *per se*. The rest is entirely devoted to photographs of the ripped bodies of lust-murder victims (printed on special calendared paper), transcripts of the testimony of the murderers as to just what they did and how they did it, and a bonus supplement, "The Poetic Nature of the Sado-Masochist," giving fourteen pages of doggerel by patients (so the author says) on the pleasures of hammering spikes into women's arteries, etc. In a third printing necessary less than two years later, Dr. de River adds an extra chapter — which he had somehow forgotten earlier — in which he discusses for the first time such minor matters, when one has photographs of mutilated corpses to reproduce, as the "Etiology, Therapy, and Prognosis" of sexual crime. Dr. de River, who was connected with the Los Angeles police department (eleven lines of other affiliations on the title-page: a record, surely) has the crust to subtitle his opus, "A Psychoanalytic Study," and both he and his publisher, Mr. Charles C. Thomas, may congratulate themselves that they have produced the most nauseating volume ever published for sick little physicians. I say this on the assumption that physicians are allowed to buy the book. Of the four copies I have ever seen, only one was in the hands of a physician: an eminent birth-controller whose interest in the subject of lust-murder was obscure. The others were the proud possessions of a hypnotic-dentist, a murder-mystery writer (whose study was on the top floor of an operating slaughterhouse, and whose special pride was his knowledge of cadaverous pathology), and an expert on the unrecorded music of Bach.

IV. DISPLACED AGGRESSIONS

The reader has now been given, as I understand it, the proper background against which to assess just what is being displaced in the following displacements of aggression. Some of these are called displacements only by courtesy, in that they restrict themselves to verbal threats rather than deeds, even though the specified object of their aggression is the woman. *A bride refuses to let her husband consummate their marriage the first night because she is menstruating. The second night she has nervous diarrhea (or a head-cold). The third night he appears at her bedside in hip-boots and a raincoat, carrying a storm lantern, and announces: "Mud or blood, shit or flood, McClanahan rides tonight!"* (Idaho, 1942. Often collected with the Jewish names Goldberg or Ginsberg.) In what is probably the original story, there is no rhyming brag but a plain threat: *A man takes his girl out for a buggy ride. He drops the reins and begins to hug and kiss her, but she refuses, saying that she is menstruating. "You know, there's another way you can satisfy me," he says, but she explains that she has piles. He drives a little further, stops the horse, gets out, picks up a rock, gets back in and says, "Now you just tell me that you got lockjaw, and I'll crush your skull!"* (1:25.) A limerick version, without any death-threat, is given in Norman Douglas' *Some Limericks* (1928), reprinted in *The Limerick* (Paris, 1953) No. 487, concerning 'the mate of a lugger' – with obvious rhymes.

No depth of callousness is too low in stories of this type if the woman can somehow be made to blame. The undisputed nadir: *A bride on her wedding night has an attack of St. Vitus dance just as she is getting into bed. The groom calls for four bellboys, has each one hold an arm or a leg, gets into position over his bride, and yells to the straining bellboys, "Let 'er go!"* (1:148. On the image of a bronchobuster [*n.b.*] riding a bucking horse.) As noted, these are called displacements of aggression only by courtesy. It is necessary to make some distinction between verbal threats and callousness on the one hand, and physical acts – on whatever pretext – on the other, such as that of the 'foolish' Englishman, noted in an earlier chapter, who grinds the ferrule of his cane in his bride's vagina to make sure it doesn't contain a hornet's nest! In a similar example, stopping at the threat, the extenuating circumstance is not folly but money (*cheat* equals *rape*), and the physical direction of the sadistic motion is reversed. Other than that, it is strictly a case for Dr. de River. *A carpenter who has put up a partition in a whore-house is told to "take it out in trade" when he asks for his promised thirty dollars pay. He tells the madam that no one in the house attracts him but her. Flattered, she lies down and he puts his thumb in her vagina and his middle finger in her anus. "What do you call that?" she asks. "That's the bowling-hold, you son of a bitch," he replies. "Now gimme my thirty dollars or I'll rip out your partition!"* (2:77 and 151.)

Seriously, how do people get laughs with jokes like that? I have remarked in the Introduction that various tellers and listeners have their 'styles' in dirty jokes. Some tell only castration stories, or scatological stories, or *principally* castration or scatological stories, and so forth. There are also anti-styles. Many people cannot endure castration stories, or any kind of dirty stories, or – over-reacting in the other direction – collapse in hysterical and unwilling laughter at stories of scatology or homosexual rape. The commonest prejudice among adults is against 'food-dirtying' themes: the snot and vomit and disgusting-food stories so commonly told by children. These are grouped with jokes on venereal disease, in Chapter 12 (Series Two), as "Narsty-Narsties." My own anti-style concerns the material in this and the four preceding sections, which I find personally unfunny and repugnant, and have only dealt with at all on the principle that one cannot refuse to discuss certain kinds of criminals on the grounds that they are too depraved. I realize that my feeling about sadistic themes pegs me immediately as a repressed sadist (with powerful homosexual or masochistic identification with the woman), but I trust there is some slight credit available for the repression.

Three stories, which I have reserved to bolster this point, are all based on the peculiar question of the repression of *speech* during intercourse. As all three pointedly combine the man's complete and unexpected silence with his callous approach and rough handling of the woman, it seems clear that there is a displacement here of sadistic guilt from the phallic area to the oral; and in this way the repression of oral sadism allows an equal and opposite freedom for phallic sadism. In the case of sexually repressed, but verbally terrifically sadistic writers, such as Swift and Carlyle, and others who might be mentioned, the trick can be seen operating in the other direction.

Two Cockney girls: "Do you know 'Arry Brown?" "Do I know 'Arry Brown! Took meself off to a pub the other night for a mug of ile for me old man. On the way 'ome, 'oo do I meet but 'Arry Brown. 'E tikes me mug of ile and drinks it, tikes me in 'is arms and kisses me; 'e ups me and 'e downs me; ins me, outs me; wipes 'is tally-whacker on me petticoat, and goes orf whistling 'Britons Never Will Be Slyves.' Do I know 'Arry Brown!" (2:50. Often circulated as a mimeographed or hektographed obscœnum during World War II, as "Do I know Americans!") In some versions the man goes off singing rather than whistling, which may be either a mistake in transmission or a signal of the end of the repressive situation. What is essentially the same story is given in *Anecdota Americana* [1927] marked 'from the Hungarian,' the editor, Mr. Joseph Fliesler, having been born in Suczawa, Austria-Hungary, in 1897. *Two peasant girls are discussing soldiers. "The strangest thing happened this morning," says one. "A soldier came into our house, where I was all alone, and without a word*

*he took off his sword and his coat and pants, and threw me on the bed
. . . . Then he got up, put on his clothes and his sword and went out
— still without a word. Lord only knows what he wanted!"* (1:85.) In
an American version, *A hotel guest rings for a chambermaid. When
she enters the room he unceremoniously throws her on the bed, has
intercourse with her, and pushes her out the door. "To this day,"* says
the maid, *"I don't know what he was ringing for."* (1:86.)

A Yiddish version, told to me by the editor of *Anecdota* in 1940,
and in any case relevant in the transmission of this story, attempts a
rational explanation of the whole scene. *A Jewish travelling salesman
in a small town hotel calls in the red-headed chambermaid, and without a word throws her on the bed and has intercourse with her. Afterwards she says, "You know, I'm not mad, but how is it you Jewish
drummers never ask a girl, the way the other fellows do? It's been the
same way with the last six Jewish drummers. They just throw me on
the bed. What's the big idea?" He takes her by the hand into the bathroom, and silently swings open the door of the medicine cabinet. Written in soap along the bottom of the mirror in Yiddish is the legend:
"Die röyte shicksa trennt. (The red-headed gentile screws.)"* As an
explanation of the man's total silence, this is self-evidently pretty weak.

Magical silence, or silence during prayer, are of course common
folk-themes (Aarne Type 1351; Thompson, *Motif-Index*, VI. 705), as
also other ritual abstentions reappearing in folktales, such as the warning to Aladdin not to let even the hem of his garment touch any of the
walls in the cavern (Hell) where he finds the Magic Lamp, on the
threat of falling instantly dead. The same is true, according to Jewish
legend, of the High Priest entering the Holy of Holies, who is to come
'near unto the altar' but not touch it, and who must wear linen
breeches to cover his nakedness, under pain of death. (*Exodus,* xxviii.
42-43.) With the joke just given, compare the title — only — of Im-
manuel Olsvanger's Yiddish joke-book, *Röyte Pomerantsen* (New
York, 1947), *i.e.* "The Red-Headed Pomeranian Woman," clearly a
folk-type in Russian-Jewish stories, like the Little Jewish Tailor or
Trickster, Yiddle with his Fiddle, the proud "Yecke" [Short-coat-wear-
ing] German Jew, and so forth. It was once widely believed, and
remnants of this belief still exist in most Western countries, that red
hair is *the mark of the Devil,* that is to say of the Devil's adultery
with the mother, or of intercourse during menstruation, since often
neither the father nor mother of a red-haired child will have hair of

that color. Thus Cain is supposed to have had red hair, implying the guilty intimacy between Eve and the Devil-Serpent, who was supposedly responsible for her sex education, just as his consort, Lilith, the female Devil, was responsible for that of Adam, and therefore hates and tries to kill in their infancy all the children of Eve. As the Devil's mark, red hair is still supposed to betoken the worst possible character in both men and women, meaning the most unrepressed expression of *id*-impulses: egoism and aggressivity in men (Judas Iscariot had red hair, we are told), and sexuality in women: *Die röyte shicksa trennt.*

An old maid finds herself pregnant. The women of the neighborhood offer various possible explanations: she may have bathed in a tub in which a man had just washed, or swallowed semen placed on some food. More realistically, one suggests that perhaps one of their husbands did it to her while she was asleep. They all agree that that must be the answer, but who? A farmer's wife speaks up: " 'Twern't Tim. 'F'twere, he'd a woke 'er." (Minn. 1946.) — *Two women are bragging about their husbands. One explains that her husband is so considerate that when he comes home late at night he tiptoes up the stairs with his shoes off, hangs up his clothes without a sound, and gets into bed without even disturbing her sleep. "Pooh!" says the other. "You call that a husband? Ptooey on such a husband! My Herman always slams the front door, no matter how late he comes home. When he comes in the room he throws his shoes on the floor with enough noise to wake the dead, and he drops his clothes all over the place. Then he comes over and slaps me on the behinder and says: "How's about it, Becky?"* (Curran, 1938, p. 69. Also, end-line: "IF *you please!*" — N.Y. 1953.)

Repression is one solution. Another, closely related, is to deny every part of the sadistic scene except the defensible normality of the punch-line. The woman in the last story above is taken in by this — that is to say, she accedes in the sadistic concept of coitus — and the listener is expected to do the same. A slap on the behinder is, of course, nothing. Some of the other displaced sadistic jokes ask one to swallow a much larger camel and strain at a much smaller gnat. The rape story, earlier, where all the carefully built up outrages of kidnapping, indecent exposure, assault, etc. etc., and finally rape, turn out at the punch-line to be "just a plain ordinary fuck!" is essentially of this type, 'where the story offers all the pleasure of the taboo act, but also offers a miraculous happy ending in which it all turns out to be an innocent mistake . . . the only kind of a story that a properly repressed sadist can really enjoy.'

A few examples will make the method clear, as also the basic insincerity of the "*CRIME does not pay*" apology in the end-line. *The wife is having a baby. The doctor calls downstairs to the husband, "Have you got a chisel?" then a mallet, corkscrew, pipe-wrench, etc. The white-faced husband finally asks, "Doc, do you figure it's a boy or a girl?" "I don't know. I can't get my instrument case open."* (Minn. 1946.) — *A man in a bar is drinking quietly, when a querulous drunk sitting next to him says, "Look at that Irishman over there. I hate the Irish! And look at that Jew. If there's one thing I hate worse than an Irishman, it's a Jew!" Etc. etc., ending with, "And what's your religion, brother?" "I'm a Quaker." "Well if there's one thing, etc. etc." The Quaker: "Fuck thee."* (N.Y. 1952. A garbled and hopelessly expurgated version, with the end-line, "Well — to Heaven with thee!" given to the *drunk*, is printed in the Canadian *Magazine Digest*, March 1953, p. 84.) This story will be treated again, with others similar, in the context of erotic and scatological vituperation and insult, in Chapter 14, "Dysphemism," in the Second Series. There has been quite a rash of jokes of this type over the last decade, and the connection with continuing political tensions and the ever-present fear of 'real' war — *i.e.* war in which this time something is liable to land *on America,* for a change, instead of always safely on the Other Guys — is made clear in the choice of the famously anti-war and anti-violent Quaker as the (suddenly violent) hero of the preceding example.

Another, collected almost as often, was the hit of the American Psychological Convention in Washington, D.C., in the summer of 1952, which went on formal record as opposed to the Jim Crow treatment of Negroes in the national capital. As remarked concerning the hornet's nest joke earlier (Fools: 2.v.1), in spite of the ultra-sensitiveness of audiences in recent years about anti-Jewish and anti-Negro jokes and phrases, even so gruesomely anti-woman a nightmare (literally) as the following will pass without particular comment — except of approval — in joke-telling sessions.

A girl is picked up by a man who takes her to his apartment. While he is changing into something more comfortable she notices that the wallpaper design is of crossed whips, and is intrigued by a large brass button marked PUSH ME. [Alice in Wonderland.] *She pushes, a secret panel slides up, and she steps into a completely outfitted torture-chamber, with whips, Iron Maidens, branding irons, and an operating table with a bucketful of damp sponges below. Suddenly her host enters behind*

*her, and the panel slides shut. He is dressed in a yellow silk dressing-
gown and his eyes are slitted evilly.* "W-w-what are you going to do
to me?" *she falters.* "I'm going to fuck you till your ears fly off!" *he
announces.* "Thank God!" (D.C. 1952.) Except for the pretense that the
end-line — which sometimes adds, "And faints" — somehow revokes
the existence of the torture-chamber, this is exactly the plot of a novel of
erotic flagellation, *The Way of a Man With a Maid,* published by Carrington in Paris about 1900, and reprinted in New York in the 1930's.
The mass production and sale of semi-erotic [!] torture-chamber illustrations without the slightest harassment by the law, by the firm of
Irving Klaw in New York throughout the 1940's and continuing, is
discussed and illustrated, with reproductions of four of Klaw's photographs and fantasy drawings of girls trussed up ready for the lust-
murder, in the newspaper, *Exposé* (New York, Oct. 1952) pp. 1 and 5.
My own editorial, "The Degenerates' Corner," in the same issue, hardly
more than touches the edge of the subject. The producers are proud of
their thousands of dollars worth of business yearly in these absolutely
sickening products of diseased minds, nor was there presumably any
law that they were breaking, till the Supreme Court's decision in the
Mishkin case in 1966, simultaneously allowing *Fanny Hill.* British
materials of this kind are illustrated — and curiously defended — in Mrs.
Gillian Freeman's *The Undergrowth of Literature* (1967).

The way out, if it is a way out, is strictly that of personal repression
— the same sort of wise stifling of spontaneous urges that makes one
refrain from picking up a jewel-like red-hot coal. Since, to speak in the
jargon, jokes are always the expression of *id* impulses and not of the
superego, repression has to be smuggled into the joke under the disguise of economy or even of a subtler form of the repressed impulse
itself. *A man offers to give a hundred dollars to hit a certain chorus-
girl on her bare buttocks. A friend who knows the girl arranges matters with her* [the 'Brown-nose Pimp' of *New York Unexpurgated,*
1966, p. 83], *and all three go up to the girl's hotel room. She lays down
on the bed with her dress up, and the man caresses her buttocks, mar-
velling at their warmth, sliding his finger into her vagina, and so
forth.* "Go ahead. What are you waiting for? Hit her!" *urges the
friend.* "Why should I? This feels wonderful, and it doesn't cost me a
thing." (1:73.) The Freudian 'economy of the libido,' and not the
economy of cash it pretends to be.

The masochist's problem is *guilt,* as Dr. Theodor Reik penetratingly
shows in *Masochism in Modern Man.* The sadist's problem is also

guilt, but he projects this guilt upon the person to whom he is sexually attracted — accusing his victim of various crimes or criminal intentions (The Wolf and the Lamb, in *Aesop's Fables*) — and is then able to punish himself in someone else's body. This may seem like a complicated way around, but it successfully avoids pain for the sadist, while keeping him happily in a violent atmosphere of pain and tears: his own by identification. I can well remember being present, as additional-dialogue writer on a musical comedy many years ago, and watching the director-star verbally brutalizing everyone onstage, the orchestra, myself, and his girl-friend sitting with him (who had had the nerve to expostulate when he reduced one of the actresses to tears). In the shambles of lacerated emotions he had created, he turned imploringly to one of his male-toadies and asked — striking himself self-pityingly or self-punishingly on the chest with both fists — "*Why do they HATE me like this?*" Beautifully condensed, in joke form: *The Masochist, pleading: "Beat me! . . . beat me!" The Sadist, sneering: "No!"* (Calif. 1952.) This may be the only solution.

V. THE PENIS

It would be too much of a simplification to pretend that the only intended use of the excessively long penis so often bragged of in jokes is to harm the woman. One goes down into the depths more circuitously than that. Like most of the sexual perversions, such as braid-cutting and coprophilia, sadism is an attempt to deny castration — invariably feared as a punishment for sexual sin. The tearing or harming of the woman's genitals with the penis or with some obvious penis symbol, such as a red-tipped branding iron, is intended to force upon her the blame for the sexual sin (as witness the fact that it is she who is being punished: *Genesis,* iii. 16), and the status of a castrated being. In this way the sadist reassures himself that *he* does not deserve the punishment of castration and that, in fact, his own body remains physically and phallically unharmed. The direct concentration on penis size, irrespective of whether or not it is used to castrate the woman, is a simpler and, fortunately, a more common neurotic method of self-reassurance against the fear of castration.

A drunk falls asleep while urinating sitting on the curb under a lamp-post. Two pranksters tie a blue ribbon around his penis. He wakes up in the morning, sees the ribbon, and says to his penis: "I don't know where you've been or what you've been doing, but I'm glad to see you won first prize." (N.Y. 1938.) In a narcissistic brag of the same type, embodying the folk notion that Negroes have specially large penises, *A Negro falls asleep under a haystack and wakes to find a blacksnake, which has crawled up his pants leg, putting its head out through his fly. "I knew you was long, and I knew you was black, but where'd you get them baby-blue eyes?"* (2:124.) The hidden element in this joke is the idea of the dangerous, fanged enemy-penis crawling up the pants leg to destroy one's own penis — the brag being a denial that this has happened — and it is often 'humorously' pointed out by men that they are in far more danger from mice, what with tight pants legs that cannot be pulled up to haul the animal out, than women are with their traditional screams and held-up skirts at the menace of the furry little phallic beast. *The Limerick* (Paris, 1953) No. 1211, gives a versified example of this fear, of a workman named Rawls who *'fell asleep in his old overalls, And when he woke up he Discovered a puppy Had bitten off both of his balls.'* (1941.) The essential feature here, of the contest of penises, has been lost sight of.

The theme of the penis spoken-to is at least as common as that of the *mentula loquens,* or speaking penis (Thompson Motif D1610.6), and often involves pet names, such as 'Oscar,' 'Junior,' or 'my friend,' generally in encouraging the penis to further sexual exploits, or in shaming it for sexual failures. *A wife asks for a divorce on the grounds that her husband has intercourse with her ten times a night. When these grounds are considered insufficient* [!] *she says, "Well I didn't want to mention it and disgrace the family, but the other night he raped my mother, and my grandmother, and my 10-year-old sister too. And then he put his eyeglasses on that thing of his and said, 'Look around and see if there's anything you missed!'"* (2:80. Often as of a Negro, who says, "*Look aroun', brudder,*" &c. N.Y.) The sadistic tone hardly needs to be observed. The use of 'any*thing*' instead of 'any*one*' (also: 'some*thing*' instead of 'some*one*') to refer to another person as a mere sexual object is a common hostile locution used by men of women, and particularly in homosexual slang. The use of the eyes as symbolizing testicles, underlined in the preceding joke by the eyeglasses, is a common symbol of long history, as in the wall-scrawls of Kilroy, which excessively overdetermine this symbolization by means of the bulging eyes, protuberant ears, and the invariably present clinging hands at both sides. (See the particularly obvious example, with a banana nose, reproduced by Richard Sterba, "Kilroy Was Here," in *American Imago,* 1948, v.181.)

The natural phenomenon of erection offers a primary reassurance of phallic integrity, and resistance to fantasied notions of castration. This point will be returned to in considering aphrodisiacs later, as the desire for renewed erection — quite apart from the desire for sexual pleasure — is a key element in the attempt to dissipate by means of aphrodisiacs the emotionally shattering effect that advancing impotence has on older men. The reassurance offered in the following story is specifically in the matter of erection, with sexual pleasure a mere background implication if present at all. *An old gentleman invites a young lady on a crowded streetcar to sit on his lap, saying that he is too old to get up and give her his seat, and by the same token too old for it to be wrong to offer his lap. After jolting along in the streetcar for a few blocks, with her bouncing on his lap, he says, "Miss, one of us will have to get up. I'm not as old as I thought I was."* (*Anecdota,* 1933, No. 415.) A few other jokes collected also carefully draw the woman's attention verbally to the fact of erection. *A nude girl refuses intercourse, saying "I'm on strike." "Me too," says her boyfriend, "but I have a feeling I'm going to get a raise, and then we'll both go to work."* (D.C. 1946. Basically only a pun.)

The sexual nature of the midget cars popular about 1930 and again since World War II as 'sports cars' has always been sensed at the folk level, though without any understanding of the underlying identification with the machine as penis and phallic power. This has become quite self-conscious in the hood and car-body designs of recent years. In the midget or 'sports' car, the individual actually *becomes* the automobile, and assimilates its motive and projective power to his own body. In one of the earliest of the midget car jokes, *A man gets into an Austin with a copy of* Lady Chatterley's Lover, *and can't get out.* (1933.) In a longer version: *A young man is out driving in an Austin with his girl. He parks and the girl spreads a blanket on the grass and lies down on it, calling to him, "Hurry up, honey, before I get over this mood." He calls back despairingly, "I can't get out of the car until I'm over this mood."* (D.C. 1944.) Even the disposition of the testicles, or rather the impossibility of disposing them, is accounted for in the Austin limerick:

There was a young fellow from Boston
Who rode around in an Austin.
There was room for his ass
And a gallon of gas,
But his balls hung outside, and he lost 'em.

(*The Limerick*, No. 1137, dating this example 1938, with an even more specifically castratory variant, dated 1950, in which the testicles are 'caught on a rock.')

The ancestor or prototype of all these Austin jokes and vehicular jokes generally can be traced back at least two centuries, as will be noted in a moment. Their essential similarity throughout is in their struggling to rationalize, by the presence of the girl on the man's lap, that riding on a horse or a jolting vehicle causes sexual excitement. This is expressed directly in the jokes given at the beginning of the section on Rape, earlier, on the girl who would "rather be raped in a Packard than jerked off in a Ford," etc. As not all persons who ride on horses or in jolting vehicles experience sexual excitement as a result, one may assume, in those who do, some reinforcement from the classic identification of riding and coitus, which will be found in almost all Western languages at least. (The German *Reiter* and French *chevaucher*, for instance; the latter specifically noted as to be avoided in polite conversation in France in Puttenham's *Arte of English Poesie*, 1589, ed. Willcock & Walker, 1936, p. 272; and the tremendous list of English slang synonyms for coitus, placed at the words *greens* and *ride* in John S. Farmer & Wm. E. Henley's *Slang and Its Analogues*, 1890–1909. Shakespeare's whole series of puns on this theme of horses, riding, and sex, while the Dauphin and his nobles wait out the night before the Battle of Agincourt, in *Henry V*, III.vii.40–72, is also very much to the point.)

The prototype joke itself has been repeatedly collected in America since 1942, in which year a bold allusion to it actually appeared on the cover of a national magazine, in a picture of a girl riding on horseback behind an Indian who is winking at the reader. *A girl driving across the desert runs out of gas. An Indian gives her a ride, sitting behind him on his pony. Every few minutes as they ride he gives a wild whooping yell that echoes across the desert. Finally he deposits her at a gas station and goes off with a last "Woo-whoo!" "What were you doing?" the station attendant asks the girl. "Nothing," she says. "I was just sitting behind him holding onto the saddle-horn." Attendant:*

"Lady! Indians ride bare-back!" (Randolph gives a version in *Pissing in the Snow,* No. 56, concerning a "McClellan saddle," collected in Missouri, 1935, from a man who had heard the story "thirty or forty years ago" in Arkansas.) Also collected in a wartime air-raid updating, during World War II, a variant in which, *A girl in London is bombed out of her house naked, and is given a ride to the hospital by a man on a bicycle. She keeps falling off as she is unwilling to press her bare breasts too hard against his back. "Here," he says, "hold onto the cross-bar, so you won't fall off." When they get to the hospital she notices that it is a girl's bike.* (N.Y. 1942. That girls' bicycles have no cross-bar, so as not to interfere with the skirt, is also used as the opening and closing comedy-hook in Jules Romains' one-act play, *La Scintillante* — The Peach — translated in Virginia & Frank Vernon's *Modern One-Act Plays from the French,* 1933, in which the curtain rises on the 'yock' comedy-scene of an intended buyer, a French ecclesiastic in his robes, examining the ladies' bicycles in a bicycle shop. To American audiences this would doubtless be even funnier, as seeming to allude to the mythical animal, the *Snarkus* or *Seat-Snuffler, which 'goes around smelling girls' bicycle-seats in the summertime.'* A related *vagina dentata* 'critter,' the *Cruncher, 'has teeth in its ass and goes around in railroad compartments biting the buttons off all the seats.'* — N.Y. 1948. Compare the *Quirk* and *Hufflah,* in Aleister Crowley's *Snowdrops from a Curate's Garden, c.* 1904, p. 121*n.*)

Both current versions of this story have been given, to point up the irrelevancy of their speciously modern references to such topical matters as gas stations, bicycles, the bombing of London in World War II, and so forth. Here is the original, from *Tom Brown's Jester* (1755, ed. 1860) p. 55–6:

> A gentleman in the country, who had three daughters, discoursing one evening on rural affairs, and the nature of vegetation, asked one of his daughters what plant or herb she thought grew the fastest? The young lady replied, asparagus; then he asked the second, who answered, a pompion or gourd; And when the same question was put to the youngest she replied the pommel of a saddle; which very much surprising the old gentleman, he desired to know what she meant, and how she could make it out? Why, said she, when I was one day riding behind our John, and the ways being so rough, that I was afraid I should fall off, he cried, "Put your hands about my waist, and

lay hold of the pommel of the saddle;" and I am sure, papa, when I first took hold of it, it was not much bigger than my finger; and in less than a minute, it was thicker than my wrist.

More closely related to brags are those jokes in which the man displays to the woman, not the fact of erection but simply his penis, again under some subterfuge or pretense of error. *A man is told to go to a whore-house at 884 West 84th Street, and instead goes to 448 West 48th Street. [Note the spoonerism-in-action.] This turns out to be a chiropodist's office, which he decides is just a front. A pretty young nurse receives him and says, "Go behind that screen and get ready." He takes out his penis, and when the nurse comes to look she says, "My god, that ain't a foot!" "You going to quibble about an inch?"* (N.Y. 1940.) — *A Highlander plans to give his girl a yard of tartan plaid for Christmas, and to make sure she likes the pattern has a kilt made of it which he wears the next time he visits her. "How do you like it?" he asks, twirling around in front of her. "It looks all right to me," she says rather surprised. "Fine," he answers, "because you're going to get thirty-six inches of it for Christmas."* (D.C. 1951.)

The persistent interest of men in making sure that each other's trouser-flies are not open, and the obnoxious friendliness with which they hasten to warn strangers of the fact, if their flies happen to *be* open, is self-evidently hostile, and the information is seldom received with thanks. The quasi-castratory boys' game of fly-ripping (displaced upward, in textbook Freudian style, to tie-ripping when disapproving elders are present) does not bother to conceal the hostility under any pretended solicitude. *Anecdota Americana* gives a tag-line, hardly a joke, in which the hostile interest is transferred to the testicles, which is very unusual except in the case of male cats or dogs, so many of whom are wantonly castrated by neurotic owners on the flimsiest excuses and with the most indecent haste. *Senator Hoare is delivering a long speech against a certain bill, standing first with his left hand and then his right in his pants pocket. His opponent rises and remarks, "The Senator from Massachusetts seems to be leaving no stone unturned to prevent the passage of this bill."* (1:164.)

The only two fly-interest jokes collected project this interest upon women, though I never heard of an authentic example of a woman warning a strange man about his open fly in the way that men so often do. Given exactly: '*Two girls sitting opposite a man in a trolley began to giggle when they noticed the fly of his trousers was open.*

"Mister," said one, "your vanity case is open." "My what?" asked he. "Your vanity case. Better close it before your lip stick drops out." (1:447. Also heard as a 'true anecdote,' ascribed to a homosexual chorus-boy at a stage rehearsal during the open homosexual period in America concurrent with World War I in Europe, but before America's entry in 1917. Another such period has followed World War II. As to the equivalence of the lipstick and penis, difficult at first to believe but perfectly well attested to by folk materials, one may mention the special lipsticks during World War II, called *puppy-pricks* by naughty girls owning them, in which, when the cap was removed, a rubber band forced the actual lip-rouge to protrude slowly by itself. The Coty two-in-one compact (1953) was composed, almost as obviously, of a flat round object containing the powder, out of which rises a cylindrical projection in which the lipstick is encased.) — *A Jew leaves his place of business open on a religious holiday to catch the trade, but goes to services himself. A woman sitting near him observes that his fly is open and whispers, "Mister, your . . . er . . . business is open." "I know, I know," he whispers back. At home later he finds his fly open, and phones up the woman to thank her. "I just found out what you were trying to tell me, about my business being open," he says. "But tell me, was the salesman in or out?"* (N.Y. 1946.)

A young man is undressing in his hall bedroom when he sees a young girl doing the same across the air-shaft. He lays his erect penis across from his window-sill to hers, and says, "Come on over." She hesitates a moment. "But how will I get back?" (1:339.) In *Anecdota* 2:101, a rationalized version is given in which a princess is searching for a man famous for his long penis, and there is a similar rationalization, on an American background, of Paul Bunyan, the Northwoods giant, who sees an Indian princess on the opposite rim of a deep canyon. Glorying, rather, in its wishful nonsense, a version has been collected, California, 1952, in which a man gets on a transcontinental train with an ironing board, which he suddenly produces when the girl in the opposite upper berth asks the formerly unanswerable, "How will I get back?" All mechanical devices that open out (like the ironing board) are standard symbols of erection, particularly the umbrella. See any women's fashion magazine. A curiously aggressive joke, difficult to place, obviously equates the unfolding top of an automobile with the mechanism of erection. *One man tells another: "I took a girl out in the car, and we parked on a lonely road, and she said to me, 'If you'll take the top down you can have anything you want.' And be-*

lieve it or not, I had that top down in seven minutes." "What's so marvellous about that?" asks the other man; "I get my top down in two minutes." "Yes, but you have a convertible." (N.Y. 1952.)

I. PHALLIC BRAG

Brags about the length of the penis are intended to reassure everyone concerned — in the story and listening to it — that his penis is not really as small as he fears: that is to say, cut off! As the concentration on the penis leads naturally into more and more homosexual avenues of interest, most jokes about measuring the penis, and bragging about some impossible length it can achieve, completely omit women from the situation, and are self-evident homosexual overtures. Actual homosexual overtures, as in public toilets, generally also begin at the urinal bank, with some admiring remark about the size of the other man's penis, or deprecating remark about one's own.

The omission of women from the scene, in jokes, and the self-evident homosexual flavor in the necessary handling, measuring, matching, and confronting of the other man's penis, have the subsidiary value of reducing the pressure of castration anxieties by removing the woman (who is simultaneously the bone of contention among males and the 'horrible example' of the dreaded punishment of castration that the victorious male will inflict), and by flattering and conciliating the more powerful male with these attentions. Jokes in which this is done without even the pretense of measuring, etc., are transferred to the chapter on Homosexuality later, in Series Two; the best-known example of this type being that in which the drunk asks the bartender to help him urinate. Chaplin uses a version of this in *City Lights,* his film containing the largest number of homosexual asides and flirtations (the exchanged cigars, the amorous drunk who pours wine into Chaplin's pants — a standard burlesque clown gag — the prizefighter who will not take off his pants in front of him, the ostrich-pose presentation of his buttocks to the robbers, etc. etc.) In the film, the excuse is not that the man is drunk, but that he is wearing boxing gloves.

A Texan in New York is very lonesome and is about to head for home when he sees a man in the railroad station wearing a ten-gallon hat and spurs. He follows him, only to lose him in the men's room, where he does not see him in the line-up at the urinals. Finally he sees his spurs under one of the booth doors, and realizes he must be sitting or his hat would show over the top of the door. From behind the door, however, come only loud splashing sounds of urination. When the man comes out, the Texan accosts him, asks if he comes from Texas, and why he sat down to urinate. The other man explains, "I just had an operation for hernia, and the doctor told me not to lift anything heavy." (D.C. 1952.) That this is a fantasy of homosexual accosting is hardly disguised — after the build-up of paranoid 'tracking one's man down' — by the absurd punch-line on penis size. This cannot, of course, be admitted of Texans; but the French — they are a funny race: *An American in Paris enters a street* pissoir, *where his penis is so long that it floats down the trough in front of the Frenchman standing next to him. The Frenchman turns to look at him in amazement, and the American decides to improve the occasion by asking where he can find a woman. "Say, bo . . . ?" he begins. The Frenchman: "C'est beau? Mon dieu, c'est magnifique!"* (N.Y. 1943.)

Coming even closer to direct accosting — which it achieves in a variant in which the Frenchman is a Frenchwoman — *An American in Paris, unable to find a whore-house, asks a gendarme to give him directions. The gendarme does not understand English very well. The American tries pidgin and pointing. "Me . . ." he says, pointing to his chest. "Ah, you weesh to eat!" says the gendarme. "No, no," says the American. He tries again, taking out a ten-dollar bill. "Ah, you weesh to gam-bol?" "No, no, no!" the American shouts in disgust, and takes out his penis. "Ah, oui oui," says the gendarme. "Wee-wee, my ass! Where the hell is the nearest whore-house?"* (N.Y. 1952.) In the heterosexual variant, *The Frenchwoman is trying to seduce the un-understanding American, and says, "Oui oui" when he finally takes out his penis. "Wee-wee, nothing! It's the biggest one in our regiment."* (D.C. 1945.)

Next after the toilet, the favorite locale for the sub-homosexual approaches and engagements of the penises of men is the barroom. There is nothing new in this. In the oldest erotic folk-ballad now extant in English, "A Talk of Ten Wives on their Husbands' Ware," dating from about A.D. 1460, and printed from the Porkington MS. No. 10 by F. J. Furnivall in *Jyl of Breyntfords Testament* (1871: Ballad Society Publications 7-a) p. 29–33, the situation is the same, though reversed, with the ten wives sitting 'at an ale,' drinking and complaining of the size and stiffness of their husbands' penises. That is to say, the scene is quasi-Lesbian, rather than male homosexual, as is now commoner at drinking places; and in a modern survival of the form of the "Talk of Ten Wives," if not of the ballad itself, called "The Whoorey Crew," even the sex of the genitals discussed has been changed to suit:

> *Three old whores from Canada*
> *Were drinking cherry wine,*
> *And their whole conversation was:*
> *"Your cunt's no bigger than mine."* (U.S. 1939.)

The lies and brags that follow are entirely similar to those with which the men at bars regale each other in the jokes now to be discussed. A version of the two opening lines of the song is given in Paul Haines' "Critique of Pure Bawdry," in the magazine *The Modern Thinker* (New York, 1933) III.290, and a related brag-song, "The Captain's Wife," in T. E. Lawrence's posthumous *The Mint* (1936), first publicly published only twenty years later.

A tramp in a saloon offers to do anything for a drink, and is bet the drink against his swallowing the contents of the cuspidor that his penis is not as long as the cat's tail. When he is told he has lost, he asks, "How did you measure that cat's tail?" "From the asshole," says the bartender. "Well then," says the tramp with dignity, "would you extend me the same courtesy?" (2:III, a version with cunnilinctus rather than the cuspidor as the losing bet: a typical anti-female equation.) Here, practically without preamble, the underlying hostility in all homosexual situations is brought to the surface, as may be seen even more clearly in the materials in the chapters on Homosexuality and Castration, in Series Two. It is curious to note that Furnivall, in publishing the "Talk of Ten Wives on their Husbands' Ware," observes in his Forewords, p. 6: 'A near relative of mine, a few years since, was greatly astonished to see a like question to that discust by the Wives, experimentally settled on some clean plates, for a bet, by a party of Welsh farmers after a market dinner at an inn on the borders.' Here, in fact rather than jest, are both the bet and the 'inn.'

One of the few jokes about the testicles is also set up as a bet at a bar, with the implied situation of men taking out their scrotums to compare, by palpation, the number of testicles present, as the real entertainment for those interested in that sort of thing. Observe the castration background, and the crucial part played, as always, by the

father-figure of the bartender. *A man who has had one testicle removed, continuously wins money in barrooms by betting that he and
the man bet with, together, have an odd number of testicles. One rainy
day when no one else comes in, he tries to bet with the bartender, but
the bartender refuses. The man keeps raising the stakes until the bartender finally agrees to bet. He has three testicles.* (N.Y. 1948. In an
earlier French version, the man doing the betting has *three* testicles, but
loses anyway. *Kryptádia,* 1907, XI. 216.) A lesser example of the
same type: *Two American sailors on shore-leave in Marseille are told
by their shipmates that all the women are whores and all the men
pimps, and that all they have to do to find a woman is to show their
penises to the first man they meet and give him a dollar.* [Compare the
gendarme joke, above.] *Not seeing any women, they go into a café, lay
their penises on the bar, and put down a dollar each. The bartender
also lays down a dollar, takes out his penis, matches them, and sweeps
up the money.* (N.Y. 1950.) Another version is given in Chapter 11,
"Prostitution," in Series Two.

It will be seen that the possession of a long penis is not necessarily
the mark of the hero, but only of the strongest and most hated: that
is to say, of the father-figure. The contests in penis length are essentially a testing of dangerous reality. The idea is to find out how strong
the father really is, in the sense of phallic power, and to vanquish him
if possible, or to conciliate him homosexually if not possible. The background figure of the woman who is really being competed for — not
just the mother, but every woman — is almost forgotten in the heat of
the contest. In an interesting illustration from a Japanese pillow-book
of the school of Kunisada (about 1850) called "The Wedding Trip,"
reproduced in F. S. Krauss' *Japanisches Geschlechtsleben* (3rd ed.,
1931) I., plate 92-c, two men are shown actually fencing with their
penises, while the woman for whom they are fighting sits in the background with her vulva exposed, nervously biting the back of her hand
as she awaits the outcome. The cover of an American humor magazine
of 1946, *The Nugget,* No. 11 (Lake Arrowhead, Calif.: Goodman Pub.
Co.) gives exactly the same scene, slightly expurgated, of course, but
including the interlocked legs of the men, and the saving grace of the
woman over whom they are fighting — with ice-cream cones! The
most ancient example of this theme is also very lightly veiled in symbols: Aaron's rod, that turns into a serpent and eats up the rods of
Pharaoh's sorcerers, in *Exodus,* vii. 12. In the irrepressible Paul Krassner's

news-sheet, *The Realist* (1967), a jousting contest with their wooden legs is suggested for two of his one-legged enemies.

It is surprising how carefully the characters in a joke can be delineated, without either the tellers or listeners identifying them for the lay-figures of father, son, mother, etc., that they so often are. One would find it difficult to miss the paternalism of the overweight and sedate patriarch, who has the last laugh on the nosey inquirer (the sexually curious child) in the following: *An Easterner in a resort hotel is intrigued by an enormously overweight, elderly Texas couple always sitting together in the lounge. He takes the opportunity of the woman being at the candy-counter one day to sidle up to the fat old man and say, "Would you forgive my inquisitiveness, sir, if I asked if you and your wife can really get together, as corpulent as you are? You don't have to answer if you don't want to, of course." "I don't mind, sonny," says the Texan in a big booming voice. "You're the fourth short-peckered Easterner that's asked me the same question."* (La Jolla, Calif. 1965, and collected earlier in less ornate form.)

In American folklore the clearest expression of the idea that the father-figure is the real possessor of the large penis so much sought after and lied about by the son, is in the jokes about the Mormons and their many wives and other personal endowments, beginning with the *double-entendre* phallic monument in Whitingham, Vermont, authentically reading: '*Brigham Young, born on this spot 1801, a man of much courage and superb equipment.*' (This is not a joke but a fact, and has been photographed by almost as many tourists as have sent home picture postcards in passing through Intercourse, Pa.) *A lady on a train is told, "That's Brigham Young. He has twenty-one wives." "Why he ought to be hung!" she says. "Lady, he is!"* (New Mexico, 1943.) — *How Mormon elders are chosen: They have to stand with their back to a three-story building, and flip a peanut completely over it with their penis.* (N.Y. 1944.) — Entrance requirement for the House of David [a bearded and presumably very virile sect]: *The applicants must strip and crawl on the beach, on their hands and knees. Those who do not leave five trails are rejected.* (*Anecdota*, 1933, No. 340.) Not assimilated to any patriarchal religious group: *A man with a penis eighteen inches long wants to join the Long Dick Club, and asks a member to put him up for election. The member turns back the lapel of his overcoat. "See that flower in my buttonhole?" he says. "Yes . . ." "Well that's the head of my prick, and I'm only the doorman."* (Calif. 1952.)

We are now entering the province of brags proper. Again, surprisingly enough, the longest penis is not necessarily the best, as is also indicated in the grudging folk-phrase topping any brag of great length: "It isn't what you've got. It's how you use it." See the very clear statements on this point headed "The Phallic Fallacy," in *Playboy* (Nov. 1967) p. 69, one from an ex-prostitute. *Three men of different nationalities are standing at a urinal. The German, who has a very large penis, flops it around boastfully and says, "You see, we are the master race." The Frenchman says, "We are known as the Lovaires."* [*i.e.,* It isn't what you've got . . .] *The Irishman, who has a small penis, says "Begorra, in my country we raise men, not pricks."* (Fla. 1949.)

In the following very interesting joke, the brag of penis length is actually only a nonsense line covering the common experience of the shrinking up of the penis into the abdomen in states of anxiety. There is also, at a different level, a sort of verbal self-castration intended to conciliate the father-judge. *A man is picked up for loitering, along with some women prostitutes. He notices that those who step up to the bar and say briskly, "I'm a whore," get off with a fine. When it comes his turn he says, "Your Honor, I'm a whore." The judge turns to an assistant and says, "Take this man in the next room and see if what he says is true." The assistant comes back and says, "Your Honor, he's no fairy. He has a penis nine inches long." "Ninety days!" The man laughs. "Lucky I didn't have a hardon, your Honor, or you'd've given me life!"* (1:461.) In a decayed version, collected California 1952, the joke ends at the man's saying "I'm a whore," with the attempt to force a laugh by the mere tempo of the telling. The peculiar notion in the original, that homosexuals never have long penises [!], is a further overdeterminant of the idea of self-castration by the submissive son.

Of completely impossible brags, two have already been given: the penis stretched across the air-shaft, at the end of the preceding section, and the Long Dick Club boutonnière, just above. As the situations in all of these are purposely made ridiculous, the whole humor must reside in the yearning overstatement of the fantasy, which means — adjusting the necessary plus & minus — the gnawing self-deprecation in fact. *Day Nurse: "Did you notice the man in Room 218 with the word* SWAN *tattooed on his penis?" Night Nurse (the next morning): "That's not* SWAN; *it's* SASKATCHEWAN!*"* (Calif. 1941.) In a variant, on the strictly homosexual situation of the 'short-arm inspection' of soldiers, *A doctor asks a soldier about a suspicious dot on his penis.* *"Where I come from," says the soldier, "all the guys have the names of* *their girl tattooed on their cocks." "But this is only a dot," says the* *doctor. The soldier sniggers. "You should see it when it spells 'Caro-* *lina'."* (D.C. 1944.)

A recent British modification, printed in the humor magazines, satirizes socialized medicine in England. *A man takes his pregnant* *wife to a government clinic. She is given a brisk examination, a tiny* *rubber-stamp is applied to her abdomen, and she is ushered out. At* *home the husband gets a magnifying glass and finally manages to* *make out the inscription:* "WHEN YOU CAN READ THIS WITHOUT A MAG- NIFYING GLASS, BRING YOUR WIFE BACK." The theme of the sarcastic inscription affixed (by whatever means) over the wife's genitals by some other man is very old. Several examples will be given at the be- ginning of the chapter on Marriage: "The Wedding Night," with note of the horns added to the lamb painted on the belly of the cuckold's wife, with which the first English jestbook, *A C. Mery Talys* (1525), ends. This is Rotunda's Motif H439.1.1, cited to various Italian *novel- lieri* of the 16th century.

At least one joke-motif on the long penis has already received folk- loristic attention: that of the penis used as a mast by a shipwrecked sailor, which has been the subject of learned inquiry in the French *Intermédiare des Chercheurs et Curieux,* in the 1880's, as *"Le Mât de* *Marseille"* (the Mast of Marseille). In the form most current in Amer- ica, *A swimmer loses the race when he sees a beautiful woman on the* *riverside, and his erection anchors him in the riverbed. "Why didn't* *you turn over and float?" he is asked. "What would I have done when* *I came to Brooklyn Bridge?"* (1:238.) Topped by: *"You call that big?* *Why once in Alaska I took out my jock to piss, got to thinking of my* *gal, and couldn't get it back in my pants. It was so cold up there in* *Alaska I had to rub it with snow to keep it from freezing, and what I* *couldn't reach with my hands I threw snowballs at!"* (1:238.) This ap- pears to be one of the few sexual brags of the tall tale variety as yet recovered, though others must unquestionably exist. Prof. Richard Dorson 'has agitated in the journals against the exclusion of such characters as Horsecock Charlie from the Bunyan material,' as usually published, but the tall tales as yet appearing in print, though they may involve themes as grandiose as prying the frozen earth loose on its axis, are in general as sexless as jelly beans. (The Paul Bunyan version of the window-sill penis story, noted above, is a recent modification and hardly authentic Bunyan.) "Horsecock Charlie's" saga is given by Prof. Dorson in the *Journal of American Folklore,* 1951, concerning *A man with an "oversized organ," who "met his death when, asleep in an upper bunk, his outsized member fell over the side and the weight pulled poor Charlie crashing to the floor."* A version of this, or a topper to it, appears in the enormously interesting American erotic animated-cartoon of the late 1920's — one of the few that exists — *Buried Treasure* (or *Abie's Buried Treasure,* the hero being Harry Hershfield's cartoon-strip character, "Abie Kabibble"), in which *the head of the hero's penis is sent searching for the woman's offered vagina, in the way that dogs are thrown a stick to retrieve.* A joke-form in which the penis is told to retrieve a thrown *herring* will be given later: fish-odors generally being an allusion to that of the vagina.

The swimmer-and-bridge story has also been collected in the decayed form of a 'height': *The height of conceit. — A flea, floating down the river with a hardon, whistling for the drawbridge to open.* (D.C. 1946.) The persistent motif of the male's supine position will be discussed later in connection with mother-in-law stories, in the chapter on Marriage. In the original or French form of the story of the swimmer, *A shipwrecked sailor floats on his back, thinks of his sweetheart, and sails home using his penis as a mast and his shirt for a sail. "But how did you steer?" he is asked. "I shoved my thumb up my ass and used my hand as a rudder."* (2:230.) The ending question-&-answer is a typical buttock-humor 'catch.' It has been suggested that there are relics of this joke in the snatches recorded in Mark Twain's *Life on the Mississippi* (1883) of the steamboat that crossed the river four times without a rudder, and the other tall tale about a barrel, the teller being encouraged to make his listeners believe him by 'showing them the knothole' — another buttock-humor catch, though Twain could count on his Victorian audience to miss it.

Gulliver has been captured by the Lilliputians, and the King orders the army to masturbate Gulliver: a royal holiday. They toil all through the Lilliputian day, with Lilliputian Red Cross nurses giving out coffee; balloon vendors, and crowds; but nothing happens. The King rides out to the midway point on Gulliver's penis and demands to know what is wrong. "I don't know, Sire," the Captain replies, "the lump passed here at three o'clock." (1:240a, p. 94.) As Swift himself noted, and obliquely commented upon, the reversal of child and parent roles in his diminutive Lilliput, by following its utopian perfections with the gross repulsiveness of the oversized Brobdingnag, it is almost unnecessary to observe the special ludicrousness of the enormous child (Gargantua) being masturbated by order of the diminutive father-figure. The end-line given is the smallest part of the intended humor. The story is sometimes presented as a formal recitation or monologue — that is to say, all build-up (or folktale) and no punch-line.

Recitations like this are quite rare, the best known being "Daniel in the Lions' Den," which is essentially a whole string of catches. (*"It tickles," said Daniel. "What tickles?" said the King. "Testicles!" cried Daniel, and they marked up one for the common people.*) A version is printed, as though in verse, in *Immortalia* (1927) p. 140–42, under the title, "The Night of the King's Castration." This is mentioned simply for the record, without any intention of urging the material into the obvious Freudian channels. Of the two other recitations collected, one also strikes the Oedipal anti-royalist note throughout, "The King of the Goddam Islands," though without mention of *castrating* the king. This, incidentally, occurs nowhere in the *Immortalia* version of "Daniel" but in the title, so powerful is the attraction of the fantasy. The last recitation collected is "Larry Turn the Crank," a burlesque lantern-slide lecture of fabulous beasts, mostly of strange scatological habits, printed in *Immortalia*, p. 153–4, again as though in verse, under the title "The Hamburg Show." An earlier and not-altogether ex-purgated version of this is given, showing that it is originally British, as "Humours of Bartlemy [St. Bartholomew's Day] Fair," in John Ashton's *Modern Street Ballads* (1888) p. 111–15. Compare also Ben Jonson's plays, *Bartholomew Fayre,* and *The Alchemist,* both produced between 1605 and 1615, in the latter of which there is the side-show or peep-show 'attraction' of a small boy with a very large penis: usually a dwarf, in fact. A vaudeville comedian told me, as a true anecdote, in New York, 1938, what is probably the mere incest-fantasy prank of *a midget who would dress up as a little boy and stand crying by the curb, appealing to the lady passers-by to help him urinate; the humor being his adult-sized penis then flopping out into the woman's hand when she helpfully unbuttoned his pants.* On the origins of the recita-tion, "The King of the Goddam Islands," also known as *The Sod's Opera,* and some of its characters, see my *The Horn Book,* p. 95–6.

As almost no area of erotic folklore in America is without a few examples, more or less vicious, about Negroes and Jews, it would be falsifying the evidence to omit those on long-penis themes, although for reasons I cannot explain — apparently centering around the anti-vaginal reference to fish — I find the second of these curiously offensive. The first has quite a history. *A Jewish ribbon salesman is gotten rid of by an anti-Semitic client with an order for "as much ribbon — any width and any color — as will reach from the end of your hook-nose to the tip of your prick!"* [Usual identification of nose and penis.] *The client comes back from lunch to find hundreds of reels of pink ribbon a yard wide being delivered at his door. He calls the factory to complain, and is told: "We want to thank you for your wonderful order to our Mr. Cohen, who, as you may not know, was born — and circumcised — in Pinsk!"* (N.Y. 1942.) Updated non-Jewish punch-line: *"Our salesman was wounded in the privates* (or: *lost the head of his prick) in Korea."* (N.Y. 1964.)

Many further jokes on circumcision will be found in the chapter on Castration themes, in the Second Series following. The leading element here, however, is certainly that of the enormous mileage, as in the original form, which, as it happens — will be found in *Joe Miller's Jests* (1739) No. 93, on 'A witty Knave coming into a Lace-shop [compare the ribbon motif, surviving for two centuries] upon *Ludgate-Hill'* in London, and asking the shopkeeper for as much lace 'as would reach from one of his Ears to the other, and measure which Way she pleased, either over his Head or under his Chin,' the point being that one of his ears 'is nailed to the Pillory in *Bristol.'* It is probably the resurrection theme, of denying and flaunting the symbolic castration — in *Joe Miller* ear-amputation, in the modern form circumcision — much more than the humorous making of profit out of the amputation of a bodily part, that has caused this century-old catch to be assimilated in its modern form to the Jew. (The *Joe Miller* motif of the method of measuring will also be found to have survived in the first joke on barroom betting given above.)

The second example also is set up on the theme of the Jew trickster, or wily beguiler, as the clever evader of castration by the *jiu-jitsu* method of seeming to accept it (in circumcision). *At an international penis contest, the Scotch contender's penis is twelve inches long, and the Frenchman's fifteen inches long. The Jew takes out a very small penis, and the judges demand to know what he is doing in a contest of this sort. Taking a dead herring out of his pocket, he throws it into the balcony, crying: "Go get it, Sammy!"* (Calif. 1941. Also collected as of a competition among Negroes.)

Another story, on the same framework, is always acted out in pantomime, with exactly the sort of contrast achieved musically in Moussorgsky's "Pictures at an Exhibition," in the characters of the heavy-treading millionaire, Samuel Goldenberg, and the quavering *schnorrer,* Schmuyle. In the present example, Goldenberg's part is played by *A big Italian boy who is mocking a little Jewish boy. "Look at my muscles!" he says, striking them with his fists. "Look at them biceps! Look at that chest! Look at them legs! What've you got? Nothing!" The little, consumptive Jewish boy opens his fly, fumbles inside (this is all acted out by the teller), and suddenly yanks out the tail of his shirt, demanding: "Where can you get a shirt like that for a dollar and eighty-nine cents?"* (N.Y. 1939.) This joke, which has been collected a number of times, is usually sprung on mixed company that has reached the saturation point with *double-entendre* jokes, or any kind of dirty jokes; and its electrifying effect is exactly what is contemplated in Westermarck's telling observation, in *The History of Human Marriage* (1922) I.419: 'We must not, of course, compare words said in public with deeds committed in secret. Persons who indulge in indecent talk would certainly shrink at performing openly the acts of which they speak.'

2. ANTI-BRAGS

The apotropaic value of belittling one's own possessions, the idea that the 'evil eye' can be averted by saying "Oh, *that* old thing!" when some article of clothing or achievement is complimented, is still widely believed in. "A poor thing, but my own." The rationalization is no longer that the squinting or envious eye, the French *guigne* or 'jinx,' might blight one's child or one's health (requiring every compliment to be followed by some such phylacterism as the Yiddish *kein-eyin-horá,* "not meaning any evil eye!" or the English "knock on wood!" and every sneeze with a "God bless you!") nor even that heavenly powers will frustrate any too boldly definite statement of intention, as about living to a certain age. Religious Jews will not, for example, state their own actual age without adding the phylacterism or formula-phrase intended to ward off evil, "— to one hundred and twenty years!" (This being the age at which Moses died, and was buried by God Himself, in *Deuteronomy,* XXXIV. 5-8, as Moses himself presumably recorded!) The ritual display of the genitals, or of hand-gestures intended to symbolize these, such as the Italian '*fa'n'gul*' (the modern American 'The Finger'), was once thought of as the most powerful of all possible ways of averting not only the evil-eye or '*guigne*' — whence the French phallic minor god or idol, 'St. Guignolet' — but even of nullifying the power of the Devil, as in Rabelais' "*Diable de Papefiguière*" story, or the English rhyming-tale, "The Gelding of the Devil," in which the Devil is put to flight by the sight of a woman's naked vulva. This is the real meaning of sexual brags. The anti-brag simply reverses this. Vague concepts on the order of 'good taste' or pip-pip British reserve are now usually substituted for the older religious determinants, but modesty is certainly the accepted form.

In jokes this is of course reversed, and the *id* is allowed a holiday of wild brags and palpable lies as to physical prowess of all types, including the sexual. The anti-brag is a curious intrusion into the usual holiday of jokes. Its wry truth — it seldom overstates the badness of the case — attempts to achieve the same reassurance as the brag, but by the more realistic method of trying to 'make a joke' of one's inadequacies and fears. The anti-brag is, then, the apotropaic joke, the *kein-eyin-horá* of humor. Its principle is: "You can't fire me — I quit," a 'game' (YCFMIQ) somehow overlooked in Dr. Eric Berne's *Games People Play* (1964), a frightening book announced, p. 69 — surely a game itself: fishing for additions? — as 'complete.' Occasionally one also finds in anti-brags a definite masochistic tone, although, as stated earlier, really masochistic jokes are almost a contradiction in terms and are extremely rare. Most of the exceptions encountered are attempts to absorb the terror of homosexual rape (by father-figure animals, such as gorillas and bulls). A similar self-mocking tone, tending toward masochism, will be found in much authentic Jewish humor, and specifically in many of the examples cited in Freud's *Wit and Its Relation to the Unconscious,* where, except in the examples of what he calls 'tendency-wit,' the real butt seems to be the teller himself, and the real pleasure that of frustration of expectation.

An undertaker is laying out the body of a man with an extremely long penis. He calls in a friend and shows it to him. "That's just like mine," says the friend. "What?" says the undertaker; "you mean to say you've got one that long?" "Well, not exactly, but it's just as dead." (Transcontinental train, U.S. 1943.) The resurrection theme here, of the dead penis that is really more alive than a live one, will be discussed much more fully in the chapter on Castration, in Series Two, with another version of a joke in which the same theme is even clearer, in its use in *making a joke* of the reality of impotence: *A man writes in his diary on his birthday: "Today I am twenty years old, and I can't bend my penis with both hands." "Today I am twenty-five years old and I can't bend my penis with both hands." And so on: thirty, thirty-five, forty, forty-five, fifty, fifty-five. Finally, at sixty: "Today I bent it. I must be getting stronger!"* (N.Y. 1952.) A Walloon version, collected in Belgium in 1902, is recorded in *Kryptádia*, VIII.42. Since, as Eric Partridge says, 'everyone has *some* French,' a translation has not seemed necessary. *Les vieux drôles ont l'habitude de dire qu'ils sont plus forts qu'à vingt ans. Si l'on les taxe d'exagération, ils répondent: "A présent, avec un doigt, je plie mon vit comme je veux. A vingt ans, mes dix doigts n'y auraient pas suffi!"*

The situation of impotence is not necessary for the anti-brag. It may also refer simply to penis size in the most self-deprecating way, in the actual moment of sexual conquest. *At a dance a woman becomes conscious of the man's extremely large erection pressing against her body, and agrees to go to bed with him. In the bedroom she observes him taking a broomhandle length out of his pocket. "See here, I thought that was your prick." "No, Ma'am, that's my decoy."* (1:248.) Vance Randolph gives a version of this in his important manuscript collection, *Pissing in the Snow, and Other Ozark Folktales* (Eureka Springs, Arkansas, 1954: Library of Congress, Music Division), a collection in which stories about insufficiently large or excessively large penises form a significantly high proportion. Randolph's story, No. 86, "The Duck Hunter's Woman," was told him in Joplin, Missouri, 1931, 'as a true story,' and credited 'to a guide on the Cowskin River, near Noel, Mo.' It attempts to rationalize the existence of the decoy penis by describing *the boy who uses it as a professional whittler of 'these here decoy ducks out of cedar wood.' When the woman finds that he does not really have "that monstrous big one,"* and that she has been had [in all senses of the term — or substitute: 'fucked', 'screwed', 'reamed,' or other hostile sexual equivalent], *'Well sir, she set up for a minute, a-staring at that thing in Elbert's hand. Then the pretty woman just fell back in bed, and laughed till the tears rolled down her cheeks. Her and Elbert tore off one more chunk, and then he went back to the carpenter shop.'*

More recent citified versions reduce the story to a wise-crack or 'quickie': *First Girl: "Hasn't he got a handsome profile!" Second Girl: "You mean halfway down? That's no profile. Believe me, those are keys!"* (1:350.) Also: *"Do you love me, Eddie, or is that just a flashlight in your pocket?"* (2:329.) The idea of the genital 'decoy' is not entirely mythical. During the compilation of my glossary of "The Slang of Homosexuality," printed in George W. Henry's *Sex Variants* (New York: Hoeber, 1941) but omitted from the post-Kinsey reprint owing to 'exigencies of space,' it was often reported — and once actually observed — that a certain plain-clothes detective on the New York 'tea-room' [toilet] squad' was winding a handkerchief around his penis as a decoy for homosexuals. One informant even stated — certainly a fantasy — that the detective was wearing a tied-on condom inflated with water, which my informant swore he would puncture! This will be discussed further in the chapter on Homosexuality in Series Two, Section 10.III, "The Short-Arm Inspection."

The 'short-arm inspection' appears in jokes almost solely as a homosexual situation of genital handling by the fearsome doctor-father. All three of the anti-brags using this situation have the tone of self-castration to avoid castration by someone else. This neurotic trick of accepting the lesser evil, and *doing it to oneself* rather than allowing it to be done or said by anyone else, is the rock-bottom reassurance against castration that the anti-brag offers. *"Why were you rejected by the army?" "One leg was shorter than the other two."* (N.J. 1942. Or: *"My middle leg doesn't touch the ground."* D.C. 1943.) — *A draft-board doctor is amazed to observe, on an otherwise well-built recruit, the smallest penis he has ever seen, and calls over another doctor to look. The recruit: "What's the matter? Haven't you ever seen an erection before?"* (Calif. 1942. This has also been collected, N.Y. 1943, as of a fat man in a shower-room. This is an attempt to rationalize the castration element, fat men being presumably eunuchoid.) The following example was collected at the same joke-telling session as the preceding, but the notes preserved do not indicate which was told first, and which was the "that-reminds-me-of-the-one-about . . . " They are self-evidently attempts at the same reassurance, in one case by means of a brag, in the other case by an anti-brag. *A man at a draft examination has a knee-length penis for which he apologizes to the doctor, saying, "I don't know what the trouble is. It's been all shrunk up for days."* (Calif. 1942.)

A few, but only a very few anti-brags exist, in which the modest self-appraisal is actually a criticism of the other party's pretentiousness or airs of power. Though the short-arm inspection of army-induction examination would seem a perfect area for sly put-downs of authority in this fashion (as in the hilarious overstatements of Kupferberg & Bashlow's *1001 Ways to Beat the Draft*, 1966), only one short-arm joke so far collected veers clearly in this direction. *An ignorant hillbilly is being examined naked for the army. The doctor prods and pokes him like human livestock, retracts his foreskin, peers into his rectum and mouth, and makes a few cryptic notes on a card. As he turns to the next recruit, the doctor says, pointing to a shelf of empty urinalysis bottles, "All right, that's all. Can you fill me one of those bottles, now?" Recruit: "From here, doc?"* (Somerville, New Jersey, 1944. As collected again, N.Y. 1965, the details as to the recruit's humiliating treatment were omitted.) This and the following story will be dealt with again later, under another context. *A man 'inquiring about the men's room at an elegant hotel, is shown with great solemnity by an attendant to the lavish lounge, furnished in period trappings of bygone splendor.' When he takes out his penis it looks so shabby by comparison that he puts it back and takes it across the street to the gas station.* (D.C. 1948.) In this splendid joke there is simply the pretense of an anti-brag. Actually it is the human being who is rejecting the gaudy pretension that attempts to overwhelm him, and not the reverse.

George Jean Nathan builds up exactly the same point, in what may even be a version of the same joke from the old music-hall days, in his "Historiette of an Episode in the Art Life of America," in *The American Spectator Yearbook* (1934) p. 210–14, in which he describes, with meticulous attention to every dollar sign, how, in the building of Rockefeller Center:

> The silvering of the 1,582 waterclosets, entrusted to the foremost interior decorators of the nation, alone cost $723,850, exclusive of the phosphorescent jade *papier de toilette* holders, designed by exclusive Fifth Avenue jewelers, which cost $83,400, [*while*] in one of the larger of the 182 men's smoking rooms, wherein each chair was equipped with a platinum and emerald cigar lighter and bordered by a Nymphenburg cuspidor bearing a likeness, in gold-leaf, of Leonardo da Vinci . . . etc. etc. . . . Nothing like it had been seen in the world before. [*And finally,*] in the $5,000,000 theatre in the $250,000,000 Rockefeller art center, the $55,000 golden curtains parted and revealed a screen on which was thrown a Hollywood movie wherein a blonde cutie got the amorous better of a brunette.

As it would be inappropriate to end this chapter on so magniloquent a note, one more example may be given, in the truer Milquetoast vein. *A man goes into a sporting-goods store to buy a jockstrap. He is embarrassed by being waited on by a lady attendant, and mutters his request with a self-conscious slur [!] on the word "jock." She misunderstands, and brings him a duck-strap for hunting ducks. "How does this work?" he inquires, baffled by it. "Well," she says, "You just stick the head in here, and then sling it over your shoulder, like this." "Who, me?"* (Calif. 1942.) For all its perfection, the punch-line is almost unnecessary here: the situation says everything. The phrase about slinging the penis 'over one's shoulder' is the standard superlative, and appears in humorous forms other than jokes, in particular in a well-known pictorial catch or trick, based on the drawing of "The Spirit of Communications," showing a statue of a naked man carrying a whole mess of spaghetti-like telephone cables, which used to appear on the cover of the New York telephone directory. *A man takes a magical potion to make his penis longer, but cannot stop its action, and must wear his penis slung over his shoulder under his coat. It begins winding around his neck and choking him, and he goes to the doctor to ask what he should do. "Look, doc," he cries, pulling open his coat suddenly and showing his problem, "what do you figure I ought to do about this?" "Well ... maybe you could get a job posing for the cover of the telephone-book."* (N.Y. 1948.) The idea of the part of the body which has a mind of its own and cannot be mastered — always essentially the penis, though compare the *kudzu* vine — is used with great effect in Terry Southern's black-humor movie, *Dr. Strangelove* (1963), in which the ex-Nazi scientist's mechanical arm keeps trying to give the Nazi salute, while his newly-Americanized human arm keeps trying unsuccessfully to stop it! (Marvellously acted by the dialect-comedian, Peter Sellers.) Parody, to the tune of "John Peel," or "The March of the Wooden Soldiers," probably dating from World War I: this is used as a chorus to the anti-gallant and anti-family verses ("The Clean Old Man") of "The Joys of Copulation."

> Do your balls hang low?
> Can you swing 'em to and fro?
> Can you tie 'em in a knot, can you tie 'em in a bow?
> Can you throw 'em over your shoulder, (*gesture*)
> Like a good American soldier? —
> Do your balls — hang — low?!

VI. POTENCY AND APHRODISIACS

The testicles are correctly considered the seat of virile power in all folk materials dealing with this point. However, as Freud has shown, castration anxieties generally center about the penis and not the testicles, being neurotically fixed in the individual's unconscious during the childhood period when the testicles are undeveloped and without pleasure 'cathexis,' or centralization of psychic energy. Certain very striking exceptions to this general rule will be noted in the chapter on Castration, in Series Two, but as there is no overpowering anxiety in the matter of the testicles, there is also no great proliferation of folk materials, jokes, etc., intended to allay such anxiety. Jokes in particular make very scant reference to the testicles. Limericks are a great deal richer in this, and chapters 2 and 14, "Organs" and "Losses," in *The Limerick* (Paris, 1953) may be consulted for the best showing of testicle humor, if the word may be applied to such grim and depressing fantasies.

The jokes on the subject that can be given here are, for the most part, paltry gag-lines. *"Papa, is that a mail plane?"* *"No, son, those are just the wheels."* (N.Y. 1945. Often published in college humor magazines in an allusive form in which *the coed asks the college boy how he can tell it's a mail plane from so far away.*) — Description of a baby boy: *"He's only three months old, but he has the strongest arms and the hardest little stomach. And bawls . . . why he bawls all day."* (1:178 and 487. Text form, Elgart, 1951, p. 112. A catch.)

The hostile element is very prominent in jokes on the testicles involving women, a hostility to be considered more fully at the beginning of the next chapter, on Women, and under "Vagina Dentata" in Series Two 13.I.6 and 13.II.4. *A mother refuses permission for her daughter to go to the ball. "Look at her belly from the last two balls!"* (1:319.) Variant: *The girl asks, "But Mother, how will I get a fellow if I don't go to balls and parties?"* *"You'll get a fellow without balls — and parties."* (1:124.) A well-known bawdy parody of William Allen Butler's *"Nothing to Wear,"* in *Harper's Weekly* (1857), still current, is based on the presumable humor of a girl who finds on her wedding night that she has married a man who has (*chorus*): *"No Balls At All!"* — *Two rat-traps are baited, one with apples and the other nuts. The husband rushes up from the cellar in the middle of*

his wife's bridge party to announce that he has caught a rat. "By the
apples?" "No, by the nuts." (About 1930. Forced; the colloquial preposition would be 'with,' not 'by.') — *"Balls!" said the Queen.* "If you
had 'em you'd be King," says the jester. (2:157, a spoilt form ascribed
to George Bernard Shaw [!] and a Lesbian actress of the period.) —
*An American actress in a London horse-cab asks the cabby if there
isn't anything he can do to make the horse go faster, as she is late.*
"No, lydy," he says. "I must save his balls for the hills." (2:120.) The
reference here appears to be simply to the testicles as a symbol of
strength — a more forthright version of, for instance, the symbolic hair
in the case of Samson. One may suspect, however, a reference to the
sadistic practice of flicking the horse's testicles with a whip. In the
Indian Patchwork (1934) of Edward & Mary Charles [Hempstead],
the matching sadism of driving the whipstock into the mare's vagina
or rectum is made the subject of a bitter note, IV.A, p. 113. This is
out-*Mother India*'ing Miss Katherine Mayo, as did also Kanhayalal
Gauba in his *H.H. or The Pathology of Princes* (Lahore, 1930), which
makes *Mother India* look like *Mother Goose.*

Potency in jokes is almost solely measured by the number of times
coitus can be engaged in without stopping. This is of a piece with the
overstatistical bias of the Kinsey Report, in which maximum is invariably equated with optimum, and, even more ridiculously succumbing to the folklore ethic, in which the speediest intercourse is actually
stated to be the most 'superior' biologically. That this will inevitably
leave the woman unsatisfied and without orgasm is, as Professor Kinsey
saw it, tough. Biology is biology. (Compare *"A pogrom is a pogrom,"*
in the section on Rape.) The actual meaning, at least in jokes, of the
urge to get through intercourse as fast as possible, is that one hates the
woman, or women, and is probably homosexual. This is an open &
shut thing, everybody knows it, and no 'biological' gobbledygook can
in the slightest obscure the point. The matching urge, to repeat intercourse as often as possible, usually involves the need for a completely
new woman, or homosexual companion, every time ('oncing'), as
the guilt over the hostility felt for any one partner makes it unpalatable
or impossible to have intercourse with the same person again. In this
sense, the Don Juan is invariably homosexual — Byron certainly was,
with his prizefighters and so on — just as the prostitute is necessarily
frigid and a man-hater, if not actually Lesbian. (All other tales they
tell you to the contrary, notwithstanding.) Something of this sort was
also clearly bothering the author of *My Secret Life.*

A doctor is asked by a male patient whether masturbation is harmful. He replies that the modern point of view is that it depends on the frequency. "Well, is three times a day too much?" "Certainly! Why don't you get yourself a girlfriend?" "I got a girlfriend." "No," says the doctor, "I mean one who understands." "She understands fine." "Then why do you have to masturbate three times a day?" "Aw, she's religious — she don't like it during meals." (2:112.) Basically the same joke: *A man feeling run down describes himself to the doctor as having sexual relations with five or more women three times every day. The doctor tells him this is the cause of his trouble. "I'm glad to hear it, Doc. I was afraid it might be the masturbation."* (2:144.) Also collected, 1943, of *A Swede who complains of severe backache, but says he does not feel it during intercourse, which he has on waking up, about 10, at noon, around 2, just before dinner, just after dinner, and on retiring. "When do you feel it?" asks the doctor. "In between times, when I yack off."* A further variant on the same situation: *Doctor: "And how often do you have intercourse with your wife?" Patient: "Three times a day." "And, ah, I suppose, with your secretary?" "Three times a day." "I see. And the maid too, no doubt?" "Three times a day." Doctor (sarcastically): "Any other women?" "Three times a day." "Great God, man, you're killing yourself! Why don't you take yourself in hand?" "Three times a day."* (Calif. 1952.) The real humor here is in the implication of the strange repetitive answers, that masturbation *does* lead to insanity.

These versions by no means exhaust the variants on this most popular of all potency jokes. The tendency, in the examples given, is to accent the man's practical idiocy, and thus slide into an acceptance of the very old quasi-castratory threat that masturbation will drive a person mad (to be 'cured' by the quasi-castratory *fact* of sterilization, lobotomy, and other surgical sub-total euthanasias). The element of sex-hatred, of oversatisfying the woman sadistically, is more prominent in two further variants, the first of which is somewhat unpleasant, but which must be given anyhow since it is the oldest version collected and on the even older three-brother frame. *The woman with the biggest vagina in the world is searching for the man with the biggest penis. She hears of three brothers in the Arkansaw hills, all of whom have fabulously large penises. She finds the first brother using his to shoo mosquitoes away. He says, "Shucks, t'ain't nothin'. You ought to see my brother's." The second brother is using his penis as a fishing pole (or plowing a field with it*). *He says, "Shucks, etc." The third brother she finds lying on his back in bed, using his penis to mash flies on the ceiling.* [Compare the sadistic young prince in Coster's *Tyl Eulenspiegel*, 1868, crushing flies on the windowpane with his thumb.] *At last! In the evening the two other brothers come home and find the woman finally satisfied, lying limp on the bed. Sitting on the floor, however, is the third brother, masturbating into a tablespoon, and pouring the semen in to fill her completely.* (Idaho, 1919. Three-brother version in *Anecdota* 2:101, but with end-line assimilated from the story of the long penis laid across the window-sills. The motif of the tablespoon occurs also in an artificial insemination limerick on a young man of Rangoon, first printed in Davis' *The International Set: A Gallery of Limerick Portraits*, Boston, 1946, No. 53; reprinted in *The Limerick*, No. 975.)

In the last variant so far collected, absolutely nothing is left but the theme of hatred. *A man goes to the psychiatrist for a variety of psychosomatic aches & pains. "All right," says the psychiatrist, "let's get down to brass tacks. How often do you have intercourse with your wife?" "Three times a week." "And what positions do you use?" "We always do it dog-fashion, Doctor — you know, on our hands and knees." "What's the big idea?" "Well how else are we both going to watch television?"* (N.Y. 1952.) Self-evidently a *new* joke, as the t.v. reference cannot have been adapted. It should be observed that new jokes are extremely rare, though professional humorists and humor collectors will generally make vague remarks about having 'made up dozens' or 'collected hundreds [sometimes thousands!] of new ones.' These usually can never be quoted when requested, or turn out to be ancient chestnuts barely repainted to pass off as new. I have mentioned, in *The Horn Book*, p. 448, the similar situation as to numerous limericks, in particular the one on Magda Lupescu ("Who came to Rumania's rescue"), of which 'it is necessary sadly to admit that the present writer has personally encountered not one, but three separate and distinct "authors" of this rhyme, one of whom — of Teutonic origin and fresh off the boat — could hardly pronounce any further words of the English language than this one limerick and his claim to authorship.'

A diabolical friend has recently attempted to put me on — in connection with the present joke concerning watching television — that he *believes* he saw a story very similar to this in the *Arabian Nights* or

Ocean of Story, about a man having intercourse with a woman from behind so they could both watch the rising sun together. (They were Zoroastrian sun-worshippers, it appears.) This is a new form of folk-lore-faking or revision: back-dating instead of up-dating. Other jokes do, of course, exist on the subject of coitus from behind, as for instance those already given of the woman who became frightened looking under the bed, and the man who found it rather nice, *"but it made the children laugh."* (Compare Freud's analysis of the dream of the 'White Wolves,' already cited at the beginning of Chapter 5.II, preceding.) Actually, the t.v. joke is derived from, or most closely related to, many older stories on coitus from behind, with the woman looking out the window (and revenge-capture versions of this) already traced to Bandello's *Novelle* (1573) IV. 27, at page 262 above.

It is a psychological fact not well known that the homosexual over-valuation of the penis is the determining factor in the homosexual's impotence with women. He construes her lack of a penis as 'proof' that castrated beings do exist, and this creates tremendous anxiety that de-prives him of potency with her. Homosexual intercourse with women is therefore commonly achieved, if at all, anally (Byron) or in posi-tions from behind in which it is possible to deny the existence of the vagina. There was even a little song (before 1950) about a well-known literary homosexual in New York who affected relations with boyish, or ignorant and inferior, women: *"My sugar is so refined, He only does it from behind."* Sir Richard Burton has made famous, in his notes to the *Arabian Nights,* a line from Mirabeau's *Errotika Biblion* (1783) in which the homosexual explains to his desperate wife that even anal intercourse with women is unsatisfactory, *because there is nothing to hold onto,* as in the saddle-horn story in the section on the Penis, earlier.

In two potency jokes, the theme of actual 'oncing' with women is made the point, the brag about the number of *times* intercourse is achieved being deflected into bragging about the number of *women.* This is classically one of the labors of Hercules. *A Southern plantation owner needs a stud male for his 250 women cotton workers who are growing restive without sexual satisfaction. He writes to a fellow planter two hundred miles down the river for the loan of his 'buck nigger.' The planter is willing, but the Negro objects to "travelling all that distance for a half an hour's work."* (2:32.) — *A Negro who is able to have intercourse thirty times a night (or with a hundred dif-*

ferent women), is only able to get up to twenty-six the night his friends are betting on him. "I can't understand it," he says later. "It went perfect at the rehearsal this afternoon." (2:139. Compare Anatole France's story, "Roland's Brag.")

These are the anti-Negro group, super-potency being presumably 'animal.' The anti-Jewish specimen: *A doctor has just delivered three women in various parts of town, all of whom name Meyer Ginsburg as the father. The fourth woman is Mrs. Ginsburg, and the doctor is amazed to find that her husband is a little wizened carpenter. He takes him aside and asks,* "How do you do it? Uptown, downtown, east side, west side, all the women claim you're the father." "It's easy, Doctor. I got a bicycle." (1:75.) The anti-Catholic specimen: *A group of sailors on a whaling ship masturbate into a tub of sperm oil. Candles are made from the oil, and a whole convent full of nuns becomes pregnant.* (Scranton, Pa. 1925. Printed in *Anecdota* 2:295.) Actual contact is notably absent here. Another shipboard example expresses the privative satisfaction, and victory over other men that is basic in all such stories, but seldom mentioned. *A sea-captain going on a long voyage takes a whore with him for his special use. The first morning she puts her head out of his cabin door, and calls to him on the bridge,* "You're going to use me before breakfast, aren't you, Captain?" *He gazes at her without speaking, turns to some passengers standing nearby, and says soulfully,* "Cunt enough for a thousand men, and it's ALL MINE!" (1:311.)

Since no one can be as potent as the potency joke pretends, its final meaning is evidently a denial of fears of impotence, or of inability to love or satisfy a woman, or even to satisfy oneself. A man who is satisfied by the first act of intercourse does not go on to the second without pause. A person who must fantasy himself or herself going on to the fiftieth or hundredth act of intercourse at a single time, obviously does not enjoy intercourse at all. This is the 'orgastic impotence' first formulated by Wilhelm Reich (*Die Funktion des Orgasmus,* 1927; not identical with the eccentric revision purporting to be a translation, published in English), and the concept is as important as Reich's pretended discovery, later, of the 'orgone' is absurd.

These repressed emotions re-emerge in the mocking of the idea of numerical potency (Kinseyism) as adding up simply to impotence. *An elderly man boasts of his ability to have intercourse seventy times a night — once in bed and sixty-nine on the floor.* (2:39.) Originally

French, and appearing in Perceau's *Histoires d'Hommes et de Dames,* (1913) p. 73, as a Marseillais brag, entitled "Pretention." This has also been collected as the answer to a riddle (really not intended to be answered) on an elderly politician in the news for marrying a secretary half his age: *"How many times does seventy go into thirty-five?"* (N.Y. 1952.) Various changes have been rung on the original theme, each time adding one more digit above sixty-nine (the French *soixante-neuf*), which is of course a reference to mutual simultaneous oragenital intercourse. *The "seventy-one": a sixty-nine with two people watching. The "seventy-two": a sixty-nine with three fingers in the anus.* And so on, including the *"thirty-four and a half,"* a Lesbian slang phrase for cunnilinctus. (All N.Y., late 1940's.) Another riddle is given here — though riddles and other miscellaneous obscœna are in general not included — because it perfectly exemplifies the concern with counting and numbers common to themes of both impotence and masturbation. *What's the difference between frustration and utter frustration? — Frustration is the first time you find you can't do it the second time. Utter frustration is the second time you find you can't do it the first time.* (N.Y. 1948.) Or the spoonerized: *Old age is when you find it takes all night to do what you used to do all night.*

Of the anti-brag type: *Two old playboys are discussing the news that men are so scarce in Paris that the women are paying $25 a night to gigolos. "But who can live in Paris on $25 a month?"* (1:369.) — *Two elderly clubmen are discussing their sex lives. "Seriously now,"* says one, *"how often do you try it?" "Once a month every month,"* says the other, *"except in July and August." "No 'r,' eh?" "No, it's not that. The man who puts me on and off goes on his vacation."* (N.Y. 1952.)

The reference to the summer months without an 'r' can be discussed in its broadest aspect only in connection with the survivals of periods of heat or rut in the human female in spring and autumn. Taken narrowly, for the moment, it may very well be a reference to the aphrodisiacal power of oysters, which, according to the mysterious medico-biological knowledge that all of us have, but none of us know where we got it, are never-never to be eaten — and we are presumably then never never to have sexual intercourse? — in May, June, July, or August, which on the one hand are too hot anyway, and, on the other hand, are fullest of sexual opportunities during the Spring Prom, summer vacation, and other modern fertility festivals. It is indeed very confusing to try to live by folklore precept. There are too many layers

of conflicting interests, ethics, and historical relics striking through
one another, to form a single consistent pattern.

One folklore belief, which, if length & strength of believing could
make a thing true would be surer than the sunrise, is that certain foods
exist which, if eaten, will cause sexual excitement and/or will ensure
sexual performance, particularly in the aged. This is believed everywhere in the world, and is also apparently believed, somewhere, of
every food in the world. The only thing wrong with it is that it is completely untrue, as is also the matching belief that there are certain
substances — such as saltpetre — which have the opposite effect. With
great perspicacity, at least one joke-frame allows of variants on both
the most famous 'aphrodisiac,' oysters, and the most famous 'anti-
aphrodisiac,' saltpetre. *A young bride feeds her husband oysters on
their wedding night, but later complains that they were not very
satisfactory: "I fed him a dozen, but only nine of them worked."*
(2:175, also, a year earlier, in Paul Haines' "A Critique of Pure
Bawdry," in *Modern Thinker*, New York, 1933, ɪɪɪ.290.) — *An old
soldier, who has not yet faded away, meets another in the street. "You
remember the saltpetre that they gave us during the war to quiet us
down?" he asks. "Yes . . ." "It's just beginning to work."* (N.Y. 1952.
Also collected in French, 1966, apparently from a humor magazine.)

*An old roué, dining with a sweet young thing, slips the headwaiter
a packet of South American yohimbin pills, telling him to put one pill
in the soup. The dinner is delayed. When he complains, he is told that
the chef accidentally put in all the pills and is waiting for the noodles
to lay down.* (2:235.) This seems to be a sophisticated version of a barnyard anecdote of which the first available date of collection is California, 1940. *A farmer gets a box of aphrodisiac pills, but decides to try
one out first on an old bull. Next morning he finds the barn kicked
all to pieces, and the cows leaning in exhaustion against the remaining
walls with their tongues hanging out, while the bull is still snorting
and stamping and eager for more. Frightened by such powerful pills
he throws the rest of them away, and goes back and tells the doctor
what has happened. "Where did you throw them?" asks the doctor
anxiously. "Down the well." "My God," says the doctor, "you didn't
drink any of the water, did you?" "No," says the farmer; "we can't
get the pump-handle down."* The motif of the aphrodisiac that acts on
inanimate objects is at least as old as the *Pentamerone* of Giambattista
Basile (1636), a collection of rococo and almost burlesque folktales in

the Bolognese dialect, including such touches as the *kiss* of the "Sleeping Beauty," aphrodisiacal or fertility brew, so powerful that the mere smell of it cooking over the fire causes all the beds in the house to have little beds, and the chamberpots underneath to have little chamberpots.

The classic aphrodisiacal or sexually 'restorative' food is the egg, and its accustomed appearance on all the breakfast tables in the land that have not yet succumbed to the wheaten lure of Crunchies, Gunkies, and Kerd (spelled backwards) is in deference to this superstition. The great antiquity of the egg as a fertility symbol hardly needs discussion here, and its use in religious and quasi-religious fertility rites such as Easter egg rolling and the Chinese storing of eggs to be eaten in their twentieth year as, naturally, aphrodisiacs. *The American who is told that an egg in his beer* [now malted milk] *will "put lead in his pencil," but who does not want one anyhow, because he has "no one to write to"* (1:299), has already been noted as a fool story. Strips of lead and zinc, and more complicated swindle devices, are similarly sold to the gullible to be worn in their shoes to "charge their batteries" (Calif. 1941.) The McAtee manuscript gives a versified 'explanatory' story called "The Triassic Ovum": *Geological discussion. "What is this Jurassic and Triassic stuff?" "I don't know about Jurassic, but the Triassic is simple. You take a hen's egg. Last night it was in the hen's ass. Tonight it's in my ass. Tomorrow night it will be in my wife's ass. Triassic!"* (McAtee, 1913, env. 7, noting its origin in a 'popular tale.')

Modern writers seriously concerning themselves with the nonsense of aphrodisiacs seem a bit ashamed of their interest, and tend to dress it up with purposeful nonsense or pretended *haut-ton*. Thus Charles F. Heartman's *Aphrodisiac Culinary Manual* (New Orleans, 1942) subtitles itself: 'Being in part, the Squire of Baudricourt's *Cuisine de l'Amour,* in use for many centuries,' though actually a translation of a quite modern work. (There is a reprint, under the title '*Cuisine D'Amour, a Cook Book for Lovers,*' New York, 1952, under the imprint of 'Boar's Head Books,' with a pig's head on an escutcheon wavy — a curious imprint considering that the publisher is Jewish; but on exactly this point of the yearning for the pig, see the opening of the following chapter, and the notes on the bacon-slicing machine in the chapter on Castration in the Second Series following.)

I have remarked elsewhere (*The Horn Book,* p. 109) that: 'The idea of the real existence of chemical aphrodisiacs — once the lowly but then-new and mysterious potatoes and tomatoes ('love-apples'), just as now the equally fallacious Spanish fly and *yohimbin* — is simply part of the standard sexual folklore of humanity. It is very significant that at least two of the three main works on the subject of aphrodisiacs have been written by proudly-practising and even proselytizing homosexuals, Magnus Hirschfeld (*Liebesmittel*, 1929, written in collaboration with Richard Linsert, and with a private supplement of erotic illustrations, usually lacking), and Norman Douglas (*Paneros*, 1930) . . . Curiously enough, the third main work on the subject, Alan Hull Walton's *Love Recipes, Old and New:* "A Study of Aphrodisiacs throughout the ages, with sections on glandular extracts, hormone stimulation and rejuvenation" (London, 1956), manages somehow, despite the modern gland-and-hormone jargon of its title, and a fourteen-page "Bibliography for the Advanced and Professional Reader," to overlook completely *both* Hirschfeld and Douglas, the two main writers on the subject, and all their works.' Newer works are the usual superficial slop, except for an illustrated series in the Japanese pharmaceutical journal *Otsuka Yakuho* (1965–66), with sexological dictionary.

Norman Douglas descended not once but twice to the subject of aphrodisiacs, and it is a pity that he did not have some good friend — among the low creatures who exploited him at the end — to give him a kick in the arse and the advice given to the homosexual King James I by his court physician, Turquet de Mayerne, according to an untraced anecdote. *The aging James was finding himself impotent, and a side-procession of handsome boys through the Royal Bedchamber, in addition to the reigning favorite, the Duke of Buckingham* (a former page-boy, whose mad extravagance brought on the English Revolution), *did not seem to restore his powers. "Do ye think a change o' diet wud do it?" the king asked Mayerne. "Not at the top end, your Majesty."* — Douglas' *Paneros* (Florence, 1930) is larded, in the American reprint, with purposely phallic decorations, such as a plateful of mixed eggs and asparagus. This is for pictorial purposes only: it is celery that is supposed to be the aphrodisiac, and then only the *root*. There is also a culminating postface-portrait of the author as an infant in a charming dress, apparently intended as humor though the joke is unclear.

Twenty years later, as his last book, finished at the age of eighty-four and published posthumously (in London, 1952), Douglas produced an actual recipe-book like Heartman's, under the title *Venus in the Kitchen, or Love's Cookery Book,* 'by Pilaff Bey,' the pseudonym being in virtue of his collaboration on this work with Giuseppe Orioli, with whom Douglas had lived for many years. The Introduction is by Mr. Graham Greene, a writer whose own works combine anal-sadistic scenes (such as falling into toilets) of high homosexual appeal, with a kind of eminently saleable religious *morbidezza* that is just now all the rage. Mr. Greene ends his Introduction with a most remarkable example of the return of the repressed: specifically of the repressed (if it *is* repressed) castration fear behind ideas of impotence and of the need for aphrodisiacal help in the first place.

There are said to be certain Jewish rabbis who perform the operation of circumcision with their thumbnail so rapidly and painlessly that the child never cries. So without warning Douglas operates and the victim has no time to realize in what purgatorio of lopped limbs he is about to awaken, among the miserly, the bogus, the boring, and the ungenerous.

Now *that* is the way to introduce a book on aphrodisiacs.

6

WOMEN

I. THE BIG INCH

HISTORICALLY, women have been the last oppressed group to make their move, nor have they actually made it yet. The Armenians and Scots have been fighting for their independence for centuries, while the destruction of the Jewish ghettos and the slave-rebellions of the Negroes in America were seriously under way by the 1770's, though it has taken the power politics of the discovery of oil and other mineral wealth in Africa to bring the Negro revolt onward now toward its culmination. Women are still frozen at the paltry assimilationist stage of hating themselves for the women that they are, and wanting to be what they can never be: *men* — pants, penis, and all the rest of it.

The great buncombe victory of the modern woman movement, as modern women imagine it to have been, was the appearance of Miss Marlene Dietrich, a German actress, fresh from her victory in the masochist film, *The Blue Angel,* at the Hollywood première of Cecil B. De Mille's *The Sign of the Cross,* on Christmas Eve, 1933, dressed in men's smoking-jacket and pants, and accompanied by another Hollywood female, a columnist, Miss Elsa Maxwell, of whom history has carefully lost track, not only dressed identically but also sporting a phoney moustache, and explaining to the press photographers that she was pretending to be Einstein! Since that time, in America and increasingly in other countries — after nearly a twenty-year cultural lag — men's clothing for women has been legal, though women's clothing can still not generally be worn publicly by men (unless pretendedly kilts or similar), apparently on the basis of the same biblical text, *Deuteronomy,* xxii. 5, which once prohibited transvestism to both sexes. On Miss Dietrich's lead, by Easter 1934, lounging pajamas, sailor pants, and even derby hats for ladies were being sported as far east as Cleveland, according to the contemporary magazines addressed to the female movie-fans, who would also, of course, wear feathers up their ass if some well-publicized movie-star or other *kitsch* royalty or nobility could be got to launch that fad as well. The real freedom for women cannot be attained by battening, in this way, on the endemic inferiority complexes (about being women) of even the most militant of them, to exploit the sheep-like and frightened unvirile imitativeness to which women can be pushed.

For the record it ought perhaps also to be mentioned that an earlier attempt to launch the pants-style for women, mildly disguised as harem-trousers or divided skirts (also known in ancient Greece some three thousand years ago, as the costumes of the surviving snake-goddess statues show), had been made by Miss Marie Dressler, at the time of World War I, in Chaplin's first movie-farce, *Tillie's Punctured Romance*. The lesbian tone given to the whole thing, and especially the finale, by Miss Dressler still seems astonishingly frank under its superficial layer of burlesque symbolisms. It remains unprecedented except for an insiders' gag-scene, miming cunnilinctus between the two female leads under the guise of setting-up exercises, in the Humphrey Bogart movie-comedy, *Beat the Devil*, in the 1950's, which was played entirely as homosexual camp. This too is not freedom.

The unconscious comedy highpoint, so far, was unquestionably reached in the spring of 1966, when an American society woman insisted upon getting married, at a florid society wedding, in pants — white, and fetchingly beruffled too, in honor of the occasion — on the grounds that she always wore pants and would not feel 'comfortable' in anything else, even for the half-hour the wedding might take. Her husband stated that he was entirely in accordance with these arrangements, and her picture, in the wedding apparel of her choice, appeared in the fashion- and society-news pages of family newspapers all over the United States, without, however, starting any fad. It is the grim and humorless sobriety that is really so shocking here. During World War II, a more lighthearted approach to the same socio-sexual reversals was taken in Great Britain, in a widely-published photograph of a long line of women factory-workers in overalls (so *necessary* for women in factories since World War I, though the men in factories just as often wear skirt-like coats) running happily toward the camera with their arms around an equal and alternate number of Scottish soldiers in kilts. One could hardly doubt, in a self-satirizing approach like this, the underlying femininity of the women and virility of the men — no matter what they might be wearing. In any case, this certainly beats all competition for transvestist gag-photographs, pants down. A similar gag-photo, but just missing the perfection of the overalls-and-kilts reversal, is featured in the Swiss-German men's magazine *Club* (1967) No. 3: p. 66–7, showing a rather epicene group of male and female models or dancers all in mini-skirts.

It is to be observed that the crucial element in all of this is the men's self-effeminization, not the women's would-be masculinization in attempting to run off with the men's pants, the late-medieval *"Kampf um die Hosen,"* or War of the Trousers. The pictorial record of this struggle is largely available in John Grand-Carteret's *La Femme en culotte* (Paris, 1899), a remarkable illustrated work published long before Marlene Dietrich was born. I have myself already had enough to say on the subject of gross penis-envy and pants, and on the prevailing fad for young women, since World War II, of skin-tight dungarees with a copper-riveted clitoris on the fly (which is 'more comfortable' of course), in *Love & Death,* p. 75–80; in my pamphlet, *On the Cause of Homosexuality* (1950); and in the brief "Notes on Masochism" first published openly in *The Compleat Neurotica* (1963) between issues Nos. 5 and 6, as a gloss on the very astonishing and completely authentic sado-masochistic "Answers to an Ad" in No. 5. As to the even more recent style, of complete male-impersonation outfits for women, with bell-bottomed trousers and fly-fronts (or even sailor-pants ballap openings, unbuttoning across the front), one assumes that the only expected advantage for the wearers is psychological. The broadest statement of the emotional problems of these girls and women is available in the psychoanalytic literature, particularly — to name but two authors exceedingly easy to read — Karl Abraham on "The Female Castration Complex" in his *Selected Papers* (1927) p. 338–69, and the fascinating and profoundly sympathetic *The Ego in Love and Sexuality* (1960) by Dr. Edrita Fried, of which a pocket-reprint exists.

What is crucial, in the social rather than the personal or neurotic sense, in all this, is not the wearing of men's clothes by women, but the *acceptance* by modern men of women wearing such clothing, topped off with slashed-bang and otherwise purposely unfeminine hair styles (actually begun after World War II in Europe, as a mark of ignominy for women who had consorted with the Nazis, and whose hair was cropped or their heads shaved). Simultaneously with accepting as sexual consorts, and even as wives, these women impersonating men and otherwise expressing gross penis-envy compulsions, many of the same men — especially the young ones — are adapting to their own use colorfully female clothing (so far as the law allows), pendant neck- and wrist-jewellery, etc., and in other ways are impersonating women. This is the so-called 'Carnaby Street' style, imported to America in the mid-1960's without any open statement that the juvenile 'Mod' gangs affecting such clothing in Britain are all frankly understood there to be homosexual.

That women would want to be men under patriarchy is not, of course, in any way surprising — pants, penis, and all the rest of it — any more than that a Negro might wish to have been born white. *What requires explanation is the men,* who can now accept — and even de- mand — these women who are visibly not women at all. For it is ob- vious that if it were found, on a broad scale, that boys and men refused to consort with girls and women dressed as boys (the Lysistrata revolt in reverse!) and that no one would marry such women, the style would immediately collapse and women would go back to their penis-envy manifestations in some less glaring and purposely provocative way. Meanwhile, what would happen to these masochistic and self-castrated young men who are already sporting women's clothes and haircuts, so far as they dare; and who would marry them? Actually, who cares? Possibly the Atom Bomb is the only solution.

Dr. Charles Winick has begun the publication of a depressing work on at least the costume and cosmetic aspects, and other exotica of this subject, under the working title, *"Dear Sir or Madam, as the Case May Be"* (preliminary article in *Antioch Review,* Spring 1963, p. 35-49), taking the point of view not that women are now preëmpting men's pants, coats, hair styles, social and economic prerogatives and the like, but that there is a 'blurring of the differences;' that men are becoming effeminized as women become masculinized, and that the two sexes are simply arriving now at a mid-point of similarity. This is certainly true, but why the social influences that effeminize men should masculinize women Dr. Winick does not explain, though he admits that: 'Today a woman could be well dressed while wearing a costume practically all of which derived from men. . . . However, a man who wore a costume practically all of which derived from women might be ar- rested for being a transvestite or might be regarded as a homosexual.' This means positively that what is happening is no 'blurring' of un- explainable origin, but that the end of men's dominance is in sight, owing to the tremendous weakening of the individual man by the Machine, and by mechanized society; and that women's activity is simply a slave-revolt, running away with the pants as banner. The "War of the Trousers," already hundreds of years old.

The entire intellectual position and historical evidence involved here, especially from the real matriarchies of the past, such as Egypt, have been masterfully mapped out, on a very broad scale, fifty years ago, in *Die weibliche Eigenart im Männerstaat* (Karlsruhe, 1921), signed by Dr. M. Vaerting; and translated into English as *The Dominant Sex* (London, 1922), now signed by the husband-&-wife team of Drs. Mathilde and Mathias Vaerting — in that order — implying that one or the other was crowded out of the first edition, or is free-loading in the second, which is *not* really sex equality. The same is true of almost all well-publicized husband-&-wife writing teams, especially certain modern historians, and I have myself been an eye-witness of one such pair going through a sort of ultra-*kitsch* literary Togetherness, for the benefit of guests, in which both sat 'writing' simultaneously on two portable typewriters, side-by-side at a long plank table. Perish forbid!

Behind the corny front, one assumes that the woman silently slogs away at all the laborious library research, or acts as their agent by means of her sex-appeal; the man does the flashy writing. Not to come too libellously close to the present day, this was certainly the case with the nature-books written (in his old age) by the great French historian, Jules Michelet, in collaboration with his wife and *inspiratrice,* Athénaïs Mialaret (Mme. Michelet), who later had the pious revenge of 'revising' the posthumous manuscripts of this tremendous stylist. (As is seldom observed, Michelet was — after Diderot's *Rameau's Nephew,* 1779, which started it all, and Carlyle's *French Revolution,* 1837, which certainly must have inspired the later historian — the creator of the modern 'stream of consciousness' style, and in serious historical works, mind you! See in particular the long dithyrambic poem-in-prose that is his history of witchcraft, *La Sorcière,* 1862, of which an excellent English translation was issued by Carrington about 1900. This type of intensely personal introspective writing derives ultimately from the Spanish and Italian picaresque writers of the early 16th century, such as Delicado and Aretino, but became common only after Carlyle and Michelet, spreading via *Les Lauriers sont coupés,* 1887, of Édouard Dujardin, to James Joyce, Céline, Henry Miller, and other lesser imitators.) The Vaertings' book, in whatever portions its authors wrote it, is an extremely important work, decades ahead of its time, and should certainly now be reprinted. We also await Dr. Winick's definitive work with sick fascination.

As to transsexual hair styles in particular — much in the news since the early 1960's, owing to the publicity-wise fad for long hair on the part of male British false-*révoltés* and bop singers chosen for their easy-to-identify-with ugliness — a pamphlet on exactly this matter had already appeared in the mid-17th century in England, *The Unlovelinesse of Love-Lockes,* by the Puritan propagandist William Prynne, bitterly attacking the *then*-current style of long hair for men, and short for women. As is well known, Prynne, for another of his writings, *Histriomastix, or The Players' Scourge* — attacking the immorality of the theatre, which was construed to involve a slur against the queen (who had appeared in a masque at court) — was sentenced by the Star-Chamber in 1634 to life imprisonment, a fine of £5,000, and to have his ears cut off at the foot of the pillory; but he stalwartly refused to wear long hair even afterwards to hide the scars.

To make all things complete, it may be added that the 'topless' or bare-breast style in America, existing recently in fact in San Francisco nightclubs (not only on the stage, which is of course ancient, but in the form of 'topless' waitresses), and attempted on public bathing beaches in America and France since 1964, is by no means intended simply to show women as attractively mammalian to appreciative males, though that is the pretense. To the contrary, it is openly thought of — by the women involved, if not by the men — as a way of matriarchally dominating or *crushing* men with the bare breasts, which are conceived of classically, at the unconscious level, especially if large, as 'female penises,' owing to the erectility of the nipples and the swelling of the breasts when in milk and during menstruation.

There is even a song on the subject, I believe, by Georges Brassens, one of the earliest of the popular singers specializing in the *facile or imaginary revolt* (as the French observers have astutely called it) of the St. Germain-des-Prés period in Paris in the late 1940's, a style now aped in America by such Katzenjammer kids as 'Bob Dylan' (Robert Zimmerman), The Mothers, the Seeds, the Freak-Outs, etc., and re-imported to France and England by 'Antoine,' the Beatles, and their further imitators, all of whom affect extremely feminine fright-wig haircuts. Brassens' song plainly concerns the New Revolt, in which a gang of maddened women go out valiantly to 'club the cops (*matraquer les flics*) with their pendulous breasts.'

This is a satirical approach, of course, but to a subject not really handled in public since the period of the legendary Greek Bacchantes and
the Vestal Virgins of Rome, Lesbian guardians of the mysteries of
earlier matriarchal religions from which patriarchy had taken over in
then-recent times, who would tear to bits any hapless male interrupting
their secret rites (of cunnilinctus? still surviving as the 'Black Mass'),
just as Venus in the guise of a rooting wild-boar kills her lover Adonis
— *i.e.,* Isis castrating Osiris and then 'searching' three days for his penis,
while he waits in Hell — and Diana, the decayed virgin relic of the
same legends, kills Actaeon by having him turned into a stag and torn
to bits by his own hunting-dogs, for the accidental crime of coming
upon this bitch-virgin bathing. The obvious parallel with 'Modesty
Blaise,' in the latest bitch-heroine movie, strangling some happily struggling masochist with a scarf (why not poisoned pussy-hairs?) strung
between her knees, need hardly be drawn here. See further: "Avatars
of the Bitch," in *Love & Death,* and the comic-strip movie, *Barbarella*
(1968), a true blast from the sewer of the unconscious.

Trained sociologists of the future may well stare uncomprehend-
ingly, unless we give them a few hints these decades, at the presumably
erotic 'cheesecake' or 'leg-art' photos which will remain on the record
in the pages of American (and imitative English, French, and German) 'men's magazines' of the 1950's and '60's, showing the ultimate
ripping apart of modern women in the two simultaneous directions
of masculinity and femininity: *dirty girls in boys' haircuts posed in
dungaree pants and bare breasts.* The paradox is even worse than appears, since, as indicated above as to the 'topless' fad of the San Francisco tit-whores, it is perhaps the breasts which are the masculine element, and the dungarees or blue jeans, modelling the buttocks attractively and often clearly outlining the vulvar groove, which are thought
of as feminine. Or at least as a sort of quasi-male intersexuality (pants
and buttocks) to help the intended male consort, or victim, master his
panic dread of the underlying (alas!) female genital anatomy, or
Gorgon Medusa, with which he will eventually be faced.

I. IDENTIFICATION WITH THE PENIS

I would repeat again that much more profound analyses of female
penis-envy are available in the psychoanalytic literature, particularly in
Karl Abraham's "Manifestations of the Female Castration Complex,"
in his *Selected Papers* (1927) p. 338–69, and no further argumentative

or theoretical preamble need be engaged in on this point. It is, further-more, unquestionable that most modern jokes on sexual themes are the creation of men and not of women, and as men are not at all shy about their pride in the possession of a penis, or the tremendous feeling of superiority it gives them over women, it is only to be expected that jokes, at least, will project upon the women who appear in them the classic textbook manifestations of penis-envy.

Actually, considering the provocations offered, at least half of the points of view ascribed to women concerning the penis are friendlier than might be expected. In case the word 'provocation' seems odd, the reader is recommended to review the jokes and folklore of the penis in the latter half of the preceding chapter, where it is made crystal clear that the basic use of the ultra-long penis so much discussed, is TO KILL THE WOMAN WITH IT. There are also endless little-boy taunts. Here is an example, from a nightclub master of ceremonies, Florida, 1951: *"That sailor over there tried to join the Waves, and he came this far (wiggling little finger) from passing the physical."* To the man this is of course a humorous insult as to the size of his penis. What is it to the woman? Another humorous example: *A doctor tells a garrulous woman who asks him where he has been, "I just delivered a baby. And, you know, the baby was born without a penis." "Ah," says the woman. "Yes," the doctor continues, "it has no penis; but in sixteen or eighteen years, it will have the finest place to put one you ever saw."* (Va., 1952.)

To agree without rancor to the fact of the existence of the penis, it is necessary for the woman — as seen in jokes — to identify herself with its possessor. *"Ah, a fine boy!" says the aunt, running her hand under the cloth. "Boy, nothing!" says the doctor. "Let go of my finger."* (1:315. Used since mid-1930's on semi-private humorous postcards with the sexes reversed in the colloquy; the minister asking, "What is the name of the boy?") — *Three sisters are bragging about their beaux. First: "We were so close last night you couldn't put your hand between us." Second: "We were so close you couldn't stick a pin between us." Third: "Piffle! My beau and I were so close together last night you couldn't tell which one of us the nuts were fastened to!"* (Idaho, 1919.) In an unusual example: *At a Norwegian picnic, when the girls had to urinate, all the men gathered in a circle around them and watched. Then the men urinated too, with the girls all watching. Next day one of the girls is merrily relating the incident to a friend. "I was so proud," she says, "when Lars took ours out."* (Calif. 1941.)

The castration anxieties in men that result in fantasies of having or wanting a very long penis, also result in fearing and hating women as dangerous and forbidden (on pain of castration), and furthermore as unworthy objects lacking penises. The preferred expression of this hatred is to harm the woman by means of the long penis, but rather than accept the guilt of admitting this, men prefer to believe that women can only receive genital pleasure if the penis erects to some absurd and exorbitant length. The whole emphasis here is on piercing and penetrating, in a quite direct sadistic sense. There is also absolutely no concern with the clitoral pressure and friction without which most women never have orgasm, for all the talk about the 'vaginal orgasm,' which merely refers to vaginal contractions during orgasm. Men refuse to admit to themselves — and not only in jokes — that women do not particularly like long penises, and are hurt physically by them. (The whole distance from the pubic bone to the sacrum is seldom more than from five to five and one-half inches in women, representing the total vaginal penetration possible without pain.) As the 'ideal' penis, which would be of moderate length but very thick, is even less common statistically than long penises over six inches — which are not actually rare — it is never mentioned in jokes or folklore at all except as an object of contempt, as in the proverbial phrase: "short and thick, like a Welshman's prick." *A woman is told that the men in the East have penises that are short and thick, while the men in the West have penises that are long and thin. She says she would prefer a man who was born in the East, but who has lived in the West a long, long time.* (D.C. 1952.) Compare: *A girl who is part Indian and part Scotch is best — she's both wild and tight.* (D.C. 1943.)

Various jokes have been given in the section on Female Fools in which the whole point is the projection upon the woman of the expectation of a penis of greater than reasonable human length, or, if sufficiently overlong, of her complaining of some irrelevancy, such as buttocks that are too small to "swing it." *Au fond* the real meaning is that the penis must be long enough to hurt her, with the pretense that this desire is masochism on the woman's part and not sadism on the man's. *A woman accepts a man's overtures when he brags of the great length of his penis, saying that he is a "real man." As he is inserting it slowly, for fear of hurting her* [sic], *she says, "Honey, I thought you said — wow! you sure are!* (Calif. 1941.) Several variants. In one, *The woman has been lent the husband of a neighbor wife. As they get into bed in the dark, she remarks, "Your wife was telling me that you had —uhh!"* (Transcontinental train, 1945.) In an almost direct statement of the masochistic idea: *The groom asks the bride on their wedding night whether things are the way she expected. "Not exactly," she says. "My sister told me it would feel just like a bevy of whales were entering me. Oh, just a minute, oh! oh! here they come!!"* (D.C. 1951.) Much of the pleasure of submitting to anal intercourse, especially by homosexuals, is masochistic in this way.

The usual brags of penis length are sometimes either made by the woman — to the presumable envy of other women — or are crucial to her choice of a man, as just above. *Three suitors are put up overnight in one bed together, while the mother and daughter listen through the wall to their conversation. The first suitor mentions the million dollars he will inherit. "That's the man for you," says the mother. The second suitor will inherit two million. "No, that's the man for you," the mother corrects herself. "All right," says the third suitor, "roll off my cock and let me get some sleep." "I'm not on your cock." "Well then it's over you, and Al is on it." "That's the man for me," says the daughter.* (2:282.) In a similar punning joke, *Three Chinese girls are bragging about the Mandarins who love them. One boasts that her lover has a dragon on his door, which is a sign of wealth. The second boasts that her lover has two dragons on his door. The third says that she has just spent a wonderful night with a man with only one dragon, but that one draggin' on the ground.* (D.C. 1944. Collected earlier, Calif. 1940, in what seems to be a rationalized version concerning Marines with dragons tattooed on their chests.) Compare also the three-sister joke, somewhat earlier, on how close together the girls and their beaux have been.

This type of brag is parodied in a joke with a pantomime punchline. *One girl mentions boastfully to another that her fiancé is going to give her a Rolls-Royce for a wedding present and that his father has a million dollars. The other counters by saying that her fiancé has a penis so long that fourteen birds can stand on it, wing to wing. Some months later they meet in a bargain basement. "What about that Rolls-Royce?" mocks the second. "Well," says the other, "it was only a Ford, and I might as well tell you that his million dollars turned out to be a little candy-store that his father owns. What about you?" "Well, seeing that you're being so honest, I'll tell you. You know what I said about my husband having a penis so big that fourteen birds can stand on it?*

Well, it's really only twelve birds, and the last one has to go like this (flapping arms like wings)." (N.Y. 1952.) Essentially this is a less covert form of an old Levantine folktale in which *A husband tests his wife's ability to keep a secret by telling her that a crow has flown out of his belly. By the time the story gets back to him, it is fifty crows — and an egg!* (Type 1381D, with references.)

Again, in case these seem too utterly modern and American, far older examples, and from other countries, can be paralleled. *Mrs. O'Reilly told Mrs. Flannagan she was mad at her for telling people that O'Reilly had a wart on the end of his penis. Mrs. Flannagan said she had said no such thing. "I only said it* felt *like he had," she explained.* (Calif. 1942.) With this compare: *A man's wife complains of the size of his penis, and he is told he must exhibit it to a jury of matrons. He objects, but in vain. All that is allowed him is that he may stand behind a screen and put his penis out through a hole to be examined. He asks the clergyman, who is very well hung, to substitute for him, but when the substitute penis is put through the hole, one of the matrons cries out: "That's the minister's; I ken't by the wart o' the point o't."* ("Some Erotic Folk-lore from Scotland," in *Kryptádia,* 1884, II. 261. The complete text is quoted below, under "Adultery," 9.III.2.) This can be traced not only to Scotland in the 19th century, but to France in the 15th, being No. 15 "La Nonne Sçavante" in the *Cent Nouvelles Nouvelles* (1461) of Antoine de La Sale, where the young monk attempts to have Brother Conrad substitute for him at the nun's window.

2. HOSTILITY AGAINST THE PENIS

In the jokes earlier, under "Female Fools," in which the woman displays an utter ignorance or pretended ignorance of the penis, a hostile tone is generally strongly in evidence in some harm or accident that befalls the penis owing to the woman's ignorance. These are penis-envy stories, to be sure, but not of the freely accepting type in which the woman is glad the penis exists and even identifies herself with its possessor. Two or three perfectly innocent acceptances have been collected, but in all of these the woman is old. In the last example she is specifically identified as the mother, which puts quite a different complexion on the matter, as the boy's desire to exhibit his penis to his mother's admiration — especially during the urination that represents *the* genital act to the child — is among the commonest of the Oedipal 'partial' urges. *A little old lady sees a penis for the first time when a boy stops to urinate by her garden gate. She throws up her hands and says, "What lovely things men will make for money!"* (From England, 1940.) — *One of three Scotch old maids finally gets married. She writes back from her honeymoon, "Eh, yon's a contrivance!"* (From Scotland, 1953.)

With this authentic Highland flavor may be compared the spurious phallic brag — full of biblical and poetic references — of Burns' letter to Robert Ainslie, of March 3rd, 1788, printed in some "1827" editions of *The Merry Muses of Caledonia,* and in my *The Horn Book* (1964), p. 148-9, but omitted from all editions of Burns' collected letters. In the Ainslie letter, after talking his common-law wife, Jean Armour, into swearing 'privately and solemnly never to attempt any claim on me as a husband, even though anybody should persuade her she had such a claim (which she had not),' Burns rewards her — she is about to give birth! — by taking 'the opportunity of some dry horse litter, and gave her such a thundering scalade that electrified the very marrow of her bones. Oh, what a peacemaker is a guid weel-willy pintle! It is the mediator, the guarantee, the umpire, the bond of union, the solemn league and covenant, the plenipotentiary, the Aaron's rod, the Jacob's staff, the prophet Elisha's pot of oil, the Ahasuerus' sceptre, the sword of mercy, the philosopher's stone, the horn of plenty, the Tree of Life between Man and Woman.' Unfortunately, Burns then takes it all back, after some further gas about having 'given her a guinea, and . . . f—d her till she rejoiced with joy unspeakable and full of glory,' by ending the letter: 'How are your soul and body putting up? A little like man and wife, I suppose. Your faithful friend, R.B.' A long synonymic flight like that rather puts into the shade even so famous a list of symbolic equivalents of the genitals as that in Freud's "Tenth Introductory Lecture to Psychoanalysis," with which compare:

A man's mother is very old and depressed. He decides to send her to a psychiatrist, explaining to him beforehand that she does not talk English. "That's all right," says the psychiatrist, "I understand Jewish perfectly." He sees the old lady, calls her Grandma, and makes her feel quite at home. "Now what's this?" he asks, holding up a spoon. "Doss iss a leffel." "Fine, fine. I knew we'd get along. And what's this (holding up a fork)?" "Doss iss a gappel." "Perfect. And this (holding up a banana)?" "Doss iss a phallic symbol." (N.Y. 1953.)

The real hostility that women often feel, as regards the penis, will not be found in jokes, since jokes are principally invented by men. What jokes express is, therefore, more often a mere projection upon the woman of the male fantasy of the desirability of a very long penis. Instead of being expressed as brags, it is expressed in the form of insults, which also subserves the uses of sex hate, which seems to be the basic emotion in most jokes about sexual relations. With only the most minor exceptions, dirty jokes involving *love* have not been encountered. I repeat: DIRTY JOKES ABOUT *love* HAVE NOT BEEN ENCOUNTERED. Some of the lines collected are really brutal cut-downs. *Man, bragging: "I'm a big fireman from Kansas City." Woman: "Well either start paying out more hose, or get closer to the fire."* (Minn. 1946.) — *A man has a penis too large for any of the girls in the brothel. "It's just like a stove-pipe," says one. He is not really displeased. "Big, huh?" he says. "No, dirty."* (2:97.) In another form, *A prostitute preparing for intercourse in an alley objects that the customer's penis is too big. "Well that's no reason to drop it in the mud," he says.* (2:21. Also collected as of the lady-teacher who keeps after school the boy nicknamed "Big Dick." — D.C. 1951.)

These have been given first to show that the penis can be objected to, no matter how long it is. It is of course more usual for the objection to be levelled against the too-short penis. *Fat woman, to fat man: "Thanks for the tip."* (Guam, 1948.) — *The bride asks the groom, "Harold dear, now that we're married, please tell me: What's a penis?" Pleased at her inexperience, he shows her. "Oh," she says, "it's just like a prick, only littler!"* (Idaho, 1952.) Also in Randolph, No. 49, "It was a Tee-Hee," Arkansas, 1930's.) The whole situation is just fantasy here, by way of getting across the hatred. Exact observation of little-known facts about intercourse can also be used in the same way. *A girl contemptuously rejects a man's proposal of marriage, saying, "What would I want with a little prick like yours? Why, it would slip out every time I sneezed." "Maybe so," says the man, "but you'd have to have the whooping cough to keep it out."* (Calif. 1942.) In a photographic joke: *A man snaps a picture of his wife's genitals as she steps out of the shower on their wedding morning. "What are you going to do with that?" she asks. "I'm going to wear it next to my heart," he says passionately. "Well then give me a photograph of yours," she says. "I'd like to get an enlargement."* (1:252.) Hardly more than a weak pun on photographic terms. A reversal of the same gag is reported of

Alfred Jarry, author of *Ubu Roi,* who died in 1907. Jarry's room had an exceptionally low ceiling, and the legs of the table and chairs were sawed off to suit. Covering a whole wall was a gigantic stone phallus from the East Indies, presented to him by Félicien Rops. When 'Rachilde,' the wife of his publisher, asked about it, remarking particularly on its size, Jarry remarked. "It's a reduction." (One of Jarry's novels, *Le Surmâle,* 1902, recently translated into English, is a science-fiction satire on the problems encountered by a supermale — *i.e.,* orgastically-impotent neurotic — who is able to repeat coitus without pause an endless number of times. Compare also F. Fleuret's *Jim Click,* 1930.)

What is usually seen in the joke about to be given is the identification of foot and penis (as also earlier, in the man who shows his penis to the chiropodist's nurse). That the long nose is believed to be a similar indicator is traditional in many countries. Of much greater interest, however, is the female-dominant situation here, to which the man responds with the underdog or masochist subterfuge of cheating (as earlier with the 'decoy' of keys, etc.), however innocently. *A woman picks up an unemployed young man with very large shoes, expecting his penis to match. In the morning he finds a five-dollar bill on the table and a note: "With my compliments . . . Buy a pair of shoes that fit you."* (2:194.) Here first published in the middle of the Depression, 1934, but also collected, 1943, of a woman who picks up a policeman with very large shoes. *Anecdota II* (1934) gives a similar employment agency joke, about *A man with a short penis who is hired by a lady writer* — "*hired, fucked, and fired in an hour.*" (2:327.)

The alternating complaints about the penis being too large or too small — which add up, of course, to the same thing — are brought together in a single brutal example: *A woman appears before the Supreme Court of Maine to ask for a divorce on the grounds that her husband's penis is too large and hurts her. The divorce is granted. The next year the same woman appears again, asking an annulment of her second marriage on the grounds that her new husband is impotent. "Well," says the judge tartly, "I dismiss the case. The Supreme Court of Maine has other business to attend to besides fitting pricks to your cunt, Madam."* (*Memorabilia,* 1911.)

Miscellaneous complaints concern such irrelevancies as the fact of circumcision (or its lack), the temperature, number, etc. of the penis. Almost any attribute can be used, or some insulting metaphoric or standard symbolic comparison, as that of *The mother who tells her daughter going out on her first date, "Every man has a rattlesnake in his pants — only it doesn't rattle."* (N.Y. 1953.) — *A Jewish woman looks through a knothole in a nudist colony fence. "Pooey," she says, "all goyim!"* (Minn. 1946.) — *First Old Maid in the art museum: "For such a big statue doesn't the Hercules have awfully small organs?" Second Old Maid: "Yes, and so* COLD *too."* (N.Y. 1952. Really a good deal older, with a possible relationship to "Le Soldat au Couvent," given in French and American forms at the beginning of the section on "Female Fools." A superstition of the middle ages has it that the devil's penis, during intercourse with human beings, is red-hot, but his semen ice-cold.) — *A tramp in tattered trousers is being given a meal by a woman in her negligée. Her breasts keep falling out, and the sight makes his penis erect through one or another of the holes in his pants as he keeps pushing it back. Discussing tramps in general at the bridge club next day, this particular tramp comes up. "That's the one," says the woman who fed him. "I've never seen a beast with so many cocks before in my life!"* (2:99. Compare the hateful jokes on the fallen-out breasts in the chapter, "The Male Approach," 4.IV, section "Breasts," earlier — a striking contrast.)

The testicles are also thought of as envied and resented by women, but there is some question as to whether this is true except in the minds of the makers of jokes. Just as most castration anxieties center around the penis and not the testicles, just so the real penis-envy of women is just that, and not testicle-envy. Both the anxiety and the envy take their rise in the period of childhood, when the testicles are small and undeveloped, and without interest of the sort present in the penis, both for its sexual use and pleasure, and for its urinary abilities, to be discussed shortly. Straight male-chauvinist brag, from *Sex to Sexty* 15:55 (1968): '*Know why, when a woman stops for a red light, she always sits there and puffs her hair? — Because she doesn't have any family jewels [i.e. testicles] to scratch.*'

A woman at the White House insists on an intercourse with the President. Guard: "You mean an interview, madam." "No, I mean intercourse! I want to see the nuts that are running the country." (N.Y. 1938.) A pretended fool joke, as is: *A woman touches a man's testicles during intercourse, and asks what they are. "Those are my nuts," he says. "Well untie the knots, and put in the rest!"* (N.Y. 1942, in Jewish dialect; Los Angeles, Calif. 1952, in Mexican dialect; N.Y. 1964, in Negro dialect, with the added encouragement: "*Dat's all good stuff!*") The concentration here on stupid mispronunciational dialect humor almost disguises this survival of the folktale of the young man, *Coypeau, who offers to sew up the girl's 'honor' for her, when she is afraid of losing it at a dance, but after a few times explains that he has no more thread, whereupon she reminds him of the two 'pelotons' — or balls of yarn — still there.* (Béroalde de Verville, *Le Moyen de Parvenir,* c. 1610, chap. 31, "Cause," given as chap. 27 in Machen's translation.) A modern French form, collected in Brittany in 1880, and printed in *Kryptádia,* II. 5–7, shows almost no variation from Béroalde's form. It is translated in *The Way of a Virgin* [1928?] p. 111–13. An echo may also be suspected in the current American semi-erotic ballad about winding up a woman's "Little Ball of Yarn." The whole theme is Aarne's Tale-Type 1542**, "The Maiden's Honor."

An astonishingly hostile story, which will be discussed again later, overdetermines the concentration on the testicles by a string of puns on the idea and word 'balls.' (Compare the motifs at Thompson's F547.6, on pubic hair, under "Remarkable Sexual Organs.") *A man marries a blonde and then wants a divorce six months later when he finds her pubic hair growing out black. When asked in court what she has to say for herself, she opens her purse, takes out a baseball, and hits her husband right between the eyes with it. The judge is about to fine her for contempt of court, but she says, "You don't understand, Judge. That's my defense. I hit him with one ball, and in two minutes his eye is black and blue. He's been banging me on the ass with two balls for six months, and when it gets the least little bit black he wants a divorce!"* (New York state, 1942.) This is evidently derived from the *contest-in-gestures* of Rabelais, II. 19, and III. 20, especially the mock religious controversy form of Aarne's Types 924A and B.

3. JEALOUSY OF MALE URINATION

The authentic extension of penis-envy on the part of women is to the ability to urinate standing, which many women do envy in men and sometimes try to imitate, with greater or less success and wetting of stockings. An important folktale on this point, collected in Picardy, and published in the first volume of *Kryptádia* (1883) p. 333, concerns *A princess who was able to urinate over the highest haycocks, to her father's great displeasure, until a clever young man took her maidenhead, after which she was not able to urinate over even an ordinary haycock and succeeded only in wetting her stockings when she tried.* An English translation is given in *The Way of a Virgin,* attributed to

Raymond Thompson but signed by 'L. and C. Brovan' ('London, 1922' [New York, c. 1928]) p. 153-7. This tale expresses with the greatest directness the idea that defloration is a kind of castration of the woman, removing any virile impulse she may have, or even any anatomical organ or special formation — the 'female phallus,' obviously — by which she seeks to express virility. In Afanasyev's *Russian Secret Tales,* No. 46, the girl only jumps over rather than pisses over haycocks, but her penis-envy is consciously the plot.

Havelock Ellis, who confesses in his autobiography to a lifelong undinist interest in women's urination, spends most of the final supplementary volume of his *Studies in the Psychology of Sex* (1928) on the case of his undinist and auto-flagellant mistress, 'Florrie,' p. 120–212, which he also submitted to Wilhelm Stekel for analysis; and on a useful historical article, p. 376–476, on undinism. Ellis' own treatment of the subject is markedly anti-analytic, as he had no desire to be cured, but he gives a very fair sampling of the analytic literature, except in the case of Karl Abraham's "Manifestations of the Female Castration Complex," in Abraham's *Selected Papers* (1927) p. 338–69, which is the *locus classicus* on penis-envy, and which evidently cast more light on the subject than Ellis was able to endure. The masochistic and undinist novel, *Gynecocracy* (1893) by 'Julian Robinson,' is probably by Havelock Ellis, to whom *Sadopaideia* (1907) by 'Cecil Prendergast' is also attributed.

The McAtee Manuscript (env. 7, 1912) gives a 'popular tale put into verse' to the following effect: *Said Sue, "When I began to run with the boys, I could piss through a fine gold ring. But now if you give me a washtub, I scarce can hit the doggoned thing."* This is clearly an American version of the kernel of the above-mentioned Picardy tale, "La Princesse que pisse par dessus les Meules," to which Ellis refers fleetingly, in his vol. v. 53, "Erotic Symbolism" (1906). The element of trying for a mark, or competing with the other sex, or even with the same sex, always appears to be present in material collected on this subject, and it is a fact that men who are not sure they can make a loud noise in urinating prefer to 'aim' for the edge of the bowl rather than disgrace themselves with a mere trickle. A similar idea of some connection between penis size and the side-phenomena of urination is to be seen in the joke in *Joe Miller's Jests* (1739) No. 122, on the subject: *'A Gentleman happening to turn up against an House to make Water, did not see two young Ladies looking out of a Window close by him, 'till he heard them giggling, then looking towards them, he asked, what made them so merry? O! Lord, Sir, said one of them,* a very little Thing *will make us laugh.'*

Mention has been made earlier of the unspoken insult to the women in the house implied by the habit of men who leave the toilet seat up after urination, and to the fact that women are aware that this is a boast of the 'superiority' of male urination in the standing position, and resent it. One joke attempts to reverse the usual insult: *A man and wife have a urination contest. They draw a line on the ground, and the husband prepares confidently to win. "Uh uh, dear," says the wife, shaking her head; "no hands!"* (N.Y. 1952.) Ellis notes in his final volume, p. 131, in discussing the standing position in urination for women: 'Last year [1927?] I saw when at Portsmouth a novel "urinette" for ladies, a quite new, up-to-date smart arrangement, without a seat; one had to stride across a boat-shaped earthenware grating. Ladies went in, and came out again with horrified faces. They simply *couldn't* they said!' These urinals for women were introduced on a wide scale, without objection, in war plants and service-women's quarters during World War II in America, and it is curious to note that they were exactly prefigured, as an erotic fantasy, in the penultimate issue, No. 17, of the erotic magazine *The Pearl* (London, Nov. 1880), in the final colloquy of a flirtatious "Drawing-Room Passe Temps": *Gent: "Is it not extraordinary that there are no public urinals for ladies?" Lady: "You men would always be standing about the doors." Gent: "But you ought to have them built like ours, you know, with the trough projecting a little further." Lady: "Butter-boat fashion, how very nice."* A story in *Voyages aux Côtes de Guinée* (1719) p. 414, reprinted in *Kryptádia,* III. 256, adapts Aesop's "Crane and Fox" (Type 60) to the War Between the Sexes. *A husband replaces the bedroom chamberpot with a narrow bottle into which his wife cannot piss. She comes to bed the next night with a funnel.*

II. THE VOICE AS PHALLUS

In an important article by Henry Alden Bunker, "The Voice as (Female) Phallus," in *Psychoanalytic Quarterly* (1934) III. 391–420, a large amount of clinical and historical material is brought together bearing on the unconscious — and sometimes not so unconscious — identification of the voice as the virile prerogative of the dominant sex. Bunker is particularly concerned with those situations in which this prerogative is 'usurped' by the female by means of virtuoso abilities in song, in powerful resonance of the speaking voice, or, basically in any kind of forthright self-expression, with the result that the woman becomes attractively dominant to some men, and repellent (the man-eating, song-singing Siren, Harpy or Rhine-maiden) to others. The guilts associated with direct and uncensored expression of thought, particularly when the thought is sexual or aggressive in content, act equally on men and on women — the Milquetoast or Dagwood has, traditionally, a weakly faint or absurdly screeching voice — but, of course, the position of men as the dominant sex in modern cultures allows and assists them to break away from the taboo more easily. Where men are in dominated situations, as in armies or on college faculties, very hedged and repressed ways of speech become habitual, as remarked upon sardonically in the punch-line or closing paragraph of Thorstein Veblen's satirical masterpiece, *The Theory of the Leisure Class* (1899).

For a woman to speak forthrightly on any subject, but particularly on any sexual subject, is presumed immediately to mark her as 'liberated,' in the sense in which Spanish-speaking peoples use the word *liberal,* of a woman, to mean simply immoral. Men would like to release, during moments of sexual passion, the demanded verbal repression put upon women; and, as is well known, they enjoy teaching taboo sex terms to women who do not know them, particularly adult women of guarded youth or foreign birth. English erotic literature — as, for instance, many of the stories in the erotic magazine, *The Pearl* (London, 1879–80) — puts into the mouths of women at orgasm whole strings of repeated erotic terms, often almost irrelevant to the action; and there is no question that these are assumed to be an exciting expression of female abandon to both the writers and readers of erotic literature, similar to men's own verbalizing of erotic tension.

The male trick, as seen in jokes, of nudging some non-sexual remark of a woman's into presumable sexual allusion, by way of erotic approach, is almost exactly matched by a similar trick ascribed to women. Except for very tough women, of powerful urges in the direction of virility, no such conversational approaches, sexual brags, or use of hostile sexual terms such as 'screw,' are really made by women in this culture, and the jokes therefore represent a fantasy on the part of the male originators and tellers of the jokes. Also, and very significantly, where most of the examples of this type of humor put into the mouths of men in the opening sections of the chapter on Men, preceding, are intended to be roughly seductive, the principal note in the examples now following, and purportedly made by women, is consistently one of hatred and rejection. All, almost without exception, are sarcastic in the extreme.

An army major answers the phone. A colored woman's voice says, "Do you all have a George Washington Jackson there?" "No." "You got a Augustus Amos Brown?" "No." "Say, you all colored?" "No," *says the major,* "I'm white but I have colored privates." "Yoo hoo! ain't you fancy!" (Calif. 1941.) This is really just a 'catch,' on the style of *phoning a tobacco-store and asking* "Have you got Prince Albert in the can?" "Yes." "Well, let him out!" which was considered the *ne plus ultra* of telephone humor in eastern Pennsylvania in the 1920's, when I was a kid. The obscenities shouted or mumbled (which is more *eerie*) at women who answer anonymous telephone calls in the night have become an increasingly common annoyance, as neurotic men lose the courage to address themselves to women in the flesh. The joke above is, of course, the female-dominant reverse of this. There are also other aggressive telephone tricks, like the schoolgirls' anonymous phone-calls to the popular boys ("I betcha can't guess who this is? — Well who would you *like* it to be?" etc.) and the phoning up of people whose names, as reversed in the directory, are made suggestive, to tell them so (*e.g.* Peter Pappas, an Oedipal favorite among children), or whose phone-numbers, if respelled by the dial-letters instead of the numbers, form taboo terms. The resistance to these annoyances, by means of unlisted numbers, resists not only this but also that urge to power (projected upon all those other people who do *not* have unlisted phone numbers) in having all those *names* at one's command, as with the fanatically 'exact' Gestapo and other secret-police files on everybody, telephone tapping, and other paranoid political devices.

The importation of the penis, or hints at the penis, into conversation by the woman, is not common even in jokes, Scatological remarks and buttock humor are more usual, probably as being less of an open sexual approach. *Professor:* "This twig is composed of bark, hardwood, and pith. You know what pith is, don't you?" *The class looks blank.* "You, Miss Brown, do you know what pith is?" "Yeth thir." (1:123.) Nightclub humor: *Master-of-Ceremonies:* "I'd like to pinch your cheeks." *Woman Singer:* "How would you like the large economy size?"

(Minn. 1946.) The first example here is presumably an 'error,' the second a reply to the male approach. Other jokes do not bother to hide the hostility of the woman's replies. *A soldier asks the cigarette girl in a nightclub, "Say, where's the piss-bucket?" "Just go through that door on the left," she says, "and down a hall till you see a sign marked 'Gentlemen.' But pay no attention to that. Go right in."* (D.C. 1943.) — *A vegetarian in a restaurant indignantly refuses the waitress's suggestion of beef tongue, on the grounds that it comes out of an animal's mouth. "Yes, sir," she says, "how about an egg?"* (D.C. 1943.)

Recent anti-political jokes have particularly emphasized anal-sadistic remarks purportedly by women. *An ex-president's wife decides to become a model for dowager styles. "But what are you going to do about that ass of yours?" says a friend. "Oh, he'll stay on the farm."* (N.Y. 1953.) In another joke on the same politician, not strictly relevant here, *The politician's daughter complains to her mother that her father has disgraced the family by saying "manure" instead of "fertilizer" in presenting medals for roses at the Ladies' Horticultural Club. "It's all right, dear," says her mother, "it's taken me years to get him to say manure."* (D.C. 1952. Randolph, *Hot Springs &c.*, Note 24.)

In an example using a far older principle of reversal, *A husband asks the doctor, to whom his wife is going for a sore throat, to try to get her to wear pants, which she refuses to do. The doctor examines her throat carefully and announces, "Madam, your trouble is caused by not wearing bloomers." "Can you really tell that by looking down my throat?" she asks skeptically. "Absolutely." "Then do me a favor, Doctor; look up my ass and tell me if my hat is on straight."* (N.Y. 1939.) The identity here between sexual freedom — the refusal to wear underwear — and verbal freedom is very clearly made. The prototype joke, in *Tom Brown's Jester* (1755, ed. 1860) p. 11, has *A doctor who refuses to prescribe for a shoemaker when the shoemaker's wife brings him a sample of her husband's urine. The doctor empties the sample bottle and urinates in it himself, saying "Take this water of mine to him and if he can fit me with a pair of boots, by looking at it, then I will prescribe for him by looking at his water."* (Motif K1955.2.)

For every joke in which the woman's importation of the sexual might conceivably be considered a flirtation, far more numerous and more striking examples of sadistic or frustrational 'punch' have been collected. As flirtations (?): *A butcher, emphasizing how fresh the veal is, says, "Lady, that calf was chasing the cow yesterday." "Maybe so, but not for milk.*" (N.Y. 1948.) — *Taxidermist, pointing to the two pet monkeys he is to stuff: "Do you want them mounted?" Lady customer: "No, just shaking hands."* (An old favorite.) — *Two girls in a café order Budweiser. Waiter: "Two Buds!" Girl: "Lucky we didn't order Country Club."* (Minn. 1946. Also collected in the decayed form of: *A girl wanted to join the yacht club, but she didn't have a yacht. So she joined the country club.* — N.Y. 1952) In comparison with these mild pertnesses, all of them essentially leaving the sexual initiative still with the man, one has, for instance the chilling anal-sadistic damp of a long obscœnum circulated in various printed and mimeographed forms since 1944, in which *A girl invited up to a bachelor's apartment is asked whether she will have port or sherry. "Sherry by all means," she says. "When I drink sherry, a thousand violins throb in my ears, my whole body glows, I am lifted on wings of ecstasy (etc. etc.) On the other hand, port makes me fart."* A cleanup, probably by a woman, on "The Fountains of Rome" (mimeo, *c.* 1965, Brown Univ.)

I. PARRYING PROPOSITIONS

The punning importation of a sexual proposition into something that the man has said is used far more often for purposes of rejecting the fictitious proposition angrily than of accepting it. A few acceptances have, however, been collected. *A woman is used to her husband coming home from work at noon to make love to her. One day he is delayed, and finally, at one o'clock, she hitches up the horse & wagon and gallops down Main Street looking for him. The tail-board of the wagon drops off, and a young man standing nearby shouts after her, "Hey, lady, don't you want your tail-board?" "Hop on here, you little mindreader!" she shouts back.* (2:193.) In a variant, reversing the sexes, *A short man in a subway crush is jammed between the breasts of two tall women talking to each other. He wriggles his eyebrows flirtatiously at one of them. "Listen, fresh guy," she rasps, "how would you like a bust in the mouth?" "Okay, you little mindreader!"* (N.Y. 1940.) The age of the original here is evidenced by the horse & wagon prop. The only other clear acceptance of the pretended proposition also involves the extra fillip of adultery: *A man with a sore throat gets to the doctor's house at lunchtime. The doctor's pretty young wife answers the door. "Is the doctor in?" the man whispers hoarsely. "No, come on in," she whispers back.* (1:19.)

For one reason or another, as will be seen, most of these propositions end in nothing. They have apparently been set up only to lead
into a 'no.' It is very difficult to say whether the jokes represent an
authentic expression of the castratory urge some women express by
disappointing the man — by being late, or delayed, by refusing him
intercourse, or, if allowing this, by *refusing orgasm* (the secret of
female frigidity) — or whether the jokes are intended to make this
reality endurable by treating it as a joke. *Scots golf coach, to Lady
Astor: "Now wull ye listen to me? Ye must put your feet further
aparrt!" "Jock, Jock, you men are all alike." (2:164.) — Stenographer,
to boss: "I dreamt about you last night." Boss: "You did?" "No, at the
last minute I lost my nerve." (N.Y. 1952. Also collected with the sexes
reversed, the man's final line being, "No, you wouldn't let me.")*

In another complex build-up of the dream of sexual relations with
the young woman employee, *A man who uses his wife's worn-out
panties for polishing his car [!] can't find any on Sunday when rum-
maging through the ragbag. Next day he asks his stenographer, "What
do you do with your panties when you wear them out?" She blushes.
"Well if I can find them afterwards, I put them in my purse." (N.Y.
1952.)* There is a nightclub variant of this, supposed to be acted out,
in which a man with obviously fake glasses asks a girl to polish the
lenses for him with her stocking-tops. (N.Y. 1963.) Girls will not un-
commonly make the friendly offer of a corner of a skirt or slip (petticoat) for this purpose — if sitting — and it is unhappily clear that the
man with eyeglasses is currently being plugged as attractive to women,
not in spite of the traditional sub-virility presumed to be connected
with weak eyes and horn-rimmed-spectacled intellectuality (the Harold
Lloyd nitwit stereotype, and standard anti-intellectual leariness), but
because of it. On the 'Great Lie' principle propounded by Hitler, and
by Machiavelli before him, heavy-rimmed glasses are currently being
peddled to men, in the usual crude doublethink of modern 'Schlock-
meister' advertising, not as sub-virile but as *super*-virile, because they
are so heavy! (One is waiting for crutches to be peddled with the same
plug.) The camp degeneracy of the advertising series of men — and
women — with eye-patches, since the 1950's, plumping for the presumed super-virility of being a castrato, is too consciously perverse to
be of interest from any folkloristic standpoint. In the White Horse
whiskey ad for *'Comes the "look-alike" generation,'* printed in *Playboy*
(Nov. 1967) p. 68, and in the *New York Times* of parallel date, al-

ready discussed in the introduction to Chapter 2.v, above, the cross-legged male, with whom the pants-wearing spread-legged female is fighting it out (including stepping on his toe!), is naturally outfitted with large dark glasses. Only people who are *hiding,* and are afraid of being seen, or who are *peeping* and are afraid of being caught, wear dark glasses except in the bright sunlight.

It is notable that the propositions and the betrayals of elaborate error maintain a surface air of male dominance and female coyness. This is not even halfway to the "voice as female phallus." Complete neurotic virility for the woman involves, in its ultimate form, a complete taking of the social and sexual initiative, *plus* the even further dominance and open hatefulness of then bringing the whole seductional situation to nothing. This seems self-contradictory, but is the only direction in which the material will be found to point. The operative element is the *desire to disappoint* on the part of the female anti-male sadist (and proto-Lesbian), matching the *desire to be disappointed* on the part of the male masochist (and proto-homosexual). The puerile screamers of the Philip Wylie anti-sex type, in their ever-popular calls-to-arms concerning 'momism' and 'matriarchy,' have always shown a complete unawareness of the profound difference between, on the one hand, the anti-sexual 'male protest' of women under male dominance, imitating men's clothing and speech for the purpose of rejecting femininity and of refusing sex to the envied and hated men; and, on the other hand, the actual maternal and ultra-female yea-saying to sex (incestuous or not) of the real matriarch under real matriarchy.

The examples given will begin with approaches to dominance, on the part of the woman, with the accent noticeably strong on the intended ultimate frustration or hate-line. *A girl pesters her escort all evening saying, "I want to get weighed." After weighing her on several scales, in drugstores, in the subway, and so forth, he takes her home disgustedly. At her door he finally asks, "Say, why did you want to get weighed so much?" "Oh," she says, "I guess I thought I was in wuve."* (Minn., 1935.) This is one of the few jokes collected which — misspelled or no — even *mentions* the subject of love. Is it really a joke about love? In a variant: *Her mother asks whether she had a good time. "Wousy."* (N.Y. 1953.) It is interesting that the instrument of frustration and insult here, as in the example on 'pith' above, is the humiliating fake-feminine vocal *impediment* of the lisp, with which

may be compared, in fact rather than in jest, the phoney Southern accent as a current feminine wile. The lengths to which this sort of
pretended impediment has historically been taken by women under
powerful patriarchies is simply incredible, for instance the pretended
limps, twists, and hands carried like sea-lion flippers among young
Victorian ladies of the 1860's, as recorded in J. Redding Ware's *Passing
English* (1909) at 'Alexandra Limp,' 'Grecian Bend,' and 'Roman Fall.'

*A minister at a house-party is shocked by the wild doings, and goes
to his room to pray. He is awakened some hours later by a light tapping at the door, and opens it to find a naked young woman standing
there. "Did you want me?" he asks stuffily. "Hell, no! I drew you."*
(2:385.) The pretense is one of acceptance, but the toughness of the
wording obviously kills any chance of that. *"Would you scream if I
raped you?" "Naw, I'm hoarse from the last twelve guys."* (N.Y. 1942.)
A come-on or a squelch? *A girl leans her bicycle against the wall of
a country post-office as she goes in for her mail. The bicycle falls over.
"Looks like your bike's tired," one of the idlers remarks. "You'd be
tired too if you'd been in between my legs as long as that bike has."*
(2:86. Collected, N.Y. 1952, with the topper, given to the man: *"Not
if I had that many nuts."*) Also in French, of a girl on horseback.

The recollection here, to the man's attention, of the girl's previous
sexual experience with other men, is the essence of the tough pose.
She is, as it were, rubbing his nose in it. On the other hand, she is also
clearly implying that she is so goddam tough and experienced that
there is no chance at all of any further sexual relations with her. One
wonders how she ever got so experienced. The real point is, her toughness and verbal freedom make her not a woman but an imitation man.
*A girl who has been speeding, sasses the traffic policeman when he
gives her a ticket. "Say," he marvels, "you're a fresh egg." "Well, I
ought to be — I was just laid an hour ago."* (2:207.) Is this an invitation to the policeman? Hardly. Another wisecrack takes care of that
possibility: *Two girls are out driving on the highway when it begins
to rain. "Go on," says the passenger, "speed it up." "Uh-uh, we can't
be fixing any tickets with the grass this wet."* (N.Y. 1946.) Based on a
much older tag-line: *"I'm not that kind of a girl, and besides the grass
is wet,"* or *" — and besides, a big red apple isn't enough."* (Scranton,
Pa. 1930's.)

Obviously this is not the way a girl would really talk who is looking to be seduced by anyone except the village goon. In a quotation

given later more at length, from Theodor Reik's *The Need to be Loved* (1963) p. 146, headed "Four-Letter Words," the crucial observation is made that the rough and obscene language affected by women who talk like this is, in most cases, not a sign of 'a low level of upbringing and education,' but an 'unconscious travesty or parody of men and their manners, and reveals a concealed and often repressed hostility to the male.' Often, as here, it is not even repressed.

Another fairly shallow rationalization is that "men like it." I can still remember with some astonishment being asked recently by a young married woman with two children — an heiress with an obviously sub-virile husband, hand-picked, whom she led around by the nose, and who connived at her adulteries with popular novelists and other characters in the 'hip' crowd — "*Say,*" (this in a voice like an ashcan being dragged over a cement floor), "*does it really excite men to hear a woman say words like 'Fuck' and 'Shit'?*" The question seems to occur to many women: Molly Bloom, in the final soliloquy in Joyce's *Ulysses,* is positive that this is exciting indeed. I am not so sure. Except for obvious male masochists, a quiet tone of voice should help.

A woman asks a man for his seat on a crowded bus, saying that she is pregnant. He gives her his seat grudgingly, but remarks that she does not look very "filled out." "Oh," she explains, "It only happened half an hour ago." (D.C. 1946.) Mocking motherhood. Similarly, from the usually pudibund *Reader's Digest* (Jan. 1943) p. 82, which allowed itself a bit of unusual latitude with the blackout humor of World War II: *During an air raid, a warden calls into the cellar of a blacked-out public shelter in London, "Any expectant mothers there?" After a brief pause, a feminine voice replies, "Hard to say. We've only been down here a few minutes."*

2. SEXUAL REJECTION

The real arena for anti-sexual speeches and rejections, put into the woman's mouth, is entered best when the man has actually made an overture. This avoids the fictitious air about angrily rejecting an overture that has not really been made at all, as in two examples taken from *Memorabilia* (1910): *A woman assaults a man, saying he insulted her by telling her she looked like a streetcar, and "No man can get on and off me for five cents."* Even more insane: *A young woman at a Grand Army of the Republic ball wears, as an apron, a small flag. An old veteran, passing by, takes hold of one corner of her apron and says emotionally, "My dear young woman, I fought many a hard battle under this flag in three of our wars." "Not under this flag!" she says, snatching it out of his hand.* These have really been reached for, and the same might be thought of the following, except for a variant that shows it actually to have been an intended overture: *A young man walking with a girl in the cool of the evening remarks, pointing to the grass, "Some dew." The girl: "But I don't. Be on your way."* (2:69.) The variant, given by McAtee (1912, env. 7) brings this into better focus: *A travelling salesman bows politely to two young women on a hotel porch, and says, "Ladies, do you fuck?" They are horrified and begin to berate him. "Excuse me, ladies," he says; "some do, and some do not."* The joke above, from *Anecdota II* (1934) is clearly a relic.

In "The Male Approach," above, a joke has been quoted — known much earlier in French — of: *A young man who is excited by watching a bull servicing a cow. He says to the farmer's daughter, who is also watching, "Believe me, I'd like to be doing what that bull is doing!" "Why don't you?" she says; "it's your cow."* (1:416.) These are the real conversational javelins into the gut, and they require the man to make the first move, and thus place himself in the disadvantageous position of the aggressor. It should be pointed out again, however, that by & large all these jokes have probably been invented by men, not by the women who are given the cutting rejections to deliver, and that they therefore represent an attempt to deal humorously with *the frightening possibility* of a sexual rejection that will seriously depress one's self-esteem. This is certainly true in the case of the men who tell them. Observe — in an example already cited — how it is possible to make a rejection even out of an acceptance if couched in sufficiently insulting terms: *He: "How's about it, honey?" She: (no answer). He: "I said how's about it?" She: (no answer). He: "Whatsamatter, ya deef?" She: "Whatsamatter, ya paralyzed?"* (N.Y. 1941.) — *A man rushes in on his fiancée with his penis out and tries to rape her. She begins berating him angrily. "Two words," he pleads, " let me say two words!" Finally, after exhausting her vocabulary of insults, she says, "Well, what's your two words, you dirty bum?" "Let go."* (1:390. Text form, N.Y. 1939.)

It is extremely important to grasp the element of *neurotic deceit* in jokes. Once one becomes aware of the surface pretenses in jokes, it is bewildering to notice how few are really what they seem. This does not refer to the necessary sudden reversal of expectation, if a laugh is to be raised, but to the difference between the real and pretended nature of the situation itself. An 'acceptance' that is really total control by the woman: *A man finds a girl asleep and begins having intercourse with her. She wakes up and begins to remonstrate. "Shall I take it out?" he asks. "Well, take it out and then put it in again a few times so I can make up my mind."* (N.Y. 1939. In Afanasyev's *Russian Secret Tales,* c. 1872, No. 36, "The Modest Lady," is very similar.) A 'proposition' that is really an insult, and an excuse for another insult topping it: *He: "How about a quick fuck?" She: "Why, how dare you speak to me like that!" He: "Don't get excited. I don't mean right now. I mean some nasty, rainy day when there's nobody else in town."* (N.Y. 1942.) A 'rejection' that is really an acceptance (of anyone but the man who asks): *A marriage-broker is told by a businesslike client that he will not marry the girl without samples of her sexual abilities. "I'm just as good a businessman as he is," the girl tells the broker. "Samples I wouldn't give him. References I'll give him!"* (1:106.)

In the later chapter on Homosexuality, in Series Two, the theme of the 'Ganymede revenge' will be discussed, with its fears of pederastic rape, and its matching fantasy of somehow harming the pedicating rapist by means of the anus. This is, however, too feminine for the virile forthrightness of the kind of sexual rejection concerned here. The final revenge must be virile too, and is achieved in pederastic rape of the man by the woman. As this is anatomically absurd, absurd situations have to be invented to encompass it, as the fantasy, reported by Lesbians, of pedicating a man by means of an elongated clitoris. (Also reported by male masochists.) That this elongated clitoris is the same over-long penis that is to be used to kill the woman in intercourse is made very plain in a castration joke often collected: *A famous playboy dies, and the undertaker phones his wife to tell her that the corpse has an erection and to ask what he should do about it. "Cut it off and shove it up his ass," she says. "That's the only place in town it hasn't been!"* (Calif. 1936. An even cruder version is given under "The Eaten Heart," 8.VIII.10, below.) Not quite so direct, in its use of various male surrogates, and in omitting the element of castration: *A woman with a rose pinned to her garter is sitting opposite two travelling salesmen on a train. "Madam," says one, "we would like to settle a bet. Is that an artificial rose or a natural rose?" "It's a natural rose," she says, "and it's watered by the spring above." Encouraged, the salesman continues:*

*"May I plant my cucumber in your spring?" "No, but you can plant
it in your friend's ass. I understand they do well in shit!"* (Idaho, 1919.
Strictly a 'sell,' and also known in France.) Both these jokes will be
considered again at the end of the chapter on Marriage, 8.VIII.10.

The theme of pederastic rape by the woman is certainly not present
at any manifest level in the following anecdote, yet its existence may
be suspected under the simple excuse of 'the flowers,' a French phrase
for menstruation. This is quoted exactly from *The Pearl*, No. 12 (June
1880) *ad fin.*, where it is given as an "Anecdote of Kate Santley": *'One
night, at the Alhambra, amongst a shower of bouquets from the boxes,
a carrot was thrown from the gallery. She coolly gathered an armful
of trophies, and after bowing again and again to the boxes, looked up
with a smile at the gods, as she said, "Excuse me taking your carrot,
now I have the flowers," and tripped off the stage amidst a storm of
applause.'*

III. OPHELIA'S CRIME

One of the things that lends credibility to the brag generally made by
homosexuals, that Shakespeare was one of them — usually on the basis
of his *Sonnets* — is the increasingly anti-woman tone of all his plays
from *Romeo and Juliet* on. Taken chronologically, *Romeo and Juliet*
is a quite early play (first published in 1597), and only the strange
scene of Capulet's cursing his daughter Juliet as a 'green-sickness car-
rion' and so forth, III.v.150–200, strikes the tone to become so prominent in later plays, as when Hamlet berates Ophelia and his mother,
and in the grotesque fulminations of Othello and Lear against women
as creatures of horse-like sexual appetite and similar. What makes this
particularly difficult to assess is the simultaneous identification that
Shakespeare, as author, clearly makes with those women in his plays —
unparalleled in dramatic literature *as women* — who speak with a
beauty and eloquence that puts to shame the male characters in the
plays in which they appear: for instance, Juliet, Portia, Cleopatra, and
Marina in *Pericles*, Act IV, who actually talks the customers out of a
whore-house, and is able, as the Bawd complains (IV.vi.4) 'to freeze
the god Priapus, and undo a whole generation.'

Enough has been said in the preceding section, and, if not, enough
will certainly be found in Dr. Bunker's article noted, "The Voice as
(Female) Phallus," to make it easy to identify these eloquent women

as quasi-men, with whom Shakespeare's identification then becomes somewhat easier to understand. That he accepts, and must accept, with their characters, the love of the men whom they love, is a fact that cannot be evaded, and Wyndham Lewis has made this femininity in Shakespeare the key to his discussion of Antony as Shakespeare's great love, in *The Lion and the Fox,* in the 1920's. The overt homosexual tone of so much in Shakespeare's plays (as for instance *Julius Caesar,* which almost omits all women characters, and *The Merchant of Venice,* with its very ambiguous closeness of the Damon & Pythias friends) is not, essentially, of interest here, nor would there be any point in discussing the self-evident homosexual submission to the noble patron in the *Sonnets,* or why the young Wriothsley ('Mr. W. H.') gave Shakespeare the then — and now — enormous sum of £1000. There is none of this in *Hamlet,* which is the crucial play, except in the strange, increasing wordage of animosity against women, that is to say women as the personification of sex, and the bringers of men into conflict. (Compare *Troilus & Cressida.*)

Ophelia's crime, for which she presumably deserves the humiliations heaped upon her by Shakespeare, will not be found anywhere in the play of *Hamlet* that we now have. About all she can be accused of is engaging Hamlet in conversation when she knows her father and the king are eavesdropping. This scene, however (III.i, opening with the words, "To be, or not to be,") has been gravely modified by Shakespeare from the Danish legend of Hamlet, even as recorded in his unquestionable source, *The Hystorie of Hamblet,* where we learn that the real intention is to test whether or not Hamlet is actually insane by having the woman (Ophelia) attempt to seduce him, on the theory, which we have already encountered, that the true fool or lunatic does not know how to perform sexual intercourse. No hint of this is given by Shakespeare, except in Polonius' obscure line, II.ii.162 (in which J. Quincy Adams was first to point out the *double entendre*), 'At such a time I'll loose my daughter to him,' which Hamlet is presumed to have overheard. (In the Danish legend his horse warns him of the plot.) But even after expurgating this part of the action, Shakespeare is as angry at Ophelia as if she had actually tried, and accuses her familiarly, in the character of Hamlet, of every immorality of which he omits to accuse his mother.

The dominant woman was, in fact, the bane of Shakespeare's own early life. His mother was the well-born and educated one in the family, his father being a butcher (*causa modestiæ*, glover). Shakespeare also married, at an early age, a much older woman, who was pregnant by him at the time, and who is suspected of having seduced him. (His willing her his 'second-best bed' is almost too well known to require mention.) His first published work, *Venus and Adonis,* in 1593, retells the legend of the matriarchal goddess who attempts to seduce a young boy, and then, in the guise of the *vagina dentata* pig with upcurled tusks, castrates him when he spurns her. The modern analytic critic, Ernest Jones, in his often rewritten *Hamlet and Oedipus* (1910–49), a work which does not in any edition acknowledge its great debt to Otto Rank's chapter on Shakespeare in his *Inzest-Motiv* (1912), explains that the excess of vilification against Ophelia is 'so wholly out of proportion to her own offence [because] in reviling her Hamlet is really expressing his bitter resentment against his mother.' (ed. 1949, p. 84.) What seems to be overlooked here is the *basis* of his resentment against his mother, which is nothing other than the projection upon her, as the dominant and seductive older female, of the sexual desire he himself feels. In a critique of Freud's interpretation of *Hamlet* ("The Matricidal Impulse," in *Journal of Criminal Psychopathology,* 1941, II. 462–4), Dr. Fredric Wertham points out the needlessness of invariably hypothesizing an 'inverted' Oedipus complex which drives the boy to reject his mother out of fear of his father's strength, and indicates the reservoir of hostility that can exist against the actually dominant mother in matriarchy, or in the mother-dominated family.

Dominance is the really nameless sin for women — unforgivable and apparently even unmentionable. Taken historically, and less narrowly than in the anatomically sexual sense, it is this horror of dominance in women that has created the ancient anti-matriarchal absurdities of an Adam who gives birth to Eve, instead of the reverse; of a Holy Family from which the mother was removed — to be put only halfway back at the Council of Ephesus, as the virgin huntress Diana (the *vagina dentata* Venus), while the worshippers of the Mother-Goddess rioted in the streets — and of even so recent an absurdity as a book, dedicated by its author, M. F. Ashley Montagu, with a motto in which he explains how he learned the 'trick' of affirming the *Natural Superiority of Women,* but into which he manages nevertheless to slip a note, p. 60, affirming that these superior creatures have, somehow, never, anywhere, succeeded in achieving matriarchal dominance over men.

It is possible to cut into this subject anywhere, by means of jokes (or any other type of folklore display), and to bring to bear on it the bland and perfect conversance with many of its most troubled depths that folk-wit exudes, as for instance the intuitive solution to the Shakespearean problem above noted usually ascribed to the late John Barrymore. *Critic: Is it your opinion that Shakespeare intended us to understand that Hamlet screwed Ophelia?" Tragedian: "I don't know what Shakespeare intended, but I always do."* (1:317.)

One of the absolute shibboleths of the late 19th century was that decent women do not smoke cigarettes. An astonishing amount of material can easily be collected on this subject, showing the tug of war between the presumed sinfulness of smoking (with burlesque queens' portraits chromolithographed on the cigarette cards) and the irrepressible urge on the part of women to partake of this hard-held male prerogative, with its every possible symbolic satisfaction of shape, hot red tip, etc., and its whole sub-sexual literature of pæans to 'My Lady Nicotine' by Arthur Machen and similar soft-baked exotics. By 1909 the battle must have been over, when it could be made into an opera-length joke in Wolf-Ferrari's *The Secret of Suzanne* (she *smoked!* and fanned the evidence up the chimney). An interesting photograph, perhaps some thirty years earlier, by the male-protest photographer Alice Austen, also kids the whole thing in a posed scene showing herself and the minister's daughter with their hair down, in petticoats and masks, smoking fake cigarettes. (Reproduced in *The Revolt of American Women,* by Oliver Jensen [and Constance Foulk], 1952, p. 24, facing an even more interesting photograph of the never-married Miss Austen and women friends in men's clothing, with a fake moustache and umbrella penis somehow overlooked by the authors, though one rhyming word of the sub-title and a page of text are devoted to Freud, p. 157, followed by two pages on women and the cigarette.)

The open secret about tobacco is that it represents the sexual prerogative of the adult male, and must not be usurped by women and children. Punitive portraits of little boys about to vomit behind the barn for the sin of smoking papa's pipe are still a routine 'humorous' subject for the covers of national magazines, and not too much knowledge of barns or boys is needed to convert the jolly symbol into the unamusing reality of the threatened punishment for masturbation or other sexual sin, with which smoking is almost openly identified. *Spinster, to flapper smoking a cigarette: "Why I'd rather be raped by a dozen men than smoke a cigarette." Flapper: "Who the hell wouldn't?"* (1920's, first recorded in a dysphemistic homosexual variant in *Anecdota* 2:60, in 1934.) In an even more exact identification, a decade before Suzanne's secret was unveiled: *Pat Ryan gives up smoking for Lent, so Mike O'Brien, at Mrs. O'Brien's suggestion, gives up intercourse till Easter. On the seventh night she wakes him gently just as he is dreaming that the Cardinal is ordaining him a Bishop. "What is it?" he asks. "Nothin', Mike, nothin'. Only I just saw Pat Ryan down behind the house schmokin'."* (*Memorabilia*, 1910, giving Pat & Mike's last names for the first time.)

The dominant vamps, and the lady and/or tigers of male fantasy have been chosen from among the women of the theatre since at least the Restoration in the late 17th century, with the beginnings of female theatrical transvestism, reaching its real height in the late 19th century of Swinburne and his lady of pain, Adah Isaacs Menken, and even more famous male-masochist–lady-sadist teams playing *Carmen*. A strong element here is probably the 'playing at pretend' so often involved in practising sado-masochist activities, almost as much as the Lesbianism or male-identification practically standard in successful women of the theatre. Critics as penetrating usually as George Jean Nathan acclaimed the apparent lusty-busty femaleness of Mae West in the early 1930's as a refreshing change from the bony epicenes of all sexes stumbling like bored jello through imported British homosexual dramas on Broadway. In folk-wit, however, Miss West was acclaimed instead as a hard, mean, dominant lady slugger, always ready with some devastating innuendo that will cut a man down to a nubbin. That this was the real character she intended to portray, and by no means that of the beef-trust beauty in the *fin de siècle* boa hat, is recorded very clearly in her movies, such as the one in which she breaks into society with a fortune inherited from a husband who has not yet consummated their marriage (quite impossible at law, as Miss West must certainly have known), lassoes her man and drags him along the ground to her boot-clad feet, with other activities more usefully to be consulted in Fuchs & Kind's *Weiberherrschaft* (4 vols. 1913–30), and possibly in my article "Avatars of the Bitch," in *Love & Death* (1949) p. 57–80.

Period pieces of the 1930's on the dominant actress theme: *An actress is out walking and steps over a manhole. One of the workmen sees she has no pants on and gooses her. "How dare you?" she purrs.*

"Lady, if your heart is as soft as your cunt, you'll forgive me." "Brother,
if your prick is as hard as your finger, come up and see me sometime."
(2:396.) Others of the type are mere puns: *The elevator boy calls out,*
"Ballroom!" "Am I crowding you, buddy?" (D.C. 1945.) — *Judge:*
"Whatever you say will be held against you." "Nuts, Judge — nuts!"
(D.C. 1943.)

With the exception of Miss West, whose private life is unimpeach-
ably normal, the dominant actress jokes are usually fathered on inter-
nationally known Lesbians. This is even more true now than in the
1930's, as Lesbianism in America again approaches a climax similar
to that of the bottom Depression year of 1932–33. In one of the current
examples: *A young man is madly in love with an actress, and takes the*
occasion of a crowded party to beg her for a night of love. "Why cer-
tainly, dahling," she says. "Go right upstairs to my bedroom, while I
get rid of these stupid people. If I'm not there in fifteen minutes —
start without me." (N.Y. 1951.) In an even crueller cut-down, *The same*
actress is being introduced to a young novelist who has expurgatorily
misspelled the erotic monosyllables in his novel. She cannot place his
name. Finally she remembers. "Oh yes, dahling — you're the boy that
can't spell fuck!" (N.Y. 1951. More detailed version in *The Limerick,*
Note 1708. The novelist in question seems to have learned since.) A
1930's joke touches the mainspring of this animosity towards men:
"Miss Lallygag," says a young man passionately, "I love you. I want
you for my wife." "All right," she says, "bring her around. Maybe I
can use her."

The sin — if we are discussing sin — is not all on one side. Lesbian
actresses with cut-throat tongues are an easy peg on which to hang the
accusation of female dominance. Consider, however, the usual stereotypes of male dominance: 'he for God, and she for God through him.'
The hardships the soldiers suffered in the Boer War, with nothing be-
tween them and the cold, hard ground but one thin native-girl. (N.Y.
1940.) This being the ideal, it is obvious that the slightest urge toward
sexual equality, in or out of bed, will be interpreted in the woman as
an urge toward dominance and an affront to a certain type of man,
usually one enmeshed in feelings of his own inferiority. Even the positions used in intercourse must be calculated to allow of the greatest
possible dominance for the man and to ensure the greatest possible subservience ('one thin native-girl') for the woman. I know of a case
where a gentleman who happened to have been a psychiatrist actually

broke off an affair with a woman on the excuse that she had, on a single occasion, asked to lie on top, and that this demonstrated virile urges that made their relationship impossible. In the same way, although the Korán says, 'Woman is your field — go into her as you will,' the Arabs have a tradition that he is accursed 'who makes heaven earth, and earth heaven.' (Compare: *Hollywood, where you can lay on the sand and look at the stars, and vice versa.* — N.Y. 1952.)

As direct expressions of the ideal of total dominance of the woman are no longer politic, jokes coming into head-on collision with the problem tend to put the expression of the ideal into the mouths of uneducated backwoodsmen and other 'inferiors': *A porter in a newspaper office gets married, and the reporters chip in to buy him a new bedspring and mattress. A few days later he brings it back. "What's the matter with it?" asks the editor. "Nothin', boss, only it feeds too fast."* (1:444.) A whole section fulminating against the innerspring mattress as ruinous of proper sexual intercourse is included in Edward Charles [Hempstead]'s *The Sexual Impulse* (1935) p. 147ff., a sex-technique manual probably more eccentric than useful. In his *Indian Patchwork* (1934), Hempstead objects, almost equally vehemently, in a passage dated January 2, 1928, to a display of books on birth control on the bookstalls of a Bombay hotel lobby, saying that when he sees Marie Stopes' book he thinks 'of the big green mantis sitting up on her hind legs and eating husband after husband as soon as he has satisfied her biological needs.' As the preceding joke might be construed to have other meanings than that of female dominance, here ascribed to it, another example on the woman's *subagitation* in intercourse makes the point entirely clear: *A hillbilly strikes up an acquaintance with a strange girl in the woods. During intercourse she begins moving her buttocks rhythmically. "What are you doin'?" asks the hillbilly suspiciously. "Just throwin' it up to you." "Never you mind. Just let it lay there, an' I'll reach for it."* (*Memorabilia,* 1910.)

Possession in common of a single wife or a single husband is a necessary condition for the dominated sex under polygamy. The emotions of the chronically unsatisfied wives of the harem are considered extremely funny in the harem-dream cartoons of the fake virile 'men's magazines,' though an entirely different set of responses are expected when the man is made the harem-animal in an occasional masochist fantasy such as H. Rider Haggard's *She* (1887) or Pierre Benoît's *L'Atlantide* (1920), movie-version as *Siren of Atlantis,* in which the dominant queen has the men kept in cages till she is ready for intercourse with them, has their tongues torn out if they beat her at chess, etc. (Motif K1237; *The Limerick*, No. 1371.)

In an *echt*-American story, our identification with, and sympathy for the male harem-beast is taken for granted, however temporary his subservient status. *A Tennessee traveller is put up overnight by a mountaineer. There is only one bed, and to save space they must sleep alternately head to heels with the mountaineer's wife and her sister. "But no foolishness," the mountaineer warns, flourishing an ancient horse-pistol which he then puts under his pillow and falls asleep. The sister-in-law, who is lying next to the traveller, slides her hand up his leg and begins fondling his penis. He points warningly to the horse-pistol, but she whispers, " 'Taint loaded," and pulls him over onto her. Then the wife, who has been watching, says "Gimme one." He points to the horse-pistol again, but she says " 'Taint loaded," and climbs over on top of him. A few minutes later the sister-in-law slides her hand up the traveller's leg again. " 'Taint loaded," he says [pointing to his penis], and turns over to sleep.* (Memorabilia, 1910.) Printed in *Anecdota* 2:283, in a version in which it is a mother who sleeps with a gun under her pillow to protect the virtue of her two daughters. Making the point of the traveller's resistance to the women's domination even plainer, in a further variant, *Nine daughters force a travelling salesman into unwilling intercourse by threatening to wake their sleeping father, who is holding a shotgun. When the fifth daughter tries to force the tired traveller, with the whispered threat, "I'll tell Papa," he says, "O.K. tell your papa. I'd rather be shot than fucked to death."* (D.C. 1943.)

The tone here is certainly one of resistance to, or of satirizing female appetite and dominance, but one cannot always be certain whether any particular harem-slave fantasy is intended as anti-woman satire or as masochist submission by the male. In the case of H. Rider Haggard, the author's acceptance of the situation as desirable is perfectly clear, as also in Robert Graves' *Watch the North Wind Rise* (1949, published in England as *Seven Days in New Crete*), a 'utopia' in which the women whip the men for pleasure in special huts, while on one page (96) the author turns into a woman while 'squatting over the fire.' At other times one cannot be too sure, as in Mr. Jerome Robbins' disgusting choreographic fantasy of a decade ago, "The Cage," a ballet concerning a cobweb matriarchate, set up with ropes attached to the skirt of the curtain, where the lady bees kick the male drone back and forth across the stage and then sting him to death by wriggling their bottoms over his face. The only cheerful note in the whole thing (which seemed to puzzle Professor Kinsey, who sat in front of me and kept scratching his head) was the implication that male masochism, however anti-woman its presentation, may perhaps be the 'cure' for homosexuality, which had been the basic subject of the preceding ballet, "The Age of Anxiety."

Real matriarchal stories go unerringly to the essence of matriarchy — the relationship to the child — and pay little attention to the stud-male's passing moment of usefulness in intercourse. There is really only one story of this type, and it is always told of a Negro woman. There is a kernel of truth here, in that owing to the breaking up of Negro families by auction sale of the men during the centuries that chattel slavery lasted in America (both before and after the signing of the Declaration of Independence), the American Negro family became, and still remains, largely centered around the mother. This explains, in part, both the frequency of Lesbianism among Negro women, and the predominant position of the term 'Mother-fucker' in the Negro contests in insult known as 'the dozens.' (See John Dollard's "The Dozens: Dialectic of Insult," in *American Imago*, Nov. 1939, 1.3–25; and especially Roger Abrahams' *Deep Down in the Jungle*, 1964.) — *A colored maid asks for a vacation to go and see her children. Mistress: "I didn't know you were married." "Well I ain't, but I ain't been neglected."* (1:65.) Published several times as a cartoon caption in the form: *"But Mandy, I thought you were an old maid." "I am, but I ain't a fussy old maid."* In an unusual concentration on the hateful and sexual elements: *The social worker finds the widow in bed with another man. "And your husband's hardly been dead a week!" "Yessum. He's dead, not me."* (2:367.) From a medical digest magazine: *Nurse: "Married?" Negro Woman: "Yes Ma'am, I been married twice." "Any children?" "Six." "All by the same father?" "Oh no, Ma'am. I had two by my first husband, two by my second, and two by myself."* (Randolph, *Hot Springs &c.*, Note 241.) Obvious, in this last, is that what is imagined in the stories to be a slur on the sexual morality of the Negro, or even an imputation of uncontrollable 'animal' passions, is actually a simple statement of the matrilocal adhering of the child to the mother, which not only was the original form of the family in human pre-history but remains that of all other mammals.

IV. FEMALE APPETITE

It was the fashion, in the repressed mid-19th century, especially in England and America, to state in so many words that men have sexual passions and that women do not. The value of an imbecility like this to a powerful patriarchal culture is self-evident. The proud apophthegm to which it was usually reduced — 'The purity of woman is the safeguard of the family' — was understood to mean *a*) that men did not have to be 'pure,' and *b*) that women were too pure to require sexual satisfaction. Any woman who felt otherwise was, by that token, impure, and not worth satisfying sexually in the first place.

The clotted moonshine of the Kinsey Report on the 'Human Male' — no Negroes or Orientals: 'Human' means *white* — insofar as it concerns women, disguises behind its columns of statistical hokum (see, in particular, its absolute removal from the sphere of statistical science in W. Allen Wallis' "Statistics of the Kinsey Report," in *Journal of the American Statistical Association,* 1949, v. 44: p. 463–84), exactly the same male-chauvinist ideal as that of patriarchal Germany or England a century ago. When some poor horny chap gets caught in a cattle-car in Montana having intercourse with a sheep — especially if it is a male sheep — and is sent to jail, he is a victim of cultural prejudices, according to Prof. Kinsey and associates. If some woman finds herself unable to arrive at orgasm when her husband withdraws, satisfied, after fifteen seconds and as many strokes (none of which involve any clitoral pressure), that is because women have not 'evolved' biologically as far as men, says Prof. Kinsey, and should not really expect to have orgasm in the first place. The principal difference between the mid-19th-century lie and the mid-20th-century lie is the statistics that have been gathered to bolster the second. There is also the striking peculiarity that where the 19th century travestied the concepts of religion to defend male heterosexuality (with prostitutes), Prof. Kinsey travestied the concepts of science to defend male homosexuality. With a bias like that, nothing he had to say about women should surprise anyone.

I. THE UNSATISFIABLE FEMALE

The folk expression of more or less this same prejudice arrives at the identical conclusion but by the opposite method: it says simply that women not only do have sexual passion, but that they have too much! — thus, that women *cannot* be satisfied sexually, and that there is no sense trying. This, you see, is exactly what Professor Kinsey says, except that it is done without statistics or 'biology.' Joke: "*Why do red-headed girls always marry such quiet, effortless men?*" "*They don't.*" (Minn. 1946.) Joke: *Three old maids went off on a tramp in the woods. The tramp died.* (1:66.) Joke: "*Dissipation? But Doctor, that's impossible. Why, he's been home every night since we were married three months ago.*" (*Amvoice,* Santa Barbara, Nov. 27, 1946, p. 3) And many more.

It does not take much intellectual penetration to see that what is being resisted here is any touch of dominance in the woman, who suddenly becomes the demonic red-head (like Judas), the *devoradora,* or eater of men, when she asks for the natural satisfaction of the orgasm that the man DOES NOT INTEND to bother to give her. Whether the excuse is that orgasm is morally (19th century) or 'biologically' (20th century) beyond her, or that no man can last long enough to give her an orgasm, is quite immaterial. The male ideal is expressed with the most staggering candor in a jocular courtroom decision to be compared with that attributed to the Supreme Court of Maine toward the beginning of this chapter: *A woman in North Dakota complains to a lawyer that her husband has his orgasm too quickly and does not satisfy her. Can she get a divorce? The lawyer looks up the law on the subject and reports to her: "Madam, there isn't a damn thing you can do about it. According to the laws of this state, when the man is through the woman is fucked."* (1:382.) As a matter of fact, that happens to be the law in *all* the states, beginning with Indiana. On the use of verbs for intercourse as meaning to cheat or be cheated — 'screw,' 'ream,' and 'diddle' are some of those, other than 'fuck,' commonly so used — see the section "Dysphemism" at the opening of the 14th chapter, in Series Two.

With the exception of the horrible joke given earlier on the iceman and the door-knob, which punishes the woman with the standard contempt of pedication for even *seeming* to complain of being unsatisfied, not a single joke has been collected among the two thousand or more examples in the present work in which a man is described as not having brought a woman to orgasm, except because of her own inadequacy. Since *not* bringing a woman to orgasm is an excessively common experience, the only explanation can be that this particular blow to a man's sexual self-esteem — not to mention the woman's! — is too serious to be carried off even in jest. Instead the guilt is completely projected upon the woman: she is accused of demanding a longer or stronger penis than can possibly exist, or a greater frequency of intercourse or passionate strength than can be expected of any man. The man's certainty of his phallic insufficiency rumbles beneath.

A woman on trial for beating her husband into insensibility explains that she had locked him out for coming home drunk, but he kept hammering on the door saying, "I'll bet you'd let me in if you knew what I'm knocking with." When she went down at once to let him in, he handed her a box of candy. (1:245. A variant represses the hateful element to a degree, and simply has *A groom knocking at his bride's door at midnight. "I bet I know what you're knocking for,"* she says. *"But do you know what I'm knocking with?"* — D.C. 1952.) In another form, *A woman on trial for beating her husband explains that he got her to come away from her work, took her upstairs, got her to take off her clothes and lie down on the bed, and then said "April fool!" and walked out. "Case dismissed," says the judge.* (1:68.) The whole point here is of course the taunt, and the man is willing to be beaten up for the opportunity to deliver it. A line that brought a tremendous laugh in one of the Marx Brothers comedies in the 1930's punishes the woman for her excess of passion with a hint at the *en brochette* empalement discussed earlier. *She: "Hold me close!" (He complies.) She: "Closer!" (He complies.) She: "Closer!" He: "If I hold you any closer I'll be in back of you."*

The one authentic sexual difference between men and women that might be used to couch some complaint against women's passion — or lack of passion, depending on which stick is being used to beat the dog — is conspicuously absent in jokes, and that is that women do not require erection to be ready for intercourse and are therefore, theoretically, 'always ready,' and can repeat intercourse immeasurably more often (and at a later age) than men. Poggio, in 1451, typifies as a 'shrewd and witty reply' (*scita facetaque responsio*) the answer given by a woman to her husband's question: *"Why, the pleasure in coitus being equally shared by both* [n.b.], *is it rather the men who solicit and pursue the women, than the women the men?" "And very rightly too,"* the wife replies. *"We are always ready and disposed for intercourse; not so with you. What would be the use of our asking you, when you are not prepared?"* (*Facetiæ*, No. 47.) This is very much in the style of the burlesque 'just-so' stories of Vignale's *La Cazzaria* (The Book of the Prick) in 1530.

Almost the only modern expression of men's insufficiency in this matter of frequency of repetition of intercourse, as compared with women, is a 'popular tale put into verse' in the McAtee manuscript (1913, env. 7): *An Irishman keeps harping on the idea that he would "like to be a Mormon, And breed a scad of little ones to bear the name O'Gorman." His wife reminds him that some Mormons have wives and concubines, as many as twenty-two, so: "Ho ho, you be a Mormon, I never heard such cheek. A Mormon, Pat, ye're crazy, with your two little fucks a week."* (Titled: "Theorick and Practick.") When the subject of repetition of intercourse comes up at all, it is either in the form of brags about the man's prowess in that direction (*The man who comes back to the drugstore three times in the same evening, buying a dozen condoms each time. "What's the matter," says the druggist, "are you ripping them?" "No, I decided to stay all night."* — 1:152), or as the ignorant expectations or almost forgivable sexual greediness of old maids at their first intercourse:

A schoolteacher in her middle forties allows herself to be seduced for the first time by the principal. She leaps out of bed and stands sobbing by the window berating herself. "Oh, how can I get up in front of those innocent children tomorrow and pretend to be worthy of teaching them, when I've been so sinful so often?" "Often?" says the principal; "I thought this was the first time." "Well, you're going to do it again, aren't you?" (N.Y. 1939.) Appetite slides imperceptibly into dominance when there is a cash payment to the man involved. The sneers of the American press, about 1900, when the importation of homosexual European noblemen to marry American heiresses had become an open scandal, were only secondarily directed at the mincing manners, foppish clothing, and catty remarks of the various imports. The primary target was invariably the heiress. A well-known joke, not traced earlier than the turn of the century, touches candidly on the question of cash payment, though at least here the sexual services are assumed to exist: *An old maid tells the young lawyer who is making her will that she has two thousand dollars, of which half is to go for her burial expenses and the other half to him if he will spend the night with her so that she will not have to die a virgin. Three days later the lawyer has not come home, and his wife goes to the old maid's house and demands, "Where's my husband?" "He's here. I decided to let the town bury me."* (*Memorabilia*, 1910. Printed in *Anecdota* 1:491.)

Bennett Cerf has printed a cleanup of this, in 1944, in which all the accent is on the money: *Two salesmen stop overnight at a farmhouse occupied by a single woman. Six months later one receives an ominous legal document. He phones his friend. "Did you by any chance make love to that girl at the farmhouse the night our car broke down?" "Why, yes." "And you gave her my name and address, didn't you?" "You're not going to get sore about that, are you?" "I'm not a bit sore. I've just heard from her lawyer. She died last week and left me the farm and $12,000 in cash."* The American salesman has reverted here to the status of the imported nobleman, who takes the cash and lets coitus go.

2. OLD MAIDS AND NUNS

Old maids in folklore are a peculiar group. Like mothers-in-law they may be suspected of being more attractive to men than the jokes imply. At least part of the parade of rejection concerning both old maids and mothers-in-law is based on their belonging to that group of *available older women* — they are assumed to be all available for the asking, and the mother-in-law may even live in the same house — but women who are dangerously similar in appearance to the real mother, and yet are not forbidden. This point will be returned to in a later section. Meanwhile it will suffice to observe the very similar treatment accorded in folklore to such dissimilar types of sacred females as old maids, harem-wives, and nuns, all of whom meet in their presumably unsatisfied sexual appetites. Where ordinary women are often enough accused of insatiability under the polite symbols of food (especially expensive food, significantly beyond the capacity of their male escorts to afford), the sexual status of the old maid, harem-wife, and nun is so central to their existence at all, that their insatiability is always stated strictly in sexual terms. The fact of the matter is that at least the last two groups often do actually transfer a good deal of their frustrated libido to over-eating. This is never mentioned in folklore, except perhaps in the stereotype of the idle-rich wife or mistress who lays on a sofa all day, reading a French novel, while toying lubriciously with a pet dog (with her stockinged foot), and 'eating chocolates.'

A few examples may be run together showing the meeting in sexual appetite of the various types of sacred women, even including the grandmother. *An old maid announces, "I'm going to buy a Ford."*

"Don't do it," says a friend. "Get a Buick. If you buy a Ford you'll get screwed." Next day she had a Ford. (1:122.) In an expurgated variant, *A man buys a car because he is told that a beautiful blonde sitting inside goes with it. He puts down his money, drives the car out of the lot, takes it out on the highway, parks, and whispers in the blonde's ear. "Uh uh," she says, shaking her head, "you got that when you bought the car."* (N.Y. 1953.) — *One of the eunuchs in a harem brags that he is the Chief Pisser. "What do you do?" "I go around the harem pissing on the sultan's wives. When one of them sizzles, I'm through for the day."* (1:22, and 409, a polite version in which a watering-pot is used. Text form: Minn. 1946.) — *A group of women are discussing how late in life a woman loses her sexual appetite. They ask Grandma, who says, "Sorry, girls, you'll have to ask somebody older than me."* (Idaho, 1920.)

Just what *is* the age when women lose their sexual appetite? Here is the answer, in a revenge for this one inalienable sexual superiority of women over men, that passes even the hostility of the 'Chief Pisser' above (who is in some versions described as an old man rather than a eunuch): *A Negro woman comes into a department store and asks for a pair of drawers. "How do you want them to button," asks the clerk, "back or side?" "It don't make no difference. They're for a corpse."* (1:55, giving 'front [?] or side.') This story is retold, in mangled Japanese dialect, and crossed with the mother-in-law theme, in "Wallace Irwin Incites Hashimura Togo to an Imitation of Irvin S. Cobb," in the *Dutch Treat Year Book* (New York, 1925) p. 11–13, from which the presumable or curtailed punch-line may be quoted as a record of what passed for humor at the time: ' *"I will take a pair of Those, price* 1$," *collapse Hon. Niggero, turning dark blue from bloshes. "Which kind shall you select?" snuggest Sails Lady, "the lock-up or the semi-detached variety?" "I are helpless to tell.'* " (The good old days?)

As will be discussed at much further length in Chapter 11.1.1, in Series Two, nuns are a survival of the priestesses of the mother-goddess cults active in Rome and Asia Minor at the time when Christianity was absorbing concepts and converts from its principal rivals, Mithraism and Judaism. The enforced chastity of the priestesses in the original cults was combined with sacred sexual licence at certain important holidays and in certain set forms, such as the Eleusinian Mysteries. With the usurping of the priesthood by men — usurping with it, and curiously retaining to this day, the women's clothing — nothing was left for the former priestesses but enforced chastity, almost without any holidays, making of them a sort of divine harem, or 'Brides of God.' As such, accusing them of unchastity and secret sexual availability became one of the prime themes of the Oedipal and rebellious humorous literature of the Renaissance. It is indicative of the very great decay into which religion has fallen in the last half century — despite its artificially-puffed recent 'revival' — that hardly a trace of this type of humor is left.

The presumable unrepressed sexuality of the Negro woman is usually brought into contrast with the chastity of the nun. *"Why do they call them nuns?" one Negro woman asks the other. "Because they ain't had none, they ain't got none, and they ain't never goin' to get none."* (Given in the McAtee ms., about 1915. More recent versions generally give a topper, such as *"No wonder they wear mourning,"* 2:61, or *"There ain't no colored nuns, is there?"* Virginia, 1952.) — *The Negro maid in a nunnery asks what the nuns do about men. "We never think about that," she is told; "we've all had saltpetre." "Well that's the trouble, honey. Why don't you try a fresh one?"* The masturbation theme will be considered shortly. *Several nuns (sometimes ministers' wives) are exchanging confidences. They decide to confess to each other their worst vice, which turns out, after a first round of confessing to fibs and other small sins, to be sex. The last one concludes, "Yes, and I like my lovers like my coffee: strong, and hot — and black. And what's your vice?" she asks belligerently of a quiet nun in the corner who has said nothing. "Me? I love to gossip."* (Minn. 1944.)

The converted prostitute (Magdalene) as nun is easily understandable historically as the sacred prostitute or orgiastic sex-priestess of the Levantine religions. The continuing identification of nun and prostitute is evident in the two following examples, more openly in the second. *After the high mass to celebrate the forgiving of Sister Mary, who has sinned with a man, Sister Katherine starts packing to leave. "I've been here for ten years," she says, "and all it's been is fucking and forgiving, fucking and forgiving. I think it's time for me to stop forgiving and do some of the fucking."* (2:377.) Note the similarity to: *A converted prostitute is beating the drum for the Salvation Army on a busy street corner: "Yes, once I lay in the arms of men. (Boom!) I sinned. (Boom!) I smoked. (Boom!) I drank gin. (Boom, boom, boom!) Night after night I gambled away my youth and happiness. But look*

*at me now! — changed (Boom!) — converted (Boom!) — washed, in
the blood of the lamb. (Boom, boom, boom!) What do I do on a Saturday night now? I stand on this street corner, beating this mother-
fuckin' drum!"* (N.Y. 1941.) In a related version she cries: *"I laid in
the arms of men. White men. Black men. Chinamen. Yes, I laid in
the arms of the devil!" Voice: "That's right sister, fuck 'em all!"*
(1:266.)

3. MASTURBATION BY WOMEN

Masturbation by women has always been a more difficult subject to
discuss than masturbation by men. Of the complex reasons for this,
two related factors can be separated out at once. First, it is economi-
cally valuable, in powerful, patriarchal cultures, for women to be sexually repressed, and any expression of sexual appetite in women is
detested and even consciously denied. Second, the female genitals are
conceived of — again under patriarchy — as a kind of inferior or castrated male genitals, lacking in attraction and narcissistic value to
women themselves. Men are proud of their own genitals. Women are
ashamed of theirs. Where men who use fantasies during masturbation
(or intercourse) remain themselves and embrace the fantasy, women
are likely to *become* the fantasy, in the sense of identifying with the
fantasied male and imagining the subjective possession of his genitals.
Few men, in masturbating, fantasy themselves as having a vagina.

Sufficient space cannot be devoted to this extremely important subject here to do it justice, and it is unfortunate that the literature is so
sparse. Two modern publications on masturbation by women both
over-react tellingly to its special taboo. In a remarkably free-spoken
pamphlet called *Auto-Erotic Practices* by 'Porter Davis' (G. Schin-
dler), published in 1950 for newsstand distribution, the title fails to
note that *all* that is discussed is auto-erotism by women. Similarly, in
"Masturbation and Love" by Ruth C. Cohn, in *Complex* No. 7 (1952),
the end-point is reached where the author finds herself saying that 'In
intercourse partners can use each other as masturbatory tools,' while
'masturbation may be experienced as tending toward fulfillment with
a real partner. . . . We have therefore to acknowledge that there are
experiences of asocial intercourse and social masturbation,' which is
periously close to saying that not only masturbation by women is not
wrong but that it is better than the real thing!

The more recent study of female orgasm behavior, by Dr. William H. Masters and Virginia E. Johnson, *Human Sexual Response* (1966) is essentially a study of female masturbation, carefully observed and photographed — from inside! As art, or neurotic infantilism, this can be of interest, as in the remarkable series of drawings by Hokusai, in his *Book of Little Flowers,* showing the child in the womb, frightened by the parents' intercourse, which it conceives of as flames and violence at the mother's orgasm, an idea crudely exploited in the eccentric psychological cult of "Dianetics" proposed by L. Ron Hubbard in the 1950's. Paraded as science, intra-vaginal photography of erotic acts is actually a worthless sort of voyeuristic activity, as the enthusiastic public acceptance of Masters' dry statistical volume — *after* the photographic sessions were over — has made very clear. That orgasm in women can only be created by clitoral friction or pressure, and that vaginal insertion and thrusting will seldom suffice, could certainly have been demonstrated (if that were the real goal) without a single photograph being required. Also, normal rather than exhibitionistic subjects could then have been studied — a significant detail, which unfortunately puts all the conclusions of the book into question. Like Kinsey's bogus extrapolations of findings in a few thousand white Protestant college-educated boys in the eastern United States (what are now called WASPS, or White Anglo-Saxon Protestants) to the 'human male' — which ought, after all, to include a few Negroes, Orientals, and perhaps Europeans! — the study of the orgasm behavior of *women who want to be photographed while masturbating* is of dubious relation to that of women in general. It is, of course, a common neurotic goal or perversion, in men, to want to watch women masturbating, or to fantasy such acts; also to watch lesbian acts, particularly cunnilinctus, between women. But the same men — and most normal women — generally think of seeing *men* masturbating (and, even more so, homosexual acts between men!) as nauseating and degrading.

Folk materials do not make these errors, but they almost invariably punish the woman, at least with pregnancy, for her autoerotic act. It is not the least significant peculiarity of the masturbation joke that women are considered to be disgraced by it, and worthy of punishment, where, in men, masturbation is the most venial of sins. Again, nuns and old maids are the butt of the accusation, and no leniency is accorded them in consideration of their frustrated state. First, the candle: *A group of sailors on a whaling ship masturbate into a tub of sperm oil. Candles are made from the oil, and a whole convent full of nuns becomes pregnant.* (Scranton, Pa. 1925. Printed in *Anecdota* 2:295; and, above, in the final section, "Potency and Aphrodisiacs," 5.vi, as an example of wholesale male potency.) The same motif, but modernized, rationalized, and Lesbianized: *The girls in a small college town where men are few have slumber-parties where they satisfy each other with a candle. One of the girls smuggles in her handsome cousin disguised as a woman, and the other girls get pregnant. "But how could it have happened?" one of the fathers asks. "I don't know, Papa. The darned old candle must have melted!"* (Idaho, 1932.) The rational element here, of the man who has been smuggled in, is of course a routine device in Boccaccio and the later Italian *novellieri* in dealing with convents. Rotunda, K1810–1858. Randolph gives a version of this joke as No. 30, "The Romping Party," recollected from Arkansas 'in the early 1890's,' with no reference to resulting pregnancies.

Second, the banana. As it is not too well known, it may be mentioned that Levantine peoples believe that the fruit of Paradise, with which Eve sinned and made Adam sin, was a banana. (The word 'apple' is not mentioned in *Genesis,* iii. 3, which says only 'fruit.') This is a far older tradition than the Sunday-school apple, and fits more reasonably with the other phallic overdeterminants in the story, such as the great tree and the serpent. One of the Moorish survivals in Spain, apparently, is the belief that a banana should not be *cut with a knife* (more recently, and with open symbolism, not be put in the refrigerator!) and that, if it is, according to the Christian rationalization of this anti-castratory cutting superstition, a picture of the crucified Christ will be seen in the cross-section — *i.e.* the three lines of the soft core. There is also a magical entertainment in which, by means of a needle & thread looped several times under the skin and then both ends brought out together, an unpeeled banana can be passed around, only to be found already sliced on opening. To balance the castratory nature of this 'entertainment' one other, more normal, may be mentioned, illustrated in Arthur Good's *Magical Experiments* (English translation, 1892) p. 191, in which a group of moustachioed French officers are seen making a banana peel itself, while it pops into a bottle from which the air has been exhausted by means of a lighted match!

At least two direct modern statements exist, both intended as humorous, in which the obvious identification of the fruit (and serpent) of Paradise is made, the first in Paul Perret's *Tableaux Vivants* (1870), one of the most natural and least frantic of modern erotica, which opens: 'It is said that the Spirit of Evil, in ancient time appeared to our Mother Eve in the form of a serpent. Do not believe it. Satan . . . presented himself to our Mother under the form of a handsome young man. That which he presented to her was not an apple, it was a prick. . . . As this history [*omitted here*] is difficult to relate to children, they tell them that this glans was an apple. It was nevertheless a prick.' Reduced to a mere wisecrack, to end *Anecdota Americana*: '*Well, if Eve had only liked bananas better we'd all still be in Paradise.*' (1:500.) A semi-private 'novelty' postcard gives this as a riddle: "*Who was the first carpenter?*" — "*Eve. She made Adam's banana stand.*" The illustration is a crude drawing in which, whatever may have been intended, the appearance is that Eve is sawing off Adam's penis with a carpenter's saw. Both Baughman (Motif J2214*b*) and Katharine Briggs & Ruth Tongue, *Folktales of England* (1965) p. 123, no. 67, give a heavily oversymbolic version of the just-so punishment story in *Genesis*, though without any reference to this of course: *Two little girls are eating their first bananas, given them by a man, in a train. Just then the train went into a tunnel*[!]. *The older sister asks the younger, "Have you begun to eat your banana yet?" "No." "Well then don't, because it makes you go blind."* Compare *The hillbilly who refuses the unknown banana, saying, "Nope, I already got too many appetites I cain't satisfy."* (N.Y. 1940.) No reference to sex in either, and yet . . .

Two old maids are buying bananas. *They are five cents each, or three for ten. "Oh well, we can always eat that one."* (*Memorabilia*, 1910. Printed in *Anecdota*, 1:446.) As a continuation of this, or sometimes with the opening that *Two old maids have been given the address of a stud-house, or male brothel, by an understanding physician. On the way they pass a barber shop behind which the barber is burning hair. "Do you think we're walking too fast?"* (N.Y. 1942.) Much other material not rising to joke form: *The sensational new banana — it pulsates!* (2:40), and the statement ascribed to the actor Pat O'Brien in answer to a question as to the plot of his new moving picture: "*It's about a nymphomaniac on a banana-ranch.*"

Miscellaneous substitute penises for female masturbation are few. It is generally either a candle or a banana, or sometimes the witch's (matriarch's) broomstick, though nothing precisely in joke form has been found on this last, which is of course inserted vaginally in order to 'fly,' not merely straddled. *A Jewish woman sends her son to the doctor with her urine specimen. On the way he drops it, and scoops up as much as he can from the sidewalk. The doctor reports that the woman is going to give birth to a litter of pigs. "Oy!" she wails, "you can't even trust a weenie these days."* (2:154. Type 1739. To compare with the pig, as a survival of matriarchal cult-worship.)

4. THE SEX MACHINE

The most hostile group of punishments of the woman for masturbation goes far beyond mere accidental impregnation. The punishment becomes, apparently, whatever the teller is most afraid of: pedicatory rape, castration, or death, or some combination of these. A joke collected several times from children: *Pat & Mike are plumbers, and are fixing the rich woman's toilet. Pat decides to use it before he goes, and finds three foot-pedals before him when he sits down. "I pushed the first one," he tells Mike, "and water sprayed up and cleaned me off. Then I pressed the second one, and a big cotton swab came up and wiped me dry." "What about the third one?" "I can't figure that one out. When I pushed on it a big rubber prick came up from beneath pumping like mad and rammed itself up my ass."* (Idaho, 1919. Also Scranton, Pa. 1927, with the less clear conclusion: "A candle came up and tapped me on the balls three times." Cf. *Kryptádia,* 1907, XI. 187.) In the following very hostile example is not so much the use of a substitute penis, as the hatred and contempt involved in doing so (compare the folk-phrase, "I wouldn't fuck her with *your* prick") and the intention, not very well disguised by the reversal at the punch-line, of killing the woman with it. *A switchman is accosted by a railroad yard prostitute and uses a metal coupling pin in intercourse with her instead of his penis. She makes no comment, and he finally asks, "Like it?" "I'm sure glad you said something," the woman replies. "Your tool's so cold I was afraid you were dead!"* (2:210.) Note that the Devil's penis is always recognizable, as being *painfully ice-cold and scaly,* in his intercourse with human beings.

Psychoanalysis has placed beyond question the necessity of identifying as a symbol of 'the imposing mechanism of the male sexual apparatus' (Freud) the complicated and indescribable machinery in various types of fantasy, such as the 'influencing machine' of the schizophrenic, and the 'time machine' and other as-yet uninvented mechanisms and planet-impregnating projectiles of science-fiction, which is the sickest literary phenomenon of our time. On the 'influencing machine' see Victor Tausk's classic article, translated into English in the *Psychoanalytic Quarterly, 1933*. On the similarity between the witchcraft mania and delusions of 'influence,' and on the extension of these in recent times to include radio waves and radar, see Jules H. Masserman's *Principles of Dynamic Psychiatry* (1946) p. 76–8. A self-controlled perpetual motion 'influencing machine,' built by a patient and intended to represent coitus when in motion, is illustrated in E. J. Kempf's *Psychopathology* (1920) p. 428. Nothing of a useful critical nature — in fact nothing but publicity gush — has yet been published on science fiction, although I have been accumulating material for this purpose for a number of years. The work of Kingsley Amis is perhaps the least bad, and a few further notes will be found in my *The Horn Book,* (1964), p. 313–31, "A Few Words on Science-Fiction." See also *Neurotica,* No. 8 (1951) "The Machine."

The relevance of the phallic machine to the rather extensive lore concerning mechanical masturbating devices for women is quite obvious. What is not so obvious is the consistent use of such machine-penises to kill the women who have the temerity to require them, from the time of Queen Pasiphaë (the Cretan Aphrodite) who hid in a mechanical cow — invented by the aeronaut Daedalus — to receive the embraces of the bull. There is a long note on published examples of the fantasy of the masturbating machine in *The Limerick* (Paris, 1953) Note 1325, as an excursus on the well-known invention of the young man of Racine, which makes a bare mention of the modern ballad of "The Great Wheel" (first collected, Cambridge, Mass. 1938, to the hymn-tune: "Oh Master, Let Me Walk With Thee") built for the benefit of the woman who 'never could ever be satisfied,' but in the end:

> *It was a case of the biter bit,*
> *There wasn't no method of stopping it;*
> *His wife was split from tail to tit —*
> *The whole damn contraption went up in shit.*

Gruesomely 'anti-gallant,' this whole sorcerer's apprentice tale ends dreadfully in a fecal explosion, which can most conveniently be described in psychoanalytic terms as an anal-sadistic substitute orgasm, in which the fucking-machine avenges its impotent creator by tearing the woman to bits. This is one of the ballads most frequently collected at present in America.

The note here of 'helpless inevitability' in the face of the Frank-ensteinian monster of the sex machine not only serves to make the machine more terrifying but also projects upon it the sadism of its background inventor. This note of inevitability is always present in jokes on mechanical themes, and now no longer has or needs the pre-Frankenstein rationalization of magic to explain it, as in the legends of the Sorcerer's Apprentice, Roger Bacon's Bronze Head (*"Time will be! — Time is! — Time was!" — Crash!!*) and the Golem of the Head Rabbi of Prague. The man who puts his penis into a cow-milking device that is inevitably set for four quarts is noted in the later chapter on Castration, subsection "Vagina Dentata," in Series Two. The female version is exactly similar. *A Philadelphia doctor who has ordered some surgical instruments accidentally receives a package from the rubber company addressed to Spain. Inside is a rubber man with an erect penis. He puts it under the bed. The servant girl finds it and says to herself, "The rich ladies can have their fun, so why can't we poor servant girls?" She puts the rubber man on the bed and gets on top. [n.b.] In embracing him she touches a spring that sets him into action, but finds after she is more than satisfied that she cannot get loose. The doctor telegraphs the company: "Rubber man screwing hired girl to death. What shall I do?" Answer: "No help for the hired girl. Rubber man wound up for twenty-four hours to fuck the Queen of Spain."* (*Memorabilia,* 1910. The lover of the Queen of Spain at the turn of the century was an American, making her the byword of female passion.) Told as a scandalous anecdote of a highborn lady of the court of Napoléon III, in *Mémoires secrètes d'un Tailleur pour Dames* (Bruxelles: Gay & Doucé, 1880), illustrated, according to the printed 'key' added to only a very few copies.

V. THE FEMALE GENITALS

I. FEAR OF THE FEMALE GENITALS

One would imagine that the overpowering attraction that the majority of men feel toward the female body would certainly, if not principally, include the female genitals. The reverse is the truth. The female genitals are accepted only after tremendous resistance based on the unwillingness to admit that there are beings without a penis.

Too much material is available in the psychoanalytic literature on the relation between castration anxiety in men, and particularly in boys, and their concept of the female genitals, to make necessary a review of the subject here. One of the most curious aspects of the matter is discussed in Freud's paper on "Fetishism" (*Collected Papers*, v.198–204,) where the partial representation of the genitals by the fetish is shown to be an attempt to deny the absence of the expected penis by concentrating on the last part of the anatomy or bit of clothing seen before the non-phallic nature of the female genitals was apprehended. 'Velvet and fur reproduce, as has long been suspected,' says Freud, 'the sight of the pubic hair which ought to have revealed the longed-for penis; the underlinen so often adopted as a fetish reproduces the scene of undressing, the last moment in which the woman could still be regarded as phallic.'

Some of the high points of the surprisingly scant belletristic and medical literature on the female genitals will be cited in the following pages. Far & away the most important is one of the most misapprehended autobiographical novels ever written, Henry Miller's *Tropic of Cancer* (Paris, 1934), which is universally accepted as a sort of sex novel or semi-pornographicum, but which is actually a towering invective against life, and in particular against sex and woman. So much so, that, as in the case of Miller's model, Céline, one must put aside moral judgment of the villainy he froths, out of gratitude for the unveiling with such monolithic power of what everyone knows but no one ever says. Almost an entire chapter of *Tropic of Cancer*, p. 109–54, the section opening with the words, 'At one-thirty I called on Van Norden,' is given over to an anti-pæan of ambivalent hatred and love of the female genitals, in which truth and madness tumble out together 'in a whirl of fragments of myth and trash,' in one long monologue comparable only to the closing pages of Joyce's *Ulysses* and "Rameau's Nephew" by Diderot, the true originator of this type of writing. Miller puts most of the passage into the mouth of 'Van Norden' (the journalist, Wambly Bald), and leaves the paragraph of greatest significance in the present context for the last, where 'Van Norden,' after almost *forty pages* of hateful disquisition on the female genitals, concludes:

It's an illusion! You get all burned up about nothing . . . about a crack with hair on it, or without hair. It's so absolutely meaningless that it fascinated me to look at it. I must have studied it for ten minutes or more. When you look at it in that way, sort of detached like, you get funny notions in your head. All that mystery about sex and then you discover that it's nothing — just a blank. Wouldn't it be funny if you found a harmonica inside . . . or a calendar? But there's nothing there . . . nothing at all. It's disgusting. It almost drove me mad.

Much more will be said later on this *'nothing,'* which is only a rather obvious way of expressing the horror of the penisless female genitals, in the chapter on Marriage, 8.III.6, "Ophelia's 'Nothing'," to which the interested reader is urged to refer. Here one is deeper than jokes.

The missing penis is never found, and Miller's ambivalent attraction and fear deepen in his later work. In *Tropic of Capricorn* (1939), in a section called "An Interlude," beginning at page 184, he drops 'Van Norden' and other speaking-trumpets, and expresses in his own voice the animus he feels against sexual intercourse and the genitals of women. Toward the end, p. 203-4, he dashes off a rhetorical hymn of perfunctory adoration, a catalogue of all the various types of female genitals in the world, only the last actually described as good, whereupon he ends suddenly, 'and these are the best of all, but whither have they flown?' Although Miller is of course not homosexual, one is reminded inevitably of Whitman's artificial passages of gas concerning fine strong women, etc., which he balances coldly against the warm catalogues of men's bodies (particularly if crippled and castrated) in which he really delights.

The reader will not be surprised, after this preamble, if most of the materials in this and the following section will be found reeking with animosity against the female genitals. I wish there were some way of avoiding this material, but there is not, and even if I were to omit it from the text it would still remain the prevailing attitude among living men, no matter what they may say during the sweet-nothing preludes. In any case, I would say again that this book is *not* intended as a showcase of my own personal emotions or bias: not in the jokes.

The anti-sexual mania of the Christian religion has always been its predominant characteristic, and remains, in the accusing and forgiving of 'sexual sin,' its principal hold over its adherents. This is in part derived from Judaism, which has always projected upon women (Eve) the sexual guilt with which the patriarch jealously taxes his sons, but nothing will be found in the earlier Jewish writings to compare to the absolute frenzy of the French and Spanish anti-woman

Catholic writers, among whom Odon of Cluny and his famous '*inter faeces et urinam nascimur*' — first-hand research, obviously — are nowhere near the worst. (Henry Miller, in *Tropic of Capricorn*, 1939, p. 196, spends half a page ringing the changes on this theme.) By comparison, the Jewish anti-menstrual regulations, in which the underlying fear is at least understandable, and the one anti-vaginal biblical passage, *Proverbs*, xxx. 15–16, are quite inconsiderable: 'The horse-leach hath two daughters, crying, Give, give. There are three things that are never satisfied, yea, four things say not, It is enough: The grave; and the barren womb; the earth that is not filled with water; and the fire that saith not, It is enough.' Rationalized already as it is (with the apologetic 'barren'), this obviously cannot be compared with the medieval Christian concept of the vagina as the *stigmata diaboli*, still surviving in, for instance, the stupid anecdotal line: *Backwoods preacher, beginning his sermon: "Will all the women in the congregation please cross their legs." (Shuffling of feet, then silence.) "All right, folks, now that the gates of Hell are closed, I can begin my sermon."* (Idaho, 1920.)

The intense conversational display of the male genitals has been sufficiently documented in earlier chapters. The female genitals, by contrast, are always to be hidden. *Girl: "I'm worried about this short skirt. I'm afraid if I bend over, someone might see my underwear. (She bends over.) There, can you see my undies?" Fellow: "No." Girl: "Well I'll bend over farther. There — can you see them now?" Fellow (gasping): "No, but I think you'd better put some on!"* (Minn. 1935.) This is also, of course, implied in the standard defense of female virtue by crossing the legs: *An old prostitute at the melodrama becomes overwrought when the villain gets the heroine backed into a corner. "Cross your legs, honey," she shouts, "and he can't do you a goddam thing!"* (Rutland, Vermont, 1940.) It may be noted in passing that the villain of the melodrama — Rudolph Rassendale, of the deathless line: *"Once aboard the lugger and the gal is mine!!"* or vice versa — was always dressed and moustached in an almost conscious representation of Satan, who has now fallen away even further to 'Mr. Coffee Nerves,' with the added indignity, in the most recent ads, of being put into science-fiction tights and jet-propelled. The late Robert Benchley left a private phonograph recording, now widely circulated, telling a story similar to that above, of an old prostitute whose heart is broken by the treatment of Little Eva in a stage performance of *Uncle Tom's Cabin,* particularly at the end where the rope that is taking her to heaven breaks and drops her on the stage "like a turd from a tall cow's ass."

2. DISPLACEMENT TO BREASTS AND BUTTOCKS

The displacement of male sexual interest from the female genitals to the breasts represents more than an oral-erotic attraction to the breasts, with all the known overtones of masochism and the return to the mother. It makes it possible to emphasize and discuss a quasi-genital area of which any childhood recollection will be one of pleasure and satisfaction, rather than the possible anxiety and horror aroused by the first realization that women do not have a penis. The buttocks — 'the larger hemispheres of the female body,' as Freud calls them in one of his few circumlocutory passages (10th Introductory Lecture) probably intended in any case as a joke — are similarly equated with the breasts, owing to their shape, and both are symbolized in dreams by 'apples, peaches and fruit in general.' Recent advertisements concerning the proper style for 'Milady's bottom,' have, for instance, referred in the necessary fractured French to the '*derrière en poire,*' with a rebus of a *pear;* and a whole bookful of illustrations — based on an unfortunate misconception of the author's meaning — have made use of the same image in a translation of Alfred Jarry's *Ubu Roi* published in London in 1951.

Folk identifications of the breasts and buttocks are not uncommon, though of course these seldom take the next step of admitting the equation with the genitals. The sexual tone of the material almost makes this unnecessary. There is also the theory, for which a good deal can be said, most clearly enounced in Ernst Klotz' *Der Mensch ein Vierfüssler* ("Man as a Quadruped," Leipzig, 1908), which notes that among the semi-quadrupeds most similar in their bodily carriage to man, such as the bear, the kangaroo, and the ape, the female is still approached from behind, as with all quadrupeds, and that one may therefore hypothesize in the earliest forms of man an original visual target identification of the buttocks and genitals of the female in sexual attraction. (See the underwear joke above.) This would also help to explain the various naso-oral sexual phenomena.

In a joke frequently printed in recent years as a 'true anecdote': *A flat-chested young actress is told to ask at the property room for "Number 906," which will be the false bust she needs. She comes back with an enormous bosom. "No, no!" shouts the director. "They gave you 609. That's Falstaff's bottom!"* (1:335, a version not using the numbers.) In *The Pearl*, No. 7, for January 1880, the same identification is made in a perfectly direct way, with the factor of sexual attraction to these attributes also present: '*When John Scott was minister of Dundee, he reproved Alick Anderson for illtreating his wife; Alick tried to justify his conduct, but the minister observed, "Oh Alick mon, there must be something wrong on both sides!" "True, very true," cried Alick, "she has neither bubbies nor buttocks!"* ' As it has already been observed sufficiently often that any reference to *death* in a joke must be interpreted as hostility, no matter how it is disguised or prevented or who is blamed; it will be enough to note in the following example that it is genital hostility that has probably here been displaced on the buttocks in the same way that genital attraction can be displaced. *A Jewish woman comes home in tears from seeing the doctor. "He told me I got tuberculosis and must die yet," she wails. "What! a big, fat woman like you?" says her husband, "that's ridiculous." He rushes to the doctor's office and begins berating him. "Now just a minute," says the doctor, "I didn't tell your wife she had tuberculosis; I told her she has too big a tokus and must go on a diet."* (1:293.)

3. WOMEN-AS-VAGINA

The actual genitals of the woman are treated with undisguised animosity. There are almost no exceptions to this. Only the fool (foreigner) is allowed to find the woman's genitals satisfactory, and that is of course the proof of his folly. *A woman falls out the window when drunk, and topples upside down into the ashcan* [!] *An Indian (or Chinaman) sees her bare legs sticking up, inserts one finger into her vagina, and turns it back and forth, smelling it appraisingly. "White man crazy, throw away squaw," he grunts. "Still good two-three years maybe."* (N.Y. 1942.) In what seems to be a variant, also based on the accusation of excessive vaginal size: *A woman wakes up with a hangover and says to her Chinese houseboy, "I guess I was pretty tight last night." "First time pretty tight. Second time pretty sloppy."* (Minn. 1946.) The further implication cannot be overlooked here that the Indian and Chinese are considered 'inferiors,' and that, as such, turning over the woman to them is of a piece with throwing her in the ashcan. This joke is set up pictorially in the sado-masochistic cartoon strip, "The Adventures of Phoebe Zeit-Geist," in *Evergreen* (April 1967) No. 46: p. 92.

The direct statement that *a woman is only a vagina* ('but a 5¢ cigar is a smoke'), and is worth nothing on any other basis, is seldom made, not because it is too ungallant and unflattering, but because it is still too much of an acceptance! Pretended 'old Spanish proverb': *"Big woman, big cunt. Little woman, ALL cunt!"* (N.Y. 1938.) The interesting subject of sexual proverbs cannot be handled here. Collections in both Yiddish and Scottish have been published separately, and there is a brief French selection in John S. Farmer's *Vocabula Amatoria* (1896) p. 223–5. Quite a number of authentic English proverbs, such as *"Fresh cunt, fresh courage,"* will be found throughout the Victorian erotic autobiography, *My Secret Life* (1888–94?), including one, of apparently Scottish origin, vol. VI, chap. 12 (ed. 1966, p. 1220) curiously typifying the genitals as having human intelligence: *"Cunt and cock are crafty coggers."* ('Cog,' to cheat or deal unfairly, as with loaded dice.)

Aside from the insults against the woman and her genitals that are based on the presumable unpleasantness of the female genital odor — which is actually intended to be a primary sexual attraction, as in all other animals and even in flowers — the palette of possible insults is obviously limited. Where not concerned with the *size* of the female genitals, as will be discussed shortly, almost nothing but explosive statements of unexplained hostility are encountered. *A woman attempts to break through the inexperienced usher's line at a theatre, insisting, "But I have a mezzanine box." "Lady, I don't care if you have brass tits; keep to the right!"* (2:85.) In a man, the ascription of metallic genitals would obviously be a compliment, as in *The Limerick,* No. 195, on the *"Young man of Madras, Whose balls were constructed of brass; When jangled together, They played "Stormy Weather," And lightning shot out of his ass!'* which practically puts him on a par with Jupiter. There is also the French phrase, *'couilles de bronze,'* said of a man of great courage; the Trinidadian 'Ironbar,' for a very virile man; and the American 'Ironballs,' for a tough general — euphemized to 'Tuffypants' [!] in a newspaper version. — *A man who says that he may look lousy but he feels good, is called*

"*Mr. Cunt,*" *on the grounds that* "*That's the only thing that looks so lousy and feels so good.*" (1:391.) As some nadir of this type of thing: *A man comes back to the clubhouse at the golf-links on a stretcher, with a golf club up his rectum. He explains that he was playing golf with his wife, and the ball landed in cowflop. He said to his wife,* "*It looks like your hole — and that's the last thing I remember.*" (N.Y. 1952.)

The crudest insult is the metonymic 'taking of the part for the whole' (too often punned upon already), in which, for instance, one refers to a boat as a 'sail,' to a sailor as a 'hand,' and to a woman as a 'cunt.' In the Van Norden passage in Miller's *Tropic of Cancer,* p. 109, already noted, several of the opening pages are spent in planting the impression of the intense contempt with which Van Norden divides all women into 'virgins' and 'cunts,' principally the latter. *A miner in San Francisco in the gold-rush days is having intercourse with a dance-hall girl sitting on a piano stool behind the curtain of one of the booths. Suddenly a hand reaches in and yanks the woman off his lap, while a voice shouts,* "*My wife! My wife!*" *The miner pulls out two guns and points them at the intruder behind the curtain, bellowing,* "*Put that cunt back!*" (1:375.) The depersonalization is very over-determined here, both the woman and her 'husband' becoming mere organs.

An important and widely circulated story on the theme of "Woman as Vagina" appears to be a good deal older than its first recording in *Anecdota* in 1927, as the heyday of the jokes on what were called 'false aids to beauty' was during the bustle period of the mid-19th century. *A man in the upper berth* [see the chapter on Marriage] *is peeping on the woman in the lower berth undressing, and sees her take off a wig, false breasts, a glass eye. She is unscrewing a wooden leg when she catches sight of the peeper.* "*What do you want?*" *she shrills.* "*You know damn well what I want. Unscrew it and throw it up here.*" (1:261. In a Spanish folktale version, Aarne Type 1379*, he asks her to throw him one buttock for a pillow.) This is a projection upon the woman of castration fears of the male type, as the deeper female castration fears are not of having parts of the body removed but of being 'sewed up.' At least two modifications of this theme have been collected: *The woman in the lower berth, who has very pro-truding teeth* [vagina dentata] *cannot sleep because of the snoring of the man in the upper berth. She bangs on the metal several times, but* *each time he wakes up, falls back asleep, and begins snoring again. Finally she bangs on the metal very hard, and the man says, "It's no use, lady. I saw you get on."* (Transcontinental train, 1945.) This covers the train element and the human rejection. The other modification concentrates on the castrated limbs, and has therefore been proper for printing in the humor magazines: *"I took that girl with the cork leg and the blonde wig and the store teeth in one of the boats on the lake last night." "You mean the one with the glass bottom?" "Gosh, I didn't notice."* (1946.)

The male castration form should be compared with the original here, though it actually belongs in a later chapter on Castration, under "Overcompensation." *A surgeon who has just performed a difficult operation unscrews the wooden hand which he has just been using. "Marvellous!" breathes the nurse. "Oh, that's nothing," says the doctor, and unscrews a wooden leg. "But how did you ever manage to overcome such handicaps, Doctor?" "Come down to my office and I'll show you." So she went down to his office and he screwed his head off.* (N.Y. 1942.) This presents itself as a mere catch, but is actually an artful denial of the possibility of castration — for men. It will be observed that where the prosthetic limbs of the woman make her undesirable and end in desexing her, the man with prosthetic limbs is a sexual superman, not to mention his other talents.

4. VAGINAL SIZE

The commonest insult concerning the female genitals is that they are too big. In jokes this represents a much more direct expression of the anxiety that every joke is intended to allay than do the long-penis jokes, which imply a solution of the problem of genital mismatching by fantastic and improbable means. Rather than admit that the penis is 'too small,' as is fearfully believed, it is far simpler to state that the vagina is 'too big.' If one reviews the rather sparse medical literature on the vagina: Martin Schurig's *Muliebria* and *Gynæcologia* (Dresden, 1729–30), *The Sexual Life of Woman* by E. Heinrich Kisch (English transl. 1910), and Robert L. Dickinson's *Human Sex Anatomy* (1933, revised ed. 1949), and a small number of lesser works, one learns simply that the muscle-tone of the vagina is reduced in women who have had a large number of children. The average tight distension in women who have had children is from two and one-quarter to two and one-half inches (the thickness of three fingers, as shown in Dickinson's *Human Sex Anatomy,* fig. 59, and interestingly prefigured in Schurig's *Gynæcologia,* p. 227). Considering the rugations inside the vagina, this measurement is not sufficiently in excess of the average diameter of the erect penis to lend much verisimilitude to the endless complaints about vaginal size.

The presumption therefore remains that the fear that the penis is insufficiently large — as demonstrated by the wishful fantasy of the large-penis jokes — has simply been projected upon the woman. In the *vagina dentata* jokes, where the opposite accusation of too tight a vagina is made, the damaged or inadequate status of the penis is again made the woman's fault. The further inconsistency of ethic is also observable that where tearing and harming the vagina with the penis, even to the point of impaling and killing the woman, is considered in jokes and other lore to be an heroic phallic feat, the vagina that does not tightly fit and sufficiently please the penis (not to mention harming it) becomes the object of insult and contempt. There is clearly a double standard in organs as well as in acts.

About the mildest joke collected on this theme is a gentle reminder of the one element of reasonableness in the whole thing: the distensibility of the vagina of the multiparous mother. *The father of triplets suggests that the obstetrician "look around a bit more. She always was a pretty roomy sort of girl."* (2:110.) Impossible exaggerations are sometimes pointed up by comparing the very large size of the vagina with the very small size of the husband's penis, and jokes on this theme will be found in a special section, "Mutual Mismatching," in the chapter on Marriage. Of pure exaggerations, the most famous is at least two hundred years old and perhaps more. *A farmer and his daughter are driving along the road in a wagon when they are held up by robbers, and everything is taken from them but some coins (or jewels) that the daughter manages to hide in her vagina. Afterwards she gives these to her father, and tries to console him for his loss. "Oh,"* he says, *"if only your mother was here, we could have saved the horse and wagon too."* (1:362, in a version on refugees from a pogrom, with the incestuous element made even more clear by having the daughter hide in her vagina the 'jewel' symbolizing virginity.) Two centuries earlier, in Thomas Hamilton, Earl of Haddington's *Select Poems* (1735) a poetized version is given under the title "The Sutler," in which: *The wife hides 'a purse as big as your fist . . . in a certain* place,' but the husband complains: ' "You've done very well, but you'd had more to brag on, If you there had conceal'd the horses and waggon".'

This has been taken to purposely absurd lengths in a peculiar joke about *A man who finds himself unable to "touch bottom" during intercourse with a prostitute. "Can't you do something about this?" he says. "It's like waving a flag in space." The woman is insulted and invites him to examine her vagina. He probes and stares and suddenly loses his footing and falls in* [Alice in Wonderland]. *He wanders for a while, and finally meets a man with a lantern whom he asks the way out. "I don't know," says the man. "I've been here two weeks looking for a team of horses."* (N.Y. 1938, also collected, 1950, with a flashlight and motorcycle instead of the lantern and horses. A unique erotic animated-cartoon movie called *Abie's Buried Treasure,* made in the late 1920's or early '30's, also opens with a scene in which a man has trouble in intercourse with a woman who later turns out to be his mother — and he to be pedicating his father — and who reaches into the vagina and finds various objects such as an alarm clock [*n.b.*] in his way.) I think it is evident that this story, in any form, is more than an exaggeration, and can only be construed as a fantasy of pregnancy and rebirth.

A delightful book of almost exactly the same sort of adventures, but frankly describing them as the experiences of a spermatozoön who becomes a child and is waiting to be born, is Marcel Arnac [Bodereau]'s fantasy, 83 *centimètres d'aventures* (1925), translated into English as *Thirty-six Inches of Adventure* (1930). At the unconscious level this theme has been explored again and again, as by 'Lewis Carroll;' in Sterne's *Tristram Shandy* (1760) and Kingsley's *Water Babies* (1863), both of which consciously bring in ideas of prebirth; in a much-anthologized story by H. P. Lovecraft (*doyenne* of the anti-fish and green-slime school of homosexual horror writing) in which a boy endlessly climbs a towering tree [birth through the father] only to find himself finally coming up out of the ground; and, in the crackpot psychology field, in Nandor Fodor's *Search for the Beloved* (1949) and L. Ron Hubbard's *Dianetics* (1950), which are so terribly concerned with the dangers of life in the womb that one wonders how they ever got out of it alive.

Even the conscious theme of womb-return has been encountered. *A yokel in a whore-house laughs when he sees the prostitute's vagina.*

"You shouldn't laugh," she says, *"you came out of one of those."* *"Yes,"* he says, *"but that's the first one I ever saw that I could get back into."* (D.C. 1944, N.Y. 1952; and, in a hostile gag-version, Minn. 1946, of *The fellow who almost killed his mother: somebody told him to go back where he came from.*) As sufficient attention has never been drawn to it for the Oedipal fantasy it is, rather than the 'bawdy poem' it is usually described as, "The Wish" by the Earl of Rochester (*d.* 1680) may be noted here. It does not appear in the facsimile reprint of the first edition of Rochester's *Poems* ('Antwerp,' 1680) recently made at Princeton, having been published first in later editions:

> *Oh, that I now cou'd by some Chymick Art*
> *To Sperm convert my Vitals and my Heart,*
> *That at one Thrust I might my Soul translate,*
> *And in the Womb my self regenerate:*
> *There steep'd in Lust, nine Months I wou'd remain*
> *Then boldly fuck my Passage out again.*

Rochester's erotic play, *Sodom,* which is unquestionably authentic in spite of scholarly pretense (as the tryout or rejected opening, "Actus Primus Scena Prima," in the *Poems,* p. 76, would alone suffice to demonstrate), is also of great psychological interest, and a fair text is fortunately available in *Kryptádia,* vol. IX (1904), also issued separately. The superior texts, in the British Museum's Harleian manuscripts and at Princeton, have not yet been released for publication. These have been edited by Mr. Terence Deakin *vis-à-vis* an even better text, in private hands in England, but publication has been delayed.

The presumably excessive female sexual appetite, which is also the main 'plot' of *Sodom* (The Prologue opens: *'Almighty Cunt, whom Bolloxinion here, Tir'd with her tedious toyl, doth quite cashier . . .'*), is often equated directly with excessive vaginal size. In the first speech in Act IV by King Bolloxinion of Sodom — presumably a caricature of the homosexual King James I of England — the usual complaint concerning vaginal size is used to excuse the king's turning to pederasty. (Mirabeau's 'explanation' of why the alternative is not pedication of women has been cited earlier.) Later in Act IV a woman is described who, starving sexually as a result of the king's proclaiming pederasty as law, has had intercourse with a horse, and who is rewarded for her excess of passion by being made 'mistress to an Elephant.'

The same sort of sardonic equation of vaginal size and passion is to be seen in a modern version of a very old story, which will be found in Poggio's *Facetiæ* (1451) No. 237. *A young man is masturbating his girl in the park with the ferrule of his umbrella. She keeps begging for more and more, and finally he exclaims, "Why you damn bitch, I've already got the whole umbrella and my arm inside. What more do you want?" "Open the umbrella!"* (2:222. Variant: *A girl complains to the man who is feeling her that his ring hurts her. He: "I'm not wearing any ring. That's my wristwatch."* 2:41.) The image of the umbrella opened rectally was used as *leitmotif* and punch-line in Jerome Weidman's *What's In It for Me?* in the 1930's, though there does not seem to be any connection with the title. The similar punishment of the egg-beater wished up the wife's rectum in the story of the three wishes will be noted further in the final section of chapter 13, on "Castration," in Series Two. It is also used as the final scene — combined with the sexual dream of the nightmare — in an unpublished American story-in-pictures, *Genesis* (New York, 1944: in my own collection), composed of three hundred erotic drawings done by an unknown master, where the pretense is made that the egg-beater, like the opened umbrella, is intended simply to satisfy, and not to punish, the unsatisfiable woman.

The original story, as given in the *Cent Nouvelles Nouvelles*, No. 12, "Le Veau," is much closer to the horse-&-wagon types. *A Dutchman is sporting with his wife under a tree in which a peasant is concealed looking for a lost calf. The Dutchman enumerates all the beauties of his wife's body aloud, saying, "Oh, I see this, and that, and that and this! Holy Mary, what a lot of things I see!" "Alas, good sir," says the peasant in the tree, "do you happen to see my calf? It seems to me I see its tail there."* Aarne Type 1355B. The modern version (in which the umbrella first appears) has been published a number of times in college humor magazines in the 1940's. *An absent-minded college professor forgets his umbrella in a hotel room, and when he gets back he finds that his room has already been taken by a newlywed couple. He is about to knock at the door when he hears the man's voice saying, "Whose little lips are these?" "Yours, dear, yours!" "And whose little teats are these?" "Yours, dear, all yours!" "Say there," the professor shouts over the transom, "when you come to the umbrella, that's mine."* (N.Y. 1940. Also collected, 1953, with a World War II barracks bag replacing the umbrella.) Note that the topper line, from the *Cent*

Nouvelles Nouvelles, about the tail — which La Sale specifically explains to refer to the woman's pubic hair — has been lost.

Mere insults concerning the size of the vagina may involve strongly symbolic comparisons, particularly in the forms given later under "Mutual Mismatching." *A girl on a date is urinating over the edge of a cliff into a lake. "Look," she says to her escort, "I peed right into that canoe down there." "That's no canoe. That's your reflection."* (2:302.) Compare: *Three men on a trip through the Canadian woods telegraph back, "Need three punts and a canoe at once." Answer: "Women on the way, but what the hell's a panoe?"* (Pa. 1935.) — *A farmer is told that a cow at the fair is worth a million dollars "because it has a cunt like a woman's." Farmer: "Well, I swan! And here I've got a woman with a cunt like a cow, and it ain't worth a nickel!"* (2:241.) Leonardo da Vinci's use of practically the same joke, but with the insult trebled, in a burlesque demonstration in his *Quaderni d'anatomia,* f.7r, n.5, that the sexual parts of a woman are, proportionately, three times as large [!] as those of a cow, has already been noted in connection with the identification of cow as mother-image in the section on "Zoöphily" earlier. The womb-return jokes above, in connection with the theme of the too-large vagina, may be considered corroborative of the identification of cow and mother.

VI. THE FEMALE CASTRATION COMPLEX

(1.) PASSIVE FORM: INFIBULATION

The psychoanalytic literature on the subject of the castration complex in women, specifically the writings of Freud, Karl Abraham, and Otto Fenichel touching on this matter, give very scant attention to the vaginal rather than phallic elements in the female castration complex. This is all the more surprising in that psychoanalytic writers have, in general, clung to the belief in a special vaginal orgasm in women, as opposed to the known and demonstrable clitoral ('phallic') orgasm. The conclusion is left to be drawn that the analytic championing of the so-called vaginal orgasm contains in itself the elements of an unconscious castrating of women; vilifying — that is to say, removing — the clitoris, calling its possibilities of excitement and satisfaction 'infantile,' and attempting to equate mental health in women with the ability to achieve vaginal orgasm in spite of the very scant supply of nerve endings in the vagina and the very great supply in the clitoris.

Like the so-called 'death-wish,' which seems to have resulted from a
combination of Freud's indubitable impotence (at the age of sixty-
four) and his desire to explain the World War in *non-economic terms,*
and which is a hopeless embarrassment to any understanding of even
the specific problems — aggression and sado-masochism — that it was
intended to solve; the idea of a special vaginal orgasm is not one of the
triumphs of psychoanalysis, and will perhaps eventually join the
'death-wish' in the innocuous desuetude into which the latter concept
has been allowed to fall since the death of Freud in 1939. A most extraordinary 'pre-analytic' side-result of this denigration of the clitoris
will be noted later in connection with the 'Halban-Narjani operation'
— really a sort of expurgated female circumcision, or extirpation of the
clitoris (by lengthening rather than removing it!) — invented and at
first championed by Princess Marie Bonaparte, later one of Freud's
most grateful friends and students, who is said to have paid the large
ransom required by the Nazis for allowing Freud to leave continental
Europe during the 1930's, to die peacefully in England in his eighties.
I will return to the 'Halban-Narjani operation' later.

It is not my purpose to expatiate here on Freud's known prejudice
against women, his allocating to them a practically 'natural' masochism (as humiliatingly accepted without question in Helene Deutsch's
volumes on women), and his peculiar and continuing references to
women in his later writings — for instance the repeated line in the
paper on "Fetishism" (1927) about the fetishist denying 'the unwelcome fact of the woman's castrated condition' — as though Freud himself shared the neurotic fantasy that women are 'castrated men.' Attention is drawn to this matter because it seems to be the real cause
of the lack of attention paid by psychoanalysis to the vaginal elements
in the female castration complex, as well as of the apparent hostility
of analysis against clitoris pleasure. While there can be no question at
all that women have, in this culture, enormous penis-envy, and do feel
that in being women they have suffered a deprivation — which may
even consciously be referred to the lack of male organs, and unconsciously to the idea that they have been cut off — women have not always lived under male dominance, nor is their character, even at present, lacking in prides and fears more basic than those rising from the
fact of having been dominated and shamed by men.

If one drops, for the moment, those ideas of castration in women which take their rise from the comparison with the anatomy of men, and considers the relation of the daughter and mother — in the same way that analysis has so carefully considered that of father and son — it becomes evident that the fantasy of bodily damage in women, as a punishment for competing sexually with the mother, which matches the fantasy of bodily damage in men as a punishment for competing sexually with the father, is not the removal of any external part of the female genitals, but rather *the fantasy that the female genitals have been sewn up* in order to prevent intercourse from taking place, or as a punishment for masturbation. A large amount of material on this repellent operation, in both the classical 'infibulation' form and as practised among certain savage tribes (usually, in later stages of social development, by the men of the tribe, as a measure of 'insuring virginity'), is presented in *Woman,* by Drs. Ploss, Bartels, and Reitzenstein, a tremendous ethnological work, translated by E. J. Dingwall.

Dr. Dingwall is also author of a work on the Renaissance fantasy of the 'chastity belt,' of the real and historical existence of which he is the principal modern proponent. The chastity belt is of course also an expression — mechanical rather than anatomical — of the same intention of closing up the woman's genitals against intercourse. So far as a perfectly impartial consideration of the evidence leads one to believe, the chastity belt has *never* had any real historical existence, and all the examples in museums (as that of the Cluny Museum: the most famous) are modern fakes. A run-down of the literature, similar to that of Dr. Dingwall, and enthusiastically accepting the infibulatory fantasy of the chastity belt as absolute fact, is Evan-Esar Levine's *Chastity Belts: An Illustrated History of the Bridling of Women* (New York, 1931), a work which, in any case, does a good deal less offensive chuckling and chortling than most of the writings on the subject.

Since the popular dissemination of literature on the chastity belt, in the last half of the 19th century, and the entering of the idea into folk-circulation, actual examples have of course been constructed and even used, usually by jealous husbands of rather low social level and obviously high neuroticism. These seldom seem to be the result of independent parallel fantasy or invention. They are of no great social importance, as the castration complex in women — more correctly, perhaps, the *infibulation* complex — is nowadays expressed on a far broader scale in a cross with that of the male, whereby surgical cuttings and removals are enacted on the woman's organs, similar to the castration and circumcision of men. See Rops' infibulatory fantasy, *Serrefesse,* with a padlock through holes bored in the *labia majora* (ear-piercing!) in G. Zwang's *Le Sexe de la Femme* (1967) p. 268.

In the Levantine patriarchies, the women are circumcised — usually by elderly women, self-elected to the work — by cutting or burning off the labia minora and clitoris. (This no doubt solves all their psychological problems of orgasm perfectly.) In America, in the last decade or two, there has been a sinister shift toward the removal of the uterus and adnexa, whether by the daughter herself in order to give up her meaningful sex life and thus ingratiate herself with her mother, or by the mother to prevent her daughter from *having* a sex life. (As in the scandalous case of the heiress, Anne Cooper Hewitt, made the subject of a chortling castration poem attributed to the Hollywood biographer of men, Gene Fowler, and given in *The Limerick,* No. 1172-9, dated 1938.) The current pattern is for the woman's hysterectomy to be recommended and performed by surgeons of the disturbed type who enjoy castrating women, after frightening them with the bogey of cancer. (The psychosurgery and sterilization of the insane are available for physicians more interested in men.)

It is grimly amusing that there is the usual double standard even in this. Where the circumcision of men, originating in the Judæo-Arab Levant, is now performed and excused in Europe and America on 'hygienic' grounds as a mere minor operation, while the castration of men is admitted to be a crime at law; the circumcision of women in the Levant is capable of arousing the most pained journalistic screams for the horrible mutilation that it so obviously is (*e.g.* H. T. Laycock's "Surgical Aspects of Female Circumcision in Somaliland," in *East African Medical* Journal, Nov. 1950; and Y. E. Hills' "Female Circumcision in the Sudan," in *Anti-Slavery Reporter and Aborigine's Friend,* London, April 1949 — articles of which the real purpose seems similar to that of publishing gruesome pictures of animals being tortured, in the comparable anti-vivisection magazines); while the 'hygienic' excuse of cancer prevention or treatment is now just as widely used to propagandize for the far more serious operations of the ablation of the breasts and womb, that are essentially nothing but the castration of women. Such operations, also, never have and never will save any woman from dying of cancer, nor even delay it very long. Furthermore, they seriously increase the woman's self-loathing in the terminal stages of the disease, and her inability to retain her image of herself as a woman. Dying women should not be tortured. Let them die clean.

Psychoanalysis recognizes the *vaginismus* type of frigidity, where the vagina goes into spasm and prevents the man from entering; but, rather than recognize in this the real expression of the castration complex of women, Dr. Fenichel for instance (*Psychoanalytic Theory of Neurosis,* 1945, p. 174) explains that this may express the 'wish . . . to break off the penis and to keep it,' although he has just finished remarking that *vagina dentata* ideas like this are the subject of many reports, but are rarely described in scientific literature. He adds: 'The anecdotes are probably based more on male castration fears and female active castration tendencies than on real occurrences.' Why the female castration tendencies do not wait, then, to express themselves until after the man is inside, but instead keep him out beforehand, is not easily explained.

Evidence will be found in the folklore of many countries for the more basic expression of the female castration complex in *the fear or threat of being sewn up or locked up vaginally.* A 'cumulative folk poem from old Persia,' quoted in an entirely different context in Evan-Esar Levine's *The Humor of Humor* (1952) p. 50, expresses this with utter clarity: '*I went upon the mountain top to tend my flock. Seeing there a girl, I said: "Lass, give me a kiss!" She said: "Lad, give me some money." I said: "My money is in my purse, my purse is in my wallet, my wallet is on my camel, and my camel is in Kerman." She said: "You want a kiss, but the kiss lies behind my teeth, my teeth are locked up, the key is with my mother, and my mother, like your camel, is in Kerman".'* ('Kiss' is patently a euphemism, since a kiss is not behind the teeth.)

In an American imitation of the well-known castratory German nursery book, Hoffmann's *Struwwelpeter* (see the final issue, No. 9, of *Neurotica,* 1951, largely devoted to this work), published under the matching title of *Slovenly Kate* in Philadelphia, 1852, and ascribed to 'Th. Hosemann' (probably a fake name intended to be confused with Hoffmann), the story of "Tell-Tale Jenny" describes how Jenny has the habit of eavesdropping and then repeating what she has heard, for which she is carried off by a horrible ogre with a tremendous hooked nose, and:

> *As soon in his cave as they're out of all hearing,*
> *He bores three great holes thro' her ears and her lips —*
> *And then a huge padlock — oh, think what an ear-ring! —*
> *Thro' each of the apertures quickly he slips.*

Now stopt is her eaves-dropping, stopt is her clack!
Oh, haste, mother, haste — she'll be lost in a crack; —
For, unless you come quickly, and snatch the child up,
The ogre, I'm certain, on Jenny will sup!

As there is no 'crack' for Jenny to be lost in, in the illustration accompanying, showing Jenny with the lock through her lips (copy in the New York Public Library), it seems probable that 'clack' and 'crack' are actually interchangeable at the end of the doggerel lines, in a way that, *if conscious,* would be considered a joke. One may also suspect that the good mother and the bad ogre, both standing over Jenny in the illustration, are merely splittings of the single mother-figure into good and bad halves, as is standard in witch tales, as the castrator of her daughter for eavesdropping — *i.e.* for the sexual sin of peeping, a frequent symbolization — exactly matches the sun-father who smiles down from the wall at the jolly tailor who castrates Struwwelpeter for sucking his thumbs. It may also be worth mentioning that 'Hosemann,' in another warning tale, of "Ned, the Toy-Breaker," gives a horrible story and drawing of a boy whose nose is made to grow 'full six feet long, and very thick,' by kneading into it the fragments of his broken toys [!], an inverted castration also used in Carlo Collodi's *Pinocchio* (1882) for the sin of lying. (Motif D1376.1.)

The approbatory view of the female genitals taken under female dominance, rather than male, is indicated in the lying-song, "Three Old Whores from Canada" quoted in the section on "Brags" in the preceding chapter, who brag about how *large* their vaginas are, with the matching denigration of the penis as small, in the "Talk of Ten Wives on their Husbands' Ware." Here we see that the brags are all reversed, the good vagina is the big one, in which birds and ships sail in and out without touching, and so forth, and any inadequacy in coitus is made the fault of the too-small penis. These implications pass the understanding of the tellers of androcentric tales, and they must reverse and rationalize them to fit them into male-dominant stereotypes: *Three women are bragging how* small *their vaginas are. One says she had to use half a jar of vaseline to permit her husband intromission; the second says she had to use a whole jar, and her husband half of another. The third says, "Excuse me girls, I've just come sick. Do either of you have a Band-Aid?"* (D.C. 1951. In a version collected N.Y. 1953, the first two women brag instead of the small sizes they require in the symbolic gloves and shoes.)

Just as the concept of the large vagina as good, under female dominance, or in Lesbianism, is ununderstandable and avoided in modern
joking tales, the dependent concept of female castration as infibulation, as a closing up of the vagina by the woman herself (or by some
punishing authority) to remove her from the sexual competition in
favor of the mother, is also ununderstandable. Where the motif occurs, it is rationalized in one way or another, for instance as an attempt
to tighten the vagina to please the man (or to preserve virginity for
his taking). *The wife of an old farmer suggests that he go and have
a set of monkey glands sewed in for a hundred dollars. Farmer: "Why
don't I send you and have the whole monkey sewed in for five hundred?"* (N.Y. 1940. See other examples of the monkey as representing
the female genitals in the chapter on Animals.) *A prostitute declares
that rather than have intercourse with a client for half her usual price,
she will "have it sewed up." "Go ahead. It could use a couple of
stitches."* (N.Y. 1942.)

A far older line, equally unfunny, which is picked up in both
Memorabilia (1910) and in the Guam mimeograph (1948) only hints
at infibulation in a way certainly veiled from the tellers: *A man explains that he bows to his tailor's daughter because she is the only
thing his tailor ever made that fits him.* On the tailor as the classic castrator (as in *Struwwelpeter,* and in the even more incredible 'scissors'
drawings in Wilhelm Busch's *Naturgeschichtliches Alphabet,* reproduced in *Neurotica* No. 9: p. 22–3), see Ferenczi's "The Sons of the
'Tailor'," in his *Further Contributions to Psycho-Analysis* (1926) p.
418–19. Ferenczi brings the tailor, as castrator, into comparison with the
barber, soldier, butcher, and doctor — the ancient fraud of the 'gentle
craft' of the shoemaker is unfortunately not punctured — but it should
be recollected that it is the needle and not the scissor that is really the
instrument of the tailor. There is also the peculiar tradition that tailors
are somehow less-than-men. On the Elizabethan stage they were caricatured frankly as homosexuals, and the punning proverb about its
requiring 'twelve tailors [to] make a man' dates from that time. The
blatantly false-heroic tailor of the 'seven-at-a-blow' folktale is also
relevant.

The best known infibulation story frankly expresses the sewing up
of the women as a punishment, but as a punishment of the man!
*Frank Harris dies and goes to Heaven. "You can have anything you
like," says Saint Peter. "Women!" Harris cries. "Sorry. We don't have*

anything like that here. We're all sexless and sing psalms instead.
You'll have to go . . . downstairs . . . for that." At the bottom of the
golden stairs Harris finds the Devil sharpening his tail and picking his
teeth with the point. "Hello, Frank," he says. "I knew you wouldn't
like it up there. But it's pretty soft down here. Two hour shifts on the
furnaces, and you can have anything you like." "Women!" Harris
shouts. The Devil snaps his fingers, and a harem of naked girls appears
lolling on pillows. Harris dives in among them but comes up again
crying, "Hey! they haven't got any holes." "Yes," says the Devil, "that's
the Hell of it." (2:392.) Also collected in a version omitting the scene
in Heaven with Saint Peter — who is, of course, God in a comedy beard
— in which *Hell is described as clouds floating by with barrels of beer*
and girls on them, while young men hopelessly fondle tremendous
erections. The barrels have holes in them, and the girls don't. (D.C.
1943.) The further development of these themes, into the frightening
'Nothing' of the female genital (*i.e.* that which lacks a penis), will be
found in the special section, "Ophelia's 'Nothing'," in the chapter on
Marriage, 8.III.6, following.

VII. PUBIC HAIR AND SHAVING

The purpose of the pubic hair is a physiological mystery. It cannot be
explained as an adventitious growth in the sense that armpit hair, for
instance, might be explained, with reference to the warmth, damp, and
friction of the armpit. This would explain only the lesser portion of
the pubic hair distributed within the crotch and gluteal cleft; while the
main growth is high over the pubic bone in front, where no such explanation will serve. There can be no question that the pubic hair is a
survival from some earlier stage of phylogenetic history. The problem
is, what function did it then serve, and serve so well that it disappeared
next-to-last of the body hair masses? The best theory so far offered is
that the human being rose to the erect position from the quadruped
and semi-erect state of, for example, the kangaroo, bear, or ape. As a
quadruped, the proto-human male would naturally approach the female from behind. (See Ernst Klotz, *Der Mensch ein Vierfüssler,*
1908; also J. R. Spinner, *Die Jungfernschaft,* 1931, both specially treating of the sexual adaptation of the quadruped position, particularly
during defloration.)

The most important determinant in sexual selection, in the semi-quadruped human, would be, as it still is among the other mammals, the sexual and genital odor of the female. This odor takes its rise from the secretions of glands just inside the opening of the vagina, and despite all folklore disclaimers and insults (particularly comparing the odor to that of fish, shrimp, or cheese), it does represent and must always have represented the most powerfully attractive of all odors to the male. In the quadrupedal position, the proto-human quadruped male approaches the combined buttock-and-genital area of the female naso-orally, sniffing the area and generally caressing it by licking before intercourse is attempted, more probably *to excite himself* than to prepare the female. The mat of pubic hair, lying forward and under the genitals in the quadruped position, would then act as a sponge to hold the odorous vaginal secretions, and only those females with a perfume reservoir of this type would be certain to attract the male and reproduce their type.

No one can fail to observe, in the present-day perfume advertisements, an absolutely conscious purveying of the perfumes on the same basis of a sexual excitant, with erotic brand-names like Tabu, Seduction, My Sin, Forbidden, Aphrodisia, Luxuria [*sic!*], and so forth; and the open suggestion that the perfume should be applied to the groove between the breasts, and to the hair areas of the armpit and the nape of the neck. The only improvement is, of course, that the natural odors of the woman are to be washed away as 'dirt,' and are to be replaced by the anal and genital secretions of deer (musk), skunks (civet), beavers (castor), and diseased whales (ambergris) at $30 an ounce. The natural secretions of the woman are free.

In the battle between the neurotic modern regression to the anal stage, expressed with the reaction-formation minus sign of an excessive interest in 'cleanliness,' white bathroom, and even kitchen fixtures, mentholated toilet paper, special 'body-odor' soaps, and 'chlorophyll' *ex votos* that make the human being (and bathroom) smell like a freshly creosoted chicken-coop, a few desperate avowals of wholesome interest in the natural body (though seldom in its natural odors) can sometimes still be found. One of these was the outburst of spring pantie-raids at coed colleges in America a few years ago and still, with the boys gathering under the girls' dormitory windows and chanting, "Throw down your panties!" and "We want sex!" This is expressing the intended meaning publicly under a very slight veil, as when the same young college men ostentatiously sport sweaters marked very large with the presumed year-number of the Class of '69. (This has been going on since 1963 at least, though the Class of '69 could not have matriculated till 1965.) As in the metonymic advertising line about sanitary napkins, the girls' panties are perhaps *"Not the best thing in the world — but next to the best!"* It is also remarkable, as seen in the completely frank folkloristic evidence, that the naso-oral phenomena of human sexual selection — involving the interest in the female pubic hair, the vaginal odor, and cunnilinctus — are accorded a much greater measure of acceptance than the actual female genitals, which the 'lack' of a penis makes neurotically fearful.

Pierre Louÿs, for example, in his privately-issued posthumous erotic works, such as *Trois Filles de leur mère* (translated into English as *The She-Devils,* Paris, 1958), his *Manuel de Civilité,* and *Pybrac,* shows himself pansexual to the highest degree, and obviously masochistic, as also in the publicly-issued *Woman and Puppet.* Yet he expresses only the standard admixture of attraction and fear in the "Song of Solomon" pæan to the female genitals (put into the mouth of the Lesbian 'slave-girl' representing himself) in the first chapter of his masterpiece, *Aphrodite,* in the 1890's:

> "It is like a flower of crimson, full of honey and of perfumes. It is like a hydra of the sea, living and soft, open at night. It is the humid grotto, the shelter always warm, the Asylum where man rests from his march toward death."
>
> The prostrate one murmured very low: "It is terrifying. It is the face of Medusa."

It was on the closing image here that the first and private American reprint of Henry Miller's *Tropic of Cancer* (New York, 1940), with its long anti-pæan against the female genitals noted earlier, was ascribed to the fictitious 'Medvsa Press,' and a title-page insigne of the vulva, with two conventionalized locks of hair and a rising line of perfume, was prepared for this edition though not used. (See the excellent analytic pages on the Gorgon Medusa, by H. A. Bunker, in *Psychoanalytic Quarterly,* 1934, III. 415–17.)

For reasons that will appear in connection with the materials themselves, jokes on the vaginal odor will be found in the opening section, on "Petting," in the following chapter. Menstruation too cannot be overlooked in this connection, though the great taboos connected with it tend to conceal its relation to the other ordinary sexually-attractive vaginal secretions and odors. Jokes on this aspect of menstruation will be found where they are essentially most logical, though perhaps least expected, in the sections on "Oragenitalism," specifically cunnilinctus, in the chapter on Marriage, 8.v.3-4, a connection to which the jokes themselves unerringly point.

As has already been noted, the jokes on the pubic hair are singularly lacking in the animosity that characterizes almost all the jokes on the actual female genitals, and more than half of those on the vaginal odor, menstruation, and cunnilinctus. Attention is drawn again to the passage from Freud's paper on Fetishism quoted at the opening of the section, "The Female Genitals," where the partialism of sexual attraction in the fetishist, accepting, for instance, only the velvet or fur or female underclothing that represent the peripheral accoutrements of the female genitals, has the effect of decreasing the anxiety with which he would look upon the non-phallic 'face of Medusa' without these veils of cloth or hair.

The mere reference to the pubic hair is sufficient to create the impression of a joke. This is true of all taboo matters, since of course it would be unnecessary (as Freud says of incest) to forbid that to which no one was attracted. *A girl comes to an artists' ball stark naked, and is turned away on the grounds that nudity is permissible but that she must represent something. She comes back wearing black gloves and shoes. "You're just as bad as you were before," says the doorman. "What are you supposed to be?" "Can't you see?" says the girl, "I'm the five of spades."* (1:64. The vaginal over-determinants of both the symbolic gloves *and* shoes are also given above in a variant on the Band-Aid joke.)

The love of men for the pubic hair, their treasuring up single pubic hairs and tufts, are frankly noted in jokes. The most florid example of this minor and almost-normal fetich is noted in David Foxon's *Libertine Literature in England, 1660–1745* (New Hyde Park, 1965) p. 16*n*, discussing Thomas Stretzer's well-known 18th-century facetia, *Merryland:* 'The name of Merryland (clearly a pun on Maryland) must be related to the Ancient and most Puissant Order of the Beggar's Benison and Merryland, a phallic club started at Anstruther, Fife, [Scotland,] in 1732 and formally inaugurated by a Code of Institutes signed on 14 September 1739. This and its offshoot, the Wig Club — the wig (perhaps more accurately a merkin) was said to have been made from the pubic hair of Charles II's mistresses, and was added to by all new members — are described in Louis C. Jones, *The Clubs of the Georgian Rakes* (New York, 1942); between them their members included George IV, four dukes, seventy-three peers and law lords of Scotland, thirty baronets and two bishops.' The ceremony of entry into the Beggar's Benison club — its name taken from a beggar's blessing recorded by Grose in 1785: '*May your prick and your purse never fail you!*' — apparently involved the initiate's *wearing* the famous merkin-wig on his head during the ceremony: namely showing his penis and masturbating publicly on a 'test-platter,' to the sound of a ceremonial trumpet. The club continued in existence until the 1890's.

The jokes seldom offer anything so ornate as to the pubic hair. *Several married men on a hunting trip are unable to sleep until the guide gives each of them a hairbrush to hold.* (2:388.) — *Two soldiers, strangers to each other, are opening their mail. "Now isn't that the most considerate wife," one of them marvels aloud; "sends me a hair right off of her snatch to remember her by." The other soldier takes the hair out of his hands, draws it through his fingers, sniffs it, and holds it to the light. "Pardon me," he says, "ain't your name Hawkins?"* (1:21.) This joke will be discussed again in the chapter on Adultery, under "Possession in Common," 9.III.2. On the magical rather than simply sentimental element in the gift of the pubic hair, compare Giovanni Sercambi's *Novelle* (written in 1374) No. 21: *A priest asks a woman for a pubic hair which will draw the woman to him. A sow's bristle is substituted, and the sow comes rushing into the church.* (Rotunda, K.1281.1*. Another example of the identification of pig and vulva.)

The hostile tone begins to creep into the jokes on pubic hair even in describing the *collectionneur fou* of these love-tokens. *A Frenchman in a bar removes a packet of pastel envelopes from his breast pocket, takes a pubic hair from each, and sniffs them lovingly, explaining to a wondering American sitting nearby just how such a collection is to be made, by plucking the hair "halfway between ze cunt and ze ass." The American makes a large collection in a hurry and goes back to the bar to show his mentor. He opens the first envelope and hands the hair to the Frenchman, saying "This was Simone — lovely!" The Frenchman takes the hair, sniffs it appraisingly, and says, "Nonononono! Too near ze ass."* (Calif. 1952.) The relationship between this story and the preceding is self-evident, as is the sub-homosexual tone of possession in common of the same woman, to be discussed much more fully at the end of the chapter on Adultery.

The mere touch of hostility noted here balloons out suddenly and viciously in a group of connected jokes: *The automobile inventor in heaven who tells God that woman is not much of an invention. "For one thing," he says, "You put the intake too near the exhaust."* (1:142. Or engineer: *"the ballroom too near the toilet." Kryptádia, XI. 138.) — A collector of petrified vulvas learns from a connoisseur, who tastes each one, that someone has cheated him and included two anuses — one Negro and the other Chinese.* (2:165.) I have seen this joke set up as a tableau at a party, using as displays, with frightening verisimilitude, dried halves of pears and apricots. Whatever is omitted here, in the direction of sadism, is caught up in a final variant including elements of cannibalism and the pig-as-vulva! *A man in very run-down condition is asked by the doctor what he eats. The man hesitates and finally admits, "I guess it's a vice I picked up in the Orient, but all I eat is fried pigs' cunts." "Well there you are," says the doctor, "you're fucking yourself to death internally."* (N.Y. 1952. Cf. Motif J2284.)

Jokes expressing actual animosity against the pubic hair are seldom as virulent, and certainly not collected anywhere near so often, as those hostile to the vagina. Actual numbers of examples on both themes should not be compared directly, as popularity of a theme is evidenced not by the number of jokes about it, but by *the number of times the jokes are collected,* and by the diverging variants that can be seen developing from them in various directions, as with the motif of *collecting* above. In one example the hostile note is struck by indirection, complaining not of the presence but of the lack of pubic hair. *A man in a whore-house asks for a virgin, but complains that the girl given him cannot be a virgin, as all the hair has been worn off her pubis. "She hasn't any wool," he says. Madam: "Wool? What do you want to do, fuck or knit?"* (Calif. 1952.)

The more common complaint, however, is of the presence of the pubic hair. *A man meets an old sweetheart of his, and observes that she still looks very young but that he didn't remember the dimple on her chin. She explains, "That's not a dimple. I had my face lifted — it's my belly-button." "Well better not have it lifted again, or you'll be wearing a curly black beard parted down the middle."* (Idaho, 1919. Various slang terms recorded in John S. Farmer & Henley's *Slang and Its Analogues,* 1890–1909, and in Henry N. Cary's *The Slang of Ven-*

ery, 1916, largely plagiarized from Farmer, give unmistakable identification of the chin-beard and female pubic hair, such as the phrase *'blending wigs'* for cunnilinctus, and *'Oom Paul'* for a cunnilinctor [on the square beard of the Boer War leader, 'Oom Paul' Kruger]. See also the remarkable list, covering nine quarto pages in Farmer & Henley, at the word *'monosyllable,'* of synonyms for the female genitals.)

A young man following a girl up the steps of a London bus tries to start a conversation with the remark, "Airy, ain't it?" "Wot did you hexpect," she replies angrily, *"hostrich feathers?"* (2:140.) — *A woman who is raising money for a political cause shows one man her knee, and he gives her ten dollars. She shows the next man her thigh, and he gives her twenty dollars. The third man, who is a White Russian general, gives her nothing, explaining that all she did was to pull up her skirt and show him Karl Marx's whiskers.* (A version in E. E. Cummings' *Eimi,* 1935, p. 309-10.) *Anecdota* 2:398, in 1934, gives a variant in which *A girl who is crazy about aviation has a picture of Lindbergh tattooed on her right thigh and Amelia Earhart on the left. She asks the young man which one he likes best. "The picture of Balboa in the middle."* In a further variant, where even the verbal initiative reverts to the woman, *A girl has "Merry Christmas" tattooed on one leg and "Happy New Year" on the other. As she leaves she says to the tattooer, "Come up and see me sometime between the holidays."* On erotic tattooing in general, see the special supplement to Albert Parry's *Tattoo,* published in *Psychoanalytic Quarterly* during the 1930's.

In one of the few jokes consciously satirizing overcompensatory pretenses: *A widow is eulogizing her husband. "He was so kind, so gentle. He never beat me. He never even touched a hair — not a hair." "What marksmanship!" the minister comments drily.* (2:182.) Compare with this the spontaneous joke, *On a Hudson River ferryboat caught between the current and the tide, and banging back & forth from side to side as it entered the ferry-slip. Voice from the crowd: "I pity his wife!"* (A real occurrence, N.J. 1942.) Two or three really hateful jokes concerning the pubic hair have also been recorded. *A tennis player, changing courts, notices that the pubic hair of a red-headed girl in the stands is not red but black. He mentions this to the second player, who says, "That's not hair, that's flies."* (2:292.) A story on the prostitution frame-situation of having no money or not enough money: *A man who has only twenty-five cents strikes a bargain with a prosti-*

tute one evening whereby she allows him to look at her genitals for this price. He is examining her carefully with his cigarette lighter in a dark alley. "What wonderful, thick hair you've got," he says. "Can you really piss through it?" "Of course." "Then you better begin right now. You're on fire." (2:169.) — A girl who is marrying a millionaire pays a doctor a thousand dollars to fix things so she'll scream and carry on like a virgin on her wedding night. Later she asks the doctor how he did it. "Simple. Knots in the hair." (The Limerick, 1953, Note 1468.)

The shaving of the woman's genitals, whether by herself or by an obstetrician on some hygienic excuse, or by a sexual partner for avowed pleasure (as in a decadent story, "Hair," in *Neurotica*, 1949, No. 5: p. 17), invariably represents a castration of the male type. A twenty-page poem called *A Genuine* [sic] *Letter from the Earl of Rochester to Nell Gwyn* (about 1730) is wholly devoted to hateful remarks about the female pubic hair, and insistence on its removal. In a 'displacement upward:' *A woman is describing a game of strip-poker in a nudist camp. "But how — ?" "We used tweezers," she says. "I lost an eyebrow."* (Minn. 1946.) In the least insulting story on actual shaving, *A man is shaving his wife's pubis to save money on the maternity hospital fee. He lathers up her pubic hair and then cannot see what he is doing. "Honey," he says, twisting his mouth grotesquely to one side, "make like this!"* (N.Y. 1940.) As with the man just above with the cigarette lighter, one may suspect the urge to harm — in this case to cut — behind the over-emphatic *fear* of harming.

The more typical shaving stories suggest it to the woman as a mere insult. *The society woman is arranging the table for a formal party when her daughter comes in and announces dramatically, "Mother, I'm a Lesbian!" "So, go upstairs and shave."* (N.Y. 1952.) In a variant, specifying the pubic hair, and therefore not rationalized with Lesbianism: *A wife threatens her husband that if he does not buy her a fur coat she will come downstairs stark naked at their next party, and does so. "Go back and take a shave," he says. "You look like a bum."* (N.Y. 1953.) — *A minister looking for a book in the rectory library notices that the young maid up on the library ladder is not wearing pants. He gives her two dollars to go and buy some. She tells another maid who immediately takes her pants off and climbs up on the ladder where the minister can see. He glances up and says, "Here, my child, here's a quarter. Go out and get yourself a shave."* (2:63 French version in *Histoires de Curés,* 1926, p. 160.) Compare "Lucy's and Kitty's Black Jocks," a British *conte-en-vers* on pubic shaving, noted in *The Horn Book,* p. 187–8, as translated from Jacques Vergier (1720), who in turn was imitating an anecdote in Béroalde de Verville's *Moyen de Parvenir* (*c.* 1610), end of chap. 42, "Diette." In all these the shaving of the woman's pubis is left neurotically incomplete, as though the man doing the shaving — or inventing the story — were overwhelmed by guilt and unable to finish the sub-castratory act.

What is so curious about this theme of shaving as an insult to the woman is that the tellers of these stories find it uncomfortably meaningless, as shown by the rationalizations about Lesbianism and fur coats, and the open symbolism of the coital ladder and the two-dollar fee in the last. It is clear, nevertheless, that it is not meaningless at all, and that the presumable pleasure in the stories involving this theme is the unspoken threat or curse of the "Blast you!" or "You be buggered!" type. In the chapter on Homosexuality, in the Second Series, the threat of pedicatory rape will be noted more at length as the ultimate insult to a man under patriarchy. In the same way this 'suggestion' of castration to the woman, this reminding her of the neurotically imagined 'unwelcome fact of the woman's castrated condition,' is the ultimate insult to a woman that men seem able to conceive.

7

PREMARITAL
SEXUAL ACTS

RELATIVELY few actors are introduced into jokes. Most of these are visibly stock characters rather than real people: men, women — husbands, lovers, wives, and prostitutes — parents and children, doctors, policemen, animals, fools. The jokes now concern their first formally recognized sexual acts: the experimentations and engagements of the premarital period of courting. Questions of interpretation, symbolism, and so forth will be touched upon far more briefly and arbitrarily in this second part of the present study. The reader who has not agreed to the viewpoint taken in the first part will not agree to it in the second part, and further argument and demonstrations would be idle. On the other hand, the running history of the War Between the Sexes that has served as theme for the introductory texts to the chapters and sections will be continued, though with somewhat less concentration, where relevant; as for instance in discussing the mother-in-law, castration, and other subjects of similar historical and psychological importance.

I. PETTING

Petting is the standard euphemism, in modern American English, for all sexual acts short of intercourse with the exception of kissing, which in the modern jargon of courtship is 'necking.' Jokes on kissing have seldom been encountered. That is to say, though hundreds of jokes on kissing have been culled, and can be culled at any time, from popular magazines, none of them accept kissing as a frankly pre-sexual act, nor discuss it in that context. Instead, 'kissing' is used as the euphemism for genital intercourse, and, as Freud remarks in a passage quoted in full at the very end of the chapter later on Prostitution, kissing is also 'in the theatre . . . permitted as a refined indication of the sexual act.' This is standard in pictorial art as well. The most popular surviving bit of 19th-century kitsch painting (or imitation thereof) is one still used, I believe, in the advertisements of 'Tabu' perfume, showing a powerful male violinist, heavily hirsute, and with his violin clutched unplayed in his hand, imprinting a suction-pump kiss on the upturned mouth of his more-than-willing lady pianist, in a way doubtless inspired by Tolstoi's shocked remarks about the 'eroticism' of Beethoven's *Kreutzer Sonata* when played by a man and a woman.

That Beethoven's music — and everyone else's, as, most obviously, that of Vivaldi or Wagner — is *specifically* an erotic expression was, of course, no secret to the composers themselves, as Beethoven's own "Heiligenstadt letter" or secret will (1802) makes perfectly articulate. In the popular arts, kissing is now strictly a euphemism, and so understood by the public, in such substitutions for franker words in a popular phrase as when the movie-comedian Bob Hope — forced to tell the absolute truth on a bet — blurts out to the provocative Paulette Goddard, "*I'd like to* kiss *you till your ears fly off!*" This is the professional humorist's approach, recorded by Max Eastman in *The Enjoyment of Laughter* (1936), where the immediate and practical question about any sex-joke being hoked up for pop-culch presentation is: "*Can you do it with* kissing?"

Petting is the adaptation of masturbatory techniques to the sexual approach. It is almost unknown among the other mammals (except the apes), where its place is taken by oragenital caresses. The more experienced sexual partner expresses the initiative by an exploratory handling of the recessive partner's body, then the quasi-sexual parts such as the breasts and buttocks, and finally the thighs and genitals, either through the clothing or bare. Shakespeare describes the activity of both sexes in the scene before the tavern after the death of Falstaff in *Henry V,* II.iii.25–40, beginning first with the dominant Hostess: 'So a' bade me lay more clothes on his feet: I put my hand into the bed and felt them, and they were as cold as any stone; then I felt to his knees, and they were as cold as any stone, and so upward and upward, and all was as cold as any stone.' (In Sir Laurence Olivier's motion-picture version, the Hostess pantomimes this in expurgated fashion, demonstrating with a man leaning his elbow on his knee, so that, at the final 'upward and upward,' she detours instead up his *arm.*) Falstaff too 'did in some sort . . . handle women.'

Inexperienced women and girls do not consider the handling of their breasts by men as more than a venial familiarity, and, in general, this is considered a proper preliminary to more 'serious' genital caresses. *A man slides his hand up a girl's leg in a bar. She slaps him.* "*No, you don't! Tits first.*" (From England, 1953. Obvious hatefulness and 'male protest,' under a formal pretext. Actually made into a limerick, N.Y. 1963, by a Two-Ton Tessie, who recited it as part of her sex-conquest spiel for the finding of masochist types.) As is not well known, but is worth recollecting, it was at one time — during the 16th and 17th centuries in Europe, and even later — a part of the perfectly formal kissing of women, publicly, with whom one was 'kissing kin,' to touch or press their breasts. This was especially done if the women were young and unmarried, in particular during the periods when the styles were (as they have now recently attempted to become again) for women to wear their breasts bare, or very much lifted and accentuated. Formal kissing no longer exists in the English-speaking countries, except among women. But anyone who has seen a young French girl line up for a whole string of two-cheek kisses, from a group of male or female school-friends, on arriving at or departing from a bus-stop or café, will realize that the formal kiss is far from dead. (The formal kiss in France is only upon the *cheeks:* the kiss on the mouth is reserved for husband or lover, and to kiss an unmarried woman on the mouth, publicly, in France, still announces that one is her lover, and is wholly unacceptable from anyone else.) I have also seen an enterprising young Frenchman, during the formality of the kiss-on-the-cheeks, charmingly recall the ancient liberty of the breasts by touching the girl's breasts alternately with his *elbows,* while kissing her alternate cheeks. *I.e.*, no hands! The girl laughed, and flipped out his tie. To a symbolic touch, a symbolic response. *A bon chat, bon rat.* No one was shocked.

Even Dean Swift, whom no one could accuse of partiality to women, allows the woman whose breasts have been pressed to escape from the sadistic trial of virginity by the lions with only the clawing of her breasts, explaining that 'Methought the whole company immediately understood the meaning of this; that the easiness of the lady had suffered her to admit certain imprudent and dangerous familiarities, bordering too much upon what is criminal.' (*The Tatler,* No. 5, 1710; omitted from the volumes of *The Tatler* published by Richard Steele, but included in Swift's *Works,* 1775, XI. 50.) Swift does not explain why the lion first 'scratched both her hands with lifting them to his nose,' but the jokes, as will be seen, indicate clearly that the masturbatory activities were mutual.

The favored locale for the mutual masturbation of the unmarried is the darkened theatre, and this is particularly suited to lowering the resistance of the woman or girl, since she knows that in so public a place the man cannot proceed to intercourse however excited he becomes. Parkbench, porch-swing, and sometimes even automobile petting is similarly done, at the girl's specific request and demand, under street lights rather than in some darker place, and what may seem to passers-by the exhibition of sexual intimacy is really, from the girl's point of view, the insuring and exhibition of her proved sexual restraint. *He: "It's so dark I can't see my hand in front of my face." She: "Don't worry. I know where it is."* (N.Y. 1944. In Elgart, 1951, p. 154.) Also presented on the formula of the 'Little Audrey,' or female-fool joke. (Little Audrey always 'laughs and laughs.') *When her boyfriend said that it was so dark he couldn't see his hand in front of his face, Little Audrey laughed and laughed, because she knew his hand* wasn't *in front of his face. — He: "Darling, I'm groping for words." She: "You won't find them there."* (N.Y. 1940. Also printed in the college-humor magazines.) Observe in both this and the preceding that the essence is the girl's mocking control.

The man's revenge indicates how manually centered, rather than coitally, the whole petting situation is: *He: "Cigarette?" She: "No, thank you. I don't smoke." "Cocktail?" "I never touch liquor." "Well, what about a stroll down Lovers' Lane?" "Please don't. What I want to do is something new, thrilling, exciting!" "O.K. Let's go over to the dairy building, and milk hell out of a couple of cows."* (N.Y. 1942.) This also has been printed in numerous college humor magazines, as the apparently 'nonsensical' punch-line sufficiently hides the obvious allusion to all the quasi-sexual elements in the milking of the cow: the handling of the mammary organs, the spirting of the milky fluid, and the *satisfaction* achieved. It also involves the identification of woman and cow, as is standard. Compare the touching comedy of married sex life, expressed in another highly popular college-humor joke on the same cow-equals-woman identification: *A farmer is milking his cow very clumsily by the light of a kerosene lamp early one winter morning. "Ouch!" says the cow; "you hurt me." "I'm sorry,"* the farmer apologizes; *"I don't know what I'm doing. I'm so tired, getting up early in the morning this way." "You* look *tired," says the cow sympathetically. "I'll tell you what I'll do. You just hang onto my teats, and I'll jump up and down."* (Printed, with phrasing, *'You just hang on,'* since the 1940's. Text: La Jolla, Calif. 1965, from the campus gay-divorcée, told at a party while simultaneously dancing the Twist, with a machine-like action and an endless *smile.*)

The woman's sexual handling of the man, as Dean Swift's reticence about the lion has shown, is thought of as far more indelicate than the man's handling of the woman, evidently because of the 'shamelessness' (*i.e.* dominance) of her taking the lead. Even Prof. Kinsey cannot quite bring himself, in his volumes on sex behavior, to use the phrase 'mutual masturbation,' but refers instead to 'petting to climax.' A curious convention is that the girl *laughs* while petting, her nervous anxiety or excitement being converted into laughter. *A young man and girl are petting in the movies. The girl keeps squealing with laughter. Manager: "What's the matter, young lady, are you feeling hysterical?" "No, he's feeling mine."* (Idaho, 1946.) Simply as a pun: *Girl, to the boy who is petting her: "Oh, I feel so silly." Boy: "Well reach in here and you'll feel nuts."* (N.J. 1942.) This has also been built up into a whole string of puns: *It's a crazy world. Turn the women upside down — they're all cracked. Turn the men upside down — they're all nuts. Turn them both upside down — they're screwy.* (N.Y. 1952.) An interesting reversal of sexes has taken place in the following: *A lady loses her glove in a bar. She sends her dog for it, and the dog comes back with the bartender's testicles.* (N.Y. 1953) Aside from the ugly and unexpected intrusion of the castration theme, compare the original, as seen in a cartoon strip by 'Caran d'Ache,' in one of the French humor magazines of the 1890's: *A hunter forgets his glove at home, and sends his dog for it. The dog comes back with the chambermaid's drawers.*

The fact of orgasm and the disposition of the semen cannot be overlooked in the jokes, because this is the focal point of much of the uneasiness about masturbation in general. The semen is thought of, somehow, as guilty evidence and to be gotten rid of. The forthright childish expedient, noted in an earlier chapter, of swallowing it and 'giving it another chance,' actually represents an attempt to destroy the evidence, and the efforts of many young men to engage in self-fellation by either bending forward or throwing the legs backward over the head during masturbation is not necessarily to be construed as a homosexual urge — certainly not as an attempt to attain some special extreme of pleasure — but rather as a narcissistic impulse of bodily re-absorption, with the emphasis clearly on avoiding the guilty 'loss.' Another aspect of auto-fellation is, of course, that the man is *supplying* the missing vagina in the form of his own mouth.

A modification of mutual orgasm to mere mutual urination: *A young couple at an exciting movie. "Suddenly they found they had pissed in each other's hand."* (2:340.) It is almost unnecessary to discuss the much greater possibilities of privacy and erotic use of moving pictures in automobiles (drive-in theatres) and homes (television), but the fare offered — which is almost solely gangster and horror movies at late hours, with the sexual material converted into violence when the cowboys wrestle lovingly with one another in leather clothing, and men gangsters slap each other (even, once in a while, a woman) across the face with guns by way of euphemized intercourse — facilitates only the most destructive possible identification of sexual intimacy as a sadistic act.

Young couple petting. Boy: "What does your father do for a living?" Girl: "He's a bill-poster." "Well here comes some paste for him." (2:341.) This is not so much a joke as a folk-phrase, which is also used of women in connection with the superstition — once almost universally believed at the folk level — that women emit a special fluid at orgasm similar to the semen in men. (See a letter on this point, in *Playboy,* Nov. 1967, p. 69, concerning a *husband* still believing this.) These fluids are identified as the essence of sexual intercourse, as for instance at law, with its concentration on questions of intromission and ejaculation in connection with marriage, adultery and rape, and it is probably this identification that makes the belief in the female ejaculation so widespread. A joke of the nasty-nasty type expressing the integral identification of semen and intercourse has been collected too often to omit: *A man and woman are petting in the balcony of a theatre (or in the grandstand at a football game). The man ejaculates in the woman's hand and she flings the semen in the direction of the orchestra pit. It lands on the bald head of the drummer, who wipes it off grimly and says to the oboist: "Say, do I look like a cunt?" "Why d'you ask that?" "Some son-of-a-bitch just threw a fuck in my face!"* (Idaho, 1946.) In one collection session, this was encountered as a sadistically drawn-out 'drunk' story, with the drunken drummer pantomiming his accident and horror, and repeating his question three or four times, with the specific intention of making the listeners feel queasy.

The whole subject of disgust in connection with the dirty joke will be treated at length in the section "Food Dirtying," in Series Two: 12.IV.2. The element of predominant interest here is that the sensation of disgust, aroused in adults (but not in children) by 'messy' substances of damp or shapeless form, thought to resemble bodily excrements of any kind, begins *only* at the instant these substances or secretions are parted from the body. Blood is the symbol of strength, life, and kinship — while it is in the veins. When spilled, it can make strong men weak to see it. In the same way, such essentially neutral substances as the naso-oral mucus or half-digested food are carried about *within* the body with no sensation of self-disgust, but become objects almost of terror when separated from the body. This point has been excellently made, though almost identifying food and feces, by Dr. Alan Dundes, in his *"Here I Sit — A Study of American Latrinalia"* (1966).

The rejection of the body which is so strong a feature of the puritan ethic, and which, with the passing of puritanism, has been continued under hygienic disguise as the fetish of 'cleanliness,' has been discussed in the last section of the preceding chapter in connection with the substitution of artificial odors (perfume) for the genital odor which is basic to sexual attraction in mammals. The natural odors of the body are advertised as dirty — the very term 'body odor' being considered so awful that even one's best friend will not pronounce it — and the artificial odors replacing them are frankly advertised as swooningly attractive sexually. The whole fabric of pretense here is very easily torn. When, for instance, the Victorian repression began to break down in the 1880's, one of the clichés of the sensational novels and melodramas was the seduction of the unsuspecting heroine by the flicking under her nose of a handkerchief, which the villain had secretly drawn through his armpit. The displacement upward of genital odor (in this case that of the male) to the armpit odor, as an aphrodisiac, is not even disguised.

Jokes about the vaginal odor, and contact with it during petting, are almost entirely lacking in the rejection usually accorded to the female genitals, and this has been noted already as a feature of jokes about the pubic hair as well. The inevitable folklore comparison of the vaginal odor with that of fish, while it partakes of the form of a slur or insult — and is so apprehended by women — is obscurely connected with the idea of fish as an aphrodisiac, and with the whole complex of mother-goddess survivals surrounding Friday as both fish-day and Venus-day, already discussed. In an anecdote given in *The Pearl,* No. 2 (August 1879), the similar odor of cheese — also, at another level, an insulting reference to the vaginal or preputial smegma — is specifically stated to be sexually exciting to the man, when a ripe cheese is found in a dark warehouse, by selecting by odor the one that gives the cheesemonger *an erection.* (Also in French 19th-century sources.) In the same way, nothing could be more unequivocal than the limerick, given in the same issue of *The Pearl* and still widely current, of the '*young curate of Eltham*': *In lanes he would linger, And play at stink-finger, And* SCREAM *with delight when he smelt 'em!*' (*The Limerick,* No. 545, from Michigan, 1935.)

The vaginal secretion and odor is even stated in one case to be identical to that thrown by other female mammals in a state of heat or sexual readiness. *A man and woman in conversation on a train observe a bull mounting a cow in a field. "How does he know she wants it?" the woman asks, and the man learnedly explains that it is all done by the sense of smell, that during a certain period of the year, etc. etc., not observing that the sight has excited the woman. On parting at their station she says, "So long, Doctor, come up and see me some time when you haven't got that cold in your head."* (2:354. Also, more flatly, "Come up and smell me some time." D.C. 1944.)

As the older of the two forms of the joke now to be given is more natural and intelligible in its action, it appears that the reference to fish has been added, as a slur, in the later version. *A young man and his girl are petting in a railroad coach in which the only other passenger is apparently blind. "Now you stop," the girl whispers, "that man across the aisle is watching us." The young man reaches across the aisle and, passing his hand in front of the other man's face, says, "Can you see, old man?" The old man sniffs a few times and then replies energetically, "No, I'm blind, but lead me to it!"* (Memorabilia, 1910. Compare: *Blind beggar, passing a fishmarket: "Hello, girls, how's business?"* — Idaho, 1932.) The bare statement of the idea, but intermediate to the later version: *A young man and his girl are petting in a railroad coach in which the only other person is the conductor, dozing nearby. The girl tells the man to stop — that the conductor may be awake. To prove he is asleep, the man holds his finger under the conductor's nose. The conductor stirs in his sleep and mutters, "Gloucester!"* (D.C. 1943.)

A later section, in the chapter on Marriage, will be devoted to the attempted demonstration that this 'man in the upper berth,' so commonly encountered on the honeymoon train, is really the father of the bride, reduced to a disembodied comedy voice. His representation here in the castrated or impuissant forms of being blind and asleep seems highly corroborative. In at least one case he is taunted in this way, *in propria persona,* with the handling of his daughter's genitals. *A young man is refused by his girl's father when asking permission to marry her. He grabs him by the nose and tweaks it (or attempts to punch him in the nose and misses).* "Hmm," *says the father, sniffing,* "you'll have *to marry her. Sit down.*" (1:334.) In the form in which the father-figure in this situation is most distant from actual father status, he is nevertheless accorded the magical omniscience and authority of the expert or demi-god: *An expert on odors is demonstrating his ability in a blindfold test at a party. He identifies pine, hickory, and other types of wood merely by sniffing them. One of the guests, who has profited by everyone else's absorption in the problem to make love to one of the women, holds his middle finger under the expert's nose.* "Hollywood," *says the expert.* (1:24.) An openly Oedipal French version of the mid-19th century has: *A cheese-merchant is testing his son's knowledge of cheeses, blindfolded, by smell. Despairing of finding a cheese the son cannot recognize, the father puts his finger into the vagina of the housemaid, who is holding the candle for them in the cellar, and challenges the son,* "And what's *this one?*" "That one is the maid!" This is clearly connected with the cheesemonger story given earlier from *The Pearl* (August 1879).

Occasionally the joke tends toward an expressed aversion to the vaginal secretion or odor. *A young man and his girl are running for the last streetcar home from the entertainment park.* "Put your fingers in your mouth and whistle to the motorman," *the girl urges.* "Not on your life," *says the young man,* "I'd rather walk." (McAtee, 1913, env. 7, a versified form titled "Finical," with the end-line, obviously inverted for the rhyme: "But put my fingers in my mouth I wouldn't for ten dollars." A form similar to the text given above is printed in *Waggish Tales,* 1947, p. 199.) *A man whose wife is angry at him and will not have intercourse with him ("the doghouse"), is advised by a friend to buy her a fur coat to get back into her good graces.* "Get her a mink coat." "She's got one of those." "Then get her a sable." "She's got one of those." "Well then, get her a Himalayan civet." "What's that?" "It's a pussy with a terrible smell." "Oh, she's got one of those!"

(N.Y. 1940.) The whole ambivalence regarding the vaginal odor is well summed up in a joke similar to the frame-situation "No Money," discussed in the chapter on Prostitution, in the Second Series. *A young man begs his fiancée to have intercourse with him, but she refuses, saying they must wait till the wedding. "Well then at least can I smell it like a dog?" he begs in desperation. That she allows him, and holds up her skirt. He takes one long whiff, and moans, "Oh honey, are you sure it'll keep?"* (N.Y. 1936.) A variant is printed in *Waggish Tales*, 1947, p. 152, in which the odor is stated to be that of the woman breaking wind. This seems to combine the Abu Hassan motif, of wind-breaking at the wedding, which is traced at the end of the chapter on Fools, and that of *The Lady and the Flea* ("All litee lady, no can catchee, shootee"), discussed in the chapter on Scatology, which is the only dirty joke on which a whole book of historical tracings — all, unfortunately, bogus — has yet been published. *The Lady and the Flea,* about 1900. (Copy: Harvard.)

II. THE PERMISSIVE FATHER

The irate father, incestuously interested in his daughter himself, who kicks downstairs with shouts of "Young puppy!" all applicants for his daughter's hand, is almost completely missing in dirty jokes. One example each has been found of *a*) the irate solution — given just above — and *b*) the actual situation implied by the 'irate father' cliché, in which the father finds the young man in intercourse with his daughter: *"Where'd you get the black eye?" "I was over at my girl's house, and we were dancing with the phonograph playing when her old man came in, and the bastard is deaf."* (1:456.) To the contrary, the father — that is to say, the *girl's* father — is depicted as ultra-permissive to the point of assisting in his daughter's seduction or abduction (by 'holding the ladder' symbolically), and any standing on his parental rights or duties of warding off the younger men makes him an immediate butt of ridicule. As fathers certainly have not been in the past, and still are not to any important degree, quite as permissive as the jokes suggest, one must assume that these represent the paradisiacal ideal, where when: *The father says, "Young man, are your intentions toward my daughter honorable or dishonorable?" The young man says, "You mean I got a choice?"* (1930's. Now frequent in public print.)

The unreal and conniving tone of the ultra-permissive father joke makes it convenient to cast the father as a fool or foreigner from whom such folly is easier to expect. *Farmer's daughter: "Daddy, the hired man broke my maidenhead." "Clumsy booger. Only last week he busted a spade."* (N.Y. 1939.) A connected joke, often collected with the preceding: *First Farmer: "That hired man of yours is a bad one! Look at his name pissed in the snow." Second Farmer: "Yup. And it's in my daughter's handwriting."* (N.Y. 1939.) The mainspring of this farmer's moral lassitude is precisely the same as that pointed out long ago by Freud as to Hamlet, who cannot revenge his father's murder because he identifies too strongly with the uncle who has killed his father and who is living in 'incestuous' intercourse with his mother.

In *Wit and Its Relation to the Unconscious* (1905), Freud gives as the main example in chapter 2, in the section on "Nonsense as a Technical Means," another lackadaisical guardian of a young girl's virginity, in this case a mere surrogate of the father — as though that would explain his permissiveness and calm. Freud is concerned in this passage with the psychodynamics of the joke and not of the participants, and is illustrating the use of nonsense in wit to indicate and deride some opposing bit of nonsense. *'A man about to go upon a journey intrusted his daughter to his friend, begging him to watch over her chastity during his absence. When he returned some months later, he found that she was pregnant. Naturally, he reproached his friend. The latter alleged that he could not explain this unfortunate occurrence. "Where has she been sleeping?" the father finally asked. "In the same room with my son," replied the friend. "How is it that you allowed her to sleep in the same room with your son after I had begged you so earnestly to take good care of her?" remonstrated the father. "Well," explained the friend, "there was a screen between them. There was your daughter's bed, and over there was my son's bed, and between them stood the screen." "And suppose he went behind the screen? What then?" asked the parent. "Well, in that case," rejoined the friend thoughtfully, "it might be possible".'* (Brill translation.)

The complete identification with the young man is even more evident in the 'foreigner' jokes of this type, which are for some reason — probably the money element — usually told as of Jews. *The businessman is berating his bookkeeper: "Last year you forged my name to checks, this year you gave away my business secrets, and now I hear you've been screwing my daughter. The next least little thing you do — out you go!"* (1:473.) This has also been collected, Calif. 1952, as of a consecutive rape of the daughter, wife, mother, and grandmother; with the father calmly drinking coffee meanwhile, and finally saying mildly: *"Some day you're going to go too far!"* That the 'too far' here really refers to the implied ultimate indignity of pedicatory rape of the father, will be noted in connection with a variant in which this occurs, in the chapter on Homosexuality, in Series Two.

One man is complaining to another about the second man's son. "Now look, I don't throw it up to you that he laid my daughter on the sofa; but what gets me is why did the son-of-a-bitch have to wipe his prick on my plush portieres?" (1:52.) A 'cleanup' of this appeared in several of the humor magazines in 1942, in which the sex element is revised into respectability by having one drunk *merely* vomit into another drunk's top hat. The importation of the complaints about money, property, and so forth can finally be understood only as an attempt to give some reason, however recalcitrant, for making any complaint at all. *Two rich manufacturers decide to treat their workers by inviting them out to their palatial estates for the weekend. One phones the other Monday morning almost in tears. "Some advice you gave me!" he shouts. "Chewing gum in my venetian blinds! Cundrums they threw into the chandeliers! Pages out of the expensive books they tore to wipe their ass on!" "You're talking?" says the other. "Forty acres I got, prime golden wheat? — FUCKED FLAT!"* (N.Y. 1940, told by the editor of *Anecdota Americana I.*)

In the end, the concentration on money and property makes the father a pimp, but this is only the case where the family is poor. Where the rich do it, as above, it is charity. The following story is given later, in a much less 'permissive' version collected by Vance Randolph: *A young man stays overnight at a farmer's house, and, unbeknownst to the farmer, as he thinks, makes love to the farmer's wife and daughter. In the morning he asks as nonchalantly as he can, "How much do I owe you?" "Wa-al, lemme see, stranger," says the farmer. "Fust there's the keep o' your horse in my stable, his fodder, and your supper. Then you had a bed for the night; you screwed my wife and daughter, and then there's the breakfast this morning. D'you think seventy-five cents would be too much? I want to be fair, y'understand."* (*Waggish Tales,* 1947, p. 117, dropping the tiresome fake-Czech accent to give the price in American money.) — *A travelling salesman is put up for the night by a farmer who warns him that if he has anything to do with his daughter it will cost him five dollars. The salesman gives the girl a quarter to say that he did not touch her, and attempts to bluster it out in the morning. The farmer reaches for a shotgun and says, "Any more nonsense out of you, and you'll marry the girl." He kicks back the mattress of the daughter's bed and points to a pan of butter with an apple hanging into it from the bedspring on a string. "See that butter?" says the farmer. "Last night it was cream."* (N.J. 1926. Text form, Minn. 1946.)

Somehow, under the excuse of money, the forbidding father is returning. In a complicated little pantomime based on bringing the forbidding situation to nothing, *A diagram is drawn consisting of a square with the four corners boxed off and marked F., D., B., and T. The teller announces that this is the floor-plan of a house and that the letters stand for Father, Daughter, Boyfriend, and Toilet. The boyfriend is being put up overnight, and naturally tries to sneak into the daughter's room. (His path is drawn on the diagram with a pencil.) But the father sticks his head out of his room in the corner, and the boy pretends to be going to the toilet instead. (New path is drawn.) Then the daughter tries, etc. etc. Finally the boy is getting desperate. (The paper is folded in four with great exactness, then torn carefully once, twice, and finally gaily into bits.) "So do you know what he did?" Victim: "No, what?" "Here, shake these pieces up." (Victim shakes them.) "That's what he did."* (N.Y. 1942. Sometimes the listener's pencil-point is broken as the punch-line. Appears to be a decayed version of Chaucer's "Reeve's Tale" and Boccaccio's IX.6, "Stumbling at the Cradle." See Aarne Types 1363-&-1544, with further references at Thompson/Rotunda K1345.)

The catch and the ridicule are obvious enough. The teller is projecting on the victim the frustration, and ego-blow of masturbation, that would otherwise have to be absorbed in the first person. In a far older catch, the victim is the father. *A young man on a train refuses the offer of a newspaper, of a cigar, and of a drink, saying, "I don't read. I don't smoke. I don't drink." Very impressed, a clergyman says, "Young man, I admire your principles. I'd like to have you meet my wife and daughter back in the next car." "I don't fuck."* (*The Pearl*, No. 18, Dec. 1880. Also *Anecdota*, 2:387.)

In the oldest mocking of the father so far collected, the strange self-castratory lengths to which the last joke goes are reversed in what is obviously an expression of the real intention. It is not that the son (disguised as the boyfriend) *refrains* from sexual intercourse; it is that he does it better than the father. *A young man is staying at his fiancée's home and her parents become worried because there is never any urine* in his chamberpot in the morning. "Go ahead, ask him," says the father to the mother, "maybe he's got some disease." The mother asks, and the boy explains that he loves the daughter so much that he goes to bed every night with an erection and has to urinate up the chimney. "Well," says the father, when the mother returns, "has he got a disease?" "Such a disease you should have!" (1:127, also Waggish Tales, p. 163, both modernizing the action by having the young man running to the bathroom constantly to put cold compresses on his erection.) The original form is told, in verse, entitled "Up the Chimney," as of 'Captain Jones of Halifax,' in The Pearl, No. 3 (Sept. 1879), ending simply with the Captain's explanation: "I feel so stiff and hot, That really I'm obliged to piss, Right up the Chimney Pot." The hateful punch-line colloquy of the husband and wife, which has become, since 1879, the presumable point of the story, is not altogether new. Poggio (1451) No. 73, gives a prototype story in which: A father and son see a young man lying drunk in the road with an erection [compare Gogol's Taras Bulba, transl. Magarshack, 1949, p. 170], and when the father points this out as a moral lesson on drunkenness, the son wonders where he can get some of that wine. The similar anecdote on Abraham Lincoln and General Grant's drunkenness (with Grant's military prowess substituted for the erection) is very well known.

The point has been touched on parenthetically, but should perhaps be made more specific, that the conflict between the young girl's father and her inevitable boyfriend is really a disguised representation of the combat between the father and his own son over the sexually desirable women of the family — both mother and daughters. One of the demonstrations of this is the group of permissive-father jokes in which the relationship, as father and son, is directly stated. A young boy who is tending cows for his father tries to seduce the neighboring farmer's little girl. "Just lemme put in an inch," he says, "and you can have old Bessie." She agrees. "One more inch and you can have old Fannie. One more and you can have old Jinnie. Oh cripes," he finally shouts, "let me shove it all in, and you can have the whole damned herd!" His father, who is hiding in the tall weeds, cries out: "Poke it to her, Johnnie! I'll help you drive the cows home." (Idaho, 1919, noting that the father's 'own gun is ready to go off.') I do not think it is pressing too hard on the identification of the cow as the mother to point out that it is she — overdetermined with three feminine names — who is really being shared, and not the 'little girl.' This is of course precisely the unconscious fantasy situation in brother-sister incest. The joke is almost identical with *Russian Secret Tales*, No. 33, "The Excitable Lady," but the even-more-excitable father's shouting frightens her away. Note also the "Johnnie Fuckerfaster" story already given under "Permissiveness," 1.VII, page 106 above.

In two other examples the father and son are again brought into parallel sexual situations, in a forthright brother-husband relationship when the girl is outside the family, and in a slightly more disguised form when sharing the mother. *A father and son are in partnership. The son seems worried and the father asks him why, reminding him that they must share their responsibilities.* "Well, Dad, since you put it that way, the stenographer is knocked up and she wants us to marry her." (1:168, with a nonsense-variant on 'female fatherhood,' in which a husband tells his wife, "*It seems the Swedish housegirl is in trouble, and she blames us.*" — 1:167.) Compare also *The partners* — this time unrelated — *one of whom telegraphs to the other about their stenographer:* "*Gertie gave birth to twins. Mine died.*" (1:286.) Here the relationship as brother-husbands is undisguised. An extraordinary passage will later be quoted in full, under "Possession in Common," 9.III.1, *ad fin.,* from Diderot's *Les Bijoux indiscrets* (1748) chap. 47, where it appears in English in the original, indicating the heavily homosexual tone of such relationships, similar to the '*skidding in on some other guy's scum*' during a gang-shag. Brother-husband relationships are extremely common at the present day, especially with unmarried girls who 'date' many men — sometimes even 'late-dating' one favored man after another on the same evening, though here the first man (the chump or sucker) seldom gets laid, and is used merely as a meal-ticket or for expensive entertainment. The mental adjustments by means of which modern men deny the polyandrous tone of such situations did not seem to be bothered with in the more cynical 18th century. Here is the obvious original of all the preceding jokes in this paragraph, from that almost-legendary source of old chestnuts, John Mottley's *Joe Miller's Jests* (1739) No. 119:

A Gentlewoman growing big with Child, who had two Gallants, one of them with a wooden Leg, the Question was put, which of the two should father the Child. He who had the wooden Leg offer'd to decide it thus. *If the Child,* said he, *comes into the World with a wooden Leg, I will father it; if not, it must be your's.*

There is more than an allusion hidden here to the primitive idea of superfetation: that, in the birth of twins etc., more than one man can be the father of the several children. Modern forms concentrate on the verbal jest. *A son who is trying to get up the nerve to pop the question to his girl, asks his father: "Dad, what did you say to Mother when you proposed?" "All I said was, 'The hell you say!' We were married the next day."* (Minn. 1946.) Very quick 'quickie' version in *Sex to Sexty* (1966) 8:41. '*Teenage proposal: "You're* WHAT?"'

If the permissive relationship with the actual son is unequivocal in these cases, that with the daughter is almost equally unequivocal in all cases. The father is presumed to identify gratefully and incestuously in the sexual relationship of the younger man with his daughter. This is hardly the way things really are, but it is evidently the way jokes wish they were. At a deeper level, this sharing of the woman by the brother-husbands involves a homosexual tone that becomes very prominent when one is aware of it — as in the central section of the chapter on Adultery: "The Relationship with the Other Man," 9.II.6 — but which should not be allowed to outweigh the consideration of Hamlet-like *incestuou*s identification, rather than homosexual, with the other man. The folk-phrase, already noted, "I wouldn't fuck her with your prick," should perhaps be revised to read, "I would." In at least one joke, the same situation of the 'cold marble floor' is encountered in both a per-missive-father and a homosexual setting, transmogrified in the latter to the 'hot desert sand.' *A Southern colonel finds his daughter in intercourse with the Yankee guest in the wine-cellar. "Daughter, wheah' is yo' South'n hospitality? Arch yo' back, honey-chile, and get that gentleman's balls off that cold mahble floor!"* (2:206, a version with the pair caught in the bushes. Text form, Calif. 1943. The 'hot desert sand' version will be found in 9.II.6, "Conniving at Adultery.") The closest approach to father-daughter incest *without* the use of guests, boy-friends, and other stalking-horses, does not manage to get past the verbal level: *A man playing golf with his wife and daughter misses an easy putt and says, "Oh, fuck!" The wife expostulates, "You ought not to talk that way in front of the child!" "Child?" He looks at the girl appraisingly. She is eighteen, pretty, and well-formed. "It seems to me you must have heard that word before," he says to her, gruffly. "Certainly, father, but never in anger."* (2:380.) Definitely a come-on, and leaving the mother and her moral shock just as definitely out.

III. POLICEMEN AND PRIESTS

What has become of the forbidding father? His functions have been separated from him and handed over to two surrogates: the policeman and priest. Historically this has certainly happened before, and a case could easily be made out for the policeman and priest never having had any other function than to protect the prerogatives of the patriarch and his successors. Aside from these, an important segment of the sexual control over the daughter remains, in jokes and in all folklore, in the hands of the mother, and this will be discussed more fully in the opening section on "The Mother-in-Law" in the following chapter.

Although certain of the states, such as Massachusetts, do actually descend to the legalistic bathos of stating that certain physical positions for the achieving of intra-vaginal coitus are, nevertheless, sodomy and therefore punishable as a crime; sexual intercourse even between unmarried persons is generally not held to be more than a misdemeanor, and — except for purposes of framing political opponents — will usually require the aggravating circumstance of public performance to lead to an arrest. (The possibility of spite-indictments on the grounds of fornication, adultery, the Mann Act, and the 'statutory rape' of young women twelve hours below the legal age of consent is a whole subject in itself.) Intercourse in parks, or in parked automobiles, creates the logical milieu for the forbidding father to do his work in the blue uniform of the policeman. *A young couple enter a police station carrying the back seat of a car. They explain that the car stalled and they got out to push, and somebody stole the car.* (*Anecdota,* 1933, p. 69. Punch-line, only, in *American Mercury,* Sept. 1939, p. 29.) Merely a pun, and with the only sin, in any case, that of the thief. This has been reworked in such a way as to turn the accusation against the lovers: *A young couple are having intercourse under their car. The next thing they know they are being arrested for obstructing traffic*[!] *"But Officer, no one can see us. We're under a car." "You mean you were. You were there so long the finance company couldn't wait, and towed away the car."* (Minn. 1946.) Moral and financial iniquity both.

The policeman is given the sop of delivering the punch-line on the understanding that he will let the young couple go. *"Whaddya doin' there?" "Just necking, Officer." "Well, put your neck back in your pants and get outa here."* (N.Y. 1941.) He may even be offered — by the jokesmith (as in *Sex to Sexty,* 1966, 8:34, cartoon) — a share in the girl: *A policeman flashes his light into the bushes on a man and girl. "Whaddya doin' in there?" Man: "Nothing." Policeman: "Then come on out here and hold this flashlight."* (N.Y. 1943.) This has been printed several times in the college-humor magazines, as has a related joke on the cab-driver, a standard voyeuristic partaker in the sexual life of the unmarried, now almost completely overlooked in jokes. *Cab-driver: "I take the next turn, don't I?" Man's voice from the back seat: "The hell you do!"* (With all of these compare *Les Cent Nouvelles Nouvelles,* 1460, No. 46, and later Italian versions cited by Rotunda, K1271.1.4.3, "Sharing the Intrigue.")

Where the policeman does not temper his justice with mercy, the even more supernal father-figure of the judge can be expected to return to permissiveness. *A policeman stumbles on a young couple making love in a graveyard, and takes them to court. The judge asks the boy what they were doing in a graveyard at midnight. "Nothing wrong, your Honor. We were just burying the old stiff." The judge turns to the girl. "And how about you?" "I was the undertaker." The judge turns angrily on the policeman. "You idiot, I fine you $25 for interfering with the burying of a* corpus delicti!*"* (Idaho, 1919.) That the judge's sympathetic identification with the young man is based on the older man's presumed impotence is intentionally evident in the joke, and other folk comparisons of impotence with death, and of the impotent penis with a corpse, will be found in the section on "Self-Castration" later, in Series Two: 13.v.

The roadhouse, rural hotel, tourist cabin, and — once, long ago — the inn, as another semi-public locale for intercourse, are also outfitted with father-figures vacillating between permissiveness and prohibition. *A couple registering at a rural hotel in Maine are asked to show their wedding license, and the man displays a fishing license to the near-sighted clerk. After they have gone upstairs the clerk examines the license more carefully, and rushes up after them shouting, "If you ain't done it, don't do it! This ain't the license fer it!"* (1:104, a variant with a travelling salesman pretending to marry the farmer's daughter with a dog license!) — *A young man registering late at night with his girl at a hotel is about to sign "John Smith and wife," when he notices about twenty John Smiths on the register already. "Go ahead," says the Negro porter, who is acting as clerk at that hour, "them is all fucktitious names too."* (2:410.) One sudden flash of animosity toward the forbidding father, showing what is really intended toward him: '*A man and wife out riding looked in vain for "The Old Log Inn" until they ran out of gas. The man got out and walked along the road until he came to a parked car in which an athletic young man was necking his girl. He stopped and asked, "How far is the Old Log Inn?" His wife found him later in the hospital.'* (Calif. 1941.)

Patriarchal religion, in the form seen in Judaism, Christianity, and Mohammedanism, is basically nothing other than a formalization, by means of a projection upon deities, and the demand for obedience to their revealed command, of the father's desired sexual control of his wives and of their female children, and the forcible exclusion of the male children from sexual activity. All three of these associated religions share in the surgical intimidation of the son by the father, just at the threshold of puberty, either in the psychological castration of circumcision at puberty (Mohammedanism), of this same operation effected at the earlier age of eight days (Judaism), or in a reminiscence of this operation — the 'blood'-sacrifice of baptism and the blood-eating of communion — in the last religion (Christianity).

As this subject has been discussed at some length in the earlier section, "The Diaper and the Scythe," nothing need be added here except to point out how this historical and social function of religion and the priest as the surrogate of the father's sexual privilege — both in the sense of upholding this privilege, and of reaping it on occasion — leads easily into the identification of the religious sexual prohibition and parental sexual prohibition ostensibly being kept separate.

Their separation is, in fact, made use of by folk materials, to ridicule the priest sexually in a way that could not be done in connection with the actual father. The humorous use of the theme of sexually sinning monk and nun has been completely standard in European folklore, certainly since the time of Boccaccio's *Decameron* in 1353, and in the *novella* literature of Italy for centuries later, at a time when Italy was in the last phase of its predominant period as both the cultural and religious center of the Western world. After the Reformation, no check or censorship was placed on the ridiculing of the Catholic clergy in Protestant countries, and if this ridicule moved on to other religious butts — such as the Puritan 'brethren and sistern' described in endless intercourse with each other, and even with horses and mares, in the Royalist drolleries of the English Civil War — this merely served to perpetuate the theme even where 'Papists' were lacking to serve as butt.

The very few jokes still to be encountered accusing the ministry of immorality, indicate by their small number — as has already been remarked concerning the jokes on nuns — the very great decay into which religion has fallen in the last half century. In the centuries when the gentry and clergy were at the height of their power, it was the gentry and clergy about whom the sexual accusations of the folktale were made to center. Even so late as the 1860's in Russia, the *papa* or 'little father' (priest) was the principal focus of sexual humor, as seen in the *Russian Secret Tales* collected by the folklorist Afanasyev, reprinted in English translation with introduction by myself (New York, 1968).

Every Sunday morning when the family was at church, Annie would be visited in bed by her lover Jock. One Sunday morning, when the coast is clear, he arrives gaily whistling "Annie Laurie." She gives him a disapproving look, and when he begins another tune she tears herself out of his arms and begins to get dressed, saying, "I'll nae fornicate wi' a mon who whustles on the Sabbath." (1:12.) This is probably the last, or one of the last, of the Puritan jokes, here driven into the Scottish provinces to seem reasonable. As already noted, a Levantine version exists, also sacrilegious, of *A man whistling in surprise when he sees another man masturbating in a mosque, and is berated by him for whistling!* (*Histoires Arabes*, pp. 23, 118.)

Also of this type is not actually a joke, but a scrap of verse with a story built up to explain it, the *cante-fable* about *A girl who is told she is being baptised (or forgiven at confession) by being laid down on a Bible, while her seducer chants:*

> *The Book of God's beneath you,*
> *The Man of God's above you.*
> *   Salvation pole*
> *   Is in your hole —*
> *Now wiggle your ass to save your soul!*

The Limerick (Paris, 1953) Note 573, gives this from an American printed source of 1928, and traces the theme of the use of the Bible in this way to Haddington's *Select Poems* (1730) No. 17, on a Scottish background, and "Off a Puritaine," in *Bishop Percy's Folio Manuscript* (about 1620; edited by Furnivall, 1867, "Loose and Humorous Songs," p. 35).

As the confessional has been the last formalization of sexual control to be transferred from the religious to the legal authority — even marriage is now more binding by the legal than by the religious ceremony alone — the confessional is the principal remaining theme of anti-religious humor. *An old woman confesses to sexual intercourse, and when the priest says, "I'm surprised at a woman of your age doing a thing like that!" she replies, "Oh, it was twenty years ago, Father, but I like to talk about it."* (Scranton, Pa. 1932. Noted also in John O'Hara's *Appointment in Samarra,* 1934.) — *A nun confesses to having been kissed by a man. "That's all right," says her confessor, "but don't let him get into your habit."* (N.Y. 1953, transmitted as one from the 'Coast.') — *A priest has a number of women confess that the grocer's new delivery boy has seduced them. He make them each put ten dollars in the poor box. The delivery boy appears last, and the priest asks angrily, "What have you got to say for yourself?" "Just this. Either you cut me in on those ten-dollar fees, or I take my business to some other parish."* (2:374.)

A more elaborate version of this has been one of the jokes most frequently encountered: *A Jewish rabbi is sitting in the confessional box with the priest to learn the principles of the Catholic religion* [!] *Two women confess to having had intercourse with their lovers, and, when questioned further, admit that it was not once but three times. As penance they are told to say three Paternosters and put ten dollars in the poor-box. Just then the phone rings and the priest is called away to give last unction to a dying man. He tells the rabbi, "You stay here and confess the rest of these people. It's Saturday night, and otherwise they won't be able to take Communion tomorrow. After all, it's all one God. Just be sure to get the ten dollars." He leaves, and the rabbi is left sitting nervously in the box. The first girl to enter confesses to having intercourse with her lover. "Three times?" says the rabbi. "Just once, Father." "You're sure it wasn't three times?" "No, Father, just once." "Well, I'll tell you what. You just say three Paternosters and put ten dollars in the poor-box, and the church will owe you two fucks."* (N.Y. 1940.) Also collected, less frequently, with the variant ending: *"Go back and do it twice more. We've got a special this week: three for ten dollars."* (D.C. 1949. In Carnoy's "Contes Picards," in *Kryptádia,* 1907, XI. 223, "Les deux pénitentes." Noted as collected in the U.S. by 1935, in my *The Horn Book,* p. 455–6, placing it on Thompson's system at J1823. Actually it is closer to J2082 or J2213.7.)

Aside from the money element, which is intended more as a libel on the Jew than on the Catholic — compare Heine's analogy of the Catholic and Protestant churches with wholesale and retail businesses, quoted at length in Freud's *Wit and Its Relation to the Unconscious,* end of chapter 2 . . . and apologized for at the beginning of chapter 3 — the main element satirized here is that *pressing* to further confessions, which has been focal in the attack on the confessional since the time of Jules Michelet in the 1840's, but which the church has never ceased to consider essential. (See the conspectus of the church's position, and bibliography of the manuals of confession, in Arthur Vermeersch, *De Castitate et de vitiis contrariis,* Rome, 1919, p. 409–13; and the extensive materials in English in *Centuria Librorum Absconditorum,* by 'Pisanus Fraxi' [Henry Spencer Ashbee], London, 1879, p. 15–300.) The same element is satirized even further in the following: *A girl is too shy to confess, so her confessor inquires by means of gestures. "Did he do this?" kissing her. "Yes, Father, and worse." "You mean he did this?" touching her breasts. "Yes, Father, and worse." Finally he has intercourse with her. "You mean that's what he did?" "Yes, Father, and worse too." "Well what worse could he do?" "He gave me the clap, Father."* (1:155.) The anterior history of this joke has already been traced in the Introduction here, section VII.

Before the disappearance of religion as an important theme of humor, the satirizing of the forbidding father-figure for any imputed sexual lapse from his own rules had extended to the logical end-point of satirizing God, in a joke told about Theodor Herzl, the founder of Zionism, who died in 1904. *Herzl's son, Hans, had been converted to Christianity, and God himself came down to earth to console him. "After all," said God, "didn't the same thing happen to My son two thousand years ago?" "Yes," replied Herzl, "but don't forget, my son was legitimate."* (*Anecdota,* 1933, No. 447.) This on the principle of *à bon chat bon rat:* only a man as great as Herzl is allowed to talk that way to God. I am told that this joke formerly circulated in Europe as a colloquy in Heaven between God and the philosopher Moses Mendelssohn, on the conversion to Christianity of his grandson Felix, the child-prodigy musician — on the model of the similar conversion of the Mozart family — but no printed source has been found for this tradition. The earliest European record of the joke is modern, in Raymond Geiger's *Histoires Juives* (1923) No. 27, where it is told without recourse to great names, of a Jew at the gate of heaven, worrying whether he will be allowed to enter.

IV. BIRTH CONTROL

The forbidding father is never represented as more ridiculous than when he attempts to force into marriage, with or without a shotgun, the young man who has made his daughter pregnant. The stage comedy, *Ruint,* by Hatcher Hughes (1925), is based entirely on the presumable humor of a family of Kentucky mountaineers out to shoot the la-de-da young man from the city by whom their daughter is thought to have been ruined. The mothers take the center of the stage, and all the men are typified as hopelessly remiss in their sexual duties of both vengeance and performance — the young man in particular, who has not even gotten beyond the first kiss before being tarred & feathered and ridden off the stage on a rail at the final curtain. The frontispiece of the printed text shows the daughter posing phallically with the shotgun herself, simultaneously preventing the young man from touching her, and revenging herself on him (in substitution for her father) for having done so. Compare Diana and Actæon, Venus and Adonis, and other closer and closer approaches to totally phallic female dominance in the telling of the same story. The musical-comedy and movie version of the life of the female sharpshooter, Annie Oakley, as *Annie Get Your Gun!* expresses all these elements in the *n*th degree, ending, as will be discussed more at length below, with an almost openly-symbolized castration of the phallic female — in order to make her, finally, become a woman and miss the target — by having the front sight of her golden rifle snipped off by a fatherly Indian with a pair of lever-action barbed-wire cutters!

In jokes, the woman's position is considered to be very much deteriorated, so far as status *vis-à-vis* the male is concerned, by pregnancy, and even more so if she is made pregnant ('got in trouble') without the man's 'doing the right thing' of marrying her. Among the various tough-guy folk recipes for handling women, of the type of: *"Find 'em, fuck 'em, and forget 'em — an' tell 'em* NOTHIN'!", the proper way of keeping a wife tamed and under control is to *"Keep her barefoot and pregnant."* (Backwoods, or fake-peasant approach.) The act of impregnation is clearly thought of as a sadistic harming of the woman by means of the penis-weapon — '*knocking her up*' — as a result of which, in another folk-phrase, she 'is poisoned' or '*falls to pieces.*' Many other folk-phrases also record this point of view, especially the adjective '*poisoned*' — meaning pregnant — noted as early as the *New Dictionary of the Canting Crew* by 'B.E., Gent.' [B. Edwards] in 1699, and as late as the anonymous erotic autobiography, *My Secret Life,* in 1888. The woman hardly appears in the jokes on pregnancy at all. The problem is strictly between the men in her life, beginning with her father.

A girl tells her father that her rich beau has made her pregnant. The father rushes to the man's address and threatens to kill him. "Now don't get excited," says the man. "I intend to do right by your daughter. If it's a boy I'll settle fifty thousand dollars on him. If it's a girl I'll settle thirty-five thousand on her. Is that fair?" "And if it's a miscarriage," says the father, *"will you give her another chance?"* (1:27.) Again the money or "Morgengabe" gives a saving tone of mere avarice to what would otherwise have to be considered ununderstandable laxity. The same situation taken from the opposite point of view: *A son tells his father, "Dad, I need ten thousand dollars. I knocked up a girl and I've got to have it." A few days later it's the second son. "I got a girl in trouble, Pop, and if I don't get her out, we're all going to be in trouble." "How much?" "Fifteen thousand." The next day the daughter comes and confesses, "Papa, I'm pregnant." "Thank God, business is picking up."* (1:27a. Randolph, *Hot Springs & Hell*, note 349.)

Freud gives four of the most famous jokes on the Jewish marriage-broker (*shadchen*) in *Wit and Its Relation to the Unconscious,* chapter 2, in the sections "Sophistic Thinking" and "Automatic Errors." Each of the jokes is uglier than the others, with the prospective bride described as a hunchback (twice), old, squinting, and with bad teeth, bleary eyes, and one leg shorter than the other. Again, as with the permissive-father joke given earlier from the same source, Freud is discussing — or appears to be discussing — the "Technique of Wit" and not its subject or tendency, which he reserves for a later chapter. The concentration on ugly and crippled wives in the examples he gives really cannot be explained, except perhaps as one of the automatic errors he is describing. He himself remarks prefatorily: 'It is perhaps only a stroke of fate that all the examples which I shall cite for this new group are again stories referring to marriage agents,' but we hardly have to accept rationalizations about 'strokes of fate' in the choice of materials — especially not from Freud. The one well-known *shadchen* story that he omits (also of Austro-Hungarian Jewish provenance, as are those he gives) supplies the sexual rather than antisexual contretemps likely to be encountered: *A marriage-broker is describing a girl in glowing terms to a prospect. "She's beautiful — edu-*

cated — fine family — money in the bank — etc. etc." The prospect is suspicious. *"If she's such a bargain,"* he asks, *"what would she want with me? What's the catch?"* *"Well, to tell you the truth,"* says the marriage-broker, *"she's just the least little bit pregnant."* (1:125.)

In *The Pearl,* No. 15 (Sept. 1880), the forbidding father is not only outwitted by the pregnancy situation, but is even tricked into the ultimate indignity of pedicatory rape. *A young woman who is afraid that her father will not consent to her marrying the man she loves, "takes the precaution" of letting herself become pregnant before broaching the subject of marriage to her father. "Egad!" he shouts, "Do you think I'll ever have that penniless puppy!" "Oh, Papa, but the puppy's had me and there's a baby coming!" the girl sobs. "Well I'm buggered!" says her father. "Father! Don't say that; we're such an unfortunate family!"* It will be observed that this swingeing young woman undertakes not only her own impregnation but also the confronting of the forbidding father more usually considered to be the suitor's task.

Except for the condom, which will be given a whole section of its own here, the *methods* of birth control are rather vague in jokes. This again demonstrates the male authorship of the jokes, as the condom is the one method of birth control — even more than withdrawal (Onan's sin, in *Genesis,* xxxviii. 9) — which puts the question of pregnancy or no pregnancy in the man's control rather than in the woman's. That women can only become pregnant during the two, or at the most three, days of and around ovulation, halfway between the menstrual periods (and now easily determinable by means of the body temperature), is almost unknown at the folk level, and it is almost tacitly assumed in jokes and other folklore that every act of intercourse not making use of birth control techniques will inevitably be followed by pregnancy. This not only is not so, it is not even a one-in-fifteen or one-in-ten chance. As a famous endocrinologist is reported to have said, "If women could become pregnant every day of their menstrual month, there would not be standing-room on earth." (We are getting there. . . .)

The problem of unwanted pregnancy is nevertheless very real, and the anxiety acute, in connection with the sexual acts of the young and unmarried. *"Let's talk about life and — er — ways to prevent it,"* one of the college men begins, in Timothy Fuller's *Harvard Has a Homicide* (1938) p. 148, a hopeful intrusion of the sexual element into a murder-mystery in a fashion discussed at some length in my book, *Love &*

Death (1949) pp. 23-4, and 65-70. This is the man's viewpoint. That of the young girl is more touchingly recorded in a little prayer first found in an eroticum, *Two Flappers in Paris*, by 'A Cantab,' apparently published in the early 1890's:

> *Oh, Blessed Virgin we believe*
> *That thou without sin didst conceive.*
> *Teach us, then, how thus believing*
> *We can sin without conceiving.*

A shorter, unrhymed form, with the flappers' prayer changed to that of a harlot, appears in the expurgated *Anecdota Americana* (1933) No. 492.

The woman's anxiety about pregnancy centers of course around the appearance or non-appearance of the expected menstruation. *What's the difference between a stenographer and a secretary? — A stenographer watches her commas, and a secretary watches her periods.* (N.Y. 1943.) — *The grouchy stenographer is all smiles one day. Boss: "What's the matter, are you sick?" Stenographer: "I'll tell the world I am!"* (1:455.) — *The comedian receives a letter: "You are not only a wonderful comedian, but as good as a doctor too. I sent my stenographer to see you, and she laughed herself sick."* (Minn. 1946.) That all of these involve the sexual exploitation of the stenographer is to be compared with the material on the concept of any woman servant or employee as an auxiliary wife, in the chapter on "The Male Approach" (4.v: "Cash on Delivery.")

In his standard work, *Abortion, Spontaneous and Induced*, Taussig points out the horrible fact that most of what is known about toxicology has been learned empirically from observing the effects of a world of poisons on the women who have taken them in the hope of procuring abortion. From a medical point of view there is probably nothing to complain of here, but one wonders why the inquiring toxicologist did not think to help the woman a little earlier, and a little differently, in her undesired pregnancy. A somewhat similar excessively practical male viewpoint is present in one of the few jokes on birth control techniques that are not wholly a rejection of coitus. *A man is bragging of having "gotten into a girl's pants" within an hour of meeting her. Another man tops this brag by describing how, while out fishing, he saw three girls in swimming naked. "I took the first one behind a bush, and after I laid her she jumped up and turned a*

somersault in the air. I asked what that was for, and she said so she
wouldn't get pregnant. Well, from then on I had one on the ground
and two in the air all the rest of the afternoon." (San Francisco, Calif.,
1945; collected with the note that the Texan telling the story accompanied the end-line 'with a rolling gesture,' probably meaning that of
hand-juggling.) The most curious aspect of this story is its apparent
reference, if only jestingly or as a fantasy, to the primitive method of
birth control practised at least in the South Seas, where the woman
ejects the semen after intercourse by means of 'hula' movements of the
pelvis, or by straining while squatting. (See the literature cited in Norman Himes' magnificently documented *Medical History of Contraception,* 1936, p. 26.) This is presented or interpreted in the present joke,
naturally, as the implied result of great male potency; and a similar
fantasy of coitus with acrobatic women is the subject of chapter 5,
"The Tumbling Twins," in an interesting American erotic work, *An
Oxford Thesis on Love* ('Taos, New Mexico' [New York], 1938), published only in mimeographed form. (Several ostensible continuations
of this work, such as *The Oxford Professor* [1950?] are not by the
same author as the original.)

The last, and the most important modern avatar of the forbidding
father is in the character of the doctor. This reaches its extreme development in the jokes about castration which are the subject of a later
chapter in Series Two, and — in fact rather than in folklore — in the
increasingly cynical use of psychosurgery and shock to reduce 'troublesome' patients, and political offenders, to a sub-human physical state.
The doctor first appears in joke materials in the milder capacity of the
'marriage counsellor,' whose activities are, however, equally castratory
at least in intent, with premarital vaginal stretchings, circumcision of
unretractable prepuces (a medical rarity), and, as the jokes see it, with
advice on birth control techniques that somehow inevitably end up in
a large, firm 'No.'

*A young bride consults the doctor as to a positive and dependable
method of birth control. He recommends an exercise which he demonstrates for her by crossing his legs and slowly shaking his head.*
(Calif. 1947.) — *A doctor tells a young bride of a simple and sure
method of birth control: orange juice. "Do you take it before or after?"
asks the bride. "Neither — instead."* (2:422.) The humor of this has
turned somewhat grim since that time, as the new temporarily steri-
lizing 'pills' being promoted in place of birth control, some of which
are required to be taken by the husband as well as the wife (see the

end of the chapter on Castration in Series Two) are actually manufactured as a citrus by-product.

The rationalizing note in both the above will not be overlooked. That is, the doctor has recommended total abstinence from sexual intercourse only because he was asked for a totally reliable contraceptive. It is significant, however, that it is the bride who is to be abstinent, as it is she who is given the advice. The husband has, presumably, other women available to him. If the doctor's privative advice is not followed, pregnancy is sure to occur. *A doctor tells an Irishwoman to put a two-gallon pot over her feet as a birth control method. She becomes pregnant anyhow, explaining that she didn't have a two-gallon pot so she used two one-gallon ones.* (1:432.) This varies the theme of what appears to be a much older joke, though first collected in 1940, of *The girl in provincial New England who is allowed to pet with her lover in bed after submitting to having both her feet put into a bundling-bag which is then tied around her waist.* [Sewing-up, or infibulation, as castration of the female, noted in the chapter on Women.] *She becomes pregnant anyhow, and when her mother taxes her with having taken her feet out of the bundling-bag, she tearfully admits, "Well, maybe one foot."* (N.Y. 1940. This has not been found in the well-known work of Henry Reed Stiles on *Bundling,* Albany, N.Y. 1859; nor in the more recent group of pamphlets on the same subject by Monroe Aurand.)

Abstinence or some equivalent self-castration is the only reliable contraceptive for the woman, as jokes see it, and the doctor and his comedy-helper, the druggist, are always there to taunt the woman when she tries anything less heroic and fails. *A woman enters a drugstore and asks to exchange a whirling douche spray for two bottles of baby food.* (1:195, given with a prologue of Negro stereotype humor on a 'negress' entering the Owl Drug Store and asking to see Mr. Owl. Compare the blackface minstrel's "Just got a job in the Eagle Laundry." "Must be some job, washing an eagle.") — *Doctor: "Go home and tell your husband . . ." Girl: "But Doctor, I'm not married." "Well then you'd better tell your lover . . ." "Why, I've never had a lover!" "All right. Then go home and tell your mother to prepare for the second coming of Christ."* (2:247.) In a variant: *The doctor stares fixedly out the window after being told that the girl has neither a husband nor a lover. "What is it, Doctor, what do you see?" "Nothing yet, but the last time this happened there was a star in the East, and I don't want to miss it."* (N.Y. 1948.)

V. THE CONDOM

This is not the place to attempt a discussion of the troubled etymology of the word 'condom,' meaning a sheath (nowadays of rubber, but originally of animal intestine) worn by the man during coitus to prevent pregnancy or disease. Most of the reliable historical information will be found in Norman Himes' *Medical History of Contraception* (1936) p. 186–206, where one of the earliest discovered uses of the word is quoted from Daniel Turner's medical work on *Syphilis* (1717) p. 74: '. . . the *Condum* being the best, if not the only Preservative our Libertines have found out at present; and yet by reason of its blunting the Sensation, I have heard some of them acknowledge, that they had often chose to risk a *Clap,* rather than engage *cum Hastis sic clypeatis* [with spears thus sheathed].' In the edition of 1724, p. 84, Turner adds that 'Dr. *Sharp,* as well as the *Wolverhampton* Surgeon, with two or three others behind the Curtain, stand Candidates with Dr. C——n, for the Glory of the invention.'

Tradition has made this Dr. Condom, here first introduced, a French physician at the court of King Charles II of England, and there is, as a matter of fact, no reason to doubt this. Charles II reigned from 1660 to 1685, leaving sufficient time for the condom to become as popular (?) as Turner's first quotation in 1717 suggests; and the name 'Condom' is, in fact, French, being that of a small town in the department of Gers, now famous for its Armagnac brandy. One presumable reference to the condom of earlier date than 1717 which may be mentioned here, only to deny, is that in *A Genuine Letter from the Earl of Rochester to Nell Gwyn,* of which a unique copy is preserved in the Dyce Collection, No. 8279, Victoria & Albert Museum, London. This is a long rhapsody in dispraise of the pubic hair of women, written in the 'nervous' and pedantic doggerel style which did not become popular until several decades after Rochester's death; but filled with extremely interesting notes and allusions concerning the pubic hair. The author — purportedly Rochester — admonishes the fifteen-year-old Nell Gwyn that she must remove her pubic hair as soon as it appears, for:

> Tho' *now* I mount thee with a Stallion's Lust,
> I *then* shall even touch thee with Disgust.
> As well one might propose a rapturous F——g

From Titillations in my Lord Mayor's Wig.
Such Horse-Hair Cundums, by their rude Contaction,
Wou'd scrub one's P——k to Death in th' Heat of Action.

Although Johannes Prinz accepts this production as authentic in his
John Wilmot, Earl of Rochester (Leipzig, 1927) pp. 145 and 175, all
serious recent critical opinion rejects it as spurious, and not on moral
grounds. The actual twenty-page pamphlet itself cannot have been
printed before 1701, as a reference to Queen Anne, p. 15*n*, proves; and
Prinz, pp. 48 and 311, proposes a date of printing 'about 1750,' which
is probably even too late. If the attribution to Rochester, who died in
1680, were credible — which it is not — it would prove the word 'condom' contemporaneous with the court of Charles II, at which Rochester flourished, and make the existence of a Dr. Condom at the same
court more than a probability. But the poem is so much inferior in style
to Rochester's real erotic works, such as *Sodom,* however interesting as
a sexological document, that the attribution is quite out of the question.
There are also the authors' completely opposed points of view: where
Rochester is the unashamed libertine, satirizing in *Sodom* a royal edict
against intercourse as the height of absurdity, the author of the *Genuine Letter* hates women and sex, and accepts any excuse to disengage
himself.

Another presumed reference to the condom by Rochester is *A
Panegyric upon Cundum,* published with attribution to Rochester and
to the Earls of Roscommon and Dorset, his contemporaries; but this
has not actually been traced earlier than an edition of their combined
works dated 1767, p. 208. In actual fact, the earliest important and authentic reference is on the title-page of a pamphlet appearing in London, 1708, under the title: *Almonds for Parrats: or A Soft Answer To
a Scurrilous Satyr, call'd, St. James's Park: With a Word or two in
Praise of Condons.* (This reference was discovered by the late Peter
Murray Hill, British bookseller specializing in this fascinating historical period before the literary repressions of the 18th century were
clamped down by Addison, Pope, and Johnson. Mr. Hill's own superlative collection of works of this period is now repositoried, for some
reason, in the library of the University of Kansas.) Fuller details as to
Almonds for Parrats will be found in Mr. Peter Fryer's popular history, *The Birth Controllers* (London, 1965) p. 24–5, noting also a reference possibly two years earlier to the bare word itself, '*Sirenge* and
Condum,' in the poem, *A Scots Answer to a British Vision,* attributed

to John Hamilton, Lord Bellhaven, in answer to a satire by Daniel Defoe. Mr. Fryer also states, p. 274, note 7, that the date 'c. 1665' which he had earlier given, in *Mrs. Grundy: Studies in English Prudery* (1963) p. 79, 'for the first appearance of the word "condom," turns out to be a wild guess,' and he apologizes for going off, as it were, half-cocked.

A number of jokes involving the condom will be found in other chapters. These include at least one reference to the skin condom — the original type — in the case of *The Englishman who buys skin condoms because he is told they are thinner than rubber and can be washed and used again, but later he complains, "They were all right, you know — thinner and all that — but I got quite a narsty note from the laundry."* (1:4.) The same idea is adapted to the rubber condom, which achieved its current tremendous popularity (see *The Accident of Birth*, 1936?, by the editors of *Fortune*) only after the successful vulcanization of rubber, and subsequent lowering of its cost, by Goodyear and Hancock in 1844. *"It's been a very bad season, hasn't it?" says one actor to another. "Yes, outside the Friars' Club they're picking up rubbers with vulcanized patches and laundry marks on 'em."* (*Anecdota*, 1933, No. 430.) — *A Scotsman loans a friend a condom, and then asks for it back later. Embarrassed, the friend says, "Why, Jock, I threw it away." "Where? Do ye think we could find it again?" "Well, hardly. I threw it out the car window on the highway." "Eh, mon, ye shouldn't ha' done it! Thot belonged to the club."* (N.Y. 1938.) On the homosexual element of such 'possession in common' — usually of the woman — see the relevant section of the chapter on Adultery, 9.III.

In the same section will be found the only modern joke collected on the use of the condom as a preventative of disease, and this is only to bring it humorously into contrast with its use as a birth control device, in the joke on *A man who is sterile loans his wife to a stranger in a hotel in a desperate effort to have her made pregnant. "She was real hot," says the stranger later, "but somehow I just couldn't get over the feeling that she might not be all right, so I used a condom."* (N.Y. 1938.) The statement on condom packages, 'Sold for prevention of disease only,' is now strictly a legal disclaimer, making possible their being sold in vending machines in public toilets (compare the Kotex vending machines in women's toilets). Originally, however, in the 18th century, the prevention of disease was the entire point as far as the man was concerned, as indicated in the quotation from Daniel Turner

(1717) on the gallants who would 'risk a *Clap,* rather than engage *cum Hastis sic clypeatis.*' (Compare also the entries in Grose's *Classical Dictionary of the Vulgar Tongue,* 1785, at 'bishop' and 'cundum,' and the advertisements in Grose's excellent folklore source, *A Guide to Health, Beauty, Riches and Honour,* 2nd ed., 1796, reproduced by Himes, p. 197–200.) Only Casanova, among the writers of the period, seems to have considered it also as a protection of the woman against undesired pregnancy.

Somewhat closer to our own day, as the commercialization of the 'New Freedom' or 'Sexual Revolution' enters its crisis phase in America in the late 1960's — as I have described at bitter length in *The Fake Revolt, or Gangsters of the New Freedom* (New York: Breaking Point, 1967) — the advertisements for hallucinatory drug accessories, sexually perverted clothing-styles, massive-volume rock-&-roll music, and 'far-out' nightclub entertainments, which bulk so large in the special newspapers of this bogus revolt, such as the *Los Angeles Free Press,* the New York *Village Voice* and *East Village Other,* begin to include advertisements for sexual apparatuses and adjuncts very much on the style of those collected by Grose in the Revolutionary 1790's. For example, this interesting item, given complete, appearing in the *East Village Other* (Nov. 1, 1967) p. 21, advertising decorated condoms, still piously 'for prevention of disease':

FRENCH TICKLERS

THE HAPCO COMPANY PROUDLY ANNOUNCES

"French Ticklers", fun, safe, re-usable, are now available. Sold only as a possible aid to marital sexual harmony and for the prevention of disease. Available in various styles. $3 for one, $2.50 each additional, postpaid, with full information. Up to six weeks for delivery. Hapco Organization [*address*]. Not sold as a contraceptive.

(On the verso is a perfectly frank drawing of a naked orgy, advertising a novel, the publisher's name being entirely absent.) The 'various styles' referred to are usually doll-like faces, composed of bits of sponge-rubber stuck on where the head of the penis will be placed, or tiny *hands,* rubber javelin-points, and other presumed 'ampallang'-style incentives to female excitement. These have, of course, no effect whatsoever, since the vagina — particularly high up, in the cervical vault, where the head of the penis strikes — has very little innervation and is largely insensitive. The 'French tickler' is actually a sort of phallic armor, or aggressive penis disguise (*'cum Hastis sic clypeatis'*), and appeals to the crackpot mystical yearnings and sexual infantilism and fears, and to the use of clothing-as-camouflage common among the drug-addicted psychopaths, or 'hippies,' who are the principal or intended audience of these newspapers, and who sometimes wear such decorated condoms as occult *protection* while 'high' on drugs. I have also seen a girl inflate them and attach them to her nipples: the breast-as-penis. The 'French tickler,' as armored condom or *ampallang*, is the perfect expression of the sadistic concept of coitus.

In spite of the total concentration on the birth control aspect of the condom in modern jokes, the prevailing tone is not one of protecting the woman, but of protecting the man from the embarrassment or forced marriage that might follow if the woman became pregnant. *A minister whose wife has had a baby explains to the bishop that "an act of God" has blessed him with a bundle from heaven and he needs a raise in salary. After the third bundle from heaven in a row, the bishop remarks diplomatically, "Rain is an act of God too, but common sense tells us to wear rubbers."* (D.C. 1944.) The few references to the woman's contraceptive benefit from the condom are all mere gags and rather satirical. *What did Kotex say to the condom? — "If you break, we both go out of business."* (N.Y. 1942.) *A woman asks to see a maternity corset. Salesgirl: "What bust?" "A condrum, you fool!"* (2:359.) — *A woman insists on being waited on by a woman attendant at a drugstore, and then asks for condoms, explaining that her husband always used to buy these, but now that he is "over there" [in the army, abroad] she has to do it herself.* (Transcontinental train, 1943.) Only a few female-fool jokes have so far been encountered as to the 'Pill.' *The girl who found they always fell out when she stood up* (La Jolla, Calif. 1965.)

Earlier, under "Pure Fools," the joke has been noted of the foreigner who does not understand the doctor's admonition to "put a condom on his organ before intercourse," and puts it on the piano instead. In a more complex version, with the fool element not so predominant, *A dumb laborer* — speaking of stereotypes! — *is given some condoms by the doctor and told, "You use these and your wife won't have any more children. But don't use them dry; wet them with a glass of water." A month later the laborer returns. "Doctor, those things you gave me were no good. I used them like you said — not dry — in a glass of water; and now when I go to the toilet, I blow balloons and make sausages, but my wife is pregnant!"* (Calif. 1952.) In a cache of novelty obscœna, collected in New York about 1915 and turned over to me by the kindness of the collector's son, a version of the same joke appears on a crumpled 3x5″ slip of paper, omitting the sausage line and the general concentration on the husband as actor, and captioned "First Prize at a Stag Party" (Béroalde's "Sea-Crab"):

> Master Barney O'Flynn wanted to give his mother a birthday present, and, in casting about to find one suitable, he decided on a toy balloon. Having bought the balloon the day before, he had to find a safe place to hide it, so he placed the balloon in the chamber and put the cover on. During the night Mrs. O'Flynn had to shed a doughnut, and as she slid over the pot and fired her wad the balloon gently bumped her stern. Then Mrs. O'Flynn screamed: "Moike, Moike, strike a light and see what I've passed!" Mike struck a light, and as Mrs. O'Flynn arose from the pot, up sailed the balloon, with Mike chasing it. After chasing the balloon around the room several times with his knife in his hand, Mike finally stabbed it, and as the explosion of the natural gas occurred Mike collapsed entirely, and exclaimed, "Begorra, I've lived for farty-seven years and this is the first time I've ever seen a phart with a skin on it!"

The drugstore situation noted just above, where the customer is embarrassed at buying condoms, is standard in both life and folklore, and it is interesting that no such embarrassment is experienced in buying toilet paper, and a good deal less in buying Kotex. This regression from the genital to the anal ('cleanliness') stage will be discussed more at length in the last chapter, "Scatology," in the Second Series. *"Gotta match?" The man asked turns out all his pockets. He has half a dozen tins of aspirin but no matches. "Whatsa matter, headache?" "No, every drugstore I went into — women attendants!"* (N.Y. 1940.) In a reversal, *A man says to a woman attendant in a drugstore, "Give me a package of aspirin, and a half a dozen condoms." "Got your nerve back, eh?" "No, I got a fucking headache."* (N.Y. 1943.) Pure hostility over the embarrassment; the dysphemistic punch-line does not even rise to the level of a pun. Wartime variant, on the rubber shortage: *A man walks into a drugstore and leans over the counter to whisper to the clerk. The clerk replies in a loud voice, "Hell, you can't even get tires."* (D.C. 1944.) There is also the question of quality — will the condoms break? — as noted earlier in the joke on *The man who came back to buy several dozen, but who was not ripping them: he had just "decided to stay all night"* (1:152); and the incest-gag of the four-year-old boy who *"knocked up the maid by puncturing all his father's condoms with a pin"* (2:331.) — *Druggist: "These rubbers are guaranteed." "But what if they break?" "Well then, er, the guarantee runs out."* (1:171.)

Several stories press the ambivalent relationship with the woman attendant in the drugstore to the point of intercourse, as is certainly implied in Grose's remarks about the 'matron of the name of Phillips, at the Green Canister, in Half-moon-street, in the Strand,' who, having 'acquired a fortune' from the sale of her 'purses' — of which the largest, called the 'bishop,' was used to contain the others — retired from the trade, but returned in 1776 when she found that the public was not well served by her successors. Casanova also has a characteristic passage where he refuses the condoms offered him by a Marseille prostitute because "the quality was too ordinary," but buys a dozen when she offers him a finer type, at three francs. *A man enters a drugstore for a cure for his persistent erection. He is embarrassed to find only a woman attendant, but explains his trouble to her when she assures him he can speak freely. "Well," he says, "I've had this hardon for three days, and it won't go down. What can you give me for it?" She disappears into the back of the store, and returns a few minutes later, saying, "I've talked it over with my sister, who's my partner here and makes up the prescriptions, and the best we can give you is the store and two hundred dollars."* (1:5 — *Memorabilia,* 1910, gives a short form where the man goes to a doctor, who replies enthusiastically and at once: *"Ten thousand dollars!"*)

In another form, action is substituted for words. *The man enters the drugstore and asks the woman clerk for a male attendant. She assures him she will not be embarrassed and he asks for condoms. "What size?" "I don't know. Do they come in sizes?" "Come in the back here," she says, taking him behind the partition to the rear of the store. "Put it in. All right. Size 7. Take it out. How many do you want?" In something of a daze he leaves the store and tells a friend all about it. The friend immediately goes to the store, pretends to be embarrassed, to want condoms and not to know his size, and is also taken into the back. "Put it in. All right. Take it out. Size 8. How many do you want?" The man waits, however, and does not withdraw till he has ejaculated. Then he says, "Oh, I don't want any right now. I just came in for a fitting."* (1:7.) In a variant: *The lady clerk calls out the size to an assistant as she measures the customer with her hand: "Size 3, Mamie; no, 4; no no, 7, Mamie; no no, 8 — Mamie, bring the mop."* (1:8.)

This has also been collected with the lady clerk actually fitting the condoms on the customer, in larger and larger sizes, until he finally says, *"Thanks, but I guess I won't need one now, after all."* (D.C. 1947.) Reduced simply to a pun: *A man with a persistent erection asks for help in a drugstore. The girl who waits on him puts acid on it, rubs it with alcohol, and tries many other things, but the erection obstinately persists until finally she puts it in cider.* (Transcontinental train, 1943.) Obviously many minds have worked on this fantasy. The motif of the *sister* of the lady druggist, or of her female assistant, Mamie, again suggests a far reminiscence of the prostitution background of the condom trade in the 18th century, and doubtless later, as recorded by Casanova and Grose.

The concealment of the condom by means of containers shaped like routine objects such as a gold-tipped cigarette or a large gold coin show by the very nature of the objects used that these date from the latter half of the 19th century (in America at least). These are still manufactured, though more or less as curiosities. The brand-names also show their *fin de siècle* origin in their similarity (Rameses, Sheiks, and so forth) to the Egyptian names given to cigarettes at that period; and, the most famous brand-name, which was long used substantively for any condom, is 'Merry Widow,' from the operetta of the same name. (When I was very young, I made a collection of the handsome aluminum box-top discs bearing this name, which I used to find in the car-parking alley on the way to school every morning, and did not learn for many years why my collection was angrily taken from me by a teacher.) Another element, beyond that of concealment, in the cigarette and coin containers, was the unutterably citified swank lent the young man by these accoutrements of virility. *The farmer tells his daughter's swain, who has been acting rough and crude to ingratiate himself with the old man, "Now you're the kind of man I want my daughter to marry — spit halfway across the room, and snot yourself on the floor —*

not one of them city slickers that blow their nose in a little rubber bag and throw it behind the sofa!" (D.C. 1944, as advice to a daughter. Printed in *Waggish Tales,* 1947, p. 168, more or less in the form given here, with the farmer congratulating the young man on not being like "those other young nincompoops" [*n.b.*])

The recurring motif of the condom thrown out the automobile or window, already mentioned twice, is logical enough in reference to the automobile but not otherwise, since this is certainly not how condoms are gotten rid of. Flushing down the toilet is actually the usual method, and this is even given official recognition in sewage disposal plants, where the increase in the appearance of condoms on the screens at every mealtime during the day, and in one long crescendo after supper, has been duly noted. The throwing motif is connected in at least two jokes with unlucky results, and it seems probable that this is a recollection of the accidental killing by a thrown or fallen object in many folktales — Thompson's Motif N331 — as for instance the killing of the demon's son by a thrown date-stone in Shahrazad's very first story in the *Arabian Nights* ("The Tale of the Trader and the Jinni").

A man is hit on the head by a used condom thrown out a third-story window. He storms into the house and demands to know who is in the room above. "My daughter," says the owner of the house. "Is she alone?" "No, my intended son-in-law is with her, why?" "No reason; I just thought I ought to tell you that your intended grandson has just had a bad fall." (*Memorabilia,* 1910. Printed in *Anecdota* 2:425, with end-line: "Come on out to the sidewalk and I'll show you your prospective grandson!") The other 'throwing' stories ending in accidents will be found in the final section of this work, Series Two, 15.v: "Anal Sadism." *A girl is told by her mother that she should allow her preferred boyfriend to have intercourse with her, and that when he leans back afterwards she should say "Well, what'll we name the baby?" and then he will have to propose. The daughter tries this method. "Well," says the man, throwing the condom out the window, "if he can get out of that we'll call him Houdini."* (1:219, text version, and the motif of the mother, from *Waggish Tales,* 1947, p. 100.) This has also been collected with a silk handkerchief used instead of a condom (Calif. 1942), which appears to be crossed with another story: *A travelling salesman out with a town girl has no condom and uses a silk handkerchief. A few years later he is passing through the same town and sees a little boy who looks exactly like himself. "Well, you're a fine little fellow," he says. "I ought to be," says the boy.*

"Mama says I was strained through a silk handkerchief." (Idaho, 1919. Also *Anecdota* 2:306.)

Similar misadventures involving the use of a condom, or makeshift condom, on the wedding night will be noted in the section "The Man in the Upper Berth" in the following chapter, and the curious identification of condom and foreskin will be discussed in the chapter on Castration, in Series Two, under "Circumcision," 13.III. The last main theme on the condom itself is that of the business of manufacturing and selling condoms, in the sense punned upon by the editors of *Fortune* in their study of the condom and general birth control industry in 1936, *The Accident of Birth*.

In quite the contrary sense, the mimeographed *Smile and the World Smiles with You* (Guam, 1948) enters a political note, headed *"News Flash": It is reported that the Democratic party is considering changing its emblem from a Donkey to a Condrum, because it stands for inflation, limits production, encourages cooperation, and gives you a feeling of security, although you know you are being screwed.* On the form here, compare the once very popular: *"Have you heard about Hitler's (or the new) secret weapon? It's Kotex: It keeps the Reds in, the Poles out, France hungry, and the U.S. without peace."* (D.C. 1943.) Combining both themes, *A condom manufacturer wants to put on a radio program with the advertisement: If You Want Children, That's Your Business; If You Don't,* THAT'S OURS! (1:397.) — *A manufacturer of 'sanitary napkins' who wants to put on a radio program, and who is refused because of the nature of his product, complains that the condom manufacturer has been allowed a program. "Yes,"* he is told, *"but they're only fucking around. You're out for blood!"* (2:96, a variant, reversing the accepted and rejected programs.) The paralleling of the condom and Kotex is very common both in fact (toilet-room vending machines) and in such lore as the riddle already noted: *What did Kotex say to the condom? — "If you break, we both go out of business."* (N.Y. 1942.) — *A man in a railroad station is annoyed by an elderly lady who asks the names and sexes of the two babies he is carrying in his arms. To all her questions he answers politely, "I don't know, Madam." Finally she snaps, "How does it happen that you don't know your own children's names, or whether they're a boy or a girl?" "I am not the father of these children, Madam,"* he replies. *"I'm a condom salesman, and these are two complaints I'm taking back to the factory."* (2:352.) See the further materials in the section "The Condom as Foreskin," under "Circumcision," in chapter 13.III.4.

What develops, from the study of the foregoing jokes on premarital sexual acts, is that courtship is not the area of anxiety for the men who make the jokes that it is for the young women who must — still, and in many ways — wait to be chosen, or else risk becoming the theoretically unwanted 'old maids.' Courtship, as the jokes see it, is something that the man can handle, preferably by a cruel exploitativeness as to woman's sexuality and hoped-for submissiveness, and by a resolute *refusal to get involved*. This is not a new disease nowadays, though I so describe it in *The Fake Revolt* (1967) p. 22–32. But it is now arriving at crisis proportions, and is now also attacking women, something it did not use to do. Sex, to be 'successful,' means seduction, preferably wholesale. The ideal is Don Juan, with his thousand-and-three female 'conquests,' which are really defeats for both parties. In one of the first of the New Freedom manuals on *The Art of Erotic Seduction* (is there some other kind?) by Albert Ellis & Roger O. Conway (New York, 1967), candidly avoiding any title-page cant as to 'Marriage,' though not promising quite so much as Vyvyan Howarth's *Secret Techniques of Erotic Delight,* and filled with elaborate techniques of pre-coital groping in parked cars and through zippered girdles — obviously a handbook for the fraternity-boy trade — one is chilled by Ellis & Conway's ruthless practicality as to the avoiding of tenderness with a 'temporary girl-friend,' p. 54–5, of whom one must 'Avoid buying sex with words of love': i.e. *Never say you love her! Why get involved?*

The New Gallantry, as can be seen, is only a step from the homosexual 'oncing' of Don Juanism, in which one is so overwhelmed by hostility and guilt, with any person with whom one has already had intercourse (and doubtless with shame at the shoddy quality of one's own performance), that one must move on precipitously to someone else the next morning. The premarital jokes float bravely on the spume and jetsam of these shallow coastal waters, with broken hearts and busted condoms for romantic scenery, before steaming out lugubriously to sink and be mired in the Sargasso Sea of marriage, in which the jokes see only disaster. One beacon-light of folkwit as to Don Juans, both male and female: *"Any man that can't find what he's looking for in a thousand women is really looking for a boy!"*

8

MARRIAGE

I. THE MOTHER-IN-LAW

MOTHERS-IN-LAW are the most curious and significant figures in all Western folk-humor. As generally understood, the mother-in-law is the *bride's* mother, and this is both historically and psychoanalytically 'correct.' Also, it is easier for a man to express himself as hating, or to laugh at jokes about other men hating the bride's mother, than hating his own. Actually, the groom's mother can almost equally fill the classic position of the mother-in-law, as the dominant and obtrusive parent at the wedding and after. The forbidding father disappears from the scene almost immediately upon the daughter's engagement being announced, nor does he generally attempt in any way to forbid or obstruct the premarital sexual adaptation of the engaged couple. The bride's father is certainly the extra man at the wedding, as his wholly preventive function beforehand would lead one to expect. This is very ancient, as is also the contradiction on which the bride's father is caught: on the one hand he must watch over his daughter's virtue (as the writer of *Ecclesiasticus* sadly bemoans), but on the other hand he must get her married off too — sometimes in a hurry and under any subterfuge, like spoiling merchandise, as in the perfectly extraordinary biblical story, in *Genesis,* xxix, of the cheating of the patriarch, Jacob, by his uncle, Laban, who palms off on him the older daughter, Leah, on his wedding night, instead of the younger and more beautiful Rachel for whom he had served without wages for seven years, and must serve yet another seven.

The father's brief reappearance, after the wedding — still in his forbidding aspect, like distant thunder troubling the feast — as the disembodied voice of "The Man in the Upper Berth," will be discussed in the following section. Meanwhile, the mother of the bride takes over from him the position of dominance over the sexual life of their daughter, in the perhaps unexpected but almost undisguised form, at least in humor, of attempting to *replace the daughter* in the daughter's own marriage bed.

There are two ways to consider this peculiar activity of the mother-in-law (which is by no means unknown in real life), depending upon whether the mother-in-law or the son-in-law is assumed to be taking the lead in their incestuous relations. The psychoanalytic position, as stated by Freud in the opening chapter of *Totem & Taboo* (1913), "The Savage's Dread of Incest," has generally been understood to assume a wholly personal and Oedipal — rather than ethnic — situation, with the son-in-law's conscious or unconscious incestuous urges toward his mother-in-law as the dynamic factor. Thus the many jokes on the subject of the mother-in-law are construed as hostile over-reactions against the real attraction felt. There can of course be no question as to the reality of the son-in-law's attraction to the woman who combines in herself characteristics of both his mother and his bride, with the added sexual opportunity — and occasion for repression — that, according to European custom, she is allowed to live with him in the same house as her daughter. Freud makes pointed mention of the 'preference that the witticisms of civilized races show for this very mother-in-law theme' as demonstrating 'that the emotional relations between mother-in-law and son-in-law are controlled by components which stand in sharp contrast to each other. I mean that the relation is really ambivalent; that it is composed of conflicting feelings of tenderness and hostility.'

All anthropological investigation, and in particular all the anthropological material that Freud cites in *Totem & Taboo,* points unmistakably to the mother-in-law as the dominant person in the situation, and it is really therefore her attraction to the son-in-law and not his to her, that is the essential feature of the problem. It is also perfectly evident that there is a real, rather than a reversed and over-reacting basis for the hostility that the son-in-law feels — which is the half of the ambivalent relationship that the incestuous explanation is inadequate to explain — when one observes the inferior position he must accept in matrilocal and matrilineal societies. There he comes to live in his mother-in-law's house, or with her clan, loses his name (clan affinity) and accepts that of the bride's mother, and sees his children — whose relationship to himself he must formally deny — reckon their descent not in his line or clan but in that of their mother and of the mother's mother. 'Matrilocal' and 'matrilineal' are words used by anthropologists who dislike admitting the existence of *matriarchy* ever or anywhere. (A startling example will be found in M. F. Ashley Montagu's publicity-oriented *The Natural Superiority of Women*, 1953, p. 6o*n*, where the author is hard put to it to explain how the superiority of women, as he sees it, has never sufficed somehow to achieve dominance over men.) But it is difficult to see in what particular — except, of course, in the dominant suffix '*-archy*' — patriarchy can be distinguished from the social organization subsumed in the words 'patrilocal' and 'patrilineal.'

In the analytic concentration on the Taboo, the Totem has been lost sight of. The point has already been made in an earlier chapter that the classic fool or nincumpoop of European folklore is similar to the average male in certain matrilineal islands of the Pacific, in that both purportedly do not understand the relationship between intercourse and pregnancy, and of the father to the child. The first important attack made on this theory of nescience, as promulgated by Sir James Frazer, was *Sex Antagonism* by Walter Heape, a book-length critique of Frazer's *Totemism and Exogamy* (1911). Heape's book, appearing in the same year as Freud's, concerns itself at great length with the question of totemism, and in particular with the fact that totemism is essentially a system of restriction on the sexual activities of men, effected by women, and a simultaneous method of excusing extra-marital pregnancy in women by reference to the so-called maternal impressions created by the sight of the totem animal. This interpretation of totemism, on which there is actually no disagreement between Frazer and Heape or anyone else, is of inestimable importance in studying the survivals of matriarchy — or, rather, their necessary conversions — in early patriarchal systems, and it is astonishing that Briffault takes almost no note of Heape's contribution, in *The Mothers*.

It will be seen that an approach such as this to the mother-in-law question is productive of enormously greater depth and richness of texture and findings than the usual expression of shotgun animosity, very late in the socio-historical day as we are, in the form of anti-mother-in-law jokes. As one example of the nadir to which this sort of thing falls — *ab uno disce omnes!* — see the scarce little anthology, A. Carel's *Les Belles-Mères: Tout ce qu'on en a dit* (Paris, 1887), heinously illustrated and including even a K.M.R.I.A. [Kiss My Royal

Irish Arse] 'culispice,' promised on the title-page, entirely in hatred and dispraise of the mother-in-law, and touching upon every possible theme in her disfavor *except* the essential one, at the folk level: that her daughter, the bride, will doubtless become exactly like her on growing older.

Jokes offer any number of interesting examples of survivals of the use of excuses of maternal impressions to explain extra-marital pregnancy, particularly where this is proved by the miscegenational body characteristics of the child. *A Southerner who has been North comes back to find his wife with a mulatto baby. She explains that while she was pregnant she was crossing a field and a Negro chased her. "Chased you?" says the husband bitterly. "It looks to me like he caught you!"* (1:284.) This is the usual modern form of such stories, but by great good fortune Poggio (1451) actually gives a form in which the excuse of the *totem animal* survives — significantly enough adduced by a 'noble and very wise old woman' (*Matrona nobili et peracuta*) — in exactly the way contemplated in Heape's remarks, p. 99, on the choosing by the adulterous mother of the totem of the unborn child: 'The anthropologist will do well to recollect that in dealing with Totemism he is dealing with a Feminine idea, and it is not easy to be assured of what and how much a woman knows, whether she be a savage or not. Is it not the fact that marital infidelity is punished with death amongst these people [the 'nescient' Central Australians]? If so, is it not also certain that a kangaroo bounding through the thicket may prove to be a very convenient excuse for illegitimate pregnancy?' Here is the almost identical story, given in Poggio's *Facetiæ* (written in Italy in 1451) No. 122:

> A Florentine, who had been abroad, came home after one year's absence, and found his wife in labor. He did not like it, suspecting some conjugal disloyalty. However, not being sure of the thing, he sought the advice of a neighbor, a noble and very wise old woman, and asked her if a child could be born to him after twelve months. She, seeing his foolishness [*i.e.* 'nescience'!] at once comforted him: "To be sure," said she; "for, if on the day she conceived, your wife happened to see a donkey, she will have borne a whole year, as asses do." The husband accepted the old woman's words, and, thanking God for having rid him of an ugly suspicion, and his wife of a grievous exposure, he acknowledged the child as his own. [Type 1362A.]

If the reader will now substitute, in the jokes that follow, this *'Matrona nobili et peracuta,'* still guarding the sexual prerogatives of her many daughters now under male dominance, in place of the usual stereotypes of the hatchet-faced mother-in-law, or the 'mother of the bride' with grandiose bosom (is that bad?) and an unstoppable tongue — a desirable quality only in male prophets and orators — a somewhat truer view of the matter of the dominant mother-in-law may appear.

I. THE FORBIDDING MOTHER

This is the matriarch in her protective aspect. But there is the other: the prohibitive aspect in which she substitutes for the forbidding father, whose prohibitions are essentially directed against the son — anybody's son — as her prohibitions are directed against the daughter. Later we will see the other side of this prohibition, where, just as the patriarch seizes all the women and drives out the younger man (who returns to kill and eat his father in the night, as Freud frighteningly posits in *Totem & Taboo,* IV. 4–5, in the never-told-tale of Old Man Noah and his Sons), just so the matriarch can turn a very dark face indeed on the sexual life of her daughters, and seize their husbands for herself.

Mother: "*Why did it take you so long to say goodnight to that young man?*" *Daughter:* "*But Mother, if a fellow takes you to the movies, the least you can do is kiss him goodnight.*" "*I thought he was going to take you to an expensive nightclub.*" *Daughter:* "*He did.*" (Joe 'Miller' Murray, *Smoker Stories,* 1942, p. 1, captioning his version: "If it had only been the Waldorf-Astoria.") *Anecdota Americana* gives an earlier form, where the girl's interest in the high cash outlay on the social date is displaced to high street numbers: *A boy takes a chorus-girl home to 168th Street, and she kisses him goodnight, saying, "Anyone who takes me all the way to 168th Street is entitled to a kiss. Next month I'm moving to 242nd Street.*" (1:105, quoting Heywood Broun's novel of the 1920's, *The Boy Grew Older.*) The baldest expression of this kind of socio-sexual calculation and materialism — best and most excruciatingly analyzed in Dr. Jules Henry's bitter anthropological examination of America, *Culture Against Man* (1963) chapter 7 — was told to me by a young butcher, between grunts, while cleaving the meat: *A man spends thirty dollars on a date with a girl, but she will not let him come into her apartment when he takes her home. She gives him his dutiful goodnight kiss in the hallway of her apartment house, among the doorbells, and turns to leave.* "Please let me come up," he begs. "Please! I'm willing to take a twenty-eight-dollar loss." (N.Y. 1953.) On *two dollars* as the traditional American fee to a prostitute — 'upstairs money,' the two-dollar bill being thus considered unlucky, as with 'the hire of a whore, or the price of a dog,' *Deuteronomy,* xxviii. 18 — see the chapter on "Prostitution," following, in Series Two. (The standard American fee has gone up to five dollars since this joke was collected, nearly twenty years ago.)

The mother is not much of a success as a forbidding parent, according to the jokes. Her authority is almost as consistently flouted as that of the father. *Mother (entering the parlor unexpectedly at midnight):* "Why, I never . . . !" *Daughter:* "Oh Mother, you must have!" (*The Owl,* 1938. Randolph, *Hot Springs &c.,* note 450, dated 1907.) — '*There were three little sisters. One said, "Mother, I'm going out with Pete to eat." "All right, darling," said her mother; "be back early." The second said, "I'm going out with Vance to dance." "All right." The third said, "I'm going out with Chuck." "Oh no, you're not," said her excited mother; "you stay right here".'* (Calif. 1942.) In another form, only the woman's indignation remains constant; even the intended rhyming alliteration has disappeared, the entire situation having changed: '*Three women, with their tiny children, visited a psychiatrist. The psychiatrist, taking them on as a group, said to the first, "You eat too much. It even shows itself in the naming of your child, Candy." "You," he said to the second, "think of nothing but money. You even called your child Penny." The third one arose, highly indignant and said, "I'm leaving. Come on, Peter".'* (Guild, *Bachelor's Joke Book,* 1953, p. 23. 'Peter' is, of course, the penis.)

The short-lived and spurious fad for Negro alliterative and assonant 'jive jargon' is recorded *in extenso* — not to say *in extremis* — in Lester Berrey & Melvin Van de Bark's *American Thesaurus of Slang: Supplement* (1947). It should be observed that alliteration belongs to the early verbal art of many cultures, and may be considered part of the linguistic childhood of languages, as of persons. See, for instance, the *Early English Alliterative Poems* of about 1360 A.D., edited by R. Morris as the first publication of the Early English Text Society in 1864. The almost wholly reduplicative vocabularies of some of the Pacific islands — *hula hula, kau kau, mau mau,* etc. — are also related by the universal origin of this process to the infantile reduplications common to many languages, such as *mama, papa, peepee, poopoo,* and the like. See further the present writer's extended monograph, *"On Sexual Speech and Slang,"* given as Introduction to the 1966 reprint of the revised volume 1 (1903–9) of John S. Farmer & William Ernest Henley's *Dictionary of Slang & Its Analogues,* along with Farmer's supplementary dictionary of French erotic slang, *Vocabula Amatoria.* More recent jokes on the expected-rhyme pattern are uncommon, though the form still remains moderately popular in bawdy 'tease-songs," such as "The Old Farmer" and "Two Irishmen, or Peter Murphy's Dog."

The flouting of the forbidding mother: *A girl is walking through the woods when a frog speaks to her. "Sweet lady, I am not really a frog at all but an ensorcelled prince. Please take me home with you, and hold me in your bosom till dawn, so that I may regain my human shape, and I will be grateful to you forever." The girl overcomes her astonishment, takes home the frog, and holds it in her bosom all night. In the morning her mother finds the young man, now in human shape, in bed with the girl, and she is told the whole story. "Well, aren't you a sweet little liar!" says the flabbergasted mother.* (Minn. 1946. Also often collected without the final scene described, ending simply: *And the next morning you'd be surprised the trouble she had making her mother believe it.*) An adaptation to the British homosexual scandals of the 1950's has a young man pick up the frog, who states merely that it is an ensorcelled 'human being,' with the ending: *"In the morning there was a handsome young prince in bed with him. — And* THAT, *my Lords, is the case for the defense!"* (N.Y. 1963, told by a young woman who later stated that she hated homosexuals as competitors for the available 'interesting men.') It should be observed that the homosexual scandals referred to here, concerning, as they did, titled perverts, resulted finally in the application, at British law, in 1967, of the freedom for homosexual acts between 'consenting male adults' which had been available in France for a century and a half under the Code Napoléon. Though the intention of the British legal relaxation, to protect aristocratic privilege even in perversion, was never stated with the vulgar directness with which I have just stated it, the bitter remark was put on the record by Hugh Fraser, M.P. (Stafford and Stone) that: 'It is a rather sad commentary that after a thousand days of this Government, there should have been no extension of freedom except to the bugger . . .' Note also that the relaxation of British law is not extended to consenting *female* adults. Lesbian aristocrats, unite!

Freud cites a child's skeptical reply, as to the biblical story of the Egyptian princess finding Moses in the bulrushes: "*That's what* SHE *said.*" These fabulous tales of the miraculous birth (or salvation) of the hero, and animal transformations, are of course very ancient. The frog story above is obviously a parody of the "Beauty and the Beast" folktale, but even in the original tale the implied mother-child relationship of Beauty to the Beast is clear, and the 'anti-magic' of sleeping all night in her bosom combines therefore not only the fantasy of rebirth (the bosom as womb, and the restorative night of sleep as pregnancy) but also that of incest with the mother. At another level, the frog cradled in the girl's bosom — significantly both 'ugly' and 'disgusting,' yet simultaneously loved and protected — is not only a symbol of the child but also of the phallus, as a male child also generally is to the mother, on the order of Lesbia's 'sparrow' in Catullus' poem, and Boccaccio's 'Nightingale.' (Day V, Tale 4.) This particular tale has also certain similarities to the present frog story, especially where *The mother and father find, in the morning, that the daughter who has been sleeping on the balcony, presumably 'to hear the nightingale . . . has caught it and is holding it in her hand.'*

The tone of open connivance here between mother and daughter is perfectly frank, and does not hide behind any pretenses of folly and so forth. Even in Boccaccio's 'Nightingale' story, for instance, *The girl is not at all respectful to her mother. She says originally that she wants to sleep on the balcony because of the heat, to which her mother replies that it is not hot. ' "Mother," said Caterina, "you ought to add 'in my opinion,' and then perhaps you would be right. But you should remember how much warmer girls are than elderly women".'* As a sexual challenge to the mother this could hardly be matched. At the dénouement, when the girl is found sleeping with her lover's penis in her hand, the mother wishes to 'scream at and insult' the young man, but only, as Boccaccio tells us plainly, because her husband is present: *'When she saw that her husband was not angered by what had happened, and when she considered that her daughter had spent a good night and had rested well* [!] *and caught the nightingale, she was silent.'*

In one very curious story, widely collected, the problem of incest breaks into the open. *A girl wants to marry one of the neighbor's sons, but her father warns her privately, "You can't marry that boy. Whatever you do, don't tell your mother, but that boy is your half-brother."*

This happens with three different boys, and the girl eventually realizes that she will not be able to marry anyone in the neighborhood, so she tells her mother. "Get your marryin' cap on, daughter," says the mother briskly. "You ain't no kin to Pa!" (N.Y. 1945, obviously of much older provenance. Davis, 1956, p. 11 gives a hillbilly version reversing the sexes.) There is a nice survival here of the basic problem of exogamy, as discussed by Freud, Frazer, and Heape, which is essentially the formal requirement that the questing male (here female) seek women elsewhere than at home in order to avoid incest within the clan (here 'neighborhood'). Compare Aarne's Tale Type 1425B, a French-Canadian story in which *the dying man learns from his wife that the reason one of their seven children has red hair is that only that one is his own.*

The wedding ceremony and feast are the last moment at which any merely prohibitive control can be exercised by either parent over the daughter. After the ceremony takes place, the formal 'consummation' of sexual intercourse is expected and even compulsory, just as it was utterly forbidden before. (Social regulation by *constraint* — in this case, contradictory constraints — never by *consent* of the governed.) The dominance of the parent can now be expressed only in openly hostile and jealous form, by actually attempting to replace the child of the same sex in the wedding bed, at the intercourse which has now finally been allowed.

Aside from peeping on the newlywed couple, the activities of this kind, of the father and of the other men present at the wedding, will be discussed in later sections of this chapter. These are in any case somewhat vague, or are presented as accidental, or as socially allowable pranks such as the *charivari*. The mother's sexual intervention is almost completely frank. First, the final prohibitiveness of the warning before the wedding, that all men are beasts, etc., here broadly satirized as hypocritical: *British mother, to her daughter the bride: "Always remember, dear, that the marital act is the most unspeakable, reprehensible thing in the world." "But Mother, you had six children." "Yes, dear. I simply closed my eyes and thought of England!"* (2:333.) In a coarser American variant: "*I draped a flag over my face and fucked for Old Glory!*" Behind the mockery, observe again the reference to the national clan.

In quite the reverse sense, the usual mother-in-law of the wedding stories is completely permissive at last, and attempts to teach the daughter how to perform intercourse, up to and including showing her by example, as in the South Pacific matriarchies where the older women *replace* the young girls in formal public sexual intercourse if the girls do not seem to have learned how to do it properly. (Domination by public humiliation.) Even the anti-sexual speech of the over-refined mother just noted can be construed as, and in fact certainly is, simply the prohibitive tail-end, or stinger, of an embarrassed attempt to impart last-minute permissive information on sex technique. This is the same situation invariably encountered in the hopeless travesty of the 'sex lecture' nowadays given to college freshmen of both sexes (separately) in America, usually by some no-nonsense staff doctor or semi-Lesbian lady gymnasium director. It is truly pathetic to observe the willingness, in fact the desperation, of the teen-aged students — at mortal grips with the sexual urges which are overpowering them from inside, both physically and psychologically — to learn something useful about sex, only to be fobbed off with what is somehow always an *anti-*sexual brainwashing, with strong emphasis on the now somewhat out-of-date themes of the dangers of pregnancy and venereal disease. The only self-respecting position of defense the young person can take is a bored I-know-all-about-it stance, which does simplify matters for the embarrassed parent or lecturer, but leaves the mists of ignorance just as thick — sometimes on both sides.

An authentic example already given (under "Female Fools," 2.IV:) *At a large women's college in Cleveland, Ohio, during the 1930's, at a sex lecture given to the girl students by one of the women teachers, the girls were invited to ask questions if there was anything they still wanted to know. One girl stood up and asked candidly: "How far does it go in?" To which the lecturer answered resolutely: "About an inch."* After which, nothing further really need be said. (Reported by one of the girls present, N.Y. 1944, with the bitter comment, "The blind leading the blind.") These phoney sex lectures are much resented by young college people, more especially by the girls who know that they desperately need authentic information. A gag-version turns the whole thing to ridicule, again by means of the pose that the girl student knows all about it: *Dean of Women, ending her passionate anti-sex lecture: "And so, girls, wherever you go, remember — you represent* Barnard. *No smoking in the streets, no shorts in the classroom, no unseemly conversation on the stairs. And above all, ask yourselves, when the men bother you, 'Is an hour of pleasure worth a lifetime of*

disgrace?' Now, are there any questions?" Voice from the back row:
"How do you make it last an hour?" (Philadelphia, 1956.)

This must be a very good joke, because I practically collapsed an
audience of several hundred people at the University of California by
telling it. This surprised me, as it has appeared several times in public
print, and I had intended it simply as a throwaway line to introduce
the question period. More than the deflation of the authority-figure of
the Dean of Women, it must be the allusion to the so-very-common
human experience that the duration of intercourse has to be measured
in minutes rather than in hours that gives it its effect. Observe again
the implication that the Dean of Women does not know this.

Bride: "Mother, I need some advice." Mother: "Yes, dear. Well, to-
night when your husband wants to get in bed with you, just remember
that men are beasts and do everything he asks." Bride: "Oh, hell,
Mother, I know all about making love. What I want to know is how
do I scramble eggs for breakfast in a double boiler?" (N.Y. 1940, earlier
1:117.) Eggs as aphrodisiacal restorative, of course. Compare the similar, not-even-hidden mockery and defiance of the tough mountain
girl's lament at the barn dance when her mother asks (taunts?) her
why she is not dancing: *"Shit, Ma! I cain't dance. When I dance I*
sweat; when I sweat I stink; and when I stink the boys won't dance
with me. Shit, Maw, I cain't dance!" (N.Y. 1938.) The dysphemistic
vulgarity in both cases is openly intended to show the girl's newly-
achieved sexual emancipation and her contempt for her mother's former dominance. 'The Voice as Female Phallus.'

2. TRYING OUT THE GROOM

In a final effort to retain her repressive sexual control over the
daughter, the mother is seen at the last in a flank attack attempting to
unsettle the prospective bridegroom's sexual attentions by various sorts
of doubts expressed as to his virility: he is too virile, he is not virile
enough; his penis is too long, too short, etc. The mother of a girl I was
once planning to marry actually wrote her daughter an anonymous
poison-pen letter — one of a series, which was found in her purse before she had a chance to mail it — reading simply: *"I hear you married*
an old fogy." This was obviously intended to be sent *after* the wedding
would be over, for purposes not entirely helpful. When I braced my
prospective father-in-law about this, and asked him what he thought

the meaning of it might be, he said it was just 'mother-love.' (As 'father-love' he had been accustomed to beating his daughter with a strap, holding her face-down on her bed.) The next girl's mother I wrestled manfully to the parlor floor, after she and her daughter had shared a few light cocktails in my home, squeezed her breasts (just to prove that Freud was all wrong), and asked her in a hoarse undertone if she was wearing pants. I hoped this time to remove all doubts as to my virility, and my not being an old fogy. However, the mother stated frigidly — from the floor — that I was some kind of a sex-fiend, that *her* husband had had his testicles tied off (to avoid pregnancies: a common sub-castratory operation in the U.S., especially in California) and *never* acted that way, and that she would refuse to come to the wedding if her daughter persisted in marrying me.

In less difficult cases (I can pick 'em!), the doubts cast upon the groom's sexual powers or equipment, whether that they are too great or too small, add up to a not very subtle way of requiring him to prove to his prospective mother-in-law — possibly *de visu et de tactu* — that what*ever* she chooses to suspect about him is not true. A heroic amount of diplomacy and restraint (as above) is apparently necessary to keep this from becoming an open flirtation with mother-daughter incest, which would of course infuriate the daughter. Thus, not only is the mother dead-set on keeping control over her daughter's sex life, after and in spite of the daughter's marriage, but she also manages to seduce the groom before the wedding (at least verbally, if her nerve fails her at the purported offer of the real thing), under the unassailable pretext of mother-love, maternal concern over her daughter's chances for marital happiness, or what-have-you. This is a very nice example of looking one way while going resolutely the other way — 'like rowing a boat' — *doublethink,* as the late George Orwell [Eric Blair] perfectly called it: the whole trick of hypocritical morality. It is very dangerous to explode these pretenses, I have found, as the exposed hypocrite has no resource but to try to destroy the person doing the exposing. See, for instance, *Rain* (1932), in the play version by Somerset Maugham and John Colton, in which the minister — made into an unspecified 'reformer' in the movie version, with his collar turned round and a string necktie added — cannot survive the discovery that he too lusts after the forbidden 'mammy-palaver' with the prostitute, Sadie Thompson, whom he has been juicily excoriating.

One of the mildest specimens included in *The Limerick* (Paris, 1953) note 18, p. 373, is a cleaned-up version of a bawdy limerick originally beginning, as encountered in *Cythera's Hymnal* in 1870:

> A young woman got married at Chester,
> Her mother she kissed and she blessed her.
> [*The clean-up continues:*]
> "This man that you've won
> Should be just loads of fun.
> Since tea he's kissed me and your sister."

This was used as a sample in the New York Sunday *News* $1,000 limerick contest, June 10, 1951, suburban edition, p. 3, with an illustration showing the bride in bed (*n.b.*) looking daggers at her mother. In the notes to my *type-facsimile* edition of Burns' *Merry Muses of Caledonia* (New Hyde Park, N.Y. 1965) p. 145, I have published, as a gloss on "Muirland Meg," who requires that the man's penis be 'As long as a sheep-foot and as great [thick] as a goose egg,' the survival of this classic 'good measure' in the modern joke giving the opposite form of the intrusive mother's sexual concern: *The bride-to-be's worried mother asks the groom if, by any chance, the men of his family are "built large," because, on the bride's side of the family, the women all are "very small." "Well," asks the groom, "is hers as big as a duck's arse?" "Of course," says the mother, a bit testily. "Well then, don't you worry," replies the groom; "mine is no thicker than a good big duck's egg."* (Chelmsford, England, 1954.)

Other jokes on these themes veer rather quickly to the uses of sex hate and a covert attack on the matriarch's own husband, by means of invidious comparisons with the daughter's prospective groom, as also with the sexual equipment of other men in general. These jokes will therefore be found in the concluding sections of this chapter, in discussing sex-hatred, and in the following chapter, "Adultery," with related jokes on the female judges or 'jury of matrons' described as examining the insufficient husband's penis in such cases.

The prohibitiveness of the parents is seen in the actual moment of change to permissiveness, upon the son's or daughter's eventual marriage, in the curious jokes in which the parents are described as peeping on the newlyweds' first intercourse. This is an evident reversal of the infinitely more common sexual peeping of the child on the parents, projected here upon the parents themselves. But in the most striking examples collected (as in the sex-hate jokes just discussed), the parents' sexual abilities — particularly the father's — are ridiculed by having the parents attempt to imitate the newlywed children's peeped-upon sexual acts, and fail, often with the saving implication that the new-fangled sexual specialties that the children are up to are just too much for their old-fashioned parents.

The newlyweds realize from sounds they hear in the next room, that the parents are listening through the wall of the bridal chamber, and decide to pack in the night and go to a hotel. The parents continue listening, confusing the sounds of packing with those of intercourse. The hastily packed suitcase will not shut and the bride whispers, "Let me sit on it." "No, I'll sit on it," says the groom. "Let's both sit on it at once," says the bride. The father pulls open the door, shouting: "This I gotta see!" (N.Y. 1940. A party record based on the same *double entendre,* entitled "It's In the Drawers," with the newlyweds trying to fit tight drawers into a dresser by smearing the runners with vaseline, etc., was issued semi-privately in Los Angeles or New York, 1943.)

The newlyweds are honeymooning at the home of the bridegroom's parents, who listen through the wall and decide to do whatever the young people do. After the young couple have had intercourse three times and are starting on the fourth, the father bangs desperately on the wall, and calls out: "Herbert, stop! You're killing your mother!" (N.Y. 1939.) What is so remarkable about this joke, which is told with the end-line in a heavy Jewish dialect, is that the father's phrasing of his own sexual failure as the son's *fault* is tantamount to an admission — whether conscious or not — that the father has been acting simply as surrogate-penis in the son's ultimate incest with the mother, at the moment of leaving his parents' family to start his own. This is also the only example collected in which the peeping parents are specifically those of the groom. Other jokes on the framework of the parents attempting to match the young couples' sexual enthusiasm and extravagancies will be found in the sections on sex-hatred.

The preliminary venture by the mother in the direction of replacing her daughter in the wedding bed is usually phrased as some ridiculing of the daughter's maidenly fears, which — to the daughter — is tantamount to mocking her inexperience, though were she to be experienced and not a virgin she would be theoretically disgraced. Either

way, the bride cannot win against the mother's domination or competition. *The young bride's old Jewish father whispers to her that he has
put a wedding present of a hundred dollar bill in one of her gloves.
She forgets about this and is getting into the taxi to leave on her honeymoon without the gloves, when suddenly she remembers and asks her
mother to run back for them* (or: *is worried about the money being
stolen, among the unprotected wedding gifts, and is found by her
mother on her wedding night wandering in the darkened dining room
searching among the gifts*). *"What is it, honey,"* says her mother;
"what do you need?" "I want my gloves, Mother." "Gloves!?" the
mother explodes; *"gloves-shmoves! Take it in your bare hand the way
I did with your father!"* (N.Y. 1952.) It may be noted that most of the
props used in these wedding-night stories are almost consciously symbolic, on the style of broad wedding-banquet toasts, hints, and leers.
The suitcase, the drawers being fitted into a dresser, and here the classic
symbol of the vaginal glove, all overdetermine the concentration on the
bride's vagina as the real *locus* of the wedding.

Letting pass, for a moment now, the theme of the dominant sexual
intrusion of the mother (or mother-in-law), which will become quite
open and unconcealed in the rest of the materials in this section, it
would be well to return temporarily to the ultimate Freudian interpretation of the mother-in-law 'problem' to uncover the deepest emotional
layer involved here. Note again that these jokes, with very few and
dramatic exceptions, have all been produced *by men*. This cannot, of
course, be proved, but it is sufficiently clear. Thus, the satirizing of the
mother-in-law's dominance over her own daughter, or over her son's
new wife, is certainly not undertaken by the originators or tellers of
the jokes (unless the tellers, at least, happen to be women) out of some
urge to defend the younger woman against the sexual control of the
older; to defend the bride, and with her the 'goodness' of women in
general, against the female ogre of the evil mother-in-law — the step-
mother or 'witch' of fairy-tales — representing the 'badness' of women,
and specifically of mothers and matriarchs.

Rather are these jokes intended to satisfy male tellers and a male
audience, and, therefore, one of the principal points of satisfaction to
all concerned may be suspected of being their expression of the hidden
sexual interest of the man in his mother-in-law, here disguised by projecting it upon *her* in the form of her intrusiveness on the wedding
day and night. Even deeper is the satirical identification of the bride

with her mother, who is, of course, the image of what the daughter will look like, be like, act like, and talk like — barring a miracle — in twenty years. This has its positive form, where the mother's sexual attractiveness is expressed as her presumed experience and sexual expertness, in advance of that of her presumably virgin daughter, the bride. In a colored cartoon, clipped from an American 'men's magazine' of the late 1950's, but unfortunately not further identified as supplied, *The groom and the bride's mother are shown sitting facing each other in a breakfast alcove in their pajamas and dressing-gowns, while the bride is coming in with the breakfast, saying enthusiastically, "I just knew you'd get along with Mother!" Under the table, unseen by the bride, the older woman has slipped off her bedroom slipper and has her bare foot thrust halfway up the groom's pajama-leg caressing him.* Compare the catch-phrase, *"I'd rather do it myelf, Mother!"*

It is clear, of course, that a man who is attracted to a certain 'type' of woman is just as likely to be attracted to her mother, if the mother is of the same type, as is very common. Under these circumstances, as Freud points out, only by means of the noisy folk-pretense that men necessarily hate and detest their mothers-in-law, is it possible (and not just in jokes) for the young husband to live in the same house with two women simultaneously: the bride and her mother. Were he to admit openly that he finds them *both* sexually attractive, he is admitting to mother-plus-daughter incest, at least as a possibility.

Even so, as noted, this is the positive form. There is also the darker, negative form, where we are dealing not with the mother's similarity to the young bride (and therefore the mother's attractiveness), but with the bride's similarity to her older mother (and therefore the bride's repulsiveness). That is what is hidden behind the contrasting of the bride's maidenly fear of sex with the mother-in-law's open avidity and curiosity; the bride's certainty that the groom's penis is too long and will surely hurt her, with the mother-in-law's certainty that it is too short and will not satisfy either her daughter or herself. In the end, however, having passed through all these humiliations, and the final danger of being replaced by her own mother (or even by the groom's mother) in her wedding bed, the bride *becomes* the mother. That is the real consummation of the marriage.

There is a well-known Oriental ceremony, formerly in use at Chinese weddings, in which the daughter-in-law is made to *crawl between the legs* of her new mother-in-law, with the 'explanation' that this symbolizes her rebirth as a daughter of the groom's mother, from between whose legs, in this way, she too has emerged. To the bride, obviously, the ceremony is just as much one of humiliation, in which she is made to crawl on the floor before and under the older woman and in close proximity to her buttocks. The rebirth is all very fine as symbol, but it is the humiliation which is the reality. After which, of course, as with any similar circumcision, or *that's-for-nothing-now-do-something* ceremonial punishment, the bride moves on to her new status, as wife and soon as mother, and may even expect someday to be allowed to humiliate other women as has been done to her. This is the standard hazing or initiation syndrome, or sado-masochistic alternation, where today's victim is tomorrow's sadist. Of the wedding-as-ordeal, almost nothing remains in the West today but the jokes.

3. THE BRIDE'S VIRGINITY

The virginity of the bride is not, nowadays in the West, the tormented *sine qua non* of marriage that it was once held to be, and still is in other cultures, as for instance among the Gypsies, with the bloodied bed-sheet of defloration (or of a killed bird whose innocence has been privately sacrificed at the last minute for that of the bride) shown publicly and proudly to the assembled guests. The actual consummation of marriage, in the first sexual act, is nowadays shifting almost imperceptibly to the *orgasm* of the bride, rather than to her defloration, as she is nowadays tacitly assumed to have been deflowered long before, doubtless in her mid- or late-teens. As brides cannot always guarantee to have an orgasm on their wedding nights, when everyone is terribly nervous, the official faking of virginity (bird's blood, screams, etc.) is now changing to the standard faking of the bride's orgasm, at which point the marriage is considered consummated by all concerned. There are still, of course, uncultivated levels at which the groom's ejaculation and orgasm consummate the marriage, as traditionally; but one really does not know where these levels are. As early as the 1930's, a comedy American wedding song by the West Indian song-writer, Andy Razaf, or in imitation of his style (in "*My Handy Man*"), was entitled "*The Swelling of the Organ and the Coming of the Bride.*" One could hardly be more explicit.

Jokes turning specifically on the question of the bride's virginity are not now often collected except in connection with the theme of the husband's having already taken it himself, or his jealousy of the 'other men' who may have preceded him in the enjoyment of the bride's favors. As such, the jokes on this theme are really those grouped in the sections, "The Man in the Upper Berth," and "The Relationship with the Other Man," in a later chapter. It is also clear, as Freud has observed in his great speculative paper, "The Taboo of Virginity" (1918), *Collected Papers,* IV. 216–35, that the demand that the bride come to the marriage altar as *virgo intacta* is simply a projection backwards in time — to the time of her birth, in fact — of the marital fidelity to which the sacrament of marriage publicly binds her from that time forward. Even though most men today no longer consciously concur in the bloodthirsty code of murderous and castratory revenges for the non-virginity of the bride, implied in the barbarous stories on these themes in the older Arabic tales (*e.g.* the frame-story of the *Arabian Nights*) and the Italian *novellieri,* particularly Boccaccio and Bandello, few men care to be required to welcome at their own weddings the known former lovers of the bride.

Very significant is the quasi-orgiastic and climactic public *kissing* of the bride by all the men present at the wedding. (Among second-generation Polish people in America there is also the even more openly symbolic *breaking of a dish* which the bride holds, by striking it with a silver coin, for the honor of the first 'kiss' or 'dance' with her; and compare also the symbolic breaking of a wineglass by the bridegroom, with his foot, at Jewish weddings.) This is an almost open survival of an implied former ritual giving-up of all sexual rights in and over the bride by all the men of the clan other than the groom, apparently by means of multiple public coitus with her, comparable to the multiple public 'kiss' still in use for this purpose. This is also an obvious opportunity for former lovers, nowadays (if they have been invited to the wedding, which the bride sometimes pointedly and tastefully avoids), to take a final, sometimes fond and sometimes angry, farewell intimacy with the bride in the allowed kiss. An unmistakable riposte or revenge on the part of the groom, under these circumstances, is to insist, himself, upon *also* kissing the former lover juicily upon the mouth. The writer nearly broke up a wedding-reception of his own by this means, and recommends it highly.

It is the unspoken homosexual implication, of pedicatory rape of the pre-marital 'adulterer' as punishment, that gives it its impact. This is the reverse of the masochistic acceptance of the wife's lover, even homosexually, by the husband, as seen in the joke with end-line *"And for me — nothing?!"* in the section "The Relationship with the Other Man" below. One of the few references that has been made to this theme is in a pictorial work on homosexuality in motion pictures, etc., *L'Erotisme d'en face* by Raymond de Becker (Paris: Pauvert, 1964; Bibliothèque Internationale d'Érotologie, No. 12) p. 210, in a caption to a still from the movie, *Vu du Pont*, in which the powerfully male Italian actor, Raf Vallone, has grabbed in his arms the rival he has caught with his woman: she meanwhile standing in the background (in her petticoat and stocking feet) with her head in her hands, registering terror or despair. De Becker remarks briefly: '*Dans "Vu du Pont," Raf Vallone se souvient de ce que l'homosexualité peut signifier aussi "outrage aux vaincus."* '

The whole complex of emotions and intimacies here is strikingly presented in a passage discussing oragenitalism — specifically fellation — in Gael Greene's once-over-lightly paperback item, *Sex and the College Girl* (New York, 1964) p. 113, quoting an unnamed young Mississippi male novelist:

> "The Southerner loves nothing more than oral activity. I guess this is because there is no oral hymen: I've been to weddings where the bride can really walk down the aisle with her placid smile of virtuous readiness, when meanwhile she has gone down on most of the male guests. There are times when you feel like kissing the bridegroom, too, the feeling being that he is doing more for you by proxy than either you or he might wish."

The meaning of the final sentence is obscure, though its homosexual tone is clear: again this is more closely related to "The Relationship with the Other Man."

The feeling of the 'rejected' lover, at the wedding, is as hostile toward the bride in the following joke as his emotion toward the groom is, essentially, one of proto-homosexual good-fellowship and polyandrous 'co-husbandry,' and perhaps even of wanting to warn him against the girl he is marrying (a hostile gesture toward the groom too, and thus 'the return of the repressed'). *A girl's former lover is pressed to say a few words of congratulation at her wedding dinner. He tries to beg off, but the bride herself insists. "Well," he says, "I don't know what to say, so I'll just offer a toast to the happy couple. — Here's to the bride: they say there's just as good fish left in the sea as were ever caught, but I doubt it! And here's to the groom: he's got her — us other fellows didn't. And here's to marriage: it's like going fishing — the fish you really want always gets away, and all you're left with is a little piece of tail."* (N.Y. 1964.) Memorabilia, 1910, gives a longer version in which the rejected suitor's disastrous frankness is again very carefully made the bride's fault:

> *A country girl threw over her lover as soon as a city chap appeared who seemed to be a good catch. In due time she was married to her latest catch. In her sense of triumph she caused her first lover to be invited to the wedding and insisted that he stay to the dinner which followed the ceremony. She was determined to humiliate him, and when congratulatory remarks were in order quietly suggested to some one that they ask him to say something. He demurred at first, but after much urging said:*
>
> *"I hardly know what to say on this happy occasion, but I will tell you of a dream I had only last night. I thought I was lying on the grass under a tree when the most beautiful bird I ever saw lit on a bough just over my head. I determined to catch it, and climbed the tree. It did not move and seemed to charm me and tempt me to pursue my purpose. I laboriously climbed out on the branch, and still it did not move. I cautiously approached it, uttering endearing words as I crawled along. At last it was within reach and I grabbed at it. To my sorrow it got away, but I got a piece of its tail."*

Underneath the open hostility and unmasking here expressed, it is observable that this is nevertheless only a verbal form or survival of the postulated ritual public intercourse of the other men present at the wedding with the bride, by means of openly alluding in this way to their former intercourse with her to which they must now bid farewell. The formal expression of this hostility is against the bride, *nota bene,* who has 'rejected' all the other men; not against the groom, with whom the former lover is constrained to comport himself as a true sportsman or 'good loser,' as in the fisherman version of the story just told. The rejected suitor is, of course, perfect for the job of unmasking, being the only person present who can offer any rational excuse, or legitimate beef, to explain the hostility of tattling on the premarital unchastity of the bride, at her own wedding. *An uneducated immigrant has been thrown over by the bride for the rich young groom. He is standing disconsolately in the corner after the ceremony, at the church, and the best man (or bride's father) attempts to cheer him up. "Don't take it so hard, old man — there's just as good fish in the sea as were ever caught." "Yah, sure," says the rejected suitor heavily, "but I hate to lose fish after I have hook in, maybe saxteen-saventeen times."* (1:487, giving the end-line only, with a group of others run together in a single paragraph, and an editorial footnote animadverting stupidly on 'the remarkable similarity of this anecdote [*sic*] to certain episodes in the work of James Joyce.')

This type of brag, or unveiling of the bride by the wrong man, is also connected with the actual poison-pen letters, to either or both of the newlyweds, as to the morals, virility, etc., of the other, nowadays sometimes enacted on the wedding day as a minor, but particularly poisonous, form of the obscene telephone call. The old-fashioned method is the most courageous: the hissed warnings in the church itself — to the groom that his bride has a lover; to the bride that the groom has a mistress . . . or a venereal disease! Among the many jealous hostilities expressed at, and in connection with, the wedding ceremony and festivities (in real life, as well as in jokes), this is merely the most open. It is, of course, quite out of date today. It is depicted, as humor, and as taking place in provincial France in 1887, on two facing pages in Marcel Arnac's novel in comic-book style, *Mémoires de Monsieur Coupandouille* (Paris, 1931) chapter vi, "Mariage;" translated as *Private Memoirs of a Profiteer* (New York, 1939), and very logically shows the groom being warned by a jealous woman, and the bride by a man.

Best friend, to the groom: "You don't want to marry that girl — everybody in Yonkers has screwed her!" Bridegroom, after a pause: "Well, uh, is Yonkers such a big place?" (1:345, also N.Y. 1939.) As collected more recently, 1966, the former male *language* prerogative, of transitive verbs for sexual intercourse — especially the violent ones, such as 'bang,' 'screw,' and 'knock,' as also 'fuck' — has now been usurped by the woman: *"She's screwed every man in Yonkers!"* This very simple but complete version not only involves the theme of sexual possession of the bride in common with all the men of the clan or community (Yonkers), but also leaves to be understood the sub-homosexual *camaraderie* of the groom with his unmarried male friends — whom he is now abandoning — which is perhaps the hidden reason for their trying to dissuade him from marriage. (A mere pun, but very popular: *The sailor who hated to get married and leave his buddies behind.* — Orangeburg, N.Y. 1942.) This is, if anything, even a bit more clear in the earliest version of the present joke found, reprinted from the British *Sporting Times* or '*Pink 'Un*,' probably of about 1910 or '20, which specifies that it is the very friend doing the warning of 'his old friend Jack' that the girl he is about to marry is a 'wrong 'un': *"Why, there's not a young man in the village that she hasn't gone wrong with!"* (*"Ah, well,"* sighed Jack resignedly, *"it's a small village, ain't it?"*), who has actually seduced the girl in the first place. (*Purple Plums,* p. 45.) ...

The most hostile form of the unveiling of the bride's premarital unchastity is of course to wait to inform the groom of it until *after* the marriage is solemnized or even consummated, and thus, at an earlier period, indissoluble ("Those whom God hath joined together let no man put asunder"). This is implied in the ritual intoning of the caution, during the Solemnization of Matrimony, according to the *Book of Common Prayer* of the Church of England: "Therefore, if any man can shew any just cause, why these two may not lawfully be joined together, let him now speak, or else hereafter for ever hold his peace." No one having *spoken,* thus 'causing a scandal,' the wedding and the consummation of marriage by sexual intercourse can proceed. *A young man tries very hard to seduce a girl on promise of marriage, but she steadfastly refuses to give herself to him till their wedding night. After making love to her then, he admits ruefully: "You know, you were right not to let me before — I never would have married you if you had." "Don't I know it," says the bride; "that's the way the last five guys fooled me!"* (N.Y. 1938.) In older forms, *The groom tells the bride he did not marry her rival because she told her mother she'd had other lovers. "What an idiot! I never told mine."* (Type 1418*.)

This joke is of unknown age, and is traditional in many European countries. One of its earliest recorded forms is the black-letter ballad, "The Shepheard and the Milkmaid" (1675), reprinted by J. Woodfall Ebsworth in *The Amanda Group of Bagford Poems* (Hertford: Ballad Society, 1880), a 'rude' supplement to his edition of *The Bagford Ballads,* vol. 3: p. 538*. In the last two stanzas, of three, the young man who is telling this tale 'of my Love and I, How we did often a milking goe;' reports:

I then did give her a kiss or two,
  Which she return'd with interest still;
I thought I had now no more to do,
  But that with her I might have my will.
But she, being taught by her crafty Dad,
  Began to be cautious and wary;
And told me, When I my will had had,
  The Divell a bit I would marry.

So marry'd we were, and when it was o'er,
  I told her plain, in the Parsonage Hall,
That if she had gi'n me my will before,
  The Divell a bit I'de a marry'd at all.
She smil'd, and presently told me her mind:
  She had vow'd she's never do more so,
Because she was cozen'd (in being too kind)
  By three or four men before so.

Whether as the modern joke, or the 17th-century tale-in-verse, this perfectly expresses every woman's hostility to the unreasonable and proprietary demand made of her, under dominant patriarchy, that she come a virgin to the embraces of a husband who is almost certainly not a virgin himself, and who would probably consider himself disgraced — as a 'he-virgin'! — if he were. This is the famous 'double standard' of 19th-century Anglo-Saxon morality, widely breaking down in the West since the 1890's and especially since World War I. It is now manifestly a dead-letter in America among a large percentage of the young people in college or who have had a college education, though even they often find it hard to allow the same 'single standard' to their own daughters later, and generally search for hygienic and emotional explanations by means of which to convince the daughters to retain — or at least to pretend to retain, so as not to embarrass the parents — the older theoretical premarital virginity. The conquest of venereal disease by penicillin since World War II, and more recently of female fertility (with results that remain yet to be seen) by means of 'The Pill' and other more-or-less foolproof methods of birth control, has made the earlier double standard of male and female virtue a dead-letter, not only in France and America, but most particularly in the Scandinavian countries, which have understood and accepted the corollary responsibility of the state — to support the woman with a child but without a husband.

The ultimate 'mock' of the whole virgin-bride concept is expressed in the character of the presumably almost-animal hillbilly (earlier, and before transporting to America, the 'Paddy-and-the-pig' comedy Irishman), who expresses the untamed yearnings of the civilized person's *id,* when, in presumably untutored backwoods innocence or crudity, he breaks all the civilized taboos and tears down and mocks everything that the civilized person — that is to say, the person who is telling the story — presumably holds holy, and does in fact consciously respect: home, mother, the flag, big-league baseball (or cricket, the *tour de France,* etc.), and his own wife's premarital virginity. *The hillbilly brings his fourteen-year-old bride back to her father the morning after the wedding. "What's the matter, Lem, warn't she up to specifications — warn't she a virgin?" "She sure was, and I ain't aimin' to stand for it. If she warn't good enough for you Hatfields, she ain't good enough for us McCoys!"* (N.Y. 1940. Or: *"If she ain't good enough for her own brothers, she ain't good enough for me!"* La Jolla, Calif. 1965.) In Elgart's *Over Sexteen* (1951) 1:100, an idiot version is given in which the hillbilly actually shoots his wife when he finds out she is a virgin, and his father agrees that he has done right. In one form or another this story seems to be very much of a favorite, and is clearly an expression of hidden chagrin that it is so difficult to find a virgin to marry these days, but expressed in Aesop's "sour grapes" parable form. (This might also be called "You Can't Fire Me, I Quit!" or YCFMIQ, one of the 'games' omitted from Dr. Eric Berne's bitterly exact but highly incomplete *Games People Play,* 1964, as is also the even more destructive form, DEHMIQRN: "Don't Even *Hire* Me, I Quit Right Now!" which is what the young man here is presumably playing.)

Vance Randolph gives a similar story, in *Pissing in the Snow,* No. 53, collected from a married woman in Monett, Missouri, 1946, who stated that it had been a common story there in the late 1930's. In this version the Arkansas boy calls off the wedding a few days before it is scheduled: *'The boy's old man wanted to know what has went wrong all of a sudden. "Paw," says the boy, "I been feeling around in Fanny's pants, and I found out she's a virgin. That's why I decided not to marry her"* . . . *"You done right, Son," says he. "If that girl ain't good enough for her own kinfolks, she ain't good enough for us, neither!"'* The whole framework is that of insults against the neighboring Arkansas, and the story is brought in with a curtain-raiser definition: *"What is a Arkansas virgin? — Well, it's a girl that can out-run all her* brothers." (Compare: "*What's virgin wool? — Wool from a sheep that could outrun the farmer.*" Scranton, Pa. 1935.) Other stories on this frame-situation of the Returned Bride, or the-morning-after-the-wedding-night, will be found in the following section, "The Honeymoon," though few which so clearly admit to the taboo against virginity and *fear* of the virgin bride. The authentic hill-dweller here caricatured does not really take any more lightly than anyone else the taboo against incest — he just is more frank about having transgressed it, or coming mighty close. Here is a real Ozark story, collected by Vance Randolph (*Pissing in the Snow*, No. 33) from another married woman, who heard it in Christian county, Missouri, about 1940:

> One time there was a fellow from Springfield come down to the James River, and some peckerwoods [hillbillies] was having a square dance. Most of them was drinking out of fruit-jars, and it looked like they was kind of a wild bunch. Soon as a set was over the fiddlers would play a few bars of "Old Horny," and then every man grabbed a girl and took her out in the brush.
>
> Pretty soon the city fellow begun to feel his cork a-bobbing, so the next time "Old Horny" come around he picked out a likely-looking girl. When they got to the brush he says "Are you married?" and the girl answered "Nope." Then he says "Do you want to do a little fucking?" and the girl answered "Yep." So she hoisted up her dress and flopped on the ground. He pulled down his pants and started to mount her. Just as the girl was a-guiding his tallywhacker home, somebody tapped the city fellow on the shoulder.
>
> "Excuse me, mister," says one of them big peckerwoods, "would you mind trading twitchets? It's pretty dark back there. I've made a mistake and picked my own sister!"

The reader will already have observed the very advanced concept of femininity — woman as 'twitchet' — that the Ozark peckerwood shares with the city fellow, as also the young lady's conversational abilities. Any way you look at it, she does have the best lines in the story. As to the incest taboo, it seems clear, from the whole *mise-en-scène* of the proposed 'swap,' that the sister was also at the point of guiding her brother's tallywhacker home, when he recognized her. In a much briefer version, collected during World War II: *Two sailors pick up two girls, and are banging them in a dark alley. One of them says to the other, "Say, Mac, do you mind swapping? I've picked up an old aunt of mine."* (San Francisco, Calif. 1943.)

From a research standpoint, the Ozark story may be considered a farce reduction of the great theme of accidental brother-sister incest, handled as tragedy in Child Ballad No. 50, "The Bonny Hind," from David Herd's manuscript collections in Scotland (1771), and very similar to the Scandinavian ballad cited by Prof. Child, "Margaret," on the daughter of the Danish king, Magnus, raped by her brother Olaf on her way home from the convent in which she has been raised. Another, probably derivative form (though Child does not observe the relationship) is Child No. 14, "Babylon, or The Bonnie Banks o' Fordie," also of Scandinavian origin, of which a Newfoundland version is passionately sung by Tom Kines, as "Banks of the Virgie-O," on his recording, *Of Maids and Mistresses* (Elektra 137, issued in New York, 1957). In this form, the brother is an outlaw or 'banished man,' and kills two of his sisters with 'his little pen-knife' for refusing to 'be his wife,' as the ballad pudibundly puts it, before he recognizes himself in the description of the long-lost brother the third sister calls for in her desperation as he is killing her. That the murders of women in the Scottish ballads represent and *are the expurgatory equivalents* of the rapes in the Scandinavian ballads from which they are derived, need not be argued here. See my pamphlet, *Love & Death: A Study in Censorship* (1949, and recently reprinted), on this whole matter of the substitution of a permissible sadism for a censored sexuality in popular culture — a substitution of which the real origins are by no means modern, and can be seen identically not only in these Scottish and Scandinavian ballads, but even more strikingly in the *Arabian Nights* and the cruel Italian *novelle* derived from them, and in classic Greek tragedy.

4. THE FEMALE CASTRATION COMPLEX

(II.) ACTIVE FORM: REVENGE

The taboo of virginity being finally and permissibly transgressed on the wedding night, the accusation of female insatiability immediately develops. Erotic literature makes use of the cliché — as lacking in factual basis as that other great cliché of erotic literature: the presumed ejaculation of a fluid by women at orgasm — that a woman is likely to feel sexual pleasure, and even experience orgasm, during the act of intercourse involving her defloration. One does not deny that this is conceivable, but it is unlikely and must certainly be statistically infrequent, and occurring only with very masochistic young women. (See: Dr. Helene Deutsch, *The Psychology of Women*, N.Y. 1944–45, vol. 1, chap. 7, "Feminine Masochism," and the writings of Dr. Karen Horney, and Princess Marie Bonaparte, especially as to fantasies of rape; also Alfred C. Kinsey, *et al., Sexual Behavior in the Human Female.*) Folklore takes this wished-for 'erotic virgin' one fantasy further, with the brides who are not only in a heaven of erotic delight on their wedding nights, but who even immediately become sexually demanding and insatiable. This is of course a straight wish-fulfillment (except at the *monetary* demanding level, where it often does take place, possibly with symbolic force); and denies both the guilt of the real pain felt by the deflowered bride, as well as other anxiety elements involved in the taboo of virginity, such as the fear of the virgin's spilt *blood,* and of the revenge in which she may engage later if not at once.

The absurdity here can also be explained in part by assimilating to the inexperienced and timorous character of the virgin bride the experienced and demanding character of the mother-in-law, as is made abundantly clear in the following old and very famous joke: *A young girl accidentally sees her fiancé urinating and is positive she can never marry him, as his penis is far too long and would hurt or kill her. Her mother persuades her to try it first, as she can then break the engagement if it is really too long. They discuss the matter with the fiancé, and all go to the bedroom. "Now, I'll put my two hands around it," says the mother, "and then if you think you can take more, you tell me, and I'll take my hands away." As intercourse progresses, the mother takes away first one hand, then the other, without waiting to be told. "Oh, Mother!" the girl finally cries, "why don't you take your hands away?"* (Idaho, 1919.) This is very similar to Novella 12 in Pietro Fortini's *Days of the Tales of the Novices* (Siena, about 1555), but without the mother-in-law element, amply present in certain other of Fortini's tales: *A shepherdess shyly asks the shepherd who is about to have intercourse with her to make a red mark on his penis with a strawberry, and to insert it only to the mark. Long after he has forgotten all about it, she whispers, "Now pass the strawberry!"* Dr. John Del Torto, who has kindly allowed me the use of his unpublished manuscript translation of Fortini's *Days,* states in his Introduction: 'The story of "passing the strawberry" . . . was collected, almost identically with Fortini's version, in California in 1951.' I have also collected it with a girl's lipstick replacing the strawberry, and the 'topper': *When the girl finally cries, "Give it all to me now!" the boy cannily replies, "No, I won't—a promise is a promise."* (N.Y. 1965.)

The same situation, on the wedding-night background, frankly burlesqued: *A young French bride is afraid that her husband will hurt her on their wedding night. Her mother promises to hide behind the bedroom door and to rush in and stop him, if the daughter calls for her. The mother hides behind the door as promised, and hears her daughter call, "Mama! Mama!" Just as she is about to break in, she hears the daughter's cry changing to: "Ma-ma, ma-MA, ma, MA, ma, MA!! ma-ma."* [Tune of the *Marseillaise*.] (Calif. 1952.) Here again, in the reference to the French national anthem — of which the opening is taken, by the way, from Mozart's 25th *Piano Concerto* (K.503): one of the most unblushing plagiarisms, by Rouget de Lisle, in musical history — there is this curious allusion to the clan or social nature of the marriage act and contract, as with the totems of Old England and Old Glory in the jokes earlier. (Compare also, strictly for the *cantefable* form, "I'll die! I'll die! I'll die-diddle-diddle, dee-die, dee-die!" ["The Campbells Are Coming"] in chapter 1, the section on Masturbation.) Unless one is to assume that all these jokes are really being written by one and the same person — perhaps Billy Rose's legendary 'wispy little geezer' in Central Park, to whom references have also been collected as the equally legendary '*crippled Negro genius, as black as the ace of spades, who* [name here any famous radio comedian] *keeps chained to the bed, by one leg, in Brooklyn, to ghost-write his stuff for him'* — there is certainly an authentic folk-theme here.

Another story, connected with that of the taking away of the hands and 'excessive' penis length, in both the general situation and in the common motif of observing the man's penis during urination, omits the mother-in-law, at least at the apparent level. *A bridegroom finds his bride unconscious on the bed on their wedding night, after she has seen him urinating in the bathroom. There is a note pinned to the pillow (or lying between her breasts), in doggerel verse:*

> *The cold-cream's on the mantle,*
> *The shoe-horn's on the shelf;*
> *I saw that great big thing of yours*
> *And I chloroformed myself.*

(*Anecdota* 2:225, with the more old-fashioned 'vaseline' for 'cold-cream.') A version collected in Washington, D.C., 1944, describes the bride as 'stretched out on the bed as stiff as a corpse, all naked,' with which may be compared the similar necrophiliac description in the famous American Negro "St. James Infirmary Blues" of the singer's farewell to his dead sweetheart in the morgue. (Also in the morbid and sentimental Brazilian movie, on the Carnival in Rio, *Black Orpheus,* which actually shows the electrocution of the Negro bride in technicolor!) It is perfectly obvious that the whole story is a mock *suicide scene* in which the bride's fear and hostility against her new husband are turned inward against herself in the classic manner of suicides.

In spite of its silly *cante-fable* poem, this story has tremendous psychological depths, indicated in *The Limerick,* Note 825, in connection with an equally silly verse about a young woman '*with a hymen in need of relief,*' who '*went to the doctor, Who prodded and shocked her, And stretched it with fingers and teeth.*' Freud, in one of his great speculative papers, "The Taboo of Virginity" (1918), *Collected Papers,* iv.217–35, discusses the peculiar psychological implications of ritual defloration, which still survives in the 'marriage counsellor's' premarital stretching, burlesqued in the limerick just quoted. Vaginismus as an expression of the bride's hostility against her husband is also discussed by Karl Abraham, the greatest theoretical writer in psychoanalysis after Freud, in the very important article, "The Female Castration Complex," in his *Selected Papers* (1927), p. 355.

One important element of the female castration complex overlooked by Abraham, or insufficiently treated in his discussion of hysterical vaginismus in frigidity, as an attempt to *keep the husband out,* is that we see here only the ultimate symptom, and must look for the cause of these manifestations in the bride's fantasies of being sewed up genitally in punishment for her sexual urges (*i.e.* for entering into sexual competition with the mother) and by way of preventing sexual acts. These fantasies are combined in women under patriarchy with elements of the more specifically male castration complex, involving fantasies of having the penis cut off, but in relation to female sexual organs (such as hysterectomy or the removal of breasts because of cancer, real or imagined). In a joke based on the wedding-night pranks to be discussed later, the castration motif of *cutting* is brought into opposition with the specifically female castration of being sewed up ("too tight"), but with the significant reversal that the mother ("too big") is not depicted as enacting the castration on her daughter but as attempting to prevent it. *As a wedding-night prank, the little sister sews the legs of the bride's pajamas [!] closed. The bride becomes hysterical when her foot will not go through, and says excitedly to her husband, "I can't get it in. You'll have to cut it open a little bit with your pocket knife." From behind the door the alarmed mother emerges screaming, "Don't cut it! Don't cut it! It'll stretch! Mine did!"* (Idaho, 1919.)

5. FEMALE FATHERHOOD

The female castration complex leads at once to the problem of Lesbianism, since Lesbianism is simply the anti-normal refuge into which the girl must flee to avoid imagined castration (infibulation) at her mother's hands for the sin of sexual competition. As with male homosexuality, the accusations against individuals and parents of the opposite sex as bad or sexually undesirable (the 'bad mother' of homosexual fiction) are not truly felt by the daughter being driven into Lesbianism, but represent gestures of feinted rejection and bogus animosity against the father, and thus all men, by way of conciliation with the mother and the evading of her expected revenge. This is a very important component in the grudge remarks about men made by neofeminists, both in and out of print, and it is always relevant to determine, in assessing such remarks, whether the woman herself actually suffered from her father or from men's domination in general, or whether she is simply faking it, in the way that male homosexuals fake their insults against their mothers, and women generally — while simultaneously imitating and trying to replace them — in order to avoid the fantasied castration at the hands of their fathers. See the particularly rich example, with proto-Nazi flute obbligatos, in the form of a Philip Wylie think-piece by the hero of Gore Vidal's homosexual novel, *The City and the Pillar* (1948) running on for nearly five pages, 237-41.

Having rejected men, with whom can the daughter marry and mate? The answer should be obvious: with the person because of whom she has rejected men — her mother. This is the passive form of Lesbianism, in which the 'butch'-consort is dominant; but it should be observed that the dominant Lesbian is also identifying herself with her mother and is lavishing on the passive partner the love she would have wished for herself from her own mother. This subject can be dealt with here only very briefly, in spite of its increasing importance in America at the present time, and though there is almost no analytic literature on Lesbianism from which meaningful insights can be drawn, except Freud's "Psychogenesis of a Case of Homosexuality in a Woman" (1920), *Collected Papers*, II. 202–31, in which *the basic cause of homosexuality* in this sexual 'retiring in favor of someone else' (*i.e.* of the parent from whom castration is feared) was first announced.

A very remarkable story, for which I am indebted for my first encounter to Mr. Osmond Beckwith, demonstrates finally how the real psychological or neurotic end-point of the jokes given above, in which the mother-in-law controls the depth of entry in her daughter's first coitus, etc. etc., is not simply the replacement of the daughter in her own wedding bed, *but of the son-in-law,* so that in effect the mother becomes her daughter's Lesbian husband. *A French lawyer at a convention in America denies the allegation that French law-cases are always about sex. "Why, take the case I'm handling right now,"* he says. *"It has no sex element in it at all: My client was in love with a girl, but she was afraid of losing her virginity and made him promise to put in just the head of his penis and to stop when he got to her maidenhead. He did exactly as he promised, but just at that moment her mother burst into the bedroom, saw what was going on, became furiously angry, and gave my client a tremendous kick in the ass that drove him right through the girl's maidenhead, all the way in. He came; the girl got pregnant; and my client claims that* THE GIRL'S MOTHER IS THE FATHER OF HER CHILD!" (N.Y. 1952. Earlier in *Kryptádia*, 1907, x. 176.)

This fantasy of 'female fatherhood,' much more gruellingly imagined, is a central element in Pierre Louÿs' *Trois filles de leur mère,* published in facsimile of the author's manuscript after his death, as no one would otherwise credit his having written it. In the climactic scene or situation, the impregnation of the mother *by one of her daughters* is achieved through the medium of semen purposely retained and excreted by the daughter rectally, after anal intercourse with her mother's lover. This is clearly the final convolution of this author's — or any neurotic male's — masochistic fantasies that women 'are really men,' have penises, can impregnate other women, etc.; and that there is therefore no danger of finding them to be 'castrated' creatures without penises on finally undressing them. As has already been noted, in the chapter on Women, this is the crucial element of the *acceptance* by modern men of women wearing men's clothing and unfeminine hair-dress, and otherwise impersonating men and expressing gross penis-envy impulsions.

As enough has been said in my book, *Love & Death* (1949) p. 78–80, on the theme of Lesbianism as nothing other than the final aspect of the dominance of the mother-in-law (the bride's mother), while her daughter responds helplessly with the frigidity or 'female impotence' which is halfway to Lesbianism; the attempt may now be made to sort out some of the folkloristic themes and elements that are blended in the 'female fatherhood' story given above. First, the element of *controlled penetration,* which has been shown in Fortini's "Passing the Strawberry" story to date from at least the 16th century in Italy. A century earlier Poggio had given, *Facetiæ,* No. 170, a *vagina dentata* story of a man who has intercourse with a girl through a hole in a board to avoid going too deep, at her request, and who then cannot get his penis out of the hole. This has already been discussed in the variant form found in the *Cent Nouvelles Nouvelles* and *Spiller's Jests,* where the *vagina dentata* element is modified to the female dominance of a jury of matrons; and will be discussed further in chapter 13, "Castration," in Series Two, concerning 'African roulette.'

In a rather insignificant modern story the question of controlled penetration is again set up as an arrangement between mother and daughter. *A girl admits to her mother to having been "fooling around" on a date, but says that the man "just maybe got about a half-inch in." On successive nights further and further progress is reported, until the daughter finally mentions that he had "put in about, er, nine inches." "You be careful," her mother admonishes her, "or that man'll rape you!"* (1:462, told in Negro dialect by way of rationalizing the fool element in the mother's connivance: a reversal, of course, of the usual prohibitiveness.) — *A little boy sleeping in an upper berth with his mother* [!] *has to go to the toilet, and on the way back, as he tells his mother, he stepped on the man in the lower berth while climbing back up. "What did he say?" his mother asks. "He didn't say anything, but I heard a lady say, 'Thank you!'"* (N.Y. 1944.) A version with an 'old Negro' stepping on a couple in a ditch, was collected in Virginia, 1952, and a versified form is given in *The Limerick,* No. 48, dated N.Y. 1946, described as happening on a riverbank. The incestuous elements in the text version are too obvious for comment.

A man is in court for a whore-house brawl. He explains that he had only one dollar and was told he could put his penis in only part way, the price being a dollar an inch. "Then along comes this son-of-a-bitch and steps on me, Judge, and runs my bill up to fourteen dollars!" (2:338, also in Negro dialect, to explain the impossibly long penis.) This theme, of not having enough money in a whore-house, will be treated more fully in the later chapter, "Prostitution," in Series Two, but it is in the present context, of controlled penetration of the frightened daughter of a dominating mother-in-law, that its true meaning is made clear. Folkloristically its genealogy is also very apparent in the present story, for, *mutatis mutandis*, this is almost precisely Poggio's No. 161, as given in Liseux' translation:

> *An itinerant quack came to Venice, on whose sign was pictured a Priapus divided, at certain intervals, by band-strings. A certain Venetian came up, and enquired the meaning of those partitions. The quack, for the fun of the thing, replied that his member was endowed with such a peculiar property, that if, with a woman, he used but the first part, he begot merchants; if the second, soldiers; up to the third, Generals; up to the fourth, Popes; his fee being proportionate to the rank and quality ordered. The dolt took his word for it, and, after a conference with his wife, brought him to his house, and bargained for a soldier. As soon as the quack had set about the job, the husband made a pretence of withdrawing, but hid himself behind the bed; when he saw the pair hard at work manufacturing the soldier agreed upon, he rushed forward, and giving the man's backside a vigorous push, so as to secure the advantage even of the fourth division: "By God's Holy Gospel," he shouted, "this will be a Pope!" fancying he had diddled the fellow.* (Type 1547. A Picard version in *Kryptádia*, 1907, x. 225, sets this up as a pretended 'government inseminator' — as also an American party-record, *c.* 1940 — in an even more obvious trio orgy.)

There can be no question that Poggio's story is also the original of *"The girl's mother is the father of her child!"* but a tremendous difference has taken place, and distance been traversed culturally, between the Lesbian overtones of the present story and Poggio's homosexual implication of pedicatory rape of the adulterer by the husband, as will be discussed further at the end of the next chapter under "The Relationship with the Other Man." It was also doubtless some return of the repressed, or purposeful erotic word-play, that led Liseux to translate Poggio's explanatory ending, *putans se socium defraudasse,* as 'diddled,' for there is no particular textual need to substitute this aggressively sexual slang term for 'defrauded.' The mother-as-father fantasy is further matched in modern jokes by the parallel fantasy of the sister-as-deflowerer, of: *The bride who explains to her husband that she has no hymen, as the result of an enema given her by her cock-eyed sister.* (2:231.) Again, the choice of such a term as 'cock-eyed' can hardly be unintentional, since the sister's aim would be just as bad if she were wall-eyed.

Even the least important element, the formal backdrop of the main story, that of the lawsuit, has been turned off into a story of its own: *A travelling salesman, approaching a farmhouse, notices the farmer's daughter leaning over the kitchen table slicing bread. He comes up silently behind her, and gets his penis into her by surprise before she knows what is happening. She becomes pregnant, and sues for support of the child. The salesman's lawyer gets him off, however, with the argument that things could have been much worse: "He could have pulled out, shot on the bread, and knocked up the whole goddam family."* (D.C. 1952.) This harks back to other fantasy ideas as to the transmission of semen and impregnation, as with *The sailors on a whaling ship who gather the semen from their masturbation in a whale-sperm bucket. Candles are made from it, along with the rest of the whale-sperm, and a whole convent full of nuns get knocked up.* (Scranton, Pa. 1925, told by children; and *Anecdota,* 2:295; the whole thing playing, of course, on the liberty of using so forbidden a word as 'sperm' if whale-sperm is meant.) Reference has already been made to this story, and (in Chapter 5.vi) to "The Sleeping Beauty," who can be awakened only by a 'kiss' in polite versions, as in Child Ballad No. 275, "The Barrin' o' the Door," a euphemism of which the meaning is made clear in the *Pentamerone's* full-blooded farcical version, in which everyone in the house, including the furniture, dishes, and chamberpot under the bed, are magically impregnated by this 'kiss.'

The extreme of potency mocked in the travelling salesman story is also perhaps intended to overcompensate for the ever-present castratory danger of coitus with the mother-figure (she who offers *food*), who is in this case supplied with a knife, as in Thackeray's parody of Goethe's

"Sorrows of Werther," where, having first met Charlotte while she 'was cutting bread and butter,' Werther finally kills himself for love of her, and:

> Charlotte, having seen his body
> Borne before her on a shutter,
> Like a well-conducted person,
> Went on cutting bread and butter.

It is not hard to see that this was the model — metre and all — of Harry Graham's "Little Willies," or *Ruthless Rhymes for Heartless Homes* (1899), so popular since, in which the principal element of what are now known as 'shaggy dog' stories was also popularized: that of a gross under-reaction, as Dr. Wolfenstein calls it, p. 151, to some bizarre, or, in the case of the "Little Willies," cruel event. This under-reaction is very appealing to the modern alienated personality which finds itself unable to react, especially with the demanded emotions of love or concern, and therefore welcomes the excuse of 'nonsense' to explain its emotional deadness.

6. INCEST WITH THE MOTHER-IN-LAW

We have now arrived at the end of the section on "The Mother-in-Law," and almost no joke has yet been given betraying any urge for sexual relationships with her, in the sense proposed by the Freudian interpretation of the mother-in-law problem. No such jokes have been collected except for a few insignificant gags: '*The stingiest Scotsman is the one who slept with his mother-in-law, to save the "wear and tear" on his pretty wife.*' (2:246.) An undated clipping from an American World War II humor magazine, similar to that from a later men's magazine already cited, shows a man with his mother-in-law on his lap while his wife looks on angrily, with the one-line caption: "*But I thought you said to make your mother feel at home.*" The popularity of one-line captions in American humor magazines, especially since the 1920's, is again very symptomatic of modern hostility and alienation: no humorous or human colloquy is attempted, and only a punch-line is given, intended to explode or destroy the person addressed.

So far as the technical incest with the mother-in-law is concerned, there is really nothing to get hold of in these gags, in the way, for instance, that Pietro Fortini's *Days of the Tales of the Novices* (written in Siena, about 1555) gives two stories, one right after the other, Novelle 4 and 5, of a young man who seduces his mother-in-law, and a mother-in-law who seduces her son-in-law, in both cases by some trickery that puts the mother in her daughter's bed at the consummation of the intended marriage. The first of these, Fortini offers as an explanation of the Italian folk-saying, "Believe Biagio," and the same will be found a century earlier in Antonio Cornazano's facetious *Liber Proverbiorum* (written before 1466) as No. 7 in the versified Latin edition — it does not appear in the Italian prose version, nor in the English translation made from this — as a long poem explaining "*Quare dicatur: Si crede Biasio.*" (Rotunda's *Motif-Index of the Italian Novella in Prose,* T417 and T417.1, notes both of Fortini's tales, adding a reference to another in which the mother-in-law is dominant, in Sermini's *Novelle,* No. 39.)

Only one English-language story has been collected of incest between son-in-law and mother-in-law. It should be observed that this *is* technically incest, exactly as though the mother-in-law were the man's own mother or sister: '*Thou shalt not uncover the nakedness of a woman and her daughter*' (*Leviticus,* xviii. 17), and Poggio gives, at No. 229, not as a jest but as "A horrible thing which took place in the Lateran Church," the story of a corpse that could not rest and rose on the eighteenth day calling for a chalice, into which, when it was brought, the dead man spat the consecrated wafer that had been given to him before death, saying: "I am damned, and endure the most excruciating torments, for that I had carnal knowledge of both mother and daughter, and never confessed myself thereof."

The English-language story has no ostensible religious element, but is based equally on a miracle — that of the endlessly elongating penis — though the tellers are not aware that this is a miraculous *punishment* (like Pinocchio's nose). *A man is walking dejectedly through the streets, and tells a Gypsy woman (or "Old Negro mammy") who accosts him, that his wife is going to divorce him because of the smallness of his penis. She gives him a magic potion and tells him to put a single drop on his penis before intercourse. Next morning his wife comes downstairs and tells her "old pipe-smoking granny" about her husband's marvellous penis. "It's that long!" she says, gesturing with both hands. The granny mutters that she won't believe it unless she sees it, and goes upstairs to the bedroom where the husband, who has overheard, has nervously poured the whole bottle on his penis. Time passes and the wife hears the granny's voice shouting far away, "Get an axe! Get an axe!" She rushes upstairs with the axe and finds her granny pinned to the ceiling by the man's penis, but as she is about to chop it down the old woman screams, "Not that! Not that! Chop a hole in the ceiling, and kiss your Granny goodbye!"* (D.C. 1952.) A shorter version, omitting the mother-in-law — *grand*mother-in-law is just that much closer to the matriarch — is given in *Kryptádia* (1884) II. 261, among "Some Erotic Folk-lore from Scotland": *'A man and woman were in each other's embraces. The man was succuba [under-neath.] His yard began to enlarge and enlarge and lift the woman. When she was nearly reaching the roof she exclaimed:*

> *"Farewell freens, farewell foes*
> *For I'm awa to heaven*
> *On a pintel's nose!"'*

It will be observed that the Scottish version specially notes, as the American version does not, the 'inferior' position taken by the man in coitus with the woman, which is so essential an element of the joke. An Arabic 'magic penis' tale is given in *Histoires Coloniales,* p. 6–8, without any matriarchal situation. This is very close to the "Long Nose" Motif D1376.1, the expurgated European form.

That the dominant relation of mother-in-law to her daughter ends not only in her replacing the husband, but in castrating him, was only to be expected. Note the great difference in the one classic tale of 'accidental' incest of a father-in-law with his son's wife, that of Judah, probably the first of the non-legendary Jews of the Bible (from whose name the word 'Jew' is taken) with Tamar, the 'levirate' wife of his sons, in *Genesis,* chapter xxxviii. In this, not only is Tamar not in any way harmed — though her husband Onan is struck dead in her arms by the Jewish god for the 'sin' to which his name has forever been connected — but she is even given twin boys, who battle in her womb [*n.b.*], by her purposeful intercourse, disguised as 'an harlot,' with her father-in-law. This story would make a great motion picture, in the Swedish manner, especially the terrific climactic scene at *Genesis,* xxxviii. 24–26; and *Deuteronomy,* xxv. 9; but has been overlooked so far by Hollywood cinéastes on the neo-religious kick. A rather amateur attempt in play form does exist, Izak Goller's *Judah and Tamar* (London: Ghetto Press, 1931; copy: Ohio State), not to be confused, of course, with the poem by Robinson Jeffers (1924).

II. WEDDING & BEDDING

The erotic jokes and leering toasts and speeches standard at weddings have obvious reasonable elements about them that need no further explanation than what is implicit in the public formalization of a sexual contract between a man and a woman, to be sealed by semi-public sexual intercourse. Definition: *"Marriage — a public admission of private intentions."* And compare the similar chiasmus of *"Kissing — uptown shopping for a downtown bargain."* (Both N.Y. 1950.) The pointed effort has been made, in the notably anti-sexual Christian religion, especially among Protestants, to drain the ceremony of the "Solemnization of Matrimony" of any clear sexual references. Thus the noble and poetic promise of the groom to the bride, *'With my whole body to thee adore,'* has been omitted for over a century from the Protestant Episcopal *Book of Common Prayer,* though the parallel (but more practical) *'With all my worldly goods to thee endow'* has been pointedly retained. As is also well recollected, the marital promise of the wife to 'love, honour and obey' her husband was changed, owing to feminist pressure during the 1920's, to the tautological 'love, honour and cherish,' precipitating a flood of mockery as in the musical-comedy and burlesque-skit title *"Love, Honor, and Oh-Baby!"* and the *double-entendre* wedding toast: *Here's to Love and Honor. They've gotten rid of Obey, but we've still got Honor; and when you've got Honor — keep on 'er!* (N.Y. 1964.)

I. THE WEDDING AS ORGY

Various ritual symbolizations have been substituted in the wedding ceremony for the sexual act itself, but these are understood by all present in a completely conscious way, and even children, if present, are assumed to be in the know, though they are limited to fake-innocent or priggish expressions, as in the joke earlier given of *A child's voice piping up at the moment when the groom is kissing the bride: "Mama, is he sprinkling the pollen on her now?"* (Footnote for history: this is a reference to the elaborate natural-history blinds as to 'birds & bees' or 'birds & flowers' by means of which sexual information was in recent decades, and still to some degree is, imparted to children.)

Any hesitancy or fumbling by the groom in such acts as finding the wedding ring or, above all, sliding it on the bride's finger — in the Jewish ritual he slides the ring, in open symbolism of coitus, up and down all the fingers of her hand while reciting the marriage formula, "Behold, thou art betrothed to me with this ring, according to the laws of Moses and Israel" — or turning up the bride's virginal white veil at the end of the ceremony and giving her their first married kiss, or (again as in the Jewish rite) stamping upon and breaking the wineglass put before him as the climax of the ceremony, is invariably met with general laughter and jesting, and mocking expressions of sympathy with the bride or offers by the other men present to take the groom's place. Invidious sartorial and sexual comparisons of the groom with the 'best man,' presumably his friend and aide, are also common; and sometimes even contests in sexual brag between them. I have myself seen a 'best man' (my own) seething with unexpressed fury that he had not 'got the girl' himself. (My fiancée also received by mail a naked photograph of herself, taken in a former lover's over-large brass bed, and captioned — as the entire message — "Remembrance of things past.")

Almost everything connected with the wedding is seized upon as the occasion for more or less broad and sometimes hostile jokes and allusions: the bride's guiding of the groom's hand and knife at the obviously symbolic first cut of the wedding cake (Canadian wedding toast: *"The Boy Scouts and the Girl Guides!"* Toronto, 1951), the throwing of her stocking and ritual blue garter (now expurgated to her bouquet) to the bridesmaids as she goes up the bedroom staircase — an open symbolization of the earlier 'loosening of the maiden girdle' and undressing of the bride (who is shown entirely naked in the superb Spanish Gypsy Romeo & Juliet motion picture, *Los Tarantos,* 1963) — the carrying of the bride across the threshold, and the 'final' leaving of the newlyweds' shoes together outside the bedroom door (formerly the bloody sheets, also an exhibitionistic 'partialism'), where facetious guests are likely to look through or pretend to look through the keyhole, and to place the newlyweds' shoes in suggestive poses for the photographer, as in the well-known 18th-century engraving, "Les Petits Pieds." (This has often been copied, particularly by Gillray, and is now finally used as springboard for whole books of caricatures showing only pairs of lovers' feet in various positions, with sardonic captions mostly turning on the woman's presumed sexual boredom, as in the title-caption, *Sam, the ceiling needs painting,* New York, 1964.)

Nowadays many of these jokes and symbolic 'partialisms' have themselves become formalized in turn, and are already traditional poses for photographs for the wedding souvenir-book (a minor kitsch industry), as for instance the cutting of the cake and the leaving of the shoes at the bedroom door, sometimes posed by the winking bride. What were originally ceremonial acts, and very serious, have thus been emptied both at the historical and simply human level of everything but their external or formal quality. The wedding shower with rice and shoes (semen, and the fertile vagina, as of "The Old Woman Who Lived in a Shoe") is a very good example of this, as the symbolic value is not always felt, except as a vague 'fertility symbol.' Meanwhile the bawdy wedding jokes, and the gag photographs (for the photographer who has posed them identically at a hundred weddings before), have come to take the place of the meaningful verbal and physical formalities of the original *rite de passage* that marriage is.

The *wedding as orgy,* with the bride taking on all the men present, is the clear historical reality behind the modern jokes. Few survivals exist in Western cultures of so remote a ritual as that posited here, though other examples of sacred or permitted public coitus of all women with all men do survive, in similarly modified 'kissing' form. For example, under the mistletoe of Christmas and Twelfth Night, to revive the dying sun at the winter solstice, when the strongest possible human 'life-magic,' namely ritual intercourse, is to be deployed. It is significant, of course, of the death-impulses of Western Christian civilization that the absurdity of attempting to ban sex from weddings — even from the wording of the marriage sacrament itself — has been evilly balanced by the simultaneous overloading of the hostile and sado-masochistic overtones of the wedding guests' audience-reaction: the weeping by the ladies present, and the charivarying and other 'practical jokes,' inflicted on the newlyweds by the men.

The few clear reminiscences of the marriage orgy still to be found are mostly in poetic (song) or pictorial form, as, in particular, "The Peasant Wedding Dance" of Pieter Breughel the Elder (about 1550), at which not only the male dancers in the foreground, but even the charmingly symbolic bagpipers, are painted with enormously evident erections. (Detroit Institute of Arts: reproduced in color as cover-sleeve for a recording of Beethoven and Mozart's *German Dances,* Counterpoint-Esoteric Records, Hollywood, Calif., about 1960, cpt-554.) Notable in the poetic form, other than the modern Scottish "Ball o' Kirriemuir," which is not specifically about a wedding, is Sir John Suckling's well-known "A Parley, between two West Countrymen, on sight of a Wedding," in his *Fragmenta Aurea,* 1646 (reprinted in *Pills to Purge*

Melancholy, ed. 1719, III.132, and in Charles Williams' & Lord David Cecil's *New Book of English Verse,* 1935, p. 302–7), which allows itself to be only gently allusive as to the sexuality of the wedding, in the 13th and final stanzas, and is really more concerned with the dialect humor of the speaker. (This is one of the earliest examples of the use of dialect — later slang — as humor, after the *Amfiparnasso* of Orazio Vecchi in 1598, and Shakespeare's stock-character Irishman, Welshman, and Scot, in *Henry V,* about the same period.) Suckling's poem is of course most famous for the two lovely lines describing the bride:

> Her Feet beneath her Petticoat,
> Like little Mice stole in and out,
> As if they fear'd the Light.

A good deal closer to the marriage orgy is the Scottish song, "The Blythesome Wedding," beginning, 'Fy, let us all to the Bridal,' in James Watson's *Choice Collection of Comic and Serious Scots Poems* (1706–11, reprinted 1869) I. 8, reprinted with the music as "The Scotch Wedding, or Lass with the Golden Hair," in *Pills to Purge Melancholy,* ed. 1719–20 and modern reprints, VI. 350. (This is not to be confused with the anti-Scottish parody, also entitled "The Scotch Wedding," in *Pills,* ed. 1719, V. 42–3, which ends with a travestied exhortation by the minister to the newly-married couple.) The real "Blythesome Wedding" is connected, both in its form and subject, and particularly in its strange personal-salvation insistence upon *named* individuals, and in its gloating descriptions of material objects and foods, with what is the principal modern orgy song, the Scottish "Ball o' Kirriemuir" (on which see my *The Horn Book,* 1964, p. 423–4, and *type-facsimile* edition of Burns' *Merry Muses of Caledonia,* New Hyde Park, 1965, pp. 178, 181, and 216–17, on "Blyth Will an' Bessie's Wedding.") In this fantasy orgy song, now very well known in America in mock Scottish dialect, the framework of a wedding has been replaced by that of a 'ball' of sinful dancing and sexual frolic.

2. CHARIVARI *VS.* CONSUMMATION

All that remains of the primeval orgy in the modern wedding is the symbolic renunciation of any right in the bride, and taking leave of any former intimacy with her, in the climactic line-up or 'gang'-kissing of the bride, by all the men present, and this has certainly lost its conscious original meaning. The hostile jokes and wedding-night pranks ('*charivari*' or 'horning'), the knowing nudges and allusions to the bride's former unchastity (at least with the groom), and the groom's (simultaneous) probable inadequacy, have become the substitute ritual: hatred and jealousy — in a word, emotional violence — replacing the now forbidden and forgotten sexual free-for-all, which would theoretically be so much more vile.

"*Did you hear about Mary? She's getting married.*" "*Married? I didn't even know she was pregnant!*" (1:487, giving the end-line only, which is also varied as: "*Who's the lucky obstetrician?*" N.Y. 1953.) In a less catty form: *The girl is displaying her baby.* "*Why, I didn't know you were married,*" *says one of the other women, counting the months backwards rapidly on her fingers.* "*I'm not,*" *says the girl.* "*This is the engagement baby.*" (*Memorabilia*, 1910.) This phrase now usually refers to a baby born less than the usual nine months after the ceremony. ("*Oh, yes,*" *says the obstetrician, to the bride's anxious question,* "*premature babies are very common — but never after the first.*" N.Y. 1965, with a long European pre-history.) The joke is also frequently encountered in a modification concerning *A young woman* (*often: Negro woman*) *who is having a difficult time with her first childbirth says to the doctor,* "*If this is what married life is like, you just go down and tell that man the engagement is off!*" (1:191.)

These are the women's jokes. In the men's jokes the accent is not on the mother-right of pregnancy, but on the unchastity to which the bride has been persuaded before the ceremony, at least by the groom, as in the "Shepheard and the Milkmaid" song of 1675, quoted earlier. "*Last night I finally persuaded my girl to say that little word 'Yes'.*" "*Congratulations, old man, when's the wedding?*" "*What wedding?*" (*Better Crops with Plant Food*, August 1941, p. 49 filler.) — *At the bachelor dinner for the groom the night before the wedding* [a particularly interesting survival, it may be remarked, essentially of didactic purpose, to teach the groom his sexual duty], *he is asked if he is going to be a man or a mouse, the difference being* "*If you're a man you'll do it the first night; if you're a mouse you'll wait till the second night.*" "*I guess I must be a louse,*" *he says.* "*I did it last night.*" (N.Y. 1938, overheard in a Radio City elevator. Guild, 1953, p. 13, gives the punchline, "*Well, boys . . . I'm way ahead of you. Meet a rat.*") This is the opposite of the nincumpoop jokes, given earlier, concerning the quintessential male fool who does not know how to take his sexual 'rights' or seize his erotic opportunities, or even how to perform intercourse.

It is surely significant that the most popular and most frequently reprinted French sex-guidance manual of recent times, *Prélude Charnel,* credited to the probably pseudonymous Robert Sermaise (about 1938?) and written in dialogue form, is entirely based on the idea of brainwashing bridegrooms into refraining from consummating their marriage on the wedding night, and to wait a few days, filled with artistic foreplay of course, and tremendous amounts of *talk* (the French '*beau-parleur*' syndrome), so that the bride shall not be, in the proudly 'sententious' opening line of the book, 'Yet another victim of masculine brutality!' (English translation as *The Fleshly Prelude,* Paris: Vendôme Press, 1939.) In a less popular sequel, *Interlude Charnel,* the author gives the show away completely — as to what is really bothering him, and what he is really peddling — by setting up an advanced course for the erotic education of the now broken-in bride, consisting of wife-swapping parties ('*parties-carrées*' or '*partouzes,*' in current French slang), in which not only the wives are swapped but the husbands also engage in homosexual acts together, or something very close.

In Anglo-Saxon folklore the classic nincumpoop, or 'muff' (French: *con,* cunt, or fool) is not so obvious a crypto-homosexual, and his evident unmanliness is considered to be simply a part of his stupidity. *The office idiot does not consummate his marriage until a week after the wedding. The next morning he comes into the office rubbing his hands together gleefully and gloating, "Oh boy, what a time I had with my wife last night!" "Why in hell did you wait so long?" he is asked. "Well, how was I supposed to know she screwed?"* (1:282, giving the end-line in the crude impersonal-generic form: "*I didn't know that she was hump!*" Compare the obviously hostile impersonalness of much homosexual slang, *e.g.*: "There goes something cool; let's cruise it." San Diego, California, 1965.) As opposed to what is usually believed and might be expected, not all women resist and resent this sort of impersonal reference to them as sexual objects. Some even accede to it, and do it to themselves at least verbally, as showing how 'tough' — *i.e.* how close to male — they really are. One such young lady told me she thought the signs on public toilets in barrooms were cowardly and coy ('*Pointers*' and '*Setters,*' etc.), and ought simply to say '*Cocks*' and '*Cunts.*' I nearly lost her friendship forever by asking, 'Which are you?' (N.Y. 1963.) In the Anglo-Hispanic 'intellectual' poetry magazine, *El Corno Emplumado,* edited in Mexico City by Margaret Randall and her husband, Sergio Mondragón, No. 22 (April 1967) inner back-cover, p. 153, under a list of "Patrons," is noted a group of eight *'female poets who, under the grouping* "CUNTS FOR CORNO" *read [poetry in public] in New York City, March 1967.'* Self-styled poetic *'cunts'* like these certainly make monkeys of men like myself, who wish to write in defense of women's right to be considered human beings, or of so gallant a feminist as Mr. Gene Marine who, in "Who's Afraid of Little Annie Fanny?" in *Ramparts* (San Francisco, February 1967) p. 26–30, speaks out almost alone against the open contempt for women now being made faddish by the 'men's magazines' with their pubic-hairless female nudes, like big-titted Chihuahua dogs, and by the underground pop-culch machinations of the 'camp'-commissars of the Homosexual International and the sick female fag-hags who help publicize them. As those of my women-readers who do *not* consider themselves 'cunts' will understand, it is very difficult to attempt to side with a sex whose self-elected spokes-women and presumed intellectuals are so desperately anxious to be shat upon.

In any real folkloristic sense, the nincumpoop or male sexual fool is not actually purported to exist at all. He is a cautionary figure, as in nursery rhymes and tales concerning children sliding on the ice or putting beans in their noses, and is set up as an object-lesson or warn-ing, as part of the sexual education of boys and young men. Al Capp's comic-strip character, the handsome hillbilly, Li'l Abner, for whom the short-skirted Daisy Mae and all other girls are frantically on the make, but who does not observe any of the sexual opportunities the cartoonist so elaborately sets up for him, is similarly intended as a roundabout cautionary tale, or immoral lesson, with overtones of masochistic jesting at oneself if one were to be (and for the times one *has* been) equally unenterprising. Another aspect of the male sexual fool or nincumpoop is that he is made to accept the guilt for the non-consummation of his marriage, though this may actually be the result — sometimes with quite conscious intention — of the sexual jeal-ousy and hostile pranks of the other men, and sometimes the women, present; especially where 'horning' or the *charivari* ('shivaree') is com-monly observed. In the *charivari,* in which the consummation of the marriage is physically prevented by noisemaking and pranks, or 'prac-tical jokes' usually connected with the newlyweds' bedroom or the wedding bed itself (as, for instance, folding its sheets in such a way that the newlyweds cannot get in), only the pretense of chortling humor covers the hostility of this ancient survival of the tribe's resistance to the girl's marriage-by-capture (the honeymoon trip). Suckling's poem, cited above, ends, for instance, with the bridesmaids delaying the consummation of the marriage by coming into the bedroom with a sack-posset (hot 'aphrodisiacal' wine drink) just as the groom is getting into bed, and with the intention of staying two hours, 'had he left the Women to't, It would have cost two hours to do't, Which were too much that Night.'

The difference between the hostilities which end in the attempted unveiling of the bride's premarital unchastity — traditionally by former and rejected lovers — and the purposeful vexations of the *charivari* type, is that one is concerned with harming the bride & groom through their sexual past, the other by preventing their sexual future, which is tantamount to preventing the marriage altogether. The bride is, of course, not as passive as the jokes would lead one to imagine, and must not be if the groom is a sexual fool. Marriage is, to her, literally 'becoming a woman' in every sense, with her own home and family and thus a sudden new measure of independence, at least from the sexual and social constrictions of life under her parents' dominance. Observe the coyness of the virgin bride changing to the proud knowingness of the wife: *A Cockney costermonger has just been married. As he and his bride climb into the cab to leave on their honeymoon, one of the groomsmen leans in and leers at them. "What abaht tonight?" he chuckles, "what abaht tonight?" "Yes," the bride shoots back at him, "and what abaht this afternoon, eh?"* (1:100.)

The over-boldness of the bride, especially premaritally, is cruelly attacked in an anecdote, rather than a joke, reported as having really happened in Scotland in the early 19th century, in the *Supplement to the Historical Portion of the Records of the Most Ancient and Puissant Order of the Beggar's Benison* (1892), which are the astonishing records of a men's sexual initiation club in Anstruther, Scotland, throughout the 18th and 19th centuries, of which an important part of the ceremony — aside from the ritual showing of the members' penises and their masturbation into a silver dish called the 'Test Platter' — was the silent examination, by the 'Knights' of the Beggar's Benison, of the sexual parts of a young town girl hired for this purpose, such young girls being known as the 'heroines' of the society. In vol. II, p. 13, at date: Candlemas, 1734, the festival of the Purification of the Virgin Mary (February 2nd) we are told:

1734. Candlemas. — 13 Knights present . . . One Feminine Gender, 17, was hired for One Sovereign, fat and well-developed. She stripped in the Closet [*i.e.* toilet], nude; and was allowed to come in with face half-covered. None was permitted to speak to or touch her. She spread wide upon a Seat, first before and then behind: every Knight passed in turn and surveyed the Secrets of Nature . . .

This is evidently only a formalized version of the standard activities of many little pre-adolescent boys, taking down the panties of the local little 'bad girl' as heroine, in cellars and under porches, sometimes with the similar formalization, of game-making, that they are 'playing doctor' and the like, but also often with a (moderate) cash payment to the little girl, as alluded to in several jokes given earlier. A very florid version of this is shown in the Italian art-movie of the 1960's, entitled "8½," in which the young boy students pay their *scudi* to survey the Secrets of Nature in the form of a grotesque dance done for them by a fat wild-woman in a shack on the dunes. This is perhaps a recollection or mock of the famous scene in Josef von Sternberg's sado-masochistic movie of the 1930's, *The Blue Angel,* which launched Marlene Dietrich as similarly showing her 'legs' to German high-school boys in a low Tingeltangel song-&-dance joint, on the style of the New Orleans jazz-&-whore houses.

The Beggar's Benison was not too fortunate in their choice of heroines, nor in the discretion of either the Knights or the girls themselves, as to what went on at the initiation ceremony. In the same year, 1734, at St. Andrew's Day (Nov. 30th) the records state, II. 14, that, of the Knights, '24 present and 4 Novices tested and frigged. Betty Wilson, 15, was hired, but a bad model and unpleasant. Resolved against such another row.' Finally, according to vol. II, p. 7, at a date not given exactly, but in the 14th year of the presidency of the Order by Dr. Charles Rogers of Fife (probably early 19th century?), at a local wedding:

it got wing [*i.e.* wind] among the Parishioners that the Bride was a heroine, and after the knot was tied, and at the departure for home, some covetous damsel shouted: — "Ah, ah! that's the B-t-h that shewed her hairy C— and A— to the gentlemen of the Beggar's Benison for Five Shillings."

This is told as a true anecdote, and may very well *be* true, or it may simply be a joke or cautionary tale recommending discretion to the Knights as to the proceedings of their phallic-worship Order. The describing of the shouting damsel as 'covetous,' and her perfect social consciousness of the members of the Beggar's Benison as 'gentlemen,' *i.e.* of the wealthy class, no matter what they might do to a girl of the poorer class available to them for cash, does suggest a true occurrence. In any case, the savoring of the coming marital consummation has here evidently turned to pure hostility, and a willingness, if possible, to impede the consummation, whether by tattletale words, or deeds, such as "*putting Novocaine in the newlyweds' vaseline*" (N.Y. 1946). Compare also the turning in of a false fire-alarm, giving the address of the newlyweds' home, so that the fire-brigade will presumably douse them with cold water, all unbeknownst, through the window of the bridal chamber. This is of course plain scatological dirtying, or 'anal sadism,' with the fire-hose supplying the urine.

A similar voyeuristic wedding-night prank is the tying of sleigh-bells to the wedding bedsprings. This has already been seen in a rationalized form in the joke on the father who ties an apple to the bedsprings over a pot of cream to spy on his daughter's suspected intimacy with her lover. In a modern version of the prank, in George S. Kaufman & Moss Hart's *The Man Who Came to Dinner* (1939), a microphone is attached to the bed and the bride & groom's intimate conversation on their wedding night is broadcast to the guests. This is again ritual public coitus, presented strictly in the form of a *charivari* prank. A phonograph recording has also been semi-publicly on sale in the U.S., early 1960's, under the title *The Sound of Love* (and pirated under other titles), giving an assortment of presumably authentical erotic grunts & groans on the part of a man and woman, with folklore supplied gratis as to the record having been made by means of a microphone hung round the neck of a multiple-orgasm nymphomaniac, though nymphomaniacs seldom have orgasm at all . . . A similar recording, as *Essai Sonore sur l'Érotisme,* Paris, 1968.

The college widow [*widow*: American dialectal term for the town prostitute, usually a grass- or other widow] *is marrying a grocer. A group of college students, her former clients, gather outside the hotel room where the marriage is being consummated. One is hoisted up to see over the transom, and the details he gives are passed along in whispers down the darkened hallway.* "He's taking off her clothes . . ." "He's taking off her clothes." "He's kissing her tits . . ." "He's kissing her tits." "Now they're in bed . . ." "Now they're in bed." *Suddenly the lookout hears the bride say,* "Oh, you're doing what no man has ever done to me before!" *The whispered report goes down the hall:* "He's fucking her in the arse . . ." "He's fucking her in the arse." (1:230.) Earlier in *The Pearl,* No. 4, Oct. 1879, of a tavern chambermaid at the "Blue Boar" marrying an ostler. The curious surviving trait of the girl's marrying a man of 'lower' social status than her former lovers is apparently to explain their hostile peeping.

3. THE MAN IN THE UPPER BERTH

The rejected suitors, unwilling to give up, with one last public kiss, their hold upon the bride, are nevertheless left behind on the honeymoon trip. A more powerful figure substitutes for them, asserting his still unalienated right to mock and to observe, even if he can no longer bring back the captured bride. This is the Man in the Upper Berth, in whose enigmatic accents — halfway between wistfulness and hatred — can be heard the last receding thunders of the forbidding father's voice.

There are a number of special elements about the railroad train that make it specially suitable as the locale of this last Oedipal conflict before the children begin their independent sex lives, formally free of parental control. The railroad train (specifically the engine) was the father- and penis-symbol *par excellence* of the later 19th century, although it has now been almost wholly superseded by the airplane and rocket. It also had until very recently its own almost-conscious literature of Oedipal adulation and defiance, not to mention the grownup toy-train fad. Aside from the train-wreck balladry of the Sweet Singer of Michigan and other folk-poets, there have been William Ellery Leonard's *The Locomotive God* — specifically intended to express and explain the author's agoraphobia (always an Oedipal problem, as with Freud himself) — the 'high iron' railroading volume of the professional photographer, Lucius Beebe; and last the most absurd movie of Hollywood's original woman-slapper, James Cagney, entitled *White Heat* (1952?), a gangster-cum-sciencefiction mélange opening with Cagney stopping a locomotive from going through a tunnel by scalding the engineer (daddy) to death with a squirt of his own live steam; continuing through epilepsy, transvestism, a gun-toting mother who avenges her son for his wife's infidelity while he is in jail, and a final mechanical parturition scene, in which Cagney and his merry men are delivered out of the belly of a milk truck (in spite of evil FBI obstetricians tracking them mercilessly along the highway to birth, with the standard radio influencing-machines of paranoia à la Dianetics), amid the tremendous metal tubes and monster grapefruit breasts of an oil refinery. There is also a closing vignette or Götterdämmerung in which Cagney explodes up a long self-consciously phallic staircase between two enormous oil-domes, screaming — meaninglessly, except in the intended symbolic sense — "*Mom, I* MADE *it!*"

Only the closing decades of a culture far gone in diseased baroque can afford such spectacles of this more-than-total celebration of phallic-mechanical death, even in the form of the later gag-images, similar, of Terry Southern's remarkable and satirical atom-bomb movie, *Dr. Strangelove* (1963). Compare also the 'James Bond' comic-strip spy movies, of most recent brew, especially the pyromaniacal *From Russia with Love,* and *Goldfinger,* which uses the identical paranoid tracing-gimmick as Cagney's *White Heat.* The folk materials in joke form being the activities of basically healthy personalities, or at least of people trying to save their mental health by these means, and not to celebrate and cash in on their mental disease, nothing will be found in them in the way of such head-on engagements with the locomotive-father or the terrifying Machine. All that can be seen in the jokes is mild and generalized, but very definite, sexual prohibitiveness emanating from everything concerned with the railroad train, except of course the frantic copulation of the pistons up ahead, a symbolization which has already been represented in satirical art more than once, especially by Jean Veber. The newlywed couple paradoxically try to leave the forbidding father behind at the church, only to find him somehow ensconced *over their heads* and mocking them in strange voices on the wedding night. This is, of course, a beautiful representation of the internalized conscience by means of which the repressive influence of the parents never ceases to prevent and upset the sexual life of their children, not only after the children's wedding but also after the parents' death or disappearance.

As to the generalized prohibitiveness of the train, the joke has already been given, in the chapter on Fools, of the bride who asks her husband if he has remembered their "intercourse tickets" or similar, because she has heard another passenger say that he has *lost his fucking tickets,*" or that if the engineer does not hurry, "*the fucking season will be over before they get there.*" These are a very exact expression of the train situation as it is experienced just below the level of consciousness: the requiring of tickets, the economic, sexual, and defecational prohibitiveness of the conductor, and especially the never succeeding in going fast enough to escape from any of this. *A woman passenger on a slow train gives birth to a baby. Conductor: "Madam, you should have known better than to get on the train in that condition." "I wasn't in that condition when I got on the train!"* (2:413). A variant given in Vardis Fisher's Mormon novel, *Children of God* (1939) p. 653-4, explains who it was that dared to impregnate her under the very eye of the conductor: she is one of Brigham Young's plural wives. The too-slow engineer can also be turned inside out and appear as impossibly overfast — again by way of sexual prohibitiveness. *A soldier is leaning out the train window at the depot to kiss his bride goodbye. The engineer has steam up, and starts the train with such a rush that the soldier misses his bride completely and kisses a cow's ass a mile and a quarter out of town.* (Idaho, 1919. Also, it will be noted, from the stronghold of the Mormon patriarchy.)

The engineer, however, is really too far away, and too absorbed in his furnaces and pistons and white-hot steam, and the other accoutrements of mechanical virility, to be more than a symbol. (One would think so, anyhow, though a greeting-card, postmarked from the Mormon capital, Salt Lake City, transcribes a highway advertising caption that almost makes one wonder: "Train wrecks few, Reason clear, Fireman never hugs Engineer — BURMA SHAVE!" Has someone been accusing them?) The conductor becomes the on-the-premises father-figure, or surrogate, with his concern about tickets, about the prevention of free rides, public eating, smoking, and petting, of private intercourse in the sleeping cars, and, of course, of forcing passengers, with an enormous seneschal's key, to "*Please refrain from flushing toilets, while the train is in the station*" (U.S. 1928, to the tune of Dvořák's "Humoresque.") His concern with petting has already been noted in the chapter on Premarital Acts, in connection with the usual piscine allegation against the female genital odor. More striking examples can be cited. *Riding on a train, a woman is fondling her man under cover of a newspaper spread on his lap. It is a hot day and they fall asleep, and a breeze blows the paper away. The conductor comes by.*

"Madam, wake up!" he says, shaking her gently. *"Your bouquet has wilted."* (Idaho, 1919. Compare: *Patient in a hospital is told not to ask the nurse for a urinal, but to say "vase." Nurse: "How big is your bouquet?"* Minn. 1946.) Boccaccio's "Nightingale."

A man with a very large penis attempts to consummate his marriage in a railroad train berth. His bride is frightened of the size of his organ. She is sure that she will make an outcry and wake the whole car, and suggests that he wait till they get into their own home. He coaxes, but to no use, and so puts his penis out the window to cool it off. In the morning he feels a pain, draws in his penis thinking it has got a cramp, and finds two mail bags hanging on it. (Memorabilia, 1910.) The theme here is that of self-castration by way of revenge, with the overcompensation of the two extra 'mail bags' as in an old pun on *Why women can't be letter-carriers.* The fearful and prohibitive bride here is more than matched by the active and sexually dominant bride of one of the most frequently collected pantomime stories. *Two newlyweds at the World's Fair can't find a hotel room. The best they can get is a single coach seat on the train to Washington. The bride sits on her husband's lap and tries to have intercourse with him, but the conductor is watching them suspiciously. When his back is turned they manage to make entry, but then he whirls suddenly and fixes them with an angry eye. "Oh, look at the trees!" says the bride, bouncing to one side and pointing out the window. "And oh! look at those houses," bouncing to the other side. "Look at that lake, and oh! look at those cows! Oh, goodie, goodie, goodie (bounce, bounce, bounce),* EVERYBODY'S *going to Washington!"* (Ohio, 1939. This is originally French: *Kryptádia,* 1907, x. 224; *Histoires d'Hommes,* 1913, p. 17. Compare, for the trick, Type 1463.)

In an *al fresco* variant, *A girl at a church picnic is having intercourse with a man sitting astraddle his lap so as not to stain her dress. The minister approaches and the man lies back hidden in the grass while the girl explains to the minister why she is sitting there. "I'm getting married pretty soon,"* she says, and *I was just thinking I'd build a house over there (moving her whole body to match the gesture), and the barn over there (gesture). But no, maybe I'd better build the barn back here (gesture), so I won't have to go over there (gesture), except for water, or riding horse-back (bounce! bounce! bounce!)* (N.Y. 1941.) Especially in this house-building version, the woman astride has achieved all the attributes of the matriarch, and is able to impugn the authority of the father-figure of minister and conductor before his very eyes. Robert Graves makes quite a point of the woman-superior position in coitus, in his male-masochist and flagellant-female 'utopia,' *Watch the North Wind Rise* (1949), an eccentric and repugnant example — to describe it as charitably as possible — of the racketeering of the woman problem now reaching some sort of climax in America.

The Man in the Upper Berth makes his first appearance on the observation platform, where his surface identity as none other but the poor, sexually-frustrated travelling salesman is also made clear. *The romantic young newlywed couples are sitting on the observation platform of the train. As night deepens one bridegroom says, "Honey, what do you say we get that Twentieth Century Limited on the rails?" And he and his bride go back to the pullman. Another groom: "Sweetheart, let's see if we can't put The Chief into Chicago by morning." Etc. Lonesome travelling salesman in the corner: "Well — guess I'll get the old hand-car greased up."* (1:417.) Back in his upper berth now: *A travelling salesman is waked up several times by a bridegroom saying, "Porter, here's a dollar. Bring us two towels." On the sixth such occasion the salesman says loudly, "Hey porter, here's fifty cents. Bring me one towel."* (2:384.)

In the later chapters on "Homosexuality" and "Castration," in the Second Series, the notion of pedicatory rape by the father, forcing the son into homosexuality, and even impregnating him with a fecal baby, will be given appropriate attention. In two examples, the Man in the Upper Berth betrays his surrogate identity as father even to the degree of allusory threats of pedicatory rape, though in both cases these are projected upon the wife, with the sub-homosexual tone of possession of her in common by both father and son. *Newlyweds on a train are protracting their preparations for intercourse while they argue whether, if the baby is a boy, they will send him to Harvard or to Yale. After an hour of this, a voice from the upper berth shouts: "Oh, shove it up her ass and send it to Princeton!"* (Calif. 1939, in a version libelling Stanford, the University of California's traditional rival, as in the anti-Stanford bawdy ballad, "The Cardinals be Damned!" Aarne Type 1430A, Motif J2060.1.) — *The newlyweds are in bed in a small hotel. A travelling salesman mistakes their door for that of the hall privy and begins rattling the knob. "What do you want?" the bridegroom shouts. "You know damn well what I want. If you ain't using both of those holes, I want one."* (2:381.) Originally a *conte-en-vers* in P.-S. Caron's *Le Plat de Carnaval* (1802) No. 13, "Les Lieux," reprinted in Barraud's *Recueil de Pièces rares et facétieuses* (1873) IV. 50,

It is to be observed that the Man in the Upper Berth does not object to the consummation of the honeymooners' marriage — only to their enjoying it, as evidenced by the folklore of the number of coital repetitions. *To avoid embarrassment the newlyweds on the train arrange to use the code phrase "Squeeze me an orange," for intercourse.* [Compare Mae West's "Beulah, peel me a grape!"] *After the fifth or sixth time, a voice from the* lower *berth says, "Go ahead and give her all the oranges you want, but stop squeezing the juice on me!"* (Pa. 1935.) Variant: *The newlyweds spend a week in their hotel room without coming down for food. The manager finally knocks at the door: "Don't you want something to eat?" Groom: "No, we're living on the fruits of love." "All right, but I'd appreciate it if you'd stop throwing the skins out the window."* (D.C. 1950.) These two variants make clear the meaning of the gesture, encountered earlier under "Petting," and "The Condom," of throwing the semen or condom at an older man, as a defiance of the forbidding father-figure with the very evidence of the forbidden sexual intimacy. Before the wedding night is over, the parental forbidding of sex will become internalized within the honeymooners, as sex hatred or rejection; the wife calling the husband inadequate ("I'm going back to Mother!") and the husband calling the wife impossible to satisfy — or just plain impossible. *On the train. The key-word for intercourse is "Scare me." After a night of this, just as the train pulls into Chicago early in the morning the bride whispers, "Scare me, honey." "Boo."* (N.Y. 1939.) This is the key to all the amenities of the honeymoon, as will be seen. (Motifs J2492-3.)

III. THE HONEYMOON

Two main themes can be separated out from the jokes on the wedding night and honeymoon that are not in any way dependent on the place of consummation — train, hotel bedroom, etc. — or in which these background elements serve merely as conveniences to the plot. These two themes represent the two characters of the bride, one of which is to change into the other by morning with the loss of her virginity, and both of which are described as equally unsatisfactory. The jokes on her maidenly reserve and ignorance (which of course turn out to be false) will be given second, since these involve the complex relationship with other men. First may be considered the theme already touched upon in the train berth, that of the insatiability of the bride and general ineptness of the groom.

A young bride puts up a rustic motto over her husband's bed: "I need thee every hour." He puts up a sign of his own: "God give me strength." (*Anecdota,* 1933, No. 258.) — *The young minister who marries a widow suggests to his bride that they kneel by the wedding bed and pray for strength and guidance. "Just pray for strength," says the widow. "I'll do the rest."* (McAtee, 1912, env. 7, versified as "Grace Before Meat.") The exact same joke is given, in translation from the Alsatian patois, in *Kryptádia,* 1884, II. 280. The idea dates in literature at least from Carew's *"A Rapture,"* (about 1639): *"My rudder with thy bold hand, like a try'd And skilful pilot, thou shalt steer, and guide My bark in Love's dark channel, where it shall Dance as the rising waves do rise and fall,"* with other reversals of the usual male and female rôles as noted earlier. From Canada, 1951: *"The Boy Scouts and the Girl Guides."*

Both sexes, as the jokes see it, complain about the other's insatiability, but the tone is quite different. The groom's complaints are always construed as reasonable, the bride's as hateful. *The young bride advises another woman not to go to a hotel for her honeymoon. "All night it was up and down, in and out; up and down, in and out — they gave us a room right next to the elevator."* (*Anecdota,* 1933, No. 207.) By comparison there is *The nervous bridegroom — all he did on his wedding night was jabber jabber jabber.* (Ohio, 1951.) — *After a week in the hotel room without going out, the groom decides to take his bride to a movie. He calls to her in the bathroom, "Honey, would you like to see* Oliver Twist?" *"No thanks, I've seen it do everything else."* (D.C. 1950.) All the various natural phenomena of famous honeymoon resorts, such as Niagara Falls, the giant redwood forests, and, especially, the hourly white-hot ejaculation of the Old Faithful geyser are used to symbolize the bride's excessive appetite and disappointment, though few references in actual joke form have been collected. *Niagara Falls: the bride's* second *big disappointment.* (N.Y. 1938.) The reference to the Falls is probably fortuitous in the following: *On the wedding morning the bride is very anxious to see Niagara Falls. The groom puts up the window shade but it is raining. They can't see the Falls, and go back to bed. Same thing the second day and third day. The fourth day the groom goes to the window, takes hold of the cord, and goes up with the shade.* (Minn. 1935.) A possible reference, specifically to the penis, has been suggested in the first and last examples in this paragraph — "up and down," and "up with the shade" — and also in the bride's first "big disappointment." I disagree with this interpretation, but give it for the sake of the record.

The most important feature of the American sexual neurosis is its regression from genital aims to earlier and more infantile goals. Regressions to anal-cleanliness compulsions in connection with sex involve excessive washing (including shampooing the head hair) and consciousness of genital and axillary odor, with deodorizing, depilating, and shaving of all parts; and also more generalized and more outwardly sadistic anality, as in the observance of strict regularity about the time of day, night, or even month; frequency, or position of intercourse. The oral regressions, in substituting food satisfaction for sex (*Dagwoodism*), are even more pervasive and more difficult to unseat, since they are basically masochistic and involve very little sadist guilt. Anal regression in men usually takes the form of a sadistic rejection of women on one pretext or another, and motion toward homosexuality. The oral regression, since it involves a masochistic dependence on the mother figure, does not exclude normal sexual relations, but may impair them when the couple engages in tearful controversy for *the right to be dependent*. The neuroticizing forces in a culture always act at least equally on women and men, though in matchingly different forms.

Three rather poor jokes are all that have been collected on the subject of food, sex, and the wedding night, where the neurosis is presented, as it were, *in statu nascendi,* as compared to its final development (also its earliest) in the food-defiling or 'purposely nasty' stories given in a later chapter. *Groom, to bride, on the morning after the wedding night:* "*What would you like for breakfast, honey?*" "*You know what I like.*" "*Yes, but you've got to eat sometime.*" (*Anecdota,* 1933, No. 202. The unexpurgated *Anecdota* 2:155 gives a variant omitting the groom and setting up the colloquy between an 'old Negro mammy' and the bride.) Note the similar oral translation of the sexual in the 'proposition': "*Shall I call you for breakfast — or just nudge you?*" (N.Y. 1940.) The following joke has been collected with both the wife and the husband as the complainant: *At the wedding breakfast the groom finds that the wife has put a head of lettuce on his plate and nothing else.* "*I just wanted to see if you eat like a rabbit too,*" *she explains.* (D.C. 1949.) This is probably the correct version, with its reference to the quick ejaculation of the rabbit, although the Guam mimeograph (1948) has the groom feeding the bride lettuce with the same explanation. If the reference is presumed to be to her sexual appetite, there is clearly an error here, as the standard animal simile in that case would be the mink.

The wedding-breakfast joke that makes the food-sex equation clearest is the prototype of the many cleaned-up variants used for public comedy: *The groom gazes soulfully at his bride in the morning, after intercourse, and says, "If you could only cook!"* (Pa. 1935.) Aside from the cleanups, there are various reversals of this, and it has become a folk-phrase. *The groom looks thoughtfully at the bride's first breakfast: scorched toast and bacon, and underdone eggs and coffee. "Hell," he says, "you can't cook either!"* (Joe 'Miller' Murray, *Smoker Stories*, 1942.) I have also seen a motion picture double-reverse of this, where the wedding-night fadeout is followed by a closeup of a fabulously perfect breakfast being cooked over a spotless stove by — as the camera draws back to reveal — the groom. He then arranges it all beautifully on a bedtray, including a little vase of flowers, tiptoes with it upstairs where his delighted bride is waiting in a fetching bedjacket, and then *accidentally* flings the whole thing in her lap. Exactly the same message is transmitted, without all the grapefruit-pushed-in-the-woman's-puss circumlocution (to which even Charlie Chaplin disgraced himself by sinking in his next-to-last motion picture, *Limelight* — the girl is hysterical, he *has* to slap her, the show must go on, etc.), in the following simplified form: *Rosie the Riveter has married a homosexual. On their wedding morning he brings in a wonderful breakfast on a tray. She looks at it, and him, and says: "If you could only fuck!"* (N.Y. 1945.) In postwar collectings, Rosie the Riveter becomes 'a Lesbian.' No error here.

I. THE NERVOUS BRIDE

The shift is very visible between the fear and taboo of virginity, not very well hidden in the preceding stories of ignorant hillbillies who refuse the bride *because* she is a virgin, and the equal or greater fear expressed as to the bride's premarital unchastity, in those jokes in which the presumably virgin bride turns out to be a sexual expert, more experienced and knowing more erotic tricks than her husband, all of which she has therefore certainly 'learned from other men.' The pre-condition of the stories of both types is ignorance — *i.e.* sexual ignorance — whether demanded in the bride or rejected in her; and the deepest expression in both types of story is the *fear of the unknown* in connection both with the wedding night and the woman or man whom one has married. In an innocent enough but very touching story, *A Negro girl is afraid to go away on her honeymoon with her new husband, and tells this to her mother. "But honey, you gotta go with him. Didn't I go on my honeymoon with Daddy?" "Sure, but you went with Daddy. I got to go with this strange man!"* (D.C. 1940.) This must be very ancient, being known in India: Motif J2463.2.

In general, however, it is to be understood that the bride's ignorance, shyness, maidenly reserve and the like are presented as a sham, intended to disguise or conceal from her husband her premarital unchastity with other men, and it is in the sudden unveiling of her nonvirginity that the principal shock to the groom is presumed to reside. This point will be returned to, in connection with the extraordinary "Sleeve Job" story in the following section. It is difficult to sort out the various types of ignorance — real and pretended — ascribed sometimes to the bride and sometimes to the groom. Those concerning the groom have been grouped earlier in the section on the male fool or nincumpoop. The ignorant bride, as just observed, tends always to be something of a fraud.

In a short story handed me for criticism by a freshman at the University of California (La Jolla) in 1964, the following burlesque passage occurred: '*"No, I've never kissed any other boy," she said, laying back and opening her mouth wide.*' When challenged on this, the young author admitted it was not original but a local 'fraternity gag.' It is clearly a spontaneous Wellerism, a type of phraseological humor well known in the older Italian literature, and imported to the English-speaking world by at least the time of Le Motteux' translation of Rabelais (1694), when, at the end of Bk. V, chap. xxix, Le Motteux extends Rabelais' simple, *"Allons de par Dieu, dist Panurge,"* to: *"Come, come, scatter no words, return'd Panurge; Every one as they like, as the Woman said when she kiss'd her Cow."* (Whole series of similar erotic and scatologic Wellerisms in English have been collected, but these being verbal humor rather than situational *jokes*, they are not included in the present volume.)

The nervous bride who didn't know whether to say "I do," "I have," or "I will" (Minn., 1946) is again not a joke but a gag-line, and is more than balanced by the cliché story combining all possible strains of ignorance: the sexual fool, the silly-ass Englishman (here Englishwoman), and those royal & noble personages who are really intended in hostile references to the 'Englishman': *The virgin daughter of a titled English family gets married. After intercourse she says to the groom, "Is this what the common people call 'fucking'?" Her husband admits it is. "Well, it's* FAR *too good for them!"* (N.Y. 1935. Also collected as of Queen Victoria asking Prince Albert, *"Do the common people do this too?"*) This is part of a whole group of folklore items stating that sexual intercourse is the only pleasure the poor can afford, and their dearest prerogative, but that the rich would take it away from them if they could. See, for example, the joke in the section on "Masturbation" earlier, about *The poor boy who explains that he has no foreskin, though he has never been circumcised, because "Rich kids have toys."* The classic expression is Robert Burns' "Poor Bodies Do Naething But Mow," in his *Merry Muses of Caledonia* (type-facsimile edition, 1965, p. 80, and my notes to that edition, pp. xiii–xiv, and 204–6, on the circumstances of Burns' writing this in 1792 as an expression of his combined sexual and rather weak political revolt).

Memorabilia gives a longer version of the "FAR too good for them" joke on the sexual ignorance of the rich and noble, dating from 1900, in which the then presumably even sillier ass than a silly-ass Englishman, a German baron, is the sexual fool: *A German baron out hunting sees on the hillside a spread umbrella, and sticking out from under it a pair of woman's legs with a pair of man's legs between them. He says to his guide, "Do you see anything on the hill?" "Herr Baron, I see an umbrella." "Do you see anything else?" "Herr Baron, I see a woman's legs sticking out under it." "Anything else?" "Herr Baron, I see a man's feet between the woman's legs." "Yes, yes, but what do you suppose they are doing?" "Herr Baron, I think they are fucking." "My God, is that thing still going on?"* The metonymic use of the feet in this way, to represent coitus, is a not uncommon theme of erotic art, as in the 18th-century "Les Petits Pieds," copied in Gillray's "Fashionable Contrasts," and most recently in *"Sam, the Ceiling Needs Painting"* (1964), a whole book of cartoons devoted to this theme. It also exists independently in Japanese erotic art, and in *Genesis,* an unpublished album (New York, 1944) in my collection, of 300 erotic drawings telling a continued story.

The shock of previous knowledge on the part of the bride is pointed up by having the groom expect her to be not only a virgin but an absolute sexual ignoramus. *An old roué marries a young girl straight from the convent school to be sure of getting a virgin. On the wedding night she gets into bed, and he approaches her in the dark and feels for her feet. "Is 'u 'ittle tootsies cold?" he begins, then suddenly and apprehensively, "why where is 'u other 'ittle tootsie?"* (1:301.) Same situation: *Old rake, young girl straight from convent school. In the lobby of the hotel where they are to spend their wedding night the bride is amazed by the beautiful unaccompanied women floating about, and asks her husband who they are. She is told that they are prostitutes, and asks what the word means. "A prostitute," he tells her, "is a woman that will sleep with any man that asks her, for fifty or a hundred dollars." "Gee," says the girl, "the priests only gave* us *an apple."* (1:307. Nicolaidès, p. 139.) — Compare: *"Wouldja for a big red apple?"* sometimes prefaced by, *"As Adam said to Eve . . . "* (In the Talmud, Midrash to *Ecclesiastes,* iv. 6, is noted a woman who prostitutes herself for apples and then distributes them among the sick. This is assuredly religious prostitution of a matriarchal type. See also *Song of Songs,* ii. 5: "Comfort me with apples, for I am sick of [with] love," a line not satisfactorily explained otherwise. Molière, in his *"School for Wives"* (1662) I.i, has a husband who is bringing up a young girl on purpose to be too innocent to cuckold him after he marries her, *e.g.* "And should one play with her at the basket, and ask her in one's turn, *What's put into't?* I'd have her answer be, *A cream tart."* (transl. 1739.) The humor naturally turns on the husband's ultimate disappointment, as in the jokes just given. The game of "the basket," here referred to, survives as "Coffeepot," described as being played for *double entendre* by a party of young men and girls in Bessie Breuer's 1930's novel, *The Daughter.*)

Knowledge of special sex techniques is *prima facie* evidence of previous knowledge in the bride. These principally include oragenital acts (as noted in the section on "Oragenitalism," following) and active motions during sexual intercourse. *The hillbilly brings the bride back to her father the morning after the wedding, saying "That up-and-down motion may come natural, but that round-and-round motion was learned!"* (1:399, as the *'cinder-shifting movement;'* also collected with the railroad phrase *'ballin' the jack.'*) The objection to the woman's motions in intercourse has already been discussed as a resistance to any hint of female dominance, or spontaneous passion. However, if these motions have been learned specially for the benefit of the groom, with some 'vegetable' or dummy male, in a marriage-counselling course, that is accepted as a sufficient gesture of subservience. But the point of the jokes on this theme is really the absurdity of the elaborate rationalizations for bridal knowledge that could only have come with experience. *The bridegroom is left limp and gasping by the sex technique of his virgin bride, and asks where she learned such tricks. She explains that she took a correspondence course in marriage while he was in the army, and when he seems incredulous she offers to demonstrate the exercises used. She lies down under a chair from which she hangs an apple and an orange, and hits each of them with her pubis with a special hip motion. Then she hangs a banana between the apple and orange, and goes through a more complicated motion to the chant: "Hit the apple, hit the orange, spin the banana, BUMP!"* (D.C. 1947, in a version adding walnuts, and finally coffee beans inserted in the bride's rectum, with the line *"grind the coffee"* instead of *"spin the banana."* A pantomime joke.) Same situation: *The bride's premarital exercise has been to put an imaginary piece of chalk in her anus and write figure-eights (or "I love you") on a blackboard in the bed. When the groom does not believe her, she lies down on the bed, puts her lipstick in her anus, and writes "Souvenir of Niagara Falls" upside down and backwards on the sheet.* (New York State, 1944. Text version, N.Y. 1953.)

In one case, the test is to be of total anatomical ignorance. *The groom asks the best man if there is any sure test of his bride's virginity, and is told to take a bucket of red paint, a bucket of blue paint, and a shovel along on his honeymoon. "Paint one ball red and one ball blue, and then if she says, 'That's the funniest pair of balls I ever saw,' hit her over the head with the shovel!"* (N.Y. 1943. Also collected D.C. 1943, with a hammer, making even clearer the intention of murdering the bride if she proves not to be a virgin.) This story is old and traditional. In Heinrich Bebel's *Facetiæ* (1514, the manuscript being dated 1508 in Bk. III.135), the parent-story of this type is given, III.108, as *"Facetiæ de simplicitate sponsæ."* In Bebel's version, which he calls an 'anecdote of Brassicanus' (the humanist Johannes Köl):

A rich peasant has just married off his daughter. At the moment when the son-in-law is about to undo the virgin knot of his shamefaced and blushing bride, he changes his mind and jumps out of bed. The astonished bride asks, "What are you do-ing, my darling?" "I'm going to get a hammer and wedge to open your virgin knot." The foolish girl became terrified, threw her arms around the neck of her crafty husband, and said naïvely: "It's not worth the trouble. There's no need of such instruments. Last year our farmhand forced it open without either a hammer or a wedge."

It will be observed that Bebel calls the bridegroom 'crafty,' implying that the whole thing is just a ruse to test his bride's virginity, exactly as in the modern story (retaining the hammer) which is almost cer-tainly derived from German sources.

The lore of the best man, or best friend of the groom, as the better man at the wedding, has already been alluded to in connection with the wedding itself, and will be discussed further under "Adultery" in the following chapter. A sidewise allusion to this relationship is clearly present in jokes on orgies, the term being broadened here to include 'foursomes' or *parties carrées,* even where the couples do not change partners at any point. In the 'gang-shag' the relationship of the men to each other is almost openly homosexual, and involving contact with each other's semen; and is much closer than the relation to the woman. *Two friends arrange a double wedding and get rooms next to each other at the honeymoon hotel. They undertake to compete in inter-course and to chalk their scores on the wall. The first man chalks up 1, then another 1, then a third; and then can do no more. In the morning the other friend and his new bride come in to look at their score, and read the three 1's as 111. "You win," says the second friend; "that's a dozen more than we could manage."* (Calif. 1941.) The same note of bragging to another man is present in *The country jay who spends his wedding night in a big city hotel. In the morning he asks for his bill and is told by the desk-clerk, "Two dollars apiece." He lays down a twenty-dollar bill.* (2:293.) The various jokes on men bragging to strangers in hotels about their wives or girlfriends, waiting passionately upstairs for them, have already been noted.

2. TRACES OF THE OTHER MAN

The traces that the other man leaves on, or even in, the bride are an ancient theme. In the older sources this generally occurs in the form of some preventive sign left by the husband, but mocked by the other man. The last story in the *Hundred Mery Talys* (1526) is of a lamb painted on the wife's belly by the jealous husband, to which (and to whom) the lover adds a pair of horns. Béroalde de Verville's *Moyen de Parvenir* almost a century later gives a version in which a saddle is added to an ass painted in the same place (Machen's translation, chap. 70, "Tale of the Painter's Ass"). Evan-Esar Levine, in his *Chastity Belts* (1931) p. 131–2, also notes the amulet form of 'this scare-belly practice,' as he calls it, in which a crucifix is hung over the wife's pubis, as in Cornazano's *Proverbii in Facetie* (1518) No. 4, "Why they say, 'Horns rather than crosses'." A modern adaptation or rationalization, in the form of a rubber-stamp on the pregnant wife's belly, has already been given, and an oragenital version also exists in which *The groom finds his bride's pubis shaved. On looking more closely at what appears to be the stubble he finds it is a tiny tattooed legend:* "DUNCAN PHYFE ATE HERE." (N.Y. 1961. The reference is to the hallmark of approval of a highway-restaurant sampling service.)

The condom affords an opportunity to adapt this theme to modern circumstances, as in the following example which is often encountered: *The day before marrying for money, a girl has one last fling with the man she really loves. He has no condom and they use the scooped-out skin of a bologna, which slips in during intercourse and cannot be retrieved. On her wedding night it comes out on her husband's penis. When he asks what it is, she says it is her maidenhead.* "Well that's the first one I ever saw with a government stamp on it!" (N.Y. 1936, or: "Where won't those bastards advertise next!" Type 1339A.) The condom that slips off during intercourse also occurs in a wedding-night story well known among children, without any reference to the other man. *On the wedding night the bridegroom uses a condom which slips off inside the bride. He fishes for it unsuccessfully with a broomstraw, which also slips in. Likewise a toothpick, with which the straw is fished for. Nine months later the baby is born wearing a raincoat and a straw hat, and carrying a cane.* (Pa. 1927, the teller ending strutting off with imaginary cane and straw hat, apparently imitating Maurice Chevalier.) In a variant tending toward the idea of punishment, the baby is not carrying a cane but is 'born with a wooden leg.' Miraculous births of this kind are an ancient theme. Rabelais' *Gargantua,* for example, I.6, is born from his mother's left ear (parodying the miraculous births of the Greek gods), crying aloud for alcoholic drink.

What is really feared, or hoped for, in these stories of possession of the wife in common with other men, and the proof of such mutual possession *de visu et de tactu,* is the meeting of another man in the body of a woman, the fantasy of 'coming in contact with a potential rival in the same sexual object,' discussed by Theodor Reik in "The Fear of Touch," in *Neurotica* (1950) No. 6: p. 3–10. He shows this to be the paramount element in such fantasies of hands-around sexual intimacy, or venereal infection, as are presented in Arthur Schnitzler's *Reigen* and in Voltaire's explanation, in *Candide* (1759) of how Dr. Pangloss caught syphilis from a maidservant, who got it from a monk, who 'caught it from an old countess, who had it from a cavalry captain, who owed it to a marchioness, who took it from a page, who had received it from a Jesuit, who, when a novice, had it in direct line from one of the companions of Christopher Columbus.' (A joke combining wholesale incest and purposeful venereal infection, exactly in this style, is given below under "Venereal Disease," in Series Two.)

The fears of infection aside, wedding-night condom stories, in which the condom or foreskin-surrogate engages the penises of both men, exactly as does the bride's vagina, are perhaps the closest to a folk statement of the idea of contact with the other men who are known or suspected to have passed through the body of the same woman. The only more direct statement encountered was not in joke form, but in a serious *complaint* concerning military college gang-shags by teenage boys, of a single Negro prostitute apparently chosen purposely for her age and extreme 'unattractiveness,' on the grounds that "*Only the first man really touches her — the rest just float in what the man before leaves behind.*" (Texas, 1950. The verbal play on 'before' and 'behind' is probably an unconscious reference to homosexual intercourse.) This is known in naval and prison slang as '*slopping down on a wet deck!*' and as '*having a buttered-bun*' in older British slang. From this it is only a short step to the conscious realization that the gang-shag is a disguised homosexual activity, with the woman simply used as a pretext or coupling-joint.

The other man's traces may range from excessive sexual aptitude on the part of the bride, as noted above, to the actual adultery on the wedding day or night. This has been used more than once as a theme in erotic literature, for example in Paul Perret's anonymous *Les Tableaux Vivants* in the late 1870's, in which a great point is made of the fact that the bride is having her last fling (but really only a sample of adulteries to come) *in her wedding gown*. She is also sitting on the toilet in company with the proto-adulterer: this is apparently felt to be an extra anal-sadistic thrust against the husband. Compare the joke toward the end of the preceding section, actually identifying woman and toilet in the tag-line, "*If you ain't using both of those holes, I want one.*" (2:381.)

The translator of Freud on *Wit,* Dr. A. A. Brill, tells, in *Psychiatric Quarterly* (1940) xiv. 732, that he collected a story five times in a single summer, probably that of 1929, from both main oceans and continents of the world, concerning *The man who finds that his bride is a remarkable swimmer. She finally explains that she had been a streetwalker in Venice.* The displacement of the bride's sexual ability to natatory needs no further comment, and this rather poor jest — actually only a pun — is still frequently collected and printed in 'men's magazines,' etc. Its popularity is clearly due to the obliquity with which it manages to state the fear of knowingness in the bride, and of her former relations with other and better men with whom the groom cannot hope to compete and whose traces he can never wipe out.

As opposed to this displacement, the whole area of fear is carefully canvassed and 'made into a joke' in a story not merely of adultery, but of multiple adultery, on the wedding night, in which the inner meaning of the bridegroom's resentment of the public kissing of the bride by all the 'other men' at the wedding is laid open as though with a cleaver. *The bride and groom are on their honeymoon trip in Paris. The groom goes down to the hotel lobby to smoke a cigar* [the same symbol used at the birth of babies] *while his bride is undressing, as she is too shy to undress while he is present. When he comes back up to their wedding suite he finds her lying stark naked in bed on top of one bellboy who is copulating with her, while a second bellboy is pedicating her from behind. She is fellating a third bellboy, and has two more by the penis, one in each hand, waiting their turn. The bridegroom is thunderstruck. "Cynthia!" he finally manages to cry out, "how could you?!" "Oh," she replies airily, releasing bellboy Number 3 with a "pop," and holding him temporarily between her shoulder and chin, "you know I've always been something of a flirt."* (2:191. Collected with the "pop!" pantomimed, N.Y. 1963.)

In a single impossible, and impossibly-detailed scene here, *all* the suspected men and intimacies of the bride's past are brought together, in a fantasy similar to that common among men, of "having all the women one has ever slept with together in one room." It is perhaps significant that the "room" referred to is usually thought of as a cocktail parlor or banqueting hall, with all the women dressed beautifully and hating one another. This fantasy has never been collected with any statement of some mass orgy to follow, as might be expected, and the fantasist as sultan of the harem of 'his women' that he has conjured up. As with the story just given, the sexual contact is really all in the past — it is the bringing of all the historically separated participants together *in one room at one time* that is the essential element of the fantasy, whether of the male harem or of the female. For it should not be overlooked — it always is! — that what looks like mass adultery or a 'gang-shag' from the male point of view, is perhaps nothing other than the enjoying of a whole harem of men, from the woman's point of view. It depends on who is the active promoter of the scene. A 'gang-shag' is presumably a gang-*rape;* but that is certainly not the case with the bride named Cynthia and her five bellboys. In a very modified form, in which nothing erotic happens or is *able* to happen, this was also the essence of the French art motion picture, *Un Carnet de Bal,* in which it is the woman who reviews and revisits all the men of her past, conjuring them up dreamily in the smoke of her cigarette (*The Secret of Suzanne*) with which the picture begins and ends.

The name 'Cynthia,' incidentally, is intended to suggest that the girl in the preceding story is of the upper class, of which the women are presumed to be 'immoral' in direct proportion to how much money their families have: money here equalling matriarchal power. In a story collected several times in France, 1960, in both French and English, much is made of the 'good family' of *The young girl who admits to her mother that she is going to have a baby, but does not know who the father is.* "*But you must know,*" the mother insists. "*How* CAN *I know,*" says the young girl of good family; "*there were twelve fellows at the surprise-party*" (French for 'wild-party' or *partouze*).

3. THE SLEEVE JOB

The false modesty of the really unvirtuous bride reaches its climax in those stories where the groom comes to some harm as a result of her simulated coyness. In its mildest expression the harm that comes to him is merely that he is refused intercourse, for which he punishes his bride in the same way. (Note: The reference to 'the spirit' in the following story is in mockery of the anti-sexual pretensions of certain Christian sects.) *The bride refuses to have intercourse with her new husband. Each time he tries on the wedding night she says, "Not yet; wait till the spirit moves me." Finally after many hours of refusing she turns to him suddenly and says, "Quick, honey, the spirit moves me." "Well, let the spirit fuck you. I've jacked off."* (D.C. 1943.) In effect very close to the French *"L'Aze te foute!"* versified in the 18th century by Piron, in which the sexually demanding woman is left to a farting jackass rather than 'the spirit.' Prose form: *Kryptádia,* x. 178; and compare *La Fleur lascive,* No. 5, from China.

The hostility here on both sides is displaced upon the intended child in two versions of the same joke collected some twenty-five years apart in Idaho. This is the reverse of the depression and mute rage that the menstruating woman feels, which is to be interpreted as her disappointment over the 'lost' child. *The newlyweds are spending their first night together in their new home. Just as the husband is about to insert his penis, the wife says, "John, darling, did you remember to lock the front door?"* [Compare *Tristram Shandy.*] *He goes down and double-checks the door. The second time she says, "John, darling, did you remember to put the cat out?" and the third time, "John, darling, did you bank the furnace?" Finally, when he comes up from the cellar, he turns his back on her in bed. Thinking perhaps she has gone too far, she says seductively, "John, darling, what shall we call our first child?" "Call him Cinders. He's laying down there on the ashpile now."* (Idaho, 1946.)

The earlier version (Idaho, 1919) attempts to rationalize the situation by basing it on ignorance rather than hostility, but imports the even more hostile element of having the groom come to physical harm. *The newlyweds do not know how to have intercourse. They decide that the woman should lie on her back and the man should masturbate in the bathroom almost till the point of orgasm, and then rush into the bedroom and make a dive for her. While this is going on, they discuss through the door what they will call the baby, and decide to call him Eli.* [It's always a boy.] *As the groom runs into the bedroom he slips on a bar of soap and crashes to the floor. He wipes himself off and recites:*

> "Well, here I slipped, and here I fell,
> And there lies Eli deader than hell!"

As more frequently collected over the last decades, this *cante-fable* story has moved on from any concern over the loss of the intended child to a strict concentration on the harm to the husband. *On the wedding night the bride is too shy to undress in front of her husband, and asks him to wait in the bathroom till she calls him. After a few minutes he calls to ask if she is ready, but she puts him off with "Just a few more minutes, dear." This is repeated several times until finally, after nearly an hour, when she whispers, "All right, dear, I'm ready," he flings open the door, rushes wildly into the room, trips on the edge of the rug, and pole-vaults out the window.* (u.s. 1943. Randolph's No. 67, "Let's Play Whammy;" Perceau's *Histoires Raides,* p. 9.)

A gruesome punishment variant of this concerns *A man who decides to 'make his own hole' when he is overcharged in a whore-house. He gets out of bed, backs away to the door, and makes a rush at the bed, intending to bore a new hole of his own in the whore's body! Instead, he trips on the carpet, pole-vaults out the window, and his penis is cut off by the broken window-glass.* (Calif. 1948.) The burlesque elements here are a bit too strong for this story to be presented, as sexual punishment tales often are, as a 'true incident,' but it is very much of the true-incident type. A version has also been collected — unfortunately with the details insufficiently recorded for reconstituting, only the tag-line having been kept — similar in framework to the "lost-condom" stories earlier, in which *The man's penis is lacerated on his wedding night by broken window-glass and the frame, when he charges through the window trying to deflower his impenetrably virgin bride. The baby is born sporting a malacca cane and wearing a cut-glass tie-pin.* (Cleveland, Ohio, 1940.) The purpose here seems to be to deny the castrational *mise-en-scène* by having any baby be born at all!

The most hateful wedding-night story or group of stories is that culminating in the mysterious "Sleeve Job," which has already been noted, in the section "Masturbation," as belonging to the class of "The Most Maddening Story in the World." Puzzle stories of this type, like the 'shaggy dog' stories which derive from them, are actually expressions of hostility against the listener. Whatever other psychological satisfactions such stories have for the teller, the listener is forced to sit or stand through a story purposely spun out in the telling as long as possible, with all sorts of absurd details and *fiorituri,* only to arrive at last at some impossible riddling climax, or, rather, lack of climax, or some worthless but elaborate pun intended to let him down hard.

All the elements of the "Sleeve Job" story are present in the various stories already given in the preceding paragraphs, involving some dangerous accident to the groom on his wedding night. The accident is either directly expressed as a castratory mishap of some kind (*e.g.* by means of broken glass), or else the penis is somehow involved in the accident, as in the 'pole-vaulting' stories, with the direct implication that the accident would never have happened to the groom except for his own excessive phallic passion. (This is a good example of throwing the blame on the victim, or 'the gun on the murdered man,' as, earlier, the Italian vendetta knife would be left between the ribs of the victim as a 'reproach,' or an 'insult to his family.') But where the teasing and delaying tactics of the tantalizing bride figure very small, and only *pour la forme,* in the earlier wedding-night stories; in the "Sleeve Job" these become a principal element. In fact, nothing else remains.

A very romantic young man meets a lovely red-headed girl in a bar. He is struck by her culture and education, and is overwhelmed to learn at last that she is an amateur prostitute. He refuses to have intercourse with her, on the grounds that that is what all her other clients do, but offers to give her the twenty dollars she has asked for, if she will go back to her room and spend the evening alone reading a good book. She is touched by his evident concern for her, and asks if he would like, instead, to have a Sleeve Job, which she never does for her clients. He agrees, but loses his nerve on the way to her room, gives her all the money he has, and tells her she must leave this terrible life and go straight. He meets her several times afterward, by accident, in various bars, but will never go to her room with her, and finally offers to marry her to reform her. She assures him, out of gratitude, that when they are married she will give him the promised Sleeve Job on their wedding night. He introduces her to his family, buys her a trousseau and an Italian sports car, and they are finally married. On the wedding night he reminds her of her promise, which she has completely forgotten. She tries to talk him out of it and suggests that they have intercourse instead, showing him her breasts and spreading open her negligée in back to try to excite him to other 'specialties.' But he insists on the Sleeve Job as promised. "Oh, all right," she says. "Go in the bathroom and cover yourself from top to bottom with soapsuds, and then come back." He covers himself with soapsuds, and rushes out of the bathroom, slips on a cake of soap, falls, kills himself, and never finds out what a Sleeve Job is. (Minneapolis, 1946.) This is very much abbreviated from the way the story was heard told, in which the pretense was also made — until the first reference to the obviously burlesque Sleeve Job — that it was a true story and had happened to the story-teller's best friend. If the teller had not himself begun cracking up in smiles at every mention of the Sleeve Job, it was obviously his intention to continue the 'true-story' pretense to the end.

Although in general, in the present work, complete variant stories have not been given, in the style of the usual folksong and folklore compilations; in the present case two complete variants will be given here, each having its important peculiarities. As the Indo-European original has also, in this case, been successfully traced, this will be given at the end, after the modern American versions, and should be compared with the first text above. The following artfully cleaned-up version was spontaneously offered to me by a ten-year-old American girl (that's *my* shaggy dog story, and I'm stuck with it!) in the presence of her astounded tourist parents, at an outdoor bar on the Boulevard Saint-Germain, in Paris, 1954. I had just told her father a joke intended to let him know in a nice way that I didn't intend to let him cheat me in business. The joke I told was perfectly 'clean' (the one about the Jewish trickster who gets the Russian Cossack to eat fish-heads to 'give him brains'), but its permissible food-dirtying elements obviously gave the little girl the cue that her own story could be told. *"Do you know what the Height of Purple Passion is?"* she challenged me. I admitted I didn't, and she told the following story in a very precise, formal way, obviously more or less by rote, as is often the case with children and women telling what they consider to be dirty stories. This casts the responsibility for the story, in a semi-conscious way — expressed in the formal exactness — on whomever they learned it from. She glanced impishly at her parents from time to time, especially at her mother, obviously enjoying their stupefaction, and her being able to get away with this story under the transparent pretext of its ending innocently in a mystery:

There was this sailor walking down the street and he met a Lady Wearing Lipstick. And she said to him, "Do you know what the Height of Purple Passion is?" And he said "No." And she said, "Do you want to find out?" And he said, "Yes." So she told him to come to her house at five o'clock EXACTLY. *So he did, and when he rang the*

doorbell, birds flew out all around the house. And they went around
the house three times and the door opened and they all flew in again.
And there was the Lady Wearing Lipstick. And she said, "Do you
still want to know what the Height of Purple Passion is?" And he
said he wanted to find out. So she told him to go and take a bath and
be very clean. So he did, and he came running back and slipped on
the soap and broke his neck. That's the end. He never found out what
it was. My girl friend Alice told me this story. It happened to some-
body she knows.

My informant was very impressed by my taking out a pencil and
saying I was going to write down her story then & there. She assisted
me in getting it just right, and when her parents got up to leave, and
went to the *caisse* to buy cigarettes, she hurriedly added that "Where
you say '*And there was the Lady Wearing Lipstick,*' you're supposed
to say: '*And nothing else!*'." (Which I think blows the gaff on the
pretended innocence of the story.) She also was rather worried about
my having written down that she was ten years old, and asked me to
correct this and say that she was only "Nine-and-a-half, *going* on ten."

This children's version has obviously added touches taken from
other folktales, such as perhaps that of the flock of birds: from "The
Swan-Maiden" or "*Peau d'Âne.*" This may, however, stem from real
observation of the Italian and other bird-lovers (in lower New York
City, for instance, where this little girl lived), who swoop their flocks
of pigeons around the roofs of the apartment-houses where they roost,
by means of long poles, oddly enough always at about five o'clock,
which is feeding time. The 'Lady Wearing Lipstick,' may be derived
by analogy from the 'Lady from Philadelphia' in Lucretia Hale's
The Peterkin Papers (1880), who has become the 'Lady with the Alli-
gator Purse' of modern children's rhymes, and also appears in various
avatars in such recent fake-folklore as the miraculously wise and patient proto-matriarch of, for instance, the 'family' motion pictures,
Mary Poppins (part animated-cartoon), *The King and I,* and *The
Sound of Music,* all of which hew slavishly to this guaranteed theme.

That the lipstick is a hidden cue to the lady's immorality is of
course clear, as with the exactly similar 'Painted Lady' in Sir James
Barrie's autobiographical *Sentimental Tommy* (1895), about which
'Painted Lady' all the sexual mystery develops for the little boy and
girl protagonists. (Compare also the same implication in the title of
James Gibbons Huneker's *Painted Veils,* 1919, largely concerned with

the sex life of women of the theatrical and musical world.) In the present story the implied immorality of the lipstick was of course made positive by the little girl informant's helpful addition of the one trait, as to the combination of *lipstick and nakedness,* which she had thought it necessary to expurgate before her parents, of whom the mother was not only — as it happens — wearing lipstick, but was also smoking and drinking in public before the child. Any of this was, not too long ago (1910–20), considered even more immoral in a woman than the wearing of lipstick. However, there is very big money in peddling habit-forming drugs such as tobacco and alcohol to adolescents and women, and killing them before their time with lung cancer and cirrhosis — the government also taking a sizeable tax cut of the profits — and propaganda millions have therefore been poured into respectabilizing smoking for women, since the 1930's, in a way that the lipstick manufacturers have not been able to match.

The most recent, and in many ways the most interesting "Sleeve Job" text was collected by Dr. Roger Abrahams from an adolescent Negro informant in South Philadelphia, about 1958–60, for his very remarkable Ph.D. thesis, developing into the courageous *Deep Down in the Jungle* (1964) p. 213–15. This text was supplied in the form of a prepared *manuscript,* which had obviously been passed from hand to hand. The additional touches in this version are almost all specifically Negro, or 'slanted' to the fantasy needs of the Negro group. The hero is stated to be 'a nigger . . . standing on the corner,' who is accosted by a white woman who asks him whether he wants a Sleeve Job. Trying to solve the mystery of what this may be, he appeals to another mysterious floating character, Old Dirty Slim, who 'was what you would call a bushwacker, a nose diver, a canyon yodler, well in other words a cocksucker, or just say that he ate pussy. He was also a puck lover, and a whore mongler. In other words he was just plain dirty Slim to everyone. So he asked Old dirty Slim, and even Slim couldn't tell him.' When, nevertheless, the hero goes to his rendezvous with the white woman, he is nervous and very tense:

> He went in looking all aroung with his hat in his hands twisting and ruffing his hat up, he heard a voice coming from the next room, saying to him to come in, where she was, when he went in to the other room, he saw a beautiful white woman laying on the couch, with white pinkish tits, with red nipples,

and a firm white body, and one leg thrown up on the top of the couch, this spreading her legs, showing her pussy, with redish brown hairs running from the crack of her ass to her nable, and around her thighs, this made him start to sweat and also made his heart beat, and to think, and to know that he was going to endure her, to seduce her, and to be love by her, not just too be love by her, but just because she was a white woman, and he had never experinced this sort of a thing, with a white woman, and mainly a sleeve job. She told him to come over to her and [not] be scared because she lived there by herself and she had know husband, and they were alone. He went to her and all he could do was to stare a[t] her taking pictures of her to remember her, and to remember the violent moments that he would spend with.

This is obviously becoming literature, in the form of a full-fledged puzzle-story, just as the term 'sleeve job' itself is now passing into the language as an allusion — still something of an insiders' gag — to any sort of mysterious or underhanded chicanery of fornicaboobery. (This last is similarly an older American gag-reference, apparently to the 'marital fraud' of intermammary coitus, and is now not to be heard among any but old-timers. Compare 'gobbledygook,' which has entered the language as meaning nonsensical talk or buncombe, since about 1940, but is originally an underworld *milieu* term for fellation, in the undisguised form 'gobble-the-goop,' *i.e.* semen. Polite etymologies have naturally been elaborated, deriving it falsely from the cry of the turkey-gobbler, etc.)

What is so curious about the "Sleeve Job" story, in its evident development in the three texts just given, from joke to folk-literature, is that it also *began* as folk-literature almost a century earlier, in France, but with very significant differences that have been strained out in the retelling. The story was apparently first printed, as having been an original recitation by Henry Monnier, the French Mark Twain, on whom see the Laffont-Bompiani *Dictionnaire biographique des auteurs,* 2nd ed. (Paris, 1964) II. 234, showing Monnier dressed in the costume of his own most famous character, the *petit-bourgeois* scrivener, M. Joseph Prudhomme, with appreciations by Gautier and Baudelaire of Monnier's perfect, almost stenographic art, as to folk-speech and scenes of popular life. The story appeared just four years before Monnier's death in 1877, under the title *"La Diligence de Lyon"* (The

Lyons Stagecoach), in a letter giving several of Monnier's jokes and recitations, signed 'Marquis de C.', in Jules Gay's bibliographical magazine, *Le Fantaisiste* (San Remo, 1873) i. 176–85, the writer noting that this story had already been mentioned in a list of Monnier's lost facetiæ in Gay's earlier magazine, *Le Bibliophile fantaisiste* (1869) p. 284. (Copies of both series: Ohio State University.) As given in *Le Fantaisiste,* the text is very long and precise as to its sexual details, but with a clear humorous intention throughout:

A young businessman, accidentally separated from his wife on his honeymoon, has missed the last train home, and is accosted in the streets of Rouen late at night by a prostitute, 'tall, slender, and with magnificent English blonde hair falling to the middle of her back in two Swiss braids. Observing the prosperous look of our businessman, she accosts him and invites him to go up to her room. "I'll be real nice," she says insidiously; "do anything you like — strip stark naked —" "Be on your way," answers the faithful husband, with the vision still in his mind of the charms of his youthful wife. "I'll do you the grand jeu [?]" "No." "Feuille de rose? [i.e. anilinctus]" "No!" "The American corkscrew?" "Old stuff — you bore me." "All right! Look, I like you. Come on, you won't have to pay anything, and we'll do the diligence de Lyon!" "No, a thousand times no! Leave me alone or I'll have you arrested".' She leaves, and he goes back to his hotel, where he dreams all night of the diligence de Lyon. Later, wondering continuously what sort of 'combination' this might be, he can no longer sleep, becomes uninterested in his wife, and finally goes back to Rouen to find the girl. She has left to take care of her dying mother in Le Havre, where he follows her, missing her by two days. He continues to follow her traces vainly: to Lille, Arras, Brussels, Antwerp. He eventually learns her name, Cornelia, from one of her friends, who suggests that Cornelia isn't the only whore in the world and would he like the friend to do the American corkscrew for him. He refuses this with horror, but offers triple pay if the girl will show him the diligence de Lyon. "I'd like to, but it's impossible. That's a specialty of Cornelia's; she's the only one who knows it. But since it interests you so much, you might as well try to find her. Like I told you, she's in Ghent now, at Hairy's place."

On he goes like the Wandering Jew, only to find Cornelia on her deathbed in the whore-house in Ghent. He forces his way in to see her, on some pretense of important family matters, and implores her, now that he has found her at last, to show him the diligence de Lyon *and cure his obsession.* [The text continues, too perfectly to attempt to paraphrase:] ' *"Que demande-tu là, mon ami? Je suis à bout de forces, expirante, et tu veux une chose que j'hésitais à faire et n'ai fait que très-exceptionellement en bonne santé?" "Ne me refuse pas. J'en suis malade et j'en deviendrais fou." "Voyons, sois raisonnable; si tu veux, nous ferons le tire-bouchon américain." "Non, non, non! ... Ce n'est pas cela! Je veux* la diligence de Lyon;" *et là-dessus il se jette au cou de Cornélie, la presse, lui fait les plus brillantes promesses, etc.* "Allons, tu y tiens tant que je vais essayer ... viens te placer à côte de moi." *Il s'installe dans le lit; Cornélie fait un effort pour se lever, mais une crise se déclare, elle retombe et ... expire, emportant son secret dans la tombe!!!!'*

The 'Marquis de C.', who saved Monnier's recitation for history, though poor Cornelia has taken her secret with her to the tomb, heads his text — for all its length — with the sub-title: *"Canvas to be developed,* and certainly meriting whatever pains one puts oneself to, on this subject." He notes that Monnier would convulse audiences of his friends with it, and that the best effect is achieved 'by multiplying and varying the voyages, and especially by correctly making use of the gag (*scie*) of the *tire-bouchon américain,* and the mirage of the *diligence de Lyon.*' (I myself don't give a damn about the *diligence de Lyon,* but I'd give anything to find out what the *tire-bouchon américain* might be ... anal digitation?) This story was obviously even more funny in a century in which street-prostitutes boiled up shamelessly at night by the hundreds, on half the public streets of London and Paris, not to mention smaller towns, with perfectly incredible offers (turning to insults if refused), as is depicted to the life in that most astonishing of all erotic autobiographies of the Victorian age, *My Secret Life,* publicly reprinted in 1966, in my Introduction to which I have given my reasons for believing it to be the work of H. Spencer Ashbee.

Puzzle-stories of this kind are also sometimes presented as practical jokes on the listener, which every shaggy dog story necessarily is, if successfully 'developed' before the listener's suspicions are aroused as to what the outcome, if any, is going to be. This brings the type rather close to the practical jokes of the '*send the fool farther*' variety, in which a new workhand, student, or recruit is sent from person to person searching vainly for a 'left-handed wrench,' the 'waybill clipper,' his 'matriculation stamp,' or 'rubber chevrons.' (Type 1296.) I have described, in *The Horn Book* (1964) p. 96–7, how I was myself victimized at a tender age by two fiendish friends, the writer known as Jack Hanley and the excellent bookseller, Timothy Trace, who, suspecting that my own private eroticism was more bibliographical than clinical, set me on a wild-goose chase — lasting for years, before the light dawned — for two non-existent sexological masterpieces, *The Art of the Tongue* and 'Heger & Dunkirk's *Lexicon of Lechery*,' both of which, I was assured, would show up my own researches in the same fields as the work of a drivelling amateur. (In case these books *do* exist, I would still welcome any details that would assist in finding them. Price no object. All is forgiven!)

The "*Diligence de Lyon*" is the sort of thing that people are prone to say 'would make a wonderful movie.' Actually it would make a terrible movie, since it has no satisfactory dénouement — which is the whole point, or anti-point, of this sort of joke; and any heavy-footed attempt to supply one will invariably mark the resultant product Class Z ('3½ stars,' as the euphemism is). This has been found true of all similar puzzle-stories attempted on the screen, for example "*So Long at the Fair*," based on Mrs. Belloc Lowndes' awful thing about the girl whose mother disappears from a Paris hotel during the Exposition, her hotel *room* disappearing as well. (This story has recently been adapted without acknowledgment into an even worse movie about an atom-bomb scientist who develops amnesia after pushing the head of a phoney peace organization out the window of his skyscraper office during a light-failure, etc. etc.; the same story being further adapted for the same actor as of an entire German prison-camp masquerading as an American veterans' hospital. What next?)

The solution to the original Paris hotel story is that the mother has died of bubonic plague, and all of Paris is in league against the daughter to keep her from finding out and thus ruining the tourist-draw at the Exposition. This early and very paranoid shaggy dog, with all its numerous and even more paranoid progeny, is not included in Brunvand's motif-index, "A Classification for Shaggy Dog Stories" (in *Journal of American Folklore,* 1963, vol. 76: p. 42–68), probably because of the attempted *solution* to the problem proposed. It is given Motif-number Z552, "The Mysterious Disappearance," by Baughman, and a text collected from a woman in Yorkshire in 1915 is given by the collectors, Katharine M. Briggs and Ruth L. Tongue in their *Folktales of England* (London, 1965) p. 98, no. 47 as "The Foreign Hotel," noting that 'Alexander Woollcott attempted to trace the source of this legend in *While Rome Burns* (New York, 1934), "The Vanishing Lady," pp. 87–94, but came to a dead end with a report in the *Detroit Free Press* in 1889.' This is close enough to the date of the actual French Expositions of the 1880's to suggest a *canard* at the expense of the hated French.

Actually, I hate to spoil the little mystery-within-a-mystery that the "disappearing hotel-room" story is in the process of becoming, with all these folklorists unable to flair or find it. But, in fact, it is nothing other than Aarne Tale Type 1406, "The Merry Wives' Wager," of which a brutal and scatological version (quite unknown to Aarne and Thompson) will be given in the chapter on "Scatology," in Series Two, 15.v.2, under the Provençal title "The *Escoumerda*," or Shit-Eater, which is *the trick of the wife who wins the prize for best fooling her husband.* The subtype of the "disappearing hotel-room" is that of Thompson's Motif J2316: '*Husband made to believe that his house has moved during his absence. The wife and her confederates transform the house into an inn with tables, signs, drinkers, etc. The husband cannot find his house.*' This is of Near-Eastern origin, appearing in the cycle of *Nasr-eddin* fool stories, which are probably the source — through the "Karaghuez" puppets — of the Levantine-Italian "Punch & Judy" shows. (Wesselski's edition, 1. 274, No. 298.) Thompson also notes a discussion of ancient French literary treatments in Joseph Bédier's *Les Fabliaux,* pp. 265–7, and 458–68; while Rotunda, at J2316, gives two versions in Italian *novelle,* as well as a Spanish form in Tirso de Molina's *Cigarrales de Toledo* (about 1630) Cig. 5. So much for the 'report in the *Detroit Free Press* in 1889.' The whole idea is, in any case, implicit in the use of backdrop and scenery changes in the theatre — as in the transportation by *genii* during one's sleep, in the *Arabian Nights,* earlier of Jesus tempted by Satan (*Matthew,* iv. 5–11) — often for purposes of comedy and mystification.

Equally supererogatory and impossibly bad is the 'solution' proposed to Monnier's joke or puzzle in a book-length story to which it was inflated, *La Diligence de Lyon,* published in Brussels, 1882, by Kistemaeckers (the main competitor of the original publisher, Gay), and signed 'Le Grand Jacques;' actually the work of Richard Lesclide, the secretary of Victor Hugo. Lesclide was evidently an occultist, as can be read between the lines of the story "The Truth about Javotte," concerning unavowed impotence disguised as occult monkeyshines, in his collection *Contes extra-galants;* and he constructs an absurd quasi-occult 'solution' to Monnier's story, which I would rather not be bothered to have to detail, to the degree that I understand it at all. It ends with an 'explosion of electricity,' of a kind now familiar to everyone who has ever sat through a Frankenstein horror-movie in which the mad scientist (but you never see a movie — except *Dr. Strangelove* — about a mad *general,* do you?) attempts to create human life by means of cheap Crookes tubes and defective rheostats. Lesclide also kills off *both* the man and the woman who have attempted the "*Diligence de Lyon,*" and the only witness who understands 'the secret of this frightful drama' rushes off on the last page without telling, promising to blow his brains out instead. The whole thing is hopeless neo-alchemical gup (as in gobbledygoop), very similar to the Arthur Machen type of 'solution' given by Cleveland Moffett to the related "Mysterious Card" story to be given immediately below.

It would perhaps be a misnomer to call Mrs. Belloc Lowndes' "Missing Hotel-Room" story an imitation of Monnier's "*Diligence de Lyon,*" and it also seems unlikely that she could have had any 'access' to Monnier's story, as they say at law. Yet the whole *mise-en-scène* of the Belloc Lowndes story, and search for the missing person, is almost exactly identical, even including the daughter who must take care of her dying mother. This is precisely the situation that causes Monnier's hero to lose track of the mysterious blonde Cornelia, in his search for the chimera of the *diligence de Lyon,* until he actually is shown, in the gruesome farce climax, climbing into her deathbed with her so that she may show him how it is done, with her dying breath. Note also the ruthless exploitation of the dying woman to serve the man's fetichistic 'needs.'

So much for the history of the "Sleeve Job," in which, as the reader will certainly have observed, it is the man who is killed, and not the woman as in Monnier's version. Of course he — or rather the listener, *who he is* — is left with the unsatisfiable obsession to haunt him, but that is not quite the same thing as being killed. Tracing a folktale historically, to the conscious art-product from which (as with folksong) it often stems, is also not the same thing as tracing it psychologically, though the same system of analogies, and comparison of similarities and differences, can be used in part. Psychological tracings involve a more particular concern with what cannot be seen at all, sometimes because it bulks too predominantly *large* in the foreground. There is a game known as "Afghanistan" employing this principle, in which the players are to find the name of a chosen locality on a map. All they know is that it is printed somewhere on the map: they don't know where. And they exhaust their patience puzzling out all the tiny little illegible hamlet names in the corners, which are never it. The name chosen is that of the main country on the map: AFGHANISTAN, which is stretched out boldly over the whole map, in the largest possible type, but letter widely separated from letter. It is invisible because its *scale* is too big. The general rule is therefore: *The one feature of any social or psychological phenomenon which most observers are likely to miss, is its* main *feature.*

The main feature of the "Sleeve Job" story in all its forms is that *it is about sex,* which is why Lesclide's and any other attempted non-sexual solution must fall absurdly to earth. More than sex, it is about a man on his wedding night, though this element is becoming lost in the most recent versions. Even Monnier sets up the protagonist's honeymoon as a mere background or anti-plot. Thus, his obsessional search for the *diligence de Lyon* is nothing other than his flight from his own honeymoon and his beloved wife. This is too big in the foreground to be visible at all. The sexuality of the story is apparently very prominent throughout, in all versions, but again, we all know very well that neither the "Sleeve Job" nor the "*diligence de Lyon*" exists at all, and that 'sleeve job' is an entirely made-up term, on the analogy of 'blow-job,' referring to fellation. (Also to a jet plane!) The story is therefore centrally concerned with sex, yet it is not about sex at all. Or, rather, it is about a kind of sex which everyone involved admits does not really exist. It is like Cleopatra's reputed erotic secrets, now 'lost,' of course. We yearn to believe that there is a kind of sex, somewhere, somehow, which will be the promised paradise of delight, and not so fraught with dangers and disappointments as the real sexuality we all know so well. Monnier's audience obviously particularly enjoyed the running admission of this, in the 'American corkscrew,' the wholly farcical counter-mystery which the hero angrily rejects, because it is 'old stuff' (*connu*), preferring to pursue the phantom of unknown sexual delight offered to him by a common street-prostitute in the night. Again, he has in fact basically rejected his wife, and the standard sexual pleasures of his honeymoon with her. Is she, perhaps, the 'American corkscrew'?

The other main feature of the "Sleeve Job" is that it is about *death*. It is of the type of those puzzle-stories in which we are typically given to understand what was in the mind of a person who has died, at the moment of his death, or in circumstances which only the dead person could know, such as the content of a dream which caused the dreamer to die of fright without waking up to leave any record. Rabelais' very well-known story of "Hans Carvel's Ring," Bk. III, chap. 28, is of this sort, though no manifest reference is made to death in this story of *The man who is given a ring by the devil, in his sleep, which will infallibly keep his wife faithful to him as long as he wears it — and who wakes up to find his finger in her vagina*. Rabelais takes this story from Poggio, No. 133, nearly a century before (an English translation had also appeared about 1535, in *Tales and Quicke Answeres*, No. 18, a decade before Rabelais' Bk. III), and it is interesting to note that Poggio tells the story about his arch-enemy, Francisco Filelfo, to whose dreams and private relations with his wife Poggio could hardly have been privy. (Compare the excruciatingly imaginary conversation in the boudoir between the Duke and Duchess of Windsor, in *Lese Majesty* [sic] by 'Norman Lockridge' [Samuel Roth], published in New York in 1952 and reprinted in pocket-form, Spring 1953, in time for the Coronation.) Short-story version in *The Best of Adam* (L.A. 1962) p. 72–9.

The deeper formal relationship of the "Sleeve Job" story with certain other puzzle-stories of unknown solution, particularly that of the department store Santa Claus, is discussed in the section on "Masturbation" in Chapter 1. Dr. Brunvand lists the "Sleeve Job" story, in his motif-index classification of shaggy dogs, as a sub-form of "The Mysterious Card (Letter)," at D510 and D510.1 (misnumbered D501.1), calling it "The Purple Passion," and noting also the variant title "My Blue Heaven," taken from a sentimental love-song of about 1930. It is also to be observed that, except for these mildly suggestive titles, *no hint of sex* occurs in the story as Brunvand describes it, as with the juvenile form of similar title collected from the little New York girl in Paris. Brunvand states merely, in fact almost antiseptically when one considers what the story is, and is really about: '*A young man somehow hears about "The Purple Passion" (or "The Sleeve Job," or "My Blue Heaven") and he tries to find out what it means. He is rejected wherever he asks and this is the cause of a miserable life for him. Just as he is about to find out what it means, he is killed in an accident.*' As

one certainly cannot suspect Dr. Brunvand of any intention to expurgate his synoptic index, the probability is that the field-collected
texts to which he had access, in the Indiana University folklore ar-
chives, have become fused with "The Mysterious Card" story below
(his D510), for which, again, his synopsis omits not only any scatological punch-line but also any reference to the situation of the groom delayed on his wedding night by his bride's shyness. For readers who
are so unwise as to *insist* on solving the mystery, I will note that "The
Sleeve Job," at least in its 20th-century versions, is developed from an
East Indian "Tunic of Nessus" story published by Prof. Thompson
(Motif K1227.4.1): *A girl tells her seducer that she cannot give herself
to him until after he bathes. She prepares the bath herself, and poisons
it.* The modern versions transform this into a puzzle or mystery merely
by omitting — or pantomiming — the final line.

4. THE MYSTERIOUS CARD

What is certainly the original form of this story, on the wedding-
night *delay* situation, has achieved the status of a modern folktale,
though its lack of a conscious solution has proved an obvious embarrassment to all tellers. In the 'obscene' version that circulates orally, the
utterly insufficient ending brings it into the shaggy dog class, where
the real pleasure to the teller is in the torturing of the listener with an
endless and unendable story. (Of the openly hostile teasing-type there
are also the "Tell us a story, Captain . . ." and "Then another ant
came in and took out another grain of wheat . . ." circular tales, and
several others on the same pattern: Types 2013 and 2320.)

*A man and wife go to Paris on their honeymoon. The man goes
down to the hotel bar to have a cigar while waiting for his bride to
undress. A woman in the bar smiles at him, takes a card from her
purse, writes something on it, gives it to him and then leaves, smiling
invitingly over her shoulder as she goes. The man looks at the card but
cannot read it as the writing is in French. He shows it to the waiter,
who turns pale and calls the manager. The manager looks at the card
and angrily orders the man to pack up and leave the hotel. He goes up
to tell his bride what has happened, shows her the card since she understands French, whereupon she bursts into tears, leaps out of bed and
begins to dress, and tells him she is going home to her mother and*

*never wants to see him again. He goes to the railroad station to leave
Paris, and meets a group of his bosom friends coming in on an excur-
sion train from London. They listen to his story, examine the card, and
then delegate a spokesman to tell him that they are going to blackball
him from his club and that none of them ever wants to see or speak
to him again. He decides to commit suicide, but a gendarme pulls him
back off the parapet of the bridge, and, on hearing his story, offers to
tell him what is on the card, assuring him that he will not arrest him
and that "Nozzing, but nozzing!" can shock a French gendarme.
They sit down on the curb to read the card, when a sudden gust of
wind blows it out of the gendarme's hand and into a sewer. They then
spend hours finding the alderman who has the key to the sewer, but
who lives halfway across Paris. They finally do get the card, and,
clutching it carefully, sit down to read it. Question: "What do you
think was on the card?" Answer: "After being down a sewer — shit!"*
(N.Y. 1940.)

Now this obviously will not do. Even allowing for all possible
pleasure in torturing the listener, that much build-up — which has here
been reduced to less than a quarter of the usual wordage — *cannot*
really end in so infinitesimal a scatological catch. Riddles and catches
turning in this ostensible fashion on the mere pleasure of throwing
some such scatological tag-line at the unsuspecting listener or butt, are
grouped in the final chapters in Series Two. One that may be given
here for its type-relation to the story just detailed was collected among
Negroes in Nova Scotia before 1925 (Fauset, p. 146, no. 20): '*A man
was going along the street and he lost a ring off his finger. He had a
cane in his hand. A woman came along and said to him, "What did
you lose?" He said, "A ring." She said, "Look on the end of your
cane." He looked on the end of his cane. What was there? — Mud.*'
(Compare cow-dung-on-the-pole story: Aarne Type 1225A.) That is
certainly the form, but it lacks almost everything else that has made
the fame of "The Mysterious Card" puzzle-story. At least two professional mystery-writers have strained themselves to discover the 'real'
answer, naturally avoiding all sexual or scatological elements for reasons discussed more fully in my monograph, *Love & Death* (1949), in
connection with the mass arts' substitution of a permissible sadism for
censored sexuality. The first attempted solution is that of Cleveland
Moffett's "The Mysterious Card," reprinted in Joseph L. French's *Masterpieces of Mystery: Riddle Stories* (1920) p. 3–43, ending with a hor-

ror-style Machenèsque solution in which the card shows the bearer's sinful soul: 'a loved face suddenly melting before your eyes into a grinning skull, then into a mass of putrefaction, then into the ugliest fiend of Hell, leering at you, distorted with all the marks of vice and shame.' (Etc.) Like Dickens' Fat Boy, Mr. Moffett evidently wants to make our blood run cold, with these tired religio-masochistic images on the style of gloating sermons by hellfire ministers and Redemptorist brothers; but he succeeds only in making us ask incredulously how the poor fool the story is about — doubtless some shoe-clerk or stockbroker's assistant — who has spent so little time in sinful Paris that he can't even read the language, can *possibly* have that sinful a soul: grinning skull, mass of putrefaction, fiend of Hell, and all that tommyrot. No, it won't do.

Ralph Straus falls back on 'pure' nonsense, calling this "The Most Maddening Story in the World," and ending with the plain statement: '*There is nothing on the card.*' (Reprinted in Philip Van Doren Stern's *The Moonlight Traveller*, 1943, p. 391–410; Straus' italics.) I must also confess that I don't know what was on the card. In fact, I do not believe there ever was any card, or that the story happened as told. Perhaps it is just an expurgated version of Monnier's "*Diligence de Lyon.*" What *does* exist is a feeling of eerieness, of fear and mystery centering around the wedding night and the intended defloration of the bride — a conscious fear not that something painful is going to happen to the woman, as is the fact, but that something inexpressible and terrible is likely to happen *to the man*. This is constant in almost every one of the stories, in most of which the bride is never deflowered at all, and the wedding and wedding night are aborted; while the bridegroom is either killed, castrated, or socially disgraced, or driven to suicide or madness. It is this concentration on some awful mystery connected with the wedding night, and striking dead or worse the heroic bridegroom who tries to brave the Forest of Thorns and Hill of Glass, and plant the fructifying 'kiss' on the lips of his Sleeping Beauty, that leads both to the suspicion of greater depth in all these stories than appears on the surface, and to the solution of the mystery itself.

Of course, within the framework of the stories as given, the solution cannot be found and is perfectly frankly not intended to be found; and the mystery is 'laughed off' as a joke at the listener's expense. Since what is feared is a *mystery,* and does not rise to the level of consciousness, all the stories about it — the "Sleeve Job," the "Mysterious Card," etc. — must necessarily end in a question mark. The story that comes closest to candor is that given at the very beginning of this section, as the key to everything which has followed, concerning the man who sets out to make *'his own hole'* in a woman's body, and ends pole-vaulting out a window with his penis cut off as punishment. If the tellers of the present group of stories could face up to this answer, or rather if they could even face the real question, they would not have to allay or resolve their anxieties by telling puzzle-stories carefully fabricated in such a way as to destroy all the evidence, or kill the only person who knows the answer, and thus remain forever unanswerable. I am indebted to Mr. Martin Gardner for an amusing current reduction of "The Mysterious Card" problem to a logical fallacy, on the 'Polack joke' pattern: *A typewritten card reading: "How to keep a Polack busy all day — (over)." The other side is identical.* (N.Y. 1968.)

An observation by Dr. Karl Abraham, in connection with the closely linked subjects of obsessive doubts and paradox-making, perfectly sums up the matter ("Transformations of Scoptophilia," in his *Selected Papers,* 1927, p. 212): 'The problems of the obsessional neurotic are always insoluble. The question which in fact he wants to ask is not *allowed* to be answered; the question which takes its place *cannot* be answered; and thus the secret is kept.'

5. THE TABOO OF VIRGINITY

And yet, the great mystery here is perhaps not altogether so insoluble as what song the Sirens sang, or what name Achilles took when disguised among the women — both of which classic questions are equally loaded with a freight of fear as to death or castration (transvestism) as the result of man's sexual attraction to woman. First, the excessive concentration on the sexual *mystery,* and its pointed setting on the wedding night, are almost enough of a hint. The 'taboo of virginity,' for it is this that we are dealing with, has been made the subject of one of Freud's greatest speculative essays, in his *Collected Papers,* IV. 217–35, and to this and to its almost equally great continuation in Karl Abraham's "Manifestations of the Female Castration Complex," in his *Selected Papers,* p. 338–69, the reader is again referred, with the strongest possible recommendation actually to look up and *read* these two remarkable papers, which (quite aside from the incidental light they cast on the present foolish jokes) represent the rock-bottom psychological framework for any real understanding of the present tortured relationships between women and men.

One point made strongly by both Freud and Abraham is that of the husband's fear of retaliation for his necessary harming of the bride in rupturing her maidenhead. This is seen in such usages as the *Morgengabe,* or gift to the bride on the morning after the wedding, for the sanguinary damage done her, still recollected in the well-known "Bell-Bottom Trousers," in the surviving line of an older song, accompanying the gift of money to the seduced girl:

"Take this, my darling, for the damage I have done;
You may have a daughter and you may have a son, &c."

Even more clear is the primitive usage of the *jus primæ noctis,* in which the bride is not deflowered by her husband at all, but by some more powerful tribal figure, such as the king or priest, or tribe matriarchs, any or all of these 'armed' with a sacred dildo; or by some more expendable stranger or slave who can be forced to run the risk. This, for instance, was the fate of the captive-hero Samson, according to the Talmudic explanation of the 'grinding' to which he is condemned by the Philistines in *Judges,* xvi. 21. Or the dangerous job of defloration can be taken on by the whole group of unmarried men of the community, as survives in the open symbolism of the present-day kissing of the bride. (Compare folktale motif K415, in which the marked culprit marks everyone else similarly, and thus escapes detection.) As already observed, the ritual group act is generally misunderstood, superficially, both in the wedding form and in its more complete modern survival as the 'gang-shag,' as mere public fun or vice; and the need of each of the men involved for the strength and public permissiveness of the *group* is overlooked. Even more surprising is the overlooking of the central and predominant position of the 'shagged' girl or kissed bride, whom the men are patently afraid, or formally forbidden, to approach *alone* (here, as well as in the early transitional patriarchies in which these customs seem to have originated), and whose 'male harem' they essentially are.

The fear of the virgin certainly still exists, even in the most highly cultured groups, or perhaps one should say particularly in such groups. Much folk and literary material could be brought together to prove this, from the transparent rationalization of Dr. Johnson's over-hearty rejection, "Maidenheads are for ploughboys!" quoted in Huneker's *Painted Veils* (1919) in connection with a very relevant scene in which a man refuses to deflower — 'make a woman of' — a more-than-willing girl; to the joke on the same situation: *A man refuses to take a girl's virginity, but offers to have an affair with her after she is no longer a virgin. "I see," she sneers, "you want somebody else to do all the dirty work, and then you'll take all the pleasure." "Sure," he replies; "I didn't dig the subway, but I ride in it."* (1:376.) If virgin girls in their late teens cannot be fooled by such quibbling — it is very common, for instance, in colleges, on the part of married graduate instructors and young professors, to whom embarrassing numbers of coed girls regularly offer their Anatomical All, along with their theme papers (this is *not* folklore) — I do not think it should fool us. The hopelessly muddled volume of literary and folklore accumulations, *The Way of a Virgin,* by 'L. and C. Brovan,' with imprint: 'London, 1922' [actually published in New York about 1930 and attributed to the independent scholar, Raymond Thompson], presents a mass of such material, though without any understanding of what any of it means, or why anyone would undertake such a volume, which is, incidentally, extremely difficult to find.

The play *Sunday in New York,* handsomely acted by Miss Jane Fonda as one of the first of the 'New Freedom' motion pictures in America (1963), turns entirely on the absurd plot situation of the rogue male or unmarried playboy who, though shown as an un-regenerate seducer who sinks to the apparently abysmal level of *telling dirty jokes* to 'warm up' or at least feel out his intended prey (this unfortunately cannot be guaranteed), nevertheless stalwartly refuses to have intercourse with her when he finds out, in bed, that she is a 'beginner.' The comedy turns, of course, on the impossibility of getting anyone else, such as her hometown fiancé, to believe in the innocence of the girl's 'white night' with the fangless wolf, since a man this frightened of female virginity — on whatever pretext of gentlemanliness, etc. — is intuitively recognized to be either an unblushing liar or a total fool. That he nevertheless does exist, or would exist if he dared to, is demonstrated by the very choice of so presumably titillating a theme for this sort of bedroom-comedy-in-reverse.

William De Morgan makes the interesting point as to paradoxical plots like these, in the afterword, "An Apology in Confidence," to his *A Likely Story* (London, 1911) p. 338, a novel turning on the fantasy theme of a painting in which all the characters are actually alive: 'Every book has a right to an assumption intrinsically improbable, to make the story go. What a flat tragedy *Hamlet* would have been without its fundamental ghost!' (He apologizes thereafter for comparing himself, at whatever distance, to Shakespeare, whom he nevertheless calls his 'giant namesake' . . .) In point of fact, the assumption that there are men unconsciously terrified of the bleeding and pain they must inflict on their virgin brides — and of the castratory 'revenge' they fear they will therefore deserve and suffer — is not in any way intrinsically improbable.

Freud cites several German literary examples, by Anzengruber and Hebbel, on the theme of the *Jungferngift,* or "Virgin's Poison," and much related material is presented in N. M. Penzer's *Poison-Damsels, and other Essays in Folklore* (London, 1952), a work unfortunately cast at a very superficial interpretive level. Most of the stories in the section "*Vagina Dentata,*" in Chapter 13, in Series Two, on Castration, are essentially of relevance here. When the castration or sub-castration of the male by the dangerous vagina is presented as the girl's defense from rape, at least a rational pretext is expressed for the man's fear of such a revenge. A story collected on various occasions in the United States, always as authentic fact, concerns *The girl who is chased by a rapist on a deserted beach, and who, when her strength gives out and she realizes she cannot outrun him, drops to the ground and stuffs her vagina with sand!* (N.Y. 1944; also La Jolla, Calif. 1965, the exact location on the shore where the event was stated to have taken place being pointed out to me, and the male culprit identified as one of the hated 'surfers' or American *lemmings,* as Dr. Jacob Bronowski has perfectly termed them.)

One of the most direct expressions of the fear of castration by the *vagina dentata* of the bride on the wedding night is that of Prosper Mérimée's mock of the Galatea legend, in the story of a man who unwittingly marries a statue by putting his ring on her finger, and who is found 'mutilated' (no details) after their wedding night. Compare the monosexual, or homosexual version of this revenge by the statue — pedicatory rape? — in the legend of *Don Juan,* especially in the form developed in Da Ponte's libretto to Mozart's opera (1787), in which the great scene of the statue of the Commander coming alive and breaking down the door to drag Don Juan off to Hell, though musically and in every other way the obvious climax of Mozart's tremendous masterpiece, was considered too frightening to end the opera there, and a terminal choral scene, with the witnesses of the tragedy beginning the usual conflicting stories and lies, had to be added. This later went to the opposite extreme, with an earthquake and eruption of Vesuvius for climax! (André Boll, in *Mozart,* Paris, 1956, p. 80.)

As to the Mérimée version, in which the destroying statue or *golem* is a woman, the author's predilection for masochistic themes of this kind is quite clear, more notably of course in *Carmen,* and in the even more masochistic adaptation of this in operatic form by Halévy (1875). This also inspired Pierre Louÿs' *Woman and Puppet,* which draws likewise from the highly masochistic La Charpillon adventure in Casanova's *Mémoires,* and in which specific mention is made of refusing intercourse to the man by means of a special canvas chastity-belt panty, of bars between the two lovers (Pyramus & Thisbe motif) while the man is forced impotently to watch his bitch-heroine have intercourse with another man, and similar sado-masochistic vacillations of this kind.

I have elsewhere expressed the tentative conclusion (in "Notes on Masochism," supplement to *Neurotica,* No. 6, 1950) that: 'Castration anxieties rising from the father or father-surrogate lead to homosexuality in the male. . . . In the same way, castration anxieties rising from the mother or mother-surrogate lead to masochism.' The reverse configuration is to be understood concerning daughters: the excessively dominant male parent produces the classic masochistic daughter (the 19th-century paterfamilias, *Mr. Barrett of Wimpole Street,* and his daughter, Elizabeth Barrett Browning); while the dominance of the female parent drives the daughter into Lesbianism or at least frigidity with men. The biographies and literary work of both Mérimée and Louÿs may be offered as presenting striking corroborations, on this aspect of male masochism. See, in particular, the biographical memoir of Mérimée by Louise Imogen Guiney, in Edmund Garrett's translation of *Carmen* (Boston, 1896), to which a good deal more could be added concerning Mérimée's career as a spy, publishing his own portrait in women's clothing as the frontispiece of the pretended 'authoress' of one of his various hoaxes. Louÿs' first and greatest success was similarly his hoax publication of pretended translations of Greek poems in praise of Lesbianism, the *Songs of Bilitis.* (It may be observed that though hundreds of women have used male pseudonyms, in 19th-century literature alone, female pseudonyms have seriously been assumed only by an infinitesimal handful of men, such as 'Fiona Macleod:' *i.e.* William Sharp, for obvious reasons.)

The point need be labored no further that the mysterious "Sleeve Job" is, at base, the fantastic fear of castration by the bride, specifically by her 'toothed vagina,' on the wedding night, at a moment when the husband is normally expecting the ordinary ecstasies of sexual intercourse, if not some unknown and unheard-of erotic specialty or 'carnal paradise' which only his bride can offer and which it is his fatality to demand. The "Sleeve Job" is therefore similar, in this hidden sense, to folktales in which — as in *Hamlet* — the secret message that the messenger carries, or object he is searching for, is the order for his own death. This is also the hidden spring of the Arabic "Appointment in Samarra" story, as of O. Henry's similar "Roads of Destiny" (*Complete Works,* 1936, p. 279–92). It has a large existence still, at the very filtered-down level of games and catches, where, for instance, the novice is sent not for the non-existent 'sky-hook' or similar, but for 'a measure of strap-oil,' which means that whoever he asks is to whip him; or where the listener is tricked into answering a riddle with the mysterious but only-too-meaningful names, "Pinch-Me" or "Kick-Me," or is made to say, "I am a monk-lock; I am a monk-key," &c.

The over-riding fear of castration is diffused throughout the complexities and castrational substitutes (total disgrace and total deprivation of love) of the "Mysterious Card" version, but in this case the dangerous fate overtakes the man not through his innocent bride, but as a result of a wild-goose chase on which he is sent by the evil temptress in the bar (Monnier's "Cornelia"). It is very clear that the 'good' bride, upstairs modestly preparing for bed, and the 'evil' temptress, downstairs flirting with strange men in the bar, are merely a splitting into two opposed characters of the combined submissiveness and hostility expected in, or projected upon, the bride. Both meet in the story of the high-society girl, "Cynthia," given earlier, who sends her bridegroom downstairs to the bar, while she has orgiastic intercourse simultaneously with five other men, or sub-men (bellboys), on her wedding night. This dividing of one complex human character, to whom one is required to respond, into *two diametrical opposites,* one of whom is wholly 'good' and therefore loved, while the other is wholly 'bad' and therefore hated, is a standard device in folktales, matching the important device — called prejudice — in human responses. The Fairy Godmother is simply the typification of everything that is loved in the mother. The Evil Witch is also the mother, but she typifies everything the mother does that is hated. Thus the Witch can be killed, burnt alive in her own oven by Hänsel & Gretel, and so forth. By dividing up one's responses in this way, it is possible to deal with complex emotions of ambivalent love and hatred for the same person, while avoiding the fear of the unknown and feelings of emotional strangulation rising from having to respond in two different ways to one and the same person.

Freud and other psychoanalytic critics have shown how this is elaborated even further in *Hamlet,* where the father-figure is divided into the entirely good Ghost (the real father) and the entirely evil uncle (the step-father), the first of whom Hamlet is lovingly to obey, and the second of whom he is to kill. But he does neither until forced to do so, and instead kills, by pure accident — though in the significant situation of being hidden behind his mother's bed-hangings — a *third* father-figure, the flatulently sententious Polonius, filled with fatherly advice, but made use of slashingly throughout the play as buffoon and butt. The "Mysterious Card" story divides the bride only into the standard two antipodal characters, of the good woman and the bad. But the point is that the evil temptress down in the bar thus really does not exist at all, anymore than does the mysterious card (compare Eve's apple?) by means of which she causes all the trouble. The evil temptress, or female devil, Lilith, is merely the bride herself in a black mask, or rather, with the virginal innocence that her husband fears will prove to be nothing *but* a mask, stripped away.

6. ophelia's 'nothing'

Finally, there is this singular matter of 'Nothing.' As presented, the preceding stories are all very long and very detailed, yet they are all eventually about nothing and end in nothing. '*There is nothing on the card.*' All the hero's search and voyaging, whether for the phantom woman herself or for the surrogate piece of paper with which she has fobbed him off, also end in nothing. But he is killed, or disgraced, or driven mad. Shattered and thunderstruck, yet all *signifying nothing.* The reader or listener, certainly, ends with nothing. One thinks of the most famous and curious *absolute* use of this word in English literature, noted by Professor Thomas Pyles, in Hamlet's "*That's a fair thought to lie between maid's legs. — Ophelia: What is, my lord? — Nothing.*" (III.ii.125.) This follows hard on the heels of Shakespeare's one & only punning pronunciation on the stage of the monosyllable 'cunt' ('country matters' or, even more clearly in the First Quarto, 'contrary matters.' In *Twelfth Night,* II.v.88, he goes no further than spelling the tabooed word out.)

I have also seen this played by the actor representing Hamlet adding to his whimsical reply, "Nothing," the gesture of putting up forefinger and thumb joined in an oval or circle representing both zero and, classically, the female genitals. (This is nowadays rationalized as meaning "O.K.," or something perfect, and presumably derives from the Italian gesture of twisting one's moustache, an even more obvious rationalization. A puffing gesture or pursing of the lips, as if kissing the air, also sometimes accompanies the hand motion: this is said to represent the unspoken appreciative word, "Perfect!" All of these holes or 'nothings' are actually the ancient apotropaic gesture representing the female genitals and intended to ward off evil, as the *Diable de Papefiguière* in Rabelais and La Fontaine is driven away in fright at the sight of the actual organ.)

At a more profound level, it must be understood that the 'nothing' that the female genital is, is not considered to be a neutral or level zero-point, but rather a definite negation or deprivation: something *should* be there, but there is nothing. This is a perfectly conscious estimation in which, in patriarchal societies, both men and women are agreed. And they assess woman as inferior (as well in their emotions as at law) simply because she is 'lacking a penis;' or think of her as a being who perhaps once had a penis but who lost it, or was deprived of it by a superior power, certainly for some sexual sin, by the standard *lex talionis* of being punished in the organ with which one has sinned: 'An eye for an eye, &c.' Woman therefore, and specifically her genital organ, is the living proof to the infantile mind, at whatever age, that the penis *can* be harmed or even totally removed. *Little boy, looking inside the panties of the little girl with whom he is playing doctor: "Gosh, you broke it right off, didn't you!"* (N.Y. 1948.)

It is this presumed demonstration that castration can really occur, with woman as the 'horrible example,' that is the primary source of the fear of woman as dangerous, especially on the wedding night, when her genital organ must be unveiled to her husband for the first time, and an even further 'nothing' added to the 'nothing' that it already is, by the husband's perforating the hymen and *'making his own hole'* in the genitals of his bride. Woman-as-hole! This is certainly the least flattering and least gallant of all estimations of 'The Sex,' and is never offered as a toast — at least not until the ladies have retired — yet it is a fundamental tenet of the almost conscious estimation of both sexes as to the difference between them. See, in this connection, the very interesting group of 'hole-as-vagina' stories in Dr. Martha Wolfenstein's *Children's Humor* (1954) p. 112, and, in fact, her whole chapter, "Riddles and the Legend of the Moron," p. 93–157, much of which is relevant here.

The deflowering of the bride is positively construed, at many levels, as depriving her once and for all of any pretensions to maleness or tomboyism. According to folk belief, for instance, she can no longer 'piss standing' or 'piss over haycocks' (the *nexus* of a well-known folktale, *Russian Secret Tales,* Nos. 46–47), after being deflowered, but can then hope for nothing more than the grudging status of being 'as good a woman as ever straddled a piss-pot.' Again, all this is very close to stating openly, and believing consciously, that to deflower the bride means to 'cut out her penis' and leave a hole. This is certainly the meaning of the sub-castratory 'female circumcision,' without which girls in the North African cultures are not considered ready for marriage, and in which the entire clitoris and most of the *labia minora* are cut or burnt off, on the pretext that this ensures that the bride will strive for vaginal rather than clitoridal sensations in intercourse and will be sure to get pregnant — as though getting pregnant were a problem in North Africa!

One of the most famous and important woman-psychoanalysts of this century, Princess Marie Bonaparte, who gave her private fortune to ransom Freud from the Nazis, so that he could die peacefully in England at the age of eighty-three, devotes a whole supplementary chapter to the "*Mutilations physiques des femmes chez les primitifs, et leur parallèle psychique chez nous,*" to conclude her remarkable study *Sexualité de la Femme* (Paris, 1951). She apparently does not consider as such a 'mutilation,' either physical or psychic, her own invention in 1924, under the asexual pseudonym, A.-E. Narjani (announced in *Bruxelles-Médical,* April 1924, and discussed in her work of 1951, p. 129–31), of an operation which she persuaded the gynecologist, Prof. Dr. Halban of Vienna, to perfect and perform, which, as she describes it, is '*une technique opératoire simple: section du ligament suspenseur du clitoris, fixation du clitoris aux plans profonds, et sa fixation en bas avec raccourcissement éventuel des petites lèvres.*'

All that can be said about this — she admits in a footnote that it was 'para-analytic and erroneous' — is that it is curiously close to the 'female circumcision' that the Arab old-wives inflict upon nubile girls, and for the same ostensible purpose: to ensure a replacement of clitoridal by vaginal eroticism in the victim.

As it happens, the principal case studied after undergoing the Halban-Narjani operation, which was actually carried out on five women before Princess Bonaparte was herself analyzed and lost interest in the subject, was that of a woman (one may guess who, perhaps) 'of a particularly reclamatory nature, who had hoped, by means of this operation, that the surgeon-father would give her the dreamed-of penis. The virility-complex of this woman was extraordinarily strong. . . . After her wound had healed, she still had to return to the only method of intercourse which had formerly satisfied her: the posture in which *she would kneel over the man lying on his back.*' (Italics supplied.) This can hardly be considered a cure of the woman's virility-complex, 'pissing over haystacks,' or whatnot, and the Halban-Narjani operation is now only one more horrible example of the operative excesses of non-psychoanalytic psychology, comparable to pre-frontal lobotomy, transorbital leukotomy (a particular horror), and other surgical atrocities, of which the value to either the patient or society has never been demonstrated, while the value to the psycho-surgeons involved — both monetarily and psychologically — is only too repulsively clear.

By way of contrast or comedy-relief, mention may be made here of the wholly *kitsch,* mass arts or pop-culch version of the same thing, in the 1940's musical comedy, later the movie, *Annie Get Your Gun,* an absolute field-day — unquestionably cynically conscious on the part of the writers — of male-protest, based mythically on the career of the female sharpshooter, Annie Oakley. Her virility-complex is made frankly the central theme, as for instance in a song-spree, "I Can Do Anything You Can Do Better Than You," in which she competes for every possible prerogative and article of clothing with the man whom she is trying to make love her. When he makes a final invidious reference to his phallic prerogative of *pants,* she responds angrily with "In your hat!", an abbreviation, as the audience is supposed to know, of the folk-phrase "Shit in your hat!" or, in full, "— and pull it over your ears, and call it curls!" Obviously something has to be done about this girl, if she is to catch a husband at all.

The Halban-Narjani operation possibly having been ruled out as too uninteresting to show in technicolor, the scriptwriters have the girl decide to lose a sharpshooting competition with the man she loves, in order to make him feel a little more like a man. But her reflexes over-mistress her, and she is simply *unable* to miss the clay ducks and hits the bull's-eye of the target every time. Comes forward at this point who but her gruff, monosyllabic American Indian proto-daddy in a blanket (really Prof. Dr. J. Bromberg Halban in redface), who takes it upon himself to correct matters. Out from under his capacious blanket he takes surreptitiously the biggest, ugliest goddam triple-action barbed-wire cutting pliers you have ever in your born days seen; grabs aholt with his perfidious Red Injun paw of Annie Oakley's superb *red-gold* rifle, presented to her by the Biggest Daddy of them all, the Emperor of Austria-Hungary, and SNIPS the front-sighting sticker-upper dooflicker off the end of her championship rifle with those ugly blue-steel pliers! Annie then cannot hit the side of a barn-door with a cannon, loses the competition, marries the guy, and they all live happily ever after. I do not think it is pressing too hard on the interpretive privilege to say that this is clearly nothing other than the plot of "The Princess Who Pissed Over Haycocks," expurgated and revised for the pop-culch audience, with the circumcision or castra-tion that 'makes a woman of her' — *i.e.* no longer an imitation man — achieved with wire-cutting pliers. Not every girl is so fortunate.

What is terrifying about deflowering one's bride, and what makes one willing to leave this messy and dangerous job, if possible, to some superior figure such as the tribal chief or marriage counsellor required to take the risk, is not so much the sin of doing anything so cruel and destructive as cutting off the bride's imaginary penis and leaving her with the hole-that-makes-her-a-woman instead. It is that the deflowered bride — all bleeding and in tears, always delaying, and often begging desperately to be let off till the next night, or forever — represents to the neurotic husband the terrifying possibility, nay certainty, that the penis can actually be lost, missing, or cut off; a belief of which the bride's own genital after defloration (and, thereafter, during menstrua-tion), visibly bleeding and *lacking a penis,* is presumed to be proof positive. That is what is so terrifying about 'nothing.'

There is also, of course, the essential matter of the bride's expected revenge, which counts for a great deal in the groom's nervous certainty that he is in an area charged with disaster. Actually, except for insensate male-protest types, most women are grateful to the man who deflowers them, even if painfully; and all are agreed in their contempt for any bridegroom who is a big enough muff (French, *con,* fool), or nincumpoop, to delay the consummation of the marriage in deference to their begging and delaying. Their resistance is biologically toned, and is intended to be overcome, as a proof that the husband is strongly male and worth mating with in the first place. Female dogs and cats can be observed engaging in the same feint. This resistance is expressed in the theme of *disappointing* the groom, or tantalizing him erotically with little or no intention of satisfying him, in all the jokes and folktales being examined here, and especially in the halfway examples leading up to the "Sleeve Job," in which, though no actual harm comes to the man, the whole atmosphere of teasing and delaying is overloaded with hostility.

Special attention should be drawn to Karl Abraham's incisive page (in his *Selected Papers,* 1927, p. 358) on just this matter of *disappointing,* as an expression in the frigid wife of repressed castration impulses against her husband. This insight brings into focus not only the problem of the presumably sexually emancipated 'cock-teaser' or 'half-virgin' before marriage, and the delays in dressing and undressing by the wife, after marriage — the humorous central theme in the present group of stories — but also the desperate form of such 'disappointing' in the wife's *refusing to experience orgasm.* Most frigidity is of exactly this wilful form, and that is the truth about this particular mystery. The wife's refusal to arrive at orgasm is not usually in response to any real harm her husband or any man has actually done her, but out of fear of punishment by her own mother for any achieved sexuality, which is presumed to have been stolen (incestuously) from the mother, or done in her despite. This does not in any way make it any the less of an almost-conscious refusal, that can be allayed only by such methods as drunkenness, or by the nervous thrill of revenging herself against the husband by having intercourse (*and orgasm*) with another man, though most men's 'technique' and equipment are very much the same.

Abraham takes the point of view, which is also taken in Freud's paper on "The Taboo of Virginity," mentioned earlier, that the bride cannot by any means be considered a completely passive participant in the creation of the fantastic fears of castration — her own, and that of the groom. In our concern with the bridegroom's fear of being castrated by the bride's 'toothed' or otherwise dangerous vagina on his wedding night, it must not be overlooked and should be emphasized again that defloration is almost consciously conceived by all parties to *be* a castration of the bride by the bridegroom's bloody penis on her wedding night, and this is the known meaning of the sentimental gloss: 'to make a woman of her.' There is therefore no reason to be surprised if she is vengeful, or that her husband fears her revenge.

Let us return finally to the question of 'Nothing,' of which the real meaning in these stories has now been discerned. As one of the commonest of defensive gestures against that which one fears is to try to laugh at it (that is, in essence, the theme of this entire book), there exists a minor theme in literature concerned with twitting and defying 'Nothing,' and with finding it enormously and inexplicably laughable, quite aside from the present group of folk-jokes. The older and classic literary pleasantries on the subject are all gathered in Dornau's *Amphitheatrum . . . joco-seriæ* (1619) and Coquelet's matched set of mock-eulogies, *Éloge de Rien,* and *de Quelque Chose* (1730). This is nowadays sometimes puffed up into a purported philosophical gesture, as in George Santayana's 'cosmic laughter' in *The Last Puritan* (1935) and his series of volumes on various 'Realms' of the less-and-less real. In the form in which this theme is now usually presented, the typically weak or homosexual *beau-parleur* or impotent *révolté* tears his way through veil after veil of philosophical mystery (or science-fiction complications) to arrive at Ultimate Truth, only to find, to his horror, that *It is Nothing* — or *There is nothing there!* — whereupon he dissolves in Cosmic Laughter as above. That this is actually a soft-focus defloration fantasy, with the fear of the finally-unveiled female genital expressed as 'laughing at nothing,' has, I think, now been made clear. That it is identical with the main plot of the "Sleeve Job" or "Mysterious Card" is also clear, though the philosophical and humorous forms are probably entirely independent proliferations.

The theme is not confined to any one language, and is the real message of much of the *avant-garde* literary nihilism of the last hundred years — from Baudelaire, Lautréamont, and Rimbaud, through Dadaism and Surrealism, to the final (?) 'Nadaist' movement, very recently, of the Colombian actionist-poet, Gonzalo Arango. (See the manifesto published in *El Corno Emplumado,* Mexico, and in the British magazine *Poetmeat,* No. 9/10, Summer 1965, p. 33–6.) In this, as in the writings of Céline and Genêt in France during World War II, the new class of *lumpen-intelligentsia* appears, or sub-intellectual 'false revolt' group, waiting and dreaming of the eventual socio-political explosion in which their nihilist fantasy or drug-induced dream of glorious 'Nothingness' can be turned into a reality. As I have noted in *The Fake Revolt* (1967) p. 26, 'The only thing real about the Fake Revolt is the explosion voicelessly promised as its final act. And it will come. For the rest, there is nothing wrong with the New Freedom . . . except that it is false, and no revolt — a revolt against nothing, and for nothing. A revolt begging for nothingness, and planning insanely to go down in the same nothingness in which it expects and intends the world to end. *Néant!* . . . The mandala or Nirvana-nothingness courted by the beatnik or hippie is the anal-sadistic Atom Bomb explosion set off by the spy. Both arrive at the identical nothingness, and are after nothing but nothingness, if by opposite paths: the infantile omnipotence in which both crawl with their pants full to the top of the world, and blow it all up in a mushroom-shaped fecal explosion.'

A collection of college-level folktales made by Mr. Richard Buehler (MS. 1964) f. 19–21, gives a quite remarkable tale — hardly a joke — transcribed from a tape-recording, which makes positive the identification of the feared 'nothing' as simply the female element or genital. Compare the joke on Frank Harris in Hell, 6.VI, at p. 388–9 above. (The informant transcribed was an Ohio State University Ph.D.:)

> Somebody told me this, that in some show this joke started to make the rounds and this broke everybody up; in fact, one show, some floorshow, had to be terminated, because everybody was breaking up [*i.e. with laughter*]. I'll tell you this and then you can understand the context. About this guy meets a girl in a bar, and she's really good looking, you know, stacked and et cetera, and she's wearing a nice low cut gown and she's really well built. Only thing seems to be strange is that one armpit's shaven. He figures, "What the hell, she's kookie [*eccentric*]," but he don't care. So, anyway, a couple of drinks, et cetera, gets — they get friendlier and finally they suggest that they go up to her apartment, so they go up there, have a couple more drinks and smooching on the couch, et cetera, and he says, "Say, baby, go into the bedroom and take your dress off."
>
> She says, "Well, I will if — "

He says, "What? Come on, baby, come on. What? Take your dress off."

She says, "Well, you've got to promise me one thing."

"Oh, baby, I'll promise you anything, anything in the world. Take your dress off."

She says, "You promise me you, you won't laugh."

"Laugh? Baby, do I look like I'm in a position to laugh? What am I gonna laugh — baby, nothing's funny, no. Come on, please, really, you know, go and take your dress off."

She says, "You promise me, you swear to me, you swear you're not gonna laugh?"

He says, "I swear, baby, I swear anything you want. I'm not gonna laugh, I'm not gonna laugh."

She says, "All right." So she goes into the other room and after a little while she says, "I'm ready."

And he rips out of his clothes and he lunges into the other room and there she is, you know. She's sitting there on the bed and he runs up to her and he looks, and there, down between her legs, nothing! Skin! No hair, nothing! You know, just complete blank, null, void, absolute zero. He looks for a second, stunned, and then, the whole insanity of the situation strikes him. It's so ridiculous and absurd that he — he just falls back and he starts to laugh. This weird laugh. This is the funniest thing he's ever seen in his life. It's this ironic joke, and he falls back in the chair and he's all convulsed with this hysterical laughter, and she comes up to him with tears in her eyes and she says, "You promised me, you said you wouldn't laugh — you weren't going to laugh, but you did laugh. Well, just for that, just for that, I'm going to piss on you." (*Raises arm.*)

Buehler refers this to Thompson Motif F547.5.7, "Extraordinary Vagina (vagina in armpit)," which notes an East-Indian congener. So simple an anatomical classification misses, however, the real point of the story. A modern French satirist — André Maurois, I believe — has written a short tale or fantasy, on the style of his science-fiction work "*1992*" (published in 1929), discussing the probable results of displacing the activity of *eating* from the mouth to the armpit. If the reference is correct, this is hardly more than a polite or expurgated anticipation or forerunner of the present tale. The normal attraction of men to the female pubis necessarily involves its being furnished with the pubic tressoria of hair, which — from the psychological point of view — allows it to remain clothed in a certain pleasant 'mystery.' As will be discussed further in the chapter on Castration, in Series Two, any concern by either sex with the shaving of the female pubic hair (as with the repugnant shaving of the female armpit hair, a displaced prudery common in the Anglo-Saxon cultures only, at present) is *per se* a neurotic symptom, being hardly more than a modification of castratory impulses against the woman herself; while the shaven female pubis naturally lacks the protective 'mystery' by means of which the male is not faced with the frightening reality of the existence of 'creatures without a penis.' As Mr. Buehler's informant puts it, in his climactic line: '. . . *there, down between her legs, nothing! Skin! No hair, nothing! You know, just complete blank, null, void, absolute zero.*'

7. MUTUAL MISMATCHING

One of the burlesque book-titles that could generally be counted on to appear in obscœna collections of the 1920's was *The Happy Marriage* by Maud FitzGerald and Gerald FitzMaud. (1:486.) Lists of this type would usually also contain such favorites as *The Life of an African Princess* by Erasmus B. Black, and *The Wildcat's Revenge* by Claude Balls; and might run to as many as twenty titles in all. An incredible compilation of these, running to two hundred and fifty-six original titles & authors, and dating in the main from Idaho, 1928, was received in 1952 through the kindness of Mr. Kenneth Larson. The possibility of any such ideal genital fitting as that of Gerald and Maud in their *Happy Marriage* has, however, always been scorned by both the tellers of jokes and the writers of manuals of 'married' sex technique. (The *un*married have to fend for themselves.) The jokesters, since their main business is the denigration of women, invariably find the vagina too large. The sex book writers, since their whole purport is to make marriage work and to smooth out its erotic difficulties, generally are concerned with the more usual problem of the vagina being too small, or, rather, the penis being 'too large' for the virgin bride.

S. H. Aurelle, in an unexpectedly practical little work, *Sex Physique Averages* (1938, Personal Problem Library, 1. p. 5–6), realistically remarks: 'The inquiries of unmarried women express fear of, rather than attraction by, excessive male [*i.e.* phallic] development. In the case of widows who have borne children, marital disappointment may be experienced from a second husband; but this is not to be looked for by the virgin bride from practically any husband.' And the very famous, though often unconsciously very funny *Sane Sex Life and Sane Sex Living* (Boston, 1919) by 'H. W. Long' [William Hawley Smith] offers as its principal original contribution to Western erotics a position for use in intercourse 'where the wife is of the "dumpy" sort, with a small mouth [!] and short fingers, while the husband is "gangling," large mouthed and long fingered.' (Chap. 8, "The Art of Love," ed. 1937, p. 126–30.)

Although most men do not marry widows with ready-made families, and those who do — such as George Washington — are generally suspected of being homosexual, the fantasy or fear of the bride with the too-big vagina is a favorite projection of the fear of having too small a penis (*i.e.* of having been 'stunted by' [castrated for] the sexual sin of masturbation). The frank statement that the husband's penis is 'too small' is often made, but seldom without the accompanying note of the wife's vagina being 'too big,' or at the very least of her sexual appetite being excessive or her attitude unvirginal and crude. *The worst insult a woman can offer a man: "Is it in?"* (2:347, noting that the question is made up of 'three words of two letters each,' that is to say, wondering how such little *things* can add up to so intolerable an insult. Compare also the parlor game, noted N.Y. 1942, of making lists of taboo words with three letters, rather than the usual four, for instance *pee, poo, tit,* &c.) *A young bridegroom shows his bride his penis and asks her if she knows what it is. "It's a wee-wee," she says. He is delighted by her innocence, and prepares to enjoy deflowering it, telling her: "Well dear, now that you're married you might as well know that the real name for it is a prick." "Oh no it isn't," she says. "I've seen plenty of pricks, and that one is a wee-wee."* (Calif. 1939. This story was suddenly quite popular again in N.Y. 1952 in a form in which *The groom tells the bride that the name of his organ is "penis." "Oh," she says, "just like a prick — only smaller."*) Randolph gives this as No. 49, "It was a Tee-hee," from Arkansas in the 1930's. Picard version in *Kryptádia* (1907) x. 27, "Interrogatoire."

As a wedding-night prank the younger sister has starched the bride's nightgown with the bottom flared upward. As the newlyweds are undressing the husband says, "Now don't you peek!" The bride, trying to get into her nightgown: "Oh, it's a little short stiff one!" The groom, blushing furiously: "You went and peeked after all!" (Idaho,

1919.) Actual measurements in inches are typical of male fears and fantasies of penis length, and evidenced in many toilet epigraphs of homosexual assignation. In two cases the wedding-night recrimination is actually measured off in this way, with the significant measurement put in the mouth of the bride. *The young husband is standing naked before the mirror in the wedding suite admiring himself.* "*Two inches more and I'd be king,*" *he says proudly.* "*Yes,*" *says the bride,* "*and two inches less and you'd be queen.*" (Calif. 1940. Compare, also from California in the mid-1930's: "*Is he queer?! If he was any queerer he'd be a Lesbian!*" Also, from "Daniel," a recitation: "*Balls!*" *said the Queen.* "*If I had 'em I'd be King.*") The husband's brag is such an obvious leadup to a denial that it must certainly be read with the minus-sign: he too is afraid that his penis is too short. *The newlyweds are undressing together for the first time in their hotel bedroom. The groom sees the bride looking at him appraisingly and, with an attempt at manly pride, puffs out his chest and beats on it saying,* "*A hundred and ninety pounds of dynamite!*" "*Yeah,*" *says the bride;* "*with a three-inch fuse.*" (D.C. 1943.)

The situation of marital undressing is still an area of anxiety for many people, especially for those with castratory notions of organ-inferiority, which they usually displace in the form of shame upon semi-sexual parts, such as abdomen or breasts, which are considered to be somewhat less (or more) than the advertised ideal. In the lower middle class in particular it was once thought a mark of particular genteelness to be able to undress while holding parts of one's clothing before one with one's teeth, or by some other agility, so that the husband or wife never saw one naked "since the day we were married." On that day, however, one *must* be seen? The same situation of marital unveiling — a reminiscence of the organ-curiosity jokes and anxieties concerning children ("Is it a boy or a girl?") — is used in the only actual joke, as opposed to mere puns, rising from the "Christine" Jorgensen self-castration scandal of 1952. *The wedding night. The wife-who-was-once-a-man looks at "her" husband and says,* "*Are you kidding? Why I cut one off bigger than that!*" Note that the one great victory of Magnus Hirschfeld's *Institut für Sexualwissenschaft* in Berlin, which was actually a propaganda organization for the furthering of homosexuality (the famous Nazi "burning of the books" was simply a tactical destruction of Hirschfeld's library and card-files to destroy the records of homosexuals and drug-addicts in the German army and Nazi hierarchy), was the modifying of German law during the 1920's to allow homosexuals of either sex and of any nationality to *marry* each other, with a ring, civil ceremony, and all. A number of American actors and literary people of the period actually went to Germany to go through this ceremony, for which the public explanation was the same 'tolerance' alleged by Denmark in the "Christine" case, and others since.

A number of jokes taper off from ideas of phallic insufficiency into the hatred of the woman, presumably for her too-large or otherwise unsatisfactory vagina, by way of a strange sub-homosexual solidarity between the husband and other male casuals of the wedding night, such as other hotel guests met in the hall or lobby (the Man in the Upper Berth) and particularly the desk-clerk or manager — patently a father-figure. The first of these to be quoted here expresses its minus as a double-plus: it is not about too small a penis but too large a penis. That this is a perfectly likely situation in real life has already been discussed. In jokes it can only be interpreted as overcompensation. (See the section of overcompensatory long penis jokes at the end of the chapter on Castration, in Series Two.) — *A young man spending his wedding night in a hotel phones down to the clerk: "This may be a strange request, but I can't get my prick in. Can you help me?" The clerk advises rubbing vaseline on his penis, but very soon the young man calls back for further advice. This time the clerk suggests heating the vaseline in a teacup and dipping his penis in this. Soon the phone rings again and the young man asks incredulously, "Can you really get your prick into a teacup?"* (Calif. 1939.)

The bride is conspicuously absent from this story. No reference whatever is made to her, except perhaps as the implied object of the preposition 'in,' in the young man's first inquiry. The whole action is between the bridegroom and the clerk, and the same is equally true in the following: *The bridegroom gives the hotel-clerk a big tip to put a dash of saltpetre in a cocktail to be sent up for his bride, and a dash of Spanish fly in his own. The bellboy gets the drinks mixed and the groom gets the saltpetre and his bride the Spanish fly. In the morning the hotel-clerk meets the groom looking completely exhausted in the lobby, and asks how the drinks worked. The groom just rolls his eyes and says, "Did you ever try to shove a pound of melted butter up a wildcat's ass with a wilted noodle?"* (N.Y. 1948. Also collected, D.C. 1952, in a version in which the groom *asks* for the saltpetre for himself, doubtless on the assumption that he is too passionate and his bride too cold. The final line is often collected without any joke, as the 'height of impossibility,' in lists of such 'heights,' which also exist in German, and in French as "*combles.*")

The drugstore clerk — the mock-doctor or doctor-*manqué* — makes a similar appearance as the 'father of the groom.' *A young man is getting married and jubilantly asks the druggist for ten cents' worth of vaseline. Next day he comes back very crestfallen and asks if he can change the vaseline for alum.* (1:459.) It will not escape the reader that the small penis has also been changed for the large vagina; and behind the friendly pathos of this story — *Anecdota I* gives it in Negro dialect to point up this element of the humor — one sees the figure of the doctor as fitter-of-parts, but always by the method of castration (in this case infibulation, or female castration, with the traditional alum). Only this interpretation will make understandable, or even endurable, the unexpectedly violent hatred expressed for the woman and her genitals in a story that starts out simply as a version of the "Is it in?" line: *A young man is trying to have intercourse with a girl behind some bushes in the park. "Is it in now, honey?" he asks. "No," she answers, "it's in the dirt." He tries again, begins thrusting, but she says, "It's in the dirt again, darling." Finally, at his suggestion, she takes hold of his penis and guides it in, but after a few thrusts the young man says, "Put it back in the dirt."* (Transcontinental train, 1943. The smoker story to end all smoker stories. Vance Randolph gives a similar tale in *Pissing in the Snow,* No. 93, "Ambrose Done All Right," quoted later here.)

By comparison, the stories specifically on the mutual mismatching of the organs are only mildly spiteful, with the concentration in every case on the punning comparison in which they are couched. Rabelais' contest-in-gestures (Aarne Type 924A): *Amenities of the divorce court. Ex-wife waves her little finger at her ex-husband, saying, "Goodbye, Shorty." He stretches his mouth as far as possible at the sides with two fingers, and says, "Goodbye, Lucy."* (2:47, a version without the nicknames, these being first collected Calif. 1940.) — *She: "It was all right, but I can't say I thought much of your organ." He: "No? Well, I didn't expect to play in an auditorium."* (2:152, also "in a cathedral.") The folk-phrases describing this contretemps always take the man's point of view — "It was like waving a flag in space (or, your arm in an empty room)." Similar lines are given to the woman only in connection with the aged or impotent husband. *Wedding toast of the latest bride of a much-married playboy: "It's been hard for some of the others, but it's pretty soft for me."* (1:385.) Only in such cases is the woman allowed to have the last word. In the present recrimination group she is invariably the butt. This is even true where the wedding situation is simply picked up at second hand: *Across the air-shaft in a hotel, a middle-aged couple* [in other versions frankly described as the parents] *see two young newlyweds playing a game where the wife tries to throw a doughnut over her husband's penis, while he tries to throw a pickle into her vagina. "Let's try it," says the middle-aged husband. "All right," says the wife, "but you'll have to get some life-savers for me to throw."* (2:368. A 1953 version has the husband top her with, *"Yes, and a watermelon for me."*) Historical note: the life-savers referred to are not the large circles of cork, but the small ones of candy. In a variant, the young couple are using marbles and dough-nuts, and when the mother suggests to the father that they play too, he says, *"O.K., you get me a dozen grapefruit, and I'll get you a few life-savers."* (D.C. 1945.)

In the most elaborate and best known of the recrimination stories on mutual mismatching, the stalking-horse of the newlywed couple is entirely omitted, for insofar as these stories really have any surface meaning at all it is in connection with married hate and old age, to which a special section will be devoted later. *Wife: "I dreamt they were auctioning off pricks. The big ones went for ten dollars and the thick ones went for twenty dollars." Husband: "How about the ones like mine?" Wife: "Those they gave away." The husband thinks this over. "I had a dream too," he says. "I dreamt they were auctioning off cunts. The pretty ones went for a thousand dollars, and the little tight ones went for two thousand." Wife: "And how much for the ones like mine?" "That's where they held the auction."* (1:413. Variants are often collected in which, instead of by size, the excellence is measured by the fame of the possessors as 'great lovers,' *e.g.* Cleopatra and Helen of Troy, or male and female movie-stars.)

The *reductio ad absurdum* of the fantasy of mutual mismatching of the genitals is found in the erotic novel *Les Bijoux indiscrets* (1748) by the French philosopher Denis Diderot, inspired by the Old French fabliau, "Le Chevalier qui faisoit parler les cons et les culs" (Barbazan-Méon, *Fabliaux et Contes*, III. 409). Diderot conceives of a country where the genital organs come in various geometrical shapes, so that one needs to match up not only male and female but also the particular shape, and where mismatching of square with triangular, etc. is the main complaint. Norman Douglas, in his *Some Limericks* (Florence, 1928) p. 58, in connection with the 'Old man of the Cape, who buggared [*sic*] a Barbary ape,' has already remarked the peculiar simili-sexual tone of the Rev. Sydney Smith's speculation or observation, in *Sketches of Moral Philosophy:* 'We generally find that the triangular person has got into the square hole, the oblong into the triangular, and a square person has squeezed himself into the round hole.' Whether or not Smith had read Diderot, and was counting on his readers' not having done so, or whether these are independent parallel fantasies, is impossible to say.

What is significant is that the whole image in both Diderot and Smith purposely implies a symbolic element to the mismatching of organs, and that is the underlying meaning of the jokes as well. What they are really referring to is *not* the genital mismatching but that of the whole lives and characters of husbands and wives out of love with each other. The genital accusations here are a reversal of the usual form of nagging, in which carping and recriminations on all sorts of irrelevant matters unconsciously add up to the complaint: "You do not perform intercourse properly." This is as true of male nags as of female, and that it is the wife who is the traditional nag is an indication of the prevailing thoughtlessness and inadequacy of husbands. Just how little use there is in off-the-cuff 'sociological' explanations of human problems is nicely pointed up by comparing this analytic cliché, as to the sexual basis of nagging, with the hopeless gibble-gabble of almost the only article on the subject, "An Anatomy of Nagging," chapter 20, in Richard Curle's *Women: An Analytical Study* (London, 1947), a bitter attack, of course.

IV. THE DOCTOR

I. THE DOCTOR AS CONFESSOR

The doctor has replaced the priest and policeman as the principal modern father-surrogate, both in *ex cathedra* prohibitions of sex and fantasies of castration as punishment for transgressing these prohibitions. It is in line with this replacement that modern medicine — which is perhaps the most backward of current sciences, most of its spectacular recent advances being in proliferation of drugs (in saleable pill-form) to kill the bacteria discovered hardly a century ago by Semmelweiss and Pasteur, with little emphasis placed on, and little progress to report in, the improvement of organic health — has been allowed to retrogress on a very wide front to such surgical barbarisms as mass-circumcision of the newborn, and psycho-surgical procedures intended to punish the insane for their presumed social (and sexual) non-adjustment to currently demanded restraints. Where medicine is allowed to enter, self-admittedly without knowledge of what it is doing, into such activities as sub-total euthanasia by means of electro-shock, or the removal of parts of the brain by means of icepicks passed into the skull through the inner corner of the eye (transorbital leukotomy, frontal lobotomy, etc.), and where we are also treated to the spectacle of the *threat* of such brainwashing used against released prisoners of war for political purposes — a great improvement over Mussolini's crude castor-oil — it is obvious that medicine, or rather surgery combined with psychiatry, has been elected to the position of sacred executioner formerly the prerogative of the butcher-priests of the early religions, with their animal victims finally substituting (as at the sacrifice of Isaac) for human.

It is almost unnecessary to point out both the castratory tone of the various punishments and other neo-religious activities being currently engaged in by medicine and psychiatry, and the contempt that their practitioners feel for any possibility of criticism in thus slipping, in actual fact, into the stereotype of the 'mad scientist' continuously flung at them since the coming out of science from under the ægis of religion in the late 17th century. (Descartes was, I believe, the last mathematical philosopher to wear his collar backwards.) So far as the present text is concerned, it is quite obvious that *all* punishments for sexual acts stem either from the doctor, or, to a lesser and disappearing degree, from the policeman & judge. Only when the joke is laid in some mythical jungle milieu is the castration or pedicatory rape (with pineapples) ordered by that now old-fashioned father-figure of 'the King.' In the chapter on Fools, earlier, judge and doctor were seen to fuse into an identical punishing figure in repressing the sexual unrepression — as folklore has it — of the idiot. In the chapter on Castration, in Series Two, only the doctor is present, replacing the sow-gelder or priestly circumciser of earlier folktales on the same theme.

The problems of the newly married are also, in jokes, placed upon the merciful and paternal lap of the physician, or 'marriage counsellor,' still not quite cut loose from his sacerdotal twin. (A number of the early 1930's sex-adjustment handbooks of technique, such as Rossiter's and Tyrer's, were actually written by clergymen.) The same is also, of course, even more true of psychiatry and general 'family counselling,' in which streamlined religion is apparently preparing to make its last stand. The forbidding father-figure who disappears underground after the engagement, rumbling only distantly at the wedding as the Man in the Upper Berth, emerges unmistakably from cover — in his capacity as sex adviser — first as the Hotel Clerk and Druggist, and finally as the Doctor. Only in the chapter on Castration will the meaning and real intention of this transmogrification be made clear, where the Doctor's answer to every sexual problem becomes boldly that of the primal Ur-Vater of the horde: "*Cut it off!*"

The newly married have their problems. Maud does not fit Gerald. Gerald does not fit Maud. The doctor makes suggestions. He asks questions. How often . . . what positions . . .? What is his answer? Like *Punch*'s advice on matrimony, his answer is invariably "Don't!" *A young couple come to the doctor after their marriage for advice, mentioning that they have had intercourse six hundred times the first year. "Far too much to-ing and fro-ing," says the doctor, and begins prescribing sedatives. They leave in a huff, explaining that they have come for advice that will assure the same number the second year.* (McAtee, 1915, env. 4.) This rather poor joke will at least serve to date the appearance of 'marriage counsellor' in American humor, though the theme certainly must date much closer, in Europe, to Tissot's madhouse horrors and threats in *L'Onanisme, ou Dissertation physique sur les maladies produites par la masturbation.* (Lausanne, 1760.) The same dim view of coital frequency is taken, at the folk level, in the proverbial statement: *If a married couple put a coin in a box every time they have intercourse the first year, and take one out every time in all the succeeding years, they will never run out of coins.* (See variants in 8.VII.1, below.)

The mocking and prohibitive tone of everything the 'marriage-counselling' doctor says is reminiscent of the left-over story, commonly printed, in which the father-figure is the army officer of an earlier day: *A soldier on a two-week wedding furlough telegraphs to his commanding officer: "It's wonderful here. Request one week's extension of leave." The reply: "It's wonderful anywhere. Return to camp at once."* (Bennett Cerf, *Pocket Book of War Humor*, 1943, p. 75.) Prohibition is for the husband. The mockery is directed against the bride. *A young bride goes to the doctor to learn more about sex after her marriage. "What is that long thing between my husband's legs?" she asks. "That's called the penis." "And what's that red knob on the end?" "That's the glans or head." "And what are those round things fourteen inches behind the head?" The doctor looks at her. "Lady," he says, "I don't know about your husband, but on me they'd be the cheeks of my ass."* (Minn. 1946. Variants: "On me they'd be hemorrhoids," or "two apples in the back pockets of my pants.") — *A pregnant young woman asks the doctor what position she will have to lie in to give birth to the baby. "The same position you were in when you started it." "My God," she exclaims, "do you mean I've got to drive around Central Park in a taxi for two hours with my feet hanging out the window?"* (2:357.) The bride is clearly competing with the doctor-father, in the matter of mockery, in both of these, but it is equally clear that his superior status is carrying the victory.

The permissive doctor or marriage counsellor, like the permissive father, is always played for something of a fool — and is thus 'destroyed' — no matter how sincerely the tellers of stories about him would like to believe in the possibility of his existence. An older example, not involving the marriage problem: *A mother asks the doctor* [now psychiatrist] *to certify her son as a lunatic and have him put in an asylum. The doctor asks what the boy has done. Lady: "At Christmas he got up at night and ate all the mince-pies in the pantry." Doctor: "Mere gluttony." Lady: "And there's something shocking to tell — the other day he threw the servant down the stairs and fucked her." "Mere depravity, Madam. Now if you had told me, instead, that your son had eaten the servant and fucked the mince-pies, there could have been no doubt as to the necessity of confining him in an asylum."* (*The Pearl*, No. 18, Dec. 1880.)

In a transitional tale the permissive father-figure is the rabbi, harking back to the centuries of sexual control and public judgment in marriage cases — like the similar control of the Catholic priest — wielded by the European rabbi with his Talmud open before him to the sex-code passages of the tractate *Sanhedrin*, or *Niddarim 20b: A young man of good family, who has been studying for several years in the great cities of Western Europe, comes back to the little town of*

Slobodka and marries his childhood sweetheart. On their wedding night he goes through a complex pre-coital routine in which, after a build-up of manual, oral, and anal sophistications, he stands up on the footboard of the bed and makes a perfect swan-dive into vaginal coitus with her. She complains to her parents and they take her husband before the local rabbi, who is tremendously shocked, floors the young man by cracking him over the head with a folio volume of the Talmud, and declares the marriage annulled. The young man appeals the case to the head rabbi at Lemberg. The father of the bride appears, and describes in detail the young man's procedure on his wedding night. The head rabbi listens carefully, stroking his beard, and finally states as his decision that the young man is within his rights and the marriage valid. "But our rabbi said — " the father begins to expostulate. "My dear man," says the head rabbi sympathetically, "what would a little rabbi in Slobodka know about fancy fucking?" (Minn. 1946. This has also been collected in Yiddish, or fake-Yiddish, with an alliterative ending on *"fentzy yentzing."*)

In a more recent version, *A Catholic changes his religion and becomes a Jew when he cannot find a priest who will absolve him from the sin of having been licked from head to toe ("around the world") in a Paris whore-house. The first rabbi whom he consults assures him that it is perfectly all right, and when told of the point of view the priests have unanimously taken, he replies, "Mine boy, what do these* goyim *know from high-class intercourse?"* (N.Y. 1953.) Complex variant, N.Y. 1963, told by a young amateur prostitute or 'party-girl' several times, of: *A girl who is turned away unforgiven from both the Catholic and Protestant religions for having committed 'the sin of sixty-nine,' and who is about to commit suicide when saved by 'a little rabbi,' who shrives her (as above), calling to her at the last moment from the shadows of the Brooklyn Bridge, "Dun't jump!"* This is the most striking example I have ever encountered of a 'favorite joke' — in this case of a highly intelligent Catholic girl who had 'lost her faith,' and was emotionally marooned, and desperate for a superior authority to which she could allow herself to submit her oral hostilities and guilts — as expressive of the teller's deepest personal problem. Compare the other examples of jokes as self-unveiling, given at the end of section II of the Introduction, neither of which was delivered with so unmistakable an air of *a cry for help.*

2. COITAL POSTURES

On the question of postures in intercourse, the usual rationalization of the 'marriage manuals' is that monogamy can still perhaps be made to work by artful variation, giving each partner the sinless illusion of many different lovers or something of the sort. As even the most versatile of practical lovers seldom use more than three or four favorite postures in intercourse, the value of the offered palette of possibilities is actually only to reassure the young and inexperienced, and the old and neurotic, both suffering from anxiety that they are very poor lovers and unable to satisfy the sexual partner. (Compare the preceding joke.) I have had occasion to discuss, in *The Horn Book* (1964) p. 63-4, some of the highpoints of the modern literature of coital posture and technique, in particular Edmond Duponchel's *Instruction libertine* — called *The Horn Book* in the English translation of the 1890's — Alphonse Gallais' *Les Paradis charnels,* and, above all others in 'the mononania of *positions,*' Dr. Josef Weckerle's *Das Goldene Buch der Liebe* (Vienna, 1907), in which last work the second volume offers no less than five hundred and thirty-one (531) non-duplicating coital positions, 'all carefully described, numbered, classified, and mnemonically titled. Duponchel and Gallais, not to mention the *Kama Sutra* and *Perfumed Garden,* are left gasping behind, if one is to judge by sheer numbers.' (The first two hundred of Weckerle's postures have been translated into English under the title *Kinesthesia of Love* 'by T. Van de Velder,' privately issued, 1937-38; and a complete translation, with introduction by the present writer, is now being readied for publication.)

To the joke-makers this is all the particular height of absurdity, and they are perhaps not far wrong. *An American and a Frenchman are arguing about how many positions for intercourse exist. The American says there are one hundred and one* [sic]; *the Frenchman insists there are only one hundred. They decide to compare notes, and the Frenchman reels off an astounding list, ending his hundred with intercourse in the ear, hanging by one toe from the chandelier, etc. "Well," the American begins, "our first way is for the woman to lay on her back and the man to lay on top of her . . ." "Oo la la!" says* the Frenchman, "ziss I nevair heard!" (2:131. Also collected, N.Y. 1953, with ending: "Aha! ze hundred and first!") The doctor now appears, in his benign disguise as 'marriage counselor,' to explain that it is all wrong whatever it is. The joke has been quoted earlier on: *The man who tells the doctor that the only position he and his wife use is on all fours from behind, because "How else are we both going to watch television?"* (N.Y. 1951.) The same mocking of the doctor as marriage counsellor is present in the cognate story of *The ignorant young couple who go to the doctor for premarital advice and are told that the posture that will best "suit their body-build is 'dog-fashion' — you know, from behind — you can do it on the floor." The next day the bride is back with a long gash in her forehead. "I got frightened looking under the bed," she explains.* (N.Y. 1946.) On the deeper element here, compare the following poetic wall scrawl which I observed a Negro high-school-girl inditing on a subway poster without any attempt at disguise, to the admiration of several other girls: *"When you and your sweetie in bed, Don't get scared, just go ahead."* (N.Y. 1953.)

The Bohannon MS. collection, *Anti-Negro Folklore* (Bloomington, Indiana, 1967) No. 23, gives the obvious last word on the subject. Note the picking-up, at the folk level, of the euphemism 'climax' for *orgasm*, from the Kinsey Report:

> This great big tall colored woman and this little bitty short colored man come into divorce court saying they want a divorce. The judge looks at them and asks them what's the matter. Is something wrong with their sex life? "Is there one of you who don't like to do it?" The colored man said, "No, she likes to do it, and I like to do it, but the trouble is the climax." The judge said, "The climax, what's the matter with the climax?" The man said, "Well, when we do it, I put my feet in her garters, then I climax and then she climaxes, but the trouble is when she climaxes she straightens her legs out and it drags my face right through it."

The allusion here to the matching of body-builds by means of special postures touches on what is actually one of the most useful possibilities in large collections of postures, and the one on which least emphasis is laid in Western manuals. (An exception is the recommendation of a special posture for the 'gangling' husband with 'dumpy' wife, quoted from *Sane Sex Life and Sane Sex Living,* above.) Other important uses of variant positions, such as the allowing of pubic or manual excitation of the woman's clitoris by the man, have finally been recognized in the popular manuals (for instance G. Lombard Kelly's *Sex Manual,* Augusta, Georgia, 1945; *Handbook for Husbands (and Wives)* by 'Porter Davis' [Gordon Schindler], El Segundo, Calif. 1949, and Dr. John Eichenlaub's *The Marriage Art,* 1961, to mention the least expensive and most frank).

The whole problem, as the jokes see it, remains strictly that of bodily mismatching, and it is evident that this is a projection on the body at large of the genital mismatching — *i.e.* erotic mismatching — actually feared. The body as phallus. *A circus midget marries the tall woman. (His friends put him up to it.) A few weeks later they ask him, "How are you getting on?" ("The tall man puts me on.") "O.K.," he says, "but there's nobody to talk to."* (1:194. Parenthetical variations, N.Y. 1952.) In a variant or reversal of this, with the fat body — which represents impotence in the folk mind — substituting for the midget body (short penis): *A fat man with a very petite wife is asked by his friends how he manages to have intercourse with her. "I just sit back in an armchair," he explains, "and move her up and down on my lap. It's just like masturbating, but you have someone to talk to."* (N.Y. 1940. In a 'quickie' version: *"Do you like masturbating?" "Naw, nobody gets fucked but me."* N.Y. 1945.)

One obscure element in much of the exotic position work in the manuals of sex technique, both Levantine and Western, is the *attempt to fly* as an ultimate sexual act, which is so prominent, for instance, in the career of Leonardo da Vinci, and in modern science fiction. Intercourse on a swing (one or both partners), on a moving animal or vehicle, and in particular the fantasy of impossible rotary motions, may be interpreted as attempts to fly, with flying identified as the supreme coitus. Particularly corroborative is the emphasis in much of the lore on this subject on the supporting of the whole weight of either the man or the woman on the penis, without the supported partner's hands or feet touching the ground. The fantasy of the sex-machine (on which see the excursus to the 'young man of Racine,' in *The Limerick,* Paris, 1953, Note 1325) is certainly connected, particularly in the achieving of rotary coital motion. The now-famous 'basket trick,' in which all these elements are brought together, was first published as an engraving without text, about 1700, and discussed in 'Doctor A.-S. Lagail's' (actually Alphonse Gallais') *Les Paradis charnels, ou Le Divin bréviaire des amants: Art de jouir purement de 136 extases de volupté* ('Priapeville,' 1903), as the sixth-from-last of the concluding 'Clowneries charnelles;' some of the others, such as the 'Judgment of Solomon,' being even more spectacular.

Entirely independently, McAtee in 1921 (env. 2) *"Supplements to Rabelais:* 1. Panurge and Faucheux discourse on *carn. cop."* describes another fantasy method of rotary coitus with the woman supported not in any basket but simply on the penis of the standing man! Whether this is a literary or a folk idea is not stated. Gallais' method, with the woman dumped into an open-bottomed basket supported on cords which are then whirled to lift and lower her, has been heard seriously described several times since 1940, as an authentic sophistication of intercourse in the bedroom (or parlor) of some rich playboy able to afford oak-beam ceilings. The following joke form — of obvious antecedents — does not appear to date earlier than 1949. *A travelling salesman brags to a farmer that he knows two hundred positions for intercourse.* "*Bet I got one you don't know,*" *says the farmer, and he takes the salesman out and shows him a hay-rig with a bottomless bushel basket attached to the rope.* "*I put the hired girl in the basket with her dress up,*" *the farmer explains;* "*then I lay underneath and pull the basket up and lower her down.*" "*But why go to all that trouble?*" *asks the salesman.* "*'Cause when I want to jazz — I spin it!*" (N.Y. 1949. The use of 'jazz' here as a verb for orgasm is most uncommon, and strengthens the theory of the origin of the mysterious word 'jism,' for semen, as a mispronunciation of 'orgasm;' in the same way that 'bull-diker,' for a Lesbian, may be traced — through various mispronunciations such as 'morphodike' — to 'hermaphrodite.')

A young sailor, inquiring from his captain about sex[!] *is told just to watch the steam turbine. Later he is asked if he gets the idea.* "*Sure do,*" *he says,* "*but how do I get my balls to twirl?*" (Minn. 1946.) What is most significant in this variant is the assimilation of the fantasy of rotary coitus to that of the sex machine. That, at a more basic level, the 'complicated and indescribable machine' is a representation of the penis itself (as noted in Freud's 10th *Introductory Lecture,* and in Viktor Tausk's "The Influencing Machine," 1919, to the utter disbelief of the sort of persons who buy 'Meccano' and 'Erector' [!] girder sets for their little boys), is expressed perfectly artlessly in this joke. The mocking of the labor-saving device idea, in the following example, may also be construed as a mechanical, *i.e.* anti-mechanical, joke.

That the stated situation is again the superiority of the farmer (natural man) over the city-bred salesman (civilized, or castrated and machine-replaced man) is probably not accidental. *A travelling salesman staying overnight at a farmhouse is proudly shown around the place by the farmer. "Built this place with my own hands," the farmer boasts, "and I made everything the* hard *way. See that floor? Didn't use no nails — the whole thing is rabbetted and dove-tailed. The* hard *way! See that ceiling? Didn't use no joists — the whole thing is hanging from a flying beam. The* hard *way!" And so forth. Finally the farmer's daughter enters the room, and the salesman looks quizzically at him. "Yup," says the farmer, "standing up in a canoe!"* (N.Y. 1944.) In a degeneration of this into a quickie: "*I just finished reading* Forever Amber *the hard way — one hand!*" (nightclub master-of-ceremonies, Minn. 1946) is recollected the remark credited to a woman, the Maréchale de Luxembourg in the 18th century, speaking of an erotic work by Count Benseval: "It can be read only with one hand." People must be getting stronger these days, as witness also the reprinting of the 4,200 pages of *My Secret Life* (New York, 1966) in "two great horse-fucking volumes," as they have been called, of over a thousand pages each.

V. ORAGENITALISM

The ultimate taboo in sex technique, in the English-language literature certainly, is that concerning the oragenital acts that are a primary routine in the sexual approach of most mammals, particularly the quadrumanes and quadrupeds in whom the sense of smell is predominant in sexual selection. The lay and even medical disapprobation of oragenital acts has been largely toned by the moral condemnation actually intended for the homosexuality or Lesbianism with which they are often connected. The legal prohibition against oragenitalism shows this very clearly, lumping it with 'sodomy,' with punishments up to twenty years, even though taking place between persons of the opposite sex, whether or not they are married to each other. How it is intended to enforce sexually intrusive laws of this type is not stated; and where public avowals of oragenital acts are thought necessary — as in divorce cases — the euphemism 'mental cruelty' has been invented to avoid criminal liability. As there are neither religious nor logical grounds for the prejudice, recourse is usually attempted to a vague 'esthetic' objection against acting 'like animals.' To this the didactic modern literature of sex technique counterposes an equally vague romantic defense, stressing the presumable similarity to the kiss, as in Van de Velde's term 'the kiss of genital stimulation, or genital kiss.' (*Ideal Marriage,* Leiden, 1926; English transl. New York, 1930, p. 169.)

The modern literature of sex technique 'in marriage' — always 'in marriage' and always notably heavy-handed — is nowhere more lacking in psychological penetration than in its persistent discussion of sexual acts in terms of what they may be expected to do for the *other* person. The moral intention here is of course laudable, but almost nowhere in this literature is there any recognition of the underlying ego-drive, and the need for it, in sexual acts. Oragenitalism in particular, when it has been treated at all in English, has almost always been discussed as a specially valuable technique for exciting the genital partner. The oral drives (nursing substitutes) almost certainly motivating the oral partner are overlooked. This is true of Van de Velde's short passage, noted above; of the references to oragenitalism in the *Encyclopedia of Sex and Love Technique* by 'Rennie Macandrew' (London, 9th ed. 1946, pp. 217–18, and 232–35) and similar works, and even in the first monograph on the subject in any language, *Oragenitalism* by 'Roger-Maxe de La Glannège' [anagram: G. Legman], (New York, 1940), which deals with the technique of cunnilinctus only. (An enlarged edition is promised.) It should be noted however, that in spite of all statements to the contrary, oragenitalism is generally engaged in to give pleasure primarily to the oral partner and not to the genital partner; and when enacted simultaneously (the 'sixty-nine,' so called from the similarity of the position of the bodies to the figures 69) the usual complaint is that "what is being done to one distracts one from what one is doing."

Jokes offer the unspoken explanation that this overlooking of the oral motivation stems from men's desire to be the recipients of oragenital caresses for their own (genital) pleasure, and that in the arguing with, and persuading of, inexperienced young women to comply with this desire, the whole matter of the woman's possible oral drives and oral pleasure is lost sight of. Even the widespread recognition that homosexuals may engage pleasurably in thousands of oragenital acts with men, without their own genitals entering at all into the sexual concurrence (although of course erection and auto-masturbatory orgasm generally take place), has not cast any broad light on the invariable relationship between orality and oragenitalism. In the case of cunnilinctus, *per contra,* as the jokes also show, the element of orality is understood to be paramount, with, for instance, dying men asking the nurse to let them perform cunnilinctus — which they have sworn to try once before they die (*n.b.*) — and invariably being revived by it. The wholly male-centered point of view of jokes is neatly demonstrated in this contradiction.

I. FELLATION BY THE BRIDE

It is assumed, of course, that the woman is ignorant of the possibility of such a thing as oragenital acts, and one of the shocks of the wedding night, in jokes, is to find her highly knowledgeable in this matter, suggesting a lack of innocence far beyond the mere loss of virginity. (In a passage which he repeats twice, calling fellation a 'repulsive propensity' and 'perverted phantasy,' Freud indicates how this desire in a woman may nevertheless arise entirely innocently, and without even the sight of animals' foreplay, as an extension of the memory of pleasure in sucking the mother's breast. *Collected Papers,* vol. III. pp. 64, 151.) *A minister, on his wedding night, comes back from brushing his teeth in the bathroom before going to bed, and finds his bride lying naked on her back in bed. He is shocked. "Why I expected to find you on your knees," he says reproachfully. "Well all right," says his bride, "but it always gives me the hiccups."* (Calif. 1942.) Or: *"I'm not that kind of a girl, and besides it always makes my head ache."* (N.Y. 1946.)

Three daughters all are married on the same day. Their parents listen at all the bedroom doors. They hear the first daughter laughing, the second crying, and the third is silent. Next morning they ask why. First daughter: "Well, you always told me to laugh when something tickled me." Second daughter: "Well, you always told me to cry when something hurt me." Third daughter: "Well, you always told me when I had my mouth full to keep it shut." (N.Y. 1942.) This is also told of *An old farmer and his two sons who go to a whore-house in town. The farmer impresses upon them the need for proper prophylaxis and asks them afterwards what they have done about it. The first son explains that he has used a regulation prophylactic kit — salve, cheesecloth bag, and all. The second son explains gruffly that he has simply poured raw whiskey over the head of his penis. "And what did you use?" he asks his father. "I just gargled with listerine," says the old man.* (Transcontinental train, 1945.)

It has been noted in the section on "Female Fools" that ignorance of the mechanism of intercourse, the hallmark of the male fool, is seldom imputed to women. The few exceptions are generally set up in order to posit the woman's ignorance of the presumably more sophisticated act of fellation. *An old roué marries an innocent virgin, but being impotent he teaches her to fellate him, explaining that that is sexual intercourse. After a few weeks he feels strong enough to attempt ordinary intercourse, but his bride shrieks, "Don't you dare to try that, you dirty degenerate!"* (1:98. Nicolaïdès, p. 117.) — *A priest offers to show a pretty young nun the "key to the kingdom of heaven," and seduces her with it. She innocently tells the mother superior, who says, "Why that lying son of Satan; for twenty years he's been telling me it was Gabriel's horn, and I've been blowing it!"* (Calif. 1952.) This story is of Italian-American provenance, and is unquestionably connected with the folktale motif K1315.1.1, "Seduction by posing as the Angel Gabriel," which Rotunda cites from Boccaccio IV.2, and other *novellieri,* with further references to Lee and Di Francia on Boccaccio's sources. (*Motif-Index of the Italian Novella in Prose,* 1942, p. 102.)

The symbol of the horn or trumpet, as indicating the penis, has not, I believe, been noted before, but it is fairly common, as in a strange erotic dream — possibly authentic — in which a man calls his penis a trumpet, and blows it to prove it when a woman insists that it is really a penis, given in *The Pearl,* No. 2 (Aug. 1879) as "Part of a Letter from Harriet Keene." The flute as a penis-symbol, and flute-playing as a term and symbol for fellation, are at least as old as the Greek *auletrides.* (See also the telephone joke, under "Tricks of the Trade," in the chapter on Prostitution, in Series Two, 11.III.4.) The term '*blowing the meat-whistle,*' for fellation, was collected too late for inclusion in my glossary of "The Language of Homosexuality," in Dr. George W. Henry's *Sex Variants* (1941), although the very common term 'blow' is of course given. That this term itself involves the metaphoric notion of a horn or trumpet, and has no actual relation to the buccal friction which is the operative element in fellation, is also quite clear, as in the catch-phrase — possibly the tag-line of a joke — "*Suck, you son-of-a-bitch; 'blow' is just a figure of speech!*" (N.Y. 1952.) Since, as noted, the activity is primarily buccal friction, and not suction, this too 'is just a figure of speech.'

2. FELLATION AS BIRTH CONTROL

The most common reference to fellation in jokes is to its use as a birth control technique. Many of these jokes are hardly more than taglines, hauling in the subject bodily for its wish-value or to allay its anxiety content (as will be seen shortly) without any real situation built up. *"If the stork brings babies, and larks bring illegitimate babies, what kind of birds don't bring any babies at all?"* "Swallows." (Calif. 1941; New Jersey, 1942.) — *The new birth control method : Gargallo. "But that's a mouthwash." "Who says it ain't?"* (1:198. Compare the joke on the farmer and his two sons, above.) Pantomime joke: *The Hollywood method of birth control (or a French abortion)* — *"Ptooey!"* (*spitting*). The Hollywood version is given in *Anecdota* 2:402 the 'French' version, Minn. 1946. The allusions to both Hollywood and France (generic term for oragenitalism: 'frenching') are both intended to imply the ultra-sophistication of the act, as with: *The American tourist who returns from a visit to France and announces: "Sexual intercourse is in its infancy in America."* (N.Y. 1942.) By the mid-1960's, with oragenital jokes and allusions prominent at the high-school level of 'hippie' lapel-buttons, and with classified advertisements in the far-out or 'underground' press on the style of *'Inexperienced young man wants fun and cunnilingus with plump lady who will teach him how,'* America is perhaps entering its sexual adolescence. I believe the 'swap-club' malady shows it is entering its sexual *decay*.

The most frequently collected reference to fellation as birth control implies the same hoaxing by the bridegroom as that in the joke on the roué, just above. *A girl is sure she can never become a mother: "I'll never learn to swallow that dreadful stuff!"* (2:223. Also a limerick version in *The Limerick*, Paris, 1953, No. 430, dated 1946.) There is an earlier version, actually a reversal, in Dr. Susruta's "Englische Erzählungen aus Indien," in *Anthropophyteia* (Leipzig, 1910) VII. 337, No. 4: *"The French are queer folk. There was a girl of this village who married a French sailor, and, when she came home after a year or two, her mother asked how it was that she was not in the family way, and she said that she really thought that it was her Man's* [German *Mann:* husband] *fault, for she always swallowed it all right."* The opening remark interestingly adumbrates the famous verse of "Mademoiselle from Armentières": *'The French they are a funny race, They fight with their feet and fuck with their face—Hinky dinky parlez-vous!'* (u.s. 1918.)

Beneath the hoaxing idea, whether by an impotent husband or simply a Frenchman (!) there is an evident reminiscence in the whole situation of the various infantile errors and theories as to the method and aperture of impregnation and birth, as discussed in Freud's *Three Contributions to the Theory of Sex* (1905). This reminiscence is clearest in the jokes, several already quoted in the opening chapter on Children, in which the child makes mock-innocent references to oragenital remarks overheard between father and mother, or father and the mother-expurgate or -surrogate of the nurse. There is also 'Little Audrey's' knowing that the baby boy's penis wasn't a whistle [*n.b.*] because she blew it and didn't get any sound—fellatory caressing of male infants by their mothers is commonly reported from many cultures other than our own, but is by no means unknown here—and, finally, the variant on *The little boy peeping through the keyhole on his sister's wedding night and saying, "God damn!—and they scold me for sucking my thumb!"* (d.c. 1943. In another version the child has been scolded for picking his nose.) A French 'novelty' ceramic piece, with the identical situation and caption-line, was encountered on public sale in Nice, 1955. Sex-kitsch!

As to the superior sophistication of fellation—never of cunnilinctus, which is presumed to be 'foreign' only in the sense of being unworthy and humiliating—there is an apparent connection between the idea of such sophistication and the use of fellation as a substitute form of intercourse during menstruation or when disease from vaginal coitus is feared. The English-language manuals of marital sex technique over the last thirty years refer only to the substitutive act of anal coitus during menstruation, but it would appear that fellation is at least as common, if only because of the absence of the pain usually accompanying infrequent anal coitus. Almost the only forthright reference to the subject, publicly published, is in an eccentric pamphlet, headed 'A Pathologic Document, *The Great Madness,* by Count Roual [*sic*] de Bretignac, Author of "The Ethnology of the Sixth Sense" and "Is Communism Inevitable?" Published by Alex Schwarzenfeld, New York' [1944]. (On page 8 Mr. Schwarzenfeld admits that he and Roual de Bretignac are 'one and the same person.') In spite of the unabashed eccentricity of the work—a "Warning to the Reader," p. 4, announcing that these pamphlets are 'the culmination of my writings, written as a guest of The Rockland State Hospital, a guest for almost six years' — Schwarzenfeld ends, p. 16, with the perfectly sane remark that 'The most insidious taboo we have placed on women is that no sex relations are possible during menstruation . . . . The result of this is to force our women into the practice of fellatio,' an observation which he unfortunately then develops to somewhat unwarranted lengths. Fellation is also very commonly offered nowadays by young virgin girls as a substitute for the feared sexual intercourse.

The joke has already been quoted in the chapter on Men, in which *The girl who denies the man intercourse on the grounds that she is menstruating, and anal intercourse because she has piles, is threatened with debraining with a rock if she says she has lockjaw.* Further connecting this set of substitutions with 'sophisticated' knowledge, a variant, D.C. 1950, includes *The man's penultimate suggestion of inter-mammary coitus, only to have the girl admit that her breasts are padded with 'falsies.'* In a much milder version of the original, the idea of sophistication is wholly in the foreground, with no mention of menstruation: *A yokel who has been to the big city takes his home-town sweetheart for a buggy-ride. On a lonely road he drops the reins and begins caressing her. "Shall I pull up my dress?" she asks timidly. "No, spit out that chewing gum."* (1:372.) This is now more usually collected in a variant on *The Indian who returns to the reservation after a visit to a big-city whore-house and is teaching his squaw the new lore he has learned there, but interrupts her to say. "Ugh, nice big cigar — smokum, no chewum."* (2:72.) The note of danger here is sometimes omitted, with his merely saying, *"No pokum — smokum."* (D.C. 1945.)

The height of elegance and sophistication in America was once traditionally Boston (*i.e.* England cut-rate, or *New* England), and the cultured Bostonian is always ridden for a fall on the usual anti-intellectual lines of the Englishman-fool stories. *A Boston aristocrat marries a chorus-girl, and sends her to England for a year to polish her manners and diction. From the railing of the homecoming ship she calls to him, "Hello, darling, have you been blue while I was gone?" "Blown, dear, blown!"* (2:174.) This is much more commonly collected than its merely grammatical humor might lead one to expect. Of the straight fool variety, the search for ultra-sophistication is seen to end in bathos: *The new discovery — a four-way girl* [the traditional number being three]. *"What's the fourth way?" the discoverer is asked. "She lets you go down on her."* (2:54.) As with cryptic references to the number 69, persistently smuggled into liquor advertising, comic-strips (Li'l Abner), magazine cartoons, and college-fraternity sweaters (since 1963!) — even in an early Chaplin film, *Easy Street* (1919) — for its oragenital allusion, the phrase 'three-way' (or even 'two-way') seems to be considered extremely naughty or advanced, in its adding the oragenital 'way' to the presumed clichés of pelvic intercourse. The idea, if not the term, can be traced to the epigram on Lyde, in the *Greek Anthology*, v.49, who accepted three men simultaneously in as many ways, as noted in *Index Limericus* (MS. 1947), to which *The Limerick* (Paris, 1953) Note 311, adds Martial's *Epigrams*, IX. 32, and a parody Purim poem (dated 1947), to the tune of "Oh, Landlord fill the flowing bowl," beginning:

> *Oh, Esther was a three-way queen,*
> *She wasn't very moral.*
> *She took the king in every way —*
> *Vaginal, anal, oral.*

A woman of the expertness and experience presumed in the fellatrix is naturally in the dominant position during the act, and the man's passive urges to have his penis caressed in this way strengthen her dominance. (The technical distinction between *fellation,* in which the oral partner is active, and *irrumation* in which — in the same act — the oral participant is passive, as indicated for instance by the positions assumed, is seldom of relevance in jokes on the subject, where the oral partner, whether a woman or a homosexual, is always considered 'active' even if performing fellation under duress.) The inevitable accompaniment of the fellatrix' dominance is the fear of phallic damage from her actions. This is seldom expressed as the direct statement that she might bite off the man's penis, though that is unquestionably what is feared. Among the clearest stories given in the chapter on Castration, in Series Two, in the section "*Vagina Dentata,*" are two — invariably told as true — in which damage of this sort is specifically described; yet in one case it is done only by accident and in the other case not by the teeth but by means of a burning cigarette. In the only joke collected where actual fellatory damage is described it is enacted only after the man is dead. *A widow goes to the morgue and cuts off the penis of her late-lamented husband. When asked why, she replies that she "had been eating that thing for years, and wanted to see what it would taste like cooked."* (D.C. 1945.) In a better known version, obviously the original, she proposes to perform pedicatory rape on his body with his own penis, on the grounds that "that's the only hole in town it hasn't been in." (Calif. 1936. See the section "The Ganymede Revenge," ending the chapter on Homosexuality, in Series Two.)

The most famous true, or allegedly true story of danger during fellation is that of Dr. James H. Snook, who testified, at his trial for the hammer-murder of Theora Hix, a student of his at the Ohio State College of Veterinary Medicine, that while parked with her in his car on a shooting-range, '. . . she grabbed open my trousers which had been buttoned up, and went down on me then, and she didn't do it very nicely and she bit me and grabbed the right hand and got hold of the privates and pulled so hard I simply could not stand it, and I tried to choke her off, and I couldn't get her loose that way, and then I grabbed her left arm and gave it a twist, and finally pulled her loose, partly, and she grabbed back again and all I could do was to hold her head up close to keep her from hurting me, and turn around and got something, and I got hold of something out of this kit and hit her with it, and I did not hit her very hard.'

The Limerick, No. 404, gives an example on the subject, and the testimony in the trial was hawked in the streets — as was not uncommon during sex trials in the U.S. in the 1920's — as a small pamphlet entitled *Dr. Snook and The Murder of Theora Hix* (Columbus, Ohio, 1929). The quotation above is from p. 24, with fuller details on cross-examination, p. 35-40, in which the point is carefully made that Miss Hix was acting for her own pleasure and not Dr. Snook's, and with the closing statement, p. 45: 'He is now in Columbus Ohio penitentiary awaiting the end.' As with other popular heroes — in certain circles — such as John Wilkes Booth and Hitler; also the Mexican revolutionary Emiliano Zapata (who 'was seen . . . riding in the mountains'); the belief is still current that Dr. Snook was never really executed, "because he was a Thirty-Third Degree Mason," and was spirited away into hiding by friends. The American sex-comedian or 'sick'-comedian, Lenny Bruce, was similarly no sooner dead in 1966, presumably of an overdose of drugs, than wall scrawls and a proposed bumper-sticker were proliferated by his ardent fans among the *révolté* college-students, reading poignantly: "LENNY LIVES!"

A story began making the rounds in the United States, also in 1966, and was in one case printed as true in a mimeographed poetry magazine, concerning: *A teeny-bopper* [very young teen-aged girl hanging around rock & roll bands] *who boldly asks all the boys in a coffee-bar whether anyone would like a 'blow-job.' One of them takes her up on the offer, and they go out behind an advertising billboard. A few minutes later he is found there, rolling on the ground in pain. The girl has bitten into his penis so hard as to leave teeth-marks, and has run away. No one ever sees her again.* (Cleveland, Ohio, 1966.) This sounds more like the Sleeve-Job than a 'blow-job.' I do not mean to imply that this story *could* not have been true originally, as I have heard both young girls and mature women confess to even more violent oral-incorporative hostility against the penis — sometimes displaced to the tongue during kissing, which may be sucked so hard as to be very painful. However, I have heard the same or a similar story told in France, in French, by high-school boys waiting for a bus. In this case, *The girl takes the boy behind the screen of an automatic photo-machine in a railroad station late at night. Her first offer is: "Give me fifty francs, and I'll show you my titties."* (Cannes, 1967; the 'fifty francs' line being taken from the latest French *jeunesse pourrie* or 'rotted youth' movie.) Possibly this *vagina dentata* teeny-bopper is wandering around the world on her 'junior year abroad'? Or possibly it is just a standard castration fantasy. The usual stories of danger in fellation are seldom direct terror-tales of this kind, or that of Dr. Snook; but displace the danger on some irrelevancy in which it is more or less successfully veiled. *A man goes to the doctor with a red rash on his penis which he thinks is venereal disease. The doctor rubs the rash off with a damp rag and says, "Tell your girl not to use so much lipstick."* (1:431. Several limerick versions.) A catch rather than a joke: "*Did you hear about the three sailors that were walking along the shore when a big wave came along and sucked them under the boardwalk?*" (N.Y. 1943. One of many sub-jokes on the various armed forces women's auxiliaries: Wacs, Waves, etc., as companions for the officers. The original female soldiers actually *bore arms* — the Amazons of antiquity, and Kerensky's palace-guard during the Russian Revolution, 1917.)

The most frequently collected, and best articulated story on fellatory 'danger' projects the whole situation into the realm of the imaginary, and the danger upon some other person than the woman. *A man who comes to a dinner party with a black eye is laughed at when he says he got it walking into a door in the dark. "Why don't you tell us who hit you?" he is asked. "All right," he says angrily, determined to make up a lie that will punish the mixed company for their disbelief. "Just as I was ready to leave I noticed a button missing from my fly. So I went and asked the lady next door to sew it on for me, and just as she was bending over to bite off the thread — her husband walked in.*" (2:428.) The printed form does not give the frame-situation of the party, which, as it were, removes the fellatory danger doubly into non-existence, by making not only the act of fellation, but the punishment for it, equally imaginary. Compare also, in *Anecdota* 1:472, the "*most perilous indoor sport: Button, Button, Here Comes My Husband.*" The "most *popular* indoor sport" is of course coitus. There seems to be some precursor of the above story being frantically pointed at in the following quotation from the 19th-century American humorist, 'Brick' Pomeroy, "How I Lost Aurelia" (reprinted from the LaCrosse, Wisc. *Democrat,* in his *Nonsense,* New York, 1868, p. 81), and, even if not, the images themselves are of striking relevance:

> The night we sat on the edge of the spring and hugged our-selves into it, I wanted to be liberal. I had nothing, so I gave Aurelia a button from my trowserloons. [He is mocking the ele-gant avoidance of the word 'pants.'] I had no knife to cut it off, so Aurelia chawed it off. And I took some of her hair, made a little string from it, and hung it around her neck. It was a charm with Aurelia's charms. She wore it near her heart. I was happy when she wore it, and often wished I was a little button with a tin top and wooden bottom so I could hang around Au-relia's neck. [Compare the masochistic ballad: "*I wish I was a diamond ring, Upon my Lulu's hand, And every time she wiped her ass, I'd see the promised land.*" — u.s. ante 1915.] It bore the marks of Aurelia's teeth, where once, in maiden medi-tation, she had squoze a tooth in it, while chawing it off!

3. CUNNILINCTUS

Cunnilinctus, usually spelled '*cunnilingus,*' is a subject of great psy-chological complexity, and justice cannot be done to it here. The most important point that can usefully be made concerning it, in connection with the jokes illustrating the folk-approach to the subject, is (as with fellation) the much greater importance in its motivation shown by oral and masochistic strivings — the desire to return to the mother's breast, or womb, and to infant dependence — than by any desire to excite the other participant by this 'technique.' In the case of the less taboo oral caressing of the woman's breasts, men are quite frank about admitting that this is done more for their own pleasure than for the woman's.

One must not, as the proverb has it, reckon without one's host. There are sexual and maternal satisfactions to the woman in oral caresses of both her breasts and genitals. There is also the peculiarity that where fellation is usually thought of as a domination of the genital partner by the oral partner, in cunnilinctus this is reversed and the oral partner (in the present frame of reference the man) is considered to be dominated by, and subservient to, the woman (the genital partner) however willingly he may have engaged in cunnilinctus, and, in fact, *because* of this willingness. Just how universal this point of view is, will be seen from the anthropological materials concerning the matrilocal Pacific islanders cited later in this section.

It must not be lost sight of that the masochistic element in cunnilinctus, which will bulk so large and even perversely in the present treatment, is essentially an encapturing for neurotic purposes of a perfectly normal mammalian erotic preliminary to which the male of the species may properly be expected to be attracted for his own pleasure. The first publicly published statement in English on cunnilinctus, in W. F. Robie's *The Art of Love* (Boston, 1921) p. 249, opens with a simple and direct statement of this attraction to cunnilinctus for the man's own pleasure, quite aside from the intended excitation of the woman: 'During the whole of my sexual experience I had a desire, when sexually excited, to bring my lips in contact with the female vulva. I knew that that method of procedure was practiced by some classes of adult persons, but I was at a loss to know whether this was a natural act or a perversion. When a child on the farm, I had often seen male animals lick the female organs, and this led me to believe that it might be natural and that my desire was only that which was experienced by every healthy man.' This passage, with its following page-and-a-half of details on cunnilinctual technique, was intended to be quoted in one of the frankest of the marriage manuals, *How to Achieve Sex Happiness in Marriage* by 'Henry and Freda Thornton' [Dr. Herman de Fremery and Mrs. Fern Hawkins McGrath], published by the Vanguard Press (New York, 1939), which does not hesitate to use the colloquial rather than Latinized scientific vocabulary of sex. The passage was, however, dropped, p. 104, along with intended paragraphs on "The Penis Kiss," "The Mutual Genital Kiss," and "Cleanliness" [! see the Table of Contents], in deference to the oragenital taboo. This is apparently still quite strong, at the publishing or pop-culch level, though oragenital acts are now widely accepted and sought at all actual *folk*-levels in the Anglo-Saxon culture, especially among adolescents and young adults. As to the continuing spread between the generations, and between sex in print and in fact, witness for example the almost total omission of this subject from Dr. John Eichenlaub's otherwise extraordinarily frank and detailed sex-technique manual, *The Marriage Art* (1961), which, as I have remarked in the Introduction to *My Secret Life* (ed. 1966) p. xliii, concerning its very popular pocket-reprint, 'is peacefully sold to non-promiscuous housewives and college girls in among the soap chips in the supermarkets, at 60¢.' (A satire on Dr. Eichenlaub's ideas appears in *Ramparts*, February 1967, pp. 8–10.) The various popular manuals of Dr. Albert Ellis on sexual subjects also give very superficial treatment to oragenital caresses — as Dr. Janet Wolfe has observed — but this omission is in part corrected in his *The Art of Erotic Seduction* (1967, one of the first of the public sex manuals to omit courageously any pious reference to 'in Marriage'), on the basis of my own work, *Oragenitalism*.

Jokes are in no doubt whatever about the male attraction to cunnilinctus, though this is alternated with resistance to the idea of cunnilinctus as a 'punishment' or domination by the woman. Where there is no question of dominance, the act is sought with a fervor which is itself the subject of several jokes. *Three chorus-girls are undressing. The first girl has the impression of a Y on her abdomen and explains that her sweetheart is a Yale man who forgot to remove his belt. The second chorus-girl has an H, for Harvard. The third girl's abdomen shows the impression of an F. Producer: "I suppose your boyfriend goes to Fordham." Chorus-Girl: "No, he's a Fire Chief. He just forgot to take off his hat."* (2:363. *Anecdota* 1:395 gives a version in which *A woman explains her scratched thighs by saying, "My husband's a Mexican and wears earrings."*) Of miscellaneous admissions of attraction by men to cunnilinctus there is the military-academy hazing trick, reported 1951, of requiring an undergraduate to answer "Yes, sir," "No, sir," or "No excuse, sir," to all questions, including the final spooneristic trick-question: "Have you ever snatched a kiss, or vice versa?" This is given in the form of a toast, in Jim Taylor's *Drop the Hook* (1952) p. 130–31: 'The other officer took out a bottle and said, "Well, *let's drink to it. A toast to the WAAC's. Here's to the kisses I've snatched and vice versa.*" ' This also, it will be noted, on a military background.

A gag-example that does not quite rise to the status of a joke expresses the idea of oral harm or danger exactly matching that feared during fellation, but projects the hostility on the female victim herself through the stalking horse of the quasi-female *Lesbian who ate up half the mattress before she found out her girlfriend had gone to the toilet.* (N.Y. 1942.) In a variant collected much later the orally-harming husband not only appears without disguise, but his hostility is directed against his only rival for oral satisfactions: *The husband who ate up the baby's foot before he found out his wife was pregnant.* (N.Y. 1950.)

One of the infrequently encountered but standard subjects of erotic art — it is one of sixteen postures of the bogus-Aretino (NOT in his *Sonetti lussuriosi,* Venice, 1526, as illustrated by Giulio Romano), often reprinted, which has also been found in an American erotic comic-book of the 1930's — is that of coitus from the side or back while the woman simultaneously nurses her child. The artist's identification with the child here, as in the usual Madonna paintings of the nursing child, is not difficult to fathom. (See further, Chapter 9.1.1, below.) In an eccentric work, *The "Marriage of Happiness" (The Revelation of Woman)* by Carl Buttenstedt, published by the author in Berlin in both German and English about 1905, a 'life-lengthening and strengthening' technique is described in which the man is to suck the non-pregnant woman's breasts during coitus until they give milk, and this will allegedly prevent her from becoming pregnant. A similar practice, when the woman is actually the mother of a nursing child, is known in American slang — without any life-lengthening or birth control rationalizations — as 'copping the baby's breakfast.'

The few reported cases of auto-fellation, or self-fellation by men, that have been studied psychiatrically, show convincingly that the satisfaction sought by the (auto-)fellator is oral and emotional rather than genital, as the penchant for fellation as a male homosexual act would also suffice to show. (*Pantomime riddle: "How does a fairy masturbate?" Teller blows out cheeks and massages his Adam's apple.* — D.C. 1951.) The orality of oragenitalism is perfectly well understood at the folk-level, and humorous reports are encountered, in connection with cunnilinctus, of the existence of a 'tongue hardon,' on which, for instance, a man chokes to death at a burlesque show while watching a strip-tease. (*Bull-eeve It Or Not,* an erotic comic-book of the early 1930's, parodying Ripley's famous strip.) The same idea is reported from California, 1932, in the form of a rather weak joke on *A man who stutters, and who, when he does so on meeting a beautiful actress, is given a pencil and paper by her to write down what he has to say.*

She explains, "I've had the experience before. Whenever men see me, their tongues get so hard they can't talk." This has been collected, more recently, in the Jerry Lewis comedy motion picture *Sailor Beware* (Paramount: 1952) in which Lewis speaks several times of being allergic to face powder and lipstick, so that when he kisses a girl his uvula swells up and becomes edematous, preventing speech — a typical burlesque comedy routine. Compare the 'definition' of *The Perfect Lover: a Frenchman with a nine-inch tongue, who can breathe through his ears.* (Arlington, Tex. 1966.)

The 'tongue hardon' is never proposed as a useful adjunct in the technique of cunnilinctus but as an embarrassment or even a danger [*n.b.*] accompanying it. Jocular descriptions of special cunnilinctual abilities do, however, include the ability to 'do double-stops' (the tongue being flicked twice on both sides of the forefinger held upright before the mouth to demonstrate this), and a sub-joke about *A man with a wart on the top of his penis who finally loses out to another man with a row of warts down the middle of his tongue.* (N.Y. 1940, from a foreign source.) Situations without 'punch-lines,' of this type, are usually rapidly made into limericks. (This one, on a man named Biddle, appears in *The Limerick,* No. 226.) The actual production of physical excrescences like this on the penis (sometimes with bells imbedded!) has been observed by anthropologists in various parts of the world, always with the explanation that it is for the women's pleasure, as with the phallic insertions of wire brushes, etc. under the general name of the *ampallang.* See earlier, on the 'French tickler,' p. 429.

It is especially the elderly man, or the presumably sub-virile 'foreigner,' who has recourse to cunnilinctus in jokes, not for his own pleasure but in order to give the woman the pleasure he is not able to offer her phallically. *An old singer is bragging that he has taken out all the chorus-girls in his show. "Oh yeah?" "Yeah; and I laid 'em all too." "Oh yeah?" "Yeah; and what's more, I satisfied 'em." "Yeah, you and your big mouth!"* (2:435.) In a touching example, *An old photoengraver is working on a "leg" photo of a beautiful actress. He looks admiringly at her seductively displayed breasts and legs, smacks his lips and says, "Why, any son-of-a-bitch that wouldn't center-field on this dame is a goddam degenerate!"* (2:412.)

The Frenchman is the traditional cunnilinctor. *During an argument an American angrily calls a Frenchman a "cock-sucker." "Sometimes," replies the Frenchman with dignity, "in ze heat of passion I kiss ze pussy. But suck ze cock — nevair!"* (2:93.) Anilinctus as an actual sex technique is seldom mentioned, though the invitation to kiss the buttocks is the most famous humorous challenge of the Western world, with a history extending back four hundred years or more. *A Frenchman is making love to an American girl. He kisses her mouth, her ears, the nape of her neck, and her breasts, and finally her belly and vulva. She becomes excited and farts, and is terribly embarrassed. "It is nozzing,"* says the Frenchman airily, *"just ze jealous asshole — he'll be next."* (D.C. 1951. In the same situation the less woman-loving American remarks only, *"Thank God for a breath of fresh air!"* N.Y. 1942. The older "Lady and the Flea" version of this, the only joke on which a whole (mock) monograph has been written, will be discussed in chapter 15," Scatology," in Series Two.) In Thomas Wolfe's *Look Homeward, Angel* (1929) p. 590-91, Wolfe describes himself shocking 'some loud pompous yokel' by means of a pretended Utopian scheme in which divorce is to be done away with, and civilization put back on its feet, by 'more and better Belly-Kissing' — needless to say, a euphemism for cunnilinctus. *Life,* Jan. 27, 1947, p. 66, photographs a Jerome Robbins ballet (his masochist 'utopian' ballet, "The Cage," has been mentioned earlier) called "Facsimile," which is practically a gag-representation of cunnilinctus, on the style of the present joke, with the male dancer kissing the female dancer in the standard upward song-pantomime progression of *toe, knee, chest* (the hand is substituted), and *nut.* Even so, the final mouth kiss, with the legs of the two dancers miming sexual intercourse — a tradition in the dance going back to Greek comedy and also retained in modern burlesque — was, according to *Life,* 'cut out in Boston because the city's censors objected.'

Despite the so-called 'New Freedom,' which is really mostly for printed books at high prices, almost the identical theatrical prudery has now been encountered twenty years later, in the pudibund San Francisco which nevertheless allows the grotesque public humiliation of women as bare-breasted waitresses in 'topless' nightclubs, and even shoe-shine joints (!) — after which one may draw the curtain. The *avant-garde* play, *The Beard, or Jean Harlow and Billy the Kid,* by the most powerful of the younger American poets, Michael McClure (concerning whom see my review in *Fact,* July 1965, vol. II, no. 4, p. 40), has been harassed nightly since 1966 owing to an oragenital act, cunnilinctus, poetically mimed onstage as the climactic scene. The newspapers referred to this discreetly as 'an act usually described in Latin.' See the illustrated text of the play in *Evergreen Review* (Oct. 1967), most of the spoken dialogue being a charade of sex hostility.

Meanwhile, the so-called '*happenings*' in both Paris and America in the 1960's (the word is Jean-Jacques Lebel's *Franglish,* or fractured-American, for the ancient extemporaneous art of *commedia dell'arte,* also known currently under the magnificent appellation of 'therapeutic psychodrama,' in the hands of Dr. Jacob Moreno), carefully include in their cynical palette of sex-exploitation kicks and nudie gag-scenes, for the far-out and deep-'in' audience of chumps, eager to believe that it is all being done under the influence of LSD (it is too, but spell that *£.s.d.!*), every type of mimed sexual scene, regularly including pretended oragenital acts. For the same price of admission, the audience could see the real thing at the private sex-exhibitions of the Rue Pigalle — and very artistically done — but the unwritten theatrical and carnival law seems to remain, "*Never wise-up a sucker.*"

An anecdote of the theatre in the 1930's tells that during the English production, under the title *The Sex Fable,* of a French play, *Le Sexe Faible* (really meaning "The Weaker Sex," but the fractured-French translation was correctly expected to draw better): *The French director — variously stated to have been Henri Bernstein or Sacha Guitry — directed the British leading actor to cross the stage to the bed where the leading lady was supposedly asleep, and to kneel by the side of the bed and kiss her tenderly on the belly. "But Mr. Bernstein," the actor objected stiffly, "I would point out to you that this lady is wearing only a nightgown." "So lift up the nightgown, my boy!"* The great leap here implied was finally made, in a hopelessly bad movie-epic of the Roman slave-revolt, *Spartacus* (1963), when the even stiffer American leading actor was persuaded somehow to kneel and kiss the belly of his pregnant wife (through her homespun skirt, my boy!) as an act of silent adoration, while the technicolor cameras rolled. Say what you will, it *is* progress. Note, however, that a similar expurgation was not observed in the hideous mass-crucifixion scene with which the same film ended.

The substitutive use of cunnilinctus as a form of intercourse leads naturally to the idea of its use as a form of birth control. Basically a joke, this is also a standard part of the salestalk of Lesbians seducing non-Lesbian girls. The foreigner (Frenchman) is almost always named in the accusation of using this method of birth control, with the even more interesting imputation of fœtophagy in the principal joke collected on this theme: *An Italian laborer is up before the court on the charge of murdering a Chinese laundryman. He invokes the Unwritten Law, but is told that the proper reaction to adultery is divorce, not murder. "But you no understand," he tells the judge desperately. "Ten years my wife she no have a kid. Every night I make 'em — but that son-of-a-bitch, he eat 'em up!"* (N.Y. 1940.) The much less poignant original is given in *The Pearl* No. 2 (Aug. 1879): *A man comes home suddenly and finds the vicar cunnilinguing his wife. "Ho! Ho!" he exclaims in a fury, "so you're the bugger who's been swallowing all my children!"* Another version is quoted in the Introduction here.

In its latest forms this joke has become a mere play on the key-word 'eat,' with its obvious oral-incorporative significance. (Bookstore clerks in New York, 1942, were, for instance, using the code-word 'PEEP' to mean 'Look at the beautiful girl who just walked into the store,' the letters spelling out the acrostic of 'Perfectly Elegant Eatin' Pussy.') *A newly-rich oil millionaire's wife hires a French chef, who drives the husband frantic with meals of snails, frogs legs, and other exotica. He comes home one evening with his mind made up to storm into the kitchen and announce that tonight supper will consist of boiled beef and mashed potatoes — or else! But the chef is not in the kitchen, and after searching everywhere he finds him in the master-bedroom cunnilinguing his wife. "How do you like that?" cries the millionaire, striking himself on the forehead — "first he fucks up my eating, and now he eats up my fucking!"* (N.Y. 1952.)

This has also been collected in a zoöphilic reversal in which: *At an isolated lumber camp the cook runs out of meat and serves up for dinner a sheep he finds behind one of the buildings. In the midst of the meal he announces what the main ingredient is, and the lumber-jacks, one and all, stop eating. "What's the matter, boys," he inquires, "did I fuck up the cooking?" "Hell no," he is told, "you cooked up the fucking."* (D.C. 1952.) In a modification for public presentation, in burlesque or nightclub work, *A magician announces that he will saw a woman in half at the waist, and two comedians throw dice (or play the finger-game of la moré) for the halves. The comedian who gets the top half shows by his facial expression that he is the loser. "Wouldn't you know I'd get the half that eats?" he says disgustedly. Then, brightening, "Some guys eat the half I don't get."* (Minn. 1946.) In none of these is the humor expected to rise from the audience's appreciation of the cross-changing rhetorical device used (the Greek *hipallage* or *chiasmus*, and Latin *submutation*). The only possible point is the insistence, in the word 'eat,' on the identity of oral strivings and oragenitalism.

4. CUNNILINCTUS AND MASOCHISM

In the jokes on cunnilinctus so far given, the masochist element is held at the unconscious level of orality, of breast-dependence; and the use of the vulva and clitoris as surrogate breast and nipple is clear in this generalized return to dependence on, and dominance by, the mother. When combined with actual castration anxieties rising from the mother, the result (in men) is masochism, in the same way that castration anxieties rising from the father lead to homosexuality. With self-evident reversals, the same formulation can be applied to the masochistic daughter of the patriarch, and the Lesbian daughter of the matriarch.

It is necessary now to consider the openly masochistic element in cunnilinctus, where this is consciously engaged in as a submission to the woman's dominance. The easiest rationalization for the joke-tellers is that the man is forced into this submission by losing a bet. *An expert pinochle-player is matched against a rich woman. He is to get $10,000 if he wins, but must "go down on" her* [the locution is also common to German] *if he loses. When he appears in his usual haunts after the game he is asked, "Well, could she play pinochle?" "Ptooey!" he says, spitting, "could that woman play pinochle!"* (N.Y. 1939.) In a similar story, much of the background remains the same — the gambling, spitting, and so forth — but the pretense of unwillingness and rejection of cunnilinctus is suddenly dropped. *A group of gamblers are irritated by a preacher who is watching them play. To get rid of him, one of the players spits noisily, saying, "Goddamit, that last cunt I sucked was certainly salty!" The preacher holds up his hand placatingly. "Peace, brother," he says, "they're all salty!"* (2:389.) — *Anecdota* 1:246 gives a rather contrived version of the same situation of gambling, with the connection between losing at cards and being 'forced' into cunnilinctus entirely spurious: *The little drummer in the poker game has been low man for the last two hours and finally throws in his cards. The game breaks up and the other players discuss what they have to do to keep their wives happy. One has to kiss her on the head before leaving, another* *on the lips, the third on the breast, the fourth on the navel. Little Drummer: "Well, I guess I'm low man again. Good night."* (1:246.) On the masochism of gambling, see *Neurotica*, No. 6: p. 11–15. Cunnilinctus is also a popular folk-'remedy' for alcoholic hangover.

Compare with this the Frenchman, earlier, and the more orally-oriented version also in *Anecdota* (1927): *"Boy was I drunk!"* a man announces. *"We had a little drink and I kissed her on the lips. Then we had another little drink and both got undressed." "Yes, yes, go on." "Then we had another drink and I kissed her on the nipples." "Yes, yes." "And another little drink and I kissed her on the belly-button." "Yes, yes!" "Oh boy, was I drunk!"* (1:441.) This is of course the standard explanation-that-is-not-an-explanation, since the whole purpose of getting drunk is to relax the inhibitions against doing what one cannot do when one is not drunk. In an unpublished American portfolio of over three hundred erotic drawings telling a continued story, under the title *"Genesis 1:27"* ('Male and female created he them'), assembled in New York, 1944, with text to match; the scores of erotic scenes masterfully depicted are invariably of simple coitus. In only one case is what even appears to be cunnilinctus implied in the foreshortening of the drawing, and in that case the text explains that the participants were too drunk to know what they were doing. This is in extreme contrast to the only other two albums of erotic art by American artists of anywhere near equal quality: *Venus Sardonica* (1929) by Mahlon Blaine, and a set of parody-illustrations to *Alice in Wonderland* (after the Tenniel drawings) signed: Friesinger, and apparently dating from the 1930's. In both of these the accent is on the most exotic and improbable erotic acts; the oral element is very prominent — as in Friesinger's parody of the Duchess in the pepper-filled kitchen 'peppering' Alice — and ordinary coitus is almost absent.

The ambivalent emotions of men in connection with the vaginal odor, alternating between the rock-bottom mammalian attraction to and by this odor and the civilized overlay of rejection on esthetic and 'sanitary' rationalizations, become even more prominent in connection with the vaginal secretions as experienced in cunnilinctus. Since the pre-coital secretion in both sexes is usually comparatively scant, the reference is most often simply to the *taste*. (A now-obsolescent slang term for a cunnilinctor was 'taster,' as noted in Henry N. Cary's *The Slang of Venery*, Chicago, 1916 — largely a plagiarism of Farmer & Henley's *Slang and Its Analogues* — in Cary's volume of synonymies, p. 139.) — *As a prank the moustache of a sleeping drunk in a barroom*

*is smeared with limburger cheese from the free lunch. He wakes up
suddenly, sniffs, sucks at a strand of his moustache and says: "I knew
I'd do that some day when I was drunk!"* (N.Y. 1945.) In Gypsy Rose
Lee's *G-String Murder* (1940?) a version of this prank is noted as a
backstage joke in the burlesque theatre, the inside of a strip-teaser's
G-string being smeared with cheese. The 'cheese' referred to is, of
course, in both cases a reference to the preputial smegma (of both
sexes), representing the vaginal secretion in its rejected aspect.

One is beginning to approach here the real problem of coital and
non-coital sexual acts, which is their use in real life as charades of
emotional expression having very little to do with physical sexuality.
In the main, cunnilinctus expresses passive-oral urges toward the remembered mother-figure and her breast, and this is just as true in the
Lesbian desire for cunnilinctus as in that of the normal male. Over-
layered on this 'unmanly' return to the womb — or as close to it as one
can reasonably get — are all the noisy protestations of dislike for the
female genitals, their odor and taste. The most extreme expression of
this kind, in pure hatred, is printed publicly in the 'sex-hate' issue of
Sex to Sexty (Fort Worth, Tex. 1966) 6:27, with the perfectly unnecessary expurgation of a single word — 'pussy,' being the plain English
term for any cat (to which the skunk family is assimilated, and in
some languages the rabbit as well) as well as for the female genitals:

> The lady found a skunk in her backyard and managed to
> lure it into a sack. Then she got on a bus and told the driver
> she had a skunk in the sack, and wanted to go to the end of the
> line and let it out. So as they rode along the odor of the swamp
> kitty permeated the whole bus. When they got to the end of the
> line, the angry bus driver hollered out, "Will the lady with the
> stinking puss[y] please get off!" . . . And five ladies crossed
> their legs and three angrily left the bus!

The most famous joke on the subject of vulvar taste or odor is one
of the most forthright acceptances of the total woman that can be
found in the whole range of English-language jokes, and represents
the crossover point between the sort of cunnilinctus that is clearly a
natural sexual approach and attraction, and the neurotic use of oragenital acts to embody profoundly masochistic impulses. *An inventor
comes to a bank, to float a loan on a process that he announces "will
make cunt juice taste like orange juice." He is thrown out at once.
A year later the banker sees the same man getting out of an enormous*

limousine while flunkies unroll a red plush carpet for him, etc. He inquires incredulously whether the man got this rich on the process with which he had approached him. "Well, no," says the inventor. "I made a change here and a change there, and I figured out a way to make orange juice taste like cunt juice, and we're thirty days behind on our shipments." (2:501, given as a special stop-press revision of 2:212, an inferior version using the genital organ and the orange instead of their juices.)

It is the habit of the sellers of erotic books — or books that are being sold as erotica, whatever their original intention may have been — to open before the customer's eyes what is thought of as the most interesting, if not the most representative, passage in the book. Authors of best-selling novels being sold at premium overprices in the bookstores of New York's Times Square and elsewhere, by this method, would perhaps be horrified if they could see which passages of their descriptive prose and dialogue are used for this sort of sales presentation. In the case of my sixty-four page monograph, *Oragenitalism,* by 'Roger-Maxe de La Glannège,' (New York, 1940), already noted, the passage most likely to be used in this way was a harmless paragraph on p. 36, discussing 'the application of liquids such as wine, orange juice, honey, brandy, melted ice-cream, *etc. ad lib.* to the vulva, either to camouflage or to enhance its characteristic taste and odor.' This is followed by a full paragraph on orange juice in particular, in what is obviously an oblique reference to the preceding joke. The text then proceeds, p. 38, to a discussion of the fruits or other food-objects inserted into the vagina during cunnilinctus (the banana being accidentally omitted!) as is reported by Karsch-Haack of the natives of Ponape in the South Pacific, using fish. This is presented simply as a sexual 'sophistication,' but it certainly involves a good deal more than that both in Ponape and elsewhere.

The dominant position of women in the matrilocal islands of the Pacific — which appear to have been operating matriarchies when Captain Cook arrived in the 1770's, and are still notably sexually permissive — is nowhere more evident than in the much greater violence or aggressiveness of the women over the men during erotic foreplay and byplay. In the Trobriand Islands, for instance, Bronislaw Malinowski observed, in The *Sexual Life of Savages* (1929) p. 334, the 'far larger scratches and marks on men than on women; and [that] only women actually lacerate their lovers.' (Could that Cleveland teeny-bopper be a Trobriander?) That protracted cunnilinctus is also *demanded* by the women in connection with this sado-masochistic scratching and biting is noted in a very significant passage by Ralph Linton on the now only recently extinct Marquesans:

> Affairs ... involved even more elaborate forms of sexual play, with the woman definitely dominant, and the man playing up to her erotic wishes. His role was to excite the woman by sucking her breasts and cunnilingus until she was excited to a high pitch and gave the signal for intercourse. These erotic preliminaries were quite devoid of tenderness [*n.b.*], and often involved scratching and biting on both sides. The sexual play was apparently of greater importance than the orgastic experience. All Marquesans were sexually potent, but the potency of the woman was dependent on these preliminaries, without which it was impossible for her to have an orgasm. (In: Abram Kardiner & Ralph Linton, *The Individual and his Society,* 1939, p. 173.)

Compare the formalized verbal insults and lacerations already noted as the 'foreplay' preceding cunnilinctus in McClure's play, *The Beard.*

Dr. Linton offers a further note on the whole oral complex of sexual relations among the Marquesans, though it is almost certain that he is in error in assuming a contraceptive intent in the technique of seminal exsufflation that he describes, in Norman Himes' *Medical History of Contraception* (1936) p. 23:

> Children were rarely born to unmarried mothers, but I think that the chances of conception were cut down mainly by the use of perversions instead of actual intercourse. The natives were extremely expert in the arts of love. However, the perversions were always practiced in private. When a group of men went out with one woman, and had intercourse with her in rapid succession, publicly, which was a common amusement, the last man had to suck semen from her vagina. This was sometimes practiced in individual intercourse as well.

The true explanation of activities of this kind can only be an extreme masochistic orality on the part of the men, matching the dominant and sadistic character of the women in matriarchal cultures. Since there can be almost no pretense that the materials inserted into the vagina and ingested by the man in cunnilinctus have any particularly sexually exciting effect on the woman, their meaning must be sought in the attraction of the men to these materials. A few of these, such as orange juice, ice-cream, alcoholic beverages, etc., are more or less neutral, and can successfully be proposed as a joke, a sophistication, or similar. When seriously practised, however, the choice of materials employed, such as oysters, suggests the special substances — almost invariably the bodily excretions, both major and minor — which are thought of as specially disgusting and humiliating, as in the case of the *last man* in the Marquesan 'gang-shag' described by Linton, in which it is perfectly evident that it is the woman who is dominating her harem-group of men, and not they who are 'raping' her.

The jokes collected for the present research also pass rapidly from the neutral foods to the presumably disgusting, as the masochist component in the man's orality takes over the whole situation. One may begin with ice cream, as the remarkable over-emphasis on milk drinks and refections is one of the most noticeable aspects of the breast-return orality of American adults. *A man's wife tells him that she knows he is "playing around" because she has found lipstick on his underwear, and that she is going to take a lover too. Some weeks later she does not come home till four A.M., and when he taxes her with infidelity she admits it boldly. "I warned you," she says; "none of your double standard for me! I have my own gigolo now, and I want you to know that he's got a penis that hangs down to his knees. And does he know where to put it, and what to do with it! And positions!? — swinging from the chandelier! And what's more, when he's all finished, for that ultra Continental touch, he fills it up with chocolate ice cream and eats it all out again!" "Hoo hah!" says her husband, "who could eat that much chocolate ice cream at three o'clock in the morning?"* (N.Y. 1953.) The man from whom this story was collected objected, on reading the manuscript version of the story, that the fact of the climactic ice cream being *chocolate* had been accidentally omitted, and observed spontaneously, 'I don't need to tell you that what the husband really means is: "Listen, you big fat clitoris, I'm not eating any of your SHIT!"'

An interesting story, collected in several forms, suggests the whole facial expression of disgust for cunnilinctus, but explains this away rather weakly as a mere chemical reaction. The *vagina dentata* fantasy is also very much in the foreground. *A client demands of the madam the "tightest girl in the whore-house." The madam privately tells one of the girls to douche with alum, later asking the client, "Well, was it tight enough?" Client, between pursed lips: "Oh, perfect!"* (2:285.) In a version in which the idea of being damaged by the vagina is even more prominent, the man involved is a minister, and the woman a choir-singer (the usual identification of nun with sacred prostitute). In the end-line, *The woman emerges from the minister's private chamber, mounts the rostrum, wriggles her eyebrows in an agony of meaningfulness, and announces: "No sermon this week."* (N.Y. 1953.) A related story omits the male actor, and in fact, all the action except for the pursing of the lips, but it points with particular strength to the *dentate* and oral-incorporative fantasies that take their rise from the easy and widespread symbolic identification of mouth and vagina — as standard as that of nose and penis. *An old maid is told by a doctor that the size of a woman's vagina can generally be told by the size of her mouth. Pursing her lips to the utmost, the old maid comments, "Is that so?"* (Transcontinental train, 1943.)

Masochist fantasies concerning cunnilinctus do not retreat even from the ingestion of the excrementitious products of the female genitals: specifically, urine and the menstrual fluid. Fantasies of eating up the child in the womb should also perhaps be included in this group, as the oral-incorporative sadism of this fantasied fœtophagy is merely the reversal of the oral masochism of ingesting the urine or menstrua. In the very remarkable, and entirely authentic, male masochist letters addressed to the classified ad of a 'STRAPPING Young Woman' and published in *Neurotica* No. 5 (1949) p. 45–64, the two principal desires expressed by the letter writers — in their masochistic phase (several of them also writing sadistic letters in answer to a different ad) — were for the satisfaction of various fetichistic and flagellatory rituals, such as being trodden on with special high-heeled shoes, and for cunnilinctus, plus urine-drinking as an extension of this ('golden fountains,' p. 56, or 'the golden shower'). As is pointed out in my necessarily very condensed reference to the subject in *The Horn Book* (1964) p. 443–5, and "Notes on Masochism," accompanying *Neurotica* No. 6 (1950), this is to be compared with the 'flapdragon' of the Elizabethan gallants, and of the English and French drinking clubs during the revolutionary period in both countries from 1776 through the 1830's and '40's.

Commentators on Shakespeare, such as Johnson and Dyce, gloss his references to the 'flapdragon' by describing the form of this in which a burning candle-end or brandy-soaked raisin is swallowed down in a toast to one's mistress. They do not, however, note Hamlet at Ophelia's grave: "*Wilt drink up vessels, eate a crocadile? I'le doo't.*" (V.i.299, in the First Quarto, 1603, only.) In later texts, the word 'vessel' — *i.e.* a chamberpot: compare Churchill's calling Mussolini Hitler's 'utensil' (a reply to Mussolini's 'Del-ano' slur on Roosevelt?) — is changed to 'eisel,' meaning vinegar. The practice, in later times, is somewhat similarly shifted to drinking champagne out of the mistress' slipper, or from a bathtub in which a chorus-girl sits. Unconsciously bringing this back to its urolagnic original — possibly by way of the following joke — the 'men's magazines' of the 1930's narrate, as scandalous and true, that the chorus-girl has filled herself with beer beforehand and urinated as she sits in the tub. The men's magazine revamping of this fantasy refers it to the alleged wine-bath of a show-girl at a contemporary party given by the impresario Earl Carroll, as depicted in a faked 'composograph' in Bernarr Macfadden's New York *Evening Graphic,* reprinted in the "Mid-Century Issue" of *Life,* January 2nd, 1950, p. 94. However, exactly the same story will be found in the turn-of-the-century manuscript *Treasury of Erotic and Facetious Memorabilia,* about 1910, also as a 'true anecdote':

> Just before Bernhardt started from Paris for her 1900 tour, the young men of her set decided it would be the thing for her to take a bath in champagne, and they would then drink her health and success in the wine hallowed by her ablutions.
>
> She consented (because of the incidental advertisement) and 100 quarts of champagne were poured into the bath-tub. The young men modestly retired and Sarah took her bath.
>
> They decided to rebottle the wine and drink it at a dinner in her honor the night before her departure. They found that they had 101 quarts of wine.

This is already an expurgation of the whole idea, hallowed as it is by the 'modest retiring' of the fast young men while Bernhardt bathes, and especially by the explanation that it was all just done for the 'incidental advertisement' (as with the theatrical producer, Florenz Ziegfeld's publicity cleanup of the whole idea somewhat later in the announced milk-bath [*n.b.*] of his showgirl wife, Anna Held, from whom he was divorced in 1913). The original is far more clearly expressed in several extant illustrations of the orgiastic drinking parties in France in the early and middle 19th century, for instance in a set of twelve sexual-scatological humorous calendar cards, in which the cards for both '8bre.' and Xbre.' (October and December) flatly identify the wine that the woman is drinking from the bottle, or pressing from grapes, with urination on the recumbent man. In the latest joke-form collected, the relationship with cunnilinctus is also stated. *At a wild party in Hollywood* [*i.e.* the American Paris] *the toast of the evening fills her slipper with champagne, then tears off her clothes and pours the wine over her breasts and pubis. The next morning the guest of honor, a director, is late at the studio. "To tell the truth," says the assistant director, "he's got a terrific hangover."* (2:185.) Also as a 'true anecdote,' of various imported movie-directors.

Cunnilinctus during menstruation is thought of as the absolute *n*th degree of perversion, in its masochistic submission to the woman. Mirabeau, for example, saves the idea for the very last page of his *Errotika Biblion* ('A Rome: De l'Imprimerie du Vatican,' 1783), "La Linguanmanie," apparently as the ultimate shock; and it is certainly used in this expectation in Aleister Crowley's fawning imitation of Baudelaire and Swinburne, *White Stains: 'The Literary Remains of George Archibald Bishop, a Neuropath of the Second Empire'* (1898) p. 106, in a poem entitled "Sleeping in Carthage," and beginning, 'The month of thirst is ended . . .' It is the mark of the difference between the pipsqueak Crowley, playing at perversion as with his other occulta and exotica, and the titan Mirabeau, grappling with the whole world-history of sex, that the latter goes on to end with the historical note that brings the whole idea suddenly into focus as a ritual act of worship of the mother-goddess, combining the most utter oral submission to the woman, representing the mother, with the terror and attraction of the life-giving, yet somehow death-dealing *blood*. Compare the strange ambivalences of *Leviticus,* xv. 19 through xvii. 14, on the sacred — yet forbidden — blood of the sacrifices, versus the 'defiling' blood of menstruation. Seen in this light, rather than as simply masochistic and perverse, cunnilinctus during menstruation is understandable as the sort of transcendent sexual rite that culminates the pre-patriarchal worship of woman now known as the Black Mass, and it is 'hardly more bizarre,' as Mirabeau concludes, 'than those libations (*semen & menstruum*) that certain women, according to Epiphanius [Hieronymus Mercurial. iv.93] offered to the gods, and thereafter swallowed.'

As I have already noted elsewhere (*The Guilt of the Templars,* pp. 124, 249), 'The entire chapter, in Freud's remarkable speculative essay, *Totem & Taboo,* on the eating or castrating of the *Ur*-father in the night (Kronos, Saturn, Noah, etc.), in the dread ceremonial of the assembled brothers, now recollected among the Semites only in the camel-eating night-feast — compare the Teutonic pig-feast, or brat-wurst festival, still existing in the American midwest — and the circumcisional Yom Kippur among the Jews, is of obvious relevance here, and says a great deal that can here only be alluded to.'

The concentration on the *blood* of the god is very conspicuous in the preaching of certain Christian sects, notably that of primitive Baptists, and it is one of the principal refinements of modern Christianity that the effort has been made to displace as much emphasis as possible from such morbid festivals and recollections as the Circumcision (January 1st) and 'Good' Friday (a euphemism for 'Bad' Friday the 13th, on which the Crucifixion is presumed to have taken place), and emphasize instead the ideas of birth and regeneration connected with Christmas and Easter. In jokes on the 'matriarchal' communion of cunnilinctus, especially during menstruation, the concentration on the blood is also very clear, rather than on any element of perverse oral submission, and it is made apparent that what is achieved in cunnilinctus is not some sex-technique excitement or *satisfaction of the woman* but an ultimate or supernal *nourishment of the man.* The blood is thought of as life-giving, *i.e.* comparable to the mother's milk, where in its negative aspect blood is considered somehow poisonous, nauseating to ingest, or even death-dealing. The perverse combination of both ideas appears in the drinking of the blood of the animals ceremonially killed in the bull-fight, as has been gloatingly described by Ernest Hemingway, insisting that it is principally women who do this behind the amphitheatre.

The most extraordinary statements ever published as to the subjective meaning or purpose of such rituals are those of Frank Reynolds, secretary of the California "Hell's Angels," an outlaw motorcycle group whose publicity has not been of the best. See, in particular, Hunter S. Thompson's *Hell's Angels* (1966) chapters 17 *ff.,* on the accusations against them of wholesale rape and drug-peddling, both of which Mr. Thompson fully details only to deny: the usual technique of journalistic 'exposés.' Frank Reynolds, however, has attempted to go on record with the inside truth about the "Hell's Angels," in *Free-*

wheelin Frank (1967), as written down by the poet Michael McClure, whose play, *The Beard,* with its climactic scene of cursing and cunnilinctus, has already been discussed. Reynolds and McClure explain very frankly in their first chapters, pp. 15–16, and 22, the meaning of the Angels' wing insignia, as first printed in *Evergreen Review* (June 1967) p. 24:

> THE RED WING PATCH — most frequently asked about, this is a mere showing of class fun-trip to us. It usually takes place during a Hell's Angel [*motorcycle*] run. You might hear a roaring voice call out: ALL RIGHT, WHO'S GOT CLASS ENOUGH TO EAT THE RED PUSSY OF THIS ANGEL MAMA? Angel mamas are nymphomaniacs who will do anything related to sex. The Angel mama at the time is menstruating, on her period, and real bloody. It is considered the nastier she is, the more class is showed by the member who goes down on her in front of everyone — at least six members — and how he goes about it, while everyone witnesses. We front to no one outside of us on this trip. This is a trip of our own. Not every member has a red wing patch, and it sure is good to lay it on [*make fun of*] a brother who does not have one. Sometimes a member has been known to barf [*vomit, from the German* werfen, *to throw* (*up*)] when bein hassled to do this. Heheheh — aghhh . . . Many brothers got their red wings off of Mama Judy. — I for one was praised after getting my red wings and told that I should get a set of red wings with a baby in the same place in which the cuntlike shape is sewn, because she was on a miscarriage at the time. It was nothin sickening about it. It was Hell's Angel soul-togetherness — our trip!

Though extremely close to immemorial matriarchal rituals, the avowed intention here is to be brave and *bad*. The final such ordeal — auto-castration — is perhaps yet to come. Note the rather strained allusion to human sacrifice or fœtophagy ('baby-eating'), apparently spontaneously re-invented and not derived from the ancient Levantine worship of Baal or Moloch, to which many references are made in the Old Testament (as in 2 *Kings,* xvii. 31, and *Jeremiah,* vii. 31) as to the *burning* of the children, though the statement of subsequent cannibalistic feasting on the sacrifices is avoided. The 'baby-eating' accusation was endlessly made against later anti-Christian groups, and is still made today against the Jews. (See my *The Guilt of the Templars*, 1966, pp. 39–41, and 102–07.)

It will be seen that there is a great deal more depth to the Hell's Angels rituals than the mere sexual bravado implied in Hunter S. Thompson's brief and antiseptic allusion (chapter 10, cited from the 'exposé' magazine, *True*) to 'the vari-colored pilots' wings: red wings indicating that the wearer has committed cunnilingus on a menstruating woman, black wings for the same act on a Negress, and brown wings for buggery.' Reynolds and McClure emphasize throughout their extraordinary document, *Freewheelin Frank,* the insistent tone of homosexual brotherhood and sexual sharing — as well as the drugtaking almost inevitably connected with the oral homosexual syndrome — involved in the oral or merely genital 'gang-bangs' or grouprapes described. They also indicate, p. 21, that the brotherhood-sign or greeting of the motorcycle group is not the usual secret handshake of fraternal organizations, but the licking of each other's tongues: 'here-I-am, brother, lick my tongue, then let's go suck a pussy of the four mamas on hand at the time, and fuckem.' A photograph of two bearded young motorcyclists, stated to be Hell's Angels, and fencing tongue-tips in this way with their mouths wide open, is printed in *The Realist* (New York, Feb. 1966) No. 64: p. 11, apparently with the intention of deriding them as homosexual: 'the Dorian Gray of the Pepsi Generation . . . the underbelly of the Great Society.' See further my discussion of the homosexual accusations against the Knights Templars in the late 13th century, *The Guilt of the Templars*, p. 96–133, whose principal difference from the Hell's Angels — so far as the public animosity against them is concerned — was that they rode horses instead of motorcycles to the Crusades.

Observe, in the first example below, the astonishingly frank *naming* of the mother, and, in the final two, the contrasting of blood-asdeath (in tuberculosis) and as the absolute elixir of life (mother's milk). *A little boy states that he knows how cunnilinctus tastes, though he has never tried it, because "Me mother saves all her old drawers for a month* [n.b.] *and then boils'em up for soup."* (2:121.) There is also an allusion to this idea in a stanza of the song "The Dirty Old Red Drawers That Maggie Wore" — a parody of "The Little Old Red Shawl My Mother Wore" — in which the same hæmophagic notion is worked in, on the style of the food-dirtying implications of "*Who* Threw the Overhauls in Mrs. Murphy's Chowder?" *Have you heard about Hitler's new secret weapon? It's Kotex. It keeps the Reds in, the Poles out, France hungry, and the U.S. without peace.* (D.C. 1943.) This is one of the few war jokes that continues to be told, as has been noted earlier. Aleister Crowley's 'month of thirst,' if not precisely stated, is certainly part of the implication here, ascribed naturally to the unrepressedly orasexual French. *A British workman accompanies a prostitute to her flat. She goes into the bathroom to prepare, and comes back saying, "I say! I'm sorry — I've come off poorly, y'know. Would you care for a drink?" "'Oo d'you think I am — Dracular?"* (N.Y. 1953. 'To come off poorly' is a British folkphrase for menstruation.) Compare the 'quickie' version of the same thing: *At the high school, what did the boy vampire say to the girl vampire? "See you next period ..."* (*Sex to Sexty*, 1965, 3:25, publicly published for newsstand distribution.)

These are the jocular forms. There are also the ugly, in which the blood is feared, and even hatefully identified with feces — the traditional opposite of mother's milk, as in Hemingway's *cagar en la leche de tu madre* ("I obscenity in the obscenity of your obscenity," as S. J. Perelman has satirized this brave dollar-a-word expurgated dysphemism), imported from sado-masochistic Spain. The following joke is very commonly collected. *A travelling salesman propositions a young woman on a train. She objects mildly that she is "unwell," but allows him to come to her berth anyhow when he says, "That's all right; I don't mind. I used to be a Marine, and you know our motto: 'Through Mud and Blood to Glory!'" Waking up the next morning he finds the train stopped at a station. He sticks his head out the window and asks a small boy (or Negro), "What station is this?" "Birmingham, suh. Who hit you in de mouf?"* (2:166.) The allusion to the American Southern town of Birmingham, and the Southern dialect pronunciation of the response, seems intended to overdetermine the reference to '*going down on*' the other person (British: '*going down to*') as meaning oragenitalism. This also exists in the parody catch-phrase, "*Go South, young man!*"

In the cognate fecal version, *A barber finds a curly blonde hair in his client's moustache. "No doubt," says the client airily; "I always kiss my wife on the head when I go to work." "Excuse me, Mr. Smith,"* says the barber, *"but you have shit all over your necktie."* (2:186.) The whole framework here is that of the usual insulting invitation to kiss one's arse, on which see the final chapters in Series Two, on Scatology.

Finally: *A prostitute parks her menstrual tampon on the night table, where her customer has laid his chaw of tobacco. In the dark both pick up the wrong one afterward. When the tobacco begins to burn her, the woman says, "You bastard, you've given me the syph!" The customer spits, and, seeing the blood, snarls, "Don't complain, you son-of-a-bitch, you've given* me *consumption!"* (2:240.) This is a very elaborate pretext, very much disguised under the stated dislike and disgust, for setting up a situation in which a man is 'accidentally' allowed to taste a woman's menstrual blood, or to sniff or chew her menstrual pad or tampon, a primitive impulse more commonly felt than admitted. Hostile impulses against the menstruating woman or the appurtenances of her menstruation are, however, frankly admitted — as for instance in the jokes and other lore about forcing or 'braining with a rock' a woman who refuses intercourse because of menstruation.

An original college-song, "Who Lit the Fuse on Little Mary's Tampax?" (obviously inspired by "Who Threw the Overhauls, &c.") was unexpectedly encountered on a tape-recording of college-songs supplied to the writer in 1962, with the statement that it included only 'old classics.' The menstrual tampon is an ancient Japanese device, brought to the U.S. by the late Dr. Robert Latou Dickinson after the 1920's earthquake, but not launched in America until the 1930's (disposable Kotex pads are also Japanese in origin). In referring to lighting its string as a 'fuse,' the implication is, of course, that the woman is to be exploded by it. Truth being stranger than fiction, as the proverb would have it, the *actual use* of Tampax menstrual tampons as fuses for bombs is suggested in an authentic quotation from a terrorist manual, in William W. Turner's "The Minutemen," in *Ramparts* (San Francisco, January 1967) p. 74, giving national publicity — for reasons unexplained — to a method of making home-made "Molotov Cocktails," ending: 'Tape a regular "Tampax" sanitary device to each bottle with masking tape.' These fire-bombs made their first general appearance in America in the summer of the same year, during the Negro riots culminating in the 'Burning of Detroit.'

In a once-over-lightly history of sex through the ages, for the tourist trade, *Physiology of Vice,* attributed to a pseudonymous 'Dr. Jaf' (the English translation here cited, Paris: Offenstadt, 1904, is remarkable for the unconscious humor of its half-hearted Anglicizing of sexual terms such as 'volupty' and 'manuary coïters'), an interesting reference is made, p. 115–17, to French homosexual clubs of both male and female courtiers in the late 17th century, at the time of Louis XIV:

Courtiers also, especially young men, established associations of the same kind even in the palace of Versailles; it was a renewal of the Order of the Templars [!] having no other motive but the most abject debauchery. The motives turned to account by the new Templars to excuse their criminal institution are contained in a pamphlet attributed to Sandras de Courtilz:

"The easy-going ways of all ladies had made their charms so despisable to youth, that one hardly knew any longer at court what it was even to look at them . . ." The impure meetings of the brotherhood took place in taverns, orgies beginning or finishing by drunkards' doings; at one of these orgies, the brotherhood, "having treated in Italian fashion [*anal intercourse*] the most handsome courtezans, took one by force, tied her arms and legs to the foot of a bed, and having put a fuse into a part of her that decency does not allow me to name, mercilessly set fire to it, taking no notice whatever of the cries of this miserable woman."

The son of Colbert [*the minister of finance*] was amongst the number of the miscreants who did this outrage. Louis XIV took energetic measures to have the culprits severely punished and more especially so, to annihilate their awful society.

It will be understood, of course, that, as opposed to the Tampax fuse in the college-song noted above, the 'fuse' here put into that part of a woman 'that decency does not allow me to name' (though it's perfectly all right to describe the atrocity involved), was presumably a real fuse or explosive. It is also important to observe that this atrocity — a century before, but in the precise style of, the Marquis de Sade's imaginings — is ascribed to a club of aristocratic *homosexual* Mohocks, the '*jeunesse pourrie*' of their century.

The ultimate apotheosis, or total acceptance of the woman as mother and mistress combined, is the following scene of death and resurrection, in a sort of travestied religious scene or ritual (which is not described, being perhaps thought of as ineffable in Holy of Holies style). The nurse or nun as priestess-prostitute is also, of course, her historical origin. *The scene is a hospital. A man is dying. The relatives are all creeping around the bed trying to get him to sign the will, but he is in a coma. They tiptoe out, leaving the young night-nurse in charge, and telling her to give him anything he wants but just to make sure he is alive to sign the will in the morning. She sits down self-*

consciously with her science-fiction magazine and a glass of instant coffee, and prepares for a long night. About three in the morning the man stirs, moans and sits up. "Nurse," he says, "nurse! I'm dying!" "Now, it's all right, sir. Just lie back and be quiet. Everything is going to be all right." "No," he says, "you can't fool me. I'm dying. I know it." "Is there anything I can do to make you more comfortable, sir?" says the nurse. He stares at her, and she comes into focus before his bleary eyes: young and pretty and plump. "Yes," he breathes, "there is something you can do for me. I've always said I'd go down on a woman before I died, and this is my last chance. What about it?" The nurse is embarrassed. "I wish you hadn't asked me that," she says; "I just happen to be having my periods." "What the hell do I care? I'll be dead by morning!" We draw the veil here for a few hours. Sunrise. The relatives come creeping back with the will, and peer into the dying man's bed to see if he is in shape to sign it. Nobody in the bed. They search high and low, but can't find him, and rush to the phone to call the morgue. Suddenly they hear a noise in the bathroom. They fling open the door, and there is the man standing at the sink in his pajama pants, shaving, and whistling "Britons Never Never Will Be Slaves" (or "The Proud Fort of Kraznahorka"). "Aren't you dying?" cry the relatives. "Dying?! One more transfusion like that, and I'll live forever!" (N.Y. 1943, from a Hungarian.) This is my favorite joke. Analyze away!

Traditionally, blood is construed not only as a sort of super-semen, in the mystical ratio of sixty drops of blood to one drop of semen (which explains the 'danger' of masturbation), but as super-milk as well: that elixir of life, or theobroma, so powerful and so dangerous that only gods may drink it and reap the gift of eternal life. In the same way, until the late 19th century, only babies and the agèd sought life and nourishment in (mother's) milk. Biographers of the poet Shelley, for instance, considered it an example of his vegetarianism and 'eccentricity' worth recording, that he once refused any nourishment after a walk in the country but 'a bowl of milk.' Proletarian writers in the present century have more than once satirized the aging oil millionaire or newspaper publisher whose best-kept secret is his buxom wetnurse. In Aldous Huxley's *After Many a Summer Dies the Swan* (1939), a fishpaste elixir of life — *i.e.* of sexual potency, without which one is 'as good as dead' — is presented in the same way, as hardly more than an unpleasant modification of the alleged wetnurse, to suit the particularly unpleasant millionaire satirized. Nothing of this sort, except the young mistress, is of course even implied in the motion-picture version, Orson Welles' masterpiece, *Citizen Kane*.

In the working-class kitsch of John Steinbeck's *The Grapes of Wrath* (1939), the good old man is nursed back to health by the even better young girl-mother. This is simply a romanticized version of the legend of the Athenian general, Cimon, nourished in prison by his daughter at her breast. (Date presumably about 460 B.C.) See Motif R81 for very full references, from many cultures. There are various 18th-century engravings of this scene reproduced in that greatest of all collections of textual and pictorial materials as to the human breast, especially female, Dr. G.-J. Witkowski's *Tétoniana* (1898–1907, in 4 vols.), vol. I, *Anecdotes,* title-page; and vol. II, *Curiosités médicales . . . sur les seins,* p. 57. The recent *Mythologie du Sein,* by 'Romi' (Paris: Pauvert, 1965) may be considered a very valuable illustrated supplement and bringing up to date of Witkowski's work. As revived during the French and American Revolutions, the legend of Cimon of Athens has been given a powerful male-protest turn, the submissive and nutritious daughter becoming instead the phallic-mother, who does not so much assist the dying man as replace him: the 'Molly Pitcher' heroine or female-warrior who pulls open her army greatcoat on the battlefield, and offers the nourishment of her breast to the dying soldier with one hand, while she fires off his cannon with the other!

Mutatis mutandis, here is certainly the great twofold mother-goddess of India, Shakta Devi, of the full and beneficent breasts in one aspect, and, in the other, the black and phallic matriarch, Kali, worshipped — as must be Lilith, the demonic anti-Eve, who kills women in childbirth — with 'obscene and bloody rites' and human sacrifice. The masochistic tone, of submission to this mother-figure or goddess, is unmistakable not only in the jokes and folklore concerning cunnilinctus (most clearly, if ambivalently, during menstruation), but in every sort of oragenitalism and by either sex. Like many if not all things in the sexual life, oragenital acts have very deep roots and deeper meanings, and cannot be understood without digging for them. In his discussion of the 'polymorphous,' or many-faceted perversions of the sexual life of the child, Freud sums up (in his 20th Lecture, *General Introduction to Psychoanalysis,* ed. 1935, p. 275) the tremendous and preponderant rôle of oral strivings, of which oragenital acts represent only the most extreme development after childhood:

If the infant could express itself it would undoubtedly acknowledge that the act of sucking at its mother's breast is far and away the most important thing in life. It would not be wrong in this, for by this act it gratifies at the same moment the two greatest needs in life. Then we learn from psychoanalysis, not without astonishment, how much of the mental significance of this act is retained throughout life. Sucking for nourishment becomes the point of departure from which the whole sexual life develops, the unattainable prototype of every later sexual satisfaction, to which in times of need phantasy often enough reverts. The desire to suck includes within it the desire for the mother's breast, which is therefore the first *object* of sexual desire. I cannot convey to you any adequate idea of the importance of this first object in determining every later object adopted, of the profound influence it exerts, through transformation and substitution, upon the most distant fields of mental life.

VI. MALE MOTHERHOOD

I. LIFE IN THE WOMB

The normal birth of children is seldom a subject of jokes, probably for the reason that it is not an area of anxiety but of happiness and self-congratulation by the parents. Even in the jokes told by children, and in the folktales dear to them, the advent of a new baby is not often construed to be the dangerous competition for the parents' love and other prerogatives that it is in fact. Most real children's jokes about childbirth are really concerned with the mystery of pregnancy, and with twitting the parents with this positive proof of their own sexuality, or rubbing their noses in the very-much-resented lies about babies being 'brought by the stork' or 'found in mother's cabbage-patch,' which latter is not so much an open symbolism as a verbal joke against the questioning child's presumed anatomical ignorance. The womb-return jokes are a duel between the father and the unborn child.

Two twins are conversing in the womb. "*Who's that bald-headed guy that comes in here every night and spits in my eye?*" (Scranton, Pa. 1930.) Afanasyev gives a story in *Russian Secret Tales* (1872) No. 7, collected in the district of Voronezh in the 1860's, with the colloquy given to two insects or animals of the kind with which children easily identify themselves, as in the adult neurotic fantasies of Kafka and Ionesco. '*A louse met a flea. "Where are you going?" "I am going to pass the night in a woman's slit." "And I am going into a woman's back-side." They parted. The next day they met again. "Well, how did you sleep?" asked the louse. "Oh, don't talk about it! I was so frightened. A kind of bald-head came to (where I was), and hunted me about. I jumped, I jumped, here and there, but he continued to pursue me. At last he spat on me and went away." "Well, gossip, there were two persons knocking about outside the hole I was in. I hid myself, and they knocked and knocked, but at last they went away"*.' In the notes to Afanasyev, apparently by Giuseppe Pitrè, in *Kryptádia* (1888) IV. 192, parallels are noted to this tale in the *contes-en-vers* of the French writers, Grécourt, *Oeuvres diverses* (Amsterdam, 1775) I. 238, "Les Deux rats;" and D'Auberval, *Contes en vers erotico-philosophiques* (Bruxelles, 1818) II. 13, "Les Trois voyageuses, ou Les Trois puces." Nicolaidès, p. 113, collected in Constantinople before 1893.

In *Forbidden Books* (Paris, 1902; reprint, New York: Roth, c. 1929, p. 181), in a note on Afanasyev's work, quoting this tale, the publisher-author, 'Carrington,' or whatever hack actually wrote this catalogue for him, remarks — obviously with some exaggeration: 'I do not be-lieve there exists a single known tongue on this earth, where the account of the night passed in the woman's vagina by some insect who is disturbed by the entry of the bald-headed (*sometimes one-eyed*) visitor is not told. How do these quips and obscene oddities travel from one language to another through generations and generations? Does the Wandering Jew tell them in his ceaseless peregrinations?' (Which is not a bad theory.)

Accounts actually of the life of the child in the womb, in the form given here of the activities or conversations of unborn twins, are at least as old as the Old Testament (the present or Ezraic recension, 5th century B.C.) and its Talmudic embroideries, in the story of Judah and his daughter-in-law, Tamar's, twin children born of their incest — Pharez and Zarah — who struggle with each other in the womb as to which is to be the firstborn. For though Zarah first 'put out his hand: and the midwife took and bound upon his hand a scarlet thread, saying, "This (one) came out first",' he then drew back his hand and 'his brother came out.' (*Genesis*, xxxviii. 27–30. Motif T575.1.3.) Simi-lar struggles and conversations in the womb, between a twin boy and girl, who finally fall in love in the classic prenatal *soixante-neuf* of twins, are made central in *83 Centimètres d'aventures* (1925) by 'Marcel Arnac' (Bodereau), translated as *Thirty-six Inches of Adventure*, which is entirely concerned with the humorous passage of the child from conception to birth. This is exactly the style also central to Laurence Sterne's *Tristram Shandy* (1760–67) and the more recent intra-uterine elucubrations of L. Ron Hubbard's *Dianetics* (1950), now dangerously popular as a psychological fad in Britain under a new appellation. (See G. Legman, "Epizootics," in *Neurotica*, 1950, No. 7: p. 11–18, a travesty.)

A joke extraordinarily reminiscent of the pretensions of "Dianetics" as to neuroses being caused by intra-uterine shocks to the child, owing to the mother's presumed attempts at self-induced abortion (this is actually illustrated in Arnac's *83 Centimètres*, with the mother planning to deject herself on her behinder from a stack of chairs and pillows, piled one on top of the other, to the floor), is alluded to in the parody, "Epizootics," in Case LS/MFT — a further allusion to the popular perversion of this advertising-acrostic as meaning "*Let's Suck, My Finger's Tired.*" This case-history and its illustrative "Epizoo-schematic" (taken from the Pennsylvania-Dutch dreambook, *Sixth & Seventh Books of Moses*), 'demonstrating basic cause of all neurosis in father's tight-fitting jockstrap,' observes — I think correctly — that Freud and Rank and *Tristram Shandy* 'may have discovered the birth-trauma, but none of them ever went as far with it as the father's left teste, did they?' In the joke — which does — *Two men are bragging as to the early date of their first recollection. One states that he can remember being in his mother's womb (sometimes with a version of the 'one-eyed visitor' joke interpolated here). The other says, "That's nothing! My father was screwing the maid alternate days, and I can remember being kept hopping from one ball to the other, trying to be born legitimate."* (N.Y. 1947.) Randolph No. 20, "A Long Time Back," gives a version of this with an Indian squaw, from Missouri, about 1940. (Baughman, X1014.1, 'polite' versions only.)

A very similar story also projects memory back to the period of life in the father's semen. *The Revolt of the Spermatozoa is caused by the father's continuously using a condom, and the realization by the eager spermatozoa that they are never going to be born at all this way. They elect a leader, and resolve that the next time they are aware the parents are having intercourse, they will all rush out of the penis together, break the condom, and impregnate their mother-to-be. The sentinels are posted, the leader waits in his great cloak under the foreskin, and when they are all sure that intercourse is in progress they storm the condom as planned. Suddenly the leader's voice rings out:* "Back! Back!! IT's SHIT!" (N.Y. 1952. Expurgated in *Sex to Sexty*, 15:43, ending "WRONG HOLE!") On the style of the organ-identification or personification type of the just-so stories, as to the origins and adventures of the sexual parts, in Antonio Vignale's *La Cazzaria* or "Book of the Prick" (1531), a work which, as I have elsewhere remarked, stands out as the most astonishing collection of erotic folk-beliefs and just-so stories in the literature of the world. (A manuscript translation into English, by the late Samuel Putnam, discussed by the translator in *Encyclopædia Sexualis,* 1936, is in my possession, and has now first been issued.) Compare the similar personification, but here identifying sex with *food,* in Burns' *Merry Muses of Caledonia* (1800, *type-facsimile* edition, 1965) p. 118, as the second stanza of "Madgie Cam to My Bed-stock," the dash-expurgations of the original being here completed:

> Cunt it was the sowen-pat,
> An' pintle was the ladle;
> Ballocks were the serving-men
> That waited at the table.

This stanza still survives among adolescents and others in America, in modernized form, as part of "The King Was in His Counting House," a brief song sometimes incorporated into the (again) Scottish "The Ball o' Kirriemuir."

A much modified version of the child's fantasy of life before birth is that of Lewis Carroll's *Alice in Wonderland* (1865) chapter 4, in which, having drunk from a mysterious unmarked bottle, Alice becomes so large — but is glad of it, as she is "quite tired of being such a tiny little thing!" — that she entirely fills the room (see Tenniel's illustration), and frightens the gruff and authoritarian White Rabbit-daddy with her size and kicking: in fact, she kicks Bill the lizard (one-eyed?), who is sent down the narrow passage of the chimney to get her, quite up the spout, and all realize they must burn down the house to get her out. (This is the child's notion of the mother's 'falling to pieces' or being completely destroyed by bearing the child, in the lack of any known or admitted method for the child to get safely out.) In Disney's revoltingly crude adaptation in animated-cartoon form, Alice is shown in this scene with her arms and legs sticking out the windows of the house-that-is-her-body, which is being set fire to at a position that can only be intended as the pubic hair — though Carroll had a horror of pubescent girls.

None of the above is for some reason discussed in Martin Gardner's otherwise superlative *Annotated Alice* (New York: Clarkson Potter, 1960) which takes cognizance of the psychoanalytic interpretations of the Alice story in its bibliography, but excludes them from the text and obviously has certain doubts about the matter, though recognizing the secret spring in Carroll's repressed pedophilia. This is not very well hidden by the purposeful 'nonsense' of the famous "Jabberwocky," in *Through the Looking-Glass* (1871), of which Humpty Dumpty, representing the author, 'explains' the well-known opening lines as *meaning:* ' 'Twas four o'clock in the afternoon, and the lithe and slimy badger-lizards — something like corkscrews — Did go round and round, and make holes like a gimblet in the grass-plot round a sun-dial.' It is not hidden at all, but almost openly expressed, in Humpty Dumpty's preferred song, chapter 6, recounting: "I sent a message to the fish: I told them 'This is what I wish'," and going on to describe the mysterious messenger who 'was very stiff and proud' who tells him to wake the little fish, who are 'in bed,' and force them (with a corkscrew) to do whatever it is that they are refusing to do. The song ends abruptly, when he "found the door was locked," and "tried to turn the handle but — " "That's all," said Humpty Dumpty. "Good-bye." Alice tries to say goodbye politely, in spite of being dropped suddenly like this, and suggests they might meet again. ' "I shouldn't know you again if we *did* meet," Humpty Dumpty replied in a discontented tone . . .'

At the ultimate pole from such repression of a not-very-difficult situation to understand, is the Earl of Rochester's boldly incestuous womb-return fantasy, "The Wish" (*ante* 1680), in his *Works,* ed. 1718, p. 112, in which, again, the curious identification of the individual with his own or his father's semen is made. This has already been quoted in full in the earlier chapter on "Women," in connection with vaginal size: 6.v.4. This is of course to be compared with Rochester's matching fantasy, as to life in the womb from the girl-child's point of view, "Written under Nelly's Picture," *Works,* p. 143, stating, of the royal courtesan, Nell Gwyn: 'She was so exquisite a Whore, That in the Belly of her Mother, Her Cunt was plac'd so right before, Her Father fuck'd them both together.' Capt. Francis Grose, in his posthumous *The Olio* (1792) p. 242, gives the apparent source of this fantasy as Spanish folk-wit, noting: 'The following verses are the work of an ancient Spanish poet:

> ' "*Eres puta tan artera*
> *Qu'en el ventre de tu madre,*
> *Tu cumistes de manera,*
> *Que te cavalgne el padre*".'

Men are very proud of their semen, as in brags about "*plastering a fly to the ceiling*" with the ejaculate when masturbating in bed on one's back. (D.C. 1952.) This may be one reason why Western women, who of course also fear the semen as the agency of making them pregnant, express such distaste for it, as is not the case, for example, in the Orient. Note for instance the crude British slang-phrase for intercourse, from the woman's point of view, "*to 'ave a bottom-wetter.*" (This term is unaccountably omitted from John S. Farmer & William Ernest Henley's (*Dictionary of*) *Slang & Its Analogues,* even in the revised and enlarged vol. 1, 1903–09, reprinted New York, 1966, with a monograph "On Sexual Speech and Slang," p. xxx–xciv, by the present writer.) Not in joke form, but simply as a sort of hostile catch-line or tag as to feminine resistance to the post-coital backwash of semen: *Wife:* "*Now don't muck about, Mr. Petherington. I can't be dipping me arse in cold water every two hours just for the likes of you!*" (London, 1954.)

An American joke makes of the profusion of the semen, instead, a cock-crow of phallic male brag: *Foggy morning on the Gloucester fishing banks. One fisherman sings out to the other, "M'wife had a baby boy!" "What'd he weigh?" "Four pounds." "Hell, you hardly got your bait back!*" (1:254.) Fears about being displaced by the ogre of the sex machine are evident in the mere pun of the following: *An Irishman in a maternity ward is worried that the thin and sickly baby he sees is his own. "No," says the nurse, pointing to a fine, chubby, baby boy, "this one is yours; the other child was born by artificial insemination." "Just what I've always heard said: 'Spare the rod and spoil the child'.*" (D.C. 1952.)

By comparison with both extremes here, the perfect norm of male pride in the male function is struck in the story of *The vaudeville actor who is very distracted while trying out before the theatre agent. "I'm sorry," he says, "I didn't hear what you asked me. I just got this telegram this morning saying my wife had triplets, and I don't know what I'm doing." "I asked you,"* says the agent, *"if you can sing." "No, I can't sing." "Dance?" "No." "Tell funny stories?" "No." "Well, what the hell* can *you do?" The actor hands him the telegram.* (Chicago, 1946.) This is matched, at least formally, by *The boy who is rejected by the army because he is not circumcised. The mother storms angrily into the army-doctor's office, and demands, "What do you want my boy for — fighting or breeding?"* (N.Y. 1944.) Part of the humor here is supposed to rise from the expurgated alliteration, and from its being so far the opposite of the probable real emotions of the mother, with the incestuous tone always present in jokes where the mother concerns herself in any way with the son's genitals or sexual life. Other stories on these themes, as also on the semen in connection with masturbation, will be found in earlier chapters.

The normality of male function begins to break down when the man expresses jealousy of any of the female prerogatives of passivity, menstruation, childbirth, etc.; or willingly allows any of his own physically male prerogatives to be usurped or even shared by the woman, for instance pants or other male clothing, or the even more significant *lying on top* habitually during sexual intercourse. It is understood of course that these matters, where they are not biologically determined (as, for instance, menstruation), are social conventions only, and that it is no more 'normal' for the man to lie on top during intercourse than for the woman, or for him to wear pants and her skirts rather than the reverse. However, where these are the socially accepted and transmitted norms for the two sexes, any insistent deviation from the one or yearning for the other is a positive sign of emotional disfunction or neurosis. This is clearly understood by everyone, even when obvious pretenses are made and rationalizations offered as to 'comfort,' etc., concerning pants for women.

Just as obviously, men who might wish to menstruate or have babies — or just stay home from work for the rest of their lives and watch television, while the pressure-cooker, dish-washing machine, and laundromat do the housework — do not have any such facile pretext of 'comfort' to hide behind, and would have to admit to funking out on their socially and biologically determined rôle. For them there is, as yet, no recourse but fantasies and jokes, or the combination of both, as in the joke-fantasy (taken seriously by many people who should know better) that men can be 'turned into women' by means of total castration and the continuous injection of female hormones to make their breasts swell slightly. Obviously men can be turned into *neuters* by the Machine, but this has as yet little status value.

The first joke reference collected as to male menstruation is in the rationalized or overcompensatory form of being caused not by an insufficiency of maleness but by an excess: '*It was said of a certain erotomaniac that he had love* [i.e. *cunt*] *on his mind so much that regularly every month he had a nosebleed!*' (*Anecdota*, 1933, No. 205.) Within twenty years this was being circulated in a franker form in which the rationalization has broken down, as in a letter from the American folklorist, the late Josiah H. Combs, from Fredericksburg, Virginia, 1952, stating: '*I once heard of a fellow who was so effeminate that he was afraid of the company of men, and that he was with women most of the time, so that his nose bled every 28 days.*' Meanwhile, a joke collected from an American college woman tells of '*A meeting between G. K. Chesterton and Lord Beaverbrook, I suppose in Piccadilly. Said the newspaperman, patting the other on the bay window, "As pregnant as ever I see, G. K." And the other wit came back, "It's too bad you can't be so once in a while, my Lord; it might stop those damn periodicals of yours".*' (Berkeley, Calif. 1941.)

As can be seen, this is presented in the form of mutual insults: one man calls the other effeminately fat, and pregnant; the other responds by implying that the man who is taunting him as effeminate is himself subject to menstruation, and thus is wholly a woman. Nevertheless, the simple idea of menstruous or pregnant men is here seen breaking into the open, significantly perhaps as a story told (twice) by a woman, who is able, as it were, to thrust the femininity she obviously considers a disability upon two famous men whom she sees as meeting 'I suppose in Piccadilly.' A similar pressing of the man toward maternity on the part of a woman is apparent in a rather similar hostile colloquy, in which however, it is only the woman *in* the joke — not telling it — who is doing the pushing: '*There was the man who dined always in the same spot, developing quite a bay window on him, till the waitress, I suppose in a flip moment, one day said to him, "I could tell you what that was if it had been on a woman." He: "It was last night. What is it?"*' (Berkeley, Calif. 1941.) In a later chapter, 13, on "Castration," in Series Two, various jokes are grouped involving operations intended to restore the man's virility, but using grafts from a woman's sexual organs, with the result that the man 'has nosebleeds every month' or 'his lip quivers when he sees a man piss,' and similar burlesqued but profound effeminizations.

2. THE MALE MOTHERHOOD OF AUTHORSHIP

The 'male motherhood' implicit in the writing of books is a very common and quite conscious form, and, by the inner logic of the art of communication, the most articulate. The few references here given, from sources in English, are far from exhausting the subject. A whole library could probably be brought together of books referring in their prefaces to the *male motherhood of authorship,* ending perhaps with one that will never be printed as planned, in which the author (a modern American writer abroad — I know him well) began: 'I am with book, and have gone ten months with it already, unable to make head or tail of this thing stirring inside me.' One of the fullest utterances on the subject is that of the remarkable but little-appreciated 17th-century satirical poet, Royalist, and drollery-compiler, Dr. James Smith, whose works would be well worth collecting and 'commentating' in a modern edition, including his extraordinary erotic parody of Marlowe, *The Loves of Hero and Leander* (1651) — noted further in Chapter 13, "Castration" — which has never been formally ascribed to him though it is probably his masterpiece. Of another of his mock-poems, *The Innovation of Penelope and Ulysses* (1658), reprinted in *Musarum Deliciæ,* 1817 and 1872, i. 265 ff., Dr. Smith writes in his "Epistle Dedicatory, to the Reader":

> Courteous Reader, I had not gone my full time, when by a sudden fright, occasioned by the Beare and Wheel-barrow on the Bank-side, I fell in travaile, and therefore cannot call this, a timely Issue, but a Mischance, which I must put out to the world to nurse; hoping it will be fostered with the greater care, because of its own innocency.

There is also the delightful simile in the preface of the laborious Edward Capell's edition of Shakespeare (1768, probably the earliest, or only, edition of Shakespeare ever set in type from a completely handwritten text prepared by the editor), in which Capell compares his labor to that of the female ostrich, whom he describes in hilariously flatfooted prose as laying her egg in the desert sands, leaving to the hot desert sun the trouble of hatching it. This comparison, and Capell's naïve style, so infuriated Dr. Johnson that he offered to ghost-write a new preface in all the virile pomposity of his own euphuistic Latinity.

The 19th century is particularly fertile in references to the male motherhood of authorship, even including one in a public speech by the homosexual politician and writer, Benjamin Disraeli, who had every reason not to speak freely, and who ventured only the deprecating simile, in a speech of November 19th, 1870: 'The author who speaks about his own books is almost as bad as the mother who talks about her own children.' (On the homosexual accusation of the real woman's 'evil motherhood,' by whatever trick imported, as here, see my pamphlet *On the Cause of Homosexuality*, 1950, p. 21–5.) The Rev. Sydney Smith (*d*. 1845) is amusingly quoted in Lady Holland's *Memoir*, I. 232, as assimilating all the perquisites of new motherhood to a poet: the straw in the street to prevent the wheels of carriages from making noise, the door-knocker tied up for the same reason, etc. '*He has produced a couplet. When our friend is delivered of a couplet, with infinite labour, and pain, he takes to his bed, has straw laid down, the knocker tied up, and expects his friends to call and make inquiries.*' But nothing can match the flinging truthfulness of Sir Philip Sidney's *Astrophel and Stella* (1591), in the opening sonnet, "Loving in Truth," of which, Sidney ends his evocation: '*Thus, great with child to speak, and helpless in my throes, Biting my truant pen, beating myself for spite: Fool! said my Muse to me, look in thy heart, and write.*'

The most total statement of the whole idea that I have encountered is at the opening of the "Preface zu den ersten zehn Editions," in *Gemixte Pickles* (Chicago, 1927), a comedy Anglo-German dialect work by 'K.M.S.' [Kurt M. Stein], author also of another volume of macaronic German-American poetry, *Die Schönste Lengevitch*. Attention has already been drawn to this passage in *The Limerick* (Paris, 1953) Note 972, as male motherhood '*in excelsis!*'

Bei den Quantitäts von neuen Books zu judgeh wo daily geadvertised werden, sollt man denken es iss a dernsight easier a Brainchild zu haben denn a neun pount Baby. In a way iss dass so, aber net entirely.

Der main Reason dafür iss becahs in dieser Line haben die Ladies plenty competition. Das andere Bissness haben sie pretty solid bei'm tail [!] und aufgesewed, but an Gehirnkindern haben sie noch kei exclusive Patent.

Indeed, da sein enny number von Gents, wo certainlich bloody Murder yelleh täten, wenn sie a Kind kriegen sollten, but wo jedes Jahr regular a Buch in die Welt bringen. A

Betschler, der Theo. Dreiser, hat a Jahr zurück even Twins in zwei Volumes gehabt, er hat aber auch zweiundsibzig Monate dran gelabored. Das war a *American Tragedy*. Die alten Authors, wo jetzt in Sets komme', wie der Balzac, die müssen ganze Litters zu oncet produced haben, und daher derifeh wir das Wort Litterature.

Notmitstanding und in shpite davon, iss es oft painvoll sowohl als dangerous der selfcontainteh Parent even von a ganz kleinen, slimmen Volume zu sein. Diesen Trouble hab ich geëxperienced . . .

If, to these perfectly straightforward expressions — and my own low-water favorite is Fred Fisher's popular song, "Daddy, You've Been a Mother to Me" (1920, revived on U.S. juke-boxes in 1950) — there were to be added that group of books in which young husbands who happen to be literary men attempt to absorb and slough off the pain of being thrust into the background by their wives' pregnancy and delivery, quite a bibliography could be developed before even beginning to integrate the materials. These extend at least from Gustave Droz' *Monsieur, Madame et Bébé* (1866) and John Habberton's *Helen's Babies* (1876), by 'Their Latest Victim;' to novelist John Fante's *Full of Life* (1952), written without falsification in the first person, and beginning with Fante describing how, '*In the quiet hours before midnight, I lay with my ear to the place and heard the trickling as from a spring, the gurgles and sucks and splashings.*' There are also such curiosa as Lawton Mackall's *Scrambled Eggs* (Cincinnati, 1920), an animal-satire on woman suffrage, with a duck named Eustace as the leading male mother.

The subliterary or amateur volumes of this type are usually presented simply as humorous manuals of comportment for new fathers. Some are amusing; most of them are pretty dull. One might mention John Gould's *Pre-natal Care for Fathers* (Brattleboro, Vt., 1941), which is better than most; *Father's First Two Years* by Fairfax Downey (1925), Maurice Holcomb & Lang Goodwin's *Poppin' a Button!* (1944), and Louis Pollock's *Stork Bites Man: What the Expectant Father May Expect* (1945). There are many more, and what is really most remarkable about them is the absolutely open hostility they express against the child — always depicted as a boy — in almost the classic primitive fashion importantly analyzed in Theodor Reik's *Ritual* (1931) p. 27–89, "Couvade and the Fear of Retaliation."

The most open and even gloating of these male motherhood manuals, so far encountered, in which the main idea seems to be beating up the baby, have been Jerome S. Meyer's *Advice on the Care of Babies* (1927), noted on the cover as 'By A Bachelor Who Can't Bear Them,' and filled with *machines* for spanking and half-killing the child — all depicted in action — and Bil Sullivan's *Babies Don't Bounce* (1947), which, under the exceedingly shallow sub-title pretense of being an "A B C of Baby Safety," squares off bravely against the boy-child with boxing gloves, in the half-title to Part 1, and proceeds to every possible home catastrophe, including of course the castrating butcher-knife, p. 21, captioned "Mother's Utensils." [!] Compare the anti-children verses, by Jan Kindler, in *The Limerick*, Note 652.

It is almost unnecessary to point out how fantasy assaults like this on the newborn child are codified and developed in the "Cautionary Tales" of the Anglo-German nursery, discussed by Ella Freeman Sharpe in *International Journal of Psycho-Analysis* (1943); in particular Dr. Heinrich Hoffmann's classic of 1845, *Struwwelpeter* (on which see *Neurotica*, No. 9, 1951), and in Col. Harry Graham's domestic-sadistic quatrains, or "Little Willies," first appearing in his *Ruthless Rhymes for Heartless Homes* (1899) by 'Col. D. Streamer,' and immediately taken up and imitated by writers like Carolyn Wells in hopes of replacing, with its pure sadistic morality, the background eroticism of the prevailing humorous verse form in English, the limerick. See the recent rhymed *sadistica* signed 'Edward Gorey.'

Male motherhood of course involves female fatherhood, though this point is seldom observed. Again, the most forthright expression of this will be found in connection with the male parturition of writing a book. Mr. Lancelot Hogben's popularized history of pictorial techniques replacing the printed word, *From Cave Painting to Comic Strip* (London, 1949), opens with the following staggeringly frank "Foreword," to which Mr. Hogben's name is signed in facsimile:

> Though my name appears on the title page as the author of this book, I cannot honestly claim to be the male parent. A suggestion of Marie Neurath was the act of fertilisation whereby I myself, and at first a little coyly, conceived the plan of a script for a picture gallery of her own choosing.

After such a beginning, no one need be surprised by the 'picture gallery,' of whoever's choosing, with its tendentious concentration on pictures of flagellation (three out of four, in color, between p. 208–9; Buster Brown laid face down on the table to be whipped by his mother, p. 222, etc.), and its principal discussion of the comic-strips, mentioned on the title-page, as a glorification of the male-dominating 'super-she's,' Superwoman and Blondie.

I would suggest as axiomatic that: *the masochist element in male motherhood is invariably best displayed where the woman figure is also present, as father.* Where the motherhood is strictly monosexual, as that of zoo attendants fighting off monkey-mothers with a pitchfork while they cuddle the pups with a rubber teat, or of campers-out without women, cooking, sewing, and making the beds for each other in the best tradition of the men's-men's-men's magazines (also of the *Saturday Evening Post:* cover, May 30th, 1953), the emphasis is of course straight anti-woman and homosexual.

3. RECTAL MOTHERHOOD

Seventeenth- and 18th-century writers were also fond of a matching scatological fancy or bit of medical folklore about the wind of farts, when restrained from their proper exit, rising as a harmful gas to the brain and there issuing in the form of madness (to wit, the book), with a further suggestion to the readers that the leaves of the book, if it displeased them, be used as the toilet paper or 'arse-wisp' this gas would originally have set to working if allowed proper exit. The relevance of this notion to male motherhood is *via* the infantile notion that impregnation is caused by intestinal gas, which the father somehow ejects into the mother, in a way possibly conceived of as similar to the cloacal intercourse of cocks and hens. Dr. Ernest Jones, in his great analytic essay on "Salt," has courageously noted the relation of this childish belief to the myth of the Annunciation, in which the locale of the Virgin Mary's impregnation is also the head, by way of the ear. The curious birth of the goddess Minerva or Athena is likewise through the head of Jupiter (in some forms of the legend through the 'thigh,' *i.e.* the buttocks, as in Beardsley's satirical illustration, which mocks this as a birth through the *calf* of the leg). This is perhaps the most famous example of the fantasy of male motherhood in literature, as the Greek and Roman deities cannot be considered ever really to have existed except as the literary creations of a priestly élite, orally transmitted by the believers. The placing of this birth in Jupiter's *head* also seems an overcompensation, or 'displacement of lower to upper,' as the standard homosexual fantasy of this kind is of the *rectal* birth of the 'male mother's' child, as will be seen below.

A most extraordinary harking-back to, or spontaneous recombustion of, the ancient 'brain-gas' theory appears to exist in a work by the German-educated physician, A. T. W. Simeons, *Man's Presumptuous Brain* (1960) p. 115, in which a special illustration in more-or-less schematic form is devoted to "The Mechanics of Evacuation," showing the actual promulgation of the fecal column and the final dropping out of the turd (shown in black), marked "End of Evacuation." Seven of the nine illustrations in this work, presumably on the misdeeds and pretentions of *Man's Presumptuous Brain,* are likewise concerned entirely with the intestinal tract, one of them (Fig. 8, p. 140) being devoted to "The Anus" and various of its problems, such as piles. It is my impression that with the exception of certain rare erotic and scatological works, in particular a modern French anti-clerical item in folio size, entitled *La Nonne,* and horribly illustrated in black-&-white, showing nuns making love and defecating in their religious costumes (compare the posed photograph of a mock-nun reading aloud to three naked girls, in *The Realist,* May 1967, No. 74: p. 11), Dr. Simeons' illustration of actual defecation and its end-product may be the only one. Would it be presumptuous to ask exactly what this has to do with the *Brain*?

An even more extraordinarily frank identification of *shitting and thinking* (as in the folk-mocking of the phrase 'sitting and thinking' with 'shitting and stinking') is that made in Dr. Jules Eisenbud's *The World of Ted Serios* (New York: William Morrow & Co., 1967), concerning an individual who Dr. Eisenbud claims can make photographic records of his own thoughts. Here is how Mr. Serios' photo-occult 'shooting' is described by Dr. Eisenbud, a psychiatrist:

> When about to shoot, he seemed rapidly to go into a state of intense concentration, with eyes open, lips compressed and a quite noticeable tension of his muscular system . . . His face would become suffused and blotchy, the veins standing out on his forehead, his eyes visibly bloodshot . . . (The proctologist would perhaps liken what was occurring to the kind of tension and pressure built up during a difficult [*bowel*] movement.)

This passage is quoted in *Popular Photography* (Chicago, October 1967) p. 137, with photographs, pp. 83, 86, showing Mr. Serios registering precisely the 'tension' or physical strain here described, actually shown as rather similar to that of a fencer at the beginning of a flying lunge. The accompanying article, by photography experts Charles Reynolds and David B. Eisendrath, indicates several rather obvious methods whereby the 'gismo' that Serios insists on holding over the camera lens — set at 'infinity' at his demand — could rather easily be loaded to contain a small reflecting optical device, namely (p. 140): 'one of the small plastic telescopes, usually containing a girlie picture, and available at many novelty shops for about 25¢.' The whole matter is perfectly summed up in Serios' shrewd question, p. 138 — which really answers itself — "How can people believe in me when no one believes in God?" They believe in him because they have lost their old irrational God, and need one.

The legend of Cimon of Athens has been mentioned at the end of the preceding section, concerning the feeding of the imprisoned or agèd father at his daughter's breast. (See Witkowski, as noted; also Albert P. Southwick's *Quizzism and its Key: Quirks and Quibbles from Queer Quarters,* Boston, 1884, p. 139, stating that a "Temple of Piety" was built by Acilius 'on the spot' where this occurred, and referring to a painting of the subject in the Boston Museum.) The fantasy of male motherhood necessarily involves the matching miracle of male lactation. Though no joking references to this have been encountered, it is stated flatly in the rabbinical commentaries on the *Book of Esther* to have been the case with Esther's uncle and foster-father, Mordecai, whose breasts grew and secreted milk so that he could nurse the heroine who was to save the people of Israel from the revenge of Haman. (Midrashic commentary on *Esther,* ii. 7.)

As it is fairly clear that Esther and Mordecai are really references to the older Levantine deities, Ishtar or Astarte and Marduk (the *Book of Esther* is not strictly canonical, nor does the name of the Jewish god, Jehovah, occur therein), this is very probably a legendary accretion concerning the male consort of the dominant mother-goddess, Astarte, taking over the female functions while she takes over the male. The whole meaning of the *Book of Esther,* beginning as it does with the humiliation of Queen Vashti for refusing to 'shew her beauty' — naked, according to the commentators — to the guests at her husband's six-months'-long orgy, and King Xerxes' resultant edict to all his dominions 'that every man should bear rule in his own house' (*Esther,* i. 10–22), can only be as a vindication of male dominance from a presumed female threat or recollection of female dominance. Such matriarchal accretions, to the Jewish form of the story, as a man who secretes milk to nourish his female foster-child, is the obvious counterpart of the legend of Cimon and his daughter. It is reminiscent of its possible divine origin — in connection with Ishtar-Astarte and Marduk — in its miraculousness, since where the legend of Cimon is based only on a natural function taken to an unusual extreme of devotion, that of Mordecai's milk is, after all, resolutely contrary to biological truth. (The standard reference in these situations to Gould & Pyle's *Anomalies and Curiosities of Medicine* is purposely omitted, as playing the rationalizers' game for them. It will in any case *not* be found to include male motherhood, though anomalous male lactation has of course been recorded.)

The jokes on male motherhood have difficulty luffing into their subject without displaying the hidden colors of unvirile or homosexual fantasy. That most commonly collected is a mere pun, first recorded by Larson in Idaho in 1918 (no. 34): *An army colonel on a very rough sea voyage gallantly gives up his accommodations in favor of a sick old woman in steerage class. Telegraphs to his wife: "Dreadful stormy passage. Deathly sick all the way. Finally gave berth to an old woman."* Again, as with Mordecai, it is the reversal that is most prominent here: the man not only gives birth to a woman but to an 'old woman' (*i.e.* mother-figure) at that. The stories now become rougher, not so much in their subject-matter as in the hostile and insulting form in which they are framed, and the violent accusations of utter imbecility, homosexuality, and the like, brought against the male butts of these stories, without any recognition of course that these men have no real existence and are conjured up by the story-tellers as the receptacles of their own confused and ambivalent emotions: hating and despising the 'male mother' on the one hand, yet yearning simultaneously for male motherhood.

A young man is fixed up by the bartender with one of the dance-hall girls. He cannot repress the idea that she may have a disease and has intercourse with her rectally instead. Later, at the bar, he asks the bartender confidentially, "Can a woman have a baby through the asshole?" A drunk standing nearby butts in: "Sure! Where do you suppose bartenders come from?" (N.Y. 1953. Also collected in an army form with punch-line, *"Where do you suppose Second Lieutenants come from?"*) Note the conversion of the boy's fears about venereal infection of himself by the woman, to a pretended concern over the possible impregnation of the woman by himself. This also involves an unconscious identification with the pedicated woman, and the notion that the man himself might therefore have the rectal baby, also known as a 'jelly baby' (*i.e.* one composed of feces) in homosexual fantasies.

In a complicated tale, of which the second half seems intended as a topper, *A homosexual with a goiter on his neck starts knitting baby clothes.* [The joke actually ends here. The rest is the topper:] *That night he makes off with a mounted policeman's horse, while two other homosexuals argue over who gets the policeman. When he comes back, the horse balks at going off with the policeman. Next morning, before taking up his knitting, the homosexual goes out and buys a pony saddle.* (2:46.) Since the implication of the neck goiter is that the homosexual is pregnant *via* fellation, the dragging in of the policeman's horse is more than an exaggeration; it is a reversion to the passive pedicatory form of homosexuality, which can more logically be pretended to cause pregnancy.

Finally, all the pretenses break down, and we are shown the situation in which a man actually has a baby, or is made to believe he is going to have a baby, by the action of some third person (doctor or wife) who must therefore be considered the imaginary father. *A physician gets rid of a hypochondriacal patient by telling him he is pregnant. He then telephones the only other doctor in town to concur in this diagnosis if the patient goes to him. After being assured by the second doctor that he is really pregnant, the man goes home and tells his wife, "I knew something awful would come of you getting on top when we make love!"* (1:54, told in Negro dialect, with end-line: *"Ah done told you what you'd do to me gettin' on top o' me like dat."*) This story is of ancient genealogy, appearing in Boccaccio's *Decameron* (1353) Day IX, Tale 3, and probably of Levantine provenance before then, being very much in the style of the fool stories of Nasr'eddin and his wife. Further very valuable references will be found in Thompson's *Motif-Index* at J2321, "Man made to believe that he is pregnant (has borne child)," and even more broadly at T578, "Pregnant man." (Note also Types 1209, 1218, 1319, 1677, and 1739.)

A French version of the following story appears in Perceau's *Histoires d'Hommes et de Dames* (1913) p. 30. *An Irishman is made to believe that grapefruit, which he has never seen before, are elephants' eggs, and that if he lays one under his belly for twenty-four hours it will hatch into an elephant that he can sell to a circus. The Widow Clancy is sceptical and gropes under the bedcovers to feel.* "B'jesus, he's right; it's hatching already! Sure I feel its trunk." (2:296. Also in the Larson MS.) This story beautifully shows the vacillation in the mind of the retailers of such jokes as to what they are really after. At the very moment of being made an utter fool, *i.e.* castrated (of both brains and virility) and effeminized, and given the rôle of the mother to play, the man's phallic integrity is still insisted upon as being able to surprise a curious woman 'under the bedcovers.' This is even more clear in the French version, which is entirely a practical joke on the woman. (Bebel, 1514, No. 148; *Kryptádia*, II. 123; Type 1218.)

The ultimate form noted by Thompson, that the fool is made to believe not that he is pregnant, but that he has actually given birth, exists currently in English in two main stories, both very often collected. *A priest of Caracas goes to the hospital with a stomach tumor. As a joke he is told that he is pregnant, and is given the baby of an unmarried girl who has died in childbirth, which he is told he has been delivered of by Cæsarean section. He brings up the baby carefully as his nephew. Years later, on his deathbed, he calls the boy to him.* "Son, there is something I must tell you. You've always called me 'Father,' but now that I'm about to die I must tell you the truth. I'm not really your father; I'm your mother!" "Then who is my father?" *says the astounded boy.* "The Archbishop of Caracas." (Fla. 1953.) This story is given decades earlier, in literary form, in Canto XII of Ezra Pound's *XXX Cantos.*

The homosexual tone, which is here evident and sardonic, is equally present in the final story collected, though much disguised: *A man wants to know what a woman really feels in childbirth. The doctor to whom he applies gives him a quart of castor-oil and securely plugs up his asshole. The man goes home, and to bed, where his increasing agonies are lightened only by the sound of an Italian organ-grinder's music down the street. The organ-grinder's monkey climbs up onto the window-sill of the man's bedroom and into bed with him, just as the man's anal plug gives way and there is a fecal explosion. Catching sight of the monkey, on coming to, the man seizes it, presses it to his breast, and cries,* "You're ugly, you're hairy, you're covered with shit, but you're mine *and I love you!*" (Berkeley, Calif. 1941, from a homosexual informant who stated he thought it was 'of 1910 vintage.') Also collected in California, 1943, from a young woman who later stated in the presence of her husband that they had intercourse only, or preferably, in a curious position in which they lay with their heads to each other's feet, the woman on top and straddling the man. This is reminiscent of Mr. Bloom's favorite sleeping position in Joyce's *Ulysses,* of which the significance is equally clear. Randolph, No. 13, "The Man That Had a Baby," gives a more recent Arkansas version of the monkey story. In the surviving Arab form of the "Fortunate Fart" story, already discussed at 2.vII.2, the Kazi gives birth to a child as a result of a 'fecund fart.' (*Histoires Arabes,* 1927, p. 256–8.) This is Thompson's Motif J2321.2, noting that it entered Europe in Basile's *Pentamerone* (1634) Day II, Tale 3, of a foolish ogre.

In the *Russian Secret Tales* collected by Afanasyev in the 1860's and published posthumously in 1872, a group of connected stories concerning male motherhood are joined together by a most important thread, not visible in the English-language versions, and that is the hostility of the wife against the husband, and her seizing of outside male prerogatives, while he is left at home to become a mother. In No. 24, "The Husband who Hatched the Eggs," the man is set to hatching the eggs (Aarne Types 1218 and 1677), not on any pretext of making money from exhibiting elephants, but because he has been sleeping lazily at home while his wife works in the fields, and a crow has carried off all the chickens while he slept. The dénouement of the story involves the wife's then *dressing in men's clothes* and pretending to be a soldier, beating her husband with a whip, for his laziness, in this disguise. He is also shown to be further unvirile by the supreme 'nincumpoop' trait of not recognizing his wife's genital organ, which she shows him, as the pretended soldier, stating that it is a wound she received in the wars. (See further the notes and analogues to all parts of this, in *Kryptádia,* IV. 196–7.) In No. 38, "The Priest Who Begot a Calf," a complicated trickster story is set up, on the situation of a priest being made to believe that he has given birth to a newborn calf which has accidentally been put, to keep it warm, by the side of the priest who is sleeping on the Dutch oven. This is similar to the creaking mechanism of the Italian organ-grinder's monkey — brought needfully though absurdly into the story given above — and may possibly be its original. The scatological *mise-en-scène* is certainly thoroughly Russian, though it does not happen to be present in this particular story of Afanasyev's.

Centrally important to the understanding of "The Husband who Hatched the Eggs" is Afanasyev's No. 27, "The Peasant who did his

Wife's Work." (Types 1408 and 1681; and found earliest in Des Périers' *Nouvelles Récréations,* No. 45, in 1558.) Though there is no question of male motherhood in this particular form, it has become the classic story of male-protest hostility in women, and is well known in English both as a tale and, I believe, as a folksong. Beginning identically as does the hatching-of-the-eggs story, the husband lazily decides one day to stay at home and do his wife's chores, which he considers to be easy, sending her out in the fields to do his work at the harvest. As punishment for his rejection of the male rôle, he arrives at a fate obviously considered even worse than — and evidently connected with — male motherhood: by a series of elaborate accidents, of the typical housework variety, he completely messes up the woman's job that he has undertaken, and finally loses all his clothes. (This trait and what follows is missing in the English-language versions.) When he dresses himself in an apron of grass 'to cover up his prick,' on the example of Adam in Eden, the mare bites off the grass apron and his genitals with it. Far from being sympathetic, the wife saves this for the final reproach on his having spoiled everything, ending, "*Ah, you son of a bitch, you've done a fine job!*" The whole story has a subordinate tone, in the choice of the household jobs the husband fails at — for instance, the cream which he spills — of involving an unspoken accusation of effeminacy or sexual impotence at the least, here rationalized as mere 'laziness.' In *Histoires Coloniales* (1935?) p. 224, a particularly full version is given, as of the fool Nasr'eddin, who ends his one-man-band household chores by giving his penis to the baby to play with. This survives in a Russian-Jewish fool story, now often told in English: *The wife who has left her foolish husband to take care of the house returns to find that he has given the baby his penis to suck. When she berates him, he replies,* "*So what* should *I give him, a knife?*" (N.Y. 1940.) Clearly connected with the Jewish story, p. 184 above, as to the man lacking a teaspoon. Note the reimportation of the castratory combination of penis-&-knife. (Type 1681B.)

Not to be overlooked is the primitive practice of *couvade,* or the 'husband's hatching,' in which the husband rather than the wife stays in bed after the birth of a child. Nothing exactly similar has been encountered in jokes. The *couvade* has been brilliantly analyzed at the deepest level, by Theodor Reik, in *Ritual* (1931) p. 27–89, "Couvade and the Psychogenesis of the Fear of Retaliation," not as the 'sympathy' with the wife's labor-pains which it purports to be, but as an expression of, or rather a socially organized defense against, the husband's hostility toward the newborn child and his jealousy of the special invalid treatment and release from work being accorded the mother at that time. Reik omits consideration of the pseudo-pregnancy of men during their wives' pregnancies, which is certainly related to the *couvade*. A superficial article on the subject, "Pregnant Papas," by Duncan Underhill, appears in *For Men Only!* (Oct. 1937) p. 83–5, in which the most interesting point is its appearance in a 'men's magazine' at all.

A close relative of mine, on the birth of his first male child — long awaited, and who was to do and be all the things in life that the father had failed at — became extremely faint, then ill, and took to his bed, with the necessary result that the parturient mother, who had had the baby at home, had to get *out* of bed the moment the doctor had left, and tend her groaning husband during his spontaneous *couvade*. The husband, who was highly neurotic in many ways, also sympathetically fainted every time he saw his wife or anyone else being given a hypodermic injection, and would babble about '*The needle!*' as he toppled over. On one occasion he did this dramatically before a fairly large audience of uninterested spectators, reeling and stumbling the whole length of a long stone hospital staircase with a baby in his arms, which he carefully deposited at the foot of the staircase before fainting. He tells this story himself, and is very proud of it.

The hostility is all inturned here, but it is visible nonetheless in the ostentatious flirting with sickness and accident. In the most remarkable joke about the relations between father and newborn child, often collected, no bones whatever are made about the hostility involved. The earliest version seems to be that given among a group of Negro "Red Bone Legends," in *Neurotica* (1951) No. 9: p. 45, by Mason Jordan Mason (said to be the pseudonym or *alter ego* of the poet, Judson Crews). In the usual form, *A drunk in a bar insists that everyone drink with him to "The papa crocodile!" On being asked why this toast, he explains solemnly, "The papa crocodile is man's best friend. The mama crocodile lays one million eggs every three months, and the papa crocodile puts on his big boots and spends all his time stamping on everyone of those goddam eggs but one. My friend," he adds, shaking his finger warningly at his interlocutor, "if it wasn't for the papa crocodile, you and me and everybody in the world would be* ASS DEEP *in crocodiles!"* One often has the feeling, in listening to or reading the remarks being currently passed about the coming 'overpopulation' of the world — of which the only logical Malthusian solution is of course to wipe everybody out with new and better atom bombs — that this drunk in the bar has made an awful lot of converts. See in particular the powerful conclusion of Eric Norden's historic interview with D.A. James Garrison, in *Playboy* (October 1967) p. 178, as to the inevitable cheapening of human life by the 'imperatives of the population explosion.'

VII. SEX AND MONEY

I. PAYMENT FOR INTERCOURSE

A minor theme here, since its importance will only appear later in the chapter on "Prostitution" in Series Two (to which the reader who has turned to the present section by accident is referred), is the matter of money and its influence on sexual acts *in marriage*. Its meaning here is as an important area and favorite expression of sexual hostility, mostly against the wife, since most of the tellers of jokes are men. At this point, the wedding and the gratifying birth of children being long past, the marriage is presumed — as seen by the joke-tellers — to have collapsed internally into the 'silent desperation' so common in many situations in modern life, and possibly throughout human history since its mistaken turning from rural naturalness and simplicity to the excessive urban agglomerations, which kill the human spirit after a period of shallow and gregarious exhilaration. Everything now, in the marriage, adds to the undercurrent of animosity between husband and wife. The concentration on money, or more particularly on its lack, is an especial irritation.

Folk proverb: "*If a married couple put a bean in a bottle for every act of intercourse during their first year, and take one out for every act in the following years, the bottle will never be emptied.*" (Boston, 1943, from an American army sergeant of Irish family background.) This looks sensible enough at first blush, but of course the hidden point is that love-making is supposed to be interesting to the married couple only during their first year together. The same folk proverb, slightly modified, collected two years later in New York, without the homey touch of the 'bean': "*If a married couple puts a penny in a jar every time, &c. &c.*" (Also with coins in a box or piggy-bank.) In changing the bean to a penny, though both are presumably only counters, the significant motion has been made toward *paying the wife for every act of intercourse*. Observe how this begins to swell in importance.

A miner who has lost his job finds that, instead of being dead broke, the family is on Easy Street. His wife actually owns four houses on their block. She has put a penny in the pig every time he had intercourse with her. "Gee, honey, you're a wonderful wife." "Yes, but you're not a wonderful husband. If you'd been true to me we could have had the saloon on the corner to boot." (2:36.) One observes that the instant the wife has or must proffer her own money she becomes acid and reclamatory. The copyright game called "Monopoly," involving real-estate manipulations of houses, money, etc., is known to be particularly popular among women and girls. The hardening of female sexuality into power-drives after the menopause, or when the husband's sexual interest has faded ("If you'd been true to me . . ."), is especially evident in the stock-market manipulations and investment portfolios of an increasing number of women, particularly in America. The photographs that are occasionally published, showing hard-faced women sitting or standing in stock-market bucket-shops, watching the posting of the day's latest quotations, compare in gruesomeness only with the photographs of sleazy middle-aged male horse-players in the betting area at American racetracks, or in PMU (*parimutuel*) bars in France. The ultimate expression is, of course, the gambling casino, as seen for instance in Las Vegas, which is a corner of Dante's Inferno that, for purposeful vulgarity and human repulsiveness — especially, as all observers have noticed, in the middle-aged women who gamble there — is, as one aghast British visitor has said, 'the only excuse necessary for the Atom Bomb.'

A man gives his wife fifty cents to put in the piggy-bank every time he has intercourse with her. One day when he needs change, and she is out, he breaks into the toy bank and finds it full of five and ten dollar bills. When he asks her about this, she says: "Do you think everybody is as stingy as you are?" (1:47.) Collected again in New York, 1938, rationalized that the money is put into a slot cut in the birth control jelly box, to buy a new tube when necessary. A great deal of folklore exists concerning the *pig,* of which the piggy-bank is not the least interesting. The pig is in all cases considered to be a female object (possibly owing to the very large number of breasts and piglets to each sow), if not representative of the vulva itself, as in the Greek term *choiros,* which means both. It is the boar — the pig-animal with upturned tusks (*vagina dentata*) — who kills Adonis by goring him significantly in the thigh or lower belly (always a euphemism for the genitals in the Bible, as in the angel's 'touching' of the 'hollow' of Jacob's thigh, in *Genesis,* xxxii. 24–5), and it is to be understood that the boar here represents the evil aspect of Adonis' mistress, Venus, who is thus *herself* killing and castrating him, as does Isis to Osiris under the rather transparent pretext of 'searching' for his penis, which only she can find because she has hidden it.

The various ritual blood-accusations against the Jews are also significantly combined with equally unfounded accusations of secret ceremonials in which the Jews gather not to drink the blood of slain Christian children, but to suck the breasts of a pig! (See propaganda woodcuts of this alleged ceremony in Eduard Fuchs' *Die Juden in der Karikatur,* München, 1921.) The midwestern American pig-eating or Bratwurst festival, in which nothing is eaten of a solid nature but the products of the pig's body (and bread), has already been noted in its similarity to the nocturnal camel-eating ceremonial, reminiscent of the killing of the *Ur-vater,* discussed in Freud's *Totem & Taboo.*

Summing up the matter briefly one may say that the pig is inevitably a female animal, closely identified with dirt (both feces and money) and with unrepressed sexuality. The ultimate degradation in Western societies is or would be to have intercourse with a pig, and especially to be caught doing so. This is made a particular climax of the riotously scatological *The Sot-Weed Factor* (New York, 1960) by Prof. John Barth. The 'exposé' magazine *The Realist* — a magazine noted for its black-humor hoaxes in gruesomely bad taste, and therefore somewhat difficult to believe — states in issue No. 75 [1967] p. 14, in *explaining* by editor Paul Krassner its most outrageous hoax of all, in issue No. 74, as to the 'neckrophiliac' defiling of the dead body of the preceding president of the United States, that one of the 'favorite jokes' of the current president, Lyndon B. Johnson, *'is about a popular Texas sheriff running for re-election. His opponents have been trying unsuccessfully to think of a good campaign issue to use against him. Finally one man suggests spreading "a rumor that he fucks pigs." Another protests, "You know he doesn't do that." "I know," says the first man, "but let's make the sonofabitch deny it".'* In such cultures as, for instance, Russia, the ultimate shame is intercourse with a mare. (*Russian Secret Tales,* Nos. 52–4, and 57.) The Western vilification of the pig stems, of course, from the Judaic prohibition of this animal as food, unquestionably as having been the totem animal of the matriarchies preceding Semitic patriarchy in the Middle East. The same is true of the 'aphrodisiacal'

fish-foods and vulviform shellfish sacred to Venus, and therefore prohibited by the Jewish dietary laws. (*Leviticus*, xi. 9–12.) Pretenses that
these prohibitions are and were originally hygienic in nature are very
recent, and are open rationalizations of the vestigial 'dietary Judaism.'

The jokes in which money has been imported into the marital sexual relation in the form of routine payments to the wife, however disguised with piggy-banks and the like, obviously imply that the wife is a
prostitute. The money thus spent is also clearly thought of as wasted,
since presumably the husband does not have to pay for his wife's favors.
I once knew a jeweller, a big harmless man, grotesquely fat, whose specialty was the repairing of ladies' wristwatches, over which he would
labor lovingly with his great banana fingers deftly operating on these
tiny mechanisms by means of tweezers and a magnifying glass. After
a period of extreme nervousness, which he realized meant he needed a
wife, he had a marriage arranged for him with a girl he had never
seen, imported specially from a Middle European country for the purpose by relatives, and *guaranteed to be a virgin*. This seemed essential
to him, as he had been assured that a girl will always love the man who
takes her virginity, a superstition which has something in it but not
much. There are also special cases, which this girl proved to be.

Immediately after the marriage she began brainwashing her husband, to the effect that he should give her little presents — mostly of
jewels, of course, since that was his trade — every time he wanted to
have intercourse with her, in order to 'make her love him more.' Eventually he pauperized himself in this way, and learned to his surprise
that the American state law under which he had married his European
bride made her the sole owner of everything he had given her. She
also took the proprietorship of his business, and offered to give him a
job as watch-repairman, at a weekly wage, not of course including any
sexual privileges with her. I believe he eventually went decently mad
and committed suicide. Everyone in town knew the story and hated the
woman, and the folktale (see elsewhere in this volume) was eventually
assimilated to her of smuggling diamonds from Holland to America
in her vagina.

Where the bean put into a bottle by newlyweds can be considered
mere score-keeping, the money put into the slot of a piggy-bank or
birth control jelly box must be considered, at a symbolic level which
is not even hidden from the participants, to be put 'into' the wife's vagina. In the same way the purse as vaginal symbol is never more clear

than when a woman with a new purse circulates through a roomful of guests demanding that each one of them throw a coin into her new purse 'for luck.' This is identical with the breaking of the Polish bride's dish, by the wedding guests striking it with silver coins for the honor of the first 'dance' with her. Any importation of money into the sexual relationship, where out-and-out prostitution cannot be admitted to, is inevitably overloaded with a freight of symbolism pointing in that direction and overdetermining the relation between the money and the vagina. Symbolism is a form of social expurgation: one says in symbols what one dare not say, or cannot bear to say in fact.

The 'waste' of money on the sexual favors of one's own wife is imported artfully into the following joke. Instead of the husband complaining of the 'time he's spent in wooing,' as in Thomas Moore's Irish song, he leaves it to the wife to complain. What is meant is, however, clear. *An Irishman does not get the nomination as alderman because of his lack of education. He tells his wife she has held him back, that he had to work to support her and the children, and that is why he had no education. "Held you back, is it?" bristles his wife; "if you'd paid as much attention to your prayer-book as you did to my bare ass, you'd be the Pope in Rome by now!"* (1:421; often collected.)

Sexual intercourse outside one's own home, and accustomed bed, is thought of as fraught with unexpected dangers. In the hotel situation, among the dangers of unfamiliarity, noise, being interrupted, and general exposure of one's lack of *savoir faire,* one of the dangers least easy to combat is the touch of money: one pays for a bed in which to lie with a woman, and this is somehow assimilated to prostitution even if the woman is one's own wife. One may also be required by the house-dick (private police) to prove that she *is* one's wife and not a prostitute, &c. *A country jay spends his wedding night in a big city hotel. In the morning he asks for his bill, and is told by the desk-clerk, "That'll be two dollars apiece." He lays down a twenty-dollar bill.* (2:293.) Under the brag of having had intercourse an impossible number of times, the joke-teller imports the standard price of a prostitute, two dollars (it's now up to five), a price so standard, in fact, that the two-dollar bill is still resisted by many people as 'bad luck,' and sometimes, frankly, as 'upstairs money.'

Observe how the dangerous sexual situation of the hotel begins to encroach adulterously on the innocent hotel guest, as in the story of "Cynthia" and her five bellboys in an earlier section. *A man leaving a hotel is charged for a room and bath, but complains that he did not use the bath.* "Well, it was there for you," *says the clerk.* "All right," *counters the man,* "here's a bill for screwing my wife — she was there for you too." "Shhh," *says the clerk,* "don't let the manager hear you. I'll fix it up with you." (Minneapolis, 1935.) A cleanup is printed in *Coronet* magazine, June 1951, p. 102, and is commonly used by masters-of-ceremonies in nightclub acts in mockery of the hotels in overpriced resort areas such as Florida. These jokes are visibly the tail-end of the dangerous situation of the wedding night, no matter where it is consummated, and other jokes concerning hotels as the sexual and prostitutory locale par excellence will be found in the chapter on "Prostitution" following, in the Second Series, where the concentration on *sex and money,* and the connection between them, is, of course, paramount.

No more terrible discovery can be made by a man than to learn that the modest bride he has married is actually an arrant whore. Pierre Louÿs quotes from the Spanish the broadly tolerant motto, "*Ayer putas, hoy comadres,*" but one observes that yesterday's whores become only today's companions — not wives. *A man comes to work the day after the wedding very worried. He explains to his friends that he forgot what he was doing and left a five-dollar bill behind the clock on the mantelpiece.* "Don't worry," *the other men console him,* "Your wife won't think anything of it. She'll think it's for household expenses." "That's not what bothers me," *says the groom.* "She gave me three dollars change!" (1:49.) *Anecdota Americana* follows this folk-version, at no. 50, with a similar story done in free verse in Thomas Burke's *Song Book of Quong Lee* (London, 1920), "Of Politicians," a title intended to excuse the story as a parable, concerning *A man who forgets himself and leaves four coins at his wedding bedside. He comes back stealthily to get them, only to find his bride* 'Biting shrewdly, with a distressing air of experience, At one of the coins.'

2. THE IDEAL WIFE

Few of the jokes in this volume have so old and clear a *formal* history as the most ruefully phrased of these discovery-stories. *A man is told by a friend that he should pick a wife who is* "An economist in the kitchen, a lady in the parlor, and a prostitute in bed." *They meet some time after the wedding and the friend asks if he is satisfied with his choice. "Well," says the newlywed, "I did what you said, but I guess I made a mistake somewhere. The woman I married turned out to be a prostitute in the parlor, a lady in the kitchen, and an economist in bed!"* (N.Y. 1953.) Proverbial sets like this are generally very old, and at least one other connected with marriage is well-known: the formula of the bride's costume, "Something borrowed, something blue, &c." (The 'blue' stands for truth: the 'troth' she is plighting.)

Bebel's *Opuscula* in 1514 give two florid formulas of this kind for the "Ideal Woman," and I believe — as will be traced further at the end of this section, and in this exact form — that these "combinations of parts" are of Levantine origin, connected perhaps with the sexual *typologies* of women given in the *Kama Sutra* of Vatsyayana and similar Arabic works. Bebel's first formula states frankly that he is trying to compound, out of the 'superior whores' of various nations, the woman who will be 'the most appetizing and agreeable in bed.' His solution is a composite woman who will have *'the little head of Prague, the breasts of Austria, the belly of France,' etc., ending with 'the feet of the banks of the Rhine* [*i.e.* dirty or muddy], *a Bavarian cunt, and a Swabian ass. Make the acquaintance of a fuckstress of this stamp, and you can lick your chops.'* This is probably not the traditional form, but a Humanistic *jeu d'esprit.* Bebel's French translator, Edmondo Fazio, in *Les Facéties érotiques de Bebelius* (1908) p. 102*n,* gives a similar, but much more polite, Italian place-name proverb, cited by Strafforello, 1. 545, which comes no closer to open sexuality than to give the *'donna perfetta'* a 'Venetian bosom.' The folk form is also given by Bebel (ed. Fazio, p. 102–3) as "The Portrait of Helen (of Troy)," stating that *'The perfect woman must have three things hard (her breasts and her ass), three soft (her hands and her belly), three short (her nose and her feet), three long (her fingers and her thighs), three black (her eyes and her cunt), three white (her legs and her neck), and three red (her cheeks and her mouth). It is said that the beautiful Helen united in herself all twenty-one of these perfections.'*

It is quite a drop from this ornate lucubration, possibly not of the perfect woman, but surely of the perfect lover, to the usual string of 19th-century literary clichés as to female beauty: the eyes to be 'limpid, mysterious pools,' neck like a swan, etc. etc. At the open-air art market in Greenwich Village in 1952, a truculent middle-aged woman artist had done a perfect satire on this, called "Ideal Beauty," in the form of a drawing of a woman's body composed of pools for eyes, a swan's neck, etc., all perfectly literally put together to prove that such an ideal beauty would be hideous indeed. It is perhaps typical of the self-hatred involved in making such a drawing, that the artist would not *sell* it — though it was exposed, presumably for sale — but stated she would make copies of it by lithography, and sold these promised lithographic copies all day. None were ever delivered.

Another descent, in the literary sense, of the original form recorded by Bebel in 1514, is the 'Dinner Sentiment' or toast given at the Scottish Beggar's Benison Society, somewhere between 1732 and 1820 (*Supplement to the Records,* 1892, p. 19): '*Three Qualities in a proper Woman: — Well-hipped, well-breasted, easy mounted.*' The clearest ancestor of the modern joke is perhaps that recorded by Richard or George Puttenham in the late 16th century. Says Puttenham (*Arte of English Poesie,* 1589, Bk. III, p. 245): '*We limit the comely parts of a woman to consist in foure points, that is to be a shrewe in the kitchin, a saint in the Church, an Angell at the bourd, and an Ape in bed, as the Chronicle reportes by Mistresse [Jane] Shore paramour to king Edward the fourth.*' This is cited in my article, "A Word on Caxton's *Dictes,*" in *The Library* (London), 1948–9, ser. 5, III. 169, adding: 'Needless to say, Holinshed's *Chronicle* (1577) III. 724–5, "reportes" nothing of the sort.'

Earlier and other examples and allusions, back to about 1550, are given in Morris P. Tilley's great *Dictionary of the Proverbs of England* (Ann Arbor, Mich. 1950) p. 747, item W702, noting in particular a version cited in Giovanni Torriano's *Italian Proverbes* (1666): '*The Italian women are Saints in the Church, Angels in the street, Devils in the house, Sirens at the windows, Magpyes at the door, and Goats in the Garden,*' suggesting that life was still being lived then in Italy as much *al fresco* as in the earlier century of Boccaccio's Nightingale. (The same proverb is alluded to by the Italian lexicographer, John Florio, in his *Second Frutes,* 1591, in abbreviated form.) Curiously enough, the first reference to the 'parlor' — still present in the modern joke form — is that of Shakespeare's rewritten form of the proverb, in *Othello* (about 1604) II.i.110: Iago's '*Come on, come on; You are pictures out of doors, Belles in your parlours, wildcats in your kitchens, Saints in your injuries, devils being offended, Players in your housewifery, and housewives* [hussies] *in your beds.*' (Adding, "*You rise to play and go to bed to work.*") This is so close to the modern form that it is possibly its direct source, which may mean that the joke is *not* to be considered as in oral transmission so far back as the 16th century

The original proverb, however, is indeed ancient, and it is this which is really being transmitted. A Hindu form dating from about the 2nd century A.D., in the scriptural law-text *Manusmrti,* III.ii.5–6, is quoted by the Austrian writer on Tantric Buddhism, now known under the monastic name of Agehananda Bharati, writing in the columns of *Playboy* (August 1966) p. 146, in a letter on the subject of prostitution and sexual ' "standards" (double *or* single) . . . The whore is attractive to the male because she reputedly knows more of the refined pleasures of sex; but once refined sexual knowledge becomes commonplace, the whore becomes increasingly redundant. The Hindu scriptures taught (1500 years ago, alas, before the rise of Gandhian puritanism) that the noble housewife should be *"grheshu lakshmi, shayaneshu veshya"* — *"in her home, the goddess of splendorous wealth; in her bed, a whore"* — admonishing the nobility to see to it that their wives learned and enjoyed the art of love, so that the prostitute became superfluous.' That is obviously both the proverb and joke, and it is significant that the reference to *money:* the 'economist in bed,' once the 'goddess of splendorous wealth,' has remained unchanged for fifteen centuries or more.

Actually, the oldest form of this sort of ringing-the-changes of praise on the character of the wife, is that of the matriarchal last chapter of *Proverbs,* xxxi. 10–31, beginning: *'Who can find a virtuous woman? For her price is far above rubies.'* (With several other monetary references.) Although attributed to King Solomon, the last two chapters of *Proverbs* are stated in their opening lines to be by other authors, and probably date from about the 6th century B.C. The final chapter, in praise of the Ideal Wife, is laid out mnemonically, as a psalm or pæan, each sentence beginning with a consecutive letter of the alphabet in Hebrew. Every possible virtue is ascribed to the wife, *except* any direct reference to her sexual charm. However, it is stated in line 28: *'Her children arise up and call her blessed; her husband also, and he praiseth her,'* which is thought to be a politely total statement of her sexual rôle. This is one of the few passages of literature this ancient still in living transmission (memorized), since all religious Jewish husbands are required to *sing* this alphabetical song, as praise of or an example to their wives, as part of the Sabbath liturgy on Friday night.

VIII. OLD AGE

1. OLD WIVES FOR NEW

The presumed impotence of the aging husband, and the probable sexual unattractiveness of the aging wife, create what are unquestionably the most anxiety-ridden years of marriage, beginning at the onset of the wife's menopause. Much of the folk material concerning male impotence actually stems from the projection on the husband of the wife's menopausal sexual collapse, especially where this simply is a continuation of the wife's lifelong female impotence, or 'frigidity' as it is usually termed, also almost always an expression of hostility against the husband, or men in general. A man in his fifties, if he is tolerably well preserved and has kept his hair — and particularly if he spends money and has other of the appurtenances of affluence: fine automobile, etc. — will, if he shows any interest, be entirely *covered,* in Western culture, by young women from eighteen to thirty years of age, with whom he comes into contact in his business or profession (such as, for instance, college teaching, or any large business office), who are more than willing to sleep with him or even set up housekeeping with him on the side, fully recognizing that he is married and probably never can or never will marry them. This is certainly an expression of the normal father-complex in such young women (especially when the man involved is 'the Boss' or employer), and also involves a certain clear rejoicing in the triumph over the mother-image that the man's wife represents.

On the other hand, a woman in her fifties — in fact, a woman in her forties — unless she is of outstanding attractiveness and personal gifts, is likely to find herself of sexual interest not only not to her husband or any other man, but also not even to herself. Except at the narcissistic level of cosmetics and 'beauty' treatments, and the endless compulsive buying of clothing and shoes (or housewares and furniture, if she identifies her body with her home) — activities always expressive of the neurotic anxiety that one is really very ugly or worthless without these assists, as the advertisers well understand and cynically exploit — almost any married woman's sexual life is likely to be prematurely ended, often in her thirties. As is well known, this will generally throw the woman back, or may be the result of her having been thrown back, upon an intrusive sub-sexual interest in her own children for the satisfaction of her emotional needs, repressively if the child is a daughter, smothering and overprotective (since necessarily non-genital) if a son. This has become classic.

The ultimate humiliation for a woman of any age is, of course, to have to pay for the sexual company of a young man or 'gigolo,' whereas a man — since essentially he has always been paying for the sexual company of women, including that of his wife — can generally carry off this humiliation by posing in his own mind as a benefactor or protective 'daddy' to the young women exploiting him. In a riddling joke, probably of European (Hungarian?) origin, but now known in the U.S. through the rich international underground of Hollywood folklore — *not* the stuff appearing in the movies — the question is put: "*What are the four times in her life that a woman blushes?*" *Answer:* "*Well, the first time, of course. Then, the first time with somebody besides her husband. And then — the first time she does it for money!*" *When the listener* bites, *and asks,* "*What about the fourth time?*" "*Oh yes, that's the first time she has to pay for it herself.*" (N.Y. 1950, attributed to the Hungarian playwright, Ferenc Molnár.)

Very much of a woman's joke is one that is the contrary of the riddle preceding, and, like it, very 'mathematical.' This is now furnished with a modern dovetail-reply or topper to a 19th century witticism which has been attributed to both Heinrich Heine and Douglas Jerrold, probably falsely in both cases since it appears in anti-clerical form in Des Périers' *Nouvelles Récréations* (1558) No. 34: *A priest is told that his housemaid should be at least fifty years old. He gets one twenty years old and another thirty.* This is also known in India. (Motif J2212.1.1.) A Rumanian form, in which the woman does the choosing, is noted at Aarne Type 1362B: '*A husband on his deathbed advises his wife to marry a man of forty. She prefers two of twenty each. It all comes to the same.*' The modern German or English form is not told as a joke, but is expressed as a bit of folk-wisdom — essentially a male brag: "*My idea of a wife at forty is that you should be able to take her to the bank, and trade her in for two twenties.*" The topper: "*Are you sure you're wired for two-twenty?*" (Kingston, Pa. 1963, sprung on me — though I had not made any such brag — with the statement that it was already an 'oldie,' by my younger sister, on learning that I planned to remarry at the age of forty-six.) As a footnote for history, 'two-twenty' is a reference to the newer and stronger 220-volt alternating current of household appliance electricity, the old-fashioned current being only 110. The hidden allusion to 'wire,' meaning the male erection, is not conscious or even known to all tellers of this joke. This was followed in the telling, though not strictly relevant, by the gag-definition that *A wife is something you screw on the bed to get the housework done.* (N.Y. 1938, and often since.) As always, the use of the neuter 'thing' in referring to a woman as sexual object is intensely hostile, and even more hostile here in that her sexuality is considered the *least* interesting part of the wife, or only a bribe!

As a matter of fact, many wives at middle age, conscious of their loss of sexual attractiveness for their husbands, try to make up for this by concentrating on cooking good meals for them, and other regressions from the genital to the oral, *including* in bed. The concentration on cooking is sometimes cattily assessed by other women as "trying to fatten him up so the young girls won't want him," or, by men, as trying to make the husband feel "too stuffed after supper to go out chasing tail." The whole matter is summed up perfectly in a Pennsylvania Dutch wall-plaque I bought in 1963 in the heart of the Pennsy-Dutch country (made notorious by the late H. L. Mencken for the close proximity there of the little towns named *Peach Bottom, Gap, Intercourse, Paradise,* and *Blue Ball*), a plaque sententiously remarking: "*Kissing don't last. Cooking do.*" As this Pennsylvania Dutch wall-plaque is stamped on the edge, 'Made in Japan,' I could not be sure the sentiment is authentic, and have changed it to read — which I am sure is at least truth if not folklore — "*Kissing do last. Cooking don't.*"

The turning in of the old wife for two new ones is also only a modernization of the 17th-century cartoon idea, to be seen in German and Dutch engravings, of "The Mill for Grinding Old Wives Into New," usually showing the old wives being dumped unceremoniously into the hopper at one end and escorted gallantly away at the other, on having been reground. In the only modern form of this, a song sometimes called "The Donnerblitz (or Donderbeck's) Machine," the husband crawls into the monster-sized sausage-making machine, which is broken; his wife, who walks in her sleep, touches the starter-button thinking it is the light-switch . . . 'And Donderbeck was meat!' Although a pretext is still retained here to cover the wife's hostility (she is innocent — she just 'walks in her sleep'), it is no longer the pretext of rejuvenating her husband in the "Old Wives Mill." Charlie Chaplin has made the Donderbeck theme into the crucial scene in his finest motion-picture satire, *Modern Times,* in which he is sucked into the accidentally-starting grinding mill and shoves his head out at various apertures calling for help, while the old machinist attempts to ease this parody birth-from-the-machine with squirts from his oil can. I have been told that a 1930's film critic, more aware than most — Parker Tyler, I believe — who referred to this scene as a 'birth-fantasy' during a public lecture at the time of its appearance, was actually hooted by his audience. As every prophet knows: *'The main thing is not to be too far ahead of the public. One year ahead is the trick for making money; ten years ahead is the trick for not making money; twenty years ahead is a sure way to get crucified.'* (Success-lecture, N.Y. 1948.)

As recently as 1963, in the pages of the *Journal of American Folklore,* well after the 'New Freedom' issue of that journal, July 1962, p. 187–265, devoted entirely to a "Symposium on Obscenity in Folklore;" a specialist in humor, Dr. Jan Brunvand, in his valuable "Classification for Shaggy Dog Stories," *JAFL,* vol. 76: pp. 45, 63, has a bit of quiet fun quoting out of context Dr. Martha Wolfenstein's Freudian discussion of a children's joke about *moth-balls* and being 'squashed,' in terms of the castration complex, though he neglects to mention anywhere that Dr. Wolfenstein's masterful two-page handling of the shaggy dog story in general, in *Children's Humor* (1954), p. 151–2, is the best and only meaningful discussion of the genre that exists. (It also is not cited in his bibliography.) Compare the related story on *golf-balls,* in the later chapter here, on Castration, under "*Vagina Dentata,*" with punch-line, "*I see you shot another golf!*" which even Dr. Brunvand would agree is concerned on a perfectly conscious level with castration fantasies.

2. IMPOTENCE OF THE HUSBAND

Too many of the jokes and witticisms on the theme of age and sexual impotence in the man are obviously jokes told mainly by men, for the conclusion to be avoided that these are mockeries of the presumed impotence of other men, by way of resisting and rebutting notions of one's own present or eventual impotence. The most perfect and elegant expression is that of the French proverb, *'Si jeunesse savait . . . ,'* equally well known in the English version: *If youth only knew; if age only could!* (Given as though a joke in *Anecdota,* 1933, no. 411.) A catty version of this, straining for wit, is attributed to George Bernard Shaw: *'Youth is too precious a gift to waste it on the young.'* Neither of these refer openly to sex, but that is what the proverb at least is cer tainly about. According to Bennett Cerf's *Try and Stop Me* (1945) p. 160, '*In London, a certain lord married a woman forty years his junior. Adele Astaire preserved for months the London* Times' *account of the ceremony, which ended with, "The bridegroom's gift to the bride was an antique pendant".*' (This was revived and went the rounds in America in 1952 on the occasion of the marriage of a well-known el derly stateman.) The subject of such real and apocryphal newspaper howlers and boners is too large to handle here, and has its own litera ture, especially in French: the volumes of Albert Aycard & Jacqueline Franck's *La Réalité dépasse la fiction* (Paris, 1955 *ff.*); and compare Fritz Spiegl's *What the Papers didn't mean to say* (Liverpool: Scouse Press, 1965). A 'department' of this kind is planned for *Kryptádia* (New Series), the Journal of Erotic Folklore being prepared for publi cation under the editorship of the present writer.

Always told as a true story nowadays, the following is assimilated to whatever much-married playboy is principally in the news. The un disguised pun is, in fact, just the sort of thing considered perfectly acceptable at wedding feasts. *Wedding toast of the latest bride of a much-married playboy:* "*It's been hard for some of the others, but it's pretty soft for me.*" Wilstach's *Anecdota Erotica* (MS. 1924: copy, NYPL 3*) and Fliesler's *Anecdota Americana* (1927) 1:385, both ascribe this to the fourth wife of Nat Goodwin, a California restaurateur; it was commonly collected as concerning Tommy Manville during the 1930's. Wilstach artlessly gives away the actual folk origin by preceding his celebrity-conscious version with the simpler riddling form: "*What did the Sultan of Turkey say to his third wife when he married her?*" "*It's pretty soft for you.*" By 1952 this was collected in Berkeley, Calif. in the then-popular 'Little Moron' format: "*Did you hear about the Little Moron who married three wives? — Two of them had it pretty soft.*" Connected with the persistent ascription of stories of this kind to named individuals are the non-joking folktales that the playboy's sumptuous wedding dinner was followed by erotic movies in technicolor, or with the bridegroom performing cunnilinctus on his bride before the assem bled guests. This is strictly in the style of the *exposé* magazines of the 1950's, and with about equal proportions of truth and embroidery. Compare, however, section 8.v.4 above, "Cunnilinctus and Masochism."

In an even milder form, verbally, but more vicious in tone, '*A young girl who had married an old man was asked how she liked liv-*

ing with him. "*Oh, it's the same thing, week in, week out,*" *she an-swered.*' (*Anecdota,* 1933, no. 498.) A humorous greeting card bought in Washington, D.C. in 1940 — long before the present conversion of 'novelty' cards of this type to the 'hate cards,' or 'sick cards' as they are euphemistically called, in both America and France — gives the matter as a little mathematical set-up. Observe the 'pessimism of impotence':

> Under 25 — Twice daily.
> 25 to 35 — Tri-weekly.
> 35 to 45 — Try weekly.
> 45 to 55 — Try weakly.
> 55 and on — Try, try, try.

(Also given in the Guam mimeograph, *Smile and the World Smiles with You,* 1948–52, p. 11.) In connection with the wedding of the elderly statesman mentioned earlier, who, presumably at the age of seventy, had married his secretary of thirty-five, the mathematical rid-dle circulated: "*How many times does* seventy *go into* thirty-five? — *Seventy times! Once on the bed and* sixty-nine *on the floor.*" (D.C. 1952. French version as "*Prétention*" in Perceau's *Histoires d'Hommes et de Dames,* 1913, p. 73.) It will be observed that oragenitalism as the last resort of the aged and impotent male is also present in the folk-tales-told-as-true of the playboy's public cunnilinctus at his wedding party. The implication is that the male tellers of such jokes and 'true' stories have fixed it in their minds, and are fixing it in the minds of their listeners, that the inevitable impotence of old age is not really so bad, as there is always the oragenital solution for satisfying the bride. Obviously it is not the satisfying of the man that is in question at all. I have been specifically told this myself, and not as a joke but as serious wisdom or advice. "You're going to have a very interesting old age," I was told, in allusion to my little manual on the technique of cunnilinc-tus, *Oragenitalism: Part I* (1940, now being revised and enlarged with the promised *Part II: Fellation and the Sixty-Nine*) — written in my early twenties when I was hardly impotent — on announcing the en-larged reissue of this, in *Fact* magazine (July 1965) vol. II, no. 4: p. 42, as 'planned in 1969, as part of the celebration of the International World's Fair of Love, to be held, I believe, in Paris in that year.'

As quite a number of people have been glad to take this reference quite seriously, I wonder if it should really be left as a joke? As a mat-ter of fact, under the title of the "First International (why not Inter-

planetary?) World's Fair of *Population Problems,*" or some such substitute for the taboo term 'LOVE,' battening on the usual insincere *kitsch*
of such manifestations, this would actually be a billion-dollar idea. One
can just see the advertisements for all the airlines: *"Fly United!"* and
"Paris in '69 — and Vice Versa!" All the bills would gladly be paid by
the contraceptive manufacturers' pavilions, Pill-peddlers, insurance
companies (toting up the future consumers on mammoth adding-
machines — or has this been done?), and the like; the main world
Churches would certainly be in favor of it, especially for the even-more-
rapidly-increasing non-white populations, as usual; and the sex-job
they would do on the entertainment midway would put a new diamond in Little Egypt's rotating belly-button, the never-to-be-forgotten
star and cynosure of the Columbian Exposition of 1892 — only this
time they would show it bare.

I am offering this idea *free* to the governments of the world. Cheap
science-fiction novelists please keep off. I do not want a dime. I do not
want a free ticket (except to the midway — to collect folklore, of
course.) I do not want the concession for the Scandinavian Bottomless-
Waitress Smörgåsbord bars, which will have to be seen to be believed.
I do not even want a 1% royalty on all paid admissions, though I admit
I deserve it. It is a gift. I particularly refuse any position as Member
of the Planning Committee. If nominated I will not run: if elected I
will not serve. This is my gift to humanity. Motto (which I have
swiped from the underground Los Angeles student movement, which
swiped it from me, who swiped it from the *Song of Songs*): MAKE
LOVE NOT WAR. Or: *'Love is strong as death.'*

Say what you will, this would certainly draw better than the current pipsqueak World Fairs of plastic sports cars (with built-in machine gun), blown-up photo *kitsch,* and deep-freeze grapefruit juice,
which are outstinking even the former garbage dumps they are planted
on in Toronto and Queens. Finally, this may not solve the world's
population problem. I admit that. In fact, just the Educational Pornographic Moving-Picture Pavilion, artistically showing what is *causing*
the population explosion (and of which I am sole owner and conces-
sionaire, though I angrily deny this as Chairman of the Planning
Committee), would probably up the said explosion right out of the
mammoth adding-machines — and among the white race this time.
But at least it's a hell of a lot better approach to the solution than the
Atom Bomb, which is the only *other* idea these latter-day Malthusians
running the world seem to have got.

3. PROSTITUTES PREFERRED

The hostile tone of the jokes about impotence deepens from here on. *An old actor marries a young bride. The next morning she apologizes for her asthma during the night. He, greatly relieved: "Oh, is that what it was? I thought you were hissing me."* (1:242.) Open references to the lack of erection which is the most alarming symptom of male impotence are very wry and self-deprecating, certainly not ascribable to anyone but men worrying about the subject. *An old man marries a young girl acrobat, so she can do a handstand while he dunks it (or: drops it in.)* (1:188.) This was revived during the 1950's at one of the final marriages of a well-known 'New Freedom' autobiographer. In another, less hopeful version: *'An old man married a young wife. They used to play around till he got an erection, then bet which way it would fall.'* (Berkeley, Calif. 1952.) In the overcompensatory vein: *An old man leaving his favorite prostitute says, "See you again in three months." "You old reprobate, don't you ever think of anything but cunt?"* (2:237.) — *An elderly roué at a brothel insists he wants his usual girl, Mamie, who happens to be occupied. The madam vainly offers him various other girls, and finally asks, "Well, what has Mamie got that the other girls don't have?" "Patience."* (N.Y. 1940, often collected.)

These references to the resort by elderly men to prostitutes are very interesting since they give the lie, quite unconsciously, to the parallel idea that the older man is necessarily impotent and cannot satisfy his wife, must have recourse to oral substitutes, etc. The resorting by the man to prostitutes comes much closer to the usual truth of the matter: that the aging wife resents and resists sexuality, which may long have been a neurotic torment to her. See, in the devastating gallows-humor of Dr. Eric Berne's *Games People Play* (1964) p. 98–131, his chapters on Marital and Sexual Games, beginning with the politely expurgated "Frigid Woman" — for the colloquial "Cock-Teaser" — and ending with "Uproar," which is only funny to those who have never lived it. The essence is, as Dr. Berne puts it in his brilliant parody of the style of *Hoyle on Whist* or *Culbertson on Contract Bridge*: 'The use made of "Uproar" [fighting] distinguishes "Frigid Woman" from "Beat Me Daddy," where "Uproar" is part of the foreplay; in "Frigid Woman," "Uproar" *substitutes* for the sex act itself. Thus in "Beat Me Daddy,"

"Uproar" is a condition of the sexual act, a kind of fetish which increases the excitement, while in "Frigid Woman," once "Uproar" has taken place, the episode is finished.' Or even more succinctly, p. 131, when he notes that these perverted games 'may be played between any two people who are *trying to avoid sexual intimacy*' (italics supplied).

A joke which at first sight appears to be on the subject of prostitution, is actually an elegant attack on the unsatisfactoriness of marriage for the husbands of wives old enough to have grown-up sons. *A young man sees his father coming out of a notorious brothel. "Father!" he says, shocked. "Son," says the father, "say nothing. I prefer the simulated enthusiasm of a paid prostitute to the dignified acquiescence of your mother."* (N.Y. 1936.) This is stylistically the best-constructed punch-line in the present volume, and is of the sort usually ascribed to Dr. Samuel Johnson, alive in folklore nearly two centuries after his death strictly as hero of all rhetorical colloquies of this kind — except this one. It has, however, its literary origins in at least Johnson's century, in the great *Dictionnaire historique et critique* (1697–1702) of Pierre Bayle, the forerunner of the Rationalist *Encyclopédie,* which, as differentiated from Bayle's magnificent one-man effort, took a whole committee to write it — as have all encyclopædias since.

In his excellent new translation of selections from Bayle (Indianapolis: Bobbs-Merrill, 1965), Prof. Richard H. Popkin remarks in a prefatory Note, p. xli–ii: 'Every student of Bayle will surely be sad to see that some of his favorite entries are missing. All sorts of fascinating articles, such as "Ovid", "Eve", "Ham", "Héloise" . . . had to be omitted, as well as the fantastically lewd one, "Quellenec".' This is on the subject of the courts of inquiry into conjugal impotence. Even more to be deprecated is the omission of Bayle's supplementary apology, or defense against his censors and detractors, *"Sur les Obscénités,"* which has been published separately by the younger Gay (Bruxelles, 1879) also as a defense — of Gay's publishing of erotica — and to which attention has been drawn, as the first recognition of the *subjective* or reflectional nature of obscenity, in Theodore Schroeder's *"Obscene" Literature and Constitutional Law* (1911), and more recently by Henry Miller. Prof. Popkin continues: 'Many articles containing some of Bayle's best bon mots were omitted. Obviously an editor must feel disheartened when he must leave out entries containing such observations as, "A girl who has been deflowered is like a wine that has lost its spirit," or "As the insensibility of a chaste wife is very disagreeable, so the ardor of a lewd mistress is a marvelous relish; this is an unfortunate cause of conjugal infidelity".' This is not *quite* the same thing — even in the more ornate prose of the two earlier English translations of Bayle made in the 1730's — as saying: "*I prefer the simulated enthusiasm of a paid prostitute to the dignified acquiescence of your mother,*" but it is stylistically very close. In the final modern descent, the joke loses even its orotund climactic line; *Anecdota Americana* (1927) 1:414, has *The son who meets his father in a brothel and begins to upbraid him.*' "*Well*," said he, severely, "*to find my own father in a place like this. Have you no respect for me? None for your marriage vows?*" "*Don't be angry, sonny,*" said the old man. "*You wouldn't have me wake up Mamma this hour of the night for a dollar, would you?*"' This is to be understood as meaning to *save* a dollar, a rock-bottom price even then.

Bayle also adds the important extra point as to the aphrodisiacal 'relish' of the 'ardor of a lewd mistress,' suggesting again that the impotence of the aging male can easily be precipitated by the frigidity of the female, at a point where she may unconsciously not want to enter her menopause alone. This is obviously a matter to be considered by the aging man who, on his side, may no longer be able to afford emotionally or physically the gallant matrimonial hammering away uselessly at the 'insensibility' of his wife, chaste as she may be, on which he may have spent ineffectual decades of love. (Mock book-title: "*I Was Ruined By My Wife's Frigidity!*") This is touched upon in perfect symbolic disguise in a perfectly proper joke, also turning on an elegant rhetorical chiasmus or spoonerism: '*A husband no longer young, attempting to carry his wife across the threshold on coming home from a romantic play, found he staggered under her weight. "I see you're not as gallant as when you were a boy," she chided him. "No," he said, "and you're not as buoyant as when you were a gal".*' (Unidentified American magazine clipping of about the 1920's.) This clearly is intended to say volumes as to what *could not* be printed in American magazines of the 1920's. The metonymic allusion to 'carrying the bride across the threshold' (which really means crossing the threshold of the bride, doesn't it?) as a further allusion to marital intercourse, is also part of the heavily coded or *lingua franca* intention of this whole 'clean' joke, which also manages neatly to indicate that it is changes in the wife's physical body that have tired the husband.

Infinitely less deft, but on precisely the same theme, and even using the same rhetorical device of spoonerism: '*Aging woman to her husband: "I'd like to do it tonight, but I'm afraid my back might peter*

out." Husband: "So would I, but I'm afraid my peter might back out".'
(Va. 1952, supplied by an aging folklorist as 'collected in the field,' but
with sinful evidences of having been concocted by himself.) A novelty
greeting card bought in Washington, D.C. 1940, makes the same allusion in the authentic if non-oral folklore form of 'friendship album'
verse:

> Friends may come, and friends may go,
> And friends may peter out.
> But you and I will always be friends —
> Peter in, or peter out!

4. APHRODISIACS AND ORGASM

References to the semen are not common in Western folklore, and
are semi-consciously considered one of the most violent flauntings of
taboo in erotic literature. In connection with male impotence, such
evidences as lack of erection, lack of seminal ejaculation, and *slowness
or inability to arrive at orgasm* become of signal interest, and none of
these can be overlooked. Even so, reference to the inability to arrive at
orgasm ('orgastic impotence') is often used to cover, or make unnecessary through negation, any reference to the taboo semen. *"What'cha
doin', Grandpaw, jerkin' off?" "No, Son, just jerkin'."* (Scranton, Pa.
1936.) This also belongs, of course, to the important group of anti-
family or anti-gallant folklore and parody, which is more common in
rhymed form, as in "Little Willie's" (sadistic but 'clean') and the
dismal recitation, "A Letter from Home," of which the climax also
attacks the enfeebled proto-father-figure of the grandfather: *"Mine's
a cheerful occupation — cracking ice for Grandpa's piles!"*

*An old millionaire who marries a chorus-girl, undertakes to have
intercourse with her three times every night or forfeit a hundred thousand dollars to her. By way of aphrodisiacal treatment he soaks his
penis in heavy cream in the privacy of the bathroom, after every act
of intercourse, to prepare himself for the next. The chorus-girl realizes
she is losing the wager and peeks through the keyhole to see how he
is beating her. "The son of a bitch!" she says, "he has a self-filler!"*
2:56, actually a reference to a type of fountain pen.) Rationalized version in *Sex to Sexty* (1966) 6:38, in which the hostile element is reduced to a travelling salesman dipping his 'talleywhacker' in a glass
of buttermilk to alleviate a bee-sting. This is first printed in Perceau's
Histoires d'Hommes et de Dames (1913) p. 48, as *"Le Bonheur con-*

tinue," entirely lacking any hateful tone, but that tone has crept in again since, in connection with venereal disease (the bee-sting?): *Two soldiers who have picked up two housemaids on their night off and have gone to a low hotel with them, go to the bathroom after intercourse to take prophylactic injections by means of army-issue tubes of mercury ointment squeezed into the penis. The girls arrange to peek over the transom, one holding the other on her back. "Better get in bed again," says the girl who can see; "they're refilling them."* (Paris, 1953.)

A young Yugoslav woman singer in New York in the 1930's told as true a long and detailed story describing *The luxuries and specialties of Viennese prostitutes, of which the climactic luxury was for the client to phone the girl two hours before he would arrive and she would fill her vagina with pebbles (or marbles) heated in boiling water and mixed with heavy cream, to be removed only the moment the client would arrive.* The boys in the phonograph store that this girl hung around, near Carnegie Hall, nicknamed her "Stroganoff" ever after, in reference to the Russian meat dish over which sour cream or yoghurt is thrown just before serving. It does not require psychoanalysis to unveil the oral regression here palpable to record-store clerks. An even more candid example of this sort of female food-fantasy, frankly mixed with sex, grass, and flowers *à la* Lady Chatterley, and heavy cream (why cream?), appears in Liza Williams' column in the irrepressibly 'free' *Los Angeles Free Press* for March 11, 1966, p. 12, beginning: 'All places marked by food and love . . .'

> I should like to sleep in a bed of Jewish doublewhipped cream cheese, squeeze it between [?] my armpits, smear it on my belly, kiss it into mounds of fleshly love. I get lost in the sensuality of food, colours, smells, textures, all the world to copulate. Grass is to sing between fingers, shove in ears, wheat to plait through hair and caress the sensitive undersides of elbow and knee.

(Now that's what *I* call preparing an interesting old age for oneself: making love smothered in cream cheese — 'like mother used to make' — and with plenty of luxurious hot baths occasionally.)

The doctor or marriage counsellor is the court of last resort for the impotent, but, like all father-figures, scant comfort. *An old man consulted a doctor because of some white discharge that had come out of his penis in the morning. "How old are you?" asked the doctor. "Seventy-two, and I haven't had intercourse with a woman for a month."*

"But you did have it a month ago?" "Yes." "That's it — you're coming." (Transcontinental train, told by a St. Louis attorney, 1943.) In a European story related to this by form in a number of ways, though actually the subject is 'female impotence' (frigidity) rather than male, *A young married woman is perturbed by her pubic hair turning a powdery red. The marriage counselor is puzzled. "How often do you have intercourse with your husband?" "Oh, just like everybody else." "Well, how often? Twice a week?" "Oh, no!" "Twice a month?" "No!" "Twice a year?" "Sometimes . . ." "I see," says the marriage counselor; "there's nothing to worry about — it's rust."* (Paris, 1959, told by a young Danish girl, whose delivery of the climactic word *"Sometimes"* was a masterpiece, done with self-deprecating squirms of pretended loathing.)

Slowness or inability to reach orgasm is a form of impotence or sex-change arriving at an earlier age than any of the others, and is usually passed off by the man involved — sometimes on himself as well as on the woman — as a nicety of his 'technique,' or as considerateness in attempting to wait for her orgasm. When, however, this is added to the inability ever to repeat intercourse in the same night, the situation is clear, especially in view of the commonness of brags as to number of *times* the autobiographical Casanovas allegedly engage in one night. (The historical Casanova gloried in the self-applied nickname or agnomen of *'Monsieur Six-fois'*: Mr. Six-times.) In actual fact, after four or five orgasms within a period of several hours a man will usually 'fire a blank,' *i.e.* emit no semen at orgasm, the seminal vesicles being empty. If he insists on continuing after this warning, the next orgasm will generally be achieved slowly and with difficulty, and be accompanied by a feeling of 'pelvic retching' and the exudation of a serous fluid resembling blood. This happens most often in very young men, for instance in their late teens, who do not know when to stop, but they generally stop there.

The 'firing of a blank' is the subject of one of Balzac's imitations, in *Les Contes drolatiques,* of the style of Boccaccio. Observe the different approach to these images in the following joke, worked up into a brief tale in the McAtee ms. (1937, Library of Congress, env. 8) entitled "One 'Catridge'." *An elderly man takes out a waitress who has 'permitted one of her breasts to repose momentarily on his shoulder' while taking his order. He holds off orgasm by the usual methods of doing multiplication in his head, viewing the landscape, etc., and by telling her a little tale about a boy and his grandfather out squirrel-*

hunting. The old man keeps aiming his rifle and putting it down again with chortles of content, but never actually shoots. Later the boy asks him why. "Well you see, sonny, it's this a-way. I love squirrel-huntin' better than anything in the world, but I had only one catridge." Less charming identifications of hunting and sex will be found in a curious and repellent story by Cyril Hume in *Collier's* magazine (1947), and throughout the African stories and reminiscences, and the bull-fighting puke of Ernest Hemingway, as is very well known. (See my *Love & Death,* 1949 and reprints, p. 86–92, in the final section "Open Season on Women.")

Dr. Roger Abrahams gives two Negro versions of the following story, in *Deep Down in the Jungle,* p. 203–5, collected in Philadelphia about 1960 — in which a great deal of emphasis is placed on the scheming of an old woman to substitute herself for a girl in a man's bed — and discusses his reasons for classifying this under Thompson and Rotunda's Motif K1317, "Lover's place usurped by another," in one of its subdivisions. Actually the story is *about* the subject indicated by its last word, and should really be classified formally as a scatological catch-tale; but in its real meaning the story is concerned with impotence, in this case female. *An old woman substitutes herself for a girl waiting for her lover in bed. She carefully says nothing during intercourse to prevent the man from recognizing the fraud, but cannot prevent herself from farting continuously out of pure enjoyment. Finally the man says, "What the hell is that stink?" "I'm sorry, sonny," she says, "I'm too old to come so I just shit."* (N.Y. 1945, told as a pretendedly real occurrence on picking up a prostitute during the London wartime blackout.)

It will be seen that the form the impotence takes here is really more male than female, since it is not old age that makes women impotent. The incestuous element is also very prominent in Abrahams' highly dysphemistic texts, in which much is made of the fact that the old woman is actually a grandmother (the girl's). The whole thing suggests a regressive identification of orgasm and defecation, at the level of a child's cloacal sexual theories. Compare the folk-phrase '*Not to know whether to shit or go blind,*' as meaning to be utterly flummoxed and confused, and not know how to react, as in Randolph's No. 100, quoted below under "The Relationship with the Other Man." The sex of the impotent person is interchangeably stated, in a less common and merely verbal variant of the present joke, to be male, which is of course more reasonable. This makes unnecessary the scatological climax, which is the most popular part, and the variant is — perhaps for that reason — seldom heard: *Prostitute, to an old man, after an hour of trying: "If you can't come, telegraph!"* (2:342, rallying an advertising slogan of the 1930's.)

5. OVERCOMPENSATIONS FOR IMPOTENCE

The overcompensatory gags as to old men having intercourse only once in several months (*"You old reprobate, don't you ever think of anything but cunt?"* 2:237) have already been mentioned. These are from the outside looking in. From the inside looking out, such *frequency* seems admirable indeed 'for a man of my years.' *Two old stage-door johnnies are discussing sex at the Lambs Club. "Do you still bother with women any more?" "Oh yes, once a month regular, except in July and August." "I suppose the heat bothers you then?" "No, that's the vacation of the man that puts me on and takes me off."* (N.Y. 1949.) This extraordinary and sub-homosexual image is also seen in the joke already given about *The unvirile rooster who never mounts the hens unless two hens get together and put him on a third.*

Randolph gives a story (*Pissing in the Snow*, No. 35) collected in Forsyth, Missouri, in 1940 from 'an elderly gentleman [who] doesn't want his name mentioned in connection with this story,' about *A man of eighty-two, 'but mighty spry for his age,' who is being kidded by the young fellows about his continuing potency. 'But Jeff just shook his head. "It ain't no fun to be old," he says, "because your memory always goes back on you ... Why, just last night I woke up with a hardon," says he, "so I roused my wife to have a little fun. But Mary says for me to shut up, because we have already done it twice, not thirty minutes before. And there was two towels laying on the floor, so I knowed she was telling the truth." Jeff looked mighty gloomy. "It's kind of sad, when a man gets so old he can't remember things like that," says he.'* (This has often been collected in various other states.)

In the Introduction to *My Secret Life,* reprinted from the original of 1888–94 in New York, 1966, in which I suggest that this remarkable Victorian sexual autobiography is the work of the erotic bibliographer, H. Spencer Ashbee, the question necessarily arises as to the veracity of such memoirs, especially in view of the anonymous author's almost excessive vaunting of his memory for sexual details of occurrences decades before. I note there: 'That the author has assimilated to his sexual potency the potency of his *memory* (probably in his fifties) is clear, as also that he is tempted to brag of his fabulous feats of memory in exactly the same way — and for exactly the same reason — that other men, suffering from similar feelings of sexual if not social inferiority, or both combined, like to tell of their "wonderful feats in coition." This type of sexually-displaced bragging, as to the power of one's memory (or the steely glance of one's eye, aim with a gun, or ability at driving a fast car), is all the more common in that the failure of memory (and coördination) is one of the commonest signs of advancing age in men, next after sexual impotence.'

It must also be axiomatic — though this is not remarked upon in the Introduction to *My Secret Life* — that all autobiographies, especially sexual, such as this one, or those of Casanova and Henry Miller, in which *actual conversations* of decades before are reported inside quotation marks, are NECESSARILY untrue, and can at best only be considered romances or autobiographical novels possibly based on actual fact. This can easily be proved by unobtrusively writing down the exact words in which any partisan of the literal truth of such memoirs states his contention in conversation, and then requesting him unexpectedly — only twenty minutes later — to repeat verbatim what he has said about the veracity of Casanova, Henry Miller, etc., while you *check him out* against the written record of what has occurred, not twenty years before but only twenty minutes. This can also be done in a tape-recorded interview, and is a very good way to lose friends.

In one case where I had the cruelty to try this, the True Believer gallantly recovered the ball with the remark: "I didn't say *I* had a photographic memory — I said Miller does!" When tried on any autobiographer himself, the matching reply would obviously be that though he has 'perfect recall' for anything that happened years before, he can remember very little now owing to the present failure not of memory but of attention, and that his *attention* was steely sharp (just like the glance of his eye, penis, etc.) in the period which his autobiography covers. This has a good deal of psychological validity to it, but does not cancel out any of the connotations of sexual bragging in autobiography — obviously undertaken in mature years — as overcompensation for fears of impotence, or as a simple sexual substitute.

Two final but perfectly pure overcompensations both import the dreaded doctor who is somehow suspected, as must be any authority-figure, of being responsible for the castration that impotence (and the equivalent death) must be considered, if only because he cannot cure the impotence complained of. This must therefore be brazened out or denied at the very moment of its being lamented. *Old gentleman of eighty, to doctor, "I think I must be getting impotent, Doctor." "Oh yes? When did you first notice any symptoms?" "Well, last night, and then again this morning."* (N.Y. 1951.) *Anecdota Americana* in 1927 gives a version (1:318) with a topper which does not seem to have survived. It follows on: '*"Well, I'm afraid there's no hope for you," the doctor replied. "You're much too old for this sort of thing." "Well, then, Doc," pleaded the old man, "give me something to take the ideas out of my mind."* Human as this plea may seem, and is, it is typically the mental position of the man just on the threshold of impotence, as the joke specifies. When impotence has actually supervened, sexual ideas are the occasion of intense anxiety and are therefore avoided by many men, though others expose themselves unwisely to continuous excitements, often on purpose — such as erotic literature and the company of desirable women — and are continuously overwhelmed by their repeated sexual failures. This is the secret problem of many self-constituted censors. Men in jail and in work and army camps, the navy, etc., similarly divide themselves rapidly into the wisely repressed and angrily unrepressed types, the second soon finding themselves in various sorts of trouble, particularly in connection with guilt feelings over homosexual practices to which they may find themselves forced, either internally or by cell-mates in prison.

It is a better solution to *avoid* impotence by regular and satisfactory intercourse with exciting women, and the full emptying of the seminal vesicles, possibly by means of anal digitation during intercourse or fellation. But this solution is of course difficult under the usual constraints of the monogamic system, for an aging married man, especially if he is not rich, except by the humiliating recourse to prostitutes. The following is usually told in long-drawn-out form, almost shaggy dog style, as an uninterrupted Joycean monologue (on which see James Moffett's valuable synthesis, "Telling Stories," with quotations from Dujardin's earlier *Les Lauriers sont coupés*, in *Etc.: A Review of General Semantics*, San Francisco, Calif. 1964, XXI. 425-50): "*Doc, I got something I want to ask you. When I was a young fellow I used to wake up in the morning with my prick like an iron bar. I couldn't push it down with both hands. I had two little girls I was screwing, and the widow down the road that I delivered ice to, that used to give me a little money on the side, but just the same — every morning — like an iron bar! Then when I had my own ice-business there was this girl in the office, and the bookkeeper, and of course my wife. But every morning, like an iron bar! Couldn't push it down with both hands. Even two years ago, when I was judging that beauty contest and delivering the champagne and everything: girls? — I had to shove 'em out of bed, and I couldn't get that thing down with both hands. But just the other day I noticed that now I can push it down with both hands. I can even push it down with one hand. Do you think I'm getting stronger, Doc?"* (N.Y. 1953.) The same joke, but less poignantly: *Two elderly gentlemen talking. "Say, do you remember during the War when they used to give us that saltpetre in our coffee, to keep us from getting horny (from thinking about women)?" "Yes, why?" "It's just beginning to work on me."* (Scranton, Pa. 1938.) The 'one-hand' joke is also encountered in France as a catch 'proving' that old men are physically stronger than young ones. As always, Randolph gives the best English-language version, *Pissing in the Snow*, No. 68, "Follow Your Leader," heard in Arkansas in the 1930's: *An old man bets with a young one as to who is the better man, and both outdrinks and out-eats him. Finally, at the whore-house, with the whores prancing about naked, the 'old booger' ties his penis in a knot, and challenges the boy to do the same!*

6. DARBY & JOAN

The interrelation of the impotent aging man with his wife varies in jokes from straight rejection (*"What's the most useless thing on Grandma? — Grandpa!"* Guam mimeo. 1948, p. 1) to an auld-lang-syne acceptance. *An old colored woman who worked while her old husband did nothing explained to those who asked her why she kept him, "I guess I just keep him for the good he used to be."* (Lexington, Ky., 1952, from a married woman.) This is only a twenty-years-later version of a well-known social worker joke: *The social worker is shocked to see the Negro woman she is interviewing slaving over her washtub to support the family while her no-good man strums happily on a banjo. "You do all the work here, don't you, Elvira?" "Guess I do, ma'm." "And he doesn't do anything, does he?" "Oh yes he do, ma'm. He makes it wuth-while!"* (Scranton, Pa. 1936.) On the matriarchal position of the woman in the Negro family, and that of the 'husband' she does not marry, see Roger Abrahams' *Deep Down in the Jungle* (1964) p. 21–30, an important statement. Dr. Abrahams consistently avoids the term 'matriarchal,' and uses 'matrifocal' instead, p. 31 *ff.*: this has the air of being a learned jest on the Negro term *'mother-fucker,'* but is seriously intended.

The preceding joke is not considered a dirty joke, as the allusion to the man's sexual duties, when he is not 'strumming his banjo,' is sufficiently covert. The musical instrument is also in all probability to be considered symbolic, the man's finger-dexterity being sexually toned in the listeners' minds. I am indebted for this insight to the most analytically-oriented of American folklorists, Alan Lomax, who has suggested in private conversation, Newport, R.I., 1964, that this is the secret of the fascination of technical excellence in guitar playing (both Spanish flamenco and as 'folksong' accompaniment) to the young people who represent almost the entirety of the neo-folksong audience and fad. The rapid and dextrous fingering of the instrument is to be assimilated directly to the fingering of the woman's vagina and clitoris, as in many older metaphoric songs about *fiddlers* as seducers; and the long-necked stringed instrument itself is often consciously posed with phallically by the crude rock-&-roll singers, though, at its most profound level, it is really a female genital symbol. See, in corroboration, the two stanzas from "Duncan Macleerie," in Burns' *Merry Muses of Caledonia* (*c.* 1800; my *type-facsimile* edition, 1965, p. 58, and note p. 182 on further examples):

> Duncan Macleerie has got a new fiddle,
> Its a' strung wi' hair, and a hole in the middle;
> An' ay when he plays on't, his wife looks sae cheary,
> Very weel done, Duncan, quo' Janet Macleerie.
>
> Duncan he play'd 'till his bow it grew greasy;
> Janet grew fretfu', and unco uneasy.
> Hoot, quo' she, Duncan, ye're unco soon weary;
> Play us a pibroch, quo' Janet Macleerie.

Compare also, in the same source, p. 53, "John Anderson, My Jo," the frankest possible complaint of the old wife to the aging husband. This song is still alive in Scotland, and Hamish Henderson, of the School of Scottish Studies, Edinburgh, has recorded in the field, in recent years, a text very similar to that given in the *Merry Muses:*

John Anderson, my jo, John,
　　When first that ye began,
Ye had as good a tail-tree
　　As any ither man;
But now its waxen wan, John,
　　And wrinkles to and fro;
I've twa gae-ups for ae gae-down,
　　John Anderson, my jo.

Burns' polite and expurgated version of this is famous only in print (*Scots Musical Museum*, III. No. 260), with its over-sentimental final stanza, as given in George Thomson's de luxe *Select Collection of Original Scotish Airs* (1793 ff.) p. 51, which, with the further references to John Anderson's bald head and snow-white hair, and the '*canty* [lively] *day*' below, is all that Burns allowed himself in glozing the above-quoted stanza of the folksong for publication:

John Anderson, my jo, John, we clamb the hill thegither,
And mony a canty day, John, we've had wi' ane anither;
Now we maun totter down, John, but hand in hand we'll go,
And sleep thegither at the foot, John Anderson, my jo!

The aged couple in bed is not, perhaps, a cheerful spectacle, but the jokes try their best to make the whole situation of impotence — and the implication of approaching death — a bit more *canty* than Burns' John and Joan 'tottering' down the hill of life to sleep together at its foot, which is not really much of a program. *The old wife is vexed with her husband's impotence and tells him to call her "Mrs. Goldfarb" from now on, since they are not lovers anymore. In his sleep he accidentally jabs her in the back with his bony knee. "Quick, Sam," she says, "call me 'Becky' and I'll turn over."* (N.Y. 1953.) The wife's unsatisfied sexual appetite, even at so late a date, is obviously part of the whole wish-fulfillment by means of which the approaching impotence of the man is to be denied, since this is after all the same wife who has appeared in so many other jokes as uninterested in sex. If the husband does not respond, other excuses than impotence can be found. *Elderly couple in bed. "Well, do something," says the wife. "Honest, Becky, I'm too tired to think of anyone."* (1:174. Repeated in the McAtee MS., env. I, "The Cynara Complex.")

An even cruder rejection is the complaint about changes in the wife's body, specifically her vagina, usually politely disguised as that she has 'lost her figure' or by reference to 'middle-age spread' of her buttocks, or just general references to gaining weight, as in the 'gallant-boy and buoyant-gal' item already quoted. The direct form, *'Revived each year for Xmas,'* is the old favorite of the guy meeting a fellow on the street, loaded with packages. *"Christmas presents?" "Yeah." "You must have a big family." "Naw, just my wife." "Boy, all those presents! What a Christmas you must have — giving her all those, and she gives you a lot, too?" "Naw, I'll probably only get the same thing I got last Christmas ... pair of carpet slippers and a piece of ass — both of them too big".'* (Brooklyn, N.Y. 1965.) This really lays it on the line, especially in the open complaint as to the unfairness of the wife's undesirable sexual return for all the husband's monetary and material *largesse.* Not only is her body undesirable, but it is also offered or available too seldom, as is implied both in the idea of Christmas or holiday sexuality and in the throwaway line, *"And she gives you a lot* [*i.e.* of sex], *too?"* She is damned if she does and damned if she doesn't. This is similar to the World War I story of *Abie Kabibble in the German prison camp who writes to his brother-in-law in America: "The food here is absolute poison — and such* small *portions!"*

In the usual impotence stories, a frequent excuse for the hostility against the wife is, first, that her appetite can never fail — untrue, of course — and second, that it is precisely her continuing appetite which shames the aging husband, who would just as lief forget about the whole thing and not be confronted with his impotence. The hostility becomes frank when the wife's sexual role is described as excessively easy, or where her erotic needs at such an age are made to seem grotesque, as those of the husband never are. *Proverb, typically as a retort to a woman accusing a man of impotence: "It's a lot easier to lay on your back with your mouth open, than to stand with your arm sticking straight out for half an hour."* (Collected in Paris, 1954, and may be a translation from the French.) Compare: *Old wife, to her husband who is urinating under a tree at a picnic: "You shouldn't stand there where people can see your thing sticking out like that." "Don't you mean 'hanging out'?"* (D.C. 1952.) Note the implied phallic jealousy of the wife, which the husband attempts to evade by deprecating his own potency. More friendly, on the face of it, but actually intended to be disgusting: *Old wife, in bed: "Sam, reach me my false teeth from the glass. I just want to* bite *you!"* (N.Y. 1946; earlier in 1:279, giving the husband's name as Meyer.) The humorous old Jewish husband and wife, she being invariably 'Becky,' have become standard in American humor since the 1920's, in response to what has ineffably been called the 'Yiddishization of American comedy,' in a think-piece on American humor in *Time* magazine, March 4, 1966, international edition, p. 26/2. (They really mean Hitler's 'Yiddification,' but are afraid to be that frank about their unfashionable anti-Semitism, even under the cover of journalistic anonymity.)

In a very interesting story for which I am indebted to Mr. Joseph Rosner, the old Jewish wife attempts, as it were, to absorb or assimilate her husband's rejection of her, by identification with him in his adultery. I wish I had been able to take this down in full, as it was delivered, as no abbreviated version can do it justice. The punch-line is the least interesting part: everything is in the situation, in true folktale fashion. (Any similarity to the names of real persons is purely coincidental.) *The wife of an aging New York brassière manufacturer learns that her husband has a mistress and is planning to leave her and go to Florida with the younger woman. She confronts him in the bedroom where he is stuffing his socks into a suitcase. "So!" she says, "Mr. Sam Plotkin is going to Florida, and he is taking with him the socks Mrs. Becky Plotkin has bought him, and also darned. But let me ask one thing of Mr. Sam Plotkin. Will this beautiful redheaded* shicksa *of his darn him his socks? Will she prepare him stuffed cabbage with sour sauce and* kasha? *Or will she lay in bed at ten* A.M. *and make goo-goo eyes at some other men across the air-shaft, while Sam Plotkin is slaving to bring in the money?" Eventually, however, the wife is reconciled to the idea of the mistress, and saves her home by insisting that the mistress be moved in, instead of her husband moving out and "throwing away money on another apartment." She accompanies them one night to the opera, and from their family box sees that their business rival, Goldfarb, is sitting in the box opposite, also accompanied by his wife and a very handsomely dressed but suspiciously non-Jewish-looking young woman. "And who, may I ask, do I see sitting there with Mr. and Mrs. Goldfarb, Sam?" Her husband shushes her, and indicates that Goldfarb has a mistress too. Mrs. Plotkin examines Goldfarb's mistress up and down through her opera-glasses, and turns back to her husband to whisper loudly: "Y'know, Sam? I like ours better."* (N.Y. 1965.)

There is an inner joke at the final line which I had better explain before *Time* magazine beats me to it, and that is that the climactic 'ours' reduces the mistress to the status of a Negro housemaid, or *schwarze,* always so referred to at bridge-table conversations. (A Negro serving-woman of any age is still called a 'wench' in the American south, and even so far north as New Jersey, though this term has long since become obsolete in England, from which it came, as is also the case with calling a Negro male servant of any age a 'boy,' the word therefore being much resented by young Negroes.) The similarities between Jews and Negroes, as persecuted groups in the West, combined paradoxically with their bitter mutual animosity and exploitations, is a subject not relevant to the present work, though the parallels are traced repeatedly in their jokes, of which the survival-value to both persecuted groups is their principal function.

The situation of the wife's accepting her husband's adultery and refusing to allow her marriage to be destroyed by it is, of course, classic in real life, being based on the material self-interest grotesquely parodied by Mrs. Plotkin. It also involves, where the 'other woman' is actually brought into the house, a close relationship with her, evidently of the type of polygamy; and the wife's effort is then, equally classically, directed to deflecting her husband's unwanted sexual attentions to the younger woman while simultaneously retaining dominance in the 'harem' as senior wife. The sister-wife relationship with the 'other' woman, and the simultaneous *superior* position of the older woman, is very overdetermined in a joke given in *The Pearl* (Feb. 1880, No. 8, *ad fin.*) entitled "A Sensible Woman": '*Mrs. Johnson going into the cellar one day, caught her husband fucking the servant girl. A short time after, finding that Kate was packing her boxes to leave, she enquired the reason. Kate: "I couldn't think of stopping, mum, after what you saw in the cellar." Mrs. J.: "Go along, girl, do you think I mind? Perhaps with what you do in the cellar, and I do upstairs, we may keep the old whoremonger at home between us".*'

The Levantine position is very frank as to the avoiding or delaying of impotence in the man by means of the regular and satisfactory continuation of sexual relations, specifically with young and attractive women. This is made very pointed in the story of King David and Abishag the Shunnamite (whence the name of this practice, as 'Shunammitism') in 1 *Kings,* i. 1–4, and ii. 13–25, where we are told: 'Now king David was old and stricken in years; and they covered him with clothes, but he gat no heat. Wherefore his servants said unto him, Let there be sought for my lord the king a young virgin: and let her stand before the king, and let her cherish him, and let her lie in thy bosom, that my lord the king may get heat . . . And the damsel [Abishag] was very fair, and cherished the king, and ministered to him: but the king knew her not.' In this context, the biblical '*knew her not*' refers of course to genital relations, meaning that King David was already impotent. Abishag is therefore still a virgin after his death when Adonijah, one of David's sons, asks the mother of the new king, Solomon, to intercede with him to allow him to marry Abishag. As this would involve admitting openly that she is still a virgin (otherwise such a marriage would be incest), and thus disgrace the memory of King David, as impotent, Solomon flies into a violent fury at this request and has Adonijah killed. In a sado-masochistic modern survival of this legendary 'getting of heat,' told as true: *A Russian noblewoman out hunting has her feet frostbitten. A moujik is seized by her equerries, his stomach is ripped open with a knife, and her feet are warmed in his dying entrails.* As frostbite is treated with cold (rubbing with snow) not with heat, this is probably a fantasy.

The Levantine position on these matters has not changed an iota since King David. (1015 B.C.) A modern prince of the East, Mr. Nubar Gulbenkian — one of my neighbors — is quoted in the London *Sunday Times,* as reprinted in the banned mimeographed anthology, *The Golden Convolvulus,* edited by Arthur Moyse (Blackburn, Lancs. 1965) p. 21; discussing his own sexual beginnings in Paris at the age of sixteen, on the demand of his father and under medical supervision. Mr. Gulbenkian concludes: 'It was upon medical advice that my father himself had one young mistress, whom he changed every year until he was eighty [*nota bene*]. He used to say, and the late Lord Evans agreed, that while it is very unkind on a young woman to have sexual relations with an old man because she loses her youth, such relations do rejuvenate the old man. This was always recognised in the harems of the East.'

7. THE RETURN TO THE SCENE OF THE HONEYMOON

It is singular to observe the candor with which jokes finally confess to the husband's impotence. The older Jewish legends (a legend is an ethnic folktale accepted at some level as true) are unanimous in ascribing all childlessness to the wife's fault, except in the case of Tamar, in

Genesis, xxxviii. 9, whose husband, Onan, purposely 'spilled it on the ground, lest that he should give seed to his brother,' and who is killed by Jehovah therefore. The more usual case is that of Sarah, the aged wife of the patriarch Abraham, who, being childless, encourages her still-potent husband to take and impregnate the handmaid, Hagar, that thus 'I may obtain children by her,' absorbing and dominating the situation exactly in the style of the Russian-American Mrs. Plotkin in the preceding story. (The same maneuver is engaged in by both of Sarah's granddaughters-in-law, Rachel and Leah, in *Genesis,* xxx. 1–10, one of the many duplicate legends or overdetermination of themes in the Bible, as with the world-holocausts of both Noah and Lot.) Only when he is ninety-nine years old, in *Genesis,* xvii. 17–25, does Abraham seem finally to admit to being less potent than at the taking and impregnating of the Egyptian *schwarze,* Hagar, fourteen years before, when he was eighty-five. For when Jehovah announces to him that at last he and Sarah will have a son, 'Then Abraham fell upon his face, and laughed, and said in his heart, Shall a child be born unto him that is an hundred years old? and shall Sarah, that is ninety years old, bear?'

The modern rejuvenating situation or ritual is not thought of as divine, though admittedly miraculous, and is quite rigid not only in the jocular folktales but also in folk-life. The husband and wife are to *return to the scene of their honeymoon,* and there the husband will be rejuvenated and will find again his former potency, though the wife is no longer expected to regain her fertility and bear, as in the Greek legend of Philemon & Baucis so similar to that of Abraham and Sarah. Compare the 'mill' that grinds wives and husbands young again, which is similarly a *return to the womb.* Many localities, more particularly in Europe than in America, are believed to have this power of rejuvenation for men, or even the curing of barrenness (now frigidity) in women, and the boatloads of what are now called, in purest kitsch-advertising lingo, 'golden-age honeymooners,' never stop arriving at the traditionally rejuvenatory sacred erotic locales, such as Paris and Venice, it being understood privately that both the husband and (sometimes) the wife have the traditional carnival right of sexual license — with 'strange women' and gondola-pushers — to make sure the magic works.

I have lived in a town, Cagnes-sur-Mer, in France, where the complete form of this sort of surviving folk belief still existed at an underground level as late as the 1930's, involving intercourse by night in a ruined chapel on a nearby hill, assimilated formally to the worship of Saint Anne (the *mother* of the Virgin Mary), but actually understood to have once been the 'chapel of the fishermen' — and thus under the protection of Venus herself — though over a mile uphill from the sea! (The level of the water was unquestionably much higher in the millennia before the worship of the Virgin drove out that of Venus [Saint Anne], almost all the old towns of the French Riviera being on hilltops.) Sacred sexual rendezvous or night locales of this type are now more generally used in all countries by young people, under the names of 'Lovers' Lanes,' than by the old for rejuvenation purposes. The Bois de Boulogne in Paris is still considered to be rejuvenatory, though the vulgar take the position that the married couples seen there at night, searching in their big automobiles for ritual sexual orgies, are mere 'wife-swappers' — as though wife-swapping were *not* an erotic ritual. That such Lovers' Lanes and sacred woods, and the sexual intercourse there indulged in, are still believed to have magical power is shown in a remarkable passage in Vance Randolph's *"Unprintable" Ozark Folk-Beliefs* (MS. 1954) p. 33–40, concerning planting rituals, in particular the Ozark method of growing mammoth watermelons, which 'takes fucking and loud grunts,' and the direct use of human semen as fertilizer, as printed in full in my anthology, *The Guilt of the Templars* (New York, 1966) p. 99–100, to which the reader is referred.

It is the old couple's golden wedding anniversary. The husband tries to show his devotion as long ago, but fails. 'As she lay before him invitingly, more or less, he attempted to induce an erection. In vain he thought of Jessie Reed, Eva Brady, and other passion-provoking Follies beauties. In vain he manipulated his withered organ. He might be interested, but the man below [n.b.] *was not. At last he shook his head sorrowfully and said, "Fifty years ago, Becky, you was ashamed. Tonight, I'm ashamed".'* (1:277.) The McAtee manuscript (1944), envelope 1, gives a version of this as "The Cynara Complex." It is also sometimes collected with the ritual situation of the return to the physical locality of the original honeymoon. *The old husband is describing to his best friend his golden honeymoon trip with his wife to the little hotel in the Thousand Lakes where they had gone fifty years before as newlyweds. "And how did it work out?" the friend asks. "Just like the first time. Only, fifty years ago she went into the bathroom and cried. This time I went into the bathroom and cried." (La*

Jolla, Calif. 1965.) The Anglo-Saxon taboo against the open expression of emotions by a man — who here admits to crying — is transgressed in this case in response to the *force majeure* of impotence, as would also be the case at the equivalent death or a funeral.

Hostile and anti-gallant variants also exist. Larson records a version from Idaho Falls, 1946, in which *The golden wedding couple 'were retracing their steps of that memorable night fifty years before. Romantically they walked arm and arm out under the stars. Finally, however, they both had to stop to take a leak. "Mirandy, darling!" he declared, with his prick in his hand, "things haven't changed a bit . . ." "Fifty years ago," she replied, "you had to stick it under a limb to keep it from squirting in your eye! Now you have to hang it* over *a limb to keep it from running into your shoe!"* ' If the punchline did not make the hostile intention sufficiently clear, the anti-gallant *mise-en-scène* of the two old lovers pissing together in the moonlight (what Burns could have done with that!) already 'telegraphs the punch' at the very beginning. Compare the non-honeymoon example on 'sticking out' and 'hanging out,' in the preceding section. The anonymous Guam mimeograph, *Smile and the World Smiles with You* (1948–52), p. 10, returns to a good-humored ruefulness: '*A couple celebrating their golden wedding went back to the same hotel they spent their honeymoon and wanted to do everything they did then.* [Note the formal ritual.] *Dad was sitting on the bed. Mother said, "Dad, can you wait until I take off my stockings?" Dad said, "Hell, Mother, I can wait until you knit a pair."*

As the numerous forms in which this joke exists indicate, this is the principal jocular approach to the theme. It represents the form that the feared situation of impotence will take, which must therefore be sloughed off or 'laughed off' by joking about it. Observe that even the magical ritual return to the honeymoon scene does not ever 'renew our days as of old' (*Lamentations,* v. 21), and the prophecy of the pæan to impotence, that is *Ecclesiastes* xii, is fulfilled: 'Remember now . . . in the days of thy youth, while the evil days come not, nor the years draw nigh, when thou shalt say, I have no pleasure in them . . . In the day when the keepers of the house shall tremble, and the strong men shall bow themselves, and the grinders [*cf.* Samson's legend] cease because they are few . . . when the sound of the grinding is low, and he shall rise up at the voice of the bird, and all the daughters of musick shall be brought low . . . and desire shall fail: because man goeth to his long home, and the mourners go about the streets. Or ever the silver cord be loosed, or the golden bowl be broken, or the pitcher be broken at the fountain ... Vanity of vanities, saith the preacher; all is vanity.'

Almost unclassifiable is the elegant story for which I am indebted to my former publisher and friend, Mr. Seymour Hacker, in which one may suspect that the 'hotel lobby' of the setting is precisely the honeymoon hotel to which the old couple have returned, searching — uselessly, as it appears — for magical rejuvenation at the Fountain of Youth or some lesser spa. *An old couple are sitting in a hotel lobby when they hear a bellboy paging "Mr. Glasscock! Paging Mr. Glasscock! Will Mr. Glasscock please call at the main desk?" A moment passes. "You know," says the old man thoughtfully, "I knew a fellow once with a wooden leg, and he could dance as well as you or I."* (N.Y. 1953.) Aside from the visible and charming association-of-ideas, there is a great deal hidden in this story which is also relevant here, such as the identification of crippledness with castration or impotence, as in the legends of the patriarch Jacob and King Oedipus. To 'compare small things with great,' the same identification is present in Ernest Hemingway's repulsive reference, in one of his final, ineffectual novels, to being 'a sucker for crips,' in connection with superannuated army officers who twiddle small smooth balls compulsively in their pockets, or old men who wish to catch at last that one big fish before they die. Compare the tremendous Captain Ahab of Melville's *Moby Dick* (1851), roaming the seas for his revenge against the great white whale who has torn off his leg, and *in the skin of whose penis* — chapter 95, following the incredible chapter on sperm-squeezing — the victorious hunter will finally clothe himself. Another rather frivolous reduction of this theme is the pirate, Captain Hook, in Barrie's *Peter Pan* (1904), whose arm has been bitten off by a crocodile who is after the other arm — the *vagina dentata* opposite of Captain Ahab's revenge — but which must always warn of its dangerous presence by the alarm clock (the conscience?) in its stomach, which it has also swallowed.

Another association-of-ideas story which should perhaps not be separated from that preceding, and which also gives evidence of being concerned with a 'golden age honeymoon' couple returning to the scene of their first consummation: *'A Grand Canyon guide told a tourist couple that the canyon grew wider by two inches each year. Thoughtlessly, the man remarked that the coloring of its cliffs was just like his wife's complexion.'* (Berkeley, Calif. 1952.)

8. FUNERALS AND MOURNING

The final denials and overcompensations of impotence continue right up to the moment of death, which, it should be emphasized again, is unconsciously considered to be identical with impotence. ("I'd just as soon be dead;" or, "It will never rise again.") This is as true in life as in jokes, and the direct sexuality of the older man is never in any case as uncharming or as socially detrimental — nor even so 'unkind on a young woman,' as soberly admitted by Mr. Gulbenkian — as the aggressive substitutes which usually replace it: miserliness, both sexual and monetary, and especially the compulsive search for the money or power which are identified with sexual potency, though the money and power already possessed cannot all be used (as with aging millionaires, generals, and politicians); also guns and hunting, and the killing of innocent animals in massive numbers. This includes the hatred of the old men for the younger and sexually potent males of the same species, whom it is arranged to have killed in the wars engineered by the old men, who also preside with police power over the draft-boards sending the young men to their death.

Compare King David's secret orders in 2 *Samuel,* xi. 2–27, sending Uriah into 'the forefront of the hottest battle,' so that Uriah shall be killed and his wife, Bathsheba, whom David has seen washing herself on the roof (as with Susanna and the avowedly impotent 'elders' in the *Apocrypha*), be available to him. It is stated, in 2 *Samuel,* xi. 27, that 'the thing that David had done displeased the Lord,' but this does not prevent the son whom he has by Bathsheba, King Solomon, from ruling after him, and having the largest harem recorded in ancient history ('he had seven hundred wives, princesses, and three hundred concubines,' all assorted 'strange women' of many nations, according to 1 *Kings* xi. 1–9), from building the Temple at Jerusalem which is the most sacred relic of the Jewish religion, and from becoming the presumed ancestor of the Christian Messiah, according to the genealogy with which the New Testament opens (*St. Matthew,* i. 6–18). This traces the birth through 'Joseph the husband of Mary,' who was not, however, the father, for 'before they came together, she was found with child of the Holy Ghost;' which reduces the whole genealogy to mere brother-husband swank. Either the genealogy or the conception via the Holy Ghost must be false. (This is the first and worst crux of New

Testament criticism, as the whole divine origin of the Christian religion stands or falls on its resolution.)

Though the death of the husband is that which must follow in logical sequence, after his impotence has announced itself in old age, there are also jokes in which this is evaded by having the wife die instead. The spouse who dies is, in fact, interchangeable: it is the hostile rejection of the marriage tie, by imagining the death of either spouse, which is crucial. *A man at his wife's funeral becomes entirely hysterical, attempting to leap into the grave, and so forth. "Calm yourself," says a friend; time will pass. A month from now, a year from now, you'll meet somebody else, and everything will be all right." "A year from now?" screams the husband. "What about tonight?"* (N.Y. 1938.) This is unquestionably and exactly descended from a story first appearing in print in English in *A Hundred Mery Talys* (London, 1526) No. 8/10, "Of the Woman that followed her fourth husband's bier and wept," the sex of the spouse who has died having been reversed during the intervening centuries. In the older version, *The widow 'made great mone and waxed very sory in so moche that her neyghbours thought she wolde swown and dye for sorow, wherfore one of her gosseps* [female relatives] *cam to her and spake to her in her ere and bad her for Godds sake comfort her self and refrayne that lamentacion.'* We are not told what the gossip says in the widow's ear, but may be sure it was similar to the advice of the friend of the husband in the modern story, for she answers: *'I wys good gosyp I have grete cause to morne, if ye knew all, for I have beryed iii. husbandes besyde this man, but ... now I am sure of no other husband and therfore ye may be sure I have great cause to be sad and hevy.'* As a matter of fact she adds that she was, at each earlier funeral, *'sure of an nother husband before the corse cam out of my house.'* That is even a little rougher than the modern tale.

In a competing publication, *Tales, and Quicke Answeres* (the modern 'snappy comebacks'), published about 1535, No. 10, the modern form is even more closely approached, when *A father suggests to his widowed daughter at her husband's deathbed that he has another, richer husband ready for her and to stop her mourning. The daughter is very displeased at this, and continues in her sorrow. The husband dies and is buried, and after his soul-mass has been sung the girl turns to her father, 'between sobbing and weeping,' and whispers in his ear, "Father, where is the same young man that ye said should be mine husband?"* Compare also the further variations on this theme in the

Italian *novelle* cited by Rotunda, K2052.4, "The oversensitive or hypocritical widow."

In a curious story collected in America only once, in 1945, from a soldier of Greek origin (as the story may also be), the widow's tears are, by an elaborate trick or misunderstanding, construed to be sexual in nature, as in numerous examples below concerning widowers. '*A woman too poor to bury her dearly beloved child finally tearfully persuaded the undertaker to place him in the coffin with another corpse. He was put between the legs of a deceased man, and at the funeral, when the mother was seen to weep copiously and was asked if she had been a dear friend of the deceased man, she replied, "No, I'm not crying for him. I'm crying for what's between his legs".*' This does not sound like an American joke at all, particularly in the desperate poverty of the mother. Observe also the identification of the male child as the (mother's) penis.

In a modern joke which omits any directly sexual reference — as do the older stories on the funeral themes — and which is therefore sometimes printed, *A husband watching anxiously at his wife's bedside during her last illness is told by her to go out and take a walk as he looks peakèd. He comes back in an hour, full of news. "Say, you know who just got engaged?" he asks. The dying woman stirs, and flutters open her eyes heavily. "Who?" "Me!"* (Heard in a nightclub, N.Y. 1964, in a 'sick-humor' act which brought down the house.) Excessive grief or tenderness at the death of a spouse is invariably assessed in folklore as false and as concealing the opposite emotion. This is Freud's theory of ambivalence exactly expressed at the folk level. Hamlet's overacting at Ophelia's grave, into which *both* he and her brother Laertes leap, V.i.272–307, struggling to see which can out-rant the other in both word & deed, by way of visible sorrow, embarrasses modern critics such as J. Dover Wilson, in *What Happens in Hamlet?* (1935) p. 269–70. But the audience unquestionably ate it up, though recognizing very well — in the jestbooks of the same period, of even greater popularity — that it was all no doubt insincere. A modern joke form (of the first text above), of theatrical or vaudeville origin, allows even the widower to admit this frankly. *A friend meets a famous actor (usually stated to be John Barrymore, the most famous Hamlet of this century), after his wife's funeral. "God," says the friend, "you certainly made a spectacle of yourself at the church, falling in a faint and dragging the corpse out of the coffin, and kissing her that way!" "That was nothing — you should have caught my act at the grave."* (Los Angeles, 1939.)

It should not be overlooked that admittedly insincere mourning at funerals is still formalized in the hiring of paid mourners or 'weepers' — often deaf-mutes — and the solemn lugubriousness that the pall-bearers evince. (Compare *Hamlet,* at Ophelia's grave, V.i.300.)

The admissions now come thick & fast, without a shred of concealment. The following story is hardly more than an insistence upon the sexual detail implied in the main type preceding: *A man's wife has died and he makes the house ring with his lamentations. The next day he is found by his brother making love to the housemaid. "What are you doing?" the brother cries, "and your wife buried not even twenty-four hours!" The widower stops only long enough to look up and shrug. "In my grief, how should I know what I'm doing?"* (1:88.) As with the archi-famous "Widow of Ephesus" story, at the end of the present section, the psychological underpinning of this story is better than it pretends to be, as it is a fact that all animals, including human beings of both sexes, easily become erotic in periods of fear or nervous strain, or, rather, that fear or any other violent emotion can easily become eroticized, either on a single occasion or habitually, which is precisely the reason for the popularity of ghost-stories and horror-films, and other sadistic entertainments such as bull-fights. In cultures that plan to survive, this connection cannot be exploited.

The contrapositive of the preceding: *A man at his wife's funeral remains outwardly very calm. One of his friends berates him. "Shame on you," says the friend, "standing there as cool as a cucumber with your hands in your pockets. Look at her mother — tearing out her hair!" "I'm tearing out my hair too, but not where you can see it."* (N.Y. 1939.) It is clear that this widower is bereaved, but the hostility of his physical response — even though turned against himself — is too violent and clear for us to think of him as really grieving for his wife. This, too, is psychologically well-founded, for not only *"We never cry for anyone but ourselves,"* as everyone will admit, but even the specific hostile tic here indicated, of tearing out one's own pubic hair in periods of impotent anger or irritation, as while being brain-baited or super-sold over the telephone, is based on correct observation of a fact seldom admitted. It is, for instance, not mentioned in Princess Marie Bonaparte's excellent article in the French *Revue de Psychanalyse* (1933) of such similar inturned hostilities as nail-biting and scratching, often in the form of long, voluptuous, but quite unconscious explorations of one's own body, from top to toe, that many people engage in while reading in armchairs or in bed.

A Jewish joke, similar to that preceding, is perhaps not relevant to the present work, but offers too clear a parallel to omit. It requires the explanation that, at the ceremony of atonement at Yom Kippur, religious Jews of both sexes recite an alphabetical catalogue of their own and all humanity's sins, beginning '*Ashámnu, bogádnu, gozálnu, dibárnu-dofie*' (We have sinned, we have transgressed, we have stolen, we have spoken evil . . .), meanwhile striking themselves with clenched fist on the breast at every word. *A woman standing in the women's balcony in the synagogue on Yom Kippur and reciting the catalogue of sins, beats herself on the pubis instead of the breast at each word. (The teller acts this out instead of saying it in words.) Her friend expostulates with her. "You're not supposed to hit yourself here; you're supposed to hit yourself here!" "Leave me alone, Yetta. I'm hitting myself where I sin the most.*" (Scranton, Pa. 1934, from a Jew of Galician Poland.) With this compare: *The Merry Widow of only a week, but dressed in bright-colored clothes, who explains to the neighbor who remonstrates with her: "Mrs. O'Randy, I vill haf you know mine pants is black. Und it's dere vere I feels it most.*" Given thus in *Anecdota Americana* (1927) 1:236, in comedy-Jewish dialect, the neighbor being Irish on the "Abie's Irish Rose" or "Cohens & Kellys" kitsch pattern. This may be a modification or 'translation' of the actual Jewish joke just given, the compiler of *Anecdota Americana* being of Hungarian-Jewish origin. The American 1930's motion-picture version of the Lehár operetta, *The Merry Widow* (1905), seems to allude to this joke, or expresses the same idea independently, in showing the change from the widow's mourning to her merriment by means of a wordless photographic shot of her wardrobe and corset-dummy, first dressed in mourning weeds of black, then suddenly whisked into flashing white. An unimportant gag-variant presents this as a riddle: "*Why do widows wear black garters?*" "*I give up.*" "*In memory of those who have passed beyond.*" (N.Y. 1953.)

As is common both in jokes and folksongs, the sex of the protagonists often is reversed in variant texts while leaving the effective identity of both perfectly clear. A very popular joke, about a Merry Widower, with the punch-line sometimes given in fractured French, is visibly derived from the preceding group, but with the attempt somehow to change the sex of the widowed spouse from female to male. The difficulty in making the change stems from the lack of a specifically *sexual* male wardrobe, comparable to the feminine garters or corsets of the widow, and the solution resorted to is of necessity rather strained. Note: *In France a condom is known politely as a "capote anglaise" or English overcoat. A foreigner in Paris, whose wife has died, wanting to buy a black overcoat in a department store, asks the floorwalker where he can find* "une capote noire." *"Certainly, sir,"* says the floorwalker, *"but may I ask why Monsieur wishes it to be black?"* "My wife has just died." *"Quelle délicatesse!"* (1:59, with the punch-line in English, as *"Such delicacy!"* and given to a lady clerk.)

In the East Indian custom of *suttee,* in which the wife is required to throw herself living into the flames of her dead husband's pyre, the identity of both spouses in the widow-widower situation is made certain in fact. In just the same way, the ancient Scandinavian warrior required his horse and sword to be buried with him; and modern man, intent on suicide, kills himself in an explosive crash in his automobile, often requiring of his wife (or friends) the involuntary *suttee* of dying in the same 'accident' with him. The Atom Bomb psychosis is of course identical, but on a national scale. (See the note in the following subsection, "The Widow of Ephesus," on the Samson complex, another name for the same *'die-with-me'* emotion.) A curious rejection of the impotence-death identification, in which the dead husband regains his potency, as it were, in and by the act of dying, is also presented as a riddle, or 'explanation' of the Indian widow's *suttee: "It's the first time in years she's seen the old man real hot."* (1:137.)

9. THE WIDOW OF EPHESUS

No joke version has been collected of the famously bitter folktale of the "Faithless Widow" or "Matron of Ephesus" (*Vidua*), which can be exactly paralleled to the original Milesian tale given in the *Satyricon* of Petronius (1st century A.D.). The best Latin text of the *Satyricon,* that edited by Michael Hadrianides (including the *Priapeia,* Amsterdam: Blaeu, 1669) p. 385–95, is heavily annotated, giving cross-references and congeners well worthy of study from beginning to end. Two complete monographs have already been devoted to this story, its peregrinations and transformations: the first by the editor of the misogynistic Schopenhauer, Eduard Grisebach, *Die Wanderung der Novelle von der treulosen Witwe durch die Weltliteratur* (Berlin, 1889), and another announced as forthcoming in 1961 by Elizabeth Brandon of the University of Houston, Texas. Brief references will be found in Thompson's *Motif-Index,* and Rotunda, at K2213.1, supplemented in Aarne's *Types of the Folktale* (ed. 1961) Type 1510, erroneously cross-referring to Type 1752* (correctly: 1352*). None of these appear to note the alleged Chinese version of the story, alluded to by the pseudonymous 'G. Froidure d'Aubigné' in his excellent article on the Milesian tales, "*Les Contes érotiques de l'ancienne Grèce,*" p. xxiii, printed as preface to J. Nicolaidès' *Contes licencieux de Constantinople* (Kleinbronn, 1906: *Contributions au Folklore Erotique,* vol. 1), and it is possible that this 'Chinese version' is a ghost, stemming from Voltaire's use of the tale in the 18th century, in the Arabizing *Zadig.* On the other hand, stories of this type are very widespread and protean, and the whole section in Thompson, T230–249, "Faithlessness in marriage," is of relevance, especially all forms of T231, "The Faithless widow," and K2213, "Treacherous wife."

It should be observed that the 'faithlessness' of the widow is a contradiction in terms, since the death of her husband has dissolved the marriage and the plighting of her troth to him. However, it is expected in all patriarchal societies that the widow shall engage in a period of mourning for her lost husband, in which the dark clothing or 'widows weeds' etc. indicate that she is not then to be considered sexually attractive, nor to engage in any sexual life during that period, even if the translethal jealousy or ostentation of the husband does not actually demand that the widow immolate herself on his pyre (*suttee*) or literally die of weeping over his tomb (Motifs T81 and T211). Though not noted in this connection by the folktale indexers, this is the identical psychological motivation of the hero Samson at his death, in *Judges,* xvi. 30, who says "*Let me die with the Philistines,*" and so arranges his suicide, in pushing down the pillars of his prison, on the roof of which three thousand of the enemy Philistines are 'sporting' at his blindness and captivity, that 'the dead which he slew at his death were more than they which he slew in his life.' The Samson complex — to give it a name — is evidently a loser's game. One of the best current examples of the underlying emotion is the "Die-With-Me" variety of purposeful automobile accident noted in the preceding sub-section. (This is one of the 'games' omitted from Dr. Eric Berne's *Games People Play.*) One must also not overlook the atom bomb, especially in the ultimate 'Doomsday Bomb' form satirized in Terry Southern's black-humor motion picture, *Dr. Strangelove* (1963), as incomparably acted by the great dialect-comedian, Peter Sellers, in the character of the bomb's inventor, whose living half is a neo-American patriot, but whose mechanical half — which tries to throttle the human half — is uncontrollably a leftover, saluting Nazi. If that doesn't say it, I don't know what can.

The gloating over the exact number of the Union dead — 'Three hundred thousand Yankees, Is stiff in Southern dust; We got three hundred thousand, Before they conquered us' — in the post-Civil War Confederate song, "The Unreconstructed Rebel" by Innes Randolph (in John H. Cox's *Folk-Songs of the South,* 1925, p. 281-2), with its grand and total humorous defiance, is similarly a boldly honest expression of the losing warrior's overpowering urge to take down as many of the enemy as possible with him, even in his inevitable defeat. There is admittedly a certain heroism about the Samson complex, to which we all answer, such as throwing one's broken sword-hilt or empty pistol at the enemy's head. (Or one's head at the enemy, as with Washington Irving's "Headless Horseman"!) But there is nothing in the situation of a dying, and presumably impotent man, leaving a widow behind, which would logically involve any such animosity against the widow.

Men do, of course, feel proprietary about women under patriarchy, consciously assessing them as sexual property. And it is clear that the patriarchal demand for the wife's required chastity to extend backward to the time of her birth — *i.e.* that she be a virgin on her wedding night — is easily extended forward in time as well, in the demand that she remain sexually 'faithful' to her husband even after he is dead. If not for the rest of her life (assuming she is not required to kill herself or die of grief at once, on his tomb), then at least for some definite and 'decent' period of mourning. The same or a lesser mourning is nowadays also expected of men, but men are not socially required to dress in 'widower's weeds' of black — a discreet armband or lapel-ribbon, at most, will do — and the idea of a given period of sexual abstinence for a man after his wife's death would be considered absurd, as is made clear in the jokes in the preceding sub-section on "Funerals and Mourning."

Nevertheless, there is something horrible about the story of the "Widow of Ephesus," and all stories like it or stemming from it; and it is intended that they be horrible. That is their job. These are cautionary stories told by men, mocking the grief of widows as hypocritical and false, and by implication warning against all women as treacherous in their sexuality even to the point of corpse-profanation. The profaning of the corpse is the climax of the story, and is the *nexus* of recognition of all its variants. As told in the *Satyricon* of Petronius, *A faithful widow will not leave her husband's tomb, and remains there for five days after all the other mourners have departed. Nearby a soldier is guarding the bodies of several crucified robbers, to prevent their friends from cutting them down and burying them. The widow and soldier meet, and while they are engaged in sexual intercourse, one of the robbers' bodies is stolen. To protect the soldier from punishment, the widow gives him her husband's body to hang on the cross in the dead robber's place.* Going this terrific anti-woman story one better is an Estonian tale collected by Aarne, in *Estnische Marchen* (FF Communications, No. 25), and summarized in Aarne-Thompson at Type 1352*, "The Woman's Coarse Act": *'The widow mourns for her husband. When the new suitor tells her to knock out the teeth of the deceased with a stone and she obeys him, he leaves her.'* At Motif T231.4 the meaning of the new husband's response to the widow's symbolic castration of the corpse of her first husband — which the new husband has himself imagined and ordered — is made more specific: *'Fearing like treatment, he leaves.'* At P214 we have the form to which all the others are really tending, in an Irish myth noted in Tom Peete Cross' *Motif-Index of Early Irish Literature* (1952): 'Wife drinks blood of slain husband.' Compare the castration of the dead Osiris by Isis: the part of the story that the Egyptian myth carefully evades.

10. THE EATEN HEART

Romantically glozed, it is not really very far to the sentimental form of the same blood-drinking in one of the most famous English ballads — and with one of the most beautiful tunes — "The Three Ravens" (Child Ballad No. 26), where a pregnant doe, representing the dead warrior's wife, 'As great with yong as she might goe,' lifts up the bloody head of the dead knight — whose sightless eyes the crows will pick — to kiss his wounds. As I have remarked, in *The Horn Book* (1964) p. 349, this is to be compared with the entirely gratuitous details which Professor Child offers as to the perverted Czar Peter the Great of Russia, slobbering over the decapitated head of "Mary Hamilton," No. 173, which is presumably historical fact, where the pregnant doe of "The Three Ravens" is fantasy.

Even more to the point, and similar in a number of traits to both the coarse Estonian folktale and the exquisite English folksong, is Child Ballad No. 269, "Lady Diamond" (also Daisy or Dysmal), of which Prof. Child gives, v. 29–34, 303, the original folktale in various international forms, as the legend of "The Eaten Heart" (Type 992, also Motif Q478.1, with references), an East Indian story concerning Rajah Rasálu in the 2nd century A.D., usually assimilated to the purported true tragedy of *Guilhem de Cabestaing, lover of a Provençal noblewoman whose husband, Ramon de Castel Roussillon, cuts out and roasts the lover's heart and gives it to his wife to eat. She commits suicide on learning what she has eaten.* This is most famously retold as Day IV, Tales 1 and 9, of Boccaccio's *Decameron* (1353), and a cadenced prose version was published by Richard Aldington in Paris, 1929, under the title *The Eaten Heart,* presumably as a parable for our time. There is also a monographic study of the forms of the legend, H. Patzig's *Zur Geschichte der Herzmäre* (Berlin, 1891), not noted by Aarne or Thompson; and compare Kristoffer Nyrop's *Sangerens Hjærte* (Copenhagen, 1908). The psychoanalytic study of this legend, as the oral-incorporative fantasy it is, remains to be made.

It should be remarked, as Thompson briefly but significantly points out, that it is not necessarily the lover's *heart* that is given to the adultress to eat in these stories, but 'Sometimes other parts of his body.' In fact, though the eating of the heart makes the story very dramatic — the heart being considered the seat of the emotions in the West, as the stomach is in the East (neither being true) — there can be little question that it is an irrelevancy, and can be and is replaced by the eating of the head or tongue, all equally a symbolization or expurgation for the forced eating of the lover's penis, which is the actual and obvious instrument of the adultery being revenged. In North Africa, a standard Arab humiliation of the living or dead enemy is the cutting off of his penis and stuffing it into his own mouth. A 'joke' version in which the widow suggests that it be stuffed into his rectum is given below.

Reference has already been made, at the end of the preceding subsection, to the myth of Isis and Osiris, in which the male god, Osiris (the Dionysus of the Greeks), is torn to bits, presumably by his enemy Typhon (who represents the ever-female Sea, according to Plutarch's *Isis and Osiris,* Sect. 33 ff.), and is left strewn in fourteen pieces. Isis lovingly gathers these up, but can find only thirteen pieces: the fourteenth piece, which is the penis, is missing, and Osiris cannot be resuscitated until this is found. Compare the curious rule, still operative among the Jewish and Catholic clergy, announced in *Deuteronomy*, xxiii. 1: 'He that is wounded in the stones, or hath his privy member cut off, shall not enter into the congregation of the Lord.' The Moslem belief, noted in my *The Guilt of the Templars*, 1966, p. 118, on the authority of Aleister Crowley, is much closer to the ancient Egyptian: 'If the body of a Mussulman is burnt he cannot go to Paradise; for the *os coccygis* [the last bone or "tail" of the spine], from which God will raise his body from the dust, is destroyed.' That Isis *is* finally able to find Osiris' penis suggests very strongly that it was she who hid it — that is, has power over it — as is also evidenced by her struggle for dominance with him, Osiris being symbolically both her son and lover. In the decayed form of this myth, as that of Venus and Adonis (particularly in Shakespeare's very masochistic poem on this classic theme), the son-lover identification has been broken. Though the mother-goddess is all loving-kindness to her son, Cupid, she castrates and kills her lover, Adonis, under the form of the groin-goring wild pig: the main matriarchal totem-animal. The legend of Diana and Actæon, who is changed to a stag and torn to bits by his own hunting-dogs in punishment for having surprised the phallic hunter-goddess bathing (*i.e.* naked, in her unwonted female aspect), retains the trait of the *tearing to bits* of the male, but this time without phallic reference.

For reasons not easily understood, Prof. Child's profoundly researched headnote, No. 269, omits any reference to what is certainly the most famous version of these cannibalistic themes in English, Shakespeare's gruesome *œuvre de jeunesse,* the blood-tragedy *Titus Andronicus,* of which the hero, in revenge for the rape of his daughter, whose tongue has also been cut out, bakes the two rapists in a pie, which he feeds at a banquet to their own mother, who is thus, as he explains to her before killing her, 'Eating the flesh that she herself hath bred.' (V.iii.62.) Compare *Deuteronomy*, xxviii. 57, on the Jewish mother during the siege, who shall eat 'her young one that cometh out from between her feet;' repeated in and probably contemporary with *Lamentations,* ii.20. There is also a modern reduction of the theme of "The Eaten Heart," significantly reversing the sexes, in the form of a folktale or song about *A girl who demands of her lover the heart of his mother to feed to her dog,* printed at the end of Jean Richepin's bitch-heroine novel, *La Glu* (Paris, 1881). I have collected this in America as the Yiddishe-momma-story-to-end-all-Yiddishe-momma-stories, with the identical final line: *The son stumbles and falls while running, carrying the torn-out heart of his mother, and the heart asks tenderly, "Did you hurt yourself, my son?"* (N.Y. 1946, from a young Jewish mother of twins.) I have not been able to determine the motif-number for this, under the Thompson system, unless it is to be connected with the Irish mythological motif, G91.1, "Man forced to eat dead father's heart goes mad," of which it might be mentioned that Ben Jonson is said to have stated the same thing, in his *Conversations* with William Drummond of Hawthornden, concerning a man who pisses on his father's grave: an ancient Roman superstition.

The position has now certainly been reached where it is possible to recognize the gruesome stories of the "Widow of Ephesus," and of her Estonian sister who knocks the teeth out of her dead husband's skull (there is a German version of this too, but it is not a legend, concerning the gold in the teeth of the Jews killed in the German concentration camps during World War II), as a projection upon the widow and her presumed 'adulterous' intentions, of a standard male fantasy of corpse-profanation and revenge. Another fantasy, also certainly relevant, is that sexual intercourse is 'weakening' to the man, but not to the woman, because he 'loses' a fluid, the semen, which she receives. This is the essence, also, of the fantasy of the *succuba,* and the physiological basis of the notion of the *vagina dentata,* in which the vagina is thought of as a mouth, sucking or biting the man's penis dangerously. It is hardly a step from this to the belief that an excess of sexual intercourse will kill a man, and that men who die have therefore doubtless been killed by their wives (vaginas), and that any kind of further indignity or even the *continuing* castration of the husband's corpse can therefore be expected from the wife, especially by way of satisfying her presumably raging sexual desires with some new man: *i.e.* the legend of the Widow of Ephesus.

The truth of the matter is probably the opposite, namely that men will certainly become prematurely impotent, after which they can also be expected to die prematurely (of a 'broken heart' or spirit), if they foolishly allow their sexual activity to be brought to a halt in late middle age — in their fifties, classically — in response to the wife's sexual rejection (not her sexual appetite!) after the menopause. In this sense it is, perhaps, true that a woman can kill her husband 'with' sexual intercourse, but in the sense exactly the opposite of that intended by folktales and jokes.

These themes have already been handled, under "The Sadistic Concept," 5.III, in one of the most popular English-language jokes now existing, which is also well known in French: *A powerfully built husband whose wife refuses to cook, or to keep the house clean, decides he will kill her by means of an excess of sexual intercourse. He fortifies himself one Friday after work with two very rare beefsteaks and a quart of wine for dinner in a restaurant, rushes home, and starts making love to her without a stop till Monday morning. When he leaves for work Monday, barely able to walk himself, the wife is spread-eagled, stark naked and dripping wet, apparently unconscious on the torn-up bed. When he gets home in the evening, he sees before entering the house that there are fresh curtains in the windows, doorstep is swept, etc., and realizes the neighbor women have come in to clean up, and lay out his wife's corpse. He enters guiltily, only to find his wife, still naked, but wearing a tiny apron and high heels, cooking a beautiful supper. "What's going on?" he says, dumbfounded; "the new curtains, supper, everything?" "Well," she says, standing on tiptoe to kiss him, "you treat me right — I'll treat you right."* (N.Y. 1938, also given as a storiette in *For Men Only,* the same year.)

This is the 'charming' version, involving only premeditated sexual murder of the wife, and it will be observed that she is described graphically as dead. In the *un*charming version, or self-punishing variant, matters take a somewhat different turn:

A man consults with a doctor friend as to a safe method of getting rid of his wife. The doctor refuses to prescribe poison, but suggests instead that the man have intercourse with his wife five or six times every night. "No woman can stand that very long," he assures the husband. "In six months she'll be dead." At the end of the stated time the doctor begins to worry, and goes to visit the friend. He finds him in a wheel-chair, his face sunken and his skin blue, all his limbs are shaking, and his face twitching and tongue hanging out as he talks. (This is all pantomimed by the teller.) Just as the doctor opens his mouth to ask how the wife is getting on, the door opens and she bounces in, wearing a short white tennis skirt and carrying a racquet and balls. "Tennis, anyone?" she asks pertly, and bounces out, the picture of health. (Also all pantomimed.) The husband looks meaningfully at the doctor, twines his shaking fingers together, and whispers gloatingly,

"She doesn't know it, but she's only got twenty-four hours left to live!"
(N.Y. 1940; collected again N.Y. 1951, ending 'two more weeks to live.')
The contrast and the transparent connection between these two stories
leaves little doubt as to the projection involved — casting the guilt for
the husband's hostility and death-wishes *upon the wife* — in the following stories in which the husband has fallen victim to his own sexual
plots, while the wife is the ruthless survivor, or Widow of Ephesus.

A wife filling out her husband's death certificate with the doctor
asks that the cause of death be stated as gonorrhea. "But he didn't die
of gonorrhea," the doctor expostulates; "it was diarrhea." *"I know,"*
says the widow; "but I'd rather have people remember him as the play-
boy he wasn't than the shitass he was." (Chicago, 1953.) The hostility
here is merely verbal, but, like Mercutio's wound, ' 'tis enough, 'twill
serve . . . A plague o' both your houses!' (*Romeo & Juliet,* III.i.100.)
The teller of this story recognized the verbal concentration as adding
up to a rather poor joke, and parlayed it with a further version of the
same rhyming pun: *A Negro soldier refuses to go and fight in Korea.*
He is asked if he is a conscientious objector, and is told that if he re-
fuses to bear arms the Provost Marshal will shoot him. "I ain't objectin'
to nothin'," he says, "but I had the gonorrhea and diarrhea both, and if
this Korea *is anything like it — go ahead and shoot!"* (Chicago, 1953.
The teller was unconscious of any hidden medical pun on *chorea,* referring to St. Vitus' dance.)

A famous middle-aged playboy dies in Florida of a heart attack, in
the midst of an orgy with three chorus-girls, and his penis stays erect
even after death. The undertakers try everything, but it will not lay
down. As a last resort they have the Negro charwoman masturbate the
corpse, but without result. They telegraph the widow in New York,
discreetly explaining the problem. Her answer comes back immedi-
ately: "Cut that thing off and shove it up his ass. That's the only place
it hasn't been yet." (N.Y. 1948. Earlier, Calif. 1936, without the 'Negro
charwoman' touch.) Compare, on the same situation, *The rich Texan*
who dies in Chicago but is too big to fit into the largest coffin available.
The undertakers phone the governor, who tells them to give the corpse
an enema, after which they can bury the remains in a cigar-box. (La
Jolla, Calif. 1965.)

A French story, also known in English, clearly shows the main element from which the story of the penis-that-survives-death is here
elaborated: the idea of pedication as the ultimate insult to a man, as

throughout the *Priapeia* and other Latin satirical poetry, particularly that of Martial. On the fantasy of auto-sodomy, implied in the anti-husband story, above, see my *The Limerick* (Paris, 1953) Note 459. Compare also the note, earlier here, on the *oral*-incorporative fantasy of "The Eaten Heart." *Two men are pissing by the side of a country road when a farm-girl passes. One of the men waggles his prick at her and says provocatively, "Say, you're from the country. What ought I to do with a cucumber like this?" "Stick it up your friend's ass," says the girl coolly; "I hear they do well in shit."* (French version, Cagnes-sur-Mer, A.-M., 1966. American version from Idaho, 1919, in 6.II.2, above.)

Until public hangings were discontinued at about the turn of the present century, it was common lore — whether true or false — that the hanged man's penis would erect at the moment of death (whence the practice in England of hanging condemned criminals in their voluminous shrouds, to hide this), and would sometimes 'piss' or ejaculate on the crowd as well; and that the penis would not become flaccid again until sunset. (As with the superstition concerning a killed snake, the most famous of all phallic symbols: *Genesis,* iii.1–5.) This is central, of course, to the story under discussion here. It is also the source of the phrase *'To die with a hardon,'* meaning to come to a bad end, and specifically to be hanged; but the phrase is nowadays sometimes thought of as meaning to be sexually potent until death, which is obviously a good end, or to die in sexual intercourse — *'la mort douce'* — which is even better, though horribly embarrassing to the survivor!

Louis Perceau, in his anonymous *Histoires d'Hommes et de Dames* (1913) p. 99, "*La Potion du vert-galant,*" gives a version of the anti-husband story clearly connected with that given above, and also involving the *'mort douce' of the aging but evergreen gallant* (in the American story: 'middle-aged playboy'), *who foolishly takes an aphrodisiacal potion, makes love to his wife three times, and to the cook four times, buggers the gardener ten times, and is in the process of raping the house dog a dozen further times when he dies. His son-in-law has to masturbate the corpse three times more before the top can be put on the coffin.* This would appear to be the original, from its date of 1913, but Vance Randolph gives a backwoods version, as "Tom Burdick's Pecker" (*Pissing in the Snow,* No. 62), which he heard told in Arkansas in 1941 by an informant who stated he had 'heard it near Fayetteville, Ark., about 1903.' This does not dispose of the probability of a French origin, but leaves the question of transmission insoluble, as always. The contrast with the French version, which has no conversational elements at all, and is all action, is illuminating. Observe also the 'mystery' ending of the Arkansas story, connected with the theme of castration (as 'punishment' for excessive sexuality), as with the "Sleeve Job" story earlier:

One time there was a fellow named Tom Burdick that fucked pretty near every woman on the creek, and so after while his health broke down. Finally old Tom died, and the neighbors come over to lay out the corpse, because there wasn't no undertakers in them days. Tom Burdick's body was laying in a pine box, but his pecker stuck up like a fence-post. Hard as a rock, too, and it stood so tall they couldn't put the lid on the coffin.

The folks never seen a corpse act like that before, and they figured Tom's pecker would crumple soon as the evening sun went down. But the goddam thing just stood there, and seemed like it was getting harder all the time. So finally Sis Hopper went and told the widow. Old lady Burdick come in the parlor where they had Tom laid out, and she seen how things was. "What do you want we should do about it?" says one of the granny-women.

The widow-woman just stared at old Burdick's pecker. "For all I care," she says, "you can cut the thing off and stick it up his ass." The folks were all surprised to hear such talk about her own husband. "Surely, you don't mean that!" says Sis Hopper, which everybody knowed she had laid up with Tom Burdick herself, whenever they got a chance. The widow Burdick looked at Sis mighty hard. "Why not?" she says. "Even when he was alive, Tom wasn't none too particular where he put it."

Poor Sis Hopper never said another word, and the widow-woman walked out of the room like she didn't have a care in the world. Them people never did tell what happened after that. But everybody could see that the coffin-lid was screwed down tight, when they buried Tom Burdick next morning.

The modern story closest to the original "Widow of Ephesus" is "Of the Burning of Old John," No. 96/100 in *A Hundred Merry Tales* (1526), also as "The Widow's Exchange" in the jestbook, *Comedians' Tales,* p. 5 (London, 1729; unique copy, Folger-Shakespeare Library), reissued as *Spiller's Jests* about 1730. This is the unacknowledged source of most of the contents of the famous *Joe Miller's Jests,* edited by John Mottley in 1739 (the rest of the contents being taken from a similar jestbook ascribed to the actress Polly Peachum, as has been shown by Evan-Esar Levine). Curiously enough, this is one of the few of the *Comedians' Tales* not reprinted in *Joe Miller* by Mottley, possibly as being too *old* a joke: *A young widow has a wooden statue of her late husband which she takes to bed with her every night, and calls Old Simon (John).One night a young man bribes her maid to put him in bed instead of the statue. 'In the Morning the Maid called at her Chamber Door, as she used to do, Madam what will you please to have for Dinner? She replied, roast the Turkey that was brought in Yesterday, boil a Leg of Mutton and Colley-flowers, and get a good Dish of Fruit. Madam, says the Maid, we have not Wood enough to dress so much Meat. If not, replied she,* you may burn *Old Simon.'* In the *Arabian Nights,* the transitional story from the "Widow of Ephesus" appears as Night 38 (Chauvin, No. 188; Elisséeff, p. 96, No. 8), "The Story of Ghanim ibn Ayyoub," concerning *Zobaïda, who buries in a tomb a wooden statue in a winding-sheet, instead of her lover, Kout al-Koloub.* (Burton, II. 45.)

Here now is the most recent version, of which the apparentage with the "Widow of Ephesus" story might not be quite so clear were it not for the intermediate version of "The Burning of Old John" in 1526 and "The Widow's Exchange" in 1729. This is given in the Larson manuscript of 'vulgar jokes,' *Odors on the Breeze* (MS. 1952) No. 13, as "The Headstone," collected from a woman related to the compiler, in Salt Lake City, Utah, 1950:

The widow could not be consoled even after her husband had been dead a year. She persistently resisted all the pleadings of her present suitor. She had a ritual, she told him, which she performed twice daily. Through the bedroom window she could see his tombstone. At dawn she always looked out and said, "Good morning, dear!" And before retiring at night she looked out and said, "Good night, darling!" Such a past devotion would not be fair to a second husband. Her suitor, however, was willing to take his chances. So at last she yielded and married him. Before going to bed, she looked out at the tombstone and said, "Good night, darling." They slept late. When at last they awoke, she looked out the window, stuck out her tongue, and cried, "Fooey on you!"

There is nothing to say about this except perhaps that Larson's *'They slept late'* is in its way as perfect as Dante's *'They read no more that day,'* which is the entirety of what is said by Dante to suggest the incest with her brother for which Francesca da Rimini is condemned to hell. Both lines are of the same sort of aposiopesis, or meaningful breaking-off, a rhetorical device not common in jokes; if the figure involved is not more correctly to be termed metonymy or synecdoche, in which one thing is said (or done) intended to suggest another — the whole groundwork of such disparate arts as that of the feint in fencing, of exhibition magic, and of symbolism both sexual and other. In the "Widow's Exchange" version of 1729, the wooden statue of the husband visibly substitutes for him, not only in being burnt to nourish the new lover — as the original "Widow of Ephesus" allows her own dead husband to be hoisted upon the crucifix to save her new lover's life — but also in the widow's bed. The implication is that the wooden statue, 'Old Simon,' is used as a sort of dildo or *olisbos,* a 'fucking-machine' for the widow's sexual gratification, though in the modern version her sexual satisfaction is only at the sentimental level, of ritual love-words spoken night and morning to her husband's tombstone. (Note that this too is a stone, *i.e.* crude statue. "Old John," in 1526, is also a statue or 'ymage of tymber,' kept in the widow's bed wrapped in a sheet.) Compare the "Sex Machine" jokes, in 6.IV.4, above.

This story exists in France in a reversal of the sexes in which *A widowered army officer expresses his astonishment that anyone can remarry after being married to a charming wife. He explains that he has had a portrait of his former wife painted for him, and has made a hole in it "just where you suppose," and makes love to the portrait while giving himself the illusion of still possessing his wife.' "Yes," added his orderly, who overheard this conversation, "but the Colonel has forgotten to tell you that he made me put my ass behind the picture!"' (His-toires d'Hommes et de Dames,* 1913, p. 53, *"Le Portrait."*) The use of the portrait as a sexual succedaneum, or *'dame de voyage,'* is perfectly frank here, as in an American version concerning *A man making love to an advertising poster of a movie-star with a hole in it, behind which is the charwoman.* (N.Y. 1936.) The relationship of this to "The Widow's Exchange" would be untraceable were it not for Perceau's French story of 1913, from which the two strains depart. *Pyramus & Thisbe?* Compare the Levantine folktales of castratory revenges, involving intercourse through a window or a hole bored in a wall: Motifs T41.1

and K1561; *Histoires Arabes,* pp. 60, 145. These are modified to the mere kissing of the buttocks, through the window, in jokes on *fensterln* or the 'night visit,' as Chaucer's "Miller's Tale," and *The Pinder of Wakefield* (1632, ed. 1956) pp. 25, 75.

The burning of the statue in "The Widow's Exchange" is also to be compared to the ritual burning of many witchcraft tokens, in all cultures, especially those intended to assure the faithfulness of a lover, as the paper-folded 'dancing dolls' (*origami* and *katagami*) of Japanese prostitutes in the late 19th century, described in De Becker's *The Nightless City,* which are finally burnt and dropped in the privy, 'over running water,' to assure the lover's return. Compare the threat of burning in Martial's *Epigrams* (1st century A.D.) VIII. 40, also in the *Priapeia,* lxxxv, concerning the statues of Priapus with the enormous wooden penis which were placed in gardens and at property limits — still surviving, with the penis draped, as the *Hermæ* or male caryatids supporting doorways in architecture — to threaten thieves or intruders with pedication, and also with castration by means of the sickle which Priapus is also sometimes shown holding (Martial, VI. 16 : *Priapeia,* xc), as likewise Father Time. According to the *Priapeia,* lxiv, and lxxxvii (identical with Catullus' *Carmina,* xx), homosexuals who would presumably enjoy being pedicated would therefore steal, and Priapus' threats were useless. Martial thus threatens the statue that if it does not drive away thieves from the grove of fig-trees — from the wood of which yonijically-fruited tree it was itself carved — it will be burnt instead.

It is clear that these statues were, in fact, survivals of the matriarchal tree-worship or 'groves' of Phœnicia, the phallic *Ashérah* against which the early Jewish religion fought bitterly, as seen in the prohibition in *Deuteronomy,* xvi. 21–2, against 'a grove of any trees' or 'any image' (*i.e.* statue) planted near the altar of Jehovah — except during the curious survival of this forbidden tree-worship at the festival of *Succoth* or Tabernacles (as in 2 *Kings,* xvii. 29–31) — and in numerous other biblical texts to be found indexed by Cruden, in the King James version, under 'grove(s)' and 'green trees.' (Compare Milady "Greensleeves" in the English folksong, and any reference to *green* — as in 'getting a green gown' — in allusion to sexual intercourse out of doors, or to the sexuality of nature: its infinite renewal and fertility.) One can still buy *kitsch*-statuettes of this pagan kind — I have one in the grove of trees behind my home — showing a glozed plaster version of the oldest and crudest form of matriarchal tree-worship, in which the carved phallic wooden statue replaces any husband: a grinning Herma with the goat-head of Pan (the Christian 'Devil') replacing bearded Hermes, on whose brow a gauze-clad nymph facing him is presumably placing a wreath, though the actual intention and original of these statues is that, under cover of the gesture with the wreath, the nymph is deflowering herself ritually on the statue's penis. In the openly diabolical or 'Black Mass' form, the woman has intercourse with the deathless erection of a hanged man, as shown in Rops' *Diaboliques,* with the Devil, in a mock of the Crucifixion.

This particular matriarchal survival, of the Gods of the Groves, in its last rococo derivative, is cast into prominence here by the hidden meaning of the original "Widow of Ephesus" story, and probably of all its descendants. For this terrific anti-woman jest or tale takes its real significance not from any of its humorous traits or elements, but from the *locale* quietly immortalized in its title. Ephesus, in Asia Minor, was the home of the great Mother-Goddess, her special site and place of worship, and remained so powerful even three centuries after Petronius' time, that, at the Council of Ephesus, in A.D. 432, it was in that city that shouting crowds demanding, "Give us our Diana of the Ephesians!" forced the elevation of the Mother-Goddess into the Christian pantheon in the quasi-divine status of the mother of the new god Jesus, the Virgin Mary, to whom are now assimilated all the attributes of Diana of Ephesus, including her miraculous virginity and her simultaneously being the goddess presiding over auspicious childbirth. (In her negative or ambivalent phase, Diana is also a brutal huntress and man-killing Amazon, and she degenerates even further in Jewish mythology into Lilith, Adam's first wife, who — as opposed to the Mother Eve — *kills* newborn babies and is now the consort of the Devil.)

That the Virgin Mary has been in a sort of theological limbo since A.D. 432, when the Ephesians forced her upon the Christian Patriarchs, is made rather evident by her having been elevated to Heaven only in 1950 — apparently as a concession to the Western emancipation of women, and as a bid for the women's vote — centuries after thousands of forgotten saints preceded her there. This is too recent to have been forgotten in turn, and it may be prophesied that if modern women's emancipation, and the power of their vote, gets any stronger, the Virgin Mary will one day soon be rediscovered to have been a member of the Holy Trinity all along (not just the 'Holy Family'), and will be allowed at last to replace the peculiar bird-goddess survival, or Holy Ghost, now substituting for her, in the more natural and credible tripartite god: Father, Mother, and Child. 'We make our gods in the image of ourselves.'

A reassessment will also have to take place, at that point, of the Crucifixion, since a Mother-Goddess will not easily have allowed a Father God no more powerful than herself to crucify her first-born son, on any pretext of saving humanity. No mother cares that much about 'humanity' in so vague and general a sense: only about her child, the actual human being. The trait of crucifixion in the tale of the "Widow of Ephesus" has also its clear significance here. The robber whose body has been stolen, and is to be replaced by that of her dead husband, has been *crucified* according to Petronius' story, not hanged on gallows as in later modernized versions. Crucifixion is, of course, a specifically Roman punishment, here in the Roman-dominated colony of Ephesus (now Smyrna, Turkey, facing Athens across the Aegean). This is emphasized pointedly and painfully in the gruesome climactic scene of mass-crucifixion of the revolted slaves by the Romans in 71 B.C. in the American motion-picture epic, *Spartacus* (1963), and is silently taken cognizance of in the relative absolution given to the Jews of the world, of the guilt for the Crucifixion, at the Oecumenical Council of Rome, in 1965 A.D.

The true butt of the joke Petronius is retailing — there is no reason to believe it is his own invention, and he himself offers it as of Near-Eastern origin — is therefore not just this one fictitious widow, but the whole surviving and at that time still very powerful remnant of human matriarchy and matriarchal worship in the Near East, specifically at Ephesus. There the cult of Diana was so strong, and so profitable to the silversmiths who made shrines for her worship, that a crowd (similar to that of A.D. 432) drove St. Paul from that city for attempting to preach Christianity there, in about A.D. 55, shouting, according to the *Acts of the Apostles,* xix. 24–34, 'all with one voice about the space of two hours . . . Great is Diana of the Ephesians,' which must have sounded to them about the way Händel's *Messiah* sounds to us. It will be observed that it was precisely in his Epistle to these woman-worshipping Ephesians, v. 3–4, 22–4, that St. Paul uniquely preached his anti-sexual crusade against 'fornication . . . filthiness, nor foolish talking, nor jesting,' and the *patria potestas* of 'Wives, submit yourselves unto your own husbands, as unto the Lord . . . let the wives be [subject] to their own husbands in everything.' (Compare the edict of Xerxes to all his dominions, after the defiance of Vashti his queen, in *Esther,* i. 22.)

Finally, though none of the commentators of Petronius or annotators of the folktale have ever emitted this suggestion, there is a striking parallel between the legend of the "Widow of Ephesus" and that of the Crucifixion itself; and there is certainly a reasonable possibility that Petronius' story is a Near-Eastern tale mocking not only matriarchy but also the mythos explaining the Crucifixion in the then-new and much disprized Christian religion. The Widow of Ephesus allows her husband to be crucified (though already dead) in order to save the life of the soldier whom she loves. Jehovah, we are told in the *Gospel according to St. John,* iii. 16, 'so loved the world, that he gave his only begotten Son,' also to be crucified by the Romans — who are now the heads of the resultant church — 'that whosoever believeth in him should not perish . . .' The contrary of the parable of the hundredth sheep gone astray, in *Matthew,* xviii. 12. Why is the sacrifice of the Widow of Ephesus considered a gruesome joke, while the sacrifice of Jehovah is sacred and magnificent? *DAMN* the 'imperatives of the population explosion'! If one member of humanity — the soldier in Ephesus, the 'hundredth sheep,' or Lot in Sodom — is not worth saving, then humanity is not worth saving.

9

ADULTERY

I. SEX HATE

F R E U D is credited with the observation that it is not our hatred of our enemies that harms us: emotions like that are exhilarating. It is our hatred for the people we really love that destroys us. This obviously has its major application on the large scale of war: the civil wars, between human beings, that all wars must be. In the present context we are concerned only with the smaller hatred between husband and wife, leading to the dissolution of marriage in the form of adultery, whether or not this is formalized in divorce. Emotions such as this are of course ambivalences, and express themselves only in alternation with the actual affection that the husband and wife really need to give or to receive, or at any rate to feel. Grouped all together as they must be, in the jokes here, they show almost none of the ambivalent love. This is part of the essential nature of jokes, since people do not joke about what makes them happy or what is sacred to them. They joke only about what frightens or disturbs them, or about the pinnacles of happiness they would like to have scaled but have failed at.

Even when jokes about marriage are essentially not hostile, a tone of violence and force is present, if not of actual sadism, by which is meant an additional or substitutive sexual pleasure rising from the violence or cruelty itself. There is a natural element in this, of dominant maleness, but it cannot be pushed very far without becoming evident sex hate. *A wife is examining herself in a new petticoat in the bedroom mirror. "Does it look all right?" she asks her husband. "It looks fine, but your pants are coming down." She casts a rapid glance at the mirror. "You're crazy," she says; "no, they're not." "Oh yes they are! I've made up my mind."* (N.Y. 1936.) This is actually intended as verbal love-making, but both parties express themselves in contrary and antagonistic terms. Compare the verbal harrying and insulting, leading to sex, in Michael McClure's *The Beard*. This is similar to the teasing of children, and especially of children by adults, in which affection can only be expressed under cover of hurting and insulting. It is the standard foreplay in the homosexual 'S. & M.' (sado-masochistic) barrooms. Much homosexual activity, and often that of adolescent boys and girls afraid of open sexuality, takes this covert violent or insulting form, and has always done so, the homosexual form as wrestling or the verbal insult-contests of 'flyting' or 'the dozens,' and the heterosexual form under such names as 'pullyhawlying' and 'rough-housing.' This has always been a favorite sexual approach with the type of tomboy girls who are frozen at the penis-envy stage in their 'teens, and who have now become — dressed in more and more frankly male-imitated pants, including fly-fronts, hip-belts, etc., as the 1960's progress — the prevailing type in America. The favorite sex-*game* of these sick females is Dr. Eric Berne's "Uproar."

Dr. Jules Henry's frightening and deeply important anthropological study of contemporary Americans as though they were far-off Patagonians, *Culture Against Man* (1963) p. 346–8, cites a pathetic family, the Portmans, in which

> Mr. Portman expresses his love for his son through throwing him around, punching him in the belly, and imitating a devouring animal. Pete [the son] cannot fail, therefore, to associate love with physical violence: to love a person is to throw him around, wallop him, and symbolically chew him up — in other words, to have fun. Pete tries a baby version of this on Elaine, his little playmate next door. Thus the toughness-love-violence combination, so common in our movies, is here built into the child's flesh and bone through the basic biological mammalian function of play.

Dr. Henry goes on to note, in terms dripping with the boiling anger he feels, that the visible result of this 'toughness-love-violence combination' is that, in America and increasingly in Americanized Europe, '*Violence is a natural resource* . . . inexhaustible and constantly increases in price — a better investment by far than diamonds!'

The hidden result is discussed by Dr. Henry elsewhere, p. 158–9: the general emotional deadness of Americans about everything except feeding their faces, and particularly about their sexuality, in which violence and shocks have increasingly to take the place of love, beginning with the anti-sexual home training in which teen-agers are given relative sexual freedom but are simultaneously warned against 'going steady,' *i.e.* falling in love. 'But though the parents are afraid of the girl's getting too deeply involved, one of the central problems in our culture is the American's difficulty in becoming deeply involved at all.' This is the groundwork, not to say the forcing-frame, of sex hate. The reference to the 'toughness-love-violence combination, so common in our movies,' also puts the finger on the most important folk-art manifestation of sex hatred, in which men slap women around, not to show anger, but to show 'love,' and by way of demonstrating how virile (?) they are. The cult made by college students, from Harvard to the University of California, in the 1960's, of the motion pictures starring Humphrey Bogart, indicates how far this has already gone. Bogart's career in this line began as the dour detective, Sam Spade, in Dashiell Hammett's *The Maltese Falcon,* in which he turns his mistress over to the police for having killed his friend, which gives the whole secret homosexual meaning of the cult. Actually these 'tough' characters played by Bogart, and his spy-movie imitators, and presumably admired by the underage cultists, are semi-mute not out of the boredom and worldly wisdom they profess, but in response to the intense emotional strangulation from which they suffer as to all emotions but hatred, particularly sex hatred. See further my discussion of *'cool'* as the new venereal disease, in the *Fake Revolt* (1967) p. 22–32.

I. SEX HATRED AND REJECTION

By 1965, an underground joke of the 1940's (first collected, D.C. 1941) had become so popular among the 'cool' set, as the emotionally-strangulated refer to themselves, that it appeared as a popular hate card, or greeting card on the self-styled 'sick-humor' kick. *All that is seen is a black background, with conversation blurb: "Kiss you? I shouldn't even be doing this!"* Essentially that is the whole Bible of the cool/sick set. In the original form of 1941, the rationalization was at least attempted that the woman who answers this to the man making love to her is his sister-in-law. Note also that it was originally specifically the woman who delivered this 'killer' or 'cut-down' line, as collected four times between 1941 and 1951. The black-backgrounded 'hate card' does not specify the speaker, of course, and allows the male observer to identify himself just as happily in the hatred. Modified version, sometimes printed in college-humor magazines of the 1940's without the opening situation specified, but given only as a he-&-she colloquy: *A man and woman are lying side by side after making love. Woman: "Why don't we get married, honey?" Man: "Who'd marry us?"* Here there is no question that it must be the man who speaks.

Other snappy comebacks on the same 'cut-down' pattern will be found in preceding chapters, especially that on "The Male Approach," and a particular 'killer' in the chapter just preceding in which, *When a man asks a woman what he should do with his penis, she tells him to "Stick it up your friend's ass. I hear they do well in shit."* The innocence or even shyness of the person 'cut down' is essential to the hostility of this type of joke, which is all punch-line or repartee, no effort being spent at all on building up a background situation. *A man refuses to take a girl dancing on their first date. "Don't you like dancing?" she asks. "No," he answers roughly; "it's just fucking set to music." A pause. "Well, what don't you like about that?" "The music."* (N.Y. 1942.) Obviously the man considers this a seductive line of approach, but a girl like that deserves somebody better. This joke has of course been made out of date by the newer dances, in which the male and female dancers are isolated from each other, though presumably in pairs, and in which the highly coital hip motions engaged in are belied by the fact that the dancers are never to touch each other. A certain amount of hateful fornicaboobery is nevertheless allowed, in rubbing buttocks with the dancers *in back,* all four dancers thus engaging in unconnected orgiastic 'buttock-adultery' with four strangers whose faces they cannot see. The particular thrill here is naturally more the hurting and rejecting of the present partner 'with whom' one is dancing, than the actual gluteal contact with strangers (as in crowded buses and subways), and dances of this type are themselves, in the words of the present joke, *'just hatred set to music.'*

Rejections of every type could be cited here. Another, connected with dancing, already given, has *A dance-hall girl who suggests to her partner that he come to her room with her. "What's in it for me?" he asks roughly. "Just a little dust from dancing."* The girl's answer seems artlessly conciliatory. Compare however the folktale noted earlier as to *The girl about to be raped on a deserted bathing beach who, at the last minute, falls to the ground and fills her vagina with sand.* These are essentially *vagina dentata* or, in expurgated form, "Poison Damsel" stories, which will be found more fully discussed in chapter 13.1, in

Series Two. As to the element of rejection or misprisal of the vagina, see chapter 6.v.1, above, "Fear and Hatred of the Female Genitals." In one slightly glozed example, a *double entendre* publicly printed more than once in 'family' humor magazines, *A man who has been planning to go on vacation to the mountains, for the trout-fishing, tells his friends in the office that he will be going instead to the seashore, because "that's his wife's whim." "Well, can't you talk her out of it?" one of the friends asks. "You don't know my wife," says the husband ruefully; "she's got a whim of iron!"* The humor, of course, lies in the unspoken allusion to the wife's genitals: actually perfectly clear in the closeness of the key-word to the ancient but still-surviving *quim,* a variant spelling of *cunt* via Chaucer's *queynte* and Andrew Marvell's *quaint* (in "To his Coy Mistress").

In particular, any attempt to make *marriage* work is almost certain to be cut down in joke form. *A woman who is always quarrelling with her husband is advised by a neighbor to treat him nicely. "Trate the man nice," says her Irish neighbor. "Whin he comes home bring him his slippers, light his pipe fer him, wear a niglijay and sit on his lap. Make the ould man comfy." The wife tries it out, and finally is cuddled up on her husband's lap and fondling him. ' "Let's go to bed, dearie?" she whispered sweetly. "We might as well," said Pat. "I'll get hell when I get home anyway".'* (1:393.) The allusion to the usual blandishments of prostitutes was very clear in this joke as late as the 1920's, but prostitution of the classic kind here alluded to — with working men sitting and drinking or playing cards in the friendly atmosphere of a brothel on a Saturday night — has largely disappeared in America, as in France, since World War II, owing to the emancipation of women in both the monetary and sexual senses.

A husband and wife have a tiff, and the wife refuses to cuddle at bedtime, so the husband reads a book while she turns over to sleep. Suddenly she wakes up feeling him put a finger in her vagina, and whirls to face him, half in anger and half willing to be reconciled. "Oh, don't worry," he says, "I was only going to wet my finger to turn the page." (1:217.) This is bloated up to a long tale concerning a young college girl who marries her professor, but who shoots him when he spends his wedding night reading Chaucer in bed [!], in the midwest humor magazine, *Calgary Eye-Opener* (undated clipping of the mid-1930's, captioned "A Night in June"). It is rather clearly descended from the most famous folktale given, or originated, by Rabelais in about 1533, "Hans Carvel's Ring," *Pantagruel,* III. 28, in which *A jealous man is given a ring by the Devil in his sleep and is told that as long as he wears it his wife will never be unfaithful to him. He wakes with his finger in her vagina.* In what is perhaps a modern reduction, in the form of a fool-story: *A woman is describing at a party the terrible dream she had. "All my teeth were suddenly gone!" she says; "I put my finger in my mouth, and there were no teeth at all!" The fool: "Are you sure you put your finger in your* mouth?" (N.Y. 1948, from a psychiatrist.) This fool, who brings out into the open the castratory element of the woman's dream, is actually none other than the ancient folk-hero, "Tooth-Breaker," the tamer of the dangerous *vagina dentata,* to whom a section is devoted in the chapter on Castration, 13.1.2, in the Second Series, and who is generally shown as the sacred fool or lunatic (the modern 'hippie'), supernaturally protected in his innocence because he has been 'touched' by God — or by the Devil, as in Rabelais' story. Precisely as in the present joke, the symbolic level is the only important one in Rabelais' tale, since it is not really meant to imply that it is by means of the husband's *finger* that the wife is to be kept faithful. The joke on turning the pages of the book has kept to the literal meaning — and long after the period when people still commonly turn pages with a moistened finger — for purposes of sexual rejection.

The classic reconciliation maneuver of sexual approach is mocked in a story appearing first in *Memorabilia* (c. 1910), and in many variant forms, of which the one most commonly collected has: *A husband and wife who have had a fight but are sleeping in the same bed because there is no other. The wife turns her back on her husband, but he turns in the same direction and tries to cuddle her from behind by drawing up his knees to "make spoons." "Get your damn knee out of my back!" she snarls. "That's not my knee, honey." A pause. After a moment the wife ventures, "It's too bad we quarrelled, isn't it?" "It's a damn shame," says the husband, and turns his back to her and goes to sleep.* (1:496, observing editorially in parenthesis: 'Of course it was his knee all the time.') This is practically a page from Dr. Berne's *Games People Play.* In the commonest variant, which ends with murder, as with the version concerning the college girl who marries her professor, *A man who has fought with his wife comes home carrying an enormous box of candy but finds she has locked him out. He bangs on the front door with the candy-box and finally she puts her head out the upstairs window and threatens to call the police if he keeps banging on the door at that hour.* "*Aw, honey,*" *he says,* "*you wouldn't talk to me like that if you knew what I was knocking with.*" *She rushes downstairs to let him in, and he hands her the box of candy. She kills him.* (N.Y. 1938.) — *Sex to Sexty,* 1966, 6:12, has this as *an armless man ringing a whore-house doorbell with his penis!*

The most touching version moves on to a more sympathetic concern with the wife's emotions, and what she feels about her married life and husband's sexual rejection. *A husband who has fought with his wife comes home determined to make up. He finds her bent over the wash-tub scrubbing, and reaches around from behind to squeeze her breasts and kiss the back of her neck. She begins to cry.* "*What's wrong, honey?*" *he says;* "*I'm sorry the way I talked to you when I left.*" "*It's not that,*" *she says helplessly.* "*It's, oh, my wash-line fell and I have to do the clothes all over again, and the baby has the measles, and now you come home drunk.*" (N.Y. 1940.) Also concerned with woman's woes: *A married woman who was too busy to answer the door when a neighbor knocks explains later:* "*The baby was suckin', the old man was fuckin', and I was readin' a book.*" (2:365.) A little prose poem expressing the same thought also exists, in the form of album-verse for summertime: '*Between the heat of the prick and the prickly heat, The baby sucking me and my husband fucking me, I'm just no good!*' This is reduced finally to: *A bride, asked what she thought of married life, replied,* "*Between the douches and the dishes, I'm in hot water all the time.*" (D.C. 1946.) Compare "No Use Rapping," at III.5, p. 800 below.

Various works on sex technique, sets of illustrations of coital postures to illustrate Aretino's *Sonnets* (18th-century imitations), show the implied position in which the woman lies on her side nursing her baby while the husband makes love to her from behind, under such mnemonic titles as "The Good Wife and Mother." Actually this is much liked by women, owing to the stimulation of the breasts being sucked simultaneously, but that is not the way the jokes would have it. It also requires a certain freedom from anti-sexual prejudice as it is, essentially, an orgy, or three-person sexual chain, and the fantasy of the artists depicting it almost certainly involves identification with the *child* (not with the father), in partaking in this way in the parental intercourse. The setting up of real orgies or trios, especially if by the husband, usually involves the fantasy of 'reliving' such a scene.

There are far more jokes and other lore concerning the wife's dissatisfaction with the husband's sexual performance and frequency than the other way around. Yet it is clear that the jokes express the usual husbands' dissatisfaction with their middle-aged wives' sexual offering, and their feeling of increasing inability and impotence as to the wives' unwelcome demands. *Woman to her husband: "If it wasn't for two things, I'd leave you." Husband: "Yes, I know. I've got one and you've got the other."* As an example of the difficulties under which a book like the present one is written, I might mention that while writing this chapter in 1966, I received an angry letter from a joke collector in Texas, telling me that I had better be nice to him because he was about to buy a collection of *twenty thousand* jokes filed by subjects, many of them 'new,' and 70 per cent 'naughty,' and giving the above as a sample. The text just quoted is, however, as transmitted to me in a letter from the American folklorist, the late Dr. Josiah Combs, dated from Fredericksburg, Virginia, January 7, 1952. (This doesn't really prove anything: it may just have taken that long for the joke to get from Virginia to Texas.)

A farm wife's setting of a dozen eggs comes off with eleven cocks to one lone hen. The farmer ridicules her for this but she replies, "I didn't intend that poor hen to suffer all her life the way you've let me." (McAtee MS. 1913, env. 7, versified as "A Deserved Retort," noting, 1944, 'based on a popular tale.') A fixed-form joke, playing on current celebrities' names, in the style of popular printed obscœna telling little stories in the form of brand-names of whiskies or tobaccos, pairs Franklin D. Roosevelt and Winston Churchill with any one of several American politicians since: *A woman's three daughters get married the same day, and all spend the first night of their honeymoons at her home. Next morning she asks them what they thought of married life. "Well," says the first, "with my husband it was just like with Churchill: 'Blood, sweat, and tears'." The second daughter says, "Mine was like Roosevelt: 'Agayne and agayne and agayne'* (or: *Four times, and I thought I'd never get him out*)." *The third daughter says, "Mine was like* [various unpopular Presidents' names are given here]: *When he thought he was in, he was out. And when he finally did get in, he didn't know what to do there.* (Or: *He was in twice, but it didn't make much difference.*)" (N.Y., and Florida nightclub, 1952–53.) This is in briefer form, in the Guam mimeograph, 1952, as a riddling question: *"Do you know why Mrs. [President] is getting a divorce? — Her husband is doing to the nation what he should be doing to her."* All sorts of changes have been rung on this, as of *The woman who demands an intercourse with the President.* "*You mean interview, don't you?*" *says the secretary.* "*No, I mean intercourse: I want to see the nuts that are running the country.*" (N.Y. 1940. Collected again, 1967, as '*the nuts that are* screwing *the country.*')

The oldest relevant joke on these punning forms has not been traced beyond the late 19th century, though the reference to florid toasts suggests it is much older. *A husband who has made a great success at a bachelor dinner with the toast,* "*To that part of woman we all love best!*" *is afraid to tell his wife the truth, and tells her he has given as a toast,* "*To that little house we all love best: the Church!*" *Disgusted with his hypocrisy she determines to tell the truth the next time his bachelor friends meet at their home, and says to them,* "*You know, gentlemen, you mustn't believe everything my husband says when he offers a toast. You remember the one you all thought was so wonderful last time? Well, he hasn't been inside one for eight years, and anyhow he fell asleep then before it was half over.*" This is certainly the original of the Roosevelt-Churchill modernization, but all that is retained, aside from the fixed verbal pun on '*in,*' is significantly the theme of the woman's sexual dissatisfaction and resultant hatred.

The husband is never seen as so unsatisfactory sexually as when he is in the process of congratulating himself on his virility. This represents a conscious understanding at the folk level that sexual brag is intended to overcompensate for feelings of sexual inadequacy, though the accusation of male inadequacy is, in jokes, almost always put into the mouth of the wife, usually in sarcastic form.

A man and his wife were sitting well down in front in a vaudeville show when a girl appeared on the stage clad only in tights. The man began to laugh so immoderately that he attracted the attention of everybody in the audience. His wife reproved him and asked what amused him so. He finally controlled himself sufficiently to whisper: "I was thinking that if I should suddenly jump over the footlights and stick it into her while she had on her tights what a scene it would make!"

His wife sulked and said nothing. After a time she burst out laughing, and kept it up until the man asked her what she was amused at. She whispered: "I was thinking that if the audience called for an encore, what a fix you would be in!" (*Memorabilia, c.* 1910, p. 58. Repeated almost exactly, *Sex to Sexty,* 1966, 5:55.)

Lest it be thought that the intention, in tracing the latest joke versions to earlier sources, is to imply that there are absolutely no 'new' jokes, here-following is an apparently *new joke* from the same most recent and astonishing source, *Sex to Sexty* (1966) 6:20. This is very much in the vein of sex hatred and dissatisfaction, with the further premium to the listener-reader that the husband who here gets his come-uppance is of the socially-sadistic type, very common in the Germanic and Anglo-Saxon cultures, who wishes to *number and classify everything* (for instance, jokes?) for the purpose of achieving an imagined 'total control.' On this key characteristic see the filler, "Any Number Can Play," in *Neurotica,* 1951, No. 8: pp. 67 and 27, to which might be added the assimilation of this almost standard trait to a certain kind of comedy patriarch, overwhelmed by the numbers of children that he has sired, as in such horribly *kitsch* items as the mock-biography of the industrial-psychologist F. B. Gilbreth, *Cheaper By the Dozen,* on the home-life of the inventor of the machine gun, Sir Hiram Maxim; also in *Life With Father, The King and I,* and *The Sound of Music,* in which the put-down of the patriarch is invariably achieved by glorifying the *really* systematic victory of the little woman who beats him at his own game: again an obvious sexual allusion.

Here is the *Sex to Sexty* story, by special permission. *'The fireman told his wife, "From now on, we're gonna do things right by bells like we do at the fire station. One bell means you meet me at the door with a big kiss. Two bells means you head for the bedroom. Three bells means we undress. Four bells mean we hit the sack, ready for action." Things went well, except suddenly she rang the bell* five *times. "What does that mean?" asked the fireman. "That means," said his wife, "for you to reel out more hose . . . you're not close enough to the fire!"'* As the attentive reader will have observed, this *brand-new* joke is simply the addition of the social-sadistic situation of 'sex life by the numbers' to a sex-hate gag or floating punch-line encountered over twenty years before in Minneapolis, 1946, in the briefer form already quoted at p. 331 above.

The actual phrasing may be compared with that in the most extreme example of the sadistic concept of coitus in English-language folklore, which is not a joke but the bawdy song or recitation, "Our Lil" (there is an even more sadistic British imitation, "Eskimo Nell," which lacks any saving grace of humor), in which the schoolteacher heroine is described as dealing out, during an epic contest in sexual intercourse with the Mexican anti-hero, One-Eyed Pete, '*Corkscrew shunts and double bunts, And tricks unknown to common cunts. But he stood firm, and topped each trick, And kept on reeling out more prick . . .*' (Ann Arbor, Mich. 1935.)

The characters are reversed only infrequently, as the dominant female or bitch-heroine seems to be too frightening (surely not too recent) to joke about. "*Oh, Henry, just think! Tonight is our wedding night.*" "*Yeh.*" "*And you're going to undress me, and press me in your arms, and take me to bed whether I want to or not.*" "*Yeh.*" "*And you're going to make love to me — love! — again, and again, and again, and again!*" "*Who, me?*" (La Jolla, Calif. 1965.) Here the man can afford to cut himself down: the woman's demands have already made him certain of his inadequacy — that is perhaps their purpose — under the disguise of submissive femininity, which is that worn by the most successful bitches.

Randolph gives the ultimate in sexual dissatisfaction stories of this kind, in *Pissing in the Snow,* No. 72, as having been told by a man in Arkansas, who 'had it from a lady at Hot Springs, Ark., in 1946:'

> One time there was a boy named Clarence, that drove the delivery wagon for Hogan's meat-market. He got to sparking a rich man's daughter named Louise, and she thought Clarence was wonderful. The rich man didn't like it much, but finally he let 'em get married. The next morning Louise was dead, and it looked like Clarence has fucked her to death in one night.
>
> About six months after that Clarence got to sparking another girl, and her name was Maisie. She thought Clarence was wonderful, too. Maisie's folks hollered like hell, but him and her run off and got married anyhow. The next morning Maisie was dead, and it looks like Clarence has fucked her to death, just like he done Louise.
>
> About six months after that Clarence got to sparking a girl named Betty, and he wants to get married right off. Betty thought about it awhile, and then she says, "Clarence let's you and me go for a walk." They went out in the woods, and Betty laid down under a tree. "Come on, Clarence," she says, "let's see what you've got." Clarence jumped onto her, and done the best he could. But it wasn't much, because his pecker was only about two inches long.

Betty didn't say nothing at the time, except that she has decided not to marry Clarence. But about ten years later, after Clarence got killed a-fighting the policemen in Okmulgee, she told Gram French all about it. "My goodness," says Gram, "what do you reckon happened to Louise and Maisie?" Betty just laughed. "I believe them girls broke their backs," she says, "a-trying to get a little fucking out of Clarence!"

2. NAME-CALLING

The inevitable divorce is preceded by direct name-callings without disguise. Both spouses find the other sexually unsatisfactory or over-demanding, and are ready to tell not only each other but the whole world all about it. One very popular story of this kind is strung on a 'dictionary definition' pattern or perversion, not common in jokes though well known in direct riddle form. *A man leaving his newly-wed bride in the morning calls back, "Goodbye, Hollyhock!" She looks up this flower in a seed catalogue to try to understand what he means and finds that the hollyhock is "gay, colorful, and beautiful." She phones her mother to tell her the lovely compliment. The mother is suspicious and suggests she look it up in the dictionary, which says instead, "rather common, does best under fences and around barns; poor in beds."* (Minn., 1946.) Randolph has a cruder version, from Pineville, Missouri, 1924, in which the girl learns from the seed catalogue that hollyhocks are *"Fine behind privies and barns, but not much good in beds."* He adds that he also 'heard it related as a "brand-new joke",' also in Missouri in 1951.

A woman demands a divorce because her husband insists on making love to her twice every night. He tells the judge he does this to get even with her for what she calls after him every morning when he leaves for work: "Bye-bye, Weenie!" Judge: "Why don't you call something back at her?" "I do. I say, 'So long, Dead ass!' " (Chicago, 1953.) The judge is clearly hauled in only for his formal permissiveness as to this exchange. Related form: *After the divorce, the wife waves to her (ex)-husband from the courthouse steps, wiggling her baby-finger at him and calls, "Bye-bye, Pinkie!" He puts both his baby-fingers in his mouth, stretching it wide, and shouts back, "So long, Lucy!"* (2:47, a version without the nicknames; the present text, N.Y. 1945.) As has already been noted more fully, under "The Male Approach," 4.1.3, the *locus classicus* of gesture-humor of this kind will be found in Rabelais' Book II. 19 and Book III. 20, on the contests in sign-language between Panurge and the Englishman, or Goatsnose, in which latter I believe the very gesture of contempt here described occurs. The tongue is sometimes stuck out as well, or the fingers waggled, at the ears or nose, as in a nude cartoon in *Playboy* (October 1967) p. 174.

The story form is the same, though without specific anatomical details, in its contrast or 'crossing,' in that of *The husband who says tenderly to his wife, everytime he goes out for a night with the boys, leaving her behind, "Farewell, mother of three," to indicate to her that her place is minding the children. She finally has enough of this and one night retorts, "Farewell, father of one."* (Paris, 1954.) Told as a translation from the Yiddish and not again collected: *A man and wife decide they must have a divorce as they cannot agree on anything, including what to do about the custody of their three children. The wife, who is willing to save her home, suggests they stay together one more year and have one more child, and then get the divorce and divide the children, two for each parent. The husband suspects a trick. "But what if we have twins?" he objects. "Hoo-hah! my twin-maker," snorts the wife. "If I had to depend on you, would I have these three?"* (N.Y. 1946.) This is to be compared with the girl's retort in the childhood classic, given in the earlier chapter on "The Male Approach," to *the boy who offers to jump over the gate to retrieve the girl's hat, though he could not lift up her nightgown the night before.* (Aarne Type 1443, heard by Thompson in Kentucky in 1906; noting a German form.) — *A man who marries a golfer's widow and makes love to her only once on their wedding night, is told by her that her first husband never "neglected her so;" repeating the same after the second and third time as well. Finally he asks her, "Say, what's par on this hole?"* (1:290, ending brutally "for *your* hole." The allusion is the same in the puns on the golfer's wife — politely the golf club-house — as "The Nineteenth Hole," golf having only eighteen holes. *Sex to Sexty*, 5:64.)

Complaints as to the size, odor, and general unsatisfactoriness of the wife's genitals, her breasts and buttocks, or those of all women, are correctly considered the most violent insults possible. It is evident that these aim strictly at the specifically sexual parts, which the man does not possess (or, in the case of the buttocks, does not consider a sexual object), and in regard to which he therefore does not feel vulnerable to any riposte. Female beauty, or rather the lack of it, is not generally bothered with in jokes, except at the level of witticisms about *"putting a paper bag" over an ugly girl's head before making love to her,* to prevent her ugliness from causing the man's erection to fail (the reason is not usually stated). Men, *per contra,* are not thought of, in this culture, as being required to be beautiful, or sexually attractive, and this is made the subject of penetrating analysis as to sexual domination in the Vaertings' important work, *The Dominant Sex* (1921). In cartoons in the public prints — as for instance the anti-woman or homosexual issue of *Sex to Sexty* magazine, No. 6 (1966), cited frequently in the present section — an obvious effort is made by the artist to make the woman as beautiful and mammiferous as possible, with the erected nipples pointedly shown, and to make the men the most disgusting possible goons, in the style of *Mad* magazine. As such goons obviously do not deserve such girls, the meaning is simply that the artist is heavily exaggerating the beauty demanded in the female and the non-beauty accepted culturally in the male, whose sexual attractiveness is to reside wholly in his virility or his money. (Money as semen, strength, or 'balls,' which the gold-digger tries to *steal.*) From this vantage point, it is easy for the man to insult the woman as falling short of the ideal beauty demanded, and as being ugly, old, fat, repulsive, and smelly in the crotch.

A man comes home to find his wife admiring herself naked in the mirror. "Do you know what the doctor told me today?" she asks. "He said I had the most perfectly formed woman's body he's ever seen." "Did he say anything about that big fat ass of yours?" "No, your name didn't even come up." (N.Y. 1952.) This is more a childish *tu quoque* than actually venomous, at least on the part of the wife. On the other hand, the excuse of the husband's 'neglect,' or his adultery (or incest), intended or achieved, allows free vent to any amount of hatred by the wife. *A young girl sees her father urinating and asks what his testicles are. "Those are the Apples of the Tree of Life," he tells her, by way of poetic concealment. She tells this to her mother, who replies, "Did he say anything about that dead branch they're hanging on?"* (N.Y. 1950.) This is related to the Garden of Eden stories, including the one in the Bible. The teller in this case, a woman, admitted it was perhaps unusual for a man to take out his testicles as well as his penis, to urinate, and added, *"Maybe they were swimming?"* This is one of the ways jokes grow and change, the adding and dropping of rationalizations being particularly common.

As to vaginal size (chapter 6.v.4 above), that of the married woman is always presumably too large, owing to child-bearing. The sex-hate issue of *Sex to Sexty*, 6:40, unexpectedly depicts *A young and pretty girl waiting in bed for her lover, who approaches the bed naked with a long board tied across his buttocks (to keep him from "falling in," according to the folk-phrase alluded to). The girl is given the aggrieved one-line caption: "Aw, come on, Boyd, it's not* THAT *bad!"* Such a situation would actually be tragic, and does in fact sometimes occur, though without any board being necessary. It is shown here, of course, utterly without sympathy and from the man's point of view, as a gratuitous insult. *A woman tells her husband that she dreamed they were having an auction of pricks. Big ones were ten dollars, little ones were fifty cents. "And how much did they get for ones like mine?" asks the husband. "Oh, those they gave away for nothing." "I had a dream too," he rejoins; "I dreamt they were auctioning off cunts. Big ones were ten dollars, and little ones were a hundred dollars." "And how much did they get for ones like mine?" "That's where they held the auction!"* (N.Y. 1938.) The jokes and fantasies comparing the vulva of a woman with that of a cow will be found in the chapter on "Prostitution," below. These are at least as old as Leonardo da Vinci's mock demonstration that the woman's organ is proportionally three times as large, in his *Quaderni d'anatomia* (before 1519), f. 7-recto, n. 5.

On any biological basis, the genital odor of the woman — as with all mammals — is the most attractive thing about her to the male, and quadruped males have in fact no other criterion of sexual choice. Every effort is made to deny this attraction, in anti-sexual cultures, and to wash away the genital odor, replacing it with similar odors under the name of 'perfume,' derived from the genital parts of other animals, such as skunks, and plants (the flowers). This is an endeavor probably more Marxian than Freudian, and as such not of interest here. I mean, the perfume-manufacturers are after the *money*, and they make their money by the running sub-vocal insult in their advertising that women naturally smell 'bad.' Most women have been brainwashed into believing this, and not a few men. It appears in jokes as the culminating insult. *A man brings home a pet monkey and the wife objects. "What will it eat?" "Anything we eat." "And where will it sleep?" "With us, of course." "But what about the smell?" says the wife. "It'll just have to get used to it, the way I did."* (N.Y. 1939.) This is also given in *Sex to Sexty*, 5:27, which likewise has the old standby, in 5:57, which appeared frequently in the similar but less frank sex-humor magazines of the 1930's, published in the midwest, showing *A blind man passing a deserted fish-market* (usually and specifically: *shrimp-stand*), *and saying "Good morning, ladies."* Perceau's *Histoires d'Hommes et de Dames* (1913) p. 95, has a connected French story, in which *A woman shrimp-seller blackmails a man by threatening to accuse him of rape, after getting him to handle the shrimps she is selling!* It is curious that it is supposed to be a reproach that a woman's genitals smell like shrimp, but has never spoiled the expensive popularity of shrimps that they smell the same way. Compare the joke earlier, under "Oragenitalism," 8.v.4, on '*making cunt-juice taste like orange-juice,*' (and vice versa), a story which gives the show away on all these culturally-toned and jocular pretenses of denying the powerful attraction to men of the vulvar odor and taste.

In *Pissing in the Snow,* No. 93, Randolph gives a complicated hoax story about *A half-witted boy at a dance who 'kept a-pestering every woman that come along, and finally they made it up to play a joke on him. A big girl named Lulu wrapped some fresh cow-shit in a piece of gunnysack, and led Ambrose out behind the barn. She laid down with the gunnysack betwixt her legs, and when he climbed on she guided his pecker right into the cow-shit. Ambrose begun to bounce up and down something wonderful, but pretty soon Lulu says, "Honey, I don't believe you've got it in very good." So then she reached her hand down to fix things. "No! No! Don't you do it!" says Ambrose, and he begun to grunt louder than ever. "If you got anything better than this, I don't want it!" ... The home folks pretty near died laughing, and some of 'em talked like the joke wasn't on Ambrose at all ...'* (Tar River, Okla. 1927, heard near Huntsville, Ark. 1910. Another of Randolph's informants stated that the 'big girl' actually was 'a man disguised in petticoats who held the cow-dung between his legs.') This has been much modified in the intervening years, and has picked up elements from the folklore of *sand* getting into a woman's vagina and preventing sexual relations — first in Perceau's *Histoires d'Hommes et de Dames* (1913) p. 47, "Les Grains de sable," in connection with cunnilinctus. *A man and woman are making love on the beach at night. The man asks, "Is it in?" "No, it's in the sand." "Now is it in?" "Oh, yes!" A moment passes, and the man says, "I don't know, I think I'll try it in the sand again."* (N.Y. 1963. Also *Sex to Sexty,* 6:21. An earlier American version, with *dirt* rather than sand, is given in 8.III.7.)

Hidden beneath all these rejections is the real and inexpugnable attraction to the woman, and specifically to her mocked and insulted genital organs. Usually told in Louisiana Cajun (Arcadian) or Canadian-French dialect: *The French trapper cannot stand domestic life and decides to desert his wife. She finds him piling his guns and traps into his canoe. "I'm leaving you," he says; "I always told you someday I would." "What am I going to do with the house and the dogs?" "Who the hell cares?" "And what am I going to do with the children?" "Stuff 'em up the crack of your ass where you got 'em!" She plays her trump card, and pulls her skirt over her head. "And what am I going to do with* THIS?" *He takes all his traps and guns out of the canoe and starts back to the house. "I'm telling you," he says,* "SOME *day I'm going to leave you!"* (Transatlantic steamship, 1963, told by an Italian-American ship's officer. In *Sex to Sexty,* 1966, 5:30.)

No more extreme spectacle of this type of marital verbal sadism has been seen in the public theatre, since the days of the Punch & Judy puppet shows, than Edward Albee's *Who's Afraid of Virginia Woolf?* (a cruel title-pun on the name of a great and suicided woman writer, which I leave for someone else to explain), one of the outstanding American theatrical successes of the 1960's, with two companies simultaneously playing it in the provinces for the hicks; also playing to record crowds in Paris in a notably bawdy-talking French adaptation by Jean Cau. Outstinking Strindberg by far, the purpose of Albee's play seems to be to make marriage so hideous to the audience that they will all turn homosexual immediately, but it may not prove to be quite so easy as that. The strangely infantile belief in the occult power of insults (*"Sticks and stones will break my bones, but names and faces never hurt me!"*) is one of the most striking points of similarity between the play and the present group of jokes, which are probably not its direct inspiration, but simply parallel folklore — and hardly more violently insulting. But then one never knows. It is certainly not drawn from real life.

The French version led to a very singular bit of feedback or cross-contamination, on the Oscar Wildean principle of 'life imitating art,' fully detailed by Gérald Limours in an article on *L' "Affaire" Robinson,* in *Le Spectacle du Monde* (Paris, Feb. 1966) p. 93–5; in which a middle-aged actress, Madeleine Svoboda, known as Madeleine Robinson, took advantage of her starring in the Jean Cau adaptation of Albee's play, opposite the actor, Raymond Gérôme, to 'add to the text insults directed against him personally, and to beat him physically with a violence unknown on the stage. All this under the eyes of the public, delighted with so much veracity.' M. Gérôme took it all like a trouper — his own part in the Albee play, truth to tell, being even more nauseous and sadistic than that of the female lead, no matter *what* she might *ad-lib* — and the story might never have been made public, except that Mme. Svoboda, flushed with her success, then undertook a one-woman crusade against fellow actresses of whom she disapproved, in particular ruining the theatrical début of the beautiful ex-strip-teaser, Rita Renoir, in *The Wind in the Sassafras,* in November 1965, by strident cat-calls at the moment when the younger woman came forward on the proscenium, with her leading man, the magnificent comedian, Michel Simon, for her first applause. *Who's Afraid of Virginia Woolf?*

Even more infantile than verbal insults and cat-calls (the French *whistle* to express disapproval in the theatre, as applauding Americans who whistle to express supreme approval have learned to their embarrassment), there is finally recourse, for purpose of sex hatred, to what has been called *the lowest of all human expressions,* the fart. All excretory functions when performed on or against another individual are understood perfectly as insults, even by infants and animals, and will be dealt with more fully in the final chapter, "Scatology," in Series Two. The *nexus* of the present example is, however, its use to express a specifically sexual hostility. This is given by Randolph, No. 87, as "Travelers Are All Fools," having been collected in Missouri in 1933 as 'an old story.' It concerns *A pretty widow-woman who refuses all the country boys because 'she says a farmer ain't no good, because he can't do nothing but shovel shit and holler "Gee!"* [to his plow-horse],' *and who gets her come-uppance from a high-class traveller to whom she gives lodging for the night when he is stopped by the rising river from going on.* ' *"Well," says he, "do you want me to treat you like my wife, or like a stranger?" The widow-woman thought awhile, and then she says, "Treat me like your wife." The man says, "All right, lady. It's your house." So then the fellow turned his back on her, let a couple of big farts, and went to sleep. The widow-woman just laid there and gritted her teeth, but she . . . never let no travelers in after that, no matter if the river is up or not.'* (A cleanup version is given below.)

Compare the riddle, "*When is the honeymoon over?*" sometimes expressed simply as a bit of proverbial wisdom: "*The honeymoon is over when the husband farts in front of his wife.*" Some families take a less rigid view of such natural events, but obviously both husband and wife must have the same privilege. This rapidly leads to such hateful abuses, if loves fades, as the rallying remarks on a spouse's fart recorded in *Sex to Sexty,* 1967, 13:49, under the heading "Windbreakers": *One Wife: Every time I let one, my husband snidely remarks, "There's a load off your mind!" Other Wife: "That's nothing; every time my husband lets one he says, "There's a big kiss for you, honey!"* This type of humor is certainly old, being nearly identical with the 17th-century witticism, recorded I believe in Thomas Dekker's *The Shoemaker's Holiday,* that the woman 'has a secret fault': *she farts in bed.* (See further "King Henry and the Miller of Mansfield," an English broadside ballad of 1655, quoted in full in Francis J. Child's *English and Scottish Popular Ballads,* 1898, v. 86, stanza 32, where the king and the miller 'with farting . . . made the bed hott.')

As usually collected, stories of the rejection of the woman by the man with whom she is in bed require some rationalization other than sex-hatred, as for instance that he is a 'nincumpoop' or sexual fool. *A traveling sales*woman *has to sleep with the farmer's big, gangling son. When they are in bed, she says, "Do you mind? I'd rather be on the other side. You roll over me and I'll roll over you, and we'll change places." Instead he gets up and runs around to the other side of the bed. She repeats the same request a few minutes later, and he runs back around the bed. "Say," she remarks, "I don't believe you know what I want at all." "Sure I do," he replies; "you want the whole damn bed, but you ain't a-gonna get it!"* (Orangeburg, N.Y., 1944.) Occasionally the necessary rationalization is mixed instead with elements from a very famous Levantine folktale on contests in stubbornness between husband and wife, which entered Europe in the 16th century through Straparola's *Piacevoli Notti,* VIII. 1, and is best known in English in comic-ballad form as "Get Up and Bar the Door." This is discussed further in the section below, "The Relationship with the Other Man."

In the present variant, *A man and woman, strangers to each other, consent to share a room in a crowded hotel if a partition is put up between the twin beds. After the light is out, the woman asks the man to get up and close the window a little. He does, and then she asks him please now to close it a little more. This is repeated several times. Finally he says, "How would you like to be Mrs. Smith just for tonight?" "Oh, I'd like that very much," she says emotionally. "Well then, get up and close the goddam window yourself!"* (N.Y. 1945.) This joke is considered to be 'clean,' as it has replaced all sexual elements with sex hatred. The man in the story is obviously not at all fooled by the woman's *manège,* and realizes — as the tellers of the story sometimes do not — that she does not want something *closed:* she wants something *opened.* (A wonderful example of Freud's "ambivalence of opposites.") The stumbling around of a man in a woman's darkened bedroom is, of course, a situation heavily freighted sexually, whatever hateful rejection is made to substitute for the expected sexual act. In Laurence Sterne's *Sentimental Journey* (1768) the book ends suddenly, halfway through the projected four volumes, with just such a scene, the man catching hold impotently of the chambermaid's —.

Though the analysis of 'clean' jokes is not within the province of the present work, a further cleanup of the preceding story might be mentioned, in which, as in all the materials just cited, the old maids' querulousness, and concern with open and closed windows, doors, and other apertures, has an equally sexual undertone. The rejection of their thus silently-offered bodies is achieved by a sort of Man in the Upper Berth, in this case going to the ultimate sex hatred of 'good-naturedly' proposing murder. *Two old maids on a train, who have never met before, argue pettily about which shall ride forward and which backward, suitcases on the seat, and so forth; and finally engage in a pitched battle as to whether the window shall be open or closed, irritating everyone else in the compartment. The conductor, whom they have summoned, is helpless to decide. "If that window is opened," says the one, "I shall catch my death a-cold." "And if that window stays shut," insists the other, "I shall suffocate." "Pardon me," says a Man Sitting in the Corner* [capitals to indicate the Mysterious Stranger, or demonic folk-hero], *"may I offer a suggestion?" The conductor agrees eagerly. "First,* OPEN *the window. That will kill one of these biddies* [sc. bitches]. *Then* SHUT *the window. That will kill the other one. And then we'll have some peace."* (Scranton, Pa. 1934. Often printed.)

3. MENSTRUATION, AND OTHER REJECTIONS

One of the commonest excuses for the wife's sexual rejection of the husband is that she is menstruating, for which she has, of course, religious authorization in the Judæo-Christian culture, the Bible specifically commanding, *Leviticus,* xx. 18 (the whole 20th chapter is well worth study): '*And if a man shall lie with a woman having her sick-*

ness, and shall uncover her nakedness; he hath discovered her fountain, and she hath uncovered the fountain of her blood: and both of them shall be cut off from among their people.' Jokes in which this is successfully countered by the man will be found in an earlier chapter under "The Sadistic Concept," his violent taking of the woman against her various protests and despite all subterfuges being considered a form of manly rape. It is relevant here only when successful in preventing intercourse — "¾ *jazztime and* ¼ *ragtime*" (*Sex to Sexty*, 5:26) — or, as in the following example, when dragged in as a pun to express sexual rejection. *Gypsy fortune-teller: "Did you ever get your hand read?" Man: "No, I don't believe in that sort of thing." "Then better take your hand out from under my skirt."* (2:287.) The sexual lore of Gypsies — also the Scottish Tinkers descended from them — in their relation with the host-populations would make a fascinating study, and is very similar to the sexual lore of Negroes *vis-à-vis* the former master race of whites.

The drunk is the sexual failure *par excellence*, though this is seldom observed at the folk level. Shakespeare's 'nose-painting and lechery,' as mutually exclusive, following the Porter's soliloquy in *Macbeth*, II.iii.-32, makes the case very clear. So do the endless sex-hatred cartoons in the public prints, showing drunks sneaking home late at night carrying their shoes guiltily in hand, while their 'neglected' wives wait to beat them over the heads, at sexless midnights, with rolling pins. The drunk has also the freedom of any sacred fool or drugged Dionysiac to handle forbidden things, such as the whole matter of menstruation and even the terrifying 'monthly rag' and other accoutrements of the woman's menstruation. (Alleged advertisement of a New York curiosity bookstore in the 1920's, as specializing in light reading: *"We specialize in weekly mags and monthly rags."*) The following burlesque skit was seen in a Florida nightclub, 1946: *The master-of-ceremonies' stooge pretends to be drunk and confides that there is a slot-machine in the ladies' toilet. "Sure there is," he insists, when the master-of-ceremonies disagrees; "where do you think I got this collar for my tux?" (Pulls out a woman's Kotex pad and hangs it around his neck, bringing down the house. Then as topper:) "Well, maybe it isn't a collar. I could use it as a simonizing rag for my car, except for these two pins." (Dangles the pad and belt-pins before the audience.) "I only went for cigarettes anyway."* People who think that 'sick humor,' or shocker nightclub acts, began with Lenny Bruce in the 1960's have never been around.

A super-salesman is being watched from behind the door by the territorial manager, who is stupefied to see the salesman run up a customer's request for a fishing rod into a whole fishing kit, hip boots and hunting clothes, an outdoor barbecue set, a new automobile, cub airplane ("for those whoppers in Canada"), and a country home to match. "How were you able to do it?" asks the manager, when the sucker has gone. "Oh, I knew he was in the right frame of mind," says the super-salesman calmly. "He originally didn't even want the fishing pole. He just came in to buy a box of Kotex for his wife." (Calif. 1952.) In an earlier defeatist version, appearing in print in the sex-humor magazine, *Calgary Eye-Opener,* in the mid-1930's, *A drugstore clerk who is given a black eye by a customer, explains that he was only trying to make a companion sale. The customer asked for a box of Kotex for his wife and the clerk suggested, as a companion sale, "a deck of cards for a dull weekend!"* The buying (or stealing) of unneeded physical objects, and the eating of unneeded foods, as a displacement of sexual dissatisfaction, is here very well understood and expressed at the folk level, and there is nothing surprising about its being, in fact, one of the main and conscious forcing-lines of Western advertising. The slogan *"Sell It with Sex!"* (especially in the case of expensive advertisements in full-full color) does not really mean what it says, but the opposite of what it says: "Sell it with the sex they *haven't got.*"

Menstruation in women is often paired, as a specifically female activity, with shaving in men, as specifically male; as in the non-joking statement, more than once encountered, that *"A man has more trouble in a lifetime, shaving every day, than a woman ever has with her monthlies. (Sometimes adding:* "I'd be willing to trade.") This also pinpoints the periodical nature of shaving, which is part of its parallel with menstruation. A well-known army triad of World War II states that a man cleans up with '*A shower, a shave, & a shit.*' (Politely: '*. . . and a haircut.*') This seems to be in the background of an odd and infrequently-collected American folk-poem, first seen in the mid-1950's — six monorhymed couplets beginning:

> Of all the dirty tricks, it really makes me rave,
> To have my wife come in to shit, when I begin to shave.
> There's just one time in all the day, when solitude I crave,
> But she insists she has to shit, at the time I have to shave.
> She sits and drops her stinking bit into that watery grave;
> I don't see why she couldn't wait until I've had my shave.

The fecal associations with the wife (while the man is presumably 'making himself clean') show that this poem has nothing in it but sex hatred. It does, of course, correctly complain of the excessive bathroom intimacy more common in cold marriages than in over-sentimental ones, despite the contrary belief.

Women have, in the last quarter century, in the Anglo-Saxon countries, undertaken the shaving of their legs in connection with wearing silk stockings, and even more commonly the shaving of their armpits. Most men resent this as an obvious usurping of a male prerogative, and among the real curiosa of our culture are the advertisements for razors for women. The similarly usurped pants, cigarette lighters, folding wallets, etc., seldom sink to such true bathos. One of the most extraordinary was an advertisement for the expensive Rolls Razor, appearing in an early issue of *Esquire* during the 1930's, at a period when it was considered a very sexy men's magazine. The advertisement showed a handsome young woman in déshabille, speaking over a telephone to a man. She is saying: "*That tip of yours was swell last night!*" The '*tip*' turns out to be, of course, that she should buy a Rolls Razor to shave herself where necessary. This advertisement deserves an "A" for effort, in trying to make what is non-sexual and even anti-sexual and perverse (sado-fetichistic) into something purportedly erotic; but the actual facts are as stated above. Men also feel erotically deprived of the secondary sexual charm of women's armpit hair, of which the sensed sexuality is precisely the reason why the Anglo-Saxon Mrs. Grundy has decreed its removal: the hairy armpit clearly resembling the hairy vulva. (Compare the joke earlier on the girl with the vagina in her armpit. 8.III.6, *ad fin.*) Girls who sometimes let their armpit hair grow to please a lover, during the winter, will nevertheless become intimidated in summer, when sleeveless dresses and bathing suits are worn, and will begin shaving again then. It is another demonstration of the *virility of the breasts* that the attempted fashion of bare breasts on bathing beaches in the 1960's *also* absurdly involves shaved armpits (thus denying their femaleness), which is hardly sexual freedom. It is, however, not common for Western women to shave the pubic hair, which they realize would be going too far; and any woman who habitually does so is to be avoided as probably dangerously neurotic. Razors for women, specifically for pubic shaving ('the bathing-suit shave'), are now being merchandised.

It happened to me quite recently to touch a number of these strings all at once, almost by accident, in visiting the sordid New York apartment of a success-oriented working-girl, who had no bathroom and had (as it later turned out) to shave her legs in the windowless kitchen sink, which would be covered with running cockroaches when one turned on the light. For reasons that escape me, I thought to tell her the joke about *The little girl and boy playing together. The little girl says, "Let's play Daddy and Mama. You shave and I'll vomit."* She responded with violent anger, and would not speak to me for the rest of the day. The cockroaches or Croton-bugs infesting most older New York apartment houses are really no one's fault: merely a symptom of the senescence of this once-great city. Women shaving — rather than reserving their femininity and 'beauty care' to the normality of armpit hair, menstruation, and so forth — is of course another matter. Those who can remember the early 1920's, before the general introduction in the West, from Japan, of disposable paper menstrual pads (later vaginal tampons, also from Japan), will recollect that men found it equally easy to be disgusted then by the "sinkful of pink water and bloody rags," when a woman would wash out her menstrual cloths monthly. In Norman Lindsay's novel *The Cautious Amorist,* in the 1920's, a specific point is made of the lone woman, cast away on a desert island with several men, requiring one of them to tear up his shirt to give her for this purpose. This was considered a very daring allusion at the time. Even today, in the backward West Indies, particularly British Trinidad, the phrase *"Tor ass clot'!"* (*Your arse cloth!*) is considered the most extreme possible insult to a woman, and its use as an ejaculation during the singing of Calypso songs or the playing of bamboo-band music — as might be *"Mother-fucker!"* by American Negroes or their imitators — is the ultimate local obscenity. It is not necessary to discuss here the ultimate British taboo-word, *"bloody!"* which can only be (like the superstition of bad luck concerning the number *thirteen*) derived from the fear of menstruation.

4. FRIGIDITY AND HENPECKING

The woman's inability to reach orgasm is not considered by the man so much as an emotional or physical loss to the woman, as an insult to himself and to his 'technique' and virility. Much of the offensive adviseering of sex-technique manuals turns on this question of practically *forcing* the woman to have an orgasm — as, for instance, by means of a vibrating-massage motor held against the clitoris during intercourse — which is an excellent shock-technique, but which cannot be the basis of a whole married life. The woman's frigidity naturally broadens into a general dislike for sexual relations, or an unwillingness to engage in them and be humiliated by her impotence. Precisely her feeling of insufficiency in the sexual role makes her unlikely or unable to accept with any calm her replacement by some more erotic woman or girl in her husband's life, if not actually in his affections; and it is a truism that frigid women are the most insanely jealous, because they know just how 'vulnerable' to other women their own rejection makes their husbands. This also explains the venomous and revindicatory greediness of most such women during the inevitable divorce following, especially if the husband can be made out the 'guilty' party, and be forced to pay. The likelihood of the frigid wife being caught in adultery, and thrown out without a settlement, is naturally slight.

An elderly husband after an evening at a risqué French farce with his wife says to her, "Come on, Martha, let's have a party." [Slang of the 1920's for sexual intercourse.] *"Go ahead," she says. Next morning she asks in a tone of interest, "How did you make out last night, John?"* (1:175, repeated verbatim in *Anecdota*, 1933, No. 176.) *Sex to Sexty*, 5:14, gives this in the form of a cartoon, showing hillbillies in intercourse — the pig sleeps in the bedroom with them — indicated by means of the usual expurgated partialism of the interlocked male and female feet, but here with the quilts courageously shown humped up as well. One-line caption: *"Pa, if I go to sleep before you get through, will you pull down my nightgown?"* As noted in my type-facsimile edition of Burns' *Merry Muses of Caledonia* (1965) p. 195, Dr. Martin Schurig — in one of the final volumes of his still classic early sexological series, *Gynæcologia, hoc est Congressus muliebris consideratio* (Dresden, 1730) — devotes a long chapter, following that *"De coitu violento, seu stupro,"* to the subject, *"De stupratio in somne,"* p. 301–67, opening with the inquiry as to whether or not intercourse with a sleeping woman is actually possible. (The present writer has demonstrated empirically, in the winter of 1964/5, that it *is* possible. Any sacrifice for research.) This excludes, of course, intercourse with a sleeping woman who is drunk as well.

The frigid woman is hated by the man. This is an absolute rule. The exception would be the man who is himself so neurotically or masochistically tainted that he welcomes the anti-sexual woman and the *mariage en blanc* with her. *"Have you seen those ice cubes with a hole in them?" "Hell, I married one!"* (N.Y. 1957. This was at the time guaranteed to be that *rara avis,* a 'new joke.') From hatred to the thought of the woman as dead, and the desire that she die, is an obvious step. *Man, to aggrieved wife: "How about a little piece [of ass], honey?" "Over my dead body!" "How else?"* (N.Y. 1953, or with punch-lines, *"As usual,"* or *"You said it!"*) The implication is the same as the joke earlier, on the man who calls his wife "Deadass" on leaving in the morning. Specifically it means that the woman will not take the trouble to move her buttocks during intercourse, and 'lays there' leaving all the necessary motion to the man; or else that she does not wriggle with anything comparable to the 'simulated enthusiasm' or *expertise* of a belly-dancer's or strip-teaser's 'bumps & grinds.' The *Paris-American Kiosk,* a tourist news magazine of 1955, gives the brief but bitter colloquy: *"Am I hurting you?" "Why?" "I thought you moved a little!"* Contradicting the idea of *orgasm as 'death.'*

Ultimately, the pretendedly dead or just-as-good-as-dead woman is dead in earnest, and the jokes imply broadly that it is the husband's 'death-wish' against her that has done her in, though we are only allowed to see him taking a last necrophiliac farewell. *A man being sentenced to jail for intercourse with his wife's body, a few hours after her death, is asked if he has anything to say in his own defense. "Honest, Judge, I didn't know she was dead. She's been like that for the last twelve years."* (1:429.) A mock-Jewish version of this has *the modern, hot-jazz, Freedom-train rabbi speaking at the "Enlighten Thy Daughter" meeting of the Ladies' Auxiliary and Bas-Mitzvah Preparation Society. "Ladies," he says in a pained but long-suffering voice, "I am sure you realize I can't discuss such matters in detail as the unfortunate member of our congregation who has been sent to the penitentiary for having intercourse with his wife's dead body by accident. But please, ladies, when making love with a good Jewish husband — please, give a little wiggle!"* (N.Y. 1963.)

The following sex-hatred story has the one clearest and longest line of descent of any tale in the present work. As presented, in the Larson MS., No. 54 (collected in Eden, Idaho, in 1932), it makes no mention of sex hatred, and is apparently entirely concerned with love. The wife's hostile or reproachful meaning is, however, its entire message.

A young couple, desperately in love, were too poor to get married. But, suddenly, a wonderful solution occurred to them: they could live on love. Certainly they had enough of that! The first morning after they were married he got up to go to work, and, since there was no breakfast, he laid her on the table and took a piece. That noon he came home, and, since there was no lunch waiting, he again laid her on the table and took a piece.

In the evening, however, he came home quite famished, and still there was no food on the table. And his sweet young wife was sitting there with her dress pulled high, her pants down, and her feet up on the oven door. "What are you doing there, Dear?" he asked. "Oh, I'm just warming up your supper, Darling!" she replied. [French: *Kryptádia,* x. 76.]

Though not traced by Aarne-Thompson (Type 1464D, noting only a modern Finnish expurgated version), the space need not be taken here to trace this to its earliest recorded form, in the Greek *Philogelos,* or *Astéia,* or Jests of Hierocles and Philagrius, somewhere before the 9th century A.D., as this has already been handled in very full detail in my *Horn Book* (1964) p. 219–22, and further in the notes to my *type-facsimile* edition of Burns' *Merry Muses of Caledonia* (1965) p. 171–4, in connection with a brief rhymed epigram set to the music of "Clout the Cauldron" in the *Merry Muses* (orig. ed. '1799' [c. 1800] p. 45), under the title, "Supper Is Na Ready":

> Roseberry to his lady says,
> "My hinnie and my succour.
> "O shall we do the thing you ken,
> "Or shall we take our supper?"
> *Fal lal, &c.*

> Wi' modest face, sae fu' o' grace,
> Replied the bonny lady;
> "My noble lord do as ye please,
> "But supper is na ready."
> *Fal lal, &c.*

Those who are interested will find a number of the intermediate 16th-century and later French texts, from which this is drawn, in my articles above-cited, and it might be added here that the sardonic touch of the excessive endearments (Lord Roseberry calling his wife his 'honey and sugar,' exactly of a piece with the 'Dear' and 'Darling' of the Idaho tale) is all that has been added in the Scottish and American form. The original — or, at least, the oldest text known — is that in the portion of the *Philogelos* attributed to Philagrius (Greek text, ed. Eberhard, Berlin, 1869) No. 244: '*A young man said to his warm-blooded wife: "Wife, what shall we do? Shall we have breakfast, or devote ourselves to Aphrodite?" She replied: "As you prefer. We haven't a bite to eat".*' Except for the change from breakfast to *supper*, the precise dry wit of the wife's mocking reply has been preserved without change for over a thousand years.

Various other jokes on themes approaching that of sex hatred will be found in the opening section of Chapter 14, "Dysphemism," in Series Two, where the he-&-she repartee has seemed less important in the jokes than the dysphemistic vulgarity and verbal violence. Physical violences, especially of the wife against the husband, are often displaced upon social proxies such as policemen, judges, etc., as in real life. In the clear or uncoded form, already given: *A man sues his wife for divorce because her pubic hair, which was blonde at their marriage, has turned black, and he demands a divorce on the grounds of fraud. As her defense she hits him suddenly in the eye with a baseball, and then says to the judge, "Look, your Honor, I hit him in the eye with one ball and it's turning black in two minutes. He's been hitting me on the ass with two balls for a year, and complains because it gets a little dark!"* (N.Y. 1942.) The 'coded' version has the scene take place before the *din-torah* (appeal to the law) of the rabbi, who replaced both judge and psychologist for the Jews of the European *shtétel* (self-contained Jewish community): *A man comes to see the rabbi, whom he finds eating his lunch of an onion and a hard-boiled egg with a Bialystoker roll, and complains to the rabbi, who continues munching his understanding, that his wife's pubic hair has turned black after being blonde since their marriage. The rabbi suddenly jams his hard-boiled egg in the complainant's eye, and says, "Look, be reasonable. I bang your eye with one egg, and immediately it turns black. You've been banging her with two eggs* [Hebrew, *baytzim*, eggs, testicles] *for months; what can you expect?"* (N.Y. 1950.) Though collected later this is probably the original, as the linguistic evidence suggests. The situation of the rabbi taking the wife's side in the *din-torah* for divorce is common in Jewish folklore, divorce being ritualistically too easy for the man. I have heard, as a 'true' story, of a rabbi felling a husband with a folio volume of the Talmud for 'driving his wife into adultery' by not making love to her often enough. (Scranton, Pa. 1938, from a young Jewish woman, unmarried.) *Se non è vero, è ben trovato.*

Mark Twain was one of the first writers to discuss the possibilities of the telephone for insulting (later obscene) communications, in "Travelling With a Reformer," in *The Man That Corrupted Hadley-burg, and other stories* (London, 1900) p. 257. Jokes seem to favor the telegram, as in the earlier example of the widow who telegraphs to the undertakers to cut off her dead husband's penis. *An American businessman in Paris writes his wife that he has met a very interesting girl dancing in the Folies Bergère, and feels he should make her his protégée or that they should adopt her. The girl has a Master of Arts degree from the University of Tours, and is only dancing naked in the Folies in order to earn enough money to go for her Ph.D. at the University of Michigan. She also has a paraplegic brother whose only support she is, and the businessman feels he ought to do something for her. His wife cables him at once:* "STOP. IF YOU CAN'T BE GOOD BE CAREFUL." *His answer is immediate:* "YOUR CABLE CAME JUST ONE HOUR TOO LATE." (N.Y. 1946.) This is very mild, everything being thrown on the situation, and the punch-line (a modern proverb) is present only out of routine. I have also heard this more recently with the girl virtuously earning her education as a topless waitress in a San Francisco nightclub, or 'Bunny' in a Playboy club (the Chicago version of the low German Tingeltangel bars).

Occasionally more detail is given. *A businessman husband telephones his wife from an Artists' and Writers' banquet to which he has been invited, and says,* "You know, dear, there's something very unexpected here. I thought it would just be drinking and speeches, but there's naked girls dancing on the tables and going under the tables with the men. What shall I do?" "If you think you can do anything," *says his wife,* "come right home." (1:312.) Combining both forms: *A New York brassière manufacturer's wife learns from a friend returning from Florida that her husband, who has gone there for a rest, has been seen helling it up with a harem of call-girls in the most expensive nightclubs. She telegraphs, hoping to touch some remnant of his business sense:* "COME HOME. WHY SPEND MONEY IN FLORIDA FOR WHAT YOU CAN GET FOR NOTHING HERE?" *Immediate reply:* "TO HELL WITH YOU AND YOUR BARGAINS."

One senses a withdrawal toward innocuousness and mere chaff in the sex-hatred stories involving letters and telegrams. This is built into the form, as implied in Mark Twain's "Travelling With a Reformer," where he wants to call the travelling reformer a jackass, but has just observed that the reformer is a powerful boxer (an early *karate*-buff, he has just struck practically dead three roughnecks who had begun to 'fling hilarious obscenities and profanities right and left' in a horse-car, some of whose timid passengers were women and children). Twain therefore 'did not say it, knowing there was no hurry and I could say it just as well some other time over the telephone.' Except for deeply disturbed individuals, or the hoaxes and 'jokes' of high-school girls and boys, obscene and threatening phone-calls, anonymous hate-mail and poison-pen letters are not the weapons of choice.

The final murder of the hated spouse, or, more often, of the adulterous lover who receives the surrogate death-blow, is common in folk-tales, especially in the older Italian *novelle* and the Levantine tales from which they stem, but is almost never encountered in jokes except on the excuse of adultery, and even there seldom in fully achieved form. The ultimate and necessary subterfuge is that of madness: the 'moron' in the moron-jokes of recent popularity, to whom everything is permitted — including murder and worse — because he gives *no* explanation at all. There has developed over the last thirty years, particularly in America, this use of a sort of folk-rationalization in humor, of comedy-insanity, far beyond what was formerly understood as the humor of 'fools,' or even of the sacred wandering Bedlam lunatics (the 'village idiot' stories), and the dwarfed and disturbed characters who have always classically been — and still are — the court-jesters, circus clowns, carnival geeks, and nightclub and vaudeville 'sick' comedians, all of whom have specifically in common their allowed and open expression of all the uglier and more anti-social parts of their own and the audience's *id*. See the end of Chapter 2, "Fools."

The best discussion so far accorded to this type of humor is Dr. Martha Wolfenstein's "Riddles and the Legend of the Moron," in her *Children's Humor* (Glencoe, 1954) p. 93–157, especially p. 126–38, which includes some very penetrating insights. Much more, however, could still be said, and should still be collected in the field of the recent 'nut' or 'bop' jokes, 'sick' jokes (there is a whole collection, of which the funniest joke is probably the title, Max Rezwin's *The Best of Sick Jokes*, New York, 1962), and elaborate *non-sequiturs* as to shaggy dogs, elephants, Martians and other interstellar displaced persons and conquistadores (collected in Dr. Charles Winick's *Outer*

Space Humor, Mount Vernon, N.Y. 1963). Occasionally these genres allow of partial rationalizations, as mere lies, nonsense, or tall-tale exaggerations, or as the temporary delirium of drunkenness or of more recent and popular hallucinatory drugs, such as hemp (marijuana) and various poisonous mushrooms (of which the most remarkable and most dangerous, the Russian Angel *amanita,* taken by the Eskimos, has fortunately not yet created a fad among *faux révolté* hippies and college students, on the style of the cynically publicized LSD, and mescal, which *create induced schizophrenia,* though this secret has been carefully kept). Also to be assimilated to the new I-ain't-responsible-because-I'm-nuts group is any humorous story with the actual *mise-en-scène* of the insane asylum itself, or any equivalent of it, such as an army induction center, a marriage counsellor's (formerly rabbi's) or physician's office, or a psychoanalyst's couch. See further the Introduction here, section III.

A fine example of this is given in the article, "Texture, Text, and Context," by Dr. Alan Dundes, in *Southern Folklore Quarterly* (1964) XXVIII. 259-61, in an extraordinary flyting or 'crossing' of horrible castration jokes *by two real informants, a husband and wife,* in which — in jocular form, *of course,* and in each other's presence — each describes a husband or wife as having castrated the other by means of a pretended foolish literalism (Thompson's Motif N13, "Husbands wager that they will be able to do what wives tell them to do"), and further pretends to be carrying around the other's cut-out organ, which is then offered 'insanely' to the listener's view:

> Three henpecked husbands determine to get back at their wives. Being henpecked, they can't really rebel, so they decide to obey their wives and to do exactly what they're told to do. A month or so later, the men are together in a bar. The first says, "Well, we were eating supper and I accidentally spilled a little tiny bit of gravy on the tablecloth. So my wife says, 'Go ahead, spill gravy all over the table!' So I did — I turned that gravy bowl over; I smeared the stuff all over the table. I sure got even with my wife!"
>
> The second says, "Well, I was comin' in the door and wind caught it, and it slammed shut. My wife, she hollers in at me, 'Go ahead, tear it off the hinges.' So I did. I ripped that damn door right off the hinges. I sure got even with my wife!"

The third one said, "We were in bed and I was trying to get my wife to make love, and I was fooling around a little and my wife, she says, 'Cut it out!' — Ever see one of these things up close?"

(This joke was told by a thirty year old male school teacher to a twenty-two year old married female folklore collector [in Lawrence, Kans. 1963]. The informant's wife was present during the joke, and when it was over she offered an alternate ending:)

"... and I was fooling around a little and my wife, she says, 'Knock it off!' [*slang for: to stop or cease*] (with the gesture of raising a hand and swinging it as if one were swinging a pendulum). "How do you put one of these things back on?"

(*Note by Dr. Dundes:*) In a version I heard in Bloomington, Indiana, in 1962. . . . The third incident is the same as in the present text except that the punchline is accompanied by a gesture in which the raconteur cups his two hands together as if concealing the detached object in question.

As the final joke in a section on "Sex Hatred," obviously this cannot be topped. The leading line, certainly, in all these insane and mock-insane variants and charades, as in the older wise-fool jokes, is the idea that one can get away with anything if only one acts crazy enough (*Hamlet, Goha the Fool, Schweik the Good Soldier*). Or else that simply and actually *being* insane is perhaps the best rationalization of all. We are now becoming aware of the dangerous anti-rational currents in modern life, as a mute and largely unconscious resistance against the pressures of society (Freud's *Civilization and Its Discontents*) and the dehumanizations of science. This is one of them.

II. THE RELATIONSHIP WITH THE OTHER MAN

It is generally overlooked that no such thing as adultery exists, in and of itself, and that this is just a name which is given to otherwise neutral and permissible sexual relations between certain socially unauthorized persons. *There is no such sexual act as adultery.* Like incest, or the sexual abuse of minors, the definition turns solely on the parental or socially determined relationship, or lack of relationship, between the

persons engaged in the sexual act. Adultery is essentially the abroga-
tion only of a social contract or, more romantically put, the betraying
of a trust. It is important to keep this salient characteristic in focus, as
otherwise the determining of when adultery does and does not take
place becomes difficult or impossible. Many a man has been killed for
being found with his shoes off and his necktie undone in another
man's wife's bedroom, without anyone being concerned with learning
or demonstrating whether physical sexual intercourse really has taken
place. The opportunity is sufficient to 'prove' the offense, and generally
to clear the husband of the accusation of murder, on what is called
the 'Unwritten Law' (the right to kill the adulterer *in flagrante
delicto*), since the testimony of the only competent witness, the wife,
as to the innocence of the relationship, cannot be expected to hold up
in court. (As opposed to the popular notion, a wife can and often does,
in such cases, testify against her husband: the law is only that she
cannot be *required* to do so.)

On the other hand, where the husband is willing to allow certain
intimacies — always short of vaginal sexual intercourse with ejaculation
of semen in the vagina (obviously a concern more with the legitimacy
of a possible child than with the exact conclusion of the adulterous
intercourse) — and where these have acquired social acceptance, extreme sexual intimacies are possible between persons, one or both of
whom may be married to someone else, without complaint by the
spouse not involved. This ranges from 'French' kissing-games among
young couples in Married Student Housing apartments at modern
universities, to the allowed games of the *'petite oie'* (mutual masturbation, oragenitalism, and vulvar intercourse without intromission) between the wives of medieval crusaders and their troubadour lovers, on
which see the important work by Robert Briffault, *Les Troubadours
et le sentiment romanesque* (1945) — now in English translation — in
supplement to his great *The Mothers*. It is curious to note that though
the same *jeux de la petite oie,* especially mutual masturbation and oragenitalism, are at present considered the sexual substitutes of choice
among unmarried young people, especially in America and France,
when the girl is unwilling to go any further; these are not now acceptable as 'less than adultery' to any normally jealous spouse.

Again, contrariwise, such absolute *curiosa* of adultery have been
created by recent centuries' progress in sexual and contraceptive techniques, as the serious legal arguing that *adultery does not take place*

if the man has worn a condom, as his penis has not actually touched the woman! Many men who would find this perfectly grotesque and absurd, can nevertheless easily be brought to agree — as in the hope of having a boy child — to the injection of another (and better) man's refrigerated semen into their wives' uterus, by way of 'artificial insemination,' as long as such pitiful social, rather than sexual, protective measures are taken, as ensuring that the wife does not know the personal identity of the donor (*i.e.* will never meet and recognize him again socially!) and making equally sure — sometimes by documents signed by the physician involved — that the donor's intelligence-quotient is above a certain minimum, that he is (or is not) a Christian, and that his skin pigmentation is not *darker* than that of the woman he is inseminating at long distance. We shall return to this point in connection with certain ancient jokes.

In countries where Carnival, Purim, or some equivalent survival of the Saturnalia is celebrated, such as the Christmas 'Office Party,' or the sort of mythical or historical solstice/equinox orgy celebrated in "The Ball o' Kirriemuir," the whole point of the festival is nothing other than the permitted sexual license, specifically to the married, as a sort of once-a-year permitted blowoff of steam. This is what is behind the present rather gauche wife-swapping binge in Protestant America. It was formerly also intended to make certain that there were few childless marriages, in the centuries before the cold and 'non-involved' mechanics of artificial insemination, and in those cultures accepting the warmer human implications of Carnival.

There emerges from these considerations the fact that 'adultery' is a fluid and culturally-controlled concept, in which the *least* important element is the woman — *adultery by the wife* being that in question — and in which the really important relationship is that between the two men: the husband and 'The Other Man.' The same is equally true in adultery *by the husband,* in which the essential question is the relationship between the wife and the 'Other Woman.' Where polygamy exists, and women live as sister-wives in harems, the principal activity of the wives is a sort of bedroom politics for the purpose of gaining status as 'head wife' over all the other wives & concubines. (See, for instance, the cruel competition of Sarah and Hagar, and later of all the various wives and sub-wives of the patriarch Jacob, in *Genesis,* chapters xvi and xxx.) The husband's or patriarch's emotions, his fertility, his sexual and social desires — as for heirs to the throne — are considered only the raw material out of which the women's competitive careers are to be carved.

This is the entire sexual history of all monarchic courts, of which the sexual servicing of European potentates as recent as Edward VII of England (in his endless decades as Prince of Wales) and of all other politicians, victorious soldiers, and millionaires before and since, is mere child's play compared to that frankly engaged in, since time immemorial, in all Levantine countries and the Orient. (See, for some astonishing examples concerning Italy and India, Harold Acton's *The Last of the Medici,* first published in Florence in the 1920's; and Kanhayalal Gauba's *"H.H." or The Pathology of Princes,* Lahore: Times of India Press, 1930.) The identical situation immediately developed in the German concentration camps during the 1940's, where it was generally not necessary to *rape* the incarcerated women — of whatever religion or nationality — large numbers of them being more than willing to jockey for small favors, food, and status by means of their pan-sexual complaisance, of a most total and unbelievably competitive sort. Things are not really so different now under monogamy, especially where the patriarch or 'boss' has any social or monetary prerogatives worth the women's fighting for. The competition is merely less frank between the legitimate wives and the career girls, *'ready, willing, and anxious to fuck their way to the top.'*

Enough examples have been given in the preceding section to make clear the inevitable relationship, at least in jokes, between sex hatred and marital infidelity — *i.e.* adultery — requiring hardly more than a spark of opportunity for the libidinal electricity to leap the gap. It is important to observe that the adultery to which the sex-hatred jokes almost invariably tend is adultery *by the husband,* since it is the husbands who are telling the jokes. The husband's adultery is considered so venial a sin, under patriarchy, under no matter what humiliating circumstances for the wife, that the adulterous element is generally lost sight of. The husband is presumably — and probably in fact — doing what any normal man would do, given the opportunity; and, if any recollection of the marital tie exists, all the emphasis is placed on the husband's boredom with or hatred for the sexually uninteresting creature who is the girl he once loved, now referred to as his 'fat, middle-aged wife.' A few further and very pointed examples can be given here, after which we will have the other side of the story: the wife's emotions about the man she married and may even have admired, who is now her perhaps equally unappetizing 'fat, middle-aged husband,' and her flight from him into a lover's arms.

The word 'love,' which has just come up almost in passing, is obviously difficult to define, nor is this the place to attempt it. A great deal of absolute bunk, practically every word of it over-subtle if not actually false, has been spread in two modern works, *The Evolution of Love* by Emil Lucka (English translation, London, 1922), and Denis de Rougemont's *Love in the Western World* (translation, 1941), both attempting to demonstrate that the idea of romantic love is somehow *modern;* the first that it rises from the German literary legend of *Tristan und Isolde,* the second that it was a medieval (French, *bien entendu*) importation from Arabic mystic poetry. In point of fact, any number of ancient Greek poets, such as the fragments of Sappho, describe the true and authentic emotion of violent love, while the *Song of Songs* (which is not actually by King Solomon, about 1000 B.C., but a Levantine epithalamium probably dating from five to eight centuries later) shows, in passage after passage, the most total picture of romantic love. One is particularly struck by the authenticity and power of the lines v. 4-7, rather spoiled by the unfortunate modern connotation of the word 'bowels' in the English translation: 'My beloved put in his hand by the hole of the door, and my bowels were moved for him . . . I opened to my beloved; but my beloved had withdrawn himself and was gone: my soul failed when he spake: I sought him, but I could not find him; I called him, but he gave me no answer.' The expurgatory nonsense that this is a 'parable of God's love for his people (*or* the church)' need obviously not detain us here. If there is any symbolism intended — and there may very well be, in such images as the lover putting in his hand by the hole of the girl's door — it is not of a religious nature. And certainly nothing in *Tristan und Isolde* or in any of the millennium-later Arab mystic poets goes so like an arrow into the real heart of the physical symptoms of the emotion of love, so lovingly anatomized as a form of *'Melancholy'* by Robert Burton (in the 17th century), as this perfect scene in the *Song of Songs.*

What is really meant by Emil Lucka and by Rougemont, and why the subject must be dealt with here, is that *marriage and love* have not been considered to be in any way connected, let alone on a *sine qua non* basis, until as recently as the early 19th century, when Balzac's *Physiology of Marriage* shows devastatingly how far at odds the emotion of love and the institution of marriage had by that time found themselves. Meanwhile, of course, if women and men could love each other with all their bodies and souls in the fifth century B.C., they could still do so — and still *were* doing so — fifteen hundred years later. But these were perhaps not the people who were getting married; or perhaps marriage, in the usual way, blunted the original frenzy of their emotion.

Though it is the habit, in Anglo-Saxon countries, to speak slightingly of cultures where marriages are still *arranged* between young people who may hardly even have met each other (not counting such marriages among royalty, where seldom mocked, though still very much the rule), the sad fact is that most marriages are not undertaken in the West, still today, for reasons of romantic love, but rather out of crude self-interest: the girl or woman in order to have her own home and social position, to be able to have the children she biologically wants, in a protected way, and to get out of her family's control (and possibly off the work-market as well); the man in order not to keep eating in restaurants all his life, to have a wife to keep house for him, and to show off to other men, and to have a 'steady lay.' Motives such as these are certainly no worse than, and not much different from, those of the *arranged* marriages of, for instance, China, and of the European Jewish culture which has disappeared since 1940. Both are marriages equally far removed from passionate love.

Many of these unfortunate people never know what they have missed, and the continuous dangling before their eyes, in books and movies and in the publicity-mounted 'private' lives of current celebrities, of the passion of violent love, serves only to frustrate and confuse them, and generally to drive them into the hypocritical pretense — especially before their children's eyes (when they are not fighting with each other!) — that they too feel this well-publicized emotion, and for their legal spouses. Adultery is the result, when this insincere and egoistically self-seeking house of cards crumbles under the impact of the authentic emotion of love, coming from outside the marriage, or even of authentic sexual passion. Just as often, too, adultery is undertaken as a *revenge* against the other spouse, not for not having loved sufficiently or devotedly enough (or even erotically enough), as is usually believed or pretended, nor even as a slap back at the other spouse's own adultery — though this is common enough — but rather for not having been able to inspire in the unloving, and now adulterous, partner the yearned-for emotion of love. That the real fault may lie in the unloving person's *inability* to love is only too clear. In any case, where adultery is the result of actual love for another person, divorce is usually immediately sought.

I. ADULTERY BY THE HUSBAND

The basic difficulty in preventing the wife or husband from learning of the 'guilty' spouse's adultery is not any technical problem in keeping the matter secret, but the immediately evident disinterest in continuing sexual relations with the rejected partner. This is phrased backwards, as it were, in an expurgated witticism in *Anecdota Americana* (1934) No. 171: '*"The reason I don't cheat," said one married man to another, "is that I find it so hard to keep up with my legitimate loving* [sc. *screwing]".*' I was told, as a true anecdote, in New York, 1964, about *A woman who tells another woman, "I'm not worried about my husband running around. I* break its neck *every morning before he leaves the house."* A remark that hostile ought to have, at the very least, an exclamation point following; but it was told in the most casual, even offhand, tone of voice. Seen from the man's point of view this is identical with the remark apocryphally attributed (at the end of the chapter, "The Male Approach," 4.v, above) to the Italian tenor Enrico Caruso, the matinée idol of the American high-society opera world of the 1900's: the period and world described in *Painted Veils* by James Gibbons Huneker. *"I never make love in the morning," Caruso is supposed to have said. "It's bad for the voice; it's bad for the health; and you never know who you might meet in the afternoon."* Most men think this is a pretty funny joke.

The organization of modern business life does not really allow of breaking into the work day with sexual activity, and the endless gags and cartoons in the men's magazines, about making love to one's stenographer on the office desk behind locked doors, during the morning 'sex-break,' are more probably to be understood as a wishful dream than as a reality. Also, most young women are not willing to agree to such totally unromantic 'quickies.' There are, of course, exceptions. The notion that *other people's sex life* takes place in an unrepressed fashion, all day long and in the most unlikely places, is a basic tenet of the sexual folk beliefs of people who, themselves, make love only in a very routine fashion in bed, after the cat and milk-bottles have been dutifully put out.

The ancient belief that confessing priests have sexual relations with the women whom they confess — or would do so, if possible — is clearly formalized in the impassable (?) nature of the wall or lattice separating the two parts of the confession booth. A similar formalization is still to be observed in many American universities, where the professors' offices — in which they are free to receive beautiful young girl students for private conferences — generally have solid doors or at least frosted windowpanes in the doors, and can be and often are locked; while the hardworking graduate students and Ph.D. candidates, who are forced to do most of the real teaching and thus liberate the professors for 'research' (so that they may Publish and not Perish), are likely to have to receive the students of both sexes in windowless little cubicles, sometimes smaller than the usual confession box, which *have no knobs on the doors* and cannot be locked or even shut! This is similar to the removal of the doors from toilet booths, in men's toilets — again in many colleges — to prevent homosexual use of the booths, which, as a matter of fact, might otherwise take place at all hours of the day.

The presumed daytime sex-lives of people in the musical and educational world — as differentiated from the mere dream of such a life in the envious business world — is of course part & parcel of the anti-intellectual stance and prejudice, especially in America. It would be going too far to say that this has no existence, in *both* worlds, but one is surprised, nevertheless, to see the arming of the anti-intellectual enemy with these accusations in, for example, the soft-focus *kitsch* dream of "The Girl in the Black Raincoat," by Professor Leslie A. Fiedler, in *Partisan Review* (Winter, 1964/5) XXXII. 35 *ff.*, in which the horny professor not only screws hell out of the willing and mysterious coed, naked as a jaybird's ass under her fetichistic black raincoat, but also appears to be sharing his delights with the Negro janitor by musing about them in blackface coon-comedy dialogue. This is really giving Norman Mailer's Greenwich Village fake-psychoanalyst-*cum*-cocksman characters, as in his powerful and valid "The Time of her Time" (in *Advertisements for Myself,* 1959), a run for their money.

As to the sex-lives of the ordinary Joe Blows of commerce and industry, these still take place traditionally at night, after working hours. *'A survey of contemporary sexual practices revealed that 20% of the men questioned, after concluding intercourse, rolled over and had a cigarette. 80% got up, dressed, and went home.'* (Berkeley, Calif., July 5th, 1947, from a well-known science-fiction writer.) This sounds exactly like the Kinsey Report approach but, as the date of collection shows, it preceded the publicity of the Kinsey Report by some time. Both, of course, respond similarly to the numerical fractionalizing or 'control approach' to the human being, created by the time-study industrial psychologists of the 1910's and since, as blisteringly typified and excoriated in Prof. John Del Torto's "The Human Machine," in *Neurotica* (1951) No. 8: p. 21–35. Since the Kinsey publications, the same numerical burlesque has been collected more and more frequently, often including other percentages such as: 2% *of the men wash,* 3% *go to the refrigerator for a snack.* (N.Y. 1953.) The 'Dagwood-complex': food satisfactions to replace the unsatisfactory or non-existent sex.

Wives are supposed to be continuously on the lookout for evidences of their husbands' infidelity. *Told in fractured-French dialect: "Pierre! You have a mistress!" "But no, my darling, I have no mistress." "Don't lie to me, Pierre, this is the third time this week you washed your feet."* (Paris, 1959.) This is in response to the stereotype of the French as a passionately sexual and animal people, who seldom bathe, and who prefer cunnilinctus to all other methods of sexual intercourse, both parts of which are untrue. One would imagine that the bidets ostentatiously present in every French hotel bedroom would give the lie to this, to tourists at least, who often use these as foot-baths (compare the joke); but this seems to have no effect, or rather the opposite effect, in implying that *"the French only wash their working parts,"* as I have heard said. (Cannes, 1966.) These notions are at least as old as World War I, during which the most famous stanza of all the hundreds to the Anglo-American army song, "Mademoiselle from Armentières," ran:

> The French they are a funny race,
> > *Parlay-voo,*
> The French they are a funny race,
> > *Parlay-voo,*
> The French they are a funny race,
> They fight with their feet
> And fuck with their face —
> > *Hinky-dinky parlay-voo!*

This must be even older than World War I, as evidenced by the reference to the foot-fighting or *savate,* no longer officially taught since about 1900. During World War II, debarking American soldiers were told in their semi-official briefing that '*The rabbits, the cows, and the women in France are all diseased.*'

The eagle eye of the wife on the husband's bodily care is of course only intended as a partialism suggesting her concern with his genitals, which 'belong' to her, in the patriarchal sense that the husband has property rights over the wife's body, and she assumes similar rights over his body as well. This is authorized in positive fashion by Paul the Apostle, in 1 *Corinthians,* vii. 4: 'The wife hath not power of her own body, but the husband: and likewise also the husband hath not power of his own body, but the wife. Defraud ye not one the other, except it be with consent . . .' These 'rights' or 'powers' cannot, of course, be enforced by the wife, since the husband's potency and erection are beyond the power of his will (or hers). *A husband comes home very late, and is undressing quietly to avoid waking his wife. She is awake, however, and is watching him through half-closed eyes. Suddenly she screams, "Meyer! where is your underwear?" "My God, I've been robbed!"* (1:342.) The sex-hate issue of *Sex to Sexty* (1966) 6:20 gives this in an interesting cartoon form showing *A man undressing and hanging his clothes in the closet while his* fat middle-aged wife *watches him from in bed. He is explaining, "Joe passed out cold, and I had to help his wife put him to bed . . ." Unknown to him but visible to the reader, he is wearing a woman's lace panties marked* "SADIE." This cannot be considered an allusion to, but is rather an unconscious feeling-of-one's-way toward, the exchange of the clothing of the sexes which has always been a part of the sexual license of Carnival. This cartoon is the rationalized form in which the clothing of the sexes is exchanged simply by *error* in connection with undressing and redressing before and after intercourse.

Part of the difficulty in hiding his adultery, on the part of the husband, is his unconscious yearning to brag of it, and thus express overtly the revenge against his wife that it is. All the errors (as above), slips of the tongue, clumsy lies, incorrect maneuvering of alibis, and other maladroitnesses by means of which the husband informs his wife of his infidelity to her, must really be considered purposeful and a form of bragging. They are in any case unnecessary, as the wife will already be aware of the husband's growing disinterest in her own sexual offering, and suspect the reason. *A man comes home from a lodge dinner and tells his wife, "The funniest thing happened. The lodge president said he'd give a new hat to any man who'd get up and say he'd been faithful to his wife since the day they were married. And not a single man got up."* Wife: *"Very funny. Where's your new hat?"* (Minneapolis, 1952.) In the opposite form: *A man rushes into his apartment shouting, "Honey, we got to move. I just found out the janitor in this place has screwed all the women but one." "Yes, I know," says his wife; "it's that stuck-up thing on the third floor."* (1:92.)

Women are expected to accept, almost as a matter of course, a sharing of the husband with the 'Other Woman' in a way that most men would consider intolerable if asked of them, as to the 'Other Man.' This battens on the essential inferiority complex with which women are purposely infected under patriarchal domination, but sometimes the biter is bit, and the woman feels *too* inferior to allow of any competition. The joke has earlier been given about *The woman who not only does not discharge the housemaid whom she finds in intercourse with her husband in the cellar, but tells her that with what she does in the cellar and the mistress does in the bedroom, perhaps they can keep the "old whoremonger" home between them.* (*The Pearl*, No. 8, Feb. 1880, *ad fin.*) This leaves the wife very much in the dominant position over the housemaid whom she is keeping, as it were, to clean up after her sexually. She denies that she is unsatisfactory: the husband's sexual appetite merely is too large. In the opposite form the housemaid has the victory, at least verbally, in the standard 'foolish literalism' of children and fools. (Note: The Swedish immigrants are considered, in the American midwest, where at one time they were at the work level of domestic servants, to be very slow-witted; as the Swiss are considered by the French, and the Germans by the Austrians, etc.) *The Swedish housemaid tells the lady of the house that the lady's husband has caught her by the washtub and "yumped" her. "What do you mean, Helga?" "Ay mean he fooked me — good!" "What did you say?!" "Ay say, 'Tank you, Mister Olson'."* (2:345.) A contest in refusal-to-understand.

Any number of folktales exist in the older collections, especially of the Italian *novellieri,* in which one person substitutes for another at an amorous assignation, usually in the dark. (Rotunda, K1840 through 1844.) It was obviously considered the height of humor for a husband to have intercourse in this way with his wife — she imagining him to be a guilty lover — or for a wife so to have intercourse with her husband, who imagines that she is someone else. *The Pearl*, No. 10 (April 1880) gives a story such as this, "Sally's Mistake," very simply as a short tale, of a pure 'accident,' and without humorous intention: *The servant-maid who walks in her sleep lies down between the husband and wife, and the husband has intercourse with her before dawn, thinking it is his wife, whom he is later surprised to find is not satisfied.* All stories such as this allow of a topper or 'double reverse,' in which *both* parties have made assignations, and therefore both the intended adultery and the intended innocent replacement go awry. *A wife learns that her husband has made overtures to the housemaid and that he plans to come to her bed that night. She replaces the housemaid, whom she sends across town on a late errand unexpectedly. Her husband 'gives her a* shtup *like she's never had before,' and when she is finally satisfied physically, and now wants her revenge, she snaps on the bedside lamp and says to him triumphantly, "I'll bet you're surprised!" "Ah sure is, Ma'm," says the Negro chauffeur in her arms.* (Cagnes-sur-Mer, France, 1955.) The real point of this story is, of course, not that the woman has been hoist with her own pétard and is humiliated by the unexpected miscegenational intercourse — that is only the top-level pretense — but that she has thus 'innocently' tasted the forbidden fruit of the far superior extra-racial intercourse, strictly owing to her husband's fault. (Rotunda K1843.2.2, citing Guicciardini, 1583, 1. 64.)

This is not the place to discuss the sexual folklore concerning the Negro *vis-à-vis* the enemy white, but a further joke can be given, obviously in the vein of that preceding, though the adulterous spouse is not the same. This joke has not been collected before about 1962, and is clearly connected with the recent resurgence of the Negro liberation movement in both Africa and the United States. *'A white employer asks his chauffeur, "What makes you niggers such good lovers?" Accommodatingly, the chauffeur tells him, "The trouble with you white folks is that you just go in there and rush, rush, rush, and before you know it, it's all over. Now the way us black folks do it, is get in there, take it easy, make long strokes, talk sweet a while, stop a while, take our time, then some more slow long strokes, nice and cool-like." The white man goes home and follows the Negro's suggestions when having intercourse with his wife. Midway, she says, "What's the matter with you today? How come you're doing it like a nigger?"'* (D. J. Bennett, "The Psychological Meaning of Anti-Negro Jokes," in *Fact* magazine, New York, March 1964, No. 2: p. 53–9, at p. 54, the author noting that he heard this joke in Texas, which has always been one of the principal anti-Negro states.)

Adultery is not, as a matter of fact, all that it is cracked up to be, and were it not for its revenge-value a good deal of it would probably never take place. Two jokes, at least, express the man's resistance to the man-among-men pose of instant and ever-ready willingness to be unfaithful to the wife one loves at the drop of another woman's pantie. *A man is telling a friend how, while his wife was out of town, the beautiful somnambulistic housemaid came into his bedroom naked in the night. "What did you do?" "What could I do? I love my wife. I turned her around and headed her back to her own bed. What would you have done?" "Exactly what you did, you lying son-of-a-bitch!"* (2:351.) The 'somnambulistic housemaid' — also in *The Pearl,* in 1880, cited just above — is a minor stock character whose purpose seems to be to accept, guiltlessly (she is asleep, after all), the guilt for the employer's sexual approaches to her, these latter being of course standard in both literature and life. Compare the night-walking chambermaid scene with which Sterne's *Sentimental Journey* (1768) abruptly ends.

The following was taken down almost verbatim from the opening of an address by an army captain to an audience of American soldiers, April 26th, 1945: *'When a soldier in the South Pacific asked his commanding officer for permission to go home and see his wife, the officer turned him down, adding, "But with all the Wacs and Waves and nurses we have down here, you should be able to get yourself a little nookie." "Sir," replied the soldier, "for two and a half years I've waved it and whacked it and nursed it; now I want to go home and have an honorable discharge".'*

2. JODY (JOE THE GRINDER)

Jody is the fellow who comes to see your wife when you aren't home. He doesn't love her; she doesn't love him. All he does is fuck her. But you keep paying the bills. They work it on the principle that *'Nobody misses a slice off a cut loaf.'* If he gives her a baby, it's your baby. You have to love it and put it through college, and get it out of jail if it turns out to be a mutt. That's Jody's work. You may be the worst parent in the world, but if the kid doesn't turn out to be the President of the United States, it's Jody's fault. The neighbors know all about it, but they won't tell you. They don't want to get INVOLVED. They tell each other, though; in fact they tell people all about it who don't even know who you are, and they're very involved in enjoying the scandal of it. They just won't tell *you*. A person can go crazy thinking about it, so what's the use? The best thing is to go and screw somebody else's wife in your spare time, while he's at work. That way *you're* Jody. It's like when you were younger: people have got to respect your sister and not get fresh with her. Meanwhile you're putting the blocks to *their* sister every Saturday night. It's hard to explain it, but it works out fair — anyhow, it's fair to everybody but you.

Who Jody is, is a mystery. People say it's the iceman or the milkman (the mailman doesn't ever seem to be Jody: he's too busy delivering the mail). But that isn't true. That's only the stuff they put in comic magazines. Jody is really the big gangling neighbor kid who's always hanging around your place, and baby-sits for you sometimes. He's your partner that's always coming over Thursdays to do the paper-work with you for next week, or to ask about going fishing Sunday. He's your best student (if you're a professor: that's K1594, K1692), the one who's going to do his thesis on your pet subject and who practically sits at your feet. He's also got a sister — Jodelle — that's your wife's best friend who's always coming around to help with the housework and things, and that you make love to in motels when your wife has her headaches. Because the truth is, let's face it: Jody is your best friend.

A man persistently refuses a theatrical agent's offer of tickets to all the finest concerts on the grounds that "Schlivovitz is playing tonight." Finally the agent loses his temper and asks, "Say, what instrument does this Schlivovitz play? I never even heard of him." "No, and you never will. He plays second saxophone in a four-piece band in a beer-joint in Newark." "So?" "So when he plays — I fuck his wife." (N.Y. 1940.) The relationship here is as distant as possible: the two men do not know or encounter each other at all. For the closer they come to knowing each other, the more the adultery with the wife comprises not only her infidelity but the betrayal by the (best) friend as well. There are also deeper levels, as will be seen below, in the section on "Possession in Common." Abrahams gives, *Deep Down in the Jungle,* p. 170, a rhymed recitation, collected from Negro informants in Philadelphia, apparently in the late 1950's, in which Jody or Joe-de-Grinder (*grind,* a British, seldom an American term for sexual intercourse) is seen to be originally a Negro typification of the wartime 'slacker' who is back home replacing the wartime hero in the bed of the wartime hero's wife.

Now in nineteen hundred and forty-four
The World War Two was over for sure.
Now a two-timing bitch with an old-man overseas,
Said, "Wake up, Jodie. Wake up, please.
This shit is over, Japan is fell."

She tries to get Jody to leave, but before he is fully awake the husband
is home and in the door, taking 'a shot of [his] bad-ass gin':

He said, "While I was overseas fighting the enemy,
    and digging that salt,
You was taking my checks and cashing them and taking
    my bitch to the Allotment Ball.
Now here's something I can't miss,
Take my motherfucking Longine off your wrist."

At no time does G.I. Joe even mention the matter of adultery: his
whole concern is, at the verbal level, with his material replacement by
Jody — the allotment checks, the ball to which he has taken his wife,
and even his wristwatch on the adulterer's wrist. The *real* replacement
objected to is of course none of these, but the substitution of Jody's penis
in the vagina that is G.I. Joe's 'property' too. This, however, is adroitly
left out of the discussion, or perhaps is symbolized as dancing at the
ball. In any case, Jody's sexual victory is a victory indeed; but he is disgraced — by the rough male code of ethics — in accepting money and
valuable presents (the wristwatch) from the woman. I remember losing
the first friend I made in France by the accident of being present at a
bank-teller's window when my friend came in escorting the young war-
widow whose lover he was, to cash the allotment check on her dead
husband's insurance. I did not speak, or greet them, or change expression, as they seemed to want to pretend I did not exist; but they would
never have anything to do with me again. Meanwhile, the husband (a
war hero) was long since heroically dead; but the disgrace of being
caught out, *as Jody,* not in bed but in the bank, was insurmountable.
Contrariwise, a woman in the same situation would not turn a hair,
and I have also been present at a bank-teller's window (in America)
where a young, highly-educated professional girl stood by while a man
she had met two days earlier cashed a large traveller's check in order
to get the money to pay the cleaning charges on her bedspread, stained

visibly with other men's semen. The man's evident masochism is not the point here, but rather the girl's perfect and unconscious aplomb.

During the 1940's a curious story went the rounds, on the West Coast, as presumably true, and also found its way, I believe, into one of the Hollywood and Broadway columnists' volumes of reprinted columns, spiced up with the stories the newspapers would not let them print, of which this was one. In it, Jody is *imported* into the adulterous situation, as it were, by the husband himself; the wife being completely innocent. *A man brings home a friend after a game of tennis, for lunch. The wife is out shopping and the man suggests that the friend take a shower while they are waiting. He then falls asleep in a hammock. The wife comes home, does not see her husband asleep in the hammock, continues upstairs where she hears the sound of water in the shower, shouts, "Hello, darling!" and, getting no answer, reaches through the shower curtain, takes hold of the man's penis and shakes it, saying, "Ding-dong, darling! I'm home." She then goes happily out and finds her husband trudging up the stairs, having been awakened by her shouting. She takes one look at him, casts a startled look back at the bathroom, dashes down the stairs and out of the house, and refuses to come home till she learns by telephone that the visitor has left.* (Los Angeles, 1940, told as absolutely true.)

This is connected stylistically, though not in subject — and yet, even there, the nexus *action* is identical: the grasping of the penis — with a story also collected as true, from numerous colleges in the U.S., since 1960. *A boy is taking a shower in a fraternity house when his parents and girlfriend arrive, unexpectedly, to visit him, and are let into the apartment by his roommate. Thinking the people he has heard entering are frat-members, the boy gets out of the shower stark naked, kicks open the bathroom door with his penis in his hand, snarling in gangster fashion, "This is a stick-up!" On seeing the assembled tableau of stupefied parents and girlfriend, he dashes out of the room, and will not return.* (Some versions have him joining the Marines, etc., which connects this story with that of the "Fortunate Fart," in Chapter 2.vii.2, above.) The deeper meaning of both these 'true' stories is their allusion to the powerful magic and anti-magic of the display of the penis in non-sexual situations. Compare the swearing of a solemn oath by 'putting the hand under the thigh,' *i.e.* upon the penis, of the person to whom the oath is sworn, in *Genesis,* xxiv. 2–9, and xlvii. 29. An American Indian form of this, in which the oath is sworn by touching and displaying one's own penis, is mentioned in Charles Erskine Scott Wood's superb and now almost forgotten collection of anti-clerical skits, *Heavenly Discourse* (1927). The usual such oath is on the testicles of which the ritual and linguistic connection with *testimony* is based on their being the *two witnesses* of sexual intercourse.

The overvaluation of the penis by all neurotics, and most crucially by homosexuals (both male and female), is of relevance here, as is also the male folk-habit of *showing the penis unexpectedly,* presumably to excite the woman to whom it is shown, but effectively as a self-reassurance against ideas of castration, a habit interestingly discussed in Prof. Steven Marcus' study of *My Secret Life,* the principal Victorian erotic autobiography, in his *The Other Victorians* (1966) pp. 114–15, 171–2. Similarly, at the turn of the 20th century, both the diminutive Frank Harris, as he himself notes in *My Life and Loves* (1922–7), a tissue of sexual lies and brags, and the 'bisexual occultist', Aleister Crowley, are known to have acted out this same charade as a regular part of their erotic approach. The idea that the sight of the penis excites the woman — especially when it is erect — was clearly a tenet of Victorian sexual folklore. Nor is it entirely false, though it operates much more surely on homosexual males suffering from castration fears, than on women. This is of course less 'magical' than the idea of the power of the display of the penis in *non*-erotic situations, when it is also more difficult to display the penis erect. The usual rationalization of such displays is in connection with urination, but the truth is plainly told in the fantasy of the little folk-quatrain (to the tune of "The Prisoner's Song"):

> If *I* had the wings of an angel,
> And the *prick* of a man that I know [*n.b.*],
> I would *fly* to the highest church-steeple,
> And *piss* on the people below!

This obviously demands comparison with the case of a young man at the University of Texas, in midsummer 1966 — an ex-Marine of six years' service, named Charles Whitman — who acted out precisely this magical ('insane') fantasy, but with a rifle with telescopic sights, with which, from the top of the college tower, he shot dead every person he saw moving on the campus, on their coming out of the buildings at lunchtime. (He had beforehand killed both his wife *and mother* with a knife.)

3. VERBAL RESPONSES TO ADULTERY

The discovery that one has been cuckolded is resisted in jokes principally in verbal fashion, since *jokes* are a literary form principally involving verbal responses, as differentiated from folktales, where the action is everything, and where the words spoken are of little importance, and seldom come to a conclusion — as jokes almost always do — in a 'punch-line' or verbal climax. The husband first resists the idea of cuckoldry and of his wife's infidelity by importing the idea into innocent contexts, obviously as a warning to her. *'Wife (to late-returning husband):* "*Is that you, John?*" *John:* "*It'd better be*".' (*Better Crops with Plant Food,* Feb. 1941, p. 49, a humorous filler in a 'house-organ' magazine.) Other favorite responses to this question, which irritates most husbands, especially on the part of a sleeping wife or mistress, are (authentically): "*No, this is Harry; move over!*" or, rather deftly, "*Sure; who were you expecting?*" (N.Y. 1963 and 1940.) The sort of trap or unveiling this is tending toward is that of *The bearded man who decides to surprise his wife by coming home one night with his beard shaved off. He crawls into bed silently and she passes a caressing hand over his face, asking, "You still here, honey?"* (N.Y. 1963; printed in *Sex to Sexty,* 1966, 5:6.)

Almost a classic in this line, and probably with much older origins, which have not been found on first search, though the crucial trait of the exchanged clothing is probably Levantine or Italian: *A policeman comes home from late duty one night, and as he is crawling into bed his wife says, "Pat, I have a terrible headache and there's no aspirin. Would you run down to the all-night drugstore and get me some?" He pulls on his clothes again in the dark and stumbles out into the night to get the aspirin. Under the first street-light he passes is another patrolman twirling his club, who looks at him in surprise and says, "O'Shaughnessy! How long have you been a Fire-Chief?"* (Ann Arbor, Mich. 1935. Very close to Rotunda, Motifs K1526 and K1549.1. Compare also Types 1360A and 1419G.) Essentially this is Poggio's No. 231/2, and Nicolaidès, p. 155, "The Holy Breeches."

Every type of evidence of the presence of the Other Man is of course eagerly searched for by the jealous and suspicious husband, though it will crush him when he finds it. *Man upbraiding his wife on coming home from work: "Who is your lover? Who is he? Who was here*

today to see you while I was out earning the money to support you?"
The wife denies everything. "Don't try to fool me. Who is he? I'm the
only man in the house: why is the toilet seat up?" (1:36, naming the
husband as Jewish, but without any reference to money.) This habit
of men's, of leaving the toilet seat up after urinating, is much disliked
by women as a reproach against their being unable (?) to 'piss standing.' The split-front toilet seat is the logical solution, and easier to keep
clean. At least two different 'men's magazines' have run almost identical cartoons in the mid-1960's showing *A man in the bathroom, in*
which the following message is written on the mirror in lipstick: "Re-
member to raise the seat, dear!" He is wiping off the toilet seat with the
"HER" towel of a prominently-marked "HIS-&-HER" towel-set. (*The*
Adam 2nd Book of Adult Stag Humor, Los Angeles, 1965, p. 36.) This
is, of course, cartoon code or shorthand for 'Piss on *her!*' A Jody version
of the towel set also exists: *Husband entering bathroom and registering*
surprise on seeing a set of three towels, not two, marked: HIS, HERS,
JOE's. (Chicago, 1958.) See, further, Chapter 6.1.3 above.

Finally, the husband examines the wife's body itself for evidences of
adultery, beginning with the partialism or evasion of these significant
towels, used for wiping away the man's externally-ejaculated semen, or
any traces of seminal 'backwash' from the woman's genitals after intercourse. These towels are also made much of in the verbal reproaches of
a certain type of jealous husband ("*You don't expect me to stand and*
hold towels while you screw all the guys on the block, do you?" — La
Jolla, Calif. 1965), sometimes with a pretended allusion to the sweat-
towels held by prizefighters' seconds. These same towels will be seen
again in the later chapter on "Prostitution," in Series Two. *A Negro*
husband comes home and finds his wife almost naked, lying exhausted
on a rumpled bed with a towel thrown over the foot. "What's goin' on,
honey?" he asks suspiciously. "I just had the misery something ter-
rible," she explains; "couldn't get outa bed all day." "An' what's dat
towel doin' there?" "I wrang it out in water to put on my head, dat's
all." He does not answer, but takes out a large razor which he begins
stropping. "What you gonna do with dat razor?" she asks nervously.
"I'm gonna shave," he says, " — EF dat towel dries out soft!" (1:356;
text-form N.Y. 1938.) Absurd as it may seem, this is nothing other than
the plot of Shakespeare's *Othello,* reduced to its essentials. (Rotunda,
K2112.6(5).1, giving references; also Thompson Motif N348, in both
cases noting the guilty handkerchief.) — *A suspicious husband finds his*
wife sitting on the lawn at a wild party. She explains she has just come

out to pee in the dark. He puts two fingers into her vagina, then draws them out and apart, and holds them up to look at them carefully. "Who the hell are you kidding?" he says; "piss don't make windows!" (2:179) The husband has gone very far, here, toward making physical contact with the 'Other Man's' genital anatomy and traces, *via* the woman's body. Physical insistences of this kind are actually if unconsciously homosexual, and will be considered more at length below, under "Possession in Common," 9.III.3.

Among the many other bitter secrets given away at last, to the public at large, in Dr. Eric Berne's *Games People Play* (1964), is the family form of what he calls the game of "Uproar" — *i.e.* prototypical father-daughter incest achieved in symbolic sadistic form, of which he specifies, p. 130-31: 'In degenerate households this game may be played in a sinister and repellent form in which father waits up for daughter whenever she goes out on a date, and examines her and her clothing carefully on her return to make sure that she has not had intercourse.' I have myself been the witness of such a scene, and the same father, according to what the girl told me, had a further set of *fioriture* on this theme (unknown even to Dr. Berne) in which he would also examine her — and her sisters — *before* they went out on dates, by suddenly pulling up their dresses as they were leaving the house, in order, as he explained, to make sure they were not 'wearing syringes in their bodies' for birth control purposes on their dates! As the girls naturally wore panties, the gruesome humor of the situation would consist of the father trying to claw their panties down — "for the same damn thing that all the other fellows want," as the girl said perfectly consciously — while the girls struggled mostly to keep their elegantly made-up hairdo's from being mussed. (Scranton, Pa. 1934.) As Dr. Berne very correctly ends, 'In the long run nature will take its course — if not that night then the next, or the one after. Then the father's suspicions are "justified," as he makes plain to the mother, who has stood by "helplessly" while all this went on.' The boyfriends here, of course, replace the Other Man.

Most of the merely verbal responses to adultery are intended, in some way, to *deny it* or somehow to explain it away, or even to make it seem 'logical.' *A husband away on a trip telegraphs his wife that he will be home that evening. When he arrives, very late, he finds her in bed with another man. He retires to a hotel and starts proceedings for divorce. The wife's father comes to see him, and arrives all smiles. "It's like I told you over the phone," he says; "I knew there had to be some*

explanation. I've been to see Elsie. She never got your telegram."
(Paris, 1959, stated to be 'a Jewish joke and very old.') What seems to
be a modification of this appeared in a Broadway columnist's stint in
1945: *A man finds his wife in a nightclub with another man.* ' *"The*
minute I turn my back," he roared, "you start running around with
some weasel! Just what have you got to say for yourself?" "I — I," she
stammered, "didn't know you ever came here!" ' Even more 'logical'
is the explanation of the husbands' adultery in the widely circulated
World War II story — not really believed by anyone to be true: *A*
group of American wives and girlfriends, learning that their men in
the army were being unfaithful to them with the Australian girls, tele-
graphed: WHAT HAVE THOSE AUSTRALIAN GIRLS GOT THAT WE HAVEN'T
GOT? *Immediate answer* (it's always immediate): NOTHING. BUT THEY'VE
GOT IT HERE. (U.S. 1944.) Many 'nincumpoop' stories, 2.11 above, turn
on the unvirile weakness of the merely verbal riposte, especially "At
Least Shut the Door!" (Rotunda J2752.1 and K1569.2.)

The elaborate device for avoiding even the direct statement of
adultery in the following story is very reminiscent of the ancient folktale concerning King Midas, who dug a hole into which he *whispered*
the secret weighing heavy on his soul: that he had the ears of a jackass.
(Grass grows out of the hole and, in its swaying, whispers the secret to
the world. — Aarne Type 782, Motif F511.2.2.) *An employer who sus-*
pects his butler of stealing his cigars shouts to him loudly in the next
room, "George, who's been stealing my cigars?" No answer. He re-
peats it more loudly. No answer. He goes into the next room and con-
fronts the butler. "George, didn't you hear me speaking to you just
now?" "No sir, there must be something wrong with the acoustics."
"Is that so? Well, you go in the next room and say something, and
we'll see if I hear you." The butler goes into the next room and shouts
at the top of his voice, "Some flat-faced son of a bitch has been screw-
ing the bejesus out of my wife!" He repeats this several times and re-
turns to the other room. "Did you hear me, sir?" "You're right,
George," says the red-faced employer; "I couldn't hear a word. Here,
have a cigar." (Minn. 1935. Motif X441.1, Type 1777A.)

This has not been traced further, but is in the line of the 'enchanted
pear-tree' stories (Aarne Type 1423; Motif K1518), by means of which
The wife and her lover commit adultery while the husband is up a tree
gathering fruit, and convince him that it is a miraculous delusion
caused by the tree. Compare of course the tale-telling tree (?) in the
Garden of Eden. The earliest version of this is given in the *Disciplina*

Clericalis (about 1108) of Pedro Alfonsi, modified with a further miracle in which *The blind husband's sight is restored during the wife's adulterous intercourse, and the wife brazenly assures him that the adultery itself is responsible for the miraculous cure, by grace of the 'goddess Venus.'* (Printed in *A Hundred Merry Tales,* ed. P. M. Zall, Lincoln, Nebr. 1963, p. 35–6, from Caxton's translation of 1484.) Alfonsi was a converted Jewish rabbi, of the real name of Mosheh Sephardi, and his tales are mostly of Jewish and Arab transmission. His conversion seems to be breaking down in the cited story, as the reference to the 'goddess Venus' suggests a Græco-Roman origin, or perhaps he was simply avoiding the sacrilege of ascribing so immoral a miracle to the Virgin Mary, to whom, otherwise, all the earlier miracles of the Magna Mater are regularly assimilated. (Motif T401.)

4. FLAGRANTE DELICTO

Let it be said, first off, that our title does not correctly translate — as is generally believed — "flagrant delectation" (*"fragrant delectation"* is the joke form), but as "flagrant crime." In Latin countries, such as France, *flagrant délit* often refers, in newspaper jargon, to such crimes as robbery. In English it now refers only to sexual intercourse, specifically adultery. We will first consider verbal responses to this classic situation, continuing those in the section preceding. All the characters speak. First the 'wronged' husband: his lines are seldom any good, for the adulterous intercourse has made a cuckold of him — equivalent to a total fool. He is now a 'jerk' (*jerk-off,* or masturbator, traditionally insane) or 'schmuck,' actually a South-Slavic term for a fool, *smok,* but identified with the Judæo-German, *Schmuck,* jewel, a euphemism for the penis as the principal ornament of a man, and very much a pejorative term, in both Yiddish and English, when applied to the man himself.

An out-of-town buyer in New York wants to get laid. A friend tells him to take the subway to Forty-Second Street, and start a conversation with the first woman that smiles at him. He becomes confused in the subway and gets out at Seventy-Second Street. A woman smiles at him in a candy-store, and they begin a conversation which ends in bed in her apartment. Suddenly they hear footsteps at the door. "Quick," cries the woman in an undertone, "it's my husband! Pretend you're fixing the clock." The buyer climbs on a chair and busies himself with the clock in the bedroom as the husband walks in. "Who's that?" "Only the man to fix the clock, dear." Obediently the buyer turns the clock hands to make it strike, and turns to smile weakly at the husband. "You son-of-a-bitch," says the husband, "I said Forty-second Street!" (1:259.) This is the husband's best verbal comeback. Actually to redeem himself he must not speak, but must *act*. (Rotunda's K1692, "Teaching the Art of Love," also in *Kryptádia*, 1883, i. 339, ii. 55; Turkish original in *La Fleur Lascive*, No. 9, "Le Chanteur.")

Contempt for the cuckold husband is paramount in the wife's verbal responses to her being caught in adulterous intercourse. *The boarder is fucking the landlady. The husband walks in unexpectedly. Landlady:* "*Look, here's big-mouth. Now everybody's going to know!*" (N.Y. 1940.) — *A man surprises his wife in bed with another man and begins berating her. She looks pityingly at him over the other man's shoulder and says, "Shut up, will you? Just look on and learn something!*" (1:89. Usually told as of Negro man and wife.) This is followed by a variant in which the husband cuts even less of a figure. No one listens to his lines at all. *A man surprises his wife in bed with another man and begins berating her:* "*To think, after all I've done for you; after I've given you only the finest of everything. Why, I took you when you were just a poor girl, and . . . say, ain't you even got enough respect to stop while I'm talking to you?*" (1:90.) Very popular, and often collected. As given in Roth's expurgated *Anecdota Americana*, 1933, No. 410, the line is addressed to the other man, not to the wife. Sometimes to both. The verbal concentration here somewhat hides the real point of this story: In most stories of adultery the point is stated, but rapidly passed, that the husband has surprised his wife and the Other Man *in flagrante*. The present story insists that he actually sees the *physical motions* of their guilty intercourse. This is the real blow to the cuckolded husband, a point of which the joke-maker has not lost sight. There exists in French a *Mock-litany for a cuckold husband:* "*Oh God, if I have to be one, at least let me not know about it. And if I have to know about it, at least let me not see it!*" (Paris, 1965, stated to be of the '*belle époque*' of the 1910's.)

Note the complete lack of any reference to the wife, and total concentration on the relationship between the two men, in an elaborate story, of wholly verbal concentration, presumably taking place in France: *Several young men are arguing as to the meaning of the phrase 'savoir-faire.' One says, "If you're screwing another man's wife and he bursts in and sees what's going on and says, 'Go ahead!' that's savoir-faire." "No," says another, "if he bursts in and says 'Go ahead!'*

and you can *go ahead —* THAT's *savoir-faire.*" (Often collected during the 1950's; printed in *Sex to Sexty,* 1966, 6:52.) This appears to be a weak modification of a singular and psychologically very true story on the same situation, but seen very much from the point of view of the adulterer's response. *A man preparing to make love to another man's wife undresses very slowly, hanging his clothes carefully over the back of the boudoir chair, and so forth. "Come on, darling, come on," says the woman; "I'm cold." "I'm coming," he says; "I'm coming," continuing slowly to take off his shoes. Suddenly there is a violent rapping at the door, and muffled shouting in a man's angry voice. "My God! My husband!" shrieks the woman; "get out of here!" Instead, the man tears off his remaining clothes and leaps into bed with her. "It's all right," he says; "I'm scared stiff."* (N.Y. 1938.)

The opposite form also exists, used as the vehicle for sex hatred instead. Same situation: *A man is in bed with a married woman, when he hears someone banging at the door, and a man's voice demanding to be let in. The woman is lost to the world, with her head thrown back, and mutters throatily, "Oh honey, kiss my tits; I'm coming."* Man: *"Kiss my ass; I'm going!"* (1:487, punch-line only, unreconstructable to anyone not knowing the story. Text-form, Cleveland, Ohio, 1939, from a young woman.) This is of ancient vintage, though its transmission is, as always, unclear. In *Les Amusements des Dames de B*** (Bruxelles)*, an anonymous scandal-work by François-Antoine Chevrier, published in 1762 with imprint 'Rouen: Pierre le Vrai,' and battening on the reputation of the city of Brussels — then, as now — for high living, fine eating, and luxurious prostitution 'for them as can afford it,' an almost exactly similar colloquy is given, the woman saying, *"Je me damnes (perds),"* and the cavalier replying, *"Je me sauve!"* which may be translated, *She: "I'm dying." He: "I'm leaving!"* This is pure vaudeville.

The adulterer's answers to the husband, rather than to the wife, are a mixture of impossible bravado and ridiculous but heartfelt explanations in the style of *The Good Soldier Schweik.* The captured adulterer is usually shown in 'men's magazine' cartoons in his underwear shorts, *causâ modestiæ* (one assumes he has put them back on, on hearing the husband banging at the door), trembling in the clothes-closet in which the burly husband has discovered him, hiding behind the wife's petticoats. It is difficult to be witty in such circumstances. The closer the adulterer comes to being actually caught *in the woman's 'arms'* (polite for *legs*), the more honorable is his position, though obviously the more dangerous. Even in such a situation, the bold *tu quoque* is possible in which the adulterer insists on the evident but unspoken point that the wife's choice of him proves that he is the better man, and that the husband's 'rights' are hollow legal relics. Compare the weak *flight-into-nonsense* of the trembling adulterer in the closet: *'Guy comes home unexpectedly; finds wife in bed sweating and palpitating. Looks in closet. Guy bare naked, holding umbrella over his head, says: "Believe it or not, I'm waiting for a streetcar".'* (N.Y. 1939, supplied as quoted from a professional humorist's files.) This punch-line has become a catch-phrase, even among people who do not know the story. *A man comes home unexpectedly, and finds his wife naked on the suspiciously rumpled bed. A big black cigar is burning in an ashtray. He himself does not smoke, and says, "Where did that cigar come from?!" The closet door opens. Out steps a big naked man who says, "Havana!"* (San Francisco, 1955.) The flight-into-nonsense as the best defense.

Obscene punch-lines are not common in this situation, the idea being in general to deny and gloss over the crucial adultery. Observe again the almost total absence of the woman from the situation. It is not that she has blotted herself out, sobbing — or palpitating, as above — under the sheets, or has taken refuge in the locked bathroom (as happens in fact), but that the sexual duel over the enjoyment of her body is strictly man's business. *Husband, to man under his wife's bed: "What are you doing under there, buddy?" "Believe it or not, mister, I'm killing a rat." "Oh, I thought maybe you were fucking it to death — your prick is out."* (Minneapolis, 1935.) Very popular, and collected endlessly over the last thirty years: *A husband comes home unexpectedly to find his wife lying naked on the bed and a strange man in the act of removing his pants. "For the last time, Madam," says the other man, rising to the occasion, "if you do not pay your gas bill at once, I shall shit on the floor."* (2:426.) This is the gas-fecal form. There is also a milk-urinary variant in which *The milkman is caught by the husband with his pants down in the wife's bedroom, his prick in his hand. He says: "Now lissen, lady, I'm tellin' ya. You're gonna pay your milk bill, or I'm gonna piss on your porch."* (N.Y. 1946, also — almost verbatim — Bloomington, Ind. 1963.) Punch-lines of this kind represent the adulterer's anal-sadistic verbal triumph, though sexually stymied. Historically they are decayed or 'nonsense' versions of Rotunda's K1517.9 (developed from K1581.5.2, originally Levantine, of the fool Bahloul in Nafzawi's *Perfumed Garden*), in which the lover pretends to be a merchant demanding payment.

The catching of the adulterous husband by the wife is not common in bawdy jokes. The situation is more generally exploited in polite humor under the standard disguise of 'kissing,' as in one verbally-oriented specimen in authentic oral transmission among children, and ascribed to the traditional arch-verbalist of folk-humor in English, Dr. Samuel Johnson the dictionary-maker. (This has also been collected as of that 'dry fart' – *pet sec,* Noah Webster; but the orotund and over-weight Johnson is preferred.) *Dr. Johnson's wife catches him kissing the maid, and says, "Oh, Samuel, I'm surprised!" "No, my dear," he corrects her, "I am surprised.* You *are astonished."* (Scranton, Pa. before 1930, told among children younger than twelve.)

5. PUNISHING THE ADULTERER

It has already been observed that most of the verbal responses to adultery are intended, in some way, to *deny it* or somehow to explain it away, or even to make it seem 'logical.' Perhaps the most perfect, and psychologically apt, example of this in all the literature of humor is a brief anecdote in *Tales, and Quicke Answers,* printed by Thomas Berthelet in London about 1535. It is No. 17, *"Of hym that was called cuckolde"*:

A certayne man, whiche upon a tyme in company betwene ernest and game was called cuckolde wente angerly home to his wyfe and sayde: wyfe, I was this day in company called kock-olde, whether am I one or nat? Syr truly, sayde she, ye be none. By my fayth (sayde he) thou shall swere so upon this boke, and held to her a boke [*the Bible*]. She denyed hit longe, but whan she sawe there was no remedy, she sayde: well sythe [*since*] I must nedes swere, I promyse you by my faythe, I will swere truly. yea do so quod he. So she toke the boke in her hande and sayd: By this boke syr ye be a cockolde. By the masse, hore, sayde he, thou lyest, thou sayste it for none other cause but to anger me. [*Note now the author's wish-fulfillment 'topper'*:]

By this tale ye may parceyve, that it is nat best at all tymes for a man to beleve his wyfe, though she swere upon a boke.

This is obviously not the same joke as the very popular modern ex-ample that follows, but there is no psychological difference, and both have a certain unmistakable poignancy despite the laugh they raise.

A man hires a private detective to follow his wife and her lover. The detective reports: "They went to the show together, then to a night-club, then to another nightclub, and came home in a taxi half-drunk. Then they went up to his apartment. I climbed up on the fire-escape and watched them through the window. They drank some more, and he chased her around the table and threw her on the hearth-rug in front of the fire and took off all her clothes with his teeth. Then he carried her into the bedroom with her pants hanging on one ankle. The shades were down in the bedroom, and so that's all I saw." "That's it!" says the husband, striking himself on the forehead; "that's IT! *Always that doubt!"* (N.Y. 1944.)

This is more common in a burlesque version in which *The final doubt remains because the detective reports, "Just as he was about to shove it in, I had my pleasure and fell off the roof."* (2:65.) This is also transmuted into a sort of modern *cante fable,* with a comedy-Chinese private detective, in order to excuse the sing-song rhyming conclusion. (Compare *"Confucius say . . ."*) The Chinese detective reports:

> I climb up tree, so I can see.
> He play with she. She play with he.
> I play with me. I fall off tree.
> So I no see. — So sorree. (N.Y. 1946.)

It will not be lost sight of that recourse is had to the private detective, however 'involved' this latter may get in what is really none of his damn business, for the purpose of gathering evidence for an eventual divorce. This is about the weakest punishment of the adulterer available in fact. In the 18th and 19th centuries in England, before enlightened legislation made such cases impossible, the trials for '*crim. con.*' (*criminal conversation:* the legal euphemism for adulterous intercourse) were the delight of the most staid British newspapers, and the delectation of their even staider readers, no matter how illegibly small the type used to print the juicier bits of evidence might be. This was essentially a form of legal pimping or extortion, with the husband benefitting monetarily from his wife's adultery, often in evidently prearranged 'badger games,' particularly set for rich and noble heirs, on the motto of Rochester's line: '*However weak and slender be the string, Bait it with* CUNT *and it will hold a King.*'

One pathetic case was that of John Bellenden Gawler, caught out in adultery in the 1790's and mulcted of most of his private fortune, a loss to which he apparently responded by losing his mind and proceeding to discover the hidden meaning of all English nursery rhymes as being secret curses in the ancient Dutch language — entirely invented by Mr. Gawler of course — against the clergy. The four volumes of examples which he published, under the pseudonym or legally-assumed name of John Bellenden Ker, as *An Essay on the Archæology of our Popular Phrases and Nursery Rhymes* (London & Andover, 1835-40), are among the rarest and most delightful of literary eccentricities in English (see further the Opies' *Oxford Dictionary of Nursery Rhymes,* 1951, p. 28), and have their real importance as being the first unexpurgated collection of children's rhymes ever published. Ker-Gawler's '*crim. con.*' case transcript is perhaps even rarer: a copy is preserved in the New York Public Library.

The most extraordinary of the '*crim. con*' cases, so far as the printed transcript is concerned, is far & away that of *Cavendish vs. Cavendish,* involving the translation into English of twelve letters 'written by the young Count de la Rochefoucault, in 1859, while attaché to the French Embassy at Rome. No pen can adequately depict their nasty licentiousness; and it would appear from allusions they contain that those from the lady to whom they were addressed were still worse.' This assessment is that of H. Spencer Ashbee, in the final volume of his bibliography of erotica, *Catena Librorum Tacendorum* (London, 1885, and reprints) p. 185-8, in connection with the rare 4-volume pornographic novel, *The Romance of Lust* (1873-6), in the final volume of which the last 26 pages are devoted to printing the Rochefoucault letters in English translation. Ashbee quotes enough to make clear that the tone is strongly masochistic and cunnilingual: '*You know that I have sucked you between the legs at those delicious moments when you made water, or when you had your monthly courses,*' *&c.* (also begging to be allowed to perform anilinctus). Why, since he finds them so 'nasty' and 'licentious,' Ashbee prints his selections at all, is obscure. His jolly hypocrisy is similar to that of the judge in the case, noted p. 185: 'When the husband's counsel handed up the letters with the sworn notary's translation he remarked that he thought they were too horribly scandalous to be read in Court. The judge scanned a few of them, and addressing the Count [*sic*], said, "I am perfectly of your opinion, my learned brother. I shall take them home and make a point of them in my address to the Jury".'

In Western folklore generally, the truly virile response to the wife's adultery is neither to get the goods on the adulterer by means of private detectives, nor — certainly not — to see how much money (or advancement in business or politics) he can be milked of on these grounds; but simply to *kill* him. If done *in flagrante delicto,* which the law accepts as being simply in the room in which both the wife and presumed adulterer are found in an advanced state of undress, most juries will let the murderer-husband go scot-free: he has invoked the 'Unwritten Law.' If, however, he murders his wife instead, even under the same circumstances, or *both* the man and woman, he will usually be found guilty of unpremeditated murder, and get a stiff jolt in jail which will finish his life. With this should be compared *The Iceman Cometh,* by Eugene O'Neill, his last play I believe, and certainly the dreariest and stupidest he ever wrote, marking the utter collapse of his talents, with the longest monologue ever delivered against women — specifically the travelling-salesman hero's wife — since the 16th century; arsled-in under the paradoxical message, "I killed her because she was so *good!*" After that, the stage was set for the viciously anti-woman and anti-sexual theatre of Tennessee Williams, Edward Albee, and the self-advertising homosexual propagandist, Jean Genet.

It is obviously far better, and in a way more logical, to express one's righteous outrage against the adulterer, not the adulteress. Since the essence of adultery is that it is a *tort* against property rights, the woman — as the property being fought over — should certainly not be harmed, though nothing prevents her being repudiated later.

This is in the line of *The Civil War joke about the Negro who refused to fight for either the North or the South, and was asked if he did not realize that it was a War to Free the Slaves. "Yessuh, Mistah Boss,"* he replied, *"ah sho' do. Yo' has often seen, has you not, two dawgs fightin' over one bone. But has yo' ever seen de bone git up an' fight?"* (Atlantic City, N.J. 1930.) We may yet live to see that *bone* 'git up an' fight!' (*Ezekiel,* xxxvii. 7–10.)

The significance of the two following stories, which are developments in violence from one another, is most particularly in the *locale* of the violence offered to the adulterer: namely his buttocks. *An English lord married to a much younger woman becomes suspicious of her going to play golf every day, and has his valet spy on her. The valet reports that she really spends her time in the woods with a handsome young golf pro. 'Then Watkins whispered something to his Lordship, and his Lordship said, "How long do you think this has been going on?" Watkins said, "Well, sir, from the freckles on his ass, I would say it has been going on all summer".'* (Guam mimeo, 1952, p. 11.) Now compare: *An English M.P. returns home unexpectedly, and when he 'softly opened the door of his wife's bedroom he saw her, or more properly her legs, high in the air, under the vigorous stroking of her lover. The Englishman seized his hunting rifle from a rack and levelled it at the offenders. "Remember, sir, you're a sportsman," softly whispered the butler. "Get him on the rise".'* (1:172. Usually delivered with unctuous Cockney self-approbation.)

The red-blooded American response is equally class-conscious and self-approbatory, but expresses its violence at the opposite end. The concern here with *front and back doors* is, probably, an unconscious link to the intended buttock-violence. *One travelling salesman on a train tells another that he has wired his wife he'll be home in an hour, and expects she'll have a fine meal on the table for him when he gets there. Others brag similarly. '"Huh," sneered another of the group. "The first thing I do when I get off the train is to buy a good baseball bat. Then I go home and ring the front bell. I run around to the back door quick, and I haven't missed a son-of-a-bitch in ten trips".'* (1:449.)

We arrive here at the in-fighting of the subject: the type of revenge against the adulterer in which not only death but *'a fate worse than death'* (for a man, *castration;* as, for a woman, *rape*) is meted out to him. This is a theme particularly often encountered in the gruesome Italian *novelle,* following and on the pattern of those of Boccaccio, particularly the *novelle* of Matteo Bandello (translated in six volumes by Payne), which are signally cruel and vengeful in the Arab-Italianate style. I have the definite impression that the original of the following recent American story appears in Bandello, but have not been able to find it. The text that follows is taken, with the permission of the editor-publisher 'Richard Rodman' (Mr. John Newbern), from *And One Flew Into the Cuckold's Nest* (Fort Worth, Tex. 1966, supplement to *Sex to Sexty* series, p. 32. Compare Rotunda K1558 and K1586.)

A farmer came home late one night and caught a traveling salesman in bed with his wife. The farmer knocked the traveling salesman cold and when he came to, he discovered himself in the barn, where the farmer had tightly clamped his little dove the girls all love in a big vice, nailed to the bench, and the handle to the vice was gone! Looking around, he saw the farmer was sharpening a large knife. "Ye gods, you're not going to cut it off!" cried the salesman. "No," said the farmer; "You can do that . . . I'm going to set the barn on fire!"

It is a toss-up whether the insistence here that the castration of the adulterer be *self*-inflicted is intended as a refusal of this revenge by the 'wronged' husband, or as a diabolical improvement.

What these stories are all driving toward, but what they curiously almost never mention, is the most ancient punishment of, and apparently almost natural biological response to, the appropriation of a desired female: the overreached or expropriated male simply hitches on, in the form of a sexual trio or chain, by engaging immediately in anal intercourse with the male who is in intercourse with the female. This can easily be observed among dogs, who sometimes form quite long writhing chains, called 'daisy-chains' among human beings. One joke only has been collected expressing this directly, and the homosexual tone in this is as strong as in the earlier "Lucky Pierre" or "Lucky Julius" story (*Kryptádia*, 1907, XI. 154). *A man finds his best friend making love to his wife. "You bastard!" he shouts, "what have you got to say for yourself?" The friend looks back over his shoulder without stopping. "What have I got to say? — Make a circle!"* (N.Y. 1947.) This matter has been mentioned earlier, in connection with the bridegroom's *resisting* the sexual mementos of earlier lovers of the bride during her formal farewell kissing of and by all the men present at her wedding. The Latin satirical poets, such as Martial, make continuous mention of this standard punishment of the adulterer, and Roman custom also seems to have symbolized the same thing in the formal punishment for adultery of having a radish (the modern *horse-*radish) stuffed up the adulterer's rectum, and he being then ridden out of town mounted backwards on a jackass. The modern tar-&-feathering and 'riding on a [fence-]rail' are a survival. Bebel's *Facetiæ* (1514) III. 161, "*De mercatore et adultera*," cites Catullus pointedly.

In issue No. 6 of *The Pearl* (Dec. 1879, *ad fin.*), an interesting folk-item of the 'typology' or 'character' form is given. This format is essentially a folk-reduction of the more ornate literary Theophrastan character, much in vogue in the late Renaissance (see the masterly bibliography by Professor Greenough), and the erotic form is at least as old as "*Les Bonnes Mœurs des Femmes*," published in the *Oeuvres* of the mountebank and haranguist, 'Bruscambille' (Rouen, 1622, also 1627, at p. 431–3, and earlier in the first of the drolleries, *La Muse Folastre* though not in the first edition of 1600: only known copy in my own collection; and in the preceding century in the *Dictz des pays joyeulx,* reprinted by Montaiglon, *Recueil de poésies françoises,* vol. v). The "Bonnes Mœurs" typified are, for instance, '*La* prudente *est celle qui a le dedans de la main velu. La* hardie *est celle qui attend deux hommes dans un trou. La* coüarde *est celle qui met la queuë entre les jambes,'* and twenty more on the same pattern. Similar modern "Farting Characters" and "Types of Men at Urinals" are commonly circulated in the form of printed 'novelties.' In exactly the same style, *The Pearl* (Dec. 1879) gives twenty "Characters of Husbands," all of which are certainly relevant to this chapter, but particularly the last:

If a husband came home and found his wife being had by another man, what would he do? That depends on his disposition.

The *Polite* husband would beg him not to draw until he'd spent.

The *Considerate* husband would offer soap, towel, and warm water, as soon as he drew.

The *Funny* husband would cry "Boh!" and tickle his arse with a feather.

The *Good Natured* husband would remark that he liked buttered buns. ['One lying with a woman that has just lain with another man, is said to have a *buttered bun.'* — Grose's *Lexicon Balatronicum* (1811), quoted in John S. Farmer & Wm. E. Henley's *Slang and Its Analogues,* rev. vol. 1 (1903-9), offset reprint, N.Y. 1966, p. 454.]

The *Ceremonious* husband would wait for an introduction.

The *Just* husband would see that he fucked fair.

The *Conceited* husband would sneer at the size of his balls.

The *Modest* husband would think his balls looked larger than his own.

The *Refined* husband would pull his shirt tail over his bottom.

The *Cautious* husband, with a large family, would ask if he had on a French letter [condom], and if not, request him to spend outside.

The *Jealous* husband would be annoyed, although he had on a French letter.

The *Suspicious* husband would make his wife wash afterwards.

The *Excitable* husband would begin to frig himself.

The *Shy* husband would blush and walk away.

The *Avaricious* husband would want to charge for it.

The *Mean* husband would look to see if he'd used his cold cream.

The *Epicurean* husband would gamahuche his wife immediately afterwards. ['Gamahuche,' a mid-19th-century French term of unknown origin — possibly from the Japanese *gamaguchi,* purse — referring to cunnilinctus. See the skit on the unusualness of the term, by Henry Monnier, in Jules Gay's *Le Bibliophile fantaisiste,* 1869, p. 282–4. It apparently lives on, much deformed, in American underworld slang, as *'lamma hutching'* (!) recorded in Roger Blake's *American Dictionary of Adult Sexual Terms,* Hollywood, 1964.]

The *Conscientious* husband would fear that he had neglected his wife.

The *Cynical* husband would be surprised that anyone should care to fuck his wife.

The *Prompt* husband would be up his arse before he could say: "Jack Robinson."

6. CONNIVING AT ADULTERY

Every variety of conniving at adultery has obviously been given, in the list preceding, in gallows-humor form. Though this 'typology' can hardly be defined as a joke, it will be observed that it makes use of pedicating the adulterer as the good, manly, roast-beef-of-Olde-England punch-line. This casts a certain light, in passing, on the technical construction of folktales or jokes in which *three* or any given number of persons respond variously to a given situation, as types rather than as individuals; the 'correct' or humorous-explosive response — representing the true response of the unrepressed *id* — being the response of the final type. This ranges from the response of the littlest Bear in "Goldilocks and the Three Bears," and that of Cinderella (as opposed to her two 'evil' sisters), to various jokes that have already been given concerning such *type* situations as the three daughters responding variously to questions about their wedding nights, or the three travelling salesmen in the preceding section, of which the manly punch-liner brains his wife's lovers with a baseball bat, without a word of warning.

Far removed are the connivers (in the dictionary sense of the term: *connive,* to feign ignorance, to shut the eyes, to pretend not to look at something distasteful or irregular; hence, to have a secret understanding with, and to abet or countenance silently). The next-to-last husband of *The Pearl's* list, the 'Cynical' husband, is developed into a joke of his own, usually delivered in heavy mock-Jewish dialect, in reference to the extreme logic-chopping and indecisive philosophizing supposedly typical of the religious or Talmudic Jew: *A New York clothing manufacturer comes home from the office early one day with a headache, and finds his partner in bed with his wife. He looks on astonished, and finally says, "Morris, I must — but you?"* (N.Y. 1940.)

As a topper to a joke given earlier, in the chapter on Marriage, of *The friend who warns the bridegroom that everybody in Yonkers has made love to the girl he is marrying, to which the conniving or acceding reply is made, "Well, is Yonkers such a big place?"* (1:345), there is *The man sitting in a bar who offers the information to a stranger that he has just married the greatest little woman in the world, giving her name and so forth. "Her!?" says the stranger, "why I used to fuck the ass off that bitch behind the pipe-organ when she sang in the choir. That girl knows more tricks on a limber prick than a monkey on a rope." The bridegroom absorbs this thoughtfully, and finally says to the bartender, "Hey, Joe, set up a couple of drinks here — friend of the wife."* (N.Y. 1952.) The husband speaks as though three-quarters drunk from the beginning, thus 'explaining' his docility. Only under the excuse of being drunk can a red-blooded American agree that he will *not* fight over what's been lost long ago anyhow. One thinks of Miss Frances Winwar (Vinceguerra)'s reply to the suit intended against her by Lord Alfred Douglas, for her published discussion of his relations with Oscar Wilde before the famous trial, that Douglas was 'suing to regain a reputation he lost in the last century.'

The relief afforded by the preceding grossly under-reactive joke, from the necessary pose of defending womanhood, the home, country, flag, mother, etc., must be very great, as it itself has a further topper, of the same anti-gallant or anti-family kind, though in this case not concerned with adultery. *Time: Just after World War II. An American in a bar in London strikes up acquaintance with two Englishmen, one of whom is deaf and the other stammers. (This is played on very heavily throughout, and in comedy-English Lord Hawhaw accent.) The stammering Englishman asks the American: "Now when you were in London during the War, did you ever go to Soho?" "Every fucking night!" The deaf Englishman: "Whatdidhesay?" "Says he went there every night. — And tell me, sir, did you ever know a Lady Esther Folkingham?" "Did I know Lady Esther Folkingham!? Not so young, but a spring in her — you know,* toujours l'amour! *— it's a won-*

der I'm alive today! 'Hot-pants Tessie,' we used to call her in the Air Force. Me and my buddies used to screw her in phone-booths. She wouldn't take money, you know; she used to pay us for it. That dame went down on everything but the Titanic." *The deaf Englishman:* "Whatdidhesay?" "He knows Mother." (N.Y. 1953.)

The woman's relations with the men she has known intimately before her marriage — or even after her widowhood or divorce — are assimilated to a kind of proto-adultery by the average man, and in a sense he is correct. He would not, of course, agree to any such estimate of his own extra-curricular and premarital affairs. All of us know at least one nauseating specimen who, after he regales us with accounts (by long-distance telephone) of how he was "drained dry — right to the marrow of the bones, brother!" by a beautiful and conscientious prostitute in some such soft-currency country as Italy or Spain, where the human ass (of both sexes) is peddled pitifully cheap; will then pull out all the *vox humana* stops on how he is now going home (marrowless) to his tidy little Southern California wife, dishwasher, and mother of his three children, whose photograph in kodachrome he cannot, at this point, be prevented from pulling out long-distance, and kissing with a loud smack. (*Sex to Sexty,* 1968, 16:64.)

Similar confidences or bragging by a married woman would be considered in even lower taste, if such a thing is possible, particularly if made to her husband concerning the earlier 'other men' in her life. These are, as it were, adulteries projected into the past, and when the woman insists upon them they are obviously substitutes for adulteries in the present. I have heard more than one bitchy young American woman describe, in recent years, entirely unrequested and unexpectedly, how she started screwing when she was eighteen, and did plenty of it; or 'sucked off' her first boy friend for x number of months, by way of protecting her virginity; how, nevertheless, she finally 'lost her cherry,' and the like. It is a fact, however, that many men will elicit such confidences, and take a painful pleasure in being excruciated by them. As with castration stories, and 'nasty-nasties,' the intention is to face oneself with the worst possible blow imaginable, for the reassurance which comes from surviving it: to show oneself that one 'can take it,' and thus there is really no danger at all. This is also the secret spring of lion-hunting, bull-fighting, mountain-climbing, and other dangerous masochistic activities of the kind. The moment of reassurance repetitively sought for is the moment right *after* the lion has sprung, bull has charged, rope has broken, and so forth, but the would-be victim somehow finds himself miraculously safe. Until the day when the mathematics of it catch up with him, and the lion or bull does *not* miss. All else failing, such persons will often end as open suicides. The case of Ernest Hemingway is almost a textbook example of the entire syndrome.

When the dangerous punishment sought is merely verbal excoriation with the details of a beloved woman's infidelity, in the style of Pierre Louÿs' *La Femme et le Pantin* and his even more masochistic privately-issued erotica, men have never had any difficulty, and will certainly not have any difficulty today, in finding a bitch-streak of this type to exploit in the average woman tittivated up in men's shirts and pants, if they lead to it by such purposeful weakness. When sexual confidences of this type seem to have been given accidentally — let alone when they are forced in a strange, gloating voice and with a shit-eating grin, on a surprised lover or husband (the full folk-phrase is *'to grin like a fox eating shit out of a wire brush'*) — the proper response or 'ploy' is to listen gravely through to the end, and then to offer, *quid pro quo,* the hidden truth about one's own life as well. Emphasizing strongly the mythical time one foolishly paid three hundred dollars in a de luxe cat-house in Rome to have three girls at once, describing all of them as being exquisitely beautiful *especially* in whatever department — bosom, buttocks, sexual complaisance, or whatnot — the female braggart being thus fenced with conversationally is particularly deficient. This never fails, and I have myself seen it run up into an epileptic fit by five o'clock in the morning. *À bon chat, bon rat.* These are dangerous games — winner take nothing. Most relationships cannot survive them and are not intended to, except on the most humiliating sado-masochistic basis. Like punch-line jokes, everything ends in tableau at that point, and no further life is conceivable for any of the participants, let alone together. These are the games that it is perhaps better not to play. Anyhow, not more than once.

Inevitably, though the struggling and the hate-relationship here is with the 'adulterous' woman herself, the sexual relationship is entirely with the other man. For it is only *his* appearance in these recollections that makes them unpalatable to the husband, lover, or other present incumbent. Were these, for instance, the recollections of the woman's own masturbatory life, the man could easily laugh them off, in the certainty that he could replace such a 'past' with something better.

When the traces he must efface are those of another man, he cannot always be sure. Nor can he always be sure of effacing them. Even the former lover sometimes feels a bit uneasy about such gratuitous confidences, out of *esprit de corps* with the chump who succeeds him. *Anecdota Americana* (1927) 1:401 gives the key story of this type. In its own words: '*Mary had lived with Jack for many months, and there was nothing she hadn't done for him, from sucking his balls to his arse. She had stopped at no licentiousness. He had screwed her and back-scuttled her. After a time, however, they had a falling-out, and parted as casually as they had come together.' Four or five months later they meet again, and he invites her up to his apartment. She refuses, explaining that she is now married. ' "And I want you to understand I told my husband everything." "You told him everything? All about the little parties we used to have, you know?" leered Jack. "Yes," said Mary. "Everything." "Well, I don't know which to admire most, your gall or your memory".'* Note that the lover is here identifying with the husband, and is even trying to defend him from the bitch he himself has rejected. The husband's position, and almost the only viable 'ploy' or defense he can take, is given as a gallant or semi-bawdy joke in a house-organ, *Better Crops with Plant Food* (March, 1941) p. 49, as a throwaway or filler: ' "*Now that I've told you about my past, do you [still] want to marry me?" "Sure, baby." "I suppose you'll expect me to live it down?" "No! I'll expect you to live up to it".'*

The husband's acting weak, *vis à vis* the wife's adultery, is the most contemptible characteristic allotted him by patriarchal folklore, and it is considered — and may even be true — that "*It's better to beat the living shit out of your wife, than to let her get away with playing around. That way she knows you care about her.*" (Given as a piece of sage advice, N.Y. 1940, to a cultivated young husband whose visible masochism led him to take the pose that his wife's nymphomaniacal adulteries with strangers that he would bring home — obviously for that purpose — were best responded to by going down to the corner drugstore meanwhile to replenish her birth control jelly!) Often seen in print is an expurgated allusion to this sort of scene. '*Sam (at picture show): "Mandy, tell dat niggah on de yuther side to take his ahm frum roun yo waist." Mandy: "Tell em yo'self; he's a puffic strangah to me".'* (*Cotton Ginners' Journal*, Aug. 1941, p. 21, filler.) The unexpurgated form, collected contemporaneously: *Mother, finding her daughter making love on the lawn (or porch swing) at a picnic:*

"Daughter, tell that man to stop jazzing you!" "Tell him yourself. I never saw him before in my life!" (N.Y. 1939.) In taunt-style: *Mother:* *"Well I never!!" "Oh, mother, you must of!"* Also, the moron-style rationalization: *An Englishman sees his wife raped before his eyes by a Frenchman in Paris, without making a move. "What's the idea?" his wife berates him afterward. "You just sat there without saying a word." "Well, what could I say? I don't know a word of French."* (2:332.) In *Kryptádia* (1884) II. 167, as a variant on "The Wagoner," given below, of a Frenchman and his wife who can't speak English.

Connected with this, is the polite but heavily-symbolized 1890's story about *The young English girl coming to France for the first time, searching through the dictionary to learn how to say "Whoa" in French, so she'll know what to scream if a French horse runs away with her.* (Paris, 1954, stated to be a classic, and obviously referring to the horse-&-carriage era.) That the runaway horse — even better, the centaur — represents the impetuous lover or 'rapist' the young girl dreams of, is only too clear to see, since she is relieved of all moral responsibility for her sexual pleasure in fantasies of rape. When this is set back one step lower, just under the threshold of consciousness, as concerning runaway horses, there is obviously no moral problem at all. The curious habit of *falling* which many young women have — even now, when there are no more runaway horses, nor tight corsets to explain fainting and swoons — must also be considered a charade on the sexual idea of 'falling from grace,' or the even less conscious identification of falling or floating (especially down staircases or off roofs, now subsumed under the idea of ski-jumps) with sexual intercourse. This was almost apotheosized in the falling of Miss Brigitte Bardot from a roof; falling, falling, draped in her hair and never landing, as the erotico-suicidal conclusion to her movie, *Private Lives.*

The acquiescent husband or 'wittol' — a term now almost as obsolete as 'cuckold' — finally appears as homosexual. *'A fag was complaining to his friend that when he got home the night before he found a man in bed with his wife. "What did you do?" his friend asked, all excitement. "Do?" said the fairy . . . "The way I slammed the door when I went out, she knew I wasn't pleased!"'* (1:310.) — *Anecdota* also gives a variant, in which, again, the wittol husband is so comically impuissant that he must be played as a homosexual. *'A fairy, who for appearances' sake had married a beautiful girl, discovered her being screwed by her employer on an office couch. He reported his indignation to a fairy friend. "I hope you got your revenge," said this latter. "I should say I did," the other* *replied. "I utterly destroyed the couch".'* (1:158.) A polite version of this was delivered in a lecture on Russian culture as seen through its literature, at Columbia University, in 1950, by a visiting psychiatrist: *A man appears on a radio tell-your-troubles program and explains that every time he gets home he finds his wife making love to the boarder on the living room couch. "Well, what do you think you ought to do about it?" asks the moderator. "That's my problem, Mr. Anthony. Do you think they could make trouble for me if I sold the couch?"* See other versions, and tracing, under "Pure Fools," 2.11, above, to Rotunda Motif *K1569.2.

The McAtee manuscript (1912, env. 4) gives what appears to be a folktale, weakly poetized under the title "The Bedwarmer," without any real punch-line, and of the classic lineage of folktales concerning shared beds and pretended sleep. *A house-guest is cold at night. The husband suggests that his wife get in bed to warm him. 'Thought he, 'twill do no harm. Wife said today her period was on.' The bed continues shaking as though with the guest's coldness. The husband shouts, "Wife, you're not warming him very quick!" She replies, her voice trailing off ecstatically as though to sleep: "E-v-e-ry-thing will be — all — all — ri — ri — ri."* This is Rotunda's Motif K1325.1, and compare also his K2059.1, the lovers who pretend to have slept all night and who 'thank God each morning for not having sinned.' Randolph gives a story on this theme, in *Pissing in the Snow*, No. 37, "Stuck in a Mud Hole":

A freighter (or wagoner) who is sleeping overnight with a farmer and his wife has intercourse with the wife by pretending to be driving his wagon in his sleep. 'The old man just opened one eye, but he seen what was going on, all right. The freighter was a-bouncing around on top of the woman, a-clucking and hollering like he was driving a team. Pretty soon the old man spoke up. "Stranger," says he, "it looks like you'll have to unload, before you can get out of that there mud hole." Now ain't that a hell of a way for a man to talk, with the old woman a-fucking a freighter right before his eyes?' Randolph notes that he collected this in 1953 from an old man who had heard it in Carroll county, Arkansas, about 1895, and who said it was a 'very old story.' It is indeed old, being No. 7 in La Sale's *Cent Nouvelles Nouvelles* (about 1460), where the husband expresses his disinterest by telling the wagoner — the identical profession (and probable pantomime) for four hundred years or more — to beware of the wife's shrewish bad temper and scratching, there being 'nothing in the world which makes her more furious' than sexual intercourse. In the Arkansas version she is simply rejected as a 'mud hole,' i.e. shit.

Another curious story is given in a later portion of the McAtee manuscript collection (1938, env. 2), as "Supplements to Rabelais: II. Justice for M. Cornecon." Again this is more a *conte* than a joke. It may also be original and not of folk provenance, but conniving at adultery can hardly be taken farther, whether as a private fantasy in literary style, or with the wholesale audience-acceptance of folktale status. *A woman complains to the judge that overuse by her husband has put corns on her sexual parts, and that these distress her. The husband replies: "Your Honor, I am not responsible for the whole of the cornefied condition. There are scaly corns that make me suspect some Breton fisherman, and tufted, woolly, and prickly ones I fear almost to mention — they may come from the Evil One himself. There are black ones that indicate traffic with a Moor; but what can I say about the yellow, and green, and purple ones? Your Honor, there are as many corns in that place as there are fleas on a fiddler's bitch; I know I didn't make 'em all."*

The moment any profit of a monetary kind, or material advantage, is expected from the wife's adultery, or when this adultery has actually been instigated by the husband for the purposes of such advantage, the situation is not really adultery but more correctly proxenetism or pimping. Folk-wit correctly assesses that what is involved here is a much higher estimate (love) of himself by the husband than of his wife or his rights of exclusivity as to her body. Since she 'belongs' to him, when her body can be sold or traded for something more valuable to him than his personal enjoyment of that body, the totally egocentric husband does not hesitate to make that sale or trade. In France, the folklore has it that it is by this means that men seek honorary decorations from lascivious governmental officers, and also that judges can thus be bribed sexually more easily than with money, if one has both 'a losing case and a beautiful wife.' In all countries it is agreed that a raise in pay or a better job can be scrounged out of the boss by offering him the use of one's wife — one use per raise. Given already as a weak pun, and too often collected for the pun to explain the popularity of the story: *During World War II a woman took a job in a 'cost-plus' factory working on the same shift with her husband, named Jack. The foreman takes her aside and tells her that the government inspectors have objected to their 'featherbedding' too many workers on the job, to get the profit percentage. "Why are you telling me all this?" she asks. "What are you getting at?" "What I'm getting at is, I'm either going to have to lay you or Jack off."* (Orangeburg, N.Y. 1944.) The 'proposition' being made here *to the wife,* that she protect her husband's job or the family income, the joke relieves the husband of any charge of direct connivance. In fact, the result of the negotiation is not stated at all, but we are left to understand that the foreman or 'straw-boss' gets what he wants. Both the pun, and the assessment of the husband, are sometimes made even more clear by having him named 'Jerk' instead of 'Jack.'

Significantly told of the massively egoistic profession of stage-actor, in which the all-powerful theatrical agent (or director) takes the place of any other boss or god: *An actor comes home to find his wife sobbing, her hair and clothing rumpled, and bruises on her arms and back. "Your agent was here," she sobs; "he insulted me, he beat me, he raped me!" "Did he leave a message?"* (N.Y. 1953.) The situation is spelled out in a variant offered simultaneously by the same teller. *An actor sits by the phone day after day, doing cross-word puzzles and waiting for his agent to call him about a booking. There is nothing to eat in the house, and finally in desperation the wife goes out to see if she can borrow some canned goods from her mother. Hours later she phones. "Hello, honey? I'm in your agent's office at the Paramount." "Well, fuck him!" "I did. You open here Thursday."* (N.Y. 1953.)

The disgracing of the husband, as less than a 'good provider,' clearly is meant to signify his unvirility: the excuse as well as the cause for his being cuckolded. This involves *the unconscious identification of money as virile power, or, conversely, of semen as money.* This is also, in large part, the explanation of the open wasting of the husband's money by hostile and hateful wives, as of the similar wasting or destroying of 'company (or government) property' by disgruntled employees. *A man in a bar is amazed to find the bartender continuously giving free drinks to everyone in the house. The bartender explains: "Did you see that fat guy in the corner, before, that went upstairs with that pretty girl?" "Yes ...?" "Well, that's the boss, and the girl is my wife. What he's doing to her, I'm doing to his business."* (N.Y. 1946, actually just a pun on the hostile meaning, of to cheat or damn, that most verbs for sexual intercourse include, especially *fuck* and *screw* in English, *baiser* in French, and *ficken* in German; on which the joke preceding, on opening at the Paramount Theatre, also turns.)

All the themes of the earlier fool stories, as to 'nincumpoops' who do not recognize the female genitals — especially of their own wives — or the act of intercourse, when they see it, also appear in connection with the weak and wittol husband, conniving at his wife's adultery, especially when this is to his own advantage. *The office fool sneaks home during working hours for a short nap, having been out gambling the night before. He comes back unexpectedly soon and confides to an office-mate, "Boy, did I just have a narrow escape! When I walked in the house, there was the boss screwing my wife. But I tiptoed out without him noticing I wasn't on the job."* (N.Y. 1940.) Impossibly weak as humor: all that is wanted is to contrive a vehicle to express the situation of withdrawing in the boss's favor from the possession of the wife. *A miner gets into the shaft-elevator chuckling out loud. "What's the joke, Sven?" asks the foreman. "Ay got good yoke on Ole," says the miner. "Ay yust find out Ole pays my wife five dollars to foke her, and I foke her for nothing."* (1:18.) Though unstated, the foreman is clearly being offered the next turn.

No English-language version, in living transmission, has been collected of the very famous European tale, Boccaccio's Day VII, Tale 7, "*Cocu, Battu et Content,*" discussed in the Introduction, section III (Rotunda: Motif K1514.4.1, giving sources), in which, *By an elaborate ruse the husband is put into his wife's clothing and in that disguise beaten by the wife's lover, who pretends in this way to reject her offered adultery. The husband comes back to bed, covered with bruises but satisfied with his wife* [*i.e.* sexually potent?] *Thus: cuckolded, beaten, and content.* The most extreme example collected of the physical humiliation of the husband, combined with the emotional humiliation of *knowing* his wife to be unfaithful, expresses the situation actually as seen from the point of view of the conniving husband or pimp. *A pimp is just getting into bed with his woman on an icy-cold winter night, when a specially good client, an out-of-town buyer, knocks at the door. The pimp climbs out on the fire-escape in his underwear, and shivers and shakes with the cold, while watching through the window-blind the client inside enjoying himself at leisure in the bed the pimp has warmed. After two hours, two 'tricks,' several drinks, and a snack in bed, the customer leaves, smoking one of the pimp's best cigars. The whore rushes to the window, and rolls in the half-frozen pimp, and starts chafing his hands and slapping his cheeks to revive him. In a trembling voice and through blue lips, the pimp asks, "Has the* SUCKER *gone yet?"* (1:78.)

Masochistic jokes of this kind will be found more common on out-and-out homosexual themes, in the following section here, III.3, particularly concerning stories transitional between the adulterous relationship with the other man and conscious homosexuality, under the title

"Masking Homosexuality." Without any physical harm actually coming to the husband, the most total humiliation to him obviously involves the adulterer's turning the tables and, instead of being pedicated in punishment by the outraged husband, outraging the husband by pedicating him instead. No joke actually going this homosexually far has been collected, but an American revision of a well-known and much older European tale comes extraordinarily close. *A man and his young bride are driving across the United States on their honeymoon trip. While camping out one night on the western desert (or stopping to change a flat tire), a Mexican bandit holds them up at gun-point, takes all their money and valuables, and then says, "And now, Señor, I am going to fuck yor' wife, and you are going to hold my balls up out of the hot sand." This done, he gallops off yodelling, leaving the newlyweds to continue their trip in silence. They drive hundreds of miles without a word being said. Suddenly the wife bursts out, "You're a hell of a man, letting him do a thing like that to me! And you not making a move to save me." "What do you mean, not making a move?" counters the husband. "Why twice, when he wasn't looking, I let his balls drop in the hot sand."* (Chicago, 1940.) Earliest in Bebel's *Facetiæ* (MS. 1508) II. 17, "*De quodam pulcherrimo vindictæ genere,*" specifying that the highwayman 'perforates' the wife 'before, behind, and above.'

In the older European version, *The husband is forced by the highwayman to hold his horse (or cloak), while the highwayman rapes his wife. Later the husband assures his wife that he made "many a dagger thrust" in the highwayman's saddle while holding his horse.* The burlesque American touch concerning the hot Mexican testicles (¡cojones furiosos!) and hotter sand, which imports the homosexual humiliation of the husband in unmistakable fashion, appears to be taken from — or should be compared with — the joke earlier given, under "The Forbidding Father," concerning *Southern hospitality: the Southern tobacco-planter who finds his daughter making love to the Northern guest on the parlor floor. "Mary Lou!" he cries, horrified; "where is yo' Southern hospitality? Arch yo' back, and get the ge'mman's balls up off that cold marble flo'!"* (2:206, and variant Calif. 1943.) The elaborate displacement of attention, from the central immorality of the situation to some ostentatiously absurd detail, is also identical in both stories. It is by means of the same mechanism, of massive under-reaction to what is essential, and total concern with misapprehended details, that shaggy dog stories achieve most of their effect.

III. POSSESSION IN COMMON

1. POSSESSION IN COMMON

As anyone who has read this far will certainly have understood by now, the present writer has little patience with journalistic blithering and the insincere exposé approach to human sexuality, to its triumphs and its far more numerous disasters. This approach seems recently to have become the special province of British journalists, dubiously exploiting the new sexual freedom in England and America by *pretending* to object to it, as in Cyril Connolly's complaining of 'the tyranny of the orgasm'(!) For example, one Malcolm Muggeridge writing a tongue-in-cheek "Down With Sex!" item for *Esquire* — a men's magazine apparently gone impotent in its old age — and an even tonguier and cheekier item, appearing in so unlikely an organ as the tourist magazine, *Holiday* (June 1966), possibly in follow-up of the far superior New Freedom piece by Clifton Fadiman, "Party of One," in the same magazine, August 1959, which I have discussed more fully in *The Horn Book*, p. 311–12. The follow-up is a particularly absurd item, "The Trouble With Starlets," by a Mr. John Fowles (much like Muggeridge in *Esquire,* but even more British), who begins by confessing that he is 'writing about a subject with which [he has] never slept' — in which case, what is his competence for complaining? — and who ends, p. 20, with an incredible burst of sympathy for the menopausals *of both sexes* whom he considers to be somehow attacked by the mere existence of pretty young girl starlets, along with an even more incredible apotheosis of the wooden statue of a chubby little naked boy or *putto* (which does not mean Italian male whore) which he has hanging over his desk, he explains, while writing about how miffed he is by seeing beautiful young women in bikini bathing-suits. This almost gives away more of what really goes into the fabrication of such propaganda pieces, behind the scenes, than is politic.

Less petty, and certainly more dangerous, there is now also the whole new tribe or crew of out-and-out literary Gangsters of the New Freedom, mostly operating out of Los Angeles, New York and London, and producing handbooks for wife-swapping and orgies, homosexuality, necrophily, etc., with phoney case-histories *à volonté* for mail-order peddling ("State age on the order-blank, please. We also supply kinky lingerie and IMPORTED high-heel boots for your *bondage* needs"), all deftly mixed or not mixed, as the case may be, with California-grown marijuana, peyotl, and LSD; and all coming on particularly strong under the banner of 'Freedom.' Needless to say, it was not for these people and what they are peddling that scores of honorable writers and publishers over the last century have gone to jail and faced professional ruin, to fight the censorship of sex. The type of bunkum think-piece produced by these gentry is seldom more offensive — at least to me — than when it presumes to concern itself with what the modern originator of this art of wowing the chumps with anti-sex and phoney-sex, the late Philip Wylie, was pleased to propagandize against under the name of 'Momism,' with clarion cries as to the presumed advancing 'Matriarchy.' (One would imagine that, under matriarchy, men would be searching for status by wearing women's clothes, and women would be out earning most of the money and dying and leaving it to the men; and not the massive reverse we see all around us as patriarchy fails.) An anti-woman attack not worth discussing further. See my *Love & Death* (1949) *ad fin.*

Utterly different is the deeply sincere article, "The Fear of Touch," in *Neurotica* (1950) No. 6: p. 3–10, written by Theodor Reik — whom I have never met — the greatest of modern lay-psychoanalysts, and author of the one finest book ever written in any language on the subject of love, and the *only* book to tell its secret, which such highly-touted attempts as Stendhal's hardly more than begin to understand. The book referred to is Reik's *Psychology of Sex Relations* (1945, reprinted by Grove Press, 1961), a title perhaps poorly chosen when one considers that its subject is actually *the emotion of love,* and the unveiling of the mystery which thousands of other writers have failed to pierce: of its genesis in the individual, and the source of its overwhelming power in those who really feel it. Were all the other books ever written on the subject of love — and particularly all the damned novels, filled with lies! — to be accidentally burnt, and this one book of Reik's preserved, not only nothing would be lost but a great deal might be gained. (I would make an honorable exception for Dr. Edrita Fried's magnificent study, *The Ego in Love and Sexuality,* New York, 1960, also reprinted by Grove Press, which is, however, mostly concerned with forms of the neurotic *inability to love,* the curse of our century.)

In his cited article, "The Fear of Touch," in *Neurotica* No. 6, Theodor Reik is concerned, as his taking-off point, with the very typically Viennese comedy-sequence *Hands Around (Reigen),* by Arthur Schnitzler, a series of gallant dialogues, each between a man and a woman, during the course of which a line of dashes interrupts the dialogue to indicate that they are engaging in sexual intercourse. Almost as though set to music like a Swiss clock *gavotte,* each participant appears (with a different partner) in two successive dialogues, and the ring of the dance is completed in the final dialogue in which one of the actors of the opening dialogue again appears. From this Reik appears to move on to other matters, and specifically to a discussion of 'neurotic patients who suffer from a fear of touch, especially from the fear of touching persons and objects which they consider possible carriers of infection.' (See further my *The Fake Revolt,* p. 22–32, on 'Cool' as *the new venereal disease.*) Reik gives a few bizarre and grotesque extensions of this, as of the man who refused to sit in movie theatres because the father of a certain Hollywood actor is supposed to have had syphilis, and 'The "touch circuit," as the patient puts it, is closed exactly as though the father of the actor had personally sat on every seat in every theater.'

Reik ends by quoting the strange reply made by the philosopher Pangloss, in Voltaire's *Candide,* when asked how he has come to be a horrible-looking old beggar, dull-eyed, covered with sores, and with the end of his nose fallen away. *"My dear Candide,"* Pangloss replied, *"you remember Paquette,. the maidservant of our august Baroness. In her arms I enjoyed the delights of Paradise which have produced the hellish tortures by which you see me devoured. She was infected with them, and she is perhaps dead of them. Paquette received this present from a most learned monk. He caught it from an old countess, who had it from a cavalry captain, who owed it to a marchioness, who took it from a page, who had received it from a Jesuit, who, when a novice, had it in direct line from one of the companions of Christopher Columbus . . ."* "Oh, Pangloss!" exclaims Candide, *"what a strange genealogy!"* And suddenly one realizes why Reik has begun with Schnitzler's *Hands Around.*

In an earlier chapter, under "Incest," the story has already been given that matches almost exactly Voltaire's satirical genealogy, tracing Dr. Pangloss' syphilis back to the companions of Christopher Columbus who are believed, probably correctly, to have brought it back from the New World: its principal cultural contribution until the Atom Bomb. Briefly detailed: *A young man in a whore-house demands that the madam supply him with a girl who has syphilis. She assures him testily that none of her girls are sick, and asks why on earth he wants such a thing. "I want to catch it so I can give it to the housemaid," he says with an evil smile. Now the madam is truly shocked. "My God!" she says, "what kind of a monster are you? What have you got against the poor girl?"* *"Nothing,"* explains the young man; *"but she'll give it to Dad. He'll give it to Mother, and she'll give it to the priest.* THAT'S *the son-of-a-bitch I'm after!"* (Transcontinental train, U.S. 1938, from a Cleveland physician.)

This joke could obviously also be given in the very relevant later chapters, "Prostitution" and "Disease," in Series Two, which is certainly its basic subject. Yet seen from the point of view of its operative *nexus* — the bearing on which the whole story turns — it has really nothing to do with prostitution, and some non-'venereal' disease such as cancer or leprosy (if these were infectious) could easily be substituted. It is essentially an incest story, and though the son explains that his revenge is directed against the man who is his mother's lover (the Hamlet complex, masterfully studied by Dr. Fredric Wertham in *Dark Legend*), the unconsciously-intended victim is probably a woman. This is implied by the specifically-intended victim being the innocent housemaid, who certainly here represents the mother that the son hates and wishes sexually to kill with his penis (by means of syphilis) for having rejected him in favor of some other lover. The same hatred of the mother, for the rejection earlier in favor of the father, the son has had to learn to control since infancy, and usually to overlayer — as does Hamlet — with dutiful love for the father-rival, or, especially as in the case of Hamlet, mere talk of such duty without being able to bring himself to perform it. But once the father has been by-passed, and the mother is discovered to be willing to accept some man *other* than the father, it is a mortal and unforgivable insult that her choice has not fallen upon her loving son.

This is a different point of view about adultery than that usually taken in jokes and folktales on the subject. It is *the parents' adultery as seen by the child*. My own experience with this is very recent, as I was first thrust into emotional recognition of it in the autumn of 1964 by the bitter answer given me by a California college girl to a rhetorical question I had asked in an informal lecture opposing the "Freedom for Pot [Marijuana]" campaign at Berkeley. (Later I decided I was wrong, and that it would be wise to wean American students *back* from LSD merely to 'pot,' since LSD *causes induced schizophrenia* as marijuana does not.)

I had inquired why student listeners really supposed their parents were supporting their bogus revolt by keeping them idle and dropping-out at college. A young girl stood up to cite the then-recent "People-opoly" sex scandals in central California, a 'life-game' on the style of the card-game, "Monopoly," in which the telephone-numbers of three ugly girls, or three male 'duds,' are exchanged for that of one live-wire; all the persons involved in the game being pledged to 'ball' (sleep with) who-ever calls to make a date, giving the password "*People-opoly*" or similar. Naturally, each person approached is assured that he or she has been traded off as a live-wire, not a dud! This is hardly more than a game-form of wife-trading or 'swapping,' except that the people being traded in, like cunt-&-prick commodities, are not necessarily married to each other. (The 'underground' or LSD press, developing in the late 1960's in America, owes most of its popularity to the *classified advertisements* car-ried for sexual orgy-clubs, and perversions and permutations of this kind, often very plainly described by the advertisers, or hidden behind allusions to 'French culture,' etc.) The girl ended her exposé by coming back to the question of the parents sending her and her fellow-students to college. "*I guess we're sent here,*" she said, including perhaps too broadly all the other students at the lecture, "*so as not to get into our parents' hair Saturday nights on their wife-swapping parties.*" As I have observed in *The Fake Revolt,* p. 19, discussing the whole matter in much more violent detail, the same young girl also tried bitterly to pose as emotionless and disillusioned, and referred contemptuously to falling in love as 'blowing your cool.'

Here Elektra speaks in no uncertain accents of her animosity against her parents' mutual adulteries, which to her mean, A) that her mother's sexual prohibitions and ideals are a hypocritical fraud; and B) that her father has rejected *her* sexually, since, in fact, he wants some woman other than her mother. Dr. Reik does not cover this point. As a matter of fact, the real subject of Reik's article is not even mentioned in it at all until the last paragraph. He leaves it to be intuited by the reader, or, rather, to well over him finally as all the pieces presented suddenly fall into place, and understanding comes gushing out just as Dr. Reik ambles slowly away. His style is thus the exact opposite of the journalistic 'nar-rative hook' or get-it-all-in-the-first-paragraph headline style, to which we have become accustomed in the last century. There is a very subtle triangulation about the way he writes. He is not interested in hitting his subject head-on, which he knows will simply shock and rebuff his listener, a lesson the present writer has found it exceptionally difficult to learn. Instead, he appears to be wandering around in pleasant circles, touching conversationally on this and on that more-or-less connected theme. And finally he shakes the listener-reader's hand, and says good-bye. And then the light goes on. Suddenly, without any grand dénouement, one is wholly aware that all the pieces have been placed, and positions given, that some ultimately tender normal need (or, rather, neurotic substitute for it) has been floodlighted under the simultaneous scrutiny of about seven attacking and enveloping pieces on the analytic chessboard, and that — for all Reik's apparent conversational casualness and wandering about, that has preceded — it is check, mate, game, and tourney. We will not see his like again.

The hint that Reik leaves in his closing paragraph, which acts as a catalyst of the whole realization of what is involved in such fantasies (or realities) of consecutive sexual intercourse, or possession in common of the same woman by more than one man, is this:

> The origin of the roundelay fantasy is the image of sharing a woman with another man, or coming in contact with another man in the same woman, and the most energetic rejection of such a fantasy. In other words, the germ of the typical fantasy is the possibility of coming in contact with a potential rival in the same sexual object. This original fantasy, whose acceptance would include the possibility of concealed homosexuality, is repressed and refused with great violence. Its re-emergence in a displaced and generalized shape leads then to the fantasy-formation of *hands-around*. If such a possibility became reality, where would it end? One, two, three men? One could meet hundreds of men in the same sexual object. The neurotic or jealous imagination follows these possibilities to infinity. *If the sexual object, the woman, is a bridge to the other man* [italics supplied], if such an unconsciously repressed possibility were admitted in thoughts . . .? A bridge can be used by many hundreds of passengers.

In hostile form — the sexual being forbidden — and evidently drawn from the usage of 'whipping-boys' in the education of princes, a very similar *hands-around of revenge* is set up in an anecdote told as true in John Aubrey's *Brief Lives* (MS. about 1680) concerning Sir Walter Raleigh 'being invited to dinner to some great person' along with his son, also named Walter, whose Oedipus complex seems to have been massive, to whom his father said:

"Thou art expected to-day at dinner to goe along with me, but thou art such a quarrelsome, affronting * * * [?], that I am ashamed to have such a beare in my company." Mr. Walter humbled himselfe to his father, and promised he would behave himselfe mighty mannerly. So away they went . . . He sate next to his father and was very demure at least halfe dinner time. Then sayd he, "I, this morning, not having the feare of God before my eies but by the instigation of the devill, went to a whore. I was very eager of her, kissed and embraced her, and went to enjoy her, but she thrust me from her, and vowed I should not, 'for your Father lay with me but an hower ago'." Sir Walter being strangely surprized and putt out of his countenance at so great a table, gives his son a damned blow over his face. His son, rude as he was, would not strike his father, but strikes over the face the gentleman that sate next to him and sayd, *"Box about: 'twill come to my father anon."* 'Tis now a common-used proverb.

This is transcribed in the edition of Aubrey's *Brief Lives* edited by Anthony Powell (London: Cresset Press, 1949) p. 326, and is followed immediately by the delicious anecdote of Raleigh's own sexual prowess: *'One time getting up one of the mayds of honor against a tree in a wood,' the girl trying vainly to fend him off with 'Nay, sweet Sir Walter! Sir Walter! At last, as the danger and the pleasure at the same time grew higher, she cried in the extacey Swisser Swatter! Swisser Swatter! She proved with child . . .'* (Note that the name 'Walter' was then pronounced without voicing the letter '*l*,' as still in *talk* or *folk*.) This anecdote was made into a catch for four voices in the 17th century. With the exception of "The Tale of Bahloul the Fool," in the Arabic *Perfumed Garden* of the Sheik al-Nafzawi (MS. Tunis, 15th century), this is one of the earliest known references to female orgasm, unmistakably described as a paroxysm or 'extacey.' Half a century after Raleigh's death in 1618, such references had become common in Restoration poetry, for example Dryden's "The Extasy," and in popular song, usually in the form of references to the woman's 'dying.'

Only when an uneasy peace has been made with the co-existence of other men, as sharers in the sexual favors of a given woman, does the woman herself reappear, under the steaming mists of the competitive relationship among the men. This is not easily achieved, and the first group of jokes here cited all concern *resistance* to possession of the woman in common. *'Driver of the Car (unfamiliar with the road): "I take the next turn, don't I?" Muffled Male Voice from the Back Seat: "Like hell you do!"'* (Dartmouth *Jack-o'-Lantern,* college-humor magazine, in *Judge,* Aug. 1942, p. 831.) Everyone here is invisible except the driver — even the road is invisible — but the woman is notably absent, except by implication under the man's refusal to share her. The stage-humorist Will Rogers often used the following line in the 1910's and '20's, in his lariat-twirling monologue act for sophisticated audiences, sometimes reversing the sexes: *"Men are funny, don't you think? I see by the papers that a man who hadn't kissed his wife for fifteen years shot the man who did."* This is supposed to be based on the murder of the architect, Stanford White, in 1906, but gets the story backwards. (*"When did Evelyn Nesbit really love Harry Thaw?" "When he shot White."* N.Y. *c.* 1930.) This is the sort of humor that later developed into the 'sick' nightclub humor of Lenny Bruce and others similar in the 1950's, with the significant difference, however, that the later humorists come out into the open with the real word hidden behind the euphemized 'kiss.'

A Texan tells the judge he wants an injunction to prevent his wife from committing adultery. "You mean you want a divorce." "Hell, no! I want an injunction. That woman is the best piece of ass in Texas." (2:335.) This to be compared with: *The man looking for advice about his marital problems, who is told, "So what if she does leave you — there's plenty of fish in the sea." "Mebbe so, Doc, but my bait ain't what it used to be."* (*Sex to Sexty,* 1966, 5:6.) Though both of these are still purely competitive, the possible superiority of other men, and the definite superiority of the woman, have already been admitted. Burlesquing the whole situation of male jealousy, and with a highly unsubtle dig at what a woman 'really amounts to': *Two prospectors going to Alaska outfit themselves, at the suggestion of the storekeeper at the Last-Chance General Store, with 'love-boards,' consisting of small pine boards cut in the outline of a woman's shape, with a fur-lined knothole in the middle. Months later one of the prospectors struggles back to civilization alone. "What happened to your partner?" "I had to kill him. I caught the son-of-a-bitch using my love-board."* (N.Y. 1949.)

The theme of 'woman as hole,' remarked upon bitterly by modern feminist writers, such as Simone de Beauvoir and Maryse Choisy, is never more clear, of course, than in connection with such masturbatory *succedanea*. The modern misogynist, Henry Miller (self-disguised for the chump-audience as a lover of sex, and orgiast, in his erotic and autobiographical *Tropics, Sexus, Nexus*, etc.), even puts into the mouth of one of the characters in *Tropic of Cancer*, 'Van Norden' — supposed to be patterned on the journalist, Wambly Bald — a discussion of *a masturbation device consisting of an apple with the core bored out, and lined with cold-cream*. Among high-school students in Scranton, about 1934, which is about the same period, a 'nasty-nasty' version of the same thing was a well-known throwaway line or gag, on one's sexual 'proposition' being rejected by one of the local high-school girls (known therefore as 'cock-teasers') on a double-date: "*Well, home to my can of hot buttered worms!*"

The captain of a sailing ship has a 'dame de voyage' *of inflatable rubber, which he has bought in a sex store in Japan, and which he keeps hidden in his quarters. He accidentally leaves it inflated on his bunk one day, when he is called to the bridge during a sudden squall, and the first mate uses it. At the end of the voyage, on returning to the sex store, the proprietor asks the captain how he liked the* dame de voyage. '*"Was she realistic?"* "I'll say she was," *answered the captain;* "so realistic she gave me a clap".' (1:354.) The unexpected infecting with gonorrhea is, of course, the crew's revenge against the captain for his superior sexual prerogatives. Even more appropriately, in the present context: *A sea-captain takes his own fat whore on board with him during a long voyage, and she sunbathes in a tiny bathing suit on the deck, under the greedy eyes of the crew, while the captain stands guard with two guns. "Cunt enough for a thousand men," he chortles, "and it's mine, all mine!"* (N.Y. 1940.) There is a sort of unconscious reply to this, in *Sex to Sexty* (1966) 5:35, in a cartoon showing *A prostitute saying to a westerner, outside a saloon, "Don't be petty, Ransley, there's enough to go around!"* This much weakens the original, in which the 'fat whore' is the earth-mother figure, à la Venus of Willersdorf, with the two-gun captain as the jealous and proprietary patriarch, and the crew as the brooding sons.

Honeymooners in an old-fashioned country hotel. During the night one of the guests starts banging on the door of their bedroom, mistaking it for the toilet. "What do you want?" calls out the husband angrily. "You know damn well what I want," comes back an equally angry male voice; "there's two holes there, if you ain't using both of them, I want one!" (N.Y. 1939. Earlier in *Anecdota*, 2:381.) For all its being set up as an accidental misunderstanding, this leaves it to the listener to fantasy not simply the sharing of the woman by the two men, but their having intercourse with her simultaneously in the 'two holes.' In the original form, given in verse in Caron's *Le Plat de Carnaval* (1802) as the 13th "Beignet," under the title *"Les Lieux à l'Anglaise,"* the adulterous situation is made clear, as the priest is having intercourse in the toilet with the wife of the man who comes knocking at the door. He is also given a topper, or retort, missing in the modern English version: *"No,"* he says, *"you can't come in; we'd be too close!"* His objection is not proprietary, as to the woman, but a rejection of the inevitable homosexual tone of any such trio orgy.

Vance Randolph gives a full-treatment transcription of a story of possession-in-common (by both sexes) rather clearly related, though without any homosexual element, at No. 100, "The Folks on Rumpus Ridge," collected from a man in Galena, Missouri in 1932, and stated by the teller to have been 'a common story in Stone county, Mo., about 1906.' Randolph observes that there are 'related yarns' in Charles M. Wilson's *Backwoods America* (Chapel Hill, N.C. 1934) p. 37–9, and in 'Norman Lockridge's' [Samuel Roth's] *Waggish Tales of the Czechs* (1947) p. 117–22. Presumably concerning backwoods 'orneriness':

One time there was an old couple that lived on Rumpus Ridge, and they had a terribly pretty daughter. It was just about dark when a stranger come along, and he says, "I have got lost, and will you let me stay all night?" They give him the spare room, and he watched careful to see where the pretty girl's bed was. After everybody had went to sleep, the town fellow sneaked over there. But the girl and her mother had traded places, so she got screwed by mistake. The old woman giggled, and the stranger was pretty mad, but there wasn't nothing he could do about it.

Pretty soon somebody come walking past in their bare feet, and the town fellow knowed the pretty girl had went back to her own bed. After while he slipped over there again, and crawled in with the pretty girl. She was glad of it, and you never seen such a shagging-match. The stranger stayed there a long time, and it was pretty near daylight when he got back to the spare room.

Next morning the old man just set in the kitchen, with a shotgun right by his chair. There wasn't much said, but the town fellow felt kind of uneasy. He eat some breakfast though, and got ready to leave. "How much do I owe you?" says he. The old farmer just looked at him. "I don't charge nobody for bed and victuals," says he, "but this here breaking up people's family is a bad business." The town fellow was shaking like holly in a high wind. "I don't care about the old woman," says the farmer, "because she's limbered enough pricks to build a bridge over James River. But Lucy is just a innocent child, and never screwed anybody but me in her whole life." With that the old man picked up the shotgun, and he cocked both hammers.

The town fellow stood there with his mouth open, and he didn't know whether to shit or go blind. But finally he says "Well, I am always willing to do the right thing [*i.e.* marry the girl]." The old farmer studied awhile, and then he let one hammer of the shotgun down easy. "Stranger," says he, "do you think three dollars is too much?" The town fellow give him the money, and then the old man let the other hammer down easy.

The pretty girl was hanging some clothes out behind the house, and she waved at the town fellow when he walked on down the road. But the town fellow never looked back. "I don't care about the money," says he, "it's the principle of the thing." And nobody likes to be scared out of a year's growth with a shotgun, neither.

All the emphasis here is on the cruel and gratuitous frightening of the town fellow, till he doesn't know 'whether to shit or go blind,' by the patriarch whose sexual rights over his daughter are more important to him than those over his wife, who has already 'limbered enough pricks to build a bridge over James River.' Even more cruel is an extremely popular story of similar punishment of the adulterer, but here the homosexual element creeps back unexpectedly in the excessive concern with the adulterer's testicles. This is true of all stories of castrating the adulterer, in particular the well-known true story of the castration of the medieval philosopher, Pierre Abélard, in the year 1118, by the henchmen of Canon Fulbert, *uncle* of Abélard's secret wife, Héloïse, which falls emotionally somewhere between the present two stories. *A midwest farmer's wife has a Swedish immigrant lover who comes to see her while her husband is working in the fields. One morning the husband comes home unexpectedly, as he has broken his rake, and the lover climbs into the chandelier over the bed to hide, his testicles unfortunately hanging over the edge. The farmer is suspicious of finding his wife in the rumpled bed, asks several questions, and finally says, "What's that hanging from the lamp?" "Oh," says the wife nervously, "that's just some sleigh-bells I put there to decorate it for Christmas." "I see," says the farmer sourly and gives the Swede's testicles a terrible crack with the rake-handle. "Yingle-yangle!" cries the Swede dolefully.* (N.Y. 1938.) Also collected with the lover hiding under the bed in a sack, and without specifying that he is struck in the testicles. *Histoires Arabes,* p. 165, gives a relic of the Levantine original: *The lover hides in a trellis, and the husband says, "Our grape-vine is sprouting balls!"* No castration. (Compare Afanasyev, No. 58.)

In all English versions there is a conscious pun on '*balls*' (testicles) and '*bells*.' The testicles are of course considered, correctly, the seat of virility, and certain presumably very virile races are believed to have extremely large testicles — combined, it should be mentioned, with small brains. Thus the American Irish, and formerly the Russian Cossacks, are known in Yiddish as *Baytzimmer,* those having large testicles, from the Hebrew *baytzim,* testicles (actually, eggs), the correct Hebrew word for the testicles being *avonim,* stones, as in *Deuteronomy,* xxiii. 1, 'He that is wounded in the stones, or hath his privy member cut off, shall not enter into the congregation of the Lord.' This rule is still operative in both the Jewish rabbinate and Catholic priesthood, and is made the subject of a special ceremony ("*Testiculos habet*") in the election of a new Pope, but has for some reason never prevented the use of male castrati in the Sistine choir and elsewhere.

Abélard, after his mutilation, not only withdrew emotionally from Héloïse, as her superb love-letters to him show, and as was only to be expected (she was seventeen years old at the time of their amour, and he forty), but was also hounded with ferocious enmity for the rest of his life by almost the entire church — though earlier one of the most famous philosophers and teachers in the West — until his final denunciation for heresy, in 1140, by the medieval politician, St. Bernard (of Clairvaux), the homosexual protector of the Knights Templars. This famous tragic story has not yet been made into a movie, probably because — despite the attraction of the castration of Abélard for the bitch-female mind today — Héloïse was anything but a bitch.

Halfway between possession-in-common and polyandry, in which the woman is frankly dominant in the situation and the various men are basically her 'studs,' are situations of a more or less prostitutory nature, which cannot be dealt with here. It is, for instance, well understood and accepted that a female prostitute will have many men as customers, but that, in addition, she has an *amant de cœur,* her pimp, to whom she gives her money and her devotion in return for presumed 'protection' and sometimes for a good deal of mistreatment. In France, and doubtless elsewhere, kept-women of the higher type will quite frankly have a '*vieux*' who pays, and a lover to whom the older man's money is siphoned off. The younger man — who is essentially a pimp — will know of the existence of the '*vieux*,' who, however, is kept ignorant of the younger man's existence if possible, as an obvious hurt to his feelings of proprietorship and virility. But what is really happening is that the presumed prostitute or kept-woman has two husbands . . . sometimes more. Full details in Doris Lilly's *How to Make Love in Five Languages* (London, 1965?), a novelized guide-book for kept-women abroad, with translated phrase-lists and warnings!

The great French encyclopedist, Denis Diderot, whose lesser writings (such as the scintillating and incredible *Rameau's Nephew*) are really his best, and who *understood women* very well, from the lowest to the highest — in order to raise a dowry for his daughter in 1772, he sold his library the following year to no one less than Catherine the Great, Empress of Russia, the Messalina of modern times — has left a very singular passage on this whole matter in his erotic novelette, *Les Bijoux Indiscrets* (1748) chap. 47, "*Le Bijou voyageur,*" or vol. II, chap. 14 of the vestpocket editions in two volumes. In this work, which is set in the framework of a mock-Oriental tale, a magic ring has the power of making women's vaginas — the '*bijoux*' in question — speak and tell their life-stories. (Thompson's Motif D1610.6.1, *pudenda loquens,* with further references in Rotunda, neither of whom cite Diderot's work.) In this particular chapter, which is the 26th service of the magic ring, the vagina of the highly-placed courtesan, Cypria, is made to speak, the woman herself being rather clearly intended as a venomous satirical portrait of Mme. de Pompadour, mistress — in every sense — of the French king Louis XV. La Pompadour is flatly stated in the second line to 'have made a fortune with her *bijou* to compare with the wealth of a Farmer-General.' The life-story told by this highly-paid vagina is not in French but in various languages, those of the countries in which Cypria has plied her informal trade: England,

Italy, Spain, and the like. It is the little-known passage *in English* in Diderot's original, which thus describes possession-in-common in the 18th century:

> A Wealthy Lord, travelling through France, dragg'd me to London. Ay! that was a man indeed! He water'd me six times a day, and as often o' nights. His prick like a comet's tail shot flaming darts: I never felt such quick and thrilling thrusts. It was not possible for mortal prowess to hold out long, at this rate; so he drooped by degrees, and I received his soul distilled through his Tarse. He gave me fifty thousand guineas. This noble Lord was succeeded by a couple of Privateer Commanders lately return'd from cruising. Being intimate friends, they fuck'd me, as they had sail'd, in company, endeavouring who should show most vigour and serve the readiest fire. Whilst the one was riding at anchor, I towed the other by his Tarse, and prepared him for a fresh trie. Upon a modest computation, I reckon'd in about eight days time, I received a hundred and eighty shot. But I soon grew tired with Keeping so strict an account, for there was no end of their broad-sides. I got twelve thousand pound from 'em for my share of the prizes they had taken. The winter quarter being over, they were forced to put to sea again, and would fain have engaged me as a tender, but I had made a prior contract with a German Count.

The tale then continues in Latin, Italian, and Franco-Spanish pidgin, Diderot announcing at the end of the chapter to his 'virtuous Lady' readers that the foreign passages preceding are 'infinitely freer than any of the clandestine books they have ever read,' meaning of course that he is challenging them to have the passages translated. That in English certainly compares strikingly with the metaphoric style of John Cleland's *Fanny Hill,* not published till the following year, 1749, though written much earlier.

2. POLYANDRY

Finally the man capitulates. Since he knows the woman is not faithful to him anyhow, he accepts his position as one husband among many 'servicing' the same polyandrous wife. The sex-hate issue of *From Sex to Sexty* (Fort Worth, Tex., 1966, 6:56) breaks out in the sudden and unexpected admission: '*Over in the oil field they have a* saying, "Don't NEVER *be jealous of a woman . . . it's better to have a quarter-interest in a gusher than to be the sole owner of a dry hole".'* (It appears we're back to *woman-as-hole.*) If the husband does not gracefully accept his position as cuckold or as wittol, the 'big, burly' brother-husbands or co-husbands are there to enforce his acceptance. *A night watchman who gets off early one night comes home to find a line of men waiting in front of his house. Through the brightly-lighted window he sees his wife making love with a 'big, burly stranger.' He makes a dash for the door, but another big man in the line grabs him: "Get in line, newcomer . . . take your turn like the rest of us!"* (Same issue of *Sex to Sexty,* 6:29.) Occasionally the news is broken to him with more sympathetic restraint by one of the brother-husbands: *'Nigger one day said to some of his boy friends, "They just about got everything rationed these days — tires, sugar, cars, and do you know that darned fool wife of mine got me rationed to twice a week?" One of the fellows said, "Shucks, that ain't so bad. I dun heard she cut some of the fellows out completely".'* (Guam mimeograph, *Smile and the World Smiles with You,* 1952, p. 4.) The admission becomes a game, easier to play of course when the co-husbandship being admitted to is mainly someone else's. *'A businessman whose wife had been running about with many men determined to bring matters to a head, so he wrote the following letter to Mr. Brown: "My dear Sir: I am fully aware of your relations with my wife. Be at my office at 2 o'clock sharp on Monday." (Answer:) "My dear Smith: Your circular letter received. Will attend conference on time".'* (1:215.)

Not in joke form, nor actually on *wife-sharing,* but tending more toward wife-*trading* as a jocular expression of marital sex hate: During the 1940's in the U.S., chain-letters were the brief fad, in which one was to send a dime to the person whose name appeared at the top of a list of five names, and five copies of the same letter to friends, with one's own name at the bottom (the trick was to *start* a chain, with one's own name fifth). The usual letter ended with the occult admonishment: "DO NOT BREAK THIS CHAIN! *It was started by an American army officer in Germany, who received $7,840 in dimes, but who broke the chain and lost it all on a single turn of a roulette-wheel.*" Parodies were immediately circulated, one of which (starting in Canada in the 1960's) asked that folklorists send copies of their latest offprints from learned journals to the poor sucker whose name, like Abou ben-Adhem's, led all the rest. The relevant parody read: "*Bundle up your wife and send* *her to the man whose name appears at the top of this list. Then cross off his name and put yours at the bottom, and send copies of this letter to five other people before midnight.* [Indicating the origin of the chain-letters in the mathematical curiosity published in Robert Ripley's syndicated "Believe it Or Not" column, "The Murder at Midnight," in which the one person who knows the murderer's name tells two other people within ten minutes, and they tell two other people, etc. By morning everyone in the world knows.] DO NOT BREAK THE CHAIN. *An American army officer who broke the chain got his own wife back! ! !"* (N.Y. 1946.)

Another version, dated 1957, ends with even more pointed rejection of one's own wife: 'You must always have faith. *Do not break this chain. One man broke the chain and he got* HIS OLD LADY *back again.'* This is quoted by Prof. Alan Dundes, in "Chain Letter: A Folk Geometric Progression," in *Northwest Folklore* (Winter 1965/66) vol. 1, No. 2: p. 14–19, with interesting analysis, also agreeing with a remark presumably paraphrased from my *The Horn Book*, p. 110, that the common male 'harem-dream' . . . 'of being "husband to all the women in the world" is particularly prevalent among those who are of an age when they are least able physically to indulge in repeated or strenuous sexual activities.' Actually, that is not what I said, and it is perilously close to being 'educated folklore.' The basic problem about sexual intercourse for men during their mature and even advanced years is not the inability to engage either in 'repeated or strenuous sexual activities' — unless, of course, they have heart 'conditions' — but, rather, the slowly increasing inability to achieve erection or *to arrive at orgasm,* which latter is often considered by the woman to be an advantage. (See the excellent description of the orgastically impotent 'phallic narcissistic' male in his earlier years — the much admired 'James Bond' or emotionless cowboy-detective-spy type in modern fantasy fiction and movies — in Ferdinand Lundberg & Marynia Farnham's *Modern Woman: The Lost Sex,* 1947, p. 332–4, importantly citing Dr. Wilhelm Reich, who first described this male 'type' as the hostile and emotionally-strangulated psychological disaster it is.)

The preceding is an example, by the way, of folklore which is not transmitted orally, but in manuscript, typescript, or print, as is much folk-poetry, album verse, pictorial 'novelties,' obscœna, and so forth. Another such form of *non-oral folklore* are the bogus letters (the parody chain-letter is essentially this), of which the milder examples are not infrequently collected and published as absolutely authentic, as in Miss Juliet Lowell's *Dere Sir*. Though usually cast in the form of complaints — to government services, insurance companies, insistent creditors, etc. — at least one bogus testimonial exists, and probably others. This was supplied in abbreviated form, as though a joke, by the folklorist the late Josiah Combs (Fredericksburg, Va. 1952): '*Farmer has nervous wife, plagued with insomnia. He orders a bottle of* Wine of Cardui. *Wife takes it, sleeps much better, takes more and more. Farmer writes to company: "Before taking your wine of Cardui, my wife was so nervous I couldn't sleep with her. After she took several bottles, anybody could sleep with her".'*

Lest it be thought that letters this pathetically ingenuous could not possibly be authentic, a collection of absolutely authentic letters received by actors, radio announcers, and other public figures — mostly about sex — has been published in France under the title *Les Perles de Vénus,* edited by Alexis Large (Paris: Denoël, 1963), with an introduction by Albert Aycard, whose own five volumes of droll newspaper errors, edited in collaboration with Jacqueline Franck, *La Réalité dépasse la fiction* (Paris: Gallimard, 1955 *ff.*) contain striking proof of the imbecilities and unconscious humor practically forced into print by the exigencies of 'writing copy' for modern newspaper production. Two earlier similar series, not quite so striking, and lacking the photodocuments in the Aycard-Franck volumes which make them particularly priceless, are *Le Musée des Erreurs, ou Le français tel qu'on l'écrit* (2 vols. 1925-8) edited by 'Curnonsky' [Maurice Sailland] and J.-Wladimir Bienstock; and two volumes, *Les Perles du Facteur* (and *Nouvelles Perles*) signed 'Jean-Charles,' published in 1959-60. Still well worth consulting is what seems to be the original volume of the kind, Mark Twain's *English As She Is Spoke* (also a Leadenhall Press imitation, *English As It Is Written*), and the *Boners* series published in the 1930's under the editorial pseudonym of 'Alexander Abingdon.' These are limited to polite items, mostly from students' answers in written schoolroom examinations. Fritz Spiegl's *What the Papers didn't mean to say* (Liverpool: Scouse Press, 1965), spine-titled "Press Clangers," goes a good deal further.

One letter in particular in Large's *Les Perles de Vénus,* p. 61, headed "*Licence d'anglais,*" is of particular interest as showing the slopping over of these merely imbecilic mash-notes to teachers, actors, etc., into the matching but anonymous poison-pen letters *by the same writers* intended to clear away competition! Compare also, in this connection, "Answers to an Ad," edited by myself, from rigorously authentic replies received to a sado-masochistic classified advertisement, published in *The Compleat Neurotica* (New York: Hacker Art Books, 1963) No. 5: p. 45–64, especially the sado-masochistically alternating letters from the identical writers, pp. 49, 52, and 56–9(!), followed by a brief analysis, *Notes on Masochism*, 3 pp., not issued in the original publication of 1949.

The acceptance of the total immorality of one's own wife is obviously difficult, and can only be admitted, even in jokes, in a tone of complete cynicism, which is far from what even the persons telling the jokes would really feel in such circumstances. *"Are you sending your wife to the country this summer? (or: to Florida this winter?)" "No, I think I'll fuck her myself."* (1:166.) This is a French joke, printed in at least one French chapbook of the 1920's, D. Acques' *"200 Monologues, &c.,"* p. 57, and was perhaps directly translated for *Anecdota.* Its cynicism is much more French than American. Far more American is the fuddle-duddle approach — I-didn't-know-what-I-wuz-doin'-becuz-I-was-drunk — by means of which all responsibility for one's own or anyone else's actions is evaded, and cast instead on the Demon Rum: *A man's wife at a football game makes a spectacle of herself, getting drunk, screaming obscene curses at the opposing team, and ending up sitting on a strange man's lap inside his raccoon coat, and bouncing up and down unmistakably. "Hey, can't you see that guy is fucking your wife?" says a friend. "Don't pay any attention," says the husband; "she's drunk." "Why in hell don't you leave her home to get drunk?" "Then everybody'd fuck her."* (Chicago, 1953.) The friend's anger and insistence doubtless analyze out as mere jealousy of the strange man in the raccoon coat — and wishing he could have a turn at the 'available' wife too — as much as identification with the husband in his disgrace. But what is the analysis of the husband's end-of-the-rope impuissance and acceding? Another version of the same joke makes his position even more clear: *Various men come up to the husband at a football game to which he has taken his wife, and while talking to him, handle his wife's breasts, buttocks, etc. The friend complains, "Say, why don't you leave your wife home?" The husband explains, "Then everybody'd fuck her."* (N.Y. 1964.) Mild cleanup in *And One Flew Into the Cuckold's Nest,* Fort Worth, Texas, 1966, p. 10, ending with the same pointed emphasis on the verb: *The husband "looked up at [the friend*] *and whimpered,* '*If I leave her at home, she* SLEEPS *with every-body!*' " Obviously just a meaningless rationalization: the husband is, and wishes to be, a spectator at his wife's quasi-adultery (as at the playing of football by *other men*), on a masochistic basis.

Of course, friends — especially best friends — are a special category in connection with adultery and the possession of women in common. It is more usual to accept a wife's adultery with a stranger — which can be written off as a mad fancy, momentary drunkenness, etc. — than with one's *best friend,* which is not only considered more likely to end in 'breaking up the marriage' through divorce, but also involves the betrayal by the friend as well as by the wife. Losing all one's faith — and all one's lovers and friends — all at once, rips the rug out from under a person in the most desperate fashion. It is better to close one's eyes if possible, or at least to make sure that only a single profound betrayal takes place at once, in any one act of adulterous intercourse. This appears to be the opposite of the message of the following joke, but the real essence of the joke is its sardonicism and absurdity. *The wife admits she has committed adultery while her husband was out of town.* "*Who was it?*" *her husband shouts;* "*was it Finkelstein?*" "*No,*" *the wife sobs,* "*it wasn't him.*" "*Was it Cohen?*" "*No.*" "*I know who it was: it was that bastard, Shapiro.*" "*No, it wasn't Shapiro.*" *A pause.* "*What's the matter — none of my friends are good enough for you?*" (2:298. Also collected more recently in a version giving the wife the punch-line: "*Don't you think I've got friends of my own?*" — N.Y. 1963.) The last word on best friends and beautiful wives: *The crusader entrusts the key of his wife's chastity belt to his best friend, and sets off for the Holy Land. Late next afternoon, already leagues from the castle, the best friend comes riding up huffing and puffing after him, waving the key.* "*Sir Ronald! Sir Ronald! You gave me the wrong key!*" (N.Y. 1938, from Mr. Joseph Fliesler, compiler of *Anecdota Americana,* original series.)

Another chastity-belt joke seems to be involved in Eric Linklater's *The Crusader's Key* (London, 1933), a novelette reissued in the U.S. in the mid-1930's with two variant illustrated dust-jackets, one being expurgated: an uncommon publishing pusillanimity. In this, *The crusader's wife throws the key of her chastity belt into the moat, to put an end to the importunities of the best friend or cavaliere servante. She then takes to overeating, for lack of any other primary pleasures, gets too fat for the chastity belt, and has to have the moat drained to find the key.* It should be mentioned again that chastity belts have never had any real existence, and are a fantasy appearing in baroque illustrations centuries after the purported era of their real use. All known examples in museums, in particular the famous chastity belt of the Musée Cluny in Paris, are post-medieval fakes. The objects contrived for the same purpose by modern neurotic husbands occasionally — usually husbands of rather low social class, and principally Italian origin — are not spontaneous inventions but are created in cognizance of the presumed existence of 'real' chastity belts. These imitations are now, and probably have always been, the only 'real' such objects in existence. On the psychology of the chastity belt, see Chapter 6.vi, p. 384 above.

This is a very good example of the folkloristic working of Oscar Wilde's paradoxical dictum (the gospel of advertising, as I have earlier remarked): '*Nature imitates Art.*' The humorous giveaway of the anatomical impossibility of such devices is in the decoration of the two apertures left for the sexually imprisoned woman's digestive needs: that in front, for urination, being frighteningly toothed; that in back, for defecation, being prettily decorated (in the Cluny Museum example) with a sort of trefoil aperture or portcullis. The principle is about the same as that used for cake-icing squeezers, and with the same presumable result. Anyone who wishes to believe that a woman would wear one of these things longer than the very first time she went to the toilet, without having a locksmith (with a headcold) come to saw it off next morning, can believe it if he wishes. The chastity belt would also be rather easy to open by removing the pin at the inevitably necessary hinge, but of course soldering it back on later would be a problem. The most elegant solution, for the woman, is implied in Linklater's story or joke. All she need do, when the husband is safely off to the Crusades, is simply have the damn thing sawed off, and go out and make love as much as she likes. When her husband returns, she presents him with the baby she has had in his absence (she can only have *one,* on this caper), and explains to him that *she became pregnant during her last intercourse with him before he left.* As he would certainly not have wanted their child (and heir) to be prevented from growing in the womb or from being born, she felt it her wifely duty to have the chastity belt sawed off. Punch-line, behind the husband's back: "*Dieu et mon droit!*" Translation: "*Fuck you, Jack.* I'm *all right!*"

A 15th-century anti-religious mocking tale which appears in the jestbook literature of most countries of Europe is still very much alive in America, the church background of the original form being changed to a golf-course. *A lawyer and a doctor are bragging about the advan-*

tages of their respective professions, ending with the ease with which their professional entrée allows them to seduce the wives of all the other club members. They finally bet on this, and sit down at the tavern on the green to count members' wives they have seduced, as they appear on the green. To their surprise they keep singing out the numbers together: "Four ... five ... six ..." and so forth. Eventually the doctor's wife and daughter appear, and he turns triumphantly to the lawyer. "See those two women?" "Sure," says the lawyer — "forty-nine, fifty!" (Minneapolis, 1935.) Other versions add that: *And then the fight began.* The verbal explosion of the punch-line here typically ends the story: that is to say, it destroys the butt (the doctor), who can have no further existence of interest to anyone. Randolph, No. 17, "The Two Preachers," gives a version much closer to the European, collected at Roaring River, Missouri, 1941. In this, the two preachers would 'holler "Amen," whenever a woman come along that one of 'em had screwed.' It ends in a fist-fight, as usual. Original in Bebel's *Facetiæ* (1508) II. 40, "*De sacerdote et ædituo.*" Doggerel 'rugby song' version in Harry Morgan's *Why Was He Born So Beautiful* (London, 1967) p. 156, "The Church Song." (Aarne Type 1781.)

The direct sharing of the wife (or husband), or offering to share, is not easy to navigate, and certain circumlocutions and mental adjustments are vital. *One wife to another: "You've been going around telling people there's a wart on the end of my husband's penis." "I did* NOT. *I only said it* FELT *like it."* (*Sex to Sexty,* 1966, 5:53.) As already observed, at the end of section 6.1.1, this is only a 'quickie' reduction of a Scottish story given in "Some Erotic Folk-lore from Scotland," in *Kryptádia,* 1884, II. 261:

A woman was dissatisfied with her husband's powers. She complained to some of her female married friends. They agreed to examine into the matter. The man was told he must exhibit what he had to a few matrons. He remonstrated, but in vain. He was however to be allowed to stand behind a screen and shew his symbol of manhood through a hole in the screen. The man in his difficulty asked the counsel of his clergyman. The clergyman undertook to get him out of the difficulty by presenting himself. Accordingly on the day fixed, the matrons placed themselves on one side of the screen and the minister on the other. He put his virility through the hole, when one of the matrons cried out, "That's the minister's; I ken't by the wart o' the point o't."

Vance Randolph gives this story (*Pissing in the Snow,* No. 75, "The Little End of Nothing"), with punch-line, given to '*old lady Wither-spoon. "Can't fool me,"* she says, *"that's old Deacon Hedgepeth's pecker!"* ' He collected this in Joplin, Missouri, in 1923. I have myself collected a version more recently (Orangeburg, N.Y., 1944) even closer to the Scottish original, ending: "*I know it by the pimple on the snout!*" which is almost a translation of the Scottish dialect form in *Kryptádia.* All forms derive ultimately from La Sale's *Cent Nouvelles Nouvelles* (MS. 1561) No. 15, "*La Nonne sçavante,*" where the young monk persuades the better-hung Brother Conrad to substitute for him at the 'short-arm' inspection at the nun's window. Such inspections still apparently exist, as bragged of in a letter on the "Phallic Fallacy," in *Playboy* (November 1967) p. 69, from an American woman, noting that she demands that her lovers 'show what they've got,' *i.e.* stand-and-deliver! Rotunda, K1848.1, gives the later Italian form of the story, in which it seems first to be assimilated to the idea of the conjugal court, or Court of Matrons, passing on the husband's potency: 'Impotent husband deceives wife by having a substitute in virility test,' citing Cynthio-Giraldi's *Hecatommithi* (1565) IX, No. 4; to which Rossell Hope Robbins, the latest editor and translator of the *Cent Nouvelles Nouvelles,* as *The Hundred Tales* (New York: Crown Publishers, 1960) p. 382, adds Malespini's *Dugocento Novelle* (1609) II. 70.

Compare also the opposite substitution, in which the woman offers her buttocks instead of her mouth to be kissed by the suitor at her window by night, in Chaucer's "The Miller's Tale," in *The Canterbury Tales* (*c.* 1390), the sexes being reversed in *The Pinder of Wakefield* (1632, ed. Horsman, Liverpool Univ. Press, 1956) p. 25–6. This is derived from, or reduced to, a popular song "Hogyn came to bowers dore," recorded in Richard Hill's *Commonplace-Book* (MS. about 1525, printed as *Songs, Carols, &c.,* ed. Dyboski, 1908, Early English Text Society, Extra Series, Vol. 101) p. 111–12. It is still done, as comedy, in the theatre (Shakespeare's *Midsummer Night's Dream*) and in cowboy movies, in a modified version in which a man expects to kiss a woman and kisses an animal instead, such as a horse or jackass, or sometimes another man's grinning and unshaven face, even a goat, as in W. C. Fields' movie comedy, *My Little Chickadee,* where he thinks it is Mae West. (Motifs K1225, K1577; *Histoires Arabes,* p. 145.)

We now come to grips with the actual offer of the wife. First, her unveiling, with the little-boy pose of "Oh, it doesn't matter!" as earlier (in the football game and raccoon coat story), "Pay no attention, she's drunk." *A house-guest at an English country home accidentally walks in on the host's wife naked in the bathtub. He rushes to apologize to the host, explaining how it happened. The host calmly twirls his moustache, and, at the end of the guest's explanation, says, "Skinny bitch, eh what?"* (2:128.) This is told mostly by women, and was collected by me in very detailed form from a doctor's wife, in New York, 1952. Its appeal to women derives from the idea many or most women have, under patriarchy, that their bodies are 'ugly' *because they do not possess the penis,* no matter what extremes they go to in the way of beauty treatments. This is the secret of the ruthless exploitation of women by fashion-peddlers, requiring something new and unsatisfactory to be bought every year; and of the hypnotized, almost zombie-like docility with which even the most domineering and bitchy women keep sheepishly following along with the 'styles,' even though they *know* they are being cynically manipulated by homosexuals who hate them. The bait held out being that they will be like all other women — thus, at least *no more ugly* than anyone else — anything can be sold to them on that basis, especially when the husband (whose 'fault' it is that they have no penis: because he has stolen it) can be hornswoggled into paying.

I do not know if my own life experience has been richer than anyone else's in *beautiful women who thought they were ugly,* but I have certainly run into a few. I will mention two, to avoid the accusation of bragging, only one of whom was a friend of my own. Gallantry requires me to omit at least two much more startling cases. A very rich American heiress, outfitted with two miserable kids and a total muff, or *con,* of a husband (whom she had married to show who had the money and WHO WAS BOSS) stayed overnight with her husband and children in an apartment in Paris in which I happened to be sub-letting space, and in true folktale fashion I walked in on her in the bathroom — not even knowing there were guests — she being naked and about to step into the bathtub. She grabbed a terrycloth towel, which she draped in front of her. "Aw, c'mon," I said, "drop the towel. I won't rape you . . . unless you ask me to." "Oh, you've seen better bodies than *this ugly thing,*" she said, slowly dropping the towel.

Same story — also true — different background: A friend of mine in New York was waiting in his girlfriend's apartment to take her to the theatre. As she did not appear, and curtain time was approaching, he went into her bedroom where he found her in a dressing-gown staring fixedly at herself in a vanity-table mirror, in which her naked breasts and body appeared like a vision of angelic loveliness. (I'm quoting.) In the silence he heard the strangest sound, which he suddenly realized was *tears* dropping on the glass top of the vanity-table. "Darling!" he said, "what's the matter?" The vision of loveliness turned to him, showing him all bare what he had been seeing only in the mirror. And she replied, squeezing the words out between tears: "I'm — so — UGLY!" I submitted this story to a tough young female of my acquaintance who handed me the key to the enigma instantly. "Men are all alike," she said. "He was just looking at her titties. *She* was looking at her soul." The girl (also the tough female) being only a harmless neurotic, the horrible 'ugliness' of her soul could surely only have been — that she was a woman, and not a man.

As is always the case, the admissions are eventually openly made, at least in jokes; everything that has been hidden and symbolized being finally blurted right out. These are always the 'best' jokes. They lack audience-participation value, since they say everything and leave nothing to be supplied by the listener; but they also get the biggest laughs. Or, rather, a different kind of laugh. For the laugh aroused when the listener suddenly sees the point *which he must supply himself* is perhaps not as loud, but those are the jokes one remembers for a lifetime. The following, too direct and vivid, are not. "*You been sleeping with my wife?*" "*Me? You're kidding. Heck no!*" "*Try her sometime . . . she's better than yours.*" (*Sex to Sexty*, 1966 5:58.) The same source gives a complicated story of folktale nature concerning *A man who buys a rooster from another man's wife but does not pay her, as she has no change. Later he says to her husband, '"Say, here's $2 for that cock I got from your wife." The other man, Sam, gazed steadily at Tom for a few seconds and replied, "It's OK, Tom, just keep it . . . I never give* YOUR *wife anything".*' (*Sexty*, 5:22.) This turns on the U.S. Southern colloquialism, 'cock,' referring to the organ or the enjoyment of the organ that a Northerner would call 'cunt,' the term apparently deriving from the Louisiana French *coquille* or *coquillage,* 18th-century French (and earlier) for a girl's genital organs or her virginity, as recorded in LeRoux' *Dictionnaire Burlesque.* What makes this particularly confusing is that 'cock' is also, of course, the principal language-word in English for the penis.

The following joke dates from World War I, at least as to its *milieu,* and it is notable that the stereotyped Negro is present as the unrepressed sexual being of white folklore. This is in accordance with the hegemony seen also in humorous postcards: Where the sexually symbolic action is not too direct, and even 'cute,' but too direct to be shown between adults, *children* are shown. Where it is not 'cute' enough for children, *little old people* are shown, who are depicted as children with white hair. Where the action is considered out-and-out vulgar, *Negroes* are shown. The final step is to show *animals*. This makes sufficiently clear the position of the Negro stereotype in white sexual folklore. *During a bombardment, two Negro soldiers find themselves in the same shell-hole together in France, though they have never met before. One of them sets out to pass the time by opening a letter from home which he had not been able to open that morning before the attack came. "Man!" he says, "how about that? My woman done sent me a hair off her pussy to keep me company!" The other Negro looks very interested, takes the hair, passes it under his nose and touches it with his tongue-tip. "Pardon me," he says, "ain't yo' name Hawkins?"* (1:21. Text-form collected N.Y. 1946. A cleanup in *And One Flew Into the Cuckold's Nest,* 1966, p. 30, is up-dated to the war in Viet Nam.) See the further congeners of this story given under "Pubic Hair," 6.VII, as to the magical use of a pubic hair to 'draw the woman to him.' (Rotunda, K1281.1.) Original in *Histoires Arabes,* p. 267: a sheepskin rug is erroneously made to fly away by similar magic!

In the relationship with the other man that is crucial to adultery, it is *the triumph over him,* rather than the sexual conquest of his wife, that is understood to be the adulterer's real thrill. This demonstrates that adultery, from the point of view of the adulterer, is a sort of Oedipal striving, with the other man's wife replacing the forbidden mother. That is to say, she would not be half so interesting if she were not 'someone else's.' The victory over her is simultaneously a victory over him. It is not necessary to insist that these are parent-surrogates that are being attacked and manipulated by the adulterer, in order to understand the attraction to the career of 'Jody.' The simple struggle for sexual status is a sufficiently deep level of motivation, if one wishes to refuse to go deeper. *Two men and their wives are on a train trip together. They pass through a tunnel. As they emerge, one of the men smirks: "Oh, boy! I just kissed your wife." "That's nothing," says the second man calmly, putting his finger under the first man's nose. "Smell!"* (1:94.) The whole folklore of trains and tunnels is nowadays being lost, especially its sexual aspects, of tunnels, of the forbidding — but outwitted — conductor-father, and his sepulchral return, as the voice in the dark (like Hamlet's ghost) of the Man in the Upper Berth. I was offered in Paris, in 1954, but could not afford, a fascinating unfolding lithograph, several *yards* long, apparently of Spanish or Portuguese origin, of the early or mid-19th century, showing a sort of "Train of Love," with the railroad cars cut open, and people making love in various positions and ways in all the cars and compartments, as also the animals in the cattle car, while the engineer buggers the fireman up ahead in the engine. It had a total and cosmic quality about it that put it quite out of the range of the usual pornographica, and I trust this unique copy has not been lost forever to research. The symbolic implications — always with 'kissing' — of the surviving "Tunnels of Love" in amusement parks, with swan-shaped boats and lovers waiting to climb aboard, and the cartoons concerning them, are hardly more than a weak echo of the sexual folklore of trains.

The duel of the doctor and lawyer (in European forms, the priest and his clerk) as to the numbers of women they have seduced, has already been given, and it is to be observed that the two men are betting, thus primarily competing, the bet being only a cash symbolization of their duel. In ultimate form: '*A man surprises his best friend screwing his wife. Says, "You're going to have to fight me for that." A regular duel. "Choose your weapons," he says. "Sorry," says the other guy; "all I know is cards, women, and booze. I'll play you gin-rummy for her. The winner gets her." The husband thinks it over. "All right. How about a dollar a point — just to make it interesting!"*' (Minneapolis, 1953, as supplied by a correspondent.) The open contempt for the woman is of course the principal element here. The Larson Manuscript, joke section, "Odors on the Breeze," No. 66, under the title, "Don't Get Discouraged!" gives a wife-sharing story of which the husband-sharing version has earlier been quoted from *The Pearl*, 1879–80. *A farmer catches the hired man and his wife 'there on his own matrimonial bed . . . hard at work knocking off a piece of ass. The hired man jumped up, buttoning his fly, and grabbed his hat. Then he began edging toward the open door. "Guess I can't stay on now!" he said apologetically. "I'll pack up and go!" "Oh, that's all right! Don't get discouraged so easy!" the old farmer reassured him, quite unperturbed. "If the two of us can't keep the old woman satisfied, why, we'll just have to hire another man!"*' (Eden, Idaho, 1932. Limerick version of this in Dr. Carlyle Ferren MacIntyre's *That Immoral Garland*, MS. 1942, on which see my *The Horn Book*, 1964, p. 452.

Few jokes that have been collected make so conspicuously clear as the following the animosity against the woman, who is thought of and treated as an *object,* coupled with an undiscriminating friendliness with all other men, and willingness to share the woman with any of them. Any greater distance from the woman, and closeness to other men (whether or not authority-figures, as here), *via* her body, can only be considered homosexuality. *A man pays a hundred dollars to "get a virgin's cherry" in a whore-house. By some accident the girl actually is a virgin, and refuses at the last moment to let him touch her (or, there is a fire), and she runs out of the house stark naked down the street. The man thunders after her in hot pursuit, and is stopped at the corner by a policeman with the standard remark, "Where's the fire, Mac?" "I don't know, officer, but if you see a naked girl running down the street —* FUCK *her! It's paid for."* (N.Y. 1948.)

Possession in common of one or more women by one or more men, instead of the one-to-one individualistic form of marriage that we are accustomed to, but which occurs in very few other animals as natural behavior, naturally involves parenthood-in-common. This was the inevitable experience of all communistic cults involving plural marriage. As a corollary, it involves a salutary reduction in hostility between the men, who are, under sexual communism, neither in competition for the women nor in any way competitively connected with the children. There are no more 'fathers': all the men are the 'uncles' of all the children, though of course the physiological relation of the mother to her child can always be demonstrated, and also cannot be severed without severe psychological danger to both. It may be prophesied that Schiller's dream or lie, in his "Ode to Joy," used as the culminating chorus of Beethoven's *Ninth Symphony* (and the equally beautiful variant form in his *Choral Fantasy*), that 'All mankind shall be as brothers: Brothers all mankind shall be,' will never be achieved, and *can* never be achieved, under either the profit system or that of monogamous marriage. It is for this reason that the first accusation invariably brought against any communistic cult or government, such as early Christianity, Soviet Russia, etc., is that all the women are available to all the men on demand (and vice versa?), that no man knows 'who his children are,' and that 'the family has been destroyed.' Meaning by this, the one-to-one monogamous family supposedly in operation in Western society, which is, in fact, a cover for largely polygamous activity by both sexes, principally by the men.

It is to be understood that the forms not only of marriage, but even of sexual intimacy, are, and would necessarily be, entirely different under other marital systems. Under avowed polygamy, for instance, as can be seen in the biblical story of the patriarch Jacob, his wives and concubines (in *Genesis,* xxix–xxx), it is perfectly common and permissible for a man to engage in sexual acts simultaneously with two women, or twenty women if he has them at his disposal. This involves not only a complete disinterest in the status emotions of the women involved, but the accepting of the simultaneous *presence* of other persons than the two immediately involved in any usual sexual act. Under our present quasi-monogamic system, the idea of having two (or twenty) girls at once is presumably the ultimate harem-dream of sexual luxury, though what it really amounts to, in practice, is being either irritated or nauseated by the Lesbian activities to which, eventually, the women in any such trio are tempted or reduced. In the same way, the possession of women in common with other men easily and immediately leads to situations that are, according to our present lights, orgies or "gang-shags," but which can also be assessed as polyandrous relations of one woman with a host of sexually subservient men. I have noted, in *The Guilt of the Templars,* p. 116–21, 'the sexual ordeals so common as *rites de passage* among adolescents, yet so little recognized (or recollected) by adults, though adolescents today leave the bold and open hints of calling their secret clubs, in signs painted in red and yellow over the door, such things as "The Cherry-Hawks" or "The Busters," which do not take much knowledge of the matter to decipher.' See further, on the phoney Sexual Revolution of exhibitionistic 'Love' and 'group-grope,' my pamphlet *The Fake Revolt* (1967) p. 26–32, which considers the moral position not relevant here.

As I note, 'the actual 3-in-1 oil orgy, involving kissing-HER-while-screwing-HIM, or screwing several other people (and the dog) simultaneously under the excuse of drugged drunkenness . . . necessarily and permutationally must involve sexual perversion.' Such orgies, 'or rather ordeals, still exist today, especially at initiations into criminal and military groups, and even among merely irregular or delinquent groups such as hoboes, kid gangs, and fraternities. Unusual sexual acts, considered "unmanly" or humiliatingly submissive, such as forced fellation by the initiate, or pedication of him (or her) by all the members present, under the name of a "gang-shag" or "gang-bang," are a common ritual ordeal to which initiates are regularly forced to submit . . . see the fantasy version of such a gang-rape, ending in the female victim's death, in the repulsive story, "Tralala," in Hubert Selby Jr.'s

Last Exit to Brooklyn (New York: Grove Press, 1964) p. 91–114, a story first appearing in *Provincetown Review,* which was banned because of it.' (*The Guilt of the Templars,* p. 116.) On the Pacific coast, Lair Mitchell describes (in the *Los Angeles Free Press,* July 15, 1966, p. 5–6) the invasion of the Xanadu, an intellectual coffee house, about 1962, by a motorcycle gang:

> One . . . evening the doors swung wide and lo! the motor-cycle gangs were upon us. Black leather jackets, dungarees, boots and trouble. Sparta had invaded Athens. . . . Jack boots clumped across the floor and delicate intellectuals shrank against the walls. . . . Every evening thereafter we were treated to the roar of motorcycles and an influx of hostile, sweating outlaw cyclists, incongruously wearing peace buttons. Some wore chains, some carried guns, and few ever seemed to bathe. Next they brought their "mermaids" — their ladies' auxiliary, so to speak — those who had passed the gang bang initiation with flying colors. Ragged girls would stumble across the room, OD'd on pills, and would fall into your lap, too dazed to know what they were doing. . . . After a few weeks neighborhood pillheads, bar drunks and narco cops followed. Gone was the easy cultured atmosphere. No more did voluptuous co-eds with long sun-burnished hair wander in. . . . The Xanadu was shabby, dirty and deserted.

I am ashamed to have to admit it, but I do not know what 'OD'd on pills' may mean. Ask your own eighteen-year-old delinquent. The point here — my own as well as Lair Mitchell's — is the impossibility of contact at any human or moral level between the young Jewish chess-players and intellectual anarchists of the Xanadu, and the irruption of proto-Nazi motorcyclists, armed with bicycle chains, guns, and peace buttons (the crucial touch of doublethink), who probably — like any other invaders from Mars — only wanted to be friendly, even bringing along their Venusian "mermaids" to share the ambiance. To Mr. Mitchell, a girl whom he knows to have been gang-banged has *got* to be 'dazed,' or as high as a kite on Mexican mushrooms, home-grown California hemp, or unspecified 'pills.' In fact, it is not so, and, to the degree that it *is* so, it is equally true of the 'voluptuous co-eds with long sun-burnished hair,' wandering in from the University of California campus, who are just as likely to be turning-on to LSD and marijuana to express their insipid anti-parental 'revolt,' *plus* a frightening and prostitutory sexual insouciance. I have known more of these than "mermaids," and know what I am talking about. See my auto-biography, *Wives & Concubines* (in preparation).

The mermaid-types, or dirty girls, cavorting around on motorcycles behind their *Lumpen-proletariat* swains, are, certainly, perishingly vain, grotesquely malleable, far gone in penis-envy, and often stupid enough to freeze rocks. But their plural sex lives do not necessitate their being either dazed or drugged, though they do of course pick up on anything their cavaliers may currently be smoking or even in-jecting. They simply take a prostitutory position similar to that of endless coeds and business girls on the make (for middle-aged business-men who can take them to the 'right' nightclubs), that there is no real difference between one act of sexual intercourse with each of *twenty* men you don't like, and twenty acts of intercourse — eventually five thousand — with *one* man you don't like: the fate, as they see it, of the 'respectable married women' they refuse to become (until later). Also, except for its intense simultaneity, the possession-in-common of a gang-bang is not emotionally so terribly different, to the girl involved, from the hard night's work of prostitutes turning fifty 'tricks,' or from the same girl's being passed from hand to hand — if I may so express it — by all the members of the group, up or down to perhaps the same number, in only a few weeks or months. This, after all, is the plural marriage of the twentieth century, in which one may suspect that the communal guilt and support of one's peers in the gang-bang is, with its hardly-hidden homosexuality, the principal part of its attraction.

Also, it is essentially a *suggestio falsi* to put the matter exclusively in terms of economic levels such as motorcycle hoodlums and their dirty girls. These are almost always of working-class backgrounds ex-cept for the few slumming homosexuals of other classes who join, and eventually take over, such groups, in the effort to be 'strong and bad.' At least, their effort is to suck up the vibrations from the unwashed proletars they consider to be strong, and whom they pose with, kissing in their fetichistic leather outfits, for the newspaper photographers, under such names as 'Hell's Angels' and the like. Essentially, all such groups are homosexual and sado-masochistic ('S.&M.') One can see exactly the same sort of plural marriages — heterosexual this time, and without the gang-bangs — engaged in by American girls of thoroughly upper-middle-class families (whom they are thus deliciously disgrac-ing of set purpose) specifically and solely with expatriate American Negroes in Paris and New York, whose cynicism in passing the girls from hand to hand is surely equally great. This too is plural marriage in the twentieth century, and anyone who doesn't like it can get off the earth. *Place aux jeunes!* PLACE AUX JEUNES!! The only people being left out of these marriages seem to be the Negro girls. The contempt and rejection that a certain kind of Negro male feels for the women of his own race is cynically detailed in John A. Williams' *The Man Who Cried I Am* (1967), of which the hero not only is repelled by Negro women and wants only white chicks, but specifically wants them to nurse him as he dies odorously and repellently of rectal cancer, doubtless intended as a symbol of something or other. It is certainly a symbol of anal-sadistic hatred of white women.

A French entertainer at an open-air 'festival' I attended in one of the outlying quarters of Paris in 1954 — nothing folkloristic: just singers and vaudevillians with microphones around their necks, and an enormous family crowd sitting on benches and chewing sweets and pissing into pop-bottles (so as not to pay another entrance fee) as at a bull-fight — delivered a story on precisely the gang-bang theme, as humor, openly trying to milk his lower-middle-class audience for *sympathie* by insisting repeatedly and offensively on the 'very good family' of the girl in his story: *A young girl,* of very good family, *tells her mother she is pregnant. Her mother is horrified. How could this happen, when did it happen, who is the father, etcetera? The young girl,* of very good family, *replies that she doesn't know how it happened because she was drunk* ['OD'd on pills'?], *that it happened at a surprise-party* — French for orgy — *at the beach, and, as to who the father is, how can she know, says this young girl of very good family, "There were eight of them!"* This joke, incidentally, did not go over very well, but it will demonstrate that 'sick comedians' were not invented by the late Lenny Bruce, nor have such been tried out yet on open-air family audiences in America, as in France a dozen years ago and more. The story is given as a Greek *proverb* by Nicolaidès, p. 66: *"When you put your bare ass in a wasps' nest, which one stings you?"*

It is particularly important to keep track in matters of this kind, in jokes as in fact, of *the emotional position taken,* especially in what concerns polygamous or polyandrous situations departing from the current and culturally-accepted norms. What may look, to the men involved or to any culturally-conditioned spectator, like a gang-bang, a dozen men 'lining up' on one drunken or helpless girl, with half the men trying to masturbate themselves into erections while waiting for their turn; may seem to the girl — the girl involved, or the girl having 'rape' fantasies of this kind — a glorious harem situation, with herself as the nymphomaniacal female monarch or Earth-Mother queen bee being 'serviced' sexually by a dozen faceless studs: the interchangeable or replaceable men.

I have been present at a public exhibition of cunnilinctus by young male members of a nightclub audience with strip-teasers on the stage — the details of the action being picked out by a master-of-ceremonies with a flashlight — at the secretly named "Blue Fox" nightclub in Tijuana, Mexico (which will be discussed further, below), during which, as I later learned, the two college women between whom I was sitting, one eighteen and one twenty-five years old, saw what was happening under totally different lights. The eighteen-year-old, a big-bosomed blonde, identified enthusiastically with the strip-teaser, and fantasied herself, as she told me later, as a sort of shameless Earth-Mother, giving emotional 'nourishment' to 'all those eager young boys' (American sailors in rented civilian clothes). The twenty-five-year-old woman also identified overwhelmingly with the naked Mexican dancer on the stage — she was half Mexican herself — but thought of the dancer as having to allow herself to be publicly 'degraded' in this way by the eager mouths of 'men she didn't even know' (!) in order, probably, to support her family. Both saw the situation as somehow connected with motherhood — it would be hard to miss this, in the intense oral centralization of the scene itself — but one took the unconscious position of the female possessor of a male harem; the other the position of a harem-slave or 'victim' of public oral rape. Which of them was right? Or, as Bacon begins his *Essayes* by inquiring: '*What is Truth?* said jesting Pilate; & would not stay for an answer.'

3. MASKING HOMOSEXUALITY

The camaraderie between the husband and the adulterer, or the brother-husbands in possession in common, is theoretically a sort of fraternizing with the enemy. But it also serves — in the not very subtle fashion of insisting on the buddy-buddy (polite for 'asshole-buddy') relation between the men — to devaluate the woman, as not really worth fighting about at all. Many a husband, in fact, does not honestly understand why he should have to engage in a death-struggle with another man (who might very well kill him, instead of the traditional reverse, as sometimes happens) over the unique proprietary rights to the sexual enjoyment of a wife he perhaps does not enjoy sexually at all, and whom he may profoundly hate. Her feelings for him are certainly made clear by her adultery. The attack on the adulterer, or the absolute refusal to share, even in the past (*hymenoclasmania:* "My wife *must* be a virgin!"), is therefore only in deference to one's own feelings of honor, self-esteem, penile insufficiency, or what-have-you. Where these are not actually called into question by the woman's adultery, she becomes no more worth fighting about than any other woman unrelated to either of the men by marriage. Men will and do fight for women in this way, but seldom to the death. That is perhaps what is meant by the cynical self-unveiling of 'Men have died and worms have eaten them, but not for love.'

The *cante-fable* known in Europe as "Der Alte Hildebrand" (Aarne Type 1360c; Motif K1556) exists in America, by way of England, but is rarely heard. Alfred Williams gives a version in *Folk-Songs of the Upper Thames* (1923) p. 293, collected about ten years earlier. The best, possibly the only, American version was published by Mellinger Henry, as heard in Cade's Cove, Tennessee, 1930 (given in various journals, and definitively in Henry's *Folk-Songs from the Southern Highlands,* 1938, p. 153, with the music), entitled "Little Dicky Whigburn." '*In London there was a spring noted for its healing qualities. The wife pretends she is sick and sends Dicky for a bottle of the water. She sings the first stanza as a signal that Dicky has gone and that the pastor can come from his hiding place.*' She prays that her husband has been sent by the Lord on "a long journey never to return," and the pastor gloats that he will eat Dicky's "eats and drink his drinks," and "This night I'll stay with his wife." '*A pedlar comes along, who has just met Dicky on his way to the spring. When he sees the pastor and hears the wife singing he understands what is up, hurries back to catch Dicky and persuades him to get in the hopsack and allow him[self] to be taken back home. As they reach the house, the pedlar sings out stanza 3,*' offering to stand by Dicky in the fight that is sure to ensue. Dicky gets out of the hopsack, and sings:

> "*Good morning, fair gentlemen all in a row;*
> *The chief of your secret I very well know.*"
> *They beat the old pastor and right straight away;*
> *They whipped Dicky's wife the very next day*
> *And Dicky and the Pedlar together did stay.*

This would make a great plot for what is now known affectionately in New York as 'the fag theatre.'

The denigration of the woman as the cause of fratricidal rivalry among men moves rapidly from a denial that the specific woman is worth the husband's fighting about (*Husband, to his partner found in adultery with his unattractive wife:* "*I must — but you?*") to a rejection of the woman by the adulterer himself. *Parting guest, at the train station after a weekend, to his host:* "*And I specially want to thank you for the use of your wife. She's the best piece of ass I ever had.*" *After the train pulls out, a fellow traveller remonstrates:* "*How on earth could you say a thing like that?*" "*Well, I had to. She was really a lousy lay, but I didn't want to hurt his feelings.*" (N.Y. 1939.) This joke, which is particularly popular and endlessly retailed in both America and France, significantly displaces the whole area of tenderness from the woman to the theoretically hated husband, or 'other man.' One is moving here very close to homosexuality, without even the intermediary chess-piece character of the pedlar in "Dicky Whigburn."

A mere gag-variant of the earlier stories on husbands overacting at their wives' graves: *A man at the funeral of a friend's wife, with whom he has been carrying on an affair, breaks into tears and finally becomes hysterical, while the husband remains impassive.* "*Calm yourself,*" *says the husband.* "*I'll be marrying again.*" (N.Y. 1942.) This is actually an almost overt statement that the person the adulterer is searching for is not really the wife but the husband. In other words, the Oedipal tone of adultery changes from an attempted heterosexual victory over the father-figure, by means of intercourse with the mother-figure (the wife), to that of a homosexual victory in disguise, the father-husband's penis being, as it were, crowded out of the mother-wife's body by that of the adulterer. The Oedipal son may also fantasy himself in this manner as pedicating (humiliating) the father in a dominant homosexual way, evidently to ward off the unconscious and threatening idea that the father will do exactly the same thing to him in punishment for his urges toward the mother. This is the crucial neurotic mechanism in homosexuality. See the introduction to Chapter 10, in Series Two, following, and my pamphlet *On the Cause of Homosexuality* (1950).

An Irishman tells the priest that he does not feel he needs forgiveness for his various adulteries, as the only married women he has relations with are Jewish. "*You're right, my son,*" *says the priest.* "*That's the only way to screw the Jews!*" (N.Y. 1940.) It is understood that the Jews being 'screwed' are not the wives but their husbands, playing on the ambiguous and hostile connotation of *screw* or *fuck:* meaning not only to engage in sexual intercourse, but also to cheat, harm, or *'ream'* (an even more hostile synonym in this sense, actually meaning: to pedicate). The punch-line here was once flung at me unexpectedly, as folk-wit, when I asked an anti-semitic six-foot Irish American how it happened, considering his anti-semitism, that both his wives to date had been undersized Jewesses, the second a cripple. Possibly I expressed my question too directly: it appears this is a leading verbal-sadistic fault of mine (according to John Clellon Holmes' "The Last Cause," in *Evergreen Review,* 1966, No. 44, reprinted in his *Nothing More to Declare,* 1967, a highly libellous biographical sketch or skit of the kind that only friends can permit themselves — an enemy would not dare). At any rate, I got a direct answer.

The approaches to homosexuality already seen in jokes concerning possession in common of the same woman may be considered part of the struggle *toward normality* when they express the Oedipal animosity against the husband (father-figure), but a succumbing to the homosexual neurosis where they make common cause with him against the woman. Even more clearly homosexual, of course, are those jokes where — under the pretexts of possession in common, adultery, or other — any concern or interest is expressed in another man's genital apparatus or activity. Such jokes are generally not thought of as masking homosexuality, but it is their function not to be too clear, while nevertheless rousing a laugh precisely by their veering close to the taboo admission of homosexual interests.

An English lord in the bathtub finds that the water is too hot and gives him an erection. The butler is very upset. "Shall I call her Ladyship, your Lordship?" "No, Jeeves, get me my baggy pants. Maybe I can smuggle THIS *one up to London."* (N.Y. 1942.) The butler is here made privy to, and accessory of, the adultery of the father-figure Englishman. There is the invisible wife being rejected, and the invisible prostitute or mistress in London being approached. But the real subject or action of the joke is simply two men observing and commenting upon the erect penis of one of them. As a matter of fact, the joke does not anywhere even specify the sex of the person in London to whom the infrequent erection is to be smuggled. But of the rejection of the wife, and her unwanted sexual demands, there can be no question. In *Sex to Sexty,* 5:44, this is given in the form of an expurgated cartoon, showing an elderly man in a bathtub and the butler as a comedy homosexual with ox-bow lips saying: *"Oh gracious, Your Lordship! Shall I rally her Ladyship?"* (The end-line is not given at all.) Observe again, following, the totally missing woman, in the concern of one man with another's sexual activity, a concern here excused by the great civilized cover-all of being drunk: '*A calisthenics fiend was passing through a park one night, and on a sudden impulse paused to do a few push-ups on the lawn. A drunk staggering by noticed him and said, "Hey, buddy, your girl's gone".*' (D.C. 1953.) The absurdity of the situation, set up only to make the punch-line possible, is very striking.

The accent here is on the *voyeurism* of the lesser male: butler, drunk, etc., representing the male-child spying on and essentially mocking the father's sexuality. A strange joke, clearly part of this group, also consists solely of voyeurism on the part of all the foreground characters, and the homosexual tone is palpable. I have even heard it delivered with the punch-line given in a flutey mock-homosexual voice. *A man loses his house key and is climbing in the window when stopped by a policeman. He assures the policeman it is his own home, and offers to show him through the house to prove it. "This is the parlor; that's my $300 turkey-fur divan. This is the dining-room, etc." He opens the door of the bedroom, and the policeman sees a man and woman in violent intercourse on the bed. "This is the bedroom," says the man calmly, "and that's my wife. Let's go downstairs and have a cup of tea." They go down to the kitchen and the man busies himself making tea. Finally the cop can't stand it any more, and says, "Say! What about that guy up there with your wife?" "Oh, him!" says the husband; "let him make his own cup of tea."* (N.Y. 1953.) Meaningless except as a refusal to admit to the understanding of the 'primal scene' of the parents' intercourse, as with the children in the Henry James story who refuse to admit that they have seen the ghost (probably the same symbol). In a variant, *the husband ends: "And you see that man on top of her? That's* ME!" The Flight into Nonsense.

Where, under any excuse, one man actually touches the body of another man in a sexually-toned situation, especially any taboo area of the other man's body, the homosexual act may be considered achieved to the degree that this is possible in jokes not consciously homosexual in nature. *A salesman stays overnight at a farmhouse and must sleep in the same bed with the farmer and his wife. Every time he has intercourse with the wife, the salesman pulls a hair from the farmer's ass to make sure he is asleep. Finally the farmer says, "Listen, I have to get up early in the morning. I don't mind you screwing my wife, but for Christ's sake, stop using my ass for a score-board!"* (2:277.) Randolph gives this as his No. 54, "Pulling Out Hairs," collected in Arkansas in 1952, from a man who stated he had 'heard it in Yell county, Ark., about 1930,' and I heard it among children in Pennsylvania then too. There is a clean-up in *And One Flew Into the Cuckold's Nest* (1966) p. 23, with *chest*-hairs! (Rotunda, K1501.2, 'Cuckold feigns to be asleep.' Observe the reversal of "The Wagoner," p. 733 above.)

A new character in American folklore is "Speedy" Pedro, or Pedro Gonzales, the 'Mexican marvel of rapidity! He is in the line of the heroic 'hard-men' of folklore, such as Brother John Henry, Paul Bunyan, Achilles, Rasputin, Tarzan, Li'l Abner, and others discussed further in *The Horn Book*, p. 227, but differs from them signally in being small, sly, insinuating, and *fast;* where they are 'hard,' powerful, and indomitable. "Speedy" Gonzales is obviously intended to represent a child, specifically the son stealing the mother from the father by guile, and accepting the standard (pedicatory) punishment for his act. A character clearly to be assimilated to "Speedy" Gonzales is introduced in the opening lines of Ken Kesey's *Jail Diary* (in *Ramparts,* San Francisco, November 1967) p. 29, as 'one of our prime heroes: *The patrol picks him up somewhere in Redwood City! In one side of the car out the other! "Catch him!" Hard to do, he's small, muscled like a wolverine, shifty as a fox, and a road-runner topknot on his head indicates the boy is* fast!!! *They get him hog tied and finally into jail . . . He's Puerto Rican, neat little moustache a black road-runner shock of hair and* fast!!! *A fireball crink shooter. "I never come down, man. I jess shoot crink and fuck, shoot crink and fuck. Can you deeg it?"* ' Nature must be imitating Art again. That is "Speedy" Gonzales. It is also "Foutindouha," the North African sexual marvel, and hero of a version of the following scatologically-oriented story told by French colonial troops. (*Histoires Coloniales, c.* 1935, p. 63.)

An American tourist travelling with his wife in Mexico has been warned against "Speedy" Gonzales, "the fastest fucker in the world." During the night, someone knocks at the hotelroom door and asks for permission to use the bathroom. It is Pedro Gonzales, of course, and the husband keeps him covered with a revolver with one hand while keeping the other tightly over his wife's cunt. This is repeated several times, until finally, owing to the draft as Pedro comes through the room, the tourist sneezes, momentarily removing his hand. Immediately he claps it back and snarls, "Where's Pedro?" "Oh, señor," says an insinuating voice, "if you want me to leave, you mos' take your feenger out of my asshole." (D.C. 1951.) Full version in Mr. Roderick Roberts'

Negro Folklore in a Southwestern "Industrial School," (MS) chapter 7, No. 10, as "Speedy Gonzales," noting: 'This story has wide currency in the white tradition. I first heard it in 1949 and have listened to at least two dozen versions since.' His text gives the final line as, *"Señor, ya gotchor finger in me asshole."* The relatively correct rendition of the Mexican accent in all forms indicates that the story probably began in the American southwest.

It should be observed that this story is nothing more than a modernization and *homosexualization* of Rabelais' "Hans Carvel's Ring." The element of the protective *hand* — taken directly from Rabelais, one suspects — disappears in another version, which arrives at out-and-out homosexual intercourse instead. *A tourist in a bar in Paris sees a Frenchman weeping into his cognac, and asks sympathetically what the trouble is. The Frenchman explains that he went home late the preceding night anxious to make love to his wife, ran into the bedroom, tore off his clothes without a word, and leapt into bed with his wife . . . "Deep, deep in ze valley of ze heaving breasts." "Well, what's wrong with that?" asks his tourist-confidant. "What ees wrong? What ees wrong, M'sieu, is zat I have found myself, instead, deep, deep in ze asshole of Jacques Le Stropp."* (N.Y. 1953.) As with the use of children, cherubic old people, Negroes, and animals; the comedy-Frenchman here, Jacques Le Stropp — who has, of course, simply replaced "Speedy" Pedro — is a sort of sexual stalking-horse, by means of which sexual acts are conceived as being engaged in that would presumably be impossible to any normal White Anglo-Saxon Protestant (WASP), and must therefore be ascribed to a Mexican, Frenchman, etc., whose ideas of normality presumably allow of greater latitude, or who are too passionately Latin, Negro, animal, or the like, to give a damn. Note also that where, at the end of the preceding section, 11.5, the pedication of the adulterer (by the "Prompt Husband," in the typology quoted from *The Pearl*) is a punishment of him or triumph over him, in its homosexual use of his body; here, in the Gonzales — Le Stropp reversal, it is a purely homosexual act which *disgraces* the active party and in which the adulterer or child triumphs (rectally, as it were) over the father.

We are accustomed in English to such phrases of rejection and contempt as '*stick it up your ass*,' with ornate variations such as ' — up the farthest corner of your ass, and give it a left-hand turn!' But in various European languages, such as French, the same contempt is also expressed by saying that one has the rejected object in one's *own* ass;

the equivalent, of course, of saying that one shits upon it. Relevant also is the joke given earlier — also ascribed to comedy-Frenchmen — of *The three bellboys in a pedicatory daisy-chain, concerning which all the surprised hotel manager can think to say is "Lucky Pierre (or Julius), always in the middle!"* Anal digitation during intercourse, or masturbation, to increase the violence of the orgasm in the man, is commonly described in pornographic literature, and is common in life as well, though it does not appear in the usual formal manuals of sex technique. That it is an evasive form of satisfying passive sexual needs on the part of the man, and that it implies the urge to be pedicated by another man during intercourse, is generally repressed from recognition as 'unmanly.' The jokes above-cited glory precisely in expressing it openly, implying not only that it is a sexual luxury ("Lucky Pierre"), but even somehow a virile triumph over the pedicating male. This is the whole unconscious rationalization of the passive homosexual.

The author of the principal Victorian sexual autobiography, *My Secret Life* (whom I argue, in the Introduction to the first openly-published edition, New York: Grove Press, 1966, to have been the erotic bibliographer, Henry Spencer Ashbee), had what would nowadays be called a particularly bad hang-up on similarly masked homosexual relationships with other men, as father-figures, with whom he would make insulated or mock-heterosexual competitive contact by means of their semen deposited in a woman's vagina. Wayland Young (Lord Kennet) puts it bluntly, from the point of view of a modern English gentleman, in *Eros Denied* (New York, 1964) p. 291: 'The author appears to have been a rich Englishman, and the unflagging length of his book reflects the unflagging length of his active life. It gives an artless picture of the sex addict, the one who can't stop, doesn't want to stop, can't think of anything else to do, is bored by having the same girl more than a week. . . . He had a kink [British for *hang-up*]: he liked to get into girls who were still full of another man's seed. It's clear that, like the sadists, such a man is only worrying about the effect on himself; this particular kink is an emblem of positively desiring no response. His obliviousness to the tears, disasters and muddles he caused with his stupid money — he did not even take a sadistic pleasure in them — makes the book painful to read. It is a compulsively long and factual account of what it is like to be a compulsive collector of physical contacts.' (This squares obviously with the identification with Ashbee, the world's greatest, *i.e.,* most compulsive, erotica collector, though I am no one to throw stones.)

Lord Kennet's book, as is — or should be — well known, is the first work in the history of the literature of the world which attempts to revindicate for the authors of serious non-fictional works the right to the same 'vulgar' or colloquial vocabulary of sex that has been made available to fiction since D. H. Lawrence's *Lady Chatterley's Lover*. In just a few lines here he has ruthlessly plucked out the heart of the mystery of the author of *My Secret Life* in a way not quite as successfully achieved in Prof. Steven Marcus' inordinately long study of the same text, *The Other Victorians* (New York: Basic Books, 1966) p. 77-196 — 120 pages of a 292-page book — especially at p. 174-5; a work which demonstrates its feckless if somewhat pre-scientific scholarship by the extraordinary lapse or resistance that it does not give a single page reference or other method of finding a single one of the seventy-seven inset quotations from the books it is quoting (some several pages in length), and the hundreds of other quotations in the text, representing nearly half the entire book. (This is not quite correct: one quoted passage is actually cited to its source, p. 183*n*, also 242. This may be due to its being in a footnote.) Compare Prof. Marcus' own interesting avowal on quotation, p. 53, that: 'To use the words of other men instead of one's own is to attempt to arrogate their strength or authority; it is furthermore a primitive device of concealment, the words and ideas of others acting as a protective cover for one's own. ... The difference between the impulse to "tell all" and the impulse to tell nothing is in such matters always difficult to maintain.'

Actual wife-trading or possession-in-common, whether in fantasy or as a sociological fact, always seems to be heavily toned homosexually. It has already been observed, concerning the absurdly didactic modern French work *Prélude charnel,* by 'Robert Sermaise,' proposing that the consummation of marriage be lengthily delayed to avoid shocking the bride, and that — as Lundberg & Farnham remark, in *Modern Woman* (1947) p. 286, concerning this bogey of "The Rape of the Wedding-Night" — the husband is 'to comport himself with the gentleness of a nurse attending a dying person, much to the disappointment of the bride, who expects some show of virility;' that the same author proceeds in a supplementary volume to suggest *parties-carrées* (in English, 'foursomes'). These are hardly more than disguised, or undisguised, homosexual affairs between the two hypothetical 'modern' husbands, via their wives' traded bodies. Perfectly frank is Robert Wolf's *Deux contes* (2 *Tales*) — the doubly-punning title laid out in phallic form — published at the author's own Isthmus Press in New York in 1928, and immediately suppressed. The two tales are "One Flesh," of a woman fantasying herself unsuccessfully as giving herself to the plumber repairing her bathroom; and "Seduction," in which the husband of a nursing wife encourages another man — their guest of an evening — to *taste his wife's milk,* then to make love to her. The other man, Johnson, cannot believe his luck:

> Then the door opened and [Ralph, the husband] came in. The covers raised from the other side. Johnson cringed from the intolerable intrusion of male fingers.
> Then he fucked, shot, bounced into her, in the saddle of her thighs. He grew limp in the wet smooth slide.
> "Let me now," Ralph was whispering. Vulgar, hairy, they lurched together. Johnson crawled slowly over and crept shame-faced out of bed.

That is what is known as laying it on the line, which is more than most writers now whooping it up for wife-trading ever do. In *Love & Death* (1949) p. 67, I note a murder-mystery, *The Smell of Money* by 'Matthew Head' (actually the art-critic, John Canaday), 'pronounced by all experts the sexiest item as yet peddled on the murder-market [at that time]. Its sex consists solely of several undescribed acts of intercourse between narrator and murderess, and a single use of the phrase "sleep with" by an elderly woman. The murderess is the wife of a sadistic homosexual, clearly described (he keeps her for trading purposes only, with a hint at seminal exsufflation in the bushes), who, for her crimes, cuts off her hands at the wrists and leaves her to bleed to death on a pink rug. He is in love with the narrator himself.' As quite a number of readers wrote to ask what is meant by 'seminal exsufflation in the bushes' (one suggesting that some pun was doubtless intended on 'blowing,' meaning fellation, and another assuming that 'bushes' referred to the female pubic hair, which was unconscious if true), the facts may be plainly stated, more in context here:

It is a common cliché in pornographic literature, and is also true in life, that a certain kind of married homosexual, or 'swinger' or 'wife-trader' (the current disguise of such neurotics), allows his wife to have intercourse with other men, in fact encourages and connives at this, and may even tote her around the world with him for just such purposes. This is, for example, the plot-gimmick of Tennessee Williams' play, *Suddenly Last Summer,* in the 1960's, in which the homosexual thus uses, as his 'bitch's blind' or bait, first his *mother,* and then, when she gets too old to attract the younger men wanted, his beautiful young mistress or bride. What the play does not, of course, specify is that while such adulterous intercourse is being concluded, the homosexual husband usually circulates in the next room, or somewhere else in the vicinity, such as under the bed (or in the bushes nearby, if out-of-doors), in order immediately thereafter to draw out the other man's semen by sucking it from the woman's vagina. There is no common slang-term for this perversion, but I have heard such a person called a 'baby-eater' by his wife.

By this roundabout method the man is able to deny, to himself at least, his homosexual urges, or powerful oral-erotic impulses toward fellation, since he has no direct oragenital relations with the other man, these being achieved or evaded by operating strictly *via* the woman's body. Oragenital urges, as Freud remarks (quoted above, at the end of Chapter 8.v.4), are always derived from relics of the nursing experience at the mother's breast — or from having been deprived of this. In the neurotic acting-out just described, it will be observed that the husband-child is simultaneously nursing at *both* parents' bodies, through the surrogate figures of his own wife and the man to whom he has offered her.

'Swingers' and 'wife-traders' are also likely to demand that their wives later give them exact anatomical details of the pleasure they have had adulterously with the other men who have been pimped to them — this being a sort of further or *verbal* sexual intercourse possible with the wife, in periods between other men — and particularly to give the husband some such formula reassurance as that "*His was bigger, but you know how to use it better.*" (N.Y. 1941.) This was quoted to me by the wife of a well-known American poet who, as aforesaid, kept her for trading purposes only. When I asked her if it was really true, she said disgustedly, "*Nah! you know; he's a poet. He* TALKS *a good fuck.*" The entire hidden meaning of the aforementioned sexual autobiography, *My Secret Life* (1888–94? reprinted New York: Grove Press, 1966), is that writer felt an overmastering neurotic certainty that his penis was smaller than that of other men — *i.e.* of his father — and engaged in a lifelong search for reassurance by having intercourse, by preference, either with young girls who would presumably not know better, or with women who had just had intercourse with another man. This is known in the U.S. Navy as 'riding (or: slopping down) a wet deck,' and Grose in 1785 recorded the British slang-phrase of similar meaning, 'to have a buttered bun.' It must be a far more common neurotic activity than is realized.

It is obviously similar to the 'gang-shag' or 'gang-bang,' which is also basically a genital relationship with all the other men present, by the possession in common of a single woman, through the actual *reliquiæ* of the other men's semen on and in the 'shagged' woman's body, and by observing the other men's naked or erect penises while they wait their turn, often masturbating while doing so, and exciting themselves by watching the man presently in action. An extraordinarily detailed scene of this kind is given in Hunter S. Thompson's exposé of the California motorcycle-gang, *Hell's Angels* (New York: Random House, 1966) end of chapter 17:

> I keep a crumpled yellow note from that night; not all of the writing is decipherable, but some of it reads like this: "Pretty girl about twenty-five lying on wooden floor, two or three on her all the time, one kneeling between her legs, one sitting on her face and somebody else holding her feet . . . teeth and tongues and pubic hair, dim light in a wooden shack, sweat and semen gleaming on her thighs and stomach, red and white dress pushed up around her chest . . . people standing around yelling, wearing no pants, waiting first second or third turns . . . girl jerking and moaning, not fighting, clinging, seems drunk, incoherent, not knowing, drowning . . . "
>
> It was not a particularly sexual scene. The impression I had at the time was one of vengeance. The atmosphere in the room was harsh and brittle, almost hysterical. Most people took a single turn, then either watched or wandered back to the party. But a hard core of eight or ten kept at her for several hours. In all, she was penetrated in various ways no less than fifty times, and probably more. At one point, when the action slowed down, some of the Angels went out and got the girl's ex-husband, who was stumbling drunk. They led him into the shack and insisted he take his own turn. The room got nervous, for only a few of the outlaws were anxious to carry things that far. But the sight of her former old man brought the girl out of her daze just enough to break the silent tension. She leaned forward, resting on her elbows, and asked him to kiss her. He did, and then groggily took his turn while the others cheered.

The *kiss* that the girl has to ask for, after having been 'penetrated in various ways no less than fifty times,' speaks volumes. Lest anyone think she was physically harmed by all this, the author — who does not believe the Hell's Angels ever actually raped anyone — adds: 'Afterwards the girl rested for a while and then wandered around the party in a blank sort of way and danced with several people. Later she was taken back for another session. When she finally reappeared I saw her trying to dance with her ex-husband, but all she could do was hang on his neck and sway back and forth. She didn't seem to hear the music — a rock-'n'-roll band . . . '

What is actually meant, as to the missing *kiss,* is that the Hell's Angels — who are famous for cunnilinctus, *à la* Aleister Crowley, on menstruating women — can nevertheless not risk the open homosexuality of oral contact with semen, in kissing a woman who has just fellated another man (or men). A tremendous point is also made at the folk-level, among male prostitutes to homosexuals — the secret profession of many if not most motorcycle gangsters — of being unwilling to kiss the fellator on the mouth. This is noted in Martial's *Epigrams* (1st century A.D.), and the matter of the *kiss* was also the crucial point in the trial of Oscar Wilde, who threw away his case and went to jail owing to not being able to resist making a flip remark, while on the witness-stand in his own behalf, as to not having kissed some male prostitute because he was 'ugly,' which was correctly seized upon by the prosecutor as meaning he would have kissed the boy if he had been cute. Note also, at the deeper level of the feared rejection, how *Salomé,* the bitch-Isolde of Oscar Wilde and Richard Strauss, grovels about on the stage with the decapitated head of St. John the Baptist, in an equally symbolic but this time castratory and sadistic consummation, screaming in pidgin-French and German that she will 'kiss' it at last.

4. RITUAL ORGIES

Although the apparent meaning of such scenes as the Hell's Angels 'gang-bang' preceding, and the current rather similar 'group-grope' of the drugged (and insane) hippies, is that of vice or cruelty; actually it would appear that these are survivals — probably by unconscious re-creation — of very ancient rituals of public sexual intercourse intended to have magical group power, as, for instance, to bring back the 'dying sun' at the winter solstice. What is now the orgiastic 'office-party' at

Christmas. As to the possibility that the survival has been real, rather than unconscious, it may be mentioned that the modern slang term '*to ball*,' meaning to have sexual intercourse, seems to be a survival, in turn, of the old name of a naked orgiastic group, the 'Ballers' or 'Buff-Ballers,' noted a century apart in England, in Pepys' *Diary* (1669) and by Grose (2nd ed., 1788), and perhaps of earlier origin in the Scottish 'witches' sabbaths' still recollected in the orgy-song "The Ball o' Kirriemuir." (On all this, see further my *The Horn Book*, 1964, pp. 231, 374–5, and 423–4.) It is also more than likely that the orgiastic scenes in the sacred sculpture and pottery of such ancient cultures as India, Greece, and Peru; also the straight trio-orgies and 'three-way girls' of, for example, the *Greek Anthology*, v. 49, "Lyde" (Latin translation in *The Limerick*, Paris, 1954, Note 311, p. 391), and certainly the unspecified sexual festivals in the tree-worship 'groves' excoriated by the Old Testament, were also essentially or originally religious ritual acts.

St. Epiphanius, Bishop of Constantia in the 4th century, in his *Panarium versus Hæresiis* (ed. Petavii, 1. 84–102, quoted by Thomas Wright, *et al.*, "The Templars and the Worship of the Generative Powers," 1865, in G. Legman, ed., *The Guilt of the Templars*, 1966, p. 249), in describing the heresy of the early Christian controversial sect of the Gnostics, states that: 'The Gnostics were accused of eating human flesh as well as of lasciviousness, and they also are said to have held their women in common, and taught that it was a duty to prostitute their wives to their guests. They knew their fellow sectarians by a secret sign, which consisted in *tickling the palm of the hand with the finger in a peculiar manner* [italics supplied]. The sign having been recognised, mutual confidence was established, and the stranger was invited to supper; after they had eaten their fill, the husband removed from the side of his wife, and said to her, "Go, exhibit charity to our guest," which was the signal for those further scenes of hospitality.' Curiously, the *tickling of the palm of the hand with the finger* — with which compare the secret handclasps and rituals of all modern fraternal organizations, and the tongue-tip fencing of the Hell's Angels! — is still very well known among American children as recently as the early 1930's in Eastern Pennsylvania, and probably still, as a secret signal between a boy and a girl, by way of asking for sexual intercourse. This must be the world's record for folkloristic survivals, absolutely at the secret 'oral' — really gestural or *non*-oral! — level.

St. Epiphanius continues (and the same thing is said of the Manichæan heretics in Prædestinati's *Adversus Hæresibus*, Bk. 1, chap. 46, according to Wright, p. 279, *n.* 8), that 'further rites practiced by the Gnostics . . . were still more disgusting, for they were said, after these libidinous scenes [of wife-sharing], to offer and administer the *semen virile* as their sacrament.' This certainly implies that the same oral-erotic and oral-neurotic need expressed in modern wife-trading, fantasied or real, of seminal exsufflation afterwards, was also current either among the Gnostics and Manichæans, *or in the fantasies of the persons so accusing them.* The eating of human flesh, mentioned in the preceding paragraph, actually refers to the presumed ritual eating of the resultant child, which is only a further expression of the same infantile oral centralization. A French orgiastic society in the 11th century in Orléans was similarly accused of this, the children born of orgies being burnt the circumcisional eighth day of life, and their ashes being ceremonially ingested. (Wright, in *The Guilt of the Templars,* pp. 255–6, 281, *n.* 17.) The attempt was made to accuse the Knights Templars of the same thing in the early 14th century (in the contemporary *Chronicles of St. Denis* and by the later Renaissance historian, Guillaume de Paradin: cited in *The Guilt of the Templars,* pp. 38–9, and 94), the Templars being said — certainly falsely — to *roast* the illegitimate children who were the presumed results of their orgies with women, in order to use 'the grease to anoint their grand statue' or idol.

Wayland Young, in *Eros Denied* (New York, 1964), p. 146*n.*, notes that the 11th-century writer, Guilbert de Nogent, stated in the same way that the Manichæan heretics used to burn the children resulting from orgies 'as soon as they were born, and bake communion bread out of their bodies.' (This is apparently the same accusation as that against the Orléans group, and probably rises from the same source, as printed in Guérard's *Cartulaire de l'Abbaye de Saint-Père de Chartres,* I. 112.) The relationship is very evident here to the blood-accusation against the Jews, which still survives in both Europe and America at a rather low cultural level. Namely, that religious Jews ceremonially kill children or use the blood of Christian virgins — the blood of their ruptured hymens, naturally — to make *matzos* at Passover [!] or to mix into the sacramental wine. This accusation has been the excuse for endless pogroms, from the Hugh of Lincoln massacre in England in the 13th century (see Chaucer's "Prioress' Tale," Marlowe's *Jew of Malta,* and Child Ballad No. 155, "Sir Hugh, or The Jew's Daughter"), to the Mendel Beiliss case in Russia in 1912, 'in which the Pope was finally obliged to intervene.' I have myself been accused of this to my face, by a Polish-American housemaid in Scranton, Pennsylvania, in 1934, whom

I was amateurishly trying to seduce, it being spring (the season of Passover) — who also wanted to *forgive* me for it, because she knew I really liked her but would be 'forced' by my religion to kill her for her hymeneal blood.

Note that the absurd touch of the *matzos* of Passover being made of the blood of the sacramental murder victim is precisely the touch which shows the survival here of the original accusation against the Manichæans and other Christian heretics, as to the baking of communion bread out of murdered children's bodies. The flat and unleavened *matzo* is, of course, the Semitic original of the sacred wafer or Host (*hostia,* sacrifice or hostage, N.B.) eaten, though not chewed, as the Eucharist or Christian Communion, which is actually the only authentic survival on a large scale of these barbaric fantasies, belonging properly to the childhood of the human race, and in which the symbolized child sacramentally killed and ingested is stated to be the Son — and only child — of God.

The terrible unconscious guilt for thus cannibalizing the god (as Freud, in *Totem & Taboo,* notes the eating in the night of the *Urfather,* Kronos, Saturn, Noah, etc., by the assembled sons, who also castrate him in the case of Noah, according to the Talmud, *Sanhedrin,* 70a), is extrojected in this way — thrown out of the consciousness of the real actors — in the form of identical accusations levelled against heretics or the heterodox, or even earlier religions, who are accused of similarly cannibalizing not the child of the god, but mere human infants, in exactly the same way. This explains why these accusations are, and will remain, perennial under Christianity, and shows the secret spring from which they derive their force: namely, from the sacrament of the Communion itself, instituted at the Last Supper, at Passover, *Matthew,* xxvi. 26–8. For it is a simple enough syllogism that if hundreds of millions of religious Christians have gathered together to eat symbolically the blood and body of the Son of God, as the supreme act of their religion, some one hundred thousand times since the Crucifixion (52 Sundays $\times$ 1900 years), then certainly the members of other religions or heretical sects may easily be suspected of similarly killing and eating the sons and daughters merely of man, as part of the worship of Moloch. (Also of Jehovah, as in the sacrifice of Isaac, *Genesis,* xxii.) The Aztecs of Mexico certainly did so, though no religion has ever recorded of itself the actual eating of the sacrificed human child.

Allusion has already been made (*The Guilt of the Templars,* p. 124, and *The Fake Revolt,* p. 29–30) to the similar oral 'possession in common' of 'ritual public cunnilinctus, of almost exactly this ordeal type, which takes place at the present time (1968) nightly — especially Saturday nights — across the border from San Diego, California, in Tijuana, Mexico, at the public night club with open access from the street, known to American students and sailors as the "Blue Fox" (its real name, which is quite different, involves a sardonic allusion to the American dollar). I have myself witnessed this, and so have hundreds of the young college men and women of San Diego, with very young American sailors, in ill-fitting civilian clothes, being urged and shamed into partaking of this ritual communion — it can hardly be called anything else — by their beer-drinking mates at the tables circling the stage on which the girl stripteasers stand offering themselves, one by one, opening and closing their knees (between, er, communicants) with all the subtle invitation of Baja California octopussy, or purple-passion squid. The color-line is also drawn, as in many churches, Negro sailors not being allowed to partake. As between the patriarchal communion of the symbolic blood-drinking and flesh-eating of the body of the god, in the Eucharist, Sunday mornings in San Diego, and the matriarchal communion of public cunnilinctus with the blatant mother-goddess stripteaser in Tijuana, Saturday nights; one may very seriously question which ceremonial is really the more primitive, and, to anyone of emotional sensibilities, more of an ordeal.'

Obviously, it is hard to decide when what appears to be simply a 'gang-bang' by current juvenile delinquents is really to be construed as an historical *ritual orgy,* in the sense earlier applied to the kissing of the bride by all the male wedding guests, 8.II.1. One extraordinary joke disguises its real implications so subtly that it has often been printed in 'family' humor magazines. *Young lady-teacher in Oklahoma: "Will anyone who has Indian blood please raise their hand." One boy raises his hand slowly. "I guess I got Indian blood." "How fascinating!" gushes the teacher; "what tribe?" "No tribe. Just one wandering Indian."* (N.Y. 1938.)

5. ARTIFICIAL INSEMINATION

Artificial insemination is nothing but permitted adultery, in which the husband withdraws in favor of the 'better man,' politely referred to (in the current euphemisms of the themselves-euphemistic Planned Parenthood and Marriage Counselling) as the 'donor.' This is the total emotional content of the subject, so far as folk-humor is concerned, and it may be doubted whether it means anything else to the parties in fact. As the deepest essential of the objection to adultery has always been not so much that the wife has intercourse with another man (which she may very well have done before her present marriage, as in the case of widows or divorcées), but that the child of such adulterous intercourse might be 'fathered-off' on the husband, it is only a proper reversal that, in the *purposeful* 'fathering-off' of artificial insemination, every absurd care must be taken to ensure that though the 'donor's' semen arrives safely and completely well up inside the wife's uterus, his penis never makes an appearance in her vagina at all. One or the other of these is the straining at a gnat while swallowing a camel, mentioned in Jesus' reprobation of the scribes and Pharisees, in *Matthew,* xxiii. 24.

Modern genetic science is called into service here, to justify activities of wife-offering and wife-trading which earlier could be rationalized only as jokes and folktales, in the discovery that the begetting of male children depends strictly on the chromosomatic heritage of the father, and that, if the woman has only daughters, it is the husband's 'fault.' What this means, in rough & ready fact, is that if a woman has three daughters in a row, and wants a son (as all women do, since, after all, a woman under patriarchy is only 'a man without a penis'), she will or should offer herself to the iceman or gas-meter reader — assuming he is a known getter of male children — on the easy adulterous principle or proverb that "*You never miss a slice off a cut loaf.*" This has been going on a long time — in fact, since before there were icemen and gas-meters — and is going on right now.

A more important element in the rich fantasy undercurrent of the relations between the sexes, at present, is that an actually *artificial* insemination would not involve the activity of the male at all, and the woman would be impregnated by the action of, let us say, electricity (the Father-God of Lightning). This idea has specially tormented highly neurotic writers and thinkers since at least the beginning of this century in the fantasy of the 'test-tube baby,' first described, I believe, in Albert Robida's more-than-total science-fiction prophecy, *Le Vingtième Siècle: La Vie Electrique* (1883–90, two rare volumes, and two even rarer supplements: *La Guerre au XXe. Siècle,* and *Voyage de Fiançailles au XXe. Siècle,* 1892, especially at p. 17). Robida's work riots in the horrible future he foresaw: prophesying, proposing, and hilariously illustrating not only test-tube babies, but also poison-gas, television, frogmen, microbic warfare, and a few other bagatelles nearly upon us, in a total and fiendishly exulting fashion that makes waste-paper of all the 'anticipations' and the literature of science fiction since.

The idea of the artificial child, or man-made life (male-mother-hood), which obviously derives from but is not the same as the older Jewish legend of the *Golem,* and the monster of *Dr. Frankenstein* of Mary Wollstonecraft Shelley (1818), has particularly seized the fancy of many writers since, beginning with Villiers de l'Isle-Adam in *L'Eve future* (1886). And even more particularly the social critic J. B. S. Haldane in *Dædalus, or Science and the Future* (1924), and in two derivative works, Aldous Huxley's *Brave New World* (1932) and George Orwell's *1984,* whose almost total plagiarisms are discussed in my *The Horn Book,* p. 314-31, at greater length. In the sense of ac-tually attempting to turn this into a reality, the French writer, Remy de Gourmont, who was restricted to a sexual activity largely consisting of animal voyeurism owing to his disfigurement by the disease lupus, frankly and masochistically envisaged "Human Parthenogenesis and the Elimination of the Male," in his *Natural Philosophy of Love* (pub-lished posthumously in 1917) chapter 7. The work with artificial im-pregnation of sea-urchins by Dr. Gregory Pincus (inventor also of the birth-control pill) since that time, has made a number of willing be-lievers leap to the conclusion that it is already a fact for human beings as well — 'in Japan,' as the folklore now has it.

A propaganda motion picture, lightly disguised as science, was made on this theme about 1950 by a French woman writer, Nicole Vedrès, otherwise operating mostly in the field of women's fashions etc., and aroused a good deal of gratifyingly shocked response on the part of male audiences. Apparently the sicker women in the audiences *loved* the idea: the state will support the babies, the whole thing once achieved is irreversible and forever, since the resultant babies can *only* be females (lacking the male genetic element, as above), and that is the end of the enemy, Man. Any necessary sex life for the remaining race of women can also doubtless be taken care of by the same Great-God Electricity, for what man can give a woman a clitoral orgasm to compare with that of the ordinary scalp-massage vibrating motor? (*Caution: It is habit-forming.*)

Men have weakly responded by trying to outflank this bogey of be-ing outmoded, replaced, and gotten rid of altogether — in fantasy at least — by the matching fantasy of the 'harem-dream' on a global scale, in which, owing to some accident, only one man is left alive on earth, and his refrigerated semen must be divided up among all the human race of women. In the fantasy sense this is tantamount to having sexual intercourse with all the women in the world, though obviously in no other sense. As noted in *The Horn Book,* p. 326, 'The absolutely open sexual statement is first made in science-fiction, I believe, in George Weston's *His First Million Women* (New York, 1934), in which Comet "Z" sterilizes all the men in the world but one, who was down in a lead-mine [Mother Earth?] – or up on the Eiffel Tower, as in the earlier *Crazy Ray* motion-picture – at the comet's passage. (Compare also another French motion-picture, the charming *Le Déjeuner sur l'Herbe,* this time mocking rather than celebrating the idea of government-controlled genetic intercourse 'for the good of the race.') This fortunate fellow is then imprisoned, and is commandeered by all the governments of the world to undertake the earth's repopulation, by the wholesale methods of artificial insemination (despite the title). The atomic version of the same thing, Pat Frank's *Mr. Adam,* did not appear until over a decade later (and the same idea is again mocked to the hilt, in Terry Southern's anti-atomic motion-picture satire, *Dr. Strangelove* in 1963). Nothing remains to be demonstrated, by Freudian or other analytic methods, after fantasy statements so very clear.' The similarly large *scale* of miraculous impregnations by Jupiter, Jehovah, and other gods is of course equally a human male fantasy.

It should not be lost sight of that, in the women's fantasy, artificial insemination gets rid of *all* the men in the world, while in the man's fantasy it gets rid only of all *other* men but the fantasist himself. This is One-Upmanship what AM, and shows plainly that artificial insemination is strictly a male idea of mechanical replacement of the impotent ('sterile' or non-male-begetting) male, which is of course also the emotional reality hidden behind these wholesale ideas of total and godlike potency, with the billion women of the world as harem.

The few jokes and folktales on these themes are – as are all bawdy jokes, basically – men's fantasy expressions and not women's, and represent the matter from the point of view of the arch-fool or nincumpoop husband being thus 'assisted,' but actually being cuckolded, by the donor, who improperly puts his penis where only his semen was desired: the synecdoche or metonymy, or part-for-the-whole, to end all such. Fliesler's *Anecdota Americana* (1927) 1:28, makes one of its few historical attempts on just this point: '*One of the earliest jokes is the tale told on the Emperor Agrippa, who, observing a slave pass the palace, was surprised to see that he was almost the image of himself. "Ho, there," the Emperor cried. "Slave, did your mother ever pass this way?"* "*No, sire, but my father did,*" *was the rejoinder. This ancient jest is repeated in various languages, with the answer sometimes:* "*My father was your father's butler*".' The variant ending proposed not only kills the joke, but would also certainly have got the slave killed for so gross an accusation, where the original has an imperturbable innocence that has made it a favorite for centuries, in the line of 'the biter bit.'

All the jokes and tales on this subject partake of an interesting and almost pre-cultural confusion as to how babies are made by their parents, what part the two parents play, and so forth. I would not go so far as to say that they hark back to a period when 'nescience of paternity' was the human situation, as it is difficult to believe that any such halcyon period ever existed, since many non-human animals (such as cows and cats) appear to know very well what they must do to become pregnant. The confusion expressed is, however, very standard in these tales, and is perhaps worth further study. Even at the most modern level, the wife's barrenness is explained, and is to be remedied, by methods that can only be called primitive. *The husky father of three strapping boys is bored by the complaints of his little bank-clerk friend who cannot get his wife pregnant, and offers to tell him a sure way.* "*You send her down to the sea for two months. You know it's often the woman's fault — run-down condition, colds, and so forth. You send her where she'll get built up, get sunshine every day, fresh air, and ten hours of undisturbed sleep every night, lots of food, eggs and fish, and the like. When she's all rested up and just can't hold herself to get back to you, send for her, get her all washed up at a Turkish bath; then, Jim, send for me!"* (1:218.)

By the standard technique already discussed, of casting upon other and 'lower' races all actions or stupidities inacceptable to the in-group of the person telling the joke, the primitivism of this ignorance as to paternity is cast on such groups as the Chinese, or American Indian. *Perplexed Chinaman:* "*Me no come. Wife no come. Baby come. How come?"* (N.Y. 1942.) — *The Indian is arrested for murdering his wife. Explains:* "*Me plant corn, come up corn. Me plant wheat, come up wheat. Me plant Indian, come up Chinaman. Me kill'em squaw.*" (Fredericksburg, Va., 1952. Much earlier in *Anecdota*, 1934, no. 423, with the Indian merely wanting a divorce.) Told as a modern Russian joke, on the Lysenko genetics controversy, in E. Haldeman-Julius' *American Freeman*, 'Feb. 1950' (1949) p. 10/6: '*Russians are telling a little joke that's concerned with . . . genetics and the rival principles of "heredity" and "environment." It goes this way: "Now take [for] example. Suppose Comrade Ivanov's wife has a baby, and the baby looks like Comrade Ivanov; that would be a demonstration of the Mendelian principle of heredity. But if the baby looks like Comrade Petrov, the next-door neighbor, then it's a triumph for Comrade Lysenko's principle of environment. See?"* This joke is in all probability American-made, as is also the case with most of the 'dumb Russian' jokes in the collection of *USSR Humor* (Mount Vernon, N.Y.: Peter Pauper Press, 1964) edited by Dr. Charles Winick, compiler also of a matching *Outer Space Humor* volume (1963), in which, similarly, very few of the jokes are authentically originated by denizens of outer space.

Not jokes, but puns or Irish bulls: *"I'm sure my husband isn't faithful to me,"* an Irishwoman remarked. *"Not one of the children look like him."* (1:30, crediting *Pins and Needles*.) — *'A man, being suspected of impotency, met a friend one day, who had railed him on it, to whom he said, "My good Sir, for all your wit, my wife was yesterday brought to bed." "What of that," said his friend, "nobody ever suspected your wife".'* (Edmund Fuller, *Thesaurus of Anecdotes*, 1942, No. 926, apparently quoting *Joe Miller's Jests*, 1739.) Roth's *Anecdota* (1933) no. 241 gives, as a throwaway line, of the kind used by nightclub and vaudeville comedians: *'I know a man who is so suspicious of his wife, that when, recently, she presented him with twins, he insisted that he recognized only one of them.'* This is connected somehow with the possession-in-common story of: *The two business partners who are both laying the stenographer. She becomes pregnant and one partner leaves town, telling the other to telegraph him whether it's a boy or a girl. The telegram:* "GERTIE HAD TWINS. STOP. MINE DIED." (N.Y. 1936.) As this seems terribly modern, fitted out as it is with stenographer, telegraph, and other recent improvements, it is edifying to compare it with its original, in *Joe Miller's Jests* (1739) No. 119; concerning the baby born *'with a wooden leg,'* and thus identifying the father, already quoted in Chapter 7.II.

Jokes turning on the question of how many months the wife has been pregnant, and whether or not the husband can thus be the father at all, also display this willful primitivism as to the whole mechanism of impregnation. The husband *wishes* to believe he is the father, rather than accuse his wife, destroy his marriage, etc. The evidence of his senses, and of the simplest sort of genetic science he believes in, must thus be denied. This has been taken so far, in England, in recent years, as to attempt the defense in court, in an accusation of adultery, that *the adulterer had worn a condom,* and had therefore never actually 'touched' the woman! If this be combined with the new ethic of the semen-donor, who also does not 'touch' the woman, but who is doing the exact opposite of wearing a condom, the legal area of adultery becomes tenuous indeed. Adultery is clearly sexual intercourse of a prohibited type — *"The wrong man in the right place,"* as the folk-definition has it (N.Y. 1946) — and any presumed concern with the parenthood of the child, the costs of its support and education (a purely modern bogey), and similar, may be considered rationalizations. The matching definition of *"Buggery: The right man in the wrong place"* (San Francisco, Calif. 1965) is seldom encountered, and clearly depends on the first definition for its spoonerism to be appreciated.

A man has been away from home for three years, and comes back to find his wife with three children and a star-boarder whom the kids call "Daddy." "Still," he says to a friend, *"who am I to condemn anybody on circumstantial evidence?"* (N.Y. 1944.) As this husband is obviously too much of a masochistic muff to live, the more popular joke on the same theme is ascribed to the comedy-Chinaman in America, whose weak acceding is part of his social condition. *The Chinese laundryman has been in America ten years and keeps sending money to his wife in China, telling the bank-clerk proudly that his wife has just had a new baby. "But, Mr. Foong,"* says the clerk, *"you've been here in America ten years." "Yes, yes,"* says the Chinaman happily; *"I got velly good fliends in China."* (N.Y. 1936.) A beautiful children's story, on the pattern of pretended naïveté: *One child tells another that her aunt has just had a baby. "But isn't your uncle in the army?"* objects the other child. *"Oh sure he is,"* says the first child airily, *"but he writes her every day." "He must have a very long pencil,"* says the second child wonderingly. (A similar version, D.C. 1947, is given in I.II.I.)

A woman entertaining a noble lover is interrupted by another lover. The nobleman is hidden in the canopy over the bed. The husband then interrupts, and the second lover is hidden under the bed. As the husband is about to ejaculate into his wife's body, she tries to draw aside and objects, "But how can we support another baby?" "The Lord above will provide," says the husband sententiously. *"The Lord above will provide, will he?"* shouts the nobleman in the canopy, *"and what about that bugger of a Baronet under the bed!"* This is a 19th-century jest-book form (still current in America) of *Les Cent Nouvelles Nouvelles,*

No. 34, of Levantine origin: *Nasr'eddin* (ed. Wesselski) 1. 271, Nicol-aidès, p. 119; *Kryptádia*, II. 167. (Types 1355A *and* C.) It is clearly a farce-reduction of the great "Entrapped Suitors," Type 1730, in the *Ocean of Story* and *Arabian Nights* (Child Ballad No. 276), dealt with further in Series Two, 15.VI.2, "Gardyloo!"

It should be carefully noted that both Thompson's and Rotunda's entire sections K1200, "Humiliating Deceptions," K1300, "Deceptions connected with Seduction and Marriage," and K1500, "Deceptions connected with Adultery," actually index a very large segment of the Italian *novelle* and other folktales, representing the main bawdy jokes of the period on sexual themes. It is of the utmost significance that these all have in common that they are based on *deceptions* in connection with sex and sexual fidelity, and often involve 'plural sex.'

Birth control devices are thought of popularly as, on the one hand, protecting young girls and overworked wives (with one child?) from unwanted pregnancies, but, on the other hand, precisely this protection is thought of as giving them the green light for every kind of 'immorality.' It has already been observed, in connection with Dr. Berne's game of "Uproar," that the lover of the daughter is, to the father, precisely the same murderously hated interloper as the lover of the wife. Many fathers, in fact, cannot give up this hatred of their sons-in-law, even after the proper legal knot is tied, nor their resentment of having been deprived of the daughter just at the moment (usually) of her finest flowering as a beautiful young woman, when she most reminds the father of the young woman he once married but who is no longer young. Most of the expressed resistance to birth control, in the century and a half now of its general dissemination since the "Diabolical Handbills," as their enemies called them, of the anarchist pants-maker, Francis Place (see Peter Fryer's *The Birth Controllers,* London, 1965), centers clearly on this ambivalent feeling that it makes 'immorality' too easy for wives and daughters, by protecting them — and the husband and father at the same time, of course — from any possibility of extra-marital pregnancy. The resistance to the prevention and cure of venereal disease by penicillin, during World War II, was based on the same jealous confusion on the part of the *patria potestas* running the world.

Two husbands whose wives are out of town are talking sex. "How do you keep your family down, Joe?" "We've got a thing upstairs in the bureau drawer. Come on, I'll show you ... My God! she's taken it with her!" (2:390.) When, however, it is a question of the man's out-of-town, or *on*-the-town, prerogatives, we have instead the dictum attributed earlier to the operatic matinée idol of the 1900's, Caruso. The Texas collection, *And One Flew Into the Cuckold's Nest* (1966) p. 19, gives what can only be considered a topper, rather than a variant, of the joke at the beginning of this paragraph: '*His wife was out of town, so he sneaked home with a blonde cutie. She refused without adequate precautions, so he said he'd get his wife's diaphragm. After looking all over for it, he fumed, "How about that? She doesn't trust me . . . she took it with her!"* If the definition of a cultivated woman is 'One who will not commit adultery in her own bed,' one wonders how to define the male type, here mocked (and yet . . .) who wants to commit adultery in his wife's diaphragm?

Jokes on birth control techniques and devices are extremely uncommon, other than those connected with withdrawal at the instant of seminal ejaculation (the sin of Onan, according to *Genesis,* xxxviii. 9–10). The devices are new, but jokes have their history. A principal form of birth control is nowadays oral intercourse: fellation of the man by the woman, the semen being disposed of by various means both natural and unnatural. (*"What bird brings the babies?"* "Storks." *"And what bird* doesn't *bring babies?"* "Swallows." — Somerville, N.J. 1943.) This is particularly practised by young girls, in both America and Europe, attempting in this way to retain their vaginal virginity while 'satisfying' their swains. I was told recently by a seventeen-year-old Southwest American girl that she had been advised to do this by her father, while a nineteen-year-old girl from Michigan was told the riddle or joke quoted just above, by her older sister, as a final bit of advice on leaving for an overnight party at a college fraternity, theoretically heavily chaperoned. Such oral techniques are supposed to have been common during the middle ages, in the relations of "Domnei" between women of superior social class and their troubadour lovers or servant-cavaliers, and were considered *not* to be tantamount to adultery. This position is still taken by a surprising number of married women, though no husband has yet been found to agree with them. *A man explains his having a black eye by saying he walked into a door in the dark. As no one will believe him, he decides to tell a better story. He then explains that when he was leaving for work in the morning he found a button missing from the fly of his pants, and went next door to ask his neighbor's wife to sew a button on for him. "And just as she was bending over to bite off the thread — her husband walked in!"* (N.Y. 1938, seldom collected since the introduction of zipper-flies.)

Artificial insemination is, in a sense, birth control in reverse, and many of its devices — such as the thermometer (of which I am the inventor) to determine the period of fertility, and the much more famous and successful Pill — can be used either to 'cause' or to prevent pregnancy on specific occasions. These two ambivalent or interpenetrating functions come into conflict in at least one story, already told in Chapter 7.v: *A man who cannot get his wife pregnant decides with her that they will go to a summer resort, that she should flirt with the man they meet there who pleases her most, and that the husband should encourage him to have a 'one-shot' affair with her, pretending to be only a friend. The project goes off as planned and the husband waits, a prey to mixed emotions, in the lobby of the resort hotel, trying to console himself with plans for the hoped-for child. An hour later he sees the substitute-father getting off the elevator and rushes up to him, greedy for the humiliating details. "How was it?" he asks. "Oh, it was great," says the other man casually, "but, you know, she was so easy to make I just couldn't get over the feeling there might be something wrong — so I used a cundrum."* (N.Y. 1938.) The psychological situation here is exactly that of the husband of any woman who goes for actual artificial insemination, and all modern cartoons on this subject, in men's magazines, humor magazines, etc., invariably imply that the physician performing the artificial insemination does or should really engage in simple intercourse with the would-be mother, rather than bother with something reminiscent of Dr. Slop's baptizing-syringe in *Tristram Shandy.*

The tracing of jokes on this theme, historically, is obviously difficult, since the subject is presumably new. However, when placed in juxtaposition with the endless folktales and jokes — even the religious legends — concerning miraculous conceptions, the similarity of approach becomes clear, especially in the continually encountered suspicion that the 'miracles' are really caused by human intervention, as with the artificially-inseminating doctor just above. In a French story, never collected in English: *A French queen who is barren makes a pilgrimage on foot from Paris to the Cathedral of Chartres, which she has been told will surely cure her barrenness. On the way, a washerwoman under a bridge hails her, and says* [speaking à la troisième personne in token of ultimate respect]: *"Is Milady making the pilgrimage to Chartres?" "Yes," says the queen, "God has cursed me with barrenness, and I am going there hoping to be cured."*

"Useless!" replies the washerwoman; "the big, strapping monk that used to do the miracles is dead." This is, of course, a lesser miracle being mocked here, than those actually promulgated in the main religious mythos. The Virgin Birth itself is also put into question, albeit a bit obliquely, in a very popular joke (already given), which is not even considered 'dirty,' though it seldom appears in public print as its sacrilege is immanent if not evident: *A girl goes to the doctor with strange symptoms she cannot understand. He examines her, sits down at his desk while she rearranges her clothes, and begins, "Now, Miss Smith, I want you to tell your fiancé . . ." "I don't have a fiancé." "Well, then, tell your boyfriend." "I don't have a boyfriend. I've never had a boyfriend." "All right, Miss Smith," he says gently, "do you mind if I look out the window? The last time this happened there was a star in the east . . ."* (Told by a young girl, Scranton, Pa. 1934.)

I have already attempted to handle this point in *The Horn Book,* p. 316, in discussing the 'test-tube baby' as the eugenic or artificially-inseminated child was originally called in science fiction, though, to be sure, an actual 'test-tube baby' would have neither father *nor* mother. 'Just as the whole new form or folk-myth of science-fiction repeats the emotional charge of earlier religio-mystic fears of the dead, and so forth, but in scientific trappings; the eugenic or test-tube baby has become the modern focus of all the earlier, and almost mute resistance to — yet simultaneous acceptance of — the folk-myth of a Virgin Birth. This could express itself earlier only obliquely or sardonically, as in the folktale or joke: *An old lady being converted from Protestantism to Catholicism, and being told of the miracle of the Virgin Birth, is asked if she has any questions. "Well," she says diffidently, "it's not really a question, but I've never been able to see the advantage over the old system."*

'At least a dozen revisions and reversals of this joke have been collected, over the last thirty years (and perhaps as many more have been missed) mostly in pictorial and cartoon form, turning on the reduplication of machines by sexo-mechanical acts, or the eugenic "marriages of the future," with a baby popping out of the machine when a coin is put into the vaguely symbolic slot.' The 'consex' idea recently.

The most recent: *A party of astronauts on Venus ask to be shown how the Venusians reproduce, and are shown a complicated machine: a button is pushed, a tape is fed into the machine with the baby's required characteristics, the wheels whir, there is a slight blue explosion, and the Venusian baby comes out the slot. "Now," says the Venusian leader, "how do you Tellurians make babies?" After a hurried confabulation, one of the female astronauts volunteers — for the sake of interplanetary relations — and the astronaut leader has intercourse with her on the table. "Very interesting," says the Venusian leader; "now, where's the baby?" "Oh, the baby won't be born for nine months yet," says the astronaut. "Well, then, what was the big hurry there at the end?"* (La Jolla, Calif. 1965; earlier on monkeys.) There is an expurgated, or perhaps only a variant form, of earlier date, in Dr. Winick's *Outer Space Humor* (1963) p. 34-5, in which the astronaut *tells,* rather than shows, how babies are made on earth. ' *"Well, how about that!" whistled the* [non-human] *guide. "That's just the way we make automobiles up here!"* ' This concerns itself only with the Our-Space/Outer-Space reversal, as do most such recent jokes, and lacks any really humorous ending.

Vasectomy — the cutting and tying off of the seminal duct — used as a birth control measure, is too new a sub-castratory technique actually to appear in jokes as yet. I was at one time the amanuensis of Dr. Robert Latou Dickinson, the American gynecologist who was one of the first to promulgate this technique, and met through him, about 1938, an anatomical-model manufacturer who insisted he was the first person on whom this operation had been done. This man, who was middle-aged, powerfully built, and handsome, made a pest of himself among the women secretaries at the New York Academy of Medicine by announcing to them — as several of them confided to me — the news of his vasectomy, coupled with the assurance that he therefore could not impregnate them, and seemed amazed that they did not all therefore sink swooningly into his arms. The idea that birth control is all right in its way, but that there is nothing like *the spice of danger,* never occurred to this modern primitive. Also, at a much deeper level, there is the tremendouly important rule, enunciated clearly for the first time in Lundberg & Farnham's *Modern Woman: The Lost Sex* (1947) in the chapter, "The Failure of Modern Sexuality," p. 271: '*The strong desire for children or lack of it in a woman has a crucial bearing on how much enjoyment she derives from the sexual act.* For the sex act is primarily concerned with having children. Women cannot make its immediate pleasure an end in itself without inducing a decline in the pleasure.'

This is the principal objection to vasectomy, the Pill, the birth control thermometer and the 'free period' which it pinpoints, and, in fact, to all methods of birth control. It also shows how completely male-oriented the birth control agitation has always been, for all its propagandistic front of 'liberating women.' Obviously no intelligent woman nowadays wants to have fifteen children: but *one* child only, in the impregnable thirty years of the sexual career of a woman, from fifteen to forty-five, is clearly not enough. Such limitation does the opposite of 'liberating' her for the personal or sexual satisfactions proposed, in limiting her sexuality to sexual intercourse, as the sexuality of men is limited. The male point of view here is made pitifully clear in the one joke — hardly more than a cartoon-gag — so far encountered on the subject of vasectomy (in *And One Flew Into the Cuckold's Nest,* 1966, p. 5): *A naked woman is sitting up in bed while her lover hides himself under the sheet, except for his penis-shaped "Kilroy" nose. She is saying placatingly to her husband, appearing suddenly in the doorway with suitcase in hand: "Don't worry, Dear! He's had a vasectomy just like you!"* That poor girl has really been brainwashed.

In the end, artificial insemination, whether human or divine, cannot be separated from the adultery it involves, simply by the *ex cathedra* statements of either law or religion, and all the less by the stumbling private subterfuges of semen-'donors,' birth control, non-vaginal intercourse, vasectomy, and the like, even including in recent decades the final and most incredible intervention in the natural sexual system: hysterectomy, the removal of the uterus itself, *as a form of birth control!* Let's try that cartoon-gag now in reverse. Does it work? *Naked woman in bed, lover, Kilroy-nose, bedsheet, husband, etc. And the wife says: "Don't worry, dear! It ain't adultery. Didn't I have a hysterectomy, just like you said?"* (Valbonne, A.-M., France, 1966.) I don't prophesy much future for that, as a joke.

The older jokes came closer to credibility in their unconscious or covert mocking of the miracles of the Annunciation and the Virgin Birth or Nativity, popularly but erroneously confused with the Immaculate Conception, which was the conception of the Virgin Mary herself by her parents, free of all 'Original' sin, a dogma for which there does not appear to be any basis in any of the Gospels. The confusion is of course based on the idea of sex as dirty, and therefore of a sexless birth or artificial conception as 'Immaculate.' The playing upon this confusion in the so-called "Grotto of the Immaculate Conception" at Lourdes, in France, where the Virgin Mary herself is stated to have appeared to a peasant girl, Bernadette Soubirous, in the mid-19th century, in a vulviform grotto, to validate this particular dogma (speaking in the local patois, so Bernadette would understand her), is one of the most recent and grotesque examples of the confusion involved and the cynicism with which it has been exploited.

Antoine de La Sale's *Cent Nouvelles Nouvelles,* or "Hundred Merry Tales" (about 1460) No. 14, "The Pope-Maker," gives the oldest known version of a story that is now known in all European cultures, concerning *A monk who seduces a girl on the pretext that he has been ordered by an angel to engender the next Pope on her body. She gives birth to a girl.* Rotunda, K1315.1, and K1315.1.1 (and 1.2), gives the whole anterior genealogy of this story, back to Boccaccio's Day IV, Tale 2, in which the seduction is achieved by posing as the Archangel Gabriel, who is, of course, the angel who announces to the Virgin Mary (in *Luke,* i. 26–38) that she has 'found favour with God' and will conceive God's son. Within a few decades of the appearance of the complete parody story in the *Cent Nouvelles Nouvelles,* it was picked up in Guardati Masuccio's *Novellino* (1476) No. 2, the girl being promised that her child will be the 'fifth Evangelist,' which comes extremely close to the biblical statement. Bebel, vol. ii. 104, and Fortini's *Notti de' Novizi,* vol. ii, even return to the Jewish locale and the Messianic promise: *A pregnant Jewish girl persuades her parents that she is to give birth to the Messiah, but gives birth to a girl.* (Thompson, Motif J2336, with further references.)

The modern story, which is as well known in Russia as in America, drops back to the mere making of a Pope, which allows more room for crude comedy. In the Russian form: *A monk seduces a peasant's wife with the peasant's knowledge, accepting payment for doing so, on the grounds that he will engender a priest, whose clerical connections will make the family rich. To do this he has merely to insert the tip of his penis, because if he inserts more the baby will be an archbishop, etc. The peasant hides (or, sometimes, is present watching), and, at the last moment, gives the priest a terrific kick in the ass, driving him completely into his wife's vagina, and shouting, "Ha! For the same money we'll get a Pope!"* (N.Y. 1940, from a Russian-Jewish delicatessen cook.) I have also collected this on two occasions with a minister and farmer replacing the monk and peasant, to Americanize the story; but the usual hero (Motif K1398; *Kryptádia,* x. 225) is the gypsy-trickster: *A hobo convinces a Kentucky mountaineer that he can make his wife give birth to a fiddler, who will make them rich by playing over the radio. The mountaineer stands behind the door during the operation, and hears the hobo fart noisily. He rushes into the bedroom shouting,*

"I said a fiddler, not a horn-player!" (White Plains, N.Y. 1942.) Further stories on this curious trait of farting during sexual intercourse will be given under "Cloacal Intercourse," in Series Two, discussing their further connection with — precisely — the myth of the Annunciation. (Compare *Russian Secret Tales,* No. 43, p. 131 above; Type 1547.)

Two further traits are present here which are perhaps worth indicating, to show the elements from which this story has been built, or into which it has been transposed, doubtless much later. First is the charming nonsense about inserting only a certain amount of the penis, which is a standard gambit in ordinary seduction. It appears full-blown in Fortini's "Passing the Strawberry" story, already noted earlier, and in many others connected with the seduction of girls who are at first unwilling, then avid for more of the penis, and finally demand more than actually exists. The other trait is that of the promised priest transmogrified into a Pope, which exists in a 'clean' story often collected in America, and intended as an obvious riposte to anti-Semitism. Its Russian parentage is very clear, as it is sometimes collected with the standard Russian-Jewish folktale characters of the trickster-tailor and the stupid Cossack, and sometimes with the Americanization of this latter as the 'Irish cop.' *An Irish policeman is bragging to a Jewish tailor that his son, Denis, is going to become a priest. "So, is there any future in it?" the tailor asks. Well, the boy can become a bishop, archbishop, even a cardinal. "So what then?" nudges the tailor. "Well," says the policeman, "them damned Eyetalians have it pretty well tied up, but, I dunno, my boy Denis — by God, he could become the Pope!" "So what then?" says the tailor. "What the hell do you want him to be," cries the policeman, "Jesus Christ?" "Vy not?" shrugs the tailor. "Vun of our boys made it."* (N.Y. 1938.) The impossible and unanswerable logic here is in the best tradition of Jewish-Talmudic paradox.

The resistance of the cuckold to the presumed advantageous or even divine or angelic impregnation of his wife is of course expressed by the devious methods described above, whereby he kicks, cheats, or otherwise 'screws' or 'reams' — *i.e.* symbolically pedicates, as punishment — the adulterer, at the very moment of the orgasm which achieves his cuckolding and the impregnation of his wife. A much simpler and more direct expression of the resistance of the husband to the whole situation of being adulterously replaced is "No Use Rapping on the Blind," which I believe to be the *cante-fable* most strongly surviving and still most commonly collected in the Anglo-American tradition. (Aarne Type 1419H, Motif K1546, noting this as Boccaccio's Day VII,

Tale 1.) Apparently the oldest known American version is that collected by Vance Randolph, No. 44, as "No Use to Rattle the Blind," heard 'near Green Forest, Ark., about 1910.' For references see Walter Anderson's *Der Schwank vom Alten Hildebrand* (Dorpat, 1931) p. 324; C. R. Baskervill, in *PMLA* (1921) XXXVI. 590–2; and Herbert Halpert, in *JAFL* (1942) LV. 137–9; also *Kryptádia* (1884) II. 115, X. 110. Boccaccio's Levantine original still survives, in *Histoires Arabes* (1927) p. 208–9, with a doggerel incantation, and the adulterer creeping on the roof.

One time there was a woman that had a good home and a baby and a new piano, but another fellow used to lay up with her while her husband was away. She told him to rattle the window-blind, and if the coast was clear she would get up and let him in. Well, one night the woman and her man was a-setting by the fire, and the window-blind begun to rattle. She was afraid he might suspicion something, because there wasn't no wind blowing. So the woman jumped up and begun to play the piano, and then she sung out:

> No use to rattle the blind,
> No use to rattle the blind,
> The baby's a-sleeping,
> Its father's a-weeping,
> No use to rattle the blind.

The woman's husband wasn't such a fool as them people thought, and he seen how things was, all right. "Get your ass out of my way," says he, and pushed her off the piano-stool. Then he begun to pound on the keys like a cyclone a-coming, and he sung out:

> No use to rattle the blind,
> No use to rattle the blind,
> The baby's a-sucking,
> And I'll do my own fucking,
> No use to rattle the blind.

Him and her just set there and looked at each other after that, but there wasn't nary a word spoke. The window-blind didn't rattle no more, neither. Some folks say the fellow that done it was so scared he run clear out of the country, and never did come back to the house where they had the new piano.

The prominence given to the *piano* in this version is apparently a rationalization of the *cante-fable* form, to explain the actors' bursting into song (as in oratorios or street-operas, now 'musical-comedies'). In other versions the man and wife are simply in bed. No reference is ever made to artificial or substitute insemination of any kind, but the curious insistence on the presence of the nursing baby — essential to the final rhyme: cf. p. 670 — makes the husband into an unwilling St. Joseph (the patron saint of cuckolds), refusing the angelic offering of the mysterious 'rapping on the blind,' when no wind is blowing. It will be recollected that, in the most naïve form of the myth of the Annunciation, shown in many primitive Italian paintings, the Virgin is impregnated by the heavenly breath insufflated into her ear by the agency of a 'Pigeon' representing the Holy Ghost, though nothing of this kind is mentioned in the *Gospel according to St. Luke,* chapter i.

As so much space has been given in the present chapter to the emotions of the husband of the adulterous wife, I may perhaps be excused for ending with a little autobiographical anecdote expressing marvellously well — it has served me nearly half a lifetime — the emotional position of the adulterer, and why to avoid it. When I was eighteen years old, in 1936, I began as a writer for the theatre in New York, a job that a relative of mine, who was a stage-comedian, got for me, trouble-shooting the dialogue of an impossible musical-comedy that later laid the biggest egg at the Palladium in London in the history of the theatre. At a certain point I was reading my script before the producer and the actors, when they all inexplicably burst out laughing. Later the comedian who had got me the job explained the mystery: while I was reading, one of the pretty young dancers or 'ponies' had walked by in her scanty costume to take a drink at the water-cooler, and my tenor voice had unconsciously dropped a full octave to a rich, virile baritone. ("The Voice as Phallus.") Taking pity on my confusion, my mentor explained to me that I was to leave the ponies strictly alone. They were all married, generally to 'bums' and drunks, and playing around with them was a mug's game. *Did I know what a mug's game was? — No. — "A mug's game," he told me, "is breaking your back at midnight, trying to make another man's wife come."*

SUBJECTS & MOTIFS

SECOND SERIES

10. HOMOSEXUALITY

SUBJECTS & MOTIFS

BIBLIOGRAPHY

INDEX